ATLANTIC

OCEAN

B A H A M A S

Camagüey Archipelago

Jigüey Bay

Ciego
de Ávila

☆ Ciego de Ávila

☆ Camagüey

Camagüey

Las Tunas

☆ Las Tunas

☆ Holguín — Nipe Bay

Holguín

Guacanayabo
Gulf

Bayamo
☆

Granma

Santiago
de Cuba

Guantánamo

☆ Guantánamo

☆ Santiago
de Cuba

Guantánamo
Bay

Guantánamo Bay
Naval Base
(U.S.A.)

Windward Passage

HAITI

JAMAICA

78°W   76°W   74°W

CUBA

ALAN WEST-DURÁN, *editor in chief*

EDITORIAL BOARD

SCRIBNER WORLD SCHOLAR SERIES

VOLUME **2**

L-Z

CUBA

ALAN WEST-DURÁN, *editor in chief*

CHARLES SCRIBNER'S SONS

A part of Gale, Cengage Learning

GALE
CENGAGE Learning

Detroit • New York • San Francisco • New Haven, Conn • Waterville, Maine • London

GALE
CENGAGE Learning

Cuba

Alan West-Durán, Editor in Chief

For product information and technology assistance, contact us at
Gale Customer Support, 1-800-877-4253.
For permission to use material from this text or product,
submit all requests online at **www.cengage.com/permissions.**
Further permissions questions can be emailed to
permissionrequest@cengage.com

While every effort has been made to ensure the reliability of the information presented in this publication, Gale, a part of Cengage Learning, does not guarantee the accuracy of the data contained herein. Gale accepts no payment for listing; and inclusion in the publication of any organization, agency, institution, publication, service, or individual does not imply endorsement of the editors or publisher. Errors brought to the attention of the publisher and verified to the satisfaction of the publisher will be corrected in future editions.

LIBRARY OF CONGRESS CATALOGING-IN-PUBLICATION DATA

Alan West-Durán, editor in chief.
   v. cm. -- (Scribner world scholar series)
   Includes bibliographical references and index.
   ISBN-13: 978-0-684-31681-9 (set : alk. paper)
   ISBN-10: 0-684-31681-1 (set: alk. paper)
   ISBN-13: 978-0-684-31682-6 (v. 1 : alk. paper)
   ISBN-10: 0-684-31682-X (v. 1 : alk. paper)
   [etc.]
1. Cuba. I. West, Alan, 1953-

F1758.C9485 2012
972.91--dc22
                                            2011012007

Gale
27500 Drake Rd.
Farmington Hills, MI, 48331-3535

ISBN-13: 978-0-6843-1681-9 (set)   ISBN-10: 0-6843-1681-1 (set)
ISBN-13: 978-0-6843-1682-6 (vol. 1)   ISBN-10: 0-6843-1682-X (vol. 1)
ISBN-13: 978-0-6843-1683-3 (vol. 2)   ISBN-10: 0-6843-1683-8 (vol. 2)

This title will also be available as an e-book.
ISBN-13: 978-0-6843-1684-0 ISBN-10: 0-6843-1684-6
Contact your Gale, a part of Cengage Learning, sales representative for ordering information.

Printed in the United States of America
1 2 3 4 5 6 7 16 15 14 13 12

Editorial And Production Staff

Executive Vice President
Frank Menchaca

Vice President and Publisher
James P. Draper

Product Manager
Stephen Wasserstein

Project Editors
Rebecca Parks, Scot Peacock

Editorial Support
Lawrence W. Baker, Sheila Dow,
Julie Mellors, Alexander Polzin,
Jennifer Stock

Editorial Assistants
Chelsea Arndt, Hillary Hentschel,
Marit Rogne

Art Director
Kristine Julien

Composition
Evi Seoud

Imaging
John Watkins

Manufacturing
Wendy Blurton

Rights Acquisition and Management
Jackie Jones, Robyn V. Young

Technical Support
Marc Faerber, Michael Lesniak, Mike Weaver

Copyeditors
Judith Culligan, Gretchen M. Gordon,
Anne C. Davidson, Jessica Hornik Evans, Michael
Levine, Mary H. Russell, David E. Salamie, Drew
Silver

Proofreaders
John Fitzpatrick, Carol Holmes, Laura Specht
Patchkofsky, Amy L. Unterburger

Translators
ASTA-USA Translation Services, Dick Cluster,
Comms Multilingual, Mark Schafer

Translation Verification
Elizabeth Campisi, Dick Cluster,
Pablo Julián Davis, Cola W. Franzen, Dawn Gable,
Lourdes Gil, Heriberto Nicolás García, Ana M.
Sanchez

Captions
Judith Culligan

Cross-References
M. Karen Bracken

Custom Graphics
XNR Productions, Inc.

Indexer
Laurie Andriot

Page Design
Kate Scheible Graphic Design, LLC

TABLE OF CONTENTS

INTRODUCTION

ew countries in the world have received the kind of political, scholarly, and journalistic attention that Cuba has throughout its history. Literally, hundreds, if not thousands, of books have been published about the largest of the Caribbean islands, including numerous biographies of Cuba's two most prominent figures, Fidel Castro and José Martí. Much of what has been written of the post-1959 revolutionary period has generated debate and controversy.

The island has demonstrated a bracing cultural vitality over its turbulent history: Cuba has been surprisingly open to foreign cultures (Africa, Europe, Asia) and yet exhibits a profound sense of nationalism. The diversity of its culture is matched by a struggle for its unfulfilled potential, burst asunder by one of the most radical revolutions in the twentieth century. Because of this dramatic re-insertion into the world stage at the height of the Cold War, Cuba is refreshingly paradoxical: Even as the country seems suspended in time or in the midst of the ruins of something that has ended, it has creatively generated a highly sophisticated cultural and social space where pre-modern religious rituals coexist with postmodern blogging, where non-market egalitarianism collides with capitalist consumption tastes.

THE COMPLEXITY OF HISTORY AND WORD CHOICE

Because of the interest and passions unleashed by their history, Cubans are "bilingual": They speak not only Spanish, but also "history as a second language," in the words of poet Dionisio Martínez. Cuban history is spelled in full caps, like tabloid headlines. There are many headlines, and this cacophony of voices and polarized interpretations challenged us as editors to create a civil dialogue and a linguistic, cultural, and conceptual translation that would present a rich, complex, and vibrant portrait of Cuba.

Currently, historical memories seem to be measured in days and weeks rather than years or decades; however, Cubans have a long memory, not surprising for a small Third World country that has had to deal with major powers (Spain, the Soviet Union, and the United States) over decades or centuries. It is this long, intricate, and sometimes troubled memory—and its many different voices—that this reference book tries to document and make intelligible to the reader.

The avalanche of literature on, by, and about Cuba reminds us of a mordant quip by American bandleader Duke Ellington: "You can say anything you want on the trombone, but you gotta be careful with words" (in Lock, p. 219). Cuban poet Virgilio Piñera, in his poem "La isla en peso" (Island in the Balance), speaks to the difficulty of defining Cuba, even for Cubans: "An entire people can perish from light or from the plague.... My people, so young, you don't know how to make order!/ My people, so divinely rhetorical, you don't know how to tell a story!/ Like light or childhood you do not have a visage" (p. 46). Ellington's advice and Piñera's poem are prudent reminders that words not only matter but have enormous resonance and implications. When the subject is Cuba sometimes words are lobbed like ideological grenades, reducing a rich symphony of voices to a shouting match between two sides.

For example, in a 2011 *New York Times* op-ed piece Cuban blogger Lizabel Mónica described how the different terms used to refer to the April 1961 U.S.-backed invasion of Cuba reflect the differing perspectives of this event. It is known in the United States as the Bay of Pigs Invasion; in Cuba it is the Battle of Playa Girón. For the Cubans, the event was a military invasion with support by the CIA: hence those who were defeated were imperialist mercenaries. For Cuban exiles, those who fought in Brigade 2506 seeking to overthrow Fidel Castro's government are seen as Cuban patriots fighting for freedom against a tyrant. While not all moments of Cuban history are so dramatically charged, it does alert us to some of the pitfalls of writing about Cuba and the hidden or not so hidden assumptions made in the words used to describe the island's history and culture. These assumptions or mistranslations of history can provoke misunderstanding, hostility, even violence.

When we speak about Cuba it should be understood as well that its meaning extends beyond the geographical territory of the island. There are over 1.2 million Cubans or Cuban-Americans in the United States, and tens of thousands living in Puerto Rico, Spain, Mexico, and Venezuela, with smaller populations scattered around the world. They constitute a significant diaspora, making important contributions in economics, culture, politics, sports, media, and ideas to a "greater Cuba." This being said, this book's emphasis is tilted toward the island, since eighty percent of the Cuban population still lives there.

WHY SO MUCH INTEREST IN CUBA?

Why so much interest in Cuba? Is it the "David vs. Goliath" political drama that erupted in 1959 that pitted a defiant Caribbean island against the most powerful nation on the planet? Is it the ideological and historical confrontation between capitalism and socialism? Is it the natural beauty of the island, which collides with its rebellious history? Is it the long relationship between Cuba and the United States, fueled by political ambition, travelers, and tourists that have seen the island as friendly neighbor, ripe fruit, or protectorate? Is it the appeal of Cuban music over two centuries, which has had a long and seductive relationship with the United States? Is it due to a persistent curiosity about a place that has been off-limits for U.S. travelers for over five decades? Is it the lure of utopian change symbolized by the Cuban Revolution?

Ever since the Enlightenment's promise of liberty, equality, and fraternity by way of the French Revolution, many thinkers have addressed the possibility of a different kind of society, free of want, exploitation, inequality, and domination. These ideals have animated many reformers and revolutionaries who seek an alternative kind of power. Cuba's utopian history is not recent, nor only related to the Marxist tradition, but rooted in both a Latin American tradition and its own longings to fulfill its national ideals, expressed by some of its key intellectual and political figures. Even the collapse of European socialism (Soviet Union and allies) between 1989 and 1991, not to mention the economic changes in China and Vietnam (opening up to global commerce, market reforms) have not completely eliminated these utopian impulses. As French philosopher Paul Ricoeur said: "A society without utopia would be dead, because it would no longer have any project, any prospective goals" (1986, p. xxi). For all their shortcomings and failures, twentieth-century revolutions, of which Cuba is clearly an example, speak the utopian language of the unfulfilled promises of the Enlightenment project. When the Berlin Wall was torn down almost everyone predicted Cuba would follow suit; some twenty-three years later the island has resisted against all odds. Conversely, those who claim that Cuba has run its course and spent its political capital, see the island from the perspective of the burgeoning group of *transitólogos* ("transitionists" often with a political agenda), those who are devising scenarios for Cuba's transition to a post-socialist society, often using comparative experiences from post-Communist Eastern Europe or ex-military regimes of Latin America. From a North American perspective, what Cuba has attempted to do over the last half century confronts us, challenging our way of looking at issues of equality, social justice, the individual and society, the commodification of daily life, race relations, North-South relations, the arts, health care, education, and politics, to name only the most visible. As editors we wanted to give more reliable tools to the reader to assess whether Cuba's lessons in these areas are positive, negative, or a mixture of both, knowing that these appraisals will shift over time.

Cuba's history, of course, did not begin in 1959 with the Revolution, and this publication is insistent in covering the Colonial period (1492–1898) and the Republican period (1902–1959) in the major articles, not only because they help illuminate the present, but because they deserve to be studied and explained in their own right. Despite its relative youth as an independent country at just a little more than a century, Cuba's roots are deep and go back centuries to Spain, Africa, Asia, the Americas, and the indigenous peoples who were the original inhabitants of the island.

A DIFFERENT KIND OF REFERENCE BOOK ON CUBA

The initial idea for this project was called an "encyclopedia," yet as the publication was conceptualized and refined the need to have a traditional type of encyclopedia with thousands of entries, biographies, etc., not only seemed repetitive of previous efforts but unnecessary. As editors we wanted to present the long view of what has made Cuba what it is today, not simply focus on the current moment.

The concept then evolved to combining a panoramic portrait of Cuba achieved through long "survey" essays, with a series of shorter and more focused "counterpoint" pieces. In this regard this reference book operates both as a mural and as a mosaic: It accentuates broad outlooks with incisive particulars. The long essays are on major topics like Economics, Food, Tobacco, Race, Sexuality, Faith, Gender, Cuban Thought and Cultural Identity, Literature, Language, and more than a dozen more. The counterpoints are associated with the big topics but focus on something specific: a date in history, a town or city, a work of art or literature, a film, a piece of music. For example, within the general category of "Sugar" (which covers the Colonial, Republican, and Revolutionary periods) there is a related article that speaks about how sugar has been represented in Cuban art, literature, song and popular culture. The topic of literature includes key counterpoints that cover important novels, poetry, or plays, like José Lezama Lima's *Paradiso* (1966) or Reinaldo Arenas's *The Color of Summer* (1991). Key works or emblems of Cuban society were selected as counterpoints. Their subject matter, perspective, and historical importance helped define Cuba's unique identity. We hope because of their brevity and themes, they offer a livelier approach to Cuba's creativity and identity.

The idea then was not to attempt an up-to-the-minute collection of information on Cuba—a thankless task, given the 24/7 information cycle—but to have the interested reader find out about the economic, historical, political, and cultural forces that have shaped Cuba and make it what it is today: from a colonial outpost in Spain's empire, to a sugar-producing juggernaut in the nineteenth century, to a troubled twentieth-century republic, and more recently an embattled revolutionary island since 1959. In an electronic age, a printed text fixes a point in time; the editors wanted that point to be a gathering place where people would be exposed to information, ideas, and knowledge that can become guides to other, renewed and multifaceted sources. Central to both long articles and counterpoints was the need to contextualize Cuba's rich history and culture to counter the simplistic, dismissive, frivolous, or shortsighted popular images of the country. Unlike a traditional encyclopedia, there is no assumption—tacit or overt—that these two volumes have all the answers about Cuba. On the contrary, the editors saw this project more along the lines of helping the reader ask the right questions about Cuba. We sincerely hope the reader will learn a great deal about the country, but more important is that consulting *Cuba* will take the reader on further journeys to explore the island's culture, history, and society with a particular discernment.

DIVERSE VIEWPOINTS

A key feature of this publication is the high participation of Cuban contributors living on the island. This was an exciting and challenging aspect of the project since it meant navigating the worlds between Cuba and the United States, always an undertaking fraught with differences, misunderstandings, and mutual suspicions. Fortunately, the drawbacks were far outweighed by their contributions; it has made the project a more rounded and nuanced view of the island's rich if sometimes baffling reality. This is not the first time scholars and artists from inside and outside the island have collaborated, but it is the first involving a major reference work in English.

In putting together an editorial team we sought to have input from the island, Cubans abroad, plus a host of Latin American, Caribbean, North American, and European scholars who are experts on the subject of Cuba. In addition, an independent historian created chronology sidebars for key articles to highlight important events. These scholars brought their decades of experience and scholarship to topics and issues that were sometimes controversial and contested. Despite the commitment to achieve consensus on difficult issues, there are perspectives in the publication that not everyone shared. Still, the authors were asked to express and discuss differences on matters that had antithetical viewpoints, and not merely take sides.

These different viewpoints have been organized to dispel some of the more hardened notions about Cuba and its people: that Cubans are anti-American, that the two sides between pro- and anti-Castro populations are monolithic blocs, that the one-party state in the island has not seen any substantial changes or reforms since the 1960s, that island Cubans do not want better relations with the United States, that Cuba's pre-1959 history should only be regarded as the prelude to the revolution led by Fidel Castro. Equally important is to recognize that not all Cubans want to leave Cuba, that post-1959 Cuba is not an unmitigated disaster, that not all Cubans in exile support the embargo (blockade), that the Cuban diaspora is pluralistic and not uniformly right-wing.

Cuba, however, elicits great passion from those who write about it, be they Cuban or not. Damián Fernández has written eloquently about this, devoting an entire book to the subject of the politics of passion and affection with regard to Cuba. In it, he warns against two dangers: seeing a false opposition between reason and emotion, especially in the political realm, and overlooking the role of emotion in analyzing the role of interests in politics. As he says: "Social life has an emotional infrastructure, and so do political systems" (p. 2). This book does not shy away from these passions or the emotional infrastructure of history; *Cuba* embraces them while avoiding the settling of scores. This emotional undertow might cause discomfort for some readers, but this discomfort reveals much about Cuba.

Given the contested terrain of Cuban history and politics, there are a great many issues on which scholars and Cubans passionately disagree: the Bay of Pigs Invasion (Batalla de Playa Girón), the Cuban Missile Crisis (Crisis de Octubre), negotiations between the U.S. and Cuban governments, immigration, the Mariel Boatlift, Cuba's involvement in Africa, the Rafter Crisis, the Helms-Burton bill, the Elián González Affair, the embargo (or *bloqueo*), congressional or executive restrictions on travel or remittances to Cuba. At a policy level there are profound disagreements on political philosophy (type of system, elections, etc.), economics (role of markets, private property, the state, entrepreneurship), human rights, reproductive rights, and privacy, among others.

These differences need not lead to despair, nor obscure the difference between information and knowledge. Information is something that can be stored, shared, used, and reused by many people; there is a public dimension to information that also lends itself to being packaged and re-articulated into "morsels" and made available to large numbers of people. Knowledge, on the other hand is more focused on an individual knower (Blair p. 2). Knowledge involves context, a bigger picture, a conceptual breadth, as well as personal-intellectual experience. While information can be compiled, knowledge requires a kind of apprenticeship through time. *Cuba* has both information and knowledge, but its editors are keenly aware that the distinction between the two can sometimes be hazy. One person's information can be deemed as just non-factual ideology by another. This does not mean that one should give up and simply conclude that gathering or disseminating information on Cuba is hopeless, or that knowledge about the country is inevitably tainted by ideological bias. It does, however, remind us that these differences are not ephemeral and challenge us to be doubly conscious of the fact that these difficulties are not going away anytime soon. It is by engaging these differences that the reader will see a more complete understanding of Cuba emerge.

THE CHALLENGE OF TRANSLATION

These differences came to the fore during the translation of work by Cuban scholars to English. The difficulty in translation was not just in the transition from Spanish to English but also in the capturing of historical or cultural nuances that might be understandable to a Cuban audience but lost on a U.S. reader. At times one word could not capture the complexity or the nuance and an explanation was necessary; this was often the case when translating (or having to explain) certain words from the Afro-Cuban religious lexicon like *orisha*, *cajón al muerto*, or *casa-templo*. In other instances it was an issue of political-historical interpretation; for example, traditionally the war between Spain and the United States in 1898 has been called the Spanish-American War or Hispanic-American War, which leaves out any Cuban agency in this matter. However, the conflict began in 1895 as the War of Independence for Cuba, and the three-year struggle was a reprise and renewal of the Ten Years' War that began in 1868; thus Cuban scholars call it more accurately the Spanish-American-Cuban War or just War of Independence.

Or when referring to the U.S. embargo, now over fifty years old, island Cubans use the word *bloqueo* (blockade), a much stronger term that evokes an image of war (with naval blockades, combat). Blockade also means that it goes beyond just a U.S.-Cuba issue and that the United States has tried to convince other countries to follow suit and support their policy. For those living in Cuba, the embargo is an act of economic warfare, used in conjunction with political and military threats to overthrow their government. So in many instances we have placed both words together to indicate these perspectives. Translation is not only a matter of linguistic difference, but cultural and/or conceptual difference, too. In this regard *Cuba* serves as a translator at all three levels.

In Paul Ricoeur's comments on translation he speaks of a state of "linguistic hospitality," where the translator "acknowledges the difference between adequacy and equivalence" and that equivalence can be achieved without total adequacy. This is where the translator can find a degree of happiness: "Linguistic hospitality, then, [is] where the pleasure of dwelling in the other's language is balanced by the pleasure of receiving the foreign word at home, in one's own welcoming house" (2006, p. 10). As editors we strove not only to create a linguistic hospitality but also a cultural and conceptual hospitality, where the reader can dwell in Cuba and where Cuba can dwell in our home as well.

As editors we proposed to "translate" what might seem untranslatable: ideas, themes, and polemics that seem unbridgeable. Cuban-American author Gustavo Pérez Firmat affirms that Cuban identity is transient, not one of essence, translational and not foundational (p. 157). If so, did the Cuban Revolution change it to a foundational identity? Or is there something about Cuba that makes it untranslatable to the United States or the new global order? Is Cuba somehow opaque in global eyes or is it a source that can shed light and understanding on important global issues and problems? As editors we would like to think the latter, while acknowledging the former.

The word "translation" always conjures up issues of faithfulness and betrayal, two words that underline much of the discourse on Cuba. For many Cubans who have left the island, the Revolution was not faithful to its original ideals and has betrayed its promises; those who have remained in Cuba see those who have departed as being unfaithful to their country, betraying its sovereignty and its utopian potential. This adherence to faithfulness or betrayal in the extra-linguistic sense (the gulf between an ideal and its realization) is echoed in the language-translation realm (bridging the gulf between two languages and cultures); both see translation as ultimately unattainable, or at best an impossible approximation, as an activity that leads to failure. Still, this pessimism does not take into account that the activity and meaning of translation (linguistic, cultural, conceptual) can be rich and enabling precisely because it is something always unfinished, something that will never be perfect. In effect, the challenge is to try again and create a new or better translation, turn it into an emblem of hope and not of failure. It is in this spirit of hope, of a linguistic, cultural, and conceptual hospitality, instead of hostility, that the editors of *Cuba* have tried to bring to its readers the rich, perplexing, and ever-changing reality of Cuba.

ACKNOWLEDGEMENTS

Any project of this magnitude requires the dedication and perseverance of many people. First, I want to thank Frank Menchaca, Executive Vice President of Gale, for proposing that it happen; it is the fifth time we have collaborated on a publication and hopefully it will not be the last. ¡Gracias, Frank! Stephen Wasserstein as Project Manager was a constant source of insight and advice, as was Jim Draper, the Publisher. Rebecca Parks, the Project Editor, was a joy to work with; her valuable comments, her patience, hard work, and equanimity were exceptional. I also want to acknowledge the invaluable editorial assistance offered by Jose Viera, Guillermo Jiménez, María del Carmen Barcia, and Manuel J. Suzarte, all in Cuba. Though I don't know them personally, I want to thank the copyeditors and the translators for their valuable work in making a difficult topic eminently readable.

The editors of this project all made this work possible: Lou Pérez, Jr., María de los Angeles Torres, César Salgado, Víctor Fowler, and Marel García-Pérez, as well as Holly Ackerman, our Contributing Editor. Their dedication to Cuba and this project have been inspiring and helped me keep my sanity. Finally, to Ester Shapiro, who shared with me on a daily basis all of the joys and frustrations of this amazing and emotional experience, while always providing insight. I dedicate this book to the memory of my mother and father, who deeply loved Cuba (and did not return after leaving in 1960) and to all Cubans, no matter where they live. To all, ¡gracias y aché!

Alan West-Duran
Editor in Chief

WORKS CITED

Blair, Ann. *Too Much to Know: Managing Scholarly Information Before the Modern Age.* New Haven, CT: Yale University Press, 2010.

Fernández, Damián J. *Cuba and the Politics of Passion.* Austin: University of Texas Press, 2000.

Lock, Graham. *Blutopia: Visions of the Future and Revisions of the Past in the Work of Sun Ra, Duke Ellington, and Anthony Braxton.* Durham, NC: Duke University Press, 1999.

Martínez, Dionisio D. *History as a Second Language.* Columbus: Ohio State University Press, 1993.

Mónica, Lizbel. "You Say Bay of Pigs, I Say…" *New York Times* (16 April 2011).

Pérez Firmat, Gustavo. *The Cuban Condition: Translation and Identity in Modern Cuban Literature.* Cambridge, U.K.: Cambridge University Press, 1989.

Piñera, Virgilio. *La isla en peso, obra poética.* Barcelona, Spain: Tusquets Editores, 2000.

Ricoeur, Paul. *Lectures on Ideology and Utopia.* New York: Columbia University Press, 1986.

Ricoeur, Paul. *On Translation.* New York: Routledge, 2006.

LIST OF CONTRIBUTORS

NORMA ABAD MUÑOZ
Writer, Advisor, Director of Radio Programs
Member, Unión de Escritores y Artistas de Cuba (UNEAC)

MARK ABENDROTH
Mentor, School of Graduate Studies
Empire State College, SUNY

HOLLY ACKERMAN
Librarian for Latin America & Iberia
Duke University

ANTONIO AJA DÍAZ
Director, Professor, Centro de Estudios Demográficos, Universidad de La Habana, Havana, Cuba
Director, Programa de Estudio sobre Latinos en Estados Unidos, Casa de las Américas

MARÍA EUGENIA ALEGRIA NÚÑEZ
Independent Scholar
Cuba

OLAVO ALÉN RODRÍGUEZ
Ethnomusicologist
Cuban, Afro-Cuban, and Caribbean Studies

CARMEN ALMODÓVAR MUÑOZ
Member
Unión de Escritores y Artistas de Cuba (UNEAC)

AURELIO ALONSO
Deputy Director

Casa de las Américas, Havana, Cuba

ALEJANDRO ANREUS
Associate Professor of Art History and Latin American/Latino Studies
William Paterson University

UVA DE ARAGÓN
Associate Director, Cuban Research Institute (retired)
Florida International University

JORGE LUIS ARCOS
Adjunct Professor of Literature
Universidad Nacional de Río Negro, San Carlos de Bariloche, Argentina

PAQUITA ARMAS FONSECA
Member, Unión de Escritores y Artistas de Cuba (UNEAC)
Member, Unión de Periodistas de Cuba

JOSSIANNA ARROYO-MARTÍNEZ
Department of Spanish and Portuguese, African and African Diaspora Studies
University of Texas, Austin

CARIDAD ATENCIO
Poet and Essayist
Researcher, Centro de Estudios Martianos de La Habana, Havana, Cuba

MARÍA DEL CARMEN BARCIA ZEQUEIRA
Senior Professor, Casa de Altos Estudios Don Fernando Ortiz, Universidad de La Habana

Senior Academic, Academia de la Historia de Cuba
Havana, Cuba

RUTH BEHAR
Professor, Department of Anthropology
University of Michigan, Ann Arbor

EMILIO BEJEL
Professor of Latin American Studies, Department of Spanish and Portuguese
University of California at Davis

CARMEN BERENGUER HERNÁNDEZ
Historian
Bibliography Specialist, Biblioteca Nacional José Martí, Cuba

MARÍA-CECILIA BERMÚDEZ
Historian, Member, Grupo de Estudios Cubanos
Unión de Escritores y Artistas de Cuba (UNEAC)

ANKE BIRKENMAIER
Professor, Department of Spanish and Portuguese
Indiana University

PETER C. BJARKMAN
Cuban Baseball Historian
www.baseballdecuba.com

MELISSA BLANCO BORELLI
Lecturer in Dance and Film Studies, Department of Dance, Film and Theatre
University of Surrey, United Kingdom

DENISE BLUM

Assistant Professor, School of Educational Studies

Oklahoma State University

VELIA CECILIA BOBES LEÓN

Professor

Facultad Latinoamericana de Ciencias Sociales, Sede México

NATALIA MARÍA BOLÍVAR ARÓSTEGUI

Writer, Researcher

Unión de Escritores y Artistas de Cuba (UNEAC)

PHILIP BRENNER

Chair, Council on Latin America

American University

P. SEAN BROTHERTON

Department of Anthropology

Yale University

RUFO CABALLERO

Former Professor, Universidad de la Habana, Havana, Cuba

Former Professor, Instituto Superior de Artes (ISA), Cuba

ANA CAIRO

Member

Unión de Escritores y Artistas de Cuba (UNEAC)

LUISA CAMPUZANO

Emeritus Professor, Facultad de Artes y Letras, Universidad de La Habana, Havana, Cuba

Founder and Director of the Women's Studies Program, Casa de las Américas

ZAIDA CAPOTE CRUZ

Instituto de Literatura y Lingüística

Havana, Cuba

DAVID C. CARLSON

Assistant Professor, Department of History and Philosophy

University of Texas-Pan American

ODETTE CASAMAYOR-CISNEROS

Assistant Professor, Department of Modern and Classical Languages

University of Connecticut-Storrs

ANA VICTORIA CASANOVA

Musicologist, Researcher, Centro de Investigación y Desarrollo de la Música Cubana

Member, Unión de Escritores y Artistas de Cuba (UNEAC), Havana, Cuba

ENVER M. CASIMIR

Visiting Assistant Professor, Latin American Studies

Gettysburg College

LUCIANO CASTILLO

Head of the Mediateca "André Bazin" of the Escuela Internacional de Cine y TV de San Antonio de los Baños

Member of the Unión de Escritores y Artistas de Cuba (UNEAC) and the Asociación Cubana de la Prensa Cinematográfica, Havana, Cuba

SIRO DEL CASTILLO

Caribbean Commissioner

Comisión Latinoamericana por los Derechos Humanos y Libertades de los Trabajadores y Pueblos (CLADEHLT)

NORMA DEL CASTILLO ALONSO

Tobacco Research Institute

San Antonio de los Baños, Artemisa, Cuba

MARIELA CASTRO ESPÍN

Director

Centro Nacional de Educación Sexual (CENESEX), Cuba

ILIANA CEPERO-AMADOR

Independent Curator

Stanford, California

MICHAEL CHANAN

Professor of Film and Video, Department of Media, Culture, and Language

Roehampton University, London

GRACIELA CHAO CARBONERO

Member, Unión de Escritores y Artistas de Cuba (UNEAC)

Havana, Cuba

JUSTO ALBERTO CHÁVEZ RODRÍGUEZ

Principal Researcher, Instituto Central de Ciencias Pedagógicas

Professor, Academia de Ciencias de Cuba

ROBERTO COBAS AMATE

Museo Nacional de Bellas Artes

Havana, Cuba

MARIO COYULA-COWLEY

Architect; Distinguished Professor, Faculty of Architecture

Instituto Superior Politécnico José Antonio Echeverría (ISPJAE/CUJAE), Havana, Cuba

GRACIELLA CRUZ-TAURA

Associate Professor, Department of History

Florida Atlantic University

MAYRA CUÉ SIERRA

Adjunct Professor

Universidad de La Habana, Havana, Cuba

JULIA CUERVO HEWITT

Associate Professor of Spanish and Portuguese, Department of Spanish, Italian, and Portuguese

Pennsylvania State University

EMILIO CUETO

Independent Scholar

MARÍA CARIDAD CUMANÁ GONZÁLEZ

Adjunct Professor, Department of Arts and Letters

Universidad de La Habana, Havana, Cuba

GUILLERMINA DE FERRARI

Associate Professor, Latin American and Caribbean Literature

University of Wisconsin-Madison

HÉCTOR DELGADO

Professional Photographer

Havana, Cuba

DANAE C. DIÉGUEZ

Assistant Professor, Department of History and Media Theory

Facultad de Arte de los Medios de Comunicación Audiovisual del Instituto Superior de Arte; Universidad de las Artes, Cuba

JORGE DUANY

Professor, Department of Sociology and Anthropology

University of Puerto Rico, Río Piedras

ILAN EHRLICH

Assistant Professor, Division of Arts, Humanities, and Wellness

Bergen Community College

VICTORIA ELI RODRÍGUEZ

Professor, Department of Musicology
Universidad Complutense de Madrid, Spain

ROSA MIRIAM ELIZALDE

Editor
Cubadebate

EUMELIO M. ESPINO MARRERO

Director of Development
Instituto de Investigaciones del Tabaco de Cuba

CARLOS ESPINOSA DOMÍNGUEZ

Assistant Professor, Department of Foreign Languages
Mississippi State University

NORGE ESPINOSA MENDOZA

Poet, Playwright, and Gay Activist
Revista Extramuros, Centro Provincial del Libro y la Literatura, Havana, Cuba

REINALDO ESTRADA ESTRADA

Research Assistant
Fundación Antonio Núñez Jiménez de la Naturaleza y el Hombre, Havana, Cuba

TONY ÉVORA

Musicologist, Painter
Valencia, Spain

ALBERTO FAYA

Singer-Songwriter, Co-Founder of the Nueva Trova Movement
Radio and Television Writer and Commentator

JORGE FEBLES

Professor and Chair of Department of Languages, Literatures and Cultures
University of North Florida

JULIE M. FEINSILVER

Senior Research Fellow
Council on Hemispheric Affairs (COHA)

ANTONIO ELIGIO FERNÁNDEZ

Independent Artist and Art Critic
Vancouver, Canada

RAÚL FERNÁNDEZ

Professor, School of Social Sciences
University of California, Irvine

SUSAN J. FERNANDEZ

Associate Professor, Department of History

University of South Florida, St. Petersburg

TOMÁS FERNÁNDEZ ROBAINA

Senior Professor and Researcher
Biblioteca Nacional de Cuba; Universidad de La Habana, Havana, Cuba

JAVIER FIGUEROA

History Department
University of Puerto Rico, Río Piedras

LUDÍN B. FONSECA GARCÍA

Director, Casa de la Nacionalidad Cubana, Bayamo, Cuba
Member, Unión Nacional de Historiadores de Cuba, Unión de Escritores y Artistas de Cuba (UNEAC), Academia de Historia de Cuba

AMBROSIO FORNET

Member
Unión de Escritores y Artistas de Cuba (UNEAC)

JORGE FORNET

Director del Centro de Investigaciones Literarias
Casa de las Américas, Havana, Cuba

VÍCTOR FOWLER CALZADA

Poet and Essayist
Member, Unión de Escritores y Artistas de Cuba (UNEAC)

CELESTE FRASER DELGADO

Associate Professor, Department of English
Barry University

REINALDO FUNES MONZOTE

Adjunct Professor, Department of History, Universidad de La Habana, Havana, Cuba
Fundación Antonio Núñez Jiménez de la Naturaleza y el Hombre

DAVID F. GARCÍA

Director of Charanga Carolina and Professor of Ethnomusicology, Music Department
University of North Carolina at Chapel Hill

GUADALUPE GARCÍA

Assistant Professor, Department of History
Tulane University

ALEJANDRO GARCIA ÁLVAREZ

Professor, Universidad de La Habana, Havana, Cuba

Member of Unión de Escritores y Artistas de Cuba (UNEAC), Academia de la Historia de Cuba, and the Asociación de Historiadores de América Latina y el Caribe (ADHILAC)

ROLANDO GARCÍA BLANCO

Researcher, Museo Nacional de Historia de las Ciencias "Carlos J. Finlay"
Member, Unión de Historiadores de Cuba, Unión de Escritores y Artistas de Cuba (UNEAC), and Academia de la Historia de Cuba

JUAN ANTONIO GARCÍA BORRERO

President, Cátedra de Pensamiento "Tomás Gutiérrez Alea"
Member, Unión de Escritores y Artistas de Cuba (UNEAC)

AUGUSTO C. GARCÍA DEL PINO CHEN

Historian
Unión Nacional de Historiadores de Cuba (UNHIC)

ORLANDO F. GARCÍA MARTÍNEZ

Independent Scholar
Cienfuegos, Cuba

MERCEDES GARCÍA RODRÍGUEZ

Principal Researcher and Senior Professor, Casa de Altos Estudios Don Fernando Ortiz, Universidad de La Habana, Havana, Cuba
Member, Academia de la Historia de Cuba, Asociación de Historiadores Latinoamericanos y del Caribe (ADHILAC), Unión de Escritores y Artistas de Cuba (UNEAC), and Unión Nacional de Historiadores de Cuba (UNHIC)

MAURO G. GARCÍA TRIANA

Historian
Unión Nacional de Historiadores de Cuba (UNHIC)

GLADYS MAREL GARCÍA PÉREZ

Senior Researcher, Academia de Ciencias de Cuba. Specialist in Women and Gender Studies
Director, Grupo de Estudios Cubanos, Unión de Escritores y Artistas de Cuba (UNEAC)

ALBERTO GARRANDÉS

Novelist and Critic
Havana, Cuba

RADAMÉS GIRO

*Independent Researcher and Principal
Editor*

Ediciones Museo de la Música, Cuba

GISELLE VICTORIA GÓMEZ

Independent Curator

*Researcher, Instituto Cubano de
Investigación Cultural (ICIC) Juan
Marinello, Havana, Cuba*

MAGDA GONZÁLEZ GRAU

Television Director

*Member, Unión de Escritores y Artistas de
Cuba (UNEAC)*

**JULIO CÉSAR GONZÁLEZ
LAUREIRO**

*Specialist in Services, Processes, and Data
Analysis, Universidad de La Habana,
Havana, Cuba*

*Member, Unión de Escritores y Artistas de
Cuba (UNEAC)*

FLORA GONZÁLEZ MANDRI

Emerson College

JULIO CÉSAR GONZÁLEZ PAGÉS

Professor

Universidad de la Habana, Havana, Cuba

GUILLERMO J. GRENIER

Professor, Department of Sociology

Florida International University

**JULIO CESAR GUANCHE
ZALDIVAR**

Essayist and Professor

New Latin-American Cinema Festival

RAMIRO GUERRA

Dancer, Choreographer, and Essayist

*Founding Director, Conjunto Nacional de
Danza Moderna de Cuba*

*Founding Member, Unión de Escritores y
Artistas de Cuba (UNEAC)*

GUSTAVO GUERRERO

Université de Cergy-Pontoise, France

LAURA G. GUTIÉRREZ

*Associate Professor, Department of Spanish
& Portuguese*

University of Arizona

PATRICK J. HANEY

Department of Political Science

Miami University, Oxford, Ohio

KATRIN HANSING

*Associate Professor, Black and Hispanic
Studies*

*Baruch College, City University of New
York*

EVGENIJ HAPERSKIJ

Council on Hemispheric Affairs

ORLANDO HERNÁNDEZ PASCUAL

*Writer, Poet, Researcher, Art Historian,
Art Critic, Havana, Cuba*

*Member, Unión de Escritores y Artistas
de Cuba (UNEAC) and International
Association of Art Critics (AICA–
Southern Caribbean)*

**RAFAEL M. HERNÁNDEZ
RODRIGUEZ**

Chief Editor

Temas. Ideología, Cultura, Sociedad

MARTA HERNÁNDEZ SALVÁN

*Assistant Professor of Spanish, Department
of Hispanic Studies*

University of California, Riverside

MAITÉ HERNÁNDEZ-LORENZO

*Adjunct Professor, Instituto Superior de
Arte, Havana, Cuba*

*Member, Unión de Escritores y Artistas de
Cuba (UNEAC)*

LINDA S. HOWE

*Associate Professor of Spanish, Department
of Romance Languages*

Wake Forest University

JORGE RENATO IBARRA GUITART

Assistant Researcher

Instituto de Historia de Cuba

GLENN JACOBS

Associate Professor of Sociology

University of Massachusetts-Boston

HÉCTOR JAIMES

*Associate Professor, Department of Foreign
Languages and Literatures*

North Carolina State University

GUILLERMO JIMÉNEZ SOLER

Lawyer, Historian

*Unión de Escritores y Artistas de Cuba
(UNEAC); Member of Academia de la*

Historia de Cuba

CATHERINE KRULL

Associate Dean, Faculty of Arts and Science

Queen's University, Canada

JENNIFER LAMBE

Department of History

Yale University

CARRIE LAMBERT-BEATTY

*John L. Loeb Associate Professor of the
Humanities, Department of History of
Art and Architecture; Department of
Visual and Environmental Studies*

Harvard University

SAUL LANDAU

Professor Emeritus

California State University, Pomona

ZOILA MERCEDES LAPIQUE BECALIS

*Member, Academia de Historia de Cuba;
Unión de Escritores y Artistas de Cuba
(UNEAC)*

*Doctora Honora of Instituto Superior de
Arte*

MARTA LESMES ALBIS

*Researcher, Instituto de Literatura y
Lingüística "José Antonio Portuondo
Valdor"*

*Professor, Universidad de La Habana,
Havana, Cuba*

JOHN M. LIPSKI

*Department of Spanish, Italian, and
Portuguese*

Pennsylvania State University

ANA M. LÓPEZ

*Associate Provost, Office of Academic
Affairs; Director, Cuban and
Caribbean Studies Institute*

Tulane University

FÉLIX JULIO ALFONSO LÓPEZ

*Professor, Colegio Universitario San
Gerónimo de La Habana, Havana, Cuba*

IRAIDA H. LOPEZ

Ramapo College of New Jersey

VIRGILIO LÓPEZ LEMUS

*Poet, Essayist, Professor, Principal
Researcher, Senior Fellow*

Academia de Ciencias de Cuba

JACQUELINE LOSS

Associate Professor, Department of Modern and Classical Languages

University of Connecticut

BONNIE ADORNO LUCERO

University of North Carolina at Chapel Hill

CARLOS M. LUIS

Retired Professor, St. John Vianney College Seminary

Art Critic, Arte al Día

WILLIAM LUIS

Gertrude Conaway Vanderbilt Chair in Spanish and Editor of Afro-Hispanic Review, Department of Spanish and Portuguese

Vanderbilt University

HUMBERTO MANDULEY LÓPEZ

Independent Scholar

Havana, Cuba

LILLIAN MANZOR

Associate Professor of Spanish; Director, Cuban Theater Digital Archive

University of Miami

INÉS MARÍA MARTIATU

Cultural Critic and Narrator

Havana, Cuba

JUAN A. MARTÍNEZ

Professor and Chair, Department of Art and Art History

Florida International University

URBANO MARTÍNEZ CARMENATE

Chairman of the Scientific Council of the Provincial Directorate of Culture

Museo Provincial Palacio de Junco, Matanzas, Cuba

FERNANDO MARTÍNEZ HEREDIA

Principal Researcher; Director General

Instituto Cubano de Investigación Cultural Juan Marinello, Havana, Cuba

LUIS MARTÍNEZ-FERNÁNDEZ

History Department

University of Central Florida

JORGE MARTURANO

Assistant Professor, Department of Spanish and Portuguese

University of California, Los Angeles

MARGARITA MATEO PALMER

Teacher, Consultant

Instituto Superior de Artes, Havana, Cuba

LUZ M. MENA

Assistant Professor, Women and Gender Studies

University of California, Davis

ROBERTO MÉNDEZ MARTÍNEZ

Member, Unión de Escritores y Artistas de Cuba (UNEAC)

Member, Academia Cubana de la Lengua

ADRIANA MÉNDEZ RODENAS

Professor, Department of Spanish and Portuguese

University of Iowa

ELIO MENÉNDEZ

Sportswriter

Havana, Cuba

JUAN MESA DÍAZ

Adjunct and Visiting Professor at Universities in Cuba, Canada, and Spain

Member, Unión de Escritores y Artistas de Cuba (UNEAC)

IVOR MILLER

Research Fellow, African Studies Center

Boston University

NANCY RAQUEL MIRABAL

Associate Professor, Latina/o Studies

San Francisco State University

NIVIA MONTENEGRO

Professor, Department of Romance Languages and Literatures

Pomona College

OSCAR MONTERO

Professor, Department of Languages and Literatures

Lehman College, City University of New York

HORTENSIA MONTERO MÉNDEZ

Curator of Cuban Art

Museo Nacional de Bellas Artes (MNBA), Havana, Cuba

DANNYS MONTES DE OCA MOREDA

Art Critic and Curator

Centro de Arte Contemporáneo Wifredo Lam and the Havana Biennial

MATÍAS MONTES HUIDOBRO

Professor Emeritus, Department of European Languages

University of Hawaii

INÉS MORALES

Florida International University

ESTEBAN MORALES DOMÍNGUEZ

Professor of Economics and Political Science, Universidad de La Habana, Havana, Cuba

Member, Unión de Escritores y Artistas de Cuba (UNEAC)

PEDRO MORALES-LÓPEZ

Professor, Universidad Pedagógica Nacional, Bogotá, Colombia

Member, Unión de Escritores y Artistas de Cuba (UNEAC), the Asociación Cultural Yoruba de Cuba, and the Asociación Colombiana para el Avance de la Ciencia

FRANCISCO MORÁN

Associate Professor of Spanish, Foreign Languages and Literatures

Southern Methodist University

NANCY MOREJÓN

Writer, Poet

Havana, Cuba

ISABEL MOYA RICHARD

Director

Editorial de la Mujer

MIRTA MUÑIZ EGEA

Professor, Universidad de La Habana; Member, Consejo Nacional de la Asociación Cubana de Comunicadores Sociales

Member, Sección de Radio y Televisión, Unión de Escritores y Artistas de Cuba (UNEAC)

ROBERT L. MUSE

Lawyer

Law Offices of Robert L. Muse

JOSHUA H. NADEL
Assistant Professor, Department of History
North Carolina Central University

CONSUELO NARANJO OROVIO
Researcher
Instituto de Historia, Consejo Superior de Investigaciones Científicas-Centro de Ciencias Humanas y Sociales-Antillas, Madrid, Spain

ROBERT C. NATHAN
Institute for the Study of the Americas
University of North Carolina at Chapel Hill

YOEL CORDOVÍ NÚÑEZ
Researcher
Instituto de Historia de Cuba

ILEANA OROZA
Lecturer, School of Communication
University of Miami

VÍCTOR JOAQUÍN ORTEGA IZQUIERDO
Writer and Journalist
President, Equipo Nacional de Historia del Deporte de Cuba
Member, Unión de Escritores y Artistas de Cuba (UNEAC); Unión de Periodistas de Cuba; Unión Nacional de Historiadores de Cuba

RICARDO L. ORTÍZ
Director of Graduate Studies; Associate Professor of U.S. Latino Literature and Culture, Department of English
Georgetown University

FRANK PADRÓN
Critic, Essayist, and Writer
Havana, Cuba

MELINA PAPPADEMOS
Assistant Professor of History & African American Studies
University of Connecticut, Storrs

SILVIA PEDRAZA
Department of Sociology and Program in American Culture
University of Michigan

LISANDRO PÉREZ
Professor and Chair, Department of Latin American and Latina/o Studies

John Jay College of Criminal Justice, City University of New York

ENRIQUE PÉREZ DÍAZ
Writer, Researcher, Editor in Chief
Havana, Cuba

GUSTAVO PÉREZ FIRMAT
David Feinson Professor of Humanities, Department of Latin American and Iberian Cultures
Columbia University

GRAZIELLA POGOLOTTI
President, Fundación Alejo Carpentier
General Counsel, Unión de Escritores y Artistas de Cuba (UNEAC)

ANTONIO JOSÉ PONTE
Writer, Vice Director
Diario de Cuba

OLGA SARINA PORTUONDO ZÚÑIGA
Professor, Universidad de Oriente
Historian, City of Santiago de Cuba

GERALD E. POYO
Professor and Chair, Department of History
St. Mary's University, San Antonio, Texas

SANTIAGO PRADO PÉREZ DE PEÑAMIL
Researcher and Television and Film Director
Televisión Cubana, Instituto Cubano de Radio y Televisión

PATRICIA PRICE
Associate Professor, International Relations
Florida International University, Miami

YOLANDA PRIETO
Professor Emerita, School of Social Science and Human Services
Ramapo College

ROLANDO PUJOL
Professional Photographer
Havana, Cuba

E. CARMEN RAMOS
Department of Art History
University of Chicago

ALBERTO RAMOS RUIZ
Festival Programmer, Festival Internacional del Nuevo Cine Latinoamericano de La Habana
Havana, Cuba

CARLOS EDUARDO REIG ROMERO
Independent Researcher, Havana, Cuba
Member, Unión de Escritores y Artistas de Cuba (UNEAC)

FRANCISCO REY ALFONSO
Historian of the Gran Teatro de La Habana
Havana, Cuba

DEAN LUIS REYES
Independent Scholar
Havana, Cuba

ARCHIBALD R. M. RITTER
Professor, Department of Economics and Norman Paterson School of International Affairs
Carleton University

PEDRO PABLO RODRÍGUEZ
Centro de Estudios Martianos de La Habana
Havana, Cuba

REINA MARÍA RODRÍGUEZ
Poet
Cuba

LAURA ROULET
Independent Scholar
Bethesda, Maryland

JORGE RUFFINELLI
Professor, Director of Department of Iberian and Latin American Cultures
Stanford University

ENRIQUE SAÍNZ
Senior Researcher
Academia Cubana de la Lengua

DAVID SARTORIUS
Assistant Professor, Department of History
University of Maryland

PAUL A. SCHROEDER RODRÍGUEZ
Professor and Chair, Department of Foreign Languages and Literatures
Northeastern Illinois University, Chicago

RICHARD SCHWEID
Independent Scholar
Barcelona, Spain

YESENIA SELIER
Center for Latin American and Caribbean Studies
New York University

ANA SERRA
Associate Professor of Spanish and Latin American Studies, Department of Language and Foreign Studies
American University

ESTER R. SHAPIRO
Associate Professor, Psychology Department
University of Massachusetts, Boston

NOHEMY SOLÓRZANO-THOMPSON
Assistant Professor of Spanish, Spanish Department
Whitman College

ARTURO SORHEGUI D'MARES
Historian
Havana, Cuba

GONZALO SORUCO
Associate Professor, School of Communication
University of Miami

ANN MARIE STOCK
Professor of Hispanic Studies and Film Studies, Department of Modern Languages and Literatures
College of William and Mary

K. LYNN STONER
Associate Professor, Department of History
Arizona State University

JEAN STUBBS
Professor, Institute for the Study of the Americas
University of London

NED SUBLETTE
Center for Postmambo Studies

MANUEL JORGE SUZARTE
Specialist, U.S.-Latin American Relations and Migratory Studies
Grupo de Estudios Cubanos; Unión de Escritores y Artistas de Cuba (UNEAC)

SUSAN THOMAS
Assistant Professor, School of Music
University of Georgia

ARACELI TINAJERO
Associate Professor
The City College of New York and the Graduate Center

MARÍA DE LOS ANGELES TORRES
Director and Professor, Latin American and Latino Studies
University of Illinois, Chicago

OMAR VALIÑO CEDRÉ
Director of the Cuban Theater Magazine Tablas

SARA VEGA MICHE
Specialist in Cuban Film and Posters
Cinemateca de Cuba

JOSÉ VEGA SUÑOL
Member, Unión de Escritores y Artistas de Cuba (UNEAC)
Holguín, Cuba

CARLOS VENEGAS FORNIAS
Instituto Cubano de Investigación Cultural Juan Marinello

Havana, Cuba

MARÍA DEL CARMEN VICTORI RAMOS
Independent Scholar
Miami, Florida

RACHEL WEISS
Professor, Department of Arts Administration and Policy
School of the Art Institute of Chicago

ALAN WEST-DURÁN
Associate Professor, Department of Languages, Literatures and Cultures
Northeastern University

ESTHER WHITFIELD
Assistant Professor of Comparative Literature, Department of Comparative Literature
Brown University

ROBERT WHITNEY
Associate Professor of History, Department of History
University of New Brunswick (Saint John)

THOMAS C. WRIGHT
Distinguished Professor, Department of History
University of Nevada, Las Vegas

OSCAR ZANETTI
Universidad de La Habana, Havana, Cuba
Member, Unión de Escritores y Artistas de Cuba (UNEAC); Academia de la Historia de Cuba

ROBERTO ZURBANO
Essayist, Editor, and Cultural Critic
Director, Fondo Editorial Casa de las Américas, Havana, Cuba

L

LANGUAGE

Essential to any understanding any nation and its culture, language is intricately involved with Cuban history and identity. Because of its colonial past, Spanish is the principal and official language of the island, but that does not mean that it was the only language spoken. Enslaved Africans brought to the island spoke languages that are still used in Cuba today, although in religious or ritual contexts, not as vernacular languages.

In what follows, three of these languages will be examined: Spanish, Lucumí, and Abakuá. Spanish in Cuba has absorbed many words from the latter two, and it is in Spanish usage where these African languages, quite transformed, can be heard in Cuban conversations.

The rich history of these three languages and their interrelationships have helped ground one of the richest literary traditions of Latin America and the Spanish-speaking Caribbean. If scholars such as Esteban Pichardo (nineteenth century), Fernando Ortiz (twentieth century), and Sergio Valdés Bernal (twenty-first century) have made major contributions to the study of Cuban Spanish, Cubans outside the island as well as its great writers such as José Martí, Alejo Carpentier, José Lezama, Nicolás Guillén, Guillermo Cabrera Infante, and Severo Sarduy have delighted readers around the world by using their highly original use of language in works of extraordinary imagination. In their hands, language is memory, creation, celebration, Cuban culture speaking.

LANGUAGE: ABAKUÁ IN CUBA AND ITS INFLUENCE ON SPANISH USAGE

Ivor Miller

A language used exclusively for ceremonial purposes by members of the Abakuá Society.

People from a variety of distinct ethnic groups of the Cross River region of southeastern Nigeria and western Cameroon were taken as slaves to the Caribbean region from the sixteenth to nineteenth centuries. Because the port from which many departed was called Old Calabar, many of them became known as *Calabarí* (and later in Cuba, *Carabalí*, reversing the *l*

and *r*), the same way that various Yorùbá subgroups became known collectively as the *Lukumí*, and various Central African Bantu groups became known as the *Congo*. One way to understand the transformation of many distinct but culturally related peoples into the Cuban Carabalí is to examine the sources for their best known cultural expression, the Abakuá initiation society and its language.

Abakuá was modeled upon the Ékpè leopard societies of the Calabar region, illustrated by the thousands of ritual Abakuá phrases based upon Ékpè codes, as documented by the Cuban folklorist Lydia Cabrera (1899–1991). The influence of Spanish is minimal, found primarily in the plural endings of words. Abakuá is an esoteric language used exclusively for ceremonial purposes that contains a mixture of various initiation dialects (called *argots* by some scholars) of the Cross River region, specifically derived from Ékpè practice.

Many West African guilds—including those for bàtá and dùndún drummers (called *Àyàn*), or the titled elders in the Ìgbo kingdom of Nri—had initiation languages unknown to non-initiates. In Cuba, many key Abakuá terms and phrases are slightly transformed from words still used in the Calabar region, where Èfìk-Ìbìbìò was the lingua franca for many distinct language communities that also practiced local variants of Ékpè. The evidence implies that many aspects of Abakuá language preceded the Middle Passage and, therefore, were not created by the historical process of transformation in the Caribbean known as creolization.

For example, *Ekório Enyéne Abakuá*, the name of the society in Cuba, is interpreted as "a group founded by a sacred mother that is called Abakuá." This phrase is understood by speakers of Qua-Éjághám in Calabar as *Ekoea Nyen Àbàkpà* (the forest is the mother of the Àbàkpà community), a meaning appreciated by Abakuá leaders. The Abakuá word *íreme* (spirit dancer) derives from the Èfìk *ídèm*; Ékue (sacred drum) derives from the Èfìk *ékpè* (leopard).

In nineteenth-century Matanzas, Abakuá members spoke a language called Suáma (Ìsú-Amá), a variant of Ìgbo. Never central to Abakuá practice, and in modern times only a memory, Suáma was displaced by Bríkamo Carabalí, Abakuá's standard ritual language. Bríkamo is held to be the language of the Usagaré (or Ùsàghàdè) community, the legendary founders of Ékpè in the estuary zone of the present-day Cameroon-Nigeria border. Abakuá say the phrase "Manyón bríkamo manyón usagaré" to indicate that Bríkamo is authentic because it comes from Ùsàghàdè. The lack of linguistic studies in this region limits outsiders' knowledge, but to the north, in the city of Ikom, *Brika mmo* means "this one is good (or authentic)," in the Nkòmè language. Because Ùsàghàdèt was recognized as a source for Ékpè teachings in the Cross River region, as the society spread regionally, so did its ritual language.

Abakuá source texts—the epic narrative of the society's creation in West Africa—were written in manuscript form in the nineteenth century and taught piecemeal in apprenticeship with masters. The performance of Abakuá language is a key element to leadership in the society. Members constantly test each other's knowledge by conversing in Abakuá, responding to one phrase with another to take the discussion further until a gap is left that the less knowledgeable person cannot fill.

The Abakuá language has influenced Cuban popular speech, as in the word *chébere* (*chévere*), which is used popularly to mean "valiant, wonderful, excellent" after *Ma' chébere*, a title of the Abakuá dignitary Mokóngo. The Abakuá terms *ekóbio* and *monína* (both meaning "ritual brother") are used as standard greetings among urban Cuban males. *Asére* (greetings) derives from the Èfìk *esiere* (good evening). Abakuá-inspired street lingo has been recorded in popular music, as in the song "Los Sitio' Asere" (Salutation to Los Sitios), which refers to a Havana barrio that is home to several Abakuá groups.

In addition, Abakuá sayings and moral codes have been translated into Spanish. For example, *Mútián keréké wasán korókó iruá/ Oreja no puede pasar cabeza* (The ear cannot surpass the head) means, in effect, that youth cannot surpass the knowledge of an elder.

The ability of scholars to understand the influence of languages from the Cross River region on the Abakuá ritual language is greatly limited by the lack of research on Cross River languages themselves. Although the Cross River is one of the most diverse linguistic regions in the world, Èfìk remains the only language to have a large dictionary, and many languages of the hinterlands have no native-speaking linguists working on them. Another issue is that historically most of the formally trained linguists working in the region were educated in Christian settings where they were trained to shy away from analyzing terms related to ancient ritual practices. Yet in the Caribbean these practices were used to organize communities during the colonial period, so understanding them is key to understanding the formative period of African presence in the Americas.

Another key issue is the tonal nature of Èfìk and other Cross River languages. Because Abakuá is not a mother tongue, but rather a set of codes learned after adolescence, the two tones of Èfìk, for example, have been lost in Cuban pronunciation. Without such knowledge and the use of diacritics to indicate tones in writing, Roman spellings of Èfìk words are either ambiguous (out of context) or meaningless. One would be unable to distinguish the Ékpè and Abakuá chieftaincy title *Mbàkàrà* and the Èfìk term *Mbàkárá*, meaning "those who govern," popularly used to mean "white man." Or to distinguish *úyò* (voice) from *ùyó* (biscuit). Or the term for the Ékpè leopard club of the Cross River region from the term for the Èkpè religious ritual among neighboring Ìgbos. Or in Éjághám, *nsí* (earth) from *nsí* (fish). Diacritics have not yet become standard in Èfìk publications, and more research is required toward this end.

BIBLIOGRAPHY

Abímbólá, 'Wándé, and Ivor Miller. *Ifá Will Mend Our Broken World: Thoughts on Yorùbá Culture in West Africa and the Diaspora.* Roxbury, MA: AIM Books, 1997.

Cabrera, Lydia. *La lengua sagrada de los ñañigos.* Miami: Colección del Chicherekú en el exilio, 1988.

Essien, Okon E. "Ibibio Orthography." In *Orthographies of Nigerian Languages,* edited by Ayo Banjo. Lagos: National Language Centre, Federal Ministry of Education, 1985.

Goldie, Hugh. *A Dictionary of the Efik Language, in Two Parts. 1. Efik and English. 2. English and Efik.* Originally published 1862. Westmead, U.K.: Gregg Press, 1964.

Manfredi, Victor. "Philological Perspectives on the Southeastern Nigerian Diaspora." *Contours: A Journal of the African Diaspora* 2, no. 2 (2004): 239–287.

LANGUAGE: LUCUMÍ

Juan Mesa Díaz

A ritual language developed in Cuba from the Yoruba language brought to Cuba by African slaves.

The Yoruba ritual language in Cuba is known as Lucumí from the terms *lùkumí* or *ùlkumí*, used very early on to refer to the Yoruba language or to the people who spoke it. Lucumí is a ritual version of the Yoruba language evolved in Cuba, used only in the rituals of the Afro-Cuban religion Regla de Ocha-Ifá; it is not spoken conversationally. Yet its influences are still profound in Cuban Spanish.

Yoruba belongs to the oral tradition of the Yoruba ethnic group, members of which were introduced to the island as slaves at the beginning of the seventeenth century from what is now known as Nigeria, Benin, and Togo. This group achieved a massive presence during the height of the sugar plantation system in western Cuba (from the end of the eighteenth century to the middle of the nineteenth century). These circumstances caused the language to be more concentrated in the areas of Havana, Matanzas, and other towns in the west-central area of the country. Here, Yoruba was associated with the religious ceremonies of the Regla de Ocha-Ifá (or Santería) and, to a lesser extent, secular activities such as dancing and music that became part of the national culture.

Yoruba is part of the dialectal continuum belonging to the Kwa subset of Benue-Congo languages. It was one of the first African languages to be codified grammatically and in a dictionary, a task undertaken by Samuel Crowther (1806–1891), a Yoruba bishop who had been freed from slavery en route to the Americas, taken to Sierra Leone and later Britain where he converted to Christianity and was ordained before returning to serve in his home country. It is a tonal language in which the mid, high, and low tones define the meaning of words. That is, the same word pronounced using a different tone can and does have a different meaning.

Yoruba has seven different vowels:

A, Ê, É, I, Ô, Ó, U

And it does not contain these letters:

C, Ñ, Q, V, X and Z

Yoruba is not studied systematically in religious communities. Many initiates try to learn the language mimetically, with no literal and only an approximate understanding of what they choose to repeat. More and more adherents insist on learning it any way they can. Learning Yoruba primarily through oral transmission has produced a plethora of spelling and pronunciation variations, in accord with the distinctive creolized Caribbean-inflected Spanish spoken by Cubans. The fact that the initial disseminators of religious texts also had very limited command of the written language resulted in several distortions in the way Yoruba in Cuba is written. These distortions are what created Lucumí from its Yoruba parent language. Lucumí's pronunciation also seems archaic, given that, due to its ritual character, it did not evolve or change over time the way its mother tongue did across the Atlantic. Regardless, the ritual language is tenacious and persists into the twenty-first century, along with its archaisms and distortions, tied to a vital and undeniably expanding religious system. It permeates popular culture on a daily basis, not only infiltrating Cuba's spoken Spanish but also quietly and continuously gaining new initiates. Some of its terms have been incorporated into popular jargon, although as of 2011 they had yet to be officially recognized by the Real Academia Española (RAE; Royal Academy of the Spanish Language).

ATTEMPTS AT CODIFICATION (AND CHANGES) IN CUBA

Anagó, a monumental book by Lydia Cabrera first published in 1957, with an introduction by Roger Bastide, represents a truly valuable attempt to survey Yoruba ritual language in Cuba. These scholars refer to the testimonial language as "words saved by faith" and "the expression of linguistic resistance" (p. 10), and they also record how and to what extent it has intermingled with Spanish. Moreover, Cabrera records the *criollo*, referring to the manner of writing down terms and expressions as they are pronounced and written in Cuba, without altering their original meaning, an invaluable contribution.

Many priests and priestesses in modern times thumb through Cabrera's book and its many typed or photocopied versions to find the meanings of terms used with ever-growing frequency in ceremonies, songs, and prayers. Other valuable contributions to the study of Lucumí include the books of Gumercindo Fernandes Portugal and the works of Cuban members of religious orders.

Due in part to the proliferation of transliterations and lack of a comprehensive standard, the worship of traditional Yoruba deities has taken on new spellings and meanings, within a Cuban context. Words from the Yoruba will be followed by a (Y), otherwise the spelling or transliteration is from Cuban spellings of Lucumí. *Ôrìsá* (Y) might be spelled *orisha* or *oricha* in Cuba. *Sàngó* (Y) might be spelled *Shangó* or *Changó*, and *Oshún* or *Ochún* are acceptable spellings of *Ósun* (Y). Cubans spell Changó, Oricha, and Ochún with a *-c*, but some still spell *orisha* with an *-s*. Likewise, the name of the Yoruba deity Iyèmojá (Y) is a combination of *iyá* (mother); *mo* (of the); *ejá* (fish), that is, *mother of the fish*. In Cuba the name of this *orisha* is spelled and pronounced Yemayá. Similarly, *Ôlòkún* (Y) in Cuba is Olokun (from the Yoruba *ôló* [master] and *òkún* [sea], that is, *master of the sea*).

The Yoruba term *èégúngún* (Y) is used to refer to the spirits of the dead but has been simplified in

Cuba to *eggun*, stressing the first syllable (**é**-gun as opposed to e-**gún**) in conformity with Spanish rules of pronunciation The expression of respect and veneration, *kábò kábíyèsí ilé* (Y) (literally *welcome home, Royal Majesty*), addressed exclusively to Changó, is pronounced and written *Kabo, kabiosile, Changó*; as a result, this deity, in a manner that approaches the secular and with the familiar tone that Cubans sometimes use, is sometimes called "Kabiosile" or simply "El Kabo," a kind of abbreviated reference to Changó.

Some Lucumí terms have been *spanishized*. This has familiarized them in a unique way; if Lucumí is already a transformation of Yoruba from Nigeria, then this represents a second-level order of transformation. For example, *àgó mo júbà* (Y) (an invocation of respect, literally *our respect*) known in Reglas de Ocha-Ifá ritual environments as *moyugba*, has been transformed and printed in the liner notes of albums by Lázaro Ros as *moyugbación*, which should imply "the act of *moyugbar*," as if "*moyugbar*" were a Spanish verb. The Lucumí "spanishized" verb *yugbonear* is derived from either the Yoruba *oyugbona* or *oyulona* (literally *the eyes of the road*), terms for a religious official responsible for guiding and helping novitiates in initiation ceremonies and who acts as a second official to the godfather or godmother. In turn, *yugbonear* means *to assume this responsibility*. In reference to these officials, *yugbonear* also takes on the Spanish forms of gender: *la oyugbona* is female and *el yugbón* is male. A similar process occurs with the word *iyawó* (novitiate, literally *married to the orisha* or *married to the religious secret*), which has generated another term to refer to the one-year period in which the novice must obey certain strict rules: *yaworaje*. The neologism in Spanish draws on the word *iyawó*, but by adding the *-raje* suffix from Spanish creates a new noun.

Modifications in the vocabulary are also found in Cuba as a result of Yoruba's feature of allowing the formation of new words by juxtaposing words or by condensing several words into one. Such is the case for *ilé Olokun*, which in Cuba refers to "the house of Olokun," or the sea; *Òkun* (Y) in Lucumí is written as *Okún*. An example of new terms created by juxtaposition can be seen with the Yoruba word *ojú*, which means *eye* (*oyú* in Cuba). Starting from this term speakers can form other words, such as *ojú ibo* (place of worship) or *ojú òrun* (visible surface of the sky). In Cuba, these words (for eye and surface) remain in their archaic versions, as *ará orun* (the heavenly ground)— from *ará* (earth) + *orun* (the realm of the eternal). Another example of juxtaposing words to form a new meaning is apparent in the place of worship, called *ibodú* (place where the sacred word descends) from *ibo* (sacred place) + *odun* (sacred breath or sacred word) or *igbodú* made up of *igba* (vessel, continent) + *odun*.

Imprecision in the interpretations of homonyms has provoked many debates and discussions. The term

apetebí ayafá (also *iyafá*) refers to the initiated woman as host of ceremonies and helper of the priest of Ifá, rooted in the word *ayafá* (*àyá* [wife] + *ifá* [the religion that gives the deity its name]). The word *àyá* has sometimes been confused with the word *àjá* (dog). The difference between both words is a subtle change in pronunciation, and their similarity has led to allegations of chauvinism against practitioners of Ifá, assuming that women are referred to as "the dogs" of Ifá. However, the true meaning of the term *apetebí* is "born and consecrated in virtue," a concept of utmost esteem.

There are also some differences between meanings of certain source words and the ones that have been preserved in Cuba, for example *tútú* (frozen) (in Cuba *tuto* [fresh]); *àpòtí* (box) (in Cuba *apotí* [chair]); *àlejó* (visit) and *àjejó* (foreigner) (in Cuba, *aleyo* [not initiated]); *oôgun* (medicine, remedy) (in Cuba *ogu* refers mostly to (witchcraft).

Ritual terminology has nourished popular language. In vernacular speech, *estar iré* (to be *iré*) means to enjoy life's bounty; obviously, the Lucumí term *iré* (good fortune) gives the idiom its meaning in Spanish. Likewise, *estar osogbo* means the opposite. If someone yells "*Ashelú!*" (police) in the street, people are bound to recognize its meaning. To feel *odara* means to be clean. *Tremendo arayé!* (Such *arayé*!) is similar to "What a problem!" Whoever "gets it from *Osá*" (an *odun* that governs, among other things, nervous problems) does so because he or she "is sick in the head."

Throughout Cuba's turbulent history, many social, academic, and intellectual groups have challenged the view of Lucumí as a national heritage; such stances were aligned with a dominant culture that denied the integral roles of African and Afro-Cuban heritage on Cuba's cultural identity. The word *Yorubá* (with stress on the last syllable in Nigeria) itself has been spanishized so that the pronunciation falls in line with Spanish rules of pronunciation. Cubans always seem to uncover the poetry in the essence of words in their fullest dimension, as in the beautiful poem by the great and very Cuban Nicolás Guillén (1902–1989).

SON NUMBER 6 (FRAGMENTS)

Yoruba I am, I weep in Yoruba
lucumí.
Because I am a Yoruba from Cuba,
I want to hoist my Yoruba lament to Cuba,
let my happy Yoruba cry ascend
out of me.

Yoruba I am;
I sing as I go,
weeping I am,
and when I am not Yoruba,
I am Congo, Mandinga, Carabalí.

BIBLIOGRAPHY

Cabrera, Lydia. *Anagó: Vocabulario lucumí (el yoruba que se habla en Cuba)*. Introduction by Roger Bastide. Havana: Ediciones C. R., 1957.

Guillén, Nicolás. *Obra Poética, 1920–1958*. 2 vols. Havana: Instituto Cubano del Libro, 1972.

Portugal, Fernandes. *Guía práctica de la lengua yorubá, en cuatro idiomas (español, inglés, portugués y yorubá)*. Havana: Editorial Ciencias Sociales, 1998.

Tratado de los odduns de Ifá: manual: Ifá en tierra de Ifá : a Ifá le corresponden los 3 días creados por Osha en la tierra. 2001. Colección En tierra de Ifá. [Cuba]: [s.n.].

LANGUAGE: SPANISH

John M. Lipski

Overview of the Spanish language in Cuba, including the formation of the Cuban dialects of Spanish.

With a population of roughly 12 million, Cuba ranks around tenth place among the world's most populous Spanish-speaking nations (eleventh if the United States is taken into consideration). Even taking into account the several million more Cubans and their Spanish-speaking descendants living outside of Cuba, speakers of Cuban Spanish represent less than 5 percent of the world's more than 400 million native Spanish speakers. Within the Spanish-speaking world, however, Cuban Spanish has played a much larger role than these numbers suggest, due to the prominence of Cuban writers, teachers, artists, athletes, activists, and politicians, who for over a century and a half have placed Cuban varieties of Spanish before a global audience. Issuing from the largest of the Antilles, the Spanish of Cuba has several unique characteristics, and at the same time it represents a dialect cluster embracing the Caribbean basin and also encompassing—due to historical settlement patterns—the Canary Islands and southwestern Spain. Outside of Cuba there are substantial numbers of Cuban Spanish speakers in Puerto Rico, Venezuela, Panama, Mexico, and Spain, but expatriate Cuban Spanish has received the greatest attention in the United States, where the majority of an estimated 1.5 million Cuban Americans continue in the early 2010s to use the language in their public and private lives.

HISTORICAL DEVELOPMENT OF SPANISH IN CUBA

The Spanish language has been spoken in Cuba since the early sixteenth century, and since then it has undergone many changes, cycling in and out of the linguistic mainstream as Cuba's fortunes waxed and waned. Although the first permanent Spanish settlements were in eastern Cuba, it was Havana that became the most important city, due largely to

colonial trade routes that dictated that ships leaving Spanish America for Spain exit via the northern Caribbean, with Havana being the final port of call before crossing the Atlantic. Deprived of officially sanctioned commercial ties with Spain, eastern Cuba often turned to contraband for its economic support, and linguistic and commercial ties with other Caribbean islands were more significant than contacts with Havana. The results are noticeable in contemporary Cuban Spanish, where the speech of the *Palestinos* (Palestinians, the modern term for Cubans from the easternmost provinces, because "Palestinians come from the East") is more similar to Dominican and Puerto Rican Spanish than to Havana's, in both vocabulary and intonation.

After Spain expanded its trade routes, Havana declined in importance and Cuban Spanish was relegated to a linguistic backwater through the end of the eighteenth century. With the Haitian revolution of the 1790s and the collapse of the French sugar-producing colony of Saint-Domingue, the Cuban sugar industry enjoyed a meteoric upsurge; later, the economy was further supplemented by commercial tobacco production. Following the Spanish-American War of 1898 and continuing through the Revolution of 1959, the United States was the largest external economic force in Cuba. Ownership of many Cuban companies by North Americans, large communities of expatriate Americans in Cuba, and frequent visits to Cuba by American tourists in the first half of the twentieth century brought many Cubans into close contact with English, particularly English terminology of sports and consumer goods. After the Revolution, Cuba's economic domination by the United States was replaced by the patronage of the Soviet Union. Thousands of Cubans studied in Eastern bloc nations, including Czechoslovakia, the German Democratic Republic, Bulgaria, and the Soviet Union, but even the obligatory teaching of Russian in Cuban schools resulted in almost no lexical borrowings or other imprints on Cuban Spanish. As of the early 2010s, the Cuban economy is subsidized by the government of Venezuela, where a type of Caribbean Spanish not unlike that of Cuba is spoken. Because this economic support does not involve large-scale displacements of either Cubans or Venezuelans, it is unlikely that Venezuelan Spanish will have any significant impact in Cuba.

Cuban Spanish was already well developed by the end of the nineteenth century, despite continued immigration from Spain, but it was during the Republican period (1902–1959) that the dialectal varieties of the newly independent nation were consolidated. The increased exposure to other varieties of Spanish occasioned by improved travel, educational systems, and mass media created a greater awareness among Cubans of the peculiarities of their forms of Spanish. During this period numerous Cuban scholars published articles and monographs on Cuban Spanish, and linguistics and philology were taught at Cuban universities, all of which underscored the fact that Cuban Spanish

■ *See also*

Education: Colonial Period

Education: Republican Period

Governance and Contestation: Colonial Period

was not simply a collection of immigrants' leftovers but rather a cohesive dialect cluster in its own right. By the time of the 1959 revolution, Cuban Spanish had taken its place among the icons of Cuban identity that were radically transformed in the ensuing years.

A large proportion of the early colonists in the Spanish Caribbean were from southern Spain, particularly Andalusia, but the two regions of Spain that supplied the largest number of immigrants to Cuba in the final century and a half of colonization were Galicia, in northwestern Spain, and the Canary Islands. Cubans began to refer to all Spaniards from the peninsula as *gallegos* (Galicians) and to the Canary Islanders as *isleños* (islanders). At the time of the Spanish-American War of 1898, almost half the white Cuban population had been born somewhere in Spain. Impressionistically, Cuban Spanish bears little resemblance to the Spanish dialect of Galicia, whereas the similarities with Canary Spanish are so striking that some observers confuse Cubans and Canary Islanders based on their speech. The congruence was enhanced by the massive emigration of Canary Islanders to Cuba in the early twentieth century; their linguistic presence is still noticeable a century later. In addition to overall patterns of pronunciation and grammar, one word that links Cuba to the Canary Islands is *guagua* (bus). Many Canary Islanders believe that this word was borrowed from Cuba, but given the presence of the term in other areas where Canary Islanders were once prominent (e.g., southeastern Louisiana, Equatorial Guinea), the opposite transfer is more likely.

When Spaniards first landed in Cuba, the island had a considerable indigenous population, mostly Arawak, with some Siboney and Taíno, but these groups left little imprint on Cuban Spanish except for numerous place-names and words that made their way from the Caribbean islands into general Latin American and even world Spanish: *batey* (plantation, yard), *conuco* (small farm), *bohío* (rustic hut), *ají* (pepper), and *huracán* (hurricane). The primary non-Hispanic linguistic influences on Cuban Spanish came from Africa and from Afro-Caribbean languages, then from China, and finally from the United States.

AFRICAN INFLUENCES IN CUBAN SPANISH

Although small numbers of sub-Saharan Africans were present in Cuba from the earliest colonial period, the strong African linguistic and cultural presence that characterizes modern Cuba only began toward the end of the eighteenth century. During most of the eighteenth century Cuba remained a neglected although not impoverished colony. The expansion of trade routes throughout the Caribbean, together with the reduced importance of the colonial treasure fleets, deprived Havana of much of its former strategic importance. Although small amounts of sugar were grown in Cuba, no Spanish-American colony could compete with the massive sugar production of the French colony Saint-Domingue (which

eventually became Haiti). As a consequence of the Haitian revolution beginning in 1791, the world's largest source of sugar disappeared almost overnight. Many French planters escaped to Cuba, and the rapid increase in world sugar prices resulted in a frenzied conversion of all available land in Cuba to sugar cultivation. To meet the skyrocketing labor demands, Cubans began to import African slaves and nominally free workers on a scale never before seen in the Spanish Caribbean. Of the estimated 750,000 to 1.2 million enslaved Africans taken to colonial Cuba, nearly 86 percent arrived during the first half of the nineteenth century.

In the first quarter of the nineteenth century, African slaves represented as much as 40 percent of the total Cuban population. If to this figure is added the large free black population, Africans and Afro-Hispanics made up well over half the Cuban population for much of the nineteenth century. The demographic distribution was not even; in the larger cities, the population was predominantly of Spanish origin, whereas in rural sugar-growing areas, the Afro-Hispanic population was in the majority.

Natives of Africa who spoke little or no Spanish were known by the term *bozal*, a Spanish word originally referring to the muzzle placed over the mouth of untamed dogs and horses and eventually to the savage beasts themselves. For much of the nineteenth century, African-born *bozales* significantly outnumbered native speakers of Spanish in many parts of Cuba, especially in rural sugar-growing areas, and they frequently communicated with one another and with overseers and other plantation workers in partially acquired Spanish. *Bozal* Spanish was familiar to most Cubans well into the twentieth century, either from firsthand experience or from the numerous imitations of *bozal* speech found in popular skits, stories, novels, and songs. With the advent of phonograph recordings, Afro-Cuban artists such as Ignacio Villa (Bola de Nieve, 1911–1971), Miguelito Valdés (1912–1978), and Celia Cruz (1924–2003) recorded popular songs using *bozal* language, and these imitations survived into the era of radio broadcasting, by which time true African-born *bozales* were exceedingly scarce. There is an ongoing debate as to whether Afro-Cuban *bozal* Spanish ever coalesced into a natively spoken and transgenerationally transmitted creole language with consistent grammatical features rather than the haphazard jumble of individual learners' approximations to Spanish. Although the demographics of rural Cuba were propitious for creolization in the early nineteenth century, the abolition of slavery in the second half of the century and the rapid incorporation of Afro-Cubans into Spanish-speaking society make it unlikely that a creolized *bozal* language lasted more than a generation, if indeed any such creolization ever took place. Some of the more common traits of nineteenth-century Cuban *bozal* Spanish include:

invariant copular verb *son* (be): "¿nuté *son* flancé, nuté *son* flancé? Si nuté *son* flancé, nuté *son* man picalo, mandito, traindó" ("are you a Frenchman? If you are a Frenchman, you are a damned scoundrel, a traitor" ["Proclama que en un cabildo de negros congos" c. 1808]);

invariant third-person singular (and sometimes) plural pronoun *elle/nelle* instead of Spanish *él* (he) and *ella* (she): "Muñeco con píritu de mueto muchacho, que *nelle* metía dientro" ("a doll with spirits of the dead inside, that she put inside" [Cabrera p. 492]);

invariant verbs based on the third-person singular: "Tú son bueno y callao, yo *va* a contá a ti una cosa" ("you are good and discreet, I'm going to tell you something" [Barnet p. 158]);

in some instances, verbs based on *ta* + verb stem: "Changó *ta vení* con el machete en la mano" ("Changó is coming with his machete in his hand" [Cruz 1974, p. x]);

occasional double negation, that is, placing *no* both before and after the verb: "*No* é mío, *no*" ("it's not mine").

These traits were not shared by all Afro-Cuban *bozales*, but they were not simply figments of (white authors') literary imagination either, because some of these elements can still be found in the speech of elderly Afro-Cubans in remote rural areas (Ortiz López), in the ritual chants of the *palo mayombe* cults (Fuentes Guerra and Schwegler), and in the trance-speech of *Santería* initiates who appear to be channeling the spirits of their *bozal* ancestors (Castellanos).

In addition to the residual presence of *bozal* Spanish in Afro-Cuban rituals, several Afro-Cuban lexical items have entered the general vocabulary; these include *chévere* (wonderful), *asere* (friend, buddy), *babalao* (Afro-Cuban priest), and *orishá* (African deity). The rites and practices of Afro-Cuban religions and secret societies, including *Santería* (Yoruba language), *Palo Mayombe* (Kikongo language), and *Abakuá* (Efik language), have contributed to the passive vocabulary of many Cubans, including nonparticipants in these rituals.

OTHER CARIBBEAN LANGUAGES IN CUBA

Beginning in the second half of the nineteenth century, when African slavery was abolished in Cuba, immigrants from other Caribbean islands arrived in eastern and central Cuba in large numbers, mostly to work on sugar plantations and other agricultural enterprises. Nearly all of these workers spoke creole languages derived from contacts between European and African languages, languages with similar grammatical structures but with words derived from former colonial speech. In the nineteenth century, many

laborers were imported from the Dutch-held Caribbean island of Curaçao, where the Afro-Hispanic creole language Papiamentu is spoken. This language bears enough similarity to Afro-Cuban *bozal* speech that some Cubans thought that Papiamentu was simply *español arañao* (tattered Spanish)—a viewpoint first offered by the Czech missionary Michael Joannes Alexius Schabel in 1704—and speakers of what was obviously a mixture of Papiamentu and Spanish appear in nineteenth-century Cuban literature simply as *bozales*. Some Papiamentu words made their way into the Afro-Cuban lexicon and still persist among some elderly Afro-Cubans; these include *agüe* (today), *yio* (son, daughter), and *aguora* (now).

The Haitian presence in eastern Cuba was once considerable, and elderly speakers of Haitian Creole can still be found in this region. Songs sung in *kreyòl* form part of the *tumba francesa* tradition among various Cuban groups of Haitian descent (Alén Rodríguez). Jamaican workers speaking creole English arrived in large numbers to work on sugar plantations; they figure prominently in the first novel of Alejo Carpentier (1904–1980), *Écue-yamba-ó* (1933). Workers from Barbados settled in coastal regions such as Baraguá, where Afro-Antillean carnival continues to be celebrated, and creole English interacts with Cuban Spanish.

CHINESE INFLUENCE ON CUBAN SPANISH

Between the middle of the nineteenth century and the first decades of the twentieth century, Cuba received more than 100,000 Chinese immigrants. The first arrivals were a response to the abolition of African slavery and the consequent demands for a replacement labor force, and Chinese workers often worked alongside former African slaves, some of whom continued to speak *bozal* Spanish. In time, an identifiable Cuban Chinese community arose, maintaining the Chinese language and culture while also speaking Spanish and participating in the Cuban lifestyle. The main cultural traces of the Chinese are found in a Cuban variant of the numbers game known as the *charada china*. Awareness of many Chinese lexical items also reached the general Cuban population, although few non-Chinese Cubans actively employed these words.

ENGLISH INFLUENCE ON CUBAN SPANISH

Despite the geographical proximity of Cuba to the United States and the strong cultural and commercial ties between the two countries, stretching from the second half of the nineteenth century through the first years of the Cuban Revolution, the English language has had very little impact on Cuban Spanish. In addition to the lexical anglicisms found throughout the Spanish-speaking world—including *chequear* (to check), *parquear* (to park), and *lonche* (lunch, especially fast food)—there are only a few uniquely Cuban words derived from English. These include *blúmeres* bloomers (woman's panties) and the now obsolete *fotingo, Ford* + the diminutive suffix -*ingo* (old dilapidated vehicle). Following the 1959 revolution, the public use of anglicisms was strongly discouraged if not outright prohibited in Cuba. An apparent exception is the terminology associated with baseball, Fidel Castro's favorite sport; Cuban sports announcers continue to employ (with Spanish pronunciation) words such as *left fielder, shortstop,* and *strike* and *foul*. One possible consequence of the shift in attitudes toward anglicisms is the Cuban pronunciation of the English expression *o.k.*, once heard as *okey*, reflecting English pronunciation, and now as *oká*, the latter being a spelling pronunciation of the letters *o* and *k*.

FEATURES OF CONTEMPORARY CUBAN SPANISH

Although Cubans themselves distinguish several regional and social varieties of Spanish, most outside observers fail to note these nuances. Speech traits common to all Cuban speakers include:

Syllable- and word-final -*s* is aspirated (pronounced like *h*) or eliminated altogether, except in the most formal recitation style. This makes *Los Estados Unidos* (the United States) sound like *Loh Ehtadoh Unido*.

In Havana and the rest of western Cuba, -*r* (and sometimes -*l*) before consonants is often converted to a copy of the following consonant; thus *porque* (because) emerges as *poqque, puerta* (door) as *puetta*, and *algo* (something) as *aggo*. In central and eastern Cuba it is not uncommon for -*r* to be pronounced as -*l* in these same contexts, especially in vernacular speech, much as occurs in Puerto Rico and the Dominican Republic. This lateralization of -*l* is not regarded favorably in western Cuba, whereas the geminated pronunciation of -*r* and -*l* often passes unnoticed in casual speech.

Word-final -*n* is given a velar pronunciation like English -*ng* in *sing*; this occurs throughout Cuba and in virtually all styles and settings, and carries no negative connotation.

In terms of grammar, Cuban Spanish shares with its neighboring Caribbean dialects the practice of forming questions without interchanging the subject and the verb, normally when the subject is a pronoun: *¿qué tú quieres?* (what do you want?) instead of *¿qué quieres tú?*

Frequent in Cuban Spanish is the combination of preposition + noun or pronoun + verbal infinitive in combinations where a conjugated subjunctive form would occur in most other dialects of Spanish: *Eso sucedió antes de yo llegar aquí [antes de que yo llegara ...]* (that happened before I arrived here); *para tú entender esto tienes que practicar más [para que tú entiendas ...]* (for you to understand this you have to practice more). This is a regional trait found elsewhere in the Caribbean and in some parts of South America and occurs in all speech styles.

Cuban Spanish contains a number of unique lexical items not found elsewhere in the Spanish-speaking world or endowed with different meanings in Cuba. A small sampling of quintessentially Cuban words includes *chucho* (light switch), *fruta bomba* (papaya), *jimaguas* (twins), and *yuma* (United States, North American).

SOCIOLINGUISTIC SHIFTS IN POST-1959 CUBA

The Cuban Revolution yielded significant shifts in sociolinguistic attitudes toward varieties of Spanish. Cuban socialism resulted in the dissolution of obvious mechanisms favoring the speech of privileged groups such as private clubs and schools and expanded educational programs and literacy campaigns in formerly marginalized areas brought ever larger numbers of Cubans into the linguistic mainstream. The formerly frequent practice of emulating peninsular Spanish speech in schools (often staffed by nuns from Spain) gave way to a greater emphasis on more naturalistic Cuban Spanish, and avowed solidarity with revolutionary principles included avoidance of speech patterns felt to reflect elitist sympathies. Although Cuban Spanish always preferred the familiar pronoun *tú* (you) over the more formal *usted*, in contemporary Cuban Spanish *usted* is increasingly rare, as are address forms such as *señor* (sir) and *señora* (ma'am) instead of *compañero/compañera* (comrade).

Changing attitudes toward popular speech patterns are also reflected in radio and television broadcasting in Cuba. Prior to the Cuban Revolution, radio and television announcers in Cuba routinely employed a highly artificial diction that bore little resemblance to spoken Cuban Spanish, particularly as regards the full pronunciation of all instances of syllable- and word-final /s/, /r/, and /l/. Moreover, the speech of educated natives of Havana was implicitly considered to be the best Cuban Spanish, although many Cubans were aware that all Caribbean varieties of Spanish often were regarded with amusement both in Spain and elsewhere in Latin America. With the triumph of the 1959 revolution, the speech traits of Fidel Castro, who is from the easternmost portion of Cuba, permeated the airwaves for hours every day, and public speakers and professional announcers throughout the island emulated many of Castro's regional traits that previously had been considered low-status. Cuban radio and television personnel in the early 2010s employ more realistic approximations to spoken Cuban Spanish, albeit with vocabulary and syntax appropriate to professional journalism. Vestiges of earlier Cuban radio and television locution can be heard on stations staffed by Cubans in the United States, including occasional clandestine shortwave radio broadcasts.

CUBAN SPANISH OUTSIDE OF CUBA

Even prior to the 1959 revolution—in fact even before Cuban independence—there were pockets of Cuban Spanish outside of Cuba, particularly in the United States. In Spanish-speaking countries, including Puerto Rico, Cuban Spanish is eventually replaced with local varieties after the first generation of immigrants. Only in the United States, where speakers of Cuban Spanish are more frequently in contact with English than with other dialects of Spanish, is there a significant retention of Cuban Spanish outside of Cuba. Beginning around the middle of the nineteenth century, Cuban nationalists—foremost among them José Martí—used the United States as a safe haven for launching revolutionary schemes. The first significant Cuban population in the United States was formed in Key West, where Cuban cigar makers established themselves as early as the 1830s. The largest permanent Cuban settlement in the United States prior to 1959 was in Tampa, where the Cuban cigar industry flourished through the first half of the twentieth century. The massive arrivals of Cubans in the second half of the twentieth century resulted in substantial Cuban communities in the greater Miami area and the metropolitan New York City area, and smaller groups in other large cities throughout the United States. Early scholarship on Cuban Spanish in the United States did not distinguish Cuban-American varieties from those spoken in Cuba; later studies have focused on the influence of English, including lexical borrowing, code-switching, and language shift. Beginning in the 1980s, research on Cuban-American Spanish took note of the increasingly diverse spectrum of regional and social dialects represented among Cubans in the United States, expanding the focus beyond Havana. Political difficulties often have encumbered the ready exchange of information about Spanish in Cuba and Cuban-American Spanish, but research in the early 2000s confirms that Cuban Spanish in the United States is not the monolithic entity it was once assumed to be; instead, it mirrors the complex and constantly evolving linguistic profile of Cuba itself.

SELECTED DISCOGRAPHY

Cruz, Celia. *Chango ta Vení* (2000).

BIBLIOGRAPHY

Alén Rodríguez, Olavo. *La música de las sociedades de tumba francesa en Cuba*. Havana: Ministerio de Cultura, 1986.

Aleza Izquierdo, Milagros, ed. *Estudios lingüísticos cubanos*. Valencia: Universitat de València, 2002.

Barnet, Miguel. *Biografía de un cimarrón*. Havana: Instituto de Etnología y Folklore, 1966.

Cabrera, Lydia. *El monte, igbo finda, ewe orisha, vititin-finda: Notas sobre las religiones, la magia, las supersticiones y el folklore de los negros criollos y del pueblo de Cuba*. Havana: Ediciones C. R., 1954.

Carpentier, Alejo. *Écue-yamba-ó*. Madrid: Editorial España, 1933.

Castellanos, Isabel. "Grammatical Structure, Historical Development, and Religious Usage of Afro-Cuban Bozal Speech." *Folklore Forum* 23 (1990): 57–84.

Choy López, Luis Roberto. *Periodización y orígenes en la historia del español de Cuba*. Valencia: Tirant lo Blanch Libros, Universitat de València, 1999.

Domínguez Hernández, Marlen, and Sergio Valdés Bernal, eds. *Le lengua en Cuba: estudios*. Santiago de Compostela, Spain: Universidade de Santiago de Compostela, 2007.

Eltis, David, Stephen Behrendt, David Richardson, and Herbert Klein, eds. *The Trans-Atlantic Slave Trade: A Database on CD-ROM*. Cambridge, U.K.: Cambridge University Press, 1999.

Fuentes Guerra, Jesús, and Armin Schwegler. *Lengua y ritos del Palo Monte Mayombe: Dioses cubanos y sus fuentes africanas*. Frankfurt: Vervuert/Iberoamericana, 2005.

García, Ofelia, and Ricardo Otheguy. "The Language Situation of Cuban Americans." In *Language Diversity: Problem or Resource?* edited by Sandra McKay and Sau-ling Cynthia Wong. Cambridge, U.K.: Newbury House, 1988.

Gómez Navia, Raimundo, and Graciela Chailloux. *De dónde son los cubanos*. Havana: Editorial de Ciencias Sociales, 2007.

Haensch, Günther, Reinhold Werner, Gisela Cárdenas Molina, and Antonio Tristá. *Diccionario del español de Cuba: Español de Cuba-español de España*. Madrid: Gredos, 2000.

Lipski, John. *Latin American Spanish*. London: Longman, 1994.

Lipski, John. "Chinese-Cuban Pidgin Spanish: Implications for the Afro-creole Debate." In *Creole Genesis, Attitudes and Discourse*, edited by John Rickford and Suzanne Romaine. Amsterdam: John Benjamins, 1999.

Lipski, John. *A History of Afro-Hispanic Language*. Cambridge, U.K.: Cambridge University Press, 2005.

Ortiz López, Luis. *Huellas etno-sociolingüísticas bozales y afrocubanas*. Frankfurt: Vervuert, 1998.

"Proclama que en un cabildo de negros congos de la ciudad de La Habana pronunció su presidente, Rey Monfundi Siliman." Havana, c. 1808.

Valdés Bernal, Sergio. *Visión geolectal de Cuba*. Frankfurt am Main: Peter Lang, 2007.

Varela, Beatriz. *Lo chino en el habla cubana*. Miami: Ediciones Universal, 1980.

Varela, Beatriz. *El español cubano-americano*. New York: Senda Nueva de Ediciones, 1992.

■ *See also*

Diasporas: Cubans
Abroad, Post-1959

Literature: Fiction in the
Special Period

LIFE ON THE HYPHEN (GUSTAVO PÉREZ FIRMAT)

Jorge Febles

The first book to deal seriously with the cultural production of Cuban Americans.

Life on the Hyphen: The Cuban-American Way (1994) is unquestionably the defining work of Cuban-American writer Gustavo Pérez Firmat (b. 1949). The book reflects his critical maturity, encompassing ideas and motifs that recur in his subsequent production. It is also a text that the author opted to rework in Spanish, translating it according to those notions he identifies in *The Cuban Condition: Translation and Identity in Modern Cuban Literature* (1989), so as to *Cubanize* it elegantly in a manner that illustrates the complexity of his dual "tongue ties," to echo the title of his 2003 study.

As Isabel Álvarez Borland correctly points out, *Life on the Hyphen* "represents Pérez Firmat's most significant contribution to the field of cultural studies" (Álvarez Borland 2004, p. 724). In this work, he demonstrates a highly personal aesthetic approach, grounded on intuition, interpretative audacity, sound research, and thoroughly assimilated critical tenets. The book, however, is not a conventional exercise in literary criticism akin to the writer's first three monographs, *Idle Fictions: The Hispanic Vanguard Novel, 1926–1934* (1982), *Literature and Liminality: Festive Readings in the Hispanic Tradition* (1986), and *The Cuban Condition: Translation and Identity in Modern Cuban Literature* (1989), a text on which he depends to a substantial degree in *Life on the Hyphen*. Nor does it equate to *Tongue Ties: Logo-Eroticism in Anglo-Hispanic Writing* (2003), a subsequent scholarly work. *Life on the Hyphen*'s impressionistic and venturesome nature may explain the book's popularity: It is a highly readable interpretation of a collective mind-set described through readily recognizable examples from a shared popular culture.

STRUCTURE

Pérez Firmat structures *Life on the Hyphen* following a method similar to the one employed in *Spiks* (1956), by Pedro Juan Soto (1928–2002), a Puerto Rican writer bent on describing the ethos of a transplanted community. In *Spiks*, a work of fiction, Soto intersperses a series of *miniaturas* (vignettes) among seven short stories depicting the anguished existence of his countrymen in New York City's Spanish Harlem in the 1950s. Similarly, Pérez Firmat inserts between the introduction and six chapters that comprise *Life on the Hyphen* six *mambos* (brief anecdotes) intended to represent the "Cuban American condition." The last of these, "Last-Mambo-in-Miami" (p. 181), is a tweaked

version of those "Bilingual Blues" that appear in his first poetry collection, *Carolina Cuban* (1987). By concluding *Life on the Hyphen* with this highly personal poem, Pérez Firmat reveals the expiatory nature of a text meant above all to depict the contradictory nature of his peers, the immigrants (or exiles) destined to "dance between two cultures," to borrow the felicitous expression used in the title of a book by William Luis.

PERTINENT THEORETICAL NOTIONS

In his introduction to *Life on the Hyphen*, "The Desi Chain," Pérez Firmat discusses relevant concepts that guide his analytical outlook. Predominant among them is his definition of the *1.5 generation*, a term he borrows from the sociologist Rubén Rumbaut. Pérez Firmat applies the concept to individuals like himself, Cuban-born baby boomers dislocated by the 1959 revolution. Brought to the United States by their parents, they walk a linguistic and cultural tightrope. They are neither wholly Cuban, as their parents are or were, nor entirely assimilated Americans, as their children are or will be. They are ABCs (American-Born Cubans) or in Pérez Firmat's terminology, CBAs (Cuban-Bred Americans). His generation, therefore, represents another link in the Desi Chain, named for the quintessential Cuban immigrant Desi Arnaz (1917–1986), whose indissoluble accent marked him as a lovable and hence tolerable alien. The reality of these denizens of *la Cuba del Norte* (Cuba of the North), Pérez Firmat's term for Miami and all the other Cuban enclaves in the United States (*Vidas,* 2000, p. 14), signifies an expansion of the translational nature of the island's culture. By translation, Pérez Firmat means not simply the act of transferring sense from one language to another, but also intralinguistic reformulations, which signify "displacement" (1989, p. 5) because even when recreating within his own language, the translator "knows that in order to pick his words, he has to keep his distance" (1989, p. 5). This stance becomes evident in *Vidas en vilo: La cultura cubanoamericana* (Suspended Lives: Cuban American Culture, 2000), the Spanish version of *Life on the Hyphen*, a reworking more than a rewording of the original that is a quite different text despite the fact that its author essentially confronts the same material, with the exception of specific fragments, a few mambos, and the logical updating of certain allusions.

SYNOPSIS

The chain envisioned by Pérez Firmat begins with Ricky Ricardo, the public face assumed by Desiderio Arnaz in order to be allowed "to love Lucy" in the iconic television comedy as well as in real life. By assuming two first names (Ricky is, after all, an affectionate nickname for Ricardo), the fictional character exemplifies domestication and, in a sense, harmless acculturation. According to Pérez Firmat, "Ricardo is the Cuban man, Ricky is the American husband. Ricky Ricardo is the Cuban-American man and husband" (1994, p. 37). In the second chapter, Pérez Firmat probes the psyche of "the-man-who-loved-Lucy"

(p. 48) by deconstructing *A Book* (1976), Arnaz's tell-all autobiography, which Pérez Firmat deems an important contribution to Cuban American culture despite its stylistic mediocrity. Pérez Firmat delves peripherally into the actor-musician's apparently unhappy life after divorcing Lucille Ball (1911–1989).

Subsequently, in accordance with the prevailing cultural studies optic, Pérez Firmat ambles freely among heterogeneous texts in search of metaphors that elucidate the intrinsic hybridity that defines immigrant creativity. Thus, he examines mambo, particularly as performed by Dámaso Pérez Prado and his orchestra, considering it a nonverbal construct that readily traverses cultures. He later reflects on the "Miami sound" of the 1970s and 1980s, focusing on groups and musicians such as Clouds, Hánsel y Raúl, and Willy Chirino (b. 1947). The latter contribute to what Pérez Firmat terms a failed Cuban American stew that does not travel well, failing to strike an international chord (p. 125). In contrast, the Miami Sound Machine, and particularly its lead singer Gloria Estefan (b. 1957) after she became a solo artist, transcends locality, but in doing so the group anticipates the inevitable merging of the Miami sound with American or Latin American popular music, hence anticipating the disappearance of the 1.5 generation.

In the last two chapters Pérez Firmat resumes his role as a literary critic in order to deconstruct two novels by Oscar Hijuelos (b. 1951), *Our House in the Last World* (1983) and *The Mambo Kings Play Songs of Love* (1990), as well as numerous poems by José Kozer (b. 1940). By juxtaposing his segments on these writers, Pérez Firmat underscores their cultural differences. Hijuelos is a CBA (he was born in New York City) who writes about Cubans from an American perspective, manipulating Spanish references awkwardly for effect, much like Hemingway did. Kozer, in contrast, is a Havana-born poet who lived and taught in New York for years yet struggled to remain faithful to his mother tongue and to an imaginary space—as Pérez Firmat asserts, "Kozer's Cuba has not existed for decades" (p. 178). Logically then, when Pérez Firmat inserts himself in the text by referring fleetingly to his own Carolina blues and intoning them afterward in "Last-Mambo-in-Miami," he emphasizes that his explications are always the inconclusive self-explanations of a "Ricky Ricardo with a Ph.D." (p. 237).

VIDAS EN VILO VERSUS *LIFE ON THE HYPHEN*

Certainly, *Vidas en vilo* replicates the bulk of *Life on the Hyphen*. Its tone, however, is much more melancholic and less anchored in linguistic exuberance. Here the hyphen—untranslatable in the sense that the Spanish *guión* does not accurately convey the cultural substance inherent in the English word—becomes *vilo*, suspension, the state of hanging in the air, whereas life, *vida*, evolves into *vidas*, a multiplicity of existences in suspended animation. Even the subtitle—"la cultura cubanoamericana"—focuses on culture rather than on a way of being, as in *Life on the Hyphen*. Finally, the 1.5 generation is transformed into the *generación media* (the generation in the middle), fragmented ideologically and culturally while inhabiting an ambivalent neverland. Pérez Firmat, who has always perceived himself as an "anglophone writer" (2003, p. 160), and who confesses, "[f]or most of my adult life, the language I have felt uneasy about has been Spanish" (p. 160), produced a far more angst-ridden text in his mother tongue. Witness the seventh chapter that he adds to the Spanish version of the book, "El sino cubanoamericano" (Cuban American Destiny), in which he speculates that his will be a generation without descendants, literary or otherwise, "no sólo la generación del medio, sino la generación sin remedio" (not only the generation in the middle, but the generation without remedy) (2000, p. 198).

As a final paradox, the lyrical conclusion to the Spanish version of *Life on the Hyphen* bears the title "Ay, mi Cuba," evoking one of those plaintive exilic songs that Pérez Firmat parodies in both books. In it, forsaking the joyful if hazardous hyphen on which his generation resides, Pérez Firmat recounts his efforts to exorcise his country's name in order to deny his diasporic condition. He strove for a month to avoid uttering the word *Cuba* or to think about the island. In order to do so, he had to live "en vilo" (in a state of suspended animation), planting in his garden for the entire period. Since then, "no pasa día en que no digo, desterrándome y desenterrándome: ¡ay! mi Cuba" (not a day goes by that I do not say, exiling and disinterring me: Oh! my Cuba) (2000, p. 199). In that sense, he develops an ambiguous kinship with Kozer, the poet who looks back too much to the island and hence defies his surroundings and immediate reality by refusing to write in English. *Vidas en vilo* thus ties at least the author's tongue to the physical space that he acknowledges will never shelter him again.

OTHER APPROACHES TO THE SAME THEME

Countless writers and scholars have sought to explicate the Cuban exile community or, for that matter, the Cuban American way. David Rieff and Joan Didion, for instance, undertook controversial outsider analyses of Miami's Cuban community, generalizing with sociopolitical intent. Alejandro Portes and Rubén Rumbaut have studied Cuban Americanness from a somewhat distanced sociological outlook, and María Cristina García historicized the Dade County community in *Havana USA: Cuban Exiles and Cuban Americans in South Florida, 1959–1994* (1997). Still others have opted for autobiographical explorations comparable to Pérez Firmat's *Next Year in Cuba: A Cubano's Coming of Age in America*. Carlos Eire's prize-winning quasi-fictional memoir *Waiting for Snow in Havana: Confessions of a Cuban Boy* (2003), Pablo Medina's *Exiled Memories* (1990), and Román de la Campa's *Cuba on My Mind: Journeys to a Severed Nation* (2000), for example, imply the desire to explain others through self, that is, to understand the psyche of generational peers through individual experiences portrayed tacitly or overtly as synecdoche. Many writers have opted to fictionalize Cuban American society and culture in order to parody, praise, or analyze it. Prominent among these are Roberto G. Fernández, Achy Obejas, Elías Miguel Muñoz, and Virgil Suárez. Finally, the scholar Andrea O'Reilly Herrera has edited two important collections that gather significant diasporic voices: *ReMembering Cuba: Legacy of a Diaspora* (2001) and *Cuba: Idea of a Nation Displaced* (2007). All these voices and numberless more who have broached the subject in essay form (e.g., Eliana Rivero, Isabel Álvarez Borland, Madeline Cámara, José Quiroga, Ruth Behar, Damián Fernández, Jorge Duany, and Iraida López) must be taken into account to develop a valid portrait of Cuban American culture. Nevertheless, Gustavo Pérez Firmat's *Life on the Hyphen* along with its Spanish version, *Vidas en vilo*, will continue to provide an essential point of departure.

BIBLIOGRAPHY

Álvarez Borland, Isabel. *Cuban-American Literature of Exile: From Person to Persona*. Charlottesville: University Press of Virginia, 1998.

Álvarez Borland, Isabel. "Gustavo Pérez Firmat." In *Latino and Latina Writers*, vol. 2. Edited by Alan West-Durán. New York: Charles Scribner's Sons, 2004.

Cámara Betancourt, Madeline, and Damián J. Fernández, eds. *Cuba, the Elusive Nation: Interpretations of National Identity*. Gainesville: University Press of Florida, 2000.

Campa, Román de la. *Cuba on My Mind: Journeys to a Severed Nation*. London: Verso, 2000.

Didion, Joan. *Miami*. New York: Simon & Schuster, 1987.

Luis, William. *Dance between Two Cultures: Latino Caribbean Literature Written in the United States*. Nashville, TN: Vanderbilt University Press, 1997.

O'Reilly Herrera, Andrea, ed. *ReMembering Cuba: Legacy of a Diaspora*. Austin: University of Texas Press, 2001.

O'Reilly Herrera, Andrea, ed. *Cuba: Idea of a Nation Displaced*. Albany: State University of New York Press, 2007.

Pérez Firmat, Gustavo. *Idle Fictions: The Hispanic Vanguard Novel, 1926–1934*. Durham, NC: Duke University Press, 1982.

Pérez Firmat, Gustavo. *Literature and Liminality: Festive Readings in the Hispanic Tradition*. Durham, NC: Duke University Press, 1986.

Pérez Firmat, Gustavo. *Carolina Cuban*. In *Triple Crown: Poems by Roberto Durán, Judith Ortiz Coffer, and Gustavo Pérez Firmat*. Tempe, AZ: Bilingual Press/Editorial Bilingüe, 1987.

Pérez Firmat, Gustavo. *The Cuban Condition: Translation and Identity in Modern Cuban Literature*. Cambridge, U.K.: Cambridge University Press, 1989.

Pérez Firmat, Gustavo. *Life on the Hyphen: The Cuban-American Way*. Austin: University of Texas Press, 1994.

Pérez Firmat, Gustavo. *Next Year in Cuba: A Cubano's Coming-of-Age in America*. New York: Anchor Books, 1996.

Pérez Firmat, Gustavo. *My Own Private Cuba: Essays on Cuban Literature and Culture*. Boulder, CO: Society of Spanish and Spanish American Studies, 1999.

Pérez Firmat, Gustavo. *Cincuenta lecciones de exilio y desexilio*. Miami: Ediciones Universal, 2000.

Pérez Firmat, Gustavo. *Vidas en vilo: La cultura cubanoamericana*. Madrid: Editorial Colibrí, 2000.

Pérez Firmat, Gustavo. *Tongue Ties: Logo-Eroticism in Anglo-Hispanic Literature*. New York: Palgrave Macmillan, 2003.

Quiroga, José. *Cuban Palimpsests*. Minneapolis: University of Minnesota Press, 2005.

Rieff, David. *Going to Miami: Exiles, Tourists, and Refugees in the New America*. Boston: Little, Brown, 1987.

Rieff, David. *Exile: Cuba in the Heart of Miami*. New York: Touchstone, 1993.

Rivero, Eliana. *Discursos desde la diáspora*. Cádiz, Spain: Editorial Aduana Vieja, 2005.

Rumbaut, Rubén G. "The Agony of Exile: A Study of the Migration and Adaptation of Indochinese Refugee Adults and Children." In *Refugee Children: Theory, Research, and Services*, edited by Frederick L. Ahearn Jr. and Jean L. Athey. Baltimore, MD: Johns Hopkins University Press, 1991.

Soto, Pedro Juan. *Spiks*. 5th ed. Río Piedras, Puerto Rico: Editorial Cultural, 1977.

LITERATURE

"Mi verso es como un puñal / que por el puño echa flor" ("My verse is like a dagger / flowering by its handle"), wrote José Martí in Versos sencillos. *Since the colonial period, creative writing and oppositional politics have been closely intertwined in Cuba as literature became the main vehicle for the expression of nationalist and antislavery sentiment in a print media heavily monitored by Spanish censorship.*

In competing literary reviews, creole reformists confronted colonial officials over the formal merits of the poetry of José María Heredia, a Byronic exile who once plotted to bring Simon Bolívar's revolution to Cuba. Progressive local writers met in private tertulias *to share drafts of abolitionist novels too controversial for print. In response, peninsular authorities sniffed out conspiracies and orchestrated trials to banish antislavery writer-activists and silence Afro-Cuban intellectuals who had mastered the protocols of poetry production and publishing. Under such repressive coloniality, belletristic practices of literature and print culture became thoroughly identified with the struggle for personal and national sovereignty and social emancipation. Martí, the revolutionary icon, is revered as much for launching* modernismo *poetics with his dazzling* versos *as for engineering the second Cuban war of independence.*

The profession of literature did not lose any of its oppositional and formal intensity when Cuba transitioned from main hub of the Spanish transatlantic trade system to flashpoint of U.S. strategic imperialism and Cold War politics. In fact, literature produced by Cubans both in the island and in exile has arguably attained the highest level of world prestige and influence possible thanks to a series of groundbreaking masterpieces. The following essays trace the developments, innovations, ruptures, and continuities in Cuban print culture and literary practices in the colonial, Republican, Revolutionary, and post-1989 periods, focusing on the areas of poetry, narrative, literary criticism, and the cultural essay.

LITERATURE: NATIONALIST AND REFORMIST LITERATURE, PRE-1850

Adriana Méndez Rodenas

Emergence of national sentiment through print culture, slave narratives, and travel writing.

In the late eighteenth century, native-born Cubans felt the first stirrings of national sentiment. The first quarter of the nineteenth century saw a shift in the growing sense of *pertenencia* (national identity). Print culture, travel writing, and other forms of literary expression played an important part in this process of collective self-definition. In response to a colonial project that absorbed Cubans within a broader peninsular identity as *españoles de ultramar* (overseas Spaniards), enlightened creole intellectuals began to separate symbolically from the metropolis. They did so by consolidating a reformist position based on two fundamental premises: political autonomy as a viable option to full-fledged independence, and an emerging cultural identity that emphasized creole values, customs, and way of life. It was through the print media that creoles first aired their sentiments of national pride in the 1830s, beginning with the *Revista Bimestre Cubana* (1831–1834) and continuing in a number of periodical publications corresponding with the boom in Cuban letters. Ultimately, colonial repression in 1844 brought about the demise of the creole enlightenment.

THE LAUNCHING OF NATIONALIST PRINT CULTURE

The establishment of the first printing press in Havana in 1735 was tied to the Crown's objective of promoting loyalty to the colonial government, a goal fostered primarily through the Sociedad Económica de Amigos del País, and, later in the century, by the official press, the Imprenta de la Capitanía General. Parallel to the rise of print culture, a generation of creole thinkers inherited the teachings of Father Félix Varela (1788–1853) as imparted in his *cátedra* (chair of philosophy) at the Seminario de San Carlos in the early 1820s. These teachings implied a growing awareness regarding the deleterious effects of the illegal slave trade. The launching of a Cuban nationalist print culture dates to 1828, when Varela, who was exiled from the island under General José Dionisio Vives, founded the newspaper *El mensagero semanal* in New York with José Antonio Saco (1797–1879) and Tomás Gener. This paper was one of the first to articulate a distinctively Cuban identity based on the resistance to the sugar culture. By the time Saco founded the *Revista Bimestre Cubana* in 1831, the institution of slavery had become one of the central concerns of creole intellectuals, now gathered as the Comisión de Literatura under the umbrella of the Sociedad Patriótica. The Sociedad had split into two factions: the autonomist faction represented by the polemicist Saco, the scholar José de la Luz y Caballero, and the cultural promoter Domingo Del Monte; and a conservative faction led by Claudio Martínez de Pinillos and Juan Bernardo O'Gaban, who opposed Saco's ideas for fostering the prosperity of the island.

Saco's writings, particularly an 1832 review of *Notices of Brazil in 1828 and 1829*, by the Irish clergyman and historian Robert Walsh, sparked a controversy over the illegal slave trade. His virulent attack on "slave traders and Spanish moneylenders" launched "the discourse of resistance against the sugar mill" (Benítez Rojo 1986, p. 21). In 1833 Del Monte attempted to form an independent Academia de Literatura Cubana, provoking a public attack by O'Gaban and an outspoken defense of the fledging institution by Saco. The arrival in Havana of the despotic captain-general Miguel Tacón in 1834 put an end to the controversy: Tacón disbanded the Academia, shut down the prestigious *Revista Bimestre Cubana*, and exiled Saco. Thus was "the first organized effort by Cuban intellectuals to mount a common front of resistance against the power of the slave traders and the saccarocracy" silenced (Benítez Rojo pp. 22–23).

■ *See also*

Cuban Thought and Cultural Identity: Costumbres in the Art and Literature of the 19th Century

Governance and Contestation: Colonial Period

Race: Slavery in Cuba

The World and Cuba: Cuba and Spain in the Colonial Period

The close of the *Revista Bimestre Cubana* led, paradoxically, to a flowering of Cuban literature during the 1835–1844 period. Antonio Benítez Rojo aptly terms the skillful maneuvering of literary expression that took place under strict government censorship "the Conspiracy of the Text" (p. 17). One could argue that Cuban literature began in 1835, the year in which the British signed a treaty with Spain calling for the Crown to end the slave trade in Cuba and its other colonies. The 1835 treaty resulted in mixed Anglo-Spanish commissions ordering the seizure of slave ships. Dr. Richard Madden, a physician sympathetic to the antislavery cause, arrived in Havana as superintendent of liberated Africans, with the mission to supervise the mixed commissions, enforce the provisions of the 1835 treaty, and guarantee the transfer of freed slaves. Madden soon became involved in the vibrant literary activity sponsored by Del Monte while promoting antislavery works abroad. He even dabbled in politics with his appeal to Del Monte to answer a questionnaire about the illegal slave trade. Within this highly charged political climate, as William Luis observes, Cuban literature emerged as a powerful "counterdiscourse which directly challenged the colonial and slavery systems" (1990, p. 27). That counterdiscourse was to permeate print culture and literary production for the remainder of the century.

After moving his *tertulia* (literary circle or salon) from Matanzas to Havana in 1835, Del Monte positioned himself at the helm of a group of writers who were soon to become the founding members of Cuban literary discourse. Under his tutelage, the pages of classic Cuban literature unfold in two distinct genres: antislavery and *costumbrista* (local color) narratives. Such works were first printed in *folletines* (serials) and in periodicals published primarily in Havana. Ramón de Palma and José Antonio Echevarría founded the first of these publications, *El Aguinaldo Habanero*, which appeared in book format in 1837, only to be discontinued because of censorship, followed by *El Álbum* (1838) and *El Plantel* (1838–1839). A fourth publication, *La Cartera Cubana* (1838–1840), was designed to escape the vigilance of Spanish colonial authorities. By 1839, however, increasing pressure led to more centrally aligned journals, such as *Faro Industrial de La Habana* (1841–1851) and *La Siempreviva* (1838–1840). Del Monte also founded *La Moda ó Recreo Semanal del Bello Sexo* (1829–1830), directed to a female audience but including articles of general interest.

ANTISLAVERY NARRATIVE

As part of his anticolonial project and in keeping with his crusade for realism inspired by the writings of Honoré de Balzac in France, Del Monte promoted a new genre: antislavery narrative. Because these works were banned in Havana, Del Monte gave a portfolio of literary works written by members of his circle to the British abolitionist Richard Madden on the eve of his departure from Cuba in 1839.

In what is surely one of the most intriguing chapters in Caribbean literary history, Del Monte secretly handed over to Madden the first productions of an authentic Cuban literature—works depicting local types and written according to a realist aesthetic—works that could not be published in Cuba given the censorship of colonial authorities. By so doing, Del Monte gave away the key to a transnational Cuban literature, in the sense that these foundational works were published outside the island borders.

The works included a selection of poems and a first-person memoir by the liberated slave Juan Francisco Manzano (1797–1854) and *Francisco: El ingenio o las delicias del campo*, a sentimental novel written in 1838 by Anselmo Suárez y Romero (1818–1878), about a love triangle among a noble field slave, the ruthless son of a white master, and a mulatto domestic slave. The portfolio also contained two pillars of the antislavery novel: "El hombre misterioso" (later named "El cura"), the second of three tales; *Escenas de la vida privada en la isla de Cuba*, by Félix Tanco y Bosmeniel, exposing the devastating effects of slavery on the planter class; and "El ranchador," a tale by Pedro José Morillas on the capture of runaway slaves by a relentless man-hunt (Lewis Galanes 1988, pp. 263–264; Luis 1990, p. 37).

Del Monte continued to promote a spectrum of literary works exposing the unjust treatment of slaves. One afternoon in 1836, before an expectant audience at his Havana salon, Manzano recited "Treinta años," a sonnet denouncing his first thirty years of life as a slave: "Treinta años ha que conocí la tierra: / Treinta años ha que en gemidor estado / Triste infortunio por doquier me asalta" (Thirty years ago I saw the earth/ for thirty years I suffered tearfully/the sad misfortunes that everywhere assault me). The poet laments not only past hardships but a future of yet more toil and struggle: "Mas nada es para mi la dura guerra / Que en vano suspirar, he soportado / Si la calculo ¡oh Dios! Con la que falta" (p. 138) (But the hard struggles I have had to endure with sighs are nothing, if I compare them—Oh God!—with what is yet to come).

Manzano's poetry, including a sequence on themes ranging from the pastoral to the nostalgic, was published in the periodicals sponsored by Del Monte and his group, including *Diario de la Habana*, *El Diario de Matanzas*, and *La Moda ó Recreo Semanal del Bello Sexo*. After gaining his freedom in 1836, Manzano published regularly in *El Aguinaldo Habanero*, *El Álbum*, *Faro Industrial de La Habana*, and *La Prensa*.

Manzano's *Autobiografía* Manzano earned literary fame and a place in the Cuban literary canon with his *Autobiografía*, which Del Monte commissioned in 1835 as part of his campaign against the institution of slavery. As the first slave-authored narrative in the Americas, Manzano's engaging account details both the injustices he suffered as a domestic slave and also his budding literary vocation under adverse circumstances. Both the fragmentary nature of the memoir and its complex editorial history render it one of the most engrossing works of Hispanic Caribbean literature. Written in a style resembling a modern stream-of-consciousness technique, Manzano carefully constructs a narrative persona based on two conflicting yet complementary motifs: the abuse he suffered as a preadolescent and the longing for freedom that eventually led the young narrator to escape from oppressive conditions. The counterpoint between oppression and liberation is carefully structured in the text, beginning with an introduction in which Manzano details the circumstances of his birth during his mother's time of service in the household of Doña Beatriz Justiz de Santa Ana and her husband Don Juan Manzano. Evoking an almost idyllic early childhood, Manzano describes his parents and siblings and his schooling up to the age of ten.

After an early apprenticeship as a tailor, the narrator goes to live with his godmother. At the age of twelve he is sent to serve the Marquesa de Prado Ameno, a transition to "la verdadera historia de mi vida" (the true story of my life), and indeed the most painful stage of his life. From this point on, the narrator documents a series of episodes that shift the tone of the memoir into a poignant antislavery statement: periods of solitary confinement in a dark, rat-infested cell; the harsh punishment received for innocently crushing geranium flowers during an afternoon walk with his mistress; and a false accusation of stealing fine poultry destined for the mistress's table, followed by a second accusation of theft when a gold coin accidentally slips between the slats of a table top. Among the many instances of abuse he suffered under the capricious Marquesa, the episode of the crushed geraniums stands out as the most arbitrary abuse of power, for it dramatizes the contrast between the narrator's melancholic and introspective nature and the irrational use of force by *mayorales* (overseers) sent to execute the mistress's wrath. Throughout the autobiography, this counterpoint between the narrator's literary bent and the rigors of slavery reinforces the image of an artist in the making, a budding poet whose sensitivity sharpens the cruelty and arbitrariness of his superiors.

Toward the latter part of the autobiography, it is the narrator's literary vocation that allows him to overcome his immediate surroundings. Manzano's literary persona is most eloquently revealed in the episode recounting how the narrator learned the alphabet at the hands of a benevolent master, D. Nicolás, during a brief interlude in Havana. Every day, the narrator enters the master's study, where he struggles to acquire the dominant means of expression; first, he memorizes books of rhetoric "like a parrot"; from here, he learns to write by painstakingly copying his master's

penmanship; finally, he perfects his craft by imitating his master's word. Writing becomes a powerful instrument of self-definition. After the Marquesa defers the much-desired goal of liberty and persistently denies his rights, the narrator ultimately decides to flee. Given the text's abrupt end, the narrator's life as a free man is left for readers to imagine, but they are told of collective efforts to free him in 1836 for the sum of 968 pesos.

Imagination as a tool for liberation is echoed in Manzano's "La visión del poeta compuesta en un ingenio de fabricar azúcar" (A Poet's Vision Composed in a Sugar Mill), a long poem providing a sentimental overview of the sugar mill as site of human suffering: "Aquí es do se encuentran reunidos / De la humana miseria los portentos" (Here is where one finds united/All signs of human misery) (p. 178). A sudden turn then shows the poet in a garden, where, in a pastoral and prophetic vision, he experiences the redeeming power of love, personified in a maternal figure mysteriously invoked so as to free himself from a constrictive paternal authority. Despite the fleetingness of this vision, the poem reads as an antidote to the *Autobiografía*, as the lyrical voice surrenders to a symbolic resolution of the evils of slavery: "¿Cómo es posible que tranquilo viva? Pues al pintar mi cruel melancolía / Que sueño, me parece todavía" (How is it possible that I continue to live in peace? Because when I convey my cruel melancholy, I feel as if I am dreaming still) (p. 190).

In contrast to Manzano's philosophical bent, Tanco's tales depict the brutality of life under slavery in a naturalist idiom. Prefaced by a note in which he affirms the impact of the black presence in Cuba, in "El niño Fernando," more popularly known as "Petrona y Rosalía," Tanco describes the lust of a white master and his son in order to highlight how the corruption of the slave system continues from generation to generation. This is shown by the repetition of sexual violence inflicted on black women. Don Antonio rapes the unfortunate Petrona, who is banished to the cane fields; his son Fernando takes advantage of Rosalía, Petrona's daughter. The story reveals that the white mistress, Doña Concepción, has engaged in a bit of artful deceit: As a means to avenge her husband's betrayal, she has taken a lover, who is Fernando's real father, thus ingeniously eluding the hint of incest, one of the primary themes of antislavery narrative, as seen in Cirilo Villaverde's *Cecilia Valdés* (1882). At the end of the tale, Petrona and Rosalía, both victims of violence as black female slaves at the mercy of their masters, die alone on the plantation. The tale ends on an ironic note, as the callous masters see this tragic event only as a loss of capital.

COSTUMBRISMO

Transforming Cuba from an island colony into an autonomous nation implied the appropriation of nature, particularly of the sugar-grinding and tobacco regions. *Costumbrista* sketches, such as Ramón de Palma's "Matanzas y Yumurí," published in *El Aguinaldo Habanero* in 1837, outlined the contours of the countryside. Cirilo Villaverde's "Excursion [sic] á la Vuelta-Abajo," first published in the 1838–1839 volume of *El Álbum*, depicts the author's return to his native Pinar del Río, a rich tobacco region threatened by the encroaching sugar industry.

Other *costumbrista* works, such as Villaverde's "Amoríos y contratiempos de un guajiro," published in *La Cartera Cubana* in April 1839, depict local types such as the *guajiro* (peasant). Such depictions helped to consolidate a sense of an insular *imagined community*, a term devised by the scholar Benedict Anderson for the geographical and social bonding that solidifies national borders. The emblematic figure of the *calesero* (coachman) is the subject of Suárez y Romero's *Francisco* and immortalized in "El Quitrín," Frédéric Miahle's lithograph of a horse-drawn carriage in which ride two demure ladies of the Havana aristocracy. Palma's romantic tale of intrigue, *Una Pascua en San Marcos*, published in *El Álbum*, fits a pedagogical discourse of the nation: In it a cuckolded Spanish officer is outsmarted by Don Claudio, a creole dandy who chases after the officer's wife while betraying his own intended, the innocent Aurora, all amid the magnificent palm groves of the Artemisa plantation. Claudio's death at the end of the novel represents a scathing critique of the listless heirs of the sugar aristocracy, a point much debated among the members of Del Monte's *tertulia*.

From the Viewpoint of Visitors Foreign travelers also participated in the incipient discourse of Cubanness. Mialhe, in his 1840 collection *Viage pintoresco alrededor de la isla de Cuba dedicado al Conde de Villanueva*, left an imprint of the *guajiro* dance, *el zapateado*. The collection included memorable views of Havana promenades and the impressive Teatro de Tacón. Also in 1840, five years after the start of the boom in Cuban letters, la Condesa de Merlin returned to Cuba, strolling through the streets of her native Havana in a gesture to recover her past. The daughter of a prominent family of the sugar aristocracy, Mercedes Santa Cruz y Montalvo was born in Havana in 1789 but resided in France during most of her adult life, returning to Cuba after the death of her husband, Count Antoine Christophe Merlin. Borrowing freely from the *costumbrista* sketches authored by Villaverde, Palma, and other members of the Del Monte circle, la Condesa de Merlin wrote a travelogue, *Viaje a la Habana* (1844), which is a romantic version of colonial life and mores. An initial encounter with the members of the Montalvo clan in the opening scenes of *Viaje a la Habana* depicts family life amid the creole aristocracy as an idyllic golden age, while her portraits of masters and slaves are tinted by her own sentimental recollection of childhood. As both insider and outsider, Merlin registers an important moment in the coming-of-age of Cuban nationality: the transition from "la raza actual de los españoles habaneros," (the

race of Havana-born natives and Spaniards) defined by their relationship to the peninsula, to a sense of interiority, "cuando aquí comenzamos á vivir no para los negocios ni para el comercio, no para la vanidad y para el público, sino para nosotros mismos, para nuestras afecciones y para nuestros placeres" (when we start to live here neither for business or commerce, neither for vainglory or public display, but rather for ourselves, for our affections and pleasures) (pp. 17, 100).

Despite her long absence from Cuba, Merlin left an indelible imprint on colonial society. A selection from her *La Havane*, a three-volume work in French that depicts creole women, their marital arrangements, and child-rearing habits, was published in serial form in the *Diario de La Habana* in September 1843. The series of letters dedicated to the French novelist and memoirist George Sand, published anonymously in *Faro Industrial de La Habana*, provoked a strong polemic in the local press regarding women's roles in colonial society.

Merlin's impressions of the bay of Havana as her ship, the *Christophe-Colomb*, sails into harbor contrasts with the views of earlier scientific explorers, such as the Baron Alexander von Humboldt, who in his *Essai politique sur l'île de Cuba* extolled the openness of the bay in comparison to similar ports in the Americas. In a now-forgotten pamphlet titled *Refutacion de un folleto intitulado Viage a la Habana ...* (1844), originally published in the *Diario de La Habana*, Félix Tanco y Bosmeniel, the most outspoken member of Del Monte's *tertulia*, denied Merlin's desire for inclusion in the "imagined community" because of her—in his view—inaccurate descriptions of the Havana coastline and urban profile. In spite of its ambivalent reception at the time, Merlin's voyage of return evokes a recurring motif in Cuban letters, a "Journey Back to the Source," as echoed in Villaverde's *Excursión a Vuelta Abajo* and Alejo Carpentier's short story "Viaje a la semilla."

In 1843 and 1844, at a time when the colonial government was battling to retain slavery on the island, it reacted violently to the Conspiración de La Escalera (Ladder Conspiracy), an alleged antislavery conspiracy among freed slaves, blacks, mulattoes, and the creole intelligentsia in Matanzas. In the cruel repression that followed, hundreds of blacks and mulattoes were tortured, imprisoned, exiled, or killed. Among the literary community, Luz y Caballero was barred from teaching for four years, Del Monte was exiled, Manzano was imprisoned and tortured, and the poet Gabriel de la Concepción Valdés (Plácido) was executed by firing squad. The flourishing of literary figures and works in nineteenth-century Cuba thus came to an abrupt end.

BIBLIOGRAPHY

Aguilera Manzano, José María. "Las corrientes liberales habaneras a través de las publicaciones periódicas de la primera mitad del siglo XIX." *Cuban Studies* 38 (2007): 125–153.

Anderson, Benedict. *Imagined Communities: Reflections on the Origin and Spread of Nationalism.* London: Verso, 1983.

Benítez Rojo, Antonio. "Power/Sugar/Literature: Toward a Reinterpretation of Cubanness." *Cuban Studies* 16 (1986): 9–32.

Bueno, Salvador. *De Merlin a Carpentier: Nuevos temas y personajes de la literatura cubana.* Havana: UNEAC Contemporáneos, 1977.

Del Monte, Domingo. *Escritos.* Edited by José A. Fernández. Havana: Cultural, 1929.

Franco, José Luciano, ed. *Autobiografía, cartas y versos de Juan Francisco Manzano.* Havana: Municipio de La Habana, 1937.

Friol, Roberto. *Suite para Juan Francisco Manzano.* Havana: Editorial Arte y Literatura, 1977.

Humboldt, Alejandro de. *Ensayo político sobre la isla de Cuba.* 1930. Edited by Fernando Ortiz, Francisco Arango y Parreño, J. S. Thrasher, et al. Havana: Fundación Fernando Ortiz, 1998.

Jensen, Larry R. *Children of Colonial Despotism: Press, Politics, and Culture in Cuba, 1790–1840.* Tampa: University Presses of Florida, 1988.

Lewis Galanes, Adriana. "El *Álbum* de Domingo Del Monte (Cuba, 1838–1839)." *Cuadernos Hispanoamericanos* nos. 451–452 (January–February 1988): 255–265.

Lewis Galanes, Adriana. *Poesías de J. F. Manzano, esclavo en la isla de Cuba.* Madrid: Betania, 1991.

Luis, William. *Literary Bondage: Slavery in Cuban Narrative.* Austin: University of Texas Press, 1990.

Luis, William, ed. *Autobiografía del esclavo poeta y otros escritos,* by Juan Franciso Manzano. Madrid: Iberoamericana, 2007.

Méndez Rodenas, Adriana. *Gender and Nationalism in Colonial Cuba: The Travels of Santa Cruz y Montalvo, Condesa de Merlin.* Nashville, TN: Vanderbilt University Press, 1998.

Méndez Rodenas, Adriana. "Tropics of Deceit: Desire and the Double in Cuban Antislavery Narrative." *Cuban Studies* 28 (1999): 83–99.

Merlin, Mercedes Santa Cruz y Montalvo. *Viaje a la Habana.* Edited by Adriana Méndez Rodenas. Doral, FL: StockCero Ediciones, 2008.

Molloy, Sylvia. *At Face Value: Autobiographical Writing in Spanish America.* Cambridge, U.K.: Cambridge University Press, 1991.

Murray, David R. *Odious Commerce: Britain, Spain, and the Abolition of the Cuban Slave Trade.* Cambridge, U.K.: Cambridge University Press, 1980.

Paquette, Robert L. *Sugar Is Made with Blood: The Conspiracy of La Escalera and the Conflict between Empires over Slavery in Cuba.* Middletown, CT: Wesleyan University Press, 1988.

Tanco y Bosmeniel, Félix. *Refutacion al folleto intitulado "Viaje a la Habana" por la Condesa de Merlin.* Havana: Imprenta de Gobierno y Capitanía General, 1844.

Tanco y Bosmeniel, Félix. "Escenas de la vida privada en la isla de Cuba." *Cuba contemporánea* 39, no. 156 (December 1925): 255–288.

LITERATURE: FICTION IN THE REPUBLICAN PERIOD

Jorge Febles

Cuban narrative production and print media from the end of the Spanish colonial period until the triumph of the Cuban Revolution.

Until the triumph of the Cuban Revolution in 1959, the predominant critical approach to the nation's literature was the positivist-inspired generational method of Salvador Bueno, Raimundo Lazo, Juan José Remos, and others. Although essayists such as Marcelo Pogolotti, in his *La república de Cuba al través de sus escritores* (The Cuban Republic Viewed through Its Writers, 1958), and José Antonio Portuondo, in *El contenido social de la literatura cubana* (Social Content in Cuban Literature, 1944), pursued a socio-historical outlook focused on representative individual voices or narrative reactions to particular states of affairs, most critics categorized writers according to timespans of fifteen to twenty years. In 1965, for example, in *La literatura cubana: Esquema histórico desde sus orígenes hasta 1964* (Cuban Literature: Historical Outline from Its Origins until 1964), Lazo synthesized literary production during the republican period by identifying three generations: an initial group comprised of writers who practiced their craft during the first two decades of the twentieth century; a second contingent that emerged about 1930; and a third that began to publish in the 1940s, came of age in the turbulent 1950s, and flourished, albeit briefly in some instances, after the triumph of the Revolution in 1959. Lazo explains that, in contrast to the earlier generations, tinged as they were by triumphal optimism or its antithesis, sociopolitical defeatism, the third generation assumed a predominantly escapist perspective, which coincided paradoxically with ideological extremism (p. 184).

PREVALENT MOTIFS

Critics largely agree on the prevailing motifs in the fictional production of Cuban writers during the first decades of the republican period. Predominant among them is the quest for national identity centering on the notion of *cubanidad* or *cubanía* (Cubanness), an elusive concept precisely because of the island's cultural diversity. Gustavo Pérez Firmat has emphasized most writers' "translation sensibility" (p. 4), which for him defines Cuban literary style and, by extension, *cubanía* itself. *Criollista* (regionalist) or *mundonovista* (New World–focused) authors intent on depicting the essence of Cuba represented Cubanness in two characteristic ways: through verbal manipulations of the vernacular (endeavors based on the naïve assumption that, in the New World, it is feasible to reinvent the linguistic wheel), and more significantly, the pursuit of an originality based on re-creation through translation

■ *See also*

Cuentos negros de Cuba (Lydia Cabrera)

Gender: Colonial Period to 1920

Governance and Contestation: The Republic: 1902–1952

The Kingdom of this World (Alejo Carpentier)

of European models. They may be counterposed after a fashion to the writers linked to *Orígenes*, the journal established in 1944 by José Lezama Lima and José Rodríguez Feo with the aspiration of making Cuban literature more cosmopolitan.

Portuondo concludes that writers of the first and second republican generations employed politics as a dominant theme. They were affected by North American interference in Cuban affairs, especially the imposition of the Platt Amendment to the Cuban constitution of 1902, which affected Cuba's rights to negotiate treaties and permitted the United States to maintain its naval base at Guantánamo Bay and to intervene in Cuban affairs. This act resulted in the institution of what some have called a *república mediatizada* (mediatized republic), since the country's sovereignty was virtually in the hands of the United States and was mediated through its interests and wishes, thus making the new nation a pseudo-republic. Hence, in their texts, novelists and short story writers repeatedly conveyed bitterness and disillusionment, while advocating for an effective governmental structure capable of administering the country properly and securing a more just society.

THE FIRST REPUBLICAN GENERATION

Despite Emilio Bobadilla's (1862–1921) acerbically naturalistic *A fuego lento* (At Low Heat, 1903), Emilio Bacardí's (1844–1922) historical narratives *Vía Crucis* (1910) and *Doña Guiomar* (1916), and Raimundo Cabrera's (1852–1923) incisive analysis of the early republic in *Sombras eternas* (Eternal Shadows, 1919), all late works by established writers, those authors who began to publish between 1905 and 1910 typify the fictional production of the first republican period. In general, they represent somewhat contrasting aesthetic attitudes and narrative interests. Seminal figures within this initial spectrum include Miguel de Carrión (1875–1929), Jesús Castellanos (1879–1912), Carlos Loveira (1882–1928), José Antonio Ramos (1885–1946), and Alfonso Hernández Catá (1885–1940). Linked by common themes, they evince in their works to a greater or lesser degree an effete *modernista* exuberance, evident particularly in linguistic affectation and erotic affinities, often combined with a measured naturalism and a positivist philosophical standpoint. Carrión and Hernández Catá, for example, wrote fiction inspired by an intention to probe clinically into the minds of their characters. In *Las honradas* (Chaste Women, 1918) and *Las impuras* (Impure Women, 1919), Carrión emulates Emile Zola's *méthode expérimentale* (experimental— i.e., scientific—method) to inquire in a *verista* (true-to-life) manner (Remos p. 291) into the psyche and moral deportment of Cuban women. In contrast, Hernández Catá, influenced by Freud and Havelock Ellis, employs a psychological realism in the stories of *Manicomio* (The Insane Asylum, 1931) and other collections, as well as in his controversial novel *El ángel de Sodoma* (The Angel of Sodom, 1929), a text that "brought him the reputation of being the first novelist to give a protagonist's role to male homosexuality in the Hispanic world" (Bejel pp. 67–68). Meanwhile, Castellanos's first novel, *La conjura* (The Conspiracy, 1908), written in florid *modernista* prose, anathematizes the social milieu that repudiates the intellectual endeavors of a misunderstood young man of science. Ramos and Loveira, by contrast, criticize vehemently in their fictional works the failed promises of the nascent Cuban state, manifest in a society ever more unjust and corrupt. Loveira, in particular, wrote angrily and in a cynical tone about Cuban institutions, national politicians, the insensitive upper bourgeoisie and U.S. meddling in the island in such defining books as *Los inmorales* (The Immoral Ones, 1919), *Generales y doctores* (Generals and Doctors, 1920), *Los ciegos* (The Blind, 1922), and *Juan Criollo* (1927), undoubtedly his best work. Pérez Firmat argues convincingly that in this quasi-picaresque narrative, the book's protagonist illustrates the evolution of the *bobo* (fool) who becomes a *vivo* (rogue), capable of obtaining wealth and power by exploiting the national flaws that Loveira invariably strove to criticize (p. 117). In parallel fashion, Ramos penned three caustic novels, analyzing Cuban reality through the first decades of the nation's existence: *Coaybay* (1927), *Las impurezas de la realidad* (The Impurities of Reality, 1931), and *Caniquí* (1936). Like Loveira's works, Ramos's texts reveal a socialist worldview—more radical in the former, less dogmatic in the latter—also manifest in other writers of this and the subsequent period.

Carrión, Castellanos, Loveira, Ramos, and Hernández Catá published their shorter fiction and essays in journals such as the weekly *El Fígaro* (1885–1934; 1943). This first generation of writers also collaborated in *Cuba contemporánea* (1913–1927), a magazine that allowed them to denounce the republic's ill state (Bueno p. 10) without forsaking their literary activities. *Cuba contemporánea* also became a forum for the second republican generation. Thus, Luis Felipe Rodríguez (1888–1947), a contemporary of the first-generation writers who practiced a more authentic *criollismo*, provided a bridge between the two eras. Rodríguez published his works in *El Fígaro*, *Letras de La Habana* and, of course, *Cuba contemporánea*. An autodidact, like most of the members of the first republican generation, Rodríguez focused his brief fictions on the Cuban countryside and on a sociopolitical reality that he perceived as critically as Loveira and Ramos, merging a learned positivist point of view with more radical revolutionary ideals. His best works—the short novel *La conjura de la ciénaga* (The Conspiracy of la Ciénaga, 1924), a definitive version of which appeared in 1937 under the title *Ciénaga*, and above all *Los relatos de Marcos Antilla* (Marcos Antilla's Stories, 1932)—evince a critical perspective voiced directly and indirectly by characters who represent with remarkable naturalness the rural environment whence they emanate.

AN ERA OF TURMOIL AND TRANSFORMATION

The progressive radicalization of Cuban politics during the 1920s and 1930s, inspired by the repressive Machado leadership, the failed revolution that ensued, the perennial discontent with U.S. interference, the ideological evolution of the island's intellectuals, racial inequalities, and the developing feminist movement, among other social factors, molded the writers of the second republican generation. Often they blended their politics with avant-garde literary forms of expression. An example of this mixture is the Protesta de los Trece (Protest of the Thirteen), which took place on 19 March 1923. Headed by poet, short story writer, and activist Rubén Martínez Villena with the purpose of voicing public concern over the illegal purchase by the Alfredo Zayas government of the Convent of Santa Clara, it involved other promising intellectuals and artists. The event led to the creation of the elitist yet largely Marxist-leaning *Grupo Minorista* (Select Group), comprised of Jorge Mañach (1898–1961), Félix Lizaso (1891–1967), Alejo Carpentier (1904–1980), Conrado Massaguer (1889–1956), Juan Marinello (1898–1977), Rubén Martínez Villena (1899–1934), and Mariano Brull (1891–1956), among others.

Writers of the second republican generation published their work in or were associated with publications that came into being during the early years of the republic: the weekly magazine *Bohemia* (began 1910; confiscated by the revolutionary government in 1960; versions still being published in Cuba and in the Cuban diaspora in the early 2010s); the monthly *Carteles* (1919–1960), the literary and cultural journal *Social* (1916–1933; 1935–1938); Renée and Sara Méndez Capote's ephemeral feminist venture *Artes y Letras* (1918); and above all, the *Revista de Avance* (1927–1930), which despite its short run defined the *minoristas* politically as well as aesthetically.

THE SECOND REPUBLICAN GENERATION

An attempt to synthesize the narrative endeavors of authors belonging to the second republican generation must focus on discernible tendencies, perceived as creative constants rather than as definitive fictionalizing methodologies. Carlos Montenegro (1900–1981) and Lino Novás Calvo (1903–1983), both of whom were engaged with immediate reality, assumed nevertheless quite different creative attitudes. Montenegro's crude realism, informed initially by patriotic ardor and by communist beliefs that he forsook later in life, is evident in several collections as well as in his prison narrative *Hombres sin mujer* (Men without Women, 1938), in which he indicts the Cuban penal system by centering the text daringly on homosexual behavior in jail. Novás Calvo, by contrast, is a far

more artful narrator whose numerous short fictions translate (to employ Pérez Firmat's notion) styles and ideas learned by reading (and in his case literally translating, since he earned a living in that fashion) English-speaking writers of the period. In stories such as "La noche de Ramón Yendía" (Ramón Yendía's Night), the author manipulates the plot to achieve intensity and maximum effect, while employing the vernacular to regionalize it. As a novelist, in 1933, he published the *bildungsroman El negrero* (The Slave Trader), a portrayal of the life of the infamous Spaniard Pedro Blanco Fernández de Trava, based essentially on *Adventures of an African Slaver* (1854), by the American Brantz Mayer.

If Montenegro and Novás Calvo reflect social and political concerns communicated, particularly in the latter case, through a sophisticated cinematic technique and an incipient magic realism, Enrique Labrador Ruiz (1902–1991) and Dulce María Loynaz (1902–1997) represent the high modernist style that coexisted with quasi-realistic fiction. In his *gaseiforme* (gas-shaped) novels such as *El laberinto de sí mismo* (The Labyrinth of Himself, 1933), and later in his *novelas caudiformes* (tail-shaped novels) such as *Trailer de sueños* (Trailer of Dreams, 1949) and *La sangre hambrienta* (Hungry Blood, 1950), Labrador Ruiz combined structural experimentation and temporal fragmentation with a decidedly Cuban space and tone, anchored firmly in popular language. Poet Dulce María Loynaz published the novel *Jardín* (Garden) in 1951. Loynaz's book, like Labrador Ruiz's works, stupefied Cuban intellectuals due to its fragmentary structure and exuberant lyricism (Davies p. 68). *Jardín* represents the aesthetic peak of the Cuban feminist literature of the time, which also includes the regionalist tales of Dora Alonso (1910–2001), Ofelia Rodríguez Acosta's (1902–1975) polemical *La vida manda* (Life Decides, 1929), and Mariblanca Sabás Alomá's (1901–1983) *La rémora* (The Hindrance, 1921).

The Afro-Cuban poetic movement of the 1920s and 1930s, inspired by European surrealism, Antillean *négritude*, and, within the island, by the anthropological and sociocultural studies of Fernando Ortiz (1881–1969), did not substantially impact narrative trends. Although novels such as Ramos's *Caniquí*, Novás Calvo's *El negrero* and Alejo Carpentier's *Ecué-Yamba-O* (1933) underscore transcultural concerns, only Lydia Cabrera (1899–1991) produced a body of work comprised mainly of short fictions and anthropological essays, all devoted to understanding, re-creating, and translating Afro-Cuban mythology and religion. Her collections *Contes nègres de Cuba* (written in French, 1936; published in Spanish as *Cuentos negros de Cuba* [Black Stories of Cuba, 1940]), *¿Por qué?* (Why? 1948), as well as the heterogeneous text *El monte* (The Wilderness, 1954) replicate the naïve tone and surreal quality endemic to myths recounted orally.

Alejo Carpentier exemplifies, undoubtedly, the pinnacle of Cuban high modernism. During the 1940s and 1950s, he published *El reino de este mundo* (The Kingdom of This World, 1949) and *Los pasos perdidos* (Lost Steps, 1953), novels that respond to his conception of *lo real maravilloso* (the marvelous real), that is, the coexistence of the commonplace and the magical, which he attributes to Latin America in its entirety, a region that had not yet exhausted its mythological potential, given the persistence of people's will to believe in the miraculous. Carpentier's application of this theory in these two books established him as a precursor in Cuban letters, along with Labrador Ruiz, Novás Calvo, and Loynaz, of Latin American magic realism.

Other important members of the second republican generation include realist writers Enrique Serpa (1900–1968), who vividly portrayed corrupt Havana in *Contrabando* (1938); Marcelo Salinas (1889–1978), who wrote the novel of social protest *Un aprendiz de revolucionario* (A Revolutionary Apprentice, 1937); and Pablo de la Torriente Brau (1901–1936), who perished during the Spanish Civil War, leaving behind the novel *Aventuras del soldado desconocido cubano* (Adventures of the Cuban Unknown Soldier, 1941) in addition to numerous short stories. They all share an essentially critical view of contemporary Cuban society.

THE THIRD REPUBLICAN GENERATION

The third republican generation came of age during the 1940s, a period when, as Lazo explains, the depressed state of the nation, unceasing corruption, and a general lack of interest in cultural affairs provoked artists either to rebel by perpetuating in their works the sociopolitical preoccupations evident among many members of the previous grouping or to assume pure aesthetic tenets that promoted escapism. As iconic leader of the latter tendency, José Lezama Lima (1910–1976) not only wrote memorable poems and essays, but perhaps more significantly edited or coedited journals that provided a space for emerging writers who shared a refined artistic outlook. Three lasted briefly: *Verbum* (three issues in 1937), *Espuela de plata* (Silver Spur, 1939–1941), and *Nadie parecía* (Nobody Seemed Like, 1942). Lezama Lima and José Rodríguez Feo (1920–1993) founded *Orígenes* (1944–1956), the most influential journal of the period. It published not only Cuban authors who shared the editors' aestheticism, but also international masters presented as models to the new generation. The first four chapters of *Paradiso*, Lezama's magnum opus published in its entirety in 1966, appeared in different issues of *Orígenes*.

Upon his departure from the journal due to editorial disagreements, Rodríguez Feo created *Ciclón* in collaboration with Virgilio Piñera (1912–1979). This influential journal lasted from 1955 until 1957, reappearing briefly in 1959. Piñera, in the interim, established himself as the most important Cuban playwright and a gifted storyteller who also wrote *La carne de René* (René's Body, 1953), a novel with homosexual implications. *Cuentos fríos* (1956) exemplifies Piñera's Kafkaesque creative method that focuses on the impermanence and absurdity of the human condition. As he does in his theatrical works, the author permeates his tales with sardonic humor, provoking disquieted laughter in readers who feel an existential angst.

The importance of *Ciclón* lies as well in the fact that it provided a forum for younger writers such as Guillermo Cabrera Infante (1929–2005), Fayad Jamís (1930–1988), and Antón Arrufat (b. 1935). Cabrera Infante, who published most of the stories that constitute *Así en la paz como en la guerra* (In Peace as in War, 1960) during the 1950s, matured as a writer after the the Revolution of 1959. A translational author in the fullest sense, his early stories enact a dialogue with William Faulkner, James Joyce, Ernest Hemingway, and other modernist writers whom he parodies frequently. Cabrera Infante also merits recognition as the founder and editor of *Lunes de Revolución* (Revolutionary Mondays), a literary supplement of the newspaper *Revolución*. From its inception on 23 March 1959, until the final issue, dated 6 November 1961, it provided a forum for aspiring authors of his generation.

Numerous other novelists and short story writers published during the 1940s and 1950s. Among the most significant are Samuel Feijóo (1914–1992), Onelio Jorge Cardoso (1914–1986), Humberto Arenal (b. 1926), Hilda Perera (b. 1926), José Lorenzo Fuentes (b. 1928), Edmundo Desnoes (b. 1930), and Lisandro Otero (1932–1998). They evince in general the generational ambivalence between egocentric aestheticism and social commitment. After the Revolution, however, they evolved toward a more committed outlook, at least during the initial years.

Were it feasible to generalize about the development of Cuban narrative during the republican period, it might be argued that, to a certain degree, it was shaped by sociopolitical circumstances. The precarious state of the mediatized republic often impelled fiction writers to examine its evolving reality with censorious eyes. In addition, many focused on the analysis of an ambiguous *cubanía*, seeking to find the essence of national identity. In doing so, they reflected the translation sensibility described so lucidly by Pérez Firmat. Others, however, sought to escape their immediate environment by surrendering to aesthetic impulses. That said, Cuban narrative in the 1898–1959 period resembles fundamentally that of most Latin American countries. Issues of identity, nation-building, political instability, marginalization, and translation of imported literary paradigms are central to the literature of the Americas throughout the first sixty years of the twentieth century.

BIBLIOGRAPHY

Bejel, Emilio. *Gay Cuban Nation.* Chicago: University of Chicago Press, 2001.

Bueno, Salvador, ed. *Antología del cuento en Cuba (1902–1952).* Havana: Dirección de Cultura del Ministerio de Educación, Ediciones de Cincuentenario, 1953.

Bueno, Salvador. *Medio siglo de literatura cubana, 1902–1952.* Havana: Comisión Nacional Cubana de la UNESCO, 1953.

Carpentier, Alejo. "Prólogo." *El reino de este mundo.* 3rd ed. Mexico City: Compañía General de Ediciones, 1971.

Chomsky, Aviva, Barry Carr, and Pamela Maria Smorkaloff, eds. *Cuba Reader: History, Culture, Politics.* Durham, NC: Duke University Press, 2003.

Davies, Catherine. *A Place in the Sun? Women Writers in Twentieth-Century Cuba.* London: Zed Books, 1997.

Fornés-Bonavía Dolz, Leopoldo. *Cuba, cronología: Cinco siglos de historia, política y cultura.* Madrid: Verbum, 2003.

Fornet, Ambrosio, ed. *Antología del cuento cubano contemporáneo.* 2nd ed. Mexico City: Era, 1970.

Lazo, Raimundo. *La literatura cubana: Esquema histórico desde sus orígenes hasta 1964.* Mexico City: Universidad Nacional Autonoma de Mee Mem, 1965.

Luis, William. *Literary Bondage: Slavery in Cuban Narrative.* Austin: University of Texas Press, 1990.

Luis, William. *Lunes de Revolución: Literatura y cultura en los primeros años de la Revolución Cubana.* Madrid: Verbum, 2003.

Martínez, Julio A., ed. *Dictionary of Twentieth-Century Cuban Literature.* Westport, CT: Greenwood Press, 1990.

Montero, Susana A. *La narrativa femenina cubana, 1923–1958.* Havana: Academia, 1958.

Pérez, Louis A., Jr. *On Becoming Cuban: Identity, Nationality, and Culture.* Chapel Hill: University of North Carolina Press, 1999.

Pérez Firmat, Gustavo. *The Cuban Condition: Translation and Identity in Modern Cuban Literature.* Cambridge, U.K.: Cambridge University Press, 1989.

Pogolotti, Marcelo. *La república de Cuba al través de sus escritores.* Havana: Lex, 1958.

Portuondo, José Antonio. *El contenido social de la literatura cubana.* Mexico City: El Colegio de México, Centro de Estudios Sociales, 1944.

Remos, Juan J. *Historia de la literatura cubana,* vol. 3. Havana: Cárdenas, 1945. Reprint, Miami: Mnemosyne, 1969.

Ripoll, Carlos. *La generación del 23 en Cuba y otros apuntes sobre el vanguardismo.* New York: Las Américas, 1968.

Romero, Cira. "Prólogo." In *Ciénaga y otros relatos,* by Luis Felipe Rodríguez. Havana: Letras Cubanas, 1984.

Smorkaloff, Pamela María. *Cuban Writers On and Off the Island.* New York: Twayne, 1999.

Souza, Raymond D. *Major Cuban Novelists: Innovation and Tradition.* Columbia: University of Missouri Press, 1976.

Thomas, Hugh. *Cuba, or, The Pursuit of Freedom.* Updated ed. New York: Da Capo Press, 1998.

LITERATURE: FICTION IN THE REVOLUTIONARY PERIOD

Alberto Garrandés

The Cuban novel and short story from 1959 to 1989.

In the thirty years after the triumph of the Revolution in 1959, Cuban narrative fiction responded to the legacies of two specific moments of readjustment in stylistic and esthetic tendencies. The first moment, rooted in the avant-garde movements of the 1920s and 1930s, remained attentive to global cultural trends but from the perspective of national self-definition. The latter moment, marked by the year 1959 and, thus, happening at the very beginning of this period within a new and unique horizon in world culture—that of the 1960s—established a new set of themes and characters inspired by visions of potential social utopias.

THE 1960s

Major sociopolitical changes kept happening in Cuba after 1959, of course. Still, the main narrative plotlines and trends of this thirty-year period were defined during the 1960s, a decade that should be thought of not just as a series of radical breaks, but as years in which intellectuals and writers came together to debate and polemicize about differing ideas Notions of social revolution and of revolution in and through culture were mixed together and debated with great urgency. However, the fact that there was a revolutionary regime wielding the full brunt of power raised pointed questions and mandates about the place of art and literature, as well as the role of intellectuals, artists, and writers, in the revolutionary process.

The so-called boom in Latin American fiction writing during that decade elevated to canonical stature a series of novels that set international standards of excellence that Cuban writers readily emulated. Still, the attractiveness of the issues, characters, and conflicts that the Revolution brought to the attention of fiction writers remained a powerful gravitational force in itself.

One can observe a synchronicity between the theoretical and intellectual debates in Cuba at the time and the new writing modes that appeared in fictional texts which almost always refer to the Cuban situation, such as *El siglo de las luces* (Explosion in a Cathedral, 1962) by Alejo Carpentier; *Tres tristes tigres* (Three Trapped Tigers, 1967) by Guillermo Cabrera Infante; *Paradiso* (Paradise, 1966) by José Lezama Lima; *Los niños se despiden* (The Children Say Goodbye, 1968) by Pablo Armando Fernández; *Biografía de un cimarrón* (Biography of a Fugitive Slave, 1966) by Miguel Barnet; *El mundo alucinante* (Hallucinations, 1969) by Reinaldo Arenas; *El viaje* (The Voyage, 1967) by Miguel Collazo; *Después de la gaviota* (After the

Seagull, 1968) by José Lorenzo Fuentes; *Memorias del subdesarrollo* (Memories of Underdevelopment, 1965) by Edmundo Desnoes; *Adire y el tiempo roto* (Adire and the Broken Time, 1967) by Manuel Granados; *Pasión de Urbino* (The Passion of Urbino, 1967) by Lisandro Otero; *El escudo de hojas secas* (The Shield of Dry Leaves, 1969) by Antonio Benítez Rojo; *Siempre la muerte, su paso breve* (Always Death, Its Brief Passing, 1968) by Reynaldo González; *Vivir en Candonga* (To Live in Candonga, 1966) by Ezequiel Vieta; *Rebelión en la octava casa* (Rebellion in the Eighth House, 1968) by Jaime Sarusky; *Condenados de Condado* (The Condemned of Condado, 1968) by Norberto Fuentes; *El regreso* (The Return, 1963) by Calvert Casey; *De donde son los cantantes* (Where the Singers Come From, 1968) by Severo Sarduy; *Circulando el cuadrado* (Circling the Square, 1963) by César López; *Los años duros* (The Hard Years, 1966) by Jesús Díaz; and *Presiones y diamantes* (Pressures and Diamonds, 1967) by Virgilio Piñera. Together these works constitute a core group or textual matrix that helped found new systems of writing and opened an interlocutive space well synched to the spirit of the 1960s .

Toward the end of the 1960s this delicate balance between commingling fictional projects and visions began to break down as aesthetico-political rulings invaded the realm of literature. An extreme dogmatism began permeating the debates over the revolutionary role of culture in the early 1970s, and muddled the counterpoint between *lo cubano* (Cubanhood) and universality that writers had viewed as a politically valid creative purpose in their previous work. Then came the very harmful regulations issued at the First National Congress of Education and Culture at the beginning of the 1970s.

THE 1970s

The term *quinquenio gris* (the Grey Five Years) refers to the first five years of the 1970s in Cuba during which Stalinist-like strictures in cultural policy smothered artistic inventiveness. However, we would need to examine all the published works of that era to determine where fiction writing turned too "grey" and officialistic and where it did not. The "grey" 1970s also saw the publication of two artistically ambitious novels by Carpentier—*Concierto barroco* (Baroque Concert) and *El recurso del método* (The Recourse to Method), both from 1974—as well as *Onoloria* (1973) by Miguel Collazo, a short masterpiece about the gifts of imagination. The 1970s also produced *El pan dormido* (The Sleeping Bread, 1975) by José Soler Puig, and Antonio Benítez Rojo's *El mar de las lentejas* (Sea of Lentils, 1979), a novel marked by the style of Carpentier and the mythical and baroque universe of the Caribbean. But these books were truly exceptional in a period when most books were characterized by a sociological perspective and by an insistent realistic style of wearisome rigidity.

The 1970s saw the official promotion, under the blunt precepts of an "official" social realism and propelled by a crude Manichaeanism, of police and crime fiction and an expansion of publishing that often amounted to nothing more than simple reprinting. But despite this, the literary environment was enlivened by two lavish novels published abroad by Severo Sarduy—*Cobra* (1972) and *Maitreya* (1978)—an author who already lived outside of Cuba, as did Guillermo Cabrera Infante—*Havana para un infante difunto* (published in English as *Infante's Inferno*, 1979)—and by fanciful short-story collections such as *Noticias de la quimera* (News of the Chimera, 1976) by Eliseo Diego; *Con los ojos cerrados* (With Eyes Closed, 1972) by Reinaldo Arenas; *Los pasos en la hierba* (Steps in the Grass, 1970) by Eduardo Heras León; *El buscador de tesoros* (The Treasure Seeker, 1971) by Rogelio Llopis; *El hilo y la cuerda* (The Thread and the Rope, 1974) by Onelio Jorge Cardoso; and *En ciudad semejante* (In a Similar City, 1970) by Lisandro Otero. Also significant were two books by Rafael Soler—*Campamento de artillería* (Artillery Camp, 1973) and *Noche de fósforos* (Night of Matches, 1974)—that, with *Tiempo de hombre* (Time of Man, 1977) by Miguel Mejides, announced the viewpoint of the Cuban narrative to come in the 1980s. During those same years, José Antonio Arocha, Manuel Cachán, and Uva de Aragón published three notable collections abroad: *El esplendor de la entrada* (The Splendor of the Arrival, 1975), *Cuentos de aquí y allá* (Stories from Here and There, 1977), and *Ni verdad ni mentira y otros cuentos* (Neither Truth nor Lie and Other Stories, 1976), respectively.

What happened in the bulk of 1970s Cuban fiction can be described as a de-dramatization of stories, a complacent mimicking of reality, and almost collective self-deception based on the myth that a literary text could enact social change, a premise drawn from the powerful contrivances of the "socialist realist" label. However, by the end of the decade, the fables began to fill up with conflicts and contradictions, and the practice of writing was reborn, not as a social mission, but as a search for artistic fulfillment.

THE 1980s

The 1980s, led by the 1980 Mariel Boatlift and its consequences, changed the panorama of Cuban narrative both on and off the island. New character types, new sources of inspiration, new horizons of expectation, and new forms of stimuli emerged; the benefits in the island were especially felt in the short story since, only with some exceptions, the novel in Cuba stayed under a mostly programmatic dynamic. Fortunately, science fiction and fantastic stories began to flourish with the work of authors such as Alberto Serret, F. Mond, Daína Chaviano, Féliz Lizárraga, and others. Various anthologies from these genres, as well as thematic collections—dealing with death, violence, love, humor—and general anthologies of the Cuban short story appeared during this time.

In 1987 two volumes of dazzling short stories by Virgilio Piñera (1912–1979) were found and published posthumously: *Muecas para escribientes* (Grimaces for Copyists) and *Un fogonazo* (An Explosion). These collections celebrated the power of pure imagination and literary play and were inspired by the oddball scenarios of Cuban everyday life. But the 1980s also produced *Colibrí* (Hummingbird, 1984) by Severo Sarduy, and *Mi llamada es* (My Calling Is, 1983) by Ezequiel Vieta, in which the experience of witnessing a historical myth—that of the figure and testimonial writings of Che Guevara, especially his *Pasajes de la guerra revolucionaria* (Passages of the Revolutionary War, 1963)—is conveyed in a highly literary manner that recalls some styles of magical realism. Other significant works included María Elena Llana's volume of short stories *Casas del Vedado* (Houses of Vedado, 1983); the stories of *Crónicas de medio mundo* (Chronicles from Middle Earth, 1984) by Alfredo Antonio Fernández; nonsensical and grotesque horror stories by Antonio Orlando Rodríguez in *Strip-tease* (1985); and the heartrending novel penned in Miami, *The Halfway House* (1987), by Guillermo Rosales. Cintio Vitier published *De Peña Pobre* (From Peña Pobre, 1980), the first of a trilogy of novels with the same name, in which the writer travels in his memory to the past as he reinvents his ideas about how history is lived. Antón Arrufat contributed a first novel, *La caja está cerrada* (The Box Is Closed, 1984), an intense and monumental work inspired by Marcel Proust.

Some of the most significant of the Cuban novels of the 1980s are *El palacio de las blanquísimas mofetas* (The Palace of the White Skunks, 1980) and *Otra vez el mar* (Once Again, the Sea, 1982) by Reinaldo Arenas; *Un tema para el griego* (A Theme for the Greek, 1982) by Jorge Luis Hernández; *Temporada de ángeles* (Season of Angels, 1984) by Lisandro Otero; *Las iniciales de la tierra* (The Initials of the Earth, 1987) by Jesús Díaz, *El cumpleaños del fuego* (Fire's Birthday, 1986) by Francisco López Sacha; *Un rey en el jardín* (A King in the Garden, 1983) by Senel Paz; and *El cazador* (The Hunter, 1985) by Raúl Luis. These works, all very different from each other, are still finding enthusiastic readers to this day. Arenas invents Pantagruelian historical fables but still makes space for meta-literary play in his writing; Hernández plays with extremely subjective focalizations of reality; Otero writes about revolutions since Cromwell's England; Díaz descends into the inner soul of characters as they begin to recognize great strains in their revolutionary convictions; Sacha and Paz study the rural and provincial environs of Cuba and tell almost magical stories; and Luis constructs metafictional artifacts with essay-like riffs and segments. *La trenza de la hermosa luna* (The Braid of the Beautiful Moon, 1987) by Mayra Montero, a Cuban author living in Puerto Rico, and two books by the Cuban-American author Roberto G. Fernández, *La vida es un special* (Life Is a Special, 1982) and *La montaña rusa* (The Roller Coaster, 1985), also enriched the Cuban novel during the 1980s.

The tone in Cuban narratives of the 1980s permeates, at least in works published on the island, several collections of short stories that still remain readable today, and in novels—some already mentioned—that tried to keep alive some of the epic and lyrical themes and elements that were part and parcel of the Cuban revolutionary process, its conflicts and its attitudes, after 1959. Thus, a system of models and types for fiction writing was assembled from an arsenal of motifs that "History" supplied not only in the "present" moment but in the revolutionary continuum born in 1959, from the clandestine struggle, the battles of the Sierra Maestra and Playa Girón, and the Literacy Campaign, to the world of rural schools, the storming of the Peruvian embassy, and the Mariel Boatlift. The last marked the launching of a double perspective now operating among Cuban writers everywhere: One outlook would remain poised on the island while the other, in a pendular-like shift, would refocus on what was happening with Cuba and Cubans abroad. This double perspective has given rise to writings where the language in which new stories of inter- or transcultural crossings are told is charged with a sort of vectorial force that challenges and redraws any formulaic notion of Cuban identity processes.

But structural erosions and aesthetic dysfunctions took their toll over time. The continuity of the narrative body introduced on the island during the 1980s is observable only in that handful of works mentioned above, and in some story collections that sidestepped the officialist expectation that literature should only function as social testimony and focused on exploring the virtual potentials in creative language, the dramatic frisson of compelling characters, and mise-en-scènes that were as rigorously fashioned as they were inventive.

Other Cuban short story writers who published during the 1980s—and some who preceded the narrative wave that followed, such as Amir Valle with *Tiempo en cueros* (Time in Skins, 1988) and *Yo soy el malo* (I Am the Bad One, 1989)—seemed to promote what could be called a "dramaturgical" trend in narrative fiction. This trend, at one point of notable interest, soon turned into a rhetorical style (now surmounted) that operated according to a set system of thematic references and clichés, Among the most notable of these works were *El niño aquel* (That Boy, 1980) by Senel Paz; *El jardín de las flores silvestres* (The Garden of Wildflowers, 1982) by Miguel Mejides; *Las llamas en el cielo* (Flames in the Sky, 1983) by Félix Luis Viera; *Descubrimiento del azul* (Discovery of Blue, 1987) by Francisco López Sacha; *Sin perder la ternura* (Without Losing Tenderness, 1987) by Luis Manuel García Méndez; *Donjuanes* (Don Juans, 1986) by Reinaldo Montero; *Se permuta esta casa* (Swap This House, 1988) by Guillermo Vidal; and *Noche de sábado* (Saturday Night, 1989) by Abel Prieto.

In conclusion, it seems that during this last period the short story generated higher creative dividends than the novel. By the end of the 1980s a new spectrum of narrative poetics and styles had arisen. The best defined styles belonged to writers already mentioned and to others such as Carlos Victoria—author of *Las sombras en la playa* (Shadows on the Beach, 1992) and *El resbaloso y otros cuentos* (The Slippery One and Other Stories, 1997)—who remain unknown on the island as they published their first collections belatedly, after leaving Cuba. Together, all these writers have contributed to renewing the panorama of the genre, revindicating the importance of relying on well-defined fictional characters instead of real-life testimonial subjects in order to fashion narrative structures that instill in the reader the progress of dramatic emotions from which springs, without a doubt, artistic fulfillment.

BIBLIOGRAPHY

Arcocha, José Antonio. *El esplendor de la entrada*. Madrid: Playor, 1975.

Aragón, Uva de. *Ni verdad ni mentira y otros cuentos*. Miami: Ediciones Universal, 1976.

Arenas, Reinaldo. *El mundo alucinante*. Mexico City: Editorial Diógenes, 1969.

Arenas, Reinaldo. *Con los ojos cerrados*. Montevideo: Editorial Arca, 1972.

Arenas, Reinaldo. *El color del verano*. Miami: Ediciones Universal, 1982.

Arenas, Reinaldo. *El palacio de las blanquísimas mofetas*. Caracas: Monte Ávila Editores, 1982.

Arenas, Reinaldo. *Otra vez el mar*. Barcelona: Argos Vergara, 1982.

Arrufat, Antón. *La caja está cerrada*. Havana: Editorial Letras Cubanas, 1984.

Barnet, Miguel. *Biografía de un cimarrón*. Havana: Instituto de Etnología y Folklore, 1966.

Benítez Rojo, Antonio. *Tute de reyes*. Havana: Casa de las Américas, 1967.

Benítez Rojo, Antonio. *El escudo de hojas secas*. Havana: Ediciones Unión, 1969.

Benítez Rojo, Antonio. *El mar de las lentejas*. Havana: Editorial Letras Cubanas, 1979.

Cabrera Infante, Guillermo. *Tres tristes tigres*. Barcelona: Seix Barral, 1967.

Cabrera Infante, Guillermo. *Havana para un infante difunto*. Barcelona: Seix Barral, 1979.

Cachán, Manuel. *Cuentos de aquí y allá*. Miami: Ediciones Universal, 1977.

Carpentier, Alejo. *El siglo de las luces*. Havana: Ediciones R., 1963.

Carpentier, Alejo. *Concierto barroco*. Havana: Editorial Arte y Literatura, 1974.

Carpentier, Alejo. *El recurso del método*. Havana: Editorial Arte y Literatura, 1974.

Casey, Calvert. *El regreso*. Havana: Ediciones R, 1962.

Collazo, Miguel. *El viaje*. Havana: Ediciones Unión, 1967.

Collazo, Miguel. *Onoloria*. Havana: Ediciones Unión, 1973.

Desnoes, Edmundo. *Memorias del subdesarrollo*. Havana: Ediciones Unión, 1965.

Díaz, Jesús. *Los años duros*. Havana: Casa de las Américas, 1966.

Díaz, Jesús. *Las iniciales de la tierra*. Havana: Editorial Letras Cubanas, 1987.

Diego, Eliseo. *Noticias de la quimera*. Havana: Editorial Arte y Literatura, 1975.

Fernández, Alfredo Antonio. *Crónicas de medio mundo*. Havana: Editorial Letras Cubanas, 1984.

Fernández, Pablo Armando. *Los niños se despiden*. Havana: Ediciones Casa de las Américas, 1968.

Fernández, Roberto G. *La vida es un special*. Havana: Ediciones Universal, 1982.

Fernández, Roberto G. *La montaña rusa*. Houston, TX: Arte Público Press, 1985.

Fuentes, Norberto. *Condenados de Condado*. Havana: Casa de las Américas, 1968.

García Méndez, Luis Manuel. *Sin perder la ternura*. Havana: Editorial Letras Cubanas, 1987.

González, Reynaldo. *Siempre la muerte, su paso breve*. Havana: Casa de las Américas, 1968.

Granados, Manuel. *Adire y el tiempo roto*. Havana: Casa de las Américas, 1967.

Guevara, Ernesto (Che). *Pasajes de la guerra revolucionaria*. Havana: Ediciones Unión, 1963.

Heras León, Eduardo. *La guerra tuvo seis nombres*. Havana: Casa de las Américas, 1968.

Heras León, Eduardo. *Los pasos en la hierba*. Havana: Casa de las Américas, 1970.

Hernández, Jorge Luis. *Un tema para el griego*. Havana: Editorial Letras Cubanas, 1982.

Jorge Cardoso, Onelio. *El hilo y la cuerda*. Havana: Ediciones Unión, 1974.

Lezama Lima, José. *Paradiso*. Havana: Ediciones Unión, 1966.

López, César. *Circulando el cuadrado*. Havana: Ediciones R, 1963.

López Sacha, Francisco. *El cumpleaños del fuego*. Havana: Editorial Letras Cubanas, 1986.

López Sacha, Francisco. *Descubrimiento del azul*. Havana: Editorial Letras Cubanas, 1987.

Lorenzo Fuentes, José. *Después de la gaviota*. Havana: Casa de las Américas, 1968.

Luis, Raúl. *El cazador*. Havana: Editorial Letras Cubanas, 1985.

Llana, María Elena. *La reja*. Havana: Ediciones R, 1965.

Llana, María Elena. *Casas del Vedado*. Havana: Editorial Letras Cubanas, 1983.

Llopis, Rogelio. *El buscador de tesoros*. Havana: Ediciones Unión, 1971.

Mejides, Miguel. *Tiempo de hombre*. Havana: Ediciones Unión, 1977.

Mejides, Miguel. *El jardín de las flores silvestres*. Havana: Ediciones Unión, 1982.

Montero, Mayra. *La trenza de la hermosa luna*. Barcelona: Anagrama, 1987.

Montero, Reinaldo. *Donjuanes*. Havana: Ediciones Casa de Las Américas, 1986.

Otero, Lisandro. *La situación*. Havana: Casa de las Américas, 1963.

Otero, Lisandro. *Pasión de Urbino*. Havana: Instituto del Libro, 1967.

Otero, Lisandro. *En ciudad semejante*. Havana: Ediciones Unión, 1970.

Otero, Lisandro. *Temporada de ángeles*. Havana: Editorial Letras Cubanas, 1984.

Paz, Senel. *El niño aquel*. Havana: Ediciones Unión, 1980.

Paz, Senel. *Un rey en el jardín*. Havana: Editorial Letras Cubanas, 1983.

Piñera, Virgilio. *Presiones y diamantes*. Havana: Ediciones Unión, 1967.

Piñera, Virgilio. *Muecas para escribientes*. Havana: Editorial Letras Cubanas, 1987.

Piñera, Virgilio. *Un fogonazo*. Havana: Editorial Letras Cubanas, 1987.

Prieto, Abel. *Noche de sábado*. Havana: Editorial Letras Cubanas, 1989.

Rodríguez, Antonio Orlando. *Strip-tease*. Havana: Editorial Letras Cubanas, 1985.

Rosales, Guillermo. *The Halfway House*. Barcelona: Salvat Editores, 1987.

Sarduy, Severo. *De donde son los cantantes*. Mexico City: Joaquín Mortiz, 1968.

Sarduy, Severo. *Cobra*. Buenos Aires: Editorial Sudamericana, 1972.

Sarduy, Severo. *Maitreya*. Barcelona: Seix Barral, 1978.

Sarduy, Severo. *Colibrí*. Barcelona: Argos Vergara, 1984.

Sarusky, Jaime. *Rebelión en la octava casa*. Havana: Instituto del Libro, 1967.

Soler Puig, José. *Bertillón 166*. Havana: Casa de las Américas, 1960.

Soler Puig, José. *El pan dormido*. Havana: Editorial Arte y Literatura, 1975.

Soler, Rafael. *Campamento de artillería*. Havana: Ediciones Unión, 1975.

Soler, Rafael. *Noche de fósforos*. Havana: Editorial Arte y Literatura, 1976.

Valle, Amir. *Tiempo en cueros*. Havana: Editorial Universitaria, Universidad de La Habana, 1988.

Valle, Amir. *Yo soy el malo*. Havana: Editorial Letras Cubanas, 1989.

Victoria, Carlos. *Las sombras en la playa*. Miami: Ediciones Universal, 1992.

Victoria, Carlos. *El resbaloso y otros cuentos*. Miami: Ediciones Universal, 1997.

Vidal, Guillermo. *Se permuta esta casa*. Havana: Ediciones Unión, 1988.

Viera, Félix Luis. *Las llamas en el cielo*. Havana: Editorial Letras Cubanas, 1983.

Vieta, Ezequiel. *Vivir en Candonga*. Havana: Ediciones Unión, 1966.

Vieta, Ezequiel. *Mi llamada es*. Havana: Editorial Letras Cubanas, 1983.

Vitier, Cintio. *De Peña Pobre*. Havana: Editorial Letras Cubanas, 1980.

LITERATURE: FICTION IN THE SPECIAL PERIOD

Odette Casamayor-Cisneros

Cuban literature's response to the economic, social, and ethical crisis caused by the collapse of the Soviet bloc in 1989.

The 1990s, known as the Special Period in Times of Peace, was characterized by the economic crisis and resulting sociopolitical changes brought about by the collapse of the Soviet Union and the socialist trading bloc, Comecon. The crisis provoked fundamental questioning of the political ideas and ethical values that grew from the revolutionary experience and brought logic to the world in which Cubans had lived since 1959. These values defined an epic conception of existence, encompassing the ideals of sacrifice, national independence, and stoic resistance to foreign and domestic enemies.

The questioning of revolutionary ideology and tradition led to an existential crisis of a kind described by Martín Hopenhayn: "to abandon the image of a possible revolution is a peculiar way to die" (p. 2). This ethical "death" presumes the loss of the ideals of historical transcendence, synthesis, and the epic, when political events lack sufficient energy of their own to "move" the contemporary subject (Baudrillard p. 4).

UNCERTAINTY AND DISILLUSIONMENT: THE LANDSCAPE OF POST-SOVIET FICTION

Uncertainty, caused by the loss of a sense of historical purpose and destiny, does not necessarily lead to disillusionment or disenchantment, but these, along with melancholy and the feeling of being disinherited, were very much in evidence after 1989 in the work of Cuban writers such as Arturo Arango (b. 1955), Abilio Estévez (b. 1954), Pedro Juan Gutiérrez (b. 1950), Leonardo Padura (b. 1955), Senel Paz (b. 1950) and Abel E. Prieto (b. 1950). Critics like Jorge Fornet have tended to privilege disenchantment over other consequences of uncertainty within the broad spectrum of contemporary writing.

Padura's protagonists are paradigmatic of Cuban post-Soviet disenchantment. During their youth, they experienced the revolutionary euphoria of the 1970s; they were educated with the idea that they were destined to work to improve Cuban society; they thought that the nation's future was in their hands. After the collapse of the Soviet bloc in 1989, they discover the sham they have been living under. They are unable to become or see the "New Man" that Che Guevara envisioned in 1965 or to save Cuba from underdevelopment. Imperialism had not been defeated and socialism had died out. In *La neblina de ayer* (The Fog of Yesterday, 2005), the characters describe the

■ *See also*

Che Guevara and the New Man

Cuban Thought and Cultural Identity: Socialist Thought

Diasporas: Introduction

Dirty Havana Trilogy (Pedro Juan Gutiérrez)

The Orígenes Group and Journal

Strawberry and Chocolate (Tomás Gutiérrez Alea and Juan Carlos Tabío)

Leonardo Padura (b. 1955) in Paris, September 2010. Cuban author Leonardo Padura uses the crime novel to convey social criticism and to express the disillusionment experienced in Cuba during post-Soviet times. ULF ANDERSEN/GETTY IMAGES

disillusionment that Cubans of this generation were experiencing as "historical fatigue" (p. 199).

A similar frustration pervades the novels and short stories of the "Ciclo de Centro Habana" (Centro Habana Series) through which Gutiérrez exposes his view of present-day Havana. Series titles are *Trilogía sucia de La Habana* (1998; *Dirty Havana Trilogy*, 2001); *El Rey de La Habana* (The King of Havana, 1999); *Animal Tropical* (2000; *Tropical Animal*, 2005); *El insaciable hombre araña* (2002; *The Insatiable Spiderman*, 2005); and *Carne de Perro* (Dog Meat, 2003). His protagonist, Pedro Juan, a contemporary of Padura's characters, is, in 1990, abandoned by family and friends, loses his journalist job, and ends up living in a building in ruins in Centro Habana. His neighbors are no longer intellectuals and well-to-do people; instead they are criminals, the defenseless poor, the unemployed, and prostitutes, whose marginality Pedro Juan adopts as an existential plan for his life.

The work of other fiction writers such as Yohamna Depestre (b. 1970), Gerardo Fernández Fe (b. 1971), Wendy Guerra (b. 1970), Pedro de Jesús (b. 1970), Orlando Pardo Lazo (b. 1971), and Ena Lucía Portela (b. 1972) differs from the disillusionment depicted by Padura and Gutiérrez. Their characters could not become disenchanted because they never had any dreams. These authors' protagonists appear to have abandoned themselves to chance, suspended in limbo before the existential void. They do not want a better future nor do they think back to the past with yearning. Born in the 1970s, these writers were brought up in the worldview of the Revolution, but they did not see its truly epic moments of the 1960s and 1970s. It was their fate to live through the bureaucratic stages of the revolutionary project, against which they learned, very early on, to brandish cynicism and skepticism as weapons.

However, the common element in the post-Soviet era is not determined so much by the particular generational experiences of all these writers, but rather by the ideological void and social uncertainty underlying contemporary Cuban life, which they addressed through their writing.

PIÑERA AND LEZAMA: WORDS OF THE MASTERS

This ideological and ethical void has some specific trends, particularly the revival of the poetry of the Orígenes group (writers associated with the literary journal *Orígenes*), which flourished in the 1940s and early 1950s. Among those poets for whom the post-Soviet crisis engendered profound frustration, *origenista* poetry suggested ways to respond. The by-then canonical *origenista* writers José Lezama Lima (1910–1976) and Virgilio Piñera (1912–1979) have not only inspired the plots of some Special Period fictions but even become characters in the works themselves. Some of these works are explicitly dedicated to them.

Lezama and Piñera frequently appear in Special Period fiction as spirits capable of adding meaning to the chaos in which the characters move. They make it possible to maintain faith in a utopia when reality holds no signs of hope. Senel Paz, in the story "El lobo, el bosque y el hombre nuevo" (The Wolf, the Woods, and the New Man, 1991)—world-renowned thanks to the film *Fresa y Chocolate* (1993; *Strawberry and Chocolate*, 1994) directed by Tomás Gutiérrez Alea from Paz's screenplay—proposes the individual withdrawal from ideological pressures and the creation of an intimate world governed by tolerance and Lezamian nostalgia. The poetic sensibility of Lezama Lima dominates La Guarida, the tiny Havana apartment in which this story's highly patriotic protagonists, the young Communist David and the gay intellectual Diego, take refuge.

In *El vuelo del gato* (The Flight of the Cat, 1999), by Abel E. Prieto, a Lezamian allegory helps the characters to resolve their debates between cunning, on

NEW VOICES IN CUBAN LITERATURE: ANTONIO JOSÉ PONTE

Antonio José Ponte (b. 1964) in Miami. Author Antonio José Ponte has become one of the most prominent literary voices in Cuba and in the Cuban diaspora. PEDRO PORTAL/NEWSCOM

Antonio José Ponte has been one of the most prominent literary and critical voices in Cuba, and subsequently the Cuban diaspora, since the 1980s. Born in Matanzas in 1964, he moved to Havana as a teenager and became known for his innovative poetry. In 1991 his *Poesía (1982–1989)* was awarded the Cuban Book Institute's National Critics' Prize, as was his *Un seguidor de Montaigne mira la Habana* (An Admirer of Montaigne Views Havana) in 1995. With the publication in 1997 of *Las comidas profundas* (Meaning to Eat), a richly metaphorical exploration of abundance and lack in Cuban culture, Ponte became increasingly visible as an essayist and cultural critic.

Ponte's 1997 poetry collection *Asiento en las ruinas* (A Seat in the Ruins) anticipates the interest in the political and theoretical implications of ruin that would underpin his later work. "Corazón de Skitalietz," a fragile romance between an astrologer and a historian in a strangely unfamiliar Havana, appeared first in Cuba and later in the United States in a collection of Ponte's stories titled *In the Cold of the Malecón* (2000), translated by Cola Franzen and Dick Cluster. Franzen also translated *Tales from the Cuban Empire* (2002), whose central story, "A Knack for Making Ruins," has been interpreted as referring to the Cuban state's manipulation of Havana. The dilapidated city and its cemetery are also the setting for Ponte's novel *Contrabando de sombras* (Smuggling Shadows, 2002).

A preoccupation with ruin and with the prerevolutionary icons of Cuban culture—José Martí, on the one hand, and the Orígenes movement, on the other—continues in Ponte's subsequent work. The 2000 reprinting in Spain of *La lengua de Virgilio* (Virgilio Piñera's Language, 1993) and the publication of *El libro perdido de los origenistas* (The Lost Book of the Orígenes Writers, 2002) established Ponte as one of the most interesting and nuanced critics of Orígenes. The meticulous demythification of Martí in *El abrigo de aire* (The Overcoat Made of Air, 2001) drew fierce criticism from the Cuban cultural establishment, as did Ponte's decision to join the editorial board of the Madrid-based journal *Encuentro de la cultura cubana*.

Over the course of the first decade of the twenty-first century, Ponte publicly spoke against the Cuban political system and its control of individuals' environmental and ideological experience; these arguments crystallized in *La fiesta vigilada* (The Supervised Party), published in 2007. That same year Ponte left the untenably hostile environment of Cuba to become editor of *Encuentro de la cultura cubana*, a position he held until 2010 when he cofounded the journal *Diario de Cuba* and published *Villa Marista en plata: Arte, política, nuevas tecnologías* (Villa Marista in Silver: Art, Politics and New Technologies) (Madrid, 2010). Ponte's work has been the subject of much scholarly attention, notably Teresa Basile's edited collection *La vigilia cubana* (2009).

BIBLIOGRAPHY

Basile, Teresa, ed. *La vigilia cubana: Sobre Antonio José Ponte* [The Cuban Vigil: On Antonio José Ponte]. Rosario, Argentina: Beatriz Viterbo Editores, 2009.

Ponte, Antonio José. *In the Cold of the Malecon*. Translated by Cola Franzen and Dick Cluster. San Francisco: City Lights, 2000.

Ponte, Antonio José. *Tales of the Cuban Empire*. Translated by Cola Franzen. San Francisco: City Lights, 2002.

Ponte, Antonio José. *La fiesta vigilada*. Barcelona: Anagrama, 2007.

Esther Whitfield

the one hand, and stoicism, on the other, between backwardness and progress, good and evil, black and white. It is the mixing of races, cultures, and ethical values, as symbolized by Lezama's metaphor of the flying cat, that saves the characters from suffering existential angst, resolving contradictions between lofty convictions inculcated in childhood under the influence of the Revolution and the routines of daily life, marked by a brutal struggle for survival during the Special Period.

These post-Soviet interpretations of Lezama Lima's work take up again the unifying and harmonious spirit of the *origenista* thought, seeing it as the quintessence of a conciliatory Cubanness. Contrarily, the presence of Virgilio Piñera in contemporary works is an allusion to an anti-*origenista* perspective, contrasting with baroque voluptuousness and the ideal of communion, which were defended by Lezama and his acolytes. An anti-*origenista* view of Cubanness is invoked in that way in *Tuyo es el reino* (1997; *Thine Is the Kingdom*, 2000), which Abilio Estévez dedicates to Piñera, whose "darkness" and "negativity" had been previously openly criticized by some members of the Orígenes group, such as Gastón Baquero (1918–1997) and Cintio Vitier (1921–2009). The ambiguous location in which this novel takes place, the Island, is described as a dark jungle, impenetrable and ever changing, unlike the translucent Lezamian world, ruled by the image. In *Tuyo es el reino*, Piñera also acts as a spiritual guide for the protagonist, Sebastián, in his life on the Island.

Also, neo-*origenismo* seems to have been accompanied by what Antonio José Ponte (b. 1964) called "the final pardon" by the authorities, after having censured the Orígenes intellectuals from the 1960s through the early 1980s. Concerned about the distortion of their legacy, in *El libro perdido de los origenistas* (The Lost Book of the *Origenistas*, 2004), Ponte offers his personal interpretation of those poets, as if from a "secret reader," apart from fads and opportunisms. His interpretation does not avoid the ideological conditioning of the *origenista* production and emphasizes the political connotations that have resulted from the official recovery of this literature.

SOCIAL MARGINALIZATION: REJECTION AND FASCINATION

Padura also pays homage to Piñera in his novel *Máscaras* (1997; *Havana Red*, 2005), through the character of a homosexual playwright who is censored during the 1970s. *Máscaras* is the third in the series of crime novels *Las cuatro estaciones* (The Four Seasons). The others are *Pasado perfecto* (1991; *Havana Blue*, 2007), *Vientos de cuaresma* (1994; *Havana Gold*, 2008), and *Paisaje de otoño* (1998; *Havana Black*, 2006).

The police detective, Mario Conde, is the protagonist in all four books. Adapting to the changes of life in Havana in the course of the series, Conde consequently becomes a private detective and rare book dealer. Nevertheless, his zeal for denouncing social ills remains unchanged; he still believes reality can be perfected. Padura uses the crime narrative to implicitly convey social criticism, in contrast to the initial stages of the Revolution, when the genre generally exalted the heroic deeds of police organizations against counterrevolutionary activities. In this respect,

Padura's perspective, also adopted by other crime writers such as Amir Valle (b. 1967), is an expression of the disillusionment experienced during post-Soviet times. Inspector Conde's attitude, however, is always distant and accusatory. Civil negligence, corrupt authorities, double standards, and the loss of ethical values are revealed as the causes of national decay. The marginal environments described are rejected by the protagonist.

Equally disillusioned with reality, Pedro Juan Gutiérrez's characters assume a different attitude toward marginalization. They embrace the same merciless existence that the former police officer criticizes. For these characters, the only possibility for survival—economic and existential—comes through cynicism, abandonment of traditional morality, and the most heartless individualism. Sexual licentiousness, alcohol, drugs, and crime complete their agenda. It is not just a matter of showing—as in Padura's detective stories—society's hidden side. In Gutiérrez's so-called dirty realism fiction, dystopia constitutes the true existential project, in which uncontrollable physical needs such as hunger and sexual urge dictate daily life. The critic Esther Whitfield calls Gutiérrez's account of post-Soviet Cuban society "zoological" (p. 108). These settings hold no hope for human improvement.

FEMALE VOICES

Along with Gutiérrez, Whitfield identifies Zoé Valdés (b. 1959) as a pioneer of this dystopic subgenre of the literature of the Special Period. Valdés's novels, mostly written during her continuing exile in Europe, also offer dark depictions of contemporary Cuba. National dystopia has always dominated her writing and is sometimes presented as a contrast to a utopian space built by the diaspora, as in *Milagro en Miami* (Miracle in Miami, 2001) and *Te di la vida entera* (1996; *I Gave You All I Had*, 1999). Her point of view is close to that of Daína Chaviano (b. 1957), who also writes from exile, painting a bitter portrait of Cuban life in novels such as *El hombre, la hembra y el hambre* (Man, Woman, and Hunger, 1998). As crude as Gutiérrez's stories, the fiction of these two authors is also notable for its female vision. In *La nada cotidiana* (1995; *Yocandra in the Paradise of Nada*, 1997), Valdés even coined the term *machismo leninismo* (machismo-Leninism), referring to the oppressive weight of male chauvinism on the post-revolutionary Cuban experience.

The discourse of Wendy Guerra is based on a similar perspective, this time from the island. In her novel, *Todos se van* (Everyone Is Leaving, 2006), she presents the post-Soviet drift through the eyes of Nieve and her mother, two women stranded in a country that many are leaving. They show how authority exercised on individual, family, and national destinies has always been patriarchal, in every period of the revolution. Like Yocandra, the protagonist of *La nada cotidiana*, Nieve was predestined to be the female version of Che Guevara's "New Man." Nevertheless, her absurd

NEW VOICES IN CUBAN LITERATURE: TERESA CÁRDENAS ANGULO

Teresa Cárdenas Angulo (b. 1970) is a poet, dancer, and storyteller who writes fiction aimed at children and adolescents, enabling them to experience history through her work. Cárdenas strips history bare, exposing the colonialist and Eurocentric seams that hold it together and revealing its old and new traps. Her work is filled with characters who have been traditionally repressed (women, blacks, girls, the elderly) who communicate in extremely expressive language. Her characters' simple stories contain anecdotes that lead the reader to the core of the tale, where suffering, scarcity, violence, and oppression have left them with wounds that must be acknowledged in order to heal and be overcome. In this manner, the characters grow in front of the viewers' eyes, coming to know themselves anew and heroically transforming their own realities. Most of Cárdenas's characters are Afro-Cubans who have been marked by the history of their race: slavery, violence, racism, and subjugation. Her books denounce the oppression to which some human beings subject others with duplicitous motives or lies, which Cárdenas is able to reveal in her moving texts. Her work is filled with extraordinary teachings frequently derived from African proverbs.

Cárdenas's literary thinking results from her perspective as a black woman. Her Afrocentric viewpoint allows her to see herself as part of an African diaspora fighting for a final emancipation, in which all people can take pride in their gender and skin color. She belongs to the group of Cuban authors who, since the 1990s, have been reexamining, through literature written for children, the relevance of Cuban reality in all its harshness, contributing to social debate by addressing topics such as racism, marginality, prostitution, and domestic violence. Cárdenas has earned national and international recognition, and her work has been translated into several languages.

Among her better-known works are *Cartas al Cielo* (Letters to Heaven, 1998), which won the David Award and the Asociación Hermanos Saíz Award in 1997 and a National Critics Award as one of the ten best books of 1998; *Maldito Solar* (Damned Tenement, 1998), winner of the Second Prize in the Delia Carrera National Poetry Competition; *Cuentos de Macucupé* (Stories of Macucupé, 2001), which won La Edad de Oro (Golden Age) Award; *Perro Viejo* (2006; *Old Dog*, 2007), which won the Casa de las Américas International Award in 2005 and a National Critics Award in 2007; and *Tatanene Cimarrón* (2006), which won the Ismaelillo Award from the Unión de Escritores y Artistas de Cuba (UNEAC; Union of Writers and Artists of Cuba).

BIBLIOGRAPHY

Cárdenas Angulo, Teresa. *Cartas al Cielo*. Havana: Ediciones Unión, 1998.

Cárdenas Angulo, Teresa. *Maldito Solar*. Matanzas: Ediciones Matanzas, 1998.

Cárdenas Angulo, Teresa. *Cuentos de Macucupé*. Havana: Cuba Gente Nueva, 2001.

Cárdenas Angulo, Teresa. *Perro Viejo*. Havana: Casa de las Américas, 2005.

Cárdenas Angulo, Teresa. *Cartas a mi mama*. Berkeley, CA: Libros Tigrillo, 2006.

Cárdenas Angulo, Teresa. *Letters to My Mother*. Translated by David Unger. Berkeley, CA: Publishers Group West, 2006.

Cárdenas Angulo, Teresa. *Tatanene Cimarrón*. Havana: Editorial Abril, 2006.

Cárdenas Angulo, Teresa. *Old Dog*. Translated by David Unger. Berkeley, CA: Publishers Group West, 2007.

Cárdenas Angulo, Teresa. *Oloyou* (bilingual ed.). Berkeley, CA: Groundwood Books/House of Anansi, 2008.

Roberto Zurbano Torres

experiences thwart the fulfillment of the revolutionary project. They differ, however, in that Yocandra, typical of Valdés's characters, converts her frustration into anti-Castro rage, while Nieve remains indifferent to traditional political and ideological positions. Her status, which could be called an ethical void, remains indeterminate in the post-Soviet chaos. This indifference is also characteristic of Ena Lucía Portela's characters. Zeta, her protagonist in *Cien botellas en una pared* (2002; *One Hundred Bottles*, 2010), personifies a final-stage position with relation to any value system based on the modern ideal of progress. Zeta's cynical indifference extends not only to economics, politics, and ideology, but also toward her own gender identification and sexual and national identity. Although, like the protagonists of Valdés, Chaviano, and Guerra, Zeta suffers under the weight of masculine authority, she makes no explicit protest against that situation. In contrast to these protagonists, neither does Zeta use her sexuality nor her body as weapons of protest in the traditional sense. Her opposition is cynical and mute. The concept of national identity also means little to the protagonist of the short story, "Una extraña entre las piedras" in the volume *Una extraña entre las piedras* (A Strange Woman among the Stones, 1999), in which Portela describes the experiences of a young Cuban woman who "migrated like the birds, when the weather changed."

DIASPORAS

Present in Cuban literature since the dawn of the nation, the dilemma of whether to stay on or leave the

NEW VOICES IN CUBAN LITERATURE: ENA LUCÍA PORTELA

Ena Lucía Portela (b. in Havana, 1972) has written four novels: *El pájaro, pincel y tinta china* (The Bird, Brush, and India Ink, 1998), *La sombra del caminante* (The Shadow of the Traveler, 2001), *Cien botellas en una pared* (One Hundred Bottles, 2002), and *Djuna y Daniel* (Djuna and Daniel, 2008), and the short story collection *Una extraña entre las piedras* (A Stranger among the Stones, 1999).

Portela is one of the few contemporary women writers who, while residing on the island, achieved international recognition. Her books have been translated into many languages, and she has won several international prizes such as Cuba's Unión de Escritores y Artistas de Cuba (Union of Writers and Artists of Cuba) Award for Novel (1997), France's Juan Rulfo Prize for Short Stories (1999) and Deux Océans-Grinzane Cavour Prize for Novel (2003), and Spain's Jaén Prize (2002).

Her works convey the state of ethical void that affected many of her contemporaries during the Special Period. Deprived of a solid traditional identity, her characters are indifferent to the chaos and the uncertainty around them. In *Cien botellas en una pared*, the young Zeta is paradigmatic; the fact that her name alludes to the last letter of the Spanish alphabet suggests that she is insignificant, on the lowest rung in the social ladder. She is totally absorbed with remaining in the "Muslim heaven . . . the sweet satisfaction of doing nothing at all, of vegging out" (p. 6) while Havana collapses under the critical conditions of the Special Period. She cannot find any effective way to escape poverty, at which she laughs irrationally, with a humor that should not be identified as mocking society but rather as self-derision, as the protagonist herself notes (Casamayor p. 5).

The body, sexuality, and gender are subjects calmly explored by Portela, who describes deliberate bodily acts typically considered to be grotesque and immoral within the traditional western imagination. Voyeurism, masochism, sadism, promiscuity, perversion, her characters fearlessly, without complaint or guilt, give themselves to these and other practices. Their behavior cannot be considered a transgression because the characters are indifferent to traditional morality and are unaware of the boundaries they supposedly violate. They are culturally conditioned sociopolitical bodies, and hunger is the essential mark of their existence during the Special Period, yet they consciously avoid participating in any negotiation that involves a relationship of power or productive fluidity. Amorphous, socially useless, and not very seductive, these bodies convey no explicit accusations or arguments against Cuban society. The female protagonist in *Una extraña entre las piedras* asserts: "To be a woman, the same as being a man, an animal, a vegetable, a mineral or an extraterrestrial, is just a fate. One is a woman no matter what, without effort, without responsibility" (Portela 1999, p. 115).

In the ethical void that pervades Ena Lucía Portela's work there is a greater radicalism: the transcending of the concepts of identity and the polarities characteristic of modern thought.

BIBLIOGRAPHY

Álvarez Oquendo, Saylin. "Negro sobre blanco: blanco sobre negro ... Y no hace falta Malévich." *Encuentro de la cultura cubana* 39 (2005–2006): 77–85.

Araújo, Nara. "Erizar y divertir. La poética de Ena Lucía Portela." In *Diálogos en el umbral*. Santiago de Cuba: Editorial Oriente, 2003.

Casamayor, Odette. "Guanajerías post-soviéticas: Apuntes ético-estéticos en torno al humor en la narrativa de Ena Lucía Portela." *La Gaceta de Cuba* 6 (November–December 2009): 3–7. Available from http://www.uneac.org.cu/gaceta/pdf/2009/gaceta2009.6.pdf.

Loss, Jacqueline. "Amateurs and Professionals in Ena Lucía Portela's Lexicon of Crisis." In *Unfolding the City in Latin America*, edited by Anne Lambright and Elisabeth Guerrero. Minneapolis: University of Minnesota Press, 2007.

Portela, Ena Lucía. "Una extraña entre las piedras." In *Una extraña entre las piedras*. Havana: Letras Cubanas, 1999.

Portela, Ena Lucía. *Cien botellas en una pared*. Edited by Iraida H. López. Doral, FL: Stockcero, 2010a.

Portela, Ena Lucía. *One Hundred Bottles*. Translated by Achy Obejas. Austin: University of Texas Press, 2010b.

Odette Casamayor-Cisneros

island has shaped the conceptualization of its national identity. The emergence in the 1990s of emigrant currents not so defined by a strictly anti-Castro position and of a calculated tolerance practiced from the island has gradually broken down the barriers between exiles and Cubans on the island, which were indestructible until the 1980s. Besides Valdés and Chaviano, other writers worthy of note are Eliseo Alberto (b. 1951), José Manuel Prieto (b. 1962), Ronaldo Menéndez (b. 1970), Jesús Díaz (1941–2002), and more recently, Ponte, Estévez, and Valle.

All the same, nostalgia continues to dominate discourse concerning the diaspora, especially in writing that originates on the island. Thus, Padura reclaims José María Heredia in *La novela de mi vida* (The Novel of My Life, 2002) as the symbol of the sorrowful Cuban condition. The novelist returns to the nineteenth-century poet's concept of the essential insularity of the Cuban condition while stressing tolerance toward emigration by post-Soviet Cubans. In general, however, only nostalgic suffering is afforded the émigré, because, from that perspective, plenitude is

NEW VOICES IN CUBAN LITERATURE: JOSÉ MANUEL PRIETO

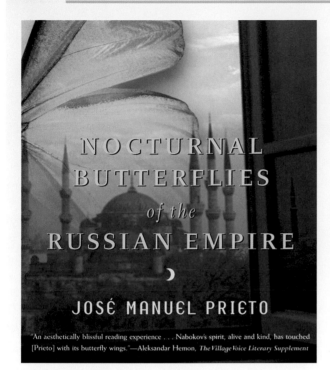

Nocturnal Butterflies of the Russian Empire. José Manuel Prieto's novel *Livadia* (1999), published in English in 2000 as *Nocturnal Butterflies of the Russian Empire*, describes a smuggler's quest to survive on the spare parts of the recently dismantled Soviet army. COVER OF U.S. EDITION OF *NOCTURNAL BUTTERFLIES OF THE RUSSIAN EMPIRE* BY JOSÉ MANUEL PRIETO. USED BY PERMISSION OF GROVE/ATLANTIC, INC.

José Manuel Prieto, born in 1962 in Havana, is an internationally renowned author of fiction and nonfiction and translator of Russian literature into Spanish. *Nunca antes habías visto el rojo* (You've Never Seen Red Like This Before, 1996), which was later revised and published in Mexico as *El tartamudo y la rusa* (The Stammerer and the Russian Girl, 2002), is Prieto's first and only collection of stories published in Cuba. The provocative lesson that emerges from the title story about the effects of western values on socialist processes is characteristic of his writing for readers in Cuba, which he left at age nineteen. This theme carried over to the first two installments of his Russian trilogy *Enciclopedia de una vida en Rusia* (Encyclopedia of a Life in Russia, 1997), a non-native informant's explanation of the idiosyncrasies of newly re-formed Russia, and *Livadia* (1999; published in English as *Nocturnal Butterflies of the Russian Empire*, 2000), a smuggler's quest to survive on the spare parts of the recently dismantled Soviet army and through the trapping of a "butterfly" through letters. In contrast, *Rex* (2007), the final part of the trilogy, is set nearly at the cusp of the twenty-first century in Marbella, Spain, where a Russian mafia family hires a Cuban tutor to civilize their son—a project that entails helping them escape the consequences of their hoax in dealing in counterfeit diamonds. Whereas the novels of Vladimir Nabokov are a crucial intertext to *Nocturnal Butterflies of the Russian Empire*, *Rex*, which has been compared by reviewers to work by literary greats such as Mikhail Bulgakov and José Saramago, is itself an amalgamation of literature that considers Marcel Proust alongside Jorge Luis Borges, Jules Verne, and H. G. Wells (Winslow 2009).

The protofictional narrator of *Treinta días en Moscow* (Thirty Days in Moscow, 2001) chronicles the changes in the Russian capital since his last stay there. In the early 2000s, Prieto again took on the role of intermediary between insiders and outsiders in his new home, New York City. Having first arrived as a prestigious fellow of the New York Public Library's Cullman Center, thanks to Esther Allen's first-rate English translations of his fiction, and articles such as the *Nation*'s "Travels by Taxi: Reflections on Cuba" (an excerpt from Prieto's *The Cuban Revolution Explained to Taxi Drivers*), Prieto became a key cosmopolitan literary and intellectual voice. Before moving to the United States, Prieto spent twelve years studying in the Soviet Union as it disintegrated to become Russia and a decade in Mexico, where he completed a Ph.D. in history.

BIBLIOGRAPHY

Prieto, José Manuel. *Nocturnal Butterflies of the Russian Empire*. Translated by Carol Christensen and Thomas Christensen. New York: Grove Press, 2000.

Prieto, José Manuel. "My Brave Face." Translated by Carol Christensen and Thomas Christensen. *Common Knowledge* 9, no. 1 (2003): 169–175.

Prieto, José Manuel. "You've Never Seen Red Like This Before." Translated by Esther Allen. *Words without Borders*. May 2005. Available from http://www.wordswithoutborders.org/article/youve-never-seen-red-like-this-before/.

Prieto, José Manuel. *Rex*. Translated by Esther Allen. New York: Grove Press, 2009.

Prieto, José Manuel. "Travels by Taxi: Reflections on Cuba." Translated by Esther Allen. *Nation* (14 December 2009). Available from http://www.thenation.com/article/travels-taxi-reflections-cuba.

Prieto, José Manuel. "Reading Mandelstam on Stalin." Translated by Esther Allen. *New York Review of Books* (10 June 2010). Available from http://www.nybooks.com/articles/archives/2010/jun/10/reading-mandelstam-stalin/

Winslow, Art. "*Rex* by José Manuel Prieto." *Los Angeles Times* (24 May 2009). Available from http://articles.latimes.com/2009/may/24/entertainment/ca-jose-manuel-prieto24.

Jacqueline Loss

presumed to be the exclusive right of those who remain in Cuba. Positions such as Portela's, which are indifferent to that polarity, are novel, striking, and convincing, although still infrequent in Cuban writing.

BIBLIOGRAPHY

Baudrillard, Jean. *The Illusion of the End*. Stanford, CA: Stanford University Press, 1994.

Buckwalter-Arias, James. *Cuba and the New Origenismo*. Woodbridge, U.K.; Rochester, NY: Tamesis, 2010.

De la Nuez, Iván, ed. *Cuba y el día después: doce ensayistas nacidos con la Revolución imaginan el futuro*. Barcelona: Mondadori, 2001.

Fornet, Jorge. *Los nuevos paradigmas: prólogo narrativo al siglo XXI*. Havana: Letras Cubanas, 2006.

Fowler, Victor. *Rupturas y homenajes*. Havana: Unión, 1998.

Hernández-Renguant, Ariana, ed. *Cuba in the Special Period: Culture and Ideology in the 1990s*. New York: Palgrave Macmillan, 2009.

Hopenhayn, Martín. *No Apocalypse, No Integration: Modernism and Postmmodernism in Latin America*. Durham, NC: Duke University Press, 2001.

Martín Sevillano, Ana B. *Sociedad civil y arte en Cuba: cuento y artes plásticas en el cambio de siglo, 1980–2000*. Madrid: Verbum, 2008.

Mateo Palmer, Margarita. *Ella escribía poscrítica*. Havana: Letras Cubanas, 2005.

Ponte Mirabal, Antonio José. *El libro perdido de los origenistas*. Seville, Spain: Librería Editorial Renacimiento, 2004.

Quiroga, José. *Cuban Palimpsests*. Minneapolis: University of Minnesota Press, 2005.

Whitfield, Esther. *Cuban Currency: The Dollar and "Special Period" Fiction*. Minneapolis: University of Minnesota Press, 2008.

■ *See also*

Cuban Thought and Cultural Identity: Socialist Thought

Education: Literacy Campaign of 1961

José Martí: Writings for and about Children

LITERATURE: CHILDREN'S LITERATURE IN CUBA SINCE 1959

Enrique Pérez Díaz

The creation of a children's literature publishing establishment after the Revolution.

Since the seventeenth century, writers and educators in Europe and later in the Americas have viewed children with a moralistic attitude that has sparked a rebellious love of books among many children and led to the writing of what have become classics of children's and youth literature. Despite a past history of school primers, readers, catechisms, and fictional works, serious literature for children and young people in Cuba had an extraordinary starting point with the publication of *La Edad de Oro* (The Golden Age), a children's magazine created by José Martí, whose first issue was dated July–October 1889. This instructive and humanist magazine, which lasted a total of four issues, constituted Cuba's best attempt to appeal to young readers. In the twentieth century, the four issues were compiled in book form, and following the triumph of the Revolution in 1959 new editions have been printed annually.

ORGANIZATIONS

Among the historical and social factors that have influenced the island's literature for children and young people since 1959 are the triumph of the Revolution and governmental efforts favoring a view of life and culture from a nonelitist perspective. In 1959 the Imprenta Nacional de Cuba (National Printing House of Cuba), headed by Alejo Carpentier, and the Editorial Nacional (National Publishing House), headed by Herminio Almendros, were founded. Massive, low-price runs of *Don Quixote*, among other works, were published.

Other influences were the Campaña Nacional de Afabetización (National Literacy Campaign) of 1961, the stocking of libraries with funds from abroad, the foundation of the Consejo Nacional de Cultura (National Culture Council) in the same year, and the establishment of the publishing houses later affiliated with the Instituto Cubano del Libro (ICL; Cuban Book Institute, founded in 1967), including Gente Nueva, specializing in literature for children and young people.

The first Forum organized in 1972 by the Ministry of Education and the National Culture Council, under the leadership of Mirta Aguirre, established guidelines for developing this branch of literature. They were based on an unbiased and innovative perspective free of moralism and indoctrination that did not shy away from using fantasy as an instrument for rewriting reality. That same year, the La Edad de Oro Prize was created, to honor the best in children's and young people's literature in the coming decades.

Contributing to the development and promotion of this literary branch were the foundation of the Ministry of Culture (1976); the Campaña Nacional de la Lectura (National Reading Campaign, 1986); the foundation in 1983 of the Cuban section of the International Board on Books for Young People (IBBY), and the emergence of its magazine *En julio como en enero* (In July as in January); and the establishment in 1985 of the Children's and Young People's Literature subsection of the Unión de Escritores y Artistas de Cuba (UNEAC; Union of Writers and Artists of Cuba) and its sponsorship of the La Rosa Blanca Prize. During the 1990s, events included the Programa Nacional para la Lectura (National Reading Program) and the Encuentros Iberoamericanos de Literatura para Niños y Jóvenes (Ibero-American Conferences on Literature for Children and Young People, 1994–1999); the Lectura Para Leer el XXI (Reading to Read the 21st Century) congresses (founded 1999), sponsored by the IBBY, continued into the new century.

ANA MENÉNDEZ

Author of one collection of short stories and three novels, Ana Menéndez was born in Los Angeles in 1970. She has worked as a journalist in Florida and California and was a columnist for the *Miami Herald*. Her first work (*In Cuba I Was a German Shepherd*) is a series of stories loosely centered around Cubans in the Miami area and presents the heartbreak and loneliness of exile without lapsing into nostalgia or stereotypes. With considerable humor and nuance, Menéndez lovingly re-creates tales that Cubans tell about the lives they led in Cuba. Their tales may or may not be true, but the emotional truth of their lives is poetically rendered.

In *Loving Che*, the narrator is a woman searching for her mother, whom she left back in Cuba after emigrating with her grandfather. Her search is further complicated by a package from a woman in Spain who claims to be her mother and that her father could have well been Che Guevara. The novel is a powerful exploration of personal identity, of familial memory intersecting with Cuba's history.

Her second novel, *The Last War*, is set in Istanbul and has nothing to do with Cuba; Menéndez, while proud of her heritage, avoids the "ethnic writer" trap of dealing with only Latino characters and situations. The main character Flash is a woman photojournalist whose husband is a war correspondent stationed in Iraq. The focus is on their marriage, love, trust, and betrayal. *Adios, Happy Homeland!* is a tale of cultural displacement that deals with the troubled history of Cuba.

BIBLIOGRAPHY

Menéndez, Ana. *In Cuba I Was a German Shepherd*. New York: Grove Press, 2001.

Menéndez, Ana. *Loving Che*. New York: Grove Press, 2003.

Menéndez, Ana. *The Last War*. New York: Harper, 2009.

Menéndez, Ana. *Adios, Happy Homeland!* New York: Grove Press, 2011.

Alan West-Durán

WRITERS

Since 1959, there have been several generations of Cuban authors writing for children and young people. Among their predecessors in the 1950s were Emma Pérez Téllez, Concepción Alzola, Hilda Perera and Alma Flor Ada. Five generations can be identified, one for each decade of the Revolution, plus three periods during the first generation.

- First Generation, 1960s. *First period*: Authors who wrote textbooks—Dora Alonso, Eliseo Diego, Félix Pita Rodríguez, Nicolás Guillén, Onelio Jorge Cardoso, Renée Potts, Renée Méndez Capote, Adelaida Clemente, Anisia Miranda, Rafaela Chacón Nardi. *Second period*: Herminio Almendros's adaptations of folklore at the National Publishing House of Cuba. *Third period*: Authors whose work appeared in periodicals such as the weekly *Pionero* (Pioneer)—Magali Sánchez, Ivette Vian, Enid Vian, Froilán Escobar.

- Second Generation, 1970s: Nersys Felipe, Julia Calzadilla, Mirta Yáñez, Waldo González, Mirta Aguirre, Albertico Yáñez, Julio Crespo, Julio Travieso, Julio Llanes, Teresita Gómez, Teresita Rodríguez, Carmen Ferrer, Olga Rodríguez Colón, Edwigis Barroso, Manuel Vázquez, Antonio Orlando Rodríguez, Joel Franz, Emilio de Armas.

- Third Generation, 1980s: Omar Felipe Mauri, Aramís Quintero, Emilia Gallego, Iliana Prieto, Eddy Díaz Souza, Luis Cabrera, Julio Blanco, José Manuel Espino, Chely Lima, Alberto Serret, Daína Chaviano, Olga Marta Pérez, Vivien Acosta, Esther Suárez, Pablo René Estévez, Mildre Hernández, Luis Caissés.

- Fourth Generation, 1990s: Teresa Cárdenas, Ariel Ribeaux, Enrique Pérez Díaz, Gumersindo Pacheco, Nelson Simón, Aurora Martínez, René Valdés, Susana Haug, Emma Artiles, Celima Bernal, Mailén Domínguez, Mirna Céspedes, Lidia Meriño, Niurki Pérez, Alberto Hernández, Reinaldo Álvarez.

- Fifth Generation, 2000s: Eldys Baratute, Yanira Marimón, Legna Rodríguez, José Linares, Alberto Peraza, Boris Mesa, Erick Adrián Pérez, Néstor Montes de Oca, José Raúl Fraguela, Rubén Rodríguez, Geovanys García, Geovanys Manso.

The 1990s were a time of changes. Although there were traditional, animist, or patriotic books before, the new texts confronted reality in another way; while continuing to promote the moral values embodied in Mirta Aguirre's work, they also dealt with contemporary problems. This literature was not as well accepted, because many readers clung to traditions and preferred less aggressive, more classical texts.

At the same time, a diaspora of Cuban authors abroad attained considerable success. They include David Chericián, Alberto Serret, Ariel Ribeaux, Chely Lima, Daisy Valls, Pablo René Estévez, Emilio de Armas, José Antonio Gutiérrez, Daína Chaviano, Andrés Pi Andreu, Cristina Rebull, Antonio Orlando Rodríguez, Emma Artiles, Gumersindo Pacheco, Roberto Pérez León, Eddy Díaz, Eduardo Frías, Eric González Conde, Luis Rafael, Ricardo Ortega, Mariela Landa, Lizet Lantigua, Froilán Escobar, Cristina Baeza, Aramís Quintero, María Aguiar, Iliana Prieto, Hilda Perera, Yanitzia Canetti, and Joel Franz Rosell. Those remaining on the island also thrived, generally with themes related to daily life.

POPULAR BOOKS AND PUBLISHERS

Among the classic books that children and young people continue to enjoy are Dora Alonso's writings, *Oros viejos* (Old Gold), by Herminio Almendros; *Flor de leyendas* (Flower of Legends), by Alejandro Casona; and *La Marcolina*, by Ivette Vian, which rose in popularity with its adaptation for television. In addition, an increasing number of young writers gained admirers in their home provinces, with the help of libraries, schools, and cultural centers. Although as of 2011 the Harry Potter books had not been published or distributed in Cuba, these stories are well known among schoolchildren, who avidly share imported copies that become available to them.

Books released by the publishers Gente Nueva, Abril, Mujer, and Unión are in great demand, and reading is encouraged from an early age. Gente Nueva puts out one million to two million copies of a hundred titles each year, including the work of many new authors. However, the books most in demand are classics: *Había una vez…* (Once upon a Time), by Herminio Almendros; *El Principito* (The Little Prince), by Antoine de Saint-Exupéry; *La Edad de Oro*; and *Diario de Ana Frank*.

These publishers constantly produce children's literature, especially by Cuban writers, and also promote up-and-coming visual artists. Many books for children and young people have been awarded prizes such as the Crítica Literaria, Casa de las Américas, El Arte del Libro, Abril, and La Rosa Blanca awards.

PROMOTION OF READING

State-subsidized low book prices make it possible for the public to buy hundreds of books. The activities of the Cuban section of the IBBY are centered on general objectives, and it determines the most needed and most feasible tasks related to the study, distribution, and publication of the best books for children and young people, the promotion of reading, friendly exchanges, and the defense, development, and consolidation of culture.

The Children's and Young People's Literature subsection of UNEAC advises on contests and panels, helps organize writers' encounters, theoretical events, and authors' soirees honoring historic or recently deceased writers. It awards the La Rosa Blanca Special Prize every five years, as well as the annual prize of the same name, in recognition of the best texts, illustrations, and integral editions. It coordinates encounters with distinguished writers, organizes plans for publishing and collections, and celebrates the International Children's Book Day with the sponsorship of the Cuban Section of the IBBY.

Institutions that promote the development of literature for children and young people are the Cuban Book Institute, the José Marti National Library, Casa de las Américas, the Juan Marinello Institute, UNEAC, the Ministry of Education, the Cuban Institute of Radio and Television, the Literature and Linguistics Institute, and the Rubén Martínez Villena Library.

Although there is no network of libraries specializing in this field, all Cuban libraries, in Havana as well as in all provinces and municipalities, have sections devoted to literature for children and young people.

One specialized publication is the magazine *En julio como en enero*, founded in 1985 by Editorial Gente Nueva with IBBY sponsorship. Other children's magazines include *Chinchila* (Chinchilla), from Editorial Cauce in Pinar del Río; *Zunzún* and *Pionero* from Casa Editora Abril in Havana; and *Barquitos del San Juan* (Small Boats of San Juan) from Editorial Vigía in Matanzas.

Among the writers' seminars are the Encuentro Nacional de Investigación y Crítica de LIJ (National Conference on Research and Criticism of Literature for Children and Young People) in Sancti Spíritus; the conference Niños, Autores y Libros: Una merienda de locos (Children, Authors and Books: A Snack for Crazies), sponsored by Editorial Gente Nueva; the conference Cuentos de la Bahía Honda (Stories of Bahía Honda) in San Pedro beach; the Encuentros Iberoamericanos de Literatura para Niños y Jóvenes (1994–1999); and the Lectura Para Leer el XXI congresses.

BIBLIOGRAPHY

Almendros, Herminio. *Oros viejos*. Havana: Gente Nueva, 2007.

Almendros, Herminio, ed. *Había una vez....* Havana: Gente Nueva, 2010.

Casona, Alejandro. *Flor de leyendas*. Havana: Gente Nueva, 2000.

Frank, Anne. *Diario de Ana Frank*. Havana: Gente Nueva, 2009.

Martí, José. *La Edad de Oro*. Havana: Gente Nueva, 2000.

Saint-Exupéry, Antoine de. *El Principito*. Havana: Gente Nueva, 2010.

LITERATURE: NONFICTION IN THE COLONIAL PERIOD

Roberto Méndez Martínez

Cuban literary critics and polemicists and their advocacy for a modern, educated nation that would assert a quintessential Cubanness in the face of the Spanish colonial presence.

During the nineteenth century, pioneers in the field of literary essays and criticism—teachers, sacred and forensic orators, memorialists, and historians—were obsessed with the idea of creating a modern and learned Cuban nation free of the consequences of colonialism. In important pieces of reflective prose, Cuban authors, though disagreeing on basic issues such as the future political relationship between the island and Spain,

the question of independence, and how to effect the transition from a slavery-based to a capitalist economy, were united on the need to promote education, the sciences, and the arts so as to establish a republic on the models of revolutionary France, Great Britain, and the United States.

The Cuban daily press was a major factor in the development of the essay and related genres. The newspaper *Papel Periódico de La Habana*, first published in 1790, voiced the concerns of a sector of *criollo* landowners who were followers of the French *encyclopédistes*, a movement of writers who promoted Enlightenment ideals. Its pages included discussions of urbanism, medicine, natural sciences, theater, and critiques of social problems. The newspaper *El Regañón de La Habana*, founded in 1800 by Ventura Pascual Ferrer (1772–1851), offered critiques of social customs and reviews of Havana's theater and other entertainments. Ferrer, who sought to uphold the aristocratic norms of neoclassicism, criticized not only audacious works of art but also popular entertainments. However, his writings are valuable for their detailed descriptions of dance, theatrical works, and fashion, which capture an emerging *criollo* culture.

The Seminary of San Carlos and San Ambrosio was the most important Cuban educational institution of the nineteenth century. During the first quarter of the century, it was the main center for intellectual debate. Father Félix Varela (1787–1853), who was closely connected to the seminary, was a

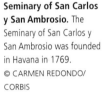

■ *See also*

Education: Colonial Period

José Martí: Political Essays

Sexuality: Republican Period

pioneering figure in Cuban education. In his writings and speeches he called for the renewal and extension of education, discussed the quest for appropriate ways to achieve independence, and, in the remarkable book *Cartas a Elpidio*, stressed the need to prepare Cuban youth from an ethical perspective to govern the destiny of the country. The first two volumes of *Cartas a Elpidio* were published in New York between 1835 and 1838, but the work remained unfinished. In Philadelphia in 1824 Varela founded the newspaper *El Habanero*, which he transferred to New York a year later and published there until 1826. The newspaper proclaimed itself "a political, scientific, and literary publication" but focused mainly on encouraging and preparing for Cuba's independence. In the following decades Cuban émigrés with similar objectives published a large number of newspapers and magazines.

The scholar José de la Luz y Caballero (1800–1862) is noted for his contributions to the cause of Cuban education. In 1838 and 1839 he played a significant part in the philosophical controversy surrounding the eclecticism of the French philosopher Victor Cousin (1792–1867). The debate among Luz, who opposed Cousin's ideas, and the brothers Manuel and José Zacarías González del Valle, Domingo Del Monte y Aponte, and other intellectuals, led Luz to publish *Impugnación a las doctrinas filosóficas de Victor Cousin* in 1840.

Domingo Del Monte (1804–1853), a poet and promoter of Cuban education and the emerging Cuban culture, is regarded as the island's most important literary critic of the nineteenth century. Famous for the literary gatherings he held in his home, he also organized notable literary magazines, among them *La Moda o Recreo semanal del bello sexo* (1829–1831) and *El puntero literario* (1830), and collaborated on others, such as *Aguinaldo habanero*, *El Álbum*, and *El Plantel*. In his writings he insists on the need to create a Cuban (as distinct from a Spanish) literature, characterized by social and ethical concerns and aesthetically linked to a sober romanticism.

LITERARY CONTROVERSIES

While in New York, Del Monte promoted the first edition of *Poesías*, by the Cuban poet José María Heredia (1803–1839). The volume's appearance fueled one of the main literary controversies of the century. The Spanish naturalist Ramón de la Sagra (1798–1871), writing in *Anales de Ciencias, Agricultura, Comercio y Artes* (1829), criticized Heredia's work on aesthetic grounds. The Cuban writer José Antonio Saco (1797–1879), writing in *El Mensajero Semanal* of Philadelphia between 18 July and 8 August 1829, responded sharply to the criticism. The controversy persisted for many months and involved other writers, such as Felix Tanco, who wrote in favor of the poet in the Cuban paper *La Aurora*, published in Matanzas. The controversy also broadened beyond aesthetics. As Fina García Marruz put it in a 1969 essay: "It was more than an issue of literary critique, it was the Cuban issue" (García Marruz 1969, p. 339).

Throughout the nineteenth century, writers debated the role of slavery in Cuba's economy and society. Because of colonial censorship, however, in most cases this debate had to be published outside of Cuba. Félix Varela's 1822 work, *Memoria que demuestra la necesidad de extinguir la esclavitud de los negros en la Isla de Cuba*, was never published during his lifetime. In leaflets on the same issue published in Europe in the 1840s and 1850s, Saco called for abolition. His crowning achievement was *Historia de la esclavitud*, the first three volumes of which were published in Paris between 1875 and 1877; the work was left unfinished upon the author's death in 1879. Del Monte, who had also called for abolition and traveled to Philadelphia in 1842 to meet with British abolitionist David Turnbull, was falsely accused by another Cuban writer of having participated in a failed slave rebellion. In August 1844 he published a letter in *Le Globe* in Paris defending himself against the accusation and expressing his belief that it was possible to abolish slavery by ending the slave trade and promoting white immigration. He spent the remainder of his life in exile.

Another controversy—more complex and more extended over time—is the one that surrounds the poet Gabriel de la Concepción Valdés (1809–1844), who wrote under the pseudonym Plácido. Despite a lack of evidence, the Spanish authorities accused the popular poet, who was famous for improvising poems at social gatherings and public events, of conspiracy and executed him by firing squad. In his essay "Dos poetas negros: Plácido y Manzano," written in Paris in 1845, Del Monte describes the executed man as someone who merely improvised verse to make a living. In debates that persisted throughout the century, intellectuals took sides on Plácido's legitimacy as a poet, with some dismissing him as primitive and others defending him as having contributed to Cuban folklore. In 1874 Pedro José Guiteras (1814–1890) published a biography of the poet in *El Mundo Nuevo* of New York, offering a measured opinion of his work.

Beginning in 1892, Juan Gualberto Gómez (1852–1933), the editor of the newspaper *La Igualdad*, encouraged an exalted image of Plácido as a patriot and intellectual, intending to transform the poet into an emblem of the blacks and mulattoes who supported the independence movement and strove at the same time for a place in the new society. In 1894 the essayist Manuel Sanguily (1848–1925) countered Gómez in three articles in which he discredited Plácido, showing an extensive knowledge of the poet's life and work. However, scholars have pointed to Sanguily's strong racial prejudice as an element of his criticism, suggesting that his emphasis on the writer's defects was far from a purely literary assessment. The controversy over Plácido persists into the twenty-first century.

The *Revista de Cuba* (1877–1884), edited by José Antonio Cortina, was an important magazine that published essays on the natural and social sciences by such remarkable writers as Rafael Montoro (1852–1933) and Enrique José Varona (1849–1933).

José Martí (1853–1895), the hero of the Cuban independence movement and an important literary figure as well, is the most wide-ranging and original essayist of the nineteenth century. His political and sociological texts, written almost entirely during his exile, were published in newspapers and magazines of various North and South American countries. "Nuestra América" was published in *El Partido Liberal* in Mexico in 1891; in other essays he analyzed the life and work of prominent thinkers and writers, as in "Emerson" (1882), "Whitman" (1887), and "Heredia" (1888). As an art critic and proponent of American modernism, he combined astute aesthetic analyses with the ethical notion that art must serve virtue.

BIBLIOGRAPHY

Bueno, Salvador, ed. *Acerca de Plácido.* Havana: Editorial Letras Cubanas, 1985.

Del Monte, Domingo. *Humanismo y humanitarismo: Ensayos críticos y literarios.* Havana: Editorial Lex, 1960.

Fernández Retamar, Roberto. *Introducción a José Martí.* Havana: Editorial Letras Cubanas, 2006.

García Marruz, Fina. "Martí y los críticos de Heredia del XIX." In *Temas martianos,* edited by Cintio Vivier and Fina García Marruz. Havana: Departamento Colección Cubana, Biblioteca Nacional José Martí, 1969.

García Marruz, Fina. *Estudios delmontinos.* Havana: Ediciones Unión, 2008.

Lezama Lima, José, ed. *El Regañón y El Nuevo Regañón.* Havana: Comisión Nacional Cubana de la UNESCO, 1965.

Martí, José. *Obras completas.* 27 vols. Havana: Social Sciences Publishing House, 1975.

Medina, Tristán de Jesús. "Cuatro laúdes." In *Narraciones,* edited by Roberto Friol. Havana: Editorial Letras Cubanas, 1990.

Mitjans, Aurelio. *Estudio sobre el movimiento científico y literario de Cuba.* Havana: Consejo Nacional de Cultura, 1963.

Saco, José Antonio. *Historia de la esclavitud desde los tiempos más remotos hasta nuestros días.* 4 vols. Havana: Departamento Colección Cubana, 1938.

Varela, Félix. *Cartas a Elpidio, sobre la impiedad, la superstición y el fanatismo en sus relaciones con la sociedad.* Facsimile ed. Miami: Editorial Cubana, 1996.

Vitier, Cintio, ed. *La crítica literaria y estética en el siglo XIX cubano.* 3 vols. Havana: Biblioteca Nacional José Martí, Departamento Colección Cubana, 1968–1974.

Vitier, Cintio. *Ese sol del mundo moral para una historia de la eticidad cubana.* Mexico City: Siglo Veintiuno Editores, 1975.

LITERATURE: NONFICTION IN THE REPUBLICAN PERIOD

Ana Cairo

Connections between the essay, public speaking, journalism, and culture from 1902 to 1959.

The essay as a genre falls into several categories, including literature, journalism, and lectures. The canon of Cuban essays begins with "Nuestra América" (Our America, 1891), by José Martí (1853–1895). Substantive and stylistic echoes of Martí's work are found in *El engaño de las razas* (The Deception of Race, 1946), by Fernando Ortiz (1881–1946); *La expresión americana* (American Expression, 1957), by José Lezama Lima (1910–1976); and "Calibán" (1971), by Roberto Fernández Retamar. The main Cuban critics who analyzed the essay as a genre are Max Henríquez Ureña (1885–1968), author of *El ocaso del dogmatismo literario* (The Decline of Literary Dogmatism, 1919); Medardo Vitier (1886–1960), author of *Apuntaciones literarias* (Literary Notes, 1935) and *Del ensayo americano* (The American Essay, 1945); and Félix Lizaso (1891–1967), author of *Ensayistas contemporáneos: 1900–1920* (Contemporary Essayists: 1900–1920, 1937). In the 1899–1959 period, marked by U.S. military occupation, followed by the declaration of the Republic of Cuba, and capped by the Cuban Revolution, Cuban writers observed and analyzed aspects of Cuban society, economy, politics, identity, and relations with the rest of the world.

FIRST DECADES OF THE REPUBLIC

Between 1899 and 1902 political themes prevailed in essay writing and public speaking. Debates about the Platt Amendment were especially important. In 1901 Juan Gualberto Gómez (1854–1933), the most famous of the black intellectual revolutionaries in the last decade of the colonial period, wrote a position paper that was one of the most important essays against the U.S amendment. In a 1935 essay, Emilio Roig de Leuchsenring (1889–1964) provided an exhaustive anti-imperialist interpretation of the history of the amendment. Parts of speeches delivered by Manuel Sanguily (1848–1925) in the Cuban Senate were used in scholastic materials for patriotic purposes. From 1944 to 1951 the politician Eduardo R. Chibás (1907–1951) had a Sunday evening radio program; upon finishing the speech "El último aldabonazo" (The Last Call), a denunciation of government corruption and plans for a coup, he shot himself. In one of the most famous prose works in Cuban history, Fidel Castro delivered *La historia me absolverá* (History Will Absolve Me), a self-defense

■ *See also*

Azúcar y población en las Antillas (Ramiro Guerra)

Cuban Counterpoint: Tobacco and Sugar (Fernando Ortiz)

Indagación del choteo (Jorge Mañach)

LANDMARKS OF THE CUBAN ESSAY DURING THE REPUBLIC

1901: Juan Gualberto Gómez (1854–1933): "Ponencia para responder al gobernador militar su comunicación sobre la Enmienda Platt" (Position Paper in Response to the Communication from the Military Governor about the Platt Amendment).

1903: Manuel Sanguily (1848–1925): "Discursos en el Senado contra el Tratado de Reciprocidad Comercial con los Estados Unidos de América" (Speeches in the Senate against the Trade Reciprocity Agreement with the United States of America).

1905: Enrique José Varona (1849–1933): "El imperialismo a la luz de la sociología" (Imperialism in the Light of Sociology).

1906: Fernando Ortiz: *Los negros brujos: Apuntes para un estudio criminal* (The Black Witches: Notes for a Criminal Study).

1916: Fernando Ortiz: *Los negros esclavos* (The Black Slaves).

1916: José Antonio Ramos (1885–1946): *Manual del perfecto fulanista: Apuntes para el estudio de nuestra dinámica político-social* (Manual for the Perfect So-and-So: Notes for the Study of Our Political-Social Dynamic).

1924: Fernando Ortiz: *La decadencia cubana* (Cuban Decadence).

1925: Julio Antonio Mella (1903–1929): *Cuba: Un pueblo que jamás ha sido libre* (Cuba: A People That Has Never Been Free).

1927: Ramiro Guerra (1880–1970): *Azúcar y población en las Antillas* (Sugar and Population in the West Indies).

1928: Jorge Mañach (1898–1961): *Indagación del choteo* (Investigation into Choteo).

1930: Mariblanca Sabas Alomá (1901–1983): *Feminismo: Cuestiones sociales; Crítica literaria* (Feminism: Social Issues; Literary Criticism).

1931: Alejo Carpentier (1904–1980): "Les points cardinaux du roman en Amérique Latine" (The Cardinal Points of the Latin American Novel).

1931: Raúl Roa (1907–1982): "Reacción versus revolución" (Reaction versus Revolution).

1934: Antonio Guiteras (1907–1935); "Programa de la Joven Cuba" (Plan for the Young Cuba).

1934: Jorge Mañach: "El estilo de la revolución" (The Style of the Revolution).

1934: Juan Marinello (1898–1977): "Notas polémicas para un ensayo: Veinticinco años de poesía cubana" (Polemic Notes for an Essay: Twenty-five Years of Cuban Poetry).

1935: Emilio Roig de Leuchsenring (1889–1964): *Historia de la Enmienda Platt: Una interpretación de la realidad cubana* (History of the Platt Amendment: An Interpretation of the Cuban Situation).

1935: Nicolás Guillén (1902–1989): *Claudio José Domingo Brindis de Salas, el rey de las octavas; Apuntes biográficos.* (Claudio José Domingo

against charges for his responsibility in the Moncada Barracks Assault (15 October 1953). While in prison Castro wrote the version of the plea that circulated clandestinely in 1954 and that is considered the political manifesto of the Cuban Revolution. "El imperialismo a la luz de la sociología" (Imperialism in the Light of Sociology; 1905), by Enrique José Varona (1849–1933), prompted theoretical debate, the impact of which extended into the twenty-first century.

In 1906 Fernando Ortiz published *Los negros brujos (apuntes para un estudio criminal)* (The Black Sorcerors [Notes for a Criminal Study]), which focuses on ethnocriminology. The work brought him prestige in Europe, Latin America, and the United States. His subsequent influential works include *Los negros esclavos* (1916), which deals with social history, building on the legacy of the nineteenth-century writers José Antonio Saco and Antonio Bachiller y Morales; *Entre cubanos: Psicología tropical* (Among Cubans: Tropical Psychology, 1913), a psychological work; and *La crisis política cubana: Sus causas y remedios* (The Cuban Political Crisis: Its Causes and Remedies, 1919), a work of political science from a liberal-left perspective. José Antonio Ramos (1885–1946), in *Manual del perfecto fulanista, apuntes para el estudio de nuestra dinámica político-social* (Manual for the Perfect So-and-So, Notes for the Study of Our Political-Social Dynamic; 1916) engages in dialogue with Ortiz, employing psychology and humor when describing characters on the political scene.

1920s–1940s

Ortiz's *La decadencia cubana* (Cuban Decadence, 1924) provided a foundation for understanding the liberal reformist projects during the period of revolutions between 1923 and 1940, when the Cuban constitution was proclaimed. In 1925, in *Cuba: un pueblo que jamás ha sido libre* (Cuba: A People That Has Never Been Free), Julio Antonio Mella (1903–1929) engaged Varona's ideas and radicalized Ortiz's denunciation of the Republican crisis. Ramiro Guerra (1880–1970) created a stir when he published *Azúcar y población en las Antillas* in serial format between May and June 1927 in *Diario de la Marina*; this work revitalized comparative economic historiography. The academic and political dispute between Ortiz and Guerra aided in the development of the social sciences, particularly in the discrepancy between the methodological foundations of their analyses of Cuban agriculture and industry.

Between October 1936 and February 1937, Roig de Leuchsenring organized a course on the history of Cuban society that was broadcast on the radio. Numerous intellectuals gave lectures in this series, prompting debate on the origins of the Cuban people, their diverse cultural heritage, forms of identity, methodological problems, comparative history, schools of research, and so on. Other projects championed by Ortiz and Roig de Leuchsenring enlisted the participation of many Cuban intellectuals. At the request of the students of the University of Havana, in 1939 several intellectuals developed a lecture series devoted to problems in the history of Cuban identity.

Brindis de Salas: King of the Octaves; Biographical Notes).

1935: Gustavo Urrutia (1881-1958): *Cuatro charlas radiofónicas* (Four Radio Talks).

1936: Pablo de la Torriente Brau (1901–1936): "Álgebra y política" (Algebra and Politics [unpublished until 1968]).

1939: Fernando Ortiz: "Los factores humanos de la cubanidad" (The Human Factors of Cubanness").

1939: Camila Henríquez Ureña (1894–1973): "Feminismo" (Feminism).

1940: Fernando Ortiz: *Contrapunteo cubano del tabaco y el azúcar* (Cuban Counterpoint: Tobacco and Sugar).

1941: Salvador García Agüero (1908–1965): *Maceo: cifra y carácter de la revolución cubana* (Maceo: Code and Character of the Cuban Revolution).

1942: Fernando Ortiz: "Por la integración cubana de blancos y negros" (For the Cuban Integration of Whites and Blacks).

1945: Medardo Vitier: *Del ensayo americano* (The Essay in the Americas).

1945: José Antonio Portuondo (1911–1996): *Concepto de la poesía* (Concept of Poetry).

1946: Alejo Carpentier: *La música en Cuba* (Music in Cuba).

1946: Fernando Ortiz: *El engaño de las razas* (The Deceit of the Races).

1947: Mirta Aguirre (1912–1980): *La influencia de la mujer en Iberoamérica* (Women's Influence in Ibero-America).

1948: Medardo Vitier: *La filosofía en Cuba* (Philosophy in Cuba).

1949: Debate between Jorge Mañach, José Lezama Lima, Cintio Vitier, and Luis Ortega.

1951: Eduardo R. Chibás (1907–1951): "El último aldabonazo" (The Last Bombshell).

1953–1954: Fidel Castro: *La historia me absolverá* (History Will Absolve Me).

1954: Lydia Cabrera (1899–1991): *El monte* (The Mountain) and "El sincretismo religioso de Cuba: Santos, orishas, ngangas, lucumís y congos" (The Religious Syncretism of Cuba: Saints, Orisha, Ngangas, Lucumíes, and Congos).

1956: Loló de la Torriente (1907–1983): *Mi casa en la tierra* (My Home on the Earth).

1956: Roberto Fernández Retamar: *La poesía contemporánea en Cuba (1927–1953)* (Contemporary Poetry in Cuba [1927–1953]).

1956: Rafael García Bárcenas: *El redescubrimiento de Dios* (The Rediscovery of God).

1957: José Lezama Lima: *La expresión americana* (Expression in the Americas).

1958: Jorge Mañach: "El drama de Cuba" (The Drama of Cuba).

1958: Cintio Vitier (1921–2009): *Lo cubano en la poesía* (Cubanness in Poetry).

The most significant of these lectures was given by Ortiz, "Los factores humanos de la cubanidad" (The Human Factors of Cubanness, 1939) in which Ortiz highlighted the culinary metaphor of the *ajiaco* (a type of stew) to facilitate understanding. This talk advanced the field of transculturation. In 1940 he took the concept further and applied intertextuality to literature and other arts in *Contrapunteo cubano del tabaco y el azúcar* (*Cuban Counterpoint: Tobacco and Sugar*), regarded as one of the premier essays of the twentieth century.

Raúl Roa (1907–1982), a disciple of the Peruvian José Carlos Mariátegui, wrote "Reacción versus revolución" (Reaction versus Revolution, 1934) in the form of a public letter employing a colloquial style, inviting the writer Jorge Mañach to a debate the ideological content of the Left and the anti-Machado Right. The end of Gerardo Machado's regime in 1933 and the nationalist actions of the revolutionary government (September 1933 to January 1934), which collapsed under a coup by Fulgencio Batista, resulted in a period of intense political violence.

Antonio Guiteras (1907–1935) proposed, in the first part of "Programa de la joven Cuba" (Plan for the Young Cuba, 1934) a theoretical reflection on the essence of the neocolonial republic; in the second part, he organized a series of measures to modernize society and guarantee effective sovereignty. Eduardo Chibás (1907–1951) in "El último aldabonazo" (The Last Bombshell) validated the second part of Guiteras's text. Fidel Castro put the ideas of both writers into action.

Pablo de la Torriente Brau (1901–1936), who was Ortiz's secretary, wrote "Álgebra y política" (not published until 1968) in the form of an epistle to his friends Raúl Roa and Ramiro Valdés Daussá. His purpose was to unravel the many factors that allowed them to state that the Revolution of 1930 was in its death throes. Ingenious in its use of systems of equations, colloquial language, and humorous and satirical resources, this vanguard work is another landmark in the Cuban essay of the twentieth century.

Despite their contributions during the two wars for independence, women were denied suffrage at the Constitutional Convention of 1901. Women's rights became one of the perpetual rallying points of Cuban intellectuals, and in 1939 women voted for and were elected as delegates to the Constitutional Convention of 1940. Mariblanca Sabas Alomá (1901–1983) wrote about women's aspirations, society, film, and art. Loló de la Torriente (1907–1983) specialized in fine arts criticism and also wrote biographical and historical essays, such as *Mi casa en la tierra* (My Home on the Earth, 1956). Lydia Cabrera (1899–1991) developed the ethnological essay in dialogue with those of Ortiz. Camila Henríquez Ureña (1894–1973) and Mirta Aguirre (1912–1980) were concerned with feminism and literary themes.

The cultural disciplines were situated amid diverse problems of renovation and modernity. In "El estilo de la revolución" (The Style of the Revolution, 1934), Jorge Mañach mixed trends from the literary and artistic vanguard with forms coming from the anti-Machado and anti-Batista political struggle. The essay circulated in the newspaper *Acción* and earned the Justo de Lara Prize in 1935, awarded to the most original and best-written text. Juan Marinello (1898–1977) wrote about the evolution of modernist poetry toward vanguard tendencies. Alejo Carpentier (1904–1980), living in exile in Paris, experimented with vanguardist narratives in 1931. Aware that the cultural interests of Latin American intellectuals were different from those of the Europeans, he engaged in a defense of the new novel. In another magisterial work he presented the evolution of Cuban music from the sixteenth century through the 1940s.

In the essays "Martí y las razas" (Martí and Race, 1941) and "Martí y las razas de librería" (Martí and the Ersatz Races, 1945), Ortiz demonstrated that Martí's thesis in "Nuestra América," that the concept of race is false, remained effective, especially after the condemnation of racism in the wording of the 1940 Constitution. In 1942, in "Por la integración cubana de blancos y negros" (For the Cuban Integration of Whites and Blacks), he offered a political, educational, and cultural strategy to slowly advance toward a fifth phase of Cuban society, in which Cuba would achieve an erasure of differentiation and in which the color of a person's skin would not matter. His essay *El engaño de las razas* (The Deception of Race, 1946) is a contribution to antifascist thinking at the international level.

In journalistic essays the poet Nicolás Guillén (1902–1989) and the architect Gustavo Urrutia (1881–1958), along with the public speaker Salvador García Agüero (1908–1965), confronted discrimination against blacks and mulattoes. They believed, like Ortiz, that political, scientific, and cultural arguments should be updated so as to systematically combat all forms of racism, prejudice, and xenophobia. The literary critic and aesthetician José Antonio Portuondo (1911–1996) wrote the notable *Concepto de la poesía* (Concept of Poetry, 1945). Roberto Fernández Retamar's *La poesía contemporánea en Cuba (1927–1953)* (Contemporary Poetry in Cuba [1927–1953], 1956) is another literary essay of note. Medardo Vitier (an interpreter of Varona) established groupings of Cuban and Latin American essayists that connected them to those in Spain. He systematized trends in Cuban intellectual thought in *Las ideas en Cuba* (Ideas in Cuba, 1938) and *La filosofía en Cuba* (Philosophy in Cuba, 1948).

In 1949 a heated literary debate on the fundamentals of poetic communication and the aesthetic dimensions of the literary vanguard between Mañach and Lezama, and joined by Cintio Vitier (1921–2009) and Luis Ortega, began in the pages of *Bohemia* magazine and continued in the national-circulation newspapers *Prensa Libre* and *Diario de la Marina*, earning a large readership. This debate was crucial for understanding the legacy of the literary avant-garde in Cuba.

1950s

In five lectures given in 1957 (*La expresión americana* [Expression in the Americas]), Lezama limned a pan–Latin American identity and evaluated the roots of Hispanic culture in interaction with native peoples. Like Lezama, Vitier gave a series of lectures in which he paired philosophical concepts with poetic images, seeking to emphasize the tradition that legitimized them. In 1988 Vitier offered a course in the Instituto Superior de Arte, which was published as *Lecciones cubanas* (Cuban Lessons, 1996). The thirty years that separated the two exercises indicated the evolution of this intellectual's theoretical position—and completed the evolution of Cuban poetry—with the mature cultural thinker modifying the passionate criteria of the young poet.

Rafael García Bárcenas, who confronted the second Batista regime starting in March 1952, was imprisoned in April 1953. While in prison, he wrote *El redescubrimiento de Dios* (The Rediscovery of God, 1956), an essay restating the philosophical search within Christian ontology. Mañach, who also angered Batista, was in exile in Spain when he was asked to write an essay denouncing the crimes of the regime. Published in Paris in 1958, "El drama de Cuba" (The Drama of Cuba) was also included in the special issue of the weekly *Bohemia* in January 1959, opening up the three-part series known as the "liberty edition." Given that the certified print run of *Bohemia* was one million copies, Mañach's work became the most reproduced essay of the twentieth century.

BIBLIOGRAPHY

Cairo, Ana. "La polémica Mañach-Lezama-Vitier-Ortega." *Revista de la Biblioteca Nacional José Martí.* (January–June 2001): 91–130. Available from http://bohemia.cu/jose-lezama-lima/polemica-ana-cairo-1.html.

Chacón y Calvo, José María. *Cartas censorias de la conquista.* Havana: Dirección de Cultura, 1938.

Chacón y Calvo, José María. *Estudios heredianos.* Havana: Editorial Trópico, 1939.

Gay Calbó, Enrique. *Orígenes de la literatura cubana: Ensayo de interpretación.* Havana: Publicaciones de la revista Universidad de La Habana, 1939.

LITERATURE: NONFICTION IN THE REVOLUTIONARY PERIOD

Linda S. Howe

Literary polemics and politics from 1959 to 1989.

Although Cuba has a strong tradition of public-minded intellectuals stretching from José Martí in the nineteenth century to Jorge Mañach, Fernando Ortiz, Juan Marinello, Enrique Varona, and Ramiro Guerra in the twentieth, the post-independence state before 1959 rarely impinged on their work. After the Revolution, the government became directly involved in all areas of cultural life—publishing, music, dance, film,

■ *See also*

The Color of Summer
(Reinaldo Arenas)

Gender: Trends in
Women's Writing after
the Revolution

The Orígenes Group and
Journal

Sexuality: The UMAP
Camps

the visual arts—greatly increasing both funding and censorship. During the ingenuous, euphoric 1960s, when the international left proclaimed solidarity with the Revolution, cultural authorities encouraged a variety of activities, although they primarily funded pro-revolutionary literature, documentary films, and graphic art. As culture became an arm of government, many intellectuals benefited from the newly created venues. They were also thrust into other public roles as educators, editors, journalists, and administrators of cultural institutions, with attendant risks.

Contemporary Cuban literary history and cultural production are inextricably linked to political and ideological battles. Pro-revolutionary writers and artists were published or produced regularly. Others experienced official chastisement or fell from grace before "rectifying" themselves ideologically or leaving the island for good. The story of how the Revolution's overarching metanarrative of national identity subsumed Cuba's literary achievements is uneven and muddled, complex and controversial.

CULTURAL PRODUCTION IN THE EARLY 1960s

The early 1960s were characterized by a push to minimize European and U.S. cultural trends, to scrutinize Latin America's colonial and neocolonial histories, and to set new ideological standards for cultural production. The United States broke diplomatic relations in January 1961, and after the CIA-backed Bay of Pigs invasion later that year failed to overthrow Castro's government, the revolution became "socialist," and Cuba developed closer ties with the Soviet Union and its Eastern European allies. The October 1962 missile crisis, which ended when the Soviets agreed to remove their offensive weapons from Cuba, and the United States agreed never to invade, reinforced nationalist and anti-imperialist sentiment on the island. By 1965, Castro had brought together all the major revolutionary groups into a unified Communist Party. The government worked to create an image of the "New Man" based on Che Guevara's and Fidel Castro's altruism and a zealously crafted revolutionary consciousness. Cuban authorities established the cultural institutions Casa de las Américas (1959), the Instituto Cubano de Arte e Industria Cinematográficos (ICAIC; Cuban Institute of Cinema Art and Industry, 1959), the Unión de Escritores y Artistas de Cuba (UNEAC; Union of Writers and Artists of Cuba, 1961), and the Consejo Nacional de Cultura (CNC; National Culture Council, 1961; became the Ministry of Culture in 1976) to generate and support new forms of cultural production and to fill the gap in official diplomacy (see Menton; Thomas 1977).

Other factors contributed to official management of Cuban culture. In 1961, Castro announced, "within the Revolution, everything; against the Revolution, nothing," and alluded to the government's right to judge an intellectual's preferred themes and subjects through "the prism of the revolutionary crystal" (pp. 20–21). That same year, Cuba held the First National Congress of Writers and Artists, in which respected literary scholar and bureaucrat José Antonio Portuondo called on writers to develop an "integrally formed national conscience" that identified with the masses (Ripoll p. 503). The distinguished University of Havana chancellor and veteran communist Juan Marinello called for a committed literature (González p. 48).

In 1959, Carlos Franqui, Guillermo Cabrera Infante, and Pablo Armando Fernández created *Lunes de Revolución*, a weekly arts and literature supplement to the newspaper *Revolución*, which Franqui had co-edited since its inception as an underground paper under the dictator Fulgencio Batista (Thomas 1971, p. 868; Szulc p. 458). A poet, art critic, journalist, revolutionary, and Castro's close ally for a time, by the early 1960s Franqui (1988) came to disagree with the Communist Party apparatus and members of the 26th of July Movement. He emigrated in 1963 and broke with the Cuban government in 1968 after Castro supported the Soviet invasion of Czechoslovakia.

In the tradition of José Rodríguez Feo's and Virgilio Piñera's literary journal *Ciclón* (1956–1959), *Lunes* writers espoused eclectic tastes and revolutionary ideals, although not adhering strictly to a given political system. In a 1961 essay in *Lunes*, Rodríguez Feo criticized writers in thrall to U.S. culture and became an entrenched revolutionary intellectual who never abandoned a global outlook on culture. Articles published by Franqui, José Lezama Lima, Cabrera Infante, and Piñera, who preferred cosmopolitan aesthetics, philosophies, and politics, elicited negative official reactions.

Some Communist Party officials attempted to rein in *Lunes de Revolución*, but it remained outside their control until 1961, when cultural bureaucrats permanently removed the *Lunes*-sponsored television documentary *P.M.* from circulation. Directed by Sabá Cabrera Infante, Guillermo's brother, the documentary depicts Havana's lively nightlife. Cultural officials argued that it was too racy and fixated on Afro-Cuban characters, creating the wrong impression of Cuban life (Menton p. 126). The fight was an extension of a 1950s rivalry between a Marxist film club and the liberals of Havana's Cine Club of the Cinemateca. The Marxist group, led by Alfredo Guevara, Julio García Espinosa, and Tomás Gutiérrez Alea, controlled the new official film institute ICAIC and prevailed over the Cinemateca, supported by Sabá Cabrera Infante, German Puig, Ricardo Vigo, and Néstor Almendros (Luis p. 17). The suppression of *P.M.*—at a time when the Bay of Pigs Invasion has just occurred—marked the beginning of the elimination of all independent cultural production, *Lunes* included. When *Lunes* ceased publication in 1961, UNEAC officials replaced it with two new journals, *La Gaceta de Cuba* and *Unión*, which continue publishing. Intellectuals associated with *Lunes* and implicated in the *P.M.* controversy were sanctioned or sent abroad as diplomats.

A HARDENING OF CULTURAL POLICY

UNEAC and Casa de las Américas now controlled literary juries. The daily paper *Granma*, official organ of the Cuban Communist Party, often denounced "unorthodox" decisions that favored aesthetics over politics. Critic, translator, and poet Heberto Padilla's problems began in 1961 with the closing of *Lunes*. An irreverent figure, in a 1967 article in *El Caimán barbudo* (The Bearded Caiman), he lambasted Lisandro Otero's award-winning novel *Pasión de Urbino* (1966) and infuriated authorities by praising Guillermo Cabrera Infante's banned novel *Tres tristes tigres* (1967; *Three Trapped Tigers*, 1971). In 1968, the UNEAC jury awarded his collection *Fuera del juego* (Out of the Game) the Julián de Casal Prize and, later, published it with a postscript by UNEAC officials protesting the prize, branding the text "diversionist." In 1971, authorities placed Padilla under house arrest (Menton pp. 135–141). In a public confession, Padilla condemned himself and fellow intellectuals, including his wife, Belkis Cuza Malé, for "crimes" against the revolution (Casal p. 462). Outraged foreign intellectuals Jean-Paul Sartre, Simone de Beauvoir, Susan Sontag, Juan Goytisolo, and Mario Vargas Llosa condemned the coerced public confession. Eventually released from custody but officially marginalized, Padilla left Cuba in 1980. In the immediate aftermath of his "confession," the First National Congress on Education and Culture established the following rules: political factors determine who works for the universities, media, and art foundations; homosexuals are barred from these institutions; literary contests will be under tight political control; and "pseudoleftist bourgeois intellectuals" who criticize the revolution must be counterattacked (Casal p. 462).

Late 1960s aesthetic and political concerns also gave birth to a new literary genre in Cuba: the *testimonio*. Initially linked to eyewitness accounts of the revolutionary struggle and the 1961 literacy campaign, in the hands of able practitioners like Miguel Barnet, it began to "novelize" personal testimony. His celebrated *Biografía de un cimarrón* (Biography of a Runaway Slave, 1966), widely imitated in Latin America, depicts the historically underrepresented voice of the former slave Montejo. Barnet published other notable testimonial novels, *Canción de Rachel* (Rachel's Song, 1969) and *La vida real* (A True Story, 1986) and several collections of poetry and essays.

The mid-1960s were also marked by repression. In 1965, officials created the UMAP camps (Military Units for the Aid of Production) and sent thousands of gays and other people considered to be nonconformists to them as punishment for deviant behavior until 1968, when they were closed due to international pressure. The so-called *quinquenio gris*, or five gray years, from 1971 to 1976 saw increased persecution of gays and other groups considered deviant. Most Cuban intellectuals and some cultural officials now agree that authorities deliberately downplayed the gravity and duration of the hard-line cultural policy. The Castro government viewed homosexuality as "bourgeois decadence" that led to sexual exploitation of youth and rampant prostitution (González; Bejel). Virgilio Piñera, playwright, poet, and major figure in the Latin American absurdist literature of the 1940s and 1950s, was a victim of the gay purges. After the revolution, he continued to publish stories and write plays, but government officials deemed his wit and "gay" lifestyle unsuitable, and he died in obscurity in 1979.

Works published in the late 1960s to late 1970s included (a) Piñera's *Presiones y diamantes* (Pressures and Diamonds, 1967), later withdrawn from bookstores; *Dos viejos pánicos* (Two Panicked Old Folks, 1968), winner of the Casa de las Américas award for theater; and *La vida entera* (A Whole Life, 1969); (b) Lezama's *Paradiso* (1966), removed then briefly returned to bookstores and not republished in Cuba until 1991, *Poesía completa* (1970), and *Oppiano Licario* (1977); (c) Nicolás Guillén's *El diario que a diario* (The Daily Daily, 1972); (d) three novels by Alejo Carpentier; (e) Antonio Benítez-Rojo's *El mar de las lentejas* (The Sea of Lentils, 1979); (f) poetry and essays by Fernández Retamar; and (g) works by Onelio Jorge Cardoso and César Leante.

A YOUNGER GENERATION

Young intellectual upstarts manifested the profound aesthetic differences that beset writers in the 1960s. Some advocated literature that was hermetic, with a rich, dense vocabulary and a modernist experimental edge; others favored realism, psychological directness, and conversational vocabulary. In the heat of the debates, writers became casualties of official moral, political, and aesthetic crusades. For example, when openly gay U.S. Beat poet Allen Ginsberg visited Cuba in 1969 to serve as poetry judge for Casa de las Américas, his irreverent remarks and behavior offended authorities, and he was thrown out. His escorts José Mario, an editor at the publishing house Ediciones El Puente, and writer Manuel Ballagas were picked up by state security and questioned.

Founded by José Mario, El Puente published work by Nancy Morejón, Eugenio Hernández Espinosa, Gerardo Fulleda León, Ana María Simo, and Manuel Ballagas, among others. In spite of the variety of its material and the enthusiasm it generated, contributors were unable to circumvent criticism and accusations about sexual orientation. Rival groups labeled them *los disolutos* (libertines) and accused them of scabrous humor, insolence, and deviant social behavior. In reality, some were homosexuals; many shared ideas, cultural interests, and friendships, but the entire group was subjected to vicious attacks (Howe 2004, pp. 35–37). Jesús Díaz, founder and editor of *El Caimán barbudo*, accused El Puente members of producing "pure" and inane literature (Mario

p. 52). Other young writers challenged El Puente's "decadent" works and drafted "Nos Pronunciamos," a manifesto published in *El Caimán barbudo* in January 1966, to reprimand its allegedly apolitical, antirevolutionary aesthetics. Echoing the rhetoric of the cultural bureaucrats Marinello and Portuondo, "Nos Pronunciamos" proposed a new, audacious literature without avant-garde pretensions and "intellectual vacillations" and singled out El Puente authors as perpetrators (Díaz Martínez pp. 116–117). As a result, José Mario was sent to UMAP and Ana Maria Simo to a mental institution, with her mother's permission. Nancy Morejón, Eugenio Hernández Espinosa, and Gerardo Fulleda León did not publish for a long time until, ostensibly, they had *reformed*. Eventually, José Mario, Ana María Simo, and Manuel Ballagas chose exile (Casal pp. 450–451).

Another young writer, Reinaldo Arenas, lived a picaresque life in Cuba, fleeing authorities to avoid arrest and hiding or smuggling his manuscripts out of the country to get them published. His works criticized official repression with intertextual references and pseudohistorical data. His gay hyperbole was not mere anger but paid homage to Lezama Lima, Piñera, and Severo Sarduy for all the crimes perpetrated against them and other iconoclastic intellectuals.

SOME WHO AVOIDED CONFLICT

Not every intellectual was in conflict with the government. For example, as director of the prestigious Casa de las Americas, Roberto Fernández Retamar oversaw its annual literary awards, which extended to all of Latin America and the Caribbean, and the publication of its journal *Casa*. Retamar envisioned the ideal literary "New Man" as a previously privileged intellectual who relinquishes egotistical and snobbish tendencies and converts his guilt over his inaction—as opposed to Castro's revolutionary deeds—into politically committed writing.

His famous 1971 essay "Calibán" revises a 1900 essay by the Uruguayan thinker Enrique Rodó, drawing on characters in William Shakespeare's *Tempest*. Rodó takes the spiritual Ariel to symbolize Latin America and its cultural elite as opposed to the crass imperialist capitalism of U.S. culture. Retamar's Calibán represents, on some level, the indigenous and multicultural, malformed, slavish, and enslaved masses of Latin America, who adeptly transgress the colonizer's rules to speak a powerful new language as an act of rebellion. He proposes a man of letters who calls for an end to Cuba's dependence on metropolitan cultural models and abandons the language as well as the conceptual and technical apparatus of Western culture. He asserts that *conversational* poets who renounce their individuality to serve the people capture the revolution's collective spirit. The essay in 1971 reiterated Castro's dictates to the intellectuals and reinforced official cultural

policies that mandated a literature that upholds the great historical struggle to break free of subjugation. At the same time, it warns against facile dismissal of Eurocentrism. Retamar illustrates how his Calibán is emblematic of myriad prominent figures in Latin American and Caribbean history, ranging from Túpac Amaru and Toussaint L'Ouverture to Pablo Neruda and Violeta Parra.

Other intellectuals of this period, Cintio Vitier, Fina García Marruz, Eliseo Diego, Pablo Armando Fernández, Lisandro Otero, and Ambrosio Fornet, like Retamar, spent all or most of their lives on the island in successful careers and produced poetry, criticism, fiction, and film scripts.

LOOSENING CONTROL

In the 1970s, Cuban cultural rigidity peaked, but after the surge of committed literature, new generations deemed social realism insufficient to remediate the suppression of prerevolutionary avant-garde, hermetic, and exteriorist literary traditions. In 1975, the First Congress of the Communist Party vowed to maintain control of the culture, beginning with the new 1976 constitution that "codified much of what had been achieved during the previous decade" (Johnson p. 146). However, in 1978, a modest dialogue with exiles began, and after the 1980 Mariel exodus of more than 125,000 Cubans, the state eased some control in an attempt to defuse criticism both off and on the island. Young writers began producing in a variety of styles by the late 1980s, including avant-garde approaches that had all but disappeared. *La Gaceta* and *Unión* changed editorial policies and started to publish Cuban-American authors.

Cuban artists, artisans, and writers found creative ways to self-publish with smaller, somewhat independent, projects. In 1985, this trend marked the birth of the unique Ediciones Vigía in Matanzas, which epitomized inclusiveness, producing handmade poetry pamphlets and scrolls and invitations to cultural events from recycled materials. Linda Howe writes:

> In 1988, Vigía's first book by Cuban writer Digdora Alonso was a response to the industrial book—the cold, schematic, impersonal texts published by Cuba's traditional presses. Vigía Press came into being because young Matanzas artists wanted to express themselves, and staff wanted to publish writers who did not find opportunities to publish elsewhere.
>
> *(2009, p. 39)*

The Matanzas writers added depth and unique local experience to Vigía's repertoire, but its eclectic tastes went on to include such well-established intellectuals and artists as Fernández Retamar, Pablo

Armando Fernández, Miguel Barnet, Carilda Oliver Labra, Zaida del Río, Eliseo Diego, Cintio Vitier, and Fina García Marruz; younger writers, such as Antonio José Ponte, Arturo Arango, and Senel Paz; iconoclastic writers Gastón Baquero, Severo Sarduy, and the Mexican poet and essayist Octavio Paz; and foreign writers, such as North Americans Emily Dickinson and Walt Whitman and Russian and Eastern European poets, such as Anna Akhmatova, Sergei Esenin, Boris Pasternak, and Wisława Szymborska.

From 1979 to 1986, repression "became less systematic and more individualized," and the "rectification process" initiated in 1986 gave intellectuals hope that government restrictions on writing, research, and publication might slowly lift. At the Fifth Congress of the Union of Communist Youth (1987), party ideologue Carlos Aldana argued for the internationalization of Cuban culture (Johnson pp. 146–147), and officials began rehabilitating ostracized intellectuals. For example, from the late 1970s through the 1980s, new positions and publication opportunities were offered to Antonio Benítez Rojo, demoted in 1970 from the directorship of Casa de las Américas Center for Library Research; Eduardo Heras León, dismissed from the editorial board of *Caimán Barbudo* for his 1971 book *Los pasos en la hierba* (Steps in the Grass); and Antón Arrufat, banned for the 1968 drama *Los siete contra Tebas* (Seven against Thebes), believed to be a veiled criticism of Raúl Castro (Johnson p. 162).

Cuban writers have attempted to flesh out these three decades of sanitized official history through memoir (Padilla's *La mala memoria* [The Bad Memory] 1988, and Antón Arrufat's *Virgilio Piñera entre el y yo* [Between Virgilio Piñera and Me], 1994); essay (Guillermo Cabrera Infante's *Mea Cuba*, 1993); film (Almendros's *Improper Conduct*, 1984); and the novel (Jesús Díaz's *Las palabras perdidas* [The Lost Words], 1996). In interviews with Emilio Bejel (1991), several Cuban writers discussed Lezama Lima's and other iconoclasts' tragicomic difficulties with cultural bureaucrats.

CONCLUSION

In Cuba, from 1959 to 1989, a centralized revolutionary narrative of national identity prioritized politics at the expense of aesthetics. The guerrilla victory transformed a small island into a giant, able to defeat the imperialist Yankees on the international Cold War stage. From 1959 to the late 1970s, potential dissidents were hounded; many homosexuals were banished to marginal posts or reeducation camps, and censorship became draconian. However, by the 1980s, the Cuban literary and cultural scene began to change, sparking new experimental artistic forms, a revaluation of previously proscribed authors (Lezama, Piñera, Lydia Cabrera), greater publication of foreign writers, and a more comprehensive engagement with Cuban-American authors. Although poetry and fiction were the most robust, most genres flourished in a vibrant literary scene.

Cuban literary history exemplifies the precarious nature of individual power in cultural politics. In the 1980s, a new generation of authors, such as Arturo Arango, Senel Paz, Abilio Estévez, Reina María Rodríguez, and Victor Fowler, began publishing their works, and, in the 1990s, a new wave of writers—Leonardo Padura, Zoe Valdés, Daína Chaviano, Antonio José Ponte, Pedro Juan Gutiérrez, José Manuel Prieto, Ena Lucía Portela, Cristina García, Oscar Hijuelos, and Mayra Montero—contributed their eclectic works to Cuba's complex canon. They show how Cubans constantly recover, reframe, rewrite, and revitalize their literary tradition.

BIBLIOGRAPHY

Arrufat, Antón. *Virgilio Piñera entre él y yo*. Havana: Ediciones Unión, 1994.

Barnet, Miguel. *Biografía de un cimarrón*. Havana: Instituto de Etnología y Folklore, 1966.

Barnet, Miguel. *Canción de Rachel*. Havana: Instituto del Libro, 1969.

Barnet, Miguel. *La vida real*. Madrid: Ediciones Alfaguara, 1986.

Bejel, Emilio. *Escribir en Cuba: Entrevistas con escritores cubanos, 1979–1989*. Rio Piedras: Editorial de la Universidad de Puerto Rico, 1991.

Benítez-Rojo, Antonio. *El mar de las lentejas*. Havana: Editorial Letras Cubanas, 1979.

Bethell, Leslie, ed. *Cuba: A Short History*. Cambridge, U.K., and New York: Cambridge University Press, 1993.

Cabrera Infante, Guillermo. *Tres tristes tigres*. Barcelona: Seix Barral, 1968.

Cabrera Infante, Guillermo. *Mea Cuba*. Mexico: Editorial Vuelta, 1993.

Casal, Lourdes. "Literature and Society." In *Revolutionary Change in Cuba*, edited by Carmelo Mesa-Lago. Pittsburgh: University of Pittsburgh Press, 1971.

Castro, Fidel. *Palabras a los intelectuales*. Montevideo: Comité de Intelectuales y Artistas de Apoyo a la Revolución Cubana, 1961.

Díaz, Jesús. *Las palabras perdidas*. Barcelona: Ediciones Destino, 1992.

Díaz Martínez, Manuel. "Poesía cubana de hoy." *Revista Canadiense de Estudios Hispánicos* 13, no. 1 (Autumn 1988): 111–125.

Foster, David William. *Gay and Lesbian Themes in Latin American Writing*. Austin: University of Texas Press, 1991.

Franqui, Carlos. *Vidas, aventuras y desastres de un hombre llamado Castro*. Barcelona: Planeta, 1988.

González, Mike, and David Treece, eds. *The Gathering of Voices: The Twentieth-Century Poetry of Latin America*. London and New York: Verso, 1992.

González, Reynaldo. *Contradanzas y latigazos*. Havana: Letras Cubanas, 1983.

González, Reynaldo. "Meditation for a Debate, or Cuban Culture with the Taste of Strawberry and Chocolate," trans. by William Rose, *Cuba Update* 15, no. 2 (May 1994): 14–19.

Guillén, Nicolás. *El diario que a diario*. Havana: Editorial Unión, 1972.

Howe, Linda. *Transgression and Conformity: Cuban Writers and Artists after the Revolution*. Madison: University of Wisconsin Press, 2004.

Howe, Linda. *Cuban Artists' Books and Prints: 1985–2009*. Winston-Salem, NC: J La'Verne Print Communications, 2009.

Johnson, Peter. "Nuanced Lives of the Intelligentsia." In *Conflict and Change in Cuba*, edited by Enrique A. Baloyra and James A. Morris. Albuquerque: University of New Mexico Press, 1993.

Lezama Lima, José. *Paradiso*. Havana: Unión, 1966.

Lezama Lima, José. *Poesía completa*. Havana: Instituto del Libro, 1970.

Lezama Lima, José. *Oppiano Licario*. Havana: Editorial Arte y Literatura, 1977.

Luis, William. "Cinema and Culture in Cuba: An Interview with Néstor Almendros." *Review: Latin American Literature and Arts* 37 (January–June 1987): 14–21.

Mario, José. "Allen Ginsberg en la Habana." *Mundo Nuevo* 34 (April 1969): 48–54.

Menton, Seymour. *Prose Fiction of the Cuban Revolution*. Austin: University of Texas Press, 1975.

Mesa-Lago, Carmelo, ed. *El caso Padilla: Literatura y revolución en Cuba: Documentos*. Miami: Ediciones Universal, 1971.

Otero, Lisandro. *Pasión de Urbino*. Buenos Aires: J. Álvarez, 1966.

Padilla, Heberto. *Fuera del juego*. Havana: Unión, 1968.

Padilla, Heberto. *La mala memoria*. Barcelona: Plaza and Janes, 1989.

Padilla, Heberto. *Self-Portrait of the Other: A Memoir*. Translated by A. Coleman, New York: Farrar, Straus & Giroux, 1990.

Padura, Leonardo. *Máscaras*. Barcelona: Tusquets, 1997.

Piñera, Virgilio. *Presiones y diamantes*. Havana: Unión, 1967.

Piñera, Virgilio. *Dos viejos pánicos*. Havana: Casa de las Américas, 1968.

Piñera, Virgilio. *La vida entera*. Havana: Contemporáneos, Ediciones Unión, 1969.

Ripoll, Carlos. *Harnessing the Intellectuals: Censoring Writers and Artists in Today's Cuba*. Washington, DC: Cuban American National Foundation, 1985.

Szulc, Tad. *Fidel: A Critical Portrait*. New York: Morrow, 1986.

Thomas, Hugh. *Cuba: The Pursuit of Freedom*. London: Eyre & Spottiswoode; New York: Harper & Row, 1971.

Thomas, Hugh. *The Cuban Revolution*. New York: Harper & Row, 1977.

LITERATURE: NONFICTION IN THE SPECIAL PERIOD

Jorge Fornet

Describes the resurgence of prose in Cuba after 1989.

In an article published in December 1968 in the Uruguayan weekly *Marcha*, Mario Benedetti (1920–2009) recognized the vigor in almost every sphere of Cuban culture after the triumph of the Revolution but noted that reflexive prose "is perhaps the only cultural area in which the Revolution finds itself at a glaring disadvantage with respect to the period prior to 1959" (p. 105). According to Benedetti, the new Cuban essay did not reach the heights attained by earlier writers such as Fernando Ortiz (1881–1969), Medardo Vitier (1886–1960), Juan Marinello (1898–1977), Raúl Roa (1907–1982), Jorge Mañach (1898–1961), and Cintio Vitier (1921–2009).

The most significant event during those years had been the recovery, through publishing, of the historical legacy of Cuban (and universal) literature. But the 1960s also produced polemics that revealed profound ideological conflicts, though they seemed to be focused on the cultural environment. With the political alignment to the Soviet Union and economic and commercial subordination to the Council for Mutual Economic Assistance (Comecon) at the beginning of the 1970s, the cultural policy of the Revolution suffered a radical turnaround that meant the end of an environment favorable to new polemics.

A NEW APEX

Although the 1980s saw thriving, creative production in literature, film, and particularly the visual arts, it was not until the following decade that the essay and criticism similarly flourished. This development was extraordinary because, with the serious economic crisis provoked by the dissolution of the Soviet Union and the Soviet bloc, a crisis of values had arisen simultaneously with a material incapacity for publishing. With the compass so altered, and without even paper for printing, it was difficult to imagine a resurrection. Curiously, the crisis generated the need to rethink the national plan and, as a consequence, gave a strong push to reflexive prose, stimulated by the climate of ideological expansion.

After a difficult start to a decade in which publications fell sharply and many periodicals ceased to exist, by the mid-1990s the first signs of editorial rebirth were visible. A peculiar form of criticism was established and spurred on by the general weakness in publishing at the time: Anthologies proliferated as a way of grouping and introducing authors. For example, in the influential *Los últimos serán los primeros* (The Last Shall Be First, 1993) the editor Salvador Redonet with great persistence and skill defined the newest generation of Cuban writers who were narrating the dramatic changes the country was experiencing. Many anthologies followed, proving the dictum that if the writers create books, the critics create literature.

By the middle of the decade, magazines whose publications had been delayed or suspended such as *Casa de las Américas* (House of the Americas), *La Gaceta de Cuba* (Cuba Gazette), *Unión* (Union), and *Revolución y Cultura* (Revolution and Culture) were revived, and others such as *Temas* (Themes) and *Contracorriente* (Countercurrent) were founded. The first of these, *Temas*, quickly became the leading journal in the social sciences, introducing debates on issues such as transition, migration, race, and sexuality, and promoting dialogue that up to then had been rare. The appearance in 1994 of the collection *Pinos nuevos* (New Pines), the result of a competition for unpublished authors, put a hundred names into circulation overnight, including a good number of essayists and critics.

The 1990s saw the continuation of work by Vitier, Roberto Fernández Retamar (b. 1930), Ambrosio Fornet (b. 1932), Reynaldo González (b. 1940), and Enrique Saínz, (b. 1941), and the emergence of Margarita Mateo Palmer (b. 1950), Víctor Fowler (b. 1960), Jorge Luis Arcos (b. 1956), Roberto Méndez, (b. 1958), Arturo Arango (b. 1955), Antonio José Ponte (b. 1964), and Alberto Garrandés (b. 1960). There was a revival of classic works by Avellaneda (1814–1873), Plácido (1809–1844), Dulce María Loynaz (1909–1997), and Mañach. The popularity of José Lezama Lima (1910–1976)—who had displaced Alejo Carpentier (1904–1980) and Nicolás Guillén (1902–1989) on the national Olympus—reached its zenith during the symposium for the fiftieth anniversary of the magazine *Orígenes* in 1994, and shortly thereafter the canon was dominated by Virgilio Piñera (1912–1979), whose work was being widely published, studied, and brought to the stage.

The foundation of the Women's Studies Program in the Casa de las Americas in 1994 definitively drove the development of gender studies in the country, a task taken on by the program's founders Luisa Campuzano (b. 1943), Mirta Yáñez (b. 1947), and Zaida Capote Cruz (b. 1967), as well as Nara Araújo (1945–2009) and Susana Montero (1952–2004). The growth of women's studies developed in parallel with a sustained growth in female prose writers at the national level.

THE ISLAND AND ITS DIASPORA

In the 1990s—building on a trend that had begun in the previous decade—the debate about the Cuban diaspora deepened. Within the inevitable ideological conflict the subject aroused, the notion prevailed that there was a single Cuban culture common to Cubans regardless of their politics and their location. Although there were stumbling blocks in the process—books that seemed unprintable on the island for the political views they put forth and authors who refused to be published in Cuba, for example—work by exiled authors appeared in national publications more frequently.

If the moderate start in the 1980s opened the door to lost classical authors such as Mañach, Lydia Cabrera (1899–1991), Lino Novás Calvo (1905–1983), Carlos Montenegro (1900–1981), Severo Sarduy (1937–1993), and Gastón Baquero (1914–1997), the breadth of the 1990s brought much access to contemporary authors (particularly fiction writers). Roberto González Echevarría (b. 1943), Gustavo Pérez Firmat (b. 1949), Oscar Hijuelos (b. 1951), Mayra Montero (b. 1952), Roberto G. Fernández (b. 1951), Eliana Rivero, Román de la Campa (b. 1948), Achy Obejas (b. 1956), and Sonia Rivera-Valdés (b. 1937) became familiar to readers of Cuban publications. Reciprocal readings and encounters between various types of intellectuals were more common, and it was not unusual to see incorporated into academic and cultural journals on the island—as part of a productive dialogue—the works of Antonio Benítez Rojo (1931–2005), Rafael Rojas (b. 1965), Iván de la Nuez (b. 1964), and Alejandro de la Fuente. Ideas produced on the island were frequently cited and discussed by intellectuals of the diaspora without denigration. Naturally, this did not mean that there were no disagreements, but rather that disagreements were examined respectfully through mutually enriching conversation.

Yet the periodical *Encuentro de la Cultura Cubana* (Encounter with Cuban Culture), founded in Madrid in 1996 by Jesús Díaz (1941–2002), demonstrated that rapprochement and dialogue could not overcome profound conflicts. Despite the fact that it included contributions from authors both inside and outside Cuba and that it espoused the idea that there is a single Cuban culture, the publication provoked disagreements and raised suspicions of intellectuals and the cultural authorities on the island.

POLEMICS

The 1990s returned vitality to polemics, a genre that had suffered particularly deeply from the dogmatism of the cultural policy that was instituted in the 1970s. After that there was an increase in the number of polemicists and subjects for discussion, from the strictly literary to the historical, social, and political.

The disappearance of real socialism in Eastern Europe, the main source of the political and ideological legitimacy and economic sustenance of the Cuban Revolution, required a rethinking of the national plan. Recovering a genealogy of the cultural debate within the revolutionary process, in 2006 the volume *Polémicas culturales de los 60* (Cultural Polemics of the '60s) appeared, compiled by Graziella Pogolotti (b. 1932). More than an archaeological work, it was a rereading and updating of disputes that, deep down, were still relevant.

One particular polemic moved the discussion like never before, uniting several generations in a rereading of the past and introducing a new form of participatory discourse—online discussion. At the beginning of 2006 a television program called *Impronta* (Stamp) was dedicated to Luis Pavón Tamayo, president of the Consejo Nacional de Cultura between 1971 and 1976, and honored those who had been directly responsible for the dogmatic, exclusionary repressive cultural policy of the 1970s. Its broadcast immediately generated an avalanche of electronic messages expressing a public condemnation that quickly took hold among intellectuals in Cuba and the diaspora. In response to the outcry, the Criterios Theoretical Cultural Center—founded by Desiderio Navarro in 2003—convened the series "Cultural Policy and the Revolutionary Period: Memory and Reflection."

Since the beginning of the 1990s the Cuban essay and criticism has seen a sustained advance related to the themes and depth of the intellectual debate, and a dialogue that includes opposing views, regardless of geographical location and ideological stance.

BIBLIOGRAPHY

Benedetti, Mario. "Situación actual de la cultura cubana." In *Cuaderno cubano*, 80–112. Buenos Aires: Schapire Editor, 1974.

Fornet, Jorge. *Los nuevos paradigmas. Prólogo narrativo al siglo XXI*. Havana: Editorial Letras Cubanas, 2006.

Instituto de Literatura y Lingüística. "José Antonio Portuondo Valdor." "Apéndice: La literatura cubana entre 1989 y 1999." In *Historia de la literatura cubana*. Vol. 3, *La revolución (1959–1988)*. Havana: Editorial Letras Cubanas, 2008.

Navarro, Desiderio, ed. *La política cultural del período revolucionario: Memoria y reflexión*. Havana: Centro Teórico-Cultural Criterios, 2008.

Pogolotti, Graziella, ed. *Polémicas culturales de los 60*. Havana: Editorial Letras Cubanas, 2006.

Redonet, Salvador, ed. *Los últimos serán los primeros*. Havana: Editorial Letras Cubanas, 1993.

LITERATURE: POETRY IN THE COLONIAL PERIOD

Enrique Saínz

The development of Cuban poetry from the early seventeenth century to the War of Independence in 1898.

The poetry of the colonial period began with the epic poem *Espejo de paciencia* (1608; The Mirror of Patience), by Silvestre de Balboa (1563–c. 1647), a Canary Islander who had settled in Cuba. Six sonnets by six different authors accompany the longer text. These works, while not high art, identify a historical moment that modern readers can better understand because of what they reveal. *Espejo de paciencia* relates the kidnapping of Bishop Fray Juan de las Cabezas Altamirano by French pirates in the island's eastern zone and the battle during which the Cubans confront the kidnappers in order to punish them for this offense. Through this poem readers come to learn about the customs and socioeconomic characteristics of Cuban society at that time.

THE EIGHTEENTH CENTURY AND THE NEOCLASSICISTS

No other Cuban poetry survives until the late eighteenth century. During the last decade of that century, three neoclassical poets appear whose works express the beliefs of the Enlightenment: Manuel de Zequeira y Arango (1764–1846), Manuel Justo Rubalcava (1769–1805), and Manuel María Pérez y Ramírez (1772–1852). Zequeira produced epic poems ("Batalla naval de Cortés en la laguna" [Cortes's Naval Battle on the Lake]), odes to nature ("Albano y Galatea"), and moralizing satires of the island's customs ("Octavas joco-serias," [Comico-Serious Octavas]). His most famous composition, "A la piña" (Ode to the Pineapple), is an example of neoclassical formalism and an emergent Cuban identity. His poetry focuses on his native soil and his Spanishness. The works of the other two neoclassical figures show the restraint, taste, and refinement that resulted from their assimilation of Spanish neoclassicism and Latin classics. The best-known examples of their work are the sonnets "A Nise bordando un ramillete" (To Nise, Embroidering a Nosegay) and "Un amigo reconciliado" (A Friend Reconciled) respectively. Other important poems by these poets are "Silva cubana" (The Cuban Woods) and "La muerte de Judas" (The Death of Judas), by Rubalcava, and "Enmanuel" by Pérez y Ramírez. These poets had ceased writing by 1820.

THE FIRST ROMANTIC PERIOD: MAJOR FIGURES

José María Heredia (1803–1839), who conspired against Spanish domination of Cuba, was the first Cuban romantic poet, and perhaps the first romantic poet in Latin American literature, although he too drew from the spirit of neoclassicism. Heredia's work is characterized most by its force and formal qualities, its passion for freedom ("La estrella de Cuba" [The Star of Cuba]), its praise of nature ("Niágara"), and its love poems ("A Emilia" [To Emilia]). The following fragment is about the famous waterfall, Niagara Falls, and shows his romantic response to nature:

> Torrente prodigioso, calma, acalla
> tu trueno aterrador; disipa un tanto
> las tinieblas que en torno te circundan,
> y déjame mirar tu faz serena,
> y de entusiasmo ardiente mi alma llena.

■ *See also*

Autobiography of a Slave (Juan Francisco Manzano)

José Martí: Writings for and about Children

Sab (Gertrudis Gómez de Avellaneda)

Versos sencillos (José Martí)

[Powerful flood, calm yourself, and silence
Your terrifying thunder; dispel some
Of the shadows that surround you.
Let me contemplate your serene face,
and my soul will fill with your ardent passion.]

Gabriel de la Concepción Valdés (1809–1844), known as Plácido, produced quite a different body of work. He was of mixed race and died at thirty-five by firing squad. Plácido had some training in the Spanish classics. His tone and style are measured, reflecting a less elevated yet still emotional kind of romanticism. Examples are "La muerte de Gessler" (The Death of Gessler), "La flor de la caña" (Flower of the Sugarcane), and "La plegaria a Dios" (Prayer to God). As with Heredia, the neoclassical aesthetic is apparent in Plácido's work. His poems include "La siempreviva" (The Evergreen); "Lo que yo quiero" (What I Love); "El hombre y el canario" (The Man and the Canary); and "El veguero" (The Tobacco Grower) In "Jicotencal," the main character (whose name, in modern times, is spelled Xicotencatl) is a pre-Columbian warrior-prince of the state of Tlaxcala, who at the urging of his elderly father the king, abandons fighting against Cortez's invading Spanish troops and instead joins them against the Aztecs. Here is the opening of "Jicotencal":

Dispersas van por los campos
las tropas de Moctezuma,
de sus diosas lamentando
el poco favor y ayuda,
mientras, ceñida la frente
de azules y blancas plumas,
sobre un palanquín de oro
que finas perlas dibujan
tan brillantes que la vista,
heridas del sol, deslumbran,
entra glorioso en Tlascala
el joven que de ellas triunfa.

[Scattered over the fields
Are Moctezuma's troops,
Complaining of their goddesses,
Who little helped or favored them.
While with a forehead plastered
By white and blue feathers,
On top of a golden carriage
Decorated with fine pearls,
So shiny, the sight of them,
Wounded by the sun, dazzles,
The young man who has won over them
Enters Tlascala, in all his triumphant glory.]

THE FIRST ROMANTIC PERIOD: MINOR FIGURES

Special mention should be given to the slave Juan Francisco Manzano (1797–1854), who wrote the heartrending *Autobiografía*, an authentic and skillful

text of extraordinary importance. His poems were collected in *Poesías líricas: Cantos a Lesbia* (Lyrical Poetry: Odes to Lesbia, 1821) and *Flores pasajeras* (Fleeting Flowers, 1839). His most famous composition, "Treinta años" (Thirty Years), describes his painful social condition with a sensibility akin to that of Spanish poet Francisco de Quevedo (1580–1645).

Another figure from this first romantic period is José Jacinto Milanés (1814–1863), who wrote emotional poems describing personal experiences. Examples are "El beso" (The Kiss), "Su alma" (Your Soul), "Mi hermano" (My Brother), "Después del baile" (After the Dance), and "El mendigo" (The Beggar). Several of his pieces present dialogues with nature, like that in "La madrugada" (Dawn). His other poems include "El sinsonte y el tocoloro" (The Mockingbird and the Cuban Trogon), "De codos en el puente" (Lying on the Bridge), "Requiescat in pace" (Rest in Peace), "Un día de invierno" (A Winter's Day), and "La fuga de la tórtola" (Flight of the Turtledove), to which following lines belong:

Si ya no vuelves, ¿a quién confío
mi amor oculto, mi desvarío,
mis ilusiones que vierten miel,
cuando me quede mirando al río,
y a la alta luna que brilla en él?

[If you don't return, to whom
Will I entrust my delirious, hidden love,
And my dreams that pour like honey
When I look at the river
And up at the moon, high in the sky,
That reflects against it.]

Among the poets of the first period is Gertrudis Gómez de Avellaneda (1814–1873), whose descriptive poetry has a formal kind of finish and metrical richness, a neoclassical inheritance. Her poems praise nature and have philosophical, religious, and erotic themes. Some are also about the act of literary creation itself. Criticized for lacking authenticity and a certain grandiloquence, her poems draw upon the Spanish masters, especially in their emotionality. Her poems "Al partir" (On Departing), "A las cubanas" (To the Women of Cuba), "A Dios" (To God), "Canto a la cruz" (Song of the Cross), "Un paseo por el Betis" (A Stroll through Betis), and "Soneto imitando una oda de Safo" (Sonnet in the Style of an Ode of Sappho), among others, are highly expressive. The following is from the initial stanza of "Al partir":

¡Perla del mar! ¡Estrella de Occidente!
¡Hermosa Cuba! Tu brillante cielo
la noche cubre con su opaco velo,
como cubre el dolor mi triste frente.

[Pearl of the sea! Star of the Occident!
Beautiful Cuba! Night's murky veil
Is drawn across your sky's refulgent trail
And I succumb to sorrow's ravishment.]

NATIVISM AND *SIBONEÍSMO*

Nativism and *siboneísmo* were literary movements led, respectively, by Francisco Pobeda (1796–1881) and Juan Cristóbal Nápoles Fajardo (1829–?), who was known as El Cucalambé. These poets were known for *Cubanizing* poetry, in the case of nativism by describing the island's natural beauties, peasant life, and customs; in the case of *siboneísmo*, by focusing on the indigenous past. Both emphases expressed an underlying romanticism. The two poets wrote in the ten-line stanza form that was popular in rural areas and was used for parties and celebrations. Their greatest strengths lie in achieving a pleasing sound, in praising the island's natural beauty, and, in the case of the *siboneístas*, in evoking an all-but-extinguished past. Some of their poems are spiritual and especially meaningful, as is the case with Pobeda's poem "La ilusión."

THE SECOND ROMANTIC PERIOD

After a lapse in poetic work from 1844 until the end of the 1850s, a rebirth occurred with the work of Rafael María de Mendive (1821–1886), which initiated what came to be known as the second romantic period. Mendive's most successful poems are "La gota de rocío" (The Dewdrop) and "La oración de la tarde" (Afternoon Prayer). Of the major poets of this second romantic period, Juan Clemente Zenea (1832–1871 is most important, especially his poems "Fidelia" and "Nocturno" (Nocturne), and his books *Cantos de la tarde* (Evensongs, 1860) and *Diario de un mártir* (Diary of a Martyr), written shortly before he was executed for his participation in the insurrection that began in 1868 (known later as the Ten Years' War). Melancholy colors his best productions, which bear the stamp of the French romantics. Openness to creative writers of other sensibilities enriched the voices of Cuban poetry in Mendive's time. His is a kind of romanticism that focuses less on the immediate, although the immediate context emerges in his dialogue with the Cuban landscape. The following stanza from "Fidelia" illustrates his poetry's qualities:

> ¡Bien me acuerdo! ¡Hace diez años
> y era una tarde serena!
> ¡Yo era joven y entusiasta;
> pura, hermosa y virgen ella!
> Estábamos en un bosque,
> sentados sobre una piedra,
> mirando, a orillas de un río,
> cómo temblaban las hierbas.

> [How well I remember!
> Ten years ago, during a serene afternoon!
> I was so young and passionate!
> A beautiful, pure virgin, she was!
> We were in a wood,
> Sitting on a rock,
> Along the riverbank,
> Watching the grass tremble.]

Joaquín Lorenzo Luaces (1826–1867) also belongs to this period, a careful wordsmith who through such poems as "Oración de Matatías" (Matathias's Prayer), "La salida del cafetal" (Leaving the Coffee Plantation), "La caída de Missolonghi" (The Fall of Missolonghi), and "Cuba, poema mitológico" (Cuba: A Mythological Poem) anticipated the work of Cuba's Parnassians. "La salida del cafetal" opens with the following:

> Tasca espumante el argentino freno,
> el bridón principeño generoso;
> enarca el cuello en ademán rifoso,
> de noble ardor y de soberbia lleno.

> [The horse champs at the silvery snaffle, mouth
>   foaming.
> Looking princely and noble,
> Arches its neck with an eager gesture,
> Full of zeal and pride.]

Luisa Pérez de Zambrana (1835–1922) closes the dialogue with the Cuban landscape that Heredia started, and in which Zenea achieved a matchless innovation. As with the latter, in Luisa Pérez there is an elegiac note, rich in its execution and authenticity, which she puts forth in her *Elegías familiars* (Family Elegies), a testimony to sorrow. One always finds in her work fluidity, taste, and delicacy of tone, as in the final stanza of her poem "Dolor supremo" (Supreme Sorrow), which was written after the death of her daughters:

> ¡oh en el silencio de la noche inmensa
> estrellas apagadas y divinas!
> ¡almas desengarzadas de mi alma!
> ¡perlas de mis entrañas desprendidas!

> [Oh, in the silence of the deep, dark night,
> Stars extinguished and divine!
> Souls that have come unstrung from my soul!
> Pearls detached from my heart!]

CUBA'S GREATEST POETS AND THE BEGINNINGS OF MODERNISM

By the end of the nineteenth century, the first manifestations of a new style appeared in the works of two great poets—José Martí (1853–1895) and Julián del Casal (1863–1893)—heirs to all the best characteristics of romanticism, and in the case of Martí, of the great Hispanic and European traditions. In 1882 the first book of poems by Cuba's greatest poet appeared, *Ismaelillo*, whose pages are novel in more than one sense and into which Martí injected the force of the Spanish-language classics. The poems in this little volume constitute an achievement without equal in the history of Cuban letters. The difference is less one of quality than of register and style, especially in the dialogue between the poet and his themes. The internal movement of objects and realities that readers see in his second book of poems, *Versos libres* (Free Verse), published posthumously, is extraordinary. Similarly meaningful and disturbing is the poet's intimate experience as conveyed in these verses, a heartfelt experience through which readers sense the extreme ethical commitment characteristic of Martí throughout his life, which nourished his gargantuan labor in organizing Cuba's War of Independence (1895–1898). In *Versos sencillos* (Simple Verses, 1891) there is a change in the register of his observations, a greater tranquility, a different way of seeing, as if the poet had found an inner peace that resolved the emotions and sufferings expressed in his earlier collections. Yet he returns to his established themes, his astonishing cosmological view, his tender and refined voice, his great love of nature, his concern for his son, his humanism, and his unyielding love of freedom, all of which are cardinal elements of his life and philosophy. An entire poetic history reaches its peak in his work, which at the same time opens itself up to other spaces and realities, which is to say, to another era. A precursor of modernism, Martí nevertheless exhibits deeply humanist concerns and maintains his distance from the preciousness and decadent flavor that pervade one wing of that movement.

In a certain sense, Julián del Casal is the antithesis of Martí, especially in the desolation, weariness, and helplessness that fill his collections: *Hojas al viento* (Leaves to the Wind, 1890), *Nieve* (Snow, 1892), and *Bustos y rimas* (Busts and Rhymes, 1893). These express a fatalistic kind of decadence that sums up the experience of a poet in hostile circumstances from which he longs to escape. The poems express suffering, an awareness of the impossible, and confrontations with an existential void. He imagines an unattainable reality, distant not in terms of space but in its nonexistence, since in no real place can he find tranquillity and gratification. His love for the city, which contrasts with his rejection of the natural world, says much about his conflict. In Martí's work, one sees the poet's view of nature as the basis for his ethics and the spirituality of his civic and literary vocations. In Casal's work, the rejection of the gifts and mysteries of the natural world reveals the secret of his sadness and anguish. The gloomy words in his best lyrics describe an extreme aesthete who cannot fully fit himself into any social context. The richness of his language is one of Casal's great contributions to Cuban national culture. These two figures, and the voices of the minor poets who were their contemporaries, close the book on the history of colonial Cuban poetry.

BIBLIOGRAPHY

Cruz-Taura, Graciella, ed. Espejo de paciencia y Silvestre de Balboa en la historia de Cuba: *Estudio, edición crítica de* Espejo de paciencia y selección documental. Madrid: Iberoamerica; Frankfurt am Main: Vervuert, 2009.

Instituto de Literatura y Lingüística. *Diccionario de la literatura cubana.* Introduction by José Antonio Portuondo. 2 vols. Havana: Editorial Letras Cubanas, 1980–1984.

Instituto de Literatura y Lingüística. "José Antonio Portuondo Valdor," Ministerio de Ciencia, Tecnología y Medio Ambiente. *Historia de la literatura cubana.* Vol. 1, *La Colonia: desde los orígenes hasta 1898.* Havana: Editorial Letras Cubanas, 2002.

Lezama Lima, José, ed. *Antología de la poesía cubana.* 3 vols. Havana: Consejo Nacional de Cultura, 1965.

Vitier, Cintio, ed. *Los poetas románticos cubanos.* Havana: Consejo Nacional de Cultura, 1962.

Vitier, Cintio. *Obras.* Vol. 2, *Lo cubano en la poesía* [1957]. Reprint, Havana: Editorial Letras Cubanas, 1998.

Vitier, Cintio. "Poetas cubanos del siglo XIX. Semblanzas" [1968]. In *Obras.* Vol. 3, *Crítica 1,* 207–249. Havana: Editorial Letras Cubanas, 2000.

Vitier, Cintio. "Recuento de la poesía lírica en Cuba: De Heredia a nuestros días" [1956]. In *Obras.* Vol. 3, *Crítica 1,* 1–34. Havana: Editorial Letras Cubanas, 2000.

LITERATURE: POETRY IN THE REPUBLICAN PERIOD

Francisco Morán

The development of Cuban poetry from the War of Independence to the Revolution of 1959.

The U.S. intervention in Cuba in 1898 was a political trauma that largely determined the intellectual and literary debates of the Republican Period (1902–1959). However, the tension between history and poetry—the crux of the literary debate—made itself felt before the intervention and reached a critical peak in early Cuban modernism, as exemplified by its most important figures: Julián del Casal (1863–1893) and José Martí (1853–1895). Casal was a poet who remained dedicated to poetry, while Martí prioritized his political activities. The war against Spanish colonialism confronted the poets with conflicting demands: a responsibility to history (requiring the subordination of literary to political activity) and a responsibility to literature (requiring devotion to poetry). Cuban literary criticism, rather unfairly and in a Manichaean manner, turned Casal and Martí into opposing poles with respect to the civic responsibility of the poet.

The imposition of the Platt Amendment by the United States worsened the frustration of intellectuals and writers, and nationalist sentiment gained strength. José Martí came to dominate political nationalism, willing to sacrifice his work for the homeland. By contrast, Casal was the epitome of the self-absorbed poet. According to Osvaldo Navarro, the contradiction between Martí and Casal was "the early warning of a disjuncture that would dialectically mark the destiny of poetry written in Cuba throughout almost the entire century" (p. 6).

See also

La isla en peso (Virgilio Piñera)

The Orígenes Group and Journal

The Poetry of Nicolás Guillén

Últimos días de una casa (Dulce María Loynaz)

Versos sencillos (José Martí)

The Martí-Casal dichotomy is expressed across the entire Republican Period. The first gesture of literary renewal, initiated by José Manuel Poveda (1888–1926) and Regino E. Boti (1878–1958), took place under the tutelage of Casal. In Poveda and Boti there is sensuality, decadence, and the desire to maintain literary autonomy. In "Julián del Casal. Canto élego" (Julián del Casal: Mournful Song) and in *Versos precursores* (Precursory Verses, 1927), Poveda pays homage to the master by taking up his decadent aesthetic. According to Cintio Vitier, Poveda takes off from the Casal of "Recuerdo de la infancia" (Childhood Memory) and "Las alamedas" (The Tree-Lined Avenues), while Boti follows upon the Casal of "La agonía de Petronio" (The Agony of Petronius) and "Mi museo ideal" (My Ideal Museum, a declaration of Casal's aestheticism). While in Poveda sound and music prevail over color and line, says Vitier, in Boti the opposite occurs. (1952, p. 69). His "Arabescos mentales" (Mental Arabesques, 1913) reveals Casal's influence in the intensity of eroticism and the central role accorded to bodies. The Martí/Casal schism would continue to play out between poets of different aesthetic orientations and within the work of each writer. Juan Marinello (1889–1977) published a single book of poems, *Liberación* (1926), with a strong modernist influence, and he took an interest in Martí the writer. But, gradually, he leaned more and more toward Martí the politician, until Marinello abandoned poetry entirely. Rubén Martínez Villena (1899–1934), author of *La pupila insomne* (The Sleepless Pupil, 1936) and one of the best poets of the 1930s, also ended up renouncing literature in order to fight the Gerardo Machado regime. His poetry is characterized by irony, pessimism, and anguish.

Marinello was an important figure of the literary herald of the Cuban avant-garde, the *Revista de Avance* (Progress Review, 1927–1930). Another poet from the magazine was José Zacarías Tallet (1893–1989), whose work, collected in *La semilla estéril* (The Sterile Seed, 1951), was characterized by colloquial turns of phrase and irony. His poem "La rumba" is one of the first examples of *poesía negra* (black poetry) written in Cuba. Regino Pedroso (1896–1983) began writing poetry with a modernist slant (*La ruta de Bagdad* [The Route to Baghdad], 1918–1923), but he turned toward social poetry. His well-known poem "Salutación fraterna al taller mecánico" (Fraternal Salutation to the Repair Shop) combines the avant-garde fascination for the machine with the social theme of work. This poem came to be considered the initiator of Cuban proletarian poetry. According to the critic María Matienzo, the significance of Pedroso's collection *Nosotros* (Us, 1933), was due to his "open militant interest" and the fact that "the poet was then a proletarian" (Matienzo 2002). From this perspective, the political value of the poetic text is what legitimated the poet's standing.

One trend within the avant-garde was the so-called pure poetry, characterized by intimism (focus on the inner life). Here, the points of contact with the so-called Generation of '27 in Spain should be noted, particularly with the work of poets such as Luis Cernuda, Federico García Lorca, and Juan Ramón Jiménez. The main exponent of pure poetry was Mariano Brull (1891–1956), who was part of the *Revista de Avance* group and who Vitier states was, in effect, "the fullest and most steadfast example we had of 'pure' poetry" (1952, p. 187). Brull's collection *La casa del silencio* (House of Silence, 1916) is characterized by an intimist note, along with echoes of Enrique González Martínez and Juan Ramón Jiménez. Mexican critic Alfonso Reyes adopted Brull's made-up word *jitanjáfora* (onomatopoeic poetry) for his verbal inventions or portmanteaux. Pure poetry in Cuba, however, constitutes a bridge between modernism and the avant-garde. Brull's most important titles include *La casa del silencio*, *Poemas en menguante* (Poems in Waning, 1928), and *Solo de rosa* (A Rose Solo, 1941). These titles suggest an oscillation between the modernist aesthetic and the avant-garde break. Readers notice this in some poems in which the linguistic innovation

José Martí (1853–1895). Author and national hero José Martí was, along with poet Julián del Casal, one of the most important figures of early Cuban modernism. HULTON ARCHIVE/GETTY IMAGES

occurs in an environment of sensuality and modernist plasticity:

> Por el verde, verde
> verdería de verde mar
> Rr con Rr
> [...] Por el verde, verde
> verdehalago húmedo
> extiéndome. —Extiéndote
>
> [On the green, green
> greenness of green sea
> Rr with Rr
> [...]
> On the green, green
> damp greenflattery
> I stretch out. —Reach out.]

("Verdehalago" [Greenflattery])

Other important figures of pure poetry are Emilio Ballagas (1908–1954) and Dulce María Loynaz (1902–1997). Author of the collection *Júbilo y fuga* (Joy and Escape, 1931), prefaced by Marinello, Ballagas was also one of the first white Cuban poets to be influenced by black poetry, in his *Cuaderno de poesía negra* (Black Poetry Notebook, 1934). (He also compiled the anthology *Antología de la poesía negra latinoamerica*, 1935.) Ballagas is possibly, after Casal, the first poet for whom homoeroticism takes a leading role in some of his most important poems, such as "Elegía sin nombre" (Nameless Elegy) and "Nocturno y Elegía" (Nocturne and Elegy). The work of Dulce María Loynaz is characterized by intimism and a sober lyricism that she maintained until the end of her life. Among her works, *Versos, 1920–1938* (Poems, 1938), *Carta de amor al rey Tut-Ank-Amen* (Love Letter to King Tutankhamen, 1938), *Juegos de agua* (Water Games, 1947), *Últimos días de una casa* (Last Days of a House, 1958), and the novel *Jardín* (Garden, 1951) stand out. In 1992 Loynaz received the Miguel de Cervantes Prize, the most prestigious prize for Spanish-language writers.

Social poetry finds one of its most significant expressions in Afro-Cuban poetry, particularly that of Nicolás Guillén (1902–1989). His *Motivos de Son* (Son Motifs, 1930) is one of the most important titles of the so-called *poesía negra*, although Guillén leaned more toward a poetic aesthetics of racial mixture. While in "Si tú supieras" (If You Were to Know) and "Sensemayá," black rhythms and language merge with ritual and stress the African note, "Balada de los dos abuelos" (Ballad of the Two Grandfathers) and "El apellido" (The Surname) bring readers to racial synthesis. The "nombre interminable, / hecho de interminables nombres" (endless name, / made of endless names) then becomes "mío, ajeno, / libre y mío, ajeno y vuestro, / ajeno y libre como el aire" (mine, alien, / free and mine, alien and yours, / alien and free as the air" ("El apellido"). From black poetry, he evolves toward one with a more radical and anti-imperialist social content. The fact that Guillén could tackle these themes without falling into the trap of mere political propaganda is demonstrated in his impressive *West Indies, Ltd.* (1934) and the unforgettable "Elegía a Jesús Menéndez" (Elegy for Jesús Menéndez). In both works he created a polyphonic orchestration of voices that, with a lyrical effectiveness uncommon in social poetry, denounces underdevelopment, imperialist intervention, political repression, and voyeuristic tourism.

A significant case in the context of social poetry that illustrates the Martí-Casal history-poetry tension is the book *La zafra* (The Harvest, 1926), by Agustín Acosta (1886–1976), a poet with roots in modernism. In an article about *La zafra*, the communist leader Julio Antonio Mella refers to it as "the first great political poem of the last period of the Republic." Directly alluding to his modernist origins, Mella warns the poet that "if he is to become what he should and can be thanks to his genius and his sensibility to the struggles of the multitude, he will have to 'kill himself' and remake himself from scratch" (p. 254). Thus, the challenge is: "Sterile vegetation and 'books for friends' or active struggle and songs for the multitude" (p. 254). Meanwhile, in 1926, Marinello (then in his pure poetry phase)—who would later predict that "the Acosta of *La zafra*" would be, without a doubt, "the one most understood, and therefore the most popular"—stated that he preferred the Acosta of *Ala* (Wing, 1915), specifically because *La zafra*'s "concern with collective problems suffers, unfortunately, from anti-aesthetic elements and oratorical emphasis" (p. 279). Here Agustín Acosta is trapped between the wing and the harvest, between Casal and Martí, between literature and politics, between Mella and Marinello.

A moment of singular importance was the visit of Spanish poet Juan Ramón Jiménez to Cuba in 1936. The "Convocatoria a los poetas cubanos" (Call to Cuban Poets) that he published in the Institución Hispanocubana de Cultural (Hispano-Cuban Cultural Institute) magazine *Ultra*, resulted in his anthology *La poesía cubana en 1936* (Cuban Poetry in 1936, 1937). Among the poets included are Virgilio Piñera (1912–1979), Angel Gaztelu (1914–1989), and José Lezama Lima (1910–1976). This anthology, together with *La poesía moderna en Cuba (1882–1925)* (Modern Poetry in Cuba [1882–1925], 1926), edited by Félix Lizaso (1891–1967) and José Antonio Fernández de Castro (1887–1951), and *Cincuenta años de poesía cubana (1902–1952)* (Fifty Years of Cuban Poetry [1902–1952], 1952), edited by Cintio Vitier (1921–2009), constitute the three most important compilations of Cuban poetry of the Republican Period.

Distancing itself from social and political themes, from Afro-Cubanism and avant-garde experimentation, the Orígenes (Origins) group arose, centered on the literary magazine of the same name and which Octavio Paz came to consider as the best Spanish-language literary magazine of its day. The well-known Havana poet José Lezama Lima was the center of the group, and the review brought together renowned writers such as Vitier, Eliseo Diego (1920–1994), Gastón Baquero (1914–1977), Fina García Marruz (b. 1923), and Lorenzo García Vega (b. 1926). The magazine also published books under the imprint of Ediciones Orígenes (Origins Editions), including many of the most important poetry collections published in Cuba: *Vísperas* (Vespers, 1953), by Vitier; *En la Calzada de Jesús del Monte* (On the Avenue of Jesús del Monte, 1949), by Eliseo Diego; and *Aventuras sigilosas* (Secret Adventures, 1945), by Lezama himself. Among other important poetry collections of the period, the following stand out: Baquero's *Poemas* (1942), García Vega's *Suite para la espera* (Suite for Waiting, 1948), García Marruz's *Las miradas perdidas* (Lost Glances, 1951), and, by Roberto Fernández Retamar (b. 1930), *Vuelta de la antigua esperanza* (Return of the Old Hope, 1959).

Lezama devised a "poetic world system" centered on poetry, characterized by his baroque style. With him, and with the Orígenes group, poetry was once again a way of life, of being in the world, as it had been before with Casal. In response to the Republican frustration, Lezama created a poetic world system centered on poetry that, for him, superseded the contingencies of history. Although he placed Martí at the center of history, his emphasis on poetry makes him gravitate toward Casal. According to Navarro, "Out of all of us, Lezama was a sort of new Casal, much more cultured and developed, but one who suffered from very similar sorts of ills" (p. 11). Thus the Martí-Casal/history-poetry tension was restaged, although here it leaned more toward the latter of these terms. Thus the search for Cubanness (principally in Lezama Lima and Vitier, the most important essayists of the group) gravitated toward the nineteenth century and specifically toward Martí and Casal. In Lezama, the inclination toward Casal is revealed, for example, in *Muerte de Narciso* (Death of Narcissus, 1937) and in *Enemigo rumor* (Enemy Rumor, 1941), in which the poetic experience is proof of being and living in the world.

Virgilio Piñera, who published in *Orígenes*, stood apart from the group, rebelling against its Catholicism and insular teleology. With an ironic style, he countered the *origenista* epiphany with the gnawing denial of an island convulsing with bodies and violence, highly eroticized, and imprisoned by water. He responded to the *orígenista* idea of salvation through poetry with the contingency of bodies. In "La isla en peso" (The Weight of the Island, 1943), Piñera attacks the consecration of the island not only by the Orígenes group but also by many other canonical Cuban poets. Besieged by the "damned circumstance of water," Cuba loses lightness and becomes heavy. Vitier's hostile reaction to the poem is the most forceful

evidence of the new and defiant view of a text that is now a classic of Cuban poetry.

When José Rodríguez Feo (1920–1993) and José Lezama Lima, the editors of *Orígenes*, severed their friendship, the former founded *Ciclón* (Cyclone), a journal joined by Piñera, who would become its most prominent figure. The military coup of 1952 put an end to the Republic. In 1959, Piñera enthusiastically saluted the *inundacíon* (as he called it) of the revolution, as did Lezama. Just a year earlier Vitier published *Lo cubano en la poesía* (Cubanness in Poetry). The Gordian knot of his reading—centering on the Cubanness of the poets he studied—is, of course, the Martí-Casal opposition. By rating Cuban poets according to the share of Cubanness assigned to them, Vitier drew margins and exclusions that strangely anticipated the powerful imposition of politics on the aesthetic that later characterized the Revolution of 1959. Therefore, it is not surprising that when the book was republished in 1970, he commented in the introduction that what was lacking in the first edition was "action." In the revised edition, he affirmed that revolutionary action had taught him that "poetry can and should embody history, with all the risks that implies." In the 1970s, Lezama Lima and Piñera would themselves personally suffer from this triumph of the light. In 1963, on the centennial of Casal's birth, Lezama Lima published "Oda a Julián del Casal," which contains his response to the violence of history, playing all his cards on Casal's empty tomb: "Our scandalous affection pursues you / and so you smile among the dead."

BIBLIOGRAPHY

Lezama Lima, José. "El 26 de julio: imagen y posibilidad." In *Imagen y posibilidad*, edited by Ciro Bianchi Ross, 19–22. Havana: Letras Cubanas, 1981.

Lizaso, Félix, and José Antonio Fernández de Castro, eds. *La poesía moderna en Cuba (1882–1925)*. Madrid: Hernando, 1926.

Marinello, Juan. "Un nuevo libro de Agustín Acosta." In *Cuba: Cultura*, edited by Ana Suárez Díaz, 278–280. Havana: Letras Cubanas, 1989.

Matienzo, María. "Poemas de Regino Pedroso." *La Jiribilla*. 75 (October 2002). Available from http://www.lajiribilla.co.cu.

Mella, Julio Antonio. "Un comentario a 'La Zafra' de Agustín Acosta." In *Escritos revolucionarios*, 254–258. Mexico City: Siglo XXI, 1978.

Navarro, Osvaldo. "Ballagas, ni más ni menos: Prólogo." In *Obra poética*, by Emilio Ballagas, 5–40. Havana: Letras Cubanas, 1984.

Piñera, Virgilio. "La inundación." *La Habana Elegante*, n.d. Available from http://www.habanaelegante.com.

Vitier, Cintio, ed. *Cincuenta años de poesía cubana (1902–1952)*. Havana: Dirección de Cultura del Ministerio de Educación, 1952.

Vitier, Cintio. *Lo cubano en la poesía*. Havana: Letras Cubanas, 1958.

LITERATURE: POETRY IN THE REVOLUTIONARY PERIOD

Virgilio López Lemus

Poetry and the Cuban poets from 1959 to 1989.

Cuban poetry is defined by the Spanish language, and this literary genre developed in specific ways between 1959 and 1989, two of which may be termed the *personal* and the *social*.

THE PERSONAL AND THE SOCIAL

In the first decade following the Revolution subjective personal poetry gave way to a collective chant about the new reality, discernable in the debates over aesthetics that appeared most in *Lunes de Revolución* (Revolution Mondays, 1959–1961), the cultural supplement of the daily paper *Revolución*. There the new poets of the colloquial generation clashed with established writers, particularly members of the famous Orígenes group led by José Lezama Lima (1910–1976) and writers of the neo-romantic movement, with José Ángel Buesa (1910–1982) at its head. The intimate, personal focus in the poetry of these groups was attacked by the newcomers who were more interested in social and political themes. Among that newcomers were Pablo Armando Fernández (b. 1929), Heberto Padilla (1932–2000), Antón Arrufat (b. 1935), and Manuel Díaz Martínez (b. 1936). The fact is, however, that it is unusual for any poet to produce a body of work that exhibits only one or the other emphasis. Some personal-focused poets explored only political themes after 1959, as in the case of Rafaela Chacón Nardi (1926–2001) and Roberto Friol (1928–2010). Other poets experimented with current trends, but not necessarily during periods of their greatest productivity.

The trend in black poetry, also called *Afro-Cuban* or *mulatto* poetry, was born at the end of the 1920s and peaked during the 1930s. Its premier figure was Nicolás Guillén (1902–1989), the so-called national poet and the poet of the Revolution. By 1959 black poetry had been superseded by other trends, but some poets assimilated its contributions and wrote texts in which blackness played an important role. The last of the pure black poets was Marcelino Arozarena (1912–1996), who wrote *Canción negra sin color* (Black Song without Color, 1960). But blackness continued to have a part in the dominant trends, particularly within colloquialism. The Cuban mythology of African roots was its principal narrative, but other traditional themes appeared in the works of mulatto women such as Excilia Saldaña (1946–1999) and white men such as Pablo Armando Fernández and Miguel Barnet

(b. 1940). Black women's poetry arose beginning in the 1960s; it often dealt with themes of gender and race, as in the works of Georgina Herrera (b. 1936) and Nancy Morejón (b. 1944), whose poem "Mujer negra" (Black Woman) is an example.

NEO-ROMANTICISM AND *ORIGENISMO*

Neo-romanticism appeared in the 1910s and 1920s. José Ángel Buesa was its champion, leading the movement until the beginning of the Revolution with his books *Diario galante* (Journal of a Gallant, 1962), published in Cuba, and *Tiempo en sombra* (Time in Shadow, 1970), in the Dominican Republic. This was the most prolific trend through the early years of the Revolution. Its central theme was erotic-amorous, using classical forms of Hispanic meter. There are traces of the neo-romantic influence in the verses of some of the new poets such as Rafael Alcides Pérez (b. 1933) and Domingo Alfonso (b. 1935). Carilda Oliver Labra (b. 1922) in *Desaparece el polvo* (The Dust Disappears, 1983) and Pura del Prado (1931–1996) in *Otoño enamorado* (Autumn in Love, 1972) continued to develop the neo-romantic trend, first in Cuba and then in the United States.

Some poets of the generations preceding the colloquial writers demonstrated avant-garde traits, such as Regino Pedroso (1896–1993), Félix Pita Rodríguez (1909–1990), and Manuel Navarro Luna (1894–1967), whose poetry was decidedly militant. Fayad Jamís (1930–1988), Roberto Branly (1930–1980), and José Álvarez Baragaño (1932–1962) approached surrealism, particularly in stylistic and lexical matters. Although certain avant-garde traits prevailed between 1959 and 1989, the avant-garde was not a truly integrated trend of the poetry of the period.

Origenismo (styles and ideas inspired by the group of poets that published in the journal *Orígenes*) also made its mark on the revolutionary years. At least eight members of the group published significant anthologies after 1959: José Lezama Lima, who published *Dador* (Donor, 1960); Virgilio Piñera (1912–1979), who wrote the very influential *La vida entera* (The Whole Life, 1969); Gastón Baquero (1914–1997), who wrote *Magia e invenciones* (Magic and Inventions, 1984) while living in Spain; Justo Rodríguez Santos (1915–1999), who published the group's first tribute to the Revolution in *La epopeya del Moncada* (The Epic of Moncada, 1963); Eliseo Diego (1920–1994), with *Los días de tu vida* (The Days of Your Life, 1977); and Octavio Smith (1921–1985). Cintio Vitier (1921–2009), one of the ideologues of the *origenistas*, and Fina García Marruz (b. 1923) leaned toward colloquialism in the book they coauthored, *Viaje a Nicaragua* (Trip to Nicaragua, 1987). Lezama Lima's prestige deepened with the publication of his poetic novel *Paradiso* (Paradise, 1966) and with the posthumous volume *Fragmentos a su imán* (The Fragments Drawn by Charm, 1977), in which he approached a conversational tone without renouncing his teleological poetics that placed the image, not the word, at the center of his creation.

The legacy of *Orígenes* was sustained by three poets: Cleva Solís (1918–1997), Roberto Friol (1928–2010), and Francisco de Oraá (1929–2010), whose works were not simple imitations. The most definable *origenista* influence was noted in poets who emerged in the 1980s, among them Raúl Hernández Novás (1948–1993), whose work is the best example of a trend that some critics called *neo-origenista*.

COLLOQUIALISM

The predominant trend in the 1960s and 1970s was colloquialism, which had developed gradually in the 1950s. Its poetry was characterized by conversational or testimonial tones, sometimes prosaic free verse, and social and urban themes, though it also incorporated intimate lines about love and family. The anthology by Roberto Fernández Retamar (b. 1930) and Fayad Jamís, *Poesía joven de Cuba* (Young Cuban Poetry, 1959), was a generational catalyst.

During that period a group from the Ediciones El Puente publishing house sustained colloquialism, distancing themselves from *origenismo* and the neoromantics. Its poet creator was José Mario (1940–2002). The movement dissolved in the mid-1970s, but not without leaving some controversies in its wake, as illustrated in the anthology *Novísimos poetas cubanos* (New Cuban Poets, 1962), which contains an anti-*origenista* manifesto prologue and also criticizes certain revolutionary poetry that its supporters called propagandist and populist.

Colloquialism developed primarily among poets born between 1925 and 1945, due to their common stylistic, formal, and thematic characteristics. Some poets who were born years earlier or later also adopted it, so it was multigenerational, and it influenced creators of various trends such as Nicolás Guillén, Ángel Augier (1910–2010), and Jesús Orta Ruiz (1922–2005), as well as a number of poets from the Orígenes Group and many younger poets who published in the 1980s.

Between 1959 and 1989 poets published their work in the cultural pages of the main newspapers and in the journals *Unión*, *La Gaceta de Cuba*, *Casa*, *El Caimán Barbudo*, and other magazines. They also made use of debate stages and media outlets for printed poetry, led primarily by the Ediciones Unión book publisher of the Writers' Union. Editorial series were printed by the state publisher, Imprenta Nacional. Some notable colloquialists such as Raúl Luis (b. 1934) and Luis Suardíaz (1936–2005) who worked in the publishing business influenced the selection of what would be published, resulting in the extension and predominance of colloquialism. Some

were less given to prosaic expression, such as Rolando Escardó (1925–1960), or testimonial, such as César López (b. 1932).

In 1968 the Cuban government instituted a cultural policy, *parametración* (parametrization), that negatively affected poetic production by setting parameters for what constituted an acceptable work. One of its consequences was the so-called Padilla affair, in which the book *Fuera del juego* (Out of Bounds, 1971) was declared to be counterrevolutionary; its author, Heberto Padilla, was briefly incarcerated, and other writers were marginalized. Given the body of works of high aesthetic value that appeared during the 1970s, it is debatable that the so-called Five Grey Years (a time of cultural repression that occurred in Cuba during the 1970s) existed for poetry in the same way that they existed for cultural policy. Regardless, the dogmatic events of these years impaired the development of the ousted poets and induced political fear in others, whose works would blossom in the 1980s with the improved cultural atmosphere. The consequences of this serious rift, more political than aesthetic, affected Cuban literary creativity for years.

The praise of Cuban nature, well represented by the work of Samuel Feijóo (1914–1992), was not compatible with the dominant external, urban trend; therefore, some poets who touched on ecological or rural matters appeared atypical until the 1980s, when a certain return to the land popularized themes that until then had been common only in oral poetry. The poets who expressed themselves in *décimas*, whether oral or written, were not integrated into urban colloquialism, though their influence can be seen in some works of the period. The themes of the popular *décima* changed little—landscapes, social life, love—but the expression of reality in constant flux was accentuated, with an emphasis on historical matters, on the contraposition of past and present, and the exaltation of the *now* of the revolutionary reality. The *décima* was important in the gradual rise of colloquialism to the degree that some so-called orthodox colloquialists such as David Chericián (1940–2002) and César López began to cultivate it. It was preserved by Orta Ruiz and other popular poets; Adolfo Martí Fuentes (1922–2002) represented it well with *Alrededor del punto* (Around the Point, 1971).

Orthodox colloquialism was overtaken in the 1980s by a multitude of styles that taken together did not reveal a single dominant trend. There was plurality in official inquiry and in content along with a renewed tropological (biblical) interest in leading to a return to pre colloquial complexity, with similarities to Orígenes or to surrealism. The influence of Lezama Lima reached its apex. In this decade notable for its poetry, the reformative impulse was multigenerational. Poets of the generation of the 1950s matured; the subsequent generations found broader perspectives, moving from an almost totalitarian colloquial aesthetic to various styles, from the realistic to the metaphysical, and from the conversational to the experimental. Poets such as Reina María Rodríguez (b. 1953), Ángel Escobar (1957–1977), Alberto Acosta-Pérez (b. 1957), Sigfredo Ariel (b. 1962), and Jesús David Curbelo (b. 1965), to name just a few, brought to Cuban poetry their youth, thematic diversity, and a yearning for expressive freedom and reform.

BIBLIOGRAPHY

Aguirre, Mirta, et al. *Poesía social de Cuba*. Havana: Editorial Letras Cubanas, 1980.

Arcos, Jorge Luis. *Las palabras son islas. Panorama de la poesía cubana, siglo* XX *(1900–1998)*. Havana: Editorial Letras Cubanas, 1999.

Augier, Ángel. *Poemas de la Revolución Cubana*. Havana: Universidad de La Habana, 1980.

Branly, Roberto. "Panorama de la joven poesía revolucionaria cubana (1959–1963)." *Anuario L/L* 1 (January–March 1967): 79–105.

Cohen, J. M. *En tiempos difíciles. Poesía cubana de la Revolución*. Barcelona: Tusquents, 1970.

Fernández, Teresa de Jesús. *Revolución: poesía del ser*. Havana: Ediciones Unión, 1987.

Fernández Retamar, Roberto. "La poesía cubana nuevamente contada." *Santiago* 9 (1972): 7–26.

García Ramos, Reinaldo Felipe, and Ana María Simó. *Novísima poesía cubana*. Havana: El Puente, 1962.

Instituto de Literatura y Lingüística. *Diccionario de la literatura cubana*. 2 vol. *Poesía*. Havana: Editorial Letras Cubanas, 1980, 1984.

Instituto de Literatura y Lingüística. *Historia de la literatura cubana*. Vol. 3, *Revolución*. Havana: Editorial Letras Cubanas, 2008.

Jiménez, José Olivio. *Estudios sobre la poesía cubana contemporánea*. New York: Las Américas, 1967.

López, César. "Poesía cubana actual: Proyecto impreciso para el fin de siglo." In *Les Langues Néo-Latines. Revue de Langues Romanes*. Paris: Société des Langues Neo-Latines, 1996.

López Lemus, Virgilio. *Palabras del trasfondo. Estudio sobre el coloquialismo cubano*. Havana: Editorial Letras Cubanas, 1987.

López Lemus, Virgilio. "Treinta años de poesía cubana (1959–1989)." *Unión* 2, no. 7 (July–September 1989): 65–70.

López Lemus, Virgilio. "Preámbulo a la poesía cubana." *Doscientos años de poesía cubana. 1790–1990. Cien poemas antológico*. Havana: Editorial Abril, 1999.

López Lemus, Virgilio. *El siglo entero. El discurso poético de la nación cubana en el siglo* XX. Santiago de Cuba: Editorial Oriente, 2008.

Marinello, Juan. "Frente a unas páginas negras." *Diario de la Marina*, 30 July 1930.

Miranda, Julio E. *Nueva literatura cubana*. Madrid: Tauros Ediciones, 1971.

Montes Huidobro, Matías, and Yara González. *Bibliografía crítica de la poesía cubana*. Madrid: Editorial Playor, 1973.

Núñez, Ana Rosa. *Poesía en éxodo, el exilio cubano en su poesía*. Miami: Ediciones Universal, 1970.

Padrón Barquín, Juan Nicolás. "Treinta años de poesía cubana (1959–1989)." *Unión* 2, no. 7 (July–September 1989): 56–64.

Souza, Jorge. *Heridos por la luz. Muestra de poesía cubana contemporánea*. Guadalajara, Mexico: Universidad de Guadalajara, 2002.

Suardíaz, Luis, and David Chericián. *La generación de los años cincuenta*. Prologue by Eduardo López Morales. Havana: Editorial Letras Cubanas, 1984.

Vitier, Cintio. *Lo cubano en la poesía*. Havana: Instituto del Libro, 1970.

LITERATURE: POETRY IN THE SPECIAL PERIOD

Marta Hernández Salván

Reina María Rodríguez

Stylistic and thematic developments in poetry since 1990.

Scholars have divided the different poetic movements of the Revolutionary period into generations starting in the 1950s with what is known as the first generation of the Revolution. In subsequent generations (from the 1980s onward) poets were more associated with the year of their birth because of their increasing ideological distance with the official revolutionary discourse. Poets from the mid-1980s through the 1990s were all born at the beginning of the Revolution between 1957 and 1967. According to Che Guevara they were supposed to embody the "New Man" of the Revolution, intellectuals who had not been soiled by bourgeois culture. The poets of this generation engaged in a cultural war over poetic styles, with the conversational style rejected and the hermetic-symbolic style becoming dominant. This dispute was part of a deeper conflict that extended to issues such as the writer's social compromise, the meaning of the act of writing, the concept of utopia, and the contradiction between nationalism and cosmopolitanism. The poets writing in the first decade of the twenty-first century (those born after 1967), by contrast, were a more heterogeneous group that distanced itself from the issues that took root in the 1980s.

BACKGROUND

The 1970s brought profound changes in poetry, with the temporary victory of conversational poetry over symbolism and hermeticism as well as introspection and intimacy in writing in general. This major trend in the poetics of the 1970s was a result of the stylistic and ideological prescriptions of the 1960s.

Since the 1960s, literary critics, theoreticians of Marxist aesthetics, and major cultural figures such as Mirta Aguirre, José Antonio Portuondo, and later Eduardo López Morales and Alberto Rocasolano discussed the question of transparency in communication, which allegedly defined relations between the writer and the people (no longer simply between the writer and the reader). This notion of transparency in writing and reading had important implications for poetry's role in society—through poetry contests, publishing, criticism, promotional mechanisms, teaching, and literary workshops.

The first signs of change were seen in the work of poets in the late 1970s—Raúl Hernández Novás, Aramís Quintero, Emilio de Armas, Jorge Yglesias—whose books still displayed traces of the hermetic style. Meanwhile, critics such as Basilia Papastamatiu (who had a weekly column on poetry in one of the country's two daily newspapers) and the young reviewers Arturo Arango and Victor Rodríguez Núñez (the editor of the cultural monthly *El Caimán barbudo*), established the analytical apparatus behind this transformation. Rodríguez Núñez, himself a poet, also compiled two emblematic anthologies of this group of poets born during a difficult decade: *Cuba: En su lugar la poesía* (Cuba: Poetry in Its Place) and *Usted es la culpable* (You Are to Blame). Rodríguez Núñez described this generation as obsessed with self-knowledge, preferring subtlety and intimacy over explicitness and declamation; they rejected superficiality and viewed their work as an antidote to populist literature. The poets in this group include Osvaldo Sánchez, Reina María Rodríguez, Marilyn Bobes, Soleida Ríos, Osvaldo Sánchez, Alex Fleires, Norberto Codina, Luis Lorente, Efraín Rodríguez Santana, Roberto Méndez, José Pérez Olivares, Ángel Escobar, and Ramón Fernández Larrea.

THE 1980s: TRANSFORMATION

The 1984 publication of *Poesía completa* (Complete Poems), by José Lezama Lima (1910–1976), provided a strong point of stylistic reference for young poets in the early 1980s. Writers were attracted to Lezama Lima's work not only for its enormous creativity and cultural depth but because it had been banned during most of the 1970s. Conversational poetry gradually declined in popularity because it had fallen into a routine of praise and denial of conflict and lacked authenticity.

The new poets adopted a style distant from the rigidity and univocality of 1970s conversational language. In the tradition of the Orígenes group of writers, their poetry was based on an exploration of the intrinsic characteristics and singularity of poetic language—hence the revived interest in authors such as Lezama and Virgilio Piñera (1912–1979), whose writings had been ignored by publishers during the so-called Five Grey Years (1971–1976) and were still partly ignored at the start of the 1980s. In addition, the new poets renounced the Revolution's heroic, exalting model on which the previous two decades of conversational poetry had been based. The antithetical and antiheroic archetype that replaced it was generally characterized by melancholy, marginality, and a lack of idealism, as well as by conceptual hermeticism. Unlike the 1970s revolutionary poetry, these works did not offer ethical prescriptions but instead focused on ways of being in the world and were influenced by post-structuralism and postmodern philosophies that led them to question some of the Revolution's most dogmatic principles. The obsession with the search for a national and cultural identity was replaced by representations of Cuba and Havana as oppressive spaces with no way out, as in Piñera's 1943 poem "La isla en peso" (Island in the Balance). Best-known members of this group are Damaris Calderón, Sigfredo Ariel, Antonio José Ponte, Emilio García Montiel, Omar Pérez, Carlos Augusto Alfonso, Sonia Díaz Corrales, Heriberto Hernández Medina, Pedro Llanes, Ismael González Castañer, Ricardo A. Pérez, Rito Ramón Aroche, Caridad Atencio, Juan Carlos Flores, and Rolando Sánchez Mejías.

Another type of poetry that appeared at this time was more humanist and lyrical, frequently written in the first person. Poets writing in this style include Norge Espinosa, Liudmila Quincoses, Frank Abel Dopico, Nelson Simón, Juan Carlos Valls, Laura Ruiz, Teresa Melo, Mariana Torres, Reynaldo García Blanco, León Estrada, Rodolfo de Jesús López Burgos, and Sonia Díaz Corrales. Some of their works have an intimist voice with a feminist or gay identity expressed in erotic or nostalgic tones. Poets in both groups eschewed the conversationalist epic tone and bluntness regarding the paroxysm of the revolutionary utopia, opting instead for more marginal voices. Their work employed minimalism, asyndeton (the omission of conjunctions from a series of related clauses), absence of punctuation, abundance of enjambments, colloquial style, metaphors, and greatly abstracted images. Some of the writings published in *Orígenes*, including those by Lezama Lima and Lorenzo García Vega, also display some of these formal characteristics, a similarity that led critics to call the 1980s poets *neo-origenistas*. Given that the change of the norm in writing can be viewed as part of the greater arc of prevailing over conversationalism, the critic Jorge Luis Arcos uses the term "post-conversationalism." In his 2010 book Arcos further identifies the poets as "post-conversational, with visible elements of a kind of neo-vanguardism" (Arcos 2010, p. 67). The generation's emblematic anthology, *Retrato de grupo* (Group Portrait), was published in 1989.

DIÁSPORA(S): RADICALIZATION

In the early 1990s the writers Rolando Sánchez Mejías, Carlos Aguilera, and Ricardo Alberto Pérez founded a literary group called Diáspora(s) and were joined immediately by Rogelio Saunders, Pedro Marqués de Armas, and Ismael González Castañer. At the colloquium "Fifty Years of *Orígenes*," held at Casa de las Américas in Havana in October 1994, Sánchez Mejías and Marqués de Armas were invited to a panel discussion called "*Orígenes* and Its Influence on New Writers." Sánchez Mejías and Marqués de Armas delivered a presentation, "Olvidar *Orígenes*" (Forgetting *Orígenes*), which announced the poets' break with Cuban literary tradition, including Orígenes itself, as well as with literary trends during the revolutionary period. The rupture was evident in their reference to a "spiritual withdrawal" and the "mortifying silence of words," in contrast to spaces in which words have been injured and are anxious to expand into infinity, "whether in the name of God, in the name of some liberating Machine of the Absolute, or in the name of the Revolution" (Sánchez Mejías 1994).

A few years after that scandalous presentation, the group's members produced a new kind of writing in works such as *Glass* and *Retrato de A. Hooper y su esposa* (Portrait of A. Hooper and His Wife), by Carlos Alberto Aguilera, which won the 1995 David Prize for Poetry; *B. B.* and *Transhumanar* (Transhumanize), by Sánchez Mejías; "Vater Pound (ode in cold metro)," by Saunders; and *Cabezas* (Heads), by Marqués de Armas, winner of the 2001 Unión Nacional de Artistas y Escritores de Cuba (UNEAC; National Union of Writers and Artists of Cuba) Prize. These authors changed the country's literary panorama, establishing meta-writing, to the extent that, while exposing or analyzing a concrete situation, their poetry is a reflection on language and its conditions or limits (essentially political). In addition, they distinguished themselves for their tendency toward experimentation, including performance art. They also created a mimeographed journal called *Diáspora(s): Documentos* (1997), distributed from hand to hand outside official publication circles. At the start of the next decade, several of its members (Sánchez Mejías, Saunders, Aguilera, and Marqués de Armas) left the country, and the group disintegrated. Its emblematic anthology is *Dossier: 26 nuevos poetas cubanos: Mapa imaginario* (Dossier: 26 New Cuban Poets: Imaginary Map), published in 1995.

OTHER VOICES

As in all literary movements, differences in poetic voices exist within these general trends. The work of Juan Carlos Flores is one of the most original of the period, particularly his collections *Los pájaros escritos* (The Written Birds), awarded the 1990 David Prize, and *Distintos modos de cavar un túnel* (Many Ways to Dig a Tunnel), winner of the 2002 UNEAC Prize. *Los pájaros escritos* had an intellectual and allegorical tone and was characterized by abundant metaphors and a melancholy caused by the loss of utopia. By contrast, the more colloquial style of *Distintos modos de cavar un túnel* emerged from a sense of marginality and the counterpoint between popular culture and intellectualism. This voice is circular, monotonous, and unproductive, symbolizing government rhetoric and the absence of civic space. Another major poet is Víctor Fowler, whose extensive oeuvre culminates in *El maquinista de Auschwitz* (The Machinist of Auschwitz), awarded the 2004 UNEAC Prize, in which the ruins of the city generate writing that has no political purpose and the search for a spirituality devoid of mysticism.

Like Fowler's work, Sigfredo Ariel's earlier work, with its contemplative tone and abstractions, later acquired a more discursive and narrative style. His vast body of work includes the notable poetry collections *Unos pocos conocidos* (A Few Acquaintances), which won the 1986 David Prize; *Hotel Central*, winner of the 1998 UNEAC Prize; and *Born in Santa Clara*, winner of the 2005 UNEAC Prize. His poems' view of daily life is often unexpected and full of precise details. Finally, Carlos A. Alfonso's unmistakable style had a fundamental influence on the poetry of the 1980s. Among his outstanding works are *Cabeza abajo* (Head Down), 1996 UNEAC prizewinner, and *El segundo aire* (The Second Wind), which was awarded the 1986 David Prize; these works are noted for their iconoclastic poetry characterized by acrimony, irreverence, and caustic language. Like Carlos A. Aguilera and Rolando Sánchez Mejías, Carlos A. Alfonso's writing is known for its biting political irony, a trait emulated by the next generation.

THE 1990s: DISPERSION

The 2001 anthology *Los parques: Jóvenes poetas cubanos* (Parks: Young Cuban Poets) begins with work by poets born in 1967, thus picking up where *Retrato de grupo* ends. In this way, the anthology implies continuity with the previous generation's emblematic work. This anthology, however, reveals stylistic diversity, the absence of a group identity, and a view of history that renounces pathos and any hierarchy of national tradition. The anthology's editors, René Coyra and Noel Castillo, insist on the instability of any collection, acknowledging that their work can only reflect its own moment. Another anthology of this generation, *Cuerpo sobre cuerpo sobre cuerpo* (Body over Body over Body, 2001), edited by Aymara Aymerich and Edel Morales, constitutes a move away from the obscurity and dogma of previous poetry and criticism toward clarity and openness.

The poets of the 1990s retreated from the battle over poetic language, which had served as a unifying element for a fundamental portion of the 1980s generation; from that time on into the early 2000s, diverse styles and thematic orientations have coincided, with the formation of no particular groups. From a historical perspective, the authors who began their literary careers in the 1980s were dealing with the remains of the repressive 1970s in Cuba, and their reaction to those traces of repression defined the search for their own style and content. In contrast, those who began in the 1990s were living in a moment when the so-called socialist camp had disappeared and their immediate reality, the Cuban Revolution, was shaken by the effects of a profound economic crisis whose influence reached the realm of ideas and values. Amid a plurality of voices, the poetry of the early 2000s has focused on themes related to identity, addressing gay and lesbian, Afro-Cuban, and feminist issues. With the establishment of the Territorial Publishing System (a network of small provincial publishing houses) in 2000, Cuban publishing has begun to recover.

CHILDREN OF THE 1970s: POET AND MENTOR REINA MARÍA RODRÍGUEZ ON YOUNG CUBAN POETS OF THE NEW CENTURY

I believe that the current shortage of poets has its roots in the 1970s, and that we are still suffering from the remains of that huge cloud, the Five Grey Years, as that time of desperation caused by orthodoxy and censorship has been called. Those born at that time have still not recovered from the damage caused by that radiation. It was a strange generation that emerged from the vacuum of an increasingly destroyed world; of few libraries, teachers, and supplies. Javier Marimón and Leymen Pérez of Matanzas; Marcelo Morales, Leonardo Guevara, Ramón Hondal and Lizabel Mónica of Havana; Pablo de Cuba and Oscar Cruz of Santiago de Cuba; José Ramón Sánchez of Guantánamo; Jamila Medina of Holguín; Legna Rodríguez of Camagüey; Luis Eligio Pérez and Amaury Carbó of Alamar—each became a night watchman: "watchman, tell me about the night," clutching the materiality of the phrase that no longer sustains any belief; just skeptical words aspiring to another route in the face of such loss (the loss of the least prodigal child, the antihero).

Javier Marimón, author of *El gatico Vasia* (The Kitten, Vasia) and *El gran lunes* (The Great Monday), an art book published by Vigía, has lived in Texas for years. Pablo de Cuba also lives there and Leonardo Guevara lives in Illinois. Marimón is more influenced by film and theater: He is interested in the visual, those new values acting upon the eye. His movements are anarchical, centrifugal (replaced by the dial of a radio that keeps reporting the same news), escaping reason; paralyzing the ego: forward, backward, insignificant desires that prattle in the text, pretending to use words not as discourses but as gestures, as speed; with a choppy

ADRIÁN CASTRO

Born in Miami in 1967, Adrián Castro is a poet, performer and interdisciplinary artist. Also a practicing *babalao* (Ifá priest), Castro weaves elements of Caribbean myth, history and music into a tapestry that is highly rhythmic, intensely spiritual, and laced with a raucous sense of humor. His Cuban-Dominican heritage is celebrated in his first book *Cantos to Blood and Honey* (1997), which also features many poems about the Ifá tradition and its orishas. Even a poem to black beans ("Symphony de Frijoles") becomes a spiritual and historical journey set to a rhumba beat. In *Wise Fish*, perhaps an allusion to Yemayá, the orisha of the oceans and motherhood, Castro examines the Afro-diasporic traditions of Cuba, Haiti, Puerto Rico, Jamaica, and Florida in his unique blend of English, Spanish, Spanglish and the ritual language of Ifá (Yoruba-Lucumí). *Handling Destiny* further explores the spiritual traditions that animate his vision, with his customary dreamy and percussive verse; it also includes an homage to Cuban percussionist and composer Mongo Santamaría. Castro's poetry reflects deeply on his multinational, plurilingual identity as a Latino author bridging Africa, the Caribbean, and South Florida.

BIBLIOGRAPHY

Castro, Adrián. *Cantos to Blood and Honey*. Minneapolis, MN: Coffee House Press, 1997.

Castro, Adrián. *Wise Fish: Tales in 6/8 Time*. Minneapolis, MN: Coffee House Press, 2005.

Castro, Adrián. *Handling Destiny*. Minneapolis, MN: Coffee House Press, 2009.

Alan West-Durán

rhythm on that containing wall of sticky cement that is the Malecón.

A little while ago I read a second yet unpublished book by Pablo de Cuba, *País sin gramática* (Country without Grammar), that revives "the incomplete" works of Lorenzo García Vega (the accursed poet of *Orígenes*), about whom Pablo de Cuba wrote his thesis. An iron structure on which to build a thematic amusement park by means of parentheses, disassociations; chains melted together with intercalated voices, parapets; betting again on the question yet to come: "who could attest—the only need—to phrases such as 'sacred family' or 'my God'" (Cuba Soria). For his part, Leonardo Guevara searches for theatricality, grandiloquence, and does not experiment with verse, but rather with body.

I had spent years waiting for the next generation because the panorama of the most recent decade of poetry on the island is fleeting, elusive, there is no sedimentation as in the 1980s and 1990s, when I heard a poet from eastern Cuba, José Ramón

Sánchez, read, "The wolf: swift cord that passes through my hatred." In his collections, *Aislada noche* (Isolated Night) and *Marabuzal* (unpublished), he asks for answers, centering: "I am stuck on an island and I don't know it" (Sánchez). In brief texts or broad panoramas, he again demands civilian poetry. In his collection, *Las posesiones* (Possessions), Oscar Cruz searches for "the most abhorrent and urgent needs . . . when everything else has abandoned me," poetry as the only salvation (Cruz).

Rural themes reappeared, not as picturesque landscape, but as savage writing. I know that there is no progression among events that are savage in character and that they do not require demonstrations; they are things that happen, that break out. In Cruz, when he is about to focus on something it becomes twisted. In his poem, "Quemaduras" (Burns), he speaks of "works by Russian authors as prizes" and then burns them. These are drastic poems, full of pain, tenderness, resentment when faced with the disappearance of the promised world, which strikes like they struck him, which he found to defend himself: "(gloves-house), (gloves-father), (gloves-land)," proposing "a physics of the absolute gesture," as Artaud proposed.

Jamila Medina published "Huecos de araña" (Spider Holes, winner of the 2008 David Prize), taking up feminist themes without nostalgia, but with daring and irony: "The woman felt the glass piercing her left foot... the woman the other... unequal above all in their moistness... Calibán, Caribbean, Caribou." Irreverent classic verses as when she uses elements of mythology, profane in her defense of the present: "Woman-fairy... woman-witch... woman-serpent... woman roof of the mouth... woman pit of the stomach."

Few poets achieve a phantasmal world with minimum brushstrokes, stutters, silences. Ramón Hondal, refined Parisian spirit, does: "The music of a hidden gesture... where there is no note" is played on a "bad piano... that errs for pleasure" ("Acordes"). Torment and impossibility leave a vacuum that defies filling, with those "lyrics... with no voice," in which, like Simone Weil, she finds "two ways of killing oneself: suicide and indifference."

In *Corrientes coloniales* (Colonial Currents, 2007), Leymen Pérez reconstructs the history of the colonial world, its lost spaces, intact beneath disaster, although his caustic voice suspects its impossible reconstruction. Meanwhile, Legna Rodríguez, in "Ciudad de pobres corazones" (City of Poor Hearts) and "Instalando me" (Installing Me) (Ácana), searches for a non lyrical subject: "a displaced subject ... who does not know where to go," and feels "that the only thing we've done until now is shut up." In "Chicle" (Chewing Gum), whose single copy was published by Mizako, she speaks of "sanitary napkin," "urethra," "the dog without a bone, without soup" and

this is her most lyrical expression. Lizabel Mónica did performance art (despite the fact that Cuban literature has not been very performative). Later on, she sought concepts as focal points: I would say that her poetry is more like a literary essay and philosophy, developing a calculated coldness.

Little has been written about Zonafranca, a group in Alamar, east of Havana, inhabited by poets who sculpt, draw and sing as part of their daily life. The rhythm of their texts comes from a square geometry composed of micro-brigade buildings made for the "New Man." Juan Carlos Flores of the previous generation—whose work includes *Los pájaros escritos* (1994), *Distintos modos de cavar un túnel* (2003), *El contragolpe* (The Counterpunch, 2009)—was the core of this project that mixes reggae, hip-hop and rap poetry with graphic and spatial structures: tradition and experimentation at the same time. Out of their "absurd realities" emerges their mystical passion in a show that asks for trust and faith.

I will mention only two: Luis Eligio Pérez breaks the pavement, consciousness; digs a ditch where drains carrying sewage appear. "Estado de guerra" (State of War) is a poetic essay in which we find another "Calzada de Jesús del Monte" (Jesús del Monte Road), his tribute to Eliseo Diego, but piercing the present reality. Amaury Pacheco wears a suit with refuse from the dollar stores and a pot on his head, a replica of Manuel de Zequeira's sombrero. "I shout curi-curi...he's a son of the people." He walks the streets wearing this outfit, repeating phrases launched from various angles is as his own persona: robotic, paraplegic.

I don't want to omit the handcrafted or digital journals such as *Arique*, published in Matanzas in the previous decade, which includes poets from that region and other latitudes; *Mar desnudo* (Nude Sea), also from Matanzas, with a very complete collection of 24 issues, featuring works by poets from all over the country, such as Marcelo Morales, whose *Cinema*, published in 1997, won the Pinos Nuevos Prize and *Materia*, published by Ediciones Unión in 2009 and awarded the Julián del Casal Prize. Other such journals include *Letra c@n acento* (Letters with @ccent), featuring various generations on the island and others who no longer live in Cuba; *Árbol invertido* (Inverted Tree), published in Ciego de Ávila by Ileana Álvarez and Francis Sánchez; the blog, *del palenque*, which offers a tribute to poet Domingo Alfonso on his 75th birthday, and has published texts of the former group *Diáspor(a)s*, in an attempt to bring its memory back from the void; *Desliz*, produced by Lizabel Mónica with criticism, essays and cultural information; and *La noria*, whose three issues have offered a broad literary spectrum including translations, produced by José Ramón Sánchez and Oscar Cruz, in eastern Cuba.

BIBLIOGRAPHY

Aguilera, Carlos A. *Memorias de la clase muerta: Poesía cubana 1988–2001*. Mexico City: Editorial Aldus, 2002.

Alfonso, Carlos, Víctor Fowler, Emilio García Montiel, and Antonio José Ponte, eds. *Retrato de grupo*. Havana: Editorial Letras Cubanas, 1989.

Arcos, Jorge Luis. *Las palabras son islas: Panorama de la poesía cubana del siglo XX (1900–1998)*. Havana: Editorial Letras Cubanas, 1999.

Arcos, Jorge Luis. *Poesía y diáspora*. Havana: Espacio Laical, 2010.

Aymerich, Aymara, and Edel Morales. *Cuerpo sobre cuerpo sobre cuerpo: Catálogo de nuevos poetas cubanos*. Havana: Editorial Letras Cubanas, 2000.

Castillo González, Noel, and René Coyra. *Los parques: Jóvenes poetas cubanos: Antología*. Cienfuegos, Cuba: Mecenas / Reina del Mar Editores, 2001.

Coyra, René. "Residuos de la fe: Para una lectura razonada de la poesía cubana de los noventas." *Cubaliteraria: Portal de Literatura Cubana* (3 September 2008). Available from http://www.cubaliteraria.cu/articulo.php?idarticulo=8664&idseccion=71&skin=2.

Cruz, Oscar. *Las posesiones*. Havana: Editorial Letras Cubanas, 2009.

Cuba Soria, Pablo de. *De Zaratustra y otros equívocos (1999–2001)*. Havana: Ediciones Extramuros, 2003.

Dorta, Walfrido. "Algunos estados, estaciones, documentos: Poesía cubana de los 80 y 90." *La Gaceta de Cuba* no. 6 (Havana) (November–December 2003).

Fowler, Víctor. "La tarea del poeta y su lenguaje en la poesía cubana reciente." *Casa de las Américas* no. 215 (Havana) (April–June 1999).

Llarena, Alicia, ed. *Poesía cubana de los años 80*. Madrid: Ediciones La Palma, 1993.

Morejón, Idalia. "Eppure si muove: Las transformaciones de la norma poética en Cuba." *Cubista*, n.d. Available from http://cubistamagazine.com/a4/040101.html.

Rodríguez Núñez, Víctor, Reina María Rodríguez, and Osmar Sánchez. *Cuba, en su lugar la poesía: Antología diferente*. Mexico City: UNAM, 1982.

Rodríguez Núñez, Víctor, ed. *Usted es la culpable*. Havana: Editorial Abril, 1985.

Sánchez, José Ramón. *Aislada noche*. Havana: Editorial Letras Cubanas, 2005.

Sánchez Aguilera, Osmar. "Poesía en claro: Cuba, años 80 (long play / variaciones)." In *Poesía cubana de los años 80*, edited by Alicia Llarena. Madrid: Ediciones La Palma, 1993.

Sánchez Mejías, Rolando. "Olvidar Orígenes." 1994. *Agulha* (poetry journal). Available from http://www.revista.agulha.nom.br/bh13sanchez.htm.

Sánchez Mejías, Rolando, ed. *Mapa imaginario: Dossier, 26 nuevos poetas cubanos*. Havana: Embajada de Francia en Cuba, Instituto Cubano del Libro, 1995.

Tápanes López, Raúl. "Poesía cubana actual: Mitos, viajes y emplazamientos medievales." *Arique* nos. 16–17 (July–December 2005). Available from http://www.cubaunderground.com/cuba-underground/ensayos/poesia-cubana-actual-mitos-viajes-y-emplazamientos-medievales?Itemid=0.

Yglesias, Jorge. *Donde irrumpe la luz: 18 poetas cubanos*. Santa Marta, Cuba: Ediciones Diálogo, 1995.

LITERATURE: PUBLISHING IN CUBA DURING THE REPUBLICAN PERIOD

Ambrosio Fornet

The development of publishing in Cuba from 1902 to 1959, including important publishing houses and publications.

Illiteracy and the absence of an adequate cultural policy prevented the development of a domestic market for the production of Cuban books for half a century. "The reason why there aren't presses (i.e., publishing houses), is not that there is nothing to publish," a bibliographer complained in 1936. "On the contrary, there is a lot that could be published, but there are no presses" (Peraza Sarausa, 1936, p. 24).

A serious conflict of a political and cultural nature was involved. In effect, once the Republic of Cuba was proclaimed in 1902, intellectuals assumed the task of instilling in the younger generations a strong sense of national identity. This is what their predecessors in Latin American countries had done once they became independent from Spain. It had to do with rescuing the not-yet-documented memory of the nation, through chronicles, biographies, and personal testimonies. "Largely compiled as part of the broader project of nation building in the newly formed republics," an expert has pointed out, "these bibliographical catalogues played a key role in constructing a foundational collective history" (Calvo 2007, p. 140).

The titles of some of the most important studies and anthologies published in Cuba between 1901 and 1905 are quite significant: *Iniciadores y primeros mártires de la revolución cubana* (Pioneers and the First Martyrs of the Cuban Revolution) and *Hombres del 68* (The Men of '68), both written by Vidal Morales, and *La revolución de Yara* (The Yara Revolution) by Fernando Figueredo. José Martí (1853–1895), "the Apostle of Cuban Independence," was profusely represented in the bibliographic repertoire of the last century, when editor Gonzalo de Quesada y Aróstegui (1868–1915) started with the publication, in 1900, of the first version of his *Obras completas* (Complete Works).

THE PUBLISHING MARKET

In talking about the challenges that faced the nascent Republic, a prestigious intellectual from that period, Enrique José Varona, used to say that without

■ *See also*

Education: Literacy Campaign of 1961

Education: Republican Period

economic development there could not be political independence, and that without education for the masses there could be no democracy. The ruling classes could never resolve those contradictions, and therefore, conditions favorable to the development of a stable and profitable publishing movement were never achieved.

In 1900 the country had a population of 1.5 million, 60 percent of whom did not know how to read or write. In 1931 a half million children, within a population already approaching 4 million, had no schools to attend, and only one of every twenty who did attend school completed the sixth grade (Foreign Policy Association 1935, p. 154). In 1950 the number of school-age children who did not attend any public or private school was almost 60 percent (Truslow 1951, p. 408). Thus a statistical paradox very typical of the colonial period was reproduced: During the 1950s illiteracy had declined to 23 percent, but the population was already about 6 million. That is to say, while the rate of illiteracy declined, the number of illiterates actually increased. "Cuba ranks high in education among the countries of Latin America," one expert observed in 1951, but "seems to have made relatively little progress in basic education during the last two decades and, in important respects, has even slipped backwards" (Truslow 1951, p. 404).

In that top-heavy society most of the country's presses and book vendors, as well as the two or three existing publishing centers, were concentrated in Havana. During the first half of the century there was only one provincial publishing house worthy of mention, not so much because of the volume of its production as because of the cultural significance of its modest catalog. It was El Arte, which Francisco Sariol founded in 1912 in the city of Manzanillo, in the former province of Oriente.

With that situation, the publishing market was just barely supported by a tiny minority, sectors that, above all, were made up of professionals and high school and university students. The booksellers' market was larger, but demand was totally covered by imported books (from Spain, Argentina, and Mexico) because only on very rare occasions were books by foreign authors published in Cuba.

THE PRODUCTION CENTERS

The only true publishing houses in existence in the country—that is to say, businesses devoted to processing and publishing books and pamphlets—were those that specialized in textbooks. Publishing was consequently aimed at a captive market made up of students at all academic levels. (There were also some special cases, such as that of the "Jesús Montero, Editor" company. It specialized in legal subjects, a fact that also guaranteed a captive market in the form of lawyers, notaries, tax assessors, and the like.) All other pub-

lishing—works not meant to be put out for general sale—was mainly produced by institutions supported by funds from the state budget (copies of these works were most often distributed at public libraries or to interested parties).

There were, then, two types of book producers: commercial and institutional publishers. The latter were responsible for the largest volume of production, if not as far as press runs were concerned, at least in terms of the number of published titles. There was a third type, of course: individual or private editions, that is to say, those whose authors would defray the costs of publishing. Those editions had very limited press runs and rarely ended up on bookstore shelves. Almost all the literary works by living authors that were published in Cuba between 1900 and 1959 were of this type. Therefore, it should not come as a surprise that some of the most important among them—short stories by Lino Novás Calvo and Virgilio Piñera, novels by Carlos Montenegro, Alejo Carpentier, Dulce María Loynaz, and Piñera—were never published in Cuba before 1960.

Editions produced by institutions benefited from what one might call the "anniversaries syndrome" (the fondness of government agencies for cultural activities to commemorate significant anniversaries). The impressive editions produced in 1927 and 1952 to commemorate the twenty-fifth and fiftieth anniversaries, respectively, of the Proclamation of the Republic serve as examples: *Evolución de la cultura cubana* (Evolution of Cuban Culture) was an eighteen-volume prose and poetry anthology commissioned by the government from critic José Manuel Carbonell, and *Historia de la nación cubana* (History of the Cuban Nation), a truly encyclopedic work in ten volumes, was entrusted to a team of experts. The most spectacular of those initiatives, headed by historian Emeterio S. Santovenia, was that of the newly formed Editorial Trópico. Over a period of eleven years—from 1936 to 1947—it published seventy volumes of works by José Martí. This collection was still incomplete at that point, finishing with seventy-four volumes. The commission created to commemorate the centennial of Martí's birth undertook a series of intense activities in the publishing field during 1953.

IMPROMPTU EDITORS

A phenomenon closely linked to the institutional publishing houses was that of individuals who were not actually publishers but voluntarily took on the function, either as sponsors or just because they were bibliophiles. They either did this independently or as advisers to a publishing house. These "impromptu editors" (Fornet 1994, p. 131) played an important role in the dissemination of national culture. The most noteworthy impromptu editor from the first half of the century was anthropologist and sociologist Fernando Ortiz (1881–1969). During the 1920s he was the driving force behind a memorable cultural project: the Colección de Libros Cubanos (Cuban Books Collection) which between 1923 and 1939 published twenty-five titles that consisted of more than forty volumes, containing a major portion of Cuban historical writing and previous literature. Each title had a prologue written by an expert in the subject matter, so that this group of books became a sort of encyclopedia on the Cuban culture of letters (including traveler's memoirs translated for the first time). These must have had a wide circulation in proportion to market capacity, since the volumes, which were bound in paperback or cloth, were sold at prices within the reach of the target sector of the public ($1.50 and $2.00, respectively).

CULTURAL, S. A.

The absolutely exceptional phenomenon known as the Colección de Libros Cubanos can only be explained by the fact that it was sponsored by Cultural, S. A., the largest publishing company in Cuba during the first sixty years of the century. This resulted from the merger of two publishing and bookseller syndicates, La Moderna Poesía (Modern Poetry) and Librería Cervantes (Cervantes Books). Specializing in textbooks, La Moderna Poesía, headed by Spanish entrepreneur José López Rodríguez, had inaugurated, as early as 1902, a collection called Biblioteca del Maestro Cubano (The Cuban Teacher's Library), that started with a panorama of the educational field in the book *La instrucción pública en Cuba* (Public School Teaching in Cuba) by philosopher and educator Enrique José Varona (1849–1933). During the 1950s Cultural S. A. included in its catalogs books aimed at teaching professionals, written by the country's best-known researchers and educators. Some of these works came to be used as official textbooks at teaching institutes in Central America and in other Caribbean countries.

OTHER PUBLISHING HOUSES

During the 1950s, other publishing concerns such as Minerva, Selecta, and Lex also published schoolbooks, research materials, and even luxurious commemorative editions such as the complete (or almost complete) works of Simon Bolívar (1783–1830), Eugenio María de Hostos (1839–1903), and José Martí.

Jesús Montero, director of the publishing house of the same name, and the poet Manuel Altolaguirre (1905–1959), founder of the small publishing firm La Verónica, both Spaniards (one of the distinguishing marks of the trade), deserve special mention. They published—just to mention two emblematic texts— *Contrapunteo cubano del tabaco y el azúcar* (Cuban Counterpoint: Tobacco and Sugar) by Fernando Ortiz and *Cuentos negros de Cuba* (Afro-Cuban Tales) by Lydia Cabrera (1899–1991), both in 1940. Also worthy of mention is Editorial Páginas, a communist party press. It published books on scientific and social subjects, particularly books by Soviet authors, and two memorable studies: *El engaño de las razas* (1946; The Deception of Race) by Fernando Ortiz and *Weyler en Cuba: Un precursor de la barbarie fascista* (1947; Weyler in Cuba: A Forerunner of Fascist Barbarism) by Emilio Roig de Leuchsenring (1889–1964).

Impromptu editors worthy of mention are those who took on the work as an extension of their duties as editors of cultural magazines, such as Carlos de Velasco and Carlos Guiral Moreno of *Cuba Contemporánea* (1913–1927; Contemporary Cuba); the group at *Revista de Avance* (1927–1930; Progress Review); and José Lezama Lima of the journal *Orígenes* (1944–1956; Origins). Ediciones Orígenes published as many as twenty-three titles (all financed by their authors).

INSTITUTIONAL PRODUCTION

Viewed with hindsight, 1910 turned out to be a significant year in the development of the Cuban publishing movement. That was the year the Academia de la Historia de Cuba (Academy of Cuban History) and the Academia Nacional de Artes y Letras (National Academy of Arts and Letters) were founded. The former, over the course of a half century, undertook an intense level of publishing activity through its publications commission (which published memoirs, drawing room discourses, and tributes, as well as classics of Cuban history, in addition to the annual *Anales*). It received a grant from the state in the 1920s for almost 700 pesos a month—quite generous at the time—and donations from some official institutions. It was the institution most involved in rescuing the nation's earlier history writings and the one that most experienced the dramatic tensions of what could be called the dialectic of memory and oblivion (Fornet 2004, p. 184).

Throughout the first half of the century there were attempts, quickly frustrated, to publish small collections of patriot biographies and chronicles on the wars for independence that were meant for a wide readership. But it was undoubtedly the Thirties Generation, as it was known, which came to power after the defeat of the rule of Gerardo Machado (1825–1933), that brought to Cuban culture a democratic breath of fresh air that would be reflected in the development of publishing. In 1935 the Office of Culture was created within the Ministry of Education and was directed over the years by distinguished intellectuals such as José María Chacón y Calvo (1893–1969) and Raúl Roa (1907–1982). It soon started to publish Cuadernos de Cultura (Cultural Collection), which offered the most comprehensive collection of Cuban authors available in Cuba until then that was within reach of the average reader, and the new Grandes Periodistas Cubanos (Great Journalists of Cuba) collection. In 1938 the Office of the City Historian (for Havana) was created, under the direction of Emilio Roig de Leuchsenring. It sponsored the Cuadernos de Historia Habanera (Havana History Collection).

The title of *cuaderno* (literally "notebook") lacked only the adjective *popular* to emphasize that its goal was to reach a wider public. This was made very clear years later with the Cuadernos de la Universidad del Aire, which gathered and published the scripts of lectures that had been read on a radio program, *La Universidad del Aire* (1933, 1949–1952; On-Air University), directed by Jorge Mañach (1898–1961).

UNIVERSITY PRESSES

A relatively late but no less important contribution to Cuban publishing was that of the University of Havana, with its Cuban Authors Library and particularly the *Obras* (Complete Works), adding up to twenty-five volumes, of two classic Cuban thinkers of the nineteenth century: Félix Varela (1788–1853) and José de la Luz Caballero (1800–1862). They were published between 1944 and 1960, under the direction of Roberto Agramonte and Elías Entralgo.

There were only two other universities in Cuba, founded in 1946 and 1948: Oriente University in Santiago de Cuba and Central University of Las Villas in Santa Clara. Some of their more significant publications during the period in question were *A propósito de* La Edad de Oro *de José Martí* (1956; Apropos of *The Golden Age* of José Martí) by educator Herminio Almendros (1898–1974) and two canonical texts by contemporary essayists: *Lo cubano en la poesía* (Cuban Identity in Poetry) by Cintio Vitier (1921–2009) and *Tratados en la Habana* (Treatises in Havana) by Lezama Lima (1910–1976), both published in 1958. Under the direction of poet and folklorist Samuel Feijóo (1914–1992), Central University of Las Villas became one of the country's most active publishing centers during the following decade.

The meager activity in the publishing arena during the first half of the twentieth century was basically supported by the efforts of certain institutions and the persistence of numerous intellectuals. Only textbooks were guaranteed a stable market. In 1959 the Cuban national printing press, Imprenta Nacional de Cuba, was created. It started its activity in 1960 by producing one hundred thousand copies of *Don Quijote de la Mancha*, which were sold in bookstores for the price of one peso. Thus, one of the long-term aspirations of Cuban intellectuals was fulfilled. They were convinced that this kind of institution, which would function under the auspices of the state, would be the equivalent of "a publishing house capable of developing Cuban culture and literary production," by subsidizing works by national authors (Smorkaloff 1987, pp. 27–28). The publishing system that came about as a consequence of this initiative fully achieved its cultural objective.

■ *See also*

Autobiography of a Slave (Juan Francisco Manzano)

The Color of Summer (Reinaldo Arenas)

BIBLIOGRAPHY

Calvo, Hortensia. "Latin America." In *A Companion to the History of the Book,* edited by Simon Eliot and Jonathan Rose. Malden, MA: Blackwell Publishing, 2007.

Foreign Policy Association. *Problemas de la nueva Cuba.* New York: Foreign Policy Association, 1935.

Fornet, Ambrosio. *El libro en Cuba; siglos XVIII y XIX.* Havana: Editorial Letras Cubanas, 1994.

Fornet, Ambrosio. "La frustración creadora: Proyectos editoriales cubanos 1900–1958." *Revista Bimestre Cubana* 20 (January–June 2004).

Peraza Sarausa, Fermín. *La imprenta y el estado en Cuba.* Matanzas, Cuba: Estrada, 1936.

Peraza Sarausa, Fermín. *Bibliografía martiana, 1853–1953.* Havana: Ediciones del Centenario, 1954.

Ricardo, José G. *La imprenta en Cuba.* Havana: Editorial Letras Cubanas, 1989.

Smorkaloff, Pamela María. *Literatura y edición de libros: La cultura literaria y el proceso social de Cuba.* Havana: Editorial Letras Cubanas, 1987.

Truslow, Francis Adams, ed. *Report on Cuba.* Washington: International Bank for Reconstruction and Development, 1951.

LITERATURE: TESTIMONIAL LITERATURE

Jorge Marturano

Overview of the Cuban tradition of testimonial writing from slave autobiography to the testimonio *vogue.*

The tradition of testimonial writing in Cuba is long, complex, and abundant. The origin of a certain body of testimonial work can be found in the autobiography of Juan Francisco Manzano (1797–1854), which initiated the antislavery narrative in Cuba in 1835, along with *El presidio político en Cuba* (The Cuban Political Prison, 1871), by José Martí (1853–1895). In narrating the firsthand experiences of slavery and imprisonment, these texts established the distinctive characteristics of the Cuban testimonial tradition, which denounces the deprivation of freedom as a method for establishing and maintaining social order. Manzano's is a marginalized voice mediated by conditions related to its publication; Martí's perspective is that of a political prisoner whose voice serves to express collective suffering. In this way, both works anticipate the role of giving voice to the people without history that is a feature of the testimonial genre during the 1960s.

THE TRAJECTORY OF CUBA'S TESTIMONIAL TRADITION

Testimonial writing takes on diverse forms, particularly if works such as memoirs, personal diaries, autobiographies, and even biographies are included. Such an inclusive definition of the testimonial tradition necessarily exceeds the limits of the *testimonio* as it was conceptualized in the 1980s—that is, a first-person account by a marginalized narrator, mediated by an editor, whose representativeness, which emanates from its political urgency, distinguishes it from autobiography. However, this broader approach restores the value of a fundamental aspect of Cuban cultural production.

Biographies in Cuba have been fundamental in establishing a genealogy of the *criollo* (Cuban) subject and in documenting the methods and forms used to construct this subject. This genealogy begins with Antonio Bachiller y Morales's *Galería de hombres útiles* (Gallery of Useful Men, 1859) and continues with Manuel de la Cruz's *Cromitos cubanos* (Cuban Picture Cards, 1892) and, later on, with the numerous biographies of Martí written during the Cuban Republic. Miguel Barnet's emblematic text *Biografía de un cimarrón* (Biography of a Runaway Slave, 1966) simultaneously takes up and reverses the role of this biographical paradigm by imbuing the narrative with the perspective and voice of a former slave—the epitome of the dispossessed and marginalized subject in Cuban society.

The long struggle for independence in Cuba generated some outstanding memoirs and autobiographies, such as *Mis buenos tiempos (memorias de estudiante)* (My Good Times [Memoir of a Student], 1891), by Raimundo Cabrera (1852–1923), as well as many diaries from the War of Independence, such as those by Máximo Gómez (1836–1905), which includes a version of Martí's last journal, and Enrique Loynaz (1871–1963). These narratives document not only extraordinary deeds but also the everyday, mundane details that are part and parcel of making history. Cuban women's autobiographical writing began with María de las Mercedes Santa Cruz y Montalvo (1789–1852), better known as the Countess of Merlin, whose works were first published in French. She also initiated a literature in exile, a genre that became important after the 1960s. Daily life during the last years of colonial society and the first decades of independent Cuba is detailed in the memoirs of Dolores María Ximeno Cruz (1866–1934) and Renée Méndez Capote (1901–1989). In their texts, family life takes on a paradigmatic and defining role within a subset of Cuban literature that extends toward the novel, as in the case of Pedro Pérez Sarduy (b. 1943). The testimonial form is more obvious in the work of Daisy Rubiera Castillo (b. 1939), for example, her *Reyita, sencillamente: testimonio de una negra cubana nonagenaria* (Reyita: The Life of a Black Cuban Woman in the Twentieth Century, 1996), which narrates the life of María de los Reyes Castillo Bueno (1902–1997) as it was told by her to her daughter (Rubiera Castillo).

All these works employ narrative techniques that make them participants in a sort of historical revisionism characteristic of testimonial literature. This pattern is apparent in the works of central figures such as Cabrera and Martí, as well as other writers whose social, racial, or gender-related marginalization contributed to the construction of a space from which to assert oneself inside the new space of the nation. Although all of these texts mentioned above establish an unequivocal relationship between representation and truth, it was the experience of imprisonment that was most important to the strengthening of the testimonial impulse.

IMPRISONMENT IN TESTIMONIAL LITERATURE

Testimonial and literary production focused on prisons constitutes a *continuum* that extends before and after the canonization of the testimonial novel and the *testimonio*. The volume of cultural production concerning the Cuban prison increased during periods of political crisis or redefinition of state power, coinciding with a need to show how the experience of individual suffering reaches the level of collective representation. Such periods of upheaval include the wars of independence, which gave rise to texts on political imprisonment, exile, and the so-called concentration camps under Spanish rule; the struggle against the government of Gerardo Machado, which was the most productive period in terms of prison testimonial writing; the 1960s, under the revolutionary regime; the crisis that brought about the Mariel Boatlift in 1980, which led to the publication of several important testimonies of the revolutionary regime's practices of political incarceration; and the 1990s, when testimonial narrative began to recount a sort of mass marginalization produced by the economic collapse characteristic of the post-Soviet period.

In the 1930s the prison became not only a space in which the conflicts of a social model in crisis were staged, but also a space for the production of literature and a catalyst for literary renewal. This factor was central in the works of such dissimilar writers as Alejo Carpentier (1904–1980), Carlos Montenegro (1900–1981), Raúl Roa (1907–1982), and Pablo de la Torriente Brau (1901–1936). In their writings imprisonment is a social, political, racial, and linguistic experience that yielded, for Montenegro, almost the entirety of his literary production, and for Carpentier, the literary experiment *Écue-Yamba-Ó* (Praise Be the Lord! 1933). During the first half of the 1930s there was a boom in testimonial prison literature, and within a relatively short period, dozens of articles published in the press by young writers such as Roa, Torriente Brau, and Aureliano Sánchez-Arango (1907–1976) condemned Machado's regime.

Torriente Brau and Montenegro were the most significant of these writers, as much for their role in the consolidation of the testimonial genre as for their work about the prison experience and its impact on the literary imagination. Of the two, the more clearly testimonial work is Torriente Brau's, which includes widely read articles and reports published in the newspapers *El mundo* and *Ahora* about Presidio Modelo (the model prison built under Machado's rule) and the situation in the rural zones. Torriente Brau's book *Presidio Modelo* (Presidio Modelo), written in 1935 but not published until 1967, is a multifaceted, heterogeneous text that was conceived not only as a narrative of the author's experience but also as an accusation of the head of the penitentiary and the institutional complicity that facilitated the creation of a penal regime ruled by terror. With an episodic structure that builds an argument similar to a public prosecutor's indictment, Torriente Brau combines different genres (autobiography, biography, geographical sketch, psychological study, forensic analysis, legal files, political landscape, fiction) in his overarching literary representation of all aspects of the prison system.

By focusing on the relationships between prisoners in his novel *Hombres sin mujer* (Womanless Men, 1938), Carlos Montenegro changed the direction of the testimonial writing that previously dealt with imprisonment in newspaper articles. Montenegro's novel, which is a fictionalization of his own prison experience, concentrates on the sexual dimension of imprisonment, describing the tension and desire created by the arrival of a new inmate at the prison. The sexual tension created by physical contact between the prisoners, and their obsession with always being watched—which turns them into sexual objects—are themes that Reinaldo Arenas (1943–1990) took up years later in *Arturo, la estrella más brillante* (Arturo: The Brightest Star, 1984), a hallucinatory testimonial about the detention camps where homosexuals and others accused of antisocial behavior were sent during part of the 1960s. Montenegro's influence can be seen most prominently in contemporary writers such as Ángel Santiesteban (b. 1966), who deals with similar themes in *Dichosos los que lloran* (Blessed Are Those Who Cry, 2006). It is worth noting, though, that many of the issues addressed by Torriente Brau and Montenegro are absent from the prison texts produced by writers of the generation that participated in the attack on the Moncada barracks in July 1953, as these works serve more as a platform for action and as affirmation of political strategies.

With the establishment of the revolutionary regime, there was an exponential increase in the number of detainees and sentenced individuals and in the number of prisons across Cuba. As a result of this situation, testimonial and autobiographical narratives after 1959 focus on the political, social, and personal aspects of incarceration. These works received little literary critical attention; their circulation and interpretation were conditioned by their political dimension, which diverted attention from their textual aspects per se. In spite of the visibility of writers such as Armando Valladares (b. 1937) and Jorge Valls (b. 1933), the texts of this period did not achieve the same effect as their Republican predecessors. Nevertheless, they are good examples of testimonial literature that introduce readers to a new dynamic both inside and outside of the prison: (political) conversion and resistance against it. In that respect, though, none of these works had the same impact as Arenas's writings or films such as *Conducta impropia* (Improper Conduct, 1984) and *Nadie escuchaba* (No One Was Listening, 1987), which are concerned with revealing subjectivities resistant to the process of revolutionary conversion.

CANONIZATION OF *TESTIMONIO*

When Barnet published *Biografía de un cimarrón* in 1966, the Revolution was still accumulating power, and Barnet's unique text signaled a change in Cuban cultural production. Despite Cuba's long tradition of testimonial writing, *Biografía* is different from all previous formulations because of the mediated nature of the narrative of Esteban Montejo, the fugitive slave and soldier during the war of independence. The editorial intervention over the voice of an exceptional yet emblematic character brings to the fore issues of representation (symbolic and political), authorship, agency, literary creation, transcription, and ideological cooptation. The originality of the text, added to Barnet's theorizing in the introduction and in "Novela testimonio: socioliteratura" (Testimonial Novel: Socio-Literature), included in *Canción de Rachel* (Rachel's Song, 1969), attracted both readers and critics to the genre. Critics emphasized the historical restoration of subjects such as Montejo, the innovative nature of the *testimonio* form, and the way *Biografía* gave prominence to the role of literature in Revolution.

Barnet published several other works that can be considered testimonial novels, which complete his fresco of Cuban history. Whereas Montejo's narrative deals with nineteenth-century plantation society up to the triumph of the War of Independence, and *Rachel* focuses on the first decades of the corrupt, decadent Republic as seen through the eyes of a dancer, *Gallego* (1981) highlights the importance of immigration in the development of the Republic, and *La vida real* (Real Life, 1984) describes the vicissitudes of Cuban economic emigrants before the triumph of the Revolution. Each of these four works is constructed in its own way, and each exposes the protean, hybrid form of the *testimonio*, as well as its political vigor. To a certain extent, this fact explains the institutionalization and canonization of *testimonio* via the introduction in 1970 of a new testimonial literature category in the literary prizes awarded by the Casa de las Américas, a Cuban cultural organization founded in the months following the Revolution to develop and strengthen cultural relations between the nations of Latin America and the Caribbean.

The Casa de las Américas *testimonio* award initially favored works that emphasized the epic dimension of militant revolutionary action. This preference was clear from the honorable mention awarded to *Girón en la memoria* (Bay of Pigs in Memory, 1971), by Victor Casaus (b. 1944), and the first prize awarded to *Aquí se habla de combatientes y de bandidos* (Here We Speak of Fighters and Bandits, 1975), by Raúl González de Cascorro (1922–1985). Beyond their individual merits, testimonial works of this type tend not to attract the attention of literary critics (especially scholars in U.S. universities) who favor texts in which the editor's place, and the subalternity and Otherness of the speaker, are obvious. Changes in the way the Casa de las Américas prize was conceived—diminishing the importance of the editor and stressing the origins and veracity of the historical sources and highlighting the text's aesthetic qualities—reflect the difficulties that any kind of institutionalization presents, especially when it produces traumatic effects in the cultural field and a glaring change in attitudes about the Revolution among an important sector of Latin American intellectuals, as it did in the 1970s.

PERPETUATION OF THE TESTIMONIAL NARRATIVE

The *testimonio*, canonized by a political gesture that gave voice to marginalized or subaltern subjects, gradually lost value among Cuban writers. Even so, the testimonial impulse in Cuban cultural production endures as much in the genre of texts that clearly owe a debt to historical, journalistic, and anthropological research as in literature that distances itself from or challenges the revolutionary enterprise. This fact can be seen in the memoirs and autobiographies of Eliseo Alberto (b. 1951) and Norberto Fuentes (b. 1943), in Arenas's *Antes que anocheza* (Before Night Falls, 1992), and in the extensive body of exile memoirs by Gustavo Pérez Firmat (b. 1949), Pablo Medina (b. 1948), and Carlos Eire (b. 1951). The testimonial function also affects literary criticism—as can be seen explicitly in Pérez Firmat's *Life on the Hyphen* (1994) and José Quiroga's *Cuban Palimpsests* (2005)—and other aspects of cultural production, as can be seen in visual arts.

Going beyond the academic debate on *testimonio*, testimonial narratives demonstrate a remarkable vitality and pertinence both as one of the richest trends of Cuban culture and as a fundamental component in the development of Cuban literature. Writers have repeatedly returned to reshape or reformulate the testimonial tradition, even reacting against it as it occurs during the 1980s. The degree to which the post-1959 Cuban revolutionary process influenced the canonization of the *testimonio* category and the testimonial form as an important feature of cultural production is clear from the institutionalization effected by the Casa de las Américas Prize. This pattern can also be seen in texts depicting the militant experience as the deciding factor in the formulation of the Revolution's "New Man," in key historical episodes such as the government's literacy campaign and the campaign to end the armed opposition against the revolutionary regime in the mountains of Escambray. This institutionalization of the testimonial literature effected during the post-Revolution period, however, had its precursor in initiatives dating from the Republican years, mostly during the 1930s and 1940s, that consisted of a special series of testimonial writing among the *Cuadernos de Cultura* (Cultural Notebooks) published by the Secretary (Ministry) of Education.

The economic crisis of the 1990s stripped all meaning from the future of the revolutionary process and redirected it toward the past. Experiences of poverty and marginalization—socioeconomic, but also spatial and cultural—became the testimonial catalyst for many contemporary Cuban narratives. This fact even applies to writers who refused to identify their works with a collective project and saw themselves documenting the breakdown of the revolutionary subjectivity. Examples include the texts of Pedro Juan Gutiérrez (b. 1950), Ángel Santiesteban (b. 1966), and Guillermo Vidal (1952–2004), for whom representation of the prison experience plays an important role, either implicitly or explicitly.

BIBLIOGRAPHY

Primary Sources

Alberto, Eliseo. *Informe contra mí mismo.* Mexico City: Aguilar, Altea, Taurus, Alfaguara, 1997.

Arenas, Reinaldo. *Arturo, la estrella más brillante.* Barcelona: Montesinos, 1984.

Arenas, Reinaldo. *Antes que anochezca.* Barcelona: Tusquets, 1992.

Bachiller y Morales, Antonio. *Galería de hombres útiles.* Havana: Instituto Nacional de Cultura, 1955.

Barnet, Miguel. *Gallego.* 1981. Havana: Letras Cubanas, 1983.

Barnet, Miguel. *Biografía de un cimarrón.* 1966. Madrid: Alfaguara, 1984.

Barnet, Miguel. *Canción de Rachel.* 1969. Havana: Letras Cubanas, 1985.

Barnet, Miguel. *La vida real.* 1984. Madrid: Alfaguara, 1986.

Cabrera, Raimundo. *Mis buenos tiempos: memorias de un estudiante*. 1891. Intro. Ana Cairo. Havana: Letras Cubanas, 1981.

Casaus, Víctor. *Girón en la memoria*. Havana: Casa de las Américas, 1970.

Castillo Bueno, María de los Reyes, and Daisy Rubiera Castillo. *Reyita, sencillamente: testimonio de una negra cubana nonagenaria*. Havana: Instituto Cubano del Libro / Prolibros, 1996.

Conducta impropia. Dir. Néstor Almendros and Orlando Jiménez Leal. Documentary. 1984.

De la Cruz, Manuel. *Cromitos cubanos*. Madrid: Editorial Saturnino Calleja, 1926.

Eire, Carlos. *Waiting for Snow in Havana: Confessions of a Cuban Boy*. New York: Free Press, 2003.

Fuentes, Norberto. *Dulces guerreros cubanos*. Barcelona: Seix Barral, 1999.

Gómez, Máximo. *Diario de campaña, 1868–1899*. Havana: Instituto del Libro, Centenario, 1968.

González Cascorro, Raúl. *Aquí se habla de combatientes y de bandidos*. Havana: Casa de las Américas, 1975.

Gutiérrez, Pedro Juan. *Trilogía sucia de La Habana*. Barcelona: Anagrama, 1998.

Loynaz del Castillo, Enrique. *Memorias de la guerra*. Havana: Editorial Ciencias Sociales, 1989.

Manzano, Juan Francisco. *Autobiografía, cartas y versos*. Havana: Cuadernos de historia habanera, 1937.

Martí, José. *El presidio político en Cuba. Último diario y otros textos*. Buenos Aires: Biblos, 1995.

Medina, Pablo. *Exiled Memories*. Austin: University of Texas Press, 1990.

Méndez Capote, Renée. *Memorias de una cubanita que nació con el siglo*. 1964. Havana: Instituto del Libro, 1969.

Montenegro, Carlos. *Hombres sin mujer*. 1938. Mexico City: Editorial Oasis, 1981.

Nadie escuchaba. Dir. Néstor Almendros and Jorge Ulla. Documentary. 1987.

Pérez Firmat, Gustavo. *Life on the Hyphen: The Cuban American Way*. Austin: University of Texas Press, 1994.

Pérez Firmat, Gustavo. *Next Year in Cuba: A Cubano's Coming-of-Age in America*. New York: Anchor Books, 1995.

Quiroga, José. *Cuban Palimpsests*. Minneapolis: University of Minnesota Press, 2005.

Santa Cruz y Montalvo, María de las Mercedes. *Mis primeros doce años*. 1831, in French. Havana: El siglo xx, 1922.

Santa Cruz y Montalvo, María de las Mercedes. *Viaje a La Habana*. 1883, in French. Havana: Editorial Arte y Literatura, 1974.

Santiesteban, Ángel. *Dichosos los que lloran*. Havana: Casa de las Américas, 2006.

Torriente Brau, Pablo de la. *Presidio Modelo*. Introduction by Ana Cairo. Havana: Ediciones La Memoria, 2000.

Torriente Brau, Pablo de la. *Testimonios y reportajes*. Introduction by Ricardo Hernández Otero. Havana: Ediciones La Memoria, 2001.

Valladares, Armando. *Contra toda esperanza*. Barcelona: Plaza & Janés, 1985.

Valls, Jorge. *Veinte años y cuarenta días*. Madrid: Ediciones Encuentro, 1988.

Vidal, Guillermo. *Las manzanas del paraíso*. San Juan, Puerto Rico: Editorial Plaza Mayor, 2002.

Ximeno y Cruz, Dolores María. *Aquellos tiempos ... Memorias de Lola María*. Havana: Imprenta y Librería El Universo, 1930.

Secondary Sources

Azougarth, Abdeslam, and Ángel Luis Fernández Guerra, eds. *Acerca de Miguel Barnet*. Havana: Letras Cubanas, 2000.

Beverley, John. *Against Literature*. Minneapolis: University of Minnesota Press, 1993.

Cairo, Ana. *La revolución del 30 en la narrativa y el testimonio cubanos*. Havana: Letras Cubanas, 1993.

Capote-Cruz, Zaida. *La nación íntima*. Havana: Ediciones Unión, 2008.

Diana, Goffredo. "Testimonio in Cuba: Limits and Possibilities." Ph.D. diss. University of Pittsburgh, 1997.

Fornet, Ambrosio. *Narrar la nación*. Havana: Letras Cubanas, 2009.

Garrandés, Alberto. *Presunciones*. Havana: Letras Cubanas, 2005.

González Echevarría, Roberto. *The Voice of the Masters: Writing and Authority in Modern Latin American Literature*. Austin: University of Texas Press, 1985.

González Laureiro, Julio César. *El camino del círculo*. Nueva Gerona, Cuba: Ediciones El abra, 2004.

Gubelberger, Georg, ed. *The Real Thing: Testimonial Discourse and Latin America*. Durham, NC: Duke University Press, 1996.

Lugo-Ortiz, Agnes. *Identidades imaginadas. Biografía y nacionalidad en el horizonte de la Guerra (Cuba. 1860–1898)*. San Juan: Editorial de la Universidad de Puerto Rico, 1999.

Molloy, Sylvia. *At Face Value: Autobiographical Writing in Spanish America*. New York: Cambridge University Press, 1991.

Rojas, Rafael. *Essays in Cuban Intellectual History*. New York: Palgrave Macmillan, 2008.

Saumell, Rafael. "El testigo problemático: narrativa carcelaria en Cuba." *Monographic Review/Revista Monográfica* 11 (1995): 207–219.

Saumell, Rafael. "1902–1959: Más narraciones entre hierros." *Encuentro de la Cultura Cubana* 20 (Spring 2001): 176–185.

Sklodowska, Elzbieta. *Testimonio hispanoamericano: historia, teoría, poética*. New York: Peter Lang, 1992.

Sklodowska, Elzbieta. "In the Web of Reality: Latin American Testimonio." In *Literary Cultures of Latin America: A Comparative History*. Vol. 2, *Institutional Modes and Cultural Modalities*, edited by Mario J. Valdés and Djelal Khadir, 197–208. Oxford, U.K.: Oxford University Press, 2004.

LUCÍA (HUMBERTO SOLÁS)

Rufo Caballero

How a film came to express the fate of a country and a culture.

The feature film *Lucía* (1968), directed by Humberto Solás (1941–2008), is one of the most important works of Cuban cinema. In weaving together three stories about three women, all named Lucía, in three different periods of Cuban history, it pays homage to all women and explores an entire century of the country's history and its struggles for independence.

The movie first tells the story of an aristocratic woman in 1895, when Cuban nationalists were battling Spanish soldiers for control of Cuba. The movie then shifts to 1933 during the regime of Gerardo Machado. The middle-class Lucía of this period runs away with a young revolutionary who is working to overthrow Machado. In the last story, set in the 1960s, the third Lucía is a young illiterate field worker newly married to a jealous man who virtually imprisons her in their home. A new teacher comes to the community and changes their lives.

With *Lucía*, his first fiction feature, Solás summed up the life of an entire country, depicting Cuba's complex history and many of its historical and contemporary problems. In 1968 Solás's artistry was at its peak, free of mannerisms, full of freshness and sensitivity; both his technique and the story itself invite imaginative and analytical thinking. In Cuba, the 1960s were a time to evaluate where the nation and its culture were going. The vigorous social imaginary coupled with the contemporary historical context made possible this affecting film that is one of the most intense and complete cultural models associated with Cuba.

The three stories of *Lucía* are connected by carefully intertwined organic dialogue and bridges. In terms of both its characters and its conflicts, the film maintains a dramatic continuity rooted in the stories' historical precision. While maintaining that continuity, Solás explores a different topic in each story, fueled by the aesthetic turmoil: the tragedy of a practically monastic Cuba, isolated and denied pleasure; skepticism in the face of a failed revolution; and the sometimes mechanical relationship between the individual and the demands of a social process. These three themes remained relevant in the political, philosophical, social, and cultural debates about Cuba conducted in the early 2000s. Solas masterfully intertwines ideological positions (always examined), symbolism, and narrative.

THE FIRST LUCÍA, 1895

The first Lucía is caught between two men, Felipe and Rafael, who to some extent represent conventions that continue to feed debate in Cuba: emancipation and instrumentality. Felipe, Lucía's brother, is the first revolutionary figure to appear in the film (followed by

■ *See also*

Gender: Colonial Period to 1920

Gender: Social Justice in the Revolutionary Period

Gender: The Women's Suffrage Movement in Cuba

Film: 1959–1989

Filmmaker Humberto Solás (1941–2008) at the Latino Film Festival in Hollywood, 2002. Humberto Solás's groundbreaking film *Lucía* (1968) explored Cuban culture and history through the stories of three women named Lucía. HECTOR MATA/NEWSCOM

Aldo, the underground fighter in the second story). Rafael, Lucía's lover, is a Spanish businessman. Lucía, like Cuba itself, is caught between the rigor of ethics and the desire for mobility (economic, social, and sensual), and the result is tragedy. Scholars often have portrayed Rafael as a traitor, and although that analysis is not incorrect, it is an oversimplification. Rafael is certainly a scoundrel: He uses Lucía to gain access to the coffee plantation and simultaneously helps to undermine the cause of independence, and he abandons Lucía during a brutal battle. (In regard to the film's symbolic settings, it should be noted that the two male characters are seen in the boarding house and on the coffee plantation.) Rafael belongs to the world of commerce. He is an intruder, someone who supposedly came to the town looking for business, for products to trade. Diametrically opposed is Felipe, the insurgent brother of Lucia. He belongs to the *cafetal* (coffee plantation), the world of production, and the land: the motherland. Felipe abandoned his house to be part of the fight against Spanish colonial government and is living now in the *cafetal*, in the wild; Rafael lives in the guesthouse, a site to people who pass, without roots. Both places and characters are symbolically opposed.

Rafael is petty and cowardly; he grovels. But from a Brechtian perspective, Rafael embodies his nature; he is an ambiguous character, born in Spain of a half-Cuban mother, who rejects politics and claims—on a verbal, rhetorical level—to love Cuba. To Lucía, Rafael represents an opportunity for pleasure, for escaping her seclusion, but when that opportunity arrives, it brings humiliation. After long, deadening years spent alone, she surrenders her virginity to Rafael when he shows only the slightest interest in her, but his real interest is finding the coffee plantation where the rebels are hiding. The symbolism is clear: Just as Lucía betrays the rebels when she reveals to Rafael the location of the coffee plantation, Cuba betrays itself when it succumbs to pleasure. This gives rise to a teleological question: Is Cuba still trapped in abstinence?

Dramatic tension infuses the story. Early on, Lucía's close friend Rafaela laments, "We're going to be old maids." After Rafael declares his love for Lucía she arrives home and throws open doors and windows; everything is bright. The girlfriends talk, laugh, and play with sensuousness and anxious expectation. Later, when the lover's betrayal is discovered, Lucía's mother Fidelina cries, "Oh, God, what darkness! What poor ventilation there is here!"

Love—the relationship with Rafael—appears to be the opportunity for Lucía's (and Cuba's) realization, but during the pitched battle at the coffee plantation Lucía's cries of longing for Rafael become cries of pain over the death of Felipe. With a sense of historical justice and an underlying fatalism, Solás's bleak vision—reprised in *Un día de noviembre* (A Day in November, 1972), *Cecilia* (1981), *Amada* (1983), *Un hombre de éxito* (A Successful Man, 1986) and

other films—determined that Lucía would become Fernandina, the dark conscience of the film (a reference to José Martí's 1895 failed Fernandina Plan to provide weapons and men in Cuba's struggle for independence). As the expression of that failure, Lucía's resentment and despair leads her to stab Rafael to death in the public square. Pathetically, Lucía returns to her seclusion and is redeemed only by tragedy.

THE SECOND LUCÍA, 1933

Solás's achievement in *Lucía* was unprecedented: It is a luminous film, stylistically brilliant, and ahead of its time in its critical view of a weakened, broken, and fading Cuba. This is particularly true in the second story of the triptych, which depicts the disappointment in the aftermath of the failed revolution of 1933, a subject Solás returned to in his vigorous adaptation of Alejo Carpentier's *El siglo de las luces* (The Century of Lights, 1992). *Lucía* is striking in its audacity in examining the collapse of a revolution—the strikes and protests, the struggle that brought down Machado, and only weeks later, the revival of corruption—just nine years after the triumph of the Revolution of 1959. At the end of this story, perhaps the best of the three, Lucía is left bewildered, doubting, staring into the camera and unable to decide whether to return to her parents' home in Cienfuegos or to resume the struggle. She is disoriented, suspended like history itself, but she also is pregnant—she carries within her the germ of another revolution.

The second story's most significant sequence occurs when Lucía and her lover Aldo party with friends (Antonio and Flora) and in their drunkenness break into an argument about the meaning of a revolution unable to cast off the evils it was meant to eradicate. There is a strong contrast between the camera angles of this scene, in which the discouraged characters are prisoners of alienation, and the photography that depicts the group dynamic during the anti-Machado strike. Another contrasting treatment is seen in the imagery of the corrupt sitting room orgy that ensnares Aldo; as the revolution morphs into an orgy, the dignity they fought for becomes degeneracy. In Solás's aesthetic, style does not support the theme; style *is* the theme. From time to time the action stops, and the dialogue lays bare his meaning with great eloquence. Solás's expressionist camera has significant counterparts in the expressionism of Cuban painters of the 1960s (Antonia Eiriz, Umberto Peña, Servando Cabrera, Acosta León, and others).

The second story confirms the urban versus rural tension present throughout the film, here expressed in spaces as diverse as the cay and the tobacconist's shop, and in the social confrontation of the city. This mobility supports the subjective expression of the second story, which is narrated by evocation, retrospective, and Lucía's memory. In the third story, subjectivity is not dispensed on the diegetic level; instead, it comes mostly from the voice of Joseíto Fernández

(1908–1979) singing his "Guantanamera" with verses adjusted to the plot of this third tale.

THE THIRD LUCÍA, 1960s

Moving from the aware and patriotic Cuban woman to the *campesina* integrated into her society and pursuing her own spiritual growth, the protagonists of *Lucía* gradually become more popularized and democratic. The third Lucía embodies the psychosocial complexity of the Revolution, the conflicts between the great ambitions, the withdrawal of those who resist the model, and the bad habits that are part of the human condition. Tomás tells his wife Lucía and the world that "he is the Revolution." He cannot see past his phallus; he cannot stand for his wife, *his* woman, to work and to learn to read and write. Tomás's machismo is a serious obstacle to the Revolution's greater goals. Here Solás addresses the tremendous conflict that emerges when ethical concerns, civic responsibilities, and personal choice are out of sync. The specter of patriarchy defines the conflict: Tomás needs possession, property, dominance, just as the father of the second story (carefully used as a point of reference, but not as a dramatic figure) needs to control the fates of the female characters. At one point Flavio scolds Tomás, "You're not going to go against a collectively beneficial measure!" Official rhetoric is ironic and even satirical, showing Solás's sardonic bent when Flavio says, "Lucía doesn't know how to read, she doesn't know how to write, she's a victim of Yankee imperialism." In subsequent years, Yankee imperialism would be blamed for most of the island's ills, modeling a politics of action-reaction that atrophied the country's development and ignoring the equally intolerable internal blockade.

None of the three Lucías is passive. The first Lucía resorts to the only action visible to her infuriated eyes: revenge. The end of the second tale finds Lucía anxious, with a thirst the viewer cannot share. The third story ends without resolution: Lucía stands in the salt marsh, angry at Tomás after admitting that she cannot live without him but neither will she yield to him. The movie closes with this complexity, softened by the gaze and the laughter of another girl. Solás ends by leaving the viewer in the grip of an emotion that endures in doubt, in the lack of certainty—if by certainty we mean a resolution of all the problems of cinema and of life.

BIBLIOGRAPHY

Caballero, Rufo, ed. *A solas con Solás. 30 años de* Lucía. Havana: Letras Cubanas, 1999.

"Los pasos y las huellas. Humberto Solás en la cultura cubana." *Cine cubano* 170 (2008).

M

THE MACHADO DICTATORSHIP FALLS: AUGUST 1933

Robert Whitney

The fight against the Machado dictatorship and the realignment of social and political forces that resulted.

The fall of the Machado dictatorship in August 1933 marked the beginning of a new phase in Cuban state formation. Prior to 1933 state politics, and Cuban sovereignty, were conditioned by the Platt Amendment. (The amendment, passed in 1901, gave the United States the right to intervene in Cuban affairs.) After Machado's ouster, the country entered a prolonged period of intense mass mobilization, and as a result, a realignment of political and social forces took place.

SOCIOECONOMIC BACKGROUND

When General Gerardo Machado y Morales (1871–1939) assumed power in May 1925, Cuba appeared to be on the path to political and economic recovery. The dramatic expansion of Cuba's sugar industry between 1914 and 1921—especially in the eastern half of the island—had brought prosperity for a few and social and economic dislocation for many. The elections of 1925 were relatively fair, and Machado rode a wave of optimism and growing nationalist sentiment. He promised to lead Cuba toward economic development and peaceful political competition. His first two years in power seemed to confirm that promise. The new president promised to protect the small sugar growers (*colonos*), establish protective tariffs for light industry, expand public works, and regulate the sugar industry by setting production quotas to control prices. Machado declared that he would diversify agriculture and that his government would not take out new foreign loans. Finally, he made the commitment to serve as president for one four-year term.

By 1926 there was no serious opposition to Machado. So confident was he about his future that he broke his promise not to run again, and most of the political elite supported him. In the fall of that year Machado's Liberal Party and the Conservative and Popular parties established an arrangement known as *cooperativismo*, which simply meant that they would support Machado's candidacy. With no opposition, Machado viewed the 1928 presidential election as an inconvenience. Yet he himself had condemned re-electionism as the source of Cuba's political turmoil. His solution to this problem was to amend the Constitution of 1901 by stipulating that he would govern until 1934. This move was too much for some of his allies. After 1928 Machado's rule increasingly depended upon repression.

Initially, opposition to Machado came from within the oligarchy. As early as 1927, prominent politicians formed the Unión Nacionalista (UN), a loose coalition of anti-reelection forces, including some from Machado's Liberal Party. UN leaders such as Carlos Mendieta (1873–1960), former president Mario Menocal (1866–1941), Carlos de la Torriente, and Roberto Méndez Peñate (1871–1934) were skilled practitioners at Plattist politics. The UN accepted the principle that ultimately the United States, not Cubans, determined the legitimacy of Cuban governments, so they tried to convince the U.S. State Department to withdraw support for Machado. American support for Machado, however, remained strong. The U.S. ambassador, Harry F. Guggenheim, did try to broker a compromise between Machado and the UN, but not to the point of removing him.

Early signs of opposition came from students at the University of Havana. Not only were students concerned about Machado's extension of term, but Machado had abolished a commission established by his predecessor, President Alfredo Zayas (1861–1934), to oversee educational reform. To make matters worse, Machado appointed a personal friend as rector of the university, a move that expressed nepotism and violated university autonomy. In response, in 1927 a group of students formed the Directorio Estudiantil Universitario (DEU; University Students Directorate).

■ *See also*

The Cuban Revolution of 1959

Economy: Republican Period

Governance and Contestation: The Republic: 1902–1952

Platt Amendment

Sugar: Republican Period

The World and Cuba: Cuba and the United States

Gerardo Machado y Morales (1871–1939) in Havana, 1930. General Gerardo Machado y Morales became president of Cuba in 1925. The fall of the Machado regime in August 1933 marked the beginning of a new phase in Cuban state formation. © CORBIS

Protests continued throughout 1928, but there was little antigovernment agitation outside the university. Machado's rule still seemed secure.

Two circumstances shifted the balance against Machado. First, from 1929 to 1934 an economic crisis drove hundreds of thousands of Cubans to ruin and hunger. Second, this economic crisis fueled both opposition to Machado and nationalist sentiment.

The world depression of 1929 hit Cuba hard. Sugar production, the measure of the Cuban economy, dropped a full 60 percent between 1929 and 1933. Throughout the early twentieth century American sugar beet growers lobbied their government to close the U.S. market to lower-priced Cuban sugar, and with the onslaught of the depression, they won their battle. The Cuban share of the U.S. sugar market dropped from 49.4 percent in 1930 to 25.3 percent in 1933. In 1924 total Cuban exports to the United States were valued at $434 million; by 1932 they stood at $80 million. Imports from the United States showed a similar decline during the same period with a drop from $290 million to $51.2 million. Cuban government revenues fell from around $90 million in 1928 to $47 million in the 1931–1932 period. By the end of the fiscal year in 1933, the Cuban government

was unable to pay many state employees. Cuba's second major export, tobacco, experienced a similar decline: Between 1929 and 1933 the export value of leaf tobacco fell 68 percent.

In response to this crisis, Cuban sugar growers reduced sugar production to counter the drop in prices. Yet world sugar production remained high, and prices continued to fall. In the spring of 1931 Cuba, along with six other nations, signed the Chadbourne Plan, an initiative intended to coordinate the restriction of world sugar production. Cuba agreed to reduce its output by 36.5 percent, Java agreed to a 10.42 percent reduction, and the European beet sugar producers accepted 15 percent. Despite these measures, the price of sugar fell by 60 percent: In 1925 the price was 2.25 cents a pound; in 1929 it was 1.72 cents, and by 1933 price bottomed out at 0.97 cents.

The social consequences of the restrictions on sugar production were disastrous, especially for wage workers and *colonos*. Larger producers could absorb the cut in production, but indebted *colonos* could not. Most *colonos* rented their land from large milling companies, and they paid rent either in the form of a percentage of their crop, in cash, or in some combination of the two. The loss of revenue from the crop restriction meant that many *colonos* could not pay rent, debts, or their workers. Soon nearly one-fourth of Cubans found themselves without work. Factories and businesses closed. There was a 50 percent reduction in state pensions, and 15 percent of state employees lost their jobs. On average, the wages of urban employees fell by 50 percent, while rural wages dropped as much as 75 percent, with some falling as low as ten cents per day during the harvest and two cents per day during the dead season. After 1930 clashes between students, workers, and the unemployed with Machado's police increased. Rural workers occupied vacant land to grow the food they needed, and cane burning became a widespread form of protest. In response, Machado suspended constitutional guarantees, and he replaced civilian governors with his military men in Pinar del Rio, Matanzas, Las Villas, Camagüey, and Oriente. Military censors watched over newspapers and other publications. By 1932 the cycle of economic crisis and political unrest fomented growing opposition and forced American diplomats to rethink their unconditional support for Machado.

THE POLITICAL CRISIS OF 1933

The political and economic crises of the 1927–1933 period generated a confrontation between Machado, who came to symbolize the evils of the Plattist state, and the rest of the population. The most articulate, if small, opposition group was the DEU. Some of Cuba's most important politicians received their baptism of fire in the DEU. Antonio Guiteras (1906–1935), Raúl Roa García (1907–1982), Aureliano Sánchez Arango (1907–1976), Eduardo Chibás (1907–1951), Carlos Prío Socarrás (1927–1964), Rubén León García, and

Manuel Antonio "Tony" de Varona (1908–1992) were all members of the DEU. The popular university professor, Ramón Grau San Martín (1887–1969), played an important role in bringing these students together to discuss and plan actions against Machado. Politically, the young men and women of the DEU were reformists, not revolutionaries. Their ideological inspiration came from Cuba's national heroes of the nineteenth century, especially José Martí, and from the United States, especially the New Deal liberalism of President Franklin D. Roosevelt. DEU manifestos typically called for civil liberties, an independent judiciary, individual rights and civic responsibilities, political pluralism, the sovereignty of the people, and a modern democratic state. Another more radical student group, the Ala Izquierda Estudiantil (Student Left Wing), also gained influence, and some of its members were members of or sympathizers with the Communist Party.

Two other opposition groups emerged during the struggle against Machado: the Communist Party (CP) and the ABC Sociedad Revolucionaria. In many ways both organizations were as much products of the crisis of 1927–1933 as they were leaders of it. The CP was formed in 1925, but its membership remained small until the early 1930s, when its ranks swelled with disgruntled workers. The CP's consistent fight against racism earned it the support of many Afro-Cuban workers. By the spring of 1933 its two unions, the Conferación Nacional Obrera de Cuba (CNOC; National Confederation of Cuban Workers) and the Sindicato Nacional de Obreros de la Industria Azucarera (SNOIA; National Sugar Workers' Union) had a national presence and CP organizers had a hard time keeping up with swelling union memberships. The ABC, in contrast, was a largely middle-class and urban organization. Its ideology was a hybrid of corporatist and fascist ideas, and it advocated a strong state that would oversee and balance competing social classes and groups. The ABC organized itself into secretive cells (A, B, C, etc.) and used insurrectionary violence (some called it terrorism) to attack Machado's police and collaborators. The ABC was more of a movement than a political party. In 1933 it was the single most popular opposition group, but this popularity stemmed less from membership size or ideology than from its confrontational and violent actions against a hated government.

It is important to highlight that with the exception of the CP, the anti-Machado groups were not revolutionaries. Despite the constant rhetoric of revolution, programmatically the UN, DEU, and ABC wanted to reform Cuba's political system, not overthrow it. They employed the language of revolution and used insurrectionary tactics because of Machado's refusal to grant meaningful reforms and his use of repression. Indeed, to one degree or another, the UN, DEU, and ABC accepted U.S. mediation as a means to oust Machado, but the refusal of American ambassadors to go that far increased the opposition's frustration with the United States. In other words, most of the opposition was not so much anti-American as it was anti-intervention, and even then these opposition groups would support U.S. intervention if it served Cuban ends. Many believed that with Roosevelt in power, U.S. ambassadors would no longer serve the narrow interests of Wall Street bankers and trusts, and they would respect Cuban sovereignty. But when U.S. ambassadors failed to meet Cuban expectations, anti-Americanism increased. Between January and April 1933 Machado and the opposition were locked in an increasingly violent stalemate, yet the United States stood by the Cuban president. With the path to reform blocked and with no help from the United States, the opposition to Machado was both universal but stalled.

The Role of Ambassador Welles When Ambassador Guggenheim's replacement, Sumner Welles, arrived in Havana in May 1933, it was clear to all that Cuba was in crisis. Welles worried that if Machado did not compromise with the elite opposition, the crisis would worsen and perhaps lead to revolution. Many in the opposition hoped that Welles, unlike Guggenheim, would use mediation to oust Machado. Much to their disillusionment, this did not happen. First, Machado unexpectedly resisted Welles's attempts at mediation. He had agreed to mediation because he thought the United States would keep him in power. But when Welles informed Machado that he would have to shorten his term by one year, the president balked. Welles then opened negotiations with the opposition in the hope of moderating their demands for Machado's immediate ouster. By 1 July 1933 the ABC, the Organización Celular Reforma Revolucionaria (OCRR), university and college professors, secondary school teachers, the UN, and the Association of Veterans agreed to participate in the mediation.

The students of the DEU, however, after considerable debate, rejected the mediation. On 16 July 1933, the DEU issued a manifesto stating that mediation undermined Cuba's right to self-determination, and it symbolized the corrupt Plattist politics of the past. The ABC split over the mediation, with a small but important segment forming the ABC Radical. The CP and its union affiliates and the Ala Izquierda Estudiantil had always rejected mediation as imperialist interference in Cuban affairs, and these groups spent their time organizing workers and students for what they hoped would be the coming revolution.

Meanwhile, mass mobilization from workers and peasants throughout Cuba did indeed threaten revolution. On 25 July 1933 a general strike swept through Havana and commerce and transport stopped in most cities and towns. Machado, the pro-mediation opposition, and the U.S. State Department did not know how to respond to this situation. Throughout July Welles tried to remove Machado before the Cuban state collapsed. Machado remained confident he could resist Welles, and in an attempt to alleviate the strike situation, he opened negotiations with the CP and CNOC: He offered both groups legality in exchange for an end to the general strike. After a heated debate within the CP's Central Committee, Machado's offer was accepted. The CP later reversed its position, but the damage was done. For decades to come many activists would never trust the CP again.

By August all that remained of the *machadato* was Machado himself. The end came when the military, fearing U.S. military intervention, put Machado on a plane for the Bahamas. Machado was quickly replaced by Carlos Manuel de Céspedes (1871–1939). But if Welles thought that Machado's departure would bring an end to Cuba's political crisis, he was mistaken.

Members of those groups and other individuals who stuck with Machado to the end were discredited, many for the rest of their political careers. Others, if they managed to break with Machado early enough, salvaged enough credibility to remain players in Cuban politics. This latter group included some representatives of the UN and some members of the Liberal, Conservative, and Popular parties. The ABC, by contrast, declined rapidly after 1933. Its uncritical acceptance of Welles's mediation destroyed its political credibility with other nationalists. In the years to come the core of the DEU would found the Partido Revolucionario Cubano (Auténtico) (PRC-A), but in the immediate aftermath of Machado's fall, the DEU dissolved into factions.

THE SHORT-TERM AND LASTING CONSEQUENCES OF MACHADO'S FALL

The short-term consequences of Machado's fall were dramatic. Cuba experienced seven years political turmoil and uncertainty. Between September 1933 and January 1934 Cuba was ruled, at least nominally, by a Provisional Revolutionary Government led by Ramón Grau San Martín. Grau's government was loose-knit coalition of nationalist and radical students, disgruntled lower-rank military officers, and a few prominent business and intellectual leaders. The provisional government promised a so-called new Cuba with social justice for all classes, protection of national industry and labor, and the abrogation of the Platt Amendment. Popular sentiment was behind Grau's government, but its actual administrative capacity to govern the country, especially outside Havana, was limited by its own internal weakness and divisions as well as opposition from entrenched political and economic interests. Indeed, in January 1934, with the backing of the United States, Grau's government was overthrown by an equally loose coalition of military and conservative forces led by a young sergeant named Fulgencio Batista y Zaldívar.

Yet despite an apparent return to the old political ways, Cuba had changed after Machado's fall. The popular experiences of mass mobilization and intense nationalist sentiment meant that after 1933, no government, no matter how conservative, could ignore (or appear to ignore) popular demands for greater political inclusion and national sovereignty. The Platt Amendment was abrogated in 1934 because even the United States had come to the conclusion that the amendment's paternalistic and neocolonialist intent was the source of much of Cuba's political instability. And despite the authoritarianism and anticommunism of Batista and other leaders, they too recognized that unions and leftists needed to be incorporated into national politics rather than simply being excluded and repressed. Consequently, by 1937, once Batista had consolidated his position within the army and state, his government legalized the CP (1938), and he increasingly courted the support of the trade union movement, much of it under communist leadership. To be sure, violence—including state-sponsored violence—plagued Cuban society after Machado's fall, but thereafter a powerful, if politically ambiguous, populist sentiment in favor of state-sponsored reform and democracy set the rules and affected the players of Cuban politics for the next thirty years.

BIBLIOGRAPHY

Aguilar, Luis E. *Cuba 1933: Prologue to Revolution*. Ithaca, NY: Cornell University Press, 1972.

Beals, Carleton. *The Crime of Cuba*. Philadelphia: J. B. Lippincott, 1933.

Benjamin, Jules. R. *The United States and Cuba: Hegemony and Dependent Development, 1880–1934*. Pittsburgh, PA: University of Pittsburgh Press, 1977.

Cabrera, Olga, and Carmen Almodóbar, eds. *Las luchas estudiantiles universitarias, 1923–1934*. Havana: Editorial de Ciencias Sociales, 1975.

Cairo Ballester, Ana. *La revolución del 30 en la narrativa y el testimonio cubanos*. Havana: Editorial Letras Cubanas, 1993.

Carrillo, Justo. *Cuba 1933: Students, Yankees, and Soldiers*. Translated by Mario Llerena. New Brunswick, NJ: Transaction Publishers, 1994.

Commission on Cuban Affairs. *Problems of the New Cuba*. New York: Foreign Policy Association, 1935.

McGillivray, Gillian. *Blazing Cane: Sugar Communities, Class, and State Formation in Cuba, 1868–1959*. Durham, NC: Duke University Press, 2009.

Pérez, Louis A., Jr. *Cuba under the Platt Amendment, 1902–1934*. Pittsburgh, PA: University of Pittsburgh Press, 1986.

Pérez-Stable, Marifeli. *The Cuban Revolution: Origins, Course, and Legacy*. New York: Oxford University Press, 1993.

Raby, David L. *The Cuban Pre-Revolution of 1933: An Analysis*. Glasgow, U.K.: Institute of Latin American Studies, University of Glasgow, 1975.

Roa García, Raúl. *La revolución del 30 se fue a bolina*. Havana: Ediciones Huracán, 1969.

Tabares del Real, José A. *La revolución del 30: Sus dos últimos años*. Havana: Editorial de Ciencias Sociales, Instituto Cubano del Libro, 1973.

Thomson, Charles. "The Cuban Revolution: The Fall of Machado." *Foreign Policy Reports* 11, no. 21 (18 December 1935): 250–260.

Thomson, Charles. "The Cuban Revolution: Reform and Reaction." *Foreign Policy Reports* 11, no. 22 (1 January 1936): 262–276.

Welles, Sumner. *Two Years of the "Good Neighbor Policy."* Washington, DC: Government Printing House, 1935.

Whitney, Robert. *State and Revolution in Cuba: Mass Mobilization and Political Change, 1920–1940.* Chapel Hill: University of North Carolina Press, 2001.

■

THE "MAMBO KING": DÁMASO PÉREZ PRADO

Tony Évora

The dynamic Cuban bandleader known as the Mambo King whose career spanned the latter half of the twentieth century.

The origin of the word *mambo* is lost in the lexicon of the African slaves who ended up in the Caribbean region. In Haiti they call vodou priests *mambo*; according to the ethnologist Fernando Ortiz, the word comes from the Congo and means "conversation." The fact is the term has floated around in Caribbean speech and has had diverse connotations. Over the course of many years, popular musicians have used the word *mambo*, along with *devil*, to identify the din or climax of the brass instruments in an untamed, restless sound.

The creator of the mambo as it is known in the early 2000s was Dámaso Pérez Prado (1916–1989), an outstanding pianist with special talent for synthesis and arranging. Though debate about who created the mambo continues, urged on by incorrect assertions, Pérez Prado was the one who established the new danceable form around 1948. The mambo was heir to a rich tradition of sound, and Pérez Prado incorporated elements of North American music to change it into something new. In mambo, the brass section achieves extraordinary effects with melody, harmony, and rhythm, backed up by saxophones that maintain syncopation and by percussion in the background.

Pérez Prado was born in Matanzas, a city east of Havana that enjoyed a certain level of culture. He grew up with his brother Pantaleón, who was also a musician. Although they came from a humble home, Pérez Prado studied classical piano and organ, and he was a standout in local groups before he moved to the capital in 1942. Once there, he earned his living playing piano. When he joined the Casino de la Playa orchestra in 1943, he earned $5 a night and an additional $2 for every musical arrangement he wrote. Pérez Prado built a solid career as an arranger for the orchestra

and other musical groups. He got the most out of the sound of every instrument. He was ambitious and realized that he needed a large orchestra, with strong brass instruments, in order to achieve the blend of sounds borrowing from Afro-Cuban and jazz rhythms.

In an early attempt to launch mambo music in Cuba, Pérez Prado recorded a demo record containing *Mambo caén* and *So caballo*, using top-class musicians who were friends. They helped him out, free of charge, because they were fascinated by his ideas, but faint-hearted musical entrepreneurs did not realize that it was something really innovative. The piano player was way ahead of his time. (A similar reception was given to Bebo Valdés when he launched his batanga rhythm, and to the *tresero* Niño Rivera, with his Cuban bebop music.)

When they ignored him in Cuba, Pérez Prado set up shop in Mexico. He rehearsed a lot and then rented the Blanquita Theater, announcing a show he called "Al son del mambo" (To the Sound of Mambo). The performance was a great success and gave Pérez Prado the platform he needed. In Mexico he experimented with different sound levels made up of two basic registers, sending the sounds of high-pitched trumpets against a wall in some recordings so that he could achieve the resonance he was wanted. (At that time, recordings made in studios used a single microphone.) His productions required excellent musicians who could hit challenging notes. He launched one composition after another, recording for RCA Victor first in Mexico, then in its studio in New York City. He was a hit: The Mambo King earned a lot of money and became famous in just a few years. More than 4 million copies of *Que rico el mambo* were sold between 1950 and 1951, an extraordinary number at the time.

Pérez Prado's most popular mambos include "Mambo no. 5," "Pianolo," "Caballo negro," "El ruletero," "Mambo en sax," "La chula linda," and "Mambo no. 8." Pérez Prado also recorded for Seeco, United Artists, Epic, and other labels. Pérez Prado's trademark was the "ugh!" he shouted at the end of most musical phrases. For all but the youngest and most fit, the mambo was very difficult to dance to, and its rapid, almost violent movements earned it a reputation as a lewd form of dance; in 1952, the cardinal of Lima (Peru) forbade all his parishioners to dance it.

But Pérez Prado is also remembered as the creator of unforgettable slow-tempo melodies such as "Cherry Pink and Apple Blossom White," with Billy Regis's trumpet suspending four long notes inside musical space before dropping off into a smooth cadence. In 1955 the song stayed at number one on the Hit Parade for ten weeks and was somewhere among the top 40 for twenty-six weeks. Pérez Prado became even more famous with "Patricia," which he brought to life with an organ and the deep bellowing of a trombone. Sales of the record reached 5 million, thanks to Federico Fellini's 1960 film *La dolce vita*, in which Anita Ekberg swings her hips to the music in pure pleasure.

■ *See also*

Music: 1945–1959

Music: Afro-Cuban Religious Influence on Cuban Popular Music

Music: Music since 1959

Pérez Prado (1916–1989), playing the bongos. During the 1940s and 1950s, Cuban bandleader and composer Dámaso Pérez Prado became known as the King of the Mambo. His best-known song, "Mambo No. 5," was first recorded in 1949. MICHAEL OCHS ARCHIVES/GETTY IMAGES

During the 1950s Pérez Prado's band appeared in several films produced in the United States and Mexico. Pérez Prado also took part in *Hotel de muchachas* (The Girls' Hotel), which was filmed in Havana in 1951. In the middle of the decade he joined Shorty Rogers to make two records that were truly exotic: *Voodoo Suite*, which combines Afro-Cuban rhythms with frenzied elements of harder pop tunes; and *Exotic Suite of the Americas*, which uses cellos and violins and is reminiscent of Nelson Riddle arrangements combined with Caribbean melodies to produce a finale of carnivalesque madness.

Pérez Prado strongly influenced two generations of North American musicians. Stan Kenton, who shared Pérez Prado's interest in trumpets, recorded Shorty Rogers's *¡Viva Prado!* which paid homage to the Mambo King. In Mexico, Benny Moré and Pérez Prado (whom Moré called *el cara de foca*, or seal face) recorded the musical themes "Anabacoa," "Pachito e' che," "Rico y sabroso," "Rabo y oreja," and other songs that formed part of the modern repertoire of the Afro-Cuban *sonero*.

Within five years, mambo fever revolutionized the work of the best Latin bands in New York City, such as those of Tito Rodríguez and Tito Puente, as well as Machito and his Afro-Cubans, a group that perfected the creative art of Pérez Prado with a kind of mambo that was faster-moving, more technical, and more to the liking of Latino dancers in Manhattan.

Pérez Prado's last public appearance was in Hollywood in September 1987, when his band played in a theater filled with mambo enthusiasts. Two years later he died of a heart attack in Mexico City at age seventy-three.

BIBLIOGRAPHY

Díaz Ayala, Cristóbal. *Música cubana. Del areyto al rap cubano*. 4th ed. San Juan, Puerto Rico: Fundación Musicalia, 2003.

Évora, Tony. *Música cubana. Los últimos 50 años*. Madrid: Alianza Editorial, 2003.

Ortiz, Fernando. *La Africanía de la Música Folklórica de Cuba*. Havana: Ministerio de Educación, 1950. Reprint, Madrid: Editorial Música Mundana Maqueda, 1998.

THE MAMBO KINGS PLAY SONGS OF LOVE (OSCAR HIJUELOS)

Héctor Jaimes

Discussion of the novel The Mambo Kings Play Songs of Love, *in light of Hijuelos's career as a writer.*

Oscar Hijuelos (b. 1951) is an American writer of Cuban descent whose works have dealt primarily with the Cuban émigré experience in the United States. Although the themes in his novels are recurrent, his approach, style, and writing technique are rich and complex. Early in his writing career, Hijuelos received the Ingram Merrill Foundation Fellowship (1982), the National Endowment of the Arts Fellowship (1985), the Rome Fellowship of the American Academy (1985), the Guggenheim Fellowship (1990), and most notably, the Pulitzer Prize in 1989 for his novel *The Mambo Kings Play Songs of Love*. This award brought Hijuelos immediate national and international recognition and afforded him the opportunity to become a full-time writer. The success of the novel was further established by its cinematic adaptation, *The Mambo Kings* (1992), directed by Arne Glimcher.

Hijuelos's works have been influenced by the stories and experiences of his Cuban-immigrant parents,

Cuban American author Oscar Hijuelos (b. 1951) in 2007. Oscar Hijuelos's 1989 novel *The Mambo Kings Play Songs of Love* won the 1990 Pulitzer Prize for fiction. The novel was later adapted into the film *The Mambo Kings*, released in 1992. ULF ANDERSEN/GETTY IMAGES

José Hijuelos and Magdelena Torrens, as well as by his own experience as a second-generation Cuban American born and raised in New York City. The immigrant theme appears in most of his novels: *Our House in the Last World* (1983), *The Mambo Kings Play Songs of Love*, *The Fourteen Sisters of Emilio Montez O'Brien* (1993), *Empress of the Splendid Season* (1999), *A Simple Havana Melody* (2002), and *Beautiful Maria of My Soul* (2010). Generally speaking, his treatment of the immigrant issue is not political, but literary. Hijuelos focuses on the nostalgia that surfaces as a consequence of cultural displacement, and he uses memory as an aesthetic tool in his handling of flashbacks, daydreams, omniscient narrators, parenthetical entries, footnotes, and even ghosts (in *Our House in the Last World*) to depict the sense of loss embedded in the immigrant experience.

Hijuelos pays great attention to the psychological development of his characters because he is more concerned with human feelings and experiences than with

■ *See also*

Diasporas: 1930s, 1940s, and 1950s

Literature: Fiction in the Revolutionary Period

The "Mambo King": Dámaso Pérez Prado

New York City

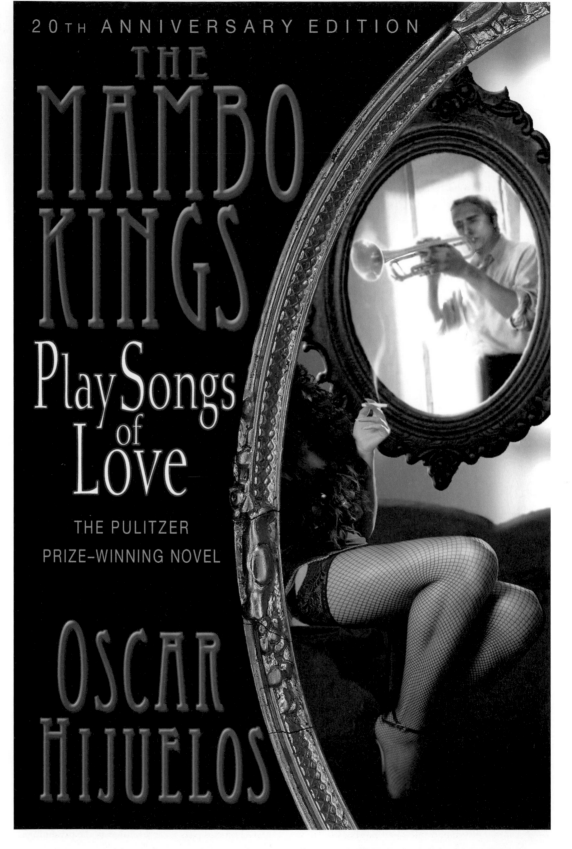

philosophical, political, or humanitarian causes. This is clear in *The Mambo Kings Play Songs of Love*, Hijuelos's second novel, which tells the story of two Cuban brothers, Cesar and Nestor Castillo, who immigrate to New York City in the late 1940s to pursue careers as musicians; although Hijuelos portrays in vivid detail the exciting lives of these two musicians, nostalgia and a sense of loss pervade the novel. Life offers the brothers many opportunities, but their own character traits seem to doom them to failure.

Rather than having chapters, the novel is divided in two parts that suggest the two sides of a record: "Side A. In the Hotel Splendour 1980" and "Side B. Sometime Later in the Night in the Hotel Splendour." This approach pays tribute to an era when famous musicians such as Tito Puente, Dámaso Pérez Prado, Machito, and Mongo Santamaría performed the best Latin music ever played in New York City. Thus, the Mambo Kings—the band that Cesar and Nestor successfully start—is the lens through which the reader views the lives of the two brothers and also a bygone era. At the beginning of the novel, Hijuelos writes: "Back then, you could walk through that park wearing your best clothes and a nice expensive watch without someone coming up behind you and pressing a knife against your neck. Man, those days were gone forever" (p. 11).

Cesar, the lead singer and an incorrigible womanizer, carries with him the weight of having left his wife—who had previously left him—and his only daughter, Mariela, back in Cuba. Similarly, Nestor's sorrow is defined by his nostalgia for Cuba and his former love, Maria, to whom he dedicates the song "Beautiful María of My Soul." His struggle as a songwriter pays off when the band performs the song on the television show *I Love Lucy*, which the Cuban bandleader Desi Arnaz produced and in which he costarred with his wife Lucille Ball. The Mambo Kings achieve immediate fame from their television appearance, but despite this success, Nestor is unable to feel comfortable in his own family. He marries Delores, a Woolworth's employee, and fathers two children, Eugenio and Leticia. At the birth of Eugenio (who narrates the beginning and end of the novel), "Nestor didn't quite know what to make of fatherhood, he felt so underprepared for manly duty in this world" (p. 112).

In keeping with the novel's record-like format and the essentially nonlinear narrative, Hijuelos conveys a sense of circularity that prevents true progress; the plot and the characters do not evolve, they revolve. Growth in the novel is impossible: Nestor's discomfort ends only with his death in a car accident while driving a drunken brother, and his death only contributes to the already pervasive emotional instability of Cesar, who dies alone in the Hotel Splendour while daydreaming of Vanna Vane, the woman with whom he enjoyed much of his fleeting success. Hijuelos describes the scene this way:

Now, in his room in the Hotel Splendour, the Mambo King watched the spindle come to the end of "The Mambo Kings Play Songs of Love." Then he watched it lift up and click back into position for the first song again. The clicking of the mechanism beautiful, like the last swallow of whiskey. When you are dying, he thought, you just know it, because you feel a heavy black rag being pulled out of you.

p. 395

A discussion of the 1992 film adaptation *The Mambo Kings* must highlight the radical difference between literature and film. The novel follows one main story but is filled with stories within stories that portray the lives of people in the United States and in Cuba. This textual complexity cannot be contained in the cinematic version, which follows the plot in a more linear fashion, but the film is enriched by visual images and music. For an American audience unfamiliar with the New York Latin scene in the 1950s, the film brings closer a little-known era. Although it fails to depict the inner lives of Cesar (Armand Assante) and Nestor (Antonio Banderas), it succeeds in bringing to the fore the luscious imagery and excitement that a live band brings to the spectator. In this way, the film does not follow the book line by line but rather narrates the trials and tribulations of two lost souls.

BIBLIOGRAPHY

Hijuelos, Oscar. *The Mambo Kings Play Songs of Love*. New York: Farrar, Straus and Giroux, 1989.

Hijuelos, Oscar. *Beautiful Maria of My Soul*. New York: Hyperion, 2010.

Jaimes, Héctor. "Oscar Hijuelos." In *Latino and Latina Writers*, edited by Alan West-Durán, María Herrera-Sobek, and César A. Salgado. New York: Charles Scribner's Sons, 2004.

MARIO CARREÑO: HIS ART AND WORLD

Carlos M. Luis

Mario Carreño's art and the social consciousness he expressed, for example, in Los cortadores de caña.

In 1943, René Portocarrero (1912–1985) began his series *Interiores del Cerro* and Wifredo Lam (1902–1982), after finishing *La jungla* (The Jungle), executed two of his most important works: *Malembo* and *La mañana verde* (The Green Morning). That same year, Virgilio Piñera (1912–1979) published his seminal poem "La isla en peso" (Island in the Balance).

Los cortadores de caña (The Sugarcane Cutters) by Mario Carreño. The painting expresses the struggle of sugarcane workers. © 2011 © 2009 ARTISTS RIGHTS SOCIETY (ARS) NEW YORK/ CREAIMAGEN, SANTIAGO DE CHILE. THE MUSEUM OF MODERN ART/LICENSED BY SCALA/ART RESOURCE, NY.

In 1943, Mario Carreño (1913–1999) was also active. He painted his oil on panel *Los cortadores de caña* (The Sugarcane Cutters). He produced different versions of this subject, using various materials and techniques, including Duco (an industrial product developed by Du Pont). Carreño also finished *Patio colonial cubano* (Cuban Colonial Patio; oil on canvas), *Desnudos* (Nudes; oil on canvas), *Tocadores de tambor* (Drummers; oil on canvas), *Pescador* (Fisherman; mixed media on board), *Fuego en el batey* (Fire in the

Sugar Workers' Town; Duco), *Los amantes* (The Lovers; oil on canvas), and *El huracán* (The Hurricane; oil on canvas). These works show Carreño's interest in changing styles, even over short periods. From the neoclassic to the cubist and the expressionist (represented by *Los cortadores de caña*), Carreño demonstrated his craftsmanship.

The works from 1943 chronicle the emergence of new subjects and a move from the use of subtle colors, as seen in *Los amantes*, to richer pigmentation, as in *El huracán* and *Fuego en el batey*. In these two works, Carreño incorporated elements of his home island's landscape, including palm trees, sugarcane, and bananas, and added other elements, such as hurricanes, as an important part of the composition. The eroticism in some of his paintings of the period, such as in *Desnudos* or *Los amantes*, illustrates a significant feature of the Cuban ethos. The introduction of folkloric subjects in some of his paintings, such as *Tocadores de tambor*, attests to the importance of nationalistic sentiments prevalent in Cuba and other Latin American countries at the time.

Along with other important paintings by Carreño, *Los cortadores de caña* was exhibited in 1943 at the Lyceum in Havana. The image of the sugarcane is a fundamental part of Cuban national identity. Another fundamental part is tobacco. Both are the subject of an important book, *Contrapunteo cubano del tabaco y el azúcar* (Cuban Counterpoint: Tobacco and Sugar, 1940), by the renowned Cuban ethnologist Fernando Ortiz (1881–1969). Carreño knew Ortiz well and was familiar with his investigation of the social and economic influence of tobacco and sugar on the Cuban identity. Carreño's sugarcane cutter expresses the struggle of the *macheteros* (cane cutters) deep in the sugarcane jungle. Painted in vivid colors, with various shades of green dominating, this painting delivers a strong statement in support of the sugar workers.

Carreño's painting was influenced by the 1926 poem by Agustín Acosta (1886–1979) titled "La zafra" (The Sugarcane Harvest). That long poem denounced the inhuman conditions that prevailed in the sugarcane industry. The influence of Acosta's poem is apparent in Carreño's work, its themes resounding throughout *Los cortadores de caña*. Carreño had an acute sense of social justice and was no stranger to the radical ideas that had pervaded Cuba since the second decade after its independence in 1902, ideas that fueled the emergence of the avant-garde. During the period between 1910 and 1939, Carreño helped develop the social and artistic ideas that began to take shape in Cuba following the early 1900s emergence of the avant-garde in Europe. Within this context, the socio historical content of *Los cortadores de caña* can be identified.

INTERNATIONAL STUDIES

Like many other painters of his generation, Carreño studied early on at San Alejandro National Academy of Arts in Havana, although he soon quit because of the stifling atmosphere of the institution. During the rule of Gerardo Machado (1925–1933), Carreño became one of the leader's opponents, executing drawings in charcoal, pastel, and pencil that conveyed the artist's political convictions. In 1932, attracted by the cultural changes that were taking place in Spain during the brief period of the Republic, Carreño attended the San Fernando Academy of Fine Arts in Madrid. In Madrid, he met Pablo Neruda (1904–1973), who would become one of his closest friends, as well as Federico García Lorca (1898–1936), Rafael Alberti (1902–1999), Manuel Altolaguirre (1905–1959), and others. In 1936, after the outbreak of the Spanish Civil War, Carreño returned to Cuba and presented an exhibition of his drawings at the Havana Lyceum.

Toward the end of 1936, Carreño also traveled to Mexico to learn from the muralists' techniques. Jaime Colson (1901–1975), a Dominican painter living at that time in Mexico, became Carreño's mentor, as did Diego Rivera (1886–1957). During this period, Carreño's style became neoclassical. He returned to Havana in 1937, but soon left for Paris, where he studied at the Académie Julian. He lived in Montparnasse, where he met Pablo Picasso (1881–1973), who suggested Carreño abandon his neoclassical style, and the surrealist painter Oscar Dominguez (1906–1957), who would also influence Carreño's career. The Jeu de Paume acquired two of his paintings after an exhibition in the Bernheim-Jeune gallery. In 1939, Carreño traveled to Italy, where he studied the Italian Renaissance masters. In 1941, he exhibited at the Perls Gallery in New York and executed some of his most monumental works, including *El nacimiento de las naciones americanas* (The Birth of the American Nations).

Carreño returned to Cuba in 1942, where he exhibited again at the Lyceum. He married Cuban millionaire and patron of the arts Maria Luisa Gómez Mena that same year, divorcing her in 1944. Also in 1944, he participated in the historic exhibition of Cuban art organized by Alfred Barr Jr. at the Museum of Modern Art in New York. His *Los cortadores de caña* was one of the highlights of the exhibition. In 1948, Carreño was invited to exhibit in Chile and then in Buenos Aires. In Santiago de Chile, he published his series *Antillanas* (West Indies), which expresses his nostalgic feelings for his native land.

POST–WORLD WAR II INFLUENCES

The 1950s witnessed intense change, with the United States emerging as the harbinger of economic expansion and new artistic ideas. Abstractionism was the new wave, and Carreño soon joined that school, incorporating within the geometric structures of his compositions certain symbolic figures rich in colors.

He took up residence in Chile in 1957, organizing the school of art at the Catholic University of Santiago and teaching art techniques and the history of Latin American painting. During his time in Chile, traveling periodically to Europe and Cuba, Carreño developed the diffuse variety of styles (with a certain inclination toward surrealism) that became the hallmark of the last stages of his career. In Chile, he married Ida González, with whom he had two daughters.

Mario Carreño's long and intense career was marked by his interest in experimentation. Using various styles, he searched rigorously for strong images. Of all his paintings, *Los cortadores de caña* is arguably his most meaningful.

BIBLIOGRAPHY

ARTNews. New York, 15–31 April (1944). Review of the exhibition of Modern Cuban Art at the Museum of Modern Art.

Carreño, Mario. *Cronología del Recuerdo*. Santiago de Chile: Editorial Antártica, 1991.

Luis, Carlos M. *Mario Carreño*. Miami: Galería Alfredo Martínez, 1999.

Mario Carreño: Exposición Retrospectiva 1939–1993. Santiago de Chile: Museo de Artes Visuales, 2004.

Sicre, José Gómez. *Cuban Painting Today*. Translated by Harold T. Riddle. Havana: Maria Luisa Gómez, 1944.

■ *See also*

Race: Free People of Color in Cuba

Race: Slavery in Cuba

Spanish-American-Cuban War: 1898

Sugar: Colonial Period

MATANZAS

Urbano Martínez Carmenate

The culture and history of Matanzas, the city known as the Athens of Cuba.

Matanzas, a maritime city 62 miles from Havana, arose on a site settled by aboriginal people who called the bay Guanima and their village Yucayo. A group of them killed some shipwrecked Spaniards who landed there around 1510, an event that gave the place its modern name (*matanza* means slaughter in Spanish). In September 1628 the Dutch corsair Peter Heyn captured the Spanish treasure fleet there. Frequent pirate attacks and smuggling prompted colonial officials to advise the king to build a fort and settle the area to counter enemy incursions and provide a shield for the capital.

Charles II issued a royal decree in 1682 to build a castle and settlement on the bay (Martínez p. 58). This work was not accomplished until 12 October 1693 when about thirty families from the Canary Islands arrived, accompanied by troops to garrison a fortress, San Carlos and San Severino de Matanzas, whose cornerstone was laid on 13 October on a site between the mouths of the two rivers. The following month, the governor of Cuba assigned the city a jurisdiction with a radius of 6 leagues, including lands that had belonged to Havana. The local *cabildo* (municipal government) started its sessions in December 1694. By September 1695 Catholic services were being held in a temporary wooden building.

THE EIGHTEENTH CENTURY

Throughout the eighteenth century Matanzas was little more than a village. The main economic activity in its surrounding areas was cattle ranching, with subsistence agriculture, tobacco, and sugar production at just a few mills. Attacks by pirates and corsairs made it necessary to build a defensive cordon around the bay. The castle of San Severino was complemented by the forts of El Morillo (1720) and San José de la Vigía (1848). Although there was little social progress in the city, the feasts of Corpus Christi and the Holy Patron, Saint Charles Borromeo, began in the eighteenth century, and theater performances started in 1747, during the celebrations of the royal oath of Ferdinand VI. The oldest known literary composition from Matanzas dates from around 1780; it included a few verses about the first local crime, which occurred around that date.

In 1793 the port was authorized to trade directly with Spanish populations, and this opportunity opened the door for socioeconomic development built on the plantation regime. The sudden appearance of trade in African slaves and the rapid rise of the sugar and coffee industries necessitated the complete refurbishment of the port in 1818. There was considerable growth in the first years after Matanzas was opened to the world, including the establishment of the first schools (1807), the arrival of the printing press and the first stirrings of journalism (1813), the establishment of the local sanitation board (1814), and the creation of a political government in 1815.

THE ATHENS OF CUBA

Between 1819 and 1867 the residents of the city and its surrounding areas lived in unprecedented splendor. Many of the most important innovations in the Cuban sugar industry were first tested in the fields around Matanzas. Steamship navigation began in 1819 with the voyage between Havana and Matanzas of the *Neptune*, the second vessel of its kind in the world and the first in the Spanish Empire (Ruíz Rodríguez p. 56). The railroad was built, and the telegraph came into use at this time. In tandem with the growth of the plantation system, the unchecked increase in the African population eventually provoked rebellions led by *cimarrones* (escaped slaves), conspiracies, and uprisings such as those at Triunvirato (1843) and La Escalera (1844), which sowed panic among the white plantation owners. In large measure, this unrest explains the failure of the Cuban independence movements between 1823 and 1830, as well as the attractiveness of reformism

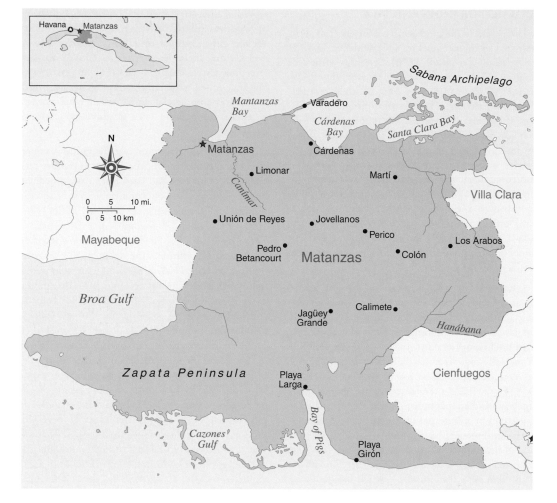

as a political option and the later enthusiasm for annexation of the island by the United States.

Matanzas became Cuba's second-largest city as a result of its demographic and economic growth driven by the sugar boom and the mills' increasing reliance on technology, as well as the rising prosperity of businesses that supported the sugar industry such as railroads, foundries, merchant emporia, and warehouses. The economic drive was duly matched by the momentum in the sphere of culture, as manifested in the fame of local institutions. *La Aurora* was known as "the prince of Cuban newspapers," and the college of La Empresa was considered the most important in the Spanish Empire. The Liceo Artístico y Literario (Artistic and Literary Lyceum, 1859), the Teatro Esteban (Esteban Theater 1863), and the Instituto de Segunda Enseñanza (Institute of Secondary Education, 1865) were among the most distinguished institutions in the colony. This intellectual constellation, coupled with a picturesque landscape (that included the Bellamar caves, the Yumurí Valley, Loma de El Pan, and the neoclassical buildings set between rivers), explain why Matanzas was designated *la Atenas de Cuba*

(the Athens of Cuba) in 1860, the same year it was connected directly by sea to New York City.

Distinguished intellectuals who lived in the area during this period included José María Heredia (1803–1839), Gabriel de la Concepción Valdés (Plácido, 1809–1844), and José Jacinto Milanés (1814–1863), poets who represented the romantic movement in Spanish literature; Domingo del Monte (1804–1853), the outstanding critic and cultural performer; the writer Cirilo Villaverde (1812–1894), who gained immortal fame with his novel *Cecilia Valdés* (1839); the painter Esteban Chartrand (1840–1884); Francisco Ximeno (1825–1891) and Juan Cristóbal Gundlach (1810–1896), notable naturalists; and the Guiteras brothers—the historian Pedro José (1814–1890) and the educators Antonio (1819–1901) and Eusebio (1823–1893). The city's printing presses produced the first regional dictionary of the Spanish-speaking Americas in 1836. The public of Matanzas applauded the greatest performers of the age, including the Austrian ballerina Fanny Elssler (1842), the soprano Adelina Patti (1856), and the pianist Teresa Carreño (1863).

THE WARS FOR INDEPENDENCE

The latter third of the nineteenth century in Cuba was dominated by the struggles for independence. During the Ten Years' War (1868–1878), Matanzas witnessed numerous conspiracies, patriots executed by firing squads, and the banning of long-standing cultural institutions that were accused of instilling the *mambí* spirit. The locals' involvement in the struggle of 1895 was much more significant. From the start, one of the most important *pronunciamientos* (declarations) of 24 February was issued in La Ignacia, within the city's jurisdiction; later, the invading force was deployed from the fields of Matanzas as the area's sugar mills succumbed to the flames of insurrectionist torches on the orders of chieftains such as Máximo Gómez (1836–1905). Ultimately the city was the target of an artillery bombardment by U.S. warships to hasten the Spanish surrender.

During this period of strife and political agitation, social and cultural life in Matanzas was undergoing important changes. Two major events took place in 1874: the founding of the local athenaeum, one of the first of these institutions in Cuba, and the first formally organized baseball game in the colony. Five years later, at the local *liceo* (high school), Miguel Faílde (1852–1921) premiered the first *danzón* performed at a Cuban institution. In 1881 twelve nations participated in an international exposition in Matanzas, the only general exhibition of its kind on the island in the nineteenth century; three years later the city hosted the first educational conference on Cuban soil. By that time the rhumba—which originated in Matanzas—was being danced at local celebrations in the poor black and free mulatto neighborhoods, and a mestizo from Matanzas, the violinist José White (1836–1918), was astounding Europe with his musical compositions. In 1878 Matanzas had been confirmed as the capital of the province of the same name, based on the new political-administrative division.

REPUBLIC AND REVOLUTION

U.S. military intervention during the war of 1895 accelerated the defeat of the Spanish and led to the occupation of the island from 1899 to 1902, when the republic was proclaimed. Matanzas lost its economic splendor with the destruction of its sugar wealth in the war. Regional statistics illustrate the catastrophe: Of the fifty-one sugar centrals that were active in the province around 1895, only seventeen were left in 1899. Sugar exports reached 352,000 tons in 1894; by 1900 they amounted to just 98,000. In the same period the population of the municipality of Matanzas declined by nearly 20 percent (González Pérez).

The republican period began with an uneven and frustrating socioeconomic process, the end result of political compromises. In the early decades of the republic, sisal was grown on the outskirts of the city of Matanzas, giving rise to a rope and cable industry. Yet the city remained mired in a peculiar lethargy, and it came to be known as the *Ciudad dormida* (Sleeping City), chiefly because of its proximity to Havana, which garnered the lion's share of manufacturing and commercial development while engaging in unfair competition with neighboring towns and cities.

Neither the economic nor the cultural achievements of the first third of the twentieth century could make up for all that had been lost in the nineteenth, but there were some outstanding figures of the early century in Matanzas such as Carlos M. Trelles (1866–1951), the Cuban bibliographer par excellence, and Carlos de la Torre (1858–1950), the renowned expert on shells and mollusks. The debut of the *danzonete*, by Aniceto Díaz (1887–1964), in 1929 was perhaps that year's most memorable success. The political struggle and insurrectionism of the 1930s helped to cultivate ideas about social justice. Strikes, collective demonstrations and rallies, and open defiance of corrupt governments raised awareness of the struggle and led to the creation of workers' unions and organizations and the maturing of other democratic associations. In 1935 at El Morrillo military agents directed by Fulgencio Batista (1901–1973) assassinated Antonio Guiteras (1906–1935), the leader of Joven Cuba (Young Cuba), a progressive organization. That same year, two major cultural institutions were founded— the Amigos de la Cultura Cubana (Friends of Cuban Culture) and the Grupo Índice; the Asociación de Artistas y Escritores Matanceros (ADAYEM, Association of Writers and Artists of Matanzas) followed in 1938 and Literary La Peña in 1945. The city scored several successes in the arts: In 1937 it hosted the Grand International Exposition of Periodical Publications; in 1941 it established the Escuela de Artes Plásticas (School of the Plastic Arts), the second of its kind in the country; in 1943 it launched the national celebration of Poet's Day, 3 March; and in 1950 the chamber orchestra (later, the symphony orchestra) was founded.

Between 1952 and 1958 Matanzas, like the rest of the nation, participated in the uprising to remove Fulgencio Batista from power. On 29 April 1956 insurrectionists attacked the Domingo Goicuría barracks in Matanzas; although the operation was a dismal military failure and most of the participants were killed, politically and morally the event served to ratchet up the pressure on the Batista regime. The people of Matanzas supported the landing of the yacht *Granma* and the actions of Fidel Castro's troops in the Sierra Maestra, and they helped build up the guerrilla groups in various areas of the province in order to advance the operations of the rebel army. This process reached its climax in 1958 with the establishment of the Enrique Hart column.

POST-REVOLUTION

After the triumph of the Revolution in 1959 Matanzas underwent a rapid transformation, especially in the social-urban dimension and in the areas of health, education, culture, and sports. Its urban footprint expanded significantly with the construction of new homes and buildings for polyclinics, hospitals, schools, cinemas, and sporting and recreational complexes. Demographic density increased even as neighborhoods and suburbs spread out in virtually all directions. In 1974 the city became the first in the country to be led by an administration of the new organs of popular power. Two years later the political/administrative organization of Cuba ratified the city of Matanzas as the capital of the province. Social indicators showed major improvements in literacy, schooling, technical training, birthrates, social security, and life expectancy of the residents of the city (*Provincia Matanzas*).

According to data from the Oficina Nacional de Estadísticas (National Statistical Office), in December 2009 the city encompassed 44.5 square kilometers and had a population of 132,678, a high percentage of whom were mixed origin or mestizos. Although Christian churches are the most visible centers of worship in the city, Matanzas is renowned for its many temple-houses that serve adherents of the popular religions of African origin. The province's historical archives contain a rich trove of records dating as far back as the colonial period that document these religions as well as slavery on the sugar and coffee plantations, whose ruins can be seen in the early 2000s around the city.

CULTURAL HERITAGE

Matanzas has many attractions of great interest to tourists, including natural features as well as archaeological and historical-cultural highlights. The Valley of Yumurí, the caves of Bellamar (Cuba's oldest tourist facility, open to the public since they were discovered in 1861), and the national park of Río Canímar are located in the environs of the city, as are the zoo, the botanical gardens, and seven museums, including the Museo Farmaceutico (Pharmaceutical Museum), which is unique in Latin America in its re-creation of a nineteenth-century French pharmacy. Also noteworthy are the castle of San Severino; the Museo de la Ruta del Esclavo (Slave Route Museum) sponsored by UNESCO and the Cuban government; the provincial Palacio de Junco (Junco Palace), which has exhibitions on regional history; and the Museo de Arte (Museum of Art), which holds valuable works ranging from etchings by Albrecht Dürer and Rembrandt to a fascinating collection of African art donated by Lorenzo Padilla (b. 1931), a Paris-based artist from Matanzas.

The city is home to the longest-running theater in Latin America, where Fanny Elssler danced in 1842; the oldest railroad station in the Americas; the legendary Palmar de Junco baseball stadium, a national monument located on the site where the sport was first played in Cuba in 1874; La Dionisia, a coffee farm established by a colonial French immigrant that is among the best preserved plantations in western Cuba; the oldest steel bridge on the island, inaugurated in 1878 over the Yumurí River; the crest of Monserrate, a natural outlook crowned by the hermitage of the same name, built by Catalans in 1875; Jesús María, a street of staircases and rich in folklore; the unique Teatro Sauto (Sauto Theater, formerly the Esteban), where famous stars, including Sarah Bernhardt (1887) and Anna Pavlova (1917), performed; and the internationally acclaimed Ediciones Vigía, founded in 1985, the only publisher in the world dedicated exclusively to producing handmade books.

BIBLIOGRAPHY

Alfonso Portillo, Pedro Antonio. *Memorias de un matancero. Apuntes para la historia de la Isla de Cuba con relación a la ciudad de San Carlos de Matanzas.* Matanzas, Cuba: Imprenta de Marzal y Cia, 1854.

Chávez Álvarez, Clara Emma. *Matanzas de rojo y negro 1952–1958.* Matanzas, Cuba: Ediciones Matanzas, 2007.

García Pérez, Gladys Marel. *Crónicas guerrilleras de Occidente.* Havana: Editorial Ciencias Sociales, 2005.

García Santana, Alicia, and Julio Larramendi. *Matanzas, la Atenas de Cuba.* Guatemala City: Ediciones Polymita, 2009.

González Pérez, José Ramón. "Aproximaciones al inicio de una historia de Matanzas en el período neocolonial (1902–1958)." Matanzas: Museo Provincial Palacio de Junco de Matanzas. Unpublished.

Martínez Carmenate, Urbano. *Historia de Matanzas. Siglos XVI–XVIII.* Matanzas, Cuba: Ediciones Matanzas, 1999.

Martínez Carmenate, Urbano. *Atenas de Cuba: Del mito a la verdad.* Havana: Ediciones Unión, 2010.

Matanzas Provincial Government. *Reseña histórica de Matanzas.* Havana: Imprenta La Revoltosa, 1941.

Pérez, Louis A., Jr. *On Becoming Cuban: Identity, Nationality & Culture.* Chapel Hill: University of North Carolina Press, 1999.

Perret Ballester, Alberto. *El azúcar en Matanzas y sus dueños en Havana. Apuntes e iconografía.* Havana: Editorial de Ciencias Sociales, 2007.

Ponte Domínguez, Francisco J. *Matanzas: Biografía de una provincia.* Havana: Imprenta El Siglo XX, 1959.

Provincia Matanzas. Santiago de Cuba: Editorial Oriente, 1978.

Ruíz Rodríguez, Raúl. *Matanzas: Surgimiento y esplendor de la plantación esclavista (1793–1867).* Matanzas, Cuba: Ediciones Matanzas, 2003.

Trelles Govín, Carlos M. *Matanzas en la independencia de Cuba.* Havana: Imprenta Avisador Comercial, 1928.

MAURICIO'S DIARY (MANOLO PÉREZ)

Víctor Fowler Calzada

Film that covers critical years in Cuban history, including the impact of the end of European socialism, the economic crisis known as the Special Period, and the attempts of Cuba to redefine its place in the contemporary world.

After an absence of twenty years, Manuel Pérez (b. 1939) returned to feature films with *Páginas del diario de Mauricio* (best known by its English translation, *Mauricio's Diary*, 2006), a film that covers the last twenty years of the Cuban Revolution. The story opens with the television broadcast of the baseball final of the Sydney Olympic Games (2000), when the Cuban team lost the gold medal to the United States, and ends with the broadcast of the victory of the Cuban women's volleyball team over Russia in the same Olympic Games. Because the plot that revolves around the main character, Mauricio, moves forward—through losses—from youthful enthusiasm toward maturity, the two Olympic events become symbolic markers in the character's life and in the transformation of the nation itself. The matches that pit the Cuban teams against these two countries hark back to the central polarity of the Cold War; thus, the defeat emphasizes the United States's role as the main antagonist in Cuba's attempts to develop an independent process, and the victory over Russia highlights the new political geography in which Cuba must pursue its social project.

Four moments in the story are critical in constructing a political reading of the narrative. The first, set at the end of the 1980s, occurs in a professional development school for workers where Mauricio is a teacher of politics. In a class on Marxist philosophy a group of students are discussing the events and consequences of the fall of the Berlin Wall. The selection of this profession for the character of Mauricio leads us to interpret him as a cog in the machine that replicates ideology. One student asks Mauricio to "show them the light," and another confesses a need for him to "raise their spirits." Mauricio's response—that they must "fully prepare [themselves] for what is coming, it's going to be hard"—can be understood only in a distinctly Cuban light: They need to reinvent a bankrupt solidarity and ideology in a context of lost connections with the socialist world, where political confrontation with the United States is a determining factor. It is here, in this classroom, that Mauricio meets the divorced mother who later becomes his wife—Mirta. When, years later, Mirta dies suddenly of an aneurism, Mauricio realizes that, with his own

daughter living in Sweden, his strained emotional relationship with Mirta's daughter Lucía is all that he has left in the country.

The second moment occurs during the events in Havana in August 1994, when Mauricio's visit to the Malecón waterfront promenade coincides with the riot that took place there. Accompanied by Lucía, his stepdaughter, he has gone to pick up a package of gifts and letters from his daughter Tatiana, which someone has brought from Sweden. He enters a building where a young protester is hiding; he may be the person who attacked a man in the street, splitting open his head. When Mauricio confronts him, asking, "What did you go to do at the Malecón?" the young man responds, "Look for a bag of stuff like they give you ... because you don't have any problems in your life, right?" For a revolutionary, particularly one such as Mauricio who teaches ideology, this is unacceptable, and he begins an argument that he eventually wins. However, the discursive position of the ideologue is fragile (recall the frustration in the young man's reply), and at Lucía's request, Mauricio ends up leading the young man out of the chaos and protecting him. For Mauricio, the combination of poverty and social inequality that motivated the protest provokes a tension that requires him to confront his social privilege as a person who travels outside the country and, therefore, has greater access to consumer goods. Learning the contents of the package sent by his daughter is less important than confirming the reality of poverty, in which even the most modest of consumer products becomes a dream and a basis for inequality. Suddenly, given two valid but opposing options (the desired gift package versus the sustenance of social solidarity, which at its most radical means renouncing the gift), Mauricio must reexamine himself and put his values to the test. The hard lesson of solidarity and renunciation defines a limitation of the revolutionary condition.

This lesson is a critical suggestion that confronts Mauricio with who he is (a cog in the machine for replicating ideology); this confrontation entails an act of learning. Then again, people can interpret any situation of this type as a conflict that disturbs the equilibrium of all the participants, who must then integrate their new understanding into behavior. The third crucial moment in the story occurs in Mexico when Mauricio meets his daughter Tatiana, who had been studying in the Soviet Union and decided after the collapse of Soviet socialism in 1991 not to return to Cuba.

The rupture with Tatiana is spread out over four temporal stages, ending with the meeting in Mexico. In the first stage, at around twenty minutes into the film, Tatiana (on vacation in Cuba) in conversation with Mauricio offers a parody of the political discourse that viewers may suppose Mauricio uses. This happens after it is revealed that Tatiana is pregnant. Halfway between the two segments, obliged as a father to face the surprise pregnancy, Mauricio talks with his daughter as the two of them watch a volleyball match. When

Tatiana extols the qualities of her partner, Mauricio, says, "It seems to me that I'm not going to be needed any more." This is an important statement that the film returns to and questions at various levels; at its end, the story refers back to this basic issue that questions the meaning of life. Because this matter is just as fundamental for the younger generation, Tatiana's parody of her father's ideologizing discourse deserves special attention:

> –Ah, Dad, so I don't have any problems? I'm young, healthy, I have a wonderful companion, we both studied what we wanted to and our future is secure. That's how it is, right? Sure, the country where we studied has been turned upside down, but…one has to be optimistic. In the end, the way the story winds up is in our hands, and everything will work itself out, here and there, in our favor.

In Tatiana's mocking and her employment of common phrases of communist rhetoric, irony simultaneously articulates the erosion of ideology and exemplifies an essence of the deep bond with her father's ideals that endures.

This bond opens up the possibility of communication between opposites (irony foreshadows the rupture) and even the rebuilding of everything in a new dimension. As a result, on his way to pick up the package and the letters that Tatiana has sent, Mauricio uses the word *rebuild* to assess his relationship with the daughter who chose another way of life and another ideological affiliation: "My relationship with Tatiana has been rebuilt with the help of time and circumstances. In the letters I have started in reply, I found a new way of understanding," the voice off screen tells us. Continuity, rupture, and rebuilding comprise the specter that floats above the meeting between father and daughter in Mexico, which is in turn a symbolic contact between opposites and a judgment on human destinies in the face of the Revolution.

The heart of their conflict is their incompatible ideas of happiness—for Tatiana, happiness is that which connects her to her family; for Mauricio, it is the task of transforming the society in which he lives. Both characters believe themselves to be happy, although they do have irritations (which they call "rocks in their shoes"). Tatiana's irritants point to a minor rebelliousness that is based on four points: understanding what "the world suffers" and not being indifferent to it; not being so blinded by "anything or anyone" that she would alter her personal life; putting her daughter and her husband first in her sphere of interests; and not being "as complacent as most people usually are over there"—an attitude that she attributes to her father's influence. Mauricio's complaints are the complaints of a political actor (not just a citizen, but a replicator of ideology) about the mistakes and failures that occur in the process of social transformation. He is someone for whom self-realization is found in his efforts to transform not only the nation, but the entire world, despite the surrenders, risks, and failures it entails (hence the happiness he finds in "being consistent"—being true to himself).

The degree of sacrifice that Mauricio and Tatiana are willing to make defines the boundary that separates the liberal from the revolutionary. After this bitter debate on the meaning of the Revolution and its fate, the film's greatest revelation (another lesson that Mauricio must learn) occurs at the end, when Mauricio appears with Lucía, his stepdaughter. Lucía's political opinions are not revealed, and on more than one occasion she is shown considering Mauricio's declarations with reserve or skepticism. Yet she has her own truth. When her own father leaves the country illegally, she stays in Cuba without offering any political explanation. When Mauricio tries to demonstrate concern for Lucía at this critical moment for her, he does it more on behalf of Mirta (his deceased wife and Lucía's mother) than for his stepdaughter. In fact, when Lucía is leaving to go say goodbye to her father and Mauricio approaches to kiss her on the forehead, she steps back, avoiding him. In contrast, in the surprising final scene, it is Lucía who twice seeks contact with Mauricio—first touching him on the arm and then squeezing his hand (the camera dwells on this last detail in a close-up).

Mauricio's Diary can be seen as a counterpoint to or rereading of Tomás Gutiérrez Alea's *Memorias del subdesarrollo* (*Memories of Underdevelopment*, 1968), given that both films deal with political judgments and positions toward the Revolution of intellectuals who produce ideology. At the same time, it is important to remember that *Mauricio's Diary*'s producer, Manuel Pérez Paredes, directed one of the most important films to define the socialist hero: *El hombre de Maisinicú* (*The Man from Maisinicú*, 1973). *Mauricio's Diary* combines the critical distance of *Memorias* with *El hombre*'s theme of sacrifice for an idea. In the film's final scene Mauricio and Lucía confess to feeling alone; they are castaways, but the camera's eye reveals the new solidarity that they have discovered. In light of their handholding and the fact that Lucía is pregnant, it is clear that Mauricio's dreams will continue—albeit in another way—as he tries to find his place in the new world order.

BIBLIOGRAPHY

Armas Fonseca, Paquita. "Páginas del diario de Mauricio: La vida no sigue igual." *La Jiribilla* 5 (29 July–4 August 2006). Available from http://www.lajiribilla.cu.

Del Río, Joel. "Páginas privadas, recuerdos compartidos." *La Jiribilla* 4 (18–24 June 2005). Available from http://www.lajiribilla.cubaweb.cu.

Del Río, Joel. "Diario polémico y a ratos impactante." *La Jiribilla* 5 (29 July–4 August 2006). Available from http://www.lajiribilla.cu.

Del Río, Joel. "Diáfano y confidencial retrato." *Portal del Cine y el Audiovisual Latinoamericano y Caribeño* (2010). Available from http://www.cinelatinoamericano.org.

Lanza, Jorge L. "Páginas del diario de Mauricio: una mirada al discurso de la nostalgia." *Calle B: Revista Cultural de Cumanayagua* (2009). Available from http://www.calleb.cult.cu.

López Saavedra, Lisbet. "Más rollo que película? El cine hoy en Cuba: su mirada a la emigración, las mujeres y los hombres." *Revista de Psicología y Humanidades.* (April 2010). Available from http://www.eepsys.com.

"Manolo Pérez habla sobre Páginas del diario de Mauricio." *Portal del Cine y el Audiovisual Latinoamericano y Caribeño.* Available from http://www.cinelatinoamericano.cult.cu.

Resik Aguirre, Magda. "La película asume el punto de vista de alguien que vive en Cuba comprometido con esta realidad. (Entrevista con Manuel Pérez, director de la película cubana Páginas del diario de Mauricio)." Interview with Manuel Perez. *La Jiribilla* (1 August 2006). Available from http://www.rebelion.org.

Reyes, Dean Luis. "Páginas del diario de Mauricio: Memorias blandas." Available from http://www.eictv.co.cu.

MEMORIES OF UNDERDEVELOPMENT (TOMÁS GUTIÉRREZ ALEA)

Paul A. Schroeder Rodríguez

A landmark film on the role of the intellectual in a revolutionary context.

Tomás Gutiérrez Alea (also known as Titón, 1928–1996) is Cuba's best-known film director and its most sophisticated theoretician. Of the dozen feature films he directed, three stand out: *Memorias del subdesarrollo* (best known by its English translation in the United States, *Memories of Underdevelopment*, 1968), *La última cena* (*The Last Supper*, 1976), and *Fresa y chocolate* (*Strawberry and Chocolate*, 1993). Because each of these films is representative of a distinct period in postrevolutionary Cuba—*Memories of Underdevelopment* corresponds to the period of triumph and affirmation of the Revolution in the 1960s, *La última cena* to the period of consolidation and institutionalization in the 1970s, and *Fresa y chocolate* to the period of economic crisis after the fall of the Berlin Wall—and because they steer clear of the double traps of revolutionary propaganda and reactionary vituperation, studying them in context helps to develop an appreciation of the political and aesthetic complexity that has characterized Cuban cultural production in general, and filmmaking in particular, since the 1960s.

DESCRIPTION OF THE FILM

In *Memories of Underdevelopment*, a film that critics consistently rank among the best Latin American films of all time, Gutiérrez Alea successfully synthesized the comic with the tragic and incorporated the formal lessons of Jean-Luc Godard, the narrative expressiveness of Sergei Eisenstein, the intellectualism of Bertolt Brecht, and the political commitment of Cinema Novo, to create a masterpiece that is not derivative, but highly original and contentious. The film, loosely adapted from Edmundo Desnoes's homonymous novel, takes place in Havana between two defining moments in post-revolutionary Cuban history: the Bay of Pigs invasion in 1961 and the Cuban Missile Crisis in 1962. Sergio (Sergio Corrieri) is an aspiring intellectual from the merchant middle class. When his wife and parents leave for the United States, he sees their departure as an opportunity to become the writer he always wanted to be. However, instead of committing himself to this task, he spends his days reflecting upon his past life and looking for love. In the end, Sergio's failure to communicate with the women he courts parallels his failure to integrate into the rapidly transforming society around him.

This synopsis, while accurate, misses the point that the main protagonist of the film is not Sergio but the viewer, who must make sense of the film's disparate and oftentimes contradictory representations of Sergio and those around him. For example, the film demystifies bourgeois individualism through a lucid character who embodies much of what is positive about bourgeois life (high level of education, cosmopolitanism, lots of free time, disposable income, and a capacity for critical thought) but also much of what is negative about it (objectification of women, compulsory heterosexuality, racism, classism, and lack of solidarity with one's fellow humans). Critics who read the film as either revolutionary or counterrevolutionary therefore ignore the structuring paradoxes that make this film an enduring classic of Cuban and world cinemas.

AESTHETICS

Memories of Underdevelopment is a collage of film material broadly divided into fiction and documentary, and each of these modes is in turn an amalgam of audiovisual styles. The most important antecedents of the film's documentary mode can be found in the newsreel production of the Instituto Cubano de Arte e Industria Cinematográficos (ICAIC, Cuban Institute of Cinema Art and Industry) and, more specifically, in the documentaries of Santiago Álvarez (1919–1998), with their signature montage of clashing images and sounds. Virtually all kinds of documents are used in *Memories of Underdevelopment*: hidden camera footage, photoessays, newsreels, television reports, radio broadcasts, newspaper clippings, and even a sociological treatise. For the fictional segments, the film draws from European sources, the more obvious ones being contemporary Italian cinema and the French New Wave.

But Gutiérrez Alea's masterful appropriation of European auteur practices should not be read as evidence of Eurocentrism on his part. Rather, his use of auteur techniques was a means to hook a specific audience—Latin American intellectuals—and not an end in itself. Thus, from the French New Wave, *Memories of Underdevelopment* appropriates Alain Resnais's continuous shifting between objective and subjective modes of narration and Godard's formal experimentation with montage and the handheld camera. From Italian contemporary cinema, on the other hand, Gutiérrez Alea appropriates Antonioni's concern with the brooding intellectual and Fellini's sympathetic portrayal of middle-aged men looking for love in all the wrong places.

Indeed, Sergio bears a striking resemblance in terms of taste, outlook, luck, and even looks to Marcello Mastroianni in *La dolce vita* (1960) and *8 1/2* (1963): a good-looking, intelligent, and cultivated man with money, time, and wit to spare. This characterization may not have been accidental, as *La dolce vita* was at the center of a 1963 debate between Alfredo Guevara, ICAIC's founding director, and Blas Roca, an orthodox Marxist politician who, in trying to impose socialist realism on Cuban artists, had criticized *La dolce vita* as an example of decadent art. In this light, *Memories of Underdevelopment* can be read as part of Gutiérrez Alea's career-long criticism of the bureaucratization of art and the revolutionary process, examples of which include his earlier *La muerte de un burócrata* (*Death of a Bureaucrat*, 1966), and his last two films, codirected with Juan Carlos Tabío: *Fresa y chocolate* and *Guantanamera* (1995).

STRUCTURE

The documentary and fictional elements in *Memories of Underdevelopment* are edited using what Eisenstein called intellectual montage, whereby the juxtaposition of shots or sequences that are dialectically opposed creates a new abstract idea, for example alienation or solidarity. The abundance of such juxtapositions also makes *Memories of Underdevelopment* a collage, which is precisely the word Gutiérrez Alea used to describe it during a cameo appearance as himself in the offices of ICAIC. The main drawback of structuring the film as a collage is that collages are taken in all at once, whereas films must be seen in time. Indeed, it is impossible to step back from a film as one would step back from a collage.

Take, for example, the way in which Noemí (Eslinda Núñez) was incorporated into the narrative. Like Elena (Daisy Granados), Noemí gets her own subtitle, but unlike Elena's narrative, which is Aristotelian and, therefore, easy to follow, Noemí's narrative is presented out of sequence and glued together only by Sergio's own fragmented imagination. Therefore, the viewer's ability to incorporate Noemí's dispersed and disconnected appearances into the film's overall narrative will be limited by his or her ability to make the necessary connections not only between relevant

and easily identifiable fragments that are close in time (easily done as the film is projected on the screen), but also between relevant fragments that are not so easily identifiable or are far apart in time (not so easily done). For example, in the opening sequence, Sergio is with Noemí at a nighttime revelry, but not shown on screen. We only find out she was with Sergio when the scene is revisited in sequence twenty-two, at which point the viewer may or may not make the connection with the opening sequence. In *Memories of Underdevelopment*, making such connections is made all the more challenging by the fact that nearly all the fictional sequences, including some of Sergio's most subjective ruminations, incorporate techniques associated with documentaries, such as the use of photographs as historical evidence, radio and television broadcasts, and hidden cameras.

THE ART AND POLITICS OF HETERODOXY

By centering its narrative on a politically underdeveloped and far from exemplary character, and by mixing fiction and documentary in ways that erase the boundaries between them, *Memories of Underdevelopment* in effect stakes an important heterodox position with respect to the Revolution's political and artistic orthodoxy, which claimed that a documentary mode of representation is intrinsically more authentic and revolutionary than a fictional mode of representation, and which called on artists to follow the precepts of socialist realism, chief among them the representation of exemplary heroes and the use of inspirational endings.

Gutiérrez Alea theorized his brand of heterodoxy in *The Viewer's Dialectic*, a collection of six essays on cinema published in 1982. The book is part film history, part film theory, and part manifesto. It includes a brief history of cinema, a discussion of what kinds of viewers have emerged from that history, a plan for how to change things, and a case study of *Memories of*

Sergio Corrieri in *Memorias del subdesarollo.* Tomás Gutiérrez Alea's 1968 film *Memorias del subdesarollo (Memories of Underdevelopment)*, starring Sergio Corrieri as an aspiring intellectual from the merchant middle class, tackles the question of how the Revolution fared in its attempt to replace bourgeois patterns of thought with socialist values. CINEGATE LTD./ NEWSCOM

Underdevelopment as a model to follow, insofar as it promotes the development of viewers' ability to think critically and for themselves by examining events from different points of views. In the film, the events thus examined are four:

1. the popular dance with Noemí (in sequences one and twenty two);
2. the farewell at the airport (in sequence two);
3. Sergio's tape-recorded argument with his wife (in sequences three and eleven); and
4. the hidden camera shots of people in the streets (in sequences four and thirty).

In each of these *double repetitions*, as Gutiérrez Alea called them, the first point of view is that of Sergio and thus helps the viewer identify with him. The second point of view is that of someone else and is shot in such a way as to help the viewer break off his or her previous identification with Sergio's point of view. At the airport, for example, the viewer is made to identify with Sergio as he bids farewell to his wife and his mother, but when the same farewell is repeated from his wife's point of view, the viewer's identification with Sergio is severed because of his visible aloofness and detachment. Ultimately, the objective of these double repetitions is to generate a critical viewing practice that will carry over to one's life outside the theater, so that viewers also take a critical attitude toward their own actions and attitudes.

More broadly, the juxtaposition of documentary and fictional parts also helps to generate a critical viewing practice by setting up a dialectic between the fictional mode's predominantly individual perspectives and the documentary mode's predominantly collective perspective. By constantly and insistently alternating these two perspectives of the Cuban Revolution, the film proposes that the truth of the Revolution is not to be found in either of these perspectives by themselves, but rather in their confrontation, and in what this confrontation suggests in a context of continuing struggles to advance a symbiotic relationship between the needs of the individual and the needs of the collective.

MEMORIES OF UNDERDEVELOPMENT AS A FILM OF THE REVOLUTION

Memories of Underdevelopment tackles the very real and timely question of how the Revolution has fared in its attempt to replace bourgeois patterns of thought and action with socialist values. In doing so, it steers clear of simplistic representations of the new order and at the same time avoids the categorical dismissal of the old. Instead, it sets in motion a dialectic between individual and collective perspectives and leaves it up to the viewer to work out possible solutions that include both personal growth and social commitment. Most of the main characters in Gutiérrez Alea's films struggle with this balancing act. In Sergio, the viewer faces

a character that has the chance to discard his old bourgeois self, with its emphasis on the individual at the expense of the collective, but fails to do so precisely because he lacks consistency—a fault he criticizes in others. However, as he goes about missing the chance to remake himself, Sergio makes some very sharp observations about the contradictions in contemporary Cuban society, and this ability to think critically is what the viewer can rescue from an otherwise disdainful character.

BIBLIOGRAPHY

Chanan, Michael, ed. *Memories of Underdevelopment, Tomás Gutiérrez Alea, Director, and Inconsolable Memories, Edmundo Desnoes, Author*. New Brunswick, NJ: Rutgers University Press, 1990.

Guevara, Alfredo. *Revolución es lucidez*. Edited by Camilo Pérez Casal. Havana: Ediciones ICAIC, 1998.

Gutiérrez Alea, Tomás. *Dialéctica del espectador*. Havana: Unión de Escritores y Artistas de Cuba, 1982.

Gutiérrez Alea, Tomás. *The Viewer's Dialectic*. Translated by Julia Lesage. Havana: José Martí Publishing House, 1988.

Gutiérrez Alea, Tomás. *Volver sobre mis pasos. Una selección epistolar de Mirtha Ibarra*. Havana: Unión de Escritores y Artistas de Cuba, 2008.

Oroz, Silvia. *Tomás Gutiérrez Alea: Los filmes que no filmé*. Havana: Unión de Escritores y Artistas de Cuba, 1989.

Schroeder, Paul A. *Tomás Gutiérrez Alea: The Dialectics of a Filmmaker*. New York: Routledge, 2002.

MIAMI

Patricia Price

Cultural landscapes of the largest urban concentration of diasporic Cubans in the United States.

A principal theme of the Cuban exile narrative holds that, over the last half century, Cubans have transformed Miami from a sleepy Anglo-American resort town to a bustling global metropolis. Whether or not Miami is a truly global city, it is undoubtedly the demographic and affective center of the Cuban diasporic population in the United States. Miami's nicknames—Havana North, the Capital of the Americas, and Little Cuba, to name just a few—indicate a relationship of close and reciprocal exchange between Miami and Cuba. This exchange has shaped the layout and use of urban spaces in Miami in distinct ways.

Urban cultural landscapes—comprising physical elements such as streets, sidewalks, commercial and residential constructions, parks, landmarks, monuments, and plazas, understood alongside the ways that urban residents use these elements—tell stories about cities and those who live in them. In this, Miami is

■ *See also*

Diasporas: Immigrant Exile Politics

Diasporas: Waves of Immigration since 1959

Education: Cuban Schools in Miami

Gloria and Emilio Estefan: Latin Music's Power Couple

Peruvian Embassy Crisis and the Mariel Boatlift: 1980

Radio: Cuban Radio in South Florida

La Virgen de la Caridad del Cobre

The World and Cuba: U.S. Culture in Cuba

no different than any other city. Yet the important demographic as well as economic, political, and cultural presence of Cuban exiles has oriented Miami's landscapes toward the Caribbean, and to a lesser extent South America and across the Atlantic to Europe, rather than gesturing inland to other U.S. cities. Miami is "a settlement of considerable interest, not exactly an American city as American cities have until recently been understood but a tropical capital: long on rumor, short on memory…referring not to New York or Boston or Los Angeles or Atlanta but to Caracas and Mexico, to Havana and to Bogotá and to Paris and Madrid" (Didion pp. 13–14).

DEMOGRAPHIC PROFILE

The metro area commonly referred to as Miami is in fact a patchwork of incorporated municipalities set within a matrix of unincorporated Miami-Dade County. Thus population count for the Miami urbanized area (a U.S. census designation), as opposed to the City of Miami proper, provides the most accurate estimate of the city's true size. With just over 5.2 million residents in 2008, the Miami urbanized area consistently ranks in the top ten largest metropolitan statistical areas in the United States.

The 2000 census found that slightly more (50.9%) of Miami's residents are foreign-born than native-born, making Miami—according to some accounts, including the United Nations—the city with the highest foreign-born population in the world. Thanks in part to immigrants, Miami is a "minority-majority" city, in which non-Hispanic whites constitute a minority population. At 82 percent in 2008, Miami-Dade County has the highest minority (almost entirely Hispanic and African American) population of the twenty-five most populous counties nationwide. The largest share—62 percent of Miami-Dade's overall population—identify as Latino or Hispanic, and within this group, a slight majority (54% in 2008) identify as Cuban or Cuban American. Miami's Cuban Americans hold power in the highest positions in local (and in some cases, state and national) government, business, media, and education, in marked contrast to other large U.S. cities with sizable Latino populations.

EXILE LANDSCAPES OF MIAMI

Although much has been written by cultural geographers and others about immigrant landscapes, next to no empirically grounded scholarship exists about specifically exile landscapes, despite the worldwide increase in people who consider themselves exiles, refugees, or otherwise displaced persons. Exiles are typically also international migrants: They have voluntarily or involuntarily left their home countries due to a fear of persecution, usually because of their political or religious beliefs or ethnicity. It is important to note that not all Cubans in Miami consider themselves to be political exiles; however, it is the first wave of Cuban émigrés who arrived in Miami from 1959 to 1980— the group that Susan Eckstein calls "the self-defined

exiles"—that has most shaped the cultural, economic, and political landscapes of Miami.

Thus, exile landscapes cannot be understood on the same terms as immigrant landscapes. At the heart of the exile experience is the loss of home and the desire to eventually return to one's home place. This loss is experienced at a variety of spatial scales, from the loss of one's literal house, to exclusion from participation in the routines of daily life in one's immediate neighborhood or village, to the exit outside the borders of one's country. Loss is also experienced temporally. The exile's experience abroad is, at least in theory, temporary, as the exile expects to return home at some point. This is fundamentally different from the condition of the immigrant, who—again, at least in theory—settles in a new land with the expectation of permanence. Recent theoretical understandings of human mobility, along with the contemporary ease of travel and communication across political boundaries, question the permanence, directionality, and totality of immigrant incorporation into host societies.

Cultural geographers understand landscapes to be ordered assemblages of elements of the built and natural world that can be scrutinized for clues to the kinds of societies that inhabited them. Landscapes, like other human constructs, prioritize some voices and visions over others. Typically, minority or oppressed populations have little visible presence in the landscape, though they may use the landscape itself to contest and perhaps overturn their subordinate status. Cultural geographers of a humanistic bent particularly emphasize the importance of home in their understanding of landscape. According to Timothy S. Oakes and Patricia L. Price, "home invokes attachment, affection, and an existential assessment of human's place on Earth, literally and figuratively speaking. Thus nostalgic landscapes can exist in dreams and memories…. Ultimately, landscapes allow humans to dwell in the world" (p. 150).

Given the primary exile theme of return home and the human imperative to belong through dwelling, it is not surprising that Cuban exiles strove to replicate in Miami the social, political, cultural, and economic worlds that existed in Cuba prior to 1959. Of course, given the selective socioeconomic character of the first waves of Cuban émigrés to Miami, only some institutions were replicated. In addition, it is not possible to transfer every last detail of a social structure intact to a new setting. Thus the landscapes crafted in Miami only selectively and partially replicated pre-1959 Cuban landscapes. Finally, return to Cuba for many remains but a dream, suffusing the landscapes of exile with a keen sense of yearning, loss, and nostalgia. While, as Ruth Behar and Lucía M. Suárez (p. 169) remark, "now and then we try to forget about geography," the fact is exiled Cubans in Miami are driven by "the desire to recover the homeland" (Grenier and Peréz, p. 88).

Residential Landscapes Although individuals of Cuban ancestry or who were born in Cuba can be found in large numbers throughout Miami's neighborhoods, Little Havana is without a doubt the symbolic ground zero of Cuban exile settlement in Miami. Like many other residential areas in Miami, Little Havana is not a formally designated neighborhood. Rather, it is a vernacular neighborhood whose exact borders exist mostly in the minds of Miamians rather than on a map of the city. Its fuzzy boundaries notwithstanding, Little Havana is roughly located west of the Miami River and downtown, south of Overtown, east of Coral Gables, and north of Coconut Grove, The Roads, and Brickell. Once a largely Jewish neighborhood called Riverside, the area became a magnet for Cuban arrivals from the early days of the exodus from the island. As with ethnic enclave neighborhoods in immigrant gateway cities throughout the United States, Little Havana served as a gateway neighborhood in a gateway city: New arrivals from Cuba encountered people from their former hometowns and provinces, they were able to use Spanish for transactions outside the home, and they could rely on their fellow countrymen and -women to assist them as they adapted to life in the United States, particularly with respect to locating employment and housing.

Though many of the early Cuban arrivals eventually moved away from Little Havana as they moved up the socioeconomic ladder, their children began to return to the old neighborhood. This occurred because they were nostalgic for the barrio of their parents and *abuelos* (grandparents) and because real estate in this close-to-downtown location became increasingly attractive from the mid-1990s as housing prices rose and traffic congestion increased throughout the greater Miami area. YUCAS (young upwardly mobile Cuban Americans) were the principal movers and shakers of the gentrification of Miami neighborhoods until about 2008, when residential real estate throughout the city tumbled in value and new construction as well as upscale renovation of existing housing stock came to an abrupt halt.

Cubans can also be found in high concentrations in the Miami neighborhoods of Hialeah, Westchester, Coral Gables, and throughout areas of unincorporated Miami-Dade County, particularly along the Southwest Eighth Street (Calle Ocho) corridor and in western portions of the county.

Commercial Landscapes Cuban exiles have left a distinctive mark on the nonresidential landscape of Miami. Some of them relocated their pre-Revolutionary Cuban businesses to landmark Miami commercial establishments. Other Cuban exiles initiated Miami-born commercial undertakings and enterprises catering to the national and international tourist trade focused on Cuban landscapes of Miami.

Urban ethnic landscapes typically highlight eating establishments and grocery stores, and here Cuban exiles are no exception. La Carreta restaurant, whose

Political expression in Miami. Miami's public spaces provide ready venues for Cubans to voice discontent over events or policies on the island. This Lincoln-Martí building in Little Havana, for example, displays large signs demanding freedom for Cuba in both English and Spanish. COURTESY OF PATRICIA PRICE

main location is on Southwest Eighth Street, was established in 1985. In 2010, it had eight branches located throughout south Florida, including one inside the Miami International Airport. Locals and visitors savor staples of Cuban-style cooking such as *rabo encendido* (oxtail stew), *lechón asado* (roast pork), and *ropa vieja* (shredded beef—literally, old clothes), accompanied by favorite Caribbean starchy sides such as *plátano maduro* (plantains), black beans and rice, and yucca.

Another landmark restaurant, Versailles, is situated just across the street and to the east of La Carreta on Southwest Eighth Street. Founded in 1971, Versailles is noted for its Cuban soul food as well as its impressive dessert selections. The ornate décor and mirrored walls create a panorama of reflected Old World finery meant to evoke the namesake French palace. The walk-up coffee window is crowded with patrons milling around at all hours of the day and night; many of them are Cuban exiles who come to talk politics and old times on the island.

To say that Miami has Cuban-oriented grocery stores, or bodegas, would be an understatement. In fact, most of the smaller grocery stores in Miami are Cuban-owned and patronized, and the items for sale are oriented to Cuban cuisine. Anglos, African Americans, and other Latinos patronizing local stores such as Presidente, La Roca, and Sedano's have to adapt to the superabundance of Cuban staples such as garlic in every form imaginable and the concomitant lack of food items not typically used by Cuban cooks, for example, American-style baking supplies.

Particularly along Calle Ocho, Cuban-themed memorabilia shops cater mostly to tourists who are bussed into Little Havana on a leg of their Miami tour. Cigar shops serve both locals and tourists, though genuine Cuban cigars are not readily available in the United States due to the U.S. trade embargo with Cuba.

Landscapes of Faith and Learning A key dimension of the Cuban exile community's conservatism is its Roman Catholic faith. Yard shrines and altars to La Virgen de la Caridad del Cobre, the patroness of Cuba and protector of sailors, are common landscape elements of Cuban-owned homes.

La Ermita de la Caridad (the Shrine to the Virgin of Charity) is located near downtown Miami. Known as "the sacred center of the Cuban Catholic community in exile" (Tweed, p. 3), its spatiality is particularly significant. The shrine houses a replica of the image of La Virgen de la Caridad, smuggled out of communist Cuba in a suitcase in 1961 (the original image is housed in a basilica outside the Cuban town of Santiago). Cuban national symbols (flags, murals, busts) abound inside the shrine and on the grounds. The shrine is located close to the shore, and the image itself is positioned so that the viewing faithful are aligned directly with Cuba, creating an affective proximity between exile worshipper and Cuban homeland.

The six-sided structure of the temple suggests both the dwellings of the indigenous Taínos and the six provinces of prerevolutionary Cuba. The cornerstone under the altar contains soil from each of these six Cuban provinces.

The Lincoln-Martí schools located throughout Cuban neighborhoods in Miami provide private K–12 education to exiles and their children and grandchildren. Founded by a Cuban exile in 1968, these schools use the Lincoln-Marti curriculum, which includes a "Cara a Cuba" history module that focuses on the glorious days on the island before Castro, and the school openly advocates freedom for Cuba. The name itself is an amalgam of U.S. president Abraham Lincoln and Cuban national hero José Martí.

Streets, Plazas, and Parks Miami's thoroughfares and public spaces provide ready venues for exile Cubans to demonstrate support for exile-specific causes and voice discontent over events or policies on the island and the mainland. In March 2010 exile celebrities Gloria and Emilio Estefan led tens of thousands of Cuban exiles in a solidarity march through the heart of Little Havana to protest the mistreatment of the Damas de blanco (Ladies in White), a group of wives and other women relatives of jailed dissidents who staged peaceful antigovernment marches in Havana.

Calle Ocho is home to what has been called the world's biggest block party. Hosted by the Kiwanis Club of Little Havana, the Calle Ocho Festival is the climax of the Carnaval Miami events. Though the Kiwanis Club of Little Havana is a primarily Cuban-led organization, the festival is pan-Latino in spirit. Over one million people from across the United States and other countries attend the festival, packing into just over twenty blocks of Calle Ocho that have been cordoned off to vehicle traffic for the event. Revelers enjoy music, food, and knickknacks from across the Americas.

As the Little Havana businesses and residences around Calle Ocho flirt with urban revitalization, artists' studios and galleries are the vanguard of gentrification. On the last Friday of every month arts patrons can hop from gallery to gallery, hear public music performances, and sample the fare of local restaurants during Little Havana's Viernes Culturales. Though Viernes Culturales is not a primarily Cuban event, many of the artists featured are Cuban, as are local establishment owners.

Little Havana abounds with memorials, plaques, parks, and public spaces dedicated to Cuban exiles and their causes. La Plaza de la Cubanidad, located at West Flagler Street and Northwest Seventeenth Avenue, pays tribute to the Cubans who drowned in attempts to escape the island in 1994. At Cuban Memorial Boulevard and Plaza (Southwest Eighth Street and Thirteenth Avenue) there are displayed a Bay of Pigs plaque, a Cuban flag, busts of José Martí and Antonio Maceo, a statue of the Virgin Mary, and a large map of Cuba mounted on a plaque. The Máximo Gómez Domino Park, located on Calle Ocho at Fifteenth Avenue, is a gathering place for mostly older male Cubans engaged in sometimes fierce domino games. Domino Park is a stop along the Miami tour bus route. Embedded in the sidewalk outside the park are stars bearing the names of Latino celebrities, echoing Hollywood with a Hispanic twist along Calle Ocho's own Walk of Fame.

Mausoleums and Museums Many Cuban exiles long to return to Cuba, but the difficult reality is that most will live out their lives in Miami and be buried there as well. Coupled with the keen sense of nostalgia and melancholy that suffuses the spirit of Cuban exiles, it is no surprise that cemeteries shape exile landscapes and discourse about Miami. José Quiroga writes, "in the symbolic grammar of Cuban discourse, Miami is a necropolis to a life that was always lived elsewhere" (p. 198). The most prominent resting place for Cuban exiles is Caballero Rivero Woodlawn Park Cemetery off Southwest Eighth Street between Southwest Thirty-second and Thirty-fourth Avenues. There lie the remains of former Cuban presidents Gerardo Machado y Morales (1871–1939) and Carlos Prío Socarrás (1903–1977), Cuban American National Foundation leader Jorge Mas Canosa (1939–1997), and a host of other notable Latinos and Miami Anglos. The cemetery also has a monument to the Unknown Cuban Freedom Fighter in the Bay of Pigs.

Museums are akin to cemeteries inasmuch as they are places where history is arrested and memories are arranged to narrate a story. Thus it is no surprise that Miami is home to several Cuban exile-themed museums. Notable among these is the Cuban Museum / Museo Cubano, dedicated to preserving and sharing Cuban culture as brought to Miami by the exiles. The house where Elián González (b. 1993) lived during his stay in Miami has been turned into a museum, Casa Elián. Maintained by Elián's great-uncle Delfín González, who lives in an apartment in the back of the house, the bungalow displays Elián's clothes and toys neatly arranged in his former bedroom and a plethora of images and memorabilia from the months in late 1999 through April 2000 when Elián lived in Miami. The so-called Freedom Tower, built in 1925 and initially serving as the *Miami News* headquarters, became a federal processing center ("Miami's Ellis Island") for newly arrived Cubans through the mid-1970s. The building's ownership changed hands several times over the years; its 2005 donation to Miami Dade College almost certainly saved it from being razed during Miami's condominium construction frenzy of the first decade of the twenty-first century. As of 2010, the Freedom Tower was a museum and gallery.

MIAMI AYER, HOY, Y MAÑANA

Exiled Cubans have made their mark on Miami, literally and affectively, and so Miami's cultural landscape reflects their past. This is true not only in the way that built environments always carry the past forward, thanks to the fixity of urban elements themselves, but also in the way that these elements were designed as references to prerevolutionary Cuba. The demographic transformation of Miami into a pan-Latino potpourri was well underway in the early twenty-first century. As of 2010, Cuban Americans struggled ever harder to maintain their position as half of the population, even in symbolically uncontested exile neighborhoods such as Little Havana, which was becoming increasingly Central and South American in flavor. As of 2010, however, the demographic transition outpaced the emotional one.

BIBLIOGRAPHY

Arreola, Daniel D., ed. *Hispanic Places, Latino Places: Community and Cultural Diversity in Contemporary America.* Austin: University of Texas Press, 2004.

Bardach, Ann Louise. *Cuba Confidential: Love and Vengeance in Miami and Havana.* New York: Random House, 2002.

Behar, Ruth, and Lucía M. Suárez, eds. *The Portable Island: Cubans at Home in the World.* New York: Palgrave Macmillan, 2008.

Curtis, James. "Miami's Little Havana: Yard Shrines, Cult Religion, and Landscapes." *Journal of Cultural Geography* 1, no. 1 (1980): 1–15.

Didion, Joan. *Miami.* New York: Simon & Schuster, 1987.

Eckstein, Susan E. *The Immigrant Divide: How Cuban Americans Changed the U.S. and Their Homeland.* New York: Routledge, 2009.

García, Maria Cristina. *Havana USA: Cuban Exiles and Cuban Americans in South Florida, 1959–1994.* Berkeley: University of California Press, 1996.

George, Paul S. *Images of America: Little Havana.* Charleston, SC: Arcadia, 2006.

Grenier, Guillermo, and Lisandro Pérez. *The Legacy of Exile: Cubans in the United States.* Boston: Allyn and Bacon, 2003.

Levine, Robert M., and Moisés Asís. *Cuban Miami.* New Brunswick, NJ: Rutgers University Press, 2000.

Oakes, Timothy S., and Patricia L. Price, eds. *The Cultural Geography Reader.* London: Routledge, 2008.

Pérez Firmat, Gustavo. *Next Year in Cuba: A Cubano's Coming-of-Age in America.* New York: Anchor Books, 1995.

Pérez Firmat, Gustavo. *Cincuenta lecciones de exilio y desexilio.* Miami: Ediciones Universal, 2000.

Portes, Alejandro, and Alex Stepick. *City on the Edge: The Transformation of Miami.* Berkeley: University of California Press, 1993.

Quiroga, José. *Cuban Palimpsests.* Minneapolis: University of Minnesota Press, 2005.

Rieff, David. *The Exile: Cuba in the Heart of Miami.* New York: Touchstone, 1993.

Tweed, Thomas. *Our Lady of the Exile: Diasporic Religion at a Cuban Catholic Shrine in Miami.* Oxford, U.K.: Oxford University Press, 1997.

MILK OF AMNESIA (CARMELITA TROPICANA/ALINA TROYANO)

Nohemy Solórzano-Thompson

A performance art piece by Carmelita Tropicana about Cuban American identity.

Carmelita Tropicana is the stage name of Alina Troyano (b. 1951), a Cuban American performance artist, playwright, and actress. Her performance art piece *Milk of Amnesia* (*Leche de amnesia*) premiered in fall 1994 at New York City's Performance Space 122 (P.S. 122). *Milk of Amnesia* is based partly on the artist's 1993 journey to Cuba. The play portrays the amnesiac main character, Carmelita Tropicana, searching for her Cuban American identity after losing her memory in an accident. She regains her memory during a trip to her native Cuba after reliving several traumatic experiences that are staged using exaggerated humor and camp. Carmelita Tropicana shares the stage with several other characters, including Pingalito Betancourt and the Writer, the most important supporting characters, and minor characters, including a horse that witnessed the conquest of Cuba and a pig that is about to be slaughtered and eaten. All of the characters are played by the same actress.

OTHER WORK

Born in Cuba, Troyano immigrated to the United States as a child in the early 1960s and grew up in New York City. Her performance art career under the stage name Carmelita Tropicana began in the early 1980s with appearances with the lesbian performance troupe WOW in the East Village. (Because most critics and audiences refer to the performance artist by her stage name, this entry also refers to her as Carmelita Tropicana.) To supplement her income, she worked as a building superintendent and was featured in Henry Gifford's New York City Boiler Tour in 2003. She performed nationally and internationally, earning positive reviews from audiences, critics, and academics. Her work received numerous awards, including an Obie for Sustained Excellence in Performance (1999), the Anonymous Was a Woman award (2005), a Cuban Arts Foundation Fellowship (2002), and three New York Foundation for the Arts awards (for play writing in 1991 and 2006; and for performance art in 1987).

Milk of Amnesia is Tropicana's only full-length solo performance and has earned her great critical and scholarly attention. Other works by Tropicana have been produced in collaboration with other artists, such as *Memorias de la Revolución/Memories of the Revolution* (1987–1988) with Uzi Parnes and *Single Wet Female* (2002–2005) with Marga Gómez. Tropicana cowrote with her half-sister, the video artist and director Ela Troyano, the award-winning short film *Carmelita Tropicana: Your Kunst Is Your Waffen* (1994).

Aside from her performance art work, Carmelita Tropicana also published critical essays about sexuality, identity, and performance, and participated in several award-winning anthologies. In 2000, Beacon Press published an anthology of her work, *I, Carmelita Tropicana, Performing between Cultures*. In the first decade of the 2000s, Tropicana regularly lectured on performance art, becoming one of the most influential contemporary performance artists.

Tropicana's work is related to that of other Latino artists such as Guillermo Gomez-Peña, Coco Fusco, and John Leguizamo. Tropicana and her peers chronicled the experience of U.S. Latinos in performances that utilized the aesthetics of U.S.-based performance art along with techniques borrowed from Latin American theater. Tropicana adapted these different techniques in order to create an innovative form of intercultural performance that the critic José Esteban Muñoz described as an artistic form that challenges dominant discourses by presenting its audience with alternative subjectivities that destabilize normative identities (Muñoz 1999).

MILK OF AMNESIA

Milk of Amnesia, like most of Tropicana's work, uses *choteo* and cross-dressing to present the audience with a transgressive Cuban American lesbian and feminist identity. *Choteo* is a form of Cuban camp that uses comedy to defuse potentially controversial subjects. In her work, Tropicana uses *choteo* and bilingual language jokes to introduce her lesbian identity. The performance makes repeated references to her libido and desire for women, but these are delivered with humor, using multiple puns that rely on knowledge of Spanish and English. Tropicana also uses *choteo* to talk about other sensitive topics such as economic problems in Cuba and the U.S. embargo.

Cross-dressing also allows Tropicana to question normative sexualities and gender roles by complicating the viewers' understanding of biological sex and desire. In *Milk of Amnesia* Tropicana effects all character changes in full view of the audience. The audience thus interprets these stage personae not as separate identities played by an actress, but rather as alter egos of the character Carmelita Tropicana. Yvonne Yarbro-Bejarano described these as "drag-on-drag metaperformances, in which the male roles are actually performed by Carmelita, not the actress that plays Carmelita" (p. 203). When the male, hyper-heterosexual Pingalito Betancourt emerges onstage, the audience sees him as Tropicana in drag and interprets his desire for women not as a heterosexual narrative, but as a humorous expression of lesbian desire. Similarly, the play introduces animal characters—a horse and a pig—to discuss political and economic problems in Cuba. Because the character Tropicana is not personally affected by either the historical genocide in the Caribbean during colonial times or the contemporary political problems of Cuba, she transforms into animals to embody their struggles. Using animals instead of human characters enriches the humor in the play and adds an additional artificial step to the drag-on-drag in order to question the construction of normative subjectivities.

Milk of Amnesia is one of the few Cuban American theater pieces that depicts a protagonist's trip to Cuba to reconnect with her heritage. The play overtly calls for reform and for solidarity between Cubans and Cuban Americans, especially with artists living on the island. Because the action takes place during the Special Period (1989–1999), a time of economic crisis in Cuba brought on by the collapse of the Soviet Union, Tropicana discusses Cuban economic difficulties, but she does not engage with Miami-based conservative politics arguing for the end of Fidel Castro's government. Tropicana carefully navigates several political camps throughout the performance to offer an alternative solution: solidarity between all peoples of Cuban descent and an end to the U.S. embargo on Cuba.

CRITICISM

Many scholars interpreted *Milk of Amnesia* as Tropicana's attempt to discuss the experience of the generation of Cuban Americans who immigrated to the United States as children. Gustavo Pérez-Firmat theorized that this generation is caught metaphorically living in the hyphen between their parents' Cuban immigrant identity and their own American experience. *Milk of Amnesia* humorously portrays this existential crisis and the need to reconcile two conflicting identities—Cuban and American—in order to heal the self.

Milk of Amnesia was staged between 1994 and 2007 in several national and international locations, including theaters in New York City and Boston; at cultural institutions, including the Institute of Contemporary Art in London, Centre de Cultura Contemporània de Barcelona, and the Hemispheric Institute of Performance and Politics in New York; and at prominent U.S. academic universities such as Yale, Duke, Brown, and Cornell.

Because of the nature of performance art, which is dependent on current events and audience reactions, variations exist from performance to performance. As with traditional forms of theater, the best way to experience performance art is to be part of its live audience. If that is not possible, the second way is to watch a taped performance, and the third way is to read the script. Unfortunately for scholars, there are few video copies of performances of *Milk of Amnesia* by Tropicana. Copies in VHS format are available from the libraries at Williams College and Stanford University (performance by Andrew Perret at P.S. 122 on 13 November 1994), Yale (performance from the 2007–2008 season), the Hemispheric Institute of Performance and Theater (2003), and the Museo del Barrio (excerpt of Pingalito Betancourt's monologue from 2008).

There are four published versions of the script of *Milk of Amnesia*. The first one, published in the scholarly journal *Drama Review* in 1995, is accompanied by an article on *Milk of Amnesia* by José Estebán Muñoz and an interview with Tropicana (Troyano) conducted by David Román. This version is the one that most closely resembles the taped performance from the premiere of *Milk of Amnesia*. The second version appeared in 1998 in the anthology edited by David Román and Holly Hughes, *O Solo Homo: The New Queer Performance*. The third is in the anthology *Latinas on Stage* (2000), edited by Alicia Arrizón and Lillian Manzor. The fourth version appears in *I, Carmelita Tropicana* (2000).

Although differences between the versions are slight, only the one in *The Drama Review* features Pingalito Betancourt's singing of "Burbujas de amor" at the end of his monologue. None of these published versions contain some of the last remarks by Tropicana before she sings Pedro Luis Ferrer's song about solidarity: In the taped performance from 1994, Tropicana first recalls all of the performance artists who have influenced her work, then jokingly discusses the relationship between the Writer character (who is boring and not adventurous) and her more fun-loving Tropicana persona, and then reads some idiomatic expressions in Spanish about Cuban ingenuity, which she translates for the audience.

BIBLIOGRAPHY

Cespedes, Karina Lissette. "Bomberas on Stage: Carmelita Tropicana Speaking in Tongues against History, Madness, Fate, and the State." In *Tortilleras: Hispanic and U. S. Latina Lesbian Expression*, edited by Lourdes Torres and Inmaculada Pertusa. Philadelphia: Temple University Press, 2003.

Garland, Leah. *Contemporary Latina/o Performing Arts of Moraga, Tropicana, Fusco, and Bustamante*. New York: Peter Lang, 2009.

Hall, Lynda. "Lorde, Anzalduá, and Tropicana Performatively Embody the Written." *Auto/Biography Studies* 15, no. 1 (Summer 2000): 96–122.

López-Craig, Tonya. "The Role of Carmelita Tropicana in the Performance Art of Alina Troyano." *Journal of Lesbian Studies* 7, no. 3 (2003): 47–56.

Muñoz, José Estebán. "No es fácil: Notes on the Negotiation of Cubanidad and Exilic Memory in Carmelita Tropicana's *Milk of Amnesia*." *Drama Review* 39, no. 3 (Autumn 1995): 76–82.

Muñoz, José Estebán. *Disidentifications: Queers of Color and the Performance of Politics*. Minneapolis: University of Minnesota Press, 1999.

Pérez-Firmat, Gustavo. *Life on the Hyphen: The Cuban-American Way*. Austin: University of Texas Press, 1994.

Román, David. "Carmelita Tropicana Unplugged." *Drama Review* 39, no. 3 (Autumn 1995): 83–93.

Solórzano-Thompson, Nohemy. "Performing Identity in Alina Troyano's *Milk of Amnesia*." *Confluencia* 12, no. 1 (Autumn 2003): 83–91.

Tropicana, Carmelita. "Milk of Amnesia / Leche de amnesia." *Drama Review* 39, no. 3 (Autumn 1995): 94–111.

Tropicana, Carmelita. "Milk of Amnesia / Leche de amnesia." In *O Solo Homo: The New Queer Performance*, edited by David Román and Holly Hughes. New York: Grove Press, 1998.

Tropicana, Carmelita. "Milk of Amnesia / Leche de amnesia." In *Latinas on Stage*, edited by Alicia Arrizón and Lillian Manzor. Berkeley, CA: Third Woman Press, 2000.

Troyano, Alina. *I, Carmelita Tropicana: Performing between Cultures*. Boston: Beacon Press, 2000.

Worthen, W. B. "Bordering Space." In *Land/Scape/Theater*, edited by Elinor Fuchs and Una Chaudhuri. Ann Arbor: University of Michigan Press, 2002.

Yarbro-Bejarano, Yvonne. "Traveling Transgressions: Cubanidad in Performances by Carmelita Tropicana and Marga Gómez." In *Reading and Writing the Ambiente: Queer Sexualities in Latino, Latin American, and Spanish Culture*, edited by Susana Chávez-Silverman and Librada Hernández. Madison: University of Wisconsin Press, 2000.

MISA CUBANA (CUBAN MASS, JOSÉ MARÍA VITIER)

Ana Victoria Casanova

A criollo mass dedicated to the Virgin patron saint of Cuba by a distinguished Cuban composer.

The *Misa cubana, a la Virgen de la Caridad de El Cobre* (Cuban Mass, for the Virgin of Charity of El Cobre), honoring the patron saint of Cuba, was created for soloists, mixed chorus, and orchestra by the composer José María Vitier (b. 1954). A particularly *criollo* style of composition is evidenced in the combination and synthesis of the traditions of the European musical form and the most autochthonous elements of Cuban music and culture to produce a contemporary expressive language.

MISA CUBANA

Comprising eleven parts, *Misa cubana* is structured in similar manner to the Ordinary of a mass, with certain additions but without abandoning the traditional form. Added to the Kyrie, Gloria, Sanctus, and Agnus Dei are the Hosanna and Salve Regina, all with their traditional liturgical texts in Latin, in accordance with Catholic masses. Three songs dedicated to the Virgin are also included, with lyrics taken from

poems by Cuban authors. These are "Déjame tomar asiento" (Let Me Take a Seat), based on a poem by Emilio Ballegas (1908–1954); "Misteriosa trasparencia" (Mysterious Transparency), taking the place of the customary Credo, with lyrics from the poet Silvia Rodríguez Rivero; and "Plegaria a la Virgen de El Cobre" (Prayer to the Virgin of El Cobre), also with lines from Rodríguez Rivero.

Many of the structural and stylistic characteristics of the mass as a musical form are found in this piece, from its epoch of grandeur up to its manifestations in the early 2000s. Vitier's mass contains elements of European classical music as well as Cuban concert music, popular music, and folkloric musical expressions linked to popular Afro-Cuban forms of religious worship. Aspects of these various types of music frequently appear at the same time in the different sections of the chorus and the orchestra. An example of this is found in Kyrie Eleison. Superimposed over a polyphonic-contrapuntal vocal dialogue between the soloist and the chorus there is, on the one hand, a concerto notion in the baroque style played by the orchestra and, on the other hand, the polytimbric and polyrhythmic discourse characteristic of the music of the popular religious celebrations of Cuban Santeria festivals, played by the percussion on *batá* drums.

Throughout the piece, tonalities and melodic ideas inspired by the baroque and classical styles merge, underscored by polyphonic and contrapuntal devices, yet transmitting a strong sense of Cubanness. The stamp of European classical music appears along with melodic inflections specific to Cuban song and the traditional interpretive style of these modalities that uses the arrangement of the first and second voices in the *dúos de trovadores* (troubadours duos). The piece also features expressive forms and rhythms characteristic of Cuban dance music such as the *contradanza*, the *danzón*, and the *son*, each with its particular *tumbaos* (collections of drum patterns), reinforced by some of the percussion instruments that traditionally accompany them.

In addition, *punto cubano*, the country music from the western and central provinces of Cuba, played in the *punto libre* style characteristic of western Cuba, plays a major role in *Sanctus*. In this section, the form of the musical language and the rhythms played on the *laúd cubano*—the chordophone typically used to interpret *punto*—join in the conversations between the orchestra and chorus at the same time that it builds on the modal shifts of the *campesino* tunes particular to this Cuban genre, with their strong Hispanic antecedents.

In the mass there is a noticeable use of instruments that originated in Cuba, including the *güiro*, the *claves*, the *cencerro*, the *tumbadora*, and the Afro-Cuban batá drums, each of which has an expressive language within the popular folkloric music of Cuba.

Misa cubana debuted in December 1996 in the Cathedral of Havana, conducted by the composer himself in a mass officiated by Cardinal Jaime Ortega.

José María Vitier (b. 1954). José María Vitier serves as conductor during a concert celebrating the birthday of Che Guevara in Havana on 13 June 2008. SVEN CREUTZMANN/GETTY IMAGES

Several of its sections were also performed in the mass offered by Pope John Paul II in the Plaza de la Revolución in Havana in January 1998 when the pope visited Cuba. Since its debut *Misa cubana* has been played on dozens of occasions in many countries, including the United States, Singapore, Israel, Spain, Italy, Denmark, England, Portugal, the Dominican Republic, Argentina, and Mexico.

JOSÉ MARÍA VITIER

A pianist and composer whose versatile and prolific work has made him one of the most distinguished contemporary composers in Cuba, José María Vitier Marruz grew up in a Havana family whose members were heavily involved in literature and the arts. His parents, the eminent poets and essayists Cintio Vitier (1921–2009) and Fina García Marruz (b. 1923), exposed him at an early age to a broad cultural panorama in which music, like literature, occupied a place of privilege.

Vitier studied piano with Margot Rojas and César López, and later studied composition with José Ardévol (1911–1981) at the Instituto Superior de Arte. Between 1983 and 1990 he led his own group, for which he composed many pieces. His goal during these years, as he defined it, was "an aesthetic project of popular concert music," nourished, according to his commentaries, "in equal measure by jazz, son, and rock from the U.S." (Martínez 1989, p. 16).

OTHER WORKS

Among his influences are, in addition to European classical music, international popular music (rock and Latin jazz), and Cuban music, including concert, popular, and folkloric. Particularly important Cuban forms are *contradanzas, danzas, danzones, trova cubana,* and the songs known as *habaneras.* His compositions are characterized by a mixture of different styles and by his abiding intention to insert the Cuban into the universal.

Vitier's catalog includes compositions for a range of instruments and performers, such as piano, piano and orchestra, soloists, orchestra and chorus, and other chamber and jazz ensembles. Many of the pieces he has written for piano are important in the contemporary Cuban repertoire, including *Danzón imaginario, Fuera del baile,* and *Danzón de fin de siglo.* These three were released on the album *Cuba dentro de un piano* (1999).

Also noteworthy is Vitier's use of texts written by himself or by Latin American or Spanish poets such as Sor Juana Inés de la Cruz (1648–1695), José Martí (1853–1895), Cintio Vitier, Rubén Darío (1867–1916), Pedro Calderón de la Barca (1600–1681), Juan Ramón Jiménez (1881–1958), and Federico García Lorca (1898–1936).

Incidental music, for dance and theater as well as for movies and television programs, is particularly important in his catalog. The soundtracks he has written include those for the films *El siglo de las luces* (The Century of Lights, 1992), *Un señor muy viejo con unas alas enormes* (A Very Old Man with Enormous Wings, 1986), *Fresa y chocolate* (Strawberry and Chocolate, 1993), *Un paraíso bajo las estrellas* (Paradise under the Stars, 1999), and *Lista de espera* (Waiting List, 2000). Particularly noteworthy are *Un señor muy viejo con unas alas enormes,* which included one of Vitier's most famous compositions; *Habanera de Ángel* (The Angel's Habanera); and *Fresa y chocolate,* which won the prize for music at the Film Festival of Asunción, Paraguay in 1994. With regard to composition for the movies, Vitier remarked:

> We should recognize … the best of Michel Legrand, John Williams, Ennio Morricone or Carmine Coppola. In Latin America we have our own movements or tendencies. As far as my work is concerned, a trace remains from every Argentine movie I see, for example, or the Brazilian movie *Ópera do Malandro* with music by Chico Buarque de Holanda, one of the most outstanding cases in point.
>
> *Reny Martínez p. 16*

In addition to *Misa cubana,* Vitier's significant works include the oratorio *Salmos de las Américas* (Psalms of the Americas, 1997), which utilizes a wide variety of texts, including prophecies from Isaiah in the Bible and Mayan prophecies collected in the *Chilam Balam,* along with quotations from Christopher Columbus's ship's log and writings by authors such as José Martí, Walt Whitman, and Pablo Neruda.

Two other important works for soloists, chorus, and orchestra had their premier in 2008: *El cantar del caballero y su destino* (The Knight's Song and His Destiny), dedicated to Che Guevara (1928–1967), with texts by Silvia Rodríguez Rivero; and the opera *Santa*

Anna, with a libretto by the Mexican novelist Carlos Fuentes, in which Vitier incorporates into the orchestra pre-Hispanic percussion instruments and *sones jarochos*, a type of music from the state of Veracruz, Mexico.

DISCOGRAPHY

Vitier, José María. *Antología de música para cine. José María Vitier* (1994).

Vitier, José María. *Misa cubana. A la Virgen de La Caridad de El Cobre* (1997).

Vitier, José María. *Cosas que dejé en La Habana* (1998).

Vitier, José María. *Salmo de las Américas. José María Vitier* (1999).

Vitier, José María, and Various Artists. *Cuba dentro de un piano* (1999).

Vitier, José María. *Melodías para el cine. José María Vitier* (2001).

BIBLIOGRAPHY

Martínez, Mayra A. *Cubanos en la música*. Havana: Editorial Letras Cubanas, 1993.

Martínez, Reny. "Un premio con alas enormes." *Revista Clave* 13 (April–June 1989): 15–16.

EL MONTE (LYDIA CABRERA)

Julia Cuervo Hewitt

Lydia Cabrera's most acclaimed book, generally referred to as the Afro-Cuban bible.

In 1954 Cuban writer Lydia Cabrera published a monumental book that was the product of many years of research on Afro-Cuban religions and lore: *El monte: Igbo-Finda, Ewe Orisha, Vititi Nfinda; Notas sobre las religiones, la magia, las supersticiones y el folklore de los negros criollos y el pueblo de Cuba* (Mount/Forest/Wilderness/Brush/ Countryside/Holy Place: Igbo-Finda, Ewe Orisha, Vititi Nfinda; Notes about the Religions, the Magic, the Superstitions and the Folklore of the Black Creoles and the People of Cuba). First published in Havana, the book was immediately praised by critics and acclaimed by Cuban writers as a seminal work on Cuban culture. It was viewed as a poetics of Cubanness, a work that explained the concept of *el monte* in the island's natural and cultural landscape and its association with Cuban society and traditions. Thanks to Cabrera's text, the notion of *el monte*, expressed for the first time in its interrelationship with Afro-Cuban beliefs, came to hold a special conceptual place in Cuban literature, as Gastón Baquero pointed out in his 10 August 1955 column "Panorama" in *Diario de la Marina*. He noted that while other American cultures worshipped the sun, in Cuba, as Cabrera's work reveals, the earth, nature, and respect for the natural surroundings are at the center of worship and of the popular lore and mythologies that formed Cuban creole culture.

A CULTURAL ICON

The concept of *el monte* in Cabrera's monumental book carved a space for African legacies in Cuba's cultural landscape and for the religious syncretism and transculturation that characterizes Cuban society. The term *el monte* in Cabrera's text refers to a complex combination of forest, brush land, wilderness, countryside, a backyard, an empty lot, a sacred space, and a holy mount where life forces coexist. It can also be any place where there is greenery, water, rocks, or metals, including a cast-iron pot full of metals (representing the orisha Oggún); water (for Yemayá and Ochún); weeds, roots, branches; or a gourd (for Osaín).

The concept of *el monte* also intersects national myths born out of the wars for independence in the nineteenth century. The term *monte* in its meaning *manigua* (thicket, brush, countryside) denotes a space of refuge for patriots during the nineteenth-century wars against Spanish colonial rule. By the twentieth century, *el monte* was charged with meanings of independence and resistance and became part of a poetics of national identity. It was with this meaning that José Martí (1853–1895), known as the Apostle of Cuban Independence, used the term *el monte* in his *Versos sencillos* (Simple Verses, 1891) to speak of a space of refuge from colonial domination. Cabrera adds religious meanings to the already significant term *el monte* in the testimonial voices of the people who forged the nation with their labor but were marginalized and negated in the national discourse. *El monte* is a text that for the first time rescues the voices of those Cuban creoles, descendants of African slaves, whose beliefs and practices survived centuries of slavery to become part of Cuba's vernacular culture.

THE CONSTRUCTION OF AN ARCHIVAL TEXT

By 1954, Cabrera had already published two collections of Afro-Cuban short stories based on her research into Afro-Cuban belief systems: *Cuentos negros de Cuba* (1936; 1940) and *¿Por qué? Cuentos negros de Cuba* (1948). *El monte* was the culmination of the time-consuming effort to document, compile, and edit religious anecdotes, practices, beliefs, rituals, remedies, myths, medicinal/spiritual cures, and, most importantly, the associations among the Cuban concept of *el monte*, the natural landscape, and Afro-Cuban cosmogony. In the introduction to *El monte*, Cabrera describes the painstaking work of uncovering facts and sorting out bits of information after long conversations with adepts and informants, some of whom tried to deceive her to prevent her from learning their

■ *See also*

Ecology and Environment: Colonial Period

Literature: Fiction in the Republican Period

Race: Slavery in Cuba

Spain's "Discovery" of Cuba: 1492

Valle de Viñales

secrets. *El monte* was the first publication in Cuba to reflect the many differences, modalities, and variations among Afro-Cuban belief systems as well as differences within the same Afro-Cuban traditions. It was the first work to explain popular misinterpretations about Afro-Cuban groups, and to explain the confusion that existed among white intellectuals in the first half of the twentieth century in Cuba about traditions, religions, and languages of African origin.

El monte was also the first study to offer a view from a religious and mythical perspective of the *ñáñigo*, or Abakuá secret society, an Afro-Cuban fraternity often wrongfully associated with criminality in Cuba. Due to the exotic images and popularity of this group, the *ñáñigo* had been the central figure of most of the literary and artistic productions of the Cuban *negrismo* movement and of Fernando Ortiz's ethnological research. In *El monte* Cabrera reveals some of the practices of the society and, through testimonial accounts, some Abakuá origin myths and rituals. The book also makes public the first photograph ever taken of a *nganga*, a secret object constructed by Congo (Bantu) sects that is believed to possess magical powers.

In this monumental archival work, Cabrera presents the information she has gathered so the differences between the major Afro-Cuban beliefs systems can be apprehended by the reader, as well as the difficulty of unraveling variations, contradictions, and syncretisms not only with European Catholicism, but also within Afro-Cuban belief systems. A summa of the different Afro-Cuban beliefs and lore on the island, *El monte* is a unique testimony to the survival of African memories, mythologies, and practices that came to form Cuba's popular culture. It is also a testimony to the survival in Cuba of African beliefs and traditions that are still practiced in Cuban society. As of the early 2000s, it is the most complete archive of Afro-Cuban myths, lore, and religious beliefs written in Cuba and of the many syncretic combinations that developed between African religions and between African and European religions and traditions.

ORGANIZATION AND CHAPTERS

Cabrera divided the text of *El monte* into twelve sections: an introduction, ten chapters divided by themes, and a dictionary of plants and their properties that makes up most of the second half of the book. The first chapter parallels the last chapter as Cabrera explains the concept of *el monte* as giver of life and the space where life-giving forces coexist, a concept shared by all Afro-Cuban belief systems. As one of her informants explained, "Everything can be found in the *monte*.... It gives us everything" (p. 13). *El monte* is the space, both earthly and divine, natural and supernatural, from which all life forces emanate and in which all forces coexist in a dynamic give-and-take in which humans also participate. It is a timeless space of life where all of the opposing principles of the cosmos converge. In the testimony of one of Cabrera's

informants, "We are children of the *monte* because life began there" (p. 13). All divinities reside there.

In the *monte*, opposite and complementary principles coexist, including the natural and the supernatural. Such coexistence is unrelated to opposition or dialectics, as it is in Western thought, but rather to sameness and simultaneity. In the *monte* (which can also be translated as *nature and life*) humans must choose between undifferentiated positive and negative paths. This choice is based on understanding and respect. In the *monte*, humans must seek to find a balance between multiple forces through proper rituals and offerings. Thus nothing is taken without giving something back. *El monte* explains in the voice of practitioners what should and should not be done, by way of numerous stories that exemplify different reasons for performing rituals.

Since *el monte* is a temporal space of simultaneity and coexisting opposite principles, it is also a space of negative forces, as Cabrera shows in the second chapter, "Bilongo." The knowledge of plants, their magic, and their mythical connections with natural and supernatural forces can provide cures but can also be used to perform a *daño*, or magic done against an individual. Proper offerings and rituals, however, can always restore balance and health. In the words of Cabrera's informant José Calazán, "Anywhere you see weeds, you will find a remedy" (p. 67). Each herb or plant, rock, or metal is associated with a life force. The force that presides over roads, doors, and destiny is Elegguá; over illnesses is Babalú Ayé, the great divine doctor; over all greenery is Osaín (for the Lucumí) or Nfinda (for followers of Congo beliefs).

The third chapter of *El monte*, "Oluwa Ewe," explains the importance of Osaín in Lucumí cosmography. This chapter is full of mythical anecdotes about Osaín and his relationship to other forces, to all *ewe*, or plants, which carefully lead the reader to the following chapter, in which Cabrera addresses the important subject of offerings to the owner of the *monte*. This chapter presents Congo (Bantu) beliefs in Cuba and the preparation of one of the most important religious power objects among Congo practitioners, a *nganga*. At this point, Baró, one of Cabrera's main Congo informants, owner of a *nganga* he named Palo-Monte-Siete-Campanas-Vira Mundo-Camposanto a la Medianoche, explains the secret ritual of constructing such a powerful magic object as well as other objects and rituals of his Congo-based belief system. Cabrera is careful to give different African religions and lore equal space in her archival documentation. Thus in chapter six Cabrera brings together both owners of the *monte*: the Lucumí Osaín and the Congo Tata Nfindo.

Having established that *el monte* is a space common and central to all Afro-Cuban belief systems, Cabrera devotes the following chapters to the two most iconic trees in Cuba, both in Afro-Cuban beliefs and in national myths. These are the ceiba tree and the royal palm. In chapter seven, Cabrera explains why the ceiba tree is the most sacred tree in Cuba. In Congo traditions it is mother Nganga, and for Lucumí adepts, it is *el monte* itself; it is mother Earth, represented by the ceiba tree. Thus, the ceiba tree is at the same time the tree of fertility and love: Ochún. Informants reveal that ceiba trees, also known as the African iroko, walk about at night conversing with each other. The ceiba is the great mother Earth, mother-*monte*, who grants children to mothers who properly ask and give the proper offering. The next chapter explains the mythical relationship of the ceiba tree to the Abakuá belief system and myths. Cabrera draws distinctions and similarities among the Abakuá and other Afro-Cuban groups. The ceiba is central to the Abakuá society's myths of origin, which trace it back to the area of Cameroon in Africa.

Cabrera devotes the next chapter to the royal palm, which for the Lucumí is the tree of Changó, the deity of thunder and lightning, the great judge, and the great king, or *Alafi*. The anecdotes here lead to the discussion in the tenth chapter, "Ukano Mambré," on the interrelationship of the royal palm and Abakuá or *ñáñigo* myths and rituals. Like the ceiba tree, the royal palm is central to Abakuá myths of origin, because it is believed that it was by the *ukano mambré* (royal palm) that the secret society of the ñáñigos, so uniquely Cuban, was originally born in Africa. Cabrera expanded the documentation about the Abakuá she used in *El monte* into a much longer study published in 1959 as *La sociedad secreta Abakuá*, written in the same testimonial format used in *El monte*.

Following the ten chapters, about midway through the book, is a dictionary of plants and their properties, their relationship to deities or natural forces, their uses for medicinal purposes or magic, and, when appropriate, the Lucumí (Yoruba) and Congo (Bantu) words for the plant. For example, for the common fruit *guayaba* (guava), Cabrera offers the scientific name, the Lucumí name, and the Congo name, identifies Elegguá as the deity that reigns over the fruit, and lists its common uses and magical properties.

CULTURAL TESTIMONY

In her introduction to *El monte* Cabrera explains that because she did not have any training in anthropological or ethnological research, she chose to simply write down what she heard and was told. Ironically, it is that lack of scientific methodology that allows the reader of *El monte* to enter and participate in the testimonial journey of Cabrera's research. In *El monte* Cabrera is the scribe who writes down what she hears, and in the role of a mediator between oral traditions and writing, she organizes and glosses what her informants tell her. For this reason *El monte* presents a vast number of different voices and varying data, sometimes contradictory, in which the subaltern voice is that of the writer who explains the material she gathers, and the authorial voices are those of her informants, some named, like Baró, Calazans, and Omi Tomi, and others anonymous.

In *El monte* Cabrera points out two essential aspects of Afro-Cuban cultural and religious tradition. First, the text illustrates the complexity of *afrocubanismo*, a term popularized by Fernando Ortiz, by showing the multiple differences between the many Afro-Cuban belief systems in Cuba. Second, *El monte* points out the linguistic instability of Spanish as the dominant language in Cuban vernacular speech. Many African words from different groups and nations were incorporated into Cuba's vernacular culture. The title of the text, *El monte: Igbo-Finda, Ewe-Orisha, Vititi Nfinda*, uses the Congo word *nfinda*, the Lucumí *ewe*, and the Spanish *monte*. The title, like the text, addresses the multilingual characteristics of Cuban colloquial speech and the complexity and syncretic coexistence of African legacies in Cuban society.

Cabrera's *El monte* rescued memories silenced in history. It carved a space in Cuban literary and cultural discourse for a non-Western mythology that provided a Cuban national poetics for writers in Cuba and in the Cuban diaspora.

BIBLIOGRAPHY

Acosta Saignes, Miguel. "El monte de Lydia Cabrera." *Revista Bimestre Cubana* 71 (1956): 286–287.

Baquero, Gastón. "Panorama." *Diario de la Marina.* Havana (10 August 1955).

Baquero, Gastón. *La fuente inagotable.* Valencia: Pre-Textos, 1995.

Cabrera, Lydia. *El monte: Igbo-Finda, Ewe Orisha, Vititi Nfinda; Notas sobre las religiones, la magia, las supersticiones y el folklore de los negros criollos y del pueblo de Cuba.* Miami: Ediciones Universal, 1975.

Cuervo Hewitt, Julia. *Aché, Presencia Africana: Tradiciones Yoruba-Lucumí en la narrativa cubana.* New York: Peter Lang Publishing, 1988.

Cuervo Hewitt, Julia. *Voices Out of Africa in Twentieth-Century Spanish Caribbean Literature.* Lewisburg, PA: Bucknell University Press, 2009.

Gutiérrez, Mariela A. *An Ethnological Interpretation of the Afro-Cuban World of Lydia Cabrera (1900–1991).* Lewiston, NY: Edwin Mellen Press, 2008.

Marks, Morton. "Exploring *El monte*: Ethnobotany and the Afro-Cuban Science of the Concrete." In *En torno a Lydia Cabrera (Cincuentenario de "Cuentos negros de Cuba")*, edited by Isabel Castellanos and Josefina Inclán. Miami: Ediciones Universal, 1987.

Novas Calvo, Lino. "*El monte.*" *Papeles de Son Armadans* 50 (1968): 298–304.

Rodríguez-Mangual, Edna M. *Lydia Cabrera and the Construction of an Afro-Cuban Cultural Identity.* Chapel Hill: University of North Carolina Press, 2004.

Ruiz de Viso, Hortensia. "La función del monte en la obra de Lydia Cabrera." In *Homenaje a Lydia Cabrera*, edited by Reinaldo Sánchez, José Antonio Madrigal, Ricardo Viera, and José Sánchez-Boudy. Miami: Ediciones Universal, 1978.

MR. RHYTHM: BENNY MORÉ

Radamés Giro

Moré credited with turning the expression of the people into song.

A long cultural history of poverty, slavery, and Afro-Cuban ritual practices, with their songs, rhythms, and dances, shaped Bartolomé (Benny) Moré (1919–1963) as he grew up in Santa Isabel de las Lajas, Cienfuegos, a municipality heavily influenced by the Bantu ethnic groups. This early inspiration through the Casino de los Congos (Congo Social Club) was singularly important to Moré's career, for in nearly all the popular music forms he practiced—*son*, rhumba, and conga—the Bantu ingredient is essential (Barnet, pp. 282–292).

In Santa Isabel de las Lajas, Moré learned to play the *yuka* and *makuta* drums from the Congo, and from the Cabildo Lucumí (Lucumí Society) in Lajas he learned the music and traditions of Regla de Ocha or Santería and how they are executed on the guitar and the *tres* (Cuban three-stringed guitar).

Harold Gramatges, winner of the Tomás Luis de Victoria Prize for Latin American Music, describes the fundamental characteristics that make Moré one of the most outstanding Cuban popular musicians of all time:

> as always occurs, in musical art arising from the wealth of folklore there are names that are established by the history of their peculiar significance. Because these are definitely names that create their own paths, propel and enrich the times, and create values that will be defined as the cultural heritage of the country. Cuba has among its most important examples an immortal name: Benny Moré.
>
> *Gramatges 1997, p. 103*

HAVANA TO MEXICO

After working with various musical groups in his hometown, in 1940 Moré moved to Havana where he played guitar in the bars to make a living, and slept in the tenements of Belén, a district renowned for the rhumba. He was in his element. He joined the Sexteto Fígaro (Figaro Sextet) of Lázaro Cordero, with whom he worked at the CMZ radio station, and in 1944 he joined the Septeto Cauto (Cauto Septet), directed by the *tresero* (Cuban tres player) Manuel "Mozo" Borgellá (1890–1960). Also in 1940 he joined the Conjunto Matamoros (Matamoros Ensemble) and began his singing career. With this group he appeared on the radio station Mil Diez, which had hosted many rising

musicians, including Celia Cruz (1924–2003), Olga Guillot (1922–2010), and Bebo Valdés (b. 1918).

In 1945 Moré traveled to Mexico with Miguel Matamoros. They debuted on 21 June in the Río Rosa cabaret with the group Son Veracruzano, directed by Raúl de la Rosa, and on the radio station XEW. After fulfilling their contract, Matamoros returned to Cuba without Moré, who stayed in Mexico. In 1946 he changed his stage name from Bartolomé to Benny and sang as a soloist or accompanied by Son Veracruzano in the Río Rosa cabaret and with the Mexican singer Lalo Montané at the Montparnasse. Later he sang with the Arturo Núñez orchestra and signed an exclusive contract with RCA Victor Mexicana to record with the orchestras of the Cubans Mariano Mercerón (1907–1974) and Dámaso Pérez Prado (1916–1989), who had started their meteoric careers in 1948 with the mambo. When Pérez Prado performed in the carnivals of Panama, he brought Moré as his singer.

Moré's own career flourished. He was accompanied by the orchestras of the Mexicans Rafael Paz and Chucho Rodríguez and that Venezuelan Aldemaro Romero (1928–2007). He performed in the Follies, at the Margo and Blanquita theaters, and in the Fénix Club and the Waikiki. He worked with the dancer Yolanda "Tongolele" Montes (b. 1932), the Cuban pianist and composer Juan Bruno Tarraza (1912–2001), and the Mexican singers María Antonia "Toña la Negra" Peregrino (1910–1982), Lalo Montané, and Pedro Vargas (1906–1989).

APPEARANCES IN FILMS AND NOVELS

Moré made his mark on many Mexican films, including *Carita de cielo* (Heavenly Face, 1946) with the Cuban starlet Ninón Sevilla (b. 1926); *En cada puerto un amor* (Love in Every Port, 1948), *Novia a la medida* (Bride Made to Measure, 1949), and *El gran campeón* (The Grand Champion, 1949) with the Cuban star Amalia Aguilar (b. 1924); *Ventarrón* (Windstorm, 1949), accompanied by the Gaona sisters; *Perdida* (Lost) with Sevilla, the Mexican composer Agustín Lara (1900–1970), and Pedro Vargas; and *Te besaré en la boca* (I Will Kiss You on the Lips, 1950), accompanied by Tarraza's orchestra. Other films include *Fuego en la carne* (Fire in the Flesh, 1949), *Cuando el alba llegue* (When Dawn Comes, 1949), *Al son del mambo* (To the Mambo Beat, 1950)—in which the Cuban singer Aurelio Yeyo Estrada dubbed the voice of Moré, who had by that time left the Pérez Prado band—and *Quinto patio* (Fifth Patio, 1950). In *El derecho de nacer* (Right to Be Born, 1951) Moré and Lalo Montané sing in voice-over. In Cuba, Moré participated in just one film, *No me olvides* (Don't Forget Me, 1956), in which he and Olga Guillot sang with the Banda Gigante band. This was his last film. All of his film appearances were brief, and he was not included in the credits. Unfortunately, he did not appear in any films with the orchestra of Dámaso Pérez Prado (Reyes Fortún, pp. 243–247).

Two films about Moré have been produced in Cuba: *Hoy como ayer* (Today Like Yesterday, 1987), by Constante "Rapy" Diego (1949–2006), produced by the Instituto Cubano del Arte e Industria Cinematográficos (ICAIC, Cuban Institute of Cinema Art and Industry) and Mexico's Instituto Mexicano de Cinematográfia (IMCINE), and *El Benny* (2006), by Jorge Luis Sánchez (b. 1960), in which Benny is portrayed by the actor Renny Arozarena (b. 1971) and the singer Juan Manuel Villa, whose voice was astonishingly similar to Moré's (Resik Aguirre, pp. 30–36). Neither of the two films is a complete biography of Moré, but rather reminiscences about his life. Of the two, *El Benny* is particularly fine.

Moré also drew the attention of novelists and poets. Guillermo Cabrera Infante (1929–2005) wrote in *Tres tristes tigres* (Three Trapped Tigers) that "on Fridays we don't have cabaret, and so we have the night free, and this Friday seemed perfect because that night

a new outdoor floor, the Sierra, had opened. So, it seemed right to hop over there to hear Benny Moré sing" (Cabrera Infante, p. 90).

In *Bolero* (1984) Lisandro Otero (1932–2008) evoked the life of Moré before and after the Cuban Revolution in the character Esteban María "Beto" Galán:

His first jazz band, with the addition of a Cuban drummer, reproduced the discovery of Dizzy Gillespie and Chano Pozo; it included a piano, five saxophones, four trumpets, three trombones, a double bass and the rest was percussion: regular drum set, bongo and conga drums, a powerful combination. In some way it was a reproduction of the Glenn Miller formula, but it was able to achieve another sound because it looked for its own style, something that didn't sound like anyone else.

Otero pp. 42–43

Benny Moré (1919-1963). Singer, bandleader, and composer Benny Moré is commemorated with a sculpture in his likeness in Cienfuegos, the capital city of the province in which he was raised. HÉCTOR DELGADO AND ROLANDO PUJOL

RETURN TO CUBA AND BANDA GIGANTE

In 1950 Moré returned to his home country. The next year he joined the orchestra of Mariano Mercerón, with whom he had performed in Mexico, as they did a stint in Santiago de Cuba. He was contracted to perform in the program *De fiesta con Bacardí* (Partying with Bacardí), which was broadcast throughout the country by Cadena Oriental de Radio (CMKW, Eastern Radio Network). The rising popular singers Fernando Álvarez (1927–2002) and Pacho Alonso (1928–1982) also worked with Mercerón's orchestra.

In Havana Moré worked for Amado Trinidad's RHC Cadena Azul (Blue Network) accompanied by the orchestra of Bebo Valdés, who by then was trying to establish his *batanga* rhythm. Later he moved to Radio Progreso (Radio Progress) with the Ernesto Duarte orchestra, but despite Moré's abilities as a singer and the fame he brought to the orchestra, Duarte only used him in the Radio Progreso broadcasts, not in his television performances or at dances. These omissions caused friction between Duarte and Moré, who knew his exclusion was discriminatory because Duarte's orchestra performed mainly in white clubs that did not admit blacks. Unfortunately, the situation ended their partnership (Martínez Rodríguez, pp. 27–28).

The time had come for a change in his music career. Moré was fascinated by the sounds of the bands that accompanied him and by the Glenn Miller records he heard at the home of Rafael Cueto (1900–1991), one of the members of Conjunto Matamoros. He was also influenced by the singing style of Orlando "Cascarita" Guerra (1920–1975), who performed with the Julio Cueva and Casino de la Playa orchestras, as well as the sounds of the Armando Romeu orchestra and the style of pianist René Hernández (1916–1987). All of them tried to combine jazz with Afro-Cuban music, as the Machito y sus Afro-Cubanos band had done in New York.

Against this background, in 1953 Moré created his Banda Gigante (Big Band), whose first members were Eduardo "Cabrerita" Cabrera, pianist and musical arranger; Miguel Franca, Santiago Peñalver, Roberto Barreto, Celso Gómez, and Virgilio Vixama, saxophonists; Alfredo "Chocolate" Armenteros, Rabanito and Domingo Corbacho, trumpets; José Miguel, trombone; Alberto Limonta, double bass; Rolando Laserie, drums; Clemente "Chicho" Piquero, bongo drums; Tabaquito, conga drums; and Fernando Álvarez and Enrique Benítez, chorus (Nasser, p. 64). He performed with his band for the first time on 3 August 1953 on the program *Cascabeles Candado*, broadcast by the Circuito CMQ radio station. They also performed on the television shows *Show de Arau* and *Papel y Tinta*. Moré's stint in Mexico had laid the foundations for his career, but it was with Banda Gigante that his singing style reached its peak.

With his orchestra Moré toured in 1956 and 1957 through Colombia, Haiti, Jamaica, Mexico, Panama, and Venezuela. In Los Angeles, California, he sang accompanied by the Luis Arcaraz orchestra. In 1958 he traveled to New York, where he performed at the Palladium accompanied by the Tito Puente orchestra (Fernández, pp. 96–97). He performed with his Banda Gigante in Havana at the Ali Bar, La Campana, Montmartre, Night and Day, the Mambí room at the Tropical, and the Sierra cabaret.

MORÉ'S STYLE AND LEGACY

By 1954 Moré was known as the *El bárbaro del ritmo* (The Wizard of Rhythm). He was famous for his compositions, in which he used simple melodic and well constructed turns that demonstrated the acute sensibility of a great composer. When performing he moved his body to the rhythm, and at times he directed the orchestra with gestures that ranged from soft to brusque, with the baton or his hat, and the orchestra responded to each of his movements.

As a singer he controlled his voice to suit the music, stretching up and down the register and even masterfully employing the middle range, sometimes with a certain nasal quality. His skill made his renditions of Ernesto Duarte's "Cómo fue" unforgettable. His original songs were performed by subsequent singers such as Mayra Caridad Valdés (b. 1956), Miriam Ramos (b. 1946), and Augusto Enríquez (b. 1961), who retained Moré's interpretations. Luis Yáñez (1920–1973) and Rolando Gómez (1924–1990), who wrote "Oh vida!" (Oh Life!), sang it exactly as Moré did, even with similar orchestration. Moré's voice overflowed when he sang his own compositions, such as the bolero "Mi amor fugaz" (My Fleeting Love), the *guajira* (traditional Cuban folk song) "Cienfuegos," the mambo "Bonito y sabroso" (Pretty and Delicious), and, above all, in tribute to his home town, "Santa Isabel de las Lajas," in the *son montuno* style.

Moré had a quality that some called charm and others called charisma. He was a unique artist who was able to perform multiple Cuban genres with absolute mastery; in the genre of rhumba, he enchanted audiences with "Rumberos de ayer" (Rumberos of Yesterday), a beautiful tribute to rhumba singers, and "De la rumba al chachachá" (From Rhumba to Cha-Cha-Cha). He also performed the *guaguancó, son, guaracha*, bolero, and mambo. These styles were always in his repertoire as the different traits of Cubans all came together in his persona. The musicologist Leonardo Acosta, who was a saxophonist for Banda Gigante, said, "musicians are very special people and it is not easy to stand before an orchestra. Moré never had a problem, although he didn't know how to sight-sing (sometimes I think he knew a little), he alone was three-quarters of the orchestra and inspiration to the other quarter" (Acosta, pp. 16–17).

Moré did not invent something new, but rather he synthesized a process that had been building within popular Cuban music and reached its zenith in him. An exceptional performer of Cuban music, Moré embodied the expression of a people turned into song.

SELECTED DISCOGRAPHY

Y hoy como ayer (1955).

El inigualable Benny Moré (1957).

Recordando a Benny Moré (1957).

Benny Moré: Así es… Benny (1958).

The Very Best of Benny Moré. Vol. 1. (1995).

20 boleros de oro: Benny Moré.

Joyas clásicas de Benny Moré.

BIBLIOGRAPHY

Acosta, Leonardo. *Elige tú, que canto yo.* Havana: Editorial Letras Cubanas, 1993.

Barnet, Miguel. *La fuente viva.* Havana: Editorial Letras Cubanas, 1998.

Cabrera Infante, Guillermo. *Tres tristes tigres.* Madrid: Editorial Seix Barral, 1970.

Fernández, Raúl. *Latin Jazz: The Perfecta Combinación/ La Combinación perfecta.* Washington, DC: Chronicle Books and the Smithsonian Institution, 2002.

Gramatges, Harold. *Presencia de la revolución en la música cubana.* 2nd ed. Havana: Editorial Letras Cubanas, 1997.

Martínez Rodríguez, Raúl. *Benny Moré.* Havana: Editorial Letras Cubanas, 1993.

Moore, Robin D. *Music and Revolution Cultural Change in Socialist Cuba.* Berkeley: University of California Press, 2006.

Nasser, Amín E. *Benny Moré.* 2nd ed. Havana: Ediciones Unión, 1994.

Otero, Lisandro. *Bolero.* Havana: Editorial Letras Cubanas, 1986.

Resik Aguirre, Magda. "Jorge Luis Sánchez: Contar historias desde la emoción." *Cine Cubano* 160–161 (April–September 2006).

Reyes Fortún, José. *El arte de Benny Moré. Ofrenda criolla II.* Havana: Ediciones Museo de la Música, 2009.

Rodríguez, Ezequiel. *Benny Moré in Memoriam.* Havana: Instituto del Libro, 1969.

MUSIC

Few countries have been blessed with the musical richness, tradition, and creativity as has Cuba. As is true in many aspects of its culture, the island's music draws on European (Spanish, mostly), African, Haitian, and North American traditions.

Cuba has boasted major musical talents: in colonial times, it was religious composer Esteban Salas; in the nineteenth century, composers Ignacio Cervantes and Manuel Saumell; and in the twentieth and twenty-first centuries, classical artists Alejandro García Caturla, Amadeo Roldán, and Leo Brouwer.

However, it is the proliferation of popular music genres that have endeared Cuban music to world audiences. Beginning in the nineteenth century, these included the contradanza, habanera, danzón, and bolero; in the twentieth century, the son, rhumba, cha-cha-chá, mambo, and Latin (Afro-Cuban) jazz were well liked.

African influences are central to Cuban music and shaped its most popular genres: danzón, son, and rhumba, the latter two essential to what is known as salsa music. Although these genres are secular, they often draw on the ritual music of religions such as Regla de Ochá (also known as Santería), Palo, Abakuá, and Arará. Cuban ethnomusicologist Fernando Ortiz called Afro-Cuban music a "resonant rum for the ears."

Cuba's ability to combine popular and classical idioms and its impressive synthesis of different styles, rhythms, and cultures are unique in capturing a past that at times has been convulsive and attuned to the nuances of contemporary street life. Cuban music is the island's memory and living history.

■ *See also*

Esteban Salas: An Eighteenth-Century Composer

Performing Arts: Bufo Theater

Performing Arts: Dance: Folkloric Dance

MUSIC: EARLY HISTORY

Zoila Mercedes Lapique Becali

Music in Cuba, from early manifestations to 1800.

The Spanish conquest and colonization of Cuba in the sixteenth century launched an encounter between the cultures originating in Spain and those of the native peoples. The Spaniards contributed the musical styles of that period, especially those of Andalusian and Castilian singers. They also contributed both military and religious music. Music was used in Catholic worship, in celebrations of the saints, commemorations and processions, sacramental rites, and festivals for the patron saints of each locale. Spanish culture of the period also contained elements of the Arab and Berber cultures, given that these had been present on the Iberian Peninsula for eight centuries.

THE ORIGINS OF CUBAN MUSIC AND DANCE

The chroniclers of the Indies cite the music of the aborigines and their instruments: *atabales*, shells (*cobo* or queen conch, and *guamo*, a conch-shell trumpet), and rattles, including the maraca and the guiro, which remained in use into modern times. Regarding dance, they mention the religious ceremonies of *areíto*, including the famous dance of the Taina woman, Anacaona. The "*son of the Mateodora*" was thought to be the first Cuban musical style. However, later research indicated it was a Santiago carnival song dating from the first half of the nineteenth century (Fuentes Matons 1981, pp. 289–290).

From the beginning of the colonial period, the Spanish imported slaves and free men of various ethnicities from Africa and Spain, including Congolese, Carabali, Mandinga, and Minas. All practiced their own music, dance, instruments, and songs in Cuba, where they were thrown together. Massive numbers of black slaves would be imported to Cuba during the reign of Charles IV (r. 1788–1808), at the request of the sugar plantation owners. With the fall of Haiti as the primary global producer of sugar, Cuba came to occupy that place in the first quarter of the nineteenth century.

The predominant musical styles of that period arrived with the Spaniards: *coplas* (improvised satirical or romantic verses) and *romance* (narrative ballads); *puntos* (a genre of improvised lyrics accompanied by picked guitars); sung *décimas* (a form consisting of eight-syllable ten-line rhyming stanzas); *villancicos* (a type of folk song sung in the local vernacular); and *seguidillas* (a lively, triple-time folk song).

In dance, the Spanish contributed the *folía* (whose name means *folly*, a rollicking triple-time dance); the sarabande (a slower triple-meter dance that originated in the Spanish colonies); the *chacona* (or *chaconne*, which originated as a quick triple-meter dance); and the *zapateo* (a tap-dance form with roots in flamenco). These dances derived from various regions in Spain, primarily in the peasant areas, together with others that disappeared in those first centuries. The Spanish *romance* prevailed and endured through subsequent centuries until today in children's games and songs (with variations) in Cuba and the Americas. The form has reemerged with romanticism, but only as poetry, not in song. The prevalent form for songs was the *décima*, a ten-line stanza used to sing peasant tunes.

The Spaniards also brought with them musicians who played the laúd (similar to the mandolin), *vihuela* (a twelve-stringed instrument with six courses of paired strings) and guitar (both five- and six-stringed versions). The guitar was the most widespread instrument in Spain at that time. Manuals for learning the *vihuela* appeared together with those for learning the guitar, since its dissemination was greater still, especially among the lower classes and sectors. Guitar players never suspected the many offspring the instrument would engender in American lands, with *criollo* versions of the *tres* (a six-stringed instrument with three courses of paired strings), the *cuatro* (consisting of four double-stringed courses), the *cinco* (with five double-stringed courses), and the *seis* (six double courses) emerging over time, along with the *charango* (a very small instrument with five double courses) and the *guitarrón* (a six-stringed bass instrument).

MUSIC IN EARLY HAVANA

This music resonated in Havana after Antón de Alaminos discovered the Windward Passage, allowing access to the north side of the island, in 1517. This is one of the reasons for the final transfer of Havana to the North Coast in 1519. Because of the natural conditions of its port, it became a base for organizing and departure for the conquest of other lands in the Americas, in addition to centralizing commerce between New Spain and Seville. And if in Spain in the sixteenth century people made music to sing in taverns and other places, it would be no less so in Havana, with its innumerable taverns and inns open day and night to provide housing and food to travelers and sailors making the *carrera de Indias*, the Indies run of cargo convoys that carried the bounty of the New World to Seville and returned with finished goods for the colonists.

FESTIVAL AND ECCLESIASTICAL MUSIC

Secular dances, some of African origin, infiltrated the religious festivals of Corpus Christi. The first reference we have is from 12 May 1570, when numerous dances and improvisations were performed within the procession, and musicians played *atabales*, fifes, *chirimías* (forerunner of the oboe), and *tambores* (Arrom 1941, p. 276). The *tarasca*—a wooden machine in the form of a many-headed serpent or a dragon, mounted on wheels and driven by men riding inside it, carrying two wooden figures seated on armchairs known as the *tarasquilla* and *tarascón* on its sides—was brought out for processions. Bull fights (conducted on horseback at the time) were held at the festivals, and it was a custom for the more notable men in the city to participate until the eighteenth century, when professional bullfighters without titles of nobility practiced the sport.

A 1642 ecclesiastical order issued in the diocesan synod prohibited indecent dances and required dances to be performed without women. Furthermore, neither altars nor nativity scenes could be built in individual homes in which dancing and musical performance took place. Starting in the seventeenth century, bishops were interested in creating music chapels in Havana and Santiago. But those who devoted themselves to liturgical music were constantly under the threat of the direst of poverty, since they were prohibited from participating in military exercises and theatrical performances.

The chapel of Santiago de Cuba was created in 1682, but it did not achieve importance until 1764, when the Havana priest Esteban Salas Castro Montes de Oca (1725–1803) arrived in the city. He had studied counterpoint and composition, plainchant, violin, and organ, in addition to philosophy, theology, and canon law. He composed masses, cantatas, hymns, salves, motets, tunes, and pastorals, along with a Stabat Mater and especially *villancicos* with beautiful lyrics taken from various Spanish and local sources. Esteban Salas's *villancicos*, cantatas, and pastorals, according to Cuban musicologist Pablo Hernández Balaguer, "represent the oldest manifestations of Cuban religious music with texts in Spanish" (1986, p. 55). Esteban Salas is the first Cuban composer to be recorded in history for his musical works, and he is a genuine representative of the New World baroque, with esthetic elements of the Spanish and Italian music of the period.

CRIOLLO CONTRADANZAS AND THEATRICAL *TONADILLAS*

Contradanzas, along with other dance genres of French origin (the minuet and waltz) burst onto the scene in Havana after being imported from Spain during the second half of the eighteenth century, and soon captivated the city's dancers. Contradanza would be all the rage from that point until the nineteenth century. The daily labors of black and mulatto musicians who constituted the musical groups of the period turned this genre into what became known as the *criollo* contradanza. Theatrical *tonadillas* (short, satirical musical comedy pieces) were performed in the Coliseo (Coliseum); this musical theater genre would influence the *teatro bufo* (comic opera) of the nineteenth century.

At the end of the eighteenth century, music from Spain and Africa were separately prominent in Cuba. Through a slow process of transculturation, they eventually blended and formed, in synthesis, Cuban music.

Discography of Esteban Salas

Villancicos de diferentes autores (entre ellos dos de Salas) (1959).

Obras de Salas (1960).

Cuatro villancicos, dos pastorelas (1983).

Veintidos obras de Esteban Salas (litúrgicas y no litúrgicas) (1995–1997).

El eco de las Indias (1997).

Música sacra en la Habana colonial (1999).

Nativité à Santiago de Cuba (2001).

BIBLIOGRAPHY

Arrom, José Juan. "Primeras manifestaciones dramáticas en Cuba (1512–1776)." *Revista bimestre cubana* 48 (1941): 276.

Carpentier, Alejo. *La música en Cuba*. 3rd ed. Havana: Letras Cubanas, 1988.

Esquenazi Pérez, Martha. *Del areíto y otros sones*. Havana: Letras Cubanas, 2001.

Fuentes Matons, Laureano. *Las artes en Santiago de Cuba*. Havana: Letras Cubanas, 1981.

Giro, Radamés, ed. *Panorama de la música popular cubana*. Havana: Letras Cubanas, 1998.

Giro, Radamés. *Diccionario enciclopédico de la música en Cuba*. 4 vols. Havana: Letras Cubanas, 2007.

Hernández Balaguer, Pablo. *Villancicos, cantadas y pastorelas de Esteban Salas*. Havana: Letras Cubanas, 1986.

Lapique Becali, Zoila. "Aportes franco-haitianos a la contradanza cubana: Mitos y realidades." In *Panorama de la música popular cubana*, edited by Radamés Giro. Havana: Letras Cubanas, 1998.

Lapique Becali, Zoila. *Cuba colonial: Música, compositors, e intérpretes*. Havana: Boloña, 2008.

Muguercia Muguercia, Alberto. *La clave xilofónica de la música cubana*. Havana: 1935.

Muguercia Muguercia, Alberto. "Teodora Ginés ¿Mito o realidad histórica?" *Revista de la Biblioteca Nacional José Martí* 3 (September–December 1971): 53–85.

Ortiz, Fernando. *La africanía de la música folklórica cubana*. Havana: Ministry of Education, 1950.

MUSIC: 19TH CENTURY

Ana Victoria Casanova

The development of Cuban musical culture in Cuba's final century as a colony.

Cuba's final century as a Spanish colony was one of the most creative and heterogeneous periods for its music. During that time, new homegrown genres crystallized, and many specifically Cuban musical styles and attitudes came to the fore, including folk music, popular music, and classical music. The diverse people of Cuba, shaped by the country's economic structures, were decisive in a complicated process of amalgamation that came to define its varied types of music.

Following the bloody 1791 slave revolt in the French colony of Saint-Domingue (present-day Haiti), causing its exit from the international market, Cuba became the world's largest exporter of coffee and cane sugar. To meet the demand for labor, Spain increased the number of Africans purchased from slave traders. Africans of diverse ethnicities, the vast majority of whom were from sub-Saharan Africa, were taken to Cuba. This traffic continued until 1886, when slavery was abolished. Parallel to the influx of Africans, and in large part due to the fear that a revolt similar to Saint-Domingue's would erupt in Cuba, a continuous immigration of whites to the island also occurred, mostly Spanish but also French and other Europeans.

The sugar industry's robust development brought great prosperity, which in turn supported a flourishing of the arts. As musical composition and performance proliferated, a national spirit emerged in them much more quickly than did notions of independence from Spain, and out of this new consciousness a Cuban personality took shape. This personality was manifested not only in the emergence of Cuban musical genres, but also in the expressive language employed in the forms inherited from Europe.

FOLK MUSIC

In the 1800s, folk musical forms appeared that, although closely linked to older Hispanic or African traditions, displayed new Cuban characteristics shaped by the sociocultural conditions in which they were reconstructed or cultivated. In addition, specifically Cuban folk expressions emerged from the complex mixture and synthesis of previously existing forms. Three major trends within Cuba's traditional or folk music should be mentioned: Hispano-Cuban music, with roots in Spain and the Canary Islands; Afro-Cuban music, of African origin; and Cuban music, born in Cuba.

HISPANIC-CUBAN MUSIC

Based on various Spanish elements introduced throughout the nineteenth century by diverse waves of immigrants, a style of singing called *punto guajiro* or *punto cubano* developed among Cuban peasants (known as *guajiros* in Cuba). The dance of the Cuban countryside, derived from several Spanish *zapateos* (dances) featuring foot stamping and tapping, was identified at the start of the century as *zapateo cubano*.

From that time the punto guajiro became known for its variety of *tonadas* (melodies), with Mixolydian or Phrygian modal structures. This variety increased even more during the course of the 1800s. The tonadas were sung in *décimas* (stanzas of ten octosyllabic lines), generally improvised by singers who were called poets, or learned by soloists. The voice was accompanied by a treble guitar called a *tiple*, or a *mandurria*. The *punto* and *zapateo* were practiced mostly by the rural population in the western part of central Cuba, but they also reached the cities and Havana, "and even

blacks improvised décimas, accompanied by the tiple, and danced zapateo: the carriage driver carried in the trunk of his *quitrín* (open carriage) the 'melancholy tiple' to accompany him in his zapateo and punto cubano" (León, p. 79).

The zapateo cubano and the tiple were out of style by the end of the century, when the *laúd*, a form of the lute, made its appearance; from that time on the laúd was the usual accompaniment for the punto, replacing the tiple and the mandurria. It was given the name *laúd campesino* or *laúd cubano*, even though some authors contend that it was nothing more than "the *contralto mandurria* born around 1880 in Spain," which was mistakenly identified at that time as the "new laúd" (Amador, p. 17).

AFRO-CUBAN MUSIC

In Cuba, Africans and their descendants gathered by ethnicity in *cabildos de nación* (ethnic group associations) in urban areas, in slave barracks on plantations, and in runaway slave communities called *palenques* (walled enclosures) in the countryside. In these spaces they preserved many musical and dance forms linked to religious as well as secular celebrations and reconstructed the African instruments and musical forms in their new Cuban sociocultural context. This activity resulted in forms of expression that differed substantially from the original African forms. On Epiphany, some cabildos were authorized to go into the streets of the cities and towns with their musical instruments and holiday dress, to dance and sing in their own style. Slaves on the plantations could play their drums, sing, and dance on their days of rest.

The many and varied kinds of Afro-Cuban folk music that proliferated during the nineteenth century included those related to the *bantú* (Bantu), *lucumí* (Yoruba), *carabalí* (Igbo-Efik), and *arará* (Fon, Ewe, and other ethnic groups from Dahomey [modern-day Benin]). Linked to bantú culture were the *makuta* religious celebrations, in which the drums of the same name were played. During the animist Regla de Palo ceremonies, *cantos de palo* were sung and *ngoma* drums were played. The *yuka* festive complex, featuring single-headed drums made from long, hollow logs, was one of the best known in that period in both urban and rural areas, because it was secular in nature. Also notable are the songs and drumming that accompany *maní*, a martial art and dance technique practiced only by men. After the first twenty-five years of the nineteenth century, the high concentration of Lucumí slaves in the western regions of Havana and Matanzas resulted in a religious festivity consisting of drumming, songs, dances, and playing of musical instruments—including the sacred *batá* drums—related to the Regla de Ocha, later known as Cuban Santería.

In the town of Regla, on the outskirts of Havana, the Abakuá secret society, called Efik-Butón, was founded in 1836. The exclusively male association was sponsored by a group of Africans of *carabalí apapá* origin and their descendants. Its members were slaves and free black men, as well as Cuban-born whites, Spaniards, and Chinese. Later on, other Abakuá chapters appeared in areas near Havana Bay, Matanzas Bay, and Cárdenas Bay. From that time on, *biankomeko* drums accompanied the songs and dances in Abakuá *plantes* (ceremonies). In various regions on the island, Cuba was also home to musical expressions linked with Arará religious festivities, featuring a *estaca* (large wooden stick) that goes into the body of a drum to tense the skin or head.

In the early 1800s, African slaves and their descendants—mostly of Bantu and Arará origin—who were the property of French settlers on eastern Cuban coffee plantations, created a music and dance form known as *tumba francesa*, as well as an association of the same name. As the century went on, these societies and their festivities spread to various parts of the country.

CUBAN MUSIC

Within Cuban folk music, dancing and dance music were particularly important. One example is the evolution and development of the musical styles known as *nengones*, which emerged in the late eighteenth century in remote rural areas of eastern Cuba. During the nineteenth century the *nengón* evolved into two of Cuba's most important musical genres: the *son*—in modern times called the *son montuno*—and the *changüí*. Likewise, new instruments appeared, including the Cuban *tres*, a kind of guitar with six strings tuned in pairs, whose playing combines the timbric concepts and the vocabulary of African drums; and the *marímbula*, a descendant of the Bantu *sanzas*;

and the first precursors of the modern-day percussion instrument known as the bongo.

Through most of the nineteenth century, writers chronicled *rumbas*, parties with their typical songs and dances, held in lower-class neighborhoods, in informal dance halls called *casas de cuna*, and among the rabble. In the urban slums that gave birth to the Cuban rhumba, various cultural elements came together, and out of their blending came rumba genres such as the *yambú* and the *guaguancó*. In rural areas with similar circumstances, the *columbia* appeared. Another form that came out of this period is the *rumba de tiempo' España* (rhumba in Spanish time), danced with mimicked gestures related to the songs performed, such as "Mamá' buela" (Grandmama) and "Lala no sabe hacer ná" (Lala Doesn't Know How to Do Anything) (León, p. 123).

POPULAR MUSIC

Cuban popular music in the nineteenth century was closely related to the emergence of Cuban ballroom dance genres and to various singing styles. The appearance at the beginning of the nineteenth century of the *contradanza cubana*, a version of the French *contredanse*, set in motion a process that would unfold, through such other dance styles as the *danza* and the *danzón*, up through the end of the century.

In the *contradanza*, dancers make arm and hand figures and shuffle their feet. The music retained its two-section form but assimilated melodic and rhythmic elements that were identifiably Cuban. It drew on working-class dance forms such as the *tumbantonio*, *culebra*, *chin-chín*, and *guabina* (León, p. 157). Street vendors' cries, known as *pregones*, and one-act plays called *sainetes* were the sources of many of the melodies, in addition to the melodic themes of arias, opera overtures, and zarzuela romances. This borrowing from other sources, so typical of the era, characterized the contradanza, and toward the end of the century was also prevalent in the danzón.

The bands that played dance halls utilized various combinations of instruments. For example, piccolo, clarinet, three violins, double bass, and percussion, for waltzes and contradanzas (Carpentier 1988, p. 112) and clarinet in C and/or B flat, valve trombone, ophicleide (brass-keyed bugle), saxhorn or cornet, two violins, double bass, *timbales*, and *güiro* (gourd) (Alén, p. 122), for groups called *orquestas típicas* or *orquestas de viento*, derived from military bands.

Charangas francesas—consisting of piano, two or four violins, double bass, *pailas*, güiro, and flute—appeared toward the close of the century. This "French-style" configuration was based on the classic French chamber music trio, composed of piano, violin, and flute, to which were added *pailas* or timbales and güiro (Alén, p. 122).

From the mid-1850s on, the word *danzón* was used to describe a square dance in which couples held flowered arches, as well as a dance in which couples embraced each other. In both cases, the music was similar to what was played for the contradanza. Later on, different music was composed that was slower, more rhythmic and more complex in its sequence of sections.

In 1877, musician Miguel Faílde (1852–1921) from Matanzas composed danzones titled "El delirio" (Delirium), "La ingratitud" (Ingratitude), "Las quejas" (Complaints), and "Las Alturas de Simpson" (Simpson Heights). They were played only informally before 1 January 1879, the date that Faílde and his band officially premiered "Las Alturas de Simpson" at El Club in the city of Matanzas (Alén, p. 127). From that moment on, the danzón definitively became the dance performed by embracing couples, moving their hips and taking short, sliding steps. This dance evolved into a rondo with five parts (ABACA), in which the *paseo*, or introduction, alternated with a first trio played by the clarinet and a second trio played by the violins, and then the close of the piece. Danzón rhythms such as the tango or *habanera* and the *cinquillo cubano* were already used in the contradanza. It spread quickly across the island, to criticism as well as acclaim. The danzón was played at dances by *orquestas típicas* and *charangas francesas*, most notably those led by Faílde, Raimundo Valenzuela (1848–1905), and Antonio Toroella (1856–1934).

Also during the nineteenth century, various styles of Cuban song were defined. In 1841, the *habanera* was born; it was described as "a contradanza . . . sung for the first time with verses expressly spoken in time to the music" (Lapique, p. 132) The first song of this type, published in November 1842, was "El amor en el baile" (Love at the Dance). Later on, this genre moved closer to the style of the romantic song, culminating in Eduardo Sánchez de Fuentes's (1874–1944) famous habanera "Tú" (You), written in 1892.

One important milestone in the evolution of Cuban song was the creation in 1851 of "La Bayamesa" (The Woman of Bayamo), with lyrics by poet José Fornaris (1827–1890) and music by Francisco Castillo Moreno and Carlos Manuel de Céspedes (1819–1874). With its typical melodic figures, its slow, three-four beat and its lyrical, romantic language, this quintessential composition became extremely popular all over the country.

In contrast was the *guaracha*, satirical, bawdy, and peppered with double entendres. Other genres—such as the *guajira* and the *criolla,* similar to Cuban country music, and the clave and the *bolero cubano*—also emerged during this century. Singing duos accompanied by guitars performed the various types of Cuban songs. Called *trovadores*, they produced a large part of the song repertory of this period.

VERNACULAR THEATER MUSIC

In the first quarter of the century, Cuban vernacular theater (equivalent to vaudeville) emerged, replacing the characters of Spanish popular theater with Cuban figures representing the country boy, the *negrito* (black fellow), the Spanish immigrant, and the mulatto woman. The famous comic actor and playwright Francisco Covarrubias (1775–1850) was a precursor of this process.

Music and dance always played a dominant role in this type of theater, through such Cuban genres as contradanzas, guarachas, habaneras, rhumbas, danzones, criollas, claves, and puntos (Martín p. 40); they also figured in sainetes and zarzuelas at the end of the century. Distinguished composers Enrique Guerrero (1818–1887), Carlos (1829–1909) and Jorge Anckermann (1877–1941), José (1855–1937) and Manuel Mauri (1857–1939), Rafael Palau (1864–1906), Hubert de Blanck (1856–1932), Guillermo Tomás (1868–1933), Ignacio Cervantes (1847–1905), Raimundo Valenzuela, and others wrote music for the Cuban vaudeville stage, and this form of theater reached its highest level with the opening of the Teatro Alhambra in Havana in 1890.

CLASSICAL OR CONCERT MUSIC

Classical or concert music in Cuba was influenced by the forms and patterns of European classicism and romanticism; the latter also conveyed the nationalist fervor so characteristic of the period. Cuban composers approached these styles in different ways, some closely following the classical or romantic models, and others simply using them as expressive elements in their pieces. Two distinguished composers who worked within classical influences were Juan París (1759–1845), successor to the religious composer Esteban Salas (1725–1803) at the Santiago de Cuba Cathedral, and Antonio Raffelin, who wrote symphonies, quartets, masses, and sacred choral music, among other works.

Other European-born genres and forms such as concertos, sonatas, symphonies, etudes, songs without words, preludes, and waltzes were written and performed on the island, and a diverse group of Cuban forms of expression were incorporated into them. In addition, concert music was made on the basis of contradanzas, danzas cubanas, and other genres that originated as ballroom dance genres. Contradanzas and danzas composed for piano and removed from the dance context appeared in the early 1800s, written by Nicolás Muñoz y Zayas, Tomás Buelta y Flores, Vicente Díaz de Comas (d. 1855), Agustín Cascantes, José Lino Fernández de Coca (b. 1830), Jorge Zequeira, Pedro Bofante, Tomás Ruiz (1834–1888), and especially pianist and composer Manuel Saumell (c. 1818–1870), among others.

Although Saumell composed some pieces for diverse vocal and instrumental combinations, among them "Plegaria" for soprano and organ and "Ave María" for voice and orchestra, his place in nineteenth-century Cuban music was assured by the more than forty contradanzas he wrote for the piano. In these compositions, in binary form with contrasting sections, Saumell showed the opposition of the parts; while the first part frequently has a language closer to classical European forms, the second part contains more Cuban, picaresque rhythms, and on occasion the composer inverts the order. "Los ojos de Pepa" (Pepa's Eyes), "La Tedezco," "El Somatén," and "La niña bonita" (The Pretty Girl) are some of his most famous contradanzas.

Quite a few composers were influenced by nationalist romanticism, evident in the expressive language and the styles they used. For example, Nicolás Ruiz Espadero (1832–1890) was a prolific composer of piano and chamber music and also the author of "Canto del Guajiro" (The Song of the Peasant) and "Canto del Esclavo" (Song of the Slave). Eminent violinist José White (1835–1918) composed outstanding pieces for violin and piano, among them "Zamacueca," "Bella Cubana" (Beautiful Cuban Woman), and "Violinesque," as well as two violin etudes and "Concierto en fa sostenido menor" (Concerto in F Sharp Minor) for violin and orchestra. Laureano Fuentes Matons (1825–1898) was the creator of *América*, the first symphonic poem composed in Cuba.

Distinguished composer and pianist Ignacio Cervantes, who also worked in the nationalist romantic style, created orchestral pieces such as *Sinfonía en do menor* (Symphony in C Minor) and *Scherzo capriccioso*; waltzes, including "Hectograph" and "La Paloma" (The Dove); and chamber music such as "Entreacto caprichoso" for string quintet and *Scherzo en fa menor* for string trio. He also wrote numerous piano pieces, including waltzes, songs without words, mazurkas, polkas, and his most outstanding work, "Serenata Cubana." In addition, he wrote more than forty danzas that were the best of the genre in the late nineteenth century. Fernando (1828–1888) and Cecilia Arizti (1856–1930) and José Manuel "Lico" Jiménez (1855–1917), the first Cuban composer of lieder and creator of a *Concierto para piano y orquesta*, were also distinguished pianists and composers during that period.

On 8 September 1807, the first opera composed in Cuba, *América y Apolo*, by an unknown composer with libretto by Manuel Zequeira y Arango (1764–1846), debuted at Havana's Teatro Principal. Subsequent authors of operas include Cristóbal Martínez Corres (1822–1842), known as the first Cuban opera composer, and Gaspar Villate (1851–1891), considered the most prolific, with works such as *Zilia, La Czarina*, and *Baltasar*, based on a drama by Cuban poet Gertrudis Gómez de Avellaneda (1814–1873). Cuban opera was marked by the dynamic patterns of bel canto and the formal and stylistic peculiarities of Italian opera, failing to bring about a truly national expression. That achievement would be accomplished in the new century.

SELECTED DISCOGRAPHY

Emilio, Frank. *Frank Emilio interpreta a Ignacio Cervantes.*

Grupo Changüí de Guantánamo. *Bongó de Monte.*

Provedo, Lucy, and José Ruiz Elcoro. *La Perla: Cantares de Cuba, Siglos XVIII y XIX* (2007).

Tieles, Cecilio. *Espadero: Obras para piano* (2006).

Various Artists. *Almendra con sabor a danzón.*

Various Artists. *Cancionero Hispano Cubano* (2005).

Various Artists. *Cervantes, cuatro pianos* (1999).

Various Artists. *Cuadernos de La Habana* (1999).

Various Artists. *Official Retrospective of Cuban Music* (1999).

Various Artists. *Serenata Cubana* (2006).

BIBLIOGRAPHY

Alén Rodríguez, Olavo. *From Afrocuban Music to Salsa.* Berlin: Piranha, 1998.

Amador, Efraín. *Universalidad del laúd y el tres cubano.* Havana: Letras Cubanas, 2005.

Carpentier, Alejo. *La Música en Cuba.* 3rd ed. Havana: Letras Cubanas, 1988.

Carpentier, Alejo. *Music in Cuba.* Minneapolis: University of Minnesota Press, 2001.

Casanova, Ana Victoria. "Influencia chopiniana en el nacionalismo musical cubano del siglo XIX." *Revista Clave* 12 (January–March 1989): 32–34.

Casanova, Ana Victoria. "La Música de Salón del Siglo XIX en Cuba: Un Panorama." In *Música Iberoamericana de Salón*, edited by José Peñin. Vol. I, 173–204. Caracas: Fundación Vicente Emilio Sojo, 2000.

Casanova, Ana Victoria. "El nacionalismo romántico de las danzas cervantinas." *Revista Clave* 1 (2001): 2–9.

Casanova, Ana Victoria. "Los Bailes de Salón del siglo XIX: Un antecedente del danzón." *Revista Digital La Jiribilla* 270 (2006).

Castillo Faílde, Osvaldo. *Miguel Faílde, creador musical del danzón.* Havana: Editora del Consejo Nacional de Cultura, 1964.

Eli Rodríguez, Victoria. "The Afro-French Settlement and the Legacy of Its Music to the Cuban People." In *Music and Black Ethnicity: The Caribbean and South America*, edited by Gerard H. Béhague. New Brunswick, NJ: Transaction, 1994.

Galán, Natalio. *Cuba y sus sones.* Valencia, Spain: Pre-Textos Literarios, 1983.

Lapique Becali, Zoila. *Cuba Colonial: Música, compositores e intérpretes, 1570–1902.* 2nd ed. Havana: Ediciones Boloña: Letras Cubanas, 2008.

León, Argeliers. *Del canto y el tiempo.* 2nd ed. Havana: Letras Cubanas, 1984.

Martín, Edgardo. *Panorama histórico de la música en Cuba.* Havana: Universidad de La Habana, 1971.

Mikowsky, Solomón Gadles. *Ignacio Cervantes y la danza en Cuba.* Havana: Letras Cubanas, 1988.

Ramírez, Serafín. *La Habana artística. Apuntes históricos.* Havana: E. M. de la Capitanía General de La Habana, 1891.

Sublette, Ned. *Cuba and Its Music: From the First Drums to the Mambo.* Chicago: Chicago Review Press, 2004.

MUSIC: 1900–1945

Olavo Alén Rodríguez

A panorama of Cuban music during the first half of the twentieth century.

The transition from the nineteenth to the twentieth century brought with it an essential transformation in the history of Cuba. The country left behind its days as a Spanish colony to become an independent republic, but this change took place amid many difficulties and adverse events, which ultimately affected the new ways of life.

The last of the three wars waged against Spain for Cuba's independence began in 1895 and ended with a partial victory for the Cubans in 1898. The victory was partial because midway through that struggle, the Spanish-American War was declared, resulting in victory for the United States in that final year. The U.S. occupation lasted until 20 May 1902, and during this time, favorable conditions were established for the United States to maintain lasting control over the economy and commerce of the entire island. Of course, this control affected the culture and new ways of life adopted by the Cubans.

TRADITIONAL AND FOLK MUSIC

At the beginning of the twentieth century, Cuba had an agricultural economy. But development in Cuba's eastern and western rural areas followed different courses during the colonial period. Two culturally dissimilar types of rural dwellers, each with its own artistic expressions, developed in these two areas. In both regions, music was the favorite art form, but each region's music had distinct features.

In the mountainous region of the east, peasant music was known as *son*, despite the fact that the primary musical genre of this area was *nengón*. In the plains of the west, the music was at first known as *Ay!* or *the Ay!* and later was given the name *punto*. Nengón exhibited a balance between earlier African and Hispanic influences, which was maintained even as the genre evolved toward the *son montuno* in one part of the Sierra Maestra, while on the other side it became the *changüí*. Because of the demographic composition in the west, punto remained stylistically closer to Spain.

The main purpose of *son* music is to accompany dancing, while that of punto is to direct the listener toward the poetic texts improvised by its performers. The rural dwellers of the west, known as *guajiros*, were closer to Havana, and through their imagery they created symbols of Cubanness that reached the theaters of the capital and from there were broadcast throughout Cuba. The new republic warmly welcomed these images and the music that accompanied them.

In the early 1900s, the image of the guajiro—dressed in white, with boots, a machete at his belt, and a *yarey* (straw hat), performing punto music by strumming his *laúd* (lute), his extemporaneous poems, and peasant *tonada* (a song or composition that is rhymed)—was the most authentic image of the liberated homeland. But its only characteristic dance, the Cuban *zapateo*, did not have sufficient strength to compete with the dance that accompanied the son, once this reached Havana and its neighboring countryside in the decades following the establishment of the republic.

The wars to liberate Cuba had always moved from east to west. The expansion of the railway, linked to the development of the sugar industry, however, took place from west to east. Traditions moved hand in hand with the movements of people provoked by these events. In this vein, perhaps the most significant event was the establishment of son in the capital, particularly beginning in the 1920s.

The son sextet, with its *tres* (Cuban guitar with three groups of two strings), bongos, *marímbula* (a Caribbean instrument derived from the African lamellophone, or thumb piano), *güiros* (hollow grooved instruments scraped with a stick), maracas, and claves, captured the attention of dancers in the west, who had been swept away by the lavish and energetic dances of the United States, such as the fox trot, ragtime, and one-step. Cuba's humble zapateo had almost been drowned out by these fashionable styles. In order to compete with U.S. musical groups, the son incorporated a seventh instrument, a trumpet, often played with a mute. Thus, in Havana, the classic son septets were born, becoming a favorite of the regular patrons of dance halls and academies throughout the country.

Many creators helped turn son into one of the most authentic expressions of what is typically Cuban. Miguel Matamoros (1894–1971), from Santiago de Cuba, gave it an urban formulation. Ignacio Piñeiro (1888–1969) brought true sonority to the septets of Havana, while Arsenio Rodríguez (1911–1970) added piano and conga drums and increased the number of trumpets, creating the famous *conjuntos cubanos* (Cuban ensembles). Among its great interpreters is the legendary Benny Moré (1919–1963). From the mid-twentieth century onward, son in the hands of Juan Formell and his band Los Van Van, as well as David Calzado and his Charanga Habanera and Elito Revé and his Charangón (among others), achieved a contemporary sound that was competitive in Latin music markets.

The son's dance form was soon more popular than other Cuban dance forms—not only rural forms, but urban ones as well. Its popularity ultimately outstripped even that of the *danzón,* which had come to be known as Cuba's national dance. For the danzón—an evolution of the Cuban *contradanza* and *danza*—to survive at all, it had to transform itself, including adopting stylistic rhythms and behaviors that had first appeared in the son. This development gave rise to the *danzonete* and the *danzón cantado*. But even those adaptations were less popular with Cuban dancers, and during this era, the danzón had to settle for a distant second to the *son*. During this time the son came to be performed commonly by professional popular music groups and not just by rural folk ensembles.

A similar process occurred with the *punto guajiro* form: Despite its being an authentic expression of Cuban peasantry, many of the musical elements arising from *punto guajiro* found a place within Cuban lyric opera and musical theater. Later, those elements were also used in radio programs and, especially, in the first phonographic recordings of Cuban music. Thus the rural *punto cubano* found a place in the hearts of urban Cuban performers. The aesthetic characteristics of the punto are found, therefore, within diverse musical genres that developed from the *canción cubana* (Cuban song). Perhaps the *guajiras* and the *criollas*, initially composed by academically trained musicians of the musical theater, are the most well-known examples.

The twentieth century and the establishment of the republic strengthened another expression of Cuban folk music that had appeared in the nineteenth century: the rhumba. This form, which emerged from the poorest class, drew upon the African musical legacy in Cuba and the social composition of its performers. Freed slaves moved into crowded urban tenements. Each family crowded into a single bedroom and shared the rest of the house with other occupants. For recreation, tenement dwellers threw parties known as *rumbas* on the patios of such houses. The end of the slave trade and slavery in 1886 disconnected Cuba from Africa, and after that the main source of black cultural nourishment was Afro-Cuban music, preserved particularly in the religious practices of former slaves and their Cuban-born descendants. This segment of the population was later culturally enriched by other impoverished and marginalized groups.

Afro-Cuban music continued to gain popularity, since the freeing of the slaves and national political independence created better conditions for it to reach other segments of the population. Its rhythms, played on typical percussion instruments, as well as its unique interpretive formulas, were attractive to intellectuals and artists. Over time this relatively elite and European-influenced sector imposed its own aesthetic criteria on Afro-Cuban music, but Afro-Cuban religious concepts, based on an Africa-derived worldview substantially different from that of the Europeans, proved equally interesting. Both the music and the ideology of Afro-Cuban music enhanced the new philosophical, religious, and artistic views of a Cuban people now free from the yoke of colonial rule.

The mood of the rhumba was different from that of Afro-Cuban music because no attempt was made to preserve and reconstruct original African elements.

The rhumba. A rhumba dancer known as Zulema performs at the Zombie Club in Havana on 16 February 1946. HULTON ARCHIVE/GETTY IMAGES

The main purpose of rhumba was to promote a party atmosphere despite the limited economic and material resources available to the partygoers. Percussion was played on household furniture, such as the side of a wardrobe, the seat of a wooden chair, or a drawer, a practice that evolved into the use of boxes and crates of different sizes. Somewhat later during this same period, makeshift drums came into use, constructed of a skin stretched over wooden staves in a barrel shape. These instruments were known as *tumbadoras,* although later on the rest of the world identified them as congas.

The music and dance of the rhumba was so influential that it expanded from the tenements and to the street during huge carnival celebrations. Throughout the first half of the twentieth century, traditional or folk music was essential to the evolution of all Cuban music, particularly popular and classical Cuban music.

POPULAR MUSIC

The development of the phonographic industry in the United States and the beginning of radio transmissions in Cuba affected the evolution of Cuban music. These technological advances created demand for folk or traditional music performed by musicians with formal training. This development was similar to the nineteenth-century evolution of the contradanza on its path to the danzón. But during the first half of the twentieth century, popular professional music for the first time caught up with many other traditional forms, such as the punto guajiro, the rhumba, and particularly the son.

The artists who performed on the radio and cut records had to be well trained, have sufficient command of their instruments, and be able to coordinate with ensemble members. Using nuance and a range of timbres, they had to make their music appeal to listeners. Traditional and folk musicians were not always able to reach this level of performance.

In previous periods, the interpretation of *danzones* was always connected to instruments that required formal training. Such was the case with the use of violins, flutes, and piano in orchestras known as *charangas francesas,* or the clarinet, trumpet, *bombardino* (a smaller tuba-like instrument), and other instruments typical of military bands, which had also found a place in the dance bands known as *piquetes típicos cubanos.* But the typical instruments used in the interpretation of *son—tres,* bongos, *marímbulas,* guiros, and claves—had been played by traditional (though formally untrained) musicians and had not been taken up by the academy. Now, however, that music was subject to the same criteria as were the conventional bands, if the music was to be broadcast on the radio or recorded. This expectation brought the levels reached by *son* groups, such as the Sexteto Habanero or even smaller singing groups such as the Trío Matamoros, in line with the professional quality of recognized danzón ensembles, such as that of the maestro Antonio María Romeu (1876–1955).

Havana was in the forefront. There, starting in the early years of the twentieth century, the U.S. record companies RCA Victor and Columbia recorded such performers of guajira music as Miguel Díaz, Antonio Domini, Antonio Morejón, Juan Pagés, Martín Silveira, Armando Rodríguez, and Miguel Puertas Salgado. They also made records of the danzón groups, including Orquesta Francesa de Tata Alfonso, the orchestra of the Teatro Alambra, the Orquesta Bambuco, the Orquesta Cubana Columbia, the Orquesta de Domingo Corbacho, and the Orquesta de Tomás Corman, along with those of Félix González, Jaime Prats, Pablo Valenzuela, Tomás Ponce Reyes, Antonio "Papaíto" Toroella, and Antonio María Romeu. Great Cuban *trova* balladeers such as Sindo Garay, Manuel Corona, Alberto Villalón, and Maria Teresa Vera were recorded, as well as opera and operetta singers such as Rosalía "Chalía" Herrera, Mariano Meléndez, Eusebio Delfín, Claudio García, and artists of the Teatro Musical Cubano (Cuban Musical Theater), such as Blanca Becerra, Arturo Feliú, Regino López, Arquímedes Pous, Guillermo Anckermann, Ramón Espigul, and Los Negritos de Palatino.

Among the recordings of *son* groups of the first half of the twentieth century, there were, in addition to the Sexteto Habanero, recordings from the Cuarteto Oriental, Son Santiaguero, Cuarteto Cruz, and Grupo Sinsonte y Vázquez. Recordings were also made of such varied groups as the Banda de Infantería, Banda Municipal, the Eliseo Grenet Orchestra, and the Luis Casas Romero Orchestra.

Musical theater and its typical stages saw the evolution of *canción cubana,* particularly because in that venue the classic Cuban song was enriched with stylistic elements taken from other manifestations of Cuban music. A good example was the Teatro Alhambra (1890–1935); the Cuban style of the music interpreted there was mixed with patriotic symbols that became strong criticisms of current politicians. Here, the musical creation of Jorge Anckermann, its director from 1911 until it closed, as well as his predecessors Manuel Mauri, Rafael Palau, and José Marín Varona, is particularly noteworthy. Other important theaters were the Teatro Cubano (previously the Molino Rojo), with the creations of Jaime Prats and Eliseo Grenet, as well as the Martí and Payret theaters, whose orchestras were directed by Moisés Simons. The Regina theater, under the baton of the composer and pianist Ernesto Lecuona, also served as an important setting for the evolution of the canción cubana during the first years of the republic, as did the Cuban zarzuelas that were later heard around the world—both those penned by Lecuona and those of other great musicians such as Rodrigo Prats and Gonzalo Roig.

The development of the *canción* within the framework of Cuban lyric theater facilitated changes in the bolero, which caused this form to reach different segments of the Cuban population. Born in the context of the *trova* ballad tradition in Santiago de Cuba, and limited until that time to guitar accompaniment, this Cuban musical genre appealed to audiences that enjoyed both lyrics and dancing. Bolero became a favorite, together with the *son*, among regular dance-hall patrons. Boleros thus entered the repertoires of popular groups of the time—*charangas, conjuntos,* jazz bands, and others—and the piano occupied an increasingly larger role in the harmony. This whole process resulted, toward the end of this era, in the appearance of a new type of bolero known as *feeling*.

The era from 1900 to 1945 as a whole can be best understood regarding Cuban music if it is divided into three stages: the first years of the republic (1902–1920); the 1920s; and the period of consolidation of popular Cuban music (1930–1950). Relatively little happened in Cuban music during the first phase; unlike the efflorescence of Cuban music in the nineteenth century, the music in this period stagnated. But the 1920s phonographic and radio industries revitalized it. Cuban music prior to the 1920s was mainly characterized by the search for new symbols of national identity within the altered context that the republic offered to the artists.

In the 1920s, Cuban music took the shape it would have for the remainder of the first half of the century. Supported by technological advances, this music became known throughout the world, earning approval from audiences in musical cultures quite unlike Cuba's. And by the 1930s, the road Cuban music would take until the 1950s had been defined. The *son*, with all its acquired urban characteristics, had reached its mature phase and had expanded—with its septets—throughout the country, in a triumphant march that bypassed even musical groups from the United States.

Between 1930 and 1950, mostly thanks to Arsenio Rodríguez from Matanzas, the first *conjuntos cubanos* appeared. Rodríguez added a piano and conga drums to the septet format and increased the number of trumpets, playing in harmonic blocks in a form similar to that of the era's jazz bands. This new type of group was better prepared than any prior form to interpret the varied genres of Cuban music, such as boleros and other types of canciones. In addition, the conjuntos cubanos could perform danzones and danzonetes and even reproduce the sounds of punto guajiro and the rhumba. The conjunto cubano later became, in the era of salsa music, one of the typical pan-Latin instrumental formats that included the *plenas, cumbias, merengues,* and other musical genres of the Spanish-speaking Caribbean in its repertoire.

The 1930s and 1940s was also the golden age of the Cuban zarzuela, a Spanish form of operetta: *María la O* (Maria the O, 1930), by Ernesto Lecuona, and *Cecilia Valdés* (1932), by Gonzalo Roig, traveled throughout the world, accompanied by popular songs such as "Tabú" and "Babalú," by Margarita Lecuona, and the "Danzón Almendra" by Abelardo Valdés. Female ensembles such as Anacaona, Renovación,

Ensueño, Hermanas González, and Indias del Caribe appeared and began competing with the many jazz-band type orchestras that were already playing the Cuban sounds, for example, the Lecuona Cuban Boys, the Timor brothers' Habana Casino, the Mariano Mercerón Orchestra, the Avilés Brothers Orchestra, the Armando Valdespí Orchestra, and Casino de la Playa.

In the 1940s, called by some the "golden age of Cuban radio," song and performance competitions became popular and strengthened the musical artistic talent of the whole country. The most important of these competitions was La Corte Suprema del Arte (the Supreme Court of Art), sponsored by the radio station CMQ. The Cuban *guaracha* (a popular dance form used in musical theater and dance halls) was enriched with the work of Ñico Saquito, and a type of *tumbao* called *mambo* began to be used in playing danzones; this form, with its shrill sound and sensuality, later became important, particularly in the work of Dámaso Pérez Prado.

The Conjuntos de Senén Suárez and Estrellas de Chapotín and the charangas Almendra, Siglo XX, Aragón, and Arcaño y sus Maravillas all appeared, as did the jazz bands Riverside, Pérez Prado Orchestra, Orquesta Cosmopolita, and the Julio Cuevas Orchestra, among others that gave a particular strength to Cuban dance music. It was in the context of Arcaño's charanga that the López brothers achieved the transformations of the danzón that later inspired the creation of the mambo by Dámaso Pérez Prado. The son septets, such as the Septeto Nacional of Ignacio Piñeiro and that of Miguel Matamoros, continued to play, and the danzón orchestras continued to rise and fall in favor among dance patrons over the decades. This period as a whole established the conditions that made possible the success of the 1950s, known as the time of the greatest blossoming in the history of Cuban popular music.

CLASSICAL OR CONCERT MUSIC

Cuban classical music in the early twentieth century reflected the notable academic training of Cuban musicians during the nineteenth century. The piano and the violin held places of esteem, but the country also had a strong academy in wind instruments, arising from the intense work carried out by its Spanish military bands.

The start of the republican era led to a search for inspiration in symbols of nationality already present in Cuba's folk and traditional music. But these symbols were very different from one another. The image and the music of the guajiro in the west monopolized musical theater and the attention of many composers, but this source was not rich. The guajiro singers improvised lyrics and called themselves poets, but they repeated the same tunes over and over. Afro-Cuban music proved more advantageous to composers of

BOLA DE NIEVE

Bola de Nieve (1911–1971) in China, 1962. Cuban musician Ignacio Villa (front right), better known as Bola de Nieve, on a tour of China in 1962. AP IMAGES/PRENSA LATINA

Born into a family steeped in Santería, Palo Mayombe, and Abakuá, and growing up in Guanabacoa, a Havana suburb rich in Afro-Cuban traditions, Ignacio Villa (1911–1971) began his musical training early. He worked as a piano accompanist first in a local cinema and then to various singers. In 1933, while touring Mexico with the singer Rita Montaner (1900–1958), he gave his first solo performance, singing "Bito Manué," adapted from Nicolás Guillén's poem. Montaner gave him the nickname *Bola de Nieve* (Snowball), ironically describing his black face and round body. His raspy voice, broad smile, waistcoat, ability to sing in several languages, and histrionic style were signatures of this exponent of the international spoken song. Villa performed throughout Latin America, Europe, and the United States. He remained loyal to the Cuban Revolution and its repudiation of racial segregation. The composer of "Tú me has de querer," and "Ay amor," his repertoire ranged from Afro-Cuban racial themes such as "Mesié Julian" to romantic material and show tunes such as "Be Careful It's My Heart."

Glenn Jacobs

Cuban classical music, but the Afro-Cuban style faced opposition amid the prevailing racial discrimination against blacks and black cultural forms. A third source

was, therefore, artificially created: An aesthetic tendency called *siboneyism* attempted to revive the music of Cuba's aboriginal past—in particular, that of the indigenous Siboney people—as the authentic music of the young Cuban nation.

The majority of the Cuban indigenous population was Taíno, however, not Siboney; the Siboneys had essentially disappeared long before the rise of the first aesthetic expressions considered Cuban and, therefore, were not able to contribute to them. Furthermore, during the time when indigenous people still lived in Cuba, there were no technologies available to preserve the sounds of their music. Academically trained musicians who visited Cuba from Europe did not take away musical scores that would have allowed the music to be preserved for posterity. Therefore, it was impossible to know how this music really sounded. Nonetheless, many musicians defended the thesis of siboneyism and created grand works based on it.

The greatest Cuban composer at the beginning of the twentieth century, Eduardo Sánchez de Fuentes (1874–1944), followed this trend. He composed a variety of operas with Cuban themes, such as *Yumurí*, *El náufrago* (The Castaway), *La dolorosa* (The Sorrowful Woman), and *Dorey*; he also created immortal songs such as "Corazón" (Heart) and his *habanera* "Tú" (You), in addition to many compositions for piano. However, this great musician, art promoter, and musicologist carefully avoided acknowledging the Afro-Cuban influence on the island's musical culture and instead attempted to demonstrate the existence of a supposed *Areíto Anacaona* (the *areíto* was a lengthy musical ritual, and Anacaona was the Taíno queen who greeted Cuba's first governor in 1511) of Siboney origin, where, he believed, the authentic and primary patriotic symbols of the nation were to be found.

Cuban intellectuals ultimately revealed the fallacy of siboneyism. Meanwhile, Afro-Cuban music had so much influence over the creative output of composers such as Amadeo Roldán (1900–1939) and Alejandro García Caturla (1906–1940), among other important creators of Cuban symphonic music, that the aesthetic trend derived from their works was later identified with *Afrocubanismo* (despite the fact that many of their compositions were inspired by Cuban, and not Afro-Cuban, music). Important Afro-Cuban symphonic works include *Motivos de son* (Son Motifs), by Roldán, and *La rumba*, by García Caturla. Operas, including *La esclava* (The Slave), by José Mauri, and *Manita en el suelo* (Little Hand on the Floor), by García Caturla, were also characterized by these Afro-Cuban influences.

In 1922, the Orquesta Sinfónica de La Habana (Havana Symphony Orchestra) was founded under the direction of Gonzalo Roig. A year later Roig created the Orquesta Filarmónica (Philharmonic Orchestra), which later came under the baton of the famous German orchestra director Erich Kleiber. The competition between these two orchestras in the capital was beneficial for the development of symphonic music in Cuba, a development that was reinforced by the work of the Pro Arte Musical Society (which brought many notable international artists to the country) and the educational work of various music conservatories, under the direction of notable maestros of the stature of Hubert de Blanck and Guillermo Tomás.

Amadeo Roldán started off with the Havana Symphony Orchestra as concertmaster and debuted many of the works that would transform Cuban music there. Together with García Caturla—who presented himself as Roldán's musical antithesis but who followed along the same path laid down by Afrocubanismo—Roldán changed the sound of classical music in Cuba. Roldán and García Caturla situated Cuban classical efforts within a musical nationalism that was enriched by adapting the most modern musical composition techniques in the world and by embracing the legacy of Afro-Cuban music and the African heritage that survived in Cuban traditional and folk music.

Roldán and García Caturla had virtually no competition during their time, but after their deaths, in 1939 and 1940, respectively, Cuban music changed again. The new path was forged by José Ardévol, a Spanish composer living in Havana, and the new aesthetic trend was guided by neoclassicism with a Cuban flavor.

As a great educator in the art of music, Ardévol surrounded himself with outstanding students of the Municipal Conservatory of Havana, and in 1942 he created the Grupo de Renovación Musical (Music Renewal Group). Ardévol's group included many important composers of the generation that followed Roldán and García Caturla, including Hilario González, Harold Gramatges, Julián Orbón, Juan Antonio Cámara, Serafín Pro, Virginia Fleites, Gisela Hernández, Enrique Aparicio Bellver, Argeliers León, Dolores Torres, and Edgardo Martín. Other composers such as Evelio Tieles Soler, Alfredo Diez Nieto, Natalio Galán, Fabio Landa, Nilo Rodríguez, Gilberto Valdés, Pablo Ruiz Castellanos, Aurelio de la Vega, Olga de Blanck, Félix Guerrero, and Carlos Borbolla also contributed to changing the sound of classical music in Cuba as the 1950s began.

SELECTED DISCOGRAPHY

Arsenio Rodríguez y su conjunto. *Arsenio Rodríguez y su conjunto* (1959–1960).

Frank Emilio Flynn y sus amigos. *Barbarísimo* (1997).

Trío Matamoros. *Trío Matamoros* (1991).

Various Artists. *Fiesta cubana: Congas y comparsas* (1991).

Various Artists. *Fiesta cubana: El bolero* (1991).

Various Artists. *Fiesta cubana: El danzón* (1991).

Various Artists. *Cuban Counterpoint: History of the Son Montuno* (1992).

Various Artists. *Son al son de Cuba* (1995).

Various Artists. *Trova tradicional cubana* (1995).

Various Artists. *Official Retrospective of Cuban Music* (1999).

Various Artists. *Grandes orquestas cubanas* (1999).

BIBLIOGRAPHY

Alén Rodríguez, Olavo. *Pensamiento musicológico*. Havana: Editorial Letras Cubanas, 2006.

Carpentier, Alejo. *La música en Cuba*. Havana: Editorial Luz-Hilo, 1961.

Collazo, Bobby. *La última noche que pasé contigo: 40 años de farándula cubana*. San Juan, Puerto Rico: Editorial Cubanacán, 1987.

Díaz Ayala, Cristóbal. *Música cubana, del areyto al rap cubano*. 4th ed. San Juan, Puerto Rico: Editorial Cubanacán, 2003.

Moore, Robin D. *Nationalizing Blackness. Afrocubanismo and Artistic Revolution in Havana, 1920–1949*. Pittsburgh, PA: University of Pittsburgh Press, 1997.

Sublette, Ned. *Cuba and Its Music*. Chicago: Chicago Review Press, 2004.

MUSIC: 1945–1958

Ned Sublette

Cuban music following World War II until the Revolution in 1959.

During World War II, noncombatant Cuba experienced a musical boom that extended into the 1950s. (By contrast, music in the United States went through a lull, which would be followed by a postwar boom.) By 1937, after years of bombs going off in public during the struggle against Gerardo Machado, a semblance of normalcy had resumed. In 1940 Fulgencio Batista became president after a relatively clean election in which he made an alliance with Cuba's large Communist Party—something possible only at that time, when the Franklin D. Roosevelt administration was promoting the image of Joseph Stalin as an ally against Nazi Germany. The war brought better economic conditions as well, as Cuba annually sold its entire sugar harvest to the United States at a high price. Musicians may not have made much money, but they had steady work. Between 1942 and 1944 the United States recording industry had been paralyzed by an American Federation of Musicians strike, making room for the first independent Cuban label, Panart (founded by recording engineer Ramón Sabat), to come to market in 1943. With the war far away, and with peace and relative prosperity at home, Cuba was dancing once again.

NEW PLAYERS, NEW STYLES

In the 1940s there were still barrio elders who had been born in Africa and brought to Cuba as slaves through the 1860s. Arsenio Rodríguez (1911–1970),

■ *See also*

The "Mambo King": Dámaso Pérez Prado

Mr. Rhythm: Benny Moré

"Queen of Salsa": Celia Cruz

a descendant of enslaved Africans, grew up in the Congo culture of Matanzas Province and first learned to play African-descended instruments. He expressed an overtly African cultural consciousness as soon as it was politically and socially possible to do so. Perhaps more than anyone else, Rodríguez made musicians conscious of the complexities of the *clave*, the rhythmic key that holds polyrhythm together.

Rodríguez also popularized the use of the *tumbadora* (conga drum) in a new instrumental format called the *conjunto*, an ensemble that expanded the *son* septet to include two (or more) trumpets and piano; later, this grouping served as a prototype for the salsa band. Whereas in the 1920s a musician could have been thrown in jail for playing *bongó* in the street, during the cultural opening of the late 1930s—despite the persistence of Cuban society's racial segregation—the drum was liberated. Rodríguez's move toward *conjunto* was countered by his friendly competitor and booking agent Antonio Arcaño (1911–1994), who added the formerly disreputable conga to his *charanga* orchestra, composed of flute, strings, and piano, creating the style he called *nuevo ritmo* (new rhythm). At La Polar and La Tropical, Havana's huge open-air beer-garden dancehalls, a discerning eye might have noticed that dancers from different barrios had different steps and that people who traveled in on the train from Matanzas to dance with Rodríguez, Arcaño y sus Maravillas, and Melodías del 40 brought still other steps.

One significant consequence of Batista's alliance with the Communists was that a Communist radio station was allowed on Cuba's busy airwaves, making for a unique chapter in hemispheric broadcasting, and Cuban musical, history. Although the station, Mil Diez, did not transmit at blowtorch power, it had repeaters across the island, and its 1010 frequency, an international clear channel, allowed it to be heard over long distances at night. Mil Diez sold commercial time but did not attract many sponsors. It had a strongly nationalist cultural policy that emphasized Cuban music, and though it paid musicians much less than the big stations, CMQ and RHC-Cadena Azul, its programming was impressive: Rodríguez's *conjunto* played live on Mil Diez at five every afternoon, and at seven came Arcaño's eighteen-piece Radiofónica.

Many singers became nationally known on Mil Diez. The new jazz-influenced romantic style called *feeling* (or *filin*) had a home there, with composers that included César Portillo de la Luz (who had his own show), José Antonio Méndez, and Ángel Díaz; singers, including Elena Burke and Omara Portuondo; and pianist Frank Emilio Flynn.

In the music-rich environment of 1940s Havana, composers and arrangers flourished. Mil Diez had an orchestra on staff, with no less than ten arrangers working under the direction of Félix Guerrero. Meanwhile, arrangers René Hernández, Dámaso Pérez Prado, and Ramón "Bebo" Valdés (b. 1918) were cultivating the styles that would soon be essential to big-band

mambo—a polyrhythmic way of scoring for jazz band that made the sax section independent from the other horns, and more rhythmic in function. When Hernández decamped to New York in 1945 to join Machito and His Afro-Cubans, Valdés took his chair in Julio Cueva's Camagüey-based big band, heard nationally on CMQ; their 1946 recording of Valdés's composition "La rareza del siglo" can be heard as an early mambo. Andrés Echevarría ("Niño Rivera"), known as a *tresero* (one who plays the *tres*, a guitar-like instrument with three wide-spaced pairs of strings, used to play a percolating rhythmic line) but also an arranger, worked with *feeling* musicians as he promoted something he called *cubibop*. Chico O'Farrill went to the United States and became an in-demand jazz arranger; his breakthrough 1948 hit, "Undercurrent Blues," was composed for Benny Goodman (1909–1986).

Arcaño y Sus Maravillas had in 1938 debuted "Mambo," a composition by Orestes López (1908–1991), the orchestra's cellist. In this case, the mambo was a final section added onto a *danzón*, with heavier rhythm. Rodríguez claimed with some justification to have been the first to do such a thing, but he never promoted the term *mambo*: he called it *diablo*. Arcaño did not brand what he did as mambo either and did not record López's "Mambo" until 1951, after Pérez Prado's success with a mambo that sounded quite different. But Orestes López's "Mambo" featured a new style of bass line by the composer's brother, Israel López (1918–2008), who was better known as "Cachao." As Bebo Valdés explained it, before Cachao Cuban music had *contratiempo* (countertime) but not syncopation. Cachao was arguably the most influential bassist of the century, and not just in Cuba: His influence extends into jazz, salsa, funk, and pop.

In 1944 Ramón Grau San Martín was elected president of Cuba and presided over the transition from World War II–era policies to Cold War anticommunism. In 1945 Cubans celebrated the Allied victory in a street party that went on for days, the crowds endlessly singing *Pin, pin, cayó Berlín! Pon, pon, cayó Japón!* (pin, pin, Berlin fell, pon, pon, Japan fell). The line was from one of many sing-along hits composed by Afro-Cuban drummer Chano Pozo (1915–1948), whose street-singing style derived from the *comparsa* groups that paraded at carnival. Pozo's music was predictive of pop songwriting to come, one based not on song structures but on what would later be called *hooks* on top of percussive grooves. As recorded on 20 June 1946, with Orlando Guerra "Cascarita" on vocals and Bebo Valdés on piano, it was a big hit for Julio Cueva's band.

Another animating feature of Cuban music was religion. Cuba's African religions were audible: on Sunday nights Radio Suaritos aired a program called *¿Qué pasa en casa? Merceditas con los batá* that featured Merceditas Valdés singing sacred Lucumí music with batá drums. A few years later, in 1948, Suaritos would be the platform from which the twenty-year-old Celina González would sing her *afro-guajira*

Opposite page:
Chano Pozo (1915–1948). Cuban percussionist Chano Pozo (center) plays the conga in 1948 with American jazz greats James Moody on saxophone and Dizzy Gillespie on trumpet. Pozo's collaboration with Gillespie ignited a period of rhythmic experimentation in African American music, as a new generation of drummers found all sorts of ways to hybridize Afro-Cuban sounds with jazz. FRANK DRIGGS COLLECTION/ GETTY IMAGES

anthem, "A Santa Bárbara," better known as "Que Viva Changó," which named an African *orishá* and its corresponding Catholic saint in the same lyric.

CUBAN MUSIC MEETS JAZZ IN NEW YORK

Some of the most notable recording dates during this era took place in New York. One was led by Pozo, whose formidable Conjunto Azul broadcast on RHC-Cadena Azul, the Cuban radio station for which he had previously worked as a bootblack. Shortly after his arrival in New York in February 1947, Pozo, together with Arsenio Rodríguez (on his first visit to New York), José Mangual, Carlos Vidal, and Miguelito Valdés, cut the first-ever recordings of barrio-style rhumba, consisting of only voice and percussion (including "Abasí," from the Calabar-descended Abakua secret men's society). This was music that RCA Victor had never wanted to record in Cuba. Three days later, Pozo recorded with Rodríguez and members of Machito's group, including the young Puerto Rican singer Tito Rodríguez. Also recorded around the same time, under the direction of René Hernández, were twelve sides by the young Olga Guillot (a former Mil Diez singer on her way to becoming one of the major stars of Cuban song), including her version of "La gloria eres tú" (José Antonio Méndez's new song, soon to be a standard).

In response to the desire by Dizzy Gillespie (1917–1993) to include congas in his music, Machito's music director and brother-in-law Mario Bauzá introduced him to Pozo, who back in Havana had already worked out how to make the congas function in jazz. Their collaboration on "Manteca" was Gillespie's biggest hit. With a nightclub entertainer's professionalism, utter self-confidence, and plenty of charisma, Pozo invented a soloist's role for the conga drum and more generally introduced U.S. musicians and audiences to the instrument. Pozo and Gillespie's collaboration ignited a great, though little remarked upon, period of rhythmic experimentation in African American music, as a new generation of drummers found all sorts of ways to hybridize Afro-Cuban with jazz. Chano Pozo, however, never saw it happen: he was shot to death in Harlem in December 1948. A host of Cuban *congueros* in the United States followed the trail he had blazed—Candido Camero, Armando Peraza, Carlos "Patato" Valdés, Francisco Aguabella, Julito Collazo, and especially Mongo Santamaría—bringing skills that jazz bandleaders and even pop singers wanted in their bands.

POSTWAR YEARS

During the 1940s the reigning diva of Cuba was Rita Montaner (1900–1958), who adopted the persona Lengualisa on her radio talk show *Mejor que me calle* (Better I Keep Quiet). During Grau's presidency, Lengualisa made daily remarks critical of government corruption. On 1 May 1948 Mil Diez was shut down by the police, and its irreplaceable collection of scores, manuscripts, and recordings disappeared. A month later, Grau's deputy Carlos Prío Socarrás won what would be Cuba's last presidential election, and Cuba sank deeper into political *gangsterismo*. That same year, broadcasting brothers Abel and Goar Mestre opened their deluxe new CMQ Radiocentro. Occupying a prime block of real estate, it made Havana's Vedado neighborhood the city's new nerve center.

The postwar years saw the flourishing of Havana's Tropicana, a casino and pleasure garden that was in competition with the Sans Souci and the Montmartre. Choreographer Rodney (Rodrigo Neira) had created a style of lavish super-revue, with themes that ranged from Haitian voodoo to Greek goddesses to (on one occasion) cocaine, headlined by top-name Cuban or international musical talent. It may have been kitsch, but it was great kitsch, and after the show there was dancing. The three venues employed hundreds of artistic personnel, including a number of top-notch musicians, who on occasion jammed with visiting jazz stars from the United States. At the Tropicana, where Montaner sang, the house band was led by Armando Romeu with Bebo Valdés on piano and Guillermo Barreto on trap drums. Two spaces with music operated at once in the huge pleasure garden. Orquesta Riverside, with Pedro Justiz ("Peruchín") as pianist and arranger and Tito Gómez on vocals, played at the Tropicana twice weekly for nine years, besides appearing every Sunday on CMQ's high-profile, Coca Cola–sponsored radio program *La Pausa que Refrezca*.

Arsenio Rodríguez left Havana to resettle in New York in 1951, where he continued to make music but had the status of cult figure rather than headliner. In his absence, the black *conjunto* style was extended and further popularized in Havana by archetypal *son* trumpeter Félix Chappotín, with singer Miguelito Cuní. Sonora Matancera, a band that had been working its way up since 1924 and was now a *conjunto*, appeared on the radio every day, where it made something of a specialty of creating simple, consistent house-band arrangements backing whatever vocalist was visiting. The band made albums with a number of singers, having their greatest success with the Puerto Rican bohemian Daniel Santos. Ultimately, the most famous of their singers would be Celia Cruz, though she became a much bigger star after leaving Cuba (and subsequently leaving Sonora Matancera).

Television came to Cuba in October 1950. The mostly white dance band Conjunto Casino did well on early Cuban television; the band also became a regular on CMQ in 1951, with the diminutive black *conguero* and dancer Carlos "Patato" Valdés as the visual star of the group. At movie houses, live variety shows took the stage between screenings, and as of 1945 the theaters were required by law to present them.

The singer Bartolomé Moré (1919–1963), who changed his name to Benny, became one of the most influential figures in Cuban music in the 1950s. He had traveled to Mexico in 1945 with a *conjunto* led by Miguel Matamoros that also included *trovador* Francisco Repilado ("Compay Segundo"). He remained there when Matamoros left, recording with various bandleaders, most spectacularly with Pérez Prado, a pianist from Matanzas with a sarcastic sense of humor and a taste for strident timbres and dissonant harmonies. The incandescent records they made in Mexico City brought the word *mambo* to the attention of the entire Hispanic world beginning in 1949, largely through the music's placement on the soundtracks of black-and-white Mexican melodramatic movies that featured sexy Cuban actresses in lurid urban settings. Moré sang with Pérez Prado in movies that were seen in Cuba.

Returning to Cuba in late 1950, Moré went to Santiago, where he sang with Mariano Mercerón's band, then was called back to Havana by Bebo Valdés in a short-lived attempt to promote a new big-band style that Valdés called *batanga*. In 1952 Moré made his Cuban theatrical debut, though it was more like a coronation. On the stage of Havana's new Teatro Blanquita, at that time one of the largest theaters in the world, in the elite neighborhood of Miramar, the long list of artists who sang with him was topped by Rita Montaner. He began his own Banda Gigante in 1953, with trombonist Generoso Jiménez serving as music director and arranger. Ostensibly modeled on the big band of famed American bandleader Glenn Miller, it showed more clearly the influence of Pérez Prado and Bebo Valdés. During the 1950s he became enshrined as the most popular Cuban singer of all time.

A DANCE WITHOUT EQUAL

People in Cuba did not dance mambo; that was a New York thing. But in 1953 the *cha-cha-chá* erupted out of Havana to sweep the world, replacing mambo's polyrhythm with something more like a beat and offering the nonvirtuosic dancer an easy, catchy step: *one-two-cha-cha-chá*. It began with a two-sided hit single by Ninón Mondéjar's Orquesta América on the Panart label: "Silver Star" and "La Engañadora," compositions by the group's violinist, Enrique Jorrín. According to the label on the disc, "Silver Star" was a *danzón*, but its chorus went, *Cha-cha-chá, cha-cha-chá, es un baile sin igual* ("... is a dance without equal"). The other side, "La Engañadora" (The Deceiver), was labeled "mambo-rhumba," but it too was a *cha-cha-chá*. By the following year, the *cha-cha-chá* had caught on everywhere, and in the United States what became known simply as cha-cha was a fundamental template for the emerging style called rock and roll.

The *cha-cha-chá* was the property of the *charangas*, with Orquesta Aragón quickly taking the lead. Founded in Cienfuegos in 1939 by bassist Orestes Aragón (d. 1962), the orchestra had worked the length and breadth of the island, learning its various styles of music, but it was frozen out of bookings in Havana

until fellow Cienfuegero and superstar Benny Moré intervened on the group's behalf. By then, Aragón had stepped down from active direction, and the group was in its second generation, led by violinist Rafael Lay. Its repertoire went well beyond the typical *danzón* of the *charanga* to incorporate *son* and other genres. When Lay went to visit *cha-cha-chá* creator Enrique Jorrín in Havana, the generous Jorrín gave him his scores to copy. Instantly Aragón had a hip new book of *cha-cha-chá*s, taken from Orquesta América, which they played with rock-solid rhythmic authority. Their recording of "El Agua de Clavelito" (RCA Victor) became a hit in the summer of 1954 at the carnival of Santiago de Cuba. Aragón rose to fame as the top *cha-cha-chá* group, and after adding Richard Egües on flute with his percussive style, the classic form of the band was complete by 1955.

With jukeboxes everywhere, the 1950s were unquestionably the golden age of the Cuban record industry. Cuban labels proliferated, while RCA Victor continued to compete. Even hard-core rhumba came into the light, a little bit: The Cuban label Puchito cut successful sides with a group called Guaguancó Matancero, subsequently known as Los Muñequitos de Matanzas, and issued an album featuring those recordings on one side and Havana rhumba group Papín y Sus Rumberos (later called Los Papines) on the other. By that time Cuban music was mainstream in the United States. Pérez Prado's slowed-down *cha-cha-chá* "Cherry Pink and Apple Blossom White" was number one on the *Billboard* chart for nine weeks in 1955. Fifty million television viewers heard Marco Rizo's *I Love Lucy* theme every week, while on the *Tonight* show, hosted by Jack Paar, the bandleader was José Melis. In New York the Palladium was blaring, and Cuban *charanguero* José Fajardo made a splash there in 1958, with Federico Aristides Soto ("Tata Güines") on congas.

HAVANA NIGHTS

In 1952 Batista took control of Cuba in a nearly bloodless military coup. Over the next few years Havana nightlife, powered by gambling, became a major economic engine and created lots of work for musicians. The peak was 1957, the year Benny Moré made some of his most famous recordings. Cachao, who had transformed Cuban music once already, recorded his first *descargas*, or, as the first album title put it, *Cuban Jam Session in Miniature*. Those Panart sides, recorded after hours with no written charts, popularized an approach that would be developed by subsequent Latin jazz musicians. Albums were being pressed domestically, and for a few years comedian-impresario Guillermo Álvarez Guedes released albums on his GEMA label. Panart had put its *cha-cha-chá* money into building a state-of-the-art recording studio, the first one in Havana.

The year 1957 began with a New Year's Day bomb that exploded in the packed Tropicana. Bebo

Valdés was sheltered by a palm tree, but it tore off the arm of a young woman. On 13 March revolutionary student groups attacked the presidential palace in Havana, provoking a gun battle that killed dozens and setting off a murderous wave of reprisals by the government against opposition figures. Oblivious to the turmoil, gangster Meyer Lansky opened his Hotel Riviera on 10 December, a high-roller's paradise that was heavily promoted in the United States on Steve Allen's NBC variety show. But people were becoming afraid even to take their children to the movies, and by the second half of 1958, things were quite tense. Fittingly for a party-commerce town, the climax came on New Year's Eve, when Batista fled the country. From 1959 to 1963, the international center of gravity of Latin music shifted away from Havana, leaving New York the unquestioned capital and pushing Puerto Ricans further forward. The image of Cuba, previously omnipresent in the United States, fell into a memory hole. But the music had already thoroughly infiltrated the styles of musicians in the United States and worldwide and continued to exert its influence.

In Cuba, an entire world was thrown to the ground. Musicians left, musicians stayed; meanwhile, entrepreneurship, support personnel, technicians, venues, replacement parts, international connections, and financial incentives disappeared. Cuban political and material culture underwent wrenching changes, preserving the stopped-in-time look of 1958 for decades to come. An exile community grew up in Miami, but it created no dance bands of note. A new Cuban music had to be created from the ashes of the old, but that took some time. Meanwhile, music in Cuba never stopped. New Year's Day 1959 was officially the first day that singer and dancer Rafael "Felo" Bacallao became a frontline member of Orquesta Aragón, a band that was beginning its third decade and would keep Cuba dancing in the 1960s.

SELECTED DISCOGRAPHY

Arcaño y sus Maravillas. *Danzón mambo 1944–1951.*

Celina y Reutilio. *Santa Bárbara.*

Conjunto Casino. *Rumba quimbumba 1941–1946.*

Cueva, Julio. *Desintegrando.*

Machito and His Afro-Cubans: *Machito and His Afro-Cubans–1941.*

Machito and His Afro-Cubans (with Miguelito Valdés). *Cuban Rhythms.*

Machito and His Afro-Cubans (with Miguelito Valdés). *Freezelandia.*

Moré, Benny. *Grabaciones Completas.*

Moré, Benny (with Pérez Prado). *El Bárbaro del Ritmo.*

Orquesta América. *Silver Star.*

Orquesta Aragón. *Mambo Inspiración: Primeras grabaciones, 1953–1955.*

Pérez Prado, Dámaso. *Kuba-mambo 1947–1949.*

Pozo, Chano. *El tambor de Cuba.*

Rodríguez, Arsenio. *Montuneando 1946–1950.*

Rodríguez, Arsenio. *Dundunbanza 1946–1951.*

Sonora Matancera. *Se formó la rumbantela.*

Sonora Matancera. *Celia Cruz en vivo CMQ v. 5, 1951–1952.*

BIBLIOGRAPHY

Acosta, Leonardo. *Descarga cubana: El jazz en Cuba, 1900–1950.* Havana: Ediciones Unión, 2000.

Contreras, Félix, ed. *Porque tienen filin.* Santiago de Cuba: Editorial Oriente, 1989.

Delannoy, Luc. *¡Caliente! Una historia del jazz latino.* Translated by María Antonia Neira Bigorra. Mexico City: Fondo de Cultura Económica, 2001.

Díaz-Ayala, Cristóbal, comp. *Enciclopedia discográfica de la música cubana 1925–1960.* Díaz-Ayala Cuban and Latin American Popular Music Collection. Florida International University Libraries. Available from http://latinpop.fiu.edu/downloadfiles.html.

English, T. J. *Havana Nocturne: How the Mob Owned Cuba—and Then Lost It to the Revolution.* New York: William Morrow, 2008.

Fajardo, Ramón. *Rita Montaner: Testimonio de una época.* Havana: Fondo Editorial Casa de las Américas, 1997.

García, David F. *Arsenio Rodríguez and the Transnational Flows of Latin Popular Music.* Philadelphia: Temple University Press, 2006.

Garriga, Silvana, ed. *Mamá, yo quiero saber…: Entrevistas a músicos cubanos.* Havana: Editorial Letras Cubanas, 1999.

Giro, Radamés. "Todo lo que usted quiso saber sobre el mambo…" In *Panorama de la música popular cubana,* edited by Radamés Giro. Havana: Editorial Letras Cubanas, 1998.

López, Oscar Luis. *La radio en Cuba.* 2nd ed. Havana: Editorial Letras Cubanas, 1998.

Lowinger, Rosa, and Ofelia Fox. *Tropicana Nights: The Life and Times of the Legendary Cuban Nightclub.* Orlando, FL: Harcourt, 2005.

Martínez, Mayra A. *Cubanos en la música.* Havana: Editorial Letras Cubanas, 1993.

Martínez Rodríguez, Raúl. *Benny Moré.* Havana: Editorial Letras Cubanas, 1993.

Padura Fuentes, Leonardo. *Los rostros de la salsa.* Havana: Ediciones Unión, 1997. English edition: *Faces of Salsa: A Spoken History of the Music.* Translated by Stephen J. Clark. Washington, DC: Smithsonian Books, 2003.

Pujol, Jordi. *Chano Pozo: El tambor de Cuba.* Barcelona: Almendra Music, 2001.

Salazar, Max. *Mambo Kingdom: Latin Music in New York.* New York: Schirmer, 2002.

Sublette, Ned. *Cuba and Its Music: From the First Drums to the Mambo.* Chicago: Chicago Press Review, 2004.

Sublette, Ned. "The Kingsmen and the Cha-cha-chá." In *Listen Again: A Momentary History of Pop Music,* edited by Eric Weisbard. Durham, NC: Duke University Press, 2007.

MUSIC: MUSIC SINCE 1959

Radamés Giro

The significant developments and musicians in both Cuba and the diaspora since the Cuban Revolution.

The dominant trend in Cuban music between 1959 and 2010 was to adopt the new techniques and expressive modes popular throughout the world, but in the first years after the triumph of the Cuban Revolution, music changed little. The most popular bands played the cabarets, theaters, and nightclubs; songs, boleros, cha-cha-chas, and the voices of the best-loved singers of the moment continued to be heard. Some well-known performers left the country, but other musicians and singers who were just as good stayed in Cuba, and the new generations produced music of indisputable quality that is enjoyed around the world.

Benny Moré (1919–1963) was the last major pre-Revolution performer on the island. The 1960s saw the establishment of several institutions that determined the future of Cuba's popular music: Casa de las Américas (House of the Americas); the Instituto Cubano de Arte e Industria Cinematográficos (ICAIC, Cuban Institute of Cinema Art and Industry); the Consejo Nacional de Cultura (National Culture Council), which became the country's cultural policy-making body; the Orquesta Sinfónica Nacional de Cuba (National Symphony Orchestra); and the Escuela Nacional de Arte (ENA, National Art School).

Cuban culture was moving toward new perspectives. In 1963 the first Cuban Music Festival featured performances of *trova*, bolero, lyrical music, *son*, rhumba, and folk music. In the same year, a forum on the Cuban musical style called *filín* (feeling) brought together singers, including Elena Burke (1928–2002) and Doris de la Torre (1932–2003), and composers who had written and performed many new songs during this period, including César Portillo de la Luz (b. 1922), José Antonio Méndez (1927–1989), Marta Valdés (b. 1934), Ela O'Farrill (b. 1930), and Ignacio Villa (Bola de Nieve, 1911–1971). The First National Trova Festival took place in Santiago de Cuba in 1962. Meanwhile, dance and music styles such as the twist, go-go dancing, the shake, the bossa nova, beat, rock, pop, and ballads became popular, but in many cases they were not used as creatively as they might have been. Rather than enriching Cuba's musical resources, they impoverished them.

The first Cuban rhythms in this period were the *pachanga*, developed by Eduardo Davidson (1925–1994), and the *mozambique*, by Pedro Izquierdo (Pello el Afrokán, 1933–2000). The *mozambique* required a group playing drums, bells, and wind instruments, and it achieved international recognition with the song "María Caracoles." Other new Cuban rhythms were the *pilón*, invented by Enrique Bonne (b. 1926) and popularized by Pacho Alonso (1928–1982) with the song "Rico pilón" (Delicious *Pilón*); and the *pa'cá*, a mixture of *son* and Venezuelan *joropo*, by Juanito Márquez (b. 1929) (Giro 2007, pp. 73–81).

A BREAK WITH THE VANGUARD

Although in the early years of the Revolution popular music followed much the same path as before, symphonic music went in quite a different direction. In 1961 the composer and guitarist Leo Brouwer (b. 1939) was invited to the Warsaw Autumn International Festival of Contemporary Music, and his participation was critical in consolidating the Cuban musical vanguard. Upon his return to Cuba, he met with several fellow musicians to discuss his experience at the festival, which he called "that transcendent resounding event" (p. 22).

The most important compositions of the 1960s include "Relieves" (Reliefs), by Carlos Fariñas (1934–2002); "Contrapunto espacial 3" (Spatial Counterpoint 3), by Juan Blanco (1919–2008); and "La tradición se rompe…pero cuesta trabajo" (Tradition Can Be Broken, but It's Hard), by Brouwer. These and other composers used serialism, electroacoustic music, spatialism, and all the techniques that were transforming classical music throughout the world—but they added a Cuban flavor. The Orquesta Sinfónica Nacional de Cuba, conducted by Manuel Duchesne Cuzán (1932–2005), performed these new works for Cuban audiences. In 1967 the Orquesta Cubana de Música Moderna (Cuban Modern Music Orchestra) was founded. It was directed by Armando Romeu (1911–2002) and comprised the most talented musicians of the time. Its music depended heavily on Afro-Cuban percussion.

Cuban dance music changed considerably after 1968. One important milestone was the addition of Juan Formell (b. 1942) to the band led by Elio Revé (1930–1997). Formell changed Revé's sound by incorporating the electric bass and the electric guitar; after that, the band no longer fit the mold of a *charanga* band. In 1969 when Formell started his own group, Los Van Van, he increased the number of violins (which played in unison with the flute), added a cello, and developed a new way of mixing the timbres of flute, electric guitar, and string bass, achieving a more complex rhythm and introducing three-part harmony by the singers. With these changes, Formell transformed the *charanga* band's traditional timbre and rhythm. In the 1980s he went one step further—in order to fill in the band's core sound, he added trombones. Formell's lyrics have always been about life in Cuba; he is a storyteller of his times. All these advances led to the development of *songo*, a blend of *son*, beat, and Yoruba music, and the only new genre in Cuban popular music since 1959.

Another significant development in Cuban music was the creation in 1969 of the Grupo de Experimentación Sonora (GES, Sound Experimentation Group)

■ *See also*

Gloria and Emilio Estefan: Latin Music's Power Couple

The "Mambo King": Dámaso Pérez Prado

of the ICAIC, led by Brouwer and consisting of Silvio Rodríguez (b. 1946), Noel Nicola (1946–2005), Pablo Milanés (b. 1943), Sergio Vitier (b. 1948), and Eduardo Ramos (b. 1946) (Sarusky, pp. 9–26). Brouwer later explained that the group worked with rock, jazz, and Brazilian music and held events in the spirit of experimentation, state-of-the-art techniques, and technical and artistic quality (p. 22).

In 1967 Casa de las Américas sponsored the First International Protest Song Conference and later established the Centro de la Canción Protesta (Protest Song Center). A new movement grew up around the center, and in 1973 the leaders of this movement—including Silvio Rodríguez, Pablo Milanés, Noel Nicola, and Eduardo Ramos—adopted the name *nueva trova* (new song movement).

One of the outstanding singer-songwriters of *nueva trova* is Silvio Rodríguez, whose songs combine poetic lyrics, melodies, and harmonies with exceptional guitar technique and singing. His songs include "La era está pariendo un corazón" (The Era Is Birthing a Heart), "Unicornio" (Unicorn), "El necio" (The Idiot), and "Cita con ángeles" (Appointment with the Angels). Another is Pablo Milanés, a renowned singer who has explored almost every popular music genre; his compositions include "No vivo en una sociedad perfecta" (I Don't Live in a Perfect Society), "Yo me quedo" (I'm Staying), and the highly original "Yolanda." Noel Nicola's songs are filled with biting satire of social conventions, hypocrisy, and pretentiousness, as seen in "Para una imaginaria María del Carmen" (For an Imaginary Maria del Carmen), "Es más, te perdono" (What's More, I Forgive You), and "Son oscuro" (Dark *Son*).

Other notable musicians who are not affiliated with *nueva trova* include the guitarist Pedro Luis Ferrer (b. 1952), who specializes in *guaracha*; his piquant Cuban style shines in "Inseminación artificial" (Artificial Insemination), "Mario Agüé," "Marucha la jinetera" (Marucha the Hooker) and "Guillermina Camarioca." The accomplished poet and singer-songwriter Amaury Pérez (b. 1953) is a guitarist with a rich harmonic palette and an impressive repertoire of songs, including "Acuérdate de abril" (Remember April), "Andes lo que andes" (Wherever You Are), "No lo van a impedir" (They Can't Stop It), and "Quédate este bolero" (Stay for This Bolero).

CUBAN BUT DIFFERENT

In 1973 the formation of Grupo Irakere brought a revolution in Cuban dance and instrumental music. The band achieved international fame with the power of its music, its skillful combination of percussion instruments (including *batá* drums) and wind instruments, and the masterful compositions and piano playing of Chucho Valdés (b. 1941). Its repertoire includes "Misa negra" (Black Mass), "Babalú Ayé," "Dile a Catalina" (Tell Catalina), and "Homenaje a Picadura (Valle de Picadura)" (Tribute to the Valley of Picadura). Irakere

had an immense influence on the development of Cuban jazz and *timba*, and on others groups such as NG La Banda, led by José Luis Cortés (b. 1951), and other bands that emerged during the 1990s. During that decade, Latin jazz, with Chucho Valdés as one of its main creators, also gained popularity around the world.

The multifaceted Bobby Carcassés (b. 1938) combines the most diverse musical styles and genres in pieces such as "Luna Wanestain" (Wanestain Moon), "Tonada a Santa Clara" (Song to Santa Clara), and "Bembedoble." Carcassés frequently uses his voice as an instrument, especially when he sings scat.

Eminent Cuban jazz musicians include the trombonist Juan Pablo Torres (1946–2005), who with his group Algo Nuevo explored elements of *son* and jazz, as did Grupo Afro-Cuba, started in 1977 by Nicolás Reinoso (b. 1939). In 1986 Fervet Opus was founded in Camagüey by Gabriel Hernández; this band played a fusion of jazz with *son*, rhumba, and considerable improvisation. Grupo Perspectiva, led by pianist Hilario Durán (b. 1953), was founded in 1994.

Among the younger Cuban jazz musicians are Emiliano Salvador (1951–1992), the most important and creative pianist of his generation, and Lilia Expósito, also known as Bellita (b. 1957), whose group Jazztumbatá displayed great originality in its vocal and instrumental treatments. Gonzalo Rubalcaba (b. 1963) heads the list of skilled Cuban jazz pianists, which also includes Roberto Carcassés (b. 1972) with his group Interactivo, Ernán López-Nussa (b. 1958), Rolando Luna (b. 1978), and Roberto Fonseca (b. 1975). Notable jazz guitarists are Jorge Luis Valdés Chicoy (b. 1955) and Carlos Emilio Morales (b. 1939); saxophonists include Paquito D'Rivera (b. 1948), César López (b. 1968), and Javier Zalba (b. 1955); and outstanding trumpet players include Arturo Sandoval (b. 1949) and Jorge Varona (1932–1988).

The Jazz Plaza Festival (later called Jazz Latino Plaza), begun in 1980, played a major role in promoting Cuban jazz. Festival performers included soloists and groups playing jazz and other types of Cuban popular music, as well as major jazz figures such as Dizzy Gillespie (1917–1993), Herbie Hancock (b. 1940), and Wynton Marsalis (b. 1961).

SALSA AND THE REVITALIZED DANCE SCENE

Salsa became an important element in 1990s dance music. Although salsa did not originate in Cuba, it soon caught the interest of Cuban musicians and dancers. The singers Oscar D'León (b. 1943), Héctor Lavoe (1946–1993), and Roberto Roena (b. 1938) and the Venezuelan group Dimensión Latina sparked that interest. D'León's performances on the island and his contact with Cuban dancers were decisive in the rise of salsa in Cuba. A joint appearance by the groups Dimensión Latina and Son 14, the latter headed by

Adalberto Álvarez (b. 1948), led to a reevaluation of salsa as a form of dance music, and it gained strength in the 1990s.

Soon other musicians and groups began playing salsa. The group Adalberto Álvarez y su Son led the way with "El regreso de María" (Maria's Return) and "Fin de semana es la cita" (Date on the Weekend); Los Van Van, led by Formell, renewed its repertoire with "La Habana no aguanta más" (Havana Can Bear It No Longer) and "Por encima del nivel" (Over the Top); Revé discovered new possibilities and revived the *changüí*, recording "Changüí campanero" (Changüí Bellringer) and "María Belén"; La Charanga Habanera had "Ricky ricón" (Richie Rick); NG La Banda offered "Échale limón" (Add Lemon) and "Que venga la fiera" (Bring on the Beast). Popular Cuban singers who embraced salsa included Issac Delgado (b. 1962), Paulito F. G. (b. 1962), and Manuel González Hernández, also known as Manolín, El Médico de la Salsa (The Salsa Doctor) (b. 1965).

Salsa is based to a large extent on *son*, an open kind of music that is capable of assimilating other rhythms. In that sense, salsa—which could be termed urban Caribbean music—can be seen as another contemporary expression of Cuban dance music (Rondón, p. 27). Manolito Simonet (b. 1961) and his band Manolito y su Trabuco, Giraldo Piloto (b. 1962) and his group Klímax, and Bamboleo have experimented with salsa, using percussion and original lyrics to create a different, if not new, type of dance music.

The music critic Leonardo Acosta (b. 1933) called *timba* "the most important phenomenon in Cuban popular music during the 1990s.... It is the first original movement in Cuban dance music since the 1950s to gain international attention. But above all, we believe that *timba* is the heir to a long tradition of popular dance music, and we should view it from that perspective" (Acosta 2004, p. 144). *Timba* brought Grupo Irakere back into the limelight. Valdes's "Aguanile" and "El guao" (The Guao, a toxic Cuban plant) exploded onto the dance floors, followed by "Ese atrevimiento" (That Daring), by Ricardo Díaz (b. 1926), and "El rucurrucu," by José Luis Cortés. These hits gave a boost to what Formell had been doing with Los Van Van.

NG La Banda made a foray into the dance scene, but the complexity and aggressiveness of its brass, as well as its highly elaborated arrangements, did not catch on with dancers; it was considered music just for listening, to the bewilderment of the musicians. If NG wanted people to dance to its music, the group had to simplify it, so it did. The music was still contemporary, but was easier to dance to.

La Charanga Habanera, which made waves with a powerful sound during its *son*-salsa period, became the emblem of *timba brava* because of its onstage image, its lyric structure, its more aggressive rap-style talk-singing, as in the choruses of "El temba" (The Temba), and its original portrayals of everyday life, as in "Qué quieres de mí" (What Do You Want from Me?).

Los Van Van. The popular Cuban band Los Van Van, led by Juan Formell (left), performs during the Peace without Borders concert in Havana's Revolution Square on 21 September 2009. © ENRIQUE DE LA OSA/REUTERS/CORBIS

A RETURN TO TRADITION: BUENA VISTA SOCIAL CLUB

Paradoxically, amid the salsa boom there was also a return to Cuban traditional music from the 1930s, 1940s, and 1950s from groups such as Sierra Maestra, Jóvenes Clásicos del Son, and the international phenomenon Buena Vista Social Club. Launched internationally in the 1999 documentary film of the same name by Wim Wenders (b. 1945), the Buena Vista Social Club popularized music from Cuba's golden age. The *son* styling of the celebrated Compay Segundo (Francisco Repilado, 1907–2003) harked back to the traditional way music had been played in Cuba's eastern provinces. With musical direction by Juan de Marcos González (b. 1954) and the U.S. guitarist Ry Cooder (b. 1947), one of Segundo's songs, "Chan chan," elevated Buena Vista Social Club to stardom. The other members of the group were guitarist Manuel Galbán (b. 1931); trumpet player Manuel Mirabal (b. 1933); laud player Barbarito Torres (b. 1956); pianist Rubén González (1919–2003); singers Ibrahim Ferrer (1927–2005; winner of the 2000 best new artist in the Latin Grammys), Omara Portuondo (b. 1930), Manuel Licea (Puntillita, 1921–2000), Pío Leiva (1917–2006), and Eliades Ochoa (b. 1946); and bassist Orlando López (Cachaíto, 1933–2009). This music was alive, not from a museum.

Another Cuban who performed traditional music that was extraordinarily popular with dancers in Cuba, parts of Latin America, and Europe was Fernando Borrego, better known as Polo Montañez (1955–2002), who had a hit in 2000 with the song "Un montón de estrellas" (A Bunch of Stars).

FOREIGN MUSIC BY CUBANS

Cubans began listening to rock in the late 1950s. The Americans Elvis Presley (1935–1977), Fats Domino (b. 1928), and Bill Haley (1925–1981), and the Argentine musicians Los Cinco Latinos, Billy Cafaro (b. 1936), and Luis Aguilé (1936–2009) were idols emulated by the Cubans Jorge Bauer, Luis Bravo (b. 1942), and Cristóbal Puga (Danny). Presley was their most significant model. The best-known Cuban rock groups in the 1960s and early 1970s were Los Astros, Los Bucaneros, Los 5-U-4, Los Dada, Los Barba, Los Magnéticos, and Ricardito y sus Cometas. Cubans first heard the Beatles in the 1970s after the ban against them had been lifted.

After 1965 rock music spread throughout Cuba. Instrumentalists were in vogue, and lyrics in Spanish practically disappeared from Cuban rock. In the 1970s, the Beatles influenced Cuban music, as did the Rolling Stones and Spanish groups such as Los Mustang, Fórmula V, and Juan y Junior. In the late 1980s a new phase was ushered in by two Cuban groups: Arte Vivo and Síntesis.

Arte Vivo, led by the guitarist and composer Mario Daly (1952–1999), played contemporary music with acoustic instruments and also performed fifteenth- and sixteenth-century Spanish *vihuela* music. Síntesis, directed by Carlos Alfonso (b. 1949), originated what might be termed Cuban rock, which was characterized by a unique timbre and vocal and instrumental treatment, an affiliation with *trova*, and the use of formal elements of Afro-Cuban music and formal resources of symphonic rock. These traits are evident in Síntesis's trilogy *Ancestros I, II,* and *III* (2005).

Cuban rock moved through diverse styles over the years: alternative rock, punk, experimental rock, rock-pop with a techno base, fusion, industrial rock, acoustic rock with flashes of country and blues. The most successful group of the 1980s was the hard rock quintet Venus, whose members sang in Spanish and wrote all their own music. The rock opera *Violente* (1987), written by the experimental musician Edesio Alejandro (b. 1958), also stands out. And then there is the highly original X Alfonso (Equis Alfonso, b. 1973), who is difficult to categorize given the diversity of his musical output.

MUSIC OF THE DIASPORA

Cuban musicians have lived in the United States since the 1930s. The best known include Mario Bauzá (1911–1993), Frank Grillo (Machito, 1909–1984), Chano Pozo (1915–1948), Miguelito Valdés (1912–1978), Chico O'Farrill (1921–2001), and Mongo Santamaría (1917–2003). Some of them performed in the bands of the Cuban musician Don Azpiazu (1893–1943) and the Spaniard Xavier Cugat (1900–1990); many of them were active during the swing and big band eras and contributed to the development of Latin jazz, especially Machito and his Afro-Cuban All Stars. Two Cuban percussionists were particularly influential: Armando Peraza (b. 1918) and Mongo Santamaría.

Peraza immigrated to the United States in 1949 and recorded with Dámaso Pérez Prado (1916–1989) during the mambo craze, then with pianist George Shearing (1919–2011) and for many years with Cal Tjader (1925–1982). He also played with Carlos Santana (b. 1947) for seventeen years. In addition to being an outstanding musician and a band leader, Santamaría—who composed "Afro-Blue," recorded by John Coltrane—was a mentor of young talent. He performed various musical genres. He was one of the first to record Regla de Ocha ritual music, on the album *Changó* (1955). In the 1970s, with the rise of Fania Records, Santamaría played with the Fania All Stars and later recorded "Ubané" (1976) with the singer Justo Betancourt (b. 1940).

The 1960s were difficult for Latin music in the United States, partly because of the break in relations between Cuba and the United States and partly because of the rise of rock and roll. The famous Palladium Ballroom in New York City—where the Puerto Rican musicians Tito Puente (1923–2000) and Tito Rodriguez (1923–1973) played mambo and cha-cha-cha and mounted battles of the bands for delighted dancers—closed its doors in 1966. The salsa boom began in the late 1960s, incorporating various Cuban rhythms (rhumba, cha-cha-cha, *son*, and *guaracha*) and popularized by a group of Puerto Rican musicians in New York that included the Palmieri brothers (Charlie, 1927–1988, and Eddie, b. 1936), Willie Colón (b. 1950), Ray Barreto (1929–2006), and Héctor Lavoe (1946–1993), and the Dominican musician Johnny Pacheco (b. 1930), who created Fania Records and worked with Celia Cruz (1924–2003) on several records during the 1970s.

After Cruz, the most well-known Cuban singer in the United States is Gloria Estefan (b. 1957), who sings pop and disco with a Latin flavor. After her 1977 debut with Miami Sound Machine, Estefan career culminated in 1984 to 1988, with songs such as "Conga," "Dr. Beat" and "Anything for You." In the 1990s she recorded several CDs in Spanish, two of which won Grammys. Other Cuban artists in Miami such as Willie Chirino (b. 1947) and Albita Rodríguez (b. 1962) made names for themselves in the United States, Cuba, and Puerto Rico.

Cuban Americans also made their mark in the rap and hip hop. Ulpidio Sergio Reyes (b. 1967), known as Mellow Man Ace, was the first successful Cuban rapper in the United States. He was followed by Don Dinero (José Manuel Guitian), Cuban Link (Felix Delgado, b. 1974), and Pitbull (Armando Christian Pérez, b. 1981), all of whom rap in both English and Spanish.

Cuban musicians in the diaspora probably had the greatest success in jazz and Latin jazz. Among the many Cuban jazz greats are Bebo Valdés (b. 1918), Chocolate Armenteros (b. 1928), Francisco Aguabella (1925–2010), and Israel "Cachao" López (1918–2008). A second generation of Cuban jazz musicians includes Arturo Sandoval (b. 1949), Paquito D'Rivera (b. 1948), Hilario Durán (b. 1953), Gonzalo Rubalcaba (b. 1963), Ignacio "El Negro" Hernández (b. 1963), and Ignacio Berroa (b. 1953). Notable younger musicians include Arturo O'Farrill Jr. (b. 1960), Omar Sosa (b. 1965), Dafnis Prieto (b. 1974), Arturo Stable, Aruán Ortiz (b. 1973), Tony Pérez, and Yosvany Terry.

RAP

Rap—a genre based on talk-singing of free or rhymed verse, accompanied by gestures and physically demanding dancing and, in its visual art form, graffiti—originated on urban streets. In Cuba it became popular in the 1990s. The best-known Cuban rap group is Amenaza (Threat, later renamed Orishas). It has an international following, and it first album, *A lo cubano* (The Cuban Way, 2000), and its video clips demonstrate the group's originality.

Bands that previously worked in other genres took up the banner of rap. NG recorded "Se la aplicaron toda" (They Gave It to Her) and "El rap de la muerta" (Dead Woman's Rap); Los Van Van produced "Esto

WHY HAS CUBAN HIP HOP RECEIVED SO MUCH FOREIGN ATTENTION?

Cuban hip hop is an expression of the global youth culture, created by and for minority people and marginalized sectors of society. Hip hop music has a way of highlighting specific social identities, and Cuban rappers, who have reached out internationally despite the U.S. embargo and overall inaccessibility to international mass media outlets, are no different. Since 2000, at least a dozen documentaries have been made by filmmakers in the United States, Canada, and Europe that feature Cuban groups such as Obsesión, Doble Filo, Anónimo Consejo, Hermanos de Causa, las Krudas, and Los Aldeanos.

Western media is attracted to agents of social unrest in undemocratic regimes, and Cuban rappers fit the bill perfectly. Mostly black youth, caught in the crosshairs of an ideology that proclaims social and racial equality and an economic situation that is at best unstable, Cuban rappers have been outspoken on issues of racism, globalization, social injustice, and inequality.

This convergence of class, age, and interest in youth culture has made Cuban rap a favorite subject of American and European academics, many of whom strongly identify with or participate in hip hop culture and who are perhaps nostalgic for a time when hip hop was more socially rebellious in their own countries.

Cuban hip hop established early partnerships with international cultural and political organizations that garnered the media attention, technical resources, and human capital essential for Cuban rappers' survival. Black Panther exiles in Cuba, such as Assata Shakur and Nehanda Abiodun, help to link Cuban rappers to international figures of black nationalism and culture.

Yesenia F. Selier

te pone la cabeza mala" (This'll Mess Up Your Head); Irakere performed "Rap de la bicicleta" (Bicycle Rap) and "El rap de la gorda" (Fat Lady's Rap); and Adalberto Álvarez y su Son recorded "Y qué tú quieres que te den" (What Do You Want Them to Give You). These groups mixed rap with reggae, blues, jazz, and *timba*.

Rap and reggaeton, the newest trends in Cuban music in the 2010s, chronicle the changes in Cuban society with lyrics about the country's history and current problems and experiences expressed in a popular, everyday language. For the defenders of Cuban identity, they represent a unique and very Cuban style.

BIBLIOGRAPHY

Acosta, Leonardo. *Del tambor al sintetizador*. 2nd ed. Havana: Editorial Letras Cubanas, 1989.

Acosta, Leonardo. *Raíces del jazz latino. Un siglo de jazz en Cuba*. Barranquilla, Colombia: Editorial La Iguana Ciega, Fundación Cultural Nueva Música, 2001.

Acosta, Leonardo. *Otra visión de la música popular cubana.* Havana: Editorial Letras Cubanas, 2004.

Águila, Víctor. *Muy personal. Pablo Milanés.* Mexico City: Zaguán Ediciones, 1990.

Alemán, Ernesto, and Guillermo Alemán. *Por quien merece amor.* Havana: Editorial Letras Cubanas, 2005.

Amer, José, ed. *Harold Gramatges.* Madrid: Fundación Autor, 1997.

Angulo, Héctor. *Toque.* Havana: Editorial Letras Cubanas, 1989.

Ardévol, José. *Música y revolución.* Havana: Ediciones Unión, 1966.

Ardévol, José. *Introducción a Cuba: La música.* Havana: Instituto del Libro, 1969.

Brouwer, Leo. *La música, lo cubano y la innovación.* 2nd ed. Havana: Editorial Letras Cubanas, 1989.

Calzadilla, Alejandro. *La salsa en Venezuela.* Caracas: Fundación Bigott, 2003.

Carpentier, Alejo. *Temas de la lira y del bongó.* Havana: Editorial Letras Cubanas, 1994.

Castellanos, Ernesto Juan, ed. *Los Beatles en Cuba. Un viaje mágico y misterioso.* Havana: Ediciones Unión, 1997.

Cedeño Pineda, Reinaldo, and Michel Damián Suárez. *Son de la loma. Los dioses de la música cantan en Santiago de Cuba.* Havana: Mercie Ediciones–Andante Editora Musical de Cuba, 2001.

Delannoy, Luc. *¡Caliente! Una historia del jazz latino.* Mexico City: Fondo de Cultura Económica, 2001.

Díaz Ayala, Cristóbal. *Del areyto al rap cubano.* 4th ed. San Juan, Puerto Rico: Fundación Musicalia, 2003.

Díaz Pérez, Clara. *Sobre la guitarra, la voz. Una historia de la nueva trova cubana.* Havana: Editorial Letras Cubanas, 1994.

Egozcue Guevara, Ela, ed. *Carlos Fariñas, pasión y luz.* Havana: Editorial Letras Cubanas, 2002.

Eli Rodríguez, Victoria, and María de los Ángeles Alfonso, eds. *Roberto Valera.* Madrid: Fundación Autor, 1998.

Eli Rodríguez, Victoria, and María de los Ángeles Alfonso, eds. *La música entre Cuba y España. Tradición e innovación.* Madrid: Fundación Autor, 1999.

Fernández, Raúl. *Hablando de música cubana.* Manizales, Colombia: Author, 2008.

Giro, Radamés. *Leo Brouwer y la guitarra en Cuba.* Havana: Editorial Letras Cubanas, 1986.

Giro, Radamés. *Música popular cubana. Breve historia a través de los géneros y otros ritmos.* Havana: Editorial José Martí, 2007.

Giro, Radamés, and Isabel González Sauto, eds. *Cincuenta canciones en años de revolución.* Havana: Editorial José Martí, 2008.

Gómez, Jorge, ed. *Canciones de la nueva trova.* Prologue by Leonardo Acosta. Havana: Editorial Letras Cubanas, 1981.

Gramatges, Harold. *Presencia de la revolución en la música cubana.* 2nd ed. Havana: 1998.

Henríquez, María Antonieta. *Lo permanente en nuestra música.* Havana: Ediciones Museo de la Música, 2008.

Hernández, Erena. *La música en persona.* Havana: Editorial Letras Cubanas, 1986.

Hernández, Isabelle. *Leo Brouwer.* Havana: Editora Musical de Cuba, 2000.

Lázaro, Luis. *Compay Segundo. Un sonero de leyenda.* Madrid: Fundación Autor, 2000.

López Sánchez, Antonio. *La canción de la nueva trova.* Havana: Atril, 2001.

Manduley, Humberto. *El rock en Cuba.* Havana: Atril, 2001.

Martín, Edgardo. *Panorama histórico de la música en Cuba.* Havana: University of Havana, 1971.

Novo Villaverde, Yolanda, and María do Cebreiro Rábade Villar. *Te seguirá mi canción del alma. El bolero cubano en la voz de la mujer.* Santiago de Compostela, Spain: University of Santiago de Compostela, 2008.

Orejuela Martínez, Adriana. *El son no se fue de Cuba. Claves para una historia 1959–1973.* Bogotá: Ediciones ACS, 2004.

Rodríguez, Silvia, and María Teresa González (Petí), eds. *Amaury Pérez.* Madrid: Fundación Autor, n.d.

Rodríguez, Silvio. *Canciones del mar.* Havana: Ojalá Ediciones, 1996.

Rodríguez Cuervo, Marta, and Victoria Eli Rodríguez. *Leo Brouwer. Caminos de la creación.* Madrid: Ediciones y Publicaciones Autor, 2009.

Rondón, César Miguel. *El libro de la salsa. Crónica de la música del Caribe Urbano.* 3rd ed. Caracas: Ediciones B Venezuela, 2007.

Roy, Maya. *Músicas cubanas.* Madrid: Ediciones Akal, 2003.

Sarusky, Jaime. *Grupo de Experimentación Sonora del ICAIC. Mito y realidad.* Havana: Editorial Letras Cubanas, 2005.

Solano, Omar. *Guía de los músicos de la salsa.* Barranquilla, Colombia: Antillas, 2002.

Vilar, Juan (Pin). *Carlos Varela.* Madrid: Fundación Autor, n.d.

■ *See also*

Cuban Thought and Cultural Identity: Socialist Thought

Governance and Contestation: The Cuban Revolution

MUSIC: *NUEVA TROVA* (NEW SONG): MUSIC OF THE CUBAN REVOLUTION

Alberto Faya

A movement of singer-songwriters addressing political and social issues that builds on traditional Cuban music while drawing on contemporary international musical influences.

The *Nueva Trova* (New Song) movement, which began in the 1960s, was integral to the evolution of Cuban music. The Spanish term *nueva trova* was adopted because the movement represented a continuity as well as a rupture with traditional *trova*. Nueva Trova combines Cuban vocal techniques characteristic of the poorest rural and urban areas, the traditional

Cuban forms *son* and rhumba, *tres* guitar techniques, and Cuban percussion with Western musical styles predominant in the 1960s, electronic instruments, and formal, literary lyrics. It drew on music from the United States (country, jazz, rock, blues, and others), Brazil, other Latin American countries, and the Caribbean, plus elements of the blues romantic song movement *filín*, which preceded Nueva Trova. The lyrics of Nueva Trova consisted of Spanish-language poetry by writers from Cuba and other countries as well as poetic texts created by singer-songwriters.

Along with these artistic influences, major events and ideas have had a strong impact on members of the Nueva Trova movement. The 1959 Cuban Revolution brought transformations in the understanding of history, social and institutional structures, civic activity, the concept of the family, the role of women, conventions related to personal relationships, and many other aspects of life. Overnight, Cubans became soldiers who defended their country and brand-new leaders of labor and political organizations. The composers and performers of the Nueva Trova movement, whose first songs appeared in the late 1960s, were supported by a broad sector of students and members of government institutions who recognized that these artists and their work were born out of the revolutionary process. Others, however, considered the members of the Nueva Trova movement troublemakers, deviants, and even counterrevolutionaries. Their songs presented a Cuban reality completely different from that of commercially promoted music and styles cultivated by the television and radio media. These postrevolutionary singer-songwriters viewed the Revolution as a capture of political power and a transformation of human beings in the realms of ethics, politics, and society. Through their music they sought cultural renewal based on revolutionary leaders' public statements. These objectives were aligned with Cuba's rich cultural heritage. The new *trovadores*, in seeking a new aesthetic, initiated a battle that remained one of the most profound in Cuban culture.

EARLY DEVELOPMENT

Among the original leading members of the Nueva Trova movement, Silvio Rodríguez (b. 1946) is one of the best-known performers in Cuba and Latin America and recognized around the world as an ambassador of Cuban music. With an unmistakable voice and a gift for poetic lyrics, Rodríguez recorded more than two dozen albums, from *Días y flores* (Days and Flowers, 1975) to *Segunda cita* (Second Date, 2010). His notable songs, which became emblematic throughout the Spanish-speaking world, include "Días y flores" (Days and Flowers). "Fusil contra fusil" (Rifle against Rifle), "Te doy una canción" (I Give You a Song), "Unicornio" (Unicorn), and "Rabo de nube" (Waterspout). Rodríguez writes about the political—an eloquent example being "Canción del elegido" (Song of the Chosen One),

about Che Guevara—as well as the personal. Considered a poet of song, Rodríguez considers the Spanish poet Federico García Lorca a mentor, as well as the Cuban national hero and writer José Martí, and the Peruvian poet César Vallejo.

The songs of Pablo Milanés (b. 1943), from Bayamo, incorporate elements of jazz and rock while keeping close and fruitful ties with traditional *trova* and *filín*. His songs, especially "Yolanda," "Amo esta isla" (I Love This Island), "Pobre del cantor" (Poverty of the Singer), "Años" (Years), and "Para vivir" (To Live), are popular throughout Latin America and Spain. He recorded more than forty albums, beginning with *Versos sencillos de José Martí* (José Martí's Simple Verses, 1973) and *Canta a Nicolás Guillén* ([Pablo Milanés] Sings Nicolás Guillén, 1975), which preserve the tone of the works of both poets. Several anthologies of Milanés's music have been released, with the participation of important singers such as Lilia Vera (Venezuela); Luís Eduardo Aute, Ana Belén, and Víctor Manuel (Spain); Chico Buarque and Milton Nascimento (Brazil); Mercedes Sosa (Argentina); and Andy Montañez (Puerto Rico). Other leading figures of the Nueva Trova movement are Noel Nicola (1946–2005), Augusto Blanca (b. 1945), Vicente Feliú (b. 1947), Miguel (Mike) Porcel (b. 1950), Sara González (b. 1951), and Pedro Luis Ferrer (b. 1952).

The Nueva Trova movement received early support from Casa de las Américas, whose director, Haydée Santamaría, encouraged young singers to join the Centro de la Canción Protesta (Protest Song Center), which was founded by U.S. cultural promoter and filmmaker Estela Bravo after the Primer Encuentro de

Silvio Rodríguez (b. 1946). Cuban folk singer Silvio Rodríguez, one of the leading members of the Nueva Trova movement, performs at the Karl Marx Theater in Havana on 29 August 2004. RAFAEL PEREZ/REUTERS/LANDOV

A Nueva Trova band. A Cuban Nueva Trova band performs in 1967. The Nueva Trova movement, which began in the late 1960s, was integral to the evolution of Cuban music. AP IMAGES/PRENSA LATINA

Canción Protesta Latinoamericana (First Latin American Protest Song Conference) in August 1967 at Casa de las Américas. In 1969, based on the initiative of Alfredo Guevara, president of the Instituto Cubano de Arte e Industria Cinematográficos (ICAIC; Cuban Institute of Cinema Art and Industry), the Grupo de Experimentación Sonora (GES; Sound Experimentation Group) was established under the direction of Leo Brouwer. Among the GES founders were Pablo Milanés, Silvio Rodríguez, Noel Nicola, Eduardo Ramos (b. 1946), Sergio Vitier (b. 1948), and Leonardo Acosta (b. 1933), joined by Emiliano Salvador (1951–1992), Pablo Menéndez (b. 1952), Sara González, and later Amaury Pérez Vidal (b. 1953), and other outstanding musicians. The GES, which remained active until 1978, had an enormous influence on Cuban music in general and the work of Nueva Trova movement members in particular. The formation of musical groups such as Mayohuacán and Moncada, supported by high school and university student organizations, and Manguaré, sponsored by the Unión de Jóvenes Comunistas (UJC; Union of Young Communists), was an innovation within the Cuban tradition. These groups explored *son* and rhumba as well as the music of South America and sparked the establishment of other groups all over Cuba.

THE NUEVA TROVA MOVEMENT AS AN ORGANIZATION

Immediately upon its emergence in the late 1960s, the Nueva Trova movement drew criticism among certain people due to its influences from rock and other foreign popular music genres. This new image featured long hair, the ready-made clothing of the common worker instead of special performance costumes, and the inclusion of lyrics that simultaneously expressed social criticism and provoked a rupture with the styles of commercial songs. The music produced by the Nueva Trova movement followed the principles set forth by Che Guevara, who called on individuals to redress past collective wrongs. The movement faced opposition from some conservative government officials that resulted in cases of exclusion, discrimination, and even banishment from the media. The young musicians of the movement were considered transgressors and even subversives by those mentioned officials who mistakingly believed that they were upholding the Revolution's principles in confronting these performers.

By the early 1970s the movement had grown considerably, with musicians in every province eager to share and publicize their work. In 1972 the Unión de Jóvenes Comunistas organized the Primer Encuentro de Jóvenes Trovadores (First Meeting of Nueva Trova Performers) in the city of Manzanillo, gathering representatives of the new musical trend from all the country's provinces. The founding declaration stated the group's belief that music played a part in the aesthetic and ideological education of the Cuban people and expressed the movement's wish to build on Cuban aesthetic traditions while struggling against imperialism and colonialism, free of any imposed outside interference.

From that year on Movimiento de la Nueva Trova (MNT) became a cultural organization with a national board of directors and branches in every province on the island that promoted regular member meetings and festivals mainly sponsored by the Unión de Jóvenes Comunistas. By 1980 the MNT had more than two thousand members, and the government gave them instruments free of charge and funded recording sessions; encounters to debate ethical, political, and aesthetic issues; and technical and musical training.

Singer-songwriters who emerged from MNT in the late 1970s and early 1980s include Santiago Feliú (b. 1962), Alberto Tosca (b. 1955), Donato Poveda (b. 1960), Anabell López (b. 1963), Xiomara Laugart (b. 1960), Carlos Varela (b. 1963), Polito Ibáñez (b. 1965), Gerardo Alfonso (b. 1958), and Frank Delgado (b. 1960). By that time many musicians had been trained at academies created in the 1960s and had started working together with the young singer-songwriters who maintained the same critical attitude as their predecessors. However, the society in which they were living was different from the one that existed during the early years of the Revolution, making a critical analysis of Cuban reality much more complex. These new musicians demanded national promotion of their music but again, in some cases, were met with new restrictions imposed by several functionaries who supposedly represented the Revolution's interests.

The newest *trovadores* wrote lyrics with more symbolism than those by their predecessors, and the musical structures of their songs were more closely associated with influences from diverse parts of the world—mostly rock music. Because their songs gave them a sort of underground status, some described them as the generation of moles. Young members of the movement established their own meeting places, separate from the ones organized by government institutions, while the MNT leadership struggled to improve ties with music distribution and promotion agencies. One document emanating from the main meeting in 1980 of all MNT members in Havana province identified a need to strengthen contacts with publicity mechanisms and the various institutions within the Ministry of Culture that promoted music. This led the Unión de Jóvenes Comunistas to create new venues such as La Casa del Joven Creador (Creative Youth Center) in Havana, which became one of the MNT's main venues.

TRANSITIONS

In 1985 the Unión de Jóvenes Comunistas, which had sponsored numerous MNT activities, decided to discontinue support of MNT and transferred those efforts to the Asociación Hermanos Saíz (Saíz Brothers Association), a new organization of young people involved in the arts. Consequently, direct attention to Nueva Trova musicians declined considerably. Although young musicians continued to absorb new influences within Cuba and popular music in general, furthering MNT's goal of promoting improvements for Cubans, they were still hampered by low interest in their work in the media.

The movement, like all of Cuba, was deeply affected by the economic crisis of the late 1980s and early 1990s, a result of the decline and collapse in 1991 of the Soviet Union. The Cuban economy, closely linked with Soviet and Eastern bloc structures, deteriorated quickly. During the so-called Special Period (1990–1994), Cuba's cultural life suffered, and support for the Nueva Trova movement musicians became very difficult to find. Institutions such as Casa de las Américas offered some backing, but these efforts were insufficient to maintain the movement as in the past. Many performers tried to make their way in Havana, and those in other provinces created new venues, such as El Mejunje in Santa Clara. Some survived by moving to other countries such as Spain, Mexico, Argentina, and the United States. Cuban singer-songwriters in Spain, including Vanito Caballero, José Luis Medina, Boris Larramendi, Pavel Urquiza, Gema Corredera, Alejandro Gutiérrez, and José Antonio Quesada, organized various groups of trovadores. One of the interesting albums produced in Spain is *Habana Abierta* (Open Havana). Some trovadores, such as Raúl Torres, Kelvis Ochoa, and David Torrens, returned to Cuba after living and working abroad. Some based their compositions on the traditional *trova* dating back to Ñico Saquito, who, with humor, ingenuity, and double entendre, sang about the Cuban reality in line with Martí's observation that humor is a whip with bells at the tip. One example of this is Frank Delgado's song, "Carta del niño cubano a Harry Potter" (A Cuban Boy's Letter to Harry Potter). Alluding to the average family's difficulties in feeding its children properly, Delgado says, "there's no magic like in Cuba, where Mother works magic three times a day."

What trovadores never lost was their love for Cuba, their desire to search for beauty, and their commitment to social and political criticism whose aim has been always to improve Cuban society. Their lyrics, while still literary, continued to evoke Cubans' daily speech patterns; their music, although influenced by world musical currents, preserved its Cuban essence.

In the late 1990s another generation of young people who had stayed on the island, kept on creating songs to express the lives they led. A movement emerging out of El Mejunje calls itself La Trovuntivitis (New-songitis); a large group in Havana called Canciones de la Rosa y la Espina (Songs of the Rose and the Thorn), joined forces with Casa de las Américas to provide venues for the newest music in the movement. Since 1997 a regular venue organized at the Pablo de la Torriente Brau Center, called A Guitarra Limpia (By Lone Guitar), was better representing the Nueva Trova movement's contemporary development. There, young talents enjoyed recognition and support for the promotion and distribution of their music. The new singer-songwriters continued to create songs that challenge the banality of commercial music and continued to address Cuban reality. Other projects such as La Guarandinga were working on children's songs.

The Nueva Trova movement, with roots in nineteenth-century Cuban culture, is an essential part of Cuban tradition. Subsequent generations continued to write and perform songs with a vision of Cuban society based on ethical principles rooted in Cuban thought, from that of José Martí and other founders of the national identity into the early twenty-first century. These songs combined political perspectives with the aesthetic heritage maintained by the poorest sectors of Cuban society and incorporated diverse cultural influences from around the world.

BIBLIOGRAPHY

Águila, Víctor. *Muy personal: Pablo Milanés*. Mexico City: Ediciones El Zaguán, 1990.

Borges Triana, Joaquín. *La luz, bróder, la luz: Canción cubana contemporánea*. Havana: Ediciones la Memoria, Centro Pablo de la Torriente Brau, 2009.

Díaz, Ariel. *La primera piedra, trovadores cubanos: El último tren*. Havana: Ediciones la Memoria, Centro Pablo de la Torriente Brau, 2009.

Giró, Radamés. *El filin: César Portillo de la Luz*. Madrid: Editorial Fundación de Autor, SGAE, 1998.

León, Carmela de. *Sindo Garay: Memorias de un trovador*. Havana: Editorial Letras Cubanas, 1990.

Sarusky, Jaime. *Grupo de Experimentación Sonora del ICAIC, Mito y Realidad*. Havana: Editorial Letras Cubanas, 2005.

MUSIC: AFRO-CUBAN RELIGIOUS INFLUENCE ON CUBAN POPULAR MUSIC

Tony Évora

The intertwining of West African deities and liturgical beliefs with Spanish words in hundreds of Cuban popular music compositions since the 1920s.

In the process of religious syncretism that took place in Cuba over several centuries, African slaves melded the European Catholic tradition with their own, enriching and strengthening it by blending Christian and African rites. The most widespread form of syncretism integrated the Catholic saints with African deities, identifying Changó with Saint Barbara, Oshún with Our Lady of Charity of El Cobre, Babalú-Ayé with Saint Lazarus, and so on.

Religious elements of Regla de Ocha (Santería), Regla de Palo Monte, and the Abakuá Secret Society were incorporated into popular dance music, including *contradanza, habanera, danza, danzón, son, guaracha,* cha-cha-cha, and bolero. This religious influence is particularly evident in *son,* the rhythm most identified with the Cuban people.

SANTERÍA OR REGLA DE OCHA IN POPULAR DANCE MUSIC

Ignacio Piñeiro (1888–1969) wrote songs in the *son* style such as the famous "Échale salsita" (Spice It Up a Bit) and other pieces enjoyed by thousands of Cubans. His 1928 song "No juegues con los santos" (Don't Play with the Saints) is about how a Santería believer identifies the saint or orisha that protects him by the color or colors of the necklace he wears:

> Mayeya, don't play with the saints,
> respect the necklaces,
> don't play with the saints....
> Don't mess with me,
> because all of us in Cuba know each other,
> whoever doesn't wear yellow
> wears blue or scarlet....
> Oribá the letter, oribabá

The pianist and composer Eliseo Grenet (1893–1950) wrote music for films and theatrical works such as *Niña Rita* (Little Rita, 1927) and for poems from *Motivos de son* (Son Motifs, 1930), by Nicolás Guillén (1902–1989). He also created the *danzones* "La mora" (The Moorish Girl) and "Las perlas de tu boca" (Pearls from Your Mouth). His compositions reflect a blending of Spanish and the ritual language of Regla de Ocha known as *Lucumí* as can be seen in his song "Espabílate" (Snap to It), famously interpreted by the great Bola de Nieve (Ignacio Villa, 1911–1971):

> Wakey wakey, sansa my coco
> Wakey wakey...
> sansa my coco uán
> and coro, coro, coro, my sansa....
> Listen to me girl, so brikina,
> emeralda, piriguanga, mazucamba,
> abariná.

From Margarita Lecuona (1910–1981) came "Babalú," a song in a slow tempo made famous by the singer Miguelito Valdés (1912–1978), who was deeply involved in the Afro-Cuban *reglas.* Known in the United States as "Mr. Babalú," Miguelito was one of the founders of the formidable Casino de la Playa orchestra in 1937. The title is a reference to Babalú-Ayé (Father of the World), the orisha associated with illness and healing, equivalent to the Catholic saint Lazarus:

> The wake is beginning
> that we make for Babalú,
> eh, give me 17 candles, to put on the cross
> Give me a string of tobacco, *mayembe* [boss],
> and a little jug of *aguardiente*
> Give me a little money, *mayengue* [chief],
> Ay, to give us luck.
> I want to ask
> that my black woman love me
> that she have money,
> and that she doesn't die.
> Ay! And I want to ask Babalú
> for a full lipped woman like you,
> that she have no other man
> and she doesn't go away... Ay!
> Babalú-Ayé, Babalú-Ayé.

Rogelio Martínez (1905–2001), the director of the group Sonora Matancera, composed "Yényere cumá." It is about a barn owl, which is used in very important sacrifices and has become a symbol of Santería. Typically, singers increase the tempo as the song moves forward:

> Yényere cumá,
> good night,
> how are you....
> Beautiful bird of the dawn.

In the 1950s the group Fajardo y sus Estrellas and the famous Aragón Orchestra recorded splendid versions separately of the *danzón* "Virgen de Regla" (The Virgin of Regla), composed by Pablo O'Farrill in 1916. With the *danzón* genre, Cuba found its national dance at the beginning of the twentieth century, as Austria had done with the waltz and Argentina the tango. The church in the municipality of Regla at the bottom of Havana Bay holds the icon of Yemayá,

Batá drummers.
Elements of traditional Cuban religions have been incorporated into the country's popular dance music. Batá drums, formerly used exclusively in religious ceremonies, are now widely played in secular settings, such as this street festival. HÉCTOR DELGADO AND ROLANDO PUJOL

equivalent to the Virgen de Regla, ruler and goddess of the waters:

> Virgin of Regla,
> pity me, pity me....
> These are my songs, cries from the soul
> a woman, blinded my existence,
> yes sir, why not,
> give me the tranquility that brings joy to my soul
> and I will not die of love.

The Matanzas musician Gilberto Valdés (1905–1971) integrated music of African origin into the symphonic music of Havana in works such as "Rumba abierta" (Open Rhumba) and "Evocación negra" (Black Evocation). He also produced various excellent *pregones* (songs based on street vendors' cries) such as "Ecó" (a parcel made of corn, occasionally with meat inside). The song references *olelé,* a food offered to the orishas, here referred to as saints:

> Ecó, ecó, ecó, ecoero
> Ecó, tamal and olelé
> ecó, ecó, ecoero

> Ecó for the black, tamal for the white
> And for the saints olelé.

Valdés also wrote "Ogguere," a lullaby with a very slow Afro-rhythm. *Ogguere* is a Yoruba word that means "soul of the earth":

> Ogguere, ogguere, ogguere....
> The six o'clock bell, rings around town
> and the black workers say their prayers.
> Ogguere go to sleep,
> that I have to do my mending
> and later I'm going to make *ecó,*
> to be bought in the slave barracks.

One of the best-known of the duets recorded by Celina González (b. 1929) and Reutilio Domínguez (1921–1971) is "Que viva Changó" (Long Live Changó), a song of the Cuban countryside with marked Lucumí or Yoruba influences. The Catholic saint Barbara is the equivalent of Changó, a much-loved deity in Cuba:

> Blessed Saint Barbara
> for you I raise my lyre

and with emotion am inspired
before your beautiful image.
Long live Changó!
With infinite will
I tear from my heart
that melodious expression
asking that from heaven
you send us your solace
and your holy blessing....
Long live Changó!

Before going into exile, the great Celia Cruz (1924–2003) sang for many years with Sonora Matancera. In "Yerbero moderno" (Modern Herbalist) she reminds listeners of the curative world of plants, a theme the Trío Matamoros developed in the 1930s in "Hojas para baño" (Leaves for Cleansing). The Regla de Ocha includes a healing component that utilizes herbs and bathing in its rituals.

A voice is heard saying,
the herbalist has arrived....
I bring sacred herb for the throat,
I bring anise for swelling.
I also bring basil for the skinny people,
and apasote for rashes,
and vetiver for those who can't see,
and with this herb you will marry.

Benny Moré (1919–1963) and Celia Cruz sang "Mata siguaraya" (*Siguaraya* Plant Shrub), created by Lino Frías, the pianist of Sonora Matancera, in a slow Afro-rhythm. The *siguaraya* is a sacred tree with egg-shaped fruit and brilliant red leaves arranged in a dome shape with spiritual power for Afro-Cubans. It is not as impressive as the huge *ceiba*, the Cuban equivalent of the African baobab, which is also a sacred tree:

In my Cuba a shrub grows
that cannot be cut without permission....
They can't be cut, because they are of the
    orisha.
that shrub grows in the forest,
that trunk has power....
That shrub is *siguaraya*.

Under the direction of Obdulio Morales (1910–1981), in the 1940s Merceditas Valdés (1928–1996) vocally illustrated several lectures about music of African origin organized by the ethnologist Fernando Ortiz. In a liturgical composition arranged by the singer herself, the flute and guitar introduce a plea to Osaín, a great friend of Changó and the orisha of medicinal herbs. He has only one foot (the right) and one arm (the left); he has one enormous ear and the other is small, and with both he hears everything.

In the 1950s the *son* singer Abelardo Barroso (1905–1972) recorded some splendid numbers with the group Orquesta Sensación. In the humorous "El brujo de Guanabacoa" (The Wizard of Guanabacoa) the singer laments the cost of divination by a *babalao*, the highest priest in Ifá, particularly when the *babalao* asks for various foods and more money:

I went to Guanabacoa,
to the house of a *babalao*,
so he would look at my house
and at me because I had bad luck.
He charged me $1.05
I only paid for the table,
the chickens, ducks and doves
weren't on the bill.
They began to look at me
the 7 pieces of coconut,
that were thrown in the air
and they began to jump
while I invoked Orula,
my Changó and Yemayá,
so they would tell me the truth
and not cheat me.
You bring me a fat rooster,
bring me cocoa butter,
bring me corn and honey
Ah! and $4.75 that I had forgotten.

The orisha Oggún is the lord of metals who lives in the forest. His color is green. He is a powerful warrior who constantly harasses the great Changó. Oggún is a central figure in the following *guaguancó*, which is one of three types of rhumbas to have survived from colonial days. Columbia and Yambú are the other two; the Columbia is the fastest rhumba, whereas the Yambú is the slowest and is danced by elderly people. Since the 1940s they are performed in humble large old houses with an interior patio and usually start with a long introduction. No additional instruments participate other than drums (or boxes), claves (two wooden sticks that are beaten in rhythm), and voices. This particular rhumba was performed by the singer Celeste Mendoza (1930–1998) from Santiago de Cuba with Los Papines (a vocal and percussion quartet founded in 1957 by brothers Luis, Alfredo, Jesús, and Ricardo Abreu).

Boys, forget your worries
I feel like enjoying myself.
Don't anyone run away
the great rhumba has begun (meaning out of
    control).
Enjoy the moment
because later you'll regret.

I went to a party of orishas, and there,
a very strong saint saved a little girl from death,
covering her with his cloak.
And I, amazed to know,
had to sing like this:
Papá Oggún, what is this?

In 1994 in Miami the brilliant bassist Cachao (Israel López, 1918–2008) recorded "Cachao's Güiro," a tribute to Obbatalá, the androgynous orisha who according to Yoruba beliefs (from Nigeria) created the human race on the orders of Olodumare (God). The recording is dominated by the exotic sound of four *chequerés*, ritual instruments made from the round fruits of the *güira* tree that are covered by a net of seeds. Following an antiphonal form, as in jazz riffs, the chorus repeats:

> Obbatalá kunawa
> Obbatalá kunawó.

ELEMENTS OF THE REGLA DE PALO MONTE OF THE CONGO

The great Cuban bandleader and composer Arsenio Rodríguez (1911–1970), a blind man who played the *tres* guitar left-handed, wrote moving boleros such as "La vida es sueño" (Life Is a Dream) and *sones* such as "Tumba palo cocuyé." His best-known number is probably the slow Afro "Bruca maniguá" (Bruca Jungle), which incorporates words from the ritual languages of Regla de Palo and Abakuá such as "carabalí," "mundele" (white man) and "bruca maniguá":

> I am Carabalí,
> of the black nation.
> Without freedom
> I cannot live.
> *Mundele* rips at my heart
> so much abuse, body so beaten. . . .
> I shall try to escape to the *bruca maniguá*!

Guillermo Rodríguez Fife (1908–1997), a guitarist from Santiago, is the author of "La negra Tomasa" (The Black Girl Tomasa), a song in the *guaracha* style (a type of satirical song). The song is also known as "Bilongo"—a wicked spell that brings bad luck:

> I am so in love
> with the black girl Tomasa,
> that when she leaves the house
> how sad I become.
> Ay, ay, ay!
> This pretty black girl
> that has put a spell on me. . . .
> The sorceress!

With "Chola Wengue" Benny Moré (who had Congolese roots) recorded a song very different from his other *sones*. In Palo Monte, Chola Wengue equates to Cachita, Our Lady of Charity El Cobre, patroness of Cuba, and the beautiful Oshún in Regla de Ocha. The Congolese also know her as Siete Ríos (Seven Rivers):

> Entonché, tonche a lamú, tonché
> now the black Congolese of the forest
> dance their *bembé*. . . .
> Chola Wengue, to Wengue Chola.

ELEMENTS FROM THE ABAKUÁ SECRET SOCIETY

The song "En la alta sociedad" (In High Society) was popularized by a recording made by María Teresa Vera (1895–1965) and Lorenzo Hierrezuelo (1907–1993) at the Radio Cadena Suaritos studios in the mid-1950s. In it, the songwriter Ignacio Piñeiro pokes fun at white people who try to make Abakuá music at a party. The *íreme* is the disguised mischievous spirit that comes to earth to ensure the religious propriety of the *ekobios* members of the sect. The íreme requires the *moruá yuansa* to compel to dance. The four drums called *Enkomo* do not produce music but their symbolic value is considerable. The *Bonkó Enchemiyá* is a long drum made from a hollowed out tree trunk with the player sitting on it while another musician beats the lower part of the drum with two sticks called *itones*. The *Anankobeko* is the name of another íreme supposed to come from the African region where the Cross River runs, right above the Biafra Bay, while *Efiméreme obón iyamba* refers to an important position in the Abakuá hierarchy. The Abakuá music is presented publicly in the *isaroko*, an exterior patio close to the *fambá* room where the secret drum ékue is kept.

> In high society
> they wanted to play *diablito* [popular term to
>   refer to Íreme],
> and a bit of singing
> they could imitate.
> When they went to play
> they sought a hundred instruments,
> their confused movements
> he didn't let them finish.
> To sing abakuá, the little maraca doesn't cut it,
> You need the *íreme, enkomo* and *bonkó*
> and the *anankobeko, efiméreme obón iyamba*.

Although the 1920 commercial recording of "Los cantares del abakuá" (The Songs of Abakuá), by Felipe Neri-Cabrera, was the first to employ Abakuá phrases, "Criolla carabalí" (Carabalí Criollo), recorded by Sexteto Habanero in 1928, appears to be the first completely Abakuá song. This composition became the model for later recordings such as those by Chano Pozo (1947), Victor Herrera (1962), and Patato and Totico (1967):

> The Sacred Fish appeared:
> Power in the river and the forest
> A king Efik authorized by Efó
> Abakuá began to work
> Aaa eee, aaa eee
> The banner Efí Abarakó are our brothers,
>   Mokóngo is valiant.
> Why do we celebrate the drum?
> Because with it the banner Bakokó Efó
> created Abakuá Efó, making us brothers.

We carry our flag proudly
Yayó eee, yayó ma-ee
Reference to the beginning of the Abakuá in
    Africa
Yayó eee, yayó ma-ee
Attention, salute the founding principle!
The drum Sése Eribo initiates the *obonekues*,
converting the people, Efí and Efó, into one.
The drum Sése is our mother
the music of the drum.
The bonkó came from Efó,
Abasí [God] loves us all.

AFRO-CUBAN RELIGIOUS ELEMENTS AFTER THE REVOLUTION

The Los Van Van orchestra, formed in 1971 by Juan Formell (b. 1942), performed a dance number titled "Soy todo" (I Am Everything), based on a poem by Eloy Machado (El Ambia). The song refers to several deities of the Ocha, Ifá, and Abakuá religions.

The last four lines refer to Changó, but some consider them to be a reference to Fidel Castro:

I am the poet of rhumba
I am the drum, the echo of the drum.
I am the mission of my roots,
the history of my land.
I am the life that is, that goes away
Ay! that goes away
I am the colors of the bundle of necklaces
so that the root doesn't die.
I am chili, I am spice.
I am the step of Changó,
the step of Obbatalá, the laugh of Yemayá
the valor of Oggún,
the ball or the spinning top of Elegguá.
I am Obba, I am Siré, Siré.

I am Aberiñán and Aberisún,
I am the answer to the crossword,
the man who gave rise to Obdebí,
the hunter of doubt.
I am the hand of truth.
I am Arere, I am conscience. I am Orula.
Who am I?
I am Arere, I am conscience. I am Orula.
Look, the time has come
to reexamine your law;
you say you are the king
show me your crown.

Cuban rappers, including Anónimo Consejo (Anonymous Advice) and Clan 537, have recorded songs with religious themes. The group Orishas dedicated a song to Elegguá and Changó, two of the main orishas, emphasizing the importance of Elegguá, who opens roads, serves as a messenger for the other orishas, and affirms the importance of truth-telling in Ifá as demonstrated in the Ifá saying, "Those who speak the truth are helped by the gods."

Son Elegguá, my saint Elegguá,
my life Elegguá, Maferefún,
King of the roads, law of my destiny,
red and black like red wine, I tell you,
who opens roads for me with his cane,
Calabash liquor, tobacco smoke,
dressed in a sack.
Who lets me see when I am sad, dull,
follow his footsteps, ask him for health
and that he keep the bad times away.
I ask the blessing to express
my feelings.
All you ask of me, consider it done,
I don't profess my philosophy about Echún,

Praise to Elegguá.
I sing for Elegguá and for Changó,
I sing the truth, I tell you.
I sing for Elegguá and for Changó,
I sing the truth, I tell you.
What I say is what I think,
what I think is what I feel.
I sing for Elegguá and for Changó,
I sing the truth.

BIBLIOGRAPHY

Díaz Ayala, Cristóbal. *Si te quieres por el pico divertir*. San Juan, Puerto Rico: Editorial Cubanacán, 1988.

Évora, Tony. *Música cubana. Los últimos 50 años*. Madrid: Alianza Editorial, 2003.

Miller, Ivor L. *Voice of the Leopard. African Secret Societies and Cuba*. Jackson: University Press of Mississippi, 2009.

Orovio, Helio. *Diccionario de la Música Cubana*. Havana: Editorial Letras Cubanas, 1992.

Sosa Rodríguez, Enrique. *Los Ñáñigos*. Havana: Casa de las Américas, 1982.

MUSIC: RITUAL MUSIC

Victoria Eli Rodríguez

Overview of the music used in rituals of the Santería, Arará, Palo, and Abakuá faiths.

The African diaspora and its continuance in the Caribbean were determining factors in the definition of Cuban culture. Africans, once separated from their natural surroundings and in a foreign environment, preserved various elements that kept them united to their past, encouraging a sense of belonging and integration into the group of origin. However, intra- and interethnic fusion and synthesis generated new

■ *See also*

Faith: Abakuá Society

Faith: Arará

Faith: Vodou

individual traits and profiles. In a complex process that extended from the sixteenth to the nineteenth centuries, Africans and their descendants, together with others of European and Asian descent and a small portion of native populations, shaped Cuba's landscape, economy, and social relations. Strong syncretism gave rise to peculiarities in speech, music, and visual arts, and played a role in both the productive and domestic spheres, as well as in entertainment and religion.

A great diversity of political and social structures, together with varied geographical and ethnic backgrounds, characterized the Africans who were brought to the Americas, particularly from West Africa. Ethnic names and labels—the latter created by slave traders and scribes—were intermixed, resulting in umbrella terms such as *Lucumí, Arará, Congo,* and *Carabalí*—to list the broadest ones—which grouped together neighboring peoples who were victims of the slave trade and whose cultural traits are recognized in Cuban musical practice.

One part of this population gathered together in urban or suburban *cofradías* (brotherhoods) and *cabildos* (councils) made up of Africans belonging to the same ethnic community or nation. Such associations enabled colonial power to exercise greater control over this segment of the population and establish mechanisms for deculturation aimed at impeding interethnic cohesion. However, the councils and brotherhoods performed important functions in terms of mutual assistance, aid, and recreation among the African population and their descendants; they developed into a tool for resistance, for preserving cultural elements and for reconstructing and reinterpreting African traditions. When slavery was abolished in Cuba in 1886, a large portion of the *cabildos* refashioned themselves as societies, brotherhoods, or house temples in order to leave behind the long-standing stigma of slave exploitation, but some conserved their former names, further reinforcing their ancestral origin.

Although African cultures did not arrive in the Americas whole cloth, all of them undertook a process of searching for a "handhold," as Argeliers León puts it, from the first moments of colonization (p. 116). Religious social conscience was, at heart, a form of "staying together," and the ancestors, deities, and primary animist expressions were resources that allowed the powers to be in situations advantageous to the individual and to be at the service of both the individual and the group (León, p. 118).

As a result of racial mixture and syncretic and transcultural processes, the main popular Cuban religions were shaped by contributions from Christianity and African religious concepts. The cosmogonic visions of Regla de Ocha-Ifá, or Santería; Regla Arará; Palo Monte; and the Abakuá (or *ñáñigo*) societies exhibit ethical and aesthetic values of African origin, converted into identifying values of the Cuban people. Such components evolved, were redefined, and expanded regionally in different contexts and among a variety of groups and social classes, adapting both to hostile settings and to situations where freedom of practice was possible.

REGLA DE OCHA-IFÁ, OR SANTERÍA

The religious system known as Ocha-Ifá, Regla de Ocha, or simply Ocha, practiced in Cuba with the generic name of Santería, is the most widespread popular religion in the country. Its popularity may be explained by the greater development achieved by the Yoruba culture in Africa by the time it fell victim to slavery, the late arrival in Cuba of individuals pertaining to this group, and the reorganization of its religious components—the cult of *orishás* (deities or gods) of the Yoruba or Lucumí pantheon, the Ifá system of oracle divination, and the beliefs and ritual world incorporating the Catholic saints. These factors help explain the persistence of these traditions and their influence in diverse segments of society.

A process of conformity and comparison took place between the legends and attributes of the orishas and Yoruba mythology—Elegguá, Ochosi, Oggún, Changó, Yemayá, Obbatalá, Oyá, Ochún, and Babalú Ayé—on the one hand, and the Catholic saints—El Niño de Atocha, Saint Norbert, San Pedro, Saint Barbara, and the Virgins of Regla, of Candelaria, of Caridad del Cobre, and San Lázaro—on the other. Followers of Santería worship these and other *orishás-santos* (deity-saint hybrids) according to criteria of constant exchange and forms of behavior.

The presentation of new initiates by their godparents, the commemoration of their date of initiation (commonly called the "saint's birthday"), offerings to the main deity of the house temple, and funeral ceremonies—all could be occasions to celebrate with music or beat the drum. Fiestas were not celebrated on established or fixed dates. Practitioners might beat the drum in celebration of certain of the Catholic holy days—for instance, on 4 or 17 December, the feast days of Saint Barbara (Changó) and Saint Lazarus (Babalú Ayé), respectively—but it was up to the believers to organize a fiesta as an act of thanks or as tribute at the request of an orisha. These situations were times for reunion and collective participation, integrating ceremonial and festive elements involving the entire house and ritual family.

In Santería a large number of prayers, offerings, and ceremonies take place accompanied by music, with interpretation through song and instruments as well as through dance. Before beginning the fiesta, a ritual musical piece called *oru de Igbodú* or *oru seco* is performed—a cycle of beats of invocation dedicated to the deities in a predetermined order that begins and closes with Elegguá, with the drummers and singers located in front of the altar of the *Igbodú* (where the orishas are found). Once this *oru* is completed, musicians move to the area of the house where the

Santería ceremony. Practitioners dance to the beat of batá drums during a Santería ceremony. Santería ceremonies are often accompanied by music and dance. Money is sometimes distributed as a sign of good luck. HÉCTOR DELGADO AND ROLANDO PUJOL

celebration will take place; they are placed in the back, near the soloist and facing the attendants, in order to promote better communication between them. The song and drum beats follow the order of the oru, in this case known as *Eyá Aranlá* (indoor celebration) or *Iban Baló* (outdoor celebration). The greatest variety of instrument types in Cuban religious ritual is found among the groups that accompany Santería's singing and dancing. In these groups, worshipers commonly use *batá* drums, *güiros*, *abwe* (or *chequeré*) and *bembé* drums; and of these, the batá drums are the most sacred.

Batá drums, like other instruments used with popular Cuban religions, are sacred objects and must be subject to ritual practices that begin with the start of their construction. Songs and prayers accompany their construction, starting with blessings and acts of purification. Once the shells of the three drums are built, consultation takes place through the *dilogún* (cowrie shells used for divination) or the *okpelé* or *opelé* (the chain of Ifá, which also serves for divination). Thus the signs and marks of each drum are defined, along with the name of the trio or batá group and other ritual aspects that will be considered after it is consecrated.

The deity Añá is found inside the drums, where it defends and protects them and gives them the power to speak, all of which intensifies special ritual practices.

This magical power is found hidden in a small leather or cloth pouch (the *añá*) that can be nailed to the interior wall of the shell or left loose; in the latter case, a peculiar sound is produced when the walls of the drum are struck and sometimes while striking the drumhead during execution. Once the añá is prepared for each instrument and corresponding marks made on the interior of the shells, a food offering is made to the drums. When the new set is completed, it must be presented to and recognized by another existing drum trio, which serves as godfather. The consecration or birth of the batá trio should be done by someone who, according to the religion, has the powers of Añá and of Osaín. The consecrated drums should be played by consecrated drummers, who receive the name *olú batá* and who must obey a series of rules concerning individual and social conduct corresponding to the hierarchical level they occupy. There are prohibitions dictated by religion and tradition that limit contact of women with the batá—women are only permitted to show their respect through greeting and dance.

REGLA ARARÁ

The religious practice of Regla Arará is very uncommon, despite the long history of Arará people, who originated from the ancient kingdom of Dahomey (today the Republic of Benin) and have been recognized since the sixteenth and seventeenth centuries. Regla Arará exhibits similarities with Santería in its ritual, magical, and religious behaviors. Like Santería, it includes initiation ceremonies, festivals, and funerals, divination, and ritual sacrifices, and it possesses a rich pantheon made up of *vodú* or *vodún* practices. After the disintegration of the old councils, the practice was reduced to certain zones of the country—particularly in Matanzas Province—or preserved in Lucumí house temples. The fiestas were conducted in accordance with the tradition of each group, but all coincided in celebrating 17 December, Saint Lazarus's Day, synchretized with Babalú Ayé among the Lucumí and with various Arará deities, emphasizing their power over health, fertility, the harvest, and family harmony. The songs, in an order similar to the Lucumí oru, are accompanied by an *ogán* (a metal idiophone), one or two rattles (*acheré* or *chachá*), and a group of three to five membranophones. Arará drums, generally large in size and cup-shaped, have a tensioning system that uses braces and pegs inside the drum shell. They are played with the hands and a stick, generating a powerful rhythmic beat and timbre.

The drums used in Arará ceremonies—like those in Santería—have great importance, because it is their music, together with song and dance, that invokes and honors the deities, calls down their presence through a state of trance, and strengthens the connections and unity among the believers. The repertoire of this group is based on the songs and beats of this religion; however, because of the strong connections among the various popular beliefs in Cuba, these rhythms can be played for Santería or Palo believers, if there are practitioners of these religions present at the fiesta. From the point of view of the ritual repertoire, the fiesta is commonly initiated with the Lucumí oru, next playing for the Arará deities, and finally closing the celebration by playing and dancing for the Palo spirits.

PALO MONTE

Regla de Palo Monte, or simply Palo, is a religious and festive practice with Bantu roots found throughout all of the western part of Cuba. A complex ritual pays tribute to the *nganga*—a recipient or vessel containing series of elements that represent the elements of nature and of man, which the practitioner of Palo hopes to dominate. The nganga unites the members of a house temple, together with the *tata nganga*, the principal figure within the Palo rite. The fiestas are carried out on anniversaries of the *prenda* or nganga, when the practitioner completes some task or when some promise must be fulfilled; they are also common during the Catholic Holy Week before Easter and on 31 December, in order to welcome the New Year. Initiation ceremonies, as occur in the other ritual practices, are performed within a closed circle of Palo practitioners, although later an open fiesta is also held.

Palo music and dance are accompanied by clapping or groups of two, three, or four congas—because of the extinction of the old *palo* drums to which a metal idiophone and shaker are added. The rhythmic designs performed by these instruments are generally short and repetitive, coinciding with the melodic structure of the song, which repeats short phrases and segments from intonations belonging to the Bantu tongues. The song is the most important musical component of Palo, to the point that many practitioners believe that Palo is performed through song. The song lyrics are the basis through which the powers of the nganga are invoked and religious action is directed. Palo songs incorporate ancient Bantu words and a language blended with Spanish words, with strong symbolic content understood only by those who know the *jerga del palero* (Palo jargon). The festive religious celebration commonly opens with the *toque* (beating) of the palo, and at the concluding moments participants can sing to the saints. Palo participants are quite reticent in describing their religious practices, but their music is found in the everyday festive practices of the Cuban people, including rhythms such as rhumba and conga.

ABAKUÁ SOCIETIES

Great organizational and ritual complexity characterizes the Abakuá (or *ñáñigo*) societies. These male-only religious brotherhoods arose in Cuba in 1836 among Africans of the Carabalí nation (from Igbo-speaking Calabar in the Bight of Biafra) and their descendants, in Havana and Matanzas provinces. Each group—referred to as a *juego* (game), *potencia* (power), or *tierra* (land) without distinction—plays part in a complicated ritual that tries to reconstruct the history of the emergence of the secret *ekpe* (or *egpa*) societies in ancient Calabar, through the mystery of a ritual or ceremonial voice. The ceremonies, or *plantes,* include the swearing-in of new members, the assumption of hierarchical posts in the governance of the society, and funeral ceremonies—*llantos* or *nyoros*—as well as the founding of new *juegos* or the disintegration of existing ones.

Two classes of instruments are used in the *plantes.* One class, of symbolic content, is made up of four percussion membranophones and an instrument called an *ékue*. The latter is the fundamental instrument of the ensemble; its sound is obtained by rubbing a rod against the drum head to reproduce the magic and ritual voice. The second class consists of the strictly musical instruments that comprise the *biankomeko* ensemble—four membranophones and three idiophones—that accompanies ritual songs, drum beats, and marches. The interpretations are based on two styles: *efó*, a slower style, and *efí*, which is more rapid. These are associated with two tribes that, according to tradition, merged in Africa in the *ekpe* society.

An important element of the celebrations is the *íremes* or *diablitos* (little devils), hooded dancers representing supernatural entities that come from the earth to participate in the plante and confirm that it is celebrated correctly. The fiesta is preceded by a secret invocation by *ékue* drum. After that, a procession of the *biankomeko* group toward the patio of the house temple begins, accompanying the singer and the chorus and in direct relation to the dance of the *diablitos*.

GENERAL ASPECTS OF MUSICAL LANGUAGE

Drumming, songs, and dance in popular Cuban religions maintain different levels of similarity and affinity with the peoples who gave rise to them; they also establish communication with deities, celebrate their presence, exchange with them, and achieve symbolic catharsis in moments of possession or trance.

According to the most orthodox criteria, all orishas, saints, deities, or ceremonial objects have their characteristic drum rhythms and songs. These individual expressions can be combined to create different rhythmic arrangements and diverse forms of vocal behaviors and dance movements. The instrumental element of the ritual acts in conjunction with the song and is able to encourage and put a halt to dancing and stimulate possession states among believers in those religions in which this behavior is part of the ceremony. When one of the dancers—in Santería or Palo—is found to be predisposed to trance, the singer, using ritual language and emphasis within the song, together with the drummer whose instrument has the deepest register of the group, establishes a true dialogue with the believer that requires him to match his movements with the rhythm of the drum, encouraging the deity to come down into his head and overcome him. At this moment the singers and drummers demonstrate their experience, increasing the intensity and rhythmic complexity of the music. The interpretation moves progressively faster and reaches the climax of the fiesta with the participation and enthusiasm of the believers. Such changes in tempo are spontaneous and follow a code determined by the actual ritual practice. The duration of each drum beat, or drum beat and song, obeys the judgment of the drummers and singers in strict relation with what takes place in the ceremony.

From the point of view of the role of the music, the instruments and the voices move in sonorous spaces defined in ranges or bands of timbre and rhythm. The groups of rhythm and timbre interpreted by the instruments can be categorized as oratorical, or speaking, since they suggest the intonations of African speech, and the believers feel certain that the drummer, through his drumming, can speak or converse with the deities. Drumming is combined in such a way that the result is perceived as a rhythmic unit made up of three tonal levels: deep, middle, and treble. The most diverse groups are traditionally performed in the deep range, where improvisation is emphasized, and this range exhibits major differences in the quality of drumming. The remaining ranges are home to more stable patterns of playing. In the early 2010s, ritual drumming in Cuba has had a reversal of functions, however, transferring improvisation back to the treble level, particularly among the young drummers who bring models from rhumba to their performances. Each form of interpretation puts the criteria of variation and stability into practice, and each range or band serves different roles of meter, rhythm, timbre, and expression. There is also a logical subordination and coordination among instruments, and among these and the voices, with elements that assume the role of a point of reference and are capable of governing the entire event. Patterns of improvisation in Santería, Arará, Palo Monte, and Abakuá are diverse, but all are subject to the models established by tradition: that is, they do not completely reflect the free will of the drummers.

The alternation between solo and chorus is another expressive characteristic in Afro-Cuban ritual music. The main singer generally begins in a treble register, and the instruments are incorporated all at once or in stages, according to the characteristic rhythm for the deity; the chorus enters without concern for any register and usually adjusts itself based on what the soloist is doing. The melodic contour of the song moves in an ascending-descending pattern based on the fundamental resonant idea or referent, whose greatest expressive tension is achieved based on the time it takes to reach the resting point of the deep sound. The oldest songs are not governed by melodic or tonal relationships, although as a consequence of the process of cultural interaction, there appears to be a tendency to replicate organizations similar to the major and minor tonal patterns, as well as the presence of pentatonic series.

Many observers are inclined to reduce the characteristics and contributions of African culture in traditional Afro-Cuban religious practice to its drumming and rhythms, describing them as monotonous, repetitive, and primitive. And certainly the repetition of brief segments is one of the characteristics of Afro-Cuban music, but this element occupies a specific place in the structure, in the same way that open forms determined by the ceremonial event in question predominate.

Within the ritual and festival space, music and dance are essential elements of integration in the religious environment. Both of these elements demonstrate and characterize devotion, and they encourage the spiritual fulfillment of the believers. Regardless of the religion in question, the fiesta is established as the participatory space par excellence in which the transmission and continuity of collective memory takes place. At the same time, it constitutes a form of identification with cultural elements originating in Africa that are fully integrated into Cuban culture.

SELECTED DISCOGRAPHY

Antología de la música afrocubana (2006).

Ros, Lázaro. *Colección Orisha Ayé* (2000–2003).

BIBLIOGRAPHY

Barnet, Miguel. *Cultos Afrocubanos. La Regla de Ocha. La Regla de Palo monte.* Havana: Ediciones Unión, 1995.

Eli Rodríguez, Victoria. "*Güiros* and *Batá* Drums: Two Instrumental Groups of Cuban Santería." In *Music in Latin America and the Caribbean: Performing the Caribbean Experience.* Edited by Malena Kuss, 71–96. Austin: University of Texas Press, 2007.

Guanche, Jesús. *Componentes étnicos de la nación cubana.* Havana: Colección la Fuente Viva, 1996.

León, Argeliers. *Del canto y el tiempo.* Havana: Editorial Pueblo y Educación, 1974.

León, Argeliers. "Continuidad cultural del africano en América." In *Anales del Caribe* 6 (1986): 115–130.

León, Argeliers. "Cómo las supervivencias africanas contribuyeron a la identificación del hombre americano." In *Tras las huellas de las civilizaciones negras en América,* 59–80. Havana: Colección la Fuente Viva, 2001.

Ortiz, Fernando. *Los instrumentos de la música afrocubana.* 5 vols. Havana: Dirección de Cultura del Ministerio de Educación, 1952–1955.

Ortiz, Fernando. *La africanía de la música folklórica de Cuba.* Havana: Editorial Cárdenas y Cía, 1950. Rev. ed. Havana: Editora Universitaria, 1965.

Vinueza, María Elena. *Presencia arará en la música folclórica de Matanzas.* Havana: Ediciones Casa de las Américas, 1989.

Vinueza, María Elena. "Tambores Arará." In *Instrumentos de la música folclórico-popular de Cuba,* edited by Victoria Eli Rodríguez, 232–246. Havana: Centro de Investigación y Desarrollo de la Música Cubana, 1997.

MUSIC: AFRO-CUBAN JAZZ

Radamés Giro

The bands and musicians integral to the fusion of Cuban music and jazz.

Though musicians and bands from the United States have traveled to Cuba since the early years of the twentieth century, it was in the 1920s with the rise of luxury hotels, nightclubs, and casinos that the presence of jazz was felt in Havana. This was when José Curbelo "put together the best Cuban jazz band of the decade" (Acosta 2001, p. 28), which—after the founding of radio station PWX in Havana in 1922—was the first to perform jazz over the airwaves. From 1930 on, jazz bands spread throughout the country. Armando Romeu (1911–2002), Gustavo Más (1918–2000), Luis Escalante (1915–1970), and Isidro Pérez (Isito) were among the first to cultivate jazz in Cuba.

THE 1940s TO THE 1970s

In 1930, Mario Bauzá (1911–1993) moved to New York and worked with the bands headed by Justo (Don) Azpiazu (1893–1943), Noble Sissle (1889–1975), Chick Webb (1909–1939), Don Redman (1900–1964), Fletcher Henderson (1898–1952), and Cab Calloway (1907–1994). In 1940, he and Frank (Machito) Grillo (1909–1984) formed the Afro-Cubans. Bauzá was a master of both Cuban music and the jazz form (especially bop). The fusion of these two idioms gave birth to Afro-Cuban jazz. Bauzá's 1943 recording *Tanga* was a great success. Bauzá's and Machito's influence on both jazz and rhythm and blues was considerable, but Mario's sustained effort over more than forty years to meld jazz with Afro-Cuban music was greater. In the second half of the 1940s, Cuban rhythms, which had previously been considered outside the frontiers of jazz, became a staple of almost every group.

But this infectious music did more. It launched Ella Fitzgerald (1918–1996) into stardom and brought Dizzy Gillespie (1917–1993) together with Cuban conga drummer Chano Pozo (1915–1948), leading to the memorable 1948 Town Hall concert in New York in which Pozo played with Gillespie's group. From then on, no jazz band was without a Cuban percussionist. Cándido Camero (b. 1921), Armando Peraza (b. 1918), Mongo Santamaría (1917–2003), Patato Valdés (1926–2007) and Carlos Vidal Bolado all worked with well-known North American jazz musicians, including Stan Kenton (1911–1979) and Cab Calloway (Stearns 1966, pp. 212–224).

In the mid-1960s, pianist and arranger René Hernández (1916–1987) left Machito's band, which declined in popularity because Hernández's arrangements had been so crucial to the Afro-Cubans' sound. In 1975, the Afro-Cubans staged a triumphal return, featuring contemporary arrangements of old numbers and with music composed by Arturo (Chico) O'Farrill (1921–2001), recording the album *Afro-Cuban Jazz Moods,* with participation by Dizzy Gillespie. The recording ended the era of the Afro-Cubans. Their reign had lasted thirty-five years.

Besides Bauzá, the other pillar of the Afro-Cuban jazz phenomenon was Chico O'Farrill. After working with various bands in Havana, he went to Mexico in 1944 and the next year returned to Havana to found Los Raqueteros del Swing and also worked with the Havana Cuban Boys group of Armando Oréfiche (1911–2000). Then he moved to New York and started his own band, using the Afro-Cubans' rhythm section (Acosta 2001, p. 74).

O'Farrill became the arranger for Benny Goodman's band, and in 1950, with the Afro-Cubans, he recorded *Afro-Cuban Jazz Suite I* with participation by Charlie Parker (1920–1955), Flip Phillips, Buddy Rich (1917–1987), Dizzy Gillespie, Mario Bauzá, Wynton Marsalis (b. 1961), Stan Kenton, Cal Tjader (1925–1982), and Count Basie (1904–1984). In 1953, O'Farrill moved on to California, where he formed another band and composed *Manteca suite,* recorded in 1954 with Dizzy Gillespie and Quincy Jones (b. 1933).

Smaller Groups, Jam Sessions The Club Cubano de Jazz, founded in 1958, brought together almost all the jazz lovers on the island of Cuba. The first

■ *See also*

Diasporas: Afro-Cubans in the Diaspora

Music: 1945–1959

New York City

theater-style jazz concert was held in 1959 in the auditorium of the Museo Nacional de Bellas Artes, but the most important jazz event after the 1960 demise of the Club Cubano de Jazz took place in 1963, with the staging of a festival in the Payret Theater, attended by the Quinteto Instrumental de Música Moderna, Free American Jazz, and the Leonardo Timor band.

Two North American jazz musicians took up residence in Havana during this time: Eddy Torriente and Mario Lagarde. They became a bulwark of Cuban jazz, with their group Free American Jazz. The most stable of all the groups, that of Felipe Dulzaides (1917–1991), also appeared at this time.

The most important groups of the era were the Quinteto Instrumental de Música Moderna (later called Los Amigos), with Frank Emilio Flynn (1921–2001) at the piano. Leopoldo (Pucho) Escalante's Noneto de Jazz also appeared in 1964, lasting until 1967. The difference between these two groups was that the Quinteto concentrated on interpretations of popular Cuban songs with jazz solos and Afro-Cuban rhythms, while the Noneto was under the influence of the sound heard in Miles Davis's and Gil Evans's *Birth of the Cool.* Both groups entered the history of Cuban jazz through their recordings.

Guitarist-composer Juanito Márquez (b. 1929) recorded several platters of Afro-Latin jazz. Another outstanding pianist was Luis Mariano Avilés (b. 1940), or "Cancañón," whose innovations in the Cuban style placed him among the greats.

Most of the Cuban jazz bands themselves had dissolved by this time, with the exceptions of the Riverside, Benny Moré's band, and the one that attracted the most interest, that of Leonardo Timor (b. 1933). Jazz continued to be played in the Tropicana night club.

Jazz Revival The Orquesta Cubana de Música Moderna was formed in 1967 in Havana, playing not only straight jazz but also Latin jazz, jazz-rock, and symphonic jazz in the tradition of Stan Kenton's progressive jazz or Gunther Schuller's Third Stream of the 1960s. The group was directed by Armando Romeu, who also contributed compositions and arrangements.

The band debuted on 12 April 1967 in the Amadeo Roldán Theater. Among its outstanding soloists were Chucho Valdés (b. 1941) on piano, Arturo Sandoval (b. 1949) on trumpet, and Paquito D'Rivera (b. 1948) on sax. The group performed at the Cuban pavilion of the Expo-'67 World's Fair in Canada and in 1970 at its first international festival, the Jazz Jamboree in Poland. Gerry Mulligan (1927–1996) and Dave Brubeck (b. 1920) were also at the Jazz Jamboree, and thanks to their influence, *Playboy* named Chucho as one of the world's leading jazz pianists along with Oscar Peterson (1925–2007), Bill Evans, McCoy Tyner (b. 1938), and Herbie Hancock (b. 1940).

Irakere In 1973, Chucho Valdés founded Irakere, and Cuban jazz took wing. Irakere was rooted in all that had come before, but with its own characteristics and with unprecedented international success for a Cuban band playing Latin jazz while based on the island. Irakere ushered in a new era for Cuban jazz that lasted into the early twenty-first century. Its strengths included its high technical level, its virtuoso soloists (Chucho, Arturo Sandoval, Paquito D'Rivera, and Carlos Emilio Morales), the powerful swing they could maintain in any rhythm, and an ability to preserve and rediscover Cuban roots in the midst of experimentation.

In 1977, Irakere played at Belgrade's Jazz Festival and Warsaw's Jazz Jamboree, along with singer Betty Carter (1929–1998) and the bands of Mel Lewis (1929–1990) and Thad Jones (1923–1986). Dizzy Gillespie, Stan Getz (1927–1991), Earl Hines (1905–1983), and David Amram (b. 1930) traveled to Havana the same year, crowning their visit with a concert in the Mella Theater. This event marked the first time since the breaking of Cuba-U.S. relations that Cuba received a delegation of jazz musicians from the United States. More important than the concert itself, however, was the encounter between the visitors and the members of Irakere.

In 1978, Irakere played Carnegie Hall alongside pianists Mary Lou Williams (1901–1981), McCoy Tyner, and Bill Evans. Stan Getz and Maynard Ferguson (1928–2006) also played with the Cuban group. Afterward they performed at the Cellar Door in Washington, D.C., and the Montreux International Jazz Festival in Switzerland.

That same year saw the production, in Havana's Karl Marx Theater, of an event called Encuentro Cuba-Estados Unidos, promoted by CBS. This concert showcased a wide variety of styles: jazz, rock, pop, country, jazz-rock, Afro-Latino jazz, rhumba, and *son.* Among the visiting artists were Billy Joel, the Fania All Stars, Rita Coolidge, Joe Zawinul, Jaco Pastorius, Billy Cobham, and the jazz-rock Weather Report featuring Wayne Shorter. Dexter Gordon (1923–1990), Woody Shaw, Hubert Laws, and Stan Getz also attended. Irakere represented Cuba.

In 1979, Irakere received a Grammy Award for the best Latin music recorded in the United States. After that, in constant reinvention, Irakere became a fixture in the vanguard of jazz in Cuba.

LATER ARRIVALS

In 1976, sax player Nicolás Reinoso (b. 1939) founded Afrocuba, and Arturo Sandoval formed his own group. Also, trombonist Juan Pablo Torres (1946–2005) and his group, Algo Nuevo, were the first in Cuba to experiment with synthesizers and other electronic instruments (a path later followed by Irakere).

The group Opus 13, led by Joaquín Betancourt (b. 1952), soon became one of the most impressive

entrants in the Jazz-Plaza festivals between 1980 and 1990. Their repertoire of Afro-Latin jazz featured brilliant arrangements and an explosive quality that could keep jazz lovers in the audience on the edge of their seats.

When stylistically versatile pianist Emiliano Salvador (1951–1992) formed his own group, he was already known as one of the great Latin jazz pianists and as a composer who could move among a great variety of Cuban musical genres. His music was characterized by coherence and equilibrium while combining the traditional and contemporary without excessive displays of virtuosity. His greatest influences were the bop, hard bop, and modal jazz of Miles Davis, John Coltrane (1926–1967), and McCoy Tyner.

As a pianist and composer, Ernán López-Nussa (b. 1958) made his name in a middle ground between classical and jazz. He began his artistic career as a member of Afrocuba, but in 1993, he created a quartet with which he participated in the Jazz-Plaza festival. Another outstanding pianist and composer was Roberto Fonseca (b. 1975).

Gonzalo Rubalcaba (b. 1963) and his group, Proyecto, thanks to unique compositions and arrangements, achieved their own original style and reputation. The group highlighted individual virtuosity, but subordinated it to the search for an idiom that emerged from Cuban roots and incorporated other elements while eschewing simple labels of Latin jazz or electronic jazz. Rubalcaba and his group mixed his explorations at the piano with an arsenal of Afro-Cuban rhythms and the use of synthesizers and computers, creating aural atmospheres that combined jazz improvisation with the use of free rhythms in constant change.

Roberto Carcassés (b. 1972), with the group called Estado de Ánimo and then with Interactivo, was a revelation right from the start. Experimental jazz and fusion led his groups to the contemporary edge of Latin jazz with an infinite range of resources, whether those of acoustic piano or those of electronic keyboards.

A Festival and a Contest In 1979, Bobby Carcassés (b. 1938) organized a series of concerts in the Casa de Cultura of Havana's Plaza de la Revolución municipality. He followed it the next year with a national jazz festival known after that as Jazz-Plaza.

Among the groups participating in subsequent years were those of Nicolás Reinoso (Sonido Contemporáneo), Emiliano Salvador, Arturo Sandoval, and Bobby Carcassés (Afrojazz), as well as Cuban jazz

Chucho Valdés. Composer, bandleader, and pianist Chucho Valdés performs with the Afro-Cuban Messengers in Havana, December 2009. SVEN CREUTZMANN/MAMBO PHOTO/GETTY IMAGES

artists of various generations and many foreign avrtists such as Dizzy Gillespie, Tania María (b. 1948), Dave Valentin (b. 1952), Ronnie Scott, Tete Montoliú (1933–1997), Charlie Haden, Max Roach (1924–2007), and Wynton Marsalis.

The 1998 Festival Internacional Jazz-Plaza also included a Concurso Iberoamericano de Jazz (Iber-Jazz'98) under the auspices of Spain's Sociedad General de Autores y Editores (SGAE) and the Fundación Autor. The contest's panel of judges, chaired by pianist and composer Chucho Valdés, conferred that year's prize on Jorge Luis Triana (b. 1958) for his piece "Reflexiones." The 1999 winner was Rolando Luna (b. 1978).

The first Concurso JoJazz (Joven Jazz [Young Jazz]) was held in 2000. Winners of this Cuban contest have included pianists Alejandro Vargas (b. 1980), Dayramir González (b. 1983), and Harold López-Nussa (b. 1983), as well as trumpet player Yasek Manzano (b. 1980). Pianists who have won international prizes include Harold López-Nussa (first prize in the Montreux International Jazz Festival in 2005) and Rolando Luna (first prize and audience prize in the solo piano competition in the same festival in 2007).

This younger generation testifies to the existence of an authentic genre of Cuban jazz. A product of the fusion of ancestral rhythms with the most contemporaneous ones, it won acceptance in Japan, Canada, the United States, and some European countries.

In October 2010, trumpet player Wynton Marsalis and the Lincoln Center Jazz Orchestra of New York performed in Havana at an event that kept musicians, music students, and the general public in a state of high expectation for four days and that could only be described as spectacular. This was the first Cuban performance by the avant-garde project Marsalis had created in 1995. Marsalis had paid a private visit to the island in 1997, which was subsequently remembered for his jamming with Cuban musicians in the Havana jazz club La Zorra y El Cuervo.

BIBLIOGRAPHY

Acosta, Leonardo. *Música y descolonización*. Havana: Editorial Arte y Literatura, 1982.

Acosta, Leonardo. *Raíces del jazz latino: Un siglo de jazz en Cuba*. Barranquilla, Colombia: Editorial La Iguana Ciega, 2001.

Backus, Rob. *Fire Music: A Political History of Jazz*. Chicago: Vanguard Books, 1976.

Berendt, Joachim E. *El jazz: De Nueva Orleáns al jazz rock*. Mexico City: Fondo de Cultura Económica, 1986.

Boggs, Vernon W. *Salsiology: Afro-Cuban Music and the Evolution of Salsa in New York City*. New York: Greenwood Press, 1992.

Cairo, Ana. *El grupo Minorista y su tiempo*. Havana: Editorial Letras Cubanas, 1978.

Calero Martín, José, and Leopoldo Valdés Quesada. *Cuba musical*. Havana: Imprenta de Molina y Compañía, 1929.

Carpentier, Alejo. *La música en Cuba*. Mexico City: Fondo de Cultura Económica, 1972.

Chediak, Nat. *Diccionario de jazz latino*. Madrid: Fundación Autor, 1998.

Delannoy, Luc. *¡Caliente! Una historia del jazz latino*. Mexico City: Fondo de Cultura Económica, 2001.

Fernández, Raúl. *Latin Jazz: The Perfecta Combinación*. San Francisco Chronicle Books in association with the Smithsonian Institution Traveling Exhibition Service, 2002.

Fernández, Raúl. *From Afro-Cuban Rhythms to Latin Jazz*. Berkeley: University of California Press, 2006.

Garriga, Silvana, ed. *Mamá, yo quiero saber… entrevistas a músicos cubanos*. Havana: Editorial Letras Cubanas, 1999.

Gerard, Charley, with Marty Sheller. *Salsa! The Rhythm of Latin Music*. Crown Point, IN: White Cliffs Media, 1989.

Giro, Radamés. *Diccionario enciclopédico de la música en Cuba*. 4 vols. Havana: Editorial Letras Cubanas, 2007.

Manuel, Peter. *Popular Musics of the Non-Western World: An Introductory Survey*. New York: Oxford University Press, 1988.

Moore, Robin D. *Nationalizing Blackness: Afrocubanismo and Artistic Revolution in Havana, 1920–1940*. Pittsburgh, PA: University of Pittsburgh Press, 1997.

Moore, Robin D. *Music & Revolution: Cultural Change in Socialist Cuba*. Berkeley: University of California Press, 2006.

Ortiz, Fernando. "Saba, samba y bop." In *Estudios etnosociológicos*. Compiled by Isaac Barreal Fernández. Havana: Editorial de Ciencias Sociales, 1991.

Roberts, John Storm. *The Latin Tinge: The Impact of Latin American Music on the United States*. New York: Oxford University Press, 1979.

Sarusky, Jaime. *Grupo de Experimentación Sonora del ICAIC: Mito y realidad*. Havana: Editorial Letras Cubanas, 2005.

Schuller, Gunther. *El jazz: Sus raíces y su desarrollo*. Buenos Aires: Editorial Víctor Lerú, 1973.

Southern, Eileen. *The Music of Black Americans: A History*. 3rd ed. New York: Norton, 1997.

Stearns, Marshall W. *The Story of Jazz*. New York Oxford University Press, 1956.

Stearns, Marshall W. *La historia del jazz*. Havana: Editorial Nacional de Cuba, 1966.

Tieles Ferrer, Cecilio. *Espadero, música y nación en Cuba colonial*. Havana: Ediciones Museo de la Música, 2007.

Ulanov, Barry. *A History of Jazz in America*. New York: Viking Press, 1952.

Waxer, Lise. *Situating Salsa: Global Markets and Local Meanings in Latin Popular Music*. New York: Routledge, 2002.

MUSIC: CUBAN ROCK

Humberto Manduley López

A half century of rock music in Cuba.

Rock and roll (later, rock) has been present in Cuba almost since its birth in the United States—it arrived on the island beginning in the mid-1950s. Given their proximity to the United States, it is no surprise that the first examples of rock in Spanish emerged in Mexico and Cuba with Los Teen Tops and Los Llópis, respectively. Through movies, radio, television, and records the genre made its mark on Cuba, primarily on youth and urban populations. Havana became the hub of the music scene, but rock and roll proliferated throughout other parts of the country. While other acclaimed musicians such as Nat King Cole and Lucho Gatica had great success playing on the island, none of rock's key stars set foot on Cuban soil. From 1956 to 1960 rock and roll fluctuated between naiveté and mimesis, with local artists emulating foreign figures. During this period Jorge Bauer (b. 1935), Luisito Bravo (1943–1998), Danny Puga (b. 1941), and Ricky Orlando (b. 1943) emerged as soloists, and groups such as Los Hot Rockers and Los Astros appeared. Vocal quartets and quintets also took up the new musical style. Later, at the height of the so-called British Invasion led by the Beatles, the combo (as an instrumental format) dominated the scene almost entirely.

STATE CENSORSHIP

Beginning in the early 1960s as part of the sociopolitical national process in Cuba, there was a virulent stigmatization of rock music that extended to a ban on playing the music on radio and television. Reasons given for the prohibition ranged from the defense of the country's musical patrimony to the rejection of any type of contamination by foreign elements. An alarming oversimplification took hold: Rock was a symptom of imperialist cultural penetration, which required (overt or surreptitious) censorship. This period of boycotts and censorship slowed the development of rock and roll in Cuba and left damaging social wounds.

During those same years the Cuban government restructured professional standards, causing a split between musicians who accepted the state guidelines for hiring artists—which renounced more rock-oriented music—and those who remained faithful to that sound and had to earn their living by other means. The professionals were guaranteed support for their performances and promotion of their work, whereas the amateurs imitated what was being played outside Cuba, performing at private parties and leaving no recordings. The amateurs were subject to political and social pressure, but maintained their connection to the genre. Groups that enjoyed the suppport of the government were Los Dada, Los Barbas, Los Novels, Los 5-U-4, Los Magnéticos, Los Centurys, and Los Bucaneros. Bands such as Los Kents, Los Pacíficos,

Sesiones Ocultas, Los Jets, Los Signos, Almas Vertiginosas, Nueva Generación, Dimensión Vertical, and Los Gnomos, however, perpetuated their music in spite of this lack of support. During this period the cult of the instrumentalist reigned supreme, and many musicians changed to more profitable or less fraught genres such as jazz and popular music.

Also noteworthy were experimental groups such as Síntesis, whose early symphonic rock became a fusion of elements from Afro-Cuban tradition and urban song, and Arte Vivo, who combined the spirit of classic concert music with free jazz and improvisation. Curiously, neither group produced direct musical heirs in the country. Except for a few isolated stories in the media (in *Perspectiva* and *Caimán Barbudo*), rock lacked a significant presence in Cuba. The symbolic end of this period was the Invierno Caliente festival in Havana in 1981, the first festival of its kind, which showed a strange imbalance: many covers and little original material.

1980s: ORIGINAL SONGS AND SPANISH LYRICS

The second half of the 1980s was dominated by Venus, a band from Havana, which was the first to have a totally original repertoire sung in Spanish. The tenuous security of performing covers gave way to a challenge: facing audiences accustomed to consuming imported rock. Venus's proposal of hard rock, and later, heavy metal, inspired bands to put their money on original material (Zeus, OVNI, Cartón Tabla, Hojo x Oja, Monserrat, Alto Mando, Metal Oscuro, Paisaje Con Río), while veteran bands such as Viento Solar, Rhodas, and Los Gens had to rethink their concepts. Spanish lyrics became the norm, making clear lyrics that were previously garbled by sometimes terrible English pronunciation and at times poor quality instruments. The Patio de María (formally known as the Casa Comunal de Cultura Roberto Branly) emerged in Havana at the end of the decade as a key location. After its closure in 2003, the Asociación Hermanos Saíz (Saíz Brothers Association) provided performance space and some support to most of the groups.

The following decade brought a generation of bands with a greater variety of styles and repertoires in Spanish: Naranja Mecánica, Extraño Corazón, Tendencia, Los Detenidos, Havana, Garaje H, Perfume de Mujer, and Anima Mundi. At the beginning of the 1990s, others chose to compose their own material but clung to English, influenced by grunge and alternative rock, along with more energetic substyles of metal: Cosa Nostra, Agonizer, Combat Noise, Mephisto, Sectarium, and Blinder. An increasing number of *trovadores* (singer/songwriters) also included rock sounds. The antecedent of performing under one's own name (Santiago Feliú, Carlos Varela, Adrian Morales) was abandoned by most of the new young singer-songwriters who took cover under group names (Superávit, Lucha Almada, Debajo). At the same time, Tanya was emerging as the only outstanding female artist.

■ *See also*

The World and Cuba: U.S. Culture in Cuba

Perfume de Mujer. The 1990s saw the emergence of a generation of Cuban bands, including Perfume de Mujer, that boasted a greater variety of styles and repertoires in Spanish. COURTESY OF ALEJANDRO VILLALÓN RENAUD

1990s: GROWTH AND RELAXATION OF STATE CONTROL

In the 1990s Cuban rock developed as a national movement and not just the isolated work of a few musicians. New styles emerged (progressive, metal, acoustic, high-profile songwriter rock, pop, fusion, punk), and there also was a gradual relaxation in the attitude of certain state institutions. Fanzines materialized—the first, *Death through Your Veins*, appeared in 1992, followed by *Ilusión, Polilla en la Sombra,El Punto Ge, Scriptorium*, and *Resistencia*—and the official media began to open up to a broad spectrum of national and foreign rock, with specialized programs and features on radio (*Sabarrrock, El Programa de Ramón, Melomanía, 58 en Rock, Disco Ciudad, Avalancha Metálica, Ad Libitum, Tiempo A, La Quinta Rueda*) and television (*A Capella, Cuerda Viva, En Confianza, Sonido Subterráneo*). There was a significant increase in the number of rock festivals throughout the country (Ciudad Metal, Metal HG, Atenas Rock, Caimán Rock, Rey Metal), and in 1998 Cubadisco took up the rock category again (a category first included in the EGREM Prizes in the 1980s) in its awards for Cuban music recordings. Interestingly, rock produced under foreign labels was not able to compete in this event or access the national distribution networks, nor could many of the independent records that are distributed irregularly at concerts or by mail.

Another way to interpret the impact rock had on the Cuban music scene is by looking at the number of musicians from diverse genres (ranging from popular to electroacoustic) who have participated or been interested in its soundscape, including Horacio "El Negro" Hernández, Frank Fernández, José María Vitier, Juan Formell, Leo Brouwer, Mike Porcell, Leonardo Acosta, Pablo Menéndez, Juan Antonio Leyva, Carlos Emilio Morales, Pedro Pablo Pedroso, Edesio Alejandro, Eudaldo Antúnez, and Pucho López.

Cuba has remained on the margin of international rock tours, hosting only a few artists beginning with Fluffy Hunter in 1957 and continuing with Rick Wakeman, Banco de Mutuo Soccorso, Fito Páez, Air Supply, Karat, Su Ta Gar, Audioslave, Sepultura, Manu Chao, Juan Carlos Baglietto, Lokomotiv GT, and Area. Events such as Havana Jam (1979) and Music Bridges (1999) saw performances by Bonnie Raitt, Weather Report, Joan Osborne, Andy Summers, Billy Joel, Trio of Doom, Indigo Girls, Peter Buck, and Jimmy Buffet, among others.

In July 2007 a key event took place: the establishment of the Agencia Cubana de Rock (Cuban Rock Agency) and its headquarters, the Maxim Rock Theater as an initiative of the Ministry of Culture. This move brought stability to the production of concerts in a venue with excellent technical conditions and accessible prices.

Hipnosis, Rice and Beans, C-Men, Escape, Tesis de Menta, Chlover, Eskoria, Jeffrey Dahmer, Porno Para Ricardo, Cry Out For, Elmer Ferrer Band, Necrópolis, Sociedad Habana Blues, Ancestor, Médula, Estigma DC, and Quantum are examples of the diverse styles of rock that existed in the early 2000s. Many cover bands, either refurbished (Los Kents, Red X, Dimensión Vertical, Los Moodys, Los Tackson) or newly minted (Magical Beat, Banda América) continued to perform as of 2010.

After more than half a century of turbulent history, in 2010 rock in Cuba was maturing, gaining a more solid conceptual form, more creative elaboration, a growing discography, and institutional support that was previously unimaginable. It was still lacking in self-referentiality (its history is not well known), and it appeared to be moving in very closed circuits with no real (or evidently real) impact on the music scene of the country. The sound of Cuban rock has been transformed since the first rock and roll of the 1950s, but it all derives from a common source—not of just the electric guitar, but an authentic need for contemporary expression.

SELECTED DISCOGRAPHY

Anima Mundi. *Jagganath orbit* (2007).

Athanai. *A Castro le gusta el rock* (2004).

Chlover. *Primer encuentro con el lado oscuro* (2009).

Combat Noise. *Frontline Offensive Forces* (2010).

Cosa Nostra. *Invisible Bridges* (1998).

Elmer Ferrer Band. *Fango's Dance* (2005).

Garaje H. *Sin azúcar* (1997).

Havana. *Puertas que se abrirán* (1997).

Hipnosis. *The Chosen One* (2004).

Los Pacíficos. *Havana 1967* (2001).

Perfume de Mujer. *Pollos de granja* (1998).

Síntesis. *Ancestros (trilogía)* (2003).

Superávit. *Verde melón* (1998).

Tesis de Menta. *Mi generación* (2006).

Various Artists. *Not Salsa, Just Brutal Music* (2008).

Zeus. *Hijos de San Lázaro* (2000).

BIBLIOGRAPHY

Manduley López, Humberto. *El Rock en Cuba*. Havana: Ediciones Atril, 2001.

MUSIC: HIP HOP

Roberto Zurbano Torres

Hip hop's development from the 1980s into the early 2000s as a characteristically Cuban music form.

Cuban hip hop is one of the most innovative cultural products to emerge from Cuba in recent decades, from a process of assimilation, appropriation, and transculturation of foreign cultural elements that resulted in a characteristically Cuban expression. Cuban hip hop began in the late 1980s with young people in the larger Cuban cities who listened to and danced to African American music played on Cuban radio at home and at parties. Combing elements of funk, pop, and rock from the 1980s and 1990s—which also had a large following among Cuban youth—hip hop

offered an attractive musical text. Cuban television and cinemas screened U.S. movies such as *Beat Street* (1984), *Breakin'* (1984), and *Breakin' 2: Electric Boogaloo* (1985) that showed young people dancing in the street with strange acrobatic movements, and Cubans imitated them.

Of the four elements of hip hop culture (rap, breaking, spoken word, and graffiti), break dancing arrived first. The first MCs (masters of ceremony, or improvisers who sing their own lyrics over a background of U.S. rap music) did not appear until the 1990s. Their lyrics were festive, challenging listeners to dance better; boasting about their gangs, their neighborhoods, or their luck with women; or displaying their knowledge of the American musicians they discovered on Cuban radio programs such as 99Jam2 and 1040, on U.S. FM radio or on U.S. television shows such as *Soul Train*, *Yo MTV Raps*, and *Showtime at the Apollo*, which could be seen in Cuba in good weather conditions via powerful homemade antennas. Young people shared this music on weekends at parties that became the scenes for performances by the first Cuban rap artists.

By 1995, in Havana alone there were more than fifty rap groups. In that year the rap promoters Rodolfo Rensoli and Balesy Rivero established Grupo Uno and organized the first Havana Rap Festival at the Casa de Cultura de Plaza (Plaza Cultural Center). Later rap festivals were held at the legendary Alamar Amphitheater, east of Havana. These festivals encouraged competition that boosted performers' professionalism and specialization and led them to create individual repertoires, more daring arrangements, and lyrics that reflected their own, highly individual realities.

RAP FESTIVALS: STAGE FOR A NEW MOVEMENT

The Havana Rap Festival in 1995 was followed by eleven successive festivals, two with no institutional support. Starting in 1998, the festival was sponsored by the Asociación Hermanos Saíz (AHS, Saíz Brothers Association), affiliated with the Young Communists Union and the Ministry of Culture. The AHS took over the selection of performers from all over Cuba and the organization of the shows at the Alamar Amphitheater and helped the best performers to turn professional by associating themselves with state enterprises. However, in 2005, the AHS withdrew its support for the festival, and two years later these annual events came to an end.

In order to secure the participation of groups each night, the festival was competitive from 1995 to 2000, when its name was changed to the Hip Hop Havana Festival. It attracted performers from all over the island and became the most important venue for Cuban rappers to make contact with rap artists, producers, and promoters from the United States, the Caribbean, Latin America, and Europe. Festival goers spread the sounds of Cuban hip hop all over the

■ *See also*

Cuban Thought and Cultural Identity: The Internet Experience in Cuba

Race: Race Relations after the Revolution

The World and Cuba: U.S. Culture in Cuba

world, and by the late 1990s, it was equal in quality and diversity to hip hop from Brazil, Spain, France, Mexico, and many other countries.

The Rap Festival was the Cuban hip hop movement's most important venue. Festivals united the movement, which became a cultural entity capable of attracting an audience, criticizing the revolutionary process from a revolutionary stance, raising consciousness of Cuba's history and racial issues, and fighting for government support. The festivals also brought to Havana international hip hop artists such as the U.S. musicians Dead Prez, Black Star (Mos Def and Tarib Kweli), Public Enemy, and the Roots, as well as Boca Floja (Mexico) and the Paperboys (Norway). The performers were joined by academics, media figures, music producers, and film and television directors from several countries.

Without government intermediaries, the festivals promoted fluid conceptual and technological exchanges between Cuban and foreign rappers. They also made the Cuban hip hop community attentive to the fact that they are part of a transnational cultural movement and that hip hop artists outside Cuba can be models for artistic, racial, community, and transnational identity in the Cuban cultural and political context.

DISCOURSE OF CUBAN RAPPERS

Cuban rappers emerged amid the Special Period—Cuba's economic crisis in the 1990s. More than material shortages, they decried the loss, deterioration, and subversion of the Revolution's utopian ideals. Most of them were young, black or mixed race, and from poor families and neighborhoods, and few had gone to college; for them, hip hop was a form of self-expression. Its critical perspective provided a forum to reject the culture's excessive Eurocentrism that disregards Cuba's own cultural forms that do not conform to Western models (e.g., Afro-Cuban religion and popular culture and Cuban body language). Although they continued to occupy a subordinate position, rappers challenged the dominant Eurocentric cultural patterns through their popular medium.

In the early 2000s, Cuban rappers were young people who described their sociocultural situation, accepted the emancipatory tradition of the Cuban Revolution in which they were formed, and critically evaluated reality, inserting racial self-evaluation and asserting race's place in Cuba's historical and cultural discourse. Rappers were not the only Cuban cultural figures who recognized and suffered from racism—musicians who played rhumba, salsa, *timba*, and *trova* did too, for example—but they were the only ones who openly and publicly rejected it. Speaking for their generation, they commented on tourism, prostitution, drugs, double standards, corruption, racial discrimination, conformism, political alienation, the market, the environment, emigration, and other issues that affect Cuba and other nations. The greater emphasis on discussing racial discrimination in Cuba was due in great measure to hip hop culture and its criticism of a circumstance that affected many rappers, most of whom were black or mixed race, who took pride in their racial identity and promoted a new aesthetic and cultural behavior.

These rappers' general discourse is the statement not of a social class, but of a quasi-marginal urban social group. The very names of Cuban rappers and rap groups demonstrate the openness with which they state their concerns and affirm their racial, cultural, religious, and ideological identities. The rappers describe a world full of social and ideological contradictions, and their lyrics are manifestos in the fight against racial discrimination; the exclusion (until 2009) of Cubans from tourist hotels and clubs; white domination of the media and society as a whole; and poverty, violence, and the resulting marginalization of city life, particularly in slums and outlying neighborhoods. Through their names, singers and groups sought a shared identity that may seem aggressive to outsiders, but for insiders was a way to articulate and defend the cohesion of a marginalized social group that consciously put forward its neighborhoods and families as settings in which to legitimize their discourse. Rap names such as Familia's Cuba Represent, Hermanos de Causa (Brothers in the Cause), Anónimo Consejo (Anonymous Advice), Doble Filo (Double Edge), Instinto (Instinct), Krudas Cubensis, EPG & B (Ghetto & Barbarito's Executive Plan), La Fabri-K (The Factory), Los Paisanos (The Countrymen), Escuadrón Patriótico (Patriot Squad), and other self-affirming labels express the desire for participation in (and transformation of) Cuban society.

Cuban rappers, both male and female, were also transnational figures because they worked with non-local codes that represented the marginal in other parts of the world, incorporating those codes into the local discourse. In other words, they operated with already transnationalized codes related to the margins. These margins—local or universal—do not always express marginality, and listeners should not confuse the marginal with being marginalized. Hip hop culture was born on the margins and although it shares some elements of marginality—violence and illegal activities, for example—at its best it expresses dissatisfaction with that world, strongly criticizing it while affirming a radical desire for social transformation.

SIGNIFICANT STAGES AND GROUPS

The founding period of Cuban hip hop (1993–1999) was characterized by social criticism that demanded the fulfillment and affirmation of revolutionary values. A massive group called for institutional support and coalesced around the Rap Festival of Alamar and around weekly gatherings in Havana where people danced and listened to hip hop music. The nascent movement thus moved from entertainment to self-awareness. Its lyrics expressed a new cultural

Primera Base. The Cuban rap group Primera Base performs during the 2001 Cuban Rap Festival in Havana. NIURKA BARROSO/AFP/NEWSCOM

reality and early forms of identity, focusing on race, marginalization, social differences, and the search for an essentially Cuban form of rap. Representative groups from this period are Amenaza (Threat), Primera Base (First Base), SBS, Orishas, Doble Filo, Obsesión (Obsession), Anónimo Consejo, Reyes de las Calles (Street Kings), Explosión Suprema (Supreme Explosion), 100% Cubano (100% Cuban), Papo Record, and Pablo Herrera.

In the second period (2000–2006), hip hop groups fully assumed a racial consciousness. The Alamar Festival was no longer competitive, and international contact in the form of outside donations and visits and exchanges with foreign groups began. Several rap groups began working officially with government-run music enterprises, and 2003 saw the creation of the Agencia Cubana de Rap (Cuban Rap Agency), to which the best Cuban rap groups are permanently contracted. Joint projects were undertaken, community work was intensified, and women in the movement began to promote gender awareness. Various alternative venues such as Almendares Park, América Theater, and La Madriguera nightclub were used, and rap groups also performed on the stages of both halls of the National Theater, the Grand Theater of Havana, the Mella Theater, and the Café Cantante (also part of the National Theater). There were appearances on the television programs *Cuerda Viva* (Strings Live), *Otros tiempos* (Other Times), and *A las doce* (At Twelve), and rap-oriented radio shows emerged,

such as *La esquina del Rap* (Rap Corner) on Radio Metropolitana. The Cuban Hip Hop Symposium was born. The movement spread within the provinces. Through international exchanges and sponsorship from foreign firms in Cuba, the technology improved, and as DJs acquired turntables, they began to occupy a more visible spot onstage, accompanying rap groups or as accomplished individual performers (some of whom were women). International tours and concerts began.

A more natural relationship developed with the market and other musicians who played jazz, *son*, *timba*, and other genres, opening the way for concerts, records, and national and international tours. The group Orishas, a fusion of rap with elements of Cuban *son*, triumphed internationally. Other models successful inside Cuba did not achieve the international recognition that Orishas gained by mixing elements of 1950s Cuban *son*, recycled in the style of Buena Vista Social Club, with the best hip hop loops. The success of Orishas obscured other important Cuban hip hop models that rejected exotic, folk, or nostalgic elements and strongly criticized Cuba's social reality, as well as experimental and contemporary fusion groups that ranged from jazz to trip hop, that featured African or Indian percussion, or that had feminist, ecologist, or Rastafarian elements. The international success of these variants was partly dependent on the social circumstances in which this music was produced and promoted. Representative groups include Instinto (Instinct), Familias Cuba Represent, Eddy

Familia's Cuba Represent. Cuban hip-hop group Familia's Cuba Represent performs during the eighth Hip Hop Havana Festival in 2002. ALEHANDRO ERNESTO/NEWSCOM

K, Mariana, Las Krudas (The Krudes), Hermanos de Causa, Free Hole Negro, and Ogguere.

The new generation (2007–2011) began amid the popularity of *reggaeton*, a genre that caused a split in the hip hop movement because it separated rappers from the critical consciousness and social concerns of rappers and turned many of them into overnight commercial and media successes whose lyrics are mostly lighthearted and evasive. In this period, there were no more Rap Festivals, little contact with institutions, and even rejection of the Agencia Cubana de Rap. Independent, nongovernmental organizations sponsored events such as the Battle of the Roosters, the Raised Fists Prize, and the Rotilla Festival of urban and alternative music. Hip hop was featured at major events broadcast by Cuban television (e.g., the Lucas Prize for video clips and the Cuerda Viva Prize for alternative music), and at the annual Cubadisco Prize, a competition among the officially recognized record labels, organized by the Ministry of Culture. At these events rappers competed among themselves and with other genres, both in the Cuban mass media and internationally.

As the Cuban rap movement spread through Cuba and its diaspora, lyrics became more critical. Hip hop groups performed at small clubs such as Tropical, El Coctel, El Barbaram, and El Karachi, all in Havana's Vedado district, and at the Rotilla Festival, the decade's only festival for alternative and urban musicians in Cuba. Representative groups from this period include Yimmy KonKlaze, Los Paisanos, Los Aldeanos (The Villagers), La Unión (The Union), Omni Zona Franca (Omni Free Zone), La Comisión

Depuradora (The Purifying Commission, Michel Extremo, Adversario (Adversary), Papá Humbertico, and Kumar y Hermanazos (Kumar and Bros.).

AGENCIA CUBANA DE RAP

By 2000, Cuban rap had achieved diversity, quality, and considerable national and international visibility. Its incisive lyrics expressed criticisms of Cuban society that were absent from Cuba's press and politically manipulated by the international press. Musicians recognized the need to become professional and maintain relations with record companies and the media to secure national and international publicity and marketing. Festival workshops demanded publication of the texts read by intellectuals and academics—mostly foreigners who identified with, recognized, and valued Cuban rap.

The movement had expanded beyond the few venues offered by cultural institutions, and members of the movement, supported by the AHS, demanded a state-run company to promote rap. This demand reached its full expression when the singer Harry Belafonte (b. 1927) met Cuban rappers during the Havana Film Festival in December 1999. Aware of Belafonte's friendship with Fidel Castro, the rappers took the opportunity to explain the movement's critical and emancipatory nature; with Belafonte's intervention, Castro became personally involved in finding a channel for incorporating rap into Cuba's cultural policy. From these negotiations, the Agencia Cubana de Rap emerged in September 2002 as part of the Ministry of Culture's Instituto Cubano de la Música (ICM, Cuban Institute of Music). In this, the government assumed the responsibility to promote rap music but not hip hop culture. Technically, an enterprise affiliated with the ICM should concern itself with music policy, but the Agencia did not have sufficient resources to deal with hip hop culture, which contains nonmusical elements.

The major achievements of the Agencia Cubana de Rap include the creation of the Asere Producciones record label (which released CDs of five of its member groups, two of which received prizes, as well as three compilation CDs); publication of *Revista Movimiento* (Movement Magazine); organization of community activities in poor neighborhoods, schools, jails, and the provinces, as well as lectures, symposiums, and annual workshops; and the production of scores of concerts and national and international tours. However, the poor technology, production, and marketing available to the Agencia were insufficient to properly promote Cuban rap inside and outside Cuba so as to demonstrate the high quality and diversity of the music.

MUSIC PRODUCTION

The true history of Cuban rap is not in the stories of its founders, critics, and performers, but rather in the records produced since 1995. These recordings—many of which were made in home studios, and some of which are poor quality—are evidence of the movement's genesis and development. Following the Cuban approach of making the best use of whatever is available, home studios became more and more sophisticated in order to produce background music and demos that could be shared among rappers and then submitted to radio stations. In time, the studios upgraded their technology and specialized in hip hop, becoming veritable underground record labels such as Real 70 (Royal 70), Esquina Caliente (Hot Corner), Machete, and Palenque. This extensive alternative record production, which began in 1995 with a CD of three songs by SBS, demonstrates Cuban hip hop's diversity of sounds, styles, and compositions. In 2008 one of these alternative recordings (*Manos a la obra* by La Fabri-K) ranked among Billboard's top 100 alternative songs.

SELECTED DISCOGRAPHY

El Adverzario. *La adverzarización* (2009).

Los Aldeanos. *La naranja se picó* (2008).

Escuadron Patriota. *Clandestino* (2007).

La Fabrik. *La Fábri-k* (2008).

Las Krudas. *Krudas Cubensis* (2003).

Kumar. *Sublevao* (2003).

Obsesión. *Un montón de cosas* (1999).

Oguere. *Llena de amor el mambo* (2007).

Orishas. *A lo Cubano* (1999).

Orishas. *Emigrante* (2003).

Los Paisanos. *Paisanología* (2004).

Cuban rapper El B. Bian Oscar Rodríguez Gala, better known as El B, performs at the Acapulco Theater in Havana on 23 April 2010. AFP/GETTY IMAGES/NEWSCOM

Papo Record. *Cabiosile* (2005).

Primera Base. *Igual que tú* (1997).

Various Artists. *Cuban Hip Hop All Stars* (2000).

Various Artists. *Con los puños arriba* (2002).

Various Artists. *Soy rapero* (2002).

Various Artists. *Asere 1* (2003).

Various Artists. *La crema del hip hop: Made in Cuba* (2005).

Various Artists. *La Comisión Depuradora* (2008).

Various Artists. *Lo nuestro* (2008).

Various Artists. *Respuesta* (2008).

SELECTED FILMOGRAPHY

Alafia, Joshua Bee, dir. *Cuban Hip Hop All Stars* (2004).

Bacallao, Ricardo, dir. *Short Radiography of Hip Hop in Cuba* (2004).

Boden, Anna, and Ryan Fleck, dirs. *Jóvenes rebeldes/Young Rebels* (2005).

Díaz, Vanessa, and Larissa Díaz, dirs. *Cuban Hip Hop: Desde el Principio* (2008).

D'Queen, dir. *ANC: Hip Hop Revolución* (2004).

Jacob-Fantauzzi, Elis, dir. *Inventos* (2004).

Pedreira, Maickel, dir. *Revolution* (2010).

Perez Rey, Lisandro, dir. *La Fabri-K, the Cuban Hip-Hop Factory* (2004).

Teodorescu, Alina, dir. *Paraíso* (2004).

Zambrano, Benito, dir. *Habana Blues* (2005).

BIBLIOGRAPHY

Agencia Cubana de Rap. *Revista Movimiento* (2004). Special series on Cuban hip hop.

Fernandes, Sujatha. *Cuba Represent! Cuban Arts, State Power, and the Making of New Revolutionary Cultures.* Durham, NC: Duke University Press, 2006.

THE MUSIC OF ERNESTO LECUONA

Olavo Alén Rodríguez

A composer, pianist, conductor, and promoter who became one of Cuba's greatest musicians.

Ernesto Lecuona (1895–1963) is the most internationally renowned of Cuban composers. He impressed many audiences, first with his exceptional piano virtuosity and later his orchestral conducting, especially of works linked to Cuban zarzuelas (musical light operettas). But he is undoubtedly best known as a composer, especially for his many popular songs, some of which, such as "Canto Siboney" (1929) and "La Comparsa," became powerful symbols of Cuban cultural identity.

THE STUDENT

Ernesto Sixto de la Asunción Lecuona Casado was born in Villa de Guanabacoa, Havana, on 6 August 1895. He studied piano first with his older sister Ernes-

Ernesto Lecuona (1895–1963). Composer, pianist, conductor, and promoter Ernesto Lecuona's respect for Cuban music and for the many artists who worked to create it were important factors in its evolution and development. FRANK DRIGGS COLLECTION/ GETTY IMAGES

tina Lecuona and then with teacher Antonio Saavedra, who prepared him for admission to the Peyrellade Conservatory. At a very early age, Lecuona met Joaquín Nin, a prominent Cuban musician, pianist, and teacher; it was during an audition for Nin that the child's exceptional gift as a pianist became apparent. As a result, Nin offered to be his teacher, and Lecuona became a student at the Conservatorio Nacional Hubert de Blanck, also in Havana. Since Nin was living in Paris at the time, he asked de Blanck himself to take on young Ernesto as his personal student until he could return to Cuba. Lecuona then studied at the Hoyo y Junco school, the Siglo XX school, and the Manuel Llerena school. He studied piano tirelessly, up to eight hours a day, adding the most difficult piano pieces to his repertoire.

In 1914, Lecuona traveled to France bearing a letter addressed to the director of the Paris Conservatory in which Hubert de Blanck recommended that Lecuona receive training. Lecuona's audition went so well, according to his biographer Carmela de León, that the judges recommended that he be offered a teaching position rather than a scholarship for study (p. 45).

Lecuona never missed a chance to learn from any musician who had something to teach him, choosing when he traveled to New York in 1916 to take classes with the well-known instructor Ernesto Berumen. By that time, however, Lecuona was so acclaimed and in such demand in concert halls that he had neither the time nor a reason to seek further instruction. The famous Cuban tenor and good friend of Lecuona, Pedro Fernández Suárez-Solar, said that when Lecuona requested lessons from French musician Robert Lortat, the teacher asked him "if it was some kind of joke" (León, p. 45).

THE PIANIST

Much was said about Lecuona's exceptional gifts as a pianist while he was a student. These gifts made him something of a legend even at the beginning of his career. People claimed that he had had surgery to extend the reach of his left hand, in order to enhance his performance of big chords. Fame followed him from a very young age and grew even stronger after his first international performance at Aeolian Hall in New York in 1916. Four years later, he completed an extensive concert tour in Spain, which led to much acclaim in that country.

In the 1920s Lecuona began to include his own work in his concerts and recitals. By then, he had already composed some of the piano works that would immortalize him. His renown as a pianist continued until the early 1930s, but his reputation as a composer gradually surpassed his fame as a performer.

Lecuona's compositions contain extremely difficult passages but were written using the conventional techniques for piano performance. These works are therefore instructive for pianists who want to learn the various rhythms of Cuban music. Lecuona himself provided the technical solution by using repetition in his works. In other words, his talent for the piano showed itself first through his performances and later through his compositions.

Lecuona performed in many of the world's best concert halls, receiving both applause of his audiences and praise from fellow musicians. For example, after hearing him play in Paris in 1928, Maurice Ravel said, "This is more than piano" (quoted in Martínez 1989, p. 32). José Iturbi told Joaquín Nin, "Neither you nor I can play that one" (quoted in Martínez, p. 32), in reference to one of Lecuona's *danzas* for piano. After hearing him in Paris, George Gershwin—to whose career Lecuona's has often been compared—presented him with the score to *Rhapsody in Blue*, so that Lecuona would add it to his repertoire. Lecuona became one of the greatest performers of this piece.

Lecuona's composing life was too engrossing for him to devote all of his time to piano. He started playing his own compositions in the concerts and recitals he gave in Cuba and abroad. But he also had a hidden motive in doing so. His compositions did not require him to devote as much time to study or practice, which gave him more time to compose, direct, and promote Cuban music.

THE PRODUCER AND THE PROMOTER

Apart from being a great artist, Lecuona was an excellent promoter of Cuban music—not only his own compositions, but also the works of many other Cuban colleagues. The concerts he organized in Cuba were a particularly important part of his efforts. He started them in the 1920s, and they continued through 1960. In reference to these concerts, the musicologist Jesús Gómez Cairo wrote: "The structure of the programs, their presence, the assiduity and systematicity they had in the musician's artistic life, and their display of theatrical techniques, make them the author's most important concert productions...Lecuona was always the organizer as well as the artistic director" (p. 35).

These concerts featured a performer for each piece, and they were organized based on a script similar to the ones used in musical theater. This permitted the creation of an important space in which to communicate with the public, which was especially important for works not typically included in musical theater repertoire.

Lecuona had a talent for programming marketable concerts, and his profits were considerable; his productions were successful, garnering great audiences for Cuban music. Maybe this was why his rivals faulted him as a mere businessman, extending this attribute by implication to his music as well. His financial success, however, did not hurt his composing at all, nor did it affect the demands he placed on himself when preparing his performances.

In his role as promoter, Lecuona made it possible for Rita Montaner to become the main artist of the Gran Compañia de Revistas Cubanas (Great Cuban Revue Company) of the Regina theater, where he was working as a director. Many other times he similarly helped performers establish themselves. Not only was he involved in discovering and hiring new talent, he was concerned about securing them fair salaries. In a letter to Gonzalo Roig on 3 November 1947 he wrote: "I just sent a telegraph to Mr. Amador asking him to send you an advance payment of 300.00 by emergency wire.... He is a reliable, responsible person, and he had assured me he would give you the advance, a very reasonable expectation" (Díaz, p. 137).

Lecuona was a successful man who shared his success with the musicians and colleagues who worked with him. His respect and admiration for Cuban music and for the many artists who worked to create it were important factors in its evolution and development, both in terms of its artistry and its financial success.

THE COMPOSER

Without doubt, Ernesto Lecuona is one of the most important composers of Cuban music. His entire oeuvre is situated between the realm of classical, academically structured music and that of professional popular music. He made good use of the advantages each has to offer. Because he was an expert in Cuban musical traditions, he utilized many of their unique rhythms, styles, mannerisms, aesthetic gestures, and projection techniques, re-creating them with his own style.

His prolific production falls into three main categories: piano pieces, musical theater, and songs. He also wrote four symphonies: *Rapsodia tropical*; *El manglar* (Mangrove Swamp), for soprano, piano, and orchestra; *Rapsodia Argentina* for piano and orchestra; and his last masterpiece, *Concierto en Rumba*. He also composed a violin and piano piece named after the traditional Cuban folk song, *Guajira*, which was inspired by Jorge Anckermann's *El arroyo que murmura* (The Whispering Brook).

Piano Pieces Lecuona's piano pieces are especially significant for Cuban music. One of his most important biographers, Orlando Martínez, refers to him as "the tropical Chopin" (Martínez, p. 77). His works are generally difficult to perform, but they are based on traditional techniques for piano performance. They are inspired by the most authentic of Cuban musical traditions, but they never are mere recitation of folk tunes. Lecuona's compositions incorporate Cuba's two main musical legacies, the Spanish and the African. Particularly noteworthy among his concert music written for the piano is his Spanish suite *Andalucía*, which has six parts: "Córdova," "Andalucía," "Gitanerías," "Alhambra," "Guadalquivir," and "Malagueña." The Spanish influence is also evident in *Ante el Escorial* (In Front of the Escorial), *San Francisco el Grande*, *Zambra Gitana* (Gypsy Flamenco), *Aragón*, *Aragonesa*, and *Gitana* (Gypsy Woman). He wrote several waltzes that became known as tropical waltzes because of their authentic Cuban elements. Some of them were very popular, such as *Vals Azul* (Blue Waltz), and others (such as *Vals en Re Bemol*) were more technical, exhibiting the qualities of great concert music. Lecuona also composed many stand-alone pieces, including *El Cisne* (The Swan, a study for the left hand), *Miniaturas*, *Zapateo y Guajira*, *Rapsodia Negra*, *La Habanera*, and *Canto del Guajiro*.

But the piano danzas are his most important works for that instrument, and the central ones form three collections. The first, published in 1923, contains one of this author's most widely known works, "La Comparsa" (The Carnival Drummers), which he wrote at age sixteen. The second was published in 1929 and contains "En tres por cuatro" (In 3/4 Time) and "Ahí viene el Chino" (Here Comes the Chinaman), among others. The third, collection (1930) contains the so-called Afro-Cuban danzas. This collection includes "La conga de medianoche" (Midnight Conga), "Y la negra bailaba" (And the Black Girl Was Dancing), and "Danza de los Ñáñigos" (Dance of the Ñáñigos).

THE MUSICAL THEATER
Lecuona wrote over fifty works for musical theater. All were great box-office hits. The first, *Domingo de piñata* (Piñata Sunday), a six-act play with a script by Mario Vitoria, opened at Havana's Teatro Martí on 9 May 1919. The last was his only opera, *El sombrero de Yarey* (The Palm-Leaf Hat), whose score was finished in the 1950s. It was never produced on stage because it had no libretto.

Between 1919 and 1929 Lecuona wrote fifteen more musical revues, including *Una Noche en Maxim's* (A Night at Maxim's), *Levántate y Anda* (Stand Up and Walk), *Radiomanía*, *La Tierra de Venus* (The Land of Venus), *Es Mucha Habana* (It's a Lot of Havana), and *Alma de Raza* (Soul of the Race). He also composed six one-act *sainetes* (farces): *La Carabana* (The Caravan), *El Triunfo de Virulilla*, *La Carrera del Amor* (The Race of love), *La Despalilladora* (The Grape Stemmer), *La Habana sin Teatros* (Havana without Theaters), and *Mi Pequeña Maldita* (My Naughty Girl). He also wrote four operettas: *Jaque al Rey* (King in Check), *Al Caer la Nieve* (When the Snow Falls), *¡Al fin . . . Mujer!* (Finally . . . Woman!), and *Mujeres* (Women).

However, Lecuona's main contribution to the world of theater was the creation of a new type of zarzuela (musical comedy) that could be defined as purely Cuban. His *Niña Rita* and *La Habana en 1830* (Havana in 1830), written in 1927, are especially important examples. Some of his zarzuelas became

Cuban classics, like *El Cafetal* (The Coffee Plantation, 1929), *El Calesero* (The Coachman, 1930), *María la O* (1930), *Rosa la China* (Rosa the Chinese Woman, 1932), and *Lola Cruz* and *Sor Inés* (1937).

SONGS
Ernesto Lecuona was an exceptional melodist. Only a few Cuban composers could compete with him in creating beautiful and original melodies; many of his songs became musical icons of the nation. His talent in creating musical themes was such that even the countermelodies used in the accompaniment are unusually significant, a technique that became a hallmark of his compositions. In addition, the rhythms he used were chosen skillfully for their Cuban flavor.

Lecuona wrote many successful songs, both within the musical theater and outside it. Some became paradigms of authentic Cuban song and were incorporated into the repertoires of the country's most notable singers. Among his many songs it is easy for Cubans and others to remember "Canto Siboney," "Como Arrullo de Palmas" (A Lullaby of Palms), "Damisela Encantadora" (The Enchanting Damsel, 1936), "Lamento Africano" (African Lament, 1919), "María la O," "Noche Azul" (Blue Night, 1927), "Para Vigo me voy" (I'm Heading to Vigo, 1955), "Se fue" (She Left), and "La Conga se va" (The Conga Line Passed By, 1927).

SELECTED DISCOGRAPHY
Fernández, Frank. *Con el alma en las manos* (2007).

Lecuona, Ernesto. *Lecuona toca Lecuona*, 2 vols., n.d.

María La O: Zarzuela Cubana de Ernesto Lecuona (1995).

Music of the Americas, Vol. IV: *Ernesto Lecuona*. Performed by Polly Ferman (1995/1998).

Noche Azul: Ernesto Lecuona y sus intérpretes (2002).

Rodríguez, Victor. *De Lecuona a Bach* (2000).

Various Artists. *100 Canciones Cubanas del Milenio* (1999).

BIBLIOGRAPHY
Díaz Pérez, Clara, and Gonzalo Roig. *De Cuba Soy Hijo: Correspondencia cruzada de Gonzalo Roig*. Madrid: Música Mundana, 1995.

Gómez Cairo, Jesús. *Ernesto Lecuona*. Havana: Letras Cubanas, 2005.

León, Carmela de. *Ernesto Lecuona: El maestro*. Havana: Editora Musical de Cuba, 1995.

Martínez, Orlando. *Ernesto Lecuona*. Havana: Unión de Escritoresy Artistas de Cuba, 1989.

N

NEW YORK CITY

Lisandro Pérez

The setting for much of Cuba's political, economic, social, and cultural history during the nineteenth century.

Until the establishment in 1886 of Ybor City, outside of Tampa, Florida, New York City housed the largest community of Cubans in the United States. In fact, throughout most of the nineteenth century, Cuban New York was the largest concentration of Latin Americans east of the Mississippi. Beyond demographics, however, New York was a premier setting for many of the transcendent events and movements that shaped the building of the Cuban nation. The metropolis on the Hudson became the place where Cubans went for an education, opportunity, or wealth, to seek refuge, start a new life or bury an old one, evade royal authority, plot revolutions, experience freedom, or buy and sell. New York took center stage as Cuba tumbled into the tumultuous decades of the separatist struggles. Virtually every major Cuban political, business, cultural, and literary figure of the nineteenth century lived, permanently or temporarily, in New York or had some relationship to the city. José Martí (1853–1895) was a New Yorker; he lived in the city for most of his adult life. He did some of his best writing there. In New York, he masterfully built a unified civilian movement to take the struggle for independence to Cuba. But the story of Cuban New York is much larger than Martí and the Partido Revolucionario Cubano (PRC, Cuban Revolutionary Party) he founded, and it started considerably before the Cuban patriot was born.

THE CUBA TRADE

As is true of most New York stories, the story of Cuban New York starts with the port. And as is true of most Cuban stories, it involves sugar. Very early in the nineteenth century, the port of New York became a critical piece in the sugar boom that transformed Cuban society. It was largely in New York that the sweet brown product of the burgeoning mills of the Havana and Matanzas regions was sold. The British occupation of Havana in 1762–1763 had opened up commerce between Cuba and London's North American colonies. Once those colonies became independent and Cuba's ascendant sugarocracy invested massively in land, slaves, and machinery to make the island the world's largest producer of sugar, Cuba had something to sell and New York was interested in buying. Manhattan and the Brooklyn waterfront housed most of the country's sugar refineries. By 1855 there were fourteen plants operating in the area. The refineries turned a handsome profit buying Cuba's raw sugar and turning it into the more marketable refined product.

While sugar was the basis of the growing trade between New York and the ports of Havana and Matanzas, other Cuban products were also involved, especially molasses, tobacco, and cigars (Albion p. 189). The exports from New York to Cuba were much more diverse. The island had to import just about everything. The sugar plantation owners bought machinery for their mills; fine linen and clothing; furnishings for their new mansions; carriages in which to ride around in Havana; and large amounts of foodstuffs, especially flour, to feed their slaves.

Throughout the first half of the nineteenth century, trade between the United States and Cuba boomed. In 1830, more than nine hundred U.S. ships entered Cubans ports. As early as 1835, the Cuba Trade, as it became known, began occupying the third or fourth spot in the total U.S. trade picture (Ely p. 458). The resulting ship traffic meant an expanded flow of passengers. From 1821 to 1850, the number of passengers arriving in New York from Cuban ports exceeded the combined number of passengers arriving from all other ports in Latin America and Spain (Lisandro Pérez 2010, p. 99).

The countinghouses that lined lower Manhattan's waterfront emerged as key players in New York's trade with Cuba. A combination of trading office, warehouse, accounting firm, credit agency, bank,

■ *See also*

Diasporas: 19th Century

José Martí: Exile in New York

The Mambo Kings Play Songs of Love (Oscar Hijuelos)

Music: Afro-Cuban Jazz

and investment managers, these mercantile establishments cultivated relations with the Cuban planters, extending them credit, acting as their shipping and commission agents, selling their sugar, managing their accounts, and purchasing goods in New York on their behalf. Merchants such as Moses Taylor became agents, bankers, and financial managers for the Cuban planters, forging links between Cuba and New York that went beyond the commercial sphere, establishing the basis for a profound and extensive exchange of not only goods and money, but also people and culture.

STUDENTS, INTELLECTUALS, AND SOJOURNERS

The Cuba Trade set the stage for a flow of Cubans to New York that started early in the nineteenth century. Spearheading that flow were boys and young men from wealthy families seeking an education and work experience, and the Manhattan countinghouses had a direct role in bringing them from Cuba. The New York merchants, at the request of their Cuban clients, would make arrangements for the sons of planters to be enrolled in boarding schools in the New York area. The countinghouses would also temporarily employ young Cuban men in their own offices, a sort of internship that would enable them to learn English and become familiar with modern business operations. In 1850 one New Yorker estimated that nearly two thousand young Cubans had already been educated in U.S. schools (Thrasher p. 425).

One of those young men was Cristóbal Madan (1806–c. 1880), whose family owned mills in the Matanzas region. His family arranged for Cristóbal to go in 1822 to New York and intern as a clerk in the Lower Manhattan countinghouse of Jonathan Goodhue, whose firm, Goodhue and Company, was engaged in the Cuba Trade. Within a period of two weeks in December 1823, the young Madan welcomed to Manhattan two of the most prominent Cuban intellectual figures of the time: the priest and philosopher Félix Varela (1788–1853) and the poet José María Heredia y Heredia (1803–1839).

Father Varela showed up on 15 December in the office of Goodhue and Company looking for Cristóbal, his former student. The priest had gone directly there from the Manhattan pier where the *Draper*, a cargo ship he had boarded in Gibraltar, had just docked. Varela was fleeing Spain, where he was persecuted for proposing a liberalization of the colonial regime in Cuba. He had not planned to travel to New York, much less remain there. But a death penalty awaited him in Havana, and although he found the cold weather nearly intolerable and English a daunting language to master, Varela stayed in New York for the next thirty years, almost to the end of his life, passing up opportunities to move to Latin American countries with warmer climates. The founder of two downtown churches and an eloquent defender of the rights of Catholics and the Irish at a time when those rights were threatened by nativists and anti-papists, the Cuban priest played a critical role in the development of the New York archdiocese (Rodríguez).

Varela's decision to remain in New York spoke volumes about the place that the city had come to occupy in the Cuban economic, political, and cultural landscapes. The closest place to Cuba was New York, and it was the city's commerce with the island that made the distance so short. Varela's decision to become a New Yorker would be repeated in subsequent decades by Cuban exiles who wished to stay close to their native island and remain active in its affairs. Only one week after the priest arrived in Manhattan, a young exiled poet from Matanzas made his way to Goodhue and Company looking for Cristóbal Madan. In the first letter José María Heredia wrote from New York, he informed his mother that "one reason I am inclined to remain here is the constant communication there is with Havana; it is where I can easily and frequently receive news of my family" (p. 90).

ANNEXATIONISM AND THE CUBAN FLAG

The importance of New York as a destination for Cubans leaving the island meant that the city was destined to become a major stage for the separatist struggles that had started unfolding by the middle of the nineteenth century. On 11 May 1850, an extraordinary event occurred in New York that symbolized the city's emerging role in the Cubans' initial stirrings to end Spanish rule in the island. That day, on the corner of Nassau and Fulton Streets, the location of the *New York Sun*, a flag, heralded on the newspaper's front page as the "Flag of Free Cuba," was unfurled. It was the first time that a piece of cloth was identified as a flag of Cuba. And it was not just any Cuban flag, but the one that remains the nation's flag in the twenty-first century. It was there, on that day, that it flew for the first time anywhere, reportedly designed and sewn in a New York boardinghouse.

It was an annexationist flag, intended to be flown in Cuba by the expeditionaries led by Narciso López (1798–1851). The López expeditions, composed largely of mercenaries and supported by Cuban and southern U.S. planters, were organized to wrest Cuba from Spanish control and annex it to the United States as a slave state. Given the long-standing relationship between the Cuban sugar producers and New York, it is not surprising that the annexationist movement was largely centered in the city. It was in New York that the annexationists published *La Verdad*, a newspaper printed in the presses of the *New York Sun* with the financial and intellectual support of Cuban sugar interests.

Among *La Verdad*'s anonymous collaborators was Cristóbal Madan, Goodhue's young intern, by this time in his forties and a lawyer who represented his family's sugar interests in both Cuba and in Manhattan. Madan led a true transnational life, dividing his time between his home in Havana, his family's sugar plantations in Matanzas, and a lavish residence near Madison Square Park, at the time one of the city's most fashionable neighborhoods. He shared that residence with his second wife, a New Yorker who was the sister of John L. O'Sullivan (1813–1895), the prominent New York Democrat and committed expansionist who coined the term *Manifest Destiny*. O'Sullivan and the editor of the *Sun*, Moses Yale Beach (1800–1868), were instrumental in persuading President James Polk to extend an offer to Madrid to buy Cuba, an offer that was flatly rejected but which represented the annexationists' interest in pursuing a more peaceful alternative to the expeditions to accomplish their goal.

The failure of both peaceful and military efforts to annex Cuba marked the decline of the annexationist movement, and by the time the U.S. Civil War began, it was practically nonexistent. For the rest of the century, New York would be the setting for many other émigré revolutionary activities and movements, most of them pursuing nothing short of total independence for Cuba. Those nationalist separatists would look back at the annexationists with contempt because of their willingness to compromise nationhood in defense of their narrow, elite economic interests. While that is not an unfair characterization, the activities of the annexationists marked the beginning of organized efforts on the part of Cubans in New York to effect changes in their homeland.

1868: WAR AND EXODUS

The war for independence that broke out in eastern Cuba on 10 October 1868 caught the Havana sugar planters by surprise. As property owners, their activism against the colonial regime had been confined to the annexationist movement or to lobbying efforts aimed at reforming the island's relationship with Madrid, but it had not extended to a potentially destructive war against Spain. Yet, when the eastern elites, based in Camagüey and in Oriente's Cauto Valley, decided that Cuba's colonial status had to be resolved with bullets, the sugar elites of Havana and Matanzas were swept up in the wake of forces they had not initiated and could not control. Cuban New York would not be the same again.

The war unleashed a wave of repression by the Spanish against those suspected of being less than loyal to the Crown. The paramilitary and fanatic *voluntarios* were responsible for carrying out a reign of terror that was especially felt in Havana. Cuban planters such as Madan, who lived in the capital and had a history of advocating changes in the colonial regime, were especially vulnerable. Fearing for their lives, many of Havana's elite families fled the country during the first months of 1869 and others were deported.

New York was overwhelmingly the principal destination of the exodus, given the long-standing relationship between the city and Havana's sugar elites, most of which had accounts with the South Street countinghouses and residences and offices in Manhattan. It was an influx that dwarfed earlier migrations of Cubans to the city, involving entire families who were leaving the island without knowing when they could return. U.S. passenger ships that usually transported primarily American visitors to and from the island were filled to capacity with Cuban families and their servants bound for the Manhattan waterfront. The Spanish government subsequently embargoed the properties of those who left, and many of them were even sentenced to death in absentia. The U.S. Census of 1870 counted 2,600 Cuban-born persons living in Manhattan alone, with more than 3,000 in what later became the five boroughs. Cuban New Yorkers far surpassed the combined total of all other Latin Americans and Spaniards living in the city (Lisandro Pérez 2010, p. 104).

The war dragged on for ten years, and during that time, and especially during its initial years, New York was the setting for intense émigré activism in support of the struggle. The elites who had previously espoused annexationism and reformism now had little choice but to embrace independence. Carlos Manuel de Céspedes (1819–1875), the easterner who initiated the war and presided over the newly formed Cuban Republic, recognized that the success of the war effort depended on political and economic support from the United States. He designated one of the exiled New York Cubans, José Morales Lemus (1808–1870), as his official representative, charging him with obtaining Washington's recognition for the rebel government and raising funds among the émigrés and sympathetic Americans to outfit expeditions to Cuba with men and military supplies. In Cuba, Morales Lemus had been a lawyer for the most prominent Cuban planter families. In his sixties when he arrived in New York with his family and servants in 1869, he died the following year in Brooklyn without accomplishing the tasks assigned to him. He was replaced as the agent of the Cuban Republic by Miguel Aldama (1821–1888), the leader of one of the most prominent and wealthy of the Havana elite families, related by marriage to Cristóbal Madan. Aldama's properties were all embargoed by the Spanish, but most of his liquid assets were deposited with Moses Taylor's countinghouse in South Street, enabling him to live lavishly in New York, as did many of the exiled planter families.

Despite the efforts by Aldama and other New York émigrés, the external support Cespedes expected never sufficiently coalesced to make any difference in the outcome of the war. Despite initial sympathetic words toward the Cuban cause by President Ulysses Grant, his administration in the end followed the policy favored by Secretary of State Hamilton Fish. Fish did not want to jeopardize U.S. relations with Spain and convinced Grant to stay neutral in the Cuban war and, even further, to order federal enforcement officials to strictly implement U.S. neutrality laws, arresting and convicting anyone found organizing expeditions to the island from U.S. soil. That antagonistic U.S. policy toward the activities of the émigrés dealt a serious blow to the ability of Aldama and other Cubans in New York to raise funds and organize expeditions on behalf of the war effort.

Despite dispatching several successful expeditions to Cuba and the heroic and selfless efforts of many, the Cubans in New York failed to provide the support necessary to sustain the war in their native island. They were hampered not just by Washington but also by disunity. During the ten years the war lasted, there were intense and destructive rivalries among Cuban New Yorkers, undermining the pro-war effort. Activists who had lived in the city since the annexationist period, such as Cirilo Villaverde (1812–1894), the writer, and his wife, the activist Emilia Casanova (1832–1897), resented the leadership role assumed by the newly arrived elites led by Morales Lemus and Aldama. The latter, as representatives of the Republic, largely excluded the longtime residents from significant roles in the campaign to support the war.

The treaty that ended the war allowed exiled Cubans to return to the island. Some of them, such as Cristóbal Madan, by now nearly seventy years old, returned with the hope of recovering their embargoed estates. It turned out to be a fruitless endeavor. Many Cuban New Yorkers chose to remain in the city, especially elites who had wisely invested the funds they had deposited in the countinghouses. Félix Govín (1826–1891), for example, invested heavily in Manhattan real estate and by the early 1880s was possibly New York's wealthiest Cuban. The Angarica family multiplied its wealth through real estate and laid roots in the city, becoming prominent leaders of a Masonic lodge. Miguel Aldama also stayed for several years after the end of the war, trying to make profitable a huge sugar refinery he had built on the Brooklyn waterfront. He failed to do so, however, and finally returned to Havana, where he died penniless. Following his wishes, his body was returned to New York to be buried next to his father in the mausoleum Miguel had purchased years before in Brooklyn's famed Green-Wood Cemetery.

For other Cuban New Yorkers—laborers, cigar workers, former slaves, domestic servants, clerks, craftsmen, and seamstresses—their migration to the city during the war meant new opportunities to improve their lives. They had nothing to recover and nothing to gain by returning to a Cuba ravaged by war. Cigar workers in particular became a growing sector of New York's Cuban community as the city's cigar manufacturing industry, originally established by German immigrants, expanded during the 1870s and 1880s, much of it devoted to the manufacture of cigars from Havana clear tobacco leaves, which had become the fashionable smokes among New Yorkers. The end of the war and the return or ruin of many of the sugar planters meant that Cuban New York became more diverse and proletarian, no longer dominated by elite interests.

JOSÉ MARTÍ AND THE PRC

José Martí arrived in New York precisely at the start of a decade: 3 January 1880. He had at least five traits in common with a previous Cuban New Yorker, Félix Varela: (1) an abiding commitment to the future of the homeland; (2) a gifted pen in service to that commitment; (3) the conviction that New York was where he needed to live if he was going to stay close to Cuba; (4) his status as a political exile, unable to return to Cuba without facing serious consequences; and (5) as had been true of Varela, Martí would spend practically the rest of his life in the city. Martí lived in New York more than fifteen years, from the time he was twenty-seven years old to shortly after his forty-second birthday. He died at that age on a Cuban battlefield, less than four months after leaving the city. The moment of his death is captured in an equestrian statue of him at Sixth Avenue and Central Park South in Manhattan.

It was in New York that Martí made the two most significant contributions that immortalized him in Cuban and Latin American history. One of those accomplishments was the creation of an enduring body of literary work. Of special importance are his *Escenas norteamericanas* (American Scenes, 1885), which chronicles life and events in the United States and was intended for a Latin American reading public. The *Escenas* reflects his intimate exposure to the best, and the worst, of what the most important city in the world had to offer. New York at the close of the nineteenth century was at the cutting edge of urban modernity, and Martí provided a unique perspective to his Latin American readers on the unfolding drama of the modern world (Rotker p. 62).

His other major accomplishment was to build a unified civilian movement that would take a sustainable armed struggle to Cuba, something no other Cuban New Yorker, or any Cuban émigré, had been able to do. Martí accomplished this with three institutions he created: (1) a network of local clubs spread throughout the Cuban diaspora; (2) the Partido Revolucionario Cubano (1892); and (3) the newspaper *Patria* (1892), edited in New York.

What was extraordinary about Martí in his political work is that he broke the mold of previous émigré activism in New York in two important ways. His movement was not elite based, but rather built from the grass roots up, especially among the cigar workers in Tampa, Key West, and New York. The other innovation of his movement was to meticulously avoid attracting the support and attention of the U.S. government and the media, a totally opposite strategy from what generations of Cuban émigrés had tried to do. Lobbying Washington and placing the cause of Cuba in the press was at the forefront of the agenda of annexationists and of New York–based leaders such as Aldama and Morales Lemus.

After his death, the wise foresight Martí had shown in avoiding U.S. attention for the Cuban cause became evident when his successors as leaders of the PRC, the longtime New Yorkers Tomás Estrada Palma (1835–1908) and Gonzalo de Quesada (1868–1915), aggressively pursued U.S. intervention in the Cuban conflict. Eventually, Washington did intervene, with disastrous consequences for Cuban sovereignty.

THE TWENTIETH CENTURY

The end of Spanish rule in Cuba, followed by a U.S. occupation and the establishment of the Cuban Republic in 1902, fundamentally changed the long-standing relationship between the island and New York, as the Platt Amendment became the basis for the development of "ties of singular intimacy" between the two countries (Pérez Jr.). In that new climate, New York reasserted itself as the premier destination for Cuban migrants. But instead of elites and cigar workers seeking to escape and overthrow Spanish colonialism, many of the Cubans arriving in New York during the first few decades of the twentieth century were part of a massive human flow, most of it temporary, that took American businesspeople and tourists to Cuba and brought to the United States, especially to the city, Cubans seeking to develop their careers, either in U.S. schools, commerce, music, and the entertainment industry or in professional sports, notably baseball and boxing (Lisandro Pérez 1994, pp. 184–188).

In the years immediately following World War II, Cuban migration to the United States increased dramatically. Not unlike the parallel flow of Puerto Ricans to New York during this period, it was largely a labor migration attracted to employment opportunities in the city's industrial and service sectors. Two novels, one by Oscar Hijuelos, *Our House in the Last World* (1983), and the other by Miguel Barnet, *La vida real* (1986; *A True Story: A Cuban in New York*, 2010) draw poignant pictures of this migration by recounting the struggles of fictional characters and families attempting to succeed in a post-war Manhattan.

After 1952 these labor migrants were joined in New York by those leaving the island due to the instability and repression created by the Batista regime. In only three years—1956, 1957, and 1958—more than forty thousand Cubans entered the United States (Lisandro Pérez 2001, p. 84). New York once again buzzed with activism directed at changing the government on the island. It would not be until after 1959 that New York's long-standing place as the premier destination for Cuban migrants to the United States would be challenged by Miami.

BIBLIOGRAPHY

Albion, Robert Greenhalgh. *The Rise of New York Port.* New York: Charles Scribner's Sons, 1939.

Barnet, Miguel. *La vida real.* Havana: Editorial Letras Cubanas, 1986. Translated by Regina Galasso as *A True Story: A Cuban in New York.* New York: Jorge Pinto Books, 2010.

Ely, Roland T. "The Old Cuba Trade: Highlights and Case Studies of Cuban-American Interdependence during the Nineteenth Century." *Business History Review* 38, no. 4 (1964): 456–478.

Heredia, José María. "Letter to María Mercedes Heredia Campuzano, New York, December 24, 1823." In *Epistolario de José María Heredia,* compiled by Angel Augier. Havana: Editorial Letras Cubanas, 2005.

Hijuelos, Oscar. *Our House in the Last World.* New York: Persea Books, 1983.

Pérez, Lisandro. "Cuban Catholics in the United States." In *Puerto Rican and Cuban Catholics in the U.S., 1900–1965,* edited by Jay P. Dolan and Jaime R. Vidal. Notre Dame, IN: University of Notre Dame Press, 1994.

Pérez, Lisandro. "La emigración y la crisis estructural de la República." *Temas* 24–25 (January–June 2001): 83–86.

Pérez, Lisandro. "Cubans in Nineteenth-Century New York: A Story of Sugar, War, and Revolution." In *Nueva York, 1613–1945,* edited by Edward J. Sullivan. New York: New-York Historical Society, 2010.

Pérez, Louis A., Jr. *Cuba and the United States: Ties of Singular Intimacy.* Athens: University of Georgia Press, 1990.

Rodríguez, José Ignacio. *Vida del presbítero Don Félix Varela.* 1878, 2nd ed. Havana: Arellano y Cía, 1944.

Rotker, Susana. *The American Chronicles of José Martí: Journalism and Modernity in Spanish America,* translated by Jennifer French and Katherine Semler. Hanover, NH: University Press of New England, 2000.

Thrasher, J. S. "Ensayo preliminar." In *Ensayo político sobre la isla de Cuba,* by Alejandro de Humboldt. Havana: Publicaciones del Archivo Nacional de Cuba, 1960.

OPERATION PEDRO PAN

María de los Angeles Torres

An operation coordinated by the U.S. government to evacuate thousands of children of Cubans opposed to Castro's revolutionary government from Cuba to the United States between 1960 to 1962.

In 1960 President Dwight D. Eisenhower signed an executive order authorizing the Central Intelligence Agency to overthrow the government of Fidel Castro (b. 1926). Part of the military organization included plans to evacuate the children of opponents of Castro; thus, the origins of the largest exodus of unaccompanied minors in the Western Hemisphere lie in military plans to overthrow the Castro government.

THE FIRST PHASE: EARLY REVOLUTION TO THE BAY OF PIGS

The original program planned to bring two hundred children out of Cuba so that their parents could fight the Castro government without worrying about their families. These parents were afraid that if they were arrested or killed their children would be left alone and in danger. The program also included young men and women who could face firing squads if they were caught in Cuba. The first phase lasted until the Bay of Pigs invasion in April 1961.

At first these unaccompanied minors received student visas through the U.S. Embassy in Havana. Harris Smith Travel Agency, a U.S.-owned business, provided travel documents to the children, who were told to tell airport officials that they had received student scholarships to study in the United States. James Baker, the headmaster of Ruston Academy, a secular private school in Havana, coordinated these efforts. In Miami, Monsignor Bryan O. Walsh, the director of the Catholic Welfare Bureau, was enlisted to care for the children.

When the United States broke diplomatic relations with the Cuban government on 3 January 1961, the embassy was closed, necessitating a new plan to obtain visa waivers for the children. Walsh was asked by the State Department and other agencies to grant blanket visa waivers to anyone under sixteen, and he arranged for the issuance of official letters from the Catholic Welfare Bureau to that effect. Minors aged sixteen to eighteen required security checks but once this was done, they too received visa waivers.

Baker organized a group of Ruston parents, teachers, and staff to distribute the visa waivers. The United States also enlisted the help of the British Embassy to facilitate the flights from Havana to Miami that stopped over in Kingston, Jamaica (at that time, a British colony). Penny Powers, a British intelligence officer who had played a role in the Kindertransport during World War II, became a point person.

Most of Baker's group was arrested days before the Bay of Pigs invasion in mid-April 1961. Up to then, 657 children and youths had come to the United States. It was, according to a post–Bay of Pigs report to President John F. Kennedy, a classified program.

Most of the organizers thought the program was over, but as the situation in Cuba became more repressive, and massive arrests, summary trials, and firing squads became common, the pressure to leave increased. Days before the Bay of Pigs invasion, the Cuban government had closed all schools. Church services were disrupted, and practicing Catholics were prohibited from participating in a series of government programs. The United States intensified its efforts to topple the regime, launching a propaganda campaign to discredit the government that included the circulation of copies of a law supposedly being considered by the Cuban government that would transfer parents' *patria potestad* (rights over their children) to the state (Elliston).

THE SECOND PHASE: THE BAY OF PIGS TO THE MISSILE CRISIS

A massive exodus from Cuba demonstrated that Cubans were voting with their feet, and immigration

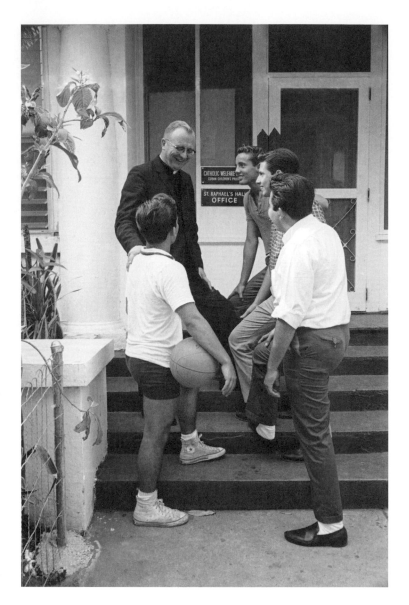

Monsignor Bryan O. Walsh with young Cuban evacuees. Monsignor Bryan O. Walsh, the director of the Catholic Welfare Bureau for the Archdiocese of Miami, chats with four Cuban boys on 17 May 1962. The boys were among thousands of Cuban minors who were brought to the United States between 1961 and 1962 as part of Operation Pedro Pan. AP IMAGES

Health, Education, and Welfare (HEW) contracted a Florida state agency, which in turn subcontracted their care to the Catholic Welfare Bureau because the majority of the children and youths were Catholic. Several smaller subcontracts were given to Jewish and Protestant agencies. Minors who did not have friends or relatives in Florida were initially placed in group homes in Florida, including in Florida City and Matecumbe, and old military barracks. As openings in church-run orphanages or foster-care families became available, children were placed. Cuban children came with a daily stipend that was higher than that paid for American children, which became an issue when the news about the Cuban children broke.

All agencies that dealt with the minors had been instructed to keep the program secret, but in March 1962 a reporter from the *Cleveland Plain Dealer* wrote a story about Cuban refugee children in Cleveland and despite pressure from the government, planned to publish it. The day before the story was to run, HEW officials gave a press conference, and the *Miami Herald* ran the story under the headline "8,000 Cuban Children Saved from Communist Brainwashing." The *Miami Herald* dubbed the program "Operation Pedro Pan."

Once the news broke, the U.S. government used the children as propaganda. In the minutes of a meeting of the Caribbean Survey Group, chaired by Attorney General Robert Kennedy, General Edward Lansdale, who had been put in charge of the Cuba project after the Bay of Pigs invasion, said of the children in the camps, "We should exploit the emotional possibilities of the 8,000 children that were under the protection of the United States" (Caribbean Survey Group). Records indicate that the discussion at this meeting led to the filming of the *Lost Apple*, a documentary that Walsh and others did not want filmed because they feared for the safety of the parents in Cuba (Torres p. 180).

By this time, the United States had shut the doors to all Cuban immigrants, including the parents of the children and youths in the United States. After the October Missile Crisis, the United States agreed not to invade Cuba and instead pressured the Castro government by refusing Cubans entry to the United States and initiating an air isolation campaign to encourage other countries not to fly in and out of Cuba. In turn, the Castro government refused to allow the minors to return home to their parents on the island. The law of "definitive abandonment" dictated that anyone who had left the island and not returned within sixty days lost his property and his right to return.

THE THIRD PHASE: THE MISSILE CRISIS TO 1965

The third phase of the program lasted until 1965, when the doors of immigration were reopened. Few records of this period have been made available to the public, but those that have suggest a mixed picture.

mechanisms were expanded. There were numerous visa waiver programs in place, including several run through the underground and administered by organizations such as International Rescue Committee, but most visa waivers given to adults and minors required a special security check, whereas Walsh's waivers did not. Once in the United States, parents were reunited with their children, a process that normally took about six months. During the second phase of Operation Pedro Pan, which lasted from the Bay of Pigs invasion in April 1961 to the Missile Crisis in October 1962, most of the fourteen thousand minors entered the United States. An exact number is difficult to obtain because even the most comprehensive lists—the airport logs—failed to record many minors who were collected at the airport by family friends.

Walsh continued to oversee the care of the children. The Children's Bureau of the Department of

Although some young men's lives were saved and those minors who were sent to boarding schools seemed to have fared better than others, there are documented accounts of sexual and emotional abuse in the orphanages where many children were placed, where letters were censored and siblings often were kept separated (Torres, Chapter Seven). Little is known about the conditions in the homes of friends and relatives of the parents. Even in the best of circumstances there would have been cultural alienation and the typical effects of prolonged separations of children and parents.

Children and minors did try to get their parents into the United States. In one case, a group in Chicago succeeded by lobbying U.S. senator Paul Douglas of Illinois to have their parents put onto cargo ships returning from Cuba (Torres p. 190). But despite efforts by the United Nations High Commissioner for Refugees to negotiate their exit permits from Cuba and pay for their flights to the United States, the U.S. government response was that for national security reasons the air embargo on Cuba had to be maintained (Airgram USUN). As pressure mounted in Cuba, Castro responded in October 1965 by opening the port of Camarioca and inviting Cuban exiles to come in boats to pick up their relatives. In response, President Lyndon B. Johnson established the Freedom Flights, twice-daily flights shuttling refugees from Cuba to the United States.

When parents finally arrived in the United States, the reunions were often tense. They were not allowed to bring their children to Miami; the federal government relocation program required that they go to live where their children had been placed, and in many instances, the children were in towns where there were few Cubans. The children had become acculturated to American ways, and parents often found it hard to re-create family relationships as they were in Cuba. There appears to be no information available on how many children and youths were never reunited with their parents. Travel back to Cuba was prohibited by both governments until 1978.

The history of Operation Pedro Pan became an arena of debate in which one side described the future robbed by the United States and the other side emphasized that the children were saved from communism. In the early 1990s, Operation Pedro Pan Group was formed to bring together the grown children of the exodus, and under the direction of Elly Chovel, it became a forum for exploring the difficult past and individual memories without the political clichés. The group also became involved in charitable work with unaccompanied refugee minors, and in 1994, members were instrumental in stopping an attempt to separate Cuban children from their parents who were detained in Guantanamo. Monsignor Walsh pleaded with politicians to advocate for the admission of entire families.

Debates about the nature of the operation reopened in 2000 when six-year-old Elián González was rescued at sea with two other survivors after their boat from Cuba sank and ten other passengers died, including Elián's mother. Elián was placed with distant relatives in Miami. A major international battle waged as his father in Cuba tried to reclaim his child and the Miami relatives refused to release him. The boy became the symbol of salvation for the exile community in Miami and in Cuba one more of the stolen children. Cintio Vitier (1921–2009), one of Cuba's national poets, declared that "a boy would save the nation." Thousands of Cubans on the island were rallied by Fidel Castro to demand that the boy be returned. He did return home to his father, six months after his rescue at sea.

The power of the myth of salvation was again at play after the 2010 Haitian earthquake when Miami Catholic Charities launched a campaign to bring Haitian children to the United States, dubbing their plan Operation Pierre Pan. At the urging of the United Nations, the program was not authorized.

There are also myths about the Pedro Pan children that have portrayed them as victims or heroes. Island-based versions such as the film *De Este Lado de la Pecera* tend to emphasize their travails. Successful businesspersons, politicians, artists, performers, and writers contribute to the mythology of the Pedro Pans, including Mel Martinez (b. 1946), the first Cuban American in the U.S. Senate; the artist Ana Mendieta (1948–1985); and the popular music performer Willy Chirino (b. 1947).

There are still many questions surrounding Operation Pedro Pan, as well as strong emotions, which have been explored in memoirs such as Carlos Eire's *Waiting for Snow in Havana* (2003) and his *Learning to Die in Miami: Confessions of a Refugee Boy* (2010), and Flora González Mandri's essay "A House on Shifting Sands." Several works of fiction on the subject have been published, among them two children's books, *Kiki, a Cuban Boy's Adventures in America* (1992), by Hilda Perera, and *The Red Umbrella* (2010), by Christina Gonzalez. Nilo Cruz's play *Hortensia and the Museum of Dreams* (2004) and Melinda Lopez's *Sonia Flew* (2009) revolve around characters who came to the United States under Operation Pedro Pan.

BIBLIOGRAPHY
Print Sources

Airgram United States Mission to the United Nations. 16 April 1965, Lyndon Baines Johnson Presidential Library, National Security Files, Cuba, Cuba Refugees #15.

Conde, Yvonne. *Operation Pedro Pan: The Untold Exodus of 14,048 Cuban Children.* New York: Routledge, 1999.

Eire, Carlos. *Waiting for Snow in Havana: Confessions of a Cuban Boy.* New York: Free Press, 2003.

Eire, Carlos. *Learning to Die in Miami: Confessions of a Refugee Boy.* New York: Free Press, 2010.

Elliston, Jon. *Psywar on Cuba : The Declassified History of U.S. Anti-Castro Propaganda*. New York: Ocean Press, 2002.

González Mandri, Flora. "A House on Shifting Sands." In *Bridges to Cuba*, edited by Ruth Behar, 76–79. Ann Arbor: University of Michigan Press, 1995.

Official Memorandum of the Caribbean Survey Group, 23 March 1962, National Archives, John F. Kennedy Files.

Rubio-Boitel, Fernando. *La pecera de La Habana: Recuento de un Pedro Pan: Desde Cuba hasta Nuevo México*. Mexico City: Ediciones del Lirio, 2009.

Torres, María de los Angeles. *The Lost Apple: Operation Pedro Pan, Cuban Children in the U.S., and the Promise of a Better Future*. Boston: Beacon Press, 2003.

Triana, Victor Andres. *Fleeing Castro: Operation Pedro Pan and the Cuban Children's Program*. Gainesville: University Press of Florida, 1999.

Nonprint Sources

Brisk, Angelica Allende. *Far from Cuba*. Television documentary. WGBH, February 2002.

Cardona, Joe, and Mario de Varona. *Flight of Pedro Pan*. Film documentary. 60 mins. Kie Films, 1999.

Escape from Havana: An American Story. Television documentary. 60 mins. *CNBC Originals*. 27 May 2010. Available from http://www.clicker.com/tv/cnbc-originals/ Escape-from-Havana:-An-American-Story-1008931/.

Viasman, Cecilia, and María de los Angeles Torres. "Pedro Pan." *All Things Considered*. National Public Radio. 3 May 2000. Available from http://www.npr.org/templates/story/story.php?storyId=1073679.

ORÍGENES GROUP AND JOURNAL

Jorge Luis Arcos

One of the most significant and controversial literary groups of twentieth-century Cuban literature.

The Orígenes group was one of the most significant and controversial literary groups of twentieth-century Cuban culture. It took its name from the last of several journals that included *Verbum* (1937), *Espuela de Plata* (Silver Spur, 1939–1941), *Nadie Parecía* (No One Seemed, 1942–1944), *Clavileño* (1942–1943), and *Poeta* (Poet, 1942–1943). The Mexican writer Octavio Paz (1914–1998) described *Orígenes* as the most important Spanish-language periodical of its time. The journal was edited by José Lezama Lima (1910–1976) and José Rodríguez Feo (1897–1958) until a split between the two resulted in two different versions of the last two issues and the emergence of *Ciclón* (Cyclone), edited by Rodríguez Feo with the assistance of the *Orígenes* dissident Virgilio Piñera (1912–1979), aggressively favoring modernity and a bolder cultural orientation.

ORÍGENES JOURNAL

Focused primarily on poetry, *Orígenes* (1944–1956) was as noteworthy as *Contemporáneos* (Contemporaries), *Sur* (South), and *Revista de Occidente* (Western Review). It attempted to resolve the dualism between national and universal culture. It strived to distinguish itself from the preceding generation, represented by the avant-garde *Revista de Avance* (Progress Review): Lezama and Cintio Vitier (1921–2009) carried on an interesting polemic with Jorge Mañach (1898–1961), one of *Revista*'s former editors-in-chief. Another of the previous generation's publications was the Marxist *Gaceta del Caribe* (Caribbean Gazette), whose first editorial, written anonymously by Mirta Aguirre (1912–1980), was the unnamed target of Lezama's first editorial in *Orígenes*.

It could be said that *Ciclón*'s editorial profile was in direct opposition to the viewpoints presented in *Orígenes*, which was also to some extent true of the weekly *Lunes de Revolución* (Revolution Mondays), except that *Ciclón*'s conflict with *Orígenes* was fueled by different aesthetic worldviews, whereas *Lunes de Revolución*, which emerged in 1959, sought to identify a publication's orientation with the Revolution's incipient official culture, a stance that put *origenistas* at risk.

THE GROUP

The Orígenes group consisted of ten poets who first achieved prominence in Vitier's anthology *Diez poetas cubanos (1937–1947)* (Ten Cuban Poets, 1948), which featured—in addition to Vitier himself—Lezama Lima, Piñera, Gastón Baquero (1914–1997), Justo Rodríguez Santos (1915–1999), Ángel Gaztelu (1914–2003), Eliseo Diego (1920–1994), Fina García-Marruz (b. 1923), Octavio Smith (1921–1987), and Lorenzo García Vega (b. 1926). The writer Roberto Fernández Retamar (b. 1930) was also frequently published in the journal, and the exiled Spanish writer María Zambrano (1904–1991), who was among the journal's most assiduous contributors, had considerable influence on the group. Her essay "La Cuba secreta" (The Secret Cuba, 1948) invested the Cuban poetry movement with a sort of philosophical metaphysics. Major painters such as Mariano Rodríguez (1912–1990) and René Portocarrero (1912–1985), the art critic Guy Pérez Cisneros (1915–1953), and the musician Julián Orbón (1912–1991) can also be considered part of the group; nevertheless, it was poetry—and specifically a poetic concept of reality—that characterized the Orígenes group and made it unique. Indeed, it was the group's painstaking poetic work that distinguished it from earlier and even contemporary tendencies (Arcos 2002).

There are two main critical approaches to this group. The more traditional viewpoint links it directly to the existence of the previously mentioned journals, through the examination of many editorials written by Lezama (Lezama Lima) and books such as Vitier's

Lo cubano en la poesía (Cubanness in Poetry, 1958). The other argues that the group's influence lasted far beyond the journal's final issue and into a new age of Cuban literature following the triumph of the Revolution in 1959. In this construct, the group had a classic period linked to its journals and another, more controversial period during which Vitier and García-Marruz were the most widely accepted group proponents (Vitier 1994; García-Marruz), all the way into the early years of the twenty-first century.

ORÍGENES IN THE REVOLUTION

In any case, opinions about the group grew more divided with the advent of that new period (Arcos 2007; Díaz). The negative criticism that began with *Ciclón* and was continued by *Lunes de Revolución* predominated until the early 1980s, thanks in part to the group's most notorious dissident, Piñera, and to the next generation, called the Fifties Generation or the first generation of the Revolution, which had new ideological tendencies that originated with *Gaceta del Caribe* and were represented by writers such as the Marxist critic Aguirre. In some sense, the triumph of the Revolution obliged the members of Orígenes to redefine their previous concept, called transcendentalist (Fernández Retamar), in light of the new political and literary context. Initially all of them enthusiastically welcomed the new revolutionary period—except for Baquero, who went into exile immediately, followed later by Orbón, Rodríguez Santos, Gaztelu, and García Vega. Very soon, however, Vitier, Diego, García-Marruz, and Smith took exception to the new government's atheist, Marxist orientation. In 1968 Vitier revealed his ideological conversion with the lecture "El violín" (The Violin), signaling the group's reinsertion into revolutionary culture, but not without reservations.

Likewise, in 1976, with the publication of García Vega's *Los años de Orígenes* (The Years of Orígenes), the group became aware of its most radical and thorough critic, this time from within. García Vega's condemnations persisted in his later memoir *El oficio de perder* (The Profession of Losing, 2004). In *El oficio de perder* García Vega begins taking apart Orígenes with a demystification of their iconography. In addition to his avant-garde aesthetic orientation and his severe criticism of the religious beliefs held by most of the group's members, García Vega injects a political analysis totally contrary to the criticisms made by *Lunes de Revolución*: García Vega attacks *origenista* capitulation to the Castro government.

Following the controversial publication of his *Paradiso* (Paradise) in 1966, the main figure of the Orígenes group, José Lezama Lima, garnered positive reception with the release of *Poesía completa* (Complete Poetry, 1970), *La cantidad hechizada* (The Enchanted Quantity, 1970), and a 1970 *Recopilación de textos* or collection of critical texts on his work published as part of Casa de las Américas' Valoración Múltiple series. However, after the public confession in 1971 of Heberto Padilla (1932–2000) (related to the 1968 publication of his prizewinning book *Fuera del juego* [Out of the Game], for which Lezama had served on the award jury), Lezama was ostracized until his death in 1976. Piñera, his ideological adversary, suffered a similar fate, as did *Lunes de Revolución* critics Padilla, Antón Arrufat (b. 1935), Pablo Armando Fernández (b. 1930), and many others. In a sense, these dramatic events reconciled Lezama and Piñera, as well as Lezama and the part of the Fifties Generation that had been most critical of the Orígenes group; aesthetic differences aside, they had all become victims of an absolute and dogmatic political power.

REHABILITATION

Following the somber 1970s, known as the dark decade or the Five Grey Years (1971–1976), the Orígenes group experienced a revival among critics in books such as *En torno a la obra poética de Fina García-Marruz* (Concerning the Poetic Work of Fina García-Marruz, 1990), *La solución unitiva. Sobre el pensamiento poético de José Lezama Lima* (The Unifying Solution: On the Poetical Thought of José Lezama Lima, 1990), and *Orígenes: La pobreza irradiante* (Orígenes: Irradiant Poverty, 1994) by Jorge Luis Arcos. The well-known critic and essayist Enrique Saínz was one of the major contributors to this reinstatement. This legitimate and necessary rehabilitation in academic studies and publications responded to the political suspicion on the part of the Marxist cultural establishment, which had mistrusted the Orígenes group's religious or "idealistic" worldview and not yet fully appreciated the group's nationalist projections.

But Orígenes' gradual reinsertion into Cuban culture, linked to international political events stemming from the end of the Cold War, made it possible for Vitier and García-Marruz to reinterpret the group on the basis of revolutionary ideological perspectives, thereby putting into effect Vitier's 1968 ideological "conversion." It was not until after 1989, when the Revolution accentuated nationalism, that these reinterpretations received official acceptance (Vitier 1994; García-Marruz). With the colloquium honoring *Orígenes*'s fiftieth anniversary, 1994 was the year when the group was fully admitted into the Revolution's academic and cultural world, and it marked the beginning of a new line of analysis by young writers, especially members of the Diáspora(s) group, as well as Víctor Fowler and Antonio José Ponte. In 2002 Ponte published *El libro perdido de los origenistas* (The Lost Book of the Origenists), having given a controversial lecture in 1994 on García Vega's *Los años de Orígenes* and Vitier's *Ese sol del mundo moral* (The Sun of the Moral World). In the same vein, Duanel Díaz released *Los límites del origenismo* (The Limits of Origenism, 2005) in Madrid, and Rafael Rojas wrote several important essays viewing Orígenes from this new perspective, not at odds with Arcos's new studies on the Orígenes group (2002; 2007).

After the 1990s, Piñera's image was rehabilitated and García Vega's critical perspective and avant-garde creativity were recognized. The same is true of Baquero. Within this multiple and sometimes contradictory process, critics reconsidered some of Vitier's emblematic texts such as *Lo cubano en la poesía* and *Ese sol del mundo moral* (published in Mexico in 1975 and in Cuba in 1995), as well as García-Marruz's *La familia de Orígenes* (The Family of Orígenes, 1997). The latter two books are the clearest representations of the authors' revolutionary and nationalistic ethical reinterpretation, which have been rebuffed by their contemporaries. In this new context, in addition to the emblematic and, in one way or another, everlasting figure of Lezama Lima, his ideological adversary Piñera reemerged vigorously, and Baquero and especially García Vega have been read and studied much more frequently.

ENDURING IMPORTANCE

But beyond these literary, ideological, and generational ups and downs, the group's internal dissidence, the multiple reinterpretations, the extra-literary interferences, and manipulation by critics, there are positive constants within the varying reactions to the Orígenes group. The most general of these is its universalist projection, which coexists with its much disputed *poética de lo cubano* (poetics of Cubanness). Another constant is the writing quality, which its members faithfully upheld despite the hostile environment. Furthermore, the group had a capacity for reinventing itself, demonstrated by Lezama, Piñera, Baquero, and García Vega. Its capacity to create a poetic system of thought within its varied personal poetic styles continued to enlighten readers at the end of the twentieth century (Arcos 1999).

Antonio José Ponte's opinion below shows how the Orígenes legacy is judged today:

> We prefer Orígenes in an open field, facing the elements, scratching at the stone of senselessness and nothingness, anxiously lost and gasping, to the improbable roads of Panglossianism. We prefer what we find in *Los años de Orígenes*, sickly pages that do not arrive at a single certainty, to the certainty we may find in *Ese sol del mundo moral*, for example.
>
> *Ponte p. 103*

This evaluation, though somewhat distant from Orígenes' essentialism or transcendentalism, and paradoxically linked to modernity, ponders Piñera's and García Vega's avant-garde, experimental vocation and projection, and reflects the affinities that the young writers of the 1990s *Diáspora(s)* group have with the once marginal or not-so-central writers in the Orígenes group. Added to this is both tendencies' radical distancing from the Revolution's ideology.

To a great extent, Lezama's protean capacity and furious singularity have saved his work from these critical ups and downs. His open thought, his heterodox worldview, his inexhaustible universality, the intensity of his imagination—his status as a "strong poet," as the American critic Harold Bloom's terms—are some of the traits that distinguish him from the other Orígenes members. The proliferation of academic studies of his work and the recognition he has received from his fellow writers attest to Lezama's work being an inexhaustible treasure. He is a classic, following Jorge Luis Borges's famous reassessment of the term, but as Bloom explains in *The Western Canon*, he is a classic who has not yet depleted his original strangeness.

The singular immersion of the *origenista* literary process within so many contexts of the Cuban Revolution (inside and outside, exiled and insular) has kept alive the controversy surrounding the Orígenes group, perhaps for too long. What should have been relegated to archaeology or a historical reference has defied deterioration because of that singularity. Nonetheless, the Orígenes group remained in the early 2000s one of the most intense and tragically polemic Cuban literary experiences, and some of its writers' works will forever be classics not only of Cuban letters, but of Ibero-American letters.

BIBLIOGRAPHY

Arcos, Jorge Luis. "Las palabras son islas." In *Las palabras son islas. Panorama de la poesía cubana del siglo XX. (1900–1999)*, edited by Jorge Luis Arcos. Havana: Editorial Letras Cubanas, 1999.

Arcos, Jorge Luis. "Los poetas de Orígenes." In *Los poetas de Orígenes*. Mexico City: Fondo de Cultura Económica, 2002.

Arcos, Jorge Luis. "*Orígenes*: Ecumenismo, polémica y trascendencia." In *La palabra perdida. Ensayos sobre poesía y pensamiento poético*. Havana: Ediciones Unión, 2003.

Arcos, Jorge Luis. "*La arena mojada* o el legado de Orígenes." In *Desde el légamo. Ensayos sobre pensamiento poético*. Madrid: Editorial Colibrí, 2007.

Bloom, Harold. *The Western Canon: The Books and School of the Ages*. New York: Harcourt Brace, 1994.

Díaz, Duanel. *Los límites del origenismo*. Madrid: Editorial Colibrí, 2005.

Fernández Retamar, Roberto. *La poesía contemporánea en Cuba (1927–1953)*. Havana: Ediciones Orígenes, 1954.

García-Marruz, Fina. *La familia de Orígenes*. Havana: Ediciones Unión, 1997.

García Vega, Lorenzo. *El oficio de perder*. Puebla, Mexico: Benemérita Universidad Autónoma de Puebla, 2004.

García Vega, Lorenzo. *Los años de Orígenes*. Buenos Aires: Bajo la Luna, 2007.

Lezama Lima, José. *Imagen y posibilidad*. Havana: Editorial Letras Cubanas, 1981.

Lezama Lima, José, and José Rodríguez Feo, eds. *Orígenes. Revista de Arte y Literatura*. Havana, 1944–1956. Facsimile ed. Introduction and author index by

Marcelo Uribe. 7 vols. Madrid: Ediciones Turner, 1989.

Ponte, Antonio José. *El libro perdido de los origenistas*. Mexico City: Editorial Aldus, 2002.

Vitier, Cintio. *Diez poetas cubanos. (1937–1947)*. Havana: Ediciones Orígenes, 1948.

Vitier, Cintio. *Lo cubano en la poesía*. Havana: Editorial Letras Cubanas, 1970.

Vitier, Cintio. *Para llegar a Orígenes*. Havana: Editorial Letras Cubanas, 1994.

Vitier, Cintio. *Ese sol del mundo moral*. Havana: Ediciones Unión, 1995.

Zambrano, María. "La Cuba secreta." In *Orígenes. Revista de Arte y Literatura. Havana, 1944–1956*, edited by José Lezama Lima and José Rodríguez Feo. Madrid: Ediciones Turner, 1989.

P

PALO MONTE AND ANCESTRAL SPIRITS: THE ART OF JOSÉ BEDIA

Orlando Hernández

The work of visual artist José Bedia and its relationship to the Afro-Cuban Palo Monte religion.

José Bedia (b. 1959) was the first Cuban artist who, in the mid-1980s, began depicting the cultural and religious world of the Palo Monte community. The originality, erudition, and respect with which Bedia approached this Afro-Cuban religious tradition, which originated in the Congo (Bakongo, Kongo, or Bantu), brought such visibility and popularity to his subject that many believe it was his sole artistic subject, which is not true; Bedia's work is extraordinarily complex and his subjects cover a much wider range.

STUDY OF INDIGENOUS CULTURES

Bedia's early works of the late 1970s deal with the old Mesoamerican Mayan and Aztec cultures and the cultures of the Lakota people and other Native American prairie communities. He later included indigenous cultures that are part of modern Mexico; Brazil's popular tradition (the Cangaceiros); heroes, patriots, and bandits from popular Caribbean mythology; Peruvian Amazon jungle cultures (the Shipibo-Conibo, the Asháninca); sub-Saharan African traditional cultures; and Afro-Cuban culture. Given the breadth of his subjects, it is clear that Bedia sought to recover and articulate the societies and groups that the old anthropology designated as primitive, savage, tribal, and premodern. According to Bedia, they have much to contribute to modernity, which he considers incomplete without them. In the early 2000s these communities are made up of both direct descendants and new followers; they represent those indigenous peoples whom European and U.S. colonizers devalued and tried in vain to

destroy, because of their false assumption that these societies resisted development and were a hindrance to progress. These religious and cultural societies, marginalized by colonialism and its so-called modernity, inspired José Bedia's art; the Afro-Cuban Palo Monte community is just one part of this indigenous universe, but because of its proximity to the artist's life, it central to his work.

It is important to note that Bedia does not address these subjects in an exploitative or opportunistic manner; that is to say, he does not simply take advantage of the aesthetic appeal of cultural expressions that are often perceived as exotic. Instead, they influenced him to the point that they change his work, his aesthetic conceptions, and even his life and beliefs. His is an unusual cross-cultural process in which the modern, so-called civilized artist attempts to assume the identity (or identities) of those societies and groups.

ENCOUNTERS AND INITIATION WITH THE PALO MONTE

At the beginning of his career, Bedia approached those societies academically, by studying relevant publications in archaeology and anthropology. Later, he encountered members of these communities directly and participated in their ceremonies. To learn more, Bedia emigrated from Cuba to Mexico in 1991 and then to the United States in 1993. But before that, the proximity of the Palo Monte religion, which was practiced in his own neighborhood in Havana, offered him the first and most influential of all his direct contacts, especially after his own 1983 *rayamiento* (initiation) as a *tata nkisi malongo* (priest) in the Briyumba Cotalima branch under the guidance of his godfather, Alberto Goicochea. With this religious initiation, Bedia began to understand, from the inside, how a traditional culture actually functions.

Also in 1983, as a member of a cultural detachment sent to Angola by the Cuban government, Bedia got a chance to meet people in the area where Palo Monte originated. After that trip he returned to Africa many times, continuing to meet and learn from groups in Kenya, Egypt, Botswana, Zambia, and South Africa.

■ *See also*

Diasporas: Cubans Abroad, Post-1959

Visual Arts: Revolutionary Period

Yaya, Yayita, Kinfuto (1992), by José Bedia. The work of artist José Bedia (b. 1959) connects nature and the spiritual world by embracing the wisdom of the ancestors, especially the ancient traditions of Africa. PRIVATE COLLECTION/PHOTO © CHRISTIE'S IMAGES/THE BRIDGEMAN ART LIBRARY

Although he learned a lot on these trips, Bedia was able to verify what he had long suspected: Much of what he was looking for in Africa was already in Cuba. Also, in 1985 Bedia apprenticed with Leonard Crow Dog, a Lakota medicine man on the Rosebud reservation in South Dakota, an experience that helped Bedia see similarities among various traditional cultures.

A BRIEF OVERVIEW OF PALO MONTE

The Rule of Palo Monte worships Nsambi or Sambi-ampungo, the Supreme Being, as well as *mpungos*, or energies in nature that have been deified, and *nfumbes*,

or spirits of the dead. The religion reached Cuba via Congolese slaves as early as the sixteenth century, but much of its philosophy entered Cuba gradually until slave trading was prohibited and then slavery itself was abolished in 1886. Over time, its adherents came to include not only slaves who were natives of the Congo and their descendants, but also Africans of different tribes and, later, Cubans of various ethnicities. Most of the ritualistic and symbolic aspects of Palo Monte were kept secret except from its initiates, as was the case with other African religious traditions that became part of Cuban culture (e.g., Rule of Ocha or Santería,

Ifá, Rule Arará, and the Abakuá Secret Society). Some rituals and symbols were described in ethnographic studies, but they rarely appeared in the visual arts. Their inclusion in Bedia's early works, which were directly about Palo Monte, was met with surprise.

MAKING VISIBLE THE INVISIBLE

José Bedia incorporated Palo Monte by depicting its *mpungos* (deities, including Sarabanda, Nsasi or Siete rayos, Nkuyo or Lucero, Mama Kalunga or Baluande, Chola Wengue, Coballende or Tata Pansua, and others) and its *nfumbes* (spirits of the dead), who up to then had been invisible, incorporeal entities. Bedia also portrayed practitioners in some of the religion's rites as well as its sacred objects, especially the *nganga* (*nkisi, kindembo, malongo*), a kettle or cauldron that is a magical receptacle made up of elements from nature, such as earth, bones, rocks, and especially *palos del monte* (wood from the forest), the origin of the most common name for the religion. He made use of its pictorial symbolism (*mpembas, patimpembas,* or simply *signatures* inscribed during rituals using plaster or white chalk) and transcribed words and phrases from the language of the ritual and from the *mambos* (songs) used during its ceremonies, incorporating them into his titles or into messages written into his works. Bedia left these words and messages in the Palero language—the Bantú spoken in Cuba (a mixture of Ki-kongo and Spanish)—untranslated, thus creating a barrier to uninitiated viewers who know nothing about these practices. By not translating the words, he showed respect for Palo Monte cultural and religious identity and he avoided trivializing beliefs associated with it.

Bedia's work exhibits a different kind of rationality, another way of understanding reality. It connects nature and the spiritual world by embracing the wisdom of the ancestors, especially the ancient people of Africa. It attempts to resolve in a different way many of the conflicts and problems that afflict modern people. José Bedia admits that his work can be seen as a kind of recycling of ancient wisdom that in modern times is fragmented and unfocused. In this sense, he feels he is its heir and transmitter. Exploration of Palo Monte helped Bedia express many historical, social, and political ideas relevant to contemporary Cuba and Cubans, including the dramas of their migrations and the feelings and concerns of Cubans inside and outside of Cuba. It has also helped the artist understand events in his own life. In this sense, Palo Monte occupies a special place in José Bedia's thought and artistic expression.

BIBLIOGRAPHY

Bedia, José. Oral history. Interview conducted by Juan Martínez, Miami, Florida, 13 February 1998. Archives of American Art, Smithsonian Institution. Available from http://www.aaa.si.edu/collections/oralhistories/transcripts/bedia98.htm.

Bedia, José. *Obra, 1978–2006.* Edited by Omar Pascual Castillo. Madrid: Galería Ramis Barquet/TURNER, 2007.

Bolívar Aróstegui, Natalia, and Carmen González Días de Villegas. *Ta Makuende Yaya y las reglas de Palo Monte.* Havana: Ediciones Unión, 1998.

Cabrera, Lydia. *El Monte. Igbo. Finda. Ewe orisha. Vititi Nfinda.* Miami: Ediciones Universal, 1975.

Cabrera, Lydia. *Vocabulario Congo.* Miami: Colección del Chicherekú en el exilio, 1984.

PARADISO (JOSÉ LEZAMA LIMA)

Jorge Luis Arcos

An all-inclusive novel of lo maravilloso natural.

The publication of the novel *Paradiso* (1966), and its unfinished sequel *Oppiano Licario* (1977), by José Lezama Lima (1910–1976), represents a singular achievement in the Latin American novel of the twentieth century. Although *Paradiso* can be read as a bildungsroman, it is also the most ambitious attempt in literature written in Spanish to express a poetic view of reality in narrative form. The novel follows the coordinates of the poetic system of the world laid out by Lezama Lima in numerous essays, including *Analecta del reloj* (1953), *La expresión americana* (The American Expression, 1957), *Tratados en La Habana* (Treated in Havana, 1958), *La cantidad hechizada* (The Bewitched Quantity, 1970), and *Imagen y posibilidad* (Image and Possibility, 1981), particularly his theory of the image.

Paradiso is the incarnation of his system in an historical image. As Lezama Lima explained, if poetry showed him the "bewitched quantity," and his essays, "the hypostasis of poetry in what I have called the imaginary eras," then his novel gave him the means to express his system within the kingdom of this world (Simón, p. 16). His poetry possessed an unusual metapoetic density, with an eros of knowledge unequaled in the Spanish language that even sacrificed lyric quality in the service of expressing a poetic image of the universe; with *Paradiso* he sought to crown in narrative form both the poetic cosmovision that infused his poetry and its discursive expression as developed in his essays. This poetic—recombinant—quality of his novel also sacrificed traditional narrative, yielding to the acquisition of poetic senses in order to interpret the whole of reality comprehensively.

PLOT

As the novel begins, the young protagonist José Cemí suffers an asthma attack, in which he is symbolically accompanied by the Catholic Trinity, as expressed

■ *See also*

Literature: Fiction in the Revolutionary Period

The Orígenes Group and Journal

Sexuality: Revolutionary Period

José Lezama Lima (1910–1976). The novel *Paradiso* (1966), by José Lezama Lima, ranks as one of the most ambitious attempts in Spanish-language literature to express a poetic view of reality in narrative form. CORTESIA/NOTIMEX/NEWSCOM

by the narrator. The following chapters develop his family's history, the mystery of friendship, Cemí's vocation for writing, and the experience of the death of his father (chapter 6); the effect that loss has on his sensitivity to the invisible world, which also is influenced by his Catholic upbringing (chapter 3); sexual initiations (chapter 8); university life as an example of the acquisition of knowledge (chapter 11); the influence of his Uncle Alberto (chapter 7), who reveals to him the carnality in words; maternal company and protection (chapter 10); dreams, the abolition of time (chapter 12) and space (chapter 13); and, finally, the decisive encounter with the poetic image through an archetypal master, Oppiano Licario (chapter 14).

The plot of the novel was well synthesized and explicated by Cintio Vitier in the second Cuban edition of the novel, which did not appear until 1991 because of the scandal that accompanied the novel's first publication in 1966, when it was removed from some bookstores and criticized as pornographic, homosexual, and even unrevolutionary. In 1988 Vitier coordinated the critical edition published that year by UNESCO's Colección Archivos and reprinted in 1996. The first five chapters and part of the final chapter, "Oppiano Licario" (1953), were originally published between 1949 and 1955 in the magazine *Orígenes*, and not identified as part of the novel. Chapters 6 through 9 were written between 1955 and 1961. Chapter 10 is dated as having been started in

January 1962—though Vitier suggests that it may have been before 1959—and certain parts of the final chapter 14 may have been written shortly before the book was sent to the printer. Vitier demonstrates that part of the first chapter of the original manuscript of *Oppiano Licario* was incorporated into chapter 11 of *Paradiso* (Lezama Lima 1996). Some have speculated that the author delayed publication of his novel until after the death of his mother in 1964. In any case, some of the final chapters were certainly completed after this date.

Through three characters, José Cemí, Ricardo Fronesis, and Foción, Lezama portrays the gradual acquisition of a poetic way of thinking and feeling in a narrative spiral that stretches from childhood to adolescence and the early years of youth, primarily through his autobiographical character, Cemí. Cemí is mesmerized by the mysterious figure of Oppiano Licario (another of the author's alter egos), the embodiment of the imago, its spatial and temporal ubiquity, its simultaneous existence in the world of history and in the otherworld, and the central subject of his poetic system of the world, resurrection.

LANGUAGE

Paradiso—and its sequel *Oppiano Licario*—is distinguished from other novels of the so-called Latin American boom by its preeminent mythopoetic projection. It does, however, share with many other novels—*Terra nostra* (Our Land, 1975), by Carlos Fuentes (b. 1928); *Bomarzo* (1962), by Manuel Mujica Láinez (1910–1984); *Adán Buenosayres* (1948), by Leopoldo Marechal (1900–1970); *Rayuela* (Hopscotch, 1963), by Julio Cortázar (1914–1984); *Conversación en la catedral* (Conversation in the Cathedral, 1975), by Mario Vargas Llosa (b. 1936); *Yo, el Supremo* (I, the Supreme, 1974), by Augusto Roa Bastos (1917–2005); *Grande sertão: Veredas* (The Devil to Pay in the Backlands, 1956), by João Guimarães Rosa (1908–1967); *Cien años de soledad* (One Hundred Years of Solitude, 1967), by Gabriel García Márquez (b. 1927); *Tres tristes tigres* (Three Trapped Tigers, 1967), by Guillermo Cabrera Infante (1929–2005)—an imperative to establish a worldview, a creative spirit, and a language, all distinctly baroque, a "language turned into nature" (Lezama Lima 1996, p. 170). This, despite the fact that at the end of his life, Lezama Lima objected to the labeling of his work as baroque (Lezama Lima 2000, pp. 245–246). He preferred the generative, open-ended, creative qualities of the baroque apart from its affiliation with a particular movement (Arcos 2007).

The critic Roberto Friol noted that "in *Paradiso* there is a *review*, a *chronicling* of the Cuban novel and the universal novel" and that "Lezama's syntax is a sum of the stages Spanish has passed through over the centuries, which he propelled in new directions" (p. 562). But the most unusual aspect of his language is, without a doubt, its roots in poetry.

POETIC AND HISTORICAL VISION OF CUBANIDAD

Paradiso espouses an ontological theory about what is Cuban (*lo cubano*) that is quite close to Lezama's notion of an historical vision developed in *La expresión americana*, which is enriched by a poetic ethos, also called *pobreza irradiante* (radiant poverty) ("A partir de la poesía," Lezama Lima 1970). The term *pobreza irradiante* became polemical due to how it was later used by fellow writers Cintio Vitier (2001) and Fina García Marruz (1997) to justify an ascetic national *telos* or purpose linked to the vicissitudes of the Cuban Revolution. Beyond its indisputable historical reference to post-1959 hardships, the term preserves meanings of religious and classical ethico-philosophical origin that Lezama Lima used to give sense to his participation in "the creative process of the nation" (Lezama Lima 1981, p. 172). It also incarnated his cultural and ethical attitude during the years of the Cuban Republic, whose history he regarded as spurious. Lezama Lima's thesis of the future incarnation of poetry in history (Lezama Lima 1981, pp. 164, 169, 170, 172, 196, 197, 198), the making of a future-conscious tradition (*tradición por futuridad*), and his notion of prophecy (Lezama Lima 1981, p. 166), certainly led to great contradictions when, in the early 1960s, he declared the Cuban Revolution the last of the "imaginary eras," Lezama's roster of great poetic epochs; still, the significance of these notions should not be reduced to this one historical event.

Lezama's ontology of *lo cubano* was similar to other ontological projects such as *mexicanidad* (Mexicanness), *españolidad* (Spanishness), *argentinidad* (Argentinness), or *peruanidad* (Peruvianness). In this regard, *Paradiso* is an intensive incursion in the search for a *cubanidad* (the essence of being Cuban), albeit quite different from that outlined by Cintio Vitier in his classic and polemical essay *Lo cubano en la poesía* (Cubanness and Poetry, 1957). Vitier's idea of an "insular teleology" (Cuba's final fate as an island culture; Vitier 1984, p. 278) should be distinguished from Lezama's, which the latter first proposed in *Coloquio con Juan Ramón Jiménez* (*Conversation with Juan Ramón Jiménez*, 1938) and which reached its peak in *Paradiso* and *Oppiano Licario*. This debate involved the dialectic between the national and the universal, which Lezama summarized in his editorial note "Razón que sea" (Whatever the Reason, 1939) with his famous phrase "the island, distinct in the Cosmos, or, same thing, the island indistinct within Cosmos" (Lezama Lima 1981, p. 198). Vitier's unilateral interpretation of Cuba's *telos* does not reflect the broad open-endedness of Lezama's vision: "to create a future-conscious tradition" (Lezama Lima 1981, p. 196) or its imbrication in the Latin American cultural history, one that is, according to Lezama, "joyously surging towards the unknown" (1981, p. 196). The theories about "historical vision" developed in *La expresión americana* and about the "imaginary eras" in *La cantidad hechizada* prevent the reduction of any of his poetic categories to a concrete historic event such as the Revolution. In this sense, there is a clear difference between Lezama's interpretation of a secret Cuba—a kind of poetically rooted, Cuban philosophical ontology, first suggested by María Zambrano in *Orígenes* in 1948—and Vitier's position. Finally, the solemnity and essentialism in Vitier's and García Marruz's poetics of Cubanness are at odds with Lezama's heterodoxy and dialogism, so full of humor and irony, and with his relativistic perspective, always open to the unpredictable. A reading of Lezama's correspondence, or his posthumous collection of poems *Fragmentos a su imán* (*Fragments Drawn by Charm*, 1977), or even *Oppiano Licario*, refutes the narrow teleological reading of Lezama by Vitier or García Marruz, notwithstanding the many valuable insights in their numerous essays on Lezama (Vitier 2001; García Marruz 1997).

LO MARAVILLOSO NATURAL

But Lezama also proposes a singular poetics in *Paradiso*—*lo maravilloso natural* (natural wondrousness) (1996, pp. 338, 516)—similar to Alejo Carpentier's *lo real maravilloso* (marvelous real), Gabriel García Márquez's *realismo mágico* (magic realism), and Juan Rulfo's notion of the porosity between this world and the next.

In *Paradiso* culture becomes nature, history becomes image, and vice versa. A sort of unifying solution between life and literature, *Paradiso* offers a knowledge derived simultaneously from wisdom and experience, a wisdom rooted in poetry, similar to the creative aporia of his friend the Spanish philosopher María Zambrano, *la razón poética* (poetic reason). Through the image of a second nature, Lezama created a supernatural just as real, vigorous, and operational as reality itself, containing a dialectic between what is closest and what is most distant, between this world and the other, or in his words, *entre lo telúrico y lo estelar* (between the telluric and the stellar). According to Lezama, *Paradiso* sought to present "the sacred character of the total journey of man" (Simón p. 27), or "the image operating in history, with the same creational power that sperm has in the siring of a child" (1981, p. 176).

In chapter 8 of *Paradiso* Lezama re-creates the discovery of sexuality in adolescence. Nevertheless, a unique vision of sexuality or creative eroticism runs through the entire novel, linked closely with his poetic category of *Eros de la lejanía* (Eros in the Distance). With *Oppiano Licario* it became evident that Lezama tried to reconcile the subject of homosexuality within the global coordinates of his poetic system of the world. A sort of *logos spermatikos* (the generative principle of the Universe, according to the Stoics) runs through *Paradiso*. This creational eroticism underpins Lezama's theory of the image and worldview. A passage from the novel helps illustrate this argument:

"This mingling of taste produced an infinite sexuality warmed by the memory of an impossible touch, which the body will blindly reconstruct in the distance and the sound of cascades" (1996, p. 88).

Lezama Lima's poetic cosmovision is fulfilled through the acquisition of several poetic senses: "*Paradiso* will be understood beyond the realm of reason. Its presence will see the birth of new senses," wrote the author (1996, p. 716). In *Paradiso*, Lezama renews poetic sensibility by devising a new poetic sensorium, term by term. He speaks of an "eros of distance" or "of knowledge," that is, the readiness to respond to stimulii or signs that beckon from a faraway "alien" realm; the vocation for relating the invisible (that which can only be perceived by trace or absence) with the visible, what is remote with what is proximate, the unknown with the known. In *Paradiso* these notions are closely linked to a creative conception of sexuality or eroticism in which nature and art seem to act in conjunction: biological and nonbiological reproduction can gestate by way of "the gaze or the grunt" or through dreams, or through an "impossible touching," while dreams open a path to knowledge or water is invested with the power of genesis, or the senses are intensely heightened, or memory becomes hyperbolic and all-knowing (as in chapter 11). One example is the magical, mysterious stillness of gazing or intent looking in the novel be it luminous, thanatic, or maternal, such as the gaze that activates the "resurrection" of the image of the Colonel while Rialta and the children play with *yaqui* pieces on the floor in chapter 7 (1996, p. 331; Arcos 1994). Overall, as the author himself noted in his novel, "everything had to *be* and had to penetrate first through the senses *before* being" (Lezama Lima 1996, p. 27; trans. Gregory Rabassa).

Beginning with Julio Cortázar's felicitous inaugural review "Para llegar a José Lezama Lima" (Approaching José Lezama Lima; Simón p. 146), *Paradiso* has amassed a copious critical bibliography (Lezama Lima 1996). In a survey carried out by *Time* magazine on the eve of the current millennium, *Paradiso* was listed among the ten most outstanding novels of the twentieth century.

BIBLIOGRAPHY

Arcos, Jorge Luis. "José Lezama Lima a través de *Paradiso*." In *Orígenes: La pobreza irradiante*. Havana: Editorial Letras Cubanas, 1994.

Arcos, Jorge Luis. "El Señor Barroco José Lezama Lima." In *Desde el légamo. Ensayos sobre pensamiento poético*. Madrid: Editorial Colibrí, 2007.

Friol, Roberto. "Paradiso En Su Primer Círculo." In *Paradiso*, by José Lezama Lima. Critical 2nd ed. Edited by Cintio Vitier. Paris: ALLCA XX, 1996.

García Marruz, Fina. "Por Dador de José Lezama Lima." In *Recopilación de textos sobre José Lezama Lima*, edited by Pedro Simón. Havana: Casa de las Américas, 1970.

García Marruz, Fina. "La poesía es un caracol nocturne." Coloquio Internacional sobre la obra de José Lezama Lima. Poesía. Espiral / Fundamentos, Madrid, Centro de Investigaciones Latinoamericanas, University of Poitiers, France, 1984.

García Marruz, Fina. *La familia de Orígenes*. Havana: Ediciones Unión, 1997.

Lezama Lima, José. *Coloquio con Juan Ramón Jiménez*. Havana: Direccion de cultura, 1938.

Lezama Lima, José. "Mitos y cansancio clásico." *La expresión americana*. Havana: Instituto Nacional de Cultura, 1957.

Lezama Lima, José. *Paradiso*. Havana: Ediciones Unión, 1966.

Lezama Lima, José. *La cantidad hechizada*. Havana: Ediciones Unión, 1970.

Lezama Lima, José. *Oppiano Licario*. Mexico: Ediciones Era, 1977.

Lezama Lima, José. *Imagen y posibilidad*. Havana: Editorial Letras Cubanas, 1981.

Lezama Lima, José. *Paradiso*. Critical 2nd ed. Edited by Cintio Vitier. Paris: ALLCA XX, 1996.

Lezama Lima, José. *Como las cartas no llegan*. Havana: Letras Cubanas, 2000.

Simón, Pedro, ed. *Recopilación de textos sobre José Lezama Lima*. Havana: Casa de las Américas, 1970.

Vitier, Cintio. "De las cartas que me escribió Lezama." Coloquio Internacional sobre la obra de José Lezama Lima. Poesía. Espiral / Fundamentos, Madrid, Centro de Investigaciones Latinoamericanas, University of Poitiers, France, 1984.

Vitier, Cintio. "Introduction." In *Paradiso*, by José Lezama Lima. Havana: Editorial Letras Cubanas, 1991.

Vitier, Cintio. *Obras 4: Crítica 2*. Havana: Editorial Letras Cubanas, 2001.

Zambrano, María. "La Cuba secreta." *Orígenes* 20 (1948): 63–69.

PERFORMING ARTS

Theater and dance have a long tradition in Cuba, a country that as early as the beginning of the nineteenth century was already one of the capitals for ballet, zarzuela, and opera. The popularity of zarzuela and opera has since faded, but since the 1959 Cuban Revolution the Cuban school of ballet is recognized as one of the most important in the world.

Folk dances of African origin were preserved outside of cultured settings until the Conjunto Folklórico Nacional de Cuba (National Folkloric Dance Troupe of Cuba) was founded in 1960; in recent decades, folk dances with Spanish roots have also been popular, and highly skilled companies have emerged. Likewise, the Conjunto Nacional de Danza Moderna (National Modern Dance Troupe) was founded at the start of the 1960s. After the Revolution, both folk dance of African origin and modern dance were promoted and their presence multiplied.

Popular dance is an element of cultural unity among Cubans. Such dances as rhumba, cha cha cha, and casino-style salsa had a major impact in the twentieth century. Casino-style salsa arose in the 1950s but achieved its fullest expression in the 1960s and 1970s.

Cuba's real-world circumstances, identity, and culture can be found in the theater. Essays trace the historic development of Cuban theater and review Bufo theater.

PERFORMING ARTS: CUBAN FORMS OF POPULAR DANCE

Graciela Chao Carbonero

The origin and development of folkloric and popular Cuban dances.

The roots of popular Cuban dances, like other expressions of traditional popular Cuban culture, have two foundations: the European and the African. Contemporary dances that originate in the different African cultures brought to Cuba by the slaves belong to the syncretic or juxtaposed faiths and are practiced in various rituals and ceremonial parties, in which dance, songs, and drums are an intrinsic part of the celebration. Some important examples are the dances dedicated to the *orishás* or saints of the Cuban Regla de Ocha or Santería of Yoruba origin; the *palo* dance of the Regla de Palo Monte of Bantu origin; the dances dedicated to the *vodunes* or *fodunes* in the Regla de Arara that originated in the culture of *ewe-fon*, a faith that was reinforced by Haitian immigration to the island after the 1920s; and the *ireme* or *diablito* dance of the Abakuá Secret Society of Calabar, now Cameroon. There are also some dances now separated from the religious element, such as the *yuca* and the *makut* from the Congo and the Haitians' *band-rara*. All of these gave rise to the rhumba complex and the various carnival-style congas.

THE RHUMBA

Rhumba is an expression of popular culture that involves a collective party disconnected from ritual. People say, "Let's go to a rhumba," when they want to play drums, sing, dance, or just participate as an observer.

The rhumba originated in the nineteenth century mostly in Havana and Matanzas, and it later spread to other cities. Its main representations are the *yambu*, an individual dance between a man and a woman that has been known as the rhumba from Spanish times and has a historic quality, as well as the mimetic rhumbas in which the dancers enact the lyrics sung by a soloist.

The most popular ones are "Mama'buela" (Mama Grandma), "Lala no sabe hacer ná" (Lala Doesn't Know How to Do Anything), "El papalote" (The Kite), and "El gavilan" (The Hawk). The last two were converted to rural versions in the province of Ciego de Avila.

Another important rhumba genre is the *guaguanco*. In the first segment, the soloist improvises lyrics that everybody listens to, and in the second segment the *capetillo* (chorus) responds and the rhumba *rompe* (breaks out) when a couple starts dancing. The guaguanco is characterized by the *vacunao*, a gesture in which the man moves his pelvis, hands, feet, or head toward the woman's pelvis, denoting the sexual act, while she covers herself with her hands in an erotic game. Several researchers believe the origin of the guaguanco is the *yuca* dance from Congo.

The *columbia* is a form of rhumba danced by men only. It is a competition: Each rhumba dancer adds or improvises variations of movements and steps that his competitor must outdo. This rhumba has rural origins, possibly in El Chucho deMena, near the town of Columbia in Matanzas (where its name comes from). Many of its steps and movement are clearly influenced by the *ireme abakuá*.

THE CONGA

The conga is a simple figurative dance that is present in carnival-float choreographies through different themes, songs, outfits, and other forms. In Havana, these include the Alacran, the Jardineras, the Bolleras, the Guaracheros de Regla. The *comparsas* of Los Hoyos, and the Paso Franco of Santiago de Cuba are other examples from elsewhere. The ballroom conga is performed by professional groups and bands and danced to by everybody at the end of a party.

POPULAR BALLROOM DANCES

The popular ballroom dances of the eighteenth and nineteenth centuries such as the *cuadrillas de Lanceros* (Lancers quadrille), the *rigodon*, the *contradanza* (contredanse), the *vals vienes* (Viennese waltz), the *polca* (polka), and the *mazurca* (mazurka) originated in Europe and were brought to Cuba and other countries of the New World. Many of these dances became part of the local folklore by being creolized (Cubanized)

■ *See also*

Enrique Jorrín and the Cha-cha-cha

Havana: Havana as Cultural Center

The "Mambo King": Dámaso Pérez Prado

Son Innovations: Arsenio Rodríguez

"Queen of Salsa": Celia Cruz

and by descending from the great city ballrooms to the small towns and popular neighborhoods.

It was unquestionably the contradanza that became the most significant. It arrived in the island in many forms: Spanish contradanza in Havana, English contredanse when the city was seized in 1762, and French contredanse in Santiago de Cuba via the mass immigration of French colonists fleeing the Haitian Revolution in the late eighteenth century. Some domestic slaves immigrated along with the French colonists and later founded the Tumba Francesa societies, where they practiced (and continue to practice into the early 2000s) the *mason*, the *yuba*, and the *frente*, which derive from ballroom dances but are accompanied by drums.

Fusion is ongoing because the same people who attend ritual parties also go to the rhumbas, dances, or popular *verbenas* for entertainment. Although they dance to different genres every time, they inadvertently and spontaneously transfer movements, steps, and subtleties from one genre to the other in perfect symbiosis.

After the musical elements and choreography of the Spanish contradanza became popular at the beginning of the nineteenth century, the dance metamorphosed into the Cuban contradanza, which gave way to the *danza*, the *habanera*, and the *danzón*, and in the twentieth century to the *danzonete*, the *danzón de ritmo nuevo*, the mambo, and the cha-cha-cha. The 1950s brought the choreography genres casino and *rueda de casino*, known in other countries as Cuban-style salsa.

The casino of the 1950s continues to develop as a choreography genre because of the dancers' creativity. Its dancers are constantly inventing new figures or incorporating steps from other Cuban dances or from foreign dances such as the twist or the lambada. It does not have its own music like other dances do. Although it appeared before salsa music, it can be danced to salsa, to a modern *son*, to a *timba*, to a *guaracha*, to a *songo* (a genre created by the musician Juan Formel), or to any other Cuban genre.

From a musical standpoint, the danzón, the danzonete, the danzón de ritmo nuevo, and the cha-cha-cha all have known creators, but in regard to their choreography, they were created and developed by the people. They are examples of traditional popular dances, which combine several elements:

Assimilation and adaptation of trendy foreign choreographies that reached the island;

Integration of elements from different Cuban dances of the same era, as occurred with the danzón and the urban son or son habanero; and

creation and generalization of new forms based on good dancers' original improvisations that contain formal, constant elements where everybody begins

the dance in a closed social dance or waltz position and follows a basic step that fits the specific style and rhythm and is done at the four eighth notes of a two-by-four beat (spins are also done at this position).

Other popular Cuban music genres such as the mambo, the *pilon*, and the Mozambique were short-lived trends because their steps and figures were not created by the masses but by choreographers or professional cabaret dancers or show dancers.

THE *ZAPATEO* AND THE *SON*

The *Zapateo*, a Cuban tap dance, was performed originally by rural people in parties called *guateques* in the eighteenth and nineteenth centuries. It is a dance in which a couple dances alone, displaying gallantry and skill. Its roots could be in Andalusia or the Canary Islands. It had local variations, but it languished in times of war during the second half of the nineteenth century and was replaced by the son at the turn of the century. With the arrival of the Republic, it was revived under the name Zapateo Nacional and performed by schoolchildren at civic and patriotic events. It is still practiced at the Fiesta de los Bandos in the town of Majagua, Ciego de Ávila.

The son originates in the mountainous regions of the east and thus has been called *montuno* (from the mountains). Some scholars believe that it comes from the *changüi* from Guantanamo, but others believe the opposite—that the changüi is a local variation of the *son montuno*. The son moved from the eastern province of Oriente to Havana in 1909, carried by soldiers. The bass and trumpet were added later to the son's instrumental band, creating sextets and septets such as the Sexteto Habanero in 1920.

Since its beginnings, the son has been danced by couples in an interlaced or waltz position. It has many variations throughout the country; some of the best known are the *sones mimeticos* from the provinces of Ciego de Avila and Las Tunas, which some musicologists consider *rumbitas campesinas* (countryside rhumbas) because, as in the mimetic rhumbas, the dancers perform movements that correspond to the lyrics but are accompanied by music typical of the son. Another variation of the son is the *sucu-sucu* typical of Isla de Pinos (now Isla de la Juventud), but without doubt the most popular son is Havana's *son habanero* (urban son), which adapted steps and figures from the danzón with freer movements of the hips and shoulders. From the musical standpoint, the son, with its montuno section, has often been incorporated into the danzón.

Few other countries besides Cuba have produced so many popular dances that have had such an impact internationally. The steps of the rhumba, conga, danzón, mambo, cha-cha-cha, and casino, often formalized for ballroom dances, can be seen in many movies and television programs all over the world.

Dancing to *son*.
Partygoers in Baracoa dance to traditional *son* music, 2 May 2005.
© BOB SACHA/CORBIS

BIBLIOGRAPHY

Balbuena Gutiérrez, Bárbara. *Las celebraciones rituales festivas en la Regla de Ocha*. Havana: Centro de Investigación y Desarrollo de la Cultura Juan Marinello, 2001.

Carpentier, Alejo. *La música a en Cuba*. Havana: Editorial Letras Cubanas, 1979.

Chao Carbonero, Graciela. *De la contradanza cubana al casino*. Havana: Editorial Adagio, 2006.

Chao Carbonero, Graciela. *El baile de y para los orishas en el Tambor de santo*. Havana: Editorial Adagio, 2008.

Ortiz, Fernando. *La Africanía de la música folklórica de Cuba*. Havana: Ediciones Cárdenas y Cía, 1950.

Pérez de la Riva, Francisco. *La Isla de Cuba en el siglo XIX vista por extranjeros*. Havana: Editorial Ciencias Sociales, 1979.

PERFORMING ARTS: DANCE: BALLET

Francisco Rey Alfonso

Development of ballet in Cuba from the nineteenth into the twenty-first century.

In Cuba, ballet is as old as the country's theatrical tradition, but its history has been plagued by an array of problems.

The opening of the Coliseum Theater, later called the Principal (Havana, 1775–1846), was a turning point in the history of Cuban culture: After that time, the island had a venue where it could properly present performances, including dance, which for decades was the least popular form of entertainment in Cuba. That attitude did not prevent the arrival of dancers of various nationalities to perform on the island, though they were unable to overcome the taint of exoticism that the *criollos* attributed to this art form. This and other prejudices made it difficult to aspire to be a dancer or choreographer. However, the influx from abroad increased as the country developed, and early on ballet artists contributed a significant work: *La fille mal gardée* (The Wayward Daughter, 1816).

THE FIRST RISE AND DECLINE

When husband and wife team María and André Pautret arrived on the scene in 1820, dance overcame its status as second-rate entertainment. At that time, it could compete even with opera. Because of these artists, the principles of *ballet d'action* as conceived by Jean-Georges Noverre (1727–1810) took root in Cuba; this aesthetic was portrayed in works such as *Médée et Jason* (Medea and Jason, 1781).

The brilliance of that period reappeared during the romantic era (1839–1866), when numerous interpretations of works typical of that style, including *La Sylphide* (The Sylph, 1841), *Giselle* (1849), and *La Esmeralda* (The Emerald, 1850), were performed. The ballet phenomenon engulfed Havana and other cities as never before, and its richness influenced other art forms. The opening of the Gran Teatro de Tacón in 1838—at the time, one of the world's best theaters—and the performances of Fanny Elssler (1841, 1842), a star whose dancing created a frenzy among Cubans, were catalysts for popular acceptance of ballet.

■ *See also*

Classical Composers: Amadeo Roldán

Havana: Havana as Cultural Center

After the romantic zenith came a decline, which was partly due to the Wars of Independence (1868–1878, 1879, 1895–1898). During the last quarter of the nineteenth century, the performances of Amalia Lepri in 1879 to 1880 stood out. Also significant were the contributions of her father Giovanni, one of the most important ballet masters of his time. Amalia Lepri's performances emphasized a characteristic of that era: the subordination of other types of performances (she danced for a zarzuela company), which continued until 1930, particularly because of the popularity of opera.

The early years of the twentieth century gave no indication of a recovery; the premiere of *Coppélia* (1904) was the only significant event prior to the performances of Anna Pávlova (1915, 1917, 1918–1919), another legend in the history of choreography and dance. The visits by Pávlova contributed to retrospective works such as *La mort du cigne* (The Dying Swan) and selections from *Raymonda* and *The Sleeping Beauty*.

THE BOOM IN STYLE

A new era dawned thanks to the Ballet School of the Sociedad Pro-Arte Musical de La Habana (Musical Pro-Arts Society of Havana, 1931–1967). The work of this society gradually changed Cubans' view of ballet as exotic, and allowed it to be practiced with institutional backing. What began modestly soon expanded, and the society ultimately launched several generations of ballet dancers and teachers.

One factor that contributed to this development was the school's association with the dancers Alicia (b. 1920), Alberto (1917–2008), and Fernando Alonso (b. 1914)—students who later became collaborators. These three talents—especially Alicia, the ultimate prima ballerina and one of the century's greatest artists—were successful both in Cuba and abroad, and their triumphs encouraged the growth of the society. Another factor was the performances by major ballet dancers and companies, contracted by the Pro-Arte Society and other organizations, such as Alicia Markova, Anton Dolin, the Ballet Caravan, the Original Ballet Russe, and the Ballet Theatre.

Both these factors prompted the creation of the country's first professional company, the Alicia Alonso Ballet (1948), known as Ballet de Cuba in 1955 and Ballet Nacional de Cuba in 1959, and considered one of the best companies in the world, and the Alicia Alonso School of Ballet (1950–1961), which established the standard for contemporary Cuban ballet training. The company and the school were two pillars in the consolidation of the art in Cuba and in the integration of Cubanness into academic ballet interpretation (Alicia), teaching (Fernando), and choreography (Alberto). Their combined work made the Alonsos the backbone of Cuban theatrical dance.

The goal of these efforts was to offer opportunities for appreciation and practice to all sectors of society and to establish an outstanding, lasting movement of national scope. Thus, despite government indifference, they brought to Cuba important ballets such as *L'après-midi d'un faune* (The Afternoon of a Faun, 1948) and complete versions of *The Nutcracker* (1953), *Swan Lake* (1954), and *Romeo and Juliet* (1956), the last two of which made their Latin American premieres in Cuba. In addition to those ballets, there were also *criollo* creations such as *Fiesta negra* (Black Fiesta, 1951), *Lydia* (1951), and *Habana 1830* (Havana 1830, 1952). In addition to Alicia Alonso, foreign collaborators such as Igor Youskevitch, Royes Fernández, Carlota Pereyra, and José Parés, and the Cubans Dulce Wohner, Lydia Díaz Cruz, Luis Trápaga, and Enrique Martínez interpreted those pieces.

During this period, besides the work of the Ballet Alicia Alonso, there were performances by the Ballet Nacional under Alberto Alonso (1950–1953), the Ballet de Cámara de La Habana (Havana Chamber Ballet) directed by Anna Leontieva (1956–1959), and the Ballet de Pro-Arte Musical.

THE CUBAN MIRACLE: THE CUBAN SCHOOL OF BALLET

The Cuban School of Ballet supported the development of the dancers known as the Four Jewels of Cuban ballet—Loipa Araújo, Aurora Bosch, Josefina Méndez, and Mirta Plá—whose triumphant performances at the Varna International Ballet Competition in 1964, 1965, and 1966 prompted the English critic Arnold Haskell to proclaim the Cuban School of Ballet the "Cuban miracle."

New names were added to this distinguished group: first, Marta García and María Elena Llorente, and later, Amparo Brito, Ofelia González, and Rosario Suárez, among others. A crop of male dancers also emerged; Jorge Esquivel and Lázaro Carreño were two of the initiators of the male dance tradition that became one of the school's distinctive traits.

Behind those dancers were important teachers such as Fernando and Alicia Alonso, Joaquín Banegas, Azari Plisetski, and the Four Jewels themselves, who were driving forces in the rapid development of Cuban ballet. Outside the company, distinguished work was done by the National School of Ballet (1961) and the Centro Pro-Danza (Pro-Dance Center, 1986)—directed by Ramona de Sáa and Laura Alonso, respectively—and other academies and training centers with inexhaustible reserves of talent. Some of their graduates include Bárbara García, Anett Delgado, and Viengsay Valdés, the prima ballerinas with the Cuban National Ballet in 2011. Such a rigorous pedagogical foundation led to Cuballet (1984) and to the Encuentros de Academias de Ballet (Ballet Academy Conferences, 1994), international courses backed by the excellence of the Cuban teaching method.

Choreography developed along with ballet technique, and leaders in choreography include Alberto Alonso, Alberto Méndez, Iván Tenorio, and Gustavo

Herrera. Méndez and Tenorio won several international competitions. In this area, Alicia Alonso also shone, particularly her revivals of great nineteenth-century works that major companies added to their repertoires.

Interest in ballet soon moved beyond the capital. In 1967 the Ballet of Camagüey was established, and ballet schools opened in several provinces, training artists who later proved their excellence. The flourishing of the art also prompted the emergence of groups that were experimental but used classical dance, with greater or lesser orthodoxy, as the basis for their projects. Examples include the Ballet Teatro de la Habana (Havana Ballet Theater, 1987–1990), directed by Caridad Martínez, and the Ballet Contemporáneo Camagüey Endedans (Camagüey Endedans Contemporary Ballet Company, 2002), directed by Tania Vergara.

This varied activity culminates in the International Ballet Festival of Havana (from 1960), an event that showcases the best that ballet has to offer with the participation of prestigious Cuban and foreign dancers and companies. These gatherings secured Cubans' interest in theatrical dance.

THE CUBAN INVASION

Consistent with such extraordinary development, in the late 1980s Cuban ballet artists spread throughout the world, and the presence of Cubans in accredited European and American troupes became common. Leading the diaspora were Carlos Acosta and José Manuel Carreño; the star dancers Xiomara Reyes, Lorna and Lorena Feijóo, Catherine Zuaznábar, Joan Boada, Julio Arozarena, Joel Carreño, Rolando Sarabia, and Taras Domitros; and various teachers, masters, choreographers, and directors, including Fernando Alonso, Loipa Araújo, Aurora Bosch, Mirta Pla, Karemia Moreno, Carlos Gacio, Pedro Consuegra, Elena Madam, and Marta García.

Thanks to the artistic and technical distinction of its artists on and off the island, Cuba has become an obligatory point of reference for the world of ballet, and its place in the world of ballet is secure. In the development of Cuban ballet, the guiding figure of Alicia Alonso stands tall; her exceptional artistic will and talent made her a living legend of dance.

The National Ballet of Cuba. Members of the Ballet Nacional de Cuba perform *Swan Lake* in 2010. © HÉCTOR DELGADO AND ROLANDO PUJOL

BIBLIOGRAPHY

Cabrera, Miguel. *Ballet Nacional de Cuba. Medio siglo de gloria.* Havana: Ediciones Cuba en el Ballet, 1998.

Gámez, Tana de. *Alicia Alonso at Home and Abroad.* New York: Citadel Press, 1972.

González, Jorge Antonio. "Apuntes para la historia del ballet en Cuba." *Revista de Música* (July 1961): 172–183.

Martin Arnold, Sandra. *Alicia Alonso: First Lady of the Ballet*. New York: Walker, 1994.

Parera, Célida. *Pro-Arte Musical y su labor de divulgación de cultura en Cuba (1918–1967)*. New York: Senda Nueva Ediciones, 1990.

Rey Alfonso, Francisco. *Grandes momentos del ballet romántico en Cuba*. Havana: Editorial Letras Cubanas, 2002.

Siegel, Beatrice. *Alicia Alonso: The Story of a Ballerina*. New York: Frederick Warne, 1979.

Terry, Walter. *Alicia and Her Ballet Nacional de Cuba*. New York: Anchor Books, 1981.

■ *See also*

Faith: Abakuá Society

Matanzas

Son Innovations: Arsenio Rodríguez

PERFORMING ARTS: DANCE: FOLKLORIC DANCE

Pedro Morales-López

Overview of Cuban folk dance.

The process that produced the Cuban people, as well as other peoples in Latin America and the Caribbean, is known as ethnogenetic fusion, a type of ethnic process that takes place when several unrelated ethnic groups with no cultural affinities merge. The convergence of dissimilar cultural elements, which acquire a new meaning in a purely pragmatic, casual, and nontheoretical manner, defines the Cuban people and their culture, including folk dance.

Cuban folk dance has three foundations: Hispanic, in its *danzas campesinas* (rural dances); African, in the dances of several popular religions (Santeria, Arara, Ganga, Palo, Abakuá); and Franco-Haitian, in vodou dances and other similar religious and recreational expressions. The rich fusion of elements from all of three of these roots and others such as Indo-American contributions has generated dances that are purely Cuban, such as *espiritismo cordonero*, rhumba, and *son*. The African and Franco-Haitian origin dances are more closely connected to Cuban religiosity. Dancing has a functional role in the *corpus* ritual; it is the means of worshipping ancestors and gods. In this ritual, this dance has two forms: the one danced by believers (whether they have been initiated or not) and the one performed by initiates while they are possessed by the supernatural entity to whom they are devoted.

A GENERAL CHARACTERIZATION

The respected dance teacher Graciela Chao summarized and categorized general characteristics of Cuban folk dance from an anthropological standpoint:

1. Folk dance is learned through imitation and is transformed through creative performance.
2. Content is crucial in folk dance.
3. Cuban folk dance is all-inclusive and involves every part of the body, with a focus on the upper body.

4. Theater and dance are closely connected in Cuban folklore, and the dancer must build and shape his character in the same professional manner an actor would. (p. 1)

The posture of the professional dancer who performs onstage and the posture of the religious dancer in a state of trance who dances in a ritual ceremony are the same: legs parallel to each other and knees flexed; upper body off-center, slightly forward; arms bent; hands below the waistline; ample relaxation of the body. This posture, accompanied by the *muelleo* (constant flexing of the knees), frees the body of its weight and allows it to easily perform movements that are centered in the upper body, particularly the upper torso.

Religious motivation is intense in the ritual environments where these dances take place. The *toques* (percussion), songs, dances, and their pantomimic language constitute a complex aesthetic, artistic, and philosophical ritual charged with symbolism and emotion. Every chanted prayer, every song, every step and its corresponding movements and variations (which require exceptional coordination), every mimed action, every shift in space (less evident in certain dances than in others)—all of these are parts of a larger prayer, a communion Cuban believers seek in order to become one with the universe.

ON STAGE

The Conjunto Folklórico Nacional (National Folk Group) and the Ballet Folklórico de Oriente, founded in the early 1960s, researched, recovered, and promoted Cuba's musical and dance traditions, disseminating them to art schools and other institutions throughout the country. Among the dances they saved are ritual dances that originated in sacred places and gained a wider audience through performances on stage, such as *Ciclo Yoruba*, *Congos Reales*, and *Abakua* from the Conjunto Folklórico Nacional's repertoire. Traditional dance styles endured mostly due to dance schools and professional companies where Cuban folk dance, singing, and percussion classes are part of the curriculum or part of the dancers' systematic training.

Modern dance techniques (such as the Cuban dance technique) are marked by the sonority, steps, movements, gestures, and the expressive attitude of the country's ritual dances. The use of the solar plexus as a center that generates a dynamic and emotional movement in the style of Isadora Duncan (1877–1927); the use of compositional levels and forms based on the so-called fall-and-recovery technique of Doris Humphrey (1895–1958); the postulates on contraction-relaxation practiced by Martha Graham (1894–1991), Anna Sokolov (1915–2000), and Merce Cunningham (1919–2009); the musicality of movement and the significance of silence supported by Mary Wigman (1886–1973)—all these contributions, as well as other influences, were integrated into Cuban dance, Cuban ballet, and Cuban musical shows. There was a mutual exchange of influence as these choreographers

Cuban National Folk Group. The Cuban National Folk Group performs during the Women in Dance International Festival in Quito, Ecuador, March 2006. RODRIGO BUENDIA/ AFP/GETTY IMAGES

incorporated elements of Cuban ritual dances, ballroom dances, carnival dances, and recreational dances in their work. The diversity in the stage choreographies of ritual dances has facilitated their spread among religious practitioners and nonpractitioners, as a form of folk projection, staging of folklore, or artistic creation inspired by the national folk language (Guerra).

In artistic creation inspired by national folk language, the artist is free to use tradition in any way he or she desires. This is true of Cuban works in various genres that have been recognized internationally, including the contemporary dance choreographies of *Súlkary* (also spelled *Súlkari*; 1971) and *Okantomí* (1970), by Eduardo Rivero (b. 1936); the ballet *El río y el bosque* (The River and the Forest, 1973), by Alberto Méndez (b. 1939); the play *Otra tempestad* (Another "Tempest," 1997), by Flora Lauten (b. 1942) with Teatro Buendía; musical pieces by Amadeo Roldán (1900–1939) and Alejandro García Caturla (1906–1940); works by the fusion group Síntesis that have been compiled in their album *Ancestros I, II, III* (2005); the novel *Cecilia Valdés* (1882), by Cirilo Villaverde (1812–1894); most of the poetry of Nicolás Guillén (1902–1989); and most of the visual art of Wifredo Lam (1902–1982) and Manuel Mendive (b. 1944).

BIBLIOGRAPHY

Balbuena Gutiérrez, Bárbara. *Las celebraciones rituales festivas en la Regla de Osha.* Havana: Centro de Investigación y Desarrollo de la Cultura Cubana Juan Marinello, 2003.

Chao Carbonero, Graciela. "Experiencias metodológicas sobre la enseñanza de las danzas folklóricas." Paper presented at V Conferencia Científica de Investigaciones sobre Arte y Cultura, Instituto Superior de Arte, Havana, 1988.

Duharte Jiménez, Rafael, and Elsa Santos García. *Hombres y dioses. Panorama de las religiones populares en Cuba.* Santiago de Cuba: Editorial Oriente, 1999.

Guerra, Ramiro. *Teatralización del folklore y otros ensayos.* Havana: Editorial Letras Cubanas, 1989.

Martiatu Terry, Inés María. *El rito como representación. Teatro ritual caribeño.* Havana: Ediciones Unión, 2000.

Morales López, Pedro. "Un desafío para la danza folklórica cubana." *danzar.cu* (Havana) 1 (April 2006): 11–12.

Ortiz, Fernando. *Los bailes y el teatro de los negros en el folklore de Cuba.* Havana: Editorial Letras Cubanas, 1981.

PERFORMING ARTS: DANCE: MODERN DANCE

Ramiro Guerra

The development of modern dance in Cuba from its beginnings in the 1950s to the early 2000s.

During the 1940s dance in Cuba encompassed a wealth of styles: folk dance rooted in the vestiges of African religions (e.g., Yoruba, Conga, Carabalí, and Arará) that racial and socioeconomic prejudices had stifled, a rich popular blossoming of ballroom dancing (*son, danzón, cha-cha-cha*), carnival festivities, and ballet.

Cuba's excellent ballet company was led by the great Cuban ballerina Alicia Alonso and her husband, Fernando Alonso, who in 1948 founded what would become the Cuban National Ballet. The company featured Cuban dancers—particularly women—as well as foreign dancers in its dance performances. Ballet training in Cuba began in 1931 at a school established

■ *See also*

Havana: Havana as Cultural Center

by the Sociedad Pro-Arte Musical de La Habana for the training of dancers and choreographers.

BEGINNINGS OF MODERN DANCE

One of the founders of modern dance, Ramiro Guerra, trained at this dancing school, studying classical ballet despite existing prejudices in Cuban culture against professional male ballet dancers. Guerra next trained with Nina Verchinina, an important figure in Col. W. de Basil's Ballets Russes, during her stay in Cuba. He went to New York to study American modern dance at the Martha Graham School and, upon returning to Cuba, decided to train dancers in the new technique, giving presentations throughout the country. In the 1950s, under the auspices of the Sociedad Nuestro Tiempo (Our Time Society), he organized a group of students and debuted works such as *Sensemayá* (with texts from the Cuban poet Nicolás Guillén) and *Llanto por Ignacio Sánchez Mejías* (Weeping for Ignacio Sánchez Mejías), based on poems by the Spanish poet Federico García Lorca. Later he traveled to Colombia, Paris, and Madrid to broaden his knowledge of dance.

Following the Revolution in 1959, Guerra became director of the Dance Department of the Teatro Nacional de Cuba (Cuban National Theater). There, with a racially diverse group of thirty dancers (ten black, ten mestizo, and ten white), he developed a repertoire that merged modern and national dance with roots in cultural explorations ongoing in previous decades in painting, literature, theater, and music. Within a year, Guerra created a repertoire of works that relied completely on music, scenery, and costumes created by Cubans, including *Suite Yoruba*, *Mulato*, *La Rebambaramba*, *El Milagro de Anaquillé* (The Miracle of Anaquillé), and *Rítmicas* (Rhythmics). The establishment of the National Council of Culture led to the formation in 1959, under the auspices of the Ministry of Education, of the Conjunto Nacional de Danza Moderna (National Modern Dance Troupe), for which Guerra choreographed several works, such as *Orfeo Antillano* (West Indian Orpheus), *Chaconna* (Chaconne), *Impromptu galante* (Gallant Impromptu), and *Medea y los negreros* (Medea and the Slave Traders). The quality and continuity in the creation of works for the repertoire made Maurice Bejart declare on a visit to Cuba, "Cuban modern dance, although it has elements of other countries, is essentially Cuban. In its search for a form of expression, it has found a way." In 1965 the Escuela Nacional de Arte (National School of Art) began to offer training in modern and folk dance.

In 1971 Guerra's avant-garde work *Decálogo del Apocalipsis* (Decalogue of the Apocalypse), combining elements of dance, music, theater, and cinema, elicited the first of that decade's examples of Cuban cultural censorship. The show's premiere at the Teatro Nacional (National Theater) was suspended, and Guerra was removed from his position as director of the dance troupe. Together with the appointment of officials from outside the world of dance to leadership posts in dance companies, these moves were an assault against the modern dance movement in Cuba. However, the seed had already taken root, and after the passing of the "gray decade with black edges" (as the 1970s in Cuba were called to refer to a particularly bleak period in Cuban cultural life), beginning in 1981 new dance groups began to appear.

NEXT GENERATION OF CUBAN CHOREOGRAPHERS

The next generation of choreographers includes several important figures who shaped the course of Cuban modern dance, beginning in the 1980s and continuing into the twenty-first century. Marianela Boán is a multiple recipient of the National Prize for Choreography and the Premio Villanueva de la Crítica Especializada (Villanueva Special Critics Award). In 1988 she created DanzAbierta, one of the country's most innovative companies, which introduced social criticism through dance as well as onstage nudity. That same year Eduardo Rivero created Danza del Caribe in Santiago de Cuba; his *Okantomi* and *Sulkary* are considered jewels of the Cuban dance repertoire. Rivero's most memorable work, *Suite Yoruba*, was the subject of the documentary *Historia de un ballet* by José Massip; the documentary won the Golden Dove Prize in Leipzig, East Germany, in 1962. In the 1990s Rosario Cárdenas devised *danza combinatoria* (combinatory dance), which made use of mathematical laws of combination and exchange toward a new freedom in choreographic composition. Her works include *Fragmentos a su imán* (The Fragments Drawn by Charm), *Dador* (Donor), and *Maria Vivan*, which bring to the stage the poetry of José Lezama Lima and Virgilio Piñera. In 1992 the dancer and choreographer Maricel Godoy founded Codanza in Holguín. *Pasajera la lluvia* (The Fleeting Rain), by Nelson Reyes, a work about homosexuality, received awards from the Unión de Escritores y Artistas de Cuba (UNEAC; Union of Writers and Artists of Cuba). Notable works by Jorge Luis Abril include *C. C. Canillitas* (The Newsboy), *El soñador* (The Dreamer), and *La goma* (The Eraser).

Others who influenced the course of modern dance in Cuba were Lidice Núñez, Julio César Iglesias, and George Céspedes. Lilian Padrón founded Danza Espiral (Spiral Dance), which hosts a biannual competition, Danzandos, for duet choreography. In 1993 Narciso Medina created a group to further explore the theatrical elements of dance; his *Metamorfosis* (Metamorphosis) received multiple international awards. He was also the organizer of the Concurso y Muestra Internacional de Video Danza Diana Alfonso (Diana Alfonso International Competition and Exhibition of Videodance), which awards prizes for onscreen Cuban dance. In Santa Clara, Ernesto Alejo founded Danza del Alma (Dance of the Soul), a male-only group that explores such subjects as sexuality, identity, marginality, and discrimination. Tania Vergara, winner of the Ibero-American Prize for choreography and the UNEAC Prize for choreography (2008), founded Endedans in Camagüey; through dance she has reinterpreted the grand female character Carmen as played by a gay transvestite. Juan Miguel Más founded Danza Voluminosa (Voluminous Dance), whose distinction is that all the dancers are overweight, thus creating another facet in the fight against discrimination. Santiago Alfonso, for many years the director and choreographer of Tropicana, the famed cabaret, created Compañía Santiago Alfonso, which experiments with vaudeville choreography. In 2010 *MalSon*, by Susana Pous, won first prize at the international event Danza del Caribe.

Since the 1980s Cuban dance has been enriched by important artists of dance from outside Cuba. Lorna Burdsall, a U.S.-born dancer who lived in Cuba from 1955 until her death in 2010, directed Danza Contemporánea de Cuba for five years. She created Así Somos (That's How We Are), a small group of dancers with a minimalist focus, whose improvisational performances in Burdsall's dance studio incorporated elements of randomness. Isabel Bustos, born in Chile and raised in Ecuador, studied dance at Cuba's Escuela Nacional de Arte. Her group Retazos (Fragments), which incorporates the dance-theater hybrid of German choreographer Pina Bausch, organized an annual event called La Habana Vieja, Ciudad en Movimiento (Old Havana, City in Movement), which featured street dancing and screenings of video dance. Other influential figures from outside Cuba are Elena Noriega of Mexico and Elfrida Mahler from the United States, who founded Danza Libre (Free Dance) in Guantánamo to work on fusing Haitian folklore found in Cuba and contemporary dance. After Mahler's death in 1999, her work was continued by the Cuban dance artist Alfredo Velásquez.

Cuba's Ministry of Culture has recognized the importance of modern dance by awarding several individuals associated with modern or contemporary dance with its prestigious national prize for dance. Award winners include Ramiro Guerra (1999), Eduardo Rivero (2001), Santiago Alfonso (2006), Lorna Burdsall (2008), and Isidro Rolando (2009). In 2003, Cuban educational television aired a twenty-one-part course on dance appreciation titled *Apreciación de la Danza* created by Ramiro Guerra.

BIBLIOGRAPHY

Guerra, Ramiro. *Teatralización del Folklore, y otros ensayos.* Havana: Letras Cubanas, 1989.

Guerra, Ramiro. *Coordenadas Danzarias.* Havana: Ediciones Unión, 1999.

Guerra, Ramiro. *Eros Baila: Danza y sexualidad.* Havana: Letras Cubanas, 2000 (winner of the Premio Alejo Carpentier).

Guerra, Ramiro. *Apreciación de la danza.* Havana: Letras Cubanas, 2003.

Guerra, Ramiro. *De la narratividad al abstraccionismo en la danza.* Havana: Centro de Investigacíon y Desarrollo de la Cultura Cubana Juan Marinello, 2003.

Guerra, Ramiro. *Calibán Danzante: Procesos socioculturales de la danza en América Latina y en la zona del Caribe.* Havana: Letras Cubanas, 2008.

Hernández, María del Carmen. *Historia de la Danza en Cuba.* Havana: Editorial Pueblo y Educación, 1980.

Hernández, María del Carmen. *El cuerpo creativo: Taller cubano para la enseñanza de la composición coreográfica.* Havana: Editorial Adagio, 2007.

Pajares Santiesteban, Fidel. *Ramiro Guerra y la danza en Cuba.* Quito, Ecuador: Casa de la Cultural Ecuatoriana, 1993.

Pajares Santiesteban, Fidel. *La danza contemporánea cubana y su estética.* Havana: Ediciones Unión, 2005.

Danza Voluminosa. Members of the dance troupe Danza Voluminosa, a Cuban troupe whose dancers are all overweight, perform the work ¿Fedra?. PHOTO BY HUMBERTO MAYOL

PERFORMING ARTS: OPERA

Francisco Rey Alfonso

The development of opera from its beginnings in 1776 to the early 2000s.

Despite its history of colonialism and underdevelopment, Cuba has always been a fertile ground for the most elaborate kind of musical theater. The construction of the first theater in Cuba, in 1775—the Coliseo (Coliseum), restored and renamed El Principal (the Principal) in 1803—was an important event in the history of Cuban performing arts, since it allowed theater to rise to higher levels. The building was inaugurated on 12 October 1776, with a performance of *Dido Abandoned* (libretto [1724] by Pietro Metastasio, with music by an unknown composer), which is thought to be the first opera ever performed in the country. Although the

■ *See also*

Havana: Havana as Cultural Center

programming for the new theater basically relied on dramatic pieces, operas also appeared on the playbill, a fact that demonstrated a *criollo* taste for that form of theater. This was the case of André Modeste Gréty's *Zémire and Azor* (1791), the first Cuban operatic production publicized in the Havana press.

RISE OF EUROPEAN OPERA IN CUBA

A French opera company from New Orleans began to put on performances in Cuba in 1800, and the presence of this troupe brought to Cuba a topic already debated in Spain, differences between Italian and French opera style. But more important to opera in Cuba than that discussion was the arrival of Spanish performers at the Principal Theater who performed there from 1810 until 1832, understandably making changes over time. Besides drama and dancing, the repertoire at the Principal consisted of operatic numbers, thanks to which scores of titles, written by the most diverse kinds of European composers, were passed on to the Cuban stage. In this respect, the premiere in North America of Wolfgang Amadeus Mozart's *Don Juan* at the Principal is notable, performed by Isabel Gamborino and Nicolás García in 1818. The soprano Mariana Galino, considered to be the first female theater star in Cuban history, also shone as a member of that cast. Those events opened the way to an operatic tradition of considerable magnitude that soon placed Cuba at the forefront of Latin America.

In 1834, the first opera company made up of Italian performers debuted in Havana. Almost every year after that, several singers would arrive from Italy and with them an ample repertoire of operas, drawn above all from Italy's most important composers, Bellini and Dinizetti, among others. This influence was reflected in every form of art, including literature; Italian dominance in music continued well into the twentieth century. That wave of singers and titles reaffirmed Cuba as a first-rate operatic stage in the New World. Such was the development achieved that, in the middle of the nineteenth century, the Tacón—a theater that opened in 1838 and took over from the Principal in 1846—was called the Cathedral of Opera in America. The phenomenon was not restricted to Havana but also showed up elsewhere in the country. Several cities erected important theaters; the goal, above all, was enjoyment of opera.

DECLINE OF EUROPEAN OPERA IN CUBA

The opera company managed by Francisco Marty (owner of the Tacón Theater at the time) from 1846 until 1850 played a fundamental role in Cuba's achieving the status of a first-rate New World operatic stage. This company had many stars, including Balbina Steffenone, Lorenzo Salvi, and Ignazio Marini. Its troupe appeared in Havana, New York City, Boston, and Philadelphia, where it presented works by Giuseppe Verdi and Giacomo Meyerbeer. Known as the golden age of Cuban opera, this period was marked by high-quality musical performers and many premieres in Cuba that were, at the same time, premieres in the New World. The soprano Concepción Cirártegui was a part of that era; she was the first Cuban to sing opera professionally (1845–1848).

Francisco Marty's dominance was undermined by the rise of the opera impresario Max Maretzek in the early 1850s. Taking advantage of Marty's neglect of his singers and offering them more money, Maretzek succeeded in attracting the performers to the United States. In this way he was able to make the United States the center of a phenomenon that until then had been centered in Cuba. That stratagem, among other factors, catalyzed opera's decline in Cuba during the second half of the nineteenth century; although the opera seasons continued in Cuba with thorough regularity, the past brilliance of the genre could no longer be achieved. After 1850, no important work premiered in the New World on a Cuban stage.

In addition to singers' preference for the United States, Cuba's wars of independence against Spanish rule (in 1868–1878 and 1895–1898) and its economic problems at the time discouraged singers. Moreover, the poor management of another leading impresario, Napoleone Sieni, contributed to the decline. During the fifteen seasons he was involved in Cuban opera—during the 1885–1904 period—Sieni did not often attract artists who were held in high esteem and his seasons generally ended in failure regardless of the composers and works he featured. The foremost performers in Cuba at that time were the Italian tenor Enrique Tamberlick (who performed there during the 1872–1873 season) and the Cuban soprano Chalía Herrera (who performed in 1899).

CUBAN INFLUENCE ON OPERA

The ups and downs experienced in the course of this history did not numb the passion that *criollo* musicians had for operatic art. That was so much the case that many of them pursued the dream of creating true opera by following the paradigmatic model par excellence: the Italian model, which was fashionable on the Continent. This was the case, in the nineteenth century, of Gaspar Villate (*Zilia* in 1877), Laureano Fuentes (*Seila* in 1895), Hubert de Blanck (*Patria* [Homeland] in 1899), and Ignacio Cervantes (*Los Saltimbanquis* [The Tumblers] in 1899), whose work, despite its Italian influence, nevertheless helped give operatic composition a Cuban flavor. The values and quantity of those works—together with what came after by José Mauri (*La esclava* [The Slave Woman] in 1921), Eduardo Sánchez de Fuentes (*Yumurí* in 1898 and *Dolorosa* [The Sorrowful Woman] in 1910), Alejandro Garcia Caturla (*Manita en el suelo* [Manita on the Ground], Natalio Galán (*Los días llenos* [The Full Days] in 1962), Héctor Angulo (*Ibeyi Añá* in 1968), Fernández Barroso (*s-XIV-69*), Roberto Sánchez Ferrer (*Van Troy*), Jorge Berroa

(*Soyán* in 1980), Juan Piñera (*Amor con amor se paga* [Love Is Paid in Love]) and others gave Cuba a special place in this art form in Latin America.

THE EARLY TWENTIETH CENTURY

During the first three decades of the twentieth century, many operatic performances took place Cuba, but their quality was low. Well-known artists performed in Cuba only occasionally; among them were the sopranos Luisa Tetrazzini (performing in 1904) and María Barrientos (in 1907). Lack of local talent came to an end, though, with the National Theater's inaugural season in 1915, presented by a troupe with some true luminaries: Juanita Capella, Claudia Musio, José Palet, Tita Ruffo, and others. But subsequent shows, on the whole, left a lot to be desired.

These deficiencies continued when another impresario, Adolfo Bracale (who managed during fifteen seasons, 1916–1930), came on the scene. Except for *coups de théâtre* when, for instance, he brought in Tina Poli-Randaccio, Tito Schipa, Hipólito Lázaro, Enrico Caruso, and others, he mostly disappointed the public with his uneven and even mediocre spectacles. The misfortunes experienced by singers and impresarios throughout those years did not, however, dampen the country's love for opera; the form still held its privileged place in Cuban life.

After the performances in Havana by the Opéra Privé de Paris in 1930 (a group of unusual quality in the country that interpreted an anthological sampling of the Russian repertoire), musical shows started to go even more into decline. From that year to the early 1960s, all that can be mentioned are the sporadic offerings presented by Cuban singers, such as those directed by the Cuban tenor Fernández Dominicis (in 1933, with Luisa María Morales, Tomasita Núñez, and others); the productions of those who sang together in the Cuban Opera Company, an initiative carried out by Juan Bonich, Gonzalo Roig, and Francisco Fernández Dominicis in 1938–1939 (along with Zoila Gálvez, Carmelina Rosell, Francisco Naya, and others); those performed under the auspices of the Pro-Arte Musical Society during the 1940s and 1950s (with Marta Pérez, José Le Matt, and others), which sometimes featured foreign guest performers (Renata Tebaldi, Victoria de los Ángeles, Fedora Barbieri, Giuseppe Campora, and others); or those of the Grupo Experimental de Ópera (Experimental Opera Group) in the 1957–1958 season, founded by Hernando Chaviano.

The foreign company contracted in 1939 by Ramón Becali should also be mentioned (with Fidelia Campiña, Robert Weede, and others). But nothing could bring vitality back to the genre, which was under siege by economic and political crises along with the advance of movies and other types of entertainment that appealed to popular taste.

OPERA DURING THE REVOLUTIONARY PERIOD

After the Revolution in 1959, the development of musical theater was governed by the state's cultural policies. To that effect, the first step the government

Eglise Gutiérrez. Cuban-born soprano Eglise Gutiérrez performs as Violetta in Giuseppe Verdi's opera *La traviata*. PHILIP GROSHONG PHOTOGRAPHY

took was to create companies, the first of which was the Teatro Lírico Nacional (National Lyric Theater) in 1963. From 1963 into the early 2000s, that collective served as the most important example of operatic interpretation in the country. The best Cuban singers in the years since the Revolution have demonstrated their talent in it: The list includes Alba Marina, Gladys Puig, Armando Pico, Ramón Calzadilla, Yolanda Hernández, Gustavo Lázaro, Emelina López, Alina Sánchez, María Eugenia Barrios, Hugo Marcos, Jesús Li, Linda Mirabal, Hilda del Castillo, Milagros de los Ángeles, and the Cuba-based Spanish singer María Remolá. The theater has also hosted numerous foreign artists. Some of its most interesting events have been the Havana International Festivals of Lyric Art, thanks to which artists of the stature of Adelaida Negri, Gian Piero Mastromei, and Pedro Lavirgen, among others, could be enjoyed.

The foreign presences that enriched the Cuban opera world during this period included performances by the Leipzig Opera (1969, 1970, 1974) and the Leipzig Municipal Theater (1979) as well as visits from several singers from Eastern Europe. This exchange allowed for the American debut in Havana of *Halka* (1971), by Stanisław Moniuszko.

Although in the late twentieth and early twenty-first centuries the Cuban operatic landscape has had various catalysts in relation to the National Lyric Theater—including the founding of Ópera de la Calle (Street Opera) in 2004, a company managed by the baritone Ulises Aquino—opera has not been able to achieve the standard seen in other parts of the world. To blame are the material and economic difficulties involved in the proper production of opera and the loss of talented performers such as Lucy Arner, Virginia Alonso, Eglise Gutiérrez, and Elizabeth Caballero, artists of international renown who have developed their careers outside Cuba.

BIBLIOGRAPHY

Carpentier, Alejo. *La música en Cuba*. México: Fondo de Cultura Económica, 1946.

González, Jorge Antonio. "Repertorio teatral cubano." *Revista de la Biblioteca Nacional* (Havana) (October–December 1951): 69–184.

González, Jorge Antonio. *La composición operística en Cuba*. Havana: Editorial Letras Cubanas, 1986.

Lapique Becali, Zoila. *Música colonial cubana (1802–1902)*. Havana: Editorial Letras Cubanas, 1979.

Parera, Célida. *Pro-Arte Musical y su labor de divulgación de cultura en Cuba (1918–1967)*. New York: Senda Nueva Ediciones, 1990.

Ramírez, Serafín. *La Habana artística*. Havana: Imprenta del E. M. de la Capitanía General, 1891.

Rey Alfonso, Francisco. *Gran Teatro de La Habana: Cronología mínima, 1834–1987*. Havana: Imprenta del Banco Nacional de Cuba, 1988.

Río Prado, Enrique. *Pasión cubana por Giuseppe Verdi*. Havana: Ediciones Unión, 2001.

Tolón, Edwin T., and Jorge Antonio González. *Historia del teatro en La Habana*. Santa Clara, Cuba: Universidad Central de Las Villas, 1961.

PERFORMING ARTS: THEATER: COLONIAL PERIOD

Carlos Espinosa Domínguez

The development of a Cuban theater from the sixteenth to the nineteenth centuries.

Little can be said about the theater found by the Spanish on their arrival in Cuba. It was limited to the *areitos*, which were not formal theatrical displays, but "a mixture of music, song, dance and pantomime applied to the religious liturgies, magical rites, epic narratives, tribal histories and large expressions of the collective will" (Ortiz p. 26). The little that is known about them comes from a few descriptions in the texts of the conquistadors.

Although researchers have uncovered the existence of a Pedro de Castilla, who, according to Rine Leal, dominated the Havana stage for six years beginning in 1570 (Leal p. 42), and a performance in 1598 of the comedy *Los buenos al cielo y los malos al suelo* (The Good to Heaven and the Bad Below) near the Castillo de la Fuerza fortress, theater did not take hold in Cuba until the eighteenth century, when *El príncipe jardinero y fingido Cloridano* (The Gardener Prince and False Cloridano, 1730–1733), by Santiago de Pita, appeared. It is of little importance that this was a version of an Italian work; it is the first dramatic text written by a Cuban. During this same period Felipe Fondesviela, the Marquis of La Torre, was governor of the island (1771–1777). He was concerned with providing Havana with promenades and entertainment locales. After his return to Spain and after waging a battle against the ecclesiastical hierarchy, the capital had its first theater, the Coliseo, at the end of the Alameda de Paula, which according to Calvert Casey was the most beautiful of the monarchy (Casey 1964a, p. 28). In addition to the Coliseo there were also were the Circo, the Extramuros, the Diorama, the Principal theaters, and later the luxurious Tacón.

For this reason, the residents of Havana enjoyed abundant and varied offerings of theater, opera, and dance beginning in 1790. This activity is reported in the pages of the *Papel Periódico de la Havana* (Newspaper of Havana), and particularly in *El Regañón de la Havana* (The Havana Arguer), where the first theater reviews were published. The founder of *El Regañón*, Buenaventura Pascual Ferrer, who was also its proprietor and only editor, also wrote a short play, *El cortejo subteniente, el marido más paciente y la dama impertinete* (The Second Lieutenant Beau, the Very Patient Husband and the Impertinent Lady, 1790–1791), which debuted when the author was eighteen years old. In her analysis of theater reviews in the *Papel Periódico*, Fina García Marruz noted that "the frequency with which the works changed and were rarely repeated suggests that a body of trained actors coexisted with a simple style of performance" (p. 281). In addition, Pascual Ferrer wrote in November 1801 that "the truth is that Havana has never had such an abundance of entertainment as it does today. Comedies, Operas, Acrobats, Mechanical Theater, wax figures, Physics Cabinets, and who knows what other things" (*El Regañón* p. 305).

The theatrical repertoire was composed of foreign texts, mostly from Spain; local writers were slow to appear, which was not unusual in countries under colonial rule. The first to emerge was Francisco Covarrubias (1775–1850), an actor who became a playwright and achieved notable success with his short plays about Cuban customs. His example was followed by other authors who used humor to make social critiques, giving rise in 1868 to a new genre, Cuban *bufo* theater. Some of the best known bufo scriptwriters were Pancho Fernández, Ignacio Sarachaga (1852–1900), and Raimundo Cabrera (1852–1923), but as Antón Arrufat has pointed out, it was a theatrical movement of authors, directors, actors, musicians, and impresarios who determined what they did on stage (p. 20). Its elements of poor taste, repetitive situations, and reduction of characters to the trio of the Negro, the mulatto, and the Spaniard were the principal limitations of bufo. However, bufo brought local characters and settings to the stage, making Cuban theater truly Cuban and developing an island taste and sensibility.

Another style of theater, so-called cultured theater, featured the works of José Jacinto Milanés (1814–1863), Gertrudis Gómez de Avellaneda (1814–1873), and Joaquín Lorenzo Luaces (1826–1867), the three best dramatists of the colonial period. Although Milanés wrote other plays, he is best known for having introduced romanticism to the Cuban stage with *El Conde Alarcos* (Count Alarcos, 1838). Gómez de Avellaneda wrote twenty plays, which proved that she was equally talented in comedy (*La hija de las flores* [Daughter of the Flowers], 1852) and tragedy (*Baltasar*, 1858). Luaces wrote three dramas and an outstanding tragedy, but his admirable talent for comedy was not fully appreciated until a century after his death, with the stage debut in 1967 of his *El becerro de oro* (The Golden Calf), a satire about opera fanatics. Together with Gómez de Avellaneda's *La hija de las flores* and José Agustín Millán's *Una aventura o El camino más corto* (An Adventure or The Shortest Route, 1842), *El becerro de oro* is among the most enduring plays written in Latin America in the nineteenth century.

In the last two decades of the nineteenth century, new theaters were built in Cuba. In Havana the Payret, the Irijoa, the Torrecillas, the Cervantes, the Albisu, and the Salón Trocha opened for theatrical productions. Provincial cities saw the construction of the Caridad (in Santa Clara), the Terry (in Cienfuegos), and the Principal (in Camagüey). Some of them hosted foreign companies as well as renowned artists such as Sarah Bernhardt (1844–1923), Benoît-Constant Coquelin, known as Coquelin aîné (1841–1909), and Tommaso Salvini (1829–1915). However, by that time, Cuban theater was undergoing a profound creative crisis. Cultured theater was a poor, contrived copy of the melodrama coming from Spain and, as Calvert Casey observed, the librettists of bufo theater were the only ones writing original theatrical works in Cuba (Casey 1964b, p. 98). As if saying goodbye along with the century, in 1899 the bufo theater offered its last season in a small hall on Galiano Street. Some months later and just blocks away, the first season opened at a new theater, the Alhambra, and a new age began for the Cuban stage.

BIBLIOGRAPHY

Arrufat, Antón. "El teatro bufo." In *La máscara y la flecha*. Havana: Ediciones Alarcos, 2007.

Casey, Calvert. "Teatro I: La Colonia: Del areíto a la ópera." *Bohemia* (11 September 1964a): 26–28.

Casey, Calvert. "Teatro II: La Colonia: De Covarrubias a los bufos." *Bohemia* (18 September 1964b): 26–28, 98.

García Marruz, Fina. "Obras de teatro representadas en La Habana en la última década del siglo XVIII, según el *Papel Periódico*." In *La literatura en el Papel Periódico de la Havana 1790–1805*. Edited by Cintio Vitier, Fina García Marruz, and Roberto Friol. Havana: Editorial Letras Cubanas, 1990.

Leal, Rine. *La selva oscura*. Vol. 1. Havana: Editorial Arte y Literatura, 1975.

Ortiz, Fernando. *La africanía de la música folklórica de Cuba*. Havana: Editorial Universitaria, 1965.

El Regañón y el Nuevo Regañón. Havana: Comisión Nacional Cubana de la UNESCO, 1963.

PERFORMING ARTS: THEATER: REPUBLICAN PERIOD

Matías Montes Huidobro

The development of Cuban theater from the War of Independence in 1898 to the Revolution in 1959.

The history of Cuban theater in the Republican period has two stages: a formative stage that started when Cuba became independent from Spain in 1898 and a development stage dating from 1939 when elections were held leading to drafting of the 1940 constitution, which was intended to strengthen the country's democracy. Theatrically, the first stage responds to a nationalist awakening through realistic mimesis; the second coincides with a period of experimentation and vanguardism launched with the founding of the Academia de Artes Dramaticas de la Escuela Libre de Havana (Dramatic Arts Academy of the Free School of Havana), led by a group of directors and actors that would transform Cuban theater.

1898–1939: BUILDING A NATIONAL THEATER

The first four decades of twentieth-century Cuban theater were years of nationalist affirmation, although the Cuban-born Alberto Insúa (1883–1963) and the Spanish-born Alfonso Hernández Catá (1885–1940), who collaborated on many works that were successfully produced in Spain as well as Cuba, reveal a Cuban stage closely linked to Spain. Gustavo Sánchez Galarraga's oeuvre is much more important and fruitful. Galarraga (1893–1934), deeply involved in the theater groups of his time, was a tireless fighter for Cuban theater; he was an advocate for bourgeois *costumbrismo* (a genre based on the depiction of customs and manners) and late romanticism. He wrote, within the limitations of that period, relatively significant plays such as *El héroe* (The Hero, 1917) and *Los hijos de Heracles* (Heracles' Children, 1924). José Cid Pérez (1906–1994), who earned much recognition, was also prolific but conventional. Ramón Sánchez Varona (1883–1962) did not write as much, but his work was of major significance. His ideas about female psychology and his characterization of conflicts and prejudice against women, put forward in *Las piedras de Judea* (The Stones of Judea, 1915), *La asechanza* (The Trap, 1918), and *La sombra* (The Shadow, 1937), demonstrate the concern of Cuban theater, and by extension the Republic, for the rights of Cuban women. Salvador Salazar (1892–1950) along with Renée Potts (1908–2000)—one of the few female playwrights of the period—were very active in the theater movement, producing mostly superficial work with occasional breakthroughs.

Works of value written by certain authors who made forays into theater should not be overlooked. One such case is that of Marcelo Salinas (1889–1978), who wrote *Alma guajira* (A Country Soul, 1928), a great example of rural theater; José Montes López (b. 1901) who wrote *Chano* (1937), an insightful exploration of the code of honor and of rural language; and Jorge Mañach (1898–1961), who wrote *Tiempo muerto* (Dead Time, 1928) a biting depiction of bourgeois apathy.

Toward the end of this period, Luis Alejandro Baralt (1892–1969) became prominent. He was one of the founders of the Teatro de Arte de la Cueva (Cavern Art Theater) in 1936 and the director of the Teatro Universitario. Two of his plays were *La luna en el pántano* (The Moon in the Marsh, 1936) and *La luna en el río* (The Moon on the River, 1938). Also worthy of mention is *La oración* (The Prayer), by Felipe Pichardo Moya (1892–1957), one of the first plays to denote the influence Spanish playwright Federico García Lorca (1898–1936) in Cuba.

However, as the most significant, brilliant, and influential figure of this entire period, José Antonio Ramos (1885–1946) should be regarded as the founder of Cuban national theater. His first plays were influenced by Spanish theater. Although his work has elements associated with melodrama and high comedy, Ramos was able to do away with all those negative components. He was ahead of all the other playwrights because of the themes he chose and his technical achievement. After *Almas rebeldes* (Rebel Spirits, 1906), Ramos's notions of social justice broke with bourgeois conventions. Despite this, his work remains a classic example of bourgeois liberalism; his temperament and his theatrical technique never allowed him to move toward Marxism. His work is marked by his concern with Cuba's future, with social injustice and the struggle of the proletariat. These concerns become evident through characters who assault each other in a kind of verbal pugilism. *Una bala perdida* (A Stray Bullet, 1907) stages a confrontation between ideology and pragmatism, which deals with the corruption of power in Ibsenian terms. *La hidra* (The Hydra, 1980) also shows Ibsen's influence. It is a naturalist analysis of a family's decadence resulting from the family's relation to political, social and financial evils. *Liberta* (1911) is a profound analysis of female psychology. It reveals female desire and the restrictions placed on it by male chauvinism. *Cuando el amor muere* (When Love Dies, 1911) also addresses the relations between genders, with much irony. In *Satanás* (Satan, 1913), the subject is more complex and theatrically innovative. Without totally abandoning Ibsen, Ramos plays with naturalism, expressionism, and Chekhovian impressionism to perform an analysis of political, financial, and erotic obscurantism in which fratricidal confrontation also makes its appearance. *Caliban Rex* (1914) is a theatrical history lesson, and *El hombre fuerte* (The Strong Man, 1915) is another study of the dynamics of power. It has a deeply theatrical presentation: a confrontation between the main character, who is blind, and his enemy, who can see, takes place on a darkened stage. It was followed by *El traidor* (The Traitor, 1915), set during the War of Independence, in which Ramos introduced the themes of treason and the search for blame, themes that came to dominate Cuban dramatic literature in the twentieth century. All of these plays lead viewers to what may be one of the most important plays in modern Cuban theater, *Tembladera* (Quagmire, 1917). In this play Ramos presents a theatrical microcosm of Cuban life. It is about the Gonsálvez de la Rosa family's long voyage into night, portraying the kinds of social confrontations that characterized the early republican period. The tentacles of patriarchy and matriarchy provoke generational and fratricidal struggles that together foreshadow the financial, political, national, and international disasters that would wreck Cuba.

Ramos does not stop at the achievements of realism in *Tembladera*. *En las manos de Dios* (In the Hands of God, 1933) is an engrossing example of expressionism; it explores the notion of a "superman" with rich theatricality and a radical approach to its subject. *La leyenda de las estrellas* (The Legend of the Stars, 1935), with its Pirandellian and metatheatrical touches, reveals a Ramos moving with the changes in the dramatic art and still growing as an artist. *La recurva* (The Hairpin Curve, 1935), a claustrophobic piece with existentialist concepts, takes place during the administration of Gerardo Machado and explores the characteristic Cuban fratricidal struggles and their fatal consequences. Ramos's later *FU-3001* (1944), about the national political demoralization, is something of an anticlimax.

POST-1939: THE MODERN THEATER

Although the second stage of Cuban theater is slated as beginning in 1939 with Carlos Felipe's writing of *Esta noche en el bosque* (Tonight in the Woods, 1939), there were signs of change from 1935 onward that began when Luis Alejandro Baralt premiered *La muerte alegre* (A Merry Death), by the Soviet playwright Nikolai Evreinov, shortly after the fall of the Machado regime. Never before had a play been performed on stage in Cuba without a prompt box or a prompter. This moment saw the beginning of a move away from strict mimetic techniques. Atemporality (timelessness) of the individual and of objects, ahistoricism (absence of concern in history) as a means of exploring universals, and scenic experimentation as a form of praxis (breaking with the traditional concept of the fourth wall and the use of incidental music by the Cuban composer Amadeo Roldán) were introduced into Cuban theater. Several teachers and directors, many of them foreign, opened up new approaches, putting directing and production on innovative paths. Although Luigi Pirandello had already entered Cuban dramatic culture with the staging of *Seis personajes en busca de autor* (*Six Characters in Search of an Author*) in 1924, his impact grew when Baralt staged, in 1936, his *Esta noche se improvisa* (*Tonight We Improvise*).

The number of important Cuban theater institutions after 1940 was impressive. The first, the Academia de Artes Dramáticas of the Escuela Libre de Havana, was established in 1940. More theaters followed: Teatro Universitario (1941), Patronato del Teatro (1942), Teatralia (1943), Farseros (1943), Academia de Artes Dramáticas (ADAD, 1945), the Academia Municipal de Arte Dramático (1947), Prometeo (1948), Las Máscaras (1949), and Los Comediantes (1950), among others. Three Cuban directors profoundly influenced the theater of the 1950s: Modesto Centeno (1914–1984), Andrés Castro (1922–2000), and especially, Francisco Morín (b. 1922), who was an innovator and staged works associated with the theater of the absurd and the theater of cruelty (for instance Genet's *The Maids*, in 1955, which administered a true shock for

avant-garde Cuban theater). The innovative ferment lasted until 1959 and brought the formal and thematic innovations of modern international theater into Cuba.

Cuban playwrights fought through difficult conditions to stage and publish their work during this period. They struggled with popular preference for foreign works, indifference to both public and private cultural organizations, lack of space to stage performances, and a general lack of interest. Nevertheless, two major playwrights emerged who had to confront these same difficulties: Carlos Felipe (1911–1975) and Virgilio Piñera (1914–1979).

Felipe started this sequence with *Esta noche en el bosque*, which has obvious Shakespearean and Pirandellian overtones and introduces chaotic, oneiric, and psychological themes and completely breaks with Ibsenian theater's laws of cause and effect. But *El chino* (The Chinaman, 1947) is where metatheatrics in Cuban playwriting began. Its scenic procedures influenced all subsequent Cuban drama in the twentieth century. Psychodrama, metatheatrics, and Cuban themes, developments that mix and blur divisions between fiction and reality and between high and low or popular culture, come together within performances that mix magical and Freudian rituals. Piñera reacted to this with a play that is another classic of national dramaturgy, *Electra Garrigó* (1948), in which the author's refashioning of Greek tragedy leads him to invent Cuban tragedy. This play is also a microcosm of Cuban life in which chauvinism and matriarchy violently confront each other on stage with a stagecraft and a language that the theater of the absurd introduced in Cuba.

Felipe made an incursion into the Havana tenements in *Tambores* (Drums, 1943). He utilized psychology, wonder, and bourgeois decadence to create a context for *Capricho en rojo* (Fantasy in Red, 1948). Under the influence of the most spectacular American theater, he conceived *El travieso Jimmy* (Mischievous Jimmy, 1949), a piece rich in subtexts, including a political subtext. *La bruja en el obenque* (The Witch in the Shroud, 1957) is a metaphoric and poetic piece while *Ladrillo de plata* (Silver Brick, 1957) is a subversive piece, in form a most conventional bourgeois theater piece, but whose subtext of sex unsettles the established order of things. However, none of these pieces had the impact that *El chino* did.

Although Piñera, too, would never surpass the success of *Electra Garrigó*, his work continued to be innovative. In *Jesús* (1948), he cubanized the biblical theme the same way he cubanized the classic premises in *Electra Garrigó*. In *Los siervos* (The Serfs, 1955), a delirious farce, he ridicules communism in a radical manner. In *La boda* (The Wedding, 1957), he almost brutally satirizes bourgeois marriage and heterosexual relations using practices of the theater of the absurd. In *Falsa alarma* (1957), he mixes the absurd with elements of the theater of cruelty. These two directions are main characteristics of twentieth-century Cuban theater. Considered as a whole, Piñera's work reaffirms the value of Cuban theater, and Piñera himself became the great icon of the Cuban theatrical avant-garde.

The list of Cuban playwrights that followed is long. Paco Alfonso (1906–1989), of the Marxist old guard, worked with socialist realism and African themes. But the highest achievement in this dramatic approach was that of Flora Díaz Parrando (1893–1992), whose *Juana Revolico* (1944) goes beyond the strictly mythical to explore Afro-Cuban culture in a naturalistic way and takes on themes, including chauvinism and social justice.

Parrando herself worked with evasion, the subconscious, and Freudian psychology in three one-act pieces: *El remordimiento* (Remorse, 1944), *Drama en un acto* (Drama in One Act, 1944) and *El Odre* (The Wineskin, 1944). This approach was shared by other playwrights: María Alvarez Ríos (1919–2010) in *La víctima* (The Victim, 1958) and Nora Badía (1921–2007) with *Mañana es una palabra* (Tomorrow Is One Word, 1947). But it was Rolando Ferrer who brought this approach to its highest point with *La hija de Nacho* (Nacho's Daughter, 1951) and later with *Lila, la mariposa* (Lila the Butterfly, 1954). Eduardo Manet (b. 1930) did something similar, but with less evanescence, in the three plays he published in a book titled *Scherzo* (1949).

Although Cuban theater took on renewed vigor in the late 1950s when new theaters appeared and new playwrights such as Roberto Bourbakis (b. 1919), Jorge Antonio González (1918–2010) and Modesto Centeno regularly staged new plays, they were soon forgotten because their works were not published. Ramón Ferreira (1921–2007), however, one of the most popular playwrights in the late 1950s, became known through a successful piece after the style of García Lorca: *Donde está la luz* (Where There Is Light, 1952). His play *El hombre inmaculado* (The Immaculate Man, 1958), a key to a better understanding of the political-historical context of the late 1950s, brought the prerevolutionary period of Cuban theater to a close.

Lastly, several playwrights made their first appearance in the 1950s, such as Matías Montes Huidobro (b. 1931), who earned the Premio Prometeo (Prometheus Prize) in 1951 for *Sobre las mismas rocas* (On the Same Rocks), a piece that anticipates the spirit of experimentation of the 1960s; and Abelardo Estorino (b. 1925), who defined his position as a predominantly realist writer with *El peine en el espejo* (The Comb in the Mirror, 1956). Within the avant-garde, Gloria Parrado (1927–1986) worked in the idioms of the absurd and the theater of cruelty in *El juicio de Aníbal* (The Judgment of Hannibal, 1958) and *La espera* (The Wait, 1958); and Antón Arrufat (b. 1935), passionately dedicated to the theater of the absurd, first became known through *El caso se investiga* (The Case Is Under Investigation, 1957). Working in a realistic manner were the following: Raúl González de Cascorro (1922–1985), whose best play is *Arboles sin raices* (Trees without Roots, 1958); Fermín Borges (1931–1987), the paragon of Cuban neorealism, who had a short career

and wrote several one-act plays (*Gente desconocida* [Unknown People, 1953], *Doble juego* [Double Play, 1954], and *Pan viejo* [Old Bread, 1954]); and lastly, Leopoldo Hernández (1921–1994), the author of several existentialist political texts marked by profound ethical conscience, among which *La consagración del miedo* (The Consecration of Fear, 1957) stands out.

In spite of the many difficulties they faced, the dramatic output of Cuban playwrights testifies to the strength of the country's theater during the Republican period.

BIBLIOGRAPHY

Arrom, José Juan. *Historia de la literatura dramática cubana.* New Haven, CT: Yale University Press, 1944.

Boudet, Rosa Ileana. *Teatro cubano: relectura cómplice.* Los Angeles: Ediciones la Flecha, 2010.

Bueno, Salvador. *Medio siglo de literatura cubana.* Havana: Publicaciones de la Comisión Nacional de la UNESCO, 1953.

Cid Pérez, José. "El teatro en Cuba republicana." In *El teatro cubano contemporáneo* Edited by Dolores Martí de Cid. Madrid: Aguilar, 1959.

Dauster, Frank. *Historia del teatro hispanoamericano.* Mexico City: Ediciones Andrea, 1966.

Escarpanter, José. "Introducción." In *Teatro*, by Carlos Felipe. Edited by José A. Escarpanter and José A. Madrigal, 11–64. Boulder, CO: Society of Spanish and Spanish-American Studies, 1988.

Espinosa Domínguez, Carlos. *Virgilio Piñera en persona.* Denver, CO: Editorial Término, 2003.

Garzón-Céspedes, Francisco. "José Antonio Ramos: una línea ascendente de rebeldía." In *Teatro*, by José Antonio Ramos, 9–20. Havana: Editorial Arte y literatura, 1976.

González Montes, Yara, and Matías Montes Huidobro. *José Antonio Ramos: Itinerario del deseo; Diario del amor.* Miami: Ediciones Universal, 2004.

Hernández Ureña, Max. "Evocación de José Antonio Ramos." *Revista Iberoamericana* 12, no. 24 (June 1947): 251–261.

Hernández Ureña, Max. *Panorama histórico de la literatura cubana.* Puerto Rico: Ediciones Mirador, 1963.

Leal, Rine. "57 años en busca de un teatro nacional ... sin encontrarlo." *Lunes de Revolución*, no. 101 (3 April 1961): 18–21.

Leal, Rine. *En primera persona.* Havana: Instituto del Libro, 1967.

Leal, Rine. *Breve historia del teatro cubano.* Havana: Editorial Letras Cubanas, 1980.

Montes Huidobro, Matías. *Persona: vida y máscara en el teatro cubano.* Miami: Ediciones Universal, 1973.

Montes Huidobro, Matías. *El teatro cubano durante la República: Cuba detrás del talon.* Boulder, CO: Society of Spanish and Spanish American Studies, 2004.

Morín, Francisco. *Por amor al arte.* Miami: Ediciones Universal, 1998.

Muguercia, Magaly. *El teatro cubano en vísperas de la revolución.* Havana: Editorial Letras Cubanas, 1988.

Portuondo, José Antonio. "El contenido político y social en las obras de José Antonio Ramos." *Revista Iberoamericana* 12, no. 24, (June 1947): 215–250.

PERFORMING ARTS: THEATER: REVOLUTIONARY PERIOD

Omar Valiño Cedré

Cuban theater after 1959.

In contrast to many other countries, the theater in Cuba is government subsidized. More than two hundred theater groups enjoy the support of a system with offices throughout Cuban territory affiliated with the National Council of Performing Arts and its provincial counterparts, all under the Ministry of Culture. This structure, developed over more than half a century, has existed in its form as of 2011 since the early 1990s.

This country of just over eleven million inhabitants subsidizes some five thousand workers and performers in theater, dance in its varied forms, circus, opera and musical and vaudeville theater, pantomime, and stage narration, among other specializations that in modern times entertain some two million spectators a year in about 36,000 performances in formal theaters and alternative spaces. Havana has about fifteen theaters, insufficient for the demands of both audiences and theater professionals. The rest of the movement is concentrated in the provincial capitals, which average three to four theaters each, for a total of fifty outside Havana. There are few theater groups based in individual municipalities. Prices are very low, and on many occasions admission is free.

In Cuba, the theater tradition is not as strong as that of other arts, such as music. Even so, there has never before been as large a theater audience, although interest is most notable in Havana and sporadic in some provincial capitals, including Matanzas, Santa Clara, Cienfuegos, Camagüey, Holguín, and Santiago de Cuba. One of the most popular genres among audiences is children's theater, in line with the government policy of promoting children's well-being.

What is far more important than the funds allocated to theater activities is the dignity afforded by others to this field of endeavor. By law and in practice, work in the theater is recognized as having the same legal and organizational status as any other labor. Consequently, the performing arts, and theater in particular, enjoy a daily presence throughout the length and breadth of the country, with corresponding influence and impact.

Most theater is centered on artistic projects, rather than companies or production units, and generally the theater director is the leader, rather than a manager or administrator. There are small, medium, and large groups and companies, as well as individual performers. The main defect is a lack of quality; even taking into account the innumerable material limitations, theatrical excellence is rarely sustained. There are, of course, exceptions affirming a relevant theatrical movement in sync with trends in Latin America, the Caribbean, and elsewhere in the world. However, such instances were too few as of 2011.

Although the network of provincial, regional, and national events showcasing Cuban productions is ample, it is smaller than is desirable, but it does exhibit a diversity of formats, concepts, and objectives. Especially interesting are the productions staged outside the usual venues, including in rural and mountain areas, where theater is offered to audiences that rarely have such an opportunity. One example is the tour known as the Cruzada Teatral Guantánamo-Baracoa (Guantanamo-Baracoa Theater Crusade).

Most of the events on the provincial level are sponsored by local groups. These include the National Theater Festival of Camagüey, held every two years and presenting the best plays debuted during the period, as well as educational, critical, and promotional activities displaying the current reality of the island's theater movement. In additional to events with national scope, Cuba hosts several international theater events, including the Matanzas Puppet Workshop, May Theater at the Casa de las Américas cultural center, and the Havana Theater Festival. In previous decades and into the early 2000s, a vast library on drama, historiography, theory, and criticism of classical and contemporary theater has been published, including the journals *Conjunto* (Collection), sponsored by Casa de las Américas, and *tablas* (stage), sponsored by the National Council of Performing Arts.

PEDAGOGY AND CRITICISM

For many people and institutions, education and training are essential, both in academic settings and elsewhere. Ever since Cuban theater began its struggle for modernity, various schools and educational programs have played a fundamental role in its development. The Higher Institute of Art (Instituto Superior de Arte, or ISA), opened in 1976, has been an important part of that process. The ISA was established on a portion of the land belonging to the National School of Art, itself founded in 1962 as a project of the Revolution, on the site of what was previously the exclusive Country Club of Havana. The Performing Arts Department was one of the first divisions established at the ISA; it later was named the Theater Arts Department because there is also a Dance Arts Department. The ISA has daily contact with the Cuban and international theater movements; it has never sought isolation in time or space, but instead actively participates in the development of new strategies and maintains the tradition of constantly questioning. Many theater performers on the national scene in the early 2000s were trained in its classrooms.

Figures such as Graziella Pogolotti, a prestigious art and theater critic with solid academic training and vast experience teaching literature, and Rine Leal, a

■ *See also*

Cuban Thought and Cultural Identity: Socialist Thought

Fefu and Her Friends (María Irene Fornés)

Playwrights of the Revolution: Abelardo Estorino and Eugenio Hernández Espinosa

scholar and theater critic, joined together to establish a university major whose effectiveness—although never perfect or beyond questioning—has had a strong influence on Cuba's theater world. Likewise, the dramatic arts major has trained many Cuban playwrights, who between 2005 and 2010 were working intensely to introduce new concepts through their writing.

There are plenty of opportunities for training. In addition to the ISA, specialized high schools in several cities—Havana, Villa Clara, Camagüey, Bayamo, and Santiago de Cuba—prepare actors. Moreover, the ISA's Media Department and the International Film School in San Antonio de los Baños concentrate on the audiovisual field rather than the dramatic arts.

THE ROAD TRAVELED

The triumph of the Cuban Revolution culminated a period that began with the establishment in 1936 of the group La Cueva (The Cave) and ended in 1958, when Raquel and Vicente Revuelta formed Teatro Estudio (Studio Theater), a theater group in the most modern sense of the term.

After 1 January 1959, there was enormous theatrical growth resulting in the foundation, with institutional backing, of groups all over the country, specializing in adult theater, children's theater, or puppet theater. This widespread activity was accompanied by creation of a theater infrastructure, restructuring of the teaching, the expansion of the various art forms, a new legal status for theater, and the growth of interest among theatergoers. Debates over art's role in society emerged and persisted, a continual source of friction, without any lasting reconciliation.

The practices of the founders of modern Cuban theater, such as Francisco Morín, were continued for a time. In the 1960s, the theater movement was dominated by Teatro Estudio, through which Vicente Revuelta introduced Konstantin Stanislavski's acting techniques and Bertolt Brecht's plays and concepts. Revuelta left Teatro Estudio and created the group Los Doce (The Twelve), which along with other groups experimented with Jerzy Grotowski's universe. With Los Doce, Revuelta staged extraordinary works, such as Lope de Vega's *Fuenteovejuna* (1619), José Triana's *La noche de los asesinos* (The Night of the Assassins, 1964), and Henrik Ibsen's *Peer Gynt* (1867). Teatro Estudio became a training ground for new directors, notably Roberto Blanco and Berta Martínez. Together, they created a repertoire of Cuban theater rich in plays, techniques, and artistic language. Among the children's theater groups (known as *guiñoles*, or puppet theater groups, given their aesthetic orientation toward the use of puppets), the Teatro Nacional de Guiñol (National Puppet Theater) laid the groundwork, under the leadership of siblings Pepe and Carucha Camejo. Their productions of Federico García Lorca's *El retablillo de Don Cristóbal* (The Farce of Don Cristóbal and the Maiden Rosita, 1931), Sergei

Prokofiev's *Peter and the Wolf* (1936), Dora Alonso's *El sueño de Pelusín* (Pelusín's Dream, 1963), José Zorrilla's *Don Juan Tenorio* (1844), and Pepe Carril's *Chicherekú* (1964) blazed new paths in theater for children as well as adults.

Following this intense growth, in the late 1960s Cuban theater started looking for new ways to reach society, while continuing to experiment in its relationship with audiences. The only group that was completely successful in this effort was Grupo Teatro Escambray (Escambray Theater Group), thanks to the solid artistic and social projection of actor and director Sergio Corrieri, which harmonized with the dominant political thinking of the 1970s that viewed art as an expressive vehicle for the masses, a kind of Greek chorus for society. Albio Paz's *La vitrina* (The Showcase, 1971) and Gilda Hernández's *El juicio* (The Lawsuit, 1973) are the best examples of dramas refracting, often critically, the new contradictions in society.

Other groups emerged throughout the 1970s with that redoubled goal of making theater a means of inquiry and expression for peripheral sectors. In Santiago de Cuba, the Cabildo Teatral Santiago (Santiago Theater Hall) reappropriated with a contemporary slant, a secular, popular street tradition known as the *theater of relations*, resulting in a foundational production: *De cómo Santiago Apóstol puso los pies en la tierra* (How Saint James Set Foot on Earth, 1974), by Raúl Pomares.

In addition to the internal crisis of the late 1960s, Cuban theater experienced a sharp loss of individual and collective creative rights in the first half of the 1970s, a consequence of errors in the conception and implementation of cultural policy. Paradoxically, the search for an art of the masses, imposed or encouraged by the agencies in charge of the cultural and ideological spheres, was one of the authentic values pursued by Cuban theater workers, but it was not based on a single, replicable formula. The result was that the 1970s left indelible scars on artists and the theater's evolution.

In the 1980s, the past's centrifugal forces were challenged by centripetal forces. By the end of that decade, a change in aesthetic tendencies was accompanied by a set of institutional and artistic transformations. Inquiry focused on the extremely complex social problems of that time and the individual's place within that context. That was the essential axis of artistic reflection in the 1980s, through a paradigmatic and strongly social praxis.

THE DRAMATURGY OF THE REVOLUTION

Actors and playwrights of the period were interested in tracing the social links between theater and the Revolution. Authors exhibited varied forms of writing, especially poetic, differences and similarities, aspects of other eras, bridges between traditions, and links between ruptures. Cuban playwriting on and off the island has told the story of individuals and groups amid utopias and contradictions, struggles

Teatro Buendía. One of Cuba's leading theater companies, Teatro Buendía, performs the play *Charenton* by Raquel Carrió at the Goodman Theatre in Chicago in 2010 as part of the Latino Theatre Festival. GOODMAN THEATRE

and conflicts. It is important to include Cuban theatrical pieces conceived and produced abroad. Even the harshest visions, on the island or off, are organic responses to the Revolution's interactions, whose indications and implications cannot be concealed.

Some outstanding figures, part of a much more extensive list, are Virgilio Piñera, Carlos Felipe, Rolando Ferrer, Abelardo Estorino, María Irene Fornés, Eugenio Hernández Espinosa, José Triana, Antón Arrufat, Héctor Quintero, José Milián, Matías Montes Huidobro, Albio Paz, Iván Acosta, Gilda Hernández, René Alomá, Freddy Artiles, Manuel Martín Jr., Rafael González, Abrahan Rodríguez, Pedro Monge, Abilio Estévez, Alberto Pedro, Nilo Cruz, Reinaldo Montero, Eduardo Machado, Raquel Carrió, Flora Lauten, Amado del Pino, Ulises Rodríguez Febles, Nara Mansur, Norge Espinosa, Caridad Svich, Abel González Melo, Yerandy Fleites, and Rogelio Orizondo.

THEATER SINCE THE LATE 1980s

In the second half of the 1980s, the arts focused on social involvement. These were times of rectification, openness, free discussion, and a wide variety of ideological and cultural influences, particularly those awakened by perestroika. An ethical breeze was blowing through Cuban society, accompanied by a return to the origins of the revolutionary process. Artists and performers did not hide their criticisms of antagonisms, imperfections, and conservative mentalities, and they turned their gaze on Cubans and their history.

After revisiting projects that had been put aside, the masters of Cuban theater (Vicente Revuelta, Roberto Blanco, Berta Martínez) joined in this spirit, while Flora Lauten founded Teatro Buendía (Good Day Theater) with the goal of renewing traditions, and that company has retained its importance into the early 2000s. Some unforgettable plays from that period are *Las perlas de tu boca* (The Pearls of Your Mouth, 1989), *Otra tempestad* (Another Storm, 1997), and *Bacantes* (Bacchae, 2001), all the result of collaboration between Raquel Carrió and Flora Lauten. In addition, of course, there was the new generation of theater workers and performers, precisely the Revolution's third generation, consisting of young people born in the late 1950s and principally the 1960s, who entered college and professional life in the 1980s, conscious of their identity and difficult mission. They recovered an organic link to the past, including tendencies that had been extinguished in the 1970s or interrupted in the late 1960s. Víctor Varela's *La cuarta pared* (The Fourth Wall, 1988) is the most indicative play of that time.

In the 1990s, theater and society accelerated their dialogue. Despite the acute economic crisis, the public—especially in Havana—joined this conversation through the stage. Now theater attempted to reflect the island's complete situation, the island as an indivisible whole, a metaphor: the island as an Island, more than a country or a nation, a form of existence. There was a resurgence of Virgilio Piñera's poetic language. Groups such as Teatro Mío (My Theater), headed by Alberto Pedro and Miriam Lezcano; later Estudio Teatral (Theatrical Studio) of Santa Clara, with Joel Sáez and Roxana Pineda; Teatro D'Dos (Theater of Two), led by Julio César Ramírez; El Ciervo Encantado (The Enchanted Deer), directed by Nelda Castillo; Teatro de la Luna (Theater of the Moon), led by Raúl Martín; Argos Teatro (Theater Argos), directed by Carlos Celdrán; and Teatro de Las Estaciones (Theater of the Seasons), headed by Rubén Darío Salazar, are representative of the work in the late twentieth and early twenty-first centuries.

The Cuban theater movement has borne witness to the many transformations experienced in the country and the world from the 1980s to the early 2000s. Theater has participated in a restructuring of all aspects of society and has undergone an evolution, contributing new forms, images, and ideas to the nation's discourse on its identity. Consequently, this explains the combination of recurrent tendencies and observable styles. On one hand, during the 1990s the father figure, ingratitude, the lack of communication between parents and children, the family, and power were all factors in the effort to achieve a stable definition of the future. On the other hand, the mechanism of deconstruction returned to the stage, supported by parody, irony, quotations, intertextuality, hyperbole, and play.

Between 2000 and 2010, there was no single dominant tendency, but instead various themes and styles presenting different and even opposing images of society. The dialogue continued between contemporary international tendencies and opposing aspects of the purest Cuban tradition. Meanwhile, a new generation strove to prevail.

■ *See also*

Cuban Thought and Cultural Identity: Costumbres in the Art and Literature of the 19th Century

Havana: Havana as Cultural Center

Performing Arts: Cuban Forms of Popular Dance

Sexuality: The Mulata Figure in the Cuban Imaginary

BIBLIOGRAPHY

Domínguez, Carlos Espinosa, ed. *Teatro cubano contemporáneo: Antología*. Madrid: Centro de Documentación Teatral y Fondo de Cultura Económica, 1992.

Dramaturgia de la Revolución. Havana: Ediciones Alarcos, 2010.

Leal, Rine. *Breve historia del teatro cubano*. Havana: Editorial Letras Cubanas, 1980.

Leal, Rine. "El teatro cubano." *Indagación* (Centro Nacional de Investigación de las Artes Escénicas) 3 (2001): 3–12.

León Jacomino, Fernando J. *De cómo el teatro santiaguero puso los pies en la tierra*. Havana: Trabajo de Diploma, Instituto Superior de Arte, 2010.

Pogolotti, Graziella, Rine Leal, and Rosa Ileana Boudet, eds. *Teatro y Revolución*. Havana: Editorial Letras Cubanas, 1980.

Tablas. Special anthology issue. 91 (December–January 2009).

Valiño, Omar. "Trazados en el agua: Para una geografía ideológica del teatro cubano de los 80–90." In *Anales de literatura Hispanoamericana*. Madrid: Universidad Complutense, Cátedra de Literatura Hispanoamericana, 1999.

Valiño, Omar. *La aventura del Escambray: Notas sobre teatro y sociedad*. Pinar del Río, Cuba: Ediciones Almargen, Editorial Cauce, 2004.

PERFORMING ARTS: BUFO THEATER

Inés María Martiatu

Comic theater with persisting racist and misogynist stereotypes.

The first performance of Cuban *bufo* was by the Bufos Habaneros (Havana Bufos) on 31 May 1868, at the Villanueva Theater. This form of theater, whose members were illiterate mulattoes and whites, had very humble origins in the Tanda de Guaracheros, in a tenement in Old Havana. This setting was starkly different from the soirees frequented by rich, educated men acquainted with the latest European trends and literature. The idea of *teatro bufo* was to imitate Madrid's comic opera and possibly the U.S. minstrel shows presented by Campbell, Christie, and Webb in Havana from 1860 to 1865 (Leal 1975, pp. 415–416). Without the slightest bit of experience, this theatrical adventure competed with the zarzuela (Spanish form of musical theater with sung and spoken dialogues), Italian opera, and melodrama.

The *guaracha* (popular music genre of song and dance with humorous themes that arose in the nineteenth century) had already established the main characters of Cuban *bufo* theater, all of which were derogatory: the *negrito* (little black man) and the *mulata* (mixed-race woman), to which were added immigrants from Spain, China, and other countries (Linares p. 100). The new theatrical form quickly gained popularity with its introduction of Cuban characters that were much preferred over the Spanish-style characters of the zarzuela.

The origins of Cuban bufo are complex. The well-known actor Francisco Covarrubias (1775–1850) had been the first to perform in blackface in the Cuban theater. He played the negrito on 14 December 1812, and 16 January 1815, sixteen years before Thomas Rice (1808–1860) created the character Jim Crow and thirty years before Daniel Decatur Emmett (1815–1904), presumed to be the author of the song "Dixie," presented the first minstrel shows (Leal 1975, p. 15). The Galician and anti-Cuban writer and slave trader Creto Gangá (1811– 1871), also known as Bartolomé José Crespo Borbón, originated the theatrical character of the negrito. In 1847, he premiered *Un ajiaco o La boda de Pancha Jutía y Canuto Raspadura* (Ajiaco Stew, or The Wedding of Pancha Jutía and Canuto Raspadura) (Leal 1975, p. 15).

Another antecedent to Cuban bufo is the portrayal of black men and women in Spain's Golden Age Theater of the late sixteenth and early seventeenth centuries, more than three hundred years before the opening of Bufos Habaneros. In Seville, black characters appeared in comedies, tragedies, mystery plays (meaning religious plays), and zarzuelas. Blacks and mulattoes performed as musicians, dancers, soloists, and singers, and also played protagonists, in plays by well-known authors such as Lope de Rueda (1510–1565), Lope de Vega (1562–1635), Alonso de Castillo Solórzano (1584–1647), and others (García Gómez p. 3).

Golden age theater presented the black man as comical and excessively talkative, just as he was portrayed in Cuban bufo well into the twentieth and twenty-first centuries. Black female characters were almost always slaves (García Gómez p. 3). Their Spanish pronunciation sounds familiar because unfortunately these same derogatory lexical distortions have been maintained by negrito characters even in the early 2000s (Ortiz p. 156). *Catedraticismo*—the term for the manner in which educated, middle-class blacks were thought to speak—is one example of the genre's racist stereotypes.

In nineteenth-century Cuban bufo, the negrito, the mulata, and the *gallego* (Spanish immigrant) pandered to certain stereotypes of the Cuban people. The characterizations of the negrito and the mulata, in this carnivalesque, idle atmosphere, concealed the reality of black men and women enslaved on the sugar plantations, the colony's economic foundation. The *bozal*, a recently arrived presumably pure black whose Spanish was poor; the *catedrático*, an educated black trying to imitate the upper class; and the *lumpen* (social delinquents) were all ridiculed. To this repertoire were added the *mulata sandunguera* (charming mulatto woman), superficial and opportunistic, and the *gallego bruto* (brutish Spaniard), who was always fooled by the negrito and the mulata (Martiatu p. 86). Leal observed, "far from extolling the national image at the start of the independence struggle, they reduced it to a marginal, cheap and vulgar vision. . . . From this stems the error, still made by some today, of equating bufo with all of Cuban theater" (Leal 1975, p. 23).

On 22 January 1869, in the middle of a performance of *El perro huevero* (The Egg-Stealing Dog), Jacinto Valdés gave a cheer for Céspedes and independence. The colonial authorities dealt out harsh punishment to the performers and the audience members who supported the nascent war of independence. The Bufos Habaneros were forced into exile and did not return to the stage until 1879, when the Zanjón Pact put an end to the war.

On 21 August 1879, the renowned Bufos de Salas, directed by Miguel Salas, appeared for the first time. They had a long-lived success, but eventually they exhausted their repertoire and fell into decline. On 10 September 1890, the original Alhambra Theater opened, presenting Salas's successor, Regino López of Asturias, with a frankly pornographic repertoire. Referring to the Alhambra, Leal wrote: "the most decisive contributions are the political revue, its conversion into a small genre, the expansion of the musical offering from the *guaracha* to complex scores" (Leal 1975, p. 52).

During this period, the character of the black man appeared as a criminal or thug, and the image of the mulata, denigrated since the early guarachas, also worsened. She was presented as loose, a prostitute, and a threat to morality, decorum, and the stability of decent families. In other words, blacks and mulattoes were portrayed as incapable of living in equality with whites. As ruling-class ideology created the image of the black man as a criminal, it did the same with the *bandido*, fueling the popularity of Manuel García, the "king of the Cuban countryside," a bandit from the late nineteenth century celebrated for stealing from the rich (Leal 1975, p. 58). These characterizations reflected Cuba's new, problematic nationality, in which the ruling class encouraged fear of blacks and a whitening of the population through immigration and refused to accept Africans and their descendants as Cubans.

On the bufo stage, the Cuban protagonists are the mulata and the negrito, despite their insulting characterizations. The immigrants from Spain and China are foreigners. Thus a concept of nationality was born, weighed down by racism, one of its most painful consequences (Martiatu p. 87). The genre lives on because offensive depictions of women, blacks, and the poor are still acceptable in the twenty-first century, and the influence of bufo on Cuban humor and in the media continues to reveal controversial aspects of Cuban society (Martiatu p. 14).

BIBLIOGRAPHY

García Gómez, Emilio. *Los negros en España*. 2005. Available from http://www.etnografo.com/negros_espana.htm.

Leal, Rine. "La chancleta y el coturno." In *Teatro bufo. Siglo XIX*, vol. 1, edited by Rine Leal. Havana: Editorial Arte y Literatura, Colección Biblioteca Básica de Literatura Cubana, 1975.

Leal, Rine. *La selva oscura. De los bufos a la neocolonia.* 2 vols. Havana: Editorial Arte y Literatura, 1975, 1982.

Leal, Rine. "Para leer a nuestros clásicos del XIX." In *Teatro del siglo XIX.* Havana: Editorial Letras Cubanas, 1986.

Linares, María Teresa. "La guaracha cubana, imagen del humor criollo." *Catauro. Revista Cubana de Antropología* (July–December 1999): 94–104.

Martiatu, Inés María. "El negrito y la mulata en el vórtice de la nacionalidad." In *Bufo y Nación. Interpelaciones desde el presente*, edited by Inés María Martiatu. Havana: Editorial Letras Cubanas, 2008.

Ortiz, Fernando. *Los negros curros.* Havana: Editorial de Ciencias Sociales, 1986.

Pozo Ruiz, Alfonso. *Los esclavos en la Sevilla del siglo XVI.* University of Seville. Available from http://www.personal.us.es/alporu/histsevilla/esclavos_sevilla.htm.

■ *See also*

Esculturas Rupestres and Other Works by Ana Mendieta

Milk of Amnesia (Carmelita Tropicana/ Alina Troyano)

The Works of Tania Bruguera

PERFORMING ARTS: PERFORMANCE ART

Lillian Manzor

The role of Cuban performance art in redefining the relationship between art and politics, challenging restrictions on freedom of expression, and engaging the public in new understandings of what art is and where it takes place.

Performance art by Cuban artists working in and outside Cuba has been influential in pushing the boundaries of what can be said and redefining the complex relationship between art and politics. Performance art is an interdisciplinary genre that borrows from different fields of visual culture such as theater, painting, video art, dance, and music as much as from politically charged daily life. It is considered an alternative practice in that it resists representational systems that are tied to repressive social systems. Two important elements of performance art are the use of the performer's body as originator of meaning and the creation of an unsettling relationship with the audience. As part of Latin American conceptualism, Cuban performance—with its strong diasporic and transnational elements—has redefined the audience as active participants and engaged in an ongoing reformulation of culture.

THE 1980s

Writer and visual artist Ana Mendieta (1948–1985) and multidisciplinary artist Leandro Soto (b. 1956) were the pioneers of Cuban performance art. Sponsored by the Cuban Ministry of Culture, Mendieta, who was born in Cuba but lived in the United States after 1961, returned to Cuba in 1981 for a performance series with the assistance of artists interested in Afro-Cuban traditions and indigenous cultures such as Soto, José Bedia (b. 1959), and Gustavo Pérez-Monzón. From 1977 to 1980, Soto

The Work of Ana Mendieta (1948–1985). Photographs by Cuban artist Ana Mendieta are exhibited at the Galleria Nazionale d'Arte Moderna in Rome, Italy, in 2010. FRANCO ORIGLIA/ GETTY IMAGES

was in Cienfuegos using materials from his environment and exploring traces of different cultures in what he called "plastic actions." Like Mendieta's pieces, these prototypes of performance art questioned institutional spaces for the making and validation of art and underscored the need to document both the process and the event. Photographs of Soto's performances were included in *Volumen Uno*, a 1981 exhibition at the Centro Internacional de Arte; however, his work was not well-received by some cultural policy makers. Around the same time (1980) the first performance festival in Cuba was held when several artists rented a beach house in Havana for the Festival de la pieza corta (Festival of the Short Piece).

Cuba entered a rectification period (1986–1990) as a response to the perceived need to set right so-called economic errors and negative tendencies such as individualism that resulted from market reforms in the early 1980s. Performance artists also sought to raise awareness of societal problems during this period. They wanted to "Revive the Revolu[tion]" (to borrow from the title of performance troupe ArteCalle's 1988 performance installation, "Reviva la Revolu") but called on society to do so. In 1986 Consuelo Castañeda and Humberto Castro (b. 1957) entered a Unión de Escritores y Artistas de Cuba (UNEAC; Union of Writers and Artists of Cuba) meeting on art and sexuality dressed in giant phalluses and threw milk at those present. Juan-Si González and others performed short, critical pieces on buses and in the streets, without any institutional mediation, allowing the spectators to take over the public spaces offered under an apparently aesthetic guise. When security agents physically repressed them, they formed the group ART-DE, an acronym for Arte Derecho and a Spanish homonym for *burning*. In 1989 the Ministry of Culture finally offered individual performance artists space in the Castillo de la Real Fuerza (Castle of the Royal Force) Museum. That same year, the conceptual photographer Arturo Cuenca (b. 1955) transformed the Castle/Museum into a symbol for "Science and Ideology," an ongoing performance that was censored by conservative bureaucrats. These forced cancellations culminated in the shutdown of the Havana Visual Arts Development Center 1990 exhibit "El objeto esculturado" (The Sculptured Object) and the six-month imprisonment of Angel Delgado, whose uninvited performance at the exhibit consisted of his defecating in a hole made in a copy of *Granma,* the national newspaper. At this moment of highest tension between institutions and performance artists, the artists decided to take over the only space left, sports. Lázaro Saavedra organized "La plástica cubana se dedica al béisbol" (Cuba's Visual Artists Play Baseball), mobilizing over fifty artists, critics, and promoters for daily ironic stagings of the clumsiest version of Cuba's national pastime.

The staging of trance/possession techniques from Afro-Cuban religious rituals is essential for understanding the development of Cuban performance art in the 1990s. Tomás González (1938–2008) developed Método de Actuación Transcendente, a method of embodying a character through trancelike techniques. Manuel Mendive (b. 1944) also used elements of Yoruba and Bantu cultures to paint naked human bodies, which then become a stage on which the muscles dance with their own energy and the energy that emanates from the street spectators.

SINCE THE 1990s

After the 1991 dissolution of the Soviet Union and thus the end of its subsidy of Cuba, the country entered a period of economic hardship that Fidel Castro called the Special Period in Time of Peace. Decentralization in the Ministry of Culture during the Special Period led to loosened institutional pressure, and artists began to enjoy more creative freedom. This development came too late for the 1980s generation, which was by now disbanded because by the 1990s most artists were living abroad without defecting, in what Cuenca coined "low-intensity exile" (quoted in Fuscó 1992, p. x). Tania Bruguera (b. 1968), one of the best-known performance artists in Cuba and in global performance circuits, emerged at this time of transition. Bruguera studied Mendieta's works to re-embody those performances in her early pieces. By bringing Mendieta back to Cuba's cultural memory in ritualistic pieces, she sought to reverse the erasure of previous generations. She slowly moved from focusing on the personal to engaging the full social body. In 2003 she founded the Cátedra Arte de Conducta (Art of Behavior Department), hosted by the Instituto Superior de Arte, an interdisciplinary program for explorations on the social and political nature of performance art. The work at the Arte de Conducta focuses on the study of behavior as the result of social structures in daily life. Like many transnational artists in the first decade of the twenty-first century who worked at different locations, Bruguera divided her time between Chicago and Havana. In Bruguera's work, the audience members often find themselves occupying the role of co-creator of the piece, thus questioning notions of authorship and defying authority. As Bruguera explained, she takes advantage of the privileged role an artist has in society to create a space in which freedom and tolerance may be negotiated.

The Havana-based theater group El Ciervo Encantado (The Enchanted Deer), founded in 1996 by actress, teacher, and director Nelda Castillo (b. 1953), also reconstructs Cuba's historical memory by bringing back works and artists that had been expunged. These performances parody topics, such as corruption, that are still off-limits. Like this group, the Cuban American performance artists Maritza Molina, Carmelita Tropicana (Alina Troyano, b. 1951), and Coco Fuscó (b. 1960) address such topics as the nature of institutions and cultural memory, exile and migration, gender and power, and sexuality. Tropicana, whose work started in feminist and lesbian circles, traveled to Cuba in 1993. Her parodical performance piece *Milk of Amnesia* shows the artist overcoming her cultural amnesia through the discovery of the collective nature of memory. Fuscó's performances, which recall Bruguera's early work, focus on the female body as a spectacle conditioned by multiple histories.

Many artists in Cuba arrive at performance art by way of pop culture styles, such as hip hop. The most influential multidisciplinary performance troupe is OMNI Zona Franca, which came together at the community center in Alamar, a housing project east of Havana. Combining oral and written elements, as well as music and the visual arts, the group achieves creative freedom paradoxically by making use of metaphors of the revolution. Forming one of the last strongholds of alternative artistic praxis in Havana, the members of this group try to infuse poetry in all of their surroundings: their stage is daily life itself. Their performance is a process borne out of their environment. Whether on the long bus ride from Havana to Alamar or in the rundown common areas of their housing projects ("Rebirth," "Communicating Vessels") or in the religious procession to the town El Rincón on the day of the St. Lazarus festivities ("For the Health of Poetry") or in their bi-monthly Friday performances or their yearly "Never-Ending Poetry Festival," they orchestrate poses and bring out the theatricality of daily gestures. As "Civic Ghosts," they work with their audience/co-participants through their simulation of reality/performance and address topics silenced or underattended by official discourse that haunt modern Cubans: the death of the *guajiro* (peasant), media disinformation, empty political slogans, the lack of beauty in everyday life, and the state-sanctioned limits to freedom of expression and movement.

There have been several performance festivals throughout the island. The first such festival, appropriately titled Primer Festival de Performance Ana Mendieta (Ana Mendieta's First Festival of Performance; Havana, 1998), was organized by the DUPP Gallery, a collective of emerging artists. These artists, guided by René Francisco Rodríguez (b. 1960), winner of the 2010 National Prize for Visual Arts, went to Jaruco in search of traces from Mendieta's nature/performance pieces there in order to reframe Cubanness in an international context. Other festivals include Puente Sur's Encuentro de Performance e Intervenciones Puente Sur (Encounter of Performance and Interventions), usually held in Mayabeque Beach (Melena del Sur), featuring installations as transformations of the physical environment; the Festival de Performance de Cienfuegos; and the Encuentro de Performance La Liebre Muerta (Dead Hare Performance Encounter) in Matanzas, whose name pays tribute to the influential German performance artist and sculptor Joseph Beuys (1921–1986), in particular to his work "How to Explain Pictures to a Dead Hare" (1965), a referent as important to contemporary performance as it was to the 1980s generation.

New technologies have expanded the modes of performance art and video art. First conceived as a way to tape and document performances, the most interesting twenty-first-century hybrid projects are by performance artists that blur the boundaries between documentary and video arts. OMNI Zona Franca was a pioneer in combining these two art forms. Important video-performance artists are Janette Chávez ("Self Censorship"), Katiuska Saavedra ("Extasis"), and the team of Javier Castro, Renier Quer, Adrián Melis, Yunior Aguiar, Celia González, Grethell Rasúa, and Luis Gárciga. This group, which emerged from Bruguera's Cátedra Arte de Conducta, works collectively but maintains individual authorship, applying new technologies to the narrative language of performance. In their quest to maintain a more direct relationship with the people with whom they work, they focus on the aesthetics of daily survival. The Circus Project: International Performance and Audiovisual Event, founded by Juan Rivero Prieto in 2003, shows performance video art and allows projects to be shared with other international artists.

Since the 1980s performance artists both in Cuba and in the diaspora have delved into the medium as a transformative gesture. They have participated in and shaped cultural policies as well as gender, sexual, and racial politics. Performance art has dared to question power and officialdom on and off the island. Whether presented live or in digital platforms, performance art has been effective in pushing the limits of artistic freedom and transforming aesthetic boundaries.

BIBLIOGRAPHY

Araoz, Raydel. "El audiovisual en el performance y el performance en el audiovisual." *Miradas*. Available from http://www.eictv.co.cu/miradas/index.

Caballero, Rufo. "Arte cubano 1981–2007: Dime lo que más te ofende." In *Agua Bendita: Crítica de arte, 1987–2007*. Havana: Letras Cubanas, 2009.

Camnitzer, Luis. *New Art of Cuba*. Rev. ed. Austin: University of Texas Press, 2003.

Camnitzer, Luis. *Didática de la liberación: Arte conceptualista latinoamericano*. Montevideo, Uruguay: Casa Editorial HUM, 2008.

Carvalho, Denise. "The World in Reverse: The Work of Maritza Molina." *Afterimage* 35, no. 4 (January–February 2008): 6–9.

Enriquez, Lazaro Yovany. "Encuentro Performance e Intervención Puente Sur." *Melena del Sur: Territorio Libre de Analfabetismo*. Available from http://www.melena.cult.cu/.

Espinosa, Magali. "Arte de conducta: Proyecto pedagógico desde lo artístico." *SalonKritik*. Available from http://salonkritik.net/.

Fuentes Rodríguez, Elvis, Glexis Novoa, Yuncikys Villalonga, and Papo Calo. *Killing Time: An Exhibition of Cuban Artists from the 1980s to the Present*. New York: Exit Art, 2008.

Fuscó, Coco. "El Diario de Miranda." *Third Text* 6, no. 20 (1992): 133–144.

Fuscó, Coco, ed. *Corpus Delicti: Performance Art of the Americas*. New York: Routledge, 2000.

Gárciga Romay, Luis. "Bifocales para un tuerto: Transgénesis y necesidad en una parte del audiovisual cubano actual." 2010. Originally published in *Arte Cubano* 2 (2009). *Proyecto Circo: Imagen y sonido*. Available from http://www.proyectocircocuba.org.

Gárciga Romay, Luis. "La gallina, el cine, el huevo, y el videoarte." 2010. *Proyecto Circo: Imagen y sonido* 1. Available from http://www.proyectocircocuba.org.

León, Glenda. *La condición performática*. Havana: Editorial Letras Cubanas, 2001.

Manzor, Lillian, and Alicia Arrizón. *Latinas on Stage*. Berkeley, CA: Third Woman Press, 2000.

Novoa, Glexis. "Cuban Performance Art of the 1980s (Chronology)." 1998. Available from http://glexis-novoa.com/index.

Posner, Helaine, Tania Brugueras, Gerardo Mosquera, and Carrie Lambert-Beatty. *Tania Bruguera: On the Political Imaginary*. Milan, Italy, and New York: Charta, 2009.

PERUVIAN EMBASSY CRISIS AND THE MARIEL BOATLIFT: 1980

Manuel Jorge Suzarte

Key events in Cuban emigration and relations between Cuba and the United States.

At the end of the 1970s relations between the United States and Cuba improved slightly under the administration of Jimmy Carter (1977–1981). Interests Section offices were opened in Havana and Washington, D.C., and U.S. businesspeople traveled to Cuba to develop commercial relations even under the continuing U.S. economic embargo or blockade. A dialogue initiated with the exile community in the United States achieved the release of political prisoners in Cuba and opened up travel for Cuban Americans; 100,000 such visitors were admitted to Cuba in 1978 and 1979. Optimism was constrained by what the United States saw as an alarming Cuban presence in Africa (particularly Angola), and by what was called a "crisis of the Soviet brigade" in Cuba, suspicion regarding Cuba's presence in Central America, and the Soviet invasion of Afghanistan. Beneath the apparent improvement in relations were differences that could lead to new tensions.

THE EVENTS AT THE PERUVIAN EMBASSY

Between October 1979 and April 1980 there were five hijackings of small Cuban crafts, the first of which was a GH-41 barge. In defiance of a previous agreement between the two nations on kidnappings, the United States did not arrest the hijackers or return them to Cuba, which raised suspicions in Cuba that the United States was promoting not only illegal departures but also terrorism—the hijacking of vessels carrying passengers and crew is an act of terrorism under international regulations (Smith pp. 200–206).

In 1979 and early 1980 there were several incidents of Cubans forcefully entering diplomatic headquarters, and in every case the embassies accepted the intruders and in some cases offered them political asylum. On 1 April 1980 a group of five people aboard a city bus crashed through the perimeter fence of the Peruvian embassy in Havana in a bid to obtain political asylum and thus be permitted to emigrate. Other attempts to break into this same embassy and the Venezuelan embassy over the preceding months had been successful—the trespassers had been offered political asylum. But in this instance, the bus crash caused the death of a Cuban police officer who had been guarding the gate of the Peruvian embassy when he was caught in crossfire as Cuban police began shooting at the bus.

The Cuban authorities immediately requested the return of the five intruders, arguing that rewarding them with grants of asylum would establish a precedent that could put the security of the diplomatic missions at risk. When Peruvian government refused and granted asylum to the Cubans, on 4 April the Cuban government withdrew police protection from the Peruvian embassy. When this news became public Cubans flocked to the embassy to seek asylum; within three days, 10,800 people had converged on the site.

The concentration of such a large number of people in such a limited space, and the inability of Peruvian diplomatic officials to meet their needs, prompted the Cuban authorities to close access to the site. A few days later, the Cuban authorities granted passes to allow people to return to their homes to await resolution of their requests for asylum; already there was a glimmer of hope that they might be allowed to leave Cuba via air to Costa Rica, Spain, or Peru, and, a few days later, via sea to Florida.

CAUSES OF THE EVENTS

News agencies and international press organizations (particularly U.S. agencies) cast the events inaccurately as a political crisis of the regime caused by deteriorating economic conditions in Cuba. Despite the structural limitations that were the legacy of Cuba's underdevelopment and limited resources (limitations reinforced by the U.S. embargo that was in effect an economic blockade), the Cuban economy had been growing steadily for the previous five years. Also, the country had been institutionalizing itself on the heels of a referendum in which a majority of Cubans had voted in favor of the socialist Constitution of 1976. The causes of the events at the Peruvian embassy lay in the complexities of the strained relations between Cuba and the United States, particularly the dynamic of migration between the two countries.

Despite the easing of tensions that allowed the opening of Interests Section offices in Havana and Washington, D.C., in September 1977 and enabled Cuban Americans to visit family in Cuba, the essential problems in the bilateral dispute—including migration issues—persisted. The family visits from Cuban emigrants (Cuban Americans and Cubans resident in the United States) that began in 1978 bolstered the migratory motivations among their relatives and in those parts of the Cuban population that identified with the North American lifestyle. Yet in 1980 immigration to the United States was essentially limited to former political prisoners with family ties in the United States.

Cuban authorities suspected that the events at the Peruvian embassy had been encouraged by U.S. political interests hostile to the Cuban revolutionary process, particularly because they had warned the Carter administration about the dangerous situation at the embassies, and had voiced their concern about the fact that there had been no immigration agreement between the two nations for the past seven years. There was no shortage of reasons to suspect the hand of the U.S. government in the embassy incident, because the United States had been behind similar events meant to destabilize the new regime in the first years of the Cuban Revolution.

After the Cuban Missile Crisis in 1962 the U.S. government canceled flights between the United States and Cuba, granted substantially fewer immigrant visas to Cubans, and began to encourage illegal departures from Cuba as a method of bringing about a political crisis that would destabilize the Cuban government. The U.S. press and political propagandists publicized these illegal departures. Fidel Castro, who concluded that the political issue of migration would continue to be used against his government, announced in 1965 that all Cubans with relatives in the United States were free to leave, and in October pleasure boats and other types of vessels were authorized to enter the small port of Camarioca to pick up relatives of Cubans living in Florida. The prospect of a massive, uncontrolled flow of immigrants arriving on the coast of Florida raised concerns in the Johnson administration, which took steps to establish the first immigration agreement between the two countries. From December 1965 to April 1973 the governments operated an air bridge between the airports of Varadero and Miami that facilitated the departure of Cubans who wanted to join family members in the United States. The Cuban Adjustment Act of 1966 waived several U.S. immigration rules for Cubans, and it preferentially made it easier for them to obtain permanent residency. To the Cuban government, this legislation is a political tool that encourages desertion and illegal departures from Cuba.

At the end of 1973, the lists of Cubans who had asked to emigrate were exhausted and the air bridge was closed. Negotiations to normalize migration to the United States failed, and there were no more departures by air. Between 1973 and 1979 the numbers of Cuban immigrants admitted to the United States decreased markedly. By 1980 the scene was set for another emigration crisis.

THE MARIEL BOATLIFT

In the midst of the crisis generated by the events at the Peruvian embassy, the Cuban government announced that the port of Mariel (west of Havana) would be opened to all those who wished to leave the country permanently, as long as boats came to pick them up. Within a few days vessels began to arrive in Cuba from Florida. From April to September 1980 about 125,000 Cubans left the port of Mariel for Florida.

This group of migrants, known as the *marielitos*, were doubly rejected and stigmatized. In Cuba the political and media discourse defined them as the underbelly of society—"scum"—and this view was shared by a significant portion of the Cuban population, who were well aware of U.S. hostility toward the Cuban revolutionary process in the preceding decades. In April and May 1980 popular marches (organized by the government) in front of the Peruvian embassy and the U.S. Interests Section offices had expressed majority support for the revolutionary political project. Political denunciations of those who wanted to emigrate from Mariel sometimes developed into charged incidents of hounding and harassment.

The arrival of the marielitos in the United States occasioned a change in Americans' assessment of them. Although the Cubans who had occupied the Peruvian embassy in hopes of being allowed to emigrate (and all those who shared this motivation) had been seen as victims of a repressive regime, as soon as they arrived on U.S. soil they were recast in the press and by several political sectors (especially Cuban American organizations) as, for the most part, undesirables—delinquents, criminals, homosexuals, and the mentally ill. In truth, most of the marielitos did not have criminal records, and many of those who did had committed crimes that were not punishable under U.S. law (for example, counterrevolutionary acts or participation in the black market).

Initially, the Carter administration tried to halt the migratory flow to stem fears of a crisis in Florida brought on by the massive wave of immigrants. The U.S. government briefly considered returning all those classified as "excludable" from entry, but in the end they accepted them, at least in part because it was a presidential election year and Carter's campaign focused on his defense of human rights. As it happened, the Mariel exodus was one of the reasons Carter lost his bid for reelection (particularly in Florida).

Because the marielitos were admitted under parolee status (a U.S. immigration status for humanitarian refugees who do not meet requirements for regular entrance), they did not benefit from the Cuban Adjustment Act and could not become permanent residents until they became eligible under a new immigration law in 1986. At the same time, some marielitos were placed in legal limbo: They were classified as *excludable* from immigrating to the United States and were detained in prison indefinitely until they could be repatriated. Under the classification "excludable" were those considered violent criminals by U.S. immigration authorities upon arrival in Florida in 1980 and those who (under parolee status) committed serious crimes on U.S. soil after 1980.

The Mariel emigrants were different from previous groups of Cuban emigrants in terms of social class, level of education, and occupation, as well as having a larger presence of black and mestizos. Only one-fifth of the marielitos were unemployed when they left Cuba, and 40 percent were manual laborers. The ratio of men to women was two-to-one, and most of the marielitos were between the ages of twenty and forty. These characteristics reflected sociodemographic changes in Cuban society that came to mark later patterns in Cuban migration and the emigrants' integration into the Cuban American community. Nearly 70 percent of Mariel emigrants live in Miami (Hernandez and Gomis; Pedraza).

SUBSEQUENT EVENTS

After the boatlift ended in September 1980, for the next fifteen years Cuba and the United States continued in their failure to normalize immigration between the two countries. In order to prevent another mass influx, in 1984 the Reagan administration negotiated immigration agreements with Cuba that included the return of the 2,746 Mariel excludables. As of 2010, 1,840 had been deported and 906 were still imprisoned awaiting deportation (Chardy p. 1A; "El Mariel 30 Years: A Quest for Freedom"). At the same time,

Mariel Boatlift.
A Cuban soldier stands beside a refugee ship at Mariel Harbor on 23 April 1980. AP IMAGES/ JACQUES LANGEVIN

the Reagan administration promised to grant up to 20,000 visas per year to Cuban immigrants, but from 1984 to 1994 only about 10 percent that allotment was granted each year. The agreement ended in May 1985 when the United States began to broadcast Radio Martí to Cuba. During the same period the U.S. Interests Section Office in Havana rejected the majority of Cubans' requests for temporary visas to visit their families in the United States, a trend that intensified at the beginning of the 1990s during the Special Period that eventually led to the Rafter Crisis of 1994.

The Mariel exodus revealed the weak points in U.S.-Cuba relations. On each side, suspicions abounded that the migration between the two countries was being politically manipulated and managed. From its Cold War perspective, the United States viewed Cuban immigration as part of the ideological fight to discredit socialism and a means of destabilizing the Cuban revolutionary government. Cuba recognized how the United States incentivized both legal and illegal departures from Cuba, and the Cuban government branded emigrants as disaffected or unpatriotic as it unburdened itself of people who did not support the Revolution or even actively opposed it. Yet, immigration crises seem to take Cuba and the United States by surprise, and they create significant political problems and end in trauma, resentment, and misunderstanding. Both Cuba and the United States stated that Mariel must not be repeated, but there was as of 2011 no certainty that it would not.

■ *See also*

Constitution of 1940

Governance and Contestation: The Republic: 1902–1952

The Machado Dictatorship Falls: August 1933

The World and Cuba: Cuba and the United States

BIBLIOGRAPHY

Books

Aja Díaz, Antonio. *Al cruzar las fronteras*. Havana: Centro de Estudios Demográficos de la Universidad de La Habana and Fondo de Población de las Naciones Unidas, 2009.

Fernández, Gastón. *The Mariel Exodus Twenty Years Later: A Study on the Politics of Stigma and a Research Bibliography*. Miami: Ediciones Universal, 2002.

Hamm, Mark S. *The Abandoned Ones: The Imprisonment and Uprising of the Mariel Boat People*. Boston: Northeastern University Press, 1995.

Masud-Piloto, Felix. *From Welcomed Exiles to Illegal Immigrant: Cuban Migration to the U.S., 1959–1995*. Lanham, MD: Rowman & Littlefield, 1996.

Pedraza, Silvia. "Cuba's Refugees: Manifold Migrations." In *Origins and Destinies: Immigration, Race, and Ethnicity in America*, edited by Silvia Pedraza and Rubén G. Rumbaut. Belmont, CA: Wadsworth, 1996.

Portes, Alejandro, and Robert Bach. *Latin Journey: Cuban and Mexican Immigrants in the United States*. Berkeley: University of California Press, 1985.

Smith, Wayne. *The Closest of Enemies*. New York: Norton, 1987.

Unión de Periodistas de Cuba. *Desafío a la desinformación*. Havana: Editora Política, 1980.

Articles

Bach, Robert, Jennifer Bach, and Timothy Triplett. "The Flotilla Entrants: Latest and Most Controversial." *Cuban Studies* 11 (July 1981–January 1982): 29–48.

Chardy, Alfonso. "Reagan-Era Accord Allows for Deportations." *Miami Herald* (26 April 2010): p. 1A.

Hernández, Rafael. "La política de los Estados Unidos hacia Cuba y la cuestión de la migración." *Cuadernos de Nuestra América* 2, no. 3 (January–June 1985): 75–100.

Hernández, Rafael, and Redi Gomis. "Retrato del Mariel: El ángulo socio-económico." *Cuadernos de Nuestra América* 3, no. 5 (January–June 1986): 124–151.

"El Mariel 30 Years: A Quest for Freedom." *Miami Herald* (18 April 2010): p. 1L.

■

PLATT AMENDMENT

David C. Carlson

A 1901 enactment by the U.S. Congress limiting the sovereignty of an independent Cuban republic.

The Platt Amendment, a 1901 enactment by the U.S. Congress written into the Cuban Constitution ahead of national independence (20 May 1902), exercised a de facto protectorate status limiting the sovereignty of an independent Cuban republic. It was used to legitimize several overt U.S. interventions into Cuba's internal affairs, and it defined terms that prescribed a fundamental Cuban concordance with U.S. interests until the amendment's formal abrogation on 29 May 1934.

PROVISIONS AND RECEPTION IN CUBA

The Platt Amendment, named after the bill's sponsor, U.S. Senator Orville Platt (1827–1905) of Connecticut, the Republican chair of the Senate Committee on Relations with Cuba, arose as a rider to the Army Appropriations Act of 1901. Yet, it represented long-standing North American ambitions to exert control and extend hegemony over Cuba that had been reiterated throughout the nineteenth century. In essence, the Platt Amendment prohibited a nominally independent Cuba from entering into treaties with foreign nations or contracting debts beyond a certain scope without the oversight and assent of the United States, thus granting the U.S. government a veto over Cuban foreign policy and delimiting Cuba's sovereignty. Article I had a military and strategic purpose akin to the Monroe Doctrine— to prevent foreign use of Cuba (the text did not acknowledge that U.S. power exercised via the Platt Amendment itself might "impair the independence of Cuba"). Article III authorized U.S. intervention

Anti-American protestors, Havana, 15 September 1933. Havana residents march in the streets after President Carlos Manuel de Céspedes is forced out of office. The next year, Cuba formally abrogated the 1901 Platt Amendment. KEYSTONE-FRANCE/GAMMA-KEYSTONE VIA GETTY IMAGES

"for the preservation of Cuban independence, the maintenance of a government adequate for the protection of life, property, and individual liberty," and in order to discharge the obligations imposed by the Treaty of Paris on the United States, which were transferred to the Cuban government. Policies of the U.S. military government in the 1899–1902 occupation were "ratified and validated" by Article IV. Article VI "omitted from the boundaries of Cuba" the Isle of Pines (today the Isle of Youth), whose status was resolved by a later (1925) agreement. Article VII directed the Cuban government to lease or sell "lands necessary for coaling or naval stations at certain specified points" that included the installation at Guantánamo Bay—the oldest foreign naval base of the United States and, since 1960, the only one in a nation with which the United States formally has no diplomatic relations. Article VIII stated "that by way of further assurance the government of Cuba will embody the foregoing provisions in a permanent treaty with the United States." Upon passage by the U.S. Congress, this legislation was required to

be introduced into the Cuban constitution, without modification, or else the U.S. occupation of Cuba would persist.

In Cuba, the Platt Amendment was opposed by many associations and veteran groups, as well as by numerous politicians, including Juan Gualberto Gómez (1854–1933) and Barolomé Masó (1830–1907). For many, the Platt Amendment betrayed the assurances in the Joint Resolution that Cuba would be left in the hands of Cubans at the end of the war with Spain. Elite opinion was divided. Some hewed to Spain and supported autonomy in the nineteenth century. Others looked to the United States as an exemplar of modernity, progress, and political liberalism, as well as a source of investment capital and know-how, and, therefore, supported U.S. influence as positive and beneficent insofar as it might propel Cuba in the same direction. Advocates of *independentismo* supported nationalist propositions of a Cuban *patria* that would stand on its own, free, independent, and sovereign. But because U.S. officials effectively left no other way to end the North

American occupation, Cuban representatives passed the measure at the Constitutional Convention Assembly in Havana by a 16-to-11 vote. Representatives who voted in favor claimed that sovereignty mediated by the United States was a step toward full independence for Cuba and preferable to a continuing U.S. military occupation.

THE MEDIATED REPUBLIC

The law made the United States the final arbiter and guarantor in Cuba's internal and external politics, and, therefore, historians have termed the 1902–1934 semi-sovereign years of dependency: the mediated republic, the Plattist republic, the pseudo-republic, and even the neocolony. Shortly before returning to the United States in 1902, the American military governor general Leonard Wood (1860–1927) wrote candidly to President Theodore Roosevelt (1858–1919): "There is, of course, little or no independence left Cuba under the Platt Amendment" (Schoultz 2009, p. 24).

Antecedent to the Platt Amendment was the 20 April 1898 Joint Resolution—the declaration of war against Spain, signed by President William McKinley (1843–1901) that included the Teller Amendment, which prohibited U.S. annexation of Cuba in the wake of the conflict. In the Teller Amendment, McKinley recognized neither the Cuban republic in arms nor the belligerency rights of the separatist rebel army, and this had led to prognostications that there were hidden imperialist motives in U.S. policy. Anti-imperialists and pro–Cuban Revolutionary Party lobbyists backed the addition of the Teller Amendment, which directed the United States to "disclaim" any "disposition of intention to exercise sovereignty, jurisdiction, or control over" Cuba "except for pacification thereof," and furthermore promised "to leave the government and control of the island to its people." With the annexation or explicit postwar control of Cuba thus blocked, *jingoes* and pro-imperialists in the United States raised the Platt Amendment as an end run around its provisions. These groups, together with North American investors, understood that there was no plausible way to rescind the obstacles to annexation, but they thought that a Cuban constituency of property owners fearful of instability and amenable to a more direct U.S. role—coupled with restrictions on the vote via property and literacy requirements—would advance their interests in the Cuban elections. Those who favored an overt U.S. role in Cuba introduced the Platt Amendment to prevent Cuba from aligning with another power and to ensure that those with commercial interests on the island would have safeguards. "Pacification" suggested that Cubans were unable to control their own affairs and promoted the paternalist view that the island was a viable state only to the degree that it furthered U.S. interests. As Senator Platt wrote in a letter to a North American investor, "the United States will always, under the so-called Platt Amendment, be in a position to straighten out things if they get seriously bad" (Schoultz 1998, p. 151).

RATIFICATION IN CUBA

After the amendment to the Cuban constitution had been passed and duly adopted, the presidential elections in Cuba saw the victory of a proponent of the new relationship, Tomás Estrada Palma (1832–1908; pres. 1902–1906), who had long favored annexation and had resided in the United States since 1877. The measure was promptly ratified in the Permanent Treaty of Cuban-U.S. relations in 1903. Estrada Palma had become head of the Cuban Revolutionary Party junta in New York after José Martí (1853–1895) departed to join the anti-colonial rebellion. Martí and other *independentistas* had organized and campaigned against annexationism, rhetorically asking, "Once the United States is in Cuba, who will drive it out?" and warning in the 1880s that it might be Cuba's "fate to have a skillful neighbor let us bleed ourselves on his threshold until finally he can take whatever is left in his hostile, selfish and irreverent hands" (Pérez 2006, p. 112). Antonio Maceo (1845–1896), killed in action during the War of Independence, had written to friends, "it is better to rise or fall without help than to contract debts of gratitude with such a powerful neighbor"(Pérez 2008, p. 175). But with the balance of forces in the post-U.S. occupation settlement shifting, nationalist propositions did not carry the day.

The Platt Amendment insinuated North American so-called soft power and legitimated the use of so-called hard power in Cuban affairs. Passage and adoption of the amendment led to the 1902 Reciprocity Treaty, which gave preferential treatment to both nations' exports: Cuban sugar entered U.S. markets at a 20 percent discount over less favored sugar exporters, and U.S. exports, capital goods, and manufactures obtained between 20 and 40 percent tariff reductions in Cuba. This agreement underpinned the post-occupation rise and consolidation of sugar monoculture and firmly established salient U.S. commercial interests and outright ownership on the island. At the end of World War I, U.S.-manufactured goods dominated Cuban markets, while 77 percent of Cuba's sugar crop went to the United States; by the early 1920s, North American capitalists controlled 60 percent of Cuba's sugar industry and fully 95 percent of production went to U.S. markets. North Americans came to dominate other key industries and services, too. The Cuban-American Treaty of February 1903 formally adopted the Platt Amendment under Article VIII and stipulated that Cuba would lease the lower portion of Guantánamo Bay to the U.S. Navy as a coaling and naval station.

INSTABILITY AND U.S. INTERVENTION

The possibility of U.S. intervention in Cuban politics became an ever-present factor in disputes and political calculations in an untested and chaotic system characterized by infighting, violence, and widespread corruption. In 1906, Estrada Palma's incumbency advantage and outright voting fraud ensured his reelection. This provoked armed rebellion by Liberal Party supporters and open calls for U.S. intervention from both sides. Estrada Palma requested intervention when it became evident that the republic's Rural Guard lacked sufficient means to repress the revolt. A second U.S. occupation of Cuba (1906–1909) ensued under Secretary of War William Howard Taft (1857–1930) and then Charles E. Magoon (1861–1920), a Minnesota judge and governor of the Panama Canal Zone. During the second occupation a permanent Cuban army was established prior to the departure of North American forces.

In 1912, the next president, Liberal José Miguel Gómez (1858–1921; pres. 1909–1913) faced an armed protest by the Independientes de Color (PIC). Many Afro-Cubans had voted for one of the principal two parties rather than the minority PIC, yet identified strongly with the 1895–1899 anti-colonial struggle against Spain and, therefore, demanded from the republic improved education, land, material conditions, an end to discrimination, and access to political office. This was not to be. Gómez, a former general of the Liberation army who had voted in favor of the Platt Amendment but nonetheless campaigned against excessive American influence, was confronted with U.S. responses to political and agrarian unrest that included a buildup of U.S. ships at Havana, Nipe, and Guantánamo Bay to "protect the lives and property of American citizens." Gómez unleashed the armed forces and militia to put down the incipient rebellion, which saw massacre and racist terror, particularly in Oriente Province. U.S. Marines fanned out by rail from Guantánamo Bay to occupy U.S.-owned sugar mills and railway properties during these disturbances.

In 1916, the Conservative president Mario García Menocal (1866–1941; pres. 1913–1921) secured reelection via vote buying and other electoral irregularities denounced by his Liberal opponents. The Liberals launched another revolt, known as la Chambelona, which led to the Platt-sanctioned intervention by U.S. Marines for a third time. Some of these troops remained in Camagüey, Nuevitas, and other areas until the early 1920s. General Enoch H. Crowder (1859–1932), special representative of the Harding administration in Cuba until 1923, inserted U.S. interests into Cuban politics in the end logic of the Platt Amendment: managing affairs through the island's political system and acquiescent politicians.

Frustration with the progress of the mediated republic and the enduring problems of Cuban society suggested that the Platt Amendment would become a whipping boy of politics and nationalist opposition to corruption, graft, political violence, and impediments to effective exercise of national sovereignty. Within Cuban politics, every political faction tried to ingratiate itself with the U.S. Embassy while assailing its opponents. Cuba became a weak state in which elite groups obtained access to political office and used it as a means to reward patronage networks, and the clases económicas were increasingly associated with foreign—principally U.S.—interests.

President Gerardo Machado (1871–1939; pres. 1925–1933) ran on a platform of presidential term limits, more equitable relationships with the United States, and repeal of the Platt Amendment. Amid steeply declining sugar prices and systemic economic and political crises exacerbated eventually by the Great Depression, Machado emerged as an authoritarian and even despotic president ruling through co-optation and political violence. Opponents responded by targeting manifestations of U.S. control in Cuba, some to express their antagonism to U.S. neocolonial hegemony, others—such as the middle-class ABC revolutionary organization that waged a terrorist campaign against Machado's Porra secret police—in the expectation that U.S. intervention would displace the increasingly unpopular autocrat. By 1933, in the midst of the Depression and an incipient social revolution in Cuba, the administration of Franklin D. Roosevelt dispatched Sumner Welles (1892–1961) to broker a change of government. A powerful U.S. fleet of thirty warships was on standby, but the Good Neighbor Policy signaled a move away from overt interventionism. Machado resigned and fled Cuba for the United States.

CUBAN ABROGATION

During the radical opposition's high-water mark, the 1933 Pentarquía (Pentarchy) chief executive council and the successive reformist government of a hundred days under Ramón Grau San Martín (1887–1969; pres. 1933–1934 and 1944–1948), Cuba abrogated the Platt Amendment. Welles recommended U.S. intervention and responded to the reformist policies and particularly the announced abrogation by withholding U.S. recognition. Ultimately, Fulgencio Batista (1901–1973) orchestrated the downfall of the government while effectively ruling through compliant caretaker presidents Carlos Mendieta (1873–1960; pres. 1934–1935), José Barnet (1864–1946; pres. 1935–1936), and Miguel Mariano Gómez (1889–1950; pres. 1936).

The Platt Amendment's formal abrogation is commonly ascribed to the 1934 Permanent Treaty signed during the presidency of Mendieta. This treaty withdrew all of the Plattist stipulations except for Article VII, the permanent lease arrangement for Guantánamo Bay. In spite of the abrogation of the Platt Amendment, the Cuban revolutionary government often responds to U.S. policy pronouncements—such as the 1996 Helms-Burton Cuban Liberty and Democratic Solidarity (Libertad) Act, in which the United States derogates to itself the determination of conditions to be met by a future Cuban government responsive to U.S. political, economic, and policy prerogatives and imperatives, and the 2004 and 2006 State Department Commission for Assistance to a Free Cuba reports that similarly outline detailed U.S. goals vis-à-vis a post-socialist Cuba—as infringements and preconditions on the effective sovereignty of Cuba redolent of the U.S.-Cuban relationship under the Platt Amendment and the first four decades of the twentieth century.

BIBLIOGRAPHY

Aguilar, Luis E. *Cuba 1933: Prologue to Revolution.* New York: Norton, 1972.

Benjamin, Jules R. *The United States and the Origins of the Cuban Revolution: An Empire of Liberty in an Age of National Liberation.* Princeton, NJ: Princeton University Press, 1990.

Hitchman, James H. "The Platt Amendment Revisited: A Bibliographical Survey." *Americas* 23 (April 1967): 343–369.

Pérez, Louis A., Jr. *Cuba between Empires: 1878–1902.* Pittsburgh, PA: University of Pittsburgh Press, 1983.

Pérez, Louis A., Jr. *Cuba under the Platt Amendment, 1902–1934.* Pittsburgh, PA: University of Pittsburgh Press, 1986.

Pérez, Louis A., Jr. *Cuba and the United States: Ties of Singular Intimacy.* 2nd ed. Athens: University of Georgia Press, 1990.

Pérez, Louis A., Jr. *The War of 1898: The United States and Cuba in History and Historiography.* Chapel Hill: University of North Carolina Press, 1998.

Pérez, Louis A., Jr. *Cuba: between Reform and Revolution.* Oxford, U.K.: Oxford University Press, 2006.

Pérez, Louis A., Jr. *Cuba in the American Imagination: Metaphor and the Imperial Ethos.* Chapel Hill: University of North Carolina Press, 2008.

Roig de Leuchsenring, Emilio. *Historia de la Enmienda Platt.* 2 vols. Havana: Oficina del Historiador de la Ciudad, 1961.

Schoultz, Lars. *Beneath the United States: A History of U.S. Policy toward Latin America.* Cambridge, MA: Harvard University Press, 1998.

Schoultz, Lars. *That Infernal Little Cuban Republic: The United States and the Cuban Revolution.* Chapel Hill: University of North Carolina Press, 2009.

Whitney, Robert. *State and Revolution in Cuba: Mass Mobilization and Political Change, 1920–1940.* Chapel Hill: University of North Carolina Press, 2001.

Williams, William Appleman. *The Tragedy of American Diplomacy.* 1959. Reprint, New York: Norton, 1988.

■ *See also*

Cuban Thought and Cultural Identity: Socialist Thought

Performing Arts: Theater: Revolutionary Period

PLAYWRIGHTS OF THE REVOLUTION: ABELARDO ESTORINO AND EUGENIO HERNÁNDEZ ESPINOSA

Maité Hernández-Lorenzo

Two approaches in the construction of new subjects and discourses within revolutionary Cuban dramaturgy.

Abelardo Estorino (b. 1925), winner of the National Prize for Literature (1992) and for Theater (2002), is considered by many critics to be the most important living Cuban playwrights. Likewise, Eugenio Hernández Espinosa (b. 1936), winner of the National Prize for Theater (2005), has been called one of the most significant playwrights of his generation. Both have developed a form of theater that works primarily through the word, accentuating a poetic realism. They began in the theater as playwrights and later, as their careers advanced, directed their own plays and those of other writers.

Both Estorino and Hernández Espinosa suffered under the strict guidelines of *parametración* (standardization), a process that resulted from the damaging and erratic cultural policy implemented by the Cuban government after the Revolution. The policy gave rise to the *Quinquenio Gris* (the Five Grey Years), which officially ran from 1971—beginning with the National Education and Cultural Congress—until 1976, the year the Ministry of Culture was founded, when the policy was reviewed and eradicated.

Estorino had been classified by critics as a transitional playwright mainly because his earliest works— *Hay un muerto en la calle* (There Is a Dead Man in the Street, 1954) and *El peine y el espejo* (The Comb and the Mirror, 1956)—were written before 1959 when the Revolution triumphed and the course of the country changed, not just politically and economically, but also socially, culturally, and in all other aspects of its citizens' lives. In contrast, Hernández Espinosa is considered an author of the Revolution because his career came together at the height of the revolutionary period. His important works include *El sacrificio* (The Sacrifice, 1961), *Los peces en la red* (Fish in the Net, 1961), and *María Antonia* (1964). The new conflicts, subjects, and social scenarios generated by the Revolution and the increasing tension between the individual and society were treated by both writers, but from different perspectives, with different expressions.

Estorino ventured into comedy with *Ni un sí ni un no* (Not a Yes or a No, 1980), puppet theater and children's theater with *La cucarachita Martina y el ratoncito Pérez* (Martina, the Cockroach, and Pérez, the Mouse, 1961), tragedy in *Morir del cuento* (Dying for a Story, 1983), theater of the absurd with *El tiempo de la plaga* (Time of the Plague, 1968), and even the classics, with *Medea sueña Corinto* (2007). Alongside his work as a playwright, he established a successful career as a director.

Estorino's body of work also accentuated his interest in and concern for individuals faced with the challenges and issues of their times. He expressed this interest through various types of theatrical discourse, by means of poetic realism, in *La casa vieja* (The Old House, 1964); parable, in *Los mangos de Caín* (Cain's Mangos, 1965); subversion of literary discourse and the construction of a metatext in *Parece blanca* (It Appears White, 1994); metaphorical self-reference as seen in *La dolorosa historia del amor secreto de don José Jacinto Milanés* (The Painful History of the Secret Love of Don José Jacinto Milanés, 1974), subsequently rewritten and restructured by the author as *Vagos rumores* (Vague Rumors, 1992); and theatrical recourse within the theater in *Morir del cuento*. Nearly all his plays have in common the familiar, intimate, closed space as the main environment in which to visualize the macro-conflicts between the individual and society.

Estorino has received various awards and recognitions, including honorable mention in the Casa de las Americas Literary Prize (1964) and a Guggenheim Foundation grant in 1997. His work has been presented in New York, Miami, Cadiz, Bogotá, Mexico City, and at numerous international festivals. In 2006 Tablas-Alarcos published in its Classical Library collection his *Teatro Completo* (Complete Theater) in two volumes. *Medea sueña Corinto* (2008) was not included in this collection.

Eugenio Hernández Espinosa rose to prominence on the national stage with the successful debut of his exemplary tragedy *María Antonia* (1964), directed by Roberto Blanco; this play was later made into a film (1991) directed by Sergio Giral. Prolific in the broad thematic scope of his production, in which various creative cycles are apparent, Hernández Espinosa places his characters into barely visible social conflicts.

His liberating, humanist works give voice to people who faced new social circumstances after the Revolution: women, blacks, and members of the lowest classes of society—groups that had been invisible but later resonated with contemporary Cuban society. He tackled gender in *María Antonia*, *La Simona* (1973), *Calixta Comité* (Calixta Committee, 1980), and *Emelina Cundiamor* (1987); race and the individual in society in *Mi socio Manolo* (My Friend Manolo, 1971), *Tíbor Galarraga* (2004), and *Alto riesgo* (High Risk, 1996); and the marginalized in *María Antonia*. With his treatment of Afro-Cuban culture and religion, through revisiting myth in *Oshún y las cotorras* (Oshún and the Parrots, 1980) and *Odebí, el cazador*

(Odebí, the Hunter, 1980), the author became an essential voice in the symphony of Caribbean literature and theater.

Contrary to the familiar, closed, and intimate space that predominates in Estorino's plays, some of Hernández Espinosa's plays (*María Antonia*, *Calixta Comité*, *Mi socio Manolo*) accentuate the opening of declaratory spaces. He reevaluates the street, the plaza, the city block, and the vulnerable courtyard as open loci where the Revolution is recaptured and positioned, where the new conflicts and new social subjects are confirmed and determined.

Hernández Espinosa's texts stand out for their high literary quality, and he makes use of popular language, oral tradition, and word play. His monologue *Lagarto Pisabonito* (Pisabonito Lizard, 1998) displays his exceptional literary skill.

Hernández Espinosa's works have been published in Cuba and abroad and have been translated into various languages. He received the Casa de las Americas Literary Prize in 1977 for *La Simona*. He has been invited as a writer and director to important international festivals in France and Spain. Several of his plays have debuted in the United States, Martinique, and Guadalupe. His collaboration in film was as a scriptwriter for *Roble de olor* (Scent of Oak, 2002), a film directed by the Cuban filmmaker Rigoberto López (b. 1947).

BIBLIOGRAPHY

Curbelo, Alberto. "El alba del negro en el teatro cubano." In *Quiquiribú Mandinga*, by Eugenio Hernández Espinosa. Havana: Editorial Letras Cubanas, Colección Repertorio Teatral Cubano, 2009.

Dauster, Frank. "Visión de la realidad en el teatro cubano." *Revista Iberoamericana* 56, nos. 152–153 (July–December 1990): 853–870.

Escarpenter, José A. "Tres dramaturgos del inicio revolucionario: Abelardo Estorino, Antón Arrufat y José Triana." *Revista Iberoamericana* 56, nos. 152–153 (July–December 1990): 881–896.

Estorino, Abelardo. *Teatro completo*. 2 vols. Colección Biblioteca de Clásicos. Havana: Editorial Alarcos, 2006.

Hernández Espinosa, Eugenio. *La Simona*. Havana: Casa de las Américas, 1977.

Hernández Espinosa, Eugenio. *María Antonia*. Havana: Editorial Letras Cubanas, 1979.

Hernández Espinosa, Eugenio. *Teatro Escogido*. 2 vols. Havana: Editorial Letras Cubanas, Colección Repertorio Teatral Cubano, 2006.

Hernández Espinosa, Eugenio. *Quiquiribú Mandinga*. 2 vols. Havana: Editorial Letras Cubanas, Colección Repertorio Teatral Cubano, 2009.

Martiatu, Inés María. "Eugenio Hernández Espinosa, una dramaturgia propia." In *Teatro Escogido*, by Eugenio Hernández Espinosa. Havana: Editorial Letras Cubanas, Colección Repertorio Teatral Cubano, 2006.

Pensamiento caribeño. Siglos XIX y XX. Prague: Universidad Carolina de Praga, Editorial-Karolinum, 2007.

Pogolotti, Graziella. "Una educación sentimental." In *Teatro completo*, by Abelardo Estorino. Colección Biblioteca de Clásicos. Havana: Editorial Alarcos, 2006.

Raza y racismo. Antología de Caminos. Havana: Editorial Caminos, 2009.

■ *See also*

Diasporas: Introduction

Faith: Judaism

Literature: Poetry in the Revolutionary Period

THE POETRY OF JOSÉ KOZER

Gustavo Pérez Firmat

The first major poet to emerge from the contemporary Cuban diaspora.

Born in Havana in 1940 to Jewish parents, José Kozer is one of the most distinctive poetic voices to have emerged from the Cuban diaspora. Although his first book of poetry, *Padres y otras profesiones* (1972), was not published until he was in his thirties, after that Kozer produced a steady stream of volumes. His work has been translated into English, Portuguese, Italian, French, and Hebrew, and has appeared in more than 250 literary magazines and anthologies. His book of poems *No buscan reflejarse*, published in Havana in 2002, was the first book since the 1970s published in Cuba by a living exiled Cuban writer.

Kozer first left Cuba in early 1958 to study at New York University and returned to the island in 1959 as a supporter of the Castro revolution. Quickly disillusioned, he left Cuba again for New York. In 1967, he began teaching at Queens College, and his unhappy first marriage dissolved the following year. In 1970, after not writing for almost a decade, he returned to poetry and began to spend summers in Spain, where he met Guadalupe Barranechea, whom he married in 1974. He and Guadalupe raised his daughter Mía and their daughter Susana while he taught and immersed himself again in Spanish. Kozer remained at Queens College until his retirement in 1995, and after living briefly in Spain, Kozer and his wife settled in South Florida.

EXILE AND MEMORY

In light of his many years of residence in New York, Kozer could be considered a Latino writer from New York, but his work makes this identification nearly impossible, for someone who comes to Kozer's poems without knowing anything about the author would be hard-pressed to locate this poet in New York. Like other exiled writers, Kozer tended to write not about the world that surrounded him but about the one he left. Although his writing makes clear that he is a Cuban-Jewish exile, it says little about the country where he has lived most of his life. The map in his work is that of Havana and particularly of Santos

Suárez, the neighborhood where he grew up. When he is not voyaging mentally to the Cuba of his childhood, his poems withdraw into his extensive readings in world literature or into the sweet security of his home, where he enumerates in loving detail the furnishings and routines that make up life inside those four walls, with little or no indication of where this home exists. The poet resides in no definable place, for he tells us: "Diaspora is *atopos* (the *no* place): no place and all places" (1999c, p. 92).

Kozer's often baroque collages of words contain the terms of the everyday household along with the world of fantasy and memory, suggesting the myriad displacing experiences of exile; the only fixed points are the poet's family, his Cubanness, and his Jewishness. He constantly returns to the past, to pre revolutionary Cuba, and to the Eastern European Jewish tradition of his parents and grandparents. Speaking of the dual Jewish and Cuban diaspora of his life, he writes that "change is not rupture because poetry connects. Each dish, each person, each member of this family constitutes another possibility. Each one of them, story, instrument, vehicle of communication ... is another basting thread of resistance, of survival, of continuity" (1999c, p. 87). In "Santos Suárez, 1956," a poem consisting of an enumeration of domestic utensils and events, a "song to casseroles," Kozer gives to the reader a string of small things: his mother's pots and pans, the noises and smells of the neighborhood, relatives who come and go. The jumbled enumeration conveys the hustle and bustle of the household. There are no large themes here, no vapid generalities about expatriation or nostalgia, for the poet is shrewd enough to let the details do the talking.

> Esta romanza
> a las marmitas, destapa: y en las tarteras,
>   serrucho
> en escabeche
> y mil glorias y mil orines el vecindario, el lebrel
> y la verja, tío
> Sidney
> que perseveró con los dijes, las alcancías, de un hijo
> mayor y el canario que
> perseveraba
> (salmodia).
>
> *Kozer 1983, p. 19*

> [This song
> to casseroles, uncover it: and in the pans,
>   swordfish
> in brine
> and the neighborhood a thousand glories and a
>   thousand urines, the greyhound
> and the grate, uncle
> Sidney
> who persevered with the trinkets, the piggy
>   banks, of an eldest son

and the canary that persevered
(psalmody).]

Translated by Gustavo Pérez Firmat

Like the world of his childhood, a poem is a universe of capacious diversity, a kind of receptacle that accommodates the most heterogeneous materials. This is why Kozer's poems are full of containers—pots, pans, vessels, vases, jars, jugs, bottles, void. Once enclosed, the void can be filled to the hilt with objects.

ACCUMULATION AND HERMETICISM

Looking upon the scriptless page as a cavity that needs to be filled with words, Kozer opts for excess rather than aridity. His poems develop by accretion or accumulation; one word generates another, one line generates another, one poem generates another, one book generates another, in a seemingly unstoppable proliferation. In his lines, occasional words and phrases are isolated, highlighted by the eccentric use of parentheses, where the punctuation segregates words that are syntactically linked—verb and predicate, matching parts, noun and adjective. In order to grasp the sense one has to read through the parentheses, thus joining syntactically phrases that are typographically distinct. For Kozer, parentheses enclose supplementary or alternative utterances: parentheses. Parentheses are the logical abode of minority discourses. As a Cuban Jewish writer, Kozer is himself parenthetical. In the title of his essay "This Is (Also) Cuba, Chaguito," the cultural specificity of Cuban Jews is signified in the parenthetical "(Also)." Kozer locates himself inside that parenthetical indication of supplementarity. Another reason for the use of parentheses is formal: Parentheses are containers, typographical casseroles, open-lidded receptacles that allow him to stuff the poem with words. Like pots and pans, parentheses are *útiles*, utensils that can be used to accumulate and keep verbal stores. Parentheses are indeed *open doors* through which additional text can enter the poem. The roundness of the containing casseroles is recovered visually in the curves of the typographical marks.

When Kozer leaves the memory world of his youth, he moves to the house that he shares with his wife and daughters, the family home in "Home Sweet Home." With the rain falling outside, the house in the poem becomes a kind of ark that shelters him and his family. From the first lines, the poem establishes a tense opposition between outside and inside, between the threatening exterior world and the domestic sanctuary.

Ya pasaron: aquellos días de verdadera
agitación.
Hay una gotera en el cuarto de la niña, dejó
de rezumar (pese a
que llueve) (llueve)
está ahí la gotera,
no rezuma, el

Bendito.
En casa, hay cinco relojes: detenidos.

Kozer 1987, p. 13

[They passed already: those days of real
agitation.
There is a leak in our daughter's room, it
   stopped
leaking (even though
it rains) (it rains)
the leak is still there
it doesn't drip,
thank God.
In the house, there are five clocks: stopped.]

Translated by Gustavo Pérez Firmat

This house seems to exist outside time and space: Because the leak has been sealed, the rain cannot come in, and because the clocks do not work, time has stood still. (A few lines later the speaker will disclose that he does not even know what month it is.) Because the opposite of *agitation* is inactivity, everything inside the house appears reduced to stillness, contrasting with the teeming neighborhood of the poet's Cuban childhood. The verbs in this stanza communicate either the cessation of activity—*pasaron, dejó*—or states of being: *hay, está*. The rain stays outside, a separation indicated by the ever-present parentheses.

Kozer's poetry constructs a geography whose confines are simply those of the Spanish-speaking world. The exclusive use of Spanish in most of his work—a Spanish so rich, capacious, and cosmopolitan that perhaps only an exile could have written it—could be seen as his effort to build a verbal edifice that will isolate him from the realities of exile. His language is supple, precise, but it does not sound quite Cuban. Kozer's Spanish has a peculiar accent, and even when he writes about Cuban subjects, his Spanish has acquired an odd international flavor. Even if the matter is Cuban, the medium is not entirely so. Or rather, it is Cuban, but it is also Spanish, Mexican, and Peruvian, and Spanglish. Bringing together words and locutions from widely dispersed regions of the Hispanic world, Kozer writes an Esperanto Spanish, a no-man's language that testifies to the author's exile condition, both a symptom of uprootedness and a shield against it. In an interview, he described the language of his poems as "absorbent, capable of absorbing all forms of language ... I am all in favor of Babel" (Mansito).

LATER WORK

As Kozer's work evolved during the 1970s and 1980s, it began to resemble the closed but not quite hermetic house of "Home Sweet Home." The straightforward conversational manner and style of his best early poems—"Te acuerdas, Sylvia," "Julio," and "Santos Suárez, 1956"—gradually gave way to dense, obscure meditations. Because the windows and doors have been closed, these poems transpire among shadows. Whereas Kozer's early poetry was notable for its joyous transparency, his poetry of this period is notable for its somber hermeticism. Kozer's always long verse-lines swell into verse paragraphs that span a page or more. In "La blanca ambigüedad de las horas" (White Ambiguity of Hours), this type of writing turns the poem into a nearly impenetrable wall of words. His language is as copious as ever, but it has become opaque, foreboding, full of enigmatic images and undecipherable references:

> La sombra del repartidor de leche nos
>   blanqueaba:
> los geranios de harina los
> enjambres de esporas
> blancas a su paso: y la
> espuma creciente de la
> palabra leche (un aviso)
> su llegada: llegó,
> consecutivo el cisma
> de la reproducción
> (cuajada, los pechos
> repletos de semillas
> el embrión de los
> sementales rojos junto
> a las madres) se nos
> llamaba órganos
> reproductores: éramos
> niños a veces (indistintos)
> de delantal (amábamos
> los tules) alguna mosca
> muerta hace poco sobre
> el ácido encaje de los
> objetos moribundos, del
> aparador: nos llaman.

Kozer 1991

> [The milk dealer's shadow whitens us:
> geraniums of flour
> the swarm of spores
> white at his step: and the
> rising froth of the
> word milk (warning)
> his arrival: he came,
> following the schism
> of reproduction
> (curdled, breasts
> full of seed
> the breeder's
> red embryo next
> to the mothers) we were
> called reproductive organs:
> children sometimes (indistinct)
> of apron (we loved
> the bulrushes) a fly

> already dead awhile on
> the acrid lace of
> dead objects, of the
> cupboard: they call us.]

Kozer 1991

In the late 1990s, for the first time, Kozer's poetry started to become permeable to the English language. In the 1999 poem "Tres de la tarde (julio)" (Three O'clock in the Afternoon, July), he not only lapses into Spanglish—"my kingdom por una cucharada de coco rayado" (my kingdom for a spoonful of grated coconut)—but also indulges in bilingual wordplay: "Matrimonial, de mattress (quiero decir) así" (Matrimonial, from mattress [I mean to say] like this) (Kozer 1999a). By the same token, in his book of prose fragments *Mezcla para dos tiempos* (1999), one of the vignettes says simply: "Rush hour, brush hour" (1999b, p. 205). These brushes with the English language would have been unthinkable in his earlier work. Even the title of the vignette "In a Station of the Metro. New York, 5 O'clock," which places the poet in an American social setting, undertakes a relocation to a here-and-now largely absent from his earlier work.

BIBLIOGRAPHY

Chavez Rivera, Armando. "Cenizas sobre Kyoto: Entrevista con el poeta cubano José Kozer." *Horizontes: Revista de la Universidad Catolica de Puerto Rico* 49, no. 96 (April 2007): 131–145.

Kozer, José. *Bajo este cien*. Mexico City: Fondo de Cultura Económica, 1983.

Kozer, José. *El carillon de los muertos*. Buenos Aires: Ediciones Ultimo Reino, 1987.

Kozer, José. "The Poetic Experience: The Logic of Chance." In *Philosophy and Literature in Latin America*, edited by Jorge J. E. Gracia and Mireya Camurati. Albany: State University of New York Press, 1989.

Kozer, José. *Prójimos/Intimates*. Translated by Ammiel Alcalay. Barcelona: Les plaquettes del Carrer Ausiàs, 1991.

Kozer, José. "Esto (también) es Cuba, Chaguito." *Papeles de Enlace* (Summer 1992): 3–4.

Kozer, José. "Dos poemas." *Crítica* 76 (June–July 1999a): 19–22.

Kozer, José. *Mezcla para dos tiempos*. Mexico City: Aldus, 1999b.

Kozer, José. "Natural Instincts." In *King David's Harp: Autobiographical Essays by Jewish Latin American Writers*, edited by Stephen A. Sadow. Albuquerque: University of New Mexico Press, 1999c.

León, Denise. "El hogar, el pan y los poemas: algunas notas sobre la poesía de José Kozer." *Espéculo: Revista de Estudios Literarios* 39 (July–October 2008).

Mansito, Nicolás. "José Kozer in Conversation with Nicolás Mansito." 28 December 2007. Available from http://jacketmagazine.com/35/iv-kozer-ivb-mansito.shtml.

Pérez Firmat, Gustavo. "Noción de José Kozer." *Revista Iberoamericana* 152–153 (July–December 1990): 1247–1256.

Reis, Roberto. "Entrevista: José Kozer." *Chasqui* 6, no. 1 (November 1976): 97.

Sefami, Jacobo. "Todo hombre es una isla: La Cuba de José Kozer." *Encuentro de la Cultura Cubana* 37–38 (Summer–Autumn 2005): 35–39.

THE POETRY OF NICOLÁS GUILLÉN

Nancy Morejón

Fundamental themes and aspects of Guillén's poetry from 1930 to 1982.

Nicolás Guillén (1902–1989) wrote numerous books of poetry that achieved world renown during his lifetime, not only in Spanish-language circles, but also among the most demanding literary critics and authors in most languages of the twentieth century. Indeed, titles such as *El son entero* (The Whole Son, 1947) and *La paloma de vuelo popular* (The Dove of Popular Flight, 1958) are among the most important books of Spanish-language poetry on both sides of the Atlantic.

THE NATIONAL POET

In his final productive decades, Guillén composed poetry considered the most elegant and essential manifestation of Cuban national identity. The Guantánamo poet Regino Boti (1878–1958) recognized Guillén's talent in 1931 and described him as a national poet, and this designation was endorsed by the Cuban people. Guillén's poetry achieved mass distribution and accolades for its excellence when his *Motivos de son* (*Son* Motifs) appeared on 20 April 1930, in "Ideales de una Raza" (Ideals of a Race), the weekly page on black themes of the newspaper *Diario de la Marina*. It was stunning, a rallying cry announcing the beginning of a literary and artistic era that was at once avant-garde and a manifestation of late nineteenth-century independence ideals. In that same year, Cuba initiated its first revolution of the twentieth century, endorsing the ideas of José Martí (1853–1895) and Antonio Maceo (1845–1896). The revolution failed, or as Raúl Roa García put it, it "faded into the din," but in its wake, great national art and literature flourished.

From April 1930 on Guillén was at the head of the Afro-Cuban movement started by scholar Fernando Ortiz (1881–1969), as it expanded the horizons of tendencies then known by several names: Afro-Cuban poetry, Negro poetry, black poetry, mulatto poetry, Afro-Caribbean poetry, Negroid poetry. These terms emphasized the ethnic element that is essential in any attempt to recapture identity. Although there are convincing rationales for each of the labels for this poetry movement, it is curious that Fernando Ortiz preferred *mulatto* and *Afro-Cuban*, because important poets of the other Spanish-speaking countries of the Greater Antilles such as the Puerto Rican Luis Palés Matos (1898–1959) and the Dominican Manuel del Cabral (1907–1999) were writing poetry of the same type at the same time. The anthropological term *Afro-Cuban*, which Ortiz applied to the period's Cuban literary history, along with its complement *Hispanic-Cuban*, convey Ortiz's interpretation of Cuban culture as the product of a process of transculturation of Spanish and African elements. Nicolás Guillén's poem "Balada de los dos abuelos" (Ballad of the Two Grandfathers) in *West Indies, Ltd.* (1934) mirrors that reality:

> Shadows only I see
> My two grandfathers accompany me.
>
> Don Federico shouts at me
> and Taita Facundo keeps quiet;
> the two dream in the night
> and wander, wander.
> And I join them.

Nicolás Guillén's first two books of poetry, *Motivos de son* and *Sóngoro cosongo* (1931), introduced a new type of Cuban poetry. From the center of this new poetry emerged the drama of the black people and their invaluable contribution to Cuban life. Some critics argued that the terms coined and employed by Ortiz and his followers were only a fad, but they actually pointed to an original way of expressing Cuba's national soul that could not be explained without considering the amalgamation of cultures brought to Cuba by African slaves.

During the first half of the twentieth century many Spanish-language critics in Cuba and the United States such as José Juan Arrom (1910–2007), Ortiz, and Boti published writings on this subject, and in the 1940s the English-language poets H. R. Hays (1904–1980) and Langston Hughes (1902–1967) explored the theme. On his return to New York after his first trip to Africa in 1929, Hughes stopped in Havana and met Guillén, and their interview was later published by editor Gustavo Urrutia in "Ideales de una Raza." Hughes and Guillén forged a friendship that was strengthened by a second meeting in Valencia during the Spanish Civil War and ended only with Hughes's death in 1967. The cultural coincidences of an Afro-American consciousness can be seen in their respective works, Hughes as the venerated king of the blues and Guillén as the genius of the *son*. Both poets channelled folk sensibility to treat colloquial language as a high form of expression.

■ *See also*

Language: Lucumí

Literature: Poetry in the Republican Period

Literature: Poetry in the Revolutionary Period

Race: Afro-Cubanía in the Republic, 1907–1959

Nicolás Guillén. Cuban poet Nicolás Guillén. HÉCTOR DELGADO AND ROLANDO PUJOL

THE *SON* AND POETIC RHYTHM

The Cuban poet and critic Cintio Vitier (1921–2009) considered the discovery of the *son* to be one of Guillén's greatest contributions to Spanish-language poetry; that innovation left a permanent mark on all Cuban poetry. Many scholars who study Guillén's work praise its rhythm, which rises out of a clear, ancestral musicality. Many major Cuban composers, including Amadeo Roldán (1900–1939), Alejandro García Caturla (1906–1940), and Silvestre Revueltas (1899–1940), noted this distinctive characteristic of Guillén's poetry and wrote musical works inspired by *Motivos de son, Sóngoro cosongo,* or *West Indies, Ltd.*

Guillén captured in his poetry the pleasure Cubans take in the use of witty comment and humor to deal with difficult (even risky or dangerous) situations by Cubanizing the Spanish metric form most common in Latin America—the romance. At the time, it was a heroic act for a poet to write verses that reflect the way many Cuban blacks (and some non-blacks) still talk and think in their everyday lives. *Motivos de son* corroborated Mirta Aguirre's statement in the 1950s that Guillén's writing was a triumph of Cuban music (Aguirre 1952). Much of his poetry

moves around this rhythmic axis. The backbone of *son* in *Motivos del son* is found in the chorus—what Cubans call the *montuno* of the *son*—whose cadence, harboring tunes, and *tumbaos* (swing) essential to Cuban identity, started to appeal to Cubans at the turn of the twentieth century.

Impressed by the poems "Rumba" and "Velorio de Papa Montero" (Wake for Papa Montero) in *Sóngoro cosongo,* written in 1931, the Spanish poet and linguist Miguel de Unamuno (1864–1936) expressed his admiration for Guillén's poems. Unamuno had been exploring the rhythmic sense and verbal music of blacks and mulattoes in the Americas from the United States to Curaçao, and he was introduced to Guillén's by his countryman, the Spanish poet Federico García Lorca (1898–1936). In Cuba, this burgeoning literary movement, born of the heat generated by *Motivos de son,* was joined by performers such as Eusebia Cosme and Luis Carbonell, who staged productions of works by poets from Cuba, Puerto Rico, and other parts of the Americas who similarly appropriated the popular urban speech of Cuba and other Caribbean cities.

The appropriation of linguistic values within a rich oral tradition incorporates an original usage of popular ritual inherent to the myths of an extremely diverse culture. Myth, as described by Miguel Barnet and Rogelio Martínez Furé, is a fundamental aspect of the mystery conveyed by the free practice of certain Caribbean religious rites (Barnet; Martínez Furé), and it attains unprecedented splendor in poems such as "Sensemayá: Canto para matar a una culebra" (Sensemayá: Song to Kill a Snake) from *West Indies, Ltd.*:

Mayombe-bombe-mayombé!
Mayombe-bombe-mayombé!
Mayombe-bombe-mayombé!

....

The snake has eyes of glass;
The snake comes and coils round a stick;
with eyes of glass, round a stick,
with eyes of glass.

....

Mayombe-bombe-mayombé!
Sensamayá, the snake...
Mayombe-bombe-mayombé!
Sensamayá, it does not move
Mayombe-bombe-mayombé!
Sensamayá, the snake...
Mayombe-bombe-mayombé!
Sensamayá, it is dead.

In the second half of the twentieth century the Argentine poet and critic Ezequiel Martínez Estrada (1895–1964) praised Guillén's national sensibility. Recognizing the patriotic feeling the poet had inherited from his father, Senator Nicolás Guillén y Urra, who had been codirector of the major liberal daily *Las Dos Repúblicas* and was killed in the

1917 civil war between conservatives and liberals, Martínez Estrada declared Guillén an independence fighter in the field of literature. Martínez Estrada applauds Guillén's use of Havana street jargon in his poetry, and notices Guillén's elegiac tone, which Martínez Estrada relates to the tragic death of the poet's father. Poems such as "Elegía camagüeyana" (Elegy for Camagüey), "Elegía a Emmett Till" (Elegy for Emmett Till), "El apellido" (My Last Name), and "Elegía a Jacques Roumain" (Elegy for Jacques Roumain) demonstrate Guillén's universalist perspective on the Atlantic slave trade and its resulting diaspora, which to this day still demands and deserves further attention and study.

FORM

Guillén's literary career began in Camagüey, where his first poems were published in the journal *Lys*. In Camagüey he wrote the poetry that appeared in his first collection, *Cerebro y corazón* (Brain and Heart), which was completed in 1922 but remained unpublished until his biographer Ángel Augier (1910–2010) published it many decades later. Guillén devoured the books in his father's library in Camagüey, soaking up the Greek classics and other important works, and proclaiming his love for Spanish metric forms, including nineteenth-century Latin American modernism, and especially the Nicaraguan Rubén Darío (1867–1916) and José Martí. *Cerebro y corazón* displays the modernist tone and style widespread at that time.

Formally, Guillén's verses are expansive, discursive, more or less reflective; in them, the poetic *I* dwells on lived experience. Following the classical style (in the Hispanic poetic tradition of Góngora, Garcilaso, Francisco de Quevedo, and Lope de Vega), the poetic *I* is actually a *we*, an almost collective monologue, stemming from the *we* of American poet Walt Whitman, and to which Cuban cultural forms are added. Guillén's poems are brief, with elliptical proposals, which he uses for satirical effect in his *sones*, epigrams, and madrigals; they form the basis of *El gran zoo* (The Great Zoo, 1967) and sections of *La rueda dentada* (The Cogwheel, 1972).

In "West Indies, Ltd.," a fluvial, prosaic, Quevedo-like poem, Guillén experimented with new poetic forms. The poem's formal style is the seed for the exceptional *Elegía a Jesús Menéndez* ("Elegy for Jesús Menéndez," 1951), in which the poet's heartbreaking anti-imperialist voice takes in a multiplicity of forms: many planes of reference and rhythms are exuberantly transposed, including the ticker tape of the New York Stock Exchange. This discourse infused by modernity, a sense of audacity, and a language taken from newspaper advertisements, reappears in one of his last collections, *El diario que a diario* (The Daily Diary, 1972). That modernistic approach was a departure from sonnets such as "A las ruinas de Nueva York" (To the New York Ruins) in *La rueda dentada*; "Che Guevara," written

in 1959 and published in *Tengo* (I Have, 1964); or the "Soneto" dedicated to the French poet François Villon, dating from 1975. Guillén was a master of form and discipline, and in successive periods—1922 to 1958 and 1959 to 1982—he expressed himself either in the traditional forms of Spanish poetry or by breaking with the classical and experimenting with an avant-garde vocation, aware of the undeniable modernity of the century in which he lived.

The poems of *Tengo*, *El gran zoo*, and *Por el Mar de las Antillas anda un barco de papel* (Over the Caribbean Sea Sails a Paper Boat, 1978), a book for children, accomplish a formal perfection. To Guillén, poetry is a powerful tool to be used in defense of noble causes; it is not light entertainment that relies on improvised inspiration, but rather on precise, exhausting work. Guillén never engaged in superfluous wordiness, pompous adjectives, or exotic cadences; indeed, as he matured his poetry became more and more synthesized and elliptical. The poem "Granma" from *Por el Mar de las Antillas anda un barco de papel* illustrates these features:

> Oh, Granma, I invoke your name!
> I approach softly.
> I touch your face.

Proclaimed a national poet at the start of his literary career, Nicolás Guillén, heir to the nineteenth-century independence ideals of the Cuban poet José María Heredia (1903–1939) and José Martí, remains in the early twenty-first century an advocate of Cuban and Caribbean culture. Devoted to the defense of the most noble causes of his time, Guillén, along with the Peruvian poet César Vallejo (1892–1938) and the Chilean poet Pablo Neruda (1904–1973), produced oeuvres that promote Latin American identities (black, Indian, mixed race) and also forged a path for later twentieth-century poets who fought oppression, economic dependence, the philosophy of dispossession, and wars of plunder. The Spanish Civil War was the first step down that path. In Valencia in 1937 Guillén joined the Partido Comunista de Cuba (PCC; Cuban Communist Party), but his membership in the party did not prevent him from devoting his life and work to the Cuban Revolution, which he saw as a succession of struggles over two centuries.

As one of the founders of the Unión de Escritores y Artistas de Cuba (UNEAC; Union of Writers and Artists of Cuba) in August 1961, Guillén came out against the Vietnam War and apartheid in South Africa and in favor of recognizing the Caribbean as the natural context of Cuban culture, within a vast Latin American dimension. He defended the Spanish language not only because it was his native tongue, but also because it had been the vehicle for magnificent literary works. According to Salvador Bueno, Guillén was the most Spanish of Cuban poets, who also fought against colonialism, a Cuban with his face toward the sun always searching for a freedom shared by all, a freedom in which, as Martí desired, people could live with full human dignity.

SELECTED WORKS BY GUILLÉN

Motivos de son. Havana: Rambla, Bouza y Compañía, 1930.

Sóngoro cosongo: Poemas mulatos. Havana: Úcar García y Compañía, 1931.

West Indies, Ltd.. Havana: Úcar García y Compañía, 1934.

Cantos para soldados y sones para turistas. Prologue by Juan Marinello. Mexico City: Masas, 1937.

El son entero; suma poética. (1929–1946). Buenos Aires: Pleamar, 1947.

La paloma de vuelo popular y Elegías. Buenos Aires: Losada, Biblioteca contemporánea collection, 1958.

Tengo. Prologue by José Antonio Portuondo. Havana: Universidad Central de Las Villas, 1964.

El gran zoo. Illustrations by Fayad Jamís. Havana: Ediciones Unión, 1967.

El diario que a diario. Havana: Ediciones Unión, 1972.

La rueda dentada. Havana: Ediciones Unión, 1972.

Por el Mar de las Antillas anda un barco de papel. Illustrations by Rapi Diego. Havana: Ediciones Unión, 1978.

Sol de domingo. Havana: Ediciones Unión, 1982.

En algún sitio de la primavera. Havana: Ediciones Unión, 2000.

Obra poética. Edited by Ángel Augier. 2 vols. Havana: Letras Cubanas, 2002.

Man-Making Words: Selected Poems of Nicolás Guillén. Translated and edited by Robert Márquez and David Arthur McMurray. 2nd ed. Amherst: University of Massachusetts Press, 2003.

BIBLIOGRAPHY

Aguirre, Mirta. *Un poeta y un continente.* Havana: Letras Cubanas, 1982.

Álvarez Álvarez, Luis. *Nicolás Guillén: Identidad, diálogo, verso.* Santiago de Cuba: Oriente, 1997.

Antuña, María Luisa, and Josefina García Carranza. *Bibliografía de Nicolás Guillén.* Havana: Instituto Cubano del Libro and Biblioteca Nacional José Martí, 1975.

Augier, Ángel. *Notas para un estudio biográfico-crítico.* 2 vols. Santa Clara, Cuba: Universidad Central de Las Villas, 1962–1964.

Augier, Ángel. *La revolución cubana en la poesía de Nicolás Guillén.* Havana: Letras Cubanas, 1979.

Barnet, Miguel. *La fuente viva.* Havana: Casa Editora Abril, 2011.

Ellis, Keith. *Cuba's Nicolás Guillén: Poetry and Ideology.* Toronto: University of Toronto Press, 1983.

Feldman, Dorothy. *Nicolás Guillén and Afro Cuban Poetry.* New York: Columbia University, 1948.

Fernández Retamar, Roberto. *El son de vuelo popular.* Havana: Ediciones Unión, 1972.

Gaetani, Francis Marion. *Nicolás Guillén: A Study on the Phonology and Metrics in His Poetry.* New York: Columbia University, 1940.

Kubayanda, Josaphat B. *The Poet's Africa: Africanness in the Poetry of Nicolás Guillén and Aimé Césaire.* New York: Greenwood Press, 1990.

Márquez, Roberto, Alfred Melon, and Keith Ellis. *Tres ensayos sobre Nicolás Guillén.* Havana: Ediciones Unión, 1980.

Martínez Estrada, Ezequiel. *La poesía afrocubana de Nicolás Guillén.* Montevideo, Uruguay: Arca, 1966.

Martínez Furé, Rogelio. *Diálogos imaginarios.* 2nd ed. Havana: Letras Cubanas, 1997.

Morejón, Nancy, ed. *Recopilación de textos sobre Nicolás Guillén.* Havana: Casa de las Américas, 1972.

Morejón, Nancy. *Nación y mestizaje en Nicolás Guillén.* Havana: Ediciones Unión, 1982.

Morejón, Nancy. *España en Nicolás Guillén.* Speech upon admission to the Academia Cubana de la Lengua. Havana: Ediciones Unión, 2005.

Roa García, Raúl. *La revolución del 30 se fue a bolina.* Havana: Huracán, Instituto Cubano del Libro, 1969.

Ruffinelli, Jorge. *Poesía y descolonización: Viaje por la poesía de Nicolás Guillén.* Mexico City: Oasis, Universidad Veracruzana, 1985.

Ruscalleda Bercedóniz, Jorge María. *La poesía de Nicolás Guillén (Cuatro elementos sustanciales).* San Juan: Universidad de Puerto Rico, 1975.

Sardinha, Dennis. *The Poetry of Nicolás Guillén: An Introduction.* London: New Beacon Books, 1976.

Smart, Ian. *Nicolás Guillén, Popular Poet of the Caribbean.* Columbia: University of Missouri Press, 1990.

Tous, Adriana. *La poesía de Nicolás Guillén.* Madrid: Cultura Hispánica, 1971.

White, Clément A. *Decoding the Word: Nicolás Guillén as Maker and Debunker of Myth.* Miami, FL: Universal, 1993.

Williams, Lorna V. *Self and Society in the Poetry of Nicolás Guillén.* Baltimore, MD: Johns Hopkins University Press, 1982.

POLITICAL PERSPECTIVES ON PRISONERS IN CUBA

Holly Ackerman

The politics behind Cuba's prison population.

Critics of the current Cuban regimes claim that the expression of open political dissent in Cuba (and not just criticism of a particular policy or the incompetence of an official) is not merely voicing an opinion on politics or governance: It can be tantamount to an expression of treason in the eyes of the Cuban state. Opposition to the Revolution and socialism is a grave offense under Cuba's concept of socialist legality since it is linked not only to conspiring to overthrow the government but also to collusion with the U.S.

government, which has openly and covertly sought to remove the revolutionary government since 1960. Hence, legality and rights stem from sovereignty. Cuba's vision of democracy is based on a majority model that requires a high degree of consensus, not one generated by minorities and opposition groups, seen as weakening national unity and majority rule (Domínguez 2009, p. 575).

The government of Cuba has been accused of detaining those who ideologically oppose them, also known as "political prisoners." The term *political prisoner* is highly charged, with shifting definitions that make it difficult to reach agreement on what a political prisoner is. From the Cuban government's perspective, these individuals are actively seeking to overthrow the government, making them not "political prisoners" but "counterrevolutionaries," "mercenaries of the United States," and "criminals." Mercenaries might seem like a truculent expression, but the fact is that opposition groups (civil, political, human rights) receive money yearly from the U.S. Agency for International Development and other U.S. government sources, disbursed by Cuban exile organizations. Ricardo Alarcón said in 2009 that "In this country, there are no political prisoners. People are in jail for crimes against the law, for being paid agents of a foreign power" (Pérez-Stable p. 128).

When the revolutionary government took power in 1959, it soon implemented many policies that brought it to a collision course both with the U.S. government as well as Cubans on the island who disagreed with these new policies. Cuba faced armed insurrection within its borders between 1959 and 1965. It also had to defeat a U.S.-sponsored invasion from outside its borders in the Bay of Pigs invasion of 1961. These acts of military aggression, combined with the economic embargo imposed by the U.S. government in 1962, created a climate in which the Cuban government felt that it was in an undeclared state of war. National security and sovereignty became preeminent concerns for a state that felt besieged economically, politically, and militarily. Cuba's concerns with national unity, territorial integrity, and social cohesion were of utmost importance.

This climate sponsored a large increase in Cuba's prison population, particularly during the years between 1959 and 1965 when the Cuban government fought armed insurrectionists. In the main, twenty thousand to forty thousand prisoners of this era were alleged to have either participated in or indirectly supported armed counterrevolutionary groups consisting of three distinct types (Thomas p. 1460; Domínguez 1978 pp. 253–254). The first type was reactionary oppositionists. Oppositionists believed that upholding continuous political order was primary and wanted to turn the political clock back to a reorganization of the pre-1959 government. These included those connected to deposed leader Fulgencio Batista, as well as those who were not directly associated with Batista

but who believed the 1958 elections were fair and valued political stability and democratic transition over armed insurrection.

The second type was the democratic revolutionary resistance (what some have called the democratic left) who fought against Batista and initially incorporated themselves into the new revolutionary regime but resumed armed activity when they disagreed with the radical drift of the new leadership. Finally, there was a large and diverse group of people rounded up as "potential security risks" in March of 1961 as the government braced for the exile invasion sponsored by the United States, which they knew was imminent. Following the defeat of the invasion at the Bay of Pigs, thousands who had been placed in preventive detention were given summary trials without due process and also entered prison with long-term sentences of up to thirty years (Ackerman; Instituto Internacional de Cooperación y Solidaridad Cubana).

Once in prison, two plans of labor and rehabilitation were eventually offered to these prisoners. The first in 1962 required hard labor, political confession, and at least the appearance of ideological conversion. The second plan, known as the Progressive Plan, was introduced in 1971 and did not require confession or the same degree of ideological incorporation into the new regime (Hamm 1989). These two plans shortened sentences and improved prison conditions for those who accepted them and considerably reduced the prison population. By 1975, this segment of the prison population had been reduced to an estimated 4,500 prisoners (Domínguez 1978, p. 254).

Those within the political penitentiary who insisted on continued resistance to the new government had few options other than to reject rehabilitation and refuse to wear the uniform of common criminals required by the government after 1962. As a consequence they served their full sentences and many spent decades clad in their underwear becoming collectively known as *plantados* (immovable or defiant ones) for their recalcitrant stance. As late as 1986, over twenty-five years after they entered prison, there were 126 documented cases of *plantado* prisoners who refused to be included in the release of over thirty-six hundred political prisoners, a deal which was brokered in 1978 between President Fidel Castro, the Carter administration, progressive Cuban exiles from the United States, and the Venezuelan Cuban community (Neier 1988; Levine).

There were still an estimated forty-three hundred prisoners that were classified by Amnesty International as "political prisoners" in Cuba in 1979. This number fell dramatically the following year as part of the release of prisoners previously negotiated under the Carter presidency. Since 1980, the number of prisoners has fluctuated between three hundred and five hundred, gradually decreasing in the first decade of the 2000s. Groups pressing for greater individual rights have been in existence since 1976, with dozens forming in the 1990s after the collapse of the Soviet Union in 1991 cut off aid from that country. Unlike the period between 1960 and 1980, sentences were much shorter, sometimes only days or weeks. This roundup and release pattern was evident in the years 1986–1988, 1995–1996, and 1998, which culminated in the release of three hundred prisoners after the pope's visit. In 2003, seventy-five people were rounded up and given sentences averaging twenty or more years. The Cuban government charged the group with receiving money from James Cason, the head of the U.S. Interests Section in Havana, conspiracy to overthrow the government, and compromising the sovereignty and territorial integrity of Cuba. Having reviewed the trial verdicts and other documents of the majority of those sentenced, Amnesty International declared that they were prisoners of conscience, imprisoned solely for the peaceful exercise of fundamental freedoms. The government and its supporters felt that the U.S. invasion of Iraq was a prelude to a similar action in Cuba. Over the years, several of the prisoners have been released, culminating with a release of fifty-two in the summer of 2010. Release of this latter group was arranged through negotiation between the state and the Cuban Catholic Church with the assistance of the Spanish government, which accepted most of those released into exile. Estimates of how many political prisoners remain vary, perhaps a hundred.

Civic and political rights in Cuba are intimately tied to the idea of sovereignty, no mere abstraction given the post-1959 history of the island. Jorge Domínguez remarked that if the European Union sovereignty is negotiable and "produces" to achieve greater goals within the entire union, for Cuba it is less negotiable and is "consumed" domestically because of the threat by the United States to its sovereignty. "To think of Cuba's future, in its future democratization and its relationship to the international community, it is essential to remember the constant presence of sovereignty and its significance as an organizing concept of its recent social and political history" (Domínguez 2009, p. 569). While significant gains have been made in terms of certain expressions of dissent, especially since 1990, future changes will largely hinge on better relations with the United States, a lifting of the embargo, or both.

■ *See also*

Governance and Contestation: The Republic: 1902–1952

BIBLIOGRAPHY

Ackerman, Holly. *Five Meanings of Cuba's Political Prisoners.* Miami, FL: Cuban Studies Association, 1998.

Amnesty International. "Cuba: Newly Declared Prisoners of Conscience." London: Amnesty International, 2004.

De Cosse, Sarah A. *Cuba's Repressive Machinery: Human Rights Forty Years after the Revolution.* New York: Human Rights Watch, 1999.

Domínguez, Jorge I. *Cuba: Order and Revolution.* Cambridge, MA: Belknap Press of Harvard University Press, 1978.

Domínguez, Jorge I. "Cuba en la comunidad internacional en los noventa; soberanía, derechos humanos y democracia." In *La política exterior de Cuba (1962–2009).* Madrid: Editorial Colibrí, 2009, pp. 567–591.

Hamm, Mark S. "Political Rehabilitation in Cuban Prisons: The Plan Progresivo." *Journal of Correctional Education* 40, no. 2 (June 1989): 72–79.

Hernández Rodríguez, Rafael. *Looking at Cuba, Essays on Culture and Civil Society.* Gainesville: University Press of Florida, 2003.

Instituto Internacional de Cooperación y Solidaridad Cubana. *El presidio político en Cuba comunista: testimonio.* Caracas: ICOSOCV Ediciones, 1982.

Levine, Robert M. *Secret Missions to Cuba: Fidel Castro, Bernardo Benes and Cuban Miami.* New York: Palgrave, 2001.

Martínez Heredia, Fernando. *Socialismo, liberación y democracía en el horno de los noventa.* Melbourne, Australia: Ocean Sur, 2006.

Neier, Aryeh. "Castro's Victims." *New York Review of Books* (17 July 1986).

Pérez-Stable, Marifeli. *The United States and Cuba: Intimate Enemies.* New York: Routledge, 2011.

Steinberg, Nik. *New Castro, Same Cuba: Political Prisoners in the Post-Fidel Era.* New York: Human Rights Watch, 2009.

Thomas, Hugh. *Cuba, or, The Pursuit of Freedom.* 1971. Rev. ed. New York: Da Capo Press, 1998.

Tulchin, Joseph S., et al., eds. *Cambios en la sociedad cubana desde los noventa.* Washington, DC: Woodrow Wilson Center, 2005.

■

THE POLITICS AND DEATH OF EDUARDO CHIBÁS

Ilan Ehrlich

The political life and dramatic death of one of Cuba's most important opposition figures from the mid-twentieth century.

Eduardo Chibás (1907–1951) was the charismatic leader of the Partido del Pueblo Cubano (Ortodoxo) from its formation in 1947 until his dramatic death in 1951. He was the most popular opposition leader during the presidency of Carlos Prío (1903–1977; pres. 1948–1952), running on a platform of social justice and the eradication of corruption within the political system. His party's slogan was "Vergüenza contra dinero" (Shame against Money), and the party used a broom as a symbol of its desire to clean out corruption. Chibás enjoyed popular support due to public confidence in his personal honesty and integrity, which were acknowledged even by his enemies (Alavés 2010, pp. 22–43; De la Osa p. 28).

THE PERSONALITY OF EDUARDO CHIBÁS AND THE COMPAÑÍA CUBANA DE ELECTRICIDAD

"Eddy," as Chibás was often called, was the most gifted orator of his generation and a consummate political showman. He maximized his appeal with a popular Sunday evening radio broadcast that reached up to 550,000 listeners, or roughly 10 percent of Cuba's population. Chibás encouraged his audience to expose examples of injustice or corruption, and every week letters poured in from all corners of the island. "As long as any Cuban suffers," he regularly reminded listeners, "I will fight for him."

In 1949, Chibás announced on his radio show that three Supreme Court judges had taken bribes from the universally scorned Compañía Cubana de

Eduardo Chibás (1907–1951), 1944. Eduardo Chibás was the most gifted orator of his generation and a consummate political showman whose popular Sunday evening radio broadcast reached up to 550,000 listeners. GEORGE SKADDING/TIME LIFE PICTURES/GETTY IMAGES

¡VERGÜENZA contra DINERO!

¡LIBERTAD ó MUERTE!

Eduardo Chibás (left; 1907–1951) and Fidel Castro (b. 1926). Fidel Castro was associated with the Ortodoxo Party during the 1940s and early 1950s. This poster may have been used during Castro's 1952 run for the Cuban legislature, which he lost. The Ortodoxo slogans appearing on the poster translate as "Shame against Money!" or "Honor against Money!" and "Liberty or Death!" © HOLLY ACKERMAN, PH.D.

Electricidad (Cuban Electric Company). The company was owned by General Electric and was infamous for charging Cubans the highest electricity prices in the Americas. Those rates had been raised again, and Cuba's Supreme Court had refused to intervene. Chibás believed exorbitant rates were especially damaging for Cuba's impoverished rural dwellers, most of whom lacked electricity. As a keen student of history and admirer of the U.S. president Franklin Delano Roosevelt, Chibás knew that the New Deal's Rural Electrification Administration had greatly reduced poverty in the U.S. countryside, and he hoped to implement a similar project one day as Cuba's president. Chibás often compared the plight of underpaid and chronically underemployed rural workers to relatively affluent urban laborers, pointing out that the former had every right to live as well as the latter.

Chibás furnished no concrete proof that the judges had behaved dishonorably, but he and most Cubans were convinced no other explanation was possible. When the outraged judges sued Chibás for slander in a court controlled by President Carlos Prío, Chibás found himself behind bars—not only for his words, but because he was Cuba's most popular opposition figure and a prime candidate to unseat Prío's party in the 1952 presidential

elections. For his part, Chibás relished the idea of political sacrifice. He wrote in defense of the people about the increase in the rates of the Compañía Cubana de Electricidad, which tripled in the 1936–1948 period, proclaiming that "To defend the Cuban people, I would proudly go to prison" (Chibás 1949, p. 75).

When Eduardo Chibás was released from prison on 4 June 1949, he was welcomed by thousands of followers, many of whom were so eager to hoist him on their shoulders, embrace him, or shake his hand that his *guayabera* (shirt) was promptly shredded. Taking in the scene surrounding the charismatic leader, the columnist Francisco Ichaso noted that Chibás possessed a "mystical presence" that inspired "quasi-religious fervor" in the thousands of people who waited for his release from the Castillo del Principe prison where he had been incarcerated. Transportation came to a halt as the demonstrators moved to a rally in support of the Ortodoxo leader in the Parque Central (Ichaso 1949, p. 76, pp. 88–89).

FRAGMENTED POLITICAL ARENA

While the incident with the Compañía Cubana de Electricidad says much about him, Chibás was more than an astute politician with a fanatical following who yearned to assist Cuba's downtrodden citizens. Chibás was unique in two important ways. First, his party, the Ortodoxos, refused to join political coalitions. In the short term, this rendered its members unelectable. Cuban politics was fragmented, and no party had received more than 50 percent of the vote since the constitution of 1940 was ratified. At the same time, deals between political parties with often widely differing platforms left many voters disillusioned, and quite a few opted to sell their votes.

In his April 1950 "Mensaje al pueblo cubano," Chibás promoted the political independence of the Ortodoxos, proclaiming, "Frente a los pactos sin ideología de la politica al uso, la ideología sin pactos de la Ortodoxia" (Contrary to pacts that sacrifice ideology in favor of political expediency, the Orthodox Party maintains its ideology without pacts). Chibás was as quick to criticize rumors suggesting a potential pact between Ortodoxo and communist parties as he was to criticize communist and government meddling in the affairs of Cuba's unions—especially the powerful Confederación de Trabajadores de Cuba (CTC, Cuban Workers Confederation). For example, he once addressed a letter to the editor of *Diario de la Marina* that stated: "We don't want the Communists to control the CTC but neither do we desire this control to fall into the hands of a group of unscrupulous politicians who are unconditionally loyal to the government and largely unconnected to the working class" (Archivo Nacional de Cuba [ANC], file 9, record 285, p. 5).

The division in the union movement persisted, and in 1947 Chibás denounced the situation (Alavés 2010, pp. 55–71). In his speech "A la Asamblea Nacional Ortodoxa," he maintained as the general line "political independence, consisting not of the celebration of national, provincial, and municipal pacts with the parties in power . . . [but] that assumes the existence of its own politics of the Ortodoxia, based on its ideology" (pp. 68–85). A Chibás supporter and parish priest, Jaime Genescá y Rovira, aptly described to Chibás the popular opinion regarding the political state of affairs at the time:

> In my continual travels I hear many workers and employees commenting on national politics and it's always the same story—they don't know who to vote for because they consider all politicians *horrible*, and for this reason everyone is hoping to sell their vote and make a little money. This is why I believe your party can offer a dignified option for the citizenry of good conscience. The party you direct only has to be slightly better or a little less bad than those we are already familiar with and you will surely obtain the votes of the good citizens who are thinking about Cuba rather than their pockets.
>
> *ANC file 36, record 1103, p. 10*

Ortodoxo Party campaign pins. The anticorruption Ortodoxo Party, founded in 1947 by Eduardo Chibás, refused to join political coalitions, which rendered many of its candidates unelectable in the short term. Chibás made a run for president in the 1948 elections, but lost. © HOLLY ACKERMAN, PH.D.

POPULAR CAMPAIGN

Chibás' second innovation was to forge such a close personal connection to his followers that voting would become an act of personal loyalty rather than a financial transaction. Chibás achieved this rapport by dispensing with the traditional barriers of formality that separated politicians and their supporters. For instance, during his 1948 presidential campaign Chibás noticed that his followers sometimes begged him to leap into their arms after he was finished speaking. Chibás obliged them with alacrity, diving head-first into a sea of hats and limbs. Afterward, this move became a regular occurrence. The journalist Enrique de la Osa wrote:

> Upon getting out of his famous automobile, Chibás would appear in rural towns and mount an open truck from which he would throw himself acrobatically into the multitude as if he wanted to bathe himself in the people of each location. The leaders of the Liberal-Democratic coalition and the [Auténtico-Republican] alliance, habituated only to the cold tactics of money, were scandalized by such demagoguery, as they called it. But Eddy trusted his political instincts in the power of a more emotional contact with the impressionable Cuban voter.
>
> *p. 468*

By May 1951, a mere twelve months before the next presidential election, a survey showed Chibás to be more than eight points ahead of his nearest challenger. Although he led in each of Cuba's six provinces and was the preferred candidate of all social classes, Chibás boasted particular loyalty among those between the ages of twenty and thirty—who favored him by a margin of more than nineteen points. Then again, Chibás had never polled more

Eduardo Chibás (1907–1951) campaign pin. Ortodoxo candidate Eduardo Chibás was considered a strong contender to win Cuba's 1952 presidential election, but he died from a self-inflicted gunshot wound in August 1951. © HOLLY ACKERMAN, PH.D.

by claiming his adversary had filched education ministry funds and invested them in Guatemalan lumber yards. Although he had no proof that Sánchez Arango owned Central American property, Chibás, whose party was perpetually short of cash, reveled in the imbroglio, believing the free publicity was worth "millions of pesos" (Conte Agüero p. 768). Chibás also assumed that the wretched state of Cuba's public schools, especially in rural areas, obviated the need to prove his allegations about Guatemalan real estate. However, when Chibás told his national radio audience on 29 July of photographs he had of decrepit school buildings, the public reacted with disappointment. They had been primed to expect lurid details of Sánchez Arango's ill-gotten Guatemalan holdings, and Chibás offered none.

THE FINAL RADIO ADDRESS

In the ensuing days, Chibás consulted Raúl Gutiérrez Serrano, Cuba's preeminent political pollster, who assured him the dip in his popularity was within the statistical margin of error and no cause for worry. But Chibás, who was normally trailed by adoring crowds as he coursed through Havana's streets, began to be heckled. During his subsequent and fateful radio address on 5 August, he compared himself to Galileo Galilei, who had been branded a "liar" and "deceiver" for lacking "physical proof" that the earth revolved around the sun (Chibás 1951, p. 96). He explained to his radio listeners:

> Last Sunday, during this same broadcast . . . I offered irrefutable proof of the enormous corruption of Prío's administration, including photos of schools and hospitals in miserable condition and contrasting them with ostentatious *fincas* and mansions of government officials who, not long ago, lived in poverty. Nevertheless . . . my words from last Sunday did not have the resonance required by such a grave situation. Cuba needs to wake up. But my knocking was not, perhaps, sufficiently strong.
>
> *p. 96*

than 35 percent of the vote, and some Ortodoxos remained skeptical of his insistence on shunning political pacts.

CONTROVERSY WITH AURELIANO SÁNCHEZ ARANGO

Rifts within the party were aggravated when Chibás became embroiled in a feud with Education Minister Aureliano Sánchez Arango (1907–1976), who was both an old enemy and a minor aspirant for Cuba's presidency from the incumbent Auténtico Party. The dispute began when Sánchez Arango falsely accused Chibás of being a coffee speculator. Chibás responded

He then emphasized that Cuba's "historic destiny" has always been frustrated by the "corruption and blindness" of its rulers. Only Ortodoxos, which shunned "transactions" and "shady deals," were fit for the task of governing (p. 96). In a stirring finale, Chibás exhorted his countrymen to "rise up and walk" and added portentously that "this is my last loud knock on your door!" (p. 96). Moments later, Chibás surreptitiously withdrew a gun from his pocket, aimed at his stomach and opened fire. Ironically, the only people who heard the shot, which was meant to ring out dramatically over the airwaves, were those who were with Chibás in the studio. Because Chibás had exceeded his time limit and been cut off, Cubans who had tuned into his show were listening to an advertisement for Café Pilon instead, unaware of what had happened.

Chibás survived the initial shot and was rushed to the hospital. Before going into surgery, he told a group of Ortodoxos: "I'm going to die, but the party must unite now more than ever. It must confront the corrupt government and pseudo-opposition" ("En Cuba, La Capital," p. 67). He survived for eleven days, all the while plotting political strategy and devouring press accounts of how his gesture was being viewed by Cuba's population. Chibás must have wondered whether widespread sympathy for him would put his party above the 50 percent threshold in the upcoming elections. Most importantly, he cherished the idea of a martyr's death that would rouse the people and secure his place in Cuban history.

Chibás's goals of a more accountable political class and less cynical electorate seemed attainable in the aftermath of his death. For one thing, corruption had become such a political byword that the ruling Auténtico Party chose to nominate Carlos Hevia, whose probity was beyond question, as its candidate for the 1952 presidential elections. Even if the Ortodoxos were defeated, Cuba probably would be better managed and more honestly administered than in the past. However, Cuba's democracy was violently uprooted by Fulgencio Batista's military coup less than three months before the voting.

BIBLIOGRAPHY

Alaves, Elena. *La Ortodoxia en el ideario americano.* Havana: Editorial de Ciencias Sociales, 2002.

Alaves, Elena. *Eduardo Chibás: clarinada fecunda.* Havana: Editorial de Ciencias Sociales, 2010.

Ameringer, Charles D. *The Cuban Democratic Experience: The Auténtico Years, 1944–1952.* Gainesville: University Press of Florida, 2000.

Archivo Nacional de Cuba (ANC). Fondo Eduardo R. Chibás. Havana.

Chibás, Eduardo R. "Por Defender el Pueblo, Iría a la Cárcel Con Orgullo." *Bohemia* 4, no. 10 (6 March 1949): 46–47, 75.

Chibás, Eduardo R. "A la Asamblea Nacional Ortodoxa." *Bohemia* (5 February 1950): 68.

Chibás, Eduardo R. "Mensaje al pueblo cubano." *Bohemia* (23 April 1950): 70–71, 98.

Chibás, Eduardo R. "Testamento Político de Chibás." *Bohemia* (26 August 1951): 96.

Conte Agüero, Luis. *Eduardo Chibás, el Adalid de Cuba.* Mexico City: Editorial Jus, 1955.

De la Osa, Enrique. *En Cuba Segundo Tiempo: 1948–1952.* Havana: Ciencias Sociales, 2005.

Ehrlich, Ilan. "Eduardo Chibás: The Incorrigible Man of Cuban Politics." Ph.D. diss., City University of New York, 2009.

"En Cuba, La Capital: El Ultimo Aldabonazo." *Bohemia* (12 August 1951): 67.

Ichaso, Francisco. "En Cuba, Política: ¡En libertad el penado 981!" *Bohemia* (12 June 1949): 76, 88–89.

Prada, Pedro. *La secretaria de la república.* Havana: Ciencas Sociales, 2001.

Rodríguez Salgado, Ramón. *Vergüenza contra dinero.* Havana: Editora Política, 2007.

Sánchez Echeverría, Lela. *La polémica infinita: Aureliano vs. Chibás y vice versa.* Bogota: Quebecor World Bogotá, 2004.

Thomas, Hugh. *Cuba: The Pursuit of Freedom.* New York: Harper & Row, 1971.

POPULAR FESTIVITIES AND CELEBRATIONS IN CUBA

María del Carmen Victori Ramos

Overview of traditional Cuban festivities.

Any festivity is the product of many elements, including the artistic—music or dance; the traditions and customs associated with each event; and the crafts and foods that make the celebration complete. The festivity emerges from a particular historical context and reflects a cultural vision of society. In any cultural context—local, national, or regional—the types of festivities and the ways they are celebrated define the traditions, thinking, and philosophy of life espoused by those who participate in them.

Throughout its five-hundred-year recorded history, the island of Cuba has witnessed a rich repertoire of festivities; some have been lost and new ones have been added. The first known Cuban festivity, Areíto, was practiced by the island's original inhabitants, the Taínos. Areíto was described by the Spaniards who conquered Cuban territory as a community celebration in which the participants dance in circles to the beat of a drum, accompanied by chanting. The purpose of the Areíto was to establish harmony between the participants and supernatural powers, thereby protecting the community. During the conquest's first decades, the Areíto gradually came into disuse, due to the extinction of the Taíno population or the interbreeding with Spaniards.

FESTIVITIES WITH SPANISH ROOTS

During the colonial and Republican periods, the most complex, complete, and valued festivities were patron saints' feast days. Each town established during the conquest was dedicated to a Catholic saint, and the day of that saint or an appearance of the Virgin Mary was generally celebrated for three days.

In addition to the religious component, celebrated in churches and processions, patron saints'

Three Kings Day parade. HÉCTOR DELGADO AND ROLANDO PUJOL

days were occasions for secular activities such as dances with popular music, traditional games of skill and gambling, and a variety of events specific to the social and cultural groups in each municipality, including singing competitions in rural areas and special children's programs. Foods and beverages typical of each place were enjoyed, and the streets and public squares were decorated. After independence, elements and symbols of the new civil, political, and social power were added, including theatrical productions and raffles to raise money for community improvement.

In spite of their deep roots, commemorations of saints' days gradually came to a halt during the first years of the Revolution. Another type of Catholic festivity took place around an altar built especially to honor a saint or the Virgin Mary. After the religious ceremony, neighbors gathered to dance, tell stories, and play different games. Although these festivities disappeared almost completely, a few have endured, mostly in remote rural areas.

FESTIVITIES WITH AFRICAN ROOTS

Also during the colonial era, the slaves brought to Cuba from sub-Saharan West Africa celebrated various religious festivities that expressed and preserved their cultural values. Many of these celebrations are maintained in the twenty-first century by the descendants of these slaves. They consist mostly of rituals honoring deities and are held in home shrines associated with the various Afro-Cuban religions.

Although outsiders are not excluded from these rituals, participation relies more on believers, relatives, friends, and guests. They follow each home shrine's calendar of rituals and in all cases are related to the day of the deity being honored.

After a difficult period in the first years of the Revolution, these celebrations gradually expanded and became more open. In many localities they replaced the saints' days and civic holidays.

There are other festivities with African roots that are mostly for fun, such as Tambor Yuka, which slaves celebrated in their barracks if the plantation owners permitted them. Considered in the early 2000s to be a peasants' holiday, this festivity survived in some rural areas. Other religious events were commemorative, such as an initiate's anniversary in Regla de Ocha or Santería, and *bembé,* a party held after a ritual activity.

CARNIVAL FESTIVITIES

Carnival festivities, introduced in Cuba during the colonial period, are a fusion of elements from many ethnicities. The characteristics vary by region and generally take place in February. The only exceptions were the *parrandas*, festivities held in December and celebrated into the early 2000s thanks to the efforts of residents in several towns and despite innumerable difficulties related to holding them on the proper date, close to Christmas, and with the appropriate characteristics. Similar festivities, such as the Feast of Corpus Christi and Epiphany, both linked to Catholic traditions, died out in the late nineteenth century. Nonreligious carnivals continued to be organized, although after 1959 they were held in the summer and adopted a uniform model based on the Santiago de Cuba carnival.

CIVIC HOLIDAYS

Verbenas were commercial fairs that included dancing to popular music and areas for games, raffles, and the sale of crafts and food. Since they were sponsored by individuals or civic groups to raise funds for community projects, after 1959 they were strictly regulated by the government and soon disappeared.

After the Revolution, political and community events were established to commemorate the creation of some community-related political institutions. One example is the annual parties put on by the Committees in Defense of the Revolution, which were held on each block and featured music, drinks, and a traditional Cuban stew known as a *caldosa* or *ajiaco*.

In summary, after 1959 there was a reduction, uniformity, and general impoverishment of traditional celebrations. Despite an initial revival of these festivals at the beginning of the twenty-first century, no new elements appeared to suggest the emergence of a new richness or variety in this important aspect of Cuban culture and society.

BIBLIOGRAPHY

Barreal Fernández, Isaac, et al. *Fiestas populares tradicionales cubanas.* Havana: Editorial de Ciencias Sociales, 1998.

Brown, David H. *Santería Enthroned: Art, Ritual, and Innovation in an Afro-Cuban Religion.* Chicago: University of Chicago Press, 2003.

Marinello, Juan. *Cultura popular tradicional cubana.* Havana: CIDCC, 1999.

POPULAR SONGS OF THE 1920s

Olavo Alén Rodríguez

Famous Cuban songs from the 1920s.

During the decade from 1920 to 1930, Cuban music experienced the culmination of a nationalist process in the arts that began before Cuba's independence from Spain in 1898 and grew stronger during the first two decades of the republic (1902–1920). At the same time, this period witnessed profound changes in aesthetic projections, instilling Cuban music with a contemporaneity that ensured its success for at least three more decades.

Cuban music acquired importance and originality not only because of its unique elements and its patriotism but also because of its beauty and the high repute it gained in other parts of the world. The essential transformations in Cuban music during the 1920s resulted at least to some degree from its need to meet the challenge of the technological changes it was experiencing.

RADIO AND THE RECORDING INDUSTRY

In 1877, Thomas Edison in the United States created a system of recording with vibrations around a cylinder, and ten years later Emile Berliner, in Europe, created the first gramophones, or lateral-cut discs. Competition between these two systems ended with the triumph of Berliner's technology and an incipient but growing demand on the part of performers to make gramophone recordings.

Musicians' demand for an increasingly secure market increased even more in 1925, when the U.S. recording companies RCA Victor and Columbia released their first discs to be played on electric phonographs. One million phonographs were sold in the United States in 1927, according to the music historian Cristóbal Díaz Ayala (p. 24).

The United States, a nation of immigrants, concentrated part of its record production on ethnic music, in order to create a large market among various nationalities in the expatriate communities in the country. Columbia and RCA Victor were the main actors in this initiative, especially in importing music from Latin America and the Caribbean. Cuba was one of the first countries to benefit from this policy, far in advance of the rest of Latin America. The incipient U.S. record industry searched Cuba for performers who could become popular in U.S. ethnic communities, and the industry also endeavored to sell records and especially its phonographs abroad, thereby assuring future markets.

The recording industry's development also had collateral effects. Columbia and RCA Victor frequently took musicians from other countries to record in the United States, and nearby Cuba had an advantage in this regard. Many musicians decided to stay in the United States for long periods, or permanently, because they found more or better sources of work there. This situation strengthened the musical capacities within immigrant communities, which in turn influenced the ethnic market and eventually the listening trends of the whole U.S. population. Thus the U.S. record industry helped make Cuban music popular throughout the world, while at the same time allowing this music to reach Cuban homes more easily.

■ *See also*

Enrique Jorrín and the Cha-cha-cha

Mr. Rhythm: Benny Moré

Music: 1900–1945

"Rita de Cuba": Rita Montaner

Radio broadcasts officially began in Cuba at 4 p.m. on 22 October 1922 (only about two years after they had begun in the United States), via the Cuban Telephone Company, a subsidiary of International Telephone and Telegraph (ITT). On that day, Station PWX broadcast a speech by the Cuban president Alfredo Zayas, preceded by the national anthem performed by the army general staff band, led by Luis Casas Romero. After that, it was all Cuban music. The diva Rita Montaner sang "Rosas y Violetas" (Roses and Violets), by José Mauri, and "Presentimiento" (Premonition), by Eduardo Sánchez de Fuentes, which were followed by the *danzón* "Princesita" (Little Princess) and "Soy Cubano" (I Am Cuban), both written by Casas Romero; the latter was performed by Mariano Meléndez. The president, good politician that he was, acted as many before him had done; he took advantage of the historic opportunity to accept $50 million from the United States, while musicians honored the occasion by giving the people new and powerful symbols of cultural identity. From the day radio began in Cuba, the country's own music dominated all its broadcasts, and it continued to do so in the first decade of the twenty-first century.

"MAMÁ INÉS," "SIBONEY," AND "EL MANICERO"

Gradually records became radio's musical mainstay, and together these media catapulted performers to fame. One example is the singer Rita Montaner, who debuted some of the most popular Cuban songs of the 1920s. Perhaps the first of those songs was "Mamá Inés," by Eliseo Grenet, who had also written—along with the composer Ernesto Lecuona—the music for the 1927 show that ushered in the zarzuela's splendor in Cuba: *Niña Rita; o, La Habana en 1830* (Young Rita; or, Havana in 1830). "Mamá Inés," written as a *tango congo*, was performed in the last act. It was Lecuona who convinced Rita Montaner to participate in the production, which opened on 29 September 1927, at the Regina theater. In blackface and dressed as a carriage driver, Rita Aurelia Fulceda Montaner y Facenda began her professional career and simultaneously became a pioneer of this theatrical form. Her performances of "Mamá Inés" were greeted by long ovations, and she was obliged to repeat the number over and over. The song remained in her repertoire for many years, was broadcast on the radio, and was recorded by Columbia.

Some months after her initial performance of "Mamá Inés," Montaner triumphed again at the Regina. Dressed as an Indian maiden, with a very short skirt and a feather in her hair, she performed in the musical review *La tierra de Venus* (The Land of Venus), with music by Lecuona. In the scene "La Gruta Siboney" (The Siboney Grotto), she sang the immortal "Canto Siboney" (Song of Siboney), which was later known merely as "Siboney." Lecuona created an instrumental arrangement of the song, and

the choreography around Montaner built up to the moment of her brilliant presentation. The memorable performance ended with her arms folded across her chest.

The song Montaner sang that is best known around the world is "El manicero" (The Peanut Vendor), written by Moisés Simons. The history of this song, which has been identified as a rhumba but is more accurately a *son pregón*, has been recounted various ways; the truth is that Montaner asked Simons to write a musical version of the typical peanut vendor's call, to perform at a show honoring Lecuona at the Regina on 30 January 1928. In May of that year, Columbia launched the sale of Montaner's records in Cuba, including "El manicero." However, the song's greatest moment was when Justo Ángel Aspiazú—from the city of Cienfuegos, known as Don Aspiazú and considered the first to popularize Cuban music in the United States—played it with his Casino Nacional de La Habana (National Havana Club) orchestra, featuring the singer Antonio Machín, at New York's Palace Theater on 26 April 1930.

Rita Montaner and Don Aspiazú were not the only well-known performers of Moisés Simons's famous tune, but other versions did not achieve the same popularity. "On July 26, 1929, it was recorded by Trío Matamoros, but it went as unnoticed as the peanut vendor himself, and never even recouped the production expenses," writes Jaime Eduardo Camargo Franco (p. 110). This is despite the fact that Miguel Matamoros, the leader of that famous trio, composed and performed several beloved songs during the 1920s.

OTHER SYMBOLS OF CUBAN CULTURE

In his *Música cubana, del areyto a la nueva trova* (Cuban Music from the Native *Areyto* to the New *Trova* Ballad), Cristóbal Díaz Ayala tells the following story.

> In 1922 Miguel [Matamoros] and his cousin Alfonso del Río were singing a serenade that resulted in failure. It rained, the woman being serenaded did not appear on the balcony, and as Miguel was putting away his guitar and getting ready to leave, he heard this conversation: at a nearby window, a girl asked, "Mama, those singers, are they from Havana?" and her mother answered, "No, dear, they're from here, from the hills," referring to the outlying neighborhoods of Santiago de Cuba. And that night, his most joyous composition was born.
>
> *p. 125*

"Son de la loma" (They Are from the Hills) became one of the most powerful musical symbols of Cuban identity and also one of Cuba's best-known pieces, inside the country and internationally, remaining so into the twenty-first century. Later in the decade, Matamoros had his first big hit with his trio:

a 1928 RCA Victor Orthophonic record of "Olvido" (Oblivion) and "El que siembra su maíz" (He Who Plants His Corn)." Díaz Ayala writes that it sold "64,000 copies in Cuba, in 90 days, a world record" (p. 120). But Trío Matamoros did not attain true fame and glory until 1930.

In the 1920s the *son montuno*—a musical genre born in and around the Sierra Maestra—was popular in Havana. Thus the genre made its way into the territory of the danzón, Victrolas, and even player pianos, with advantages that may have determined its ultimate success. Musical groups hired to play the *son*—composed of a guitar, a *tres* guitar, a *botija* or a *marimbula*, bongos, claves, and maracas—did not need musicians with academic musical training—unlike the danzón bands, in which piano, violins, and flute dominated. Furthermore, the *son*'s syncopated rhythms were conducive to dancing, not only in the slow, measured tempo of *danzón*, but also in a much faster manner. This gave dancers the chance to show their prowess, and the tempo was similar to the U.S. dance styles invading Havana. Later on, these sextets added a trumpet, often played muted, thus establishing the well-loved *son* septets that were even closer to the sound of U.S. bands.

Sextets and septets performed many *sones* and songs that attained national popularity. The Sexteto Habanero had hits with numbers such as "A la loma de Belén" (On the Hill of Belén) and "Elena la cumbanchera" (Elena the Reveler), by Gerardo Martínez, and "Bururú Barará," by Felipe Neri, both members of the band. In 1926 Ignacio Piñiero joined the Sexteto Occidente, whose director and lead singer was María Teresa Vera, and he composed the emblematic "Suavecito" (Softly) three years later.

Cuban *trovadores,* or balladeers, also recorded some hits in the 1920s. The fierce hurricane that strafed Havana in 1926 inspired Sindo Garay to write the well-known "El ciclón y la palma" (The Hurricane and the Palm Tree). At that time, María Teresa Vera and Manuel Corona sang one of Garay's great songs, "Longina," composed in 1918. In 1923 they incorporated "Santa Cecilia" (Saint Cecilia) into their repertoire; Corona had written it the previous year, and for a long time he considered it his favorite song. The duo was hired in 1922 by RCA Victor, and on a subsequent trip to New York, they recorded for Columbia with the Sexteto Occidente. Vera commented that "The recordings came out almost without interruption. It's the first time I got so much money for singing" (quoted in Calderón, p. 54). In this period they sang "Cabo de la guardia" (Corporal of the Guard), "Esas no son cubanas" (Those Are Not Cuban Women), and "Papá Montero." Others whose songs lived beyond the 1920s include Eusebio Delfín, who in 1924 wrote "Y tú qué has hecho" (And What Have You Done), known in Cuba and around the world as "En el tronco de un árbol" (In the Trunk of a Tree).

The 1920s were a time of great changes for Cuban music, when it acquired the modernity to project many of its legitimate traditions into the future. Authentic traditions were presented in a new way, and this made it possible to achieve international success.

SELECTED DISCOGRAPHY

100 canciones cubanas del milenio (1999).

Borja, Esther. *Esther Borja canta a dos, tres, y cuatro voces* (2004).

Fornés, Rosita. *Éxitos de ayer y de siempre* (2004).

Mis cincuenta preferidas (2001).

BIBLIOGRAPHY

Alén Rodríguez, Olavo. *De lo afrocubano a la salsa.* Havana: Ediciones Artex, 1994.

Alén Rodríguez, Olavo. *From Afrocuban Music to Salsa.* Book and CD. Berlin: Piranha Musik Production & Verlag, 1998.

Calderón, Jorge. *María Teresa Vera.* Havana: Editorial Letras Cubanas, 1986.

Camargo Franco, Jaime Eduardo. *"El manicero," el rey de los pregones.* Barranquilla, Colombia: Publicaciones Comerciales, 2002.

Díaz Ayala, Cristóbal. *Música cubana del areyto a la nueva trova.* San Juan, Puerto Rico: Editorial Cubanacán, 1981.

Díaz Ayala, Cristóbal. *Discografía de la música cubana.* Vol. 1. San Juan, Puerto Rico: Fundación Musicalia, 1994.

Fajardo Estrada, Ramón. *Rita Montaner: Testimonio de una época.* Havana: Fondo Editorial Casa de las Américas, 1998.

Q–R

"QUEEN OF SALSA": CELIA CRUZ

Raúl Fernández

The career of Celia Cruz and her influence on Latin American musical culture.

Celia Cruz (1924–2003), the great Cuban salsa singer, was one of the most popular Latin American musical figures of the twentieth century. An examination of her career reveals six elements of her extraordinary influence.

CRUZ'S UNDERSTANDING OF POPULAR TASTE

Celia Cruz had an exceptional knack for recognizing popular trends in dance music. This talent allowed her to make major contributions to the musical heritage of Cuba and the Spanish-speaking Caribbean.

One challenge in the world of popular music is ascertaining whether one tune or another will receive mass approval and become a hit. Ever-changing musical tastes and their unpredictability go with the popular music territory. A few exceptional musicians have possessed the ability to capture riffs, phrases, and melodies that grabbed the immediate attention of listeners and dancers. In the realm of Cuban popular dance music, Celia Cruz was such a musician.

Cruz was not merely a vocalist with a great voice who just happened to record a large number of hits, including "Burundanga," "Sopa en botella," "Caramelo," "Quimbara," and "Yerbero Moderno." She personally selected each of the tunes that became a hit, often against the advice of composers and promoters who wanted her to record something else. She studied the lyrics and music of the songs brought to her attention, sang them to herself, and made her own decisions about which to record. One such song was composed in *bembé*, or 6/8 rhythm, by Oscar Bouffartique,

a violinist, pianist, and music teacher well-known to professional musicians but neither a successful composer nor a household name with the public. Although using bembé in popular songs was deemed risky—the rhythm was considered too slow and, perhaps worse, was identified with near-hermetic sacred Afro-Cuban religious ceremonies—Cruz insisted on recording Bouffartique's "Burundanga," which immediately became one of the emblematic recordings of 1950s Havana.

Cruz's carefully selected *sones* and *guarachas* (popular Cuban song genres) became so popular throughout the Caribbean basin that they eventually became part of the cultural heritage, not just in Cuba but in major Caribbean cities known for their musical tradition—Ponce, Puerto Rico; Puerto Plata, Dominican Republic; Veracruz, Mexico; Cartagena and Barranquilla, Colombia; and Puerto Limón, Costa Rica.

CRUZ AND CUBAN BROADCASTING

Cruz's contribution to Cuban music dates back to the beginning of her career in the 1940s when she sang for Havana radio station Mil Diez. In the mid-1940s the newly legalized Partido Socialista Popular (PSP) launched a radio station that came to be known, because of its location in the radio bandwave (1010 AM), as Mil Diez. Historians of Cuban popular music generally acknowledge that Mil Diez programming signified a major change in the music available on the radio. The station featured music styles, orchestras, and artists that had not previously had access to the airwaves. It had no commercial interruptions and projected a populist style, which appeal to the Cuban public. It was on Mil Diez that the composers associated with the *movimiento del "feeling"* ("feeling" movement) first performed their songs; jazz also became a regular part of the daily programming, which emphasized the latest innovations in dance music popular among working-class listeners. Antonio Arcaño's *danzón de nuevo ritmo*, Arsenio Rodríguez's *son montuno*, and the popular Afro-sones. Arcaño y sus Maravillas, Arsenio Rodríguez, and the Trío Matamoros with Benny Moré were among the prominent artists whose music was often broadcast

■ *See also*

Cuban Singers in the United States

Diasporas: Afro-Cubans in the Diaspora

Miami

Music: Afro-Cuban Religious Influence on Cuban Popular Music

Celia Cruz (1924–2003). The Cuban-born queen of salsa, Celia Cruz, came to embody the essence of Afro-Cuban popular music and "tropical" dance music throughout Latin America. CHRISTIAN AUGUSTIN/ACTION PRESS/ ZUMA PRESS/NEWSCOM

by Mil Diez. Moreover, all the music on Mil Diez was live; no recorded music was broadcast.

Cruz was part of Mil Diez's select roster of artists. She sang accompanied by the station's band, directed by notable Cuban conductor and violinist Enrique González Mantici, and featuring the young *bongosero* Ramón "Mongo" Santamaría. Through Mil Diez the Cuban public listened for the first time to Cruz's deep contralto voice. Some of her live performances have survived, mostly in the form of Afro-sones such as "El cabildo de la Mercé," "Pa' congrí," "Tuñaré," and "Mi Iyale." The popularity of Cruz and the rest of the Mil Diez performers led other major radio stations to develop similar programming, often hiring musicians away from Mil Diez. By the end of the 1940s, Cuba's musical panorama had changed substantially, thanks in part to Cruz and the other artists who made their start at Mil Diez.

INTRODUCTION OF AFRO-CUBAN MUSIC TO A WHITE AUDIENCE

In the 1950s, Celia Cruz helped transform the sound of the Sonora Matancera, an ensemble that acted as a musical bridge, bringing an Afro-sone light to white dancing audiences.

One the oldest of the Cuban *son conjuntos* ("Cuban sound" bands), the Sonora Matancera played music with a slow-to-medium tempo. It was a simple sound that allowed the ensemble to accompany various singers over the years. The Sonora sound, always played on the beat, did not have the syncopated accents and off-beats that characterized Arsenio Rodríguez's conjunto. In the argot of Cuban musicians, while both Arsenio and the Sonora were high-quality ensembles, Rodríguez's group was compact and energetic, a *conjunto macho*. La Sonora, by contrast, was a *conjunto hembra* ("feminine" band), and a conservative one at that, perhaps the last conjunto to add conga drums in the late 1940s. Other musicians referred to the Sonora Matancera as *música fácil* (easy listening), *música para*

blancos (music for whites), or even more negatively *música de caballitos* (merry-go-round music). Music connoisseurs of the 1940s and 1950s claimed that black Cubans never danced to the Sonora Matancera. And it was indeed the case that the Sonora Matancera, an all-black ensemble, played largely for audiences at white Spanish society events, including the Sociedad Artística Gallega (Galician Artistic Society) and other society functions.

After joining La Sonora, Cruz chose catchy *guaracha* tunes played at a fast pace, adding her rhythmic vocal improvisations and restrained *sabrosura* (flavor). As the composer and musician Ned Sublette has noted, Cruz made the Sonora sound blacker (p. 575); at the same time, she was not one of the local *locas* like Juana Bacallao who wore a platinum wig fifty years before Cruz dared do the same. Cruz did not drink or smoke and did not engage in the daring theatrics of other female performers of the time such as Bacallao and, later, La Lupe. These qualities made her nonthreatening to white Havana society. Thus, for the first time, a black female singer from a working-class Havana neighborhood became a leading entertainer at sedate Spanish dance locations in Havana.

CREATION OF A TRANSNATIONAL POPULAR MUSICAL CULTURE

Through her voice, music, and songs, Celia Cruz transnationalized Latin American folklore and music to create a greater sense of Pan-American unity. Cruz was a fan of all Latin American popular music, especially Venezuelan and Colombian folkloric compositions, and the songs of Colombia's Lucho Bermúdez. She recorded songs from all over Latin America, including the Brazilian tune "Usted Abusó," the *ranchera* "Tú y las nubes," and the Peruvian "Toro Mata." She added her passion for Latin American folklore and traditions to the Cuban-Caribbean core of her music. Her most successful recordings with Johnny Pacheco, Willie Colón, and Papo Lucca were mixtures of Cuban guarachas, Dominican *merengues*, Puerto Rican *bombas*, and songs from Mexico, Peru, Colombia, and elsewhere. These mixtures became the essence of the new concept of salsa, which served to build bridges among various Latino communities, especially in the United States. Salsa also became a form of cultural defense against the dominant and diluting influences of the easy pop and rock music originating in the United States.

Cruz transformed the Peruvian classic "Fina Estampa" into a Latin American hit, and she made "A papá" into much more than just another bomba by Mon Rivera. Through her direct artistic intervention, she contributed to the development of a Latin American feeling of unity centering on salsa and Cuban music. In the last three decades of her career, Cruz used her performances and recordings to become an ambassador for Latin American music as audiences around the world learned to identify her shout of *Azúcar!* as emblematic of the sound of salsa.

CIRCUMSPECTION ABOUT GENDER ISSUES

Though Cruz was a musical innovator, her contributions to the emerging debate over issues of feminism and gender representation were largely symbolic and limited by her perception of what the market could bear. Throughout her life, Cruz maintained a polished conservative appearance and carefully managed her public image. Thus, in matters pertaining to the public representation of black women's sexuality or issues related to race relations, she was circumspect and market-savvy.

Curiously, at the beginning and at the end of her career, she was involved in performances that touched on the subject of beautiful black female bodies—in both cases, through a traditional male gaze. After her work at Mil Diez, Cruz appeared at Havana's Teatro Fausto in *Sinfonía en blanco y negro* (Symphony in White and Black), a show choreographed by the famed Roderico Neyra, with music by Bobby Collazo. Other performers included vocalists Elena Burke and Xiomara Alfaro. The show featured a group of attractive young *mulatas* (mulattas, or mixed-race women) dancing to popular hits sung by Cruz. The show was a great success, running for two years, during which time it was renamed *Mulatas de Fuego*. An idiomatic translation might be "Hot Chocolates," the original Spanish conveying a "hot" sexuality that is both gendered and racialized as not white and not black. The show's title was another expression of that persistently fetishized Cuban icon, the mulata. According to those who saw it, the beautiful mulatas performed nicely choreographed, highly sexualized, provocative dances. Cruz's accompaniment of the show's stellar attractions cast her almost in the role of observer, allowing her to keep her distance physically and figuratively, while singing with her usual and proper *sandunga* (grace and elegance).

More than fifty years later, while Cruz was struggling with the last stages of terminal cancer, she released a CD and DVD featuring "La Negra tiene tumbao." Much had changed in half a century: nudity, sexual tension, and erotic fantasies characterized the song's video. However, Cruz's performance recalled in many ways her earlier supporting role for the dancing *mulatas*. In "La negra tiene tumbao," she also maintains her distance; she is not a participant in the video itself. Her role is that of an observer whose singing provides commentary on the body of the model-like black woman featured in the short segment, praising the way she moves and walks. In spite of these obvious parallels, Cruz's participation this time was subtly but significantly different. Her fame and advanced age—she was over eighty years old when the video was produced—graced her with a grandmotherly aura and the calm authority for commenting directly and effusively on the beauty of the model she affectionately calls *negrita*.

For some in the Cuban-American community, Cruz went too far by participating in this steamy video. But she and her advisers understood that the video was a way to reach and sell to a younger generation that had grown up in the worlds of hip hop and MTV. In the same vein, the strongly sexualized portrayal of the young woman in the video may have offended those holding on to a more progressive representation of gender. Yet, as Monika Gosin has suggested, Cruz's "La Negra tiene tumbao" saluted, albeit in a limited way, the spice, sexiness, and positive self-image of black women (p. 162). In any case, it may have been unrealistic to expect her, after a sixty-year career and in the twilight of her life, to suddenly abandon her tried-and-true sense of the market in favor of the critical perspective of the academy.

The same dictates applied in connection with issues of black pride: Insofar as Cruz addressed this theme, it had more to do with market conditions than with political consciousness. Cruz was interpreted differently by different audiences, and she carefully managed these differences. Thus, she was careful not to publicize among her white Cuban American fans in Miami her 1970s performance with the Fania All-Stars in Zaire on the occasion of the Ali-Foreman heavyweight championship "Rumble in the Jungle." But she also had a powerful audience base among Latin Americans of color in New York, Los Angeles, Puerto Rico, the Dominican Republic, Colombia, Venezuela, Peru, Panama, Ecuador, and elsewhere. Those audiences went into a frenzy when they interpreted her "Bemba Colorá," as a sardonic recognition of the shared blackness of all African-descended peoples of the Americas.

Decades earlier, Cuban poet Nicolás Guillén's political poem "Negro Bembón" had lovingly reproached black people for their self-consciousness about their physical features. It may well be that Cruz, in a less politically conscious way, struck a similar note with "Bemba Colorá," while reaching a much broader audience. Because of the powerful market response to the song, she made "Bemba Colorá" one of her signature performance pieces.

CONTRIBUTION TO THE GROWTH AND DEVELOPMENT OF LATIN JAZZ

Cruz professed not to care for jazz. In the late 1970s, she expressed her disappointment when the Cuban band Irakere received a Latin music Grammy award for which she had also been nominated. While she had no standing in the world of Latin jazz, the growth of the genre in South America was made easier after Cuban dance music had taken root there, allowing local musicians in many countries to absorb its rhythmic elements. While the styles of Machito and Arsenio Rodríguez found a home in the United States, the laid-back, less syncopated sound of Cruz and her backup band, the Sonora Matancera, were popular in Mexico and South America. Cruz thus played an important, although perhaps unwitting, role in connecting Afro-Cuban rhythms to Latin jazz. She helped lay the foundation that allowed generations of younger musicians to experiment and develop new avenues for this music of the Americas.

BIBLIOGRAPHY

Aparicio, Frances. "The Blackness of Sugar: Celia Cruz and the Performance of (Trans)Nationalism." *Cultural Studies* 13, no. 2 (April 1999): 223–236.

Fernández, Raúl. *Latin Jazz: The Perfect Combination.* San Francisco: Chronicle Books, 2002.

García, David. *Arsenio Rodríguez and the Transnational Flows of Latin Popular Music.* Philadelphia: Temple University Press, 2006.

Gosin, Monika. "'Other' than Black: Afro-Cubans Negotiating Identity in the United States." In *Una ventana a Cuba y los estudios cubanos/A Window into Cuba and Cuban Studies,* edited by Rodrigo Lazo, Ivette N. Hernandez, and Sara Johnson. San Juan, PR: Ediciones Callejón, 2010.

López, Oscar Luis. *La Radio en Cuba.* 2nd ed. Havana: Letras Cubanas, 1998.

Sublette, Ned. *Cuba and Its Music: From the First Drums to the Mambo.* Chicago: Chicago Review Press, 2004.

Recordings and Videos

Cruz, Celia. *Celia Cruz con la Sonora Matancera* (1967).

Cruz, Celia. *Cruz & Colón* (1977).

Cruz, Celia. *Azúcar Negra* (1993).

Cruz, Celia. *An Extraordinary Woman . . . Azúcar!* DVD. (2003).

Cruz, Celia, Johnny Pacheco, Justo Lucca, and Papo Betancourt. *Recordando El Ayer* (1976).

Puente, Tito, and Celia Cruz. *With Celia Cruz* (1969).

RACE

As in much of the Americas, notions of race are historically linked to the institution of slavery. Cuba is no exception. One of the last countries in the Western Hemisphere to abolish slavery (1886), Cuba has struggled with this legacy even as it has embraced its African heritage as being central to Cuban culture.

Cuba, paradoxically, has been called the whitest and blackest island in the Caribbean: whitest because a large segment (from 50 to 70 percent) is of European descent, especially compared to the French- and English-speaking Caribbean where whites are less than 5 percent of the population; blackest because in certain manifestations of its culture (religion, music, folklore, language) it shows profound African influences. Cuba also had a significant population of free people of color even during times of slavery.

Upon its independence, Cuba sought to define itself. People of African descent and a small, but significant, Chinese community became more important in delineating Cuba's cultural and national identity. Black writers, scholars, and artists began to have an increasing voice in the national dialogue, even if, as a group, black, Chinese, and mestizo populations often felt the brunt of discrimination and poverty.

The Revolution of 1959 made large strides for black and mixed-race Cubans by eliminating many public barriers to discrimination: in the workplace, education, health, and public spaces (beaches, parks, clubs, etc.). However, subtler forms of discrimination persisted, aggravated by the collapse of the Soviet Union and subsequent economic crises.

RACE: INTRODUCTION

Alan West-Durán

An overview of how race is viewed in Cuba, especially from the perspective of Fernando Ortiz's concept of transculturation and later views that challenge it.

Like all societies that were once slave states, Cuba was divided along class, gender, and especially racial lines. Notions of citizenship were racialized in colonial times, when Spanish *casta* paintings and racial classificatory regimes detailed an obsessively minute taxonomy based on the amounts of European, African, Chinese, and indigenous ancestry that a person had. When Cuba became independent, the racial classifications were simplified to black, white, and mixed race (mulatto, mestizo). Yet, like other societies in the region, Cuban society is affected by *shadeism,* and it has a plethora of terms to capture even slight variations in skin tones and features.

For much of the twentieth century Cuba, like Brazil, was depicted as a racial democracy—a view later largely discredited. Yet many scholars have pointed out that the island never was segregated to the extent associated with Jim Crow in the United States and that racial and cultural mixing was much more prevalent in Cuba than in the United States. Others have argued that the so-called one-drop rule functioned differently in Cuba: In the United States one drop of black blood made an individual black; in Cuba it worked in opposite fashion, to a degree, depending on how light the person's skin appeared.

Many Cuban scholars do not use the term *Afro-Cuban* to refer to Cubans of African descent, arguing that the term is redundant and that it elevates a racial marker above national and cultural relevance—Cubanness. The term is used as an adjective to refer to Afro-Cuban religions or Afro-Cuban music, though some scholars prefer *religiones cubanas de descendencia africana* (Cuban religions of African descent). To refer to persons, Cuban scholars typically use the terms *negros y mulatos* (blacks and mulattoes) and *negros y mestizos* (blacks and mestizos) and, subsequently, *cubanos de descendencia africana* (Cubans of African descent) and *cubanos de color* (Cubans of color). These terms reflect Cubans' way of looking at race, which is to see it within a national or cultural context, rather than through a racial lens.

This perspective and much of this terminology derives from the work of Fernando Ortiz (1881–1969), a Cuban scholar and ethnologist who wrote about matters *Afro-Cuban*—a term he coined. Ortiz argued that Cuba's multiracial society was the product of *transculturation* (another term he coined), a process distinct from the notion of the melting pot. In transculturation two or more cultures come together in a historical conjuncture to produce something uniquely Cuban without entirely losing their original (European, African, Asian) identities. Although the term usually is used to describe racial mixing in Cuba, it is also useful in describing Cuban religions, food, music, and other cultural phenomena that are the product of historical transformation and mixing (Ortiz 1995). The process of transculturation can take centuries, and it often happens as a result of less than innocent circumstances; for example, the Afro-Cuban religion Regla de Ocha (Santería) that combines elements of European, African, and Arabic cultures came into being in a context of slavery and resistance to the imposition of Catholicism. For transculturation to be effective the different components should be on an equal footing, which was not the case in Cuba under colonialism, slavery, and undemocratic regimes.

Ortiz's use of transculturation locates Cuba racially in terms of *exceptionalism*, codified by José Martí's insistence that Cuba's patriotism and the struggle for independence transcended race. Martí vigorously denied that race existed (from a scientific standpoint). Ortiz's *Martí y las razas* (Martí and the Races, 1941) and *El engaño de las razas* (The Deceptions of Race, 1946)

can best be understood in the context of World War II and the twentieth-century eugenics and Nazi racism; undoubtedly, when compared to Germany under the Third Reich, Cuba seemed a racial paradise. Perhaps Ortiz had in mind the toxic effects of racial segregation in the United States, a country he knew well, having lived in Washington, D.C., for two years. In *El engaño de las razas* Ortiz, like Martí, argued that the notion of race lacks scientific rigor: For Ortiz, race was a scientific hoax, a social swindle, and an intellectual fraud.

Ortiz's exceptionalist view held sway for decades, and for some scholars, it continued to do so in the twenty-first century. To his credit, Ortiz said that without black people there would be no Cuba. Other perspectives on Cuban racial identities and histories have been categorized as Marxist and black nationalist (Sawyer pp. 21–35). The Marxist viewpoint holds that racial disparities are caused by class oppression and that ending formal and social obstacles to integration (in education, public areas, beaches, clubs and the workplace) leads to the elimination of racism. The black nationalist perspective argues that so-called color-blind advances in Cuba end up perpetuating racist stereotypes and institutions that do not improve the plight of black and mestizo Cubans. All three theories have their advantages, to be sure, but they each have significant flaws: Exceptionalism overlooks historical patterns of exclusion and discrimination, Marxism downplays the more subtle ways that racism manifests itself outside formal channels (or worse, undermines them from within), and the black nationalist view tends to underappreciate the enormous advances made by Cubans of African descent since 1959.

Reliance on these perspectives—particularly exceptionalism and Marxism, which are more prominent in Cuba—had the effect of limiting the empirical research on race that is needed to ground more theoretical approaches and implement public policy. Since the mid-1980s, however, there has been an increase in the literature on the subject from scholars both on the island (Tomás Fernández Robaina, Pedro Serviat, María del Carmen Barcia Zequeira, Esteban Morales, Jesús Guanche, and Rogelio Martínez Furé) and abroad (Alejandro de la Fuente, Ada Ferrer, Aline Helg, Rebecca Scott, Alejandra Branfman, Carlos Moore, and Robin Moore). The scholar Mark Sawyer has argued that the term *inclusionary discrimination*, coined by the Brazilian scholar Edward Telles, sums up a more complex reality that recognizes the coexistence of racial inclusion and exclusion. Key historical moments or crises, regime changes, transnational events, and racial ideologies condition the types (and degrees) of inclusion and exclusion over time. For example, the Spanish-American-Cuban War (1895–1898) was a breakthrough for black and mestizo Cubans in terms of inclusion, but after independence progress stagnated, and with the explosive uprising in 1912, the violence visited on Cubans of African descent was an extreme measure of exclusion.

Not surprisingly, the most trenchant criticisms and observations on race in Cuba emanate not from the social sciences but from the arts. Rappers such as Soandry del Río (formerly of Hermanos de Causa) and the duo Anónimo Consejo chronicle the daily lives and travails of black and brown Cubans. The visual artists Belkis Ayón (1967–1999), María Magdalena Campos Pons (b. 1959), Alexis Esquivel (b. 1968), and Juan Roberto Diago (b. 1971) all are adamant in their denunciations of racism, but as they carefully examine the intricacies of what it means to be of African descent in contemporary Cuba, they do not agree on racial assumptions of personal and collective identity. Campos Pons's *Tríptico I* (from *When I Am Not Here/Estoy Allá*, 1996) consists of three large Polaroid self-portraits: The left panel shows her in white face, with "Patria Una Trampa" (Homeland a Trap) written on her chest; the middle panel shows her with true-to-life skin tones, her face partially obscured by a thicket of sticks; the right panel depicts her as mixed race, with her eyes closed, and written on her chest in English, "Identity Could Be a Tragedy." The title of the piece indicates Campos Pons's bicultural reality (having lived roughly half her life in Cuba, half in Boston) and also the intense dialogue in Cuba and the United States about race and identity, which her body mediates. The left panel illustrates how race is defined in Cuba: Culture and nation trump racial difference, hence she appears in white face, a visual reminder of Frantz Fanon's *Black Skin, White Masks* (1952). The right panel embodies the pitfall of identity politics in the United States and of whitening seen as tragedy. Between trap and tragedy is the central image, where the artist's face is difficult to make out and appears fragmented. Perhaps this middle photo avoids the excesses of the right and left panels, but it offers no consolation: The illusions and elisions of race remain stubbornly elusive, and yet the traumas of racialized history remain inscribed on the body. If the body speaks the truth, in the spirit of Fanon, it will do so as a question, challenging Cuba's most cherished notions of self, society, race, and culture. Artists and scholars need each other in order to untangle these blind spots of history. To understand the shifting and often volatile social text that is race in Cuba, "the subjective realm of 'cultural memory' and the 'truth claim' of objective scholarship" need to be brought together (Ramsey p. 27).

BIBLIOGRAPHY

De la Fuente, Alejandro, ed. *Queloides: Race and Racism in Contemporary Cuban Art*. Pittsburgh, PA: Mattress Factory, 2010.

Marti, José. "Mi Raza." In *Cuba, Nuestra América los Estados Unidos*. Mexico City: Siglo XXI, 1973.

Ortiz, Fernando. *El engaño de las razas*. 1946. Havana: Instituto Cubano del Libro, 1975.

Ortiz, Fernando. *Cuban Counterpoint: Tobacco and Sugar*. Durham, NC: Duke University Press, 1995.

Ortiz, Fernando. *Martí humanista*. Havana: Fundacion Fernando Ortiz, 1996.

Ramsey, Guthrie P., Jr. *Race Music Black Cultures from Bebop to Hip Hop*. Berkeley: University of California Press, 2003.

Sawyer, Mark Q. *Racial Politics in Post-Revolutionary Cuba*. Cambridge, U.K.: Cambridge University Press, 2006.

RACE: SLAVERY IN CUBA

María del Carmen Barcia Zequeira

Slavery as practiced in Cuba from 1492 to 1886.

The origins of slavery in Cuba go back to the period of the Conquest. Slavery had existed long before then on the Iberian Peninsula, so there was nothing unusual about the Spaniards bringing a labor force from Africa to the New World. From that time forward, over a period that spanned some four hundred years, slavery left its mark on the island's economic, social, and cultural life.

ORIGINS

The first slaves to arrive in Cuba were known as *ladinos*. They received this name because they spoke Spanish, having lived on the Iberian Peninsula for many years. Those who arrived directly from Africa were known as *bozales* (muzzled ones) because they spoke only their native tongue.

The ethnic names in the documentary record point to specific African origins: the oldest ones found as of 2011 include the Mina, Mandinga, Ensensa, Kasanga, Biafara, Kalu, Zape, and Congo. Nevertheless, throughout that four-century period, Africans from many different groups arrived in Cuba, and more than eighty denominations of origins have been identified (Guanche pp. 312–333). The predominant groups arriving on the island were those embarking from the port of Calabar (known as the Carabalí), along with the Congo (Bantu) and Lucumí (Yoruba). Children born in Cuba of African parentage were called *criollos*.

In order to be sold, the slaves were classified into different groups. The most expensive of the lot, known as the *pieces of Indies*, were roughly eighteen to thirty-five years old; next came the *mulecones*, who were between twelve and eighteen years old; and the *muleques*, who were under twelve years old. Two *mulecones* were considered equivalent to one *piece of Indies*, and three *muleques* were equivalent to two *mulecones*. In the eighteenth century, the *pieces of Indies* fetched prices that ranged between 280 and 300 pesos. This sum rose steadily, except when the English patrols were intensified and there were more slave

CHRONOLOGY OF EVENTS

1510s: First slaves brought to Cuba.

1520: Three hundred slaves brought to Cuba to work the Jaugua gold mine.

1533: First slave uprising in Cuba at the Jobabo mines.

1708: Royal decree permits slaves to purchase freedom, attaining status of *cortados*.

1727: Slave uprising at Quiebra-Hacha sugar mill west of Havana.

1740: Havana Company granted monopoly on slave trade.

1789: New slave code promulgated.

1789: All Cuban ports opened to slave trade.

1791: Haitian slave uprising begins.

1811: Spain abolishes slave trade, except to Cuba.

1812: Aponte Rebellion.

1817: Spain signs a treaty with England agreeing to end the slave trade to Cuba.

1825: Guamacaro slave rebellion in Matanzas Province.

1842: Regulations on slaves promulgated.

1843: Carlota leads slave rebellion at Triumvirato sugar mill in Matanzas; *La Escalera* (the Conspiracy of Ladders), also in Matanzas; "black and brown" battalions terminated.

1868–1878: Ten Years' War leads to the liberation of tens of thousands of slaves.

1870: Segismundo Moret's Free Wombs Law grants freedom to the children of slaves.

1880: Masters Law passed.

1886: Slavery abolished in Cuba.

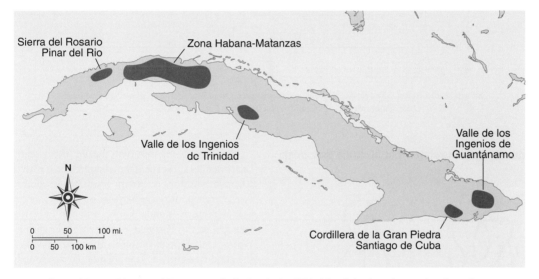

Major Zones of Plantation Development in Cuba in the Nineteenth Century

SOURCE: Roura Alvarez, Lisette and Teresa Angelbello Izquierdo. "El bohío: vivienda esclava en las plantaciones cubanas del siglo XIX." Boletín del Gabinete de Arqueología 6, no. 6 (2007): p. 137.

uprisings, or after the enactment of the Piracy Laws in 1865 and the Free Wombs Law of 1870 (Bergad et al. pp. 162–173).

Slaves were branded with irons as if they were cattle, an inhumane practice known as *carimbar* that lasted from the sixteenth century until 1784. The Spanish Crown was paid a tax of thirty-three pesos for each branded servant.

SLAVE DEMOGRAPHY

The first slaves arrived in Cuba in 1513. Within twenty-nine years, the island had more Indians and blacks than whites. The aboriginal population, who were slaves until 1552, declined in numbers, while both the free and the nonfree black populations continued to increase. By 1607, there were more blacks than whites in Havana, and they made up 45 percent of the total population of the island (Macías pp. 21, 34).

The importation of slaves continued until 1870, the year in which the last known consignment of black Africans was recorded (Franco p. 389). It is estimated that approximately nine hundred thousand Africans arrived in Cuba. They were unevenly spread throughout the island and from the 1820s onward were considerably more numerous in the western region.

The slave traffic was originally conducted by settlers authorized on a case-by-case basis by the king of Spain. In the eighteenth century, there were three companies engaged in the slave trade: the French East India Company, between 1701 and 1713; the British South Sea Company, between 1713 and 1739; and the Royal Company of Havana, from 1740 onward.

Figure 1

Price of slaves in Cuba, aged 15 to 40, 1790–1875

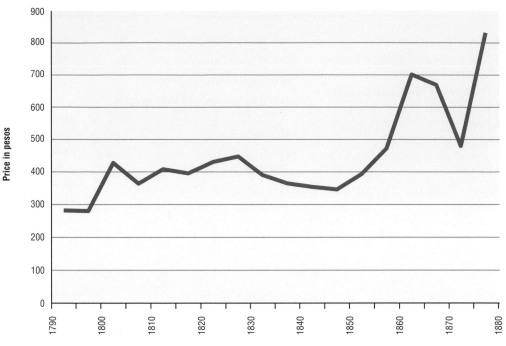

SOURCE: Laird Bergad, Fe Iglesias García, and Maria del Carmen Barcia. *The Cuban Slave Market, 1790–1880*. Cambridge, U.K.: Cambridge University Press, 1995.

Symbols applied to slaves that illustrate their origin

Applied in 1717 to Africans introduced in Santiago de Cuba

Mark on the slaves of the Compañia de Jesús in Havana

Mark on the slaves of the Real Compañia de Comercio de la Habana

Figure 2   SOURCE: Jorge Ibarra Cuesta.

In 1789, the African slaves trade were liberated. After 1820, when the slave trade became illegal in Cuba, slaves continued to be imported illegally not only from Africa, but from the United States and the Lesser Antilles, Jamaica in particular.

Africans were captured during tribal warfare. Their enemies subsequently exchanged them with traffickers for weapons or luxury goods, whereupon they were crammed into slave barracks on the African coast, such as those at Ajouda, Gorée, and San Luis, which belonged to the Portuguese, French, or English slave traders, and shipped onward (Boubacar pp. 55–76). The conditions for the transatlantic voyage were horrific, and many slaves did not survive the journey: They were crammed together; they were hungry and thirsty; many fell ill; and one out of seven perished (Mettas vol. 2, p. 382). When illegal traffickers were intercepted, they preferred to toss their human cargo at sea in order to make the evidence of their crime disappear. During periods when the trade was legal, the slaves disembarked at the main ports and were transferred to depots in order to be classified and sold. In areas where the slave trade was illegal, they were smuggled through places that were not closely guarded and then sent directly to the mills, coffee farms, or prearranged locations.

SLAVE LABOR

The work performed by the slaves during those four centuries was quite diverse. Some tasks were intensive, such as building forts or toiling on plantations that produced for the global market; others tasks, linked to services and household chores, were not as abusive, even though these slaves, too, were not exempt from punishment.

Estimated numbers of Africans arriving in Cuba, 1785–1865

Figure 3

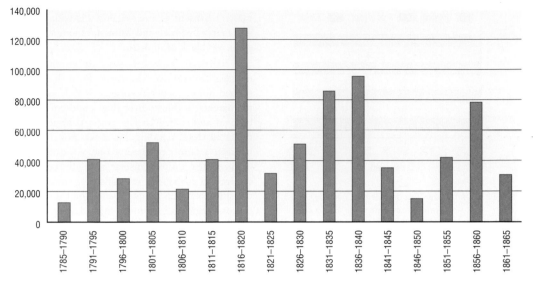

SOURCE: Eltis, David. *Economic Growth and the Ending of the Transatlantic Slave Trade*. New York: Oxford University Press, 1987, p. 245.

Since the conquest of the island was mainly urban in character, slaves worked mostly in the cities and their outskirts during the first two centuries of the colony. As the estates and villas laid up their store of wealth, they had to protect themselves from attack by marauders and pirates. Fortresses were built to protect the treasure fleets gathered in Havana that transported riches from the New World to Spain. Slaves who belonged to the king himself were brought in for the construction, while other slaves belonging to the landed oligarchy were leased, since leasing slaves was a way for the masters to make money with no effort whatsoever. At the beginning of the seventeenth century, one hundred slaves were leased for such work. (Macías p. 35). Those who were engaged in building the fortresses and other engineering works, such as the Zanja Real, and managed to survive this hard labor emerged as trained blacksmiths, stonecutters, carpenters, or masons, and their masters could demand a high wage for their work. Slave labor was also used in the copper mines of Santiago del Prado, in the eastern region of the island. Exploitation of this use began with eighty Africans, but by 1620 the mine engaged 339, of whom 35.4 percent were female. This operation ended in the mid-seventeenth century.

Slaves were also used for other kinds of work: laying roads, clearing estates, cultivating the land, and tending herds; they served as shepherds, water carriers, carters, stevedores, peddlers and vendors, cart-pullers, and public criers. They also performed duties deemed to be beyond the pale, such as that of executioner, for which criminals were usually employed. Black women, whether slave or free, were used as innkeepers, washerwomen, seamstresses, and

Percent of the Cuban population by region and social class, 1827

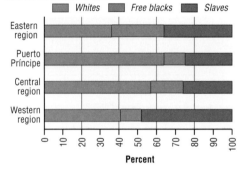

SOURCE: *Cuadro estadístico de la Siempre Fiel Isla de Cuba, correspondiente al año 1827*. Havana: Viudas de Arazoza y Soler, 1829.

Figure 4

prostitutes, a profession that allowed many slaves to obtain their liberty. Women also sold fruits and foodstuffs in the byways. Many a soldier and sailor escorting the treasure fleet on its Havana leg would mingle with them in order to find lodging, food, clean clothes, and cheap sex; these relationships contributed to the rise of mestizo families.

With the crops, flocks, and herds they managed to raise and by stashing away part of their wages, some slaves—women in particular—were able to save enough money to purchase their freedom. In due course, some became the owners of properties and houses in their own right; others were freed by the grace of their masters, in recognition of their integrity. Concessions of this sort were typically granted in the

Percent of the Cuban population by region and social class, 1862

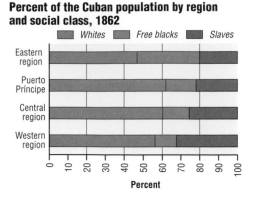

Whites | *Free blacks* | *Slaves*

SOURCE: Armíldez de Toledo, Conde de. *Noticias estadísticas de la Isla de Cuba en 1862*. Havana: Imprenta del Gobierno, Capitanía General y Real Hacienda, 1864.

Figure 5

Percent of the Cuban population by region and social class, 1846

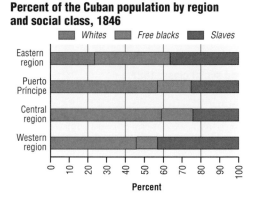

Whites | *Free blacks* | *Slaves*

SOURCE: *Cuadro estadístico de la Siempre Fiel Isla de Cuba, correspondiente al año 1846*. Havana: Imprenta del Gobierno y Capitanía General, 1847.

Figure 6

master's last will and testament, and thus they were documented. A slave who reported a conspiracy might also be freed, as would women who bore more than twelve live children, a highly fraught achievement in an age characterized by high infant mortality rates.

Spanish legislation on slavery was not as punitive as French or English laws and provided for some degree of license. Manumission, for instance, established a price for the slave that was unaffected by the market's ups-and-downs and gave the slave the opportunity to purchase his or her liberty in cash or on a payment plan (Perera Díaz and Meriño pp. 44–72).

MARRIAGE AND FAMILY

Another special feature was the institution of marriage between slaves, established in the belief that this fostered docility. By law, masters were supposed to encourage marriage and sell their slaves in such

a manner as to preserve the bond between couples (Barcia pp. 51–58). They could marry without their master's consent or even against his will; they could also marry free men and women, as long as their skin color was black or mulatto.

Marriage, however, was just another method of social control over the slaves. Even though it prescribed unions between couples, it did not recognize the parents' authority over their children, who could be used and sold. Marriage was a contract that gave the family legal standing, but it was not the only way to create a family or preserve one. Africans tended to legalize their unions, insofar as many criollo slaves engaged in consensual relationships. Since most relationships between couples were not formalized, the census recorded the status of most slaves as single.

Family relationships were based on blood but also on affinity. The same roof and hearth might shelter children, parents, and grandparents, as well as godparents, godchildren, and *taitas* (persons of acknowledged social prestige), *caravelles* (persons who had come over on the same ship), and *cofrades* or brothers (those who belonged to the same religious group). There were nuclear, extended, and mixed families, and most were matrifocal, although some were headed by men. Despite the fragmentation of families implicit in being the legal chattel and under the control of another person, slaves still managed to obtain news about their relatives and in a general way to assert family solidarity and their guardianship over young children and elderly parents (Barcia pp. 166–180).

METHODS OF SOCIALIZATION

The socialization patterns of blacks were essentially expressed through three types of groupings: the African *cabildos* (or councils), the Catholic *cofradías* (or brotherhoods), and the military battalions of *morenos* and *pardos* (blacks and browns). The first of these institutions arose as a method for colonial administration, but as it evolved it also served other interests, establishing economic and client relationships, as well as ethnic and parental alliances. Since the cabildo functioned rather like a large family, it was able to meld its religious beliefs with those of the hegemonic system, thus giving rise to new transcultural systems.

These were urban groups whose membership consisted of free blacks (Africans with a similar ethnic origin). But they were also joined by their criollo children and a few slave members of the cofrades (fraternities). Their presence in Havana and Santiago de Cuba dates back to the sixteenth century; by 1755, there were twenty-one of these groups in the capital. The Catholic cofradías of browns and blacks also created a space that convened the black and mulatto elites, including the battalion officers, some of whom belonged to African cabildos. The cabildos and the fraternities were cross-linked with other social groups, as evidenced by the parental networks in these spaces and the existence of militia members.

Black and brown troops had existed since the sixteenth century. Toward the end of the English occupation, in 1763, they were reorganized in order to protect the island from similar attacks. Each battalion had four hundred militia members and twelve officers, directed by a military staff. These units assembled one-third of the free blacks and mulattoes, who enjoyed certain privileges, such as the right to bear arms and enjoy military privileges. To be a member of a battalion was symbol of social prestige.

After the 1770s, the battalions engaged with distinction in many extraterritorial actions and maneuvers, generally, however, without obtaining the recognition they deserved. The battalions were extinguished in 1844, when they were deemed to be politically dangerous after some of their members participated in the conspiracy of La Escalera.

TOWARD THE PLANTATION ECONOMY

The island of Cuba has produced sugar since the sixteenth century. During that early phase, production was geared for supplying local needs. In 1595, the Law on Privileges of Sugar Mills, which benefited the producers, was approved. In that same year, one thousand slaves were brought to the island. In 1600, the king extended a large loan to seventeen sugar-mill owners in Havana, although the actual number of sugar mills in the area was approximately twice that. In 1661, there were approximately twenty thousand slaves working in the cane fields (García p. 19). Due to the wars in Europe, the price of sugar on world markets rose steadily between 1680 and 1739, and the cattle ranches were demolished to make way for sugar mills. The Havana Company was established in tandem with this process in 1740 and secured the concession to import Africans, while also marketing sugar and other products.

Although the English occupation of Havana lasted only one year, it encouraged the entry of blockade-runners and broke the Spanish trading monopoly. By 1779, a market for Cuban sugar had consolidated in the United States. These elements created the conditions that allowed Cuba to replace the production of Saint-Domingue after the rebellion of 1791.

Despite the level of development that the institution of slavery had reached on the island in the nineteenth century, it was rooted only in certain limited areas, and Cuba was never a plantation colony. The rest of the country had ranches, haciendas, estates, and small farms, with diverse methods of production.

PLANTATION AREAS OF THE ISLAND OF CUBA

Before the Haitian Revolution (1791–1804), Cuba had 486 mills and three coffee estates. It exported an average of 9,000 metric tons of sugar a year. It had 32,077 slaves, constituting 18 percent of the population of the island, many of whom were engaged in services, including

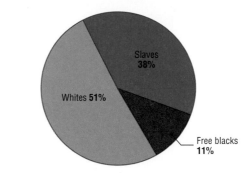

Marriages conducted in Havana, 1827

SOURCE: *Cuadro estadístico de la Siempre Fiel Isla de Cuba correspondiente al año 1827.* Havana: Viudas de Arazoza y Soler, 1829.

Figure 7

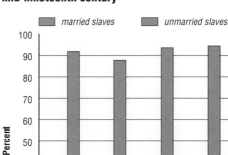

Percent of married and unmarried slaves according to the census of the mid-nineteenth century

SOURCE: Spanish Colonial census figures of 1841, 1846, 1861, 1870.

Figure 8

household chores. At that time, Saint-Domingue appeared to be the most prosperous of all the European colonies. It had 793 mills, 3,117 coffee estates, and 789 cotton farms. It was the largest producer of sugar and coffee for world markets. All this wealth was produced by 434,419 slaves, who made up 88 percent of the total population (Yacou p. 12).

The Haitian insurrection swept away the slave plantations, and the great landowners of Cuba stepped up to seize whatever advantage they could under the circumstances. Within ten years, Cuban coffee production had risen from 2,000 to 40,000 hundredweights (quintals) a year (Pérez de la Riva p. 28), and Cuba replaced Saint-Domingue as the top supplier of sugar on world markets.

Figure 9

Slave population (1774-1877)

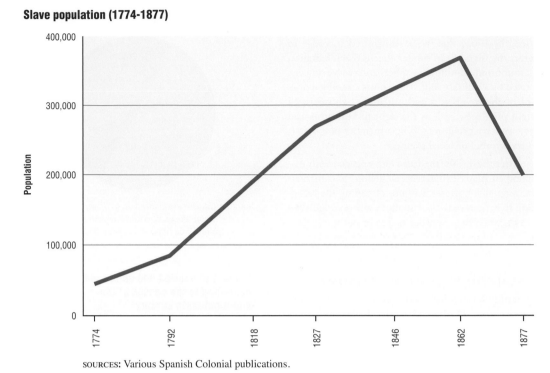

SOURCES: Various Spanish Colonial publications.

Despite this development, the percentage of the Cuban population who were slaves never surpassed the comparable figure for Haiti, even though the number kept rising until 1862 due to the remarkable expansion of the sugar factories, and, to a lesser extent, of the coffee estates. During this stage, slaves were not found only on the great plantations. They were quite prominent in the household arena and in the sectors of services, ranches, small holdings, and even the tobacco plantations.

WORK ON THE PLANTATION

Labor discipline and controls on the plantations were extreme and broke the traditional organizational and social forms of the African population, which had to adapt to new relationships and ways of life, with an impact on everything from dietary habits to parental relationships and even religious beliefs. Every aspect of life was regulated, planned, and controlled, in order to produce slaves who were, from their masters' point of view, another expensive piece of machinery that was expected to cover its own costs and strengthen the bottom line. Slaves were bought, sold, depreciated, and discarded, like any object.

The roster of blacks on a labor crew was known as a *dotación* (endowment) whose size would vary as a function of the cultivated areas on the farm, depending on how state-of-the-art the factory was. The more highly mechanized the mill or coffee farm, the greater the number of slaves required in order to grow the coffee or sugarcane. A sugar press generally had eighty slaves, while a semi-mechanized mill

might have as many as three hundred, and a fully mechanized mill might have twice that number. The largest coffee estates had between one hundred and two hundred slaves.

Work during the harvest and milling season went on without a break for approximately ten days at a time. Occasionally, a work break would land on a Sunday, providing a technical pause to clean the equipment and stave off fermentation, which would entail costly losses of sucrose. Similar processes, albeit less complex ones, took place in the coffee fields. As soon as the harvest was in, the maintenance and repair work began, both at the factories and in the growing areas; the pressure of work became less intense, although the slaves were always kept busy (Moreno Fraginals vol. 2, pp. 25–29).

Daily activities were governed by the number of bells: nine to start work, nine to mark the lunch hour, and nine to stop work. Different bell strikes were used for other specific activities. The bells were installed in a high place, such a belfry tower built for that purpose, or on the roof of the tallest building. These structures could also serve as a panopticon to oversee the slaves (Moreno Fraginals vol. 2, pp. 29–38).

The plantations had highly structured power and control systems. The masters delegated oversight to their managers and the *mayoral* (overseer), who in turn had various *contra-mayorales* (assistant overseers), who were slaves selected on the basis of two factors: the master's trust and the crew's respect. These men thus had both a real and symbolic importance, since they were the direct embodiment of power; paradoxically,

Labor sectors of slaves (1827–1862)

Figure 10

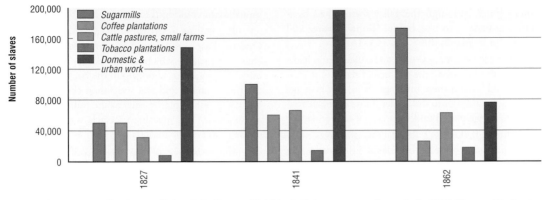

SOURCE: *Cuadro estadístico de la Siempre Fiel Isla de Cuba, correspondiente al año 1827*. Havana: Viudas de Arazoza y Soler, 1829; Armíldez de Toledo, conde de: *Noticias estadísticas de la Isla de Cuba en 1862*. Havana: Imprenta del Gobierno, Capitanía General y Real Hacienda, 1864.

even though they were appointed to watch and control the slaves' labor and to punish them when there were infringements, they maintained relationships with the *cimarrones* (runaway slaves) and on many occasions were the actual promoters of uprisings.

MAINTENANCE AND REPRODUCTION OF SLAVES

Because slaves were expensive and their productive work was highly valuable, they needed to be maintained in optimal physical shape. Every year, they were provided with two changes of clothing, and their dwellings were temperate. The food was plain, but rich in calories. The main staples for their two daily meals were *tasajo* (salt-cured meat), codfish (also cured), and starches (plantains, yams, manioc, etc.). They were also given corn, flour, and rice.

On the large sugar mills and coffee estates, the meals were cooked at a central location. At the smaller ones, supplies were distributed and cooked by the servants themselves, who also ingested large amounts of sugar in a variety of forms: *raspadura* (cane juice candy), syrup, molasses, and *guarapo* (cane juice) (Moreno Fraginals vol. 2, pp. 57–63). During the early phases, near their thatch huts and subsequently in the vicinity of their barracks, the slaves cultivated their *conucos*, tiny strips of land on which they raised hogs and poultry and grew root crops, which helped supplement their diet or could be sold either on the premises of the sugar mill or coffee estate or elsewhere.

The slaves were issued clothing modules referred to as their *esquifación* (skiffs). The first set of clothes was issued at the beginning of the harvest. For men it consisted of trousers, a shirt, and a wool cap; for women it was a dress, a scarf, and a cap. The second set was issued at the end of the milling season and was similar to the first, except that a straw hat was issued instead of the wool cap. They were also given a flannel jacket and a

wool blanket, which was supposed to last the entire year. The skiff did not include footwear, since shoes were used only by urban slaves. Black field hands were prey to chiggers, an insect that burrows underneath the skin and produces boils that could get infected and prevent a person from walking (Moreno Fraginals vol. 2, pp. 63–66).

Domestic and urban slaves lived in their master's home, although occasionally they had their own or rented rooms. Field hands lived in huts known as *bohíos*, which were frequently grouped into hamlets or *barracones* (barracks). The latter term was used rather ambiguously, because it sometimes referred to the slave's hut, while at other times it referred to his or her residence in the *barracón* (Pérez de la Riva 1975, p. 22). Until the end of the eighteenth century, estate owners barely gave a second thought to the location of their slave dwellings because the crews were small and easily controllable (Roura Alvarez and Angelbello Izquierdo 2007, p. 140). But thereafter, the situation began to change, due to the rising number of slaves and the need to assert tighter control over them. At that point, the *bohíos* began to be concentrated in specific locations and in some cases were replaced by *barracones*. In any event, the slave houses were built near the factory areas, because this got slaves to the workplace faster (Roura Alvarez and Angelbello Izquierdo 2007, p. 149).

On most of the very large sugar mills and coffee estates, the bohío was always the slave's home, and, as can be seen in many engravings of the period, they were located in places that facilitated surveillance. At the El Padre coffee estate, the slave dwellings were surrounded by a high wall (Roura Alvarez and Angelbello Izquierdo 2007, p. 146).

Some of the larger and more developed mills had large barracones built around a patio, while others used the galley format. Some mills used barracones to house single slaves, and bohíos for the married ones, but sometimes there were rooms in the central building to house the married slaves. As of 2007 no barracks built around a patio had been found on the coffee estates, although the galley format had been found, as had, of course, bohíos (Roura Alvarez and Angelbello Izquierdo 2007, pp. 143–147).

Virtually all the sugar mills and coffee estates had a criollo house for raising the children of slaves. The children would remain there until age seven, at which age they were inducted into the lighter chores of the plantation. They were placed under the care of elderly slaves.

Although the 1842 Regulations on Slaves mandated that slaves were to be housed in barracks, the bohíos continued to be the predominant method of housing, because the barracks were an expensive solution. In 1852, the city of Cárdenas had 221 sugar mills, of which only 98 had barracks, 73.5 percent of which were built out of stone or brick (Barcia Zequeira 2009, p. 216).

With regard to the slave rebellions in Matanzas, in 1825, regulations were enacted that prescribed that barracks should be built for enclaves with more than thirty slaves. Although some landowners heeded this provision, it failed to quell the escapes and uprisings, as shown by the rebellions that occurred between 1843 and 1844 in this area.

PUNISHMENT AND SLAVE RESISTANCE

Punishing a slave was the master's right, and the range of punishments was broad (jail, shackles, chains, knouts, pillories, stocks, and the lash), and there were other, more torturous forms of brutality, such as scorching with hot plates, pulling teeth, and chopping off hands and genitals. The most common practice was to exceed the permissible number of lashes, which regulations set at twenty-five, but the intensity of the punishment could lead to the death of the slave.

The law included some horrendous provisions. One of these was known as *escarmiento* (exemplary chastisement), in which the death penalty could be inflicted by garrote, shooting in the back, or hanging; the head, hands, and feet were then chopped off for display in public places, such as the mill hamlets or at a crossroads. This macabre spectacle was an assertion of the power of the masters.

The resistance of the slaves could take many forms. Tools got broken; masters were poisoned; there were abortions and suicides, parricides, and matricides. There were *cimarrones* (escaped urban and rural slaves), both individuals and groups, and uprisings. The methods of resistance were usually prompted by food shortages, inadequate clothing, and above all excessive work and punishments.

The rural cimarrones organized themselves in *palenques* (stockades or wooden forts), which is to say, groups who lived in a collective manner. Between 1796 and 1854, they were persecuted and hounded by quadrilles of six men or parties of twenty-five men, directed by a rancher who used trained dogs to capture them. Upon being identified by the master, the slave was returned; otherwise, slaves were remanded to the *cimarrón* deposit, where they could be rented out for all kinds of jobs. The palenques were located in remote, unpopulated, and inaccessible areas; despite this, some of them communicated among themselves. The most important ones are El Frijol (The Bean), Todos Tenemos (We All Have Some), Vereda de San Juan (St. John's Lane), Calunga, and Vuelta Pariente (Kin's Return) (La Rosa Corzo 1991, p. 224). The cimarrones gradually declined in number after the 1840s, when, paradoxically, the largest of all the slave rebellions, known as La Escalera, took place.

Slave rebellions occurred after the revolution in Saint-Domingue, which led to a decree calling for the expulsion of French and English slaves who had been imported after 1790. Some uprisings were linked to the activities of the free blacks, as occurred in the conspiracies of Aponte in 1812 and La Escalera (1843–1844). Along with the latter, the most important conspiracy took place in Guamacaro in 1825. Both areas are in Matanzas, a region of huge plantations.

In 1843, there was an uprising that included the so-called endowments of eleven sugar mills, one coffee estate, a ranch, and slaves working on the Cárdenas-Bemba railroad. A female slave called Polonia had reported that a large-scale conspiracy was underway and that on the first day of Christmas 1844 the slaves of six other mills would rise in rebellion. The repression began at once, targeting slaves, who made up more than one-fourth of the participants in the conspiracy, as well as free blacks and mulattoes, who accounted for nearly three-fourths.

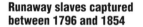

Runaway slaves captured between 1796 and 1854

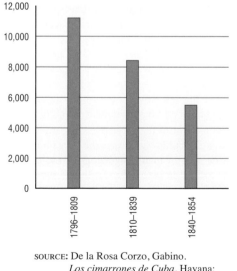

SOURCE: De la Rosa Corzo, Gabino. *Los cimarrones de Cuba.* Havana: Editorial Ciencias Sociales, 1988, p. 94.

Figure 11

After the conspiracy of La Escalera, the free black and brown battalions were suppressed, and controls over slave crews and subalterns in the cities were tightened. The historical annals record this as a "year of hidings," a reference to the use of whips for inflicting the punishments.

THE ABOLITION OF SLAVERY

Slavery was abolished on the island of Cuba in 1886, after a drawn-out process whose first stirrings came in 1811, when two deputies, the Mexican Miguel Guridi y Alcocer (1763–1828) and the Spaniard Agustín Argüelles (1776–1843), brought up the issue at the Cortes. For the owners of the great plantations, the slave labor force was a critical input that they obtained through massive importation; to them the abolition of slavery was simply inconceivable, and they continued to import slaves illegally after the legal trade was suppressed in 1818. They dismissed the analysis of Félix Varela (1788–1853) and José Antonio Saco (1797–1879) with regard to the extinction of slavery, evaded the Treaty of 1835 between Spain and Great Britain, and delayed the implementation of the Criminal Law.

By the 1860s, plantation owners were convinced that the end of slavery was near, but they now attempted to deal with the issue within a framework of economic and political reforms that the imperial metropolis refused to grant. Accordingly, they headed off Manuel Becerra's abolitionist project and grudgingly accepted the Law of Free Wombs drafted by Segismundo Moret (1833–1913).

The Ten Years' War brought a new twist to the story. The abolition of slavery had been decreed at the Assembly of Guáimaro, in 1869, in a definitive document that was signed on 23 December 1870. This emancipation was valid only in the insurrectionist camp. The Moret Law was enacted almost simultaneously. Under the Masters Law, enacted in 1880, all slaves were to be emancipated by 1889, but the infamous institution was finally and definitively abolished six years later, in 1886.

The mill owners themselves were virtually unaffected, but more than two hundred thousand blacks and mulattoes who became free men and women now found themselves in a precarious situation, free by law but with a freedom that guaranteed them no economic benefits. The brand of slavery would continue to mark Cuba's history for many years to come.

BIBLIOGRAPHY

Barcia Paz, Manuel. *Con el látigo de la ira: Legislación, represión, y control en las plantaciones cubanas, 1790–1870.* Havana: Editorial de Ciencias Sociales, 2000.

Barcia Zequeira, María del Carmen. *Burguesía esclavista y abolición.* Havana: Editorial de Ciencias Sociales, 1987.

Barcia Zequeira, María del Carmen. *Los ilustres apellidos: Negros en Havana colonial.* Havana: Editorial Boloña, 2008.

Barcia Zequeira, María del Carmen. *La otra familia.* Santiago de Cuba: Editorial Oriente, 2009.

Bergad, Laird, Fe Iglesias García, and María del Carmen Barcia. *The Cuban Slave Market, 1790–1880.* Cambridge, U.K.: Cambridge University Press, 1995.

Boubacar, Barry. *El reino de Waloo: Senegal antes de la conquista.* Havana: Editorial de Ciencias Sociales, 2008.

Cantero, Justo G. *Los ingenios: Colección de vistas de los principales ingenios de azúcar de la isla de Cuba.* Havana: Imprenta La Cubana, 1857.

Chateausalins, Honorato B. *El vademécum de los hacendados cubanos, o guía para curar la mayor parte de las enfermedades: Obra adecuada a la zona tórrida y muy útil para aliviar los males de los esclavos.* New York: G. F. Bunce, 1831.

Childs, Matt D. *The 1812 Aponte Rebellion in Cuba and the Struggle against Atlantic Slavery.* Chapel Hill: University of North Carolina Press, 2006.

Eltis, David. *Economic Growth and the Ending of the Transatlantic Slave Trade.* New York: Oxford University Press, 1987.

Franco, José Luciano. *Comercio clandestino de esclavos.* Havana: Editorial de Ciencias Sociales, 1980.

García, Gloria. *Conspiraciones y revueltas: La actividad política de los negros en Cuba (1790–1845).* Santiago de Cuba: Editorial Oriente, 2003.

García Rodríguez, Mercedes. *Entre haciendas y plantaciones: Orígenes de la manufactura azucarera en La Habana.* Havana: Ciencias Sociales, 2007.

Guanche, Jesús. *Africanía y etnicidad en Cuba.* Havana: Editorial Adagio, 2009.

Humboldt, Alejandro de. *Ensayo político sobre la isla de Cuba.* Havana: Cultural S.A., 1930.

La Rosa Corzo, Gabino. *Los cimarrones de Cuba.* Havana: Editorial de Ciencias Sociales, 1988.

La Rosa Corzo, Gabino. *Los palenques del oriente de Cuba: Resistencia y acoso.* Havana: Editorial Academia, 1991.

Le Riverend, Julio. *Historia económica de Cuba.* Havana: Ediciones R., 1971.

Lucena Salmoral, Manuel. *Los códigos negros de la América Española.* Madrid: Ediciones Unesco, Universidad de Alcalá, 1996.

Macías, Isabelo. *Cuba en la primera mitad del siglo VII.* Seville, Spain: Escuela de Estudios Hispano-Americanos de Sevilla, 1978.

Meriño Fuentes, María de los Angeles, and Aisnara Perera Díaz. *Matrimonio y Familia en el ingenio: Una utopía posible: La Habana (1825–1886).* Havana: Editorial Unicornio, 2007.

Mettas, Jean. *Repertoire des expéditions négrières françaises au XVIIIe siéle.* Edited by Serge Daget and Michèle Daget 2 vols. Paris: Société Française d'Histoire d'Outre-Mer, 1978–1984.

Moreno Fraginals, Manuel. *El Ingenio: Complejo económico social cubano del azúcar.* 3 vols. Havana: Editorial Ciencias Sociales, 1978.

Paquette, Robert. *Sugar Is Made with Blood: The Conspiracy of La Escalera and the Conflict between Empires over Slavery in Cuba.* Middletown, CT: Wesleyan University Press, 1988.

Perera Díaz, Aisnara, and María de los Ángeles Meriño. *Para librarse de lazos, antes buena familia que buenos brazos: Apuntes sobre la manumisión en Cuba.* Santiago de Cuba: Editorial Oriente, 2009.

Pérez de la Riva, Francisco. *El café: Historia de su cultivo y exportación en Cuba.* Havana: J. Montalvo, 1944.

Pérez de la Riva, Juan. *El barracón y otros ensayos.* Havana: Editorial Ciencias Sociales, 1975.

Roura Alvarez, Lisette, and Teresa Angelbello Izquierdo. "El bohío: Vivienda esclava en las plantaciones cubanas del siglo XIX." *Boletín del Gabinete de Arqueología* 6 (2007): 136–150.

Scott, Rebecca. *Slave Emancipation in Cuba: The Transition to Free Labor, 1860–1899.* Princeton, NJ: Princeton University Press, 1985.

Yacou, Alain. "L'émigration á Cuba des colons français de Saint-Domingue au course de la Révolution, 1789–1815." Ph.D. diss. University of Bordeaux, 1975.

■ *See also*

Aponte Rebellion: 1811–1812

Racial Uprising and Massacre: 1912

Spanish-American-Cuban War: 1898

Ten Years' War: 1868–1878

RACE: FREE PEOPLE OF COLOR IN CUBA

Alan West-Durán

Afro-Cubans and Cuban society before the abolition of slavery.

Despite the totalizing nature of African bondage in Cuba, slavery was not a monolithic system. During the centuries of slavery on the island, Cuba had a considerable number of what were called free people of color. They constituted from 15 to 20 percent of the population from 1492 to 1886, when slavery ended. The presence of this large population was a notable difference between Cuba and the English- and French-speaking Caribbean and the United States and helps explain the unique racial dynamics of Cuba. These have been more fluid and perhaps less exclusionary, although slavery in Cuba was no less cruel, destructive, and exploitative than elsewhere. The large number and percentage of free people of color was related to rates of manumission and to a system known as *coartación* (limit, as in limiting the period one was enslaved), which enabled slaves to negotiate with their masters a price for their freedom, to be paid in installments, usually over several years. At times *cabildos* (mutual aid societies) helped to finance the freedom of family members. Manumission and coartación were more common in the cities, where slaves had greater economic opportunities to perform extra work for pay that would enable them to purchase their freedom. Rural slaves who had *conucos* (plots of land they were allowed to cultivate) and could sell their crops were able to do likewise. There was also a group of people known as *emancipados* captured from the illegal slave trade after the 1820s and temporarily held as slaves for a fixed term—usually seven years—before being given their freedom. It is estimated that these captured illegal slaves numbered 25,660 between 1824 and 1866 (Klein p. 198).

The free population of color prevailed in the manual trades; an 1846 census reveals that they were the majority of tailors, seamstresses, masons, builders, workers, carpenters, shoemakers, cooks, washerwomen, undertakers, and coach drivers (Paquette p. 107). Among musicians this population dominated, and there was a small group of tavern owners. Some became landowners and a few even owned slaves. However, their presence was underrepresented in education, commerce, government, and the higher echelons of the Catholic Church. Proof that a close relationship existed between the enslaved and the free people of color is the following: Between 1825 and 1829, at the height of the plantation system in Cuba, in six parishes of Havana, almost one-fifth of all marriages registered were between free persons and slaves (Castellanos and Castellanos p. 84).

LIMITED SOCIAL MOBILITY

Free people of color formed cabildos, a type of mutual aid society that goes back to the *cofradías* (religious brotherhoods) in Spain. They were usually referred to as *cabildos de nación* (*nación* being understood as ethnic or linguistic group or people—that is, the Africans in Cuba). These voluntary associations are known to have existed as early as the mid-sixteenth century and helped their members adjust to the shock of the new cultural, economic, and social realities created by forced migration and enslavement. Cabildos were usually organized along ethno-linguistic lines and helped preserve African languages, customs, and other aspects of African heritage. They also ensured decent burial for the deceased, assisted their brethren who ran afoul of the law, helped the indigent and the sick, and hosted social and religious events.

Many free people of color participated in the military, in units known as Batallones or Compañías de Pardos (mixed-race) y Morenos (blacks). By 1770 roughly one-third of the Spanish army stationed in Cuba was composed of pardos and morenos (Castellanos and Castellanos 1988, p. 87). In many instances when security was paramount, slaves fought for Cuba, as was the case during the defense of Havana against the invasion of the British (1762–1763). As a result of their bravery against the British, hundreds of slaves were set free. Service in these units was an instrument of social mobility that many officers and, to a lesser degree, enlisted men used to acquire property and give their children an education.

The free population of color was adamant about education and a significant minority acquired primary and secondary education. However, going to university was much more difficult, requiring a document proving purity of blood, basically a certificate of whiteness. Aside from the bureaucratic entanglements, the process was costly. And of course it meant that a person of color applying for

Cuba population figures from 1774 to 1899

Table 1

Year	Total	White	Slaves	Free Non-Whites
1774	171,620	96,440 (56%)	38,879 (23%)	36,301 (21%)
1792	272,300	153,559 (56%)	64,590 (24%)	54,151 (20%)
1827	704,486	311,051 (44%)	286,492 (41%)	106,492 (15%)
1841	1,007,624	418,291 (42%)	436,495 (43%)	152,838 (17%)
1861	1,396,530	793,484 (57%)	370,553 (27%)	232,493 (17%)
1877	1,509,291	1,032,435 (68%)	211,247 (14%)	265,609 (18%)
1899	1,572,797	1,067,254 (68%)		505,543 (32%)

Urban Slaves: 20%; Rural Slaves: 80%
In 1857: 1% of owners had 25% of slaves; 4% of population owned slaves

SOURCE: Kenneth Kiple, *Blacks in Colonial Cuba, 1774–1899*; Franklin Knight, *Slave Society in Cuba During the Nineteenth Century*, University of Wisconsin Press, 1970, pp. 134–135.

such a document had to be a very light pardo, that is, someone who could pass for white. Still, quite a few pardos did manage to become lawyers, dentists, and doctors.

This limited social mobility, however, did not compensate for Cuba's racial inequalities. A pardo's success meant rejecting any black or biracial identity and allowing himself to be whitened by administrative or legal decree. The human and psychological price must have been great—not to mention that many darker-skinned Cubans did not have even this possibility, particularly those who were enslaved (Castellanos and Castellanos 1988, p. 92).

THE LADDER CONSPIRACY

The free population of color was an intermediary population between whites and slaves, and despite the designation *free*, they never had the same freedoms as whites. For example, they were not permitted to hold important positions in government or the Church. In their public interactions they had to show deference to whites (ceding the sidewalk or taking off their hats), and there were prohibitions on alcohol and the right to marry whites. At certain times, this population was seen as a danger by white ruling elites, and limitations were always placed on their relationships with their enslaved brethren. A dramatic measure of the fear experienced by whites was the repression unleashed in response to the so-called Conspiración de La Escalera (Ladder Conspiracy) in 1844, in which the greatest punishment was inflicted on the free population of color. More than eighty people were executed, including renowned poet Gabriel de la Concepción Valdés (known as Plácido); some three thousand others were imprisoned or banished (Paquette p. 229). The Escalera repression also motivated many free people of color to return to Africa (Howard p. 14).

In the nineteenth century, with the British ending of the slave trade (1807) and subsequently slavery itself (1834–1838), the price of slaves of Cuba dramatically increased (quadrupling between 1845 and 1861), causing a considerable reduction in the rate of manumissions and coartaciones. This situation was, in part, offset by the importation of Chinese indentured servants, which began in 1847.

THE STRUGGLE FOR INDEPENDENCE

By 1868, Spain was seeking a way to gradually abolish slavery, but rebel forces issued their *Grito de Yara* (Cry of Yara, 10 October 1868), which dramatically made independence and abolition its central demands. Free Cubans of color (and the cabildos) were highly supportive of the independence struggle, and many became famous leaders: Quintín Bandera (1833–1906), Guillermo Moncada (1841–1895), Policarpo Pineda (Rustán; 1839–1872), Flor Crombet (1851–1895), and José Maceo (1848–1896). The most prominent was Antonio Maceo (1845–1896), who led Cuban insurrectionists in the Ten Years' (or Great) War (1868–1878), the subsequent Guerra Chiquita (Little War, 1879–1880), and the Spanish-American-Cuban War (1895–1898), and is now a national hero. Maceo's military skills were legendary and well known outside Cuba (many African Americans named their children after him). Spain's colonial regime increased surveillance, harassment, and imprisonment of free Cubans of color but also offered enticements (such as amnesty for desertion), particularly to slaves, who were promised freedom if they fought for Spain. The pro-independence struggle did not succeed before the abolition of slavery in 1886, but sixteen thousand former slaves who fought with the rebels were freed, and between 1870 and 1875, colonial authorities freed over fifty thousand slaves. Free people of color had a considerable influence on the economy and culture of nineteenth-century Cuba before abolition.

BIBLIOGRAPHY

Castellanos, Jorge, and Isabel Castellanos. *Cultura Afrocubana*. Vol. 1, *El Negro en Cuba, 1492–1844*. Miami, FL: Ediciones Universal, 1988.

Castellanos, Jorge, and Isabel Castellanos. *Cultura Afrocubana*. Vol. 2, *El Negro en Cuba, 1845–1959*. Miami, FL: Ediciones Universal, 1990.

Ferrer, Ada. *Insurgent Cuba: Race, Nation, and Revolution, 1868–1898*. Chapel Hill: University of North Carolina Press, 1999.

Howard, Philip A. *Changing History: Afro-Cuban Cabildos and Societies of Color in the Nineteenth Century*. Baton Rouge: Louisiana State University Press, 1998.

Klein, Herbert S. *Slavery in the Americas: A Comparative Study of Virginia and Cuba*. Chicago: University of Chicago Press, 1967.

Paquette, Robert L. *Sugar Is Made with Blood: The Conspiracy of La Escalera and the Conflict between Empires over Slavery in Cuba*. Middletown, CT: Wesleyan University Press, 1990.

■ *See also*

Racial Uprising and Massacre: 1912

RACE: RACIAL ISSUES DURING THE TRANSITION TO INDEPENDENCE

Fernando Martínez Heredia

Race in Cuba from 1886 to 1895 and during War of Independence (1895–1898); the foundation of the Republic, the transformation of the black in Cuba to the black Cuban, democratic policy, conservative society, and racism between 1898 and 1907.

The seventeen-year process of abolishing slavery in Cuba ended in 1886. It was shaped by economic, political, and social motives, but, for many, after the Ten Years' War (1868–1878), slavery could not continue. In the new era of full capitalism, blacks were still needed, now as paid workers; in general, they remained in the regions where they had been slaves. An 1881 royal order eliminated the prohibition against interracial marriage. Although this act initiated the end to legal racism, the administration of justice, education, and other colonial affairs remained discriminatory. The new modes of production did not require a merciless, racist caste system as had been the rule earlier, but blacks and mulattoes—one-third of the population of Cuba—now experienced racism based on social custom. As a result, they faced profound disadvantages.

THE STRUGGLE FOR RACIAL EQUALITY AMONG NEWLY FREE CUBANS

For the newly freed after 1886, it was now normal to have families, move freely off their farms, hire themselves out as workers, or seek other forms of income—to have their own economy—and to aspire to or own a home and hold certain rights. New motivations drove their work ethic, and they added their consumption to the market. The dismal weight of the enslaved masses on the moral deterioration of social standing for free blacks was reduced, and it was easier for relationships and mutual esteem to progress. But although the economic position of a minority placed them among the middle class or lent those in the lower classes a higher sense of security in their lives, the cultural status of nonwhites was the lowest in Cuban society. Science, much influenced by trends of Positivism, determined that nonwhites were inferior beings, with the only debate being whether this inferiority was biological or social.

For their part, Cuban blacks and mulattoes had to try to escape from the bottom of society through work, personal achievement, advancement of their children, the rejection of cultural practices that were considered barbaric or backward, and the assumption of behaviors and goals connected to white ideals. For some blacks, this was not feasible, but for all of them it was now a tempting possibility. Several sectors joined forces, establishing mutual-aid and trade associations. The Directorio Central de Sociedades de Color (Central Directory of Societies of Color), founded in 1887 and the most famous of these associations, was a unique expression of the new struggles for racial equality and for equality under the law. Activists denounced racist acts, demanded compliance with the law, created awareness, and mobilized people, in addition to promoting education and other actions. Juan Gualberto Gómez (1854–1933), the son of slaves but educated in France and Spain, became the most famous propagandist and defender of this cause as director of the newspaper *La Fraternidad* (The Brotherhood) and leader of the Directorio Central.

Colonial policies toward blacks and mulattoes had a preventive political component, with tacit acknowledgment that they could seek satisfaction for their demands through a new revolution. The Partido Liberal Autonomista (Liberal Autonomist Party), which claimed to represent the sons of the island and had some influence, shared in the racism of the time. Meanwhile, in the spiritual realm, the island experienced the formation of the Cuban identity through the emergence of a political sort of patriotism that referred to the *Grito de Yara*, the uprising in the eastern town of Yara that sparked the Ten Years' War, as its precursor. In the legend of the Yara uprising, blacks were primary actors who had lived and fought on equal footing with whites and who contributed heroes and martyrs to the cause. Among the separatists, racism was considered shameful or outright rejected.

JOSÉ MARTÍ'S CUBAN REVOLUTIONARY PARTY

At the beginning of the 1890s, José Martí (1853–1895), who was an exile in the United States, created an illegal political party in order to carry out a new revolutionary proposal: the Partido Revolucionario Cubano (Cuban Revolutionary Party). Martí's party took as its starting point the country's enormous cultural potential and called on Cubans to reject conservatism and evolutionism, throw out the old colonialism, and obstruct the crystallization of a new colonialism, founding what Martí referred to as a new republic. He proposed closing the doors to U.S. expansionism in the Caribbean and Latin America and urged Cubans to win not only their independence but also their national freedom, as well as to initiate a social policy that strongly favored the majority.

Martí emphatically exhibited his advanced antiracist beliefs in the face of the scientific racism that flourished at the time. But he could not forget that racism existed, and he formulated a strategy to combat it. He maintained strong practical ties with associations and individuals of color, both among expatriates such as himself and on the island. His project was not gradualist: He called on all Cubans—and expressly nonwhites—to create a free and just nation, and to satisfy their demands in the process. Juan Gualberto Gómez became the delegate of Martí's party on the island while the latter was in exile.

THE MULTIRACIAL NATURE OF THE REVOLUTION OF 1895

The conspirators that planned the Revolution of 1895 were multiracial. The Directorio Central threw itself into subversive activities. Activists, contacts, and leaders were of all colors; the same occurred in the uprisings that began on 24 February. Antonio Maceo (1845–1896), a mulatto from the eastern part of the island, was a hero who was converted into a symbol. His famous Baraguá protest, in which he refused to recognize a solution other than absolute independence, was at the center of the Mambi legend. Maceo's arrival in April 1895 was decisive in spurring thousands of people from the eastern part of the island to join the war. The invasion across the country, which he directed alongside Máximo Gómez (1836–1905), another important military figure from the Ten Years' War, turned Maceo into a great political leader on a national scale.

Blacks and mulattoes went to war en masse; it has been estimated that they made up 60 percent of combatants. As Martí foresaw, the organized revolutionary violence constituted a gigantic school for the creation of values (including antiracism), capabilities, and citizenship for the participants, the collaborators, and the families of patriots. The development that those who were beginning to be Cubans achieved through armed struggle was much greater than would have been achieved if independence had been established through a long-term evolutionary progression and also essentially different. The experiences, feelings, and ideas of the revolutionary war caused racism to recede significantly. For nonwhites, it was an especially positive event. It provided them with an identity that they shared with all Cubans, without feeling *less than*,

an identity that was not bestowed upon them. The insurrection gave them much more recognition than did contemporary social life, and their political activities represented an enormous leap with respect to their limited prior civic experience and the scope of their earlier demands.

The behavior of the blacks and mulattoes in the conflict was extraordinary. They rivaled whites in terms of discipline, bravery, sacrifice, and commitment. They faced up to the hardships of an all-out war, which caused massive death and devastation in the country. From the beginning, there were nonwhite sergeants and officers involved, making it the first truly multiracial army in the Americas. For several decades after the war, veterans constituted a prestigious civic figure in Cuba. Veterans included whites, mulattoes, and blacks, who came together for the first time on matters of reputation. One of the most important accomplishments of the Revolution of 1895 was the transformation of blacks in Cuba into Cuban blacks.

LINGERING STRAINS OF RACISM

However, the issue of race did not disappear. Within the revolutionary camp, racism continued and was expressed as contempt, double standards, and manifest injustices; many insurrectionary forces were guilty of these practices, while others tolerated them. This trend was undoubtedly due to the cultural character of the racism that had been established in Cuba. But these conditions were also related to the social and political conservatism that existed within the heterogeneous insurrectionary camp, which managed to counterbalance the radical wing. In any case, racism was morally condemned in a republic at arms that prohibited all references to persons other than *citizen*. But all revolutions involve holdovers, and not just changes.

As a result of the Spanish-American-Cuban War of the summer of 1898, Cuba was subjected to a military occupation that lasted until May 1902. This condition meant a step back in terms of the race issue. The United States was then at the height of its racist history, so it was inevitable that Americans would reinforce Cuban racists and would try to transfer some of their ideas and institutions to the island. But the most negative thing about the U.S. action was more general. By imposing cutbacks and forcing the dissolution of the most fundamental institutions of the revolution, guide and ally of the new dominant postwar neocolonial regime of the United States decisively contributed to the diminishing or adulteration of the achievements of the Cuban revolution, including those related to race and racism. The result was specific and the effects clear, but it was also part of a bigger national frustration.

THE IMPACT OF THE REVOLUTION ON NONWHITES

Understanding the race issue in Cuba from that point forward entails considering the affiliations in which it is inscribed. For example, the revolution impacted poor whites, blacks, and mulattoes in at least four ways: (1) it increased personal capacities and stimulated a search for social betterment; (2) it effected positive changes to self-esteem; (3) it led to changes in attitudes with respect to the nature of the existing order and its omnipotence, and in ideas related to political and social systems; and (4) it caused Cubans to self-identify as citizens and as members of social groups, which included the identification of *others* and of potential enemies.

The new Republican reality brought with it limitations and adaptations of those four impacts. Two facts contributed to this: (1) the Revolution of 1895 knocked down certain hierarchies but maintained many others and did not delegitimize the unrestricted nature of commercial relationships and capitalist property that had been spread throughout Cuba; and (2) from 1898 on, there was a strong campaign in favor of adherence to the law and compliance with the social hierarchy. Poor Cubans thus experienced a complicated process of tension and contradiction. The increase in their self-esteem and personal potential and their expectations for upward mobility were to a large degree unsatisfied; however, their exercise of citizenship was vigorous and enduring, and their conception of politics and social life was modernized according to advanced democratic ideals. Cuban blacks and mulattoes inscribed their specificities within a society in which individual affirmation and group identity, social protest, political activity, and submission to the rules of a system were largely restored.

THE SOCIAL CONSTRUCTION OF RACE AND RACISM IN CUBA

The social construction of race and racism in Cuba entered into a new period. The weight of nationalism in the Republican racial construct was not determined by a plan from above. There were strong popular components, and it formed part of a national construct molded through pressure, negotiation, and conflict among the various social groups. In this new age, relationships based on racial equality gained ground on a national scale, and ideas about these relationships were much more inclusive. Reasons for this change include:

1. Nonwhites won these achievements through large-scale participation in the great crucible of war, and the conviction that they had won rights was affirmed.
2. Interracial alliances were developed in the political and social struggles of the revolution and the Republic; these also tended to endure, although with new content, and interracial bonds based on these shared experiences were created.
3. The main contemporary ideology was Mambi nationalism, which proclaimed antiracism and equality. The Mambi

ideology was legitimized due to its practice as part of national exploits, and it was invoked later in the face of Republican realities.
4. The legal order and political system of the first Republic favored the full assumption of citizenship by nonwhites and their presence in civic life, although this was limited.
5. Nonwhites appealed to all means at their disposal to climb the social ladder: education, work, association, political participation, and the image of members of the national community.
6. The exploitation of free work could not make broad use of antiblack racism when the expanding economy received an enormous mass of white immigrants, and workers' associations became more and more interracial.

Racism persisted, nonetheless, in the new circumstances for the following reasons:

1. It was already solidly culturally implanted in the collective conscience of the population, with everyday mechanisms for its reproduction.
2. The results of the Revolution of 1895 did not affect the foundations of the social system of domination supported by racism. Under the Republican order, racism could be tapped, and it was used to gain advantages in the fields of exploitation and domination.
3. The neocolonial bourgeois Republican system was politically liberal and socially conservative. Racism was a social element that could feasibly be used as a conservative trump card due to its cultural establishment and its supposed natural, rather than socially constructed, foundations.
4. The shared beliefs in civilization and progress served to draw attention away from the Mambi ideology and to legitimize the new order. These included the theory of white superiority and the belief in the advantages and inevitability of *whitening* Cuba, beliefs that held that education, economic solvency, and European ideas and customs were the yardstick of superiority or merit.
5. The enormous influence of the United States in Cuba favored the persistence of racism and, to some degree, its exacerbation.

A PERIOD OF RACIAL CONFLICT AND ADJUSTMENT

Racism in the first Republic brought the country closer to one of the mainstream Western attributes of the period: colonialist, imperialist racism, based on ideas

LEADERS OF THE PARTIDO INDEPENDIENTE DE COLOR (PIC)

Evaristo Estenoz Corominas (1872–1912) and Pedro Ivonet Dofourt (1860–1912) were the most popular leaders of the Partido Independiente de Color (PIC; Independent Party of Color), a political party comprising almost entirely African former slaves. Ivonet had fought in the Cuban War of Independence under Antonio Maceo (1845–1896) and ascended to the rank of colonel. Estenoz also fought in the War of 1895 and participated in the invasion. He was a construction foreman, and his intervention helped to end the 1899 construction workers' strike.

On 7 August 1908 Estenoz, Ivonet, and others founded the Agrupación Independiente de Color (Independent Color Union), which later became the PIC. The party was granted legal status by the U.S. occupation government, but in 1910 it was deemed to be an illegal group when Congress approved Martín Morúa Delgado's amendment that prohibited political parties with single-race membership. Nevertheless, the party continued its activities, securing superior court orders to stop the police from interfering. Because of that, there were rumors of an agreement between Estenoz and Ivonet and President José Miguel Gómez (1858–1921) to legalize the party if it supported Gómez's reelection. A sham armed protest was planned to facilitate repeal of the amendment before the 1912 election, but the president, fearful of the possibility of a third intervention by the United States, ordered the killing of Estenoz and Ivonet to prevent them from revealing how they had been deceived. During the rebellion in Oriente Province, Estenoz, Ivonet, and between 4,000 and 6,000 nonwhite Cubans were killed by government forces.

To date, there has been no objective assessment of Estenoz and Ivonet's political party, which provided a new, unique option that was never contemplated before—or after—in the countries of Latin America and the Caribbean with mainly black and white populations.

BIBLIOGRAPHY

Betancourt, Juan René. "Evaristo Estenoz." In *El negro ciudadano del futuro*. Havana: Cárdenas y Compañía, 1960.

Castro Fernández, Silvio. *La masacre del Partido Independiente de Color*. Havana: Editora Política, 2007.

Estenoz, Evaristo. "A mis amigos." *El Nuevo Criollo* (1905): 2.

Estenoz, Evaristo. "Carta abierta." *El Triunfo* (20 February 1908): 9.

Fuente, Alejandro de la. "Black Autonomous Mobilization: PIC." In *A Nation for All: Race, Inequality, and Politics in Twentieth-Century Cuba*. Chapel Hill: University of North Carolina Press, 2001.

Portuondo Linares, Serafín. *Los independientes de color*. Havana: Dirección de Cultura, 1950.

Tomás Fernández Robaina

---

of racial superiority and the "white man's burden." With this step, the Cuban regime abandoned important advances in social conscience, the fruit of the process of conflict described above. Consequently, the regime reduced its capacity to channel the population through hegemony and thus demonstrated its inability to assert any claim to existence as anything more than a minor partner or servant. This abandonment of its own culture on the part of the dominant-dominated generally creates a proclivity to seek legitimacy in resemblance to the metropolitan model.

The demands of nonwhites for political participation were, in large measure, satisfied—despite strong limitations—and they used it over and over to gain or claim social spaces. However, they did not attempt to modify the new structure of race and racism to a detectable extent. Two widespread beliefs took on decisive weight in guiding civic behavior and political judgments: (1) the refusal to offer any pretext for U.S. intervention; and (2) the unconditional unity of all Cubans as a requirement for maintaining the nation and upholding an image that would counterbalance the supposed inability to exercise self-government. These beliefs were systematically brandished as a way to accuse black and mulatto activists of not being patriotic when their demands for greater equality or improvement in the circumstances of their social group offered a real or apparent challenge to the existing order.

The Republic was clearly experiencing a permanent state of conflict: It was neocolonial, postrevolutionary, nationalist, liberal, bourgeois, democratic, an exploiter of labor, and a supporter of profound social inequalities. Important principles and necessary practices stood in opposition to one another, as did institutions and ideologies. Therefore, nationalism, racism, democracy, and sovereignty were at work simultaneously. Each of these aspects has its specific history within the period, as well as a specific history of relationships, contradictions, and conflicts among them.

During its first five years, the Republic experienced a difficult adjustment in terms of the race question, between the new relationships and institutions born from the revolution and the civic practices of 1898 to 1902, on one hand, and the profound racism established in the nineteenth century as one of the elements that constituted Cuban culture, on the other. Together with the modes of production and modernity, this racism had at first been ironclad and shared; later, it was an aspect of conservatism in the late colonial period. The great revolution struck a hard blow to the foundations of racism in the last five years of the nineteenth century. But there was always a contradiction in a significant portion of the interpersonal relationships. From 1902 to 1907, the race issue was part of a reassuring return to order in a country that was being reconstructed, with a republican political environment that was plagued with inconsistencies, a liberal economic environment, and a conservative social environment.

NEW FORMS OF PROTEST AND ACTIVISM

Racial protest took on new content and new forms. It reclaimed the fruits of the revolution in terms of rights, work, respect, land, strict equality before the law, and changes that would open to nonwhite Cubans areas that were previously forbidden to them. During this period, activists worked through the print media, political parties, and antiracist civic associations and certain allied organizations. The fact that the protesters were veterans lent the movement prestige, and they sought to be a force for pressure and negotiation. The movement allied itself or took part in other protests or broader claims from the poor, salaried workers, artisans, or neighbors. It was natural for the racial protest to classify itself as Cuban, to brandish patriotism, and to feel democratic. It could not be repressed or openly rejected, and it was a school for its participants, but it did not achieve great success. Meanwhile, the Republican police persecuted and repressed so-called black witches, and some educated Cubans supported scientific racism.

The attempt to reelect President Tomás Estrada Palma (1832–1908) met with widespread rejection and led to a brief civil war in August 1906 and a second U.S. intervention from September 1906 through January 1909. Many blacks and mulattoes (many of them veterans) participated in the August events. This disturbance brought popularity to the Partido Liberal (Liberal Party), which had contended with the Partido Moderado (Moderate Party) of Estrada Palma. The Partido Moderado would soon become the Partido Conservador (Conservative Party) under the bipartisan system of the first Republic. Liberal leaders tried to take advantage of their status as the supposed representatives of the old Mambi forces, nationalism, and everyday people. Many black and mulatto activists saw the Partido Liberal as an organization that favored their desires and interests. They soon learned that, despite notable differences, both parties respected the status quo of discrimination and racial prejudice.

During the constitutional debates of 1900 to 1901, the military governor of Cuba, Leonard Wood (1860–1927), in a report to his superiors, called Juan Gualberto Gómez—the prestigious civil rights leader, meritorious revolutionary, and close companion of Martí—a "lazy Negro." In 1906, the first governor, William H. Taft (1857–1930)—who later became president of the United States—used Juan Gualberto Gómez as interlocutor in his conversations with the opponents of Estrada Palma. In his autobiography, Juan Gualberto Gómez recounts that one day Taft told him, "And you don't know that my main job in Cuba is to talk to you?" (Gómez p. 169). Throughout the second intervention, Governor Charles E. Magoon (1861–1920) was aided by a small consulting commission of Cubans and Americans, and he named Juan Gualberto Gómez, the only nonwhite in the group, as its secretary. But U.S. military intelligence officials, who at the time were investigating suspicious blacks and mulattoes in Cuba, most of them veterans, used three terms interchangeably in their reports: black, poor, and liberal. As occurs when one works on the ground, they found themselves looking at truly novel problems.

BIBLIOGRAPHY

Barcia Zequeira, María del Carmen. *Capas populares en Cuba (1880–1930)*. Havana: Editorial Ciencias Sociales, 2005.

Batrell Oviedo, Ricardo. *Para la historia: Apuntes autobiográficos*. Havana: Seoane y Álvarez, 1912.

Carbonell, Walterio. *Crítica, cómo surgió la cultura nacional*. Havana: Editorial Yaka, 1961.

De Armas, Ramón. *La Revolución pospuesta: Destino de la revolución martiana de 1895*. Havana: Centro de Estudios Martianos, 2002.

De la Fuente, Alejandro. *A Nation for All: Race, Inequality, and Politics in Twentieth-Century Cuba*. Chapel Hill: University of North Carolina Press, 2001.

Fernández Robaina, Tomás. *El negro en Cuba, 1902–1958*. Havana: Editorial Ciencias Sociales, 1990.

Ferrer, Ada. *Insurgent Cuba: Race, Nation, and Revolution, 1868–1898*. Chapel Hill: University of North Carolina Press, 1999.

Gómez, Juan Gualberto. *Por Cuba libre*. Havana: Office of the City Historian, 1954.

Helg, Aline. *Our Rightful Share: The Afro-Cuban Struggle for Equality, 1886–1912*. Chapel Hill: University of North Carolina Press, 1995.

Herrera, José Isabel (Mangoché). *Impresiones de la Guerra de Independencia*. Havana: Editorial de Ciencias Sociales, 1948.

Historia y memoria: Sociedad, cultura, y vida cotidiana en Cuba, 1878–1917. Havana: Centro de Investigación y Desarrollo de la Cultura Cubana Juan Marinello; Ann Arbor: University of Michigan, 2003.

Ibarra Cuesta, Jorge. *Patria, etnia, y nación*. Havana: Editorial Ciencias Sociales, 2007.

Iglesias Utset, Marial. *Las metáforas del cambio en la vida cotidiana: Cuba, 1898–1902*. Havana: Ediciones Unión, 2003.

Maceo, Antonio. *Ideología política: Cartas y otros documentos*. Havana: Editorial de Ciencias Sociales, 1998.

Martí, José. *Obras completas*. Havana: Editorial Nacional de Cuba, 1963–1965.

Martínez Heredia, Fernando. *Andando en la Historia*. Havana: Ruth Casa Editorial, Instituto Cubano de Investigación Cultural Juan Marinello, 2009.

Martínez Heredia, Fernando, Rebecca J. Scott, and Orlando García Martínez. *Espacios, silencios, y los sentidos de la libertad: Cuba entre 1878 y 1912*. Havana: Ediciones Unión, 2001.

Pérez, Louis A., Jr. *Cuba between Empires, 1878–1902*. Pittsburgh, PA: University of Pittsburgh Press, 1983.

Pérez Guzmán, Francisco. *Radiografía del Ejército Libertador, 1895–1898*. Havana: Editorial Ciencias Sociales, 2005.

Portuondo Zúñiga, Olga, and Michael Max P. Zeuske Ludwig, eds. *Ciudadanos en la nación*. Santiago de Cuba: Oficina del Conservador de la Ciudad; Alemania, Germany: Fritz Thyssen Stiftung, 2002.

Scott, Rebecca J. *Degrees of Freedom: Louisiana and Cuba after Slavery*. Cambridge, MA: Belknap Press of Harvard University Press, 2005.

RACE: AFRO-CUBANÍA IN THE REPUBLIC, 1907 TO 1959

Melina Pappademos

Afro-Cubans' contributions to the Cuban republic and their struggle for social and economic equality.

In 1893, on the eve of Cuba's third and final anticolonial war against Spain (1895–1898), the nationalist poet and philosopher José Martí (1853–1895) forecasted an end to historic racial tensions in Cuba. In his essay "Mi raza" (My Race), he predicted the disappearance of race as a primary marker of social worth after independence. Despite enduring a centuries-old colonial system of entrenched social inequities, Martí exalted the will of the Cuban people to prevail over inequality after national independence and to build a meritocracy of deeply held cultural and moral commitments:

> In Cuba, there will never be a racial war. The Republic cannot go backwards. Ever since the day of redemption for Negroes in Cuba, ever since the declaration of independence in Guáimaro on April 10, civil rights, granted by the Spanish Government for political expedience, were already practiced prior to Cuba's independence and cannot now be denied. . . . Merit, the manifest and continuous evidence of culture, and inexorable trade will eventually unite all men. In Cuba, there is much greatness, in both Negroes and whites.

Martí's words were a call to dismantle the social and economic strictures that placed blacks and whites on an uneven playing field. The gradual disappearance of widely held beliefs about blackness and whiteness, he argued, would allow the birth of a harmonious national community. Martí's philosophy (which was at least partially inspired by the decisive participation of Afro-Cuban foot soldiers and officers in the anticolonial insurgency) placed Afro-Cubans at the forefront of an egalitarian national identity. Yet Martí also appreciated the unique, double burden that Afro-Cubans shouldered in Cuba's transition from colony to independent republic: the legacy of their subordination as Cuban colonials under Spanish rule and their racial marginalization in a climate that privileged Europeanness at the expense of the African descended. Presciently, he cautioned that without a fundamental reconsideration of the meanings of blackness and whiteness, the nation's (and in particular, Afro-Cubans') prospects for more stable and equitable social relations would remain burdened by the albatross of a racialist colonial past. Although Martí's writings have since inspired generations of Cubans of all colors to imagine an inclusive Cuban nation, in 1893 these ideals were an unreliable predictor of what would happen after Cubans achieved independence in 1898. Throughout Cuba's republican period (1902–1959), though Afro-Cubans struggled to improve their socioeconomic position and participated in all aspects of Cuban historical development, they continued to face formidable barriers to their rightful share of the nation's resources.

THE POLITICAL SPHERE

Freedom from Spanish colonialism in 1898 afforded all Afro-Cuban men new political status as full citizens of the Republic and, in 1901, equipped them with the right to vote. (Cuban women were granted suffrage in 1934.) Yet Afro-Cubans continued to be deeply frustrated by economic barriers and ongoing racial exclusions. Their disillusionment with the egalitarian ideal of Cuban racelessness that Martí and others had eloquently espoused rested largely on the fact that their participation in electoral democracy did not bring an equitable distribution of social and economic opportunities. There was a narrow window of opportunity for Afro-Cubans after colonialism, and a small number of them emerged as civic leaders and public officials. This first generation of Afro-Cuban leaders hailed from the ranks of veterans of the Liberation Army. Men such as the generals Juan Gualberto Gómez (1854–1933), Silverio Sánchez Figueras (1852–1915), and Genoroso Campos Marquetti (1874–1966), as well as Rafael Serra (1858–1909), represented a corps of Afro-Cuban civic activists who parlayed their fame as leaders in the wars of independence into civil service posts and government office after colonialism ended. After securing local, regional, and national administrative posts, they worked with Afro-Cuban newspapers, clubs, civic associations, unions, and multiracial public schools to enhance their political power and influence.

Notwithstanding their aspirations to advance despite racial marginalization, Afro-Cuban leaders supported the structures of republican governance, and this bias led them to eschew overt racial consciousness

■ *See also*

Cuban Thought and Cultural Identity: The Various Ways of (Not) Being Cuban

Music: Afro-Cuban Religious Influence on Cuban Popular Music

Racial Uprising and Massacre: 1912

and to support elitist bourgeois liberal values. Rather than espousing racial nationalism, cross-class Afro-Cuban unity, or Afro-Cuban political mobilization, in their public appearances and in newspapers this small sector of highly visible Afro-Cuban leaders professed a belief in progressivism, liberal democracy, and bourgeois respectability. They endorsed reform rather than fundamental change of socioeconomic structures or cultural norms, arguing that this was the most sensible way to advance the race. Further, they insisted that Afro-Cubans' self-identification with their African past and with allegedly savage Africanist cultural practices harmed Afro-Cubans' interests. Most Afro-Cuban civic and political leaders agreed that Afro-Cubans needed to adopt modern, so-called civilized values such as self-abnegation, refinement, civility, respectability, order, industry, and thrift. As the Afro-Cuban politician Rafael Serra counseled in 1904, by pursuing formal education, professional training, and legal marriage, Afro-Cubans in independent Cuba could advance socially and economically and leave behind outmoded, Africanist "savage practices" (El negro Falucho). Even as Afro-Cuban leaders demonstrated their own fitness for public service and political responsibility, they lectured that the island's Afro-Cuban population overall needed to work to improve their level of civilization. Some Afro-Cuban leaders, such as Lino D'Ou (1871–1939), called for an end to racial discrimination in public spaces. D'Ou was an important political figure who in his lifetime was a *mambí* (an anticolonial rebel army soldier) general, a member of the House of Representatives, a Freemason, a journalist, and an Abakuá (an African-derived, male secret society). He proposed that discrimination be outlawed in public areas and the workplace.

This group of relatively successful Afro-Cuban leaders was only a tiny fraction of the island's total Afro-Cuban population; data enumerated in 1907, 1919, 1931, and 1943 and published in the 1943 census states that in this period Afro-Cubans constituted between 25.6 and 29.7 percent of the island's total population (Junta Nacional del Censo p. 741). Afro-Cubans made up a large voting block in a highly competitive political arena, and Afro-Cuban support was important for all politicians, irrespective of color, to win political office. Although Afro-Cubans supported many different parties and subscribed to a variety of political ideologies, few Afro-Cuban candidates ran on dominant political parties' tickets and even fewer held leadership positions within the parties. More often than not they failed to win political office in proportion to the total Afro-Cuban electorate: In 1905, only four out of sixty-three representatives to the House were Afro-Cuban; in 1908 the number increased to fourteen blacks or mulattoes elected to Congress— about 15 percent of the total number elected that term (de la Fuente p. 64). This low level of representation limited their access to political favors and appointments, including access to lucrative public-sector jobs.

MILITANCY AND GOVERNMENT REPRESSION

The vast majority of Afro-Cubans suffered from lack of employment opportunities. They were generally blocked from professional and private schools, and they lacked adequate medical care and housing. As the Afro-Cuban labor activist Evaristo Estenoz (1872–1912) wrote in 1908, "Barely established, the Republic has turned our [black] concerns to anger, and done so to a greater extent and under worse conditions than in the most offensive moments of colonialism" (Linares p. 24). Data published in the 1907 census demonstrates that whites were more literate, possessed more professional and academic titles, and secured more lucrative employment than Afro-Cubans. Whites were also much less likely to be incarcerated (see Office of the Census of the United States 1907, pp. 135, 206, 233). Although Afro-Cubans flourished in the manual trades (e.g., as masons, shoemakers, and tailors), they were vastly underrepresented as professionals (e.g., as lawyers, physicians, civil engineers, and teachers) (de la Fuente p. 116).

Given their bleak prospects, some Afro-Cubans were moved to militancy. By 1908, Estenoz, the Liberation Army Colonel Pedro Ivonet (1860–1912), and other activists founded the Partido Independiente de Color (PIC, Independent Party of Color). Despite the PIC's struggle to increase Afro-Cubans' access to public-sector employment and administrative offices, the party was largely unsuccessful in elections. In 1910 the government's opposition to the party as a dangerous example of autonomous Afro-Cuban mobilization resulted in the arrest of Estenoz and public attacks on the legitimacy of the organization. On 14 February 1910 the Senate passed the Morúa Amendment as a state-sponsored deterrent to Afro-Cuban political mobilization. Authored by an Afro-Cuban senator, Martín Morúa Delgado (1856–1910), the Morúa Amendment outlawed political parties and independent groups made up "exclusively of people of one race or color" (see Helg 1995, p. 165).

Notwithstanding the government's efforts to suppress racial mobilization, in 1912 Afro-Cuban frustration boiled over and members of the PIC rose up in protest against their marginalization. From May to August 1912, primarily in Oriente Province, several hundred *independentistas* occupied foreign property and engaged in military skirmishes with the Cuban army to protest both the Morúa Law and their exclusion from the rewards of Cuban political life. The so-called Race War of 1912 began on 20 May 1912, the official ten-year anniversary of the Republic's founding, and ended almost three months later, after PIC leaders and thousands of Afro-Cuban civilians had been killed by Cuban and U.S. armed forces and white civilian brigades. Whites set ablaze the thatched-roof shacks of Afro-Cuban citizens and hanged, decapitated, castrated, stabbed, and shot them in mass numbers. In one horrific account of the massacre, a white volunteer in Santiago de Cuba sported a bloody bag of ears lopped off of the heads of his slaughtered victims (Helg 1995, pp. 207–224).

CUBANIDAD AND THE POLITICS OF RACE

Government repression of Afro-Cuban activism in the first decade of the republic assumed global dimensions. Cuban intellectuals, such as the University of Havana law professor Francisco Carrera y Justiz (1857–1947), asserted a new political identity rooted in an imagined Cuban modernity that they defined in opposition to both the archaic practices of Spanish colonialism and the controlling and civilizing impulses of U.S. domination (see Zavala pp. 1–5). They hoped that in a global hierarchy the new Cuban nation would be distinguished for its noteworthy achievements of civilization. For example, Carrera argued that all modern polities adopted good government, which made them superior to inert, antimodern societies that rejected civilization. As he theorized, "Races that do not struggle—such as, for example, the Indian and the Black—exist in Asia, Africa, and America as an immutable stagnation, fighting *against* civilization" (Carrera y Justiz pp. 9–10; italics added).

Carrera asserted a modern *cubanidad* (Cubanness) that drew on white supremacist ideals as he faced both U.S. domination of his native Cuba and the island's rapidly shifting social demography. After 1900 the influx of black Antillean laborers who came to work in Cuba's rapidly expanding sugar industry—a by-product of North American economic investments in the fledgling republic—raised Cuban legislators' concerns over the island's increasing *black* (those who self identified or who were identified as being of African descent) presence. White immigration, they believed, would safeguard white domination. In 1902, during the first U.S. occupation of the island (1898–1902), the military government passed legislation to restrict the immigration of nonwhites, and in 1906 the Law of Immigration and Colonization was passed to encourage the settlement of families and day laborers from Spain (the Canary Islands) and other European nations (Sweden, Norway, Denmark, and Italy) (see Helg 1990, p. 54).

The early twentieth century was a period of intensive movement of people and ideas in the Americas. The mass immigration of Jamaican and other British West Indian workers to Cuba from about 1898 to 1929 brought Garveyism to Cuba. The Jamaican Marcus Garvey (1887–1940) founded the Universal Negro Improvement Association (UNIA) in his home country in 1914, and soon after he traveled to New York City to internationalize the organization. The UNIA quickly established chapters throughout the world, including in Cuba, where members were mostly anglophone Antillean immigrants and, to a lesser degree, native-born blacks.

Concentrated in the island's eastern region among first- and second-generation British West Indians who lived there, the UNIA was a significant presence in Cuba. When Garvey visited the island in 1921, he was officially received by Cuban statesmen as well as leaders of the prominent Afro-Cuban elite society Club Atenas (Giovannetti p. 13).

Antillean immigrant workers in Cuba were subject to antiblack violence, and their presence (and its perceived threat to Cuban employment) fanned racist antagonisms toward the social and economic progress of native-born Afro-Cubans. The third decade of the Cuban republic saw intense repression of Cubans of African descent, particularly those who practiced African-derived dance, music, and religions. Antiblack sentiments and violence accompanied republican political upheaval, such as the 1933 founding of the Ku Klux Klan Kubano (Cuban Ku Klux Klan), an act contemporaneous with the Cuban revolution of that same year. Historians have documented several incidences of violence against Afro-Cubans during the 1930s, as a political response to their perceived support of Gerardo Machado (1871–1939), who was ousted by the 1933 revolution, including deaths by hanging and shooting (see Guridy p. 55). As part of the fear of Afro-Cuban cultural and religious practices *comparsas* (a choreographed, carnival music and dance procession) were banned from carnival celebrations from 1913 to 1937.

This period also saw the rise of Cuban anthropology and eugenics and the scholarly disembodiment of Afro-Cubans, as demonstrated by the early career of the attorney, politician, anthropologist, and criminologist Fernando Ortiz y Fernández (1881–1969). Ortiz devoted the early years of his career to researching Afro-Cuban sociopsychopathology, and in 1906 he published *Hampa-afrocubana: los negros brujos* (Afrocuban Underworld: Black Witchdoctors). Although Ortiz later advanced profoundly influential theories about the nature of Cuban national identity (in 1937 he founded the Society for Afro-Cuban Studies), in this early work he argued that Cuban exceptionalism rested on its African legacy and that Cubans of African descent were inherently criminal, a view he later rejected. Other once-respected but now discredited scientists of the era such as Israel Castellanos took measurements of the lips, nose, hair texture, speech, and cranium of African-descended Cubans in an effort to prove their social and intellectual inferiority. The scientific movement to categorize, rank, and socially engineer populations was by no means limited to Cuba. The era's scientists in Latin America, the Caribbean, and elsewhere espoused eugenicist theories and gathered human data to support these theories, and their findings were recognized and widely respected by their colleagues (see Stepan).

In contrast, Rómulo Lachatañere (1909–1952) was the most prominent Afro-Cuban intellectual to

Marcus Garvey (1887–1940), c. 1920. Jamaican nationalist leader Marcus Garvey was the founder of the Universal Negro Improvement Association (UNIA), which had a large following in Cuba during the 1920s. MPI/ GETTY IMAGES

study African-derived religions, and his *O Mío Yemayá* (1938) and *Manual de Santería* (1942) were pioneering studies. His article "Some Aspects of the Black Problem in Cuba" (1942), originally published in English, supports scholars who publicly confronted the problem of antiblack racism in Cuba. It also criticizes those who labeled these scholars racists because of their willingness to openly address racial inequality. The article discusses the delicate and often silenced issue of color hierarchies among the African descended in Cuba, based on their differing phenotypes, namely their facial features and lighter or darker skin tones.

ECONOMIC CRISIS

As republican Cubans joined the family of nations, they were keenly aware that they bore the burden of proving to an international community their ability to act as moderns. This requirement was exacerbated by U.S. dominance in Cuban political and economic affairs; indeed, the U.S.-sponsored Platt Amendment to the Cuban Constitution (1902) gave the United States carte blanche to "stabilize" the island in the event of domestic turmoil and unrest. Further, one contemporary scholar argues that on the eve of the Great Depression in 1929 the United States had more than $1 billion invested in Cuban sugar, public utilities, railways, mines, tobacco, hotels, factories, government debt, and real estate (Jenks).

Cuban–North American trade relations and Cuba's economic dependence on the production and exportation of sugar helped to undermine the island's economy during the republican period, especially during the boom/bust cycles of the 1920s, 1930s, and 1950s. In fact, Cubans were so dependent on North American trade that by the time the 1929 economic crisis put millions of North Americans out of work and onto the streets, Cubans had already suffered the effects of instability and severe economic downturn. By the end of the 1920s many Cubans were underemployed or were unpaid for months at a time; among the worst affected were agricultural workers, who disproportionately were Afro-Cubans and immigrant Antilleans. Even without an economic crisis, production in the sugar industry always slowed to a trickle during the *tiempo muerto* (dead time), which could last six or more months every year. During the off season workers had to eke out a living at other poorly remunerated jobs.

The extended economic crisis of the 1920s helped to fuel open rebellion in the 1930s. By August 1933 the island was paralyzed by a general strike. Cuban workers in communication, transportation, utilities, agriculture, and the media declared a work stoppage that was quickly followed by a revolt of the Cuban military's officers and rank and file soldiers. Unable to control the masses of workers and the military, President Gerardo Machado y Morales (1925–1933) conceded defeat and fled Cuba for the Bahamas on 12 August 1933. The work stoppage and the Sergeants' Revolt steered the island in a new political direction and helped to break Cuba's political subjugation to the United States, most notably when the hated neo-colonialist Platt Amendment was abrogated in 1934 by then-president Ramón Grau San Martín. Social issues took on new dimensions as artists, intellectuals, women, labor, and youth groups entered the political arena and agitated for economic opportunities and national advancement and explored the nature and implications of *cubanidad* (Cubanness) for the island's disparate social sectors.

CULTURAL PRODUCTION

One example of revived nationalist concerns, new social pronouncements, and the changing face of Cuban identity came on the eve of the 1933 Revolution when the Afro-Cuban journalist Gustavo Urrutia (1881–1958) convinced Havana's most conservative daily newspaper, *El Diario de la Marina*, to run a weekly column devoted to the so-called black question. In the column titled "Ideals of a Race," Urrutia aired Afro-Cuban concerns and informed *El Diario*'s predominately white readership about issues that were pertinent to Afro-Cubans. The column was short-lived, running from 1928 to 1931, but it resurfaced under Urrutia's editorship a few years later as "Harmonies." The new title reflected the period's volatility and rising racial tensions. Urrutia hoped that an open discussion of race would support national advancement, which he and others believed depended on racial unity and tranquil relations among the island's socioeconomic sectors. Urrutia also produced four radio broadcasts in December 1935 aimed at an audience of Afro-Cubans. The *cuatro charlas radiofónicas* (four radio chats)—which were aired in the midst of a global *black vogue* movement that saw the rise of the songstress Rita Montaner (1900–1958), the *danses sauvages* of Josephine Baker (1906–1975), and *negritud* philosophies and cultural production—espoused racial pride, black authenticity, racial purity, and elements of anticolonialism (see Urrutia de Quiroz pp. 1–20).

In the late 1920s and early 1930s *Afrocubanismo* (Afrocubanism) emerged as one of the most influential (if not widely accepted) Cuban cultural forms of the twentieth century. As distinct from the primarily racial, economic nationalism espoused by the Afro-Cuban activist Juan René Betancourt (1918–1976)—embodied by his Organización Nacional de Rehabilitación Económica (ONRE, National Organization for Economic Rehabilitation)—Afrocubanism aimed at discovering cultural forms and expressions that were uniquely Cuban and celebrated the island's African legacy by constructing an artistic genre that emphasized syncopation and alliterative sounds. Adherents and interpreters of Afrocubanism also cast African influences in Cuba as exotic, hypersexual, unrefined, bestial, and differentiated from European influences in Cuban culture. Finally, the Afrocubanist movement embraced nationalist ideals, suggesting in particular that African influences served the Cuban nation by vivifying Cuban cultural production (see Arredondo).

This art/aesthetic movement popularized cultural forms such as rhumba dance and *afrocubanista* poetry. The white *Afrocubanista* poet Ramiro Guirao (1908–1949) published many Afrocubanist works in his *Órbita de la poesía afrocubana* (Orbit of Afro-Cuban Poetry, 1938). The mulatto *afrocubanista* poet Nicolás Guillén's *Sóngoro Cosongo* (1931) and his later work made him one of the most celebrated artists and public intellectuals of the twentieth century. Guillén (1902–1989) worked variously as a journalist, typographer, political activist, and writer; the son of a politician, he also had a brief stint as a politician in the 1940s. Guillén wrote incisively about issues of race (with essays on Lino D'Ou and Rómulo Lachatañeré) but above all was an integrationist who predicted that due to their solidarity, Cubans eventually would exhibit full national unity, which he described as a "Cuban

color"; he was avid in defining Cuba as a mestizo or mulatto nation and culture. A colleague and friend of the American poet Langston Hughes, Guillén was sympathetic toward the Cuban Revolution and for these views was appointed president of the Unión de Escritores y Artistas de Cuba (Union of Writers and Artists of Cuba) in 1961.

THE LABOR MOVEMENT

As Afrocubanism has been framed as the most significant aspect of Afro-Cuban activism in twentieth-century Cuba, far less attention has been given to black leaders in the Cuban labor movement, despite the depth of their political influences. The labor movement gained momentum during the economic crisis of the 1920s and early 1930s, when tens of thousands of workers experienced underemployment, layoffs, and loss of benefits. During this time many of the island's most vocal labor organizations were founded, including the Federación Nacional de Torcedores (National Federation of Cigar Workers), the Confederación Nacional Obrera de Cuba (CNOC, National Confederation of Cuban Workers), the Sindicato Nacional de Obreros de la Industria Azucarera (SNOIA, National Sugar Workers' Union), and the Unión de Obreros y Empleados de Plantas Eléctricas (Electrical Plant Workers' and Employees' Union). The Cuban Communist Party was also active in the 1930s and 1940s in the fight against racial discrimination. Afro-Cubans took leadership roles in organized labor and mobilized the predominantly Afro-Cuban workforces of large-scale industries such as the sugar, tobacco, and port industries. The best-known labor leaders were Lázaro Peña (1911–1974) in tobacco, Aracelio Iglesias Díaz (1901–1948) in shipping docks, and Jesus Menéndez (1911–1948) in sugar. Peña, Iglesias, and Menéndez were among the founders of the Confederación de Trabajadores de Cuba (CTC, Confederation of Cuban Workers) in 1939. Menéndez also founded the provincial federation of the CTC in Las Villas Province. Peña was a delegate to the Central Latinoamericano de Trabajadores (CLAT, Confederation of Latin American Workers) in 1938 and later served as secretary general of the CTC in the early 1960s. These Afro-Cuban labor leaders' militancy came at a high personal cost. Menéndez was murdered in January 1948, allegedly for publicly criticizing President Ramón Grau San Martín (1944–1948) and for convincing sugar workers to conduct a work stoppage during the 1948 *zafra* (sugar harvest). In October of that same year Iglesias, then the leader of the Federación Obrera Marítima Local del Puerto de La Habana (Federation of Maritime Workers of Havana Port), was also shot to death for his labor activities (see Riera Hernández pp. 203–208).

THE CUBAN REVOLUTION

Labor mobilization was one of many intense political currents in Cuba during the 1940s and 1950s. Economic crises, U.S. domination of Cuban politics

JUAN RENÉ BETANCOURT: THE FIGHT AGAINST RACISM

From the time he was a young man, Juan René Betancourt (1918–1976) focused on the social and cultural problems faced by Cubans of African descent. In 1940, as secretary of culture for the Federation of Black Societies of Camagüey, he incorporated economic advancement into the struggle against discrimination. He founded the Business Cooperative Movement, with the goal of opening businesses where Afro-Cubans would be able to work and acquire goods, while establishing themselves as members of the greater society.

In 1954 Betancourt delivered a tribute to Juan Gualberto Gómez, a fighter for Cuban independence and for racial equality, on the centenary of Gómez's birth. In 1955, he published his *Doctrina Negra* (Black Doctrine) in which he evaluates the historical, social, cultural, and religious legacy of Africans and their descendants. In this work he sets out, in the form of questions and answers, his racial ideology, which was based on the concept that blacks should think of themselves first as black people as much as Cubans, since thinking of themselves as just Cuban had achieved nothing for them as a community, though it may have done so for some individuals. According to Betancourt, there were many black leaders, but only two leaders of blacks: José Antonio Aponte (killed in 1812 in a slave revolt) and Evaristo Estenoz (a founder of a black political party, murdered in 1912). Betancourt founded the National Economic Rehabilitation Organization for the Negro in 1954. Its goal was financial investment in

businesses, building construction, and other projects so that blacks could be provided with jobs. Once Batista fell from power (1959), Betancourt took over the head office of the Cuban Federation of Black Associations. He called on the revolutionary government to state exactly what its antiracist policy would be. He published *El negro: Ciudadano del futuro* (The Black Man: Citizen of the Future) in 1959, with a preface by the historian Elías Entralgo. In addition to new material, the book included articles that Betancourt had published in the magazine *Bohemia* and the newspaper *Revolución*. Because his way of fighting racism differed from the government's and because of his openly anti-Communist position, the government forced him out of Cuba in 1960. After that, he lived in New York City with his wife and their two U.S.-born children. There he went on to devote himself more to the fight against Cuba's dominant ideology, which is why his most significant antiracist writings are still unknown to large sectors of Cuban society.

WORKS BY JUAN RENÉ BETANCOURT

Doctrina Negra. Havana: P. Fernández, 1955.

"La integración nacional." In *Cuadernos de la Universidad del Aire* (Havana) (November 1956).

"Fidel Castro y la integración nacional." *Bohemia* 51, no. 7 (15 February 1959): 122–123.

El negro: Ciudadano del futuro. Havana: Cárdenas, 1959.

and economy, and increasing repression by President Fulgencio Batista (1940–1944, 1952–1958) radicalized Cubans. Yet, Batista himself was mixed-race, and some credit him with integrating the armed forces of the country, particularly its officer corps. During his second presidency many Afro-Cuban societies and organizations received government support and there were a few black and mestizo high-ranking officials in his administration, which led to the erroneous notion that the anti-Batista struggle was largely a white affair. Perhaps the most significant movement to emerge at this time was the nationalist, anti-Batista 26th of July movement, led by Fidel Castro (b. 1926). Known as *los barbudos* (the bearded ones), these revolutionaries were primarily young, middle-class, and educated; a significant number of the 26th of July combatants and members of the underground were Cubans of African descent. They launched their first armed attack against Batista's army in 1953 and nearly six years later succeeded in ousting Batista from power. He fled the island on 31 December 1958, and on 1 January 1959 the Cuban Revolution triumphed.

Following explicit early pronouncements by the revolutionary government on radical structural change

and issues of social equality, the revolutionary press paid special attention to the plight of Afro-Cubans. On 19 January the newspaper *Revolución* published "¡Negros No … Ciudadanos!" (Not Blacks, Citizens!), referring to the new, preferred political identity of the African descended. The piece featured several photos depicting blacks in everyday situations and their comments on a variety of topics ranging from workplace conditions, wages, and unemployment, to housing and the inhumanity of Havana's infamous *solares* (slum) housing. Several of the elderly Afro-Cuban women featured lamented the difficulty of their roles as primary caregivers for their grandchildren (Hernández Artigas). Interestingly, issues of race and racial discrimination were not mentioned, as if to underscore the point that these subjects were citizens with problems of concern to all Cubans, irrespective of race. Also clear in the article is the idea that a common history shared by Cubans of all colors is integral to the new government's claimed humanist foundation, which built on the edict of a raceless Cuban nation advanced by José Martí almost seven decades earlier. This notion of a shared Cuban identity was further developed by intellectuals such as the eminent Afro-Cuban historian Walterio Carbonell (1920–2008).

In his *Cómo surgió la cultura nacional* (On the Origin of National Culture, 1961), Carbonell examined Spanish and Africanist components in national culture and highlighted African diasporans' unique political and economic contributions to Cuban historical development.

On 7 February 2003, when Fidel Castro spoke at Havana's Karl Marx Theater at the annual Conference on Pedagogy, one point he emphasized was that the Revolution had not yet solved the issue of "socioeconomic differences in the Cuban population"; the race question, specifically discrimination, was still a problem. The Cuban head of state suggested that eliminating Cuba's historic racial segregation had not adequately addressed racial discrimination; despite the revolutionary state's racial integration of schools, work centers, beaches, and recreational public spaces as one way to advance structural equality, the Revolution had not completely eliminated persistent racist ideologies in Cuba. A clearer picture of the racial politics of the republican period helps to explain why discrimination remained a factor in Cuban society after 1959—contemporary race relations in Cuba were visible in the archive of its racial past.

BIBLIOGRAPHY

Arredondo, Alberto. *El negro en Cuba*. Havana: Editorial Alfa, 1939.

Carbonell, Walterio. *Crítica: cómo surgió la cultura nacional*. Havana: Editorial Yaka, 1961.

Carrera y Justiz, Francisco. *El Municipio y la cuestión de razas*. Havana: La Moderna Poesía, 1904.

de la Fuente, Alejandro. *A Nation for All: Race, Inequality, and Politics in Twentieth-Century Cuba*. Chapel Hill: University of North Carolina Press, 2001.

El negro Falucho. "Ser o no ser." *El Nuevo Criollo* (19 November 1904). Reprinted in Helg, *Our Rightful Share: The Afro-Cuban Struggle for Equality, 1886–1912*. Chapel Hill: University of North Carolina Press, 1995.

Giovannetti, Jorge. "The Elusive Organization of 'Identity': Race, Religion, and Empire among Caribbean Migrants in Cuba." *Small Axe* 10, no. 1 (March 2006): 1–27.

Guridy, Frank. "'War on the Negro': Race and the Revolution of 1933." *Cuban Studies* 40 (2009): 49–73.

Helg, Aline. "Race in Argentina and Cuba, 1880–1930." In *The Idea of Race in Latin America, 1870–1940*, edited by Richard Graham. Austin: University of Texas Press, 1990.

Helg, Aline. *Our Rightful Share: The Afro-Cuban Struggle for Equality, 1886–1912*. Chapel Hill: University of North Carolina Press, 1995.

Hernández Artigas, José. "¡Negros No ... Ciudadanos!" *Revolución* (19 January 1959).

Jenks, Leland. *Our Cuban Colony*. New York: Vanguard Press, 1928.

Junta Nacional del Censo. *Informe general del censo de 1943*. Havana: P. Fernández y Cía, 1945.

Lachatañeré, Rómulo. *Oh, mio Yemaya!!: Cuentos y cantos negros*. Havana: Editorial de Ciencias Sociales, 1992.

Lachatañeré, Rómulo. *Manual de Santería*. 2nd ed. Havana: Editorial de Ciencias Sociales, 2007.

Linares, Serafín Portuondo. *Los independientes de color. Historia del partido independiente de color*. Havana: Editorial Librería Selecta, 1950.

Martí, José. "Mi raza." *Patria* (16 April 1893).

Office of the Census of the United States. *Census of the Republic of Cuba, 1907*. Washington, DC: Author, 1907.

Riera Hernández, Mario. *Historial obrero cubano, 1574–1965*. Miami: Rema Press, 1965.

Stepan, Nancy Leys. *"The Hour of Eugenics": Race, Gender, and Nation in Latin America*. Ithaca, NY: Cornell University Press, 1990.

Urrutia de Quiroz, Gustavo E. *Cuatro charlas radiofónicas*. Havana: n.p., 1935.

Zavala, Iris. *Colonialism and Culture: Hispanic Modernisms and the Social Imaginary*. Bloomington: Indiana University Press, 1992.

RACE: RACE RELATIONS AFTER THE REVOLUTION

Esteban Morales Domínguez

Attempts to deal with racism in Cuba after 1959.

Racism thrived in Cuba before 1959, due to the legacy of Spain's pro-slavery colonial regime. Racism persisted under the U.S. intervention on the island during the first years of the twentieth century, and by both the republican and dictatorial governments that ruled the country. The Revolution that triumphed in 1959, therefore, inherited this problem, one of the most complex in Cuban society. Despite the broad social policies that were implemented in the more than fifty years that followed, blacks and mestizos remained at a disadvantage with respect to whites in many aspects, and manifestations of racism persisted among a portion of the Cuban population. This remained true despite the fact that racial equality was declared a right, as indicated in Articles 41, 42, and 43 of Chapter VI of the Constitution of the Republic, in effect since 1976 (Constitution of the Republic of Cuba pp. 20–21).

ONE OF THE MOST COMPLEX PROBLEMS

Until 1959, Cuban society—with a significant proportion of black and mestizo residents—was made up of an economically powerful minority, a minuscule middle class, and a large mass of poor workers and peasants. Blacks and mestizos occupied the lowest positions in society: They had the least access to wealth and the lowest quality of life. Blacks in particular made up the mass of the poorest and most neglected, and they endured the heaviest discrimination due

■ *See also*

Cuban Thought and Cultural Identity: Socialist Thought

Economy: Special Period

Faith: Afro-Cuban Religions and Revolution

Governance and Contestation: The Cuban Revolution

to the color of their skin (one peculiarity of Cuban racism is that it operates on a color scale). Cubans do not practice just one type of racism, however, since this phenomenon has specific regional characteristics. In the eastern part of the country, specifically in Santiago de Cuba where there is a significant black population, the perception of racial identity is different than in Havana or in Holguín, where the black population is smaller; a light-skinned person of mixed race would be considered white in Santiago but not in Havana. This situation creates relatively different circumstances, perspectives, paths, and spaces for social mobility.

Until the middle of the 1980s, the racial issue was almost always approached with fear of provoking social divisions; its analysis has been avoided, making it impossible to resolve the problem of racism and thereby strengthen cultural and national identity. For these and other historic reasons, in the early 2000s, there remained people in Cuba who chose not to listen or speak about the issue. Historically, the subsumption of race under the umbrella of national unity formed a negative dynamic, which delayed the necessary grappling with racism and related racial issues.

In January 1959, Fidel Castro was already addressing the problem of racism, categorizing it as a blight to be rooted out of Cuban society. His speeches demanded justice, above all else, for blacks and mestizos in the workplace, but also socially and culturally. Some found his ideas worrisome, while others responded with joy. For blacks and mestizos, Castro represented the hope that racial inequities would be addressed. But for those whites who foresaw the Revolution's process of radicalization, Castro's position was one reason to escape the country. These divergent responses demonstrated the sharp social sensitivities around the problem.

However, beginning with Castro's declarations, substantial political changes began to occur for the poor in Cuba, and within that class, for blacks and mestizos. These political changes brought about a profound shift in Cuban culture and consciousness.

This struggle to change inherited attitudes and culture was apparent in the Revolution's early support for a cultural campaign directed at the recovery and preservation of African values within Cuban culture. These efforts included the founding of the Ballet Folklórico Nacional (National Folkloric Ballet) of the Instituto de Etnología (Institute of Ethnology) within the Academia de Ciencias (Academy of Sciences) and the rediscovery of the work of Fernando Ortiz (1881–1969) and the carnival festivals, with the strong presence of the traditional *comparsas* (carnival societies), among other initiatives (Hoz).

The Revolution created all manner of opportunities never before seen by this sector of society: jobs, free education and health care, equal pay, a broad social security system, and improved living conditions.

For the first time, blacks appeared in all labor sectors on a massive scale and had access to universities and other centers of study. Some took on civil service jobs, and in general they participated broadly and with distinction in the social, economic, and cultural life of the country.

Despite the development of a highly humanistic social policy, however, there were problems that limited blacks and mestizos from capitalizing on the opportunities opened to them by the Revolution. Poverty had been experienced by whites, but wealth had never been open to blacks, and the historical starting points for whites, blacks, and mestizos were very different. This disparity in wealth put blacks and mestizos at a disadvantage in making use of the opportunities offered by the new social policies. Skin color, therefore, continued to operate as a strong factor in social differentiation, which aggravated the situation of blacks and mestizos—regardless of the continued existence or not of racism. These differences were not considered by those formulating social policy.

In 1962 the Second Declaration of Havana affirmed, rather idealistically, that the problem of racism had been resolved. The social environment that began to prevail and the egalitarian social policies that offered opportunities generally, also produced a considerable improvement in the quality of life for blacks and mestizos. In the midst of this situation, organizations for blacks and mestizos—which had provided an important space for coming together and achieving representation and which had roots dating back to the social struggles of blacks in the nineteenth century—began to disappear. Such organizations began to be considered unnecessary, since the new state and the administration of the revolutionary government had taken charge of the cause they had represented. Over the years, debate has raged over the wisdom of the historic decision by blacks and mestizos to accept the dissolution of those organizations and place their struggle to achieve their proper place in Cuban society in the hands of the government.

For a long period, many Cubans stopped seeing race as a problem that would hold back the social development of blacks and mestizos, as it had done before. The creation of social, political, and mass organizations whose by-laws did not limit membership based on skin color contributed to this attitude and climate.

A NEW CULTURE REQUIRING PROMOTION

In a speech closing the First Congress of the Communist Party of Cuba in 1975, Fidel Castro proclaimed Cuba to be an Afro–Latin American country. This, along with the country's cooperative medical missions to Africa, its participation in the Angolan War of Liberation, and particularly its fight against apartheid in South Africa and for the liberation of Nelson Mandela, had a strong impact on self-esteem within the country, among blacks in particular. At the same time, the general population felt itself to be part of a historic chapter in the struggle for equality and social justice in the world.

The opening of schools for African children on Isla de la Juventud (Isle of Youth), together with campaigns related to social equality, also contributed to an atmosphere in which the race issue was seen as a matter that was being solved. Cubans, regardless of their color or social origin, joined together in revolutionary tasks; began attending day care, schools, universities, and military training together, sharing in all the struggles, dangers, and successes of those years.

The cultural change within the country was important, despite the persistence of stereotypes, discrimination, and racism. This change was clearly expressed in the increase in interracial marriages and racial mixing in other areas of social and cultural life. This environment made it difficult for the Cuban media to present the race problem with objectivity and clarity.

All these developments led to a new culture of togetherness and solidarity, lending credibility of the official discourse that in Cuba racial problems did not exist. But this is not to say that the message was accepted by everyone. A tiny segment of the black intelligentsia warned that the race problem had not disappeared, that it lived on within white hegemony, and that the concept of culture that was being defined still did not correspond to what Cuba's blacks and mestizos needed to achieve, a view that was shared by many citizens, in particular blacks and mestizos.

Nevertheless, Cuba's attainments in economic, political, and social life through the middle of the 1980s established a clear and hopeful picture of a country nearing an optimum level of solutions on all planes of life domestically, with racism in particular disappearing. In addition, the prevailing environment, especially the political environment, was not conducive to a discussion of these issues within Cuban society.

Around the middle of the 1970s, a process of economic recovery began, particularly in the 1975–1985 period, in which average annual economic growth exceeded 4 percent (Morales Domínguez 1996). This trend indicated that the Cuban economy and the society in general had entered a period in which it had overcome its historical difficulties in meeting the needs for the bulk of the population. When the socialist countries, particularly the Soviet Union, became Cuba's primary trading partners, these advantageous economic relations contributed to Cuba's economic growth and were decisive in the favorable outcomes for the Cuban economy during those years.

Through these relationships, many Cubans—in particular blacks and mestizos—acquired scientific training and social experience by undertaking studies abroad. A broad and beneficial scholarship program

contributed greatly to the emergence of a black and mestizo intelligentsia in Cuba. These groups had never had the opportunity to receive training at such a rate under the preferential rules that the Republic had imposed prior to 1959, when wealthy white families were the only ones able to send their children abroad to study, particularly in the United States. A paradox of the embargo, one that was especially positive for Cuban blacks and mestizos, was that it attempted to contain Cubans inside the borders of the island; this situation stimulated the widespread acquisition of international, and particularly scientific, experience, to which most Cubans had never before had access. The population's quality of life rose noticeably, including that of a significant number of blacks and mestizos.

In 1986, Raúl Castro, second secretary of the Cuban Communist Party, declared the need to include more women, young people, and blacks within the party. As a result, a type of quota was established for entry into the organization. Many of the party's grassroots organizations (without properly analyzing the proposal and distorting its purposes) allowed young people, blacks, and mestizos—male and female—to join in order to comply with what was considered to be a mandate from the authorities. This mandate was soon forgotten, however, and it became apparent that this approach was not the best way to achieve representation of blacks and mestizos in the party or in any other organization or segment of national life.

DIFFICULTIES AFTER THE MID-1980s

Beginning in the second half of the 1980s, the disintegration of the socialist bloc countries began. In addition, the U.S. embargo against Cuba intensified when the United States passed new laws, known as the Torricelli Act (1992) and the Helms-Burton Act (1996), which penalized ships landing at Cuban ports and foreign companies doing business with Cuba. These factors, together with weaknesses in the Cuban economy, inaugurated a dramatic period in Cuban society, which found itself in a profound economic crisis.

That crisis entailed serious socioeconomic hardship, and blacks and mestizos suffered the most. The historical starting point of nonwhites, and the force with which the culture of poverty reproduced its survival mechanisms, acted against blacks and mestizos and revealed that these groups had not been able to forge a stable lifestyle or take advantage of the numerous opportunities for advancement put in place by the Revolution. Based on this dynamic, blacks and mestizos continued to be the least favored in the labor market, especially in terms of the quality of job opportunities and income.

In addition, the economic measures adopted in response to the crisis, including Cuba's acceptance of foreign investment and representatives from foreign companies, as well as the development of foreign tourism, did not benefit blacks and mestizos to the same extent as Cubans of other racial origins. They remained at a disadvantage in terms of access to the best jobs, since generally the new economy did not incorporate them on equal footing. Many, affected by their critical family situations, abandoned their university studies. The crisis of 1989 to 1994, and the profound social effects that came with it, led many Cubans to the conviction that it had been unrealistic to think they had seen a solution to the issue of the differing standards of living among the three racial groups (whites, mestizos, and blacks), as well as racial prejudice, discrimination, and racism. Clinton Adlum observed:

> Blacks and mestizos were and continue to be those who receive the fewest remittances from abroad, since they make up only 15% of Cuban emigrants to the United States, which is the country from which most remittances are sent to Cuba. This figure sets out an important difference in relation to the political agendas with which the present is judged in the process of debating the future course for Cuba.
>
> *p. 15*

In addition, blacks and mestizos tended to emigrate later, at a time when the United States was no longer a country of great opportunity, and did not have the support of family living in the United States. Most emigrated in the 1980s, carrying the stigma of the Mariel Boatlift on their backs, forming part of a group of Cubans considered to be less educated and to have less desirable lifestyles, social behavior, and manners unacceptable for U.S. society. These emigrants were thus at a disadvantage in helping their family members back in Cuba.

The economic crisis brought the race issue to the fore, with all the drama of a problem held to have been solved, but which had not truly been. It became clear that racism had not disappeared as had been assumed, nor was it disappearing at the pace that many imagined; rather, it had merely been hidden, waiting for the right moment to reappear. Cuba, without trying, had become a case study, clearly showing that to defeat racism it was not enough to defeat the foundations of capitalism or to unfurl an egalitarian social policy. Racism was a multifaceted problem that could only disappear when the culture that gave birth to it disappeared. As long as this did not happen, the danger always existed that racism would reemerge, as was occurring in the early 2000s in Cuba.

Many Cubans saw they had been idealistic and naïve in declaring the racial problem resolved. Fidel Castro himself, in a September 2000 speech in New York City, referred to the problem when he stated, "we have taken a long time to discover … that marginality, and with it racial discrimination, is something that, in fact, is not overcome with one law, or with ten laws, and even after forty years we have not been able to stamp it out" (quoted in Morales Domínguez 2011, p. 6).

Fidel Castro continued to refer to the problem, bringing to bear his concept of objective discrimination. Raúl Castro discussed racism in his speech closing the Eighth Congress of the Unión de Jóvenes Comunistas (Union of Communist Youth) in 2010. In the speech, he expressed the concern among Cuba's political leaders that the struggle against racism in Cuba had not ended, but in fact had started anew.

In a 1995 study carried out in Havana and Santiago de Cuba by the Centro de Antropología (Anthropology Center) of CITMA (Ministerio de Ciencia, Tecnología, y Medio Ambiente), 75 percent of respondents agreed that racial prejudice continued to be common on the island. In three Havana neighborhoods, the survey results indicated that 58 percent of whites considered blacks to be less intelligent, 69 percent affirmed that blacks did not have the same values and level of decency as whites, and 68 percent were opposed to interracial marriage (Alvarado 1996).

From that point forward, a battle began to overcome a new era of racism. The problem was not new, and the battle did not promise to be brief. A system of stereotypes, discrimination, and racism were built upon a foundation of as yet unresolved inequalities, the involuntary or voluntary ignorance of a large segment of the Cuban people, and the cynical attitudes still held by many people—all in the context of the contradictions of a socioeconomic model that had not yet achieved its goals. In sum, it is a complex system in which the problem exists as a burden inherited from the past, but also worsens in response to societal problems and tensions. This turns racism into a challenge that threatens to reestablish itself in the collective conscience of Cuban society.

RACE IN THE EARLY 2000s

As of 2011, official figures were not available, but in trying to assess Cuba's racial composition, both among party cadres and organizations, and especially in the Asamblea Nacional del Poder Popular (National Assembly of the People's Power), confirmed the substantial participation of blacks and mestizos. This situation differed greatly from the one reported in the 1981 census.

Racism in Cuba, like elsewhere, has a strong subjective component and is steeped in ignorance; many people become aware of the problem only when confronted directly with the issue. In many cases, they realize that they are themselves racist or have expressed racist attitudes without having been conscious of it before. People perceive or sense racism differently depending upon their age, class background or family upbringing. For example, young Cubans experience it largely in terms of the importance their parents place on it. Cubans born at the beginning of the Revolution find it difficult to tolerate interracial couples, whereas such couples are considered normal among generations born in the 1970s and afterward.

Racial hatred, open animosity toward those of a different color, and resistance to sharing common spaces with persons of another race are not normally observed in Cuba. In fact, Cubans possess a certain anti-discriminatory ethic, and those who feel prejudice often hide it, because they are aware that having such sentiments is socially unacceptable. Since racism is often hidden, it becomes important to discuss the issue openly and through every available medium in order to properly address it (Catasus Cervera and San Marful Orbis p. 236, tables 43 and 47).

In accordance with the dynamic whereby unresolved social problems find their own political expression, Cuban civil society has begun to generate alternative institutional arenas to deal with outside the formal political system. An example is the group Color Cubano, which emerged under the sponsorship of the Unión de Escritores y Artistas de Cuba (UNEAC; Union of Writers and Artists of Cuba) and generated momentum in addressing the race issue. This organization led to a broader treatment of the issue with the creation of the Comisión de Lucha contra el Racismo y la Discriminación Racial (Commission for Struggle against Racism and Racial Discrimination) within UNEAC, supported the effort through culture. Another organization, the Comisión Nacional para los Estudios Raciales en Cuba (the National Commission for Racial Studies in Cuba), established within the National Library, focused on the study and assessment of the issue.

Between the mid-1980s and the first decade of the 2000s, a growing cultural production has reflected the problems of racism in Cuba, including documentaries, articles, books, theatrical and audiovisual works, rap music, paintings, monuments, commemorations, and more. This array of work suggests that the issue was being addressed culturally as never before—not only in terms of the recovery of Afro-Cuban traditions (work that had begun long before) but also in a frank treatment of the racial issue and its contemporary challenges. Scientific research was also conducted. There was, in addition, an immense and valuable body of historiography, as well as the production of other books closely tied to the racial issue from a historical perspective. Far fewer, however, are the works that offered a contemporary treatment of the race issue, its challenges, and possible solutions in Cuban society today.

In addition, a profusion of groups, community projects, and nongovernmental institutions have addressed the issue of racism, for example, the Cofradía de la Negritud (Brotherhood of Blackness), the Comité Ciudadano por la Integración Racial (Citizens Committee for Racial Integration), Observatorio Critico (Critical Observatory), and others with ties to nongovernmental organizations, such as UNEAC's Comisión de Lucha contra el Racismo y la Discriminación Racial. These groups seek alternative approaches in the fight against racism and racial discrimination.

In Cuba, racism has an underlying economic component since black people are associated with poverty. The state, in its various forms, therefore made numerous efforts to confront racism by addressing poverty issues. These efforts include the Liberty Project (personally directed by Fidel Castro), which sought to open branch libraries in poor neighborhoods (although due to the economic difficulties of the Special Period, only around thirty of these were established). The same can be said for supplemental nutrition programs for underweight children, which were launched in 1997 on the basis of the Cuban Communist Party's study of the impact of the "special period," and which still operate. State-supported efforts included the opening of the Talleres de Transformación Integral del Barrio (Workshops for Comprehensive Neighborhood Transformation) in marginal locations, a program in place since 1990, and the creation of neighborhood cafeterias that served subsidized meals, primarily to low-income senior citizens. Because of Cuba's history, all measures to combat poverty also aim at the advancement of the black population, or endeavor to prevent this population from sinking further.

POSITIONS FOR CONFRONTING RACISM

Not everyone who is concerned with racism in Cuba takes the same position regarding the issue and its causes and solutions. Two fundamental positions can be identified. One position considers racial problems in Cuba to be the responsibility of the Cuban government. Advocates of this line of thought argue that racism results from the lack of a human rights policy, democracy, and civil liberties for blacks. They maintain that revolutionary leaders, particularly Fidel Castro, have not paid attention to the racial problem with a view to solving it. On the race issue, advocates of this position are considered to be dissident, and upon reading their documents, one observes a tendency to minimize the accomplishments of the Revolution with regard to Cuban blacks and mestizos. This group assumes that the solution of the racial problem depends on a change in the Cuban political regime. (see Madrazo Luna, CIR Feeds 2010 and 2011).

The other position—which does not imply a total overhaul or abandonment of socialism—begins with the recognition of the advances achieved by the Revolution. Adherents of this view note the Revolution's mistakes in addressing racism: the lack of a broader debate about race, the absence of the issue in programs taught in educational institutions, and the failure to consider skin color as a variable of social differentiation in Cuba. This is compounded by the lack of a statistical system that would better reflect social and economic problems among blacks and that would permit more objective research on the subject. Despite the previous flaws, those who hold this position believe that Cuban blacks have made a great deal of progress and that if the Revolution had not taken place, blacks would have had to carry their own revolution to achieve the position they have today. For those who adhere to this position, the solution lies in deepening socialism and developing a discussion in which problems of race form part of the process of improving Cuban society. They do not look to changing the Cuban political regime as a solution; such a change would not benefit blacks, as they do not see such a drastic change as being motivated by an anti-racist objective.

The new battle against racism in Cuba involves a struggle between these two positions and the efforts of each group to change Cuban society. Both groups deploy their actions within a framework of political tolerance on the part of the Cuban government. As a result, the confrontation is not violent in nature, but peaceful. It is, rather, a mutual observation and interpretation by the opposing sides.

The principal challenges faced by both groups are: eliminating the ignorance that still prevails regarding the topic of race in Cuba; achieving greater inclusion of black leaders and important persons in history books and to strengthen the study of Africa, Asia, and the Middle East; and promoting the study of human history as a process simultaneously involving the diverse groups that make up the species (otherwise, Africa would be a story not of development but solely of crisis). Race consciousness—still lacking in Cuban society—must be strengthened in order to encourage self-esteem among blacks, to put the subject of race in its rightful place within Cuban education at all levels, and to achieve an increase in the level of institutional attention to this issue.

Two books, Pedro Serviat's *El problema negro en Cuba y su solución definitiva* (The Black Problem in Cuba and Its Definitive Solution, 1986) and Carlos Moore's *Castro, the Blacks, and Africa* (1988), define the two opposing positions without offering a solution to the issues facing Cuba in the early 2000s. The first fails because there is no such thing as a definitive solution to the black problem in Cuba, and the second because it tends to advocate positions that do not overcome the trap of racism; specifically Moore's position is that of black nationalism, which in Cuba is often viewed as separatist and racist.

Unfortunately, advocates of the first position may distance themselves from a direct and genuine struggle against racism in Cuba in order to bring about a political confrontation. Such a confrontation would lead them to adopt an attitude of separation from the struggle and from offering their efforts to attain a society within which blacks and mestizos truly achieve the position that they deserve, one that no nonwhite group enjoys in any society of the Americas.

BIBLIOGRAPHY

Adlum, Clinton. *Anuario CEAP*. Havana: University of Havana, 1997–1998.

Agüero, Sixto Gastón. *Racismo y mestizaje en Cuba*. Havana: Editorial Lid, 1959.

Alvarado, Juan Antonio. "Relaciones raciales en Cuba: notas de investigacion." *Temas* 7 (July–September 1996): 37–43.

Alvarado, Juan Antonio. "Estereotipos y prejuiciso raciales en tres barrios habaneros." *Revista América negra* 15 (December 1998): 89–118.

Castro, Raúl. "Discurso de clausura del VIII Congreso de la UJC." *Granma* (2010): 2.

Castro Ruz, Fidel. *Noticias de hoy*, 6 January 1959; *Revolución*, 31 January, 23 January, 18 March, 6 February 1959; *FNTA*, 9 February 1959; *Noticias de hoy*, 24 March 1959; *Revolución*, 23 March 1959; "Diario de la Marina," 29 March 1959; *Revolución*, 26 March 1959.

Castro Ruz, Fidel. *Las ideas son el arma esencial en la lucha por la humanidad*. Havana: Oficina de Publicaciones del Consejo de Estado, 2003. 27–30.

Catasus Cervera, Sonia, and Eduardo San Marful Orbis. "La población por color de la piel." In *Informe ONE*, chap. 15, 235–239. Havana: Oficina Nacional de Estadísticas, 2006.

Constitution of the Republic of Cuba. Havana: Editora Política, 2003.

Duharte Jiménez, Rafael, and Elsa Santos García. "Cuba y el fantasma de la esclavitud." *Revista América negra* 15 (December 1998): 199–216.

Espina Prieto, Mayra. *Políticas de atención a la pobreza la desigualdad: Examinando el estado de la experiencia cubana*. Buenos Aires: Consejo Latinoamericano de Ciencias Sociales, 2008.

Fernández Robaina, Tomás. *Cuba: Personalidades en el debate racial*. Havana: Editorial Ciencias Sociales, 2007.

Fuente, Alejandro de la. "Raza, desigualdad y prejuicio en Cuba." *Revista América negra* 15 (December 1998): 21–42.

Fuente, Alejandro de la. *Una nación para Todos: Raza, desigualdad, y política en Cuba, 1900–2000*. Madrid: Editorial Colibrí, 2000.

Girardi, Giulio. *El ahora de Cuba: Tras el viaje de Juan Pablo II*. Madrid: Editorial Nueva Utopía, 1998.

González, Ana Margarita, and Rafael Hojas Martínez. Interview with Esteban Morales Domínguez. *Trabajadores* (14 December 2009): 7.

Guanche, Jesús. "Etnicidad y racialidad en la Cuba Actual." *Revista América negra* 15 (December 1998): 43–66.

Hormilla, Helen H., and Dixie Edith. "Sombras que no siempre se ven." *Revista Bohemia* 102, no. 12 (4 June 2010): 29–36.

Hoz, Pedro de la. *África en la Revolución cubana: Nuestra búsqueda de la más plena justicia*. Havana: International Conference on Culture and Development, 2005.

Madrazo Luna, Juan Antonio. "Por una Revolución Ética." CIR Feed, 10 December 2010.

Madrazo Luna, Juan Antonio. "Mujer ante el espejo." In *Negra Cubana tenía que ser*, CIR Feed, 15 February 2011.

Montejo Arrechea, Carmen V. *Sociedades negras en Cuba, 1878–1960*. Havana: Centro de Investigación y

Desarrollo de la Cultura Cubana Juan Marinello, Editorial Ciencias Sociales, 2004.

Moore, Carlos. *Castro, the Blacks, and Africa*. Los Angeles: Center for Afro-American Studies, University of California, 1988.

Morales Domínguez, Esteban. *Economía y política del conflicto Cuba–Estados Unidos en los umbrales del siglo XXI*. Havana: Economía y Desarrollo, 1995.

Morales Domínguez, Esteban. "Economía y política del conflicto Cuba–Estados Unidos." *Revista economía y desarrollo* 3–4 (1996): 50–67.

Morales Domínguez, Esteban. "Un modelo para el análisis de la problemática racial cubana contemporánea." *Revista catauro* 6 (July–December 2002): 52–93.

Morales Domínguez, Esteban. *Cuba: Algunos desafíos del color*. Havana: Editorial Ciencias Sociales, 2006. 65–100.

Morales Domínguez, Esteban. *Cuba: Color de la piel, nación, identidad, y cultura: ¿Un desafío contemporáneo?* Havana: Editorial Ciencias Sociales, 2007. 163–189.

Morales Domínguez, Esteban. *Desafíos de la problemática racial en Cuba*. Havana: Editorial Fernando Ortiz, 2007.

Morales Domínguez, Esteban. *La problemática racial en Cuba: Algunos de sus desafíos*. Havana: Editorial José Martí, 2011.

Morales Domínguez, Esteban, Carlos Batista, and Kanako Yamaoka. *The United States and the Reinsertion to International Economy of Cuba: Triangular Analysis*. Joint Research Program Series, no. 126. Tokyo: Institute of Developing Economies, 1999.

Pérez, Esther, and Marcel Lueiro, eds. *Raza y racismo*. Havana: Editorial Caminos, 2009.

Pérez-Sarduy, Pedro. "¿Que tienen los negros en Cuba?" *Revista América negra* 15 (December 1998): 217–232.

Sawyer, Mark Q. *Racial Politics in Post-Revolutionary Cuba*. New York: Cambridge University Press, 2006.

Torres-Cuevas, Eduardo. *En busca de la cubanidad*. 2 vols. Havana: Editorial de Ciencias Sociales, 2006.

Zabala, María del Carmen, ed. *Pobreza, exclusión social, y discriminación racial en América Latina y el Caribe*. Buenos Aires: Consejo Latinoamericano de Ciencias Sociales, Editores Siglo del Hombre, 2008.

RACE: THE CHINESE IN CUBA

Mauro G. García Triana

The importance of the Chinese component in the Cuban nation.

Race matters in Cuba typically refer to the experiences of people of African descent, whereas the Chinese presence is rarely acknowledged. People from Europe, Africa, and to a lesser extent Asia participated in the creation of the Cuban nation. Between 1847 and 1874 about 150,000 Chinese were brought to Cuba when abolition of slavery on the island was in sight and the need to increase the supply of cheap labor became apparent. This traffic came to an end when a Chinese imperial commission's investigation discovered acts of abuse and resolved to discontinue the practice. Later, between 1900 and 1959, about 32,000 Chinese migrated to Cuba. As of February 2011, it was estimated that there were fewer than one hundred native-born Chinese in Cuba. There was perhaps between 2,500 and 3,000 first-, second-, and third-generation Chinese or mixed-race descendants; more remote descendants, with more limited Chinese ancestry, were estimated to number between 50,000 and 70,000 Cubans (Yion Lee; Eng Herrera).

The Chinese contributed greatly to securing Cuba's independence. Between 2,000 and 7,000 Chinese participated in the Ten Years' War (1868–1878), and they enriched the Cuban Liberation Army's spirit of rebellion and combat morale (Pérez de la Riva 2000, pp. 166–167). From 1860 to 1880 Asian laborers accounted for 15 percent of Cuba's total labor force, and they were crucial for economic development as a whole and for the growth of the sugar industry and the railroads in particular (Pérez de la Riva 1996, p. 281). Chinese immigrants influenced the island's eating habits, creating vegetable gardens throughout the island. Between 1865 and 1870, free Chinese immigrants began to arrive from the United States. These so-called California Chinese contributed capital and invigorated the Chinese community's economy, and they promoted Chinese culture by opening theaters in the provinces of Havana, Matanzas, and Las Villas. The Chinese theaters introduced to Cuba tonal forms that inspired composers such as Miguel Faílde (1852–1921), the creator of the *danzón* (a Cuban music genre); José Urfé (1879–1957); Ernesto Lecuona (1895–1963); and Osvaldo Farré (1902–1985). They contributed the Chinese trumpet, an instrument which in the twenty-first century is considered authentically Cuban, to the characteristic Carnival conga of Santiago de Cuba. Two exemplary Chinese-Cuban artists are the surrealist-cubist painter Wifredo Lam (1902–1982) and the poet Regino Pedroso (1896–1983).

Although the immigrants maintained strong ties with their native land, the vast majority of Chinese immigrants (over 90%) were male and overwhelmingly from the province of Guangdong (*Revista Económica* 1878, p. 97; Pérez de la Riva 1996, p. 23). The phenomenon of racial discrimination inherent to multiethnic, classist societies such as Cuba presented complex challenges to the young Chinese community. Due to family and demographic circumstances, most free Chinese partnered with black, mulatto, or white women. The resulting mixed-race population was not considered legitimately Chinese and could not join clan or regional associations. Ancestral loss of culture in the mixed-race population accelerated the assimilation of mixed-race individuals into Cuban society (Rodríguez Ruiz 2000, pp. 103–105).

■ *See also*

La Jungla and the Artistic Development of Wifredo Lam

Sugar: Colonial Period

Chinatown in Havana. About 150,000 Chinese laborers were brought to Cuba in the mid-nineteenth century. Thousands more migrated to Cuba between 1900 and 1959, resulting in the establishment of Chinese businesses, schools, newspapers, and associations in Havana and other cities.
HÉCTOR DELGADO AND ROLANDO PUJOL

Nevertheless, Chinese businesses, institutions, bilingual schools, newspapers, and associations flourished. For example, the Chung Wah Casino, established in 1893, carried out charity works and cultural and educational activities. The Chinese population in Cuba had a dual civic participation in political affairs, both in Cuba and in China; the Chee Kung Tong Republican Party (known as the *tríadas*, or triads), for instance, favored the overthrow of the Manchu and the Qing dynasties (though despite its name, it was not a political party). Other groups supported the Nationalist Party led by Sun Yat Sen (1866–1925) and later by Chiang Kai-Shek, or, like the Alianza Protectora de Obreros y Campesinos (Protective Alliance of Workers and Peasants), sympathized with the left or the Communists. All of the associations worked together during the second Sino-Japanese War (1937–1945) toward the common goal of ending the Japanese occupation of China. The victory of the Chinese Revolution revived immigration to Cuba (3,000 people between 1950 and 1959) and polarized the Cuban Chinese community between Chiang Kai-Shek's pro-nationalists (Taiwan, Hong Kong) and Mao Zedong's pro-Communists (China) (García

Triana p. 17). However, the Alianza closed in 1955 due to lack of funding.

Until 1959, the mass of Chinese-Cuban descendants experienced an environment of dual belonging (and sometimes, rejection): Regarding those born to a Chinese father and a Cuban mother, the Cuban society gradually assimilated them yet rejected them because of their skin color and the Cuban wealthy elite simultaneously excluded and drew them. Consequently, as time passed, fewer individuals knew Chinese, understood Chinese music and opera, or maintained Chinese religious life (most of them were either Catholic or Protestant). Although the Chinese are part of Cuban society, they have not been spared social exclusion and discrimination. Examples include the events following Andrés Chiu Lión's death in 1926, the 1934 Fifty Percent Law (which targeted not only Chinese but Spaniards, Jamaicans, and Haitians), and discrimination that followed the Sino-Soviet split in 1965.

Historically, the Chinese have identified themselves as white in Cuba's social structure even though their birth records classify them as mixed-race, which is ambiguous and dissociated from blackness. Racial mixing over time has contributed to Cuban Chinese affirmation of Cuban identity, even when they maintain family ties in China or when they belong to ethnic-based cultural and social associations.

An anthropological study of seventy-two persons in Havana's Chinatown in 2000 showed that 20.8 percent were native-born Chinese, 50.7 percent were first-generation descendants, and 28.5 percent were second-generation descendants. Eighty percent were men and 20 percent were women. Descendants had very little knowledge of the Chinese language; only 19.4 percent claimed any knowledge of it. Overall, 57.1 percent participated in associations and 42.8 percent did not. Of the respondents, 46.4 percent reported no religious affiliation, 32.1 percent reported Christian beliefs, 17 percent reported Afro-Cuban beliefs, and 3.5 percent reported other beliefs, including ancestor worship (Rodríguez Ruiz pp. 103–126).

The 1959 Cuban Revolution and the economic measures that followed seriously harmed the Chinese community, which not only was affected by class divisions but also suffered from a lack of full integration into the Cuban nation for complex reasons explored above. The division between the Cuban and Chinese governments that resulted from the Sino-Soviet rupture in 1965 led to a wave of prejudice and discrimination against Chinese-born Cubans and their descendants that lasted until the 1980s. Although the Revolutionary Offensive of 1968 did not specifically target the Chinese, this liquidation of most of the private businesses that had survived previous nationalizations hit the Chinese community hard. Thousands of Chinese-born residents and Chinese-Cubans left Cuba (mostly for Miami and New York) after 1959, and between 1960 and 2010 there were no new waves of Chinese immigration to Cuba.

During the second half of the 1980s, the Cuban authorities supported the revival of Chinese associations, which enrolled descendants and carried out programs that promoted the Chinese community's pride in its ethnic origins and ancestry, along with Chinese culture, arts, and traditions. In 1993 the Grupo Promotor del Barrio Chino (Chinatown Development Group) was established and educational institutions, including the Escuela de Lengua y Artes China (School of Chinese Language and Arts), were founded. Chinese associations and families were given restaurant licenses, and new Chinese stores opened, offering typical Chinese products that had been available previously in stores throughout Cuba. These trends coincided with a period of notable advance in governmental relations between Cuba and China, which became stronger than ever. Immigrants from the cradle of one of the world's greatest civilizations, it appears, continued to revitalize the Chinese side of Cuba.

BIBLIOGRAPHY

Baltar Rodríguez, José. *Los chinos de Cuba*. Havana: Fundación Fernando Ortiz, 1997.

Eng Herrera, Pedro J. (historian on the Chinese community in Cuba), interviewed by Mauro G. García Triana, 9 February 2011.

García Triana, Mauro. "Los Chinos de Cuba y los Nexos entre las dos Naciones." *Boletin Problemas Filosóficos* 2 (July 2003): 17.

García Triana, Mauro, and Pedro Eng Herrera. *The Chinese in Cuba, 1847–Now*. Lanham, MD: Rowman & Littlefield, 2009.

López, Kathleen. "One Brings Another: Formation of Chinese Communities in Cuba." In *The Chinese in the Caribbean*, edited by Andrew Wilson. Princeton, NJ: Markus Wiener, 2004.

López-Calvo, Ignacio. *Imaging the Chinese in Cuban Literature and Culture*. Gainesville: University Press of Florida, 2009.

Pérez de la Riva, Juan. *Demografía de los culíes chinos (1853–1874)*. Havana: Pablo de la Torriente, 1996.

Pérez de la Riva, Juan. *Los culíes chinos en Cuba*. Havana: Ciencias Sociales, 2000.

Revista Ecónomica (Havana, 1878).

Rodríguez Ruiz, Pablo. "Relaciones interétnicas e interraciales en el barrio Chino de La Habana." *Revista Catauro* 2, no. 2 (2000): 103–126.

Yion Lee, Carlos (president, Min Chin Tang Society of Cuba), interviewed by Mauro G. García Triana, 10 February 2011.

RACIAL UPRISING AND MASSACRE: 1912

David Sartorius

A widespread and violent response to a protest in Oriente Province by Cuba's first black political party, which killed thousands of Afro-Cubans.

In May and June 1912 violence was initially unleashed against members of the Partido Independiente de Color (PIC, Independent Party of Color), a black political party in Cuba and the first of its kind in the Americas. After the party had been banned by a 1910 law, members in Oriente Province organized an armed protest against their exclusion from upcoming elections. The idea of armed protest was common in Cuba, at least in the first years of the Republic: A group, party, or movement would take a group of armed followers to an area and issue a declaration to the press, thereby pressing the government to negotiate. But instead of dialogue, the PIC's protest was met by a fierce backlash that involved the army, the rural guard, and the police, as well as white vigilantes and the U.S. military. Provoked by press reports of a race

■ *See also*

Governance and Contestation: The Republic: 1902–1952

Platt Amendment

Race: Free People of Color in Cuba

Race: Racial Issues during the Transition to Independence

CHRONOLOGY OF EVENTS

1902: Association of African-descended veterans organized.

1905: Liberal Party leader Enrique Villuendas assassinated; Liberals boycott election; President Estrada Palma and his Moderate Party win.

1906: Rebellion breaks out; President Estrada Palma requests U.S. intervention and resigns, handing government over to Secretary of War William Howard Taft as "U.S. Governor of Cuba"; President Theodore Roosevelt sends U.S. forces to Cuba; Taft replaced by Charles E. Magoon.

1908: Partido Independiente de Color (PIC) founded; Liberal General José Miguel "El Tiburón" Gómez elected president.

1909: U.S. forces withdraw from Cuba; leaders of the PIC arrested.

1910: The Morúa Law bans political parties based on race or religion.

1912: May: PIC holds demonstrations demanding repeal of the Morúa Law; General Carlos Mendieta uses machine guns against demonstrators in Oriente, killing or wounding 150 people.

1912: June: Public property torched by protestors as violence spreads; with congressional support, President Gómez declares martial law; warships *Washington* and *Rhode Island* arrive at Havana to protect U.S. interests; U.S. Marines move on Oriente; PIC leader Evaristo Estenoz killed by troops.

1912: July: PIC leader Pedro Ivonet killed while "trying to escape."

1913: Conservative General Mario G. Menocal elected president; PIC prisoners released.

1915: Government grants full amnesty for PIC members.

war against white Cubans, the crackdown became indiscriminate, targeting a broader spectrum of Afro-Cubans irrespective of their political affiliations. Estimates of the number of Afro-Cubans killed in 1912 vary from 2,000 to 5,000 (Helg p. 225). The conflict fundamentally altered the terms on which Cubans of color participated in public and political life, and it exposed the limits of the racially inclusive ideals of Cuban nationalism in the early Republican period.

REPUBLICAN HOPES AND FRUSTRATIONS

The promise of national independence had dimmed for Cubans of African descent in the first decade of the twentieth century, particularly for those who had fought in the war against Spain and for those who sought improved economic and political opportunities. The PIC organized in the political context of a fragile new national state that drew on the example of the nineteenth-century struggle for independence to promote a patriotic ideology privileging national unity over racial solidarity. Thus, political organizing around voting blocs—and through clientelistic networks established by veterans—held promise in the early Cuban Republic. An association of African-descended veterans of the War of Independence (1895–1898) organized a committee in 1902 to lobby for increased representation in public employment. However, organizing along racial lines—even with the goal of addressing the inequalities that compromised the idea of "a nation for all"—drew suspicion for amplifying social divisions.

Establishing a black political party further divided Afro-Cuban activists, and the formation in 1908 of the PIC, led by Evaristo Estenoz (1872–1912), came in the wake of defeats for black political candidates in local elections. Blacks in Cuba belonged to different political parties, and even during the independence struggle, Cubans of color were annexationists, autonomists, and pro-independence. The party identified

its base of support in black members of the Liberal Party and veterans, but with another weak showing in the national elections later in 1908, it was open to alliance with the Conservative Party, which recognized the potential for mounting a unified challenge to Liberal power. Indeed, Estenoz, a former labor leader, a captain in the Cuban liberation army, and a Liberal Party supporter, had found himself supported by Conservatives at crucial moments prior to 1912. With party branches in many cities throughout the island and a limited-run newspaper, *Previsión*, the PIC advocated for more public jobs for Afro-Cubans and an end to racial discrimination and inequality. It also favored expanded education, land and labor reform, penitential and judicial reform, and the abolition of the death penalty. It opposed the Platt Amendment, which sanctioned U.S. intervention in Cuba, while simultaneously seeking support from U.S. officials for its political and electoral project. Given this opposition to the Platt Amendment and the racial politics of the United States at the time, it is intriguing that the PIC was formed and registered as a party under the Leonard Wood administration that occupied Cuba from 1906 to 1908.

With the congressional elections of 1910 on the horizon, the black Liberal senator and longtime writer and activist Martín Morúa Delgado (1856–1910) introduced legislation barring groups of any single race or color from constituting a political party. Morúa was motivated in part by Cuban nationalist ideology and in part by worries of an all-white party forming in response to the PIC, and when the bill passed he was rewarded by the Liberal president José Miguel Gómez (1858–1921) with an appointment making him the first Afro-Cuban cabinet member. The Morúa Amendment also stated that parties could not be formed by reason of birthright, wealth, or profession. In effect, the law channeled Cuban politics into the confines of a strictly economic struggle, effectively closing options for cultural or identity politics (Fowler Calzada pp. 89–90).

PIC members were arrested and detained during 1910 until elections had ended. The Liberal Party's attempts to cultivate black support—notably, through visits by the president and vice president to black associations in Cuban cities—did not stop many Afro-Cubans from deserting the party, nor did those gestures subdue individuals who were frustrated by Morúa's legal defeat of the PIC. After 1910, despite internal divisions and occasional, lukewarm signals from the government suggesting negotiation, members of the PIC became even more openly critical of President Gómez and of the shortcomings of the Cuban Republic, and they advocated a more confrontational political position than those supported by black Liberals and civic-minded veterans; most party-affiliated black politicians did not back the PIC.

PROTEST AND RETRIBUTION

The goal of the three-day armed protest organized by the PIC in May 1912 was to force President Gómez to repeal the Morúa law and legalize the party again. Led by Estenoz, the *Previsión* journalist Pedro Ivonet (1860–1912), and local party leaders, several hundred *independientes* gathered in southern Oriente Province and threatened to destroy foreign-owned property. It is understandable that the large U.S.-owned estates were a focus for frustrations, for they had transformed the province's diversified agricultural economy in the years following independence. Many Afro-Cubans had migrated to Oriente after 1898 with hopes of acquiring land and finding prosperity, but along with Afro-Cubans native to the region, many of whom had played formidable roles in the wars for independence, they were constrained by substantial land purchases by U.S. companies. New sugar and fruit plantations, enclave towns, and a railroad network had transformed rural Oriente and its potential for the kind of land tenancy and cultivation sought by the peasantry. Underrepresented in the professions, public jobs, and regional politics, the African-descended population understood the significance of Estenoz and the PIC to the region, and so did the Cuban government: For some, fear of widespread resistance justified extending the violence directed at the protesters to all Afro-Cubans living in the province (though many *independiente* supporters were protected by Liberal politicians and local mayors).

The response by the government and by ordinary citizens was immediate and virulent. White Cubans organized local militias to protect their families and communities across the island and, if necessary, to travel to Oriente to suppress PIC activities. The full-scale backlash that escalated across the island no longer specifically targeted party members; instead, there were attacks on any Afro-Cubans suspected of fomenting what was labeled a race war. In one gruesome episode, General Carlos Mendieta (1873–1960) killed or wounded 150 peaceful Afro-Cubans on 31 May in a simulated battle intended to show journalists the efficiency of the new machine guns. *Independientes* responded on 31 May and 1 June by challenging rural guards in the black-majority town of La Maya, burning several buildings in the process. Chaos developed as *independientes* dispersed to Oriente's extensive mountains and forests. Many white families living in the countryside sought refuge in cities, and rural schools were suspended.

On 5 June Congress approved President Gómez's request to suspend constitutional guarantees of public association in Oriente for forty-five days in order to restore order. General José de Jesús "Chuchito" Monteagudo (1861–1914) organized four thousand soldiers, rural guards, and volunteers in Oriente as military authority assumed control of the police and justice systems and imposed strict limits on civil liberties. Private citizens organized into militias also committed acts of violence against Afro-Cubans—helped in no small part by the government's distribution of nine thousand rifles to mayors throughout Oriente. The murders of Afro-Cubans were conspicuously public: Black men were hanged from trees, dismembered, and shot in broad daylight. Black women suffered similar fates, and some women, even though they could not formally join the PIC, were arrested for their involvement in the protest.

The role of the press in the unfolding of events cannot be understated. Inflammatory reports of black rebellion fomented popular anxieties and government action. In Santa Clara, cautionary news reports even preceded planned PIC activities. The idea of a race war initiated by Cubans of African descent had a long history on the island. In the aftermath of the Haitian Revolution, fears of a similar slave uprising in Cuba posited race war as the worst scenario that could befall the plantation society. The presence of black insurgents in the independence movement prompted regular accusations that anticolonial conflicts were fundamentally racial conflicts. The presence of Haitian (and other West Indian) migrant laborers in Oriente and the French surnames of some PIC leaders fueled spurious associations with Haiti. National and local newspapers drew on racist tropes of black *brujos* (sorcerers) and rapists to denounce the race war, and they exaggerated the real and potential damage and violence done by the protesters. They created perceptions that the multiracial pact of Cuban nationalism had been broken by Afro-Cubans in the PIC and that a violent crackdown was necessary to restore order to the island. With frequent invocations of public opinion challenging the intentions of the 20 May protest, out of fear or conviction many black associations, as well as the national veterans' council, condemned the actions of the PIC before the events turned bloody.

Although the heart of the conflict was in eastern Cuba, PIC members in other Cuban cities and towns were also arrested, even though the absence of multiple protests on 20 May confirmed that there had been no nationwide demonstration planned. A handful of *independientes* in Santa Clara Province roamed the countryside. Those led by Simeón Armenteros cut telephone and telegraph lines near Cienfuegos, but there were no other reports of unrest or property damage outside of Oriente. Sugar and tobacco workers in Havana Province were rounded up on vague suspicions or rumors, and prominent veterans, activists, and journalists were arrested in the city of Havana. White militias joined the multiracial rural guards, policemen, and soldiers in Matanzas and Camagüey to patrol town and countryside to detain suspects. In Pinar del Río arrests proliferated despite the local PIC leaders' condemnation of the armed protest, and an attempted escape by several prisoners there resulted in a confrontation that left six people dead. The activity outside of Oriente may have been limited in part by the low level of PIC support in rural areas, where persistent poverty, rather than the demands of urban veterans, drove political agendas and patron-client networks that sometimes crossed racial lines.

Invoking the Platt Amendment's provision that threats to North American property justified direct intervention, U.S. companies complained that their property was endangered, which prompted the U.S. government to send three warships of marines to Oriente, ostensibly to prevent aggression that had not yet occurred. To the frustration of the Cuban government, around one thousand marines landed and protected railroads and estates for approximately one month. Two ships remained in Havana harbor until 1 July.

U.S. interests in Cuba were not the only parties that asked for help from the United States. Since 1910 PIC leaders had sought the interceding pressure of the United States to repeal the Morúa law. Estenoz himself had threatened damage to U.S. estates in order to draw U.S. attention to *independiente* demands. He had also asked the United States to intervene militarily in the crackdown (to avoid further bloodshed), but the United States was highly reluctant because it had already done so twice (1898–1902 and 1906–1908), and to do so a third time in barely fifteen years would mean admitting that Cuba was incapable of self-governance and that the island would require a permanent U.S. military presence. Instead of pacifying Cubans, the arrival of North American troops provoked resentment from Gómez, heightened popular anxiety about the scale of the conflict, and informed the Cuban government's decision to distribute arms to Protestant missions and foreign properties. In short, the U.S. presence eclipsed possible peaceful resolutions to the conflict and enabled Cubans themselves to concentrate on violent repression, rather than preventive action, in the name of national strength. Other foreign observers decried the indiscriminate violence they witnessed, even as they doubted their power to stop it. As the French consul in Santiago noted,

Monteagudo's terror in the countryside would "hand over all these unfortunate and inoffensive black day laborers, rural workers, coffee pickers, cane cutters, herdsmen, and servants to the pitiless executioners of the military administration's dirty work. I tremble for this black flesh" (Helg p. 222).

It is difficult to identify the center of gravity for the wave of violence that engulfed Cuba in 1912. The justice minister, provincial governors, mayors, and Gómez himself all intervened at some point to urge other authorities to respect the rights of Afro-Cubans unaffiliated with the PIC. Indeed, Gómez may have tacitly supported the initial *independiente* protest as a strategy to pressure Congress to repeal the Morúa law, but as the conflict broadened he could control neither the violence nor its political consequences. For PIC members, such support proved illusory as killings, arrests, and the destruction of homes and farms continued apace; as political debates raged, so too did the bloodshed.

By the end of June most of the PIC leaders had been killed, the government had declared the uprising finished, and negotiations of amnesty for the surviving suspected protesters had stalled. More than 2,000 individuals remained accused of rebellion, and hundreds of individuals were still detained in Santiago de Cuba and Guantánamo. Estenoz had been shot and killed on 27 June near Alto Songo, and Ivonet was shot dead near El Caney on 18 July. Their bodies were publicly displayed in Santiago, sending a powerful message of retribution and warning against similar protests in the future; they were buried in common graves to avoid the possibility of memorial sites that might publicly document the atrocities that had occurred.

AFTERMATH AND SIGNIFICANCE

The events of 1912 and the dissolution of the PIC marked a turning point in Afro-Cuban political organizing in the Cuban Republic. Most of the so-called rebels arrested in May and June 1912 were released fairly quickly because there was insufficient evidence to convict them of wrongdoing. Beginning late in 1912, an amnesty campaign led by Daniel Fajardo Ortiz, a journalist for the Santiago newspaper *El Cubano Libre*, threatened to reanimate accusations of racial antagonism, but ultimately it secured the release of the Guantánamo PIC leader Eugenio Lacoste in September 1913 and other remaining prisoners the following month.

The periodic circulation of rumors of black conspiracy in the following years suggests that the fears that animated the 1912 repression continued to have significant symbolic political value. The war against Afro-Cubans reversed the political fortunes of the Liberal Party, as the 1912 election brought Conservatives to national power for the next twelve years, and Liberals were long held answerable for the massacre. More significantly, black voters remained an important bloc within Cuba's political system. Although most Afro-Cubans continued to support the Liberals, they also participated actively in Conservative, Communist, Ortodoxo, and Auténtico Party politics in subsequent decades, and the parties aspired to consider the racial composition of the slate of candidates they put forward in elections. The relocation of racial politics after 1912 to a public sphere that valued civic virtue was by no means automatic, given the frightening use of the press and public spaces in mobilizing violence. Yet the continued strength of Afro-Cuban social and recreational clubs and politically engaged journalism challenged stereotypes about black inferiority and insurmountable racial divisions. The Morúa law remained in effect and the PIC never reconstituted itself after 1912, but Afro-Cubans neither disappeared from politics nor abandoned struggles to give concrete meaning to the race-transcendent ideals of the Cuban nation.

BIBLIOGRAPHY

Castro Fernández, Silvio. *La masacre de los independientes de color en 1912*. Havana: Editorial de Ciencias Sociales, 2002.

De la Fuente, Alejandro. *A Nation for All: Race, Inequality, and Politics in Twentieth-Century Cuba*. Chapel Hill: University of North Carolina Press, 2001.

Fermoselle, Rafael. *Política y color en Cuba: La guerrita de 1912*. Montevideo: Editorial Geminis, 1974.

Fernández Robaina, Tomás. *El negro en Cuba (1902–1958)*. Havana: Editorial de Ciencias Sociales, 1990.

Fowler Calzada, Victor. "Contra el argumento racista." *Encuentro de la Cultura Cubana* 53–54 (Summer–Fall 2009): 82–98.

Helg, Aline. *Our Rightful Share: The Afro-Cuban Struggle for Equality, 1886–1912*. Chapel Hill: University of North Carolina Press, 1995.

Meriño Fuentes, María de los Ángeles. *Una vuelta necesaria a mayo de 1912*. Havana: Editorial de Ciencias Sociales, 2006.

Pérez, Louis A., Jr. "Politics, Peasants, and People of Color: The 1912 'Race War' in Cuba Reconsidered." *Hispanic American Historical Review* 66 (August 1986): 509–539.

Portuondo Linares, Serafin. *Los independientes de color: Historia del Partido Independiente de Color*. Havana: Publicaciones del Ministerio de Educación, 1950.

RADIO

Cuba was one of the first countries in the Americas to get radio. Over the years, it has produced many popular and memorable radio programs. Radio was a basic vehicle for presenting content—particularly Cuban music—that popularized cultural values. Cuban radio's enormous creativity can be seen in its establishment of the radio drama format, which quickly spread across national borders to the rest of Latin America.

Starting in 1959, the elimination of private ownership of radio stations and commercial messages was the starting point for transformation. All radio stations were united into a single public service system, in which cultural content and social interest prevailed. Today, Cuba's radio signals, including the international Radio Habana Cuba, reach virtually the entire country. In addition, Internet radio broadcasts exist.

Cuban radio of the diaspora—whose history is essentially political—has developed mostly in southern Florida. The most recent effort is Radio Martí, financed by the U.S. government. Since its founding, Radio Martí has been a source of conflict between the two countries. As a whole, radio programs produced by Cuban Americans in southern Florida have served as an important vehicle of cultural unification, preservation of historical memory, and regional Latinization.

RADIO: BEGINNINGS AND DEVELOPMENT

Norma Abad Muñoz

The development of radio in Cuba from the first station in 1922 to the programs of the first decade of the twenty-first century.

Radio broadcasting in Cuba dates back to 1922, when on 9 April the Cuban Telephone Company, a subsidiary of the International Telephone and Telegraph Corporation, announced its plan to build a radio station. On 13 May, Cuban Telephone informed the public that for this purpose, a tower atop the station's main building, 161 feet above street level, had been completed.

THE BEGINNINGS

Yet, the first station on air, on 22 August 1922 with permission granted by the Department of Communications (under the Secretariat of Government), was radio station 2LC, owned by the Cuban musician

■ *See also*

Television: Beginnings and Development

and composer, Luis Casa Romero. With nightly broadcasts, Cuba positioned itself as the first Latin American country to establish radio broadcasting. It was not until 10 October that the Cuban Telephone Company inaugurated its radio station, PWX, which had broadcasting capabilities far superior to 2LC, though it did not broadcast everyday.

The establishment of these stations, especially 2LC, which had only modest equipment, thrilled amateur (ham) radio operators and technicians. Small broadcasters began to proliferate, with stations helping each other without regard to personal profit. In 1922 brochures on wireless telephony with instructions on building radiotelephonic receivers appeared, and in the next year, there were books and correspondence courses on radiotelephony. Agents in Cuba from Victor Talking Machine Company and Columbia Phonograph Records expanded their sales stock with popular music recordings and devices, including radio receivers.

On 12 February 1923, by presidential decree, criteria and regulations for radiotelegraphic and radiotelephonic services were approved. Small station owners strove to increase their broadcasting power. The year ended with a total of thirty-one radio stations established, the majority of which were in Havana (López pp. 526–527). On 2 July 1925, legislation creating the Communications Ministry, which included the Radiotelephony Division, was approved. By 1926, radio broadcasting of commercials had begun.

At the start of the 1930s there were sixty-one radio stations in the country, forty-three of them in Havana (López pp. 529–530). Among them were CMBC, founded on 15 December 1929 with the call letters 2 AF (which later became the popular Radio Progreso), and CMCB, previously 2 OH, inaugurated on 18 July 1928 (which became CMQ on 12 March 1933).

COMMERCIAL RADIO

The period of experimentation and fascination with the launch of radio broadcasting ended quickly. The 1930s ushered in profound social, political, and economic crises in Cuba; its destabilizing effects shook the country from end to end. Radio broadcasting, nevertheless, remained hugely popular, and its repeated commercials influenced consumption. Many sponsors continued to advertise, but their influence became secondary to the overpowering push by the industrial sector, which took over its products' advertising campaigns. Cigar, beer, and soap companies took center stage, with the latter becoming dominant.

The most successful radio stations were able to secure financing to undertake cutting-edge construction and technical modifications. New studios were inaugurated, with luxurious and comfortable sound stages. Studio audiences and their applause and background noise became an integral part of radio shows, though at times listeners found them irritating. The decade ended with thirty-four

medium wave stations and ten shortwave stations in Havana, and a total of ninety stations throughout Cuba (López pp. 532–534).

Popular programs of the time include *La voz del aire* (The On-Air Voice), a satirical news program; *La corte suprema del arte* (The Supreme Court of Art), which launched stars of radio, theater, television, and film; the very famous *Las aventuras de Chan Li Po* (The Adventures of Chan Li Po), a detective serial; *Universidad del Aire* (On-Air University), which championed culture; *Hora Múltiple* (Variety Hour), the first of many variety programs; and *La novela radial* (The Radio Serial), the original radio soap opera.

In the 1940s radio continued to expand. Cuba had eighty-two stations, forty-four of them in Havana (Radiomanía, 1948 pp. 80–81). During that decade RHC-Cadena-Azul (Blue Network) was established on 1 April 1940; Mil Diez (One Thousand Ten, or 1010) on 1 April 1943; Radio Reloj (Clock Radio) on 1 July 1947; Union Radio on 6 October 1947; and CMBF on 25 April 1948. It was the decade of programs such as *El suceso del día* (The News of the Day), in which possibly the first version of the song "Guantanamera" was sung; Clavelito's *El vaso de agua* (The Glass of Water); *El rincón criollo* (Traditional Corner); *La bolsa del saber* (The Bag of Knowledge); *La tremenda corte* (The Tremendous Court); *Los tres Villalobos* (The Three Villalobos), *Leonardo Moncada*; and two *radionovela* (radio soap opera) legends—*La novela del aire* (The Story of the Airwaves) and *El derecho de nacer* (The Right to Be Born).

The spectacular competition between the radio businessmen Amado Trinidad Velasco and Goar Mestre Espinosa began in the 1940s. During the first half of the decade, Trinidad dominated the airwaves with his RHC Cadena Azul, the country's only broadcaster with a national telephonic network. In October 1943 Mestre and his two brothers purchased a majority of the shares of CMQ, at that time a national chain of four stations. CMQ had been the most popular network in Cuba until 1941, when it was surpassed by RHC Cadena Azul.

Trinidad's strategy was to pay high wages to all his staff—not just the on-air talent—and he poured his personal fortune, estimated at more than 2 million pesos, into the fierce battle he waged for domination of Cuban radio. Testimony to his success was RHC Cadena Azul's achievement of a 65 percent share of the national audience in 1943, compared to CMQ's 15 percent (López p. 176). A year later, a new building and studio was opened on Paseo del Prado; it became known as the Palace of Radio. There was no control over expenditure and little exercise of business sense at RHC Cadena Azul, and the cult of personality around Trinidad himself (he was compared to King Midas, and he came to believe it) was one of the factors that brought down the business. Trinidad failed to see the crisis that was coming. By 1945 there was an exodus of high-quality artists to Mil Diez, even though they received lower wages there.

In 1942, Goar Mestre returned to Cuba from the United States, where he had graduated in 1936 with a degree in business administration from Yale University. He returned as the exclusive representative for Vostov Production and founded a large advertising agency that sponsored several radio programs on RHC Cadena Azul, while at the same time purchasing spots on CMQ. In 1943 he bought out the shares of Miguel Gabriel, one of CMQ's two owners, and became the station's general manager. In response to Trinidad's Palace of Radio, he conceived of the Radiocentro project. The cornerstone of the industrial complex was laid on 3 March 1946, and Radiocentro, S.A., was inaugurated on 12 March 1948 at 23rd and L Streets in the El Vedado neighborhood. This development was the most comprehensive step forward for the Latin American radio industry at the time, and Mestre became president of the Asociación Interamericana de Radiodifusión (AIR; Inter-American Broadcasting Association), an organization of more than three thousand stations on the continent.

The impact of CMQ would soon make itself felt. The July 1949 survey by the Asociación de Anunciantes de Cuba (Cuban Association of Advertisers) showed CMQ as having fourteen of the twenty most listened-to programs. Notably, this survey does not include the popular program *El Derecho de Nacer* (The Right to be Born), which had gone off the air in April of that year.

In sum, Cuban radio had become a network weaving together many threads: the print press, advertising agencies, radio reporters, newly created publications, systems of purchasing of radio spots and of hiring of artists, firms, and manufacturers, as well as politicians in power.

DEVELOPMENT AND EXPANSION: THE 1950s

In 1950 Havana had thirty-one medium wave radio stations and fifteen shortwave stations. There were sixty-one stations outside Havana, most of them affiliates of the three dominant networks: RHC-Cadena Azul, CMQ, and Unión Radio. Cadena Oriental de Radio (Eastern Radio Network) broadcast mostly to the former province Oriente (Betancourt and Oliva pp. 173–176). The RHC-Cadena Azul and CMQ networks battled ferociously for listeners, but RHC had already gone into bankruptcy. On 24 October 1950 Unión Radio began television broadcasting in Cuba, and CMQ followed suit on 18 December, though regular broadcasts would only begin on 11 March 1951.

In the 1940s and 1950s there were two main types of radio programs: news and radio novelas Forty-six news programs were broadcast in the early 1950s throughout the island, twenty-three of them from Havana (El Periodismo pp. 188–191). The most popular were broadcast by CMQ, Unión Radio,

and Radio Progreso, as well as Guido García Inclán's "Newspaper of the Air" on COCO-CMCK.

CMQ dominated the radio serials; no other broadcaster could compete. Its afternoon programming schedule broadcast ten radio serials, and evenings were capped off by two adventure serials: *El Capitán Banderas* (Captain Banderas) and *Leonardo Moncada*, originally by Leovigildo Díaz and later taken over by Enrique Núñez Rodríguez; it ran for nearly two decades. Most serials lasted from ten to twenty minutes and were named after the sponsoring soap-manufacturer's product. They aired one after another, grouped into two programming blocks with the two best serials bookending those blocks of programming with thirty-minute slots, differentiating them from the other shows. Iris Dávila's *Divorciadas* (Divorcées), which was known for its social content, was broadcast from 11:30 a.m. to noon, followed by Armando Couto's *Los tres Villalobos*, an adventure series. In the evening, Caridad Bravo Adams's *La novela del aire*, a romantically themed radio novela, was scheduled in the 8:30 slot. These serials, along with news programs, musical variety programs, and comedy shows, were typical of the programming on a typical day in April 1953, Monday through Saturday. Sunday programming took a rest from news and music, and in the evenings aired two popular programs: radio theater and *La Universidad del Aire*.

La tremenda corte. The popular radio show *La tremenda corte* was broadcast in Cuba from the 1940s through the 1960s. The program starred Aníbal de Mar (center), shown here with writer Caridad Bravo Adams (left) and station owner Amado Trinidad Velasco. COURTESY OF THE CUBAN HERITAGE COLLECTION, UNIVERSITY OF MIAMI LIBRARIES, CORAL GABLES, FLORIDA

When a coup on 10 March 1952 brought General Fulgencio Batista to power, censorship and political reprisals hung over media broadcasting. Armed struggle against Batista's rule began on 26 July 1953 with the revolutionaries' assault on the Moncada headquarters, and on 2 December 1956 the Granma expedition led by Fidel Castro disembarked for the southeast coast of Cuba. The Revolution had begun. The first stage of the invasion occurred in the Sierra Maestra. By the time Castro entered the Sierra, there was one radio for every six households in Cuba, the second-highest density in Latin America. Cuba already had a sophisticated radio culture that would serve the insurrectional forces in their struggle against Batista.

On 24 February 1958 Radio Rebelde (7RR) was officially inaugurated in the Sierra Maestra. It was a shortwave station whose effectiveness at communicating a political agenda was immediately evident. As the advance of the rebel army expanded the war to other territories and provinces, shortwave radio stations were set up along the way and became part of the Cadena de la Libertad (Freedom Network) that also included all networks operating on the continent. On one hand, there were the internal communications among the revolutionary forces, for which forty stations were in operation; on the other, stations on the outside, such as Venezuela's Indio Azul (Blue Indian), communicated directly with the Sierra Maestra (the general command). In Central and South America, commercial stations (e.g., Venezuela's Radio Continental, Colombia's Radio Caracol, and Argentina's LR1-Radio el Mundo, among others) rebroadcast programs and information originally aired by Radio Rebelde.

FROM COMMERCIAL TO PUBLIC SERVICE RADIO

The triumph of the Revolution on 1 January 1959 opened up a new, transitional stage in Cuban radio broadcasting that lasted until 16 November 1960. On 12 January 1959 the Circuito Nacional Cubano network (formerly owned by Batista) and its twelve stations were seized by the government. In subsequent months, two more networks (Unión Radio and Cadena Oriental de Radio) were also taken over, as well as some stations that supported the former leader.

By 20 March 1960 the majority of small- and medium-sized broadcasting stations made up the Frente Independiente de Emisoras Libres (FIEL; Independent Front of Free Radio Stations), whose purpose was to broadcast news about the incipient revolutionary process. From July through early October, the national Radio Progreso network, Circuito CMQ, and Radiocentro were all seized. On 16 November 1960, with the backing of FIEL, state radio appeared, promoting new political and social goals.

Cuba, an archipelago containing over 109,886 square kilometers (42,400 sq mi), with a population estimated at 6,734,776 in 1959, had 98 medium wave radio stations and 5 national networks in January of that year. About 32 percent of the stations were in Havana (Bracero p. 395). Medium-sized and small stations, which accounted for the majority, had equipment of highly irregular quality, and their broadcast coverage areas were limited. Wide areas of silence hung over the country; only 50 percent of Cuban territory received coverage, and this mainly in the larger cities. Extensive rural areas, including the mountains in the western, eastern, and central parts of the country, had no coverage.

The 1960s were crucial in Cuban radio broadcasting, ushering in profound changes not only in the technical and structural area but also in content. Units were upgraded so that better equipment and locations could improve transmission quality and coverage. Work on the ideological content of the broadcasts became a priority; the leading role of the people in achieving significant social changes in order to defend the country against aggression of all kinds was stressed and became more cohesive. The new style of communications was direct, rational, and, most importantly, sought to mobilize the population.

Furthermore, after thirty-five years of growth, radio advertising came to an end. Beginning 22 February, with a deadline of 19 March 1961, all advertising was to end. No Cuban radio or television stations were permitted to air commercials to promote the sale of any product whatsoever. No less important was the prohibition on sensationalist or yellow journalism in news broadcasts. The mass media of the Revolution were meant to positively contribute to the development of character, both collective and individual. Vulgarity, harsh or disrespectful remarks, and remarks in bad taste were all forbidden.

The Ministry Council Law of 24 May 1962 created the Instituto Cubano de Radiodifusión (ICR; Cuban Broadcasting Institute), later renamed the Instituto Cubano de Radio y Televisión (ICRT; Cuban Radio and Television Institute), which oversaw both radio and television broadcasts throughout the national territory. Its primary goals were to contribute to the formation and development of the new social values and to improve the quality of news, educational, cultural, and entertainment programming. In 1994 its purpose, roles, and powers as an organization for central administration were made even more specific.

MAIN STRUCTURAL CHANGES

Among the salient structural changes were those made to national networks. On 24 February 1968 CMQ changed its name to Radio Liberación (Liberation Radio). Radio Progreso was maintained, and Radio Rebelde was promoted as a national network for news, sports, and entertainment programming after it was given the facilities confiscated from Circuito Nacional Cubano (Cuban National Circuit).

CMBF, which since its creation in 1948 had focused on classical music with specialist commentary, and whose reach had been restricted to Havana, was transformed into a national station that carried broadcasts twenty-four hours a day. Radio Reloj, known for broadcasting only news and frequently announcing the time of day, became a national station in September 1961 when it added the Cadena Oriental de Radio's relay stations.

Radio Habana Cuba, officially inaugurated on 1 May 1961, was a shortwave station broadcasting beyond the country's borders in nine different languages. With a variety of news and cultural programming, it was formed for the purpose of promoting a Cuban account of the nation's sociopolitical transformation and reporting the Cuban government's official positions. Radio Enciclopedia, established on 7 November 1962, provided continuous programming featuring instrumental music and cultural commentary. It was converted into a national network on 19 June 1984.

Changes to radio broadcasting were based on the rational use of existing capacities, and their aim was to expand national coverage. By 1968 the country had forty radio stations, one of which had international reach. Five were national, eight provincial, and the rest local. However, the most significant changes of the period were in program content.

PROGRAM CONTENT

Three national radio stations carried the bulk of programming: CMQ (later Radio Liberación), Radio Progreso, and Radio Rebelde. Traditionally, CMQ gave more time to dramatic programs.

The reassignment of broadcasting hours in order to better meet the country's needs particularly benefited programs targeted at farmers and children. Dramatizations in the form of soap operas, short stories, and theatrical pieces established new trends, and high-quality programs appeared and enjoyed long runs. *Fiesta a las nueve* (9:00 Party) followed the tradition of the great musical comedy shows; it was first presented on 1 April 1961 and ran until late 1968. *La novela de las dos* (2:00 Soap Opera), named for its starting time, was first broadcast in 1962 and was still on the air in 2011. *Alegrías de Sobremesa* (After-Dinner Delights), which began in 1963 and was still broadcast in 2011, featured humorous scripts by Alberto Luberta highlighting the essence of Cuban traditions and scenes of daily life and presented performances by popular Cuban musicians. *Nocturno* (Nighttime), which came on the air for the first time on 2 August 1966 sought to tune in to developments in the world of international music. It was marked by the work of announcers both from Cuba and abroad and by its emphasis on poetry. Though the show was meant for a broad audience, young people adopted it as their own.

Programs introduced between 1970 and the mid-1980s included *Formalmente informal* (Formally Informal, 1971), an interview show; *Tu novela de amor* (Your Love Story, 1979), whose name indicates

its content; and *Haciendo Radio* (Doing Radio, 1984), a comprehensive news magazine.

In children's programming, *Tía tata cuenta cuentos* (The Storytelling Nanny) and *La cajita de música* (Little Music Box) achieved an extraordinary level of popularity. In addition, for some eighteen years, classes devoted to musical education for the country's primary schools were broadcast by Radio Rebelde; this idea came from Cuca Rivero, who wrote the scripts and directed the shows.

Dramatic programming took on a cultural role in the broadest sense. Offerings from around the world took their place alongside those from Cuba. Cuban and Latin American stories were featured in a daily slot on the afternoon program schedule. On Sunday nights *Teatro* (Theater) offered representative pieces of that genre. Radio novelas evolved in the 1970s: The romantic element did not disappear, but childish, affected melodrama in romantic conflict did. Although all three national networks were broadcasting radio serials in 1980, Radio Liberación and Radio Progreso were airing the greatest number of them.

Dramatic programming of the most important works of Cuban and world literature—in serials, short stories, and theatrical pieces—had a strong influence on the cultural development of the listening audience. The public became familiar with the writers and bookstore sales rose. This was reinforced by the program *Tu amigo el libro* (Your Friend, the Book), which included commentary on the week's featured book and dramatization of selected passages.

Cultural programming also elevated listeners' appreciation of music. In 2009, some 80 percent of the musical numbers broadcast were the work of Cuban composers and performers, and there were more than one thousand music programs on the radio nationally (ICRT; Instituto Cubano de Radio y Televisión, 2010). From the early days of Cuban radio broadcasting, music programs enjoyed high ratings, and those devoted to national music have been important to the preservation and defense of Cuban identity, as well as the very survival of musicians (who receive royalties every time one of their numbers is broadcast) and their works in the national memory. In addition to classical and instrumental music, Cuban radio offers numerous programs devoted to jazz, international rock, Latin American music, and specialized genres such as boleros or what was later known as world music.

News programs, built around the development of professional journalists and a broad array of topics, constitute another basic component of daily programming. Although strictly speaking, Cuba has no community radio, the stations in the cities fulfill that role in areas hard to reach or with special characteristics (e.g., mountains, fishing regions, cattle ranches). The broadcasting of sports events and specialized sports programs also has become a significant part of Cuban radio. Radio Rebelde, in its role as a national broadcaster, airs the most important national and international sporting events.

OTHER CHANGES

At the end of the first quarter of 1984 Radio Liberación was closed down, and some of its dramatic programs were moved to Radio Progreso. Some staff members were relocated to Radio Rebelde, and the rest became the staff for the program production entity Radioarte, which specialized in providing dramas for provincial and local stations.

During 1987 Cuban radio broadcast a total of 325,414 hours, 37,325 of them on national stations, at a power of 1,309.2 kilowatts. At the end of 2000, there were 1 international, 6 national, 17 provincial, and 43 municipal stations. Each day 2,769 radio programs were broadcast, for a total of 1,138 hours. Nationwide, programming was 38.3 percent music, 38 percent news, 14.2 percent variety, and 9.5 percent dramas. The dramas consisted of 374 programs, of which 171 were stand-alone shows and 203 were serials. Soap operas totaled sixty-five (ICRT 2010).

By 2010 the Cuban radio system was made up of 96 stations, of which 1 (Radio Habana Cuba) was international, 7 were national, 16 were provincial, and 72 municipal. Digitization of the system was advancing as financing permitted. Of all the stations in existence, 64 had a web site and 6 were streamed over the Internet; the Cuban radio portal provides a listing and links to these stations. National coverage approached 98 percent. Cuban radio was broadcasting more than 4,000 programs every week, and more than 501,000 hours per year (ICRT 2010).

Radio broadcasting had a presence in Cuban life for almost nine decades, providing both information and entertainment, and a reliable defense against dangers of any kind. With the radio Cubans know they are not alone, and their voice is also heard.

BIBLIOGRAPHY

Betancourt, Enrique, and Raúl Oliva, eds. *Anuario Artístico*. Havana: Authors, 1951.

Bracero Torres, Josefa. *Silencio … Se Habla*. Havana: Editorial Pablo de la Torriente Brau (Unión de Periodistas de Cuba), 2007.

Instituto Cubano de Radio y Televisión (ICRT). *Informe a los Diputados a la Asamblea Nacional del Poder Popular*. Havana: Author, 2005.

Instituto Cubano de Radio y Televisión (ICRT). *Informe a la Asamblea Nacional del Poder Popular*. Havana: Author, 2010.

López Fernandez, Oscar Luis. *La Radio En Cuba*. Havana: Editorial Letras Cubanas, 1981.

El periodismo en Cuba: Libro conmemorativo del Día del Periodista. Vol. 16. Havana: n.p., 1951.

Radiomanía (Havana) 8, no. 10 (October 1948).

Salwen, Michael. *Radio and Television in Cuba*. Ames: Iowa State University Press, 1994.

RADIO: COMMERCIAL AND CULTURAL PROGRAMMING IN CUBA

Mayra Cué Sierra

Commercial radio as a cultural platform in Cuba through the 1950s.

The national radio broadcasting system was launched on 22 August 1922 by Luis Casas Romero (1882–1950), a Cuban and owner of the radio station 2LC. Between 1922 and 1959, Cuba's broadcasting system was driven by the U.S. electronics industry and communications companies allied with local businesses. The system was strengthened by the growing number of radio receivers, phone lines, and short wave frequencies in Cuba, which contributed to the achievement of national and international reach, as well as commercial, communications, and cultural practices and circuits that made Cuba a leader in Latin American broadcasting.

ARTISTIC APPROPRIATION AND CULTURAL-EDUCATIONAL UNDERTAKINGS

From its early replication of foreign formats and broadcasts as well as traditional approaches derived from the theater, Cuban radio evolved toward original production of its own. The creation of radio theater sets stimulated acting, scenery, and a direct relationship between artists and audience, giving rise to a new kind of cultural practice. Some productions were broadcast from important theaters, helping to diversify artistic projects as well as relationships between artists and media.

Cuban radio assimilated a broad range of cultural and media patterns; it was allied with the press, film, and theater, interweaving activities and disciplines. Its programming favored the dramatic arts, information, and advertising, bringing together the popular and the classical, the foreign and the local.

RADIO MILESTONES OF THE 1930s

From the 1930s on, the lack of a solid film industry put radio at the center of Cuba's culture industry. Cuban radio's formats, genres, and products led to standardized and homogenized content, creating formulas meant to appeal to mass audiences. Meanwhile, radio programming reflected the profound cultural transformation taking place in Cuban society and expressed an artistic and ideological opposition, derived from Cuban and more broadly Latin American sources, to Anglo-Saxon culture. During the 1930s, educational and cultural practices arose that would prove long-lasting features of Cuban society.

Beginning in 1930, lectures on experimental psychology were broadcast, as were classes on foreign languages and a variety of other educational subjects, and military band and symphonic orchestra concerts, including those performed by students at music conservatories and academies. In 1931, many Cuban *zarzuelas* (light operas) were broadcast from the stage of the Teatro Martí. Beginning in 1932, such programs as *La Universidad del Aire* (The University of the Airwaves) offered people a chance to improve themselves, and *La hora juvenilia* (The Children's Hour) broadcast regional folk music performed by children. In *La hora Siboney* (The Siboney Hour), Gustavo Sánchez Galárraga and Ernesto Lecuona, with an orchestra of fifty teachers, debuted Cuban *zarzuelas* on Cuban radio. During this decade, RCA Victor sponsored radio broadcasts in Cuba of New York's Metropolitan Opera season. A celebration of the 800th performance of *La hora múltiple* (The Variety Hour)—a model for radio drama and music shows—brought Cuba's entire Philharmonic Orchestra together with prestigious composers and performers in the first contest of traditional Cuban song.

From Santiago de Cuba in 1933, Félix Caignet debuted *Las aventuras de Chan Li Po* (The Adventures of Chan Li Po), the first detective series written by Cubans. In 1934, Radio Agrícola Nacional (National Agriculture Radio), a channel supported by the Secretariat of Agriculture, was launched as a public service on a global scale. By 1935, competitions of art aficionados provided talent for radio shows, and *La hora Sensemayá* (The Sensemayá Hour) analyzed ethnology and folklore while performing music of African origin. Beginning in 1936, the Philharmonic Orchestra broadcast Sunday concerts from the Teatro Auditórium and the Havana Amphitheater to the eastern part of Cuba over a radio network based in the capital.

In 1937, radio became the epicenter of Cuban culture. The rebroadcast of *The Adventures of Chan Li Po* in Havana unleashed an unprecedented phenomenon in Cuban entertainment, with the production of the country's first sound film based on that story. *La corte suprema del arte* (The Supreme Court of Art), a contest for amateurs, turned into a nationwide, popular artistic movement that had an impact on the entire society and influenced the film *La aventura peligrosa* (The Dangerous Adventure); *La hora Bacardi* (The Bacardi Hour) broadcast the first operas recorded in radio studios. *El concurso de los Precios Fijos* (The Precios Fijos Contest), sponsored by the Havana department store Precios Fijos (Fixed-Price), inaugurated the dramatic serial or soap opera. Audiciones Emerson broadcast *La derrota de compay Gallo* (The Downfall of Brother Rooster) live from Teatro Martí, and the Secretariat of State sponsored weekly programs about cultural values from the nations of the Americas. These unique offerings developed beyond their specific content, leading to the formation of companies focused on cultural, educational, or training material.

In 1939, radio stations CMZ (daytime) and COX (nighttime) were launched by the Negociado de Radiodifusión del Cuerpo de Cultura del Ejército Nacional (the Radio Broadcasting Department within the Army's Culture Corps). These stations offered select Cuban and foreign music, dramatizations, and educational, historical, recreational, and practical programming to students and teachers in civilian-military academies and to all citizens. The subsequent transfer of these stations to the Ministry of Education expanded their cultural reach for decades.

THE DEVELOPMENT OF NEW TYPES OF PROGRAMMING

Radio featured adaptations of literary, theatrical, and movie works, while also producing original, scripted shows. The latter became a prime vehicle for serial narratives, broadcast live, featuring melodrama and romance for all ages, both inside and outside Cuba's borders. Music programming broadcast a wide range of genres as well as instrumental and vocal formats, sometimes creating fusions or hybrids. Themes, plots, and conventions drawn from film, audio recordings, and print all found their way into radio programming. Contests and spectacles organized by businesses and hotels were also broadcast, and the transmission of sporting events emerged as a cultural practice.

Faced with the deterioration of radio management as a result of excessive competition, various elements in Cuban society demanded legislation to regulate the practices of radio and communications companies. Cuba's Secretariat of Communications oversaw radio's artistic quality and tried to eliminate vulgarity and poor taste. The Educational and Cultural Administration within the Ministry of Education took charge of the guidance and oversight of all cultural, educational, scientific, and artistic activities throughout society.

NEW BUSINESS MODELS AND COMPETITION, 1940s–1950s

In 1943, the renowned CMQ-Radio, founded by Miguel Gabriel and Angel Cambo and boasting the most powerful transmission signal of any station in Cuba, was partially acquired by the Mestre Espinosa brothers, who revamped it. The subsequent founding of Radio Reloj (information and advertising) and CMBF Onda Musical (instrumental music) added new variety to the broadcast dial; this diversification increased still further when another cultural landmark appeared in the same decade: the people's station, known as "the 1010," after its frequency. The station was purchased by the Partido Socialista Popular (People's Socialist Party) by means of a fund-raising drive.

The most powerful Cuban broadcasters became concentrated in ownership and competed for audiences and advertisers, putting artists under contract and raiding one another for talent: RHC Cadena Azul (Blue Network), founded by Amado Trinidad Velasco, the only radio magnate from outside Havana, began broadcasting in the province of Villa Clara and organized a multi-provincial network from the capital of Santa Clara. RHC Cadena Azul wrested primacy in Cuban broadcasting away from CMQ. This rivalry stimulated the production of radio dramas, cultural revues, Cuban and Latin American popular music, rural culture shows, the simultaneous hiring of Latin American theater and movie stars by radio stations, theaters, and cabarets, and rising salaries for radio talent. In 1948, two events helped CMQ retake the lead for good: the inauguration in the Vedado district of the Radiocentro building—an icon of modern construction, technology, radio programming, and sound recording—and the premiere of *El derecho de nacer* (The Right to be Born) by Caignet, which instantly became a model for the sentimental soap opera on radio across all of Latin America.

During the 1950s, several genres (radio novelas, *aventuras, zarzuelas, radioteatros*) gained popularity on both Latin radio and television. Also a broader range of programming developed, sales of Cuban scripts and recordings in the region increased, and the first movie versions of Cuban sentimental stories were created. Broadcasters such as Radio Progreso, owned by the Fernández family, gave priority to hiring foreign artists and established its own record label, expanding its musical offerings and promoting music from across Latin America. During this period, Unión Radio, owned by Gaspar Pumarejo Such, and CMQ Radio, with all its owners except Miguel Gabriel, contributed to the basic legacy of Cuba's first television broadcasters.

THE IMPACT OF CUBAN RADIO

Cuban commercial radio burst into the private realm with its reach and immediacy. Its impact affected a large and far-flung audience from many social sectors, the majority of whom were semiliterate or illiterate, creating an utterly unprecedented cultural and communications phenomenon. Cuban radio refashioned U.S. and European genres and formats, creating a Latin American model based on traditional sensibilities and emphasizing the region's historical and cultural roots.

Radio's technological novelty, assimilation of cultural frameworks and expressions, and application of media and market research provided differing levels of profit to all its actors and social agents and positioned it as a force within the region. The Cuban radio industry mixed cultural content and messages, established new aesthetic approaches, and transmitted Cuban and other Latin American cultural production throughout the region. Cuban radio became the industrial, organizational, and creative template for the programming, performances, production, and management, and the agent of significant cultural, symbolic, communications, and marketing exchanges. Radio's commercial and advertising growth and its star-entertainment-spectacle system did not cancel out its vast cultural, educational, socializing, and informational influence. A proper appreciation of Cuban commercial radio

helps to preserve a treasure trove of Latin American practices and traditions that endure in the collective memory and in the popular imagination of the region.

BIBLIOGRAPHY

Archives of Cuban Radio of Institute of Radio and Television. La Habana (1930–1959).

Bracero Torres, Josefa. *Silencio ... se habla.* Havana: Editorial Pablo de la Torrente Brau, 2007.

Cubarte: El portal de la cultura cubana. Available from http://www.cubarte.cult.cu/.

Cué Sierra, Mayra. "Senderos de amor: La génesis del modelo latino de la telenovela." Ph.D. diss., University of Havana, 2007.

Dávila Mune, Iris. *El melodrama: Un caso en tela de juicio y en torno al serial en delirio de periodista.* Havana: Ediciones Unión, 2007.

González Martínez, Víctor J. "La industria cultural cubana y la gestión del grupo Mestre Espinosa." Ph.D. diss., University of Havana, 2009.

López Fernández, Oscar Luís. *La radio en Cuba.* 3rd ed. Havana: Editorial Letras Cubanas, 2002.

Salwen, Michael B. *Radio and Television in Cuba: The Pre-Castro Era.* Ames: Iowa State University Press, 1994.

RADIO: CUBAN RADIO IN SOUTH FLORIDA

Gonzalo Soruco

The Cuban exiles' power of radio and ideology.

In June 1959, the Cuban government began expropriations of land and businesses owned mostly by U.S. companies. Washington retaliated by ending purchases of Cuban sugar, which for years had been the island's principal earner of foreign exchange. When Fidel Castro received military equipment from the Soviet Union, the long and close relationship between the island and the United States came to an end. Worried about the direction of the Cuban Revolution, the U.S. government put into effect a strategy that had served it well since the end of the World War II. It was a program of covert action that required the formation of an opposition front of disaffected Cubans, a carefully orchestrated communications campaign delivered through clandestine radio, the creation of a covert intelligence organization within Cuba, and the preparation of a paramilitary force outside Cuba.

RADIO SWAN

Like a previous action that had successfully toppled the government of Guatemala in 1954, the campaign against Castro began in Greater Swan Island, near the coast of Honduras, where the CIA installed a 50-kilowatt radio transmitter. Radio Swan, which went on the air on 17 May 1960, joined a number of

■ *See also*

Bay of Pigs Invasion: 1961

Cuban Embargo

Cuban Thought and Cultural Identity: The Internet Experience in Cuba

Diasporas: Introduction

Miami

pirate and clandestine radio stations operated by Cuban exiles located in Florida and around the Caribbean—presumably aided by the CIA—that since 1959 had bombarded the island daily with messages that encouraged Cubans to armed insurrection against Castro and sabotage of government facilities (Wasburn p. 38). Radio Swan's programming, produced by the CIA and various groups of Cuban exiles, included propaganda as well as "music, soap operas, religion, news, and political polemics" (Soley and Nichols p. 178).

The propaganda campaign failed, and the April 1961 intervention was an embarrassment referred to in U.S. history books as "the Bay of Pigs fiasco." The CIA blamed the Cuban exiles it had hired for the "Swan radio fiasco" (Gleijeses p. 6), but the failures belonged to the CIA, which had failed to understand the Revolution and the Cuban people. General Maxwell Taylor, who chaired a Cuban Study Group to determine why the invasion failed, described the problems with the message broadcast by Radio Swan as one of the contributing factors: "In the first place, these groups talked over much about their activities in Miami and the hard fight they were conducting along Biscayne Boulevard. . . . [The] Cuban programs became the fulcrum where the political ambitions of Cuban exiles in Miami were presented to the other Cubans in Miami. Finally, each program fought for 'scoops'" (cited in Soley and Nichols p. 179). Not surprisingly, the credibility and reputation of Radio Swan began to wane.

Another clandestine radio station that aired messages similar to Swan's was Tony Varona's Radio Cuba Independiente, the voice of the Frente Revolucionario Democratico (FRD, Democratic Revolutionary Front), which transmitted from a cabin cruiser sailing off the coast of Cuba. Its programs were taped in Miami (Szulc and Meyer). Others included La Voz de Cuba Libre, a clandestine radio station transmitting from Puerto Rico; Radio General Maceo, sponsored by the Alianza Nueva Democrática; Radio Americas, the voice of the Frente Obrero Revolucionario Democratico Cubano (FORDC, Labor Revolutionary Democratic Front of Cuba); and Radio Cuba Libre, WGBS, sponsored by the Committee for the Liberation of Cuba. WGBS boasted that its programs were designed to refute daily the communist propaganda.

Castro quickly responded to the propaganda onslaught. In the early 1960s a powerful radio station in Havana, Radio Progreso, began to air a program titled "Radio Free Dixie" that incited blacks in the United States to commit acts of violence and sabotage (cited in Soley and Nichols p. 182). Robert F. Williams, a black civil rights leader who found political asylum in Cuba, was a regular host of "Radio Free Dixie," calling for black insurrection in the United States.

One aspect of the propaganda plan for Cuba was correct—selection of radio as the medium. Radio in Cuba was very popular, and most Cubans had one or more receptors. In the 1950s Cuba had the most advanced and creative broadcasting industry of the Americas (Rivero). Naturally, after the failure of the Bay of Pigs invasion, Cuban exiles who had worked in radio picked up where Radio Swan had left off.

RADIO, POLITICS, AND CUBANISMO

In an article published by the *Miami Herald* in 1983, the news director for Florida's WRHC, Tomás Regalado (from 2009, the mayor of Miami), highlighted the importance of Spanish-language radio to arriving Cubans, not only during the early days of the exile, but also during the Mariel Boatlift (Regalado), when the details of events and names of arrivals that were vital to the community were quickly communicated by radio. This news was equally important to Cubans still living in Cuba, who listened to the broadcasts for the lists of Cubans arriving in Florida.

The media also controlled the message. The radio stations, managed by capable Cuban personalities such as Salvador Lew and Armando Pérez-Roura, served the exiles' political agenda well and helped to control the ideological purity of the message that reached the public sphere. From the 1960s, using the language of the Cold War, Miami's Cuban radio maintained a uniform, militantly anti-Castro message, and any deviation from the orthodoxy was met with violence. For example, on 30 April 1976, WQBA broadcaster Emilio Milian was badly hurt by a bomb that had been placed under the hood of his car because he had advocated dialogue with the Castro government (Frederick p. 33). In Miami, the medium became the guard dog of the political power structure rather than its watchdog.

The battle for the hearts and minds of the Cubans in the island, and for ideological purity among the exiles in Miami, was fought over the airwaves by several groups, some funded by the U.S. government and some funded by the exiles themselves. The most prestigious was the U.S. government's Voice of America (VOA), whose programs reached around the world. After the Bay of Pigs, the VOA began to broadcast "Cita con Cuba" every evening for one hour. As part of Operation Mongoose, the CIA funded an additional sixty stations that broadcast propaganda to the island in order to "continue to encourage low risk, simple sabotage, and other forms of active and passive resistance" (cited in Schoultz p. 400). By the 1980s, commercial radio stations owned or managed by Cuban exiles had significant audiences in Cuba (Veciana-Suarez 1982).

CUBAN-OWNED STATIONS

The story of how the first Cuban-owned radio station in Miami was born was told by Salvador Lew in *Hogar Club* (p. 6). On 31 December 1972, Alberto Villalobos invited Lew, who had been a classmate and friend of Castro at the University of Havana, and Lazaro Asencio to celebrate the New Year at Centro Vasco (a well-known Cuban-owned Spanish restaurant) and discuss the possibility of purchasing a radio station. But it was not until 15 November 1973 that the purchase of

WRIZ was finalized and the first Cuban-owned station was launched. Its call letters and slogan became WRHC-1560 AM "Cadena Azul," in honor of the famous Cuban network of the same name. For the next three years the station ranked number one in Dade and Broward counties, obtaining 15 percent of the audience (Lew). Its programming included "La Noche y Usted" with Marta Flores, "La Guantanamera" with Flores and Willy Leiva, and "Peña Azul" with Salvador Lew.

In the early 1960s, the first station to target the Spanish-language market of Miami was WQBA-1140 AM, better known as "La Cubanisima" (The Most Cuban). In 1966 Susquehana Broadcasting executives realized the importance of that market and purchased the 1140 AM radio station. It soon became the most popular Spanish-language station in the region, and it remained so for years, with Tomás Garcia-Fusté as vice president of programming and Agustín Tamargo and Raúl Tapanes as political analysts and entertainers. "Radio Reloj," a copy of a popular Cuban program that broadcast news every hour on the hour, was broadcast daily from 10:00 p.m. to 1:00 a.m. under the direction of Salvador Lew. The morning edition was broadcast from 5:00 to 9:00 a.m. under the direction of Jorge Bourbakis. Radio personalities who launched their careers on "La Cubanisima" include journalist Bernadette Pardo (daughter of the former Castro ally José Pardo Llada); reporters to the stars Mauricio Zelic and Lilly Estefan; journalist and editor María Elena Rodríguez; journalist Marta Flores; and meteorologist John Morales. Its FM station (WQBA107.5 FM), "Super Q," was the first bilingual station in the market (Veciana-Suarez 1987, p. 85). In the first decade of the 2000s it was known largely as a Latin music station. In the early 1960s, competing with "La Cubanisima" for the Cuban exile audience was WFAB, "La Fabulosa." Tomás Regalado cut his career as a reporter at this station, reporting on the Freedom Flights. By the 1970s Spanish-language radio stations run or owned by Cuban exiles included WQBA-1140 AM and 107.5 FM; WFAB; WCMQ-1210 AM and 92.3 FM; QWAQI-710 AM; WRHC-155 AM; and WOCN-1450 AM and 103 FM.

In 1984 a group of Cuban American investors—one of whom was Maria Pérez-Roura, the wife of Radio Mambí's Armando Pérez-Roura—formed Unión Radio, Incorporated, which bought WOCN-1450 AM. Its programming concentrated largely on news and talk shows with a political slant. In 1985 Mambisa Broadcasting Company, formed in Miami by the president and associates of Cosmo Communications, a maker of clocks, radios, and telephones, purchased the English-language station WGBS and created WAQI-710 AM, popularly known as Radio Mambí. According to Ann Louise Bardach, the manager and part owner of Mambí, Armando Pérez-Roura is the high priest of Cuban radio and "king maker in exile politics" of Miami: "[Over] the years, Pérez-Roura has offered a hospitable welcome to some of the most notorious characters in the exile community.

Convicted terrorists such as Orlando Bosh and disgraced politicians like Demetrio Pérez are often heard on Mambí" (Bardach p. 104). Pérez-Roura played a strategic role during the Elián González debacle.

Mambí exerted political influence on exile issues, for example, the early 2000 custody case of six-year-old Elián González, which captivated the nation. González's mother had drowned while crossing the strait between Cuba and the United States, and the Immigration and Naturalization Service placed the boy with his Miami relatives. An international custody battle ensued when Elián's father and the Cuban government demanded the child's return. Pérez-Roura used his radio program to galvanize the Cuban-American community, demanding that Elián stay in the United States. In addition to Pérez-Roura, other figures at Mambí exerted considerable political influence in the exile community. The *Miami Herald* reported that Marta Flores, one of Mambí's star reporters, known as "Reina de la Noche" (Queen of the Night), "pocketed thousands of dollars from campaigns in the 1990s from her advertising agency Mar-Flo, a practice considered unethical but not illegal" and that "Everyone from Gov. Jeb Bush to State Rep. Marco Rubio has visited her studio" (Corral p. A1). Another of Mambí's stars, Ninoska Pérez Castellón, gained fame while working for the powerful Cuban American National Foundation, which is dedicated to the overthrow of the communist government in Cuba.

WWFE 670 AM, "La Poderosa" (the Powerful One), is owned by the Cuban American Jorge A. Rodriguez. Raquel Regalado, wife of Tomás Regalado, coanchored a daily morning show, "Lo que otros no dicen" (What Others Won't Say), as well as "Panorama." The station's programming is highly political and has been accused of intolerance (Balmaseda).

When they began broadcasting, "La Cubanisima" (WQBA) in the 1970s and Radio Mambí (WAQI) in the mid-1980s attracted big audiences with their mostly political programs, but in order to retain and enlarge their audiences they began to air more general programs. The WQBA's popular "Micrófono Abierto," broadcast daily from 9:00 a.m. to 12:00 p.m., included interviews, chat, and news, along with information of local events. These stations attracted audiences with Cuban music and popular singers such as Celia Cruz, Albita, and Gloria Estefan. As the *Miami Herald*'s Ana Veciana-Suarez pointed out, "Cuban radio, and later television, became the preservers of Cuban culture, customs and values" (1988, p. 5A).

RADIO MARTÍ

In May 1985 U.S.-government-owned Radio Martí, a brainchild of the Reagan administration, began broadcasting to the island. The effects of Radio Martí on island audiences were questionable. Research has shown that the effects of propaganda, and particularly international propaganda, are limited, affecting mostly audiences already predisposed to believe the message (DeFleur and

Radio Martí. Radio newscasters Pedro De Pool (left) and Sonia Barriel deliver the news on 24 January 2007 at the Radio/ TV Martí studios in Miami, Florida. JOE RAEDLE/AFP/ GETTY IMAGES/NEWSCOM

Dennis). Radio Martí is largely an ideological symbol that binds the executive branch of the U.S. government with the Cuban exiles of south Florida (Nichols). Radio Martí's broadcasts were a political victory for the right wing of the Cuban American community and its political leader, the businessman Jorge Mas Canosa (1939–1997), director of the powerful Cuban American National Foundation, who had demanded that the U.S. government become more involved in the fight with Fidel Castro. At first, some of Radio Martí's programs such as "Tempranito y de Mañana" had an audience in Cuba, but Radio Martí lost listeners first when its signal was blocked by Cuba and later with the development of technologies that offered new options for cultural consumption in Cuba (e.g., the Internet, computer games, pirated movies, and TV soap operas). Moreover, the Cuban government reorganized its cultural infrastructure in order to give the people the same entertainment that Radio Martí offered: more music and more radio novellas. In 1994 the *Miami Herald* published a "Cuba poll" by CID-Gallup— undoubtedly flawed—that showed that 10 percent of those interviewed "listened to Radio Martí the most" ("How Cubans Responded to Questions" 1994). It was not coincidental that these data were collected during the *período especial* (Special Period), when poverty in Cuba was at an all-time high. A 2009 study by the U.S. government's Government Accountability Office estimated that TV Martí programs reached audiences of less than 1 percent of Cubans on the island (Adams).

In 2004 the credibility and professionalism of Radio and TV Martí was called into question when it was revealed that the George W. Bush administration had paid several newspaper reporters from *El Nuevo Herald* for commentaries on the Martí network. *El Nuevo*'s publisher, Jesús Díaz, dismissed three reporters; six others involved in the controversy were not disciplined. The incident sparked animosity between the newsrooms of the sister newspapers *El Nuevo Herald* and the *Miami Herald* and ignited debate about the fundamental role of journalism in a democratic society (Seelye).

MASS MEDIA AND CULTURE

People use the media to survey their environment, to connect with others, to maintain their cultural ties, and to be entertained (Katz, Gurevitch, and Haas). Upon their arrival in Miami, the exiles needed to find places to live and shop, to connect with others like themselves, and to get news about friends and relatives they left behind. Miami's Cuban radio met these needs. Aside from setting the political agenda, Cuban radio in Miami became a source of unity, a means of maintaining history, culture, and symbolism, and above all, a means of maintaining the language.

In the new millennium, Cubans account for slightly over 50 percent of Miami-Dade's Hispanic population. They are becoming politically diverse, and new debates, such as the debate about Venezuela's Hugo Chávez, have changed the political discourse somewhat. In 1998 the Cuban jazz musician Chucho Valdés and his group Irakere were able to perform in Miami without significant problems. A decade earlier, the performance of a play by Dolores Prida had to be canceled after the theater received bomb threats. Prida, a New York playwright, had once called for diplomatic relations with Cuba (Veciana-Suarez 1988). After that an increasing number of island artists appeared on Miami stages and on local television. The fact that radio personalities such as Francisco Aruca (who hosted "Yesterday in Miami") and Edmundo García ("The Night Moves") attract Cuban American audiences who would prefer to deal openly with Castro is also an indication of change. In 2003, for example, García interviewed the pro-democracy dissident Osvaldo Payá via telephone from Havana and had callers question him directly ("Best Spanish-Language Radio Personality" 2003). García also rankled some anti-Castro factions in Miami by interviewing Ricardo Alarcón, the president of the Cuban parliament, and by criticizing the political intolerance of local Spanish-language radio and television personalities.

In the early 2000s Miami is a Latin American city where Spanish is spoken as often—or more often—than English, and where music from Latin America, and particularly from the Caribbean, fills the streets. It owes much of its character to the Cuban exiles who worked and fought hard to make it their own. Their victories did not include the downfall of Castro, but they managed to change the way Americans perceived them. Yet, Cuban radio in the first decade of the twenty-first century followed the path of other media in the United States. WQBA and WAQI, once the pride of the exiles, were purchased by corporations in Dallas and Los Angeles, which in turn were bought in 2004 by Univision Communications Incorporated ("Federal Government Approves Univision Deal" 2003).

BIBLIOGRAPHY

Adams, David. "Time to Scrap TV Marti, Critics Say." *St. Petersburg Times* (16 February 2009). Available from www.tampabay.com/.

Balmaseda, Liz. "Radio Station Glued to the Past." *Miami Herald* (19 November 2001): 1B.

Bardach, Ann Louise. *Cuba Confidential: Love and Vengeance in Miami and Havana*. New York: Random House, 2002.

"Best Spanish-Language Radio Personality." *Miami New Times* (15 May 2003).

Corral, Oscar. "Women on Airwaves Setting Agenda on Cuban Issues." *Miami Herald* (8 May 2006): A1.

DeFleur, Melvin L., and Everette E. Dennis. *Understanding Mass Communication*. Boston: Houghton Mifflin, 1981.

"Federal Government Approves Univision Deal to Buy Hispanic Broadcasting Corp." *Los Angeles Daily News* (23 September 2003).

Forment, Carlos. "Political Practice and the Rise of the Ethnic Enclave: The Cuban-American Case, 1959–1979." *Theory and Society* 18 (1989): 47–81.

Frederick, Howard. *Cuban-American Radio Wars: Ideology in International Telecommunications*. Norwood, NJ: Ablex, 1986.

Gleijeses, Piero. "Ships in the Night: The CIA, the White House and the Bay of Pigs." *Journal of Latin American Studies* 27, no. 1 (February 1995): 1–42.

"How Cubans Responded to Questions." *Miami Herald* (18 December 1994): 37A.

Katz, Elihu, Michael Gurevitch, and Hadassah Haas. "On the Use of the Mass Media for Important Things." *American Sociological Review* 38, no. 2 (1973): 164–181.

Lew, Salvador. "La Historia de WRHC: Como Surgió la Primera Emisora Cubana en los Estados Unidos." *Hogar Club* n.d. Photocopy available in University of Miami's Cuban Heritage Collection. Updated 2002. Abbreviated version available from http://www.cadenaazul.com/.

Nichols, John S. "When Nobody Listens: Assessing the Political Success of Radio Martí." *Communication Research* 11, no. 2 (April 1984): 281–304.

Regalado, Tomás. "How the Community Is Served by Spanish-Language Radio." *Miami Herald* (22 October 1983): A25.

Rivero, Yeidy M. "Havana as a 1940s–1950s Latin American Media Capital." *Critical Studies in Media Communication* 26, no. 3 (2003): 275–293.

Rodriguez, David. "Edmundo García contra la mentira (María Elvira Salazar)." 8 April 2010. Available from http://www.kaosenlared.net/.

Schoultz, Lars. *That Infernal Little Cuban Republic: The United States and the Cuban Revolution*. Chapel Hill: University of North Carolina Press, 2009.

Seelye, Katherine Q. "Miami Publisher Steps Down over Payments to Reporters." *New York Times* (4 October 2006): A16.

Soley, Lawrence C., and John S. Nichols. *Clandestine Radio Broadcasting: A Study of Revolutionary and Counterrevolutionary Electronic Communication*. New York: Praeger, 1987.

Szulc, Tad, and Karl E. Meyer. *The Cuban Invasion: The Chronicle of a Disaster*. New York: Ballantine Books, 1962.

Veciana-Suarez, Ana. "Latin Radio Solicits Tips from Cuba." *Miami Herald* (30 November 1982): 2.

Veciana-Suarez, Ana. *Hispanic Media, USA: A Narrative Guide to Print and Electronic Hispanic News Media in the United States*. Washington, DC: Media Institute, 1987.

Veciana-Suarez, Ana. "Spanish Broadcasters Wield Growing Clout, Stations Provide Community Service, Voice for Émigrés." *Miami Herald* (2 February 1988): 5A.

Wasburn, Philo C. *Broadcasting Propaganda: International Radio Broadcasting and the Construction of Political Reality*. Westport, CT: Praeger, 1992.

■ *See also*

Television: Soap Operas

RADIO: SOAP OPERAS

Norma Abad Muñoz

The broadcasting of radio soap operas in Cuba, with particular emphasis on El derecho de nacer, *a seminal radio soap opera whose regional significance continued after its 1948 premiere.*

By 1930, just eight years after the official launch of the first radio station in Cuba, sixty radio stations were broadcasting across the island, most of them

The film cast of *El derecho de nacer* (The Right to Be Born). The series *El derecho de nacer,* which premiered on Cuban radio in 1948, became a model for the sentimental soap opera throughout the Americas as well as the basis for two films. © HOLLY ACKERMAN, PH.D.

concentrated in the capital. Between 1930 and 1932 radio dramas were introduced, an original concept in radio that was to have great significance in the development of Cuban radio broadcasting. Radio *novelas* (soap operas) soon became a permanent feature on the Cuban radio dial. None was more popular or more influential—throughout Latin America—than *El derecho de nacer* (The Right to Be Born), which premiered in 1948.

DEVELOPMENT OF THE GENRE

In Havana in the 1930s theater celebrities started taking leading roles and working as directors in the new radio shows. Two successful figures were Enriqueta Sierra, who put together and directed the first radio theater programs, and Marcelo Agudo, who did the same with comedies. They selected works, typically from Spanish theater, and adapted them to the available transmission time. In 1932 Félix B. Caignet (1892–1976), a renowned journalist, composer, and poet from the eastern part of the island, introduced children's literature to radio programming

on CMKC in Santiago de Cuba. Caignet recounted the adventures of *Chilín y Bebita* and *Chilín y Bebita y el enanito Coliflor* (Chilín, Bebita, and the Dwarf Cauliflower). In 1934 Caignet wrote original radio scripts for the serial *Las aventuras de Chan Li Po* (The Adventures of Chan Li Po) daily broadcasts of which, beginning with "La serpiente roja" (The Red Serpent), began in January 1937, in the 8:00–8:30 p.m. time slot. The title character was a sagacious Chinese private detective who made two expressions famous: "tell me everything—absolutely everything" and "patience—much patience." Each serial, which incorporated dialogue, sound effects, and music, was fifteen to twenty episodes long, with plots conceived as a unified whole. Recognizing the differences between theater and radio, Caignet incorporated the narrator as a character in the plot so that listeners could "see with their ears." Each episode built sufficient dramatic intensity to leave radio listeners eager to tune in the next day. The serial had extraordinary success from the very beginning, and its provincial author became exceedingly popular.

The serials that followed *Chan Li Po* gained a nationwide audience. In 1938 Caignet wrote *El monstruo en la sombra* (The Monster in the Shadow), a program that shocked the public and marked the first time Cuban radio dealt with the major social problem of heroin use. Denouncing the criminal activity of dealers and warning against this scourge of the nation's youth, the serial was a call to action. However, with this and a few other exceptions, radio theater of the late 1930s was criticized for having run out of original ideas and affecting listeners in negative ways.

Beginning in 1939 and continuing into the 1940s, the major development in Cuban radio was the introduction of soap operas. In late 1939 a fifteen-minute show, *La novela radial* (The Radio Soap Opera), was created, with the writer Reinaldo López del Rincón in charge of adapting scripts. From 1939 to 1945 the novelist and essayist Alejo Carpentier (1904–1980), who acquired radio broadcasting experience during an eleven-year exile in France, won acclaim for his original scripts and adaptations of great works of international literature for one-hour broadcasts. *La novela del aire* (The Soap Opera of the Air), written by Caridad Bravo Adams (1908–1990), who was born in Mexico to Cuban parents, emerged in 1941. Adams later gained fame as a writer of *telenovelas*, the television successor to radio novelas. In October 1941 Caignet presented the dramatized version of "Aladdin and His Marvelous Lamp," whose target audience was children but which appealed to all ages.

In 1942 and 1943 an increasing amount of airtime was devoted to soap operas, such as *La novela del hogar* (The Home Soap Opera) and *La novela Palmolive* (The Palmolive Soap Opera), by a diverse array of scriptwriters, notably Leandro Blanco, José Ángel Buesa, and Antonio González. By the mid-1940s soap operas, with their elements of passion, romance, and unattainable love, dominated the air waves. Popular shows by Caignet included *El precio de una vida* (1944), *El derecho de nacer* (1948), and *La novela del aire* (1949); by Leandro Blanco, *La novela Palmolive* (1945, 1946) and *La novela del aire* (1947); and by Arturo Liendo, *La novela guajira* (1950).

AN ENDURING INFLUENCE

El derecho de nacer, which ran for 314 episodes and earned the highest ratings of any Cuban radio soap opera, triggered an uproar. Caignet struck a nerve as his story unveiled realities that people pretended not to know. He dared to address the subject of a woman who becomes pregnant out of wedlock and who is then stigmatized and repudiated by her family. He dared listeners to consider how far an illustrious family might go to safeguard its honor. Caignet frames the story as a condemnation of the pregnant woman's parents for trying to force her to abort the baby. He addresses the theme of religious faith in terms of conviction, submission, and spiritual refuge. Above all, Caignet's story exalts the black race through the key character of Mamá Dolores.

El derecho de nacer immediately crossed national boundaries and had an unprecedented regional impact, with themes that remained relevant into the twenty-first century. A pioneering program, *El derecho de nacer* established new guidelines for radio and eventually television media in Latin America and Spain. It had barely ended in Cuba when it was already being broadcast in other countries through their own productions—Venezuela (1949), Puerto Rico (1949), Panama (1951), Colombia (1951), Brazil (1951), Mexico (1951), Ecuador (1952), Nicaragua (1952), as well as El Salvador, Peru, Spain, and the United States (in Pasadena, California)—with ratings in these countries even higher than those reported in Cuba (50.63%). In some countries, such as Puerto Rico, Nicaragua, and Brazil, it was broadcast twice a day. Colombia broadcast it over seven radio stations simultaneously. Brazil broadcast it over Radio Nacional de Río de Janeiro three times a week in the evening and rebroadcast it in the morning. During the novela's broadcast run, weekly supplements such as *Radio teatro* (Radio Theater), published in Río de Janeiro in 1952, and *Radio Guía* (Radio Guide), published in Cuba, printed summaries of episodes of *El derecho de nacer*.

For Caignet, Mexico became a second homeland, and two important film versions of *El derecho de nacer* were made there. The first, which premiered at the Orfeón movie theater in Mexico City in 1952, starred Jorge Mistral, Gloria Marín, Martha Roth, and Lupe Suárez. The second version, which premiered in 1966 at the city's Roble cinema and starred Aurora Bautista, Julio Alemán, Maricruz Olivier, and Eusebia Cosme, won six ONIX awards from the Instituto de Cultura Cinematográfica de la Universidad Iberoamericana (Institute of Cinematographic Culture of the Ibero-American University). At the time of the film's premiere, *El derecho de nacer* was also being broadcast on Mexican radio and television.

Radio shows and their writers, 1944–1950

Year	Drama Title	Author
1944	*El precio de una vida*	Félix B. Caignet
1945	*La novela Palmolive*	Leandro Blanco
1946	*La novela Palmolive*	Leandro Blanco
1947	*La novela del aire*	Leandro Blanco
1948	*El derecho de nacer*	Félix B. Caignet
1949	*La novela del aire*	Félix B. Caignet
1950	*La novela guajira*	Arturo Liendo

Table 1   SOURCE: Agrupación de la Crónica Radial Impresa.

Aurora Bautista in El derecho de nacer (1966). Spanish actress Aurora Bautista starred in the 1966 film version of the Cuban radio drama *El derecho de nacer* (The Right to Be Born). DIGITAL PRESS PHOTOS/ NEWSCOM

Radio broadcasts of *El derecho de nacer* have occurred many times in the years since 1948. A telenovela version was broadcast in 1958 on Cuba's CMQTV, in Puerto Rico in 1959, and in Peru in 1962. Three were created in Brazil (1964, 1978, and 2001); one in Venezuela (1966); and three in Mexico (1966, 1981, and 2001). In 1988, forty years after its release, it was re-recorded in Cuba by director Oscar Luis López, with strict adherence to the original scripts, not only as a tribute to the author and to the anniversary, but also as a historic preservation of an invaluable work of radio drama. In a survey conducted by the Associated Press in 2008 among Mexican television experts, *El derecho de nacer* was chosen as the best (out of ten) Latin American soap operas of all time.

The original radio soap opera *El derecho de nacer* has been criticized for its melodrama, the script's poor literary quality, and pretentiousness. But the radio novela must be understood in its historical context, and though Caignet was not a writer of subtlety, he was imaginative and persuasive. It is worth noting that the *novelón* (protracted serial) *El collar de lágrimas* (The Necklace of Tears), by José Sánchez Arcilla, had a three-year run of 965 episodes that started before, continued alongside, and extended after *El derecho de nacer*. Its title became an expression of popular mockery for several generations.

In Cuba after 1959, radio soap opera writers were expected to imbue the genre's traditional format, whether in original scripts or adaptations of world literature, with content that contributed to cultural development. *Tu novela de amor* (Your Soap Opera of Love), which first aired in 1979, was extremely popular, as were *La novela de las dos* (The Two O'clock Soap Opera) and *La novela cubana* (The Cuban Soap Opera). Successful writers in the genre include Eliseo Iglesias Novoa, Manuel Ángel Daranas, Marcia Castellanos Parra, and Joaquín Cuartas, who was recognized as the most important dramatic author. His soap opera *Cuando la vida vuelve* (When Life Returns, 1996), a work of homage to Caignet, achieved the highest ratings in Cuba, comparable only to *El derecho de nacer*.

BIBLIOGRAPHY

López, Oscar Luis. *La radio en Cuba*. Havana: Editorial Letras Cubanas, 1981.

RAFTER CRISIS: 1994

Antonio Aja Díaz

A mass sea exodus by Cubans seeking entry into the United States that led to U.S.-Cuba migration agreements.

The rafter crisis of August 1994, an exodus of nearly thirty-seven thousand Cubans by sea seeking entry into the United States, was a significant episode in the history of relations between the Cuba and the United States. The term *balseros* (rafters) has long been used to refer people who, without government authorization, attempt

CHRONOLOGY OF EVENTS

1980: Mariel Boatlift brings an estimated 125,000 Cuban refugees to Florida.

1989: Berlin Wall falls, marking the end of the Cold War.

1991: Soviet Union ends its subsidies to Cuba and withdraws its troops; the Soviet Union collapses.

1993: Cuba legalizes possession of U.S. dollars and eases travel restrictions on exile visits to Cuba.

1994: July: U.S. Coast Guard rescues thirty-one survivors from the *13 de Marzo*, which sank off Havana with the loss of thirty-five lives.

1994: August: Castro proclaims open emigration policy, provoking another boat lift; the Coast Guard picks up 32,000 Cubans at sea and takes them to Guantánamo Bay.

1994: September: U.S. and Cuba agree to allow a minimum of 20,000 visas to Cubans annually.

1995: May: U.S. and Cuba reach a new emigration agreement.

1996: U.S. Congress passes Cuban Adjustment Act, creating special immigration procedures that allow Cubans to become permanent residents after one year, and Helms-Burton Act, hardening economic embargo of Cuba.

to leave Cuba by sea in a homemade raft or small boat. During the Cuban economic crisis of 1990 to 1994, a result of the disintegration of the Soviet Union, Cuba's main sponsor, and disappearance of the East European socialist bloc, an increasing number of Cubans sought emigration as a solution to economic difficulties. During the second half of 1993, the Cuban government took measures to mitigate the social effects of the economic crisis, including the legalization of holding U.S. dollars and allowing increased trips to Cuba for Cubans who had left the country legally. Until August 1994 those leaving by sea had to elude Cuban patrols or if intercepted face criminal charges of *salida ilegal del país* (illegal departure from the country), which carried prison sentences and fines. Faced with growing unrest, in August the government temporarily ceased to enforce the law against departure, and the number of rafters swelled.

In the late 1980s and especially at the beginning of the 1990s, Cuban public opinion on emigration grew more favorable. The decision to emigrate was made with greater ease, encouraged by communication with those who had already emigrated. Cubans no longer took a negative view of income in addition to one's basic salary, and thus the privilege of being in a position to receive foreign currency remittances represented one way to make ends meet. As Antonio Aja noted in 2009, between 1985 and 1994, the number of Cubans involved in illegal departures, including those who arrived in the United States and those whose attempts were thwarted, was 82,500, out of which over 60,000 cases took place between 1991 and 1994.

Cubans who attempt raft voyages fall into three categories: those who leave in fragile craft with little planning or knowledge of the sea; those who have made preparations to maximize their chances of survival despite having inadequate craft; and those who hire smugglers with fast boats, greatly increasing the cost but also offering the greatest chance of survival. During the period from 1991 through July 1994, according to Holly Ackerman and Juan Clark (1995), 30 to 40 percent fell in the first category, 50 to 60 percent in the second, and 3 to 5 percent in the third. Cubans who

attempt the crossing, particularly those in makeshift craft, encounter serious physical danger. Many of the rafts lack adequate steering mechanisms, and strong currents can set them adrift for days. A prolonged journey on the open sea exposes rafters to the risk of dehydration, starvation, sunburn by day and hypothermia by night, and shark attacks. Rough seas easily swamp rafts or wash rafters overboard. As told in firsthand accounts, the strain of the experience can induce significant mental distress that sometimes results in trauma that continues even after rescue. (Resources that include firsthand accounts of rafters' experiences are gathered in *The Cuban Rafter Phenomenon: A Selected Bibliography*, at the Web site of the Duke University Libraries.)

CRISIS AND RESOLUTION

In the new wave of emigration that took place from January to September 1994, some 36,900 people left, with numbers peaking in August. These emigrants, representing a continuation of the Cuban emigration pattern since the Mariel Boatlift, a mass exodus that occurred in 1980, were mostly young white males with high school or college educations. The pressure exerted by the phenomenon of illegal departures, including the hijacking of three large government boats, triggered social unrest. When the Cuban government responded by ceasing to enforce laws against departures, the United States was faced with receiving thousands of illegal Cuban immigrants.

At the same time that demand for emigration was growing, immigration pathways to the United States became more restricted and more complicated. U.S. authorities in south Florida continued to admit Cuban rafters while maintaining their policy of restricting visas that would allow Cubans to immigrate legally. Undocumented Cubans who arrived by sea would be admitted, even those who committed crimes in order to leave Cuba, including theft of ships, kidnapping, and even murder. Although most rafters left in small rowboats or homemade vessels, there were increasing incidents of aircraft and ship theft starting in 1991 until early August 1994. On 5 August, the

***Balseros*, August 1994.** *Balseros* leave Cojimar, a fishing village near Havana, on makeshift rafts in the hope of reaching Florida. © J.B. RUSSELL/SYGMA/ CORBIS

Cuban government announced that the government would not interfere with illegal departures by sea to the United States if the United States did not take any measures to deter those who committed crimes to facilitate their departures. On 8 August a new kidnapping and murder took place as part of an attempt to depart for the United States; this event caused Cuba to announce that it would not continue respecting U.S. borders while the U.S. government incited the violation of those same borders.

In view of these events, the United States changed its enforcement of Cuban immigration policy completely. The Clinton administration announced that the country would not admit the rafters, distancing itself from the position of the Carter administration in 1980 and marking the first time the United States had taken real steps to discourage illegal Cuban immigration. The government feared the consequences that the wave of immigrants might have on south Florida and on the country as a whole. Moreover, the ability of the Cuban government to permit a mass exodus was seen as politically intolerable and as possibly affecting Bill Clinton's chances of reelection.

The U.S. Coast Guard intercepted the rafters and placed them at the U.S. Naval Base at Guantánamo Bay. By preventing the rafters from reaching U.S. territory they were precluded from having access to the terms of the Cuban Adjustment Act of 1966. That federal law allows Cubans—including those arriving outside of recognized ports of entry—who have been inspected and admitted or paroled into the United States after 1 January 1959 and have been physically present for at least one year; and are otherwise admissible to the United States to apply for permanent residence regardless of caps on immigration. The approximately thirty thousand Cubans at Guantánamo Bay as well as other U.S. military bases in Panama were clustered in inadequate conditions without a defined immigration status. As Ackerman and Clark note, official sources from the United States and Cuba estimate very few casualties during the period of U.S. Coast Guard interception, whereas death rates during the previous period are estimated at 25 percent or more.

In September 1994 the United States and Cuba held negotiations in New York on open migration, and on 9 September they signed a new immigration agreement that put an end to the crisis. The Cuba-U.S. Migration Accord refers primarily to the control of illegal immigration from Cuba to the United States by sea. The United States agreed to return all Cubans trying to enter the country who were intercepted at sea, and Cuba agreed to readmit them and to take no punitive actions against them. A supplemental agreement announced on 2 May 1995 in Washington and Havana allowed the Cubans being held at Guantánamo to enter the United States. The U.S.-Cuba Migration Accords of 1994 and 1995 established legal and orderly emigration, awarding a minimum of twenty thousand visas to Cuban immigrants.

Compliance with the 1994 accords established a legal, orderly, and regular flow of immigrants, and illegal departures became partially controlled while the Cuban Adjustment Act remained in force. Cubans who met no other immigration criteria were given the opportunity to apply for an immigration visa by registering for a lottery. Family and household members of those who had already been granted visas as immigrants had an increased likelihood of gaining visas themselves for the purposes of family reunification.

SINCE 1994

The implementation of the accords largely stopped the mass exodus. But although no further migratory explosions from Cuba to the United States occurred between 1994 and 2010, the accords did not stop departures completely. Departure and arrival locations changed to prevent capture, and after 1995 smugglers were used with much greater frequency. The *Ruta del Sur* (southern route), established in the late 1990s and early twenty-first century, involves smuggling humans in fast boats to Mexico or Honduras and then overland to the U.S.-Mexico border. Almost all Cuban emigrants who manage to reach U.S. soil by eluding the Coast Guard are admitted to the United States and then can become permanent residents one year later under the Cuban Adjustment Act. The Cuban-American community has used its organized political power to support the

continued admission of Cuban immigrants into the United States.

Furthermore, a flow of legal immigrants to the United States began to be established, the social and demographic composition of which could be selectively guided by the United States to target sectors key to Cuba's future, such as young people and professionals. Many in Cuba viewed the U.S. government's selective admission regarding Cuban immigrants as a policy of hostility toward the Cuban revolutionary government. Enforcement of the Cuban Adjustment Act acquired new nuance after 1995, because the Migration Accords limited the actions the United States could take in regard to individuals captured at sea. In 2003 the George W. Bush administration suspended talks on immigration under political pressure from the vocal anti-Castro, conservative Cuban-American faction based in Miami, but under President Barack Obama the dialogue resumed in 2009; by early 2011, four meetings had been held.

BIBLIOGRAPHY

Ackerman, Holly, and Juan M. Clark. *The Cuban Balseros: Voyage of Uncertainty.* Miami: Policy Center of the Cuban American National Council, 1995.

Ackerman, Holly, Damian Fernández, and María Domínguez, guest eds. Special Section: *The Cuban Balsero Crisis Ten Years Later. Latino Studies* 3, no. 3 (November 2005): 372–428. Available from http://www.palgrave-journals.com/lst/journal/v3/n3/index.html#ar.

Aja, Antonio. "Agosto del '94 y el proceso migratorio cubano." *Areito* (Miami) 5 (1995).

Aja, Antonio. "La emigración ilegal desde Cuba hacia los Estados Unidos y sus motivaciones." *Cuadernos de Nuestra América* (Havana) (January–June 1996).

Aja, Antonio. "Cuban Emigration in the 1990s." *Cuban Studies* 30 (2000):1–25.

Aja, Antonio. *Al Cruzar las Fronteras.* Havana: CEDEM, 2009.

Boswell, Thomas D. *A Demographic Profile of Cuban Americans.* Miami: Cuban American National Council, 1994.

The Cuban Rafter Phenomenon: A Selected Bibliography. Compiled by Holly Ackerman. Duke University Libraries. Latin American and Caribbean Studies. Available from http://library.duke.edu/research/subject/guides/lastudies/bibliographies/cuban_rafter_phenomenon.html.

The Cuban Rafter Phenomenon: A Unique Sea Exodus. Electronic resource. Coral Gables, FL: University of Miami Digital Library Program, 2004. Available from http://balseros.miami.edu/.

Greenhill, Kelly M. *Weapons of Mass Migration: Forced Displacement, Coercion, and Foreign Policy.* Ithaca, NY: Cornell University Press, 2010.

Hernández, Rafael. "Cuba y los cubano-americanos: El impacto del conflicto EE.UU.-Cuba en sus relaciones presentes y futuras." *Cuadernos de Nuestra América* (Havana) 12, no. 23 (1995): 4–47.

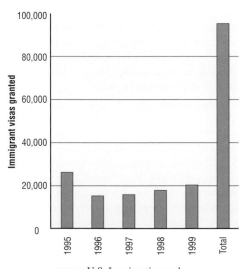

Immigrant visas granted between 1995–1999 by the United States in compliance with the Migration Accords of 1994

SOURCE: U.S. Immigration and Naturalization Service, *Statistical Yearbook of the Immigration and Naturalization Service, 1998.* Washington, D.C.: U.S. Government Printing Office, 2000. Available from http://www.dhs.gov/xlibrary/assets/statistics/yearbook/1998/1998yb.pdf

Figure 1

Martín, Consuelo. "Perspectivas teórica psicosocial para el estudio de la familia cubana emigrada." *Anuario*, CEAP. University of Havana, 1995.

Martínez, Milagros, Antonio Aja Diaz, Blanca Morejón, et al. *Los balseros cubanos: Un estudio a partir de las salidas ilegales*. Havana: Editorial de Ciencias Sociales, 1996.

Pedraza, Silvia, and Rubén G. Rumbaut. *Origins and Destinies: Immigration, Race, and Ethnicity in America*. Belmont, CA: Wadsworth, 1996.

EL RAPTO DE LAS MULATAS AND THE ARTISTIC DEVELOPMENT OF CARLOS ENRÍQUEZ

Carlos M. Luis

Carlos Enríquez's development as an expressionist painter and his El rapto de las mulatas.

The career of Carlos Enríquez (1900–1957) was marked by controversy due to the artist's anarchic personality and the eroticism of many of his paintings and drawings. He was born the son of a respected doctor, who sent him to school in the United States to study engineering. Enríquez instead decided to attend the Pennsylvania Academy of Fine Arts, where he met painter Alice Neel (1900–1984), in 1924. The two married the following year and moved to Havana; the couple separated in 1930.

While in Havana, Enríquez began to paint his first portraits, which came to represent an important part of his artistic oeuvre. By that time he had adopted an expressionistic style with strong sexual overtones that earned him a reputation as a pornographer. An exhibition of eight of his oil paintings in the Exposición de Arte Nuevo (1927) was condemned as "exaggerated realism" and removed from the show. In 1930, another exhibition of his drawings was censored for the same reason and had to be transferred to the office of his friend, the historian Emilio Roig de Leuchsenring. Between 1930 and 1933, during a stay in Europe, Enríquez became interested in surrealism, and he may have met the French-Cuban dada and surrealist painter Francis Picabia (1879–1953). Picabia, like Enríquez, was an *enfant terrible*, and his use of superimposed images in renditions of the female figure was a technique adopted by Enríquez. In 1934, an exhibition at the Lyceum Havana of Enríquez's paintings, which he had produced in Madrid the previous year, was closed on opening night.

In the early 1930s, Enríquez became interested in Cuban myths and legends, taking his work in a new direction, which he outlined in a magazine article, "El criollismo y su interpretación plástica" (The Pictorial Interpretation of the *Criollo* Style, 1935). By then he had finished one of his most important works, *El rey de los campos de Cuba* (The King of the Cuban Fields, 1934), dedicated to Manuel García, the so-called Cuban Robin Hood. In 1936, Enríquez coined the term *romancero criollo* (*criollo* romance) to describe his art.

In 1938, *El rapto de las mulatas* (The Kidnapping of the Mulatto Women) received an award at the second National Exhibition of Painting and Sculpture. A year later, Enríquez published the first in his novel trilogy, *Tilín García*, which depicts in realistic terms the violent and erotic lives of Cuban peasants. (His second and third novels, *La vuelta de Chencho* and *La feria de Guaicanama*, were written in 1942 but not published until 1960.) In 1939, he moved to his small house in the outskirts of Havana, which he called *El hurón azul*; it became a mythic place of the Cuban artistic life.

At the end of 1943, Enríquez traveled to Mexico, where he met the painters Diego Rivera (1886–1957), who opened his exhibition at the Palacio de Bellas Artes, and José Clemente Orozco (1883–1949), with whom he practiced mural painting. On his return to Cuba, Enríquez gave a lecture on surrealism at El Frente Nacional Antifascista at the opening of an exhibition of drawings by his friend the painter Marcelo Pogolotti (1902–1988). The next year he traveled to Haiti, where he studied the island's folklore and incorporated it into his drawings. In 1947, he designed the scenery for the ballet *Antes del alba*, by Hilario González, and illustrated *El son entero*, a collection of poems by Nicolás Guillén (1902–1989). By that time Enríquez's heavy drinking was taking a toll on his health: His work after 1950 was not as successful as what he produced in the 1930s and 1940s. He died in 1957 at his beloved *El hurón azul* on the day before the opening of an exhibition of his work at the Lex gallery in Havana.

THE MASTERPIECE *EL RAPTO DE LAS MULATAS*

Enríquez's *El rapto de las mulatas* (1930) is unquestionably one of the great paintings of his generation, showing the artist at the peak of his powers. Enríquez's technique and figures convey the artist's knowledge of the Renaissance masters, for example, the eroticism of Peter Paul Rubens and the expressionism of the Spanish Renaissance painter El Greco, along with the general Renaissance interest in depicting the dramatic moment. But in technique Enríquez's approach borrows mostly from the late-nineteenth-century expressionists' work, for example, Edvard Munch's *The Scream* (1893). From

■ *See also*

Sexuality: The Mulata Figure in the Cuban Imaginary

Visual Arts: Republican Period

the early stages of his career, Enríquez was inclined to find a language of his own, distancing himself from the dictates of academic painting. In *El rapto de las mulatas*, Enríquez focuses on the male subjugation of the female figure, arranging the figures in such a way as to fuse male dominance and female vulnerability. *El rapto de las mulatas* illustrates Enríquez's expressionistic technique, which places the action in the scene second to the artist's treatment of it.

His bold use of colors communicates the effect of a voluptuous personality attempting to play an active part inside his paintings. A close look at *El rapto* reveals the ecstasy of the woman being abducted, in contrast with the ferocity of her kidnappers. The painting is unified by the superb rendition of the contrasting attitudes of the three characters into a single scene full of dramatic suggestion. Similarly, in his novel *Tilín García* Enríquez demanded that the reader confront the crude reality of the peasant's life. In both cases, the active participation of the viewer and the reader emphasize Enríquez's skill in rendering of human passions.

After several decades, Enríquez's uninhibited expression still maintains its initial impact. Many of his drawings that portray lesbian scenes or nudes belong to a long tradition of erotic art. His unpublished illustrations of the poems of Pietro Arentino (1492–1556), based on Giulio Romano's original drawings in the private collection of Jorge Fernández de Castro and his wife Marta, are a testament to his stormy imagination. His use of color anticipated the styles of the 1950s and 1960s in many ways. His willingness to so directly express human lubricity and violence makes him a unique figure in the Cuban art world.

BIBLIOGRAPHY

Colectivo de Autores. *El Hurón azul: Un hurón diferente.* Havana: Directorio Estudiantil Universitario, 1986.

Guillén, Nicolás. *El son entero.* Buenos Aires: Editorial Pleamar, 1947.

Luis, Carlos M. *Carlos Enríquez: Themes and Variations.* Miami, FL: Museo Cubano de Arte Cultura, 1986.

Luis, Carlos M. "Violencia y sexualidad en la obra de Carlos Enríquez." In *El Oficio de la Mirada: Ensayos de Arte y Literatura Cubana.* Miami, FL: Ediciones Universal, 1998.

Martínez, Juan. *Carlos Enríquez: The Painter of Cuban Ballads.* Miami, FL: Cernuda, 2010.

Pogolotti, Graziella. *Carlos Enríquez: Exposición Retrospectiva, 1900–1957.* Havana: Museo Nacional, 1979.

Sánchez, Juan. *Carlos Enríquez.* Havana: Editorial Letras Cubanas, 1996.

Valls, Jorge. *Carlos Enríquez: Algo que decir.* Miami, FL: Alfredo Martínez Gallery, 1997.

THE RATION SYSTEM IN CUBA

Mirta Muñiz Egea

Rationing as an integral element of Cuban social and economic policy and its effects on the nation and its people.

Rationing is a controlled distribution system that wartime economies adopt as a survival strategy. In Cuba rationing is accomplished through the *libreta de abastecimiento* (ration booklet). The *libreta*, as it is generally called, is to be understood as the government's intention to guarantee an equitable minimum level of consumption; this level includes a basic basket of staple goods, consisting of items that are generally subsidized or whose sale is regulated and priced so as to be accessible for persons on an average salary. After fifty years of existence of the *libreta,* the Cuban government proposed to eliminate it. In a speech on 16 April 2011, Raúl Castro stated that the government would move from subsidizing products in general to aiding people who are unable to sustain themselves.

STRUCTURE AND JUSTIFICATION OF RATIONING

Every household in Cuba is provided with a *libreta*, which contains information on the number of family members, as well as their differentiating indicators, such as age, pregnancy, or illness (diabetes, AIDS, cancer, and others duly attested to with a medical certificate). Purchases take place along a circuit of neighborhood distribution points, such as grocery stores, dairy stores, butcher shops, food stalls, and produce stands. Within the government, the Ministry of Internal Commerce (MINCIN) is directly responsible for the *libreta*. Rationing is a complex system that says much about the quality of a country's agriculture or its potential for importing food, the system of international relations within which a small country aims to generate a development plan, the public health system, social cohesion, institutional responses to crises, and generally speaking, issues as basic as whether or not social policies safeguard citizens.

Along with rationing in Cuba, it is also possible to freely purchase food on parallel markets or at hard-currency stores (although at noticeably higher prices), at the networks of cafeterias or restaurants (state-owned or private), and other sales points in Cuba. Furthermore, lunch is offered at a very low cost at workplaces, schools, and neighborhoods, and for low-income elderly people as part of the Family Food System. In recent years, however, the types of food aid offered at worker cafeterias have been decreasing and are disappearing.

■ *See also*

Cuban Embargo

Cuban Thought and Cultural Identity: Socialist Thought

Economy: Revolutionary Period

Economy: Special Period

Food: Food Shortages and Gender

Governance and Contestation: The Cuban Revolution

Opposite page:
El rapto de las mulatas by Carlos Enríquez (1900–1957). *El rapto de las mulatas* (The Kidnapping of the Mulatto Women), one of Carlos Enríquez's most famous works, exhibits a unique blending of sexuality and violence. The painting won an award at the second National Exhibition of Painting and Sculpture in 1938. COLECCIÓN MUSEO NACIONAL DE BELLAS ARTES, LA HABANA, CUBA

Empty shelves. The dairy section of this grocery store in Havana, photographed in 2009, offered a minimal selection of milk and butter, and little else. STEVEN L. RAYNER/NATIONAL GEOGRAPHIC/GETTY IMAGES

REASONS BEHIND RATIONING

The first controls over supplies appeared in March 1962. The system has endured into the early 2000s and is possibly the longest-lasting of its kind in history. Two main factors are considered to have led to its adoption. The first is the hostility of the U.S. government to the Revolution in 1959 and subsequent attempts to undermine the Cuban economy:

- burning the sugarcane fields;
- sabotaging manufacturing centers;
- eliminating the sugar quota;
- suspending oil supplies;
- refusing to refine oil from the Soviet Union, and
- the Bay of Pigs invasion in April 1961.

To this list must be added the breaking of diplomatic ties between Cuba and virtually every other government in Latin America, and Cuba's expulsion from the Organization of American States (OAS) in January 1962. This measure, adopted under pressure by the United States, deprived Cuba of all nearby markets, with the exception of Mexico and Canada, which did not support the policy. Since then Cuba was forced to use costly Cuban ships or to pay high shipping fees to cover the return of empty transports from non-U.S. ports (USDA 1998). Some researchers refer to this as a virtual tax, and they estimate that it increased the cost of importation of goods up to 30 percent (Kirkpatrick; Garfield).

The second factor is the increase in the purchasing power of the population due to the social justice measures implemented under the Revolution. These measures include land reform (1959); cuts in rents and an urban reform law (1960), which transferred ownership of housing to the occupants; price freezes on staple items in the basic basket; free education and health care services; and a massive literacy campaign in 1961, which led to greater access to skilled jobs. Insofar as they did not lead to an increase in the supply of goods, these measures made it necessary to take steps to prevent hoarding and speculation.

ECONOMIC FRAMEWORK OF RATIONING

Beginning in the late nineteenth century, the United States was Cuba's main trading partner, accounting for over 80 percent of Cuban exports and imports. By the late 1950s, according to the U.S. Department of Agriculture's (USDA) *Cuba's Food and Agriculture Situation Report*, "U.S. interests owned a significant portion of Cuban resources: 25 percent of Cuba's land (75 percent of arable land), 50 percent of the sugar and rum industries, and 90 percent of the transportation and electrical services, plus significant cattle, banking, oil, tobacco, and mining interests" (USDA 2008, p. 7). The United States provided over 70 percent of imports and over 60 percent of exports to that market. The sugar industry was Cuba's main source of revenue (nearly 80 percent of total exports and 40 percent of national income); it can thus be stated that U.S. capital controlled the Cuban economy. The cutbacks in the yearly sugar quota negotiated with the United States, followed by the quota's total cancellation in March 1961, delivered a tough economic blow against the fledgling revolutionary government. Just months before, in January 1961, the United States broke off diplomatic ties with Cuba. When the U.S. Congress approved the Foreign Assistance Act on 4 September 1961, it established the principle that no aid should be provided to the current government of Cuba, and it authorized the president to implement a partial or full embargo on trade between the two countries. A total economic embargo was imposed by presidential decree on 7 February 1962. (What is known in the United States as an embargo is viewed by Cubans as a *bloqueo,* or blockade.) In March 1962 Cuba launched its rationing system, which remains in effect as of 2011.

The first rationing measure followed the U.S. suspension of lard shipments in June 1961. At the time Cuba had one of the world's highest per capita levels of consumption of this product. The Soviet Union offered to send 10,000 tons of fats, and in July Cuba implemented rationing. Shoes were the first manufactured article to be rationed: Children's shoes were recorded in the school booklet and adult shoes in the food products booklet.

THE PARALLEL MARKET

Between 1971 and 1989 the so-called flexible sale system was introduced, which meant the implementation of a system of coupons for optional rationing of manufactured goods. For instance, a coupon might be valid for a dress, but it could also be used for a bolt of cloth; thus consumers could choose between the two. The twofold purpose behind this arrangement was to encourage manufacturing output by developing national industry and small local manufacturers and to allow new and additional consumption at prices that were differentiated from those of the rationing system. Thus two rationing systems existed: one for manufactured goods and another for food.

Boxed cigarettes were the first product to be placed on the parallel market. To this end, the right to obtain cigarettes at the regulated price (20 and 25 centavos) was frozen for citizens who were sixteen years or older in 1971, and cigarettes began to be sold without any restrictions whatever at prices that ranged from 1.60 to 2.40 pesos per pack. The objective was to avoid taking on new rationing commitments while helping capture the cash circulating in the economy. In March 1968, during what was called the Revolutionary Offensive, the government passed Ley 1076, which nationalized all private businesses (more than 58,000 throughout the country). From that date forward, 100 percent of business activity was managed by the state. This measure, which was implemented even though the state lacked the organizational capacity to efficiently take on the management of all business, led to serious market distortions. In order to achieve some kind of equilibrium, the government eventually found

it necessary to enact various alternatives, such as the so-called San Germán Plan, which used coupons to divide the population into purchasing groups so as to manage access to goods in a structured fashion. Sales systems were also implemented to satisfy particular requirements, such as clothing and footwear for workers, infant clothing, and hotel and diplomatic supplies.

In 1970 Cuba's full capacities and energy were directed toward the Ten Million Ton Sugar Harvest, an officially declared goal. The basic revenue of the state was geared toward defense and investment, and imports of consumer goods were practically eliminated. Even though this was the largest harvest in Cuban history (8.5 million tons), the harvest fell short of the goal, and the equivalent of one year of wages was left circulating in the economy, without any possibility of increasing the supply of available products. Rationing had no response to this situation. A swine flu epidemic in 1971 prompted the slaughter of five hundred thousand hogs in barely a month, throwing the economy and consumption further out of equilibrium just when the negative impact of the previous year's harvest was at its worst (Silveira and Pérez). According to William Blum in his 1995 book *Killing Hope: U.S. Military and CIA Interventions since World War II,* one of the individuals involved claimed that strains of the swine flu virus had been introduced to the island in a covert CIA operation.

IMPACT OF THE END OF THE SOCIALIST BLOC

Cuba's economy had become interwoven with those of other socialist countries, particularly the Soviet Union. The nature of trade and cooperative relationships with these countries made the first half of the 1980s the best years of the Cuban ration booklet. Output increased, there were stable deliveries, and wages translated into increasing benefits on the free markets, making the ration booklet increasingly unnecessary. Nevertheless, between 1987 and 1989 U.S. trade laws ratcheted up the pressure of the *bloqueo* against Cuba. In 1989 the crisis of socialism intensified in the Eastern Bloc. When the Soviet Union collapsed in 1991, the last pillar of external support for development of the Cuban system vanished along with it.

The beginning of the complex process of transformation in the Soviet Union and the ultimate implosion of the Soviet system had a far-reaching impact on Cuba: on import and exports markets (over 80 percent of the total for each), and on financial and economic assistance, and fuel supplies (nearly 100 percent of Cuba's oil came from the Soviet Union). This change sank the entire Cuban economy into depression, led to the demise of the parallel markets, and left the ration booklet as the only means of survival. Through the Torricelli Act in 1992, the United States reinforced the embargo and furthered the isolation of Cuba.

Cuba launched an economic reform process in 1994, which began with the free circulation of hard currencies, the development of an internal foreign exchange market, and the establishment of an export promotion program. In September 1995 the government approved a new law addressing foreign investment. The U.S. *bloqueo* was ratcheted up yet again through the Helms-Burton Act of 1996, which actually amplified its extraterritorial scope and meant that even the president of the United States could not modify it (only suspend its implementation for periods of six months). One of the consequences of the Helms-Burton Act was to ward off potential partners and steady investment, which has had an underdeveloping effect on Cuba.

OTHER CONSIDERATIONS

The *libreta*, and its persistence, is one of the issues most widely debated by critics of the Cuban Revolution, who see it as epitomizing the incapacity of the socialist system to feed the country's population. Such critiques tend to disregard the causes that led to the ration booklet and instead focus on the booklet itself, viewing it as the only recourse for the Cuban citizen to put food on the table. But Cuban rationing occurred within an immediate context in which many people became the owners of their own homes (due to the 1961 Urban Reform Law), while rents remained low for those tenants who actually paid rent, and there were no evictions. Furthermore, the education and public health systems are free (and geared toward reducing infant mortality, protecting vulnerable groups, and raising the population's standard of living). To isolate rationing from this context is to lose sight of the complexity of the scenario from which Cuba—as an underdeveloped, single-crop, single-export country—has attempted to retool its economy and gear it toward a development model that is not subordinate to the influence of the United States.

The enduring presence of the *libreta* must be understood in the context of several factors:

1. the refusal of First World countries (and economies) and many international development financing organizations to engage in trade with Cuba or extend credit;
2. the aging of the technological infrastructure inherited from the prerevolutionary period, and the impossibility of repairing or renewing it after 1959;
3. the technological incompatibility between these inherited technologies and that came later from the Eastern Bloc;
4. the aging of the technological infrastructure that originated in the Eastern Bloc and the impossibility of repairing or renewing it after 1989, which means that on three different occasions in less than fifty years Cuba was forced to undertake massive industrial and technological investments;
5. the terms of trade, from 1989 to the present, for raw materials, finished products (including food), and technology, which generally speaking have been at higher-than-market prices, without loans on favorable terms, and from distant places (which increases transportation costs).

To have engaged in all these efforts without plunging society into chaos is, the opinion of the critics notwithstanding, an achievement that was built precisely on the ration booklet. Nevertheless, if the *libreta* is considered from this perspective a symbol of resistance and social cohesion, it is also a manifestation of the errors and shortcomings of the solutions chosen, particularly the concentration of land under state ownership and of production in large-scale state enterprises (farms whose losses are covered by the state, given its promise to maintain full employment and equity at all costs).

The key points of criticism of this model are:

1. it provided few incentives for producers
2. it failed to increase productivity;
3. it led to a decline in the quality of products;
4. it served to excuse wastefulness and the deviation of resources;
5. it led to continuous losses due to transportation and storage problems;
6. it spawned a huge bureaucratic apparatus;
7. it limited the independence of producers and local management;
8. it encouraged arbitrary decision making; and
9. it led to a disconnection between agricultural production and end-consumption.

TWENTY-FIRST-CENTURY DEVELOPMENTS

Cuba is at a critical juncture in terms of managing a series of measures to increase its food output and, accordingly, to move toward the extinction of the ration booklet. President Raúl Castro has insisted that doing so will be possible only to the extent that national agricultural production increases. Despite economic troubles (aggravated in 2008 by damage from three hurricanes, Ike, Gustav, and Paloma), the state has maintained the policy of segmenting consumption in order to protect vulnerable groups, and, as noted by Raúl Pérez (2009), has implemented quite a number of health programs in order to improve or eliminate nutritional problems, in particular those related to anemia due to iron deficiencies.

Results of a 2001 survey on habits in food consumption indicated that daily calorie consumption, which between 1992 and 1993 had fallen abruptly to 1,863 (the USDA recommends 2,100 to 2,300), had risen to an average of 2,480. Nevertheless, Conner Gorry reported in 2009 that these calories were coming disproportionately from sugar and carbohydrates,

with a deficiency in protein, whole grains, fruits, and vegetables. As a result Cuba is manufacturing vitamin-enriched food products, many of which are incorporated into school meals. Other such products are among those mandated by regulations and distributed through the ration booklet or available in foods that can be freely purchased. The report "Hunger and Malnutrition in the Countries of the Association of Caribbean States (ACS)" (2005) states that "Cuba and Belize show a low level of LBW [low birth weight] (6 percent), which is lower than the average observed in the most industrialized nations" (CEPAL p. 11). Likewise, José Juan Ortiz, a UNICEF official, has noted that Cuba is the only country in Latin America that does not have severe malnutrition (Ravsberg 2010). The 2010 report of the Food and Agriculture Organization of the United Nations includes Cuba on its list of countries with low malnutrition rates for preschoolers, at under 5 percent, with minimal differences between regions, and on a par with developed countries.

Even though in the early 1990s Cuba's indicators were pointing in the direction of chaos and famine, by 2011 the biggest problem was that Cubans must dedicate a high percentage of their income to food. Some sources place the figure as high as 60 percent. In fact, where excessive weight loss had been one of the most serious health problems for the population, since the late 1990s the main risk has been that of obesity and its related illnesses.

BIBLIOGRAPHY

Álvarez, José. *Overview of Cuba's Food Rationing System.* EDIS document FE482, a publication of the Department of Food and Resource Economics, Florida Cooperative Extension Service, UF/IFAS, University of Florida, Gainesville. July 2004. Available from http://edis.ifas.ufl.edu/fe482.

American Association for World Health (AAWH). *Denial of Food and Medicine: The Impact of the U.S. Embargo on Health and Nutrition in Cuba.* March 1997.

Amnesty International. *The U.S. Embargo against Cuba: Its Impact on Economic and Social Rights.* London: Author, 2009.

Blum, William. *Killing Hope: U.S. Military and CIA Interventions since World War II.* Monroe, ME: Common Courage Press, 1995.

Bradlee, Benjamin C. *Conversations with Kennedy.* New York: Pocket Books, 1976.

Castro Ruz, Fidel. *Ideología, conciencia y trabajo político, 1959–1986.* Havana: Editora Política, 1986.

CEPAL, Social Development Division. "Hunger and Malnutrition in the Countries of the Association of Caribbean States (ACS)." Coordinated by Rodrigo Martínez. Santiago, Chile. September 2005. Available from http://www.eclac.org/publicaciones/xml/1/26901/sps11_LCL2374_eng.pdf.

Food and Agriculture Organization, United Nations. *Country Profiles: Cuba.* 2010. Available from http://ftp.fao.org/es/esn/nutrition/ncp/cubmap.pdf.

Cuban ration booklet. The Revolution brought Cubans education, health care, housing, and food, which the state made available through a ration system that included subsidies, price controls, and distribution programs at workplaces and schools. © HOLLY ACKERMAN, PH.D.

Franklin, Jane. *Cuba and the United States: A Chronological History*. Melbourne, Australia: Ocean Press, 1997.

Garfield, Richard. *The Impact of Economic Sanctions on Health and Wellbeing*. Relief and Rehabilitation Network paper 31. London: Overseas Development Institute, 1999.

Gorry, Conner. "Cubans Team Up for Better Nutrition." *MEDICC Review* 11, no. 4 (Fall 2009): 20–22.

Hernández, Rafael. *Looking at Cuba: Essays on Culture and Civil Society*. Translated by Dick Cluster. Gainesville: University Press of Florida, 2003.

Kirkpatrick, Anthony F. "Role of the USA in Shortage of Food and Medicine in Cuba." *Lancet* 348 (1996): 1489–1491. Available from http://www.cubasolidarity. net/Kirkpatrick-lancet.pdf.

Miranda Bravo, Olga. *Cuba/USA: Nacionalizaciones y bloqueo*. Havana: Editorial de Ciencias Sociales, 1996.

Muñiz, Mirta, and Arnaldo Vega. *El pan cierto de cada día: Consideraciones sobre el racionamiento*. Havana: Pablo de la Torriente Editorial, and Buenos Aires: Nuestra América, 2003.

Murray, Mary. *Cruel and Unusual Punishment: The U.S. Blockade against Cuba*. Melbourne, Australia: Ocean Press, 1993.

Pérez, Louis A., Jr. *Cuba: Between Reform and Revolution*. 4th ed. New York: Oxford University Press, 2011.

Pérez, Raúl. "The Public Health Sector and Nutrition in Cuba." *MEDICC Review* 11, no 4 (Fall 2009): 6–8.

Premat, Adriana. "Small-Scale Urban Agriculture in Havana and the Reproduction of the 'New Man' in Contemporary Cuba." *Revista Europea de Estudios Latinoamericanos y del Caribe* 75 (October 2003): 88–99. Available from http://www.cedla.uva.nl/50_publications/ pdf/revista/75RevistaEuropea/75Premat.pdf.

Ravsberg, Fernando. "UNICEF: Cuba, sin desnutrición infantile." Interview with José Juan Ortiz, UNICEF representative in Havana. BBC Mundo (26 January 2010). Available from http://www.bbc.co.uk/mundo/ cultura_sociedad/2010/01/100126_1823_unicef_ cuba_gz.shtml.

Rodríguez-Ojea, Arturo, Antonio Berdasco Santa Jiménez, and Mercedes Esquivel. "The Nutrition Transition in Cuba in the Nineties: An Overview." *Public Health Nutrition* 5, no. 1A (2001): 129–133.

Silveira Prado, Enrique A., and Alfredo Pérez Amores. "Historia del Agroterrorismo de Estados Unidos de América contra Cuba." *REDVET: Revista electrónica de Veterinaria* 11, no. 03B (2010). Available from http:// veterinaria.org/revistas/redvet/n030310B/0310B_ HV05.pdf.

Spadoni, Paolo. *Failed Sanctions: Why the U.S. Embargo against Cuba Could Never Work*. Gainesville: University Press of Florida, 2010.

U.S. Department of Agriculture (USDA), Economic Research Service. "Cuba's Agriculture: Collapse & Economic Reform," *Agricultural Outlook* AGO-255, October 1998. Available from http://www.ers.usda. gov/publications/agoutlook/oct1998/.

U.S. Department of Agriculture (USDA), Office of Global Analysis. *Cuba's Food and Agriculture Situation Report*. March 2008. Available from http://www.fas. usda.gov/itp/cuba/CubaSituation0308.pdf.

RAÚL CORRALES: PHOTOGRAPHER OF THE REVOLUTION

Iliana Cepero-Amador

Raúl Corrales, a leading Cuban photographer and one of the most influential photojournalists in the depiction of the first years of the Cuban Revolution.

Sardonic and sharp, straightforward and amusing, Raúl Corrales (1925–2006) was a gifted storyteller, but it was as a photographer that his brilliance shone. And though his photographic career spans nearly half a century of Cuban political and social history, it is the pictures he took during the first years of the Revolution that make Corrales one of the most important Latin American photographers of the twentieth century.

BACKGROUND AND EARLY CAREER

Corrales's origins were humble. The son of an immigrant farm worker from Galicia, Corrales spent his early years in a small town in the countryside. When his family moved to Havana, Corrales undertook several jobs, selling fruit, cleaning cutlery, and shining shoes (Sarusky p. 7). For a time, he served as a valet to the popular Mexican actor and singer Jorge Negrete during his performances in Cuba. While working as a bellboy at the elegant café-restaurant El Carmelo in the posh Vedado neighborhood in 1938 to 1939, Corrales sold American magazines such as *Look*, *Time*, and *Life*. As he became familiar with American photojournalism, two photographers stood out for him: Walker Evans and Dorothea Lange (Sarusky p. 7). He saw the way social inequalities were depicted in their pictures, as well as a sense of human dignity, and years later he strove to expose the same quality in his own subjects.

Corrales saved money and bought a small 127-millimeter Baby Black camera and with it took pictures on the streets of Havana. Because he did not have enough money to print them, he examined his negatives with a magnifying glass. In 1944, while working as a cleaner for an advertising agency (the Cuba Sono Film), Corrales was given a photo assignment because he was the only person in the office with a camera. Although he took only one picture, it was good enough to earn him a staff position. Once fully immersed in professional photography, Corrales learned the proper techniques of developing and printing negatives.

According to Corrales, the Cuba Sono Film provided him with a photographic education and strongly political subjects (interview with author, November 2005). As a propaganda agency of the Partido Socialista Popular (PSP), the Cuba Sono Film offered photographic, film, and audio services to the workers' movement and to the PSP political campaigns. Among other subjects, Corrales covered the port trade union, where he absorbed the communist ideas that determined both his future political sentiments and his photographic choices.

In the late 1940s and 1950s, Corrales worked for several newspapers, including *Noticias de Hoy* and *Última Hora* (both run by the Communist Party), and fashionable magazines such as *Bohemia* and *Carteles*. In 1957, his ascending career landed him a job as the head of photography at the prestigious publicity agency Siboney.

REVOLUCIÓN AND *INRA*

By 1959, Corrales was a well-known and respected reporter. His credentials could not have been better suited for the new government: He was a remarkable photographer, and his political leanings were undoubtedly leftist. It was a logical development that Corrales would play a significant role in the propagandistic machinery of the new regime (see Cepero pp. 232–238). However, by this time he had developed a corpus of work that represented the individual as both the conveyer of ideological tenets and the receptacle of conflicting emotions.

Since the very beginning of the Revolution, Fidel Castro had had a clear idea of the importance of propaganda as a tool in the maintenance of political power. Considering the scarcity of televisions in Cuba in the early 1960s, it fell to the press to provide the public with practical and immediate news. Castro transformed *Revolución* (an underground newspaper during the Batista regime) into the official organ of his revolutionary government, and it became a sanctioned space where Castro's regime exerted a fair amount of editorial control and through which they communicated the changes unfolding across the country.

Once *Revolución* had achieved the status of most official publication, Corrales became a staff member. The twenty-eight-page large-format paper was the true chronicle of everyday life in the Revolution, reporting daily on events throughout the island. The periodical frequently displayed full-page photographs illustrating every government decision and law. News was presented in a highly direct manner, drawing on the principles of billboard advertising to reach all segments of the population, including those who were illiterate.

By 1959, Corrales had become head of the photography department of the Instituto Nacional de Reforma Agraria (INRA; National Institute for Agrarian Reform). Castro, then prime minister, proposed to Corrales that he create a visual magazine that would provide in-depth coverage of the reform program and carry reports that would be rejected by bourgeois media outlets because of their radical political connotations. Castro had an issue of *Life* magazine near him, and he told Corrales that he wanted the magazine's format and

visual concept to be similar to *Life*. In a country such as Cuba with high levels of illiteracy among the urban and rural poor (whom Castro depended upon for support), it was crucial that the images be primary. Photography had to secure the Revolution's credibility with the people and to persuade them that Castro's new ideology was essential for the survival of the revolutionary process.

Following that principle, the magazine called *INRA* dealt mostly with economic issues—and political ones, to a lesser extent—by displaying large black-and-white or color photographs that were explained by a brief text. Corrales's managerial talent was a decisive factor in the magazine's success. In order to foster competition, photographers were not paid a fixed salary; instead, their remuneration depended on whether their work was selected for publication and on the importance attributed to an image. As in *Revolución*, *INRA*'s best picture went on the cover and the best news item appeared in the middle pages. Corrales made these choices, aided by Minister of Industry Che Guevara (1928–1967) when the subject was production and industrialization. The magazine covered the photographers' expenses when they traveled to the countryside for their reports. With this strategy, photographers could devote themselves entirely to their work, without financial constraints; these work conditions produced excellent photographs and what Castro most wanted—great receptivity.

CASTRO'S PHOTOGRAPHER

In another move of political self-promotion, Castro designated Corrales and Alberto Korda (1928–2001) his personal photographers. (Korda was the photographer of *Guerrillero heroico*, the iconic image of Che Guevara.) The two men accompanied Castro on his travels around the country and overseas, ensuring the meticulous deployment of information Castro wanted publicized. They also produced an array of rather intimate pictures of the leader, before Castro closed the window on his personal life.

Corrales stayed close to Castro for two years. In January 1960, he documented the symbolic hike made by the commander-in-chief, his entourage, and members of the Milicias Revolucionarias (Revolutionary Militias) to Minas de Frío in the Sierra Maestras (stronghold of the Castro and Guevara rebel armies during the Batista regime). In a bold maneuver of archival fiction, Corrales conceived the series of photographs as a reenactment of life in the hills during the years of the guerrilla struggle against Batista.

Corrales used a 35-millimeter camera and natural light, which allowed him to capture the spontaneity and freshness of rapidly unfolding events. This period was marked by Castro's long speeches and public mobilizations on an almost daily basis, and that political context explains the recurring subject of popular rallies in Corrales's work. Two photographs are truly memorable for their pictorial design. The first is *Sombreritos* (Little Hats), which was taken during a 1 May celebration in 1960, and depicts the masses parading in small groups. The picture resembles Tina Modotti's famous photographs, echoing the stylistic devices from the New Vision movement in the 1920s such as dynamic vantage points and a graphic quality determined by the geometry of the composition.

The second is *Primera Declaración de la Habana* (First Havana Declaration, 1960), which was so uniquely framed that it was printed on Cuba's 10 peso bill. Corrales recounted the story behind that picture several times. Castro called him to the platform to take a photograph that would encompass him and the crowd below. Assessing the difficulty of the task, Corrales had no choice but to gently ask two ministers to move from their seats so he could get the correct angle for the shot. The result became the iconic photograph of the Cuban Revolution, one that combines Castro's political authority with the unconditional devotion of his people. Corrales always boasted that many of his colleagues tried to imitate the famous take but failed because none of them had enough political weight "to get two ministers out of their chairs" (interview with author, November 2005; Sarusky p. 7).

Archetypal images such as *La Caballería* (Cavalry, 1960) helped to foster a sense of victory—a myth fashioned by the official discourse. The photograph depicts the arrival of guerrillas on the lands formerly belonging to the United Fruit Company. Dressed in full uniform and wearing straw hats, some of the soldiers hoist Cuban flags. The scene's triumphant tone is supported by a composition that brings to mind a historical painting: A dramatic, wide sky serves as a heroic backdrop for the row of fighters, whose placement is hierarchical (the highest-ranking individuals, the chiefs of the INRA, are located in the center). This is no ordinary group; their faces can be seen and recognized. These are the victors of the *epic feat*, a term the government used to identify the Revolution.

PORTRAITS OF COMMON PEOPLE

In addition to such overtly ideological work, Corrales also displayed a distinct sensitivity and profound lyricism in his portrayal of ordinary people. Inspired by the dignity of Dorothea Lange's and Walker Evans's subjects, Corrales composed portraits in which the humanity of the models trumps overtly ideological messages. *Malagón* (1959) and the series *The Band of New Rhythm* (1962) are clear examples of that trend.

Malagones were members of a countryside militia organized by Castro in 1959 in the Pinar del Río province to expel ex-Batista military forces in the area. Their name derives from their leader, Leandro Rodríguez Malagón. In *Malagón* Corrales presents a sixty-year-old soldier in bright daylight from a low angle. Conferring on him a sculptural form, Corrales transformed his model into a timeless icon of bravura and righteousness.

The Band of New Rhythm, taken during the chilling days of the Cuban Missile Crisis, is mostly based on close-ups of male torsos, hands, and musical instruments. In quasi-abstract compositions, the photos present men's backs, stained and worn clothes,

Raúl Corrales (1925–2006). Raúl Corrales, one of Cuba's most prominent photojournalists, broke with the established practice in which the photographic subject is seen up close, instead giving the leading role to details and objects in the foreground. © ALEJANDRO ERNESTO/CORBIS

and a bizarre combination of Russian submachine guns with clarinets, trumpets, and drums. These models were not members of the military, but musicians who had been mobilized and sent to strategic locations throughout the country. Corrales focuses on the specific symbols that synthesize the seriousness of the situation and the essentially upbeat nature of the Cuban people: Even under threat of nuclear war, these men were able to play music. The poetry conveyed in these images expresses in visual terms the fusion of art and politics at the core of any revolutionary process, and it serves as a plea for hope in the darkest of circumstances.

The duet *El Sueño* (The Dream) and *La Pesadilla* (The Nightmare), photographed during Castro's trip to Venezuela in 1959, offers an allegorical dimension to the directness of the revolutionary iconography of the early 1960s. The historical situation was simple: It was very late at the Cuban embassy in Caracas, and Castro's bodyguards were exhausted. In *El Sueño* a guard sleeps in a folding bed. In the tidy room, the man's gun rests on the top of a cabinet next to a delicate vase. The juxtaposition of elements within the frame is what gives this picture its symbolic breadth. Above the cabinet hangs a canvas depicting the naked torso of a woman. The real sleeping man and the painting of the naked woman are located on the same axis, suggesting a carnal desire felt by the bodyguard beyond his political duties.

The same psychological element permeates *La Pesadilla*. In this minimal composition another guard is sleeping on a couch, and above him there is a painting of a long-haired man with his back turned to us—he seems lost in the middle of nowhere and his fear and confusion can be read as a projection of the inner fears that might emerge in the guard's dreams. In a tentatively Freudian manner, Corrales seems to represent the anxiety harbored within this man's unconscious. In doing so, he may be suggesting that before uniforms and ideologies, common humanity, in all its complexity, should be considered first.

In producing one of the most solid photographic oeuvres of the Cuban revolutionary era, Corrales not only created archetypical images of what a political hero should look like, but also demonstrated that despite political leanings, these bearers of ideology are also people. Like the viewers of these photographs, the depicted subjects wrestle with anxiety, confusion, and desire.

After a short but intense period of documenting the feverish and complex beginnings of Castro's revolution, Corrales continued taking pictures for himself and worked in the Office of Historical Affairs of the Council of State of Cuba, where he was in charge of preserving and organizing the Revolution's photographic legacy. He never considered himself a great photographer; instead, he felt he was merely a privileged witness to an unrepeatable historical event.

BIBLIOGRAPHY

Cepero, Iliana. "Myths and Realities: Cuban Photography of the 1960s and 1970s." In *Cuba: Art and History from 1868 to Today*, edited by Nathalie Bondil. Montreal: Montreal Museum of Fine Arts; New York: Prestel Publishing, 2008.

Corrales, Raúl, in interview with the author, November 2005.

Sarusky, Jaime. "Raúl Corrales." In *Cuba: La imagen y la historia*, by Raúl Corrales. Cuba: Ediciones Aurelia, 2006.

RELOCATION OF THE AUDIENCIA TO CUBA, 1799–1801

Bonnie Adorno Lucero

The history behind and causes of the shift of the Spanish imperial administrative center in the Caribbean.

In 1801, the Audiencia of Santo Domingo was relocated to Puerto Príncipe, Cuba. Santo Domingo was the principal city in the Spanish colony of the same name (modern-day Dominican Republic) as part of the island of Hispaniola, shared with its western neighbor the French colony of St. Domingue (modern-day Haiti). Spanish administrators moved the Audiencia in response to a myriad of political and social transformations, most notably the French Revolution, the subsequent wars between France and Spain, the Haitian Revolution, and the expansion of Haitian control to the eastern portion of Hispaniola. Spain's cession of Santo Domingo to France in the 1795 Treaty of Basel was made effective only in 1799 when the Haitians under Toussaint Louverture (1743–1803) seized it, forcing the Audiencia out. The transfer marked the beginning of a new era. As the Spanish Empire began to crumble, Cuba remained the ever-faithful isle, Pearl of the Antilles.

The first Spanish administrative institution established in the Americas, the Audiencia of Santo Domingo was created in 1511 by a royal decree by King Ferdinand V (king of Castile 1474–1504; king of Aragon as Ferdinand II, 1479–1516). Operation of the Audiencia was delayed because of tensions between Ferdinand and the governor of Hispaniola, Diego Colón y Moniz Perestrello (r. 1509–1514), son of Cristóbal Colón (Christopher Columbus), over his defiant attitude toward authorities in Spain. On 14 September 1526, Emperor Charles I (r. 1500–1558) issued a decree to reestablish the Audiencia, this time within the newly created Viceroyalty of New Spain.

■ *See also*

Azúcar y población en las Antillas (Ramiro Guerra)

Governance and Contestation: Colonial Period

Havana: Atlantic Center of Shipping, Commerce, and Building

CHRONOLOGY OF EVENTS

1511: Ferdinand V creates the Real Audiencia of Santo Domingo.

1526: Emperor Charles I reestablishes the Audiencia within the Viceroyalty of New Spain.

1786: Spain creates Audiencia of Caracas, limiting the Audiencia of Santo Domingo to the Caribbean and Florida.

1791–1804: Haitian Revolution.

1795: Spain signs the Treaty of Basel, ceding Santo Domingo to France.

1799: Spanish forces withdraw from Hispaniola; Audiencia moves to Santiago de Cuba.

1800: Audiencia moves to Puerto Príncipe.

1838: Audiencia of Havana is created.

The main purpose of the Audiencia was the administration of justice. It was headed by a president, called the governor, who simultaneously acted as the captain general of the administrative unit called the captaincy. The Audiencia exercised two main functions: civil hearings presided over by *oidores* (judges), and criminal proceedings, heard by *alcaldes de crimen* (criminal magistrates). This was one of the most important governing institutions in colonial Spanish America.

JURISDICTION OF THE AUDIENCIA

The jurisdiction of the Audiencia of Santo Domingo initially encompassed the Caribbean and the coastal mainland of Venezuela and Florida. Audiencias proliferated during the sixteenth century as new territories were conquered. They were created in Mexico in 1527, Panama in 1538, Guatemala and Lima in 1543, Guadalajara and Bogotá in 1548, Chacras (modern Sucre, Bolivia) in 1559, and Quito and Concepción in 1565 (Spain/Council of the Indies 1846, pp. 157–176). Several others were established in the seventeenth and eighteenth centuries, including one in Santiago (1609, replacing Concepción), Buenos Aires (1661, re established 1783), Caracas (1786), and Cuzco (1787). By the late eighteenth century, the Audiencia of Santo Domingo had jurisdiction over the Caribbean islands, Florida, and the mainland provinces of Maracaibo and Guyana.

The massive territorial expansion undertaken by the Spanish Crown during the sixteenth century resulted in the increasing neglect of Santo Domingo. Indeed, as gold poured out of Mexico and silver out of Peru, Spanish settlers eagerly sailed to the mainland to seek their fortune. Santo Domingo, by comparison, did not seem a very lucrative or attractive place for settlers. Its economy was dismal, lacking the precious metal and mineral deposits of the mainland and relying largely on cattle ranching and contraband trade. Moreover, the island lacked a steady labor force due to the decline of its indigenous populations.

Sparse population and inadequate military protection made Santo Domingo particularly vulnerable to piracy and foreign attack. These problems culminated in the devastating attack by Sir Francis Drake in January 1586, which destroyed the city of Santo Domingo and left Spanish control over the island weakened. Throughout the seventeenth century, French settlements threatened Spanish dominion over Hispaniola, until finally the western third of the island was ceded to France on 20 September 1697 in the Treaty of Ryswick.

Spain retained control of the eastern two-thirds of Hispaniola, and the Audiencia continued to function, but the rapid economic success of the French colony of St. Domingue soon began to overshadow the sparsely populated and economically stagnant east. Quite simply, by the eighteenth century, the Spanish colony paled in comparison to its western neighbor, St. Domingue—then the world's largest sugar producer, and one of the most important centers of the slave trade.

Neither France nor Spain was content to share the island. With the outbreak of the French Revolution in 1789, and the subsequent political turmoil enveloping Europe, the tenuous Spanish hold over Santo Domingo was dealt a final blow. Emboldened by military success against the Prussians and Austrians, who had failed in their attempted invasion of France in 1792, the French National Convention guillotined Louis XVI on 21 January 1793. When Spain in January and England in February joined the coalition against France, the French swiftly declared war on each.

CONSEQUENCES OF THE FRENCH REVOLUTION

France and Spain battled in Europe and the Caribbean. In Europe, the French invasion of the Iberian Peninsula ignited the War of the Pyrenees, which lasted from March 1793 to July 1795. French troops engaged in combat with Spain on two fronts in the eastern and western Pyrenees Mountains. The French advanced first on the eastern front, defeating the Spanish in November 1794 and driving them back into Catalonia, after which stalemate ensued. On the western front, French armies seized control of northwestern Spain by early 1795.

French military successes prompted Spanish capitulation and the signing of the Treaty of Basel on 22 July 1795. Spain ceded Santo Domingo to the French in return for French respect for prewar Spanish territorial boundaries. This concession reflected the peripheral place of Santo Domingo within the Spanish

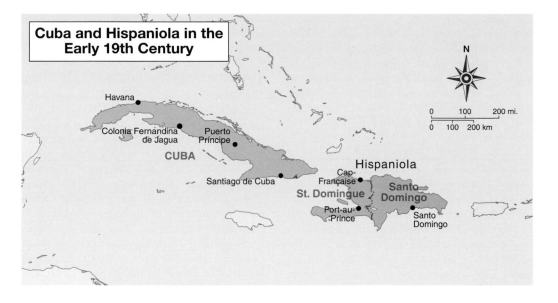

Cuba and Hispaniola in the Early 19th Century

Empire. Although the French ambassador proposed the devolution of the Louisiana Territory instead of the cession of Santo Domingo, the Spanish initially declined this offer. Years later, however, they reconsidered, and Spain unsuccessfully attempted to exchange Louisiana for the return of Santo Domingo. Spain also recognized the French revolutionary government in the treaty. Spanish recognition of revolutionary France would be viewed with tragic irony thirteen years later in 1808 with the Napoleonic invasion of Spain and sequestration of Ferdinand VII. This provoked the crisis of legitimacy that would cost Spain its mainland possessions in the Americas.

While the execution of the French monarch, Louis XVI, engendered war in Europe, the Declaration of the Rights of Man and Citizen, proclaimed on 26 August 1789 by the French National Assembly, provoked unrest in the French colony of St. Domingue. A delegation of free people of color, including Julien Raimond (1744–1801) and Vincent Ogé (c. 1755–1791), traveled to Paris in October 1789 to demand equal rights. The newly elected French Constituent Assembly sought to exploit the tensions between recently *nouveaux livres* (freed slaves) and free men of color, who had been vying for political equality with whites since the 1780s. The assembly extended citizenship rights only to the latter in March 1790, hoping to further divide the two groups. Ogé returned to St. Domingue in July of the following year to take a more forceful approach.

Taking up arms, Ogé organized a contingent of several hundred men in his hometown of Dondon, south of Cap Française (modern Cap Haitien or Okap). He petitioned the Provincial Assembly of Cap Française to extend citizenship rights to all. When his demands were not met, he led an uprising. After initial successes, he was captured and executed in 1791 along with his coconspirator Jean-Baptiste Chavannes and nineteen

others. The torture and execution of Ogé made him a martyr of the struggle for the rights of people of color in St. Domingue. Although he was not an opponent of slavery, his followers took up arms and allied with slaves against white discrimination. On 22 August 1791, a slave rebellion erupted in St. Domingue, engulfing the entire colony by the following year. The demands for rights by free people of color had transformed into a slave rebellion (Dubois pp. 80–90).

THE HAITIAN REVOLUTION

Emerging from an "unthinkable" slave uprising, the Haitian Revolution, as this rebellion would later be called, shook the entire Atlantic world to its core (Trouillot p. 73). The political and social tumult of revolution made the colony an ideal candidate for the extension of European hostilities. Indeed, St. Domingue became another arena of contention between the British and Spanish against the French. White planters in St. Domingue sought British support against the French, to quell the slave uprising and restore racial order. At the same time, certain rebel leaders, including General Toussaint Louverture, Georges (Jorge) Biassou (1741–1801), and Jean François Papillon (Juan Francisco) (d. 1820), initially supported the Spanish, whose forces in Hispaniola included two regiments from Cuba, some of which would remain on the island until 1799. (The deployment of the regiments of Havana and Santiago in Hispaniola during the Spanish offensive there created the need for defensive reinforcements in Cuba, which was met by the deployment of both white and *pardo* [mulatto, mixed-race] battalions across the island [Kuethe pp. 143–144]. These battalions were in charge of overseeing prisoners taken during the war with France from 1793 to 1795 [Ferrer pp. 184–185].)

Louverture shifted his loyalty back to France in May 1794 with the French promise to abolish slavery in St. Domingue. He also successfully expelled the British from the island by 1798. The defeat of British and Spanish forces by the powerful Haitian general and the French victory on the European front was not enough, however, to reestablish French sovereignty in Hispaniola. Regional factionalism in St. Domingue and the lofty aspirations of Louverture to unite the island and free all slaves significantly undermined French authority.

The transfer of Santo Domingo from Spanish to French sovereignty was also complicated by a number of logistical factors. Although Santo Domingo was officially in French hands by 1795, a clause in the Treaty of Basel permitted the continuation of Spanish governance from Santo Domingo during a transition period of unspecified length (Pan-American Scientific Congress 1917, p. 615). Moreover, the Treaty of Basel required Spain to provide transportation to remove military and government personnel as well as settlers who wished to emigrate from the island. Upon the arrival of Spanish evacuation ships in December 1795, the peace was refused because the French lacked the manpower to replace the Spanish. Instead, the ships carried away families who wanted to emigrate, along with the remains of Christopher Columbus. A further delay to the transfer of sovereignty was a treaty proposed by Spain to exchange Louisiana for the return of Santo Domingo, an offer formally rejected by the French in June 1796 (Schaeffer pp. 51–52).

The Spanish would not leave Hispaniola until 1799, when Toussaint Louverture consolidated his rule over the island. By 1798, all troops and territory in St. Domingue were controlled by two men: Louverture and André Rigaud. These men had been allies since 1794 and had repelled the British invasion together. Negotiating the terms of the British withdrawal with the two Haitian generals, Governor Comte d'Hédouville undermined Louverture's position of authority vis-à-vis Rigaud, thus sowing seeds of contention between the two. In the War of the South (1798–1800), Louverture crushed Rigaud, who upon defeat fled to Santiago de Cuba and subsequently found exile in France. Louverture thereby consolidated his control over the western third of Hispaniola. Marching east, he sought to unify the island. Upon reaching Santo Domingo, he made effective the cession of the Spanish territory. During this campaign, he forced the Spanish officials to flee (Dubois pp. 231–236). Toussaint's conquest also provoked massive emigration of white elites, many of whom found a new home in Cuba (Schoenrich pp. 33–44).

During the civil war in St. Domingue, the Audiencia moved to Santiago de Cuba, by the royal decree of 17 March 1799. Shortly thereafter, it was transferred to Puerto Príncipe under a decree of 31 July 1800, and within a year had become established there. With the creation of the Audiencia of Havana in 1838, the jurisdiction of the Audiencia of Puerto Príncipe was limited to the central and eastern provinces of Cuba; in 1853 it was abolished and was later replaced by the Audiencia of Camagüey in 1868.

THE INCREASING IMPORTANCE OF CUBA

The French and Haitian Revolutions pushed the Audiencia out of Santo Domingo, but why did Spain choose to move it to Cuba? In the late eighteenth century, Cuba experienced a dramatic economic boom as the island's sugar industry developed. Sugar had a late start in Cuba. The mass production through plantation agriculture and slave labor gained momentum only in the late eighteenth century as other Caribbean sugar economies peaked and began their decline. With its closest competitor (St. Domingue) obliterated by the Haitian Revolution, Cuba became the world's largest sugar producer almost immediately. With the elimination of St. Domingue forcing prices higher, Cuban planters enjoyed substantial profits.

The rise of sugar in Cuba meant increased slave imports. Fearing that the significant population of color on the island would threaten the racial order, white Cubans realized the importance of Spanish colonial rule in maintaining peace and ensuring the continuation of slavery. The Haitian Revolution had transformed the New World's most profitable colony into the poorest country in the hemisphere, a spectacle that disturbed wealthy Cuban planters.

In 1812, the first major slave rebellion, the Aponte Rebellion, erupted in Cuba. It began in Puerto Príncipe, and the leader José Antonio Aponte reputedly owned portraits of the Haitian revolutionaries Henri Christophe, Toussaint Louverture, Jean François, and Jean-Jacques Dessalines. This terrified Cuban slaveholders (Childs pp. 1–4). Fear of further slave revolts and the development of another Haiti in Cuba reinforced elite Cuban loyalty to Spain. The loyalty of white Cuban slaveholders became even more meaningful in the first decade of the nineteenth century as mainland Spanish America challenged Spanish rule. Cuba remained faithful.

If independence meant slave revolt and the execution and mutilation of elites, then white Cubans preferred stability under Spanish rule. Spanish policy in Cuba in the wake of the Haitian Revolution hinged on two related policies: brutal suppression of slave resistance, which became increasingly intensified throughout the nineteenth century, and careful control the island's racial composition. The latter was fostered by establishing white settlements throughout the island in the early nineteenth century, such as San Fernando de Nuevitas (near Camagüey) in 1818 and Colonia Fernandina de Jagua (Cienfuegos) in 1819 (Ferrer pp. 132–133).

The transfer of the Audiencia from Santo Domingo to Cuba marked a new period in Spanish imperial history and Cuban history. It signified the rising political and economic importance of Cuba within the Spanish Empire. It also fomented new social dynamics and racial tensions on the island. It highlighted Spain's tenuous hold over its New World possessions but solidified Cuban loyalty to the disintegrating empire, a hold that would face serious challenge only in the final decade of the nineteenth century.

BIBLIOGRAPHY

Childs, Matt D. *The 1812 Aponte Rebellion in Cuba and the Struggle against Atlantic Slavery.* Chapel Hill: University of North Carolina Press, 2006.

Cordero Michel, Emilio. *La revolución haitiana y Santo Domingo.* Santo Domingo: Editora Nacional, 1968. 4th ed., Santo Domingo: Ediciones UAPA, 2000.

Dubois, Laurent. *Avengers of the New World: The Story of the Haitian Revolution.* Cambridge, MA: Harvard University Press, 2004.

Ferrer, Ada. "Cuba en la sombre de Haití: Noticias, sociedad y esclavitud." In *El rumor de Haití en Cuba: Temor, raza y rebeldía, 1789–1844*, edited by Dolores González-Ripoll, Consuelo Naranjo, Ada Ferrer, et al. Madrid: Consejo Superior de Investigaciones Científicas, 2005.

Kucthc, Allan J. *Cuba, 1753–1815: Crown, Military, and Society.* Knoxville: University of Tennessee Press, 1986.

Pan-American Scientific Congress. *Proceedings of the Second Pan-American Scientific Congress, Section VI: International Law, Public Law and Jurisprudence,* James Brown Scott, Chairman. Washington, DC: Government Printing Office, 1917.

Schaeffer, Wendell G. "The Delayed Cession of Spanish Santo Domingo to France, 1795–1801." *Hispanic American Historical Review* 29, no. 1 (1949): 46–68.

Schoenrich, Otto. *Santo Domingo: A Country with a Future.* New York: Macmillan, 1918.

Spain/Council of the Indies. "Titulo Quince. De las Audiencias y Chancillerias Reales de las Indias." In *Recopilación de leyes de los reynos de las Indias* [1681]. 5 vols. Madrid: Imprenta y Librería de Don Ignacio Boix, 1846.

Trouillot, Michel-Rolph. *Silencing the Past: Power and the Production of History.* Boston: Beacon Press, 1995.

"RITA DE CUBA": RITA MONTANER

Tony Évora

One of Cuba's best-loved singers and actresses of the first half of the twentieth century.

The singer and actress known affectionately as "Rita de Cuba" by her countrymen achieved fame in the first half of the twentieth century for her passionate singing, particularly of Afro-Cuban songs. Rita Montaner (1900–1958) was born in Guanabacoa, near Havana, to a mulatto mother and a white pharmacist father. At age four she started studying music under the guidance of her mother. In 1910 Montaner joined the Peyrellade Conservatory, where she studied solfège, theory, harmony, and piano. Montaner's marriage to a white lawyer, Alberto Fernández Díaz, secured her entry to high society. Their sons Domingo Alberto and Rolando were born in 1919 and 1921, respectively.

CAREER

In 1922 Montaner participated in the first concerts of so-called typical music organized by the composer Eduardo Sánchez de Fuentes (1874–1944), who had persuaded her husband to let her perform. This event marked the beginning of a professional career that ranged from Afro-Cuban music to opera and European theater. Montaner's mezzo-soprano voice and wide range was greatly admired; even the simplest song was transformed when she performed it.

Hers was the first female voice to be heard on Cuba's national radio, which was launched on 10 October 1922. She soon achieved fame with her versions of Eliseo Grenet's "Mamá Inés" and "Siboney," a song that celebrates the passion of a member of the native tribe that occupied central Cuba at the time of the Spanish conquest, which was written by Ernesto Lecuona (1895–1963). "Mamá Inés," which Montaner recorded in 1929, owes its popularity mainly to its contagious rhythm and its memorable chorus, "todos los negros tomamos café" ("all of us black people drink coffee"). Later, Montaner performed the works of composers such as Gonzalo Roig (1890–1970), Jorge Anckermann (1877–1941), and Amadeo Roldán (1900–1939).

In 1926 while on vacation in New York City, Montaner underwent an emergency appendectomy. Once recovered, she was invited to participate in a concert in aid of the blind, which was staged at the Plaza Hotel; during this performance she was discovered by a representative from the Schubert Follies, who offered her a contract to tour throughout the United States.

From the early 1930s on and no longer married, Montaner assumed the bohemian lifestyle of an artist. She went to Paris with her lover, the actor Paco Lara, and there she attained great success with the song "El manicero" (The Peanut Vendor), which had been written for her by Moisés Simons. This song invites ladies not to go to bed before having first tasted the street vendor's peanuts.

In 1931 she made her debut in New York starring in Al Jolson's production *Wonder Bar*, then toured the United States with the company for the next year. The following year, Montaner quit Jolson's company and returned to Cuba.

In March 1933 she performed in the Mexican theaters Politeama and Iris, where her artistic partnership with the pianist and singer Ignacio Villa

■ *See also*

Music: Afro-Cuban Religious Influence on Cuban Popular Music

The Music of Ernesto Lecuona

Popular Songs of the 1920s

Rita Montaner (1900–1958). The voice of singer and actress Rita Montaner was beloved in Cuba during the first half of the twentieth century. COURTESY OF THE CUBAN HERITAGE COLLECTION, UNIVERSITY OF MIAMI LIBRARIES, CORAL GABLES, FLORIDA

(1911–1971) began; it was Montaner who gave Villa the nickname "Bola de Nieve" (Snowball), which followed him for the rest of his life. As quoted in Aldo Martínez-Malo, Villa related:

> The day of her debut in the Politeama theater of Mexico, in 1933, she introduced me as "the black guy that comes with me." I was not expecting it, and I did not know what to do. She went on the stage with a radiant smile and introduced me as "the extraordinary Cuban performer, Bola de Nieve." She pushed me over to the mic and told the band: "Play 'Vito Manué tú no sabe ingle.'" Being so fat and of such dark a complexion, I had a real impact on the audience. They gave me an ovation.

p. 104

In the next year Montaner married the sportsman Ernesto Estévez and shot her first movie in Mexico, *La noche del pecado* (The Night of Sin). In June 1934 she made her debut in the revue show *La tentación del trópico* (The Lure of the Tropics) in the Maipo theater in Buenos Aires, where she caused a great sensation.

In the 1940s Montaner began performing in Cuban theater and Spanish zarzuela as well as sketch comedy. When singing vernacular works, she stylized *chusmería criolla* (Cuban vaudeville) in numbers such as "El golpe de Bibijagua" (The Blow of Bibijagua), "El marañon" (The Cashew), and "Ponme la mano Caridad" (Touch Me, Caridad). Her radio program became a hit. When television arrived in Cuba she launched her show *Rita and Willy*, in which she acted alongside Guillermo Álvarez Guedes (b. 1928).

In 1948 she appeared in the movie *María la O* based on Lecuona's zarzuela. She worked for nine years in the Tropicana cabaret, and in 1954 she played the leading role in the film *La única* (The One and Only). After her television program was censored because of its criticism of Fulgencio Batista's regime, Montaner returned to the theater. Showcasing her great lyrical abilities, she sang the part of Madame Flora in Gian Carlo Menotti's opera *La médium* (The Medium, 1946) at the Hubert de Blanck conservatory.

MONTANER'S STYLE

Montaner's mysterious and tragic tone when singing African music made hearing her performances of Gilberto Valdés's Afro-Cuban songs such as "Ogguere," "Tambó," and "Ile-nko-Ilé-nbé" a memorable experience. Indeed, these songs can be sung successfully only by a singer with a refined technique, enormous confidence, and great skill and rhythm—all of which Rita possessed in abundance—as well as a sensitivity that Montaner turned into nostalgia. Her voice was like a cry of protest against the racial discrimination that pervaded Cuban society. Unfortunately, this impassioned type of singing damaged her vocal cords.

Montaner had an untamed temper and did not suffer fools. When asked her opinion she would go straight to the point, and she took affronts badly, acquiring notoriety for her violent and mocking temper. On one occasion, while having a heated argument with a theater owner, she is quoted as having said: "the audience is here to see me—not you or your theater. I have to respect them" (Martínez-Malo p. 123). On stage, however, she was different: In front of an audience she became the great artist.

Montaner was connected to Afro-Cuban religion, having been initiated into Lucumí. Many stories circulated about how she could not decide on an orisha (spirit) and how she rejected the oracle's advice to be initiated with a particular orisha. In the end, and facing death, Montaner bowed to pressure and chose to be initiated into the Regla de Ocha, but the oracle told her that the orisha had refused her, and she had to choose another. But it was too late; she died of throat cancer at age fifty-eight. This story may be just the stuff of legend, but some Santería practitioners point to Montaner's experience as an example of the iron will of the orishas, who have no mercy for those who displease them.

After Montaner's death, the maestro Lecuona, who had been her friend at the Peyrellade Conservatory when they were young, discussed her 1927 acting debut in *Niña Rita* and *La tierra de Venus*. He is quoted in Martínez-Malo as saying:

In the first play we included the famous "Mamá Inés," and in the second one we added "Siboney." Rita was a real success. Her name gained rapid-increasing popularity. She made a lot of records. Later, she took part in some of my plays, such as in the opening of *Rosa la China*, with lyrics written by Sánchez Galarraga and the music written by me.

Her education was astonishing, she would talk about anything. She took in everything she read and heard. Further, whatever her beautiful eyes caught sight of, she never forgot. Her name was synonymous with glory, announcing her meant a full theater in advance. I was by her side during her illness. I brought her a headscarf and a fan as presents. She took my arm and walked with me around the room, she was quite amused. I was there with her from nine until two, but when I left I was sad, depressed. Two days later I heard of her death on the radio. It was seven a.m. It was a blow to the head, to the heart, and to the soul.

p. 110

BIBLIOGRAPHY

Martínez-Malo, Aldo. *Rita. La única*. Havana: Abril, 1988.

Moore, Robin D. *Nationalizing Blackness*. Pittsburgh, PA: University of Pittsburgh Press, 1997.

SAB (GERTRUDIS GÓMEZ DE AVELLANEDA)

Adriana Méndez Rodenas

The first antislavery novel written in the Americas.

Gertrudis Gómez de Avellaneda (1814–1873), author of the first antislavery novel in the Americas, is one of the most prominent writers of transnational Cuban literature. Born in Camagüey of a Spanish naval officer and a Cuban mother, Gómez de Avellaneda is best known for her sonnet "Al partir" (Farewell to Cuba), which describes her departure from Cuba in April 1836 (Servera pp. 12, 14). After a brief residence in Seville, Gómez de Avellaneda established herself in Madrid, where she became a leading poet and playwright.

Her most significant contribution to Cuban letters is *Sab* (1841), a classic of the antislavery genre because of its daring portrayal of a mulatto slave in love with his white mistress and its depiction of a crucial transition in plantation society, the demise of the small plantation before the onslaught of the sugar industry and foreign commercial interests. Gómez de Avellaneda's sentimental treatment of masters and slaves is echoed in a series of antislavery novels by writers affiliated with Domingo del Monte (1804–1853), who spearheaded the first national literary movement in Cuba under the banner of Balzacian-style realism during the crucial years between 1835 and 1844. Gómez de Avellaneda's novel is aligned with a broader continental tradition of female-authored abolitionist narrative (Davies pp. 16–17), anticipating *Uncle Tom's Cabin* (1852), by Harriet Beecher Stowe, a novel protesting slavery in the U.S. South (Picón Garfield pp. 52–53).

Sab figures prominently in Spanish American romanticism for its bucolic depiction of landscape, expanding an emerging discourse of Cuban nationalism to the interior of the island. Set in Gómez de Avellaneda's native province of Puerto Príncipe (modern Camagüey), the novel centers on Sab, an eponymous character who is "enslaved" not only by his abject social condition but also by his all-consuming love for Carlota, the delicate daughter of a creole planter, Don Carlos, whose considerable wealth diminishes as a result of swift changes in the plantation system. Bidding for Carlota's hand is the rapacious Enrique Otway, who sees in Carlota a means to move up the social ladder, prodded as he is by his father's ambitions as an established British businessman in Cuba. While the Otways represent British commercial interests, Carlota's father stands for the small plantation owner whose losses are a direct result of the boom in the sugar industry during the first quarter of the century, when bigger and more technologically advanced *factorías* spread over Cuba's western provinces (Moreno Fraginals pp. 20–24). Carlota's doomed marriage to Otway warns against a mercantilist hold on the nation, while countering as well the del Monte group's allegiance to British abolitionists.

The economic context of the novel serves as backdrop for a complicated tale of romantic intrigue. Sab's frustrated love for Carlota, expressed in the language of sublimated eroticism, is matched by Carlota's infatuation for Enrique, which blinds her to his opportunism and ruthlessness. As a prototypical romantic hero, the passionate Sab counters Otway's calculated conquest of Carlota; the two male characters stand at opposite ends in the novel's economy of desire. A third subplot complicates the struggle over Carlota's hand. Teresa, an orphaned cousin adopted by Carlota's family, balances Carlota's role as romantic heroine by becoming a silent rival for Enrique's affection. To reinforce her abolitionist message, Gómez de Avellaneda establishes a series of contrasts between race and ethical temperament: Otway, the white Anglo-Saxon, emblematizes the "dark" or "inferior" soul, while Sab, the mulatto slave, represents the "light" or "superior" spirit (Gómez de Avellaneda p. 50). Sab is the only character capable of altruistic sacrifice for the object of his love. A similar pattern emerges around the two female figures, since Teresa's reserve is countered by Carlota's vulnerability

■ *See also*

Cecilia Valdés (Cirilo Villaverde)

Gender: Colonial Period to 1920

Literature: Nationalist and Reformist Literature, pre-1850

Race: Slavery in Cuba

and impetuousness. Despite the differences between these women, the tragic fate allotted them is portrayed as a consequence of sharing the same fundamental flaw: rivalry over the hapless Enrique.

The triangular love plot sparks an analogy sustained throughout the novel: Because romantic love is depicted as a form of abjection, the social condition of women is compared to that of the slave, a message inscripted in the climactic scene of the novel. On the eve of Carlota's fated marriage, Sab offers Teresa a winning lottery ticket that would make her rich and hence attractive to the ambitious Otway, thus thwarting Carlota's hopes but preventing her union with the materialistic Otway (Gómez de Avellaneda p. 153). In a daring countermove, Teresa refuses Sab's gift, offering herself as his future spouse instead, with the promise of escape to another shore and a more open society (Gómez de Avellaneda p. 151). Seduced by Teresa in word if not in fact, Sab rejects this offer but accepts Teresa's proposal to give the ticket away to Don Carlos as guarantee of Carlota's dowry, thus sealing her fated marriage to Otway. Teresa's practical grasp of matters of the heart unravels the conflicting web of love interests but leaves intact the novel's central concern: the contradiction between Sab's immense capacity for love and the constraints of the slavery system that thwart such exuberant emotion. Despite the fact that his sublime passion makes him the perfect match for Carlota, Sab is left to mourn the obstacles represented by his race and the stigma of slavery.

At the end of the novel Teresa, from her sojourn in a convent, gives Carlota a letter that Sab had written to her just before he died, clearly intended to reach his beloved by means of Teresa's intervention. Echoing other nineteenth-century precursors such as Madame de Staël (1766–1817) and George Sand (1804–1876), Gómez de Avellaneda strikes against the gender conventions of the age, particularly the institution of marriage, in which women are reduced to "[p]obres y ciegas víctimas!" (poor and blind victims!), mere slaves forced to bow down before their masters (Gómez de Avellaneda p. 212). Woman's collective duty under the yoke of patriarchy is seen as worse than the slave's, since each woman must submit "until death do us part," whereas the slave nourishes the hope of purchasing his freedom (Gómez de Avellandeda p. 212). The novel thus subverts the code of romantic passion: Sab is Carlota's slave both literally and symbolically, as, out of love, he wishes nothing but "*vivir y morir en su servicio*" (to live and die in her service) (Gómez de Avellaneda p. 23). Likewise, Carlota is a victim of her own desires and unwise choice of erotic object. Only Teresa sidesteps the constrictions of the prevailing gender system by her voluntary surrender to a religious life (Picón Garfield pp. 65–66). The novel's economy of desire matches, at a textual and symbolic level, its critique of the hegemony of the sugar plantation.

Given its abolitionist and feminist messages, the novel articulates an early yet constitutive stage in the formation of Cuban nationalism. Similar to Cirilo Villaverde's *Excursión a Vuelta Abajo* (1838; 1842), a memoir recounting the author's return trip to his native Pinar del Río in order to commemorate the region's natural beauty and once-prosperous tobacco industry, Don Carlos sets out for the region of Cubitas, a fictional district of agricultural pasturelands in decline caused by massive deforestation and the spread of industrialized mills during the 1830s sugar boom (Moreno Fraginals). Cubitas represents *Cuba pequeña*, the interior of the island, where autochthonous values, customs, and peoples reside, a pastoral site where local communities evolve marked by a strong sense of *pertenencia*, or rootedness in place (Benítez Rojo 1986, p. 15); hence, the use of the diminutive ending in Cubitas is meant to highlight the growth of a community into *civitas*, or a communal way of life. The novel dramatically shows how the peaceful mores and social ties of *Cuba pequeña* are threatened by the encroachment of *Cuba grande*, the economic interests of the sugar plantation, with its all-consuming ambition for land, foreign capital, and the use and abuse of human labor (Benítez Rojo 1986, pp. 15–16). As in other Spanish American masterpieces, such as Jorge Isaacs's *María* (1867), the tropics appear here as a region of exceptional bounty and beauty, as seen in the proliferation of native flora and fauna, including the *cocuyo*, or night-flying insect, and the reference to native products, such as the *casabe*, a bread made out of root vegetables which was a staple of the diet of the Taínos, the primary indigenous tribe in Cuba (Gómez de Avellaneda pp. 89–90).

To what extent does Sab represent a future national subject? Described as "*un mulato perfecto*" (Gómez de Avellaneda p. 15), an even blend between African and European elements, the protagonist appears as a racial composite: "*su color de un blanco amarillento con cierto fondo oscuro*" (his skin color of a yellowish white mixed with a certain dark background) (Gómez de Avellaneda p. 16) tends to give him, according to some, a suspicious racial ambiguity (Sommer p. 118). The character's hybridity, along with his role as individualized romantic hero, reinforces the trope of transculturation, as his own eloquent self-fashioning makes clear: "*Pertenezco a esa raza desventurada sin derechos de hombres . . . soy mulato y esclavo*" (I belong to that unfortunate race without any human rights . . . I am a slave and a mulatto) (Gómez de Avellaneda p. 19). By making Sab a national prototype, and, at the same time, the emblem of miscegenation, Gómez de Avellaneda affirms a link of solidarity among all marginalized sectors (Picón Garfield p. 66), hence anticipating the future "*Cuba mulata*," an ideology premised on racial blending and equality prevalent during the *Afrocubanista* movement of the 1930s and 1940s.

Aligned with other nineteenth-century foundational fictions that allegorize romantic love as a way to construct national identities (Sommer), the sublimated romance between Sab and Carlota reimagines the nation in more inclusive terms. Indeed, *Sab* anticipates the theory of transculturation of Fernando Ortiz (1881–1969), which proposes that blending two cultures forms a third, integrated whole. This is best seen in one of the pivotal scenes, in which Don Carlos and his family go to the region of Cubitas to visit Sab's adopted mother, an indigenous wisewoman named Martina. Hiding in a cave, which is suggestive of the veritable erasure of indigenous culture from the map of the nation, Martina, a descendant of a Taíno cacique or chief, retells his legend to the creole family gathered there. The light that mysteriously appears across the night sky in the region of Cubitas is really the cacique's tormented soul, which comes to haunt his oppressors as a last act of defiance (Gómez de Avellaneda p. 92). Martina's and Sab's speeches end in a prophetic vision in which the blacks carry out the vengeance declared by their indigenous forebears (Gómez de Avellaneda p. 93). The invisible kinship between Martina and Sab underlines the gesture of inclusion premised by the novel, as the sickly grandson under Martina's care serves as a symbol for the birth of a nation, parallel to Eugenio, a minor character and Don Carlos's only male heir, whose sickly constitution suggests a critique of the reformist project represented by Domingo del Monte and other enlightened creoles.

Once Martina's folktales conclude, the family sits down to a banquet where master and slave, man and woman, white and black, English and creole, enjoy a communal feast in celebration of peaceful *convivencia* (coexistence), hence suspending, for a brief epiphany, the racial tensions surrounding them (Gómez de Avellaneda p. 110). The banquet scene participates in that collective "desire for the nation" underscored by racial, social, and cultural harmony, "a utopian project of co-existence to compensate for a fragmented, unstable, and conflictive Antillean identity" (Benítez Rojo 1989, p. 28).

The same utopian impulse surfaces toward the end of the novel, when a broken-hearted Sab returns to Martina's cave, on the eve of Carlota's and Otway's marriage and before his own imminent end. In parallel fashion, Carlota returns to the region of Cubitas after Teresa reveals to her the contents of Sab's epistle, mourning for Sab in much the same way as his adopted mother, Martina (Gómez de Avellaneda p. 214). Whereas earlier the mysterious light had been associated with the return of the cacique ancestor, now, local superstition associates it with Martina's ghost, only to make a sudden shift, as the figure reveals the quiet presence of Carlota, who pays homage to Sab in his final resting place. Although their union was impossible given existing class and racial boundaries, the lovers are united at the end in the mythical time/ space of a (future) imagined nation: "*¿habrá podido olvidar la hija de los trópicos, al esclavo que descansa en una humilde sepultura bajo aquel hermoso cielo?*" (could

the daughter of the tropics ever forget the slave who rests in a humble grave beneath such a glorious sky?) (Gómez de Avellaneda p. 217).

In comparison to the cycle of antislavery novels produced by the Del Monte circle, particularly Anselmo Suárez y Romero's *Francisco* (written 1839; published 1880), Gómez de Avellaneda presents here an original image of Cuban nationality, a tripartite blending of races and cultures (Taíno, Spanish, and African), which serves to reconcile, albeit symbolically, the tragic outcome of romantic love. As is the case with Cirilo Villaverde's *Cecilia Valdés* (1882), the blending of races is the cornerstone of Cuban nationality. Toward the end of the novel, both the last descendant of the creole aristocracy and the lone survivor of Taíno ancestors suffer the same fate, leaving Sab as racial hybrid to represent a nation-in-the-making. For some critics, the protagonist's tragic death suggests an ambivalence regarding the inclusion of the black in an integrated project of nationhood. While Sab's outcry against the institution of slavery does not propose a literal end to the system (Kirkpatrick p. 157), it does show the effects of racial difference on both blacks and whites, thus marking its ethical import in Cuban literature. Sab, Teresa, and Carlota, along with the mythical Martina, configure a collective identity founded on alterity and difference (Picón Garfield p. 79), a symbolic matrix emerging out of passionate exchange among three dominant races. In contrast to creole reformism emblematized in the image of Don Carlos's sickly male offspring, the novel suggests a union, albeit precarious, among its various constituents, revising Spanish American foundational fictions and projecting as well a pan-Caribbean desire for inclusion.

Critics have commented on the affinities between author and protagonist, as if Gómez de Avellaneda projected her own marginal condition as a female writer onto Sab's agonized awareness (Sommer p. 115; Davies p. 15). Like Sab, Gómez de Avellaneda was, despite her greatness, unfortunate in love, as revealed in her *Autobiografía y cartas* (Autobiography and Letters, reprinted 1996), an ardent collection of love letters documenting her vehement yet unrequited passion for her first love, the Spanish lawyer Ignacio Cepeda, letters which span from her early period in Seville to the time of Cepeda's marriage (1839–1854) (Mata-Kolster p. 176). At the height of her literary fame and after another failed romantic interlude, Gómez de Avellaneda married Pedro Sabater in 1846 and was widowed the same year. Nine years later, she married Domingo Verdugo, whose appointment as governor of Santiago facilitated the couple's return to Cuba in 1859 (Servera pp. 27–28, 34–36).

The stellar rise of Gómez de Avellaneda's literary career in the Madrid of the 1840s and 1850s was due primarily to her success as a playwright; *Baltasar* (1858), considered "her last dramatic work, has been judged indisputably the best of her plays"

Gertrudis Gómez de Avellaneda (1814–1873). Gertrudis Gómez de Avellaneda, author of *Sab*, the first antislavery novel in the Americas, is one of the most prominent writers of transnational Cuban literature. FOTOSEARCH/ GETTY IMAGES

(Mata-Kolster p. 177). This prolific author also contributed to a typically romantic genre—the historical romance—with *Guatimozín, el último emperador de Méjico* (1845), only giving it a transamerican twist by shifting the setting from ancient Greece to pre-Conquest Mexico, hence formulating the past as pageant.

As a novelist, Gómez de Avellaneda continued her earlier depiction of women's social condition in *Dos mugeres* (Two Women) (1842–1843), a work denouncing adultery. Despite her literary fame, in 1852 she was denied a place in the Real Academia Española de la Lengua (Servera p. 31). She met similar resistance upon her return to her native island in 1859, where she had to defend her right to be included as a Cuban writer in an anthology of local poets compiled by the editors of *El Fanal* and *El Siglo*, two periodical publications in her native Camagüey. In Cuba, she directed *Album cubano de lo bello y lo bueno* (Cuban Album of the Beautiful and the Good), a bi-monthly publication that, despite its relatively short life (from February to August 1860), played a crucial role in addressing societal expectations of gender (Picón Garfield p. 19). Masterpieces of early feminist historiography, Gómez de Avellaneda's articles on "La mujer" (Woman), published in the *Album*, astutely assessed women's place in world history. One of her legends, "El cacique de Tumerqué," recounts an episode from early colonial history (Picón Garfield p. 49), while "El aura blanca" is set in Camagüey; the novel *El artista barquero o los cuatro cinco de Julio* (The Boatman Artist or the Four Fifth of July), published in Havana in 1861, returns to the theme of women's redemption through virtue (Servera p. 37; Picón Garfield pp. 48–49).

After the death of her husband, Gómez de Avellaneda returned to Madrid in 1864, where she prepared an edition of her complete works. Significantly, she left out *Sab, Dos mugeres,* and *Guatimozín* from the 1869–1871 Madrid edition, an exclusion explained as a form of self-censorship, based on her understanding that none of these works would pass through the stringent Spanish censor (Picón Garfield p. 49), but that Servera attributes to her growing nationalist sentiment (pp. 48–49). Traditionally, Gómez de Avellaneda's place in Cuban literature has been designated by prefacing her maternal last name with the article "la," an ingrained but annoying patriarchal gesture which diminishes the stature of her genius. In "Al partir," Gómez de Avellaneda inscribes an image of Cuba that is not only visual but auditive: "*tu dulce nombre halagará mi oído*" (your sweet name will ring flatteringly to my ear) (Sarduy p. 20). May readers echo this famous verse in order to acknowledge her rightful place in the Cuban canon by granting her the full stature of her name: Gómez de Avellaneda.

BIBLIOGRAPHY

Araújo, Nara. "Raza y género en *Sab*, o el juego de los espejos." In *El alfiler y la mariposa. Género, voz y escritura en Cuba y el Caribe*, 39–49. Havana: Editorial Letras Cubanas, 1997.

Araújo, Nara. *Visión romántica del Otro: Estudio comparativo de Atala y Cumandá, Bug-Jargal y Sab*. Mexico City: Universidad Autónoma Metropolitana, 1998.

Benítez Rojo, Antonio. "Power/Sugar/Literature: Towards a Reinterpretation of Cubanness." *Cuban Studies* 16 (1986): 9–31.

Benítez Rojo, Antonio. *La isla que se repite: El Caribe y la perspectiva posmoderna*. Hanover, NH: Ediciones del Norte, 1989.

Bravo Villasante, Carmen. *Una vida romántica: La* [sic] *Avellaneda*. Barcelona: EDHASA, 1967.

Davies, Catherine. "Introduction." In Gertrudis Gómez de Avellaneda, *Sab*. Edited by Catherine Davies. Manchester, U.K.: Manchester University Press, 2001.

Gómez de Avellaneda, Gertrudis. *Sab*. Havana: Consejo Nacional de Cultura, 1963. Reprint, edited by Mary Cruz, 1976. Havana: Editorial Letras Cubanas, 1983. Reprint, edited by José Severa. Madrid: Editorial Cátedra, 1999. Reprint, edited by Catherine Davis. Manchester, U.K.: Manchester University Press, 2001.

Kirkpatrick, Susan. *Las románticas: Women and Subjectivity in Spain, 1835–1850*. Berkeley: University of California Press, 1989.

Luis, William. *Literary Bondage: Slavery in Cuban Narrative*. Austin: University of Texas Press, 1990.

Mata-Kolster, Elba. "Gertrudis Gómez de Avellaneda (1814–1873)." In *Latin American Writers*, vol. 1, edited by Carlos A. Solé and Maria Isabel Abreu. New York: Charles Scribner's Sons, 1989.

Méndez Rodenas, Adriana. "Mujer, nación, y otredad en Gertrudis Gómez de Avellaneda." In *Cuba en su imagen—Historia e identidad en la literatura cubana*. Madrid: Editorial Verbum, 2002.

Moreno Fraginals, Manuel. *The Sugar Mill: The Socioeconomic Complex of Sugar in Cuba, 1760–1860*. Translated by Cedric Belfrage. New York: Monthly Review Press, 1976.

Picón Garfield, Evelyn. *Poder y sexualidad: El discurso de Gertrudis Gómez de Avellaneda*. Amsterdam: Rodopi Press, 1993.

Sarduy, Severo. "Tu dulce nombre halagará mi oído." In *Homenaje a Gertrudis Gómez de Avellaneda—Memorias del simposio en el centenario de su muerte*, edited by Rosa M. Cabrera and Gladys B. Zaldívar. Miami, FL: Ediciones Universal, 1981.

Servera, José. "Introducción." In Gertrudis Gómez de Avellaneda, *Sab*. Edited by José Servera. Madrid: Editorial Cátedra, 1999.

Sommer, Doris. "*Sab*, C'est Moi." *Foundational Fictions: The National Romances of Latin America*. Berkeley: University of California Press, 1991.

SANTA CLARA'S LEONCIO VIDAL PARK

María-Cecilia Bermúdez

The Leoncio Vidal Park, heart of the urban, social, and cultural life of Santa Clara.

Santa Clara was founded in 1689 by eighteen families who moved from the Villa de Remedios to the region in the center of Cuba called *Cubanacán* by the Taíno indigenous group. The origin of the Leoncio Vidal Park lies in the Spanish colonial regulations that established that each new village had to leave a barren plot of land to be converted into a Plaza de Armas (Arms Square). In its historic evolution, this central square would become the heart and lungs of the city.

The new settlers cared for that 17,222 square-foot area and constructed *bohíos* (huts) around it, centering their civil life in the Casa Consistorial (town hall) and their spiritual life in the church. By the mid-seventeenth century there were rustic streets around the square and an area used for the sale of produce that came to be known as Plaza del Mercado (Market Square).

The physical and aesthetic development of the area prospered with the establishment of the 1812 constitutional government in Spain, which decreed that the square be named Plaza de la Constitución (Constitution Square) and ordered that it be paved and decorated with flowerboxes filled with ornamental plants protected by iron grilles, as well as a pyramid, which was later demolished.

Successive remodeling included limiting the points of access; adding gas lighting, fountains with sculptures that represented the seasons of the year, and the first monument; reorganizing the surrounding streets; building La Glorieta, a polygon-shaped gazebo where the Tarragona barracks' musical band played concerts, and the *pérgola* semicircular colonnade covered with plants. These improvements revived the site that became known as Plaza de Recreo (Recreational Square).

The transformations of the park during the twentieth century, even though undertaken for aesthetic and cultural purposes, had deep social consequences (Cabrera-Cuello p. 25). The first improvement, in 1922, redistributed the flowerboxes and separated the paved areas into four concentric paths that reflected the racist attitudes prevalent during that period: Blacks were segregated to the outer and narrowest path, whereas whites enjoyed the central areas lined with individual comfortable iron seats. The second remodeling, in 1959, joined the paths, thereby eliminating those racial barriers in both practical and social terms.

MILITARY AND POLITICAL HISTORY

Vidal Park is unusual for having served the nation's interests as the site of three of Cuba's most important military battles as well as the Spanish colonial government's cruel repressive policies and the Cuban people's insurrections and political activities during its struggle for a real independence. Because of its strategic location at the center of the island, Santa Clara was of military interest to both sides during the nineteenth-century emancipation wars. Spain had turned this town into a powerful fortress, with elite troops and barracks especially around the Plaza de Armas (García-González 1999, pp. 30–31), while the commander in chief of the Mambi revolutionary army, Generalissimo Máximo Gómez (1836–1905), quartered his troops in the area.

In 1876, during the Ten Years' War, Gómez, relying on the strong underground intelligence network in Santa Clara, ordered Manuel "Titá" Calvar-Oduardo (1827–1895), to show strength against the Spaniards by commandeering the town's supplies and rallying the despairing population.

Twenty years later, during the Independence War, Gómez again ordered an attack on Santa Clara, this time to be led by Brigadier Leoncio Vidal-Caro (1864–1896). At different times in the park's history, both men carried out their missions and reached the center of the city, though Vidal and his assistant, Corporal Ramón Brito, were killed by Spanish rifle fire. In his memory, the park was named after him (García-González 1999; Rodríguez-Altunaga).

In 1897, the park witnessed the dramatic consequences of the Spanish Captain-General Valeriano Weyler's policy of concentrating peasant families in towns where military garrisons were established. In Santa Clara, thousands of sick and hungry men, women, and children wandered the streets and squares; 6,000 of them were buried in just one day. It has been estimated that this policy caused the deaths of 150,000 to 200,000 Cubans (Torres-Cuevas and Loyola pp. 370–371).

■ *See also*

Governance and Contestation: Insurrection, 1952–1959

Guerrillero Heroico (Alberto Korda)

Spanish-American-Cuban War: 1898

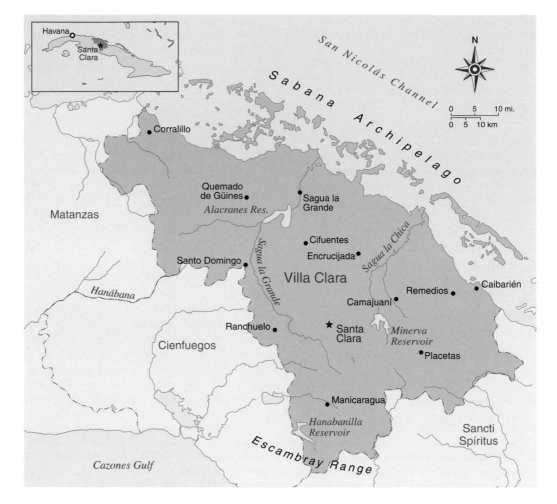

Among many *Santaclareños* who supported the nineteenth-century independence movement through intelligence work and the foundation of revolutionary clubs were Tomás González, considered the first intelligence agent from Santa Clara (García-González 1999, pp. 9–10); Luis Eduardo del Cristo (1821–1871); Miguel-Gerónimo Gutiérrez (1822–1871); Manuel García-Garófalo Morales (1853–1931); Antonio (1845–1870) and Guillermo (1847–1871) Lorda-Ortegosa and their families; Carolina Rodríguez-Suárez (1829–1899); and Eduardo Machado-Gómez (1838–1877).

In the period from 1902 to the battle led by Ernesto "Che" Guevara (1928–1967) in 1958, the Leoncio Vidal Park was the site of political and patriotic activities, strikes, student demonstrations, and revolutionary actions for freedom and social justice (García-Pérez pp. 55–58).

In response to the coup d'état on 10 March 1952, various groups gathered in the park and outside the city hall and demanded that the mayor give them guns to fight against the military coup and in support of the democratically elected government led by

the Partido Auténtico. Students from the Instituto de Segunda Enseñanza de Santa Clara (Institute of Secondary Education) and other schools went on strike, and their protest in the park was soon joined by people from all over the city. From that time on, these young people—known as the Fifties Revolutionary Generation—became an insurrectional force among students and other sectors, despite the government's brutal repression of them (Choy-Rodríguez and García-Bertrand pp. 28–29).

During the Battle of Santa Clara in December 1958, the park was one of the sites of the revolutionaries' third and decisive battle to defeat Fulgencio Batista's dictatorship. The Directorio Revolucionario 13 de Marzo (13 March Revolutionary Board) and the Movimiento Revolucionario 26 de Julio (26 July Revolutionary Movement) forces jointly led by Guevara fought all over the city. They overpowered the troops and armaments sent in an armored train by Batista's army and captured the Palacio del Gobierno Provincial (provincial government headquarters) and the Gran Hotel, later the Santa Clara Libre Hotel, both located across from the park (Fernández-Mell pp. 361–380).

In the early 2000s, the hotel facade remained pitted with bullet holes from the battle.

Between 30 December 1958 and 1 January 1959, all army and police positions surrendered except those in the park, where sharpshooters continued their resistance until the end (Guevara 1977, pp. 253–267). Among the many citizens of Santa Clara who participated in the revolutionary movement were Agustín Gómez-Lubián (1937–1957) and Margot Machado (b. 1909) and her sons Quintín (1931–1986) and Julio (1933–1957) Pino-Machado.

Two monuments to this historic struggle were erected: one at the spot where the armored train was overrun and a mausoleum honoring Guevara, those who fought against the Batista regime, and other internationalist fighters. In front of the mausoleum, which is located in Santa Clara's Plaza de la Revolución (Revolution Square), stands a bronze statue of Guevara.

MONUMENTS IN AND NEAR VIDAL PARK

The city's cultural, social, and patriotic history is remembered in sculptures, monuments, and the buildings that surround the park. The Obelisco, built in 1886, was the park's first monument. A four-sided column made of grey granite from Boston, it honors Juan Martín de Conyedo (1687–1761) and Francisco Hurtado de Mendoza (1724–1803), two priests who devoted their lives to education and public health.

Marta Abreu Arencibia (1845–1909), a patriot from Santa Clara, was recognized for her philanthropic work and dedication to Cuba's fight for freedom and against U.S. control after the Republic of Cuba was founded. She gave a large part of her fortune to the independence struggle and established schools, hospitals, homes, and the first public laundries (Anido pp. 8–9). With her husband and fellow patriot Luis Estévez-Romero (1850–1909), she built the Teatro La Caridad (La Caridad Theater) on one of the corners facing the park, with the goal of financing charity work with its profits. Well-known artists and architects helped to create the complex, which included dance rooms, clubs, and a confectionery. Because of its architectural and artistic value and the noble aims that motivated its creation, the theater was declared a national monument in 1991. A monument was built in 1924 honoring Marta's social conscience and patriotism. It depicts her sitting, holding the book *Desde Yara hasta Baire* (From Yara to Baire), written by her husband in 1899. The bronze statue, created by French sculptor August Millard, has a granite base on which are depicted her activities and the coat of arms of Santa Clara.

That same year, a bust of Brigadier Leoncio Vidal-Caro was placed in front of the mayor's office. On the other side stands La Farola, an iron column topped with a light in the form of a Phrygian cap,

which symbolizes the Cuban nation, honoring Vidal's assistant, Corporal Ramón Brito, who died at his side in battle in 1896.

The bust of the priest Alberto Chao, known as "Padre Chao," pays tribute to the priest's educational and charity work, and above all, his self-denying dedication to help the people rounded up in Santa Clara during the reconcentration period in 1895. The white marble bust was sculpted in Italy and unveiled in 1927. A small street with access to the park is also named after him.

The Glorieta, remodeled in 1911, is a veritable embodiment of Santa Clara's culture. There, the Santaclareños sang Cuba's national anthem for the first time. Since then the gazebo has been the traditional site of the municipal band's frequent concerts, featuring classics of Cuban and universal music.

One of the sculptures in Vidal Park represents a boy holding a broken boot from which water flows. It represents the boys who traveled with U.S. Civil War soldiers, playing drums and carrying water in their boots for lack of another container. The J. L. Mott Company of New York was commissioned to install the sculpture in a fountain in 1925 (González-Rodríguez p. 38). It was destroyed in 1959, but sculptor José Delarra created a bronze replica, *El niño de la bota infortunada* (The Boy with the Leaking Boot), which was placed in the original spot during Santa

Clara's three-hundredth anniversary festivities. In addition, two granite blocks respectfully recall the battle for independence commanded by General Calvar in 1876 and the 1990 declaration of Vidal Park as a national monument.

Many of Santa Clara's most outstanding educators, artists, and writers of the nineteenth and twentieth centuries are honored by monuments, street names, plaques, and the names of educational and social institutions: teacher Nicolasa Pedraza-Bonachea (1770–1868); engineer Herminio Leiva-Aguilera (1836–1897); mural painter Domingo Ravenet (1905–1969); painters Jorge Arche (1905–1957), Eduardo Abela (1889–1965), Ernesto González-Puig (1913–1988), and Lesbia Vent-Dumois (b. 1932); poet Emilio Ballagas (1908–1954); orator Severo Bernal (1918–1990); sociologist, philosopher, and professor Gaspar Jorge García-Galló (1906–1992); writer Onelio Jorge Cardoso (1914–1986); painter and folklore specialist Samuel Feijóo (1914–1992); professor, politician, and diplomat Juan Marinello (1898–1977); musicians and composers Agustín Jiménez-Crespo and Carlos Fariñas-Cantero (1934–2002); painter Aida-Ida Morales (b. 1931), singer Moraima Secada (1930–1984); and actress Eslinda Núñez (b. 1943).

BUILDINGS IN AND NEAR THE PARK

In the nineteenth and twentieth centuries *santaclareños* created cultural, social, educational, and political institutions and associations that needed to be centrally located. To this end, they constructed buildings around Vidal Park whose designs were remodeled continually adapting to the social changes and architectural styles of each period, from colonial to neoclassical, art deco, and postmodern, bringing about the eclectic character of this historic site.

The Casa de la Cultura Juan Marinello is an arts center housed in a mansion built in 1922 for the Liceo Artístico y Literario (Arts and Literary Center), a cultural institution founded in 1869 that played a significant role in the wars of independence. In 1869, the publication *El Liceo* was launched there with the collaboration of prestigious artists and writers, but in response to the revolutionary spirit of the institution, the Spanish government took over the building to house its troops. As a result, Liceo members joined either the underground struggle or the independence insurrection (Rodríguez-Altunaga p. 187). After the 1895 war, it was reborn with the 1898 publication of *El Pueblo* (The People), and it sponsored literary soirees, free educational programs for workers and their children, public speaking and literature classes, and a library. In the early twenty-first century the Casa de la Cultura continued to broaden and deepen the Liceo's traditions.

The radio station CMHW is located in the former town hall where Santa Clara's early leaders first attempted to govern the city (Barroso-Horta, Castro-González, and Acosta-Pujols p. 18). The structure underwent a series of improvements until it was finally replaced by a modern two-story building with a European-style clock in its tower, the tolling of which can be heard in and near the park.

Cuba's 1902 Constitution resulted in the creation of a provincial government whose headquarters was located in the former armory. In 1922, it was remodeled with other buildings in the Vidal Park area. Later, the building was used for the Biblioteca Provincial Martí (Martí Provincial Library), which hosted innumerable cultural and patriotic events, including the annual ceremonies for the El Beso de la Patria Award (Kiss of the Homeland) and the José Martí Contest, as well as the interment ceremony on 17 October 1997 for Che Guevara and the other guerrilla fighters found thirty years after their assassination on 9 October 1967 in Bolivia.

The Museo de Artes Decorativas (Museum of Fine Arts) has a colonial architecture modeled on nineteenth-century Cuban houses, with a cobblestone yard surrounded by traditional *portales* (arcades) that provide shade and separate the adjoining rooms. Restored when it became a museum, the building contains a collection that includes two card tables crafted in New York by the French cabinetmaker Charles-Honoré Lannuier (Kenny pp. 242–249).

The Instituto de Santa Clara, later the Preuniversitario Osvaldo Herrera, is the city's oldest secondary school, with more than a century of educational, cultural, and patriotic tradition. It was established by royal decree on 2 September 1882 as the Instituto de Segunda Enseñanza (Editorial Cubana pp. 34–35). After its founding, it had a large student population that, along with its teaching staff, became the basis for secondary education in Cuba's central region. It also offered classes free of charge to workers and other citizens on nights and Sundays.

Located in a building whose grand architecture complements the patriotic and cultural history contained in its walls, the school nurtured teachers and students who were leaders of the student and revolutionary movement. They included Osvaldo Herrera (1933–1958), who lost his life while fighting the Batista regime, and Rodolfo de las Casas (1936–1969), a distinguished revolutionary figure (Choy-Rodríguez and García-Bertrand pp. 76–79).

There are also old and new buildings with recreational facilities and services around the park. Hotels, restaurants, coffee shops, art galleries, banks, post and business offices, stores, houses, and schools are linked by shaded *portales*, creating an invisible chain surrounding Vidal Park—that historic, harmonious, and *criollísimo* (very Cuban-Criollo) site that has embraced Santa Clara's cultural, social, and urban life for more than three centuries.

BIBLIOGRAPHY

Anido, Alberto. *Marta Abreu de Estévez*. Santa Clara, Cuba: Colección Escambray, 1993.

Barroso-Horta, Lourdes, María de los Ángeles Castro-González, and Maily Acosta-Pujols. *Fondos de identidad villaclareña*. Havana: Editora Historia, Instituto de Historia de Cuba, 2009.

Castro Ruz, Fidel. "Una introducción necesaria." In *El Diario del Che en Bolivia, Noviembre 7, 1966 a Octubre 7, 1967*, by Ernesto Guevara, pp. vii–xxix. Havana: Instituto del Libro, 1968.

Castro Ruz, Fidel. "Discurso pronunciado en la velada solemne en memoria del comandante Ernesto Che Guevara el 18 de octubre de 1967." In *Ernesto Che Guevara: Obras, 1957–1967*, vol. 1, 11–24. Colección Nuestra América. Havana: Casa de las Américas, 1970.

Cabrera-Cuello, Migdalia. *Una villa entre dos ríos. Aspectos de Santa Clara Colonial*. Santa Clara, Cuba: Editorial Capiro, 2004.

Choy-Rodríguez, Armando, and José A. García-Bertrand. "Memorias del Instituto de Segunda Enseñanza de Santa Clara. Lucha contra la tiranía batistiana." *Opus Habana* 12 (2009).

Cristóbal-García, Ángel. *El Parque Vidal*. Santa Clara, Cuba: Colección Escambray, 1993a.

Cristóbal-García, Ángel. *El Teatro La Caridad*. Santa Clara, Cuba: Colección Escambray, 1993b.

Editorial Cubana. *Las Villas. Álbum-Resumen ilustrado*. Havana: Author, 1941.

Fernández Mell, Oscar. *Días de combate*. Havana: Colección Uvero, Instituto del Libro, 1970.

García-González, Luis A. *Al pie del tamarindo*. Santa Clara, Cuba: Colección Escambray, 1993.

García-González, Luis A. *La inteligencia mambisa en Santa Clara*. Santa Clara, Cuba: Editorial Capiro, 1999.

García-Pérez, Gladys Marel. *Cuando las edades llegaron a estar de pie*. Havana: Editorial Letras Cubanas, 1978.

González-Rodríguez, Susadny. "El niño y su bota infortunada." *Sol y Son* 117, no. 6 (December 2009–January 2010): 38.

Guevara, Ernesto Che. *Escritos y discursos*. Havana: Editorial Ciencias Sociales, 1977.

Guevara, Ernesto Che. *Pasajes de la guerra*. Havana: Editora Política, 2004.

Kenny, Peter M. "Opulence Abroad: Charles-Honoré Lannuier's Gilded Furniture in Trinidad de Cuba." In *American Furniture 2004*, edited by Luke Beckerdite. Fox Point, WI: Chipstone Foundation, 2004.

Kenny, Peter M., Frances F. Bretter, and Ulrich Leben. *Honoré Lannuier, Cabinet Maker from Paris*. New York: Metropolitan Museum of Art, 1998.

Pérez, Louis A., Jr. *On Becoming Cuban. Identity, Nationality, and Culture*. New York: Ecco Press, 1999.

Pérez-Cabrera, Freddy. "Teatro La Caridad, testigo excepcional de la cultura villaclareña." *Granma* (September 8, 2010): 14.

Rodríguez-Altunaga, Rafael. *Las Villas. Biografía de una provincia*. Havana: Imprenta El Siglo XX, 1955.

Torres-Cuevas, Eduardo, and Oscar Loyola-Vega. *Historia de Cuba 1492–1898. Formación y Liberación de la Nación*. 2nd ed. Havana: Editorial Pueblo y Educación, 2002.

SANTIAGO DE CUBA

Olga Sarina Portuondo Zúñiga

*History and significance of Cuba's second major city,
from the colonial era to the twenty-first century.*

Santiago de Cuba, the second-most important city
in the Cuban archipelago and capital of the province
of the same name, is located in the southeast part of
the island. It lies on the east side of a deep bay surrounded by mountains. The source of the Cauto River
lies nearby, and the region is dominated by the massive Sierra Maestra mountain range, which includes
the Gran Piedra (Great Rock). The defining feature of
the area is its rugged topography. Santiago de Cuba
was the starting place for native Arawak (sub-Taíno)
settlements.

COLONIAL ERA

After Diego Velázquez de Cuéllar completed the
conquest of the island of Cuba, he founded Villa de
Santiago in July 1515. Santiago was the capital of the
government possession of the island of Fernandina
(Cuba), part of the viceroyalty of La Española. The first
expeditions to conquer the North American continent
departed from there. In 1522 Santiago was given the
status of city, with its church designated a cathedral,
headquarters of the diocese of Cuba. The first African
slaves arrived in its port. Once its gold was exhausted

and the natives decimated, the city shrank in population. Havana, because of its geographical advantages,
became the effective capital of the island of Cuba from
the mid-sixteenth century on. Residents of Santiago,
faced with attacks by privateers and pirates, demanded
fortifications. The few inhabitants devoted their time
to extensive livestock farming. There was a line of continuity among *encomenderos* (individuals, generally
conquistadors, awarded grants by the Crown giving
them control over land and the right to exact tribute
from its indigenous inhabitants) and hacienda owners,
who engaged in a contraband commerce tolerated by
imperial officials.

During the sixteenth century the Spanish began
mining copper deposits in Cardenillo Mountain. In
1599 slaves under Crown administration performed
extraction of the mineral to supply the artillery foun-
dry in Havana and founded the towns of Santiago del
Prado (El Cobre) and San Luís del Caney (as an indigenous reservation) in the early seventeenth century,
both of which would exert economic and social influence on the daily life of Santiago de Cuba. From 1607
on, the city served as the colonial administrative center
of the Eastern (Oriental) Department (containing
the jurisdictions of Baracoa and Bayamo), which the
Crown created in an effort to suppress black-market
activities.

The government of Pedro de la Roca y Borja
(1639–1643) undertook the building of the castles of
San Pedro de la Roca (El Morro) and La Estrella, and
the battery of Santa Catalina. The port actively served
as a base for *criollo* corsairs. After the occupation of

**Map of Santiago de
Cuba**

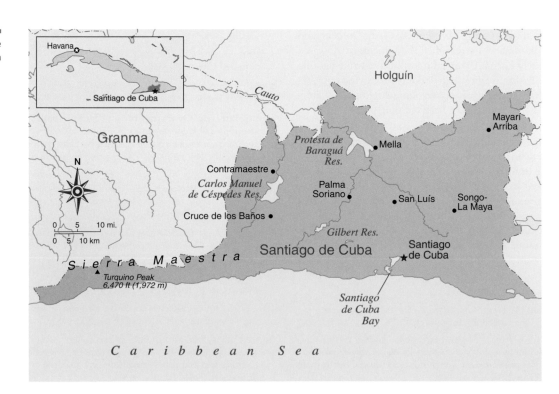

CUBA

Jamaica by the English in 1655, colonists from that island took refuge in Santiago. In 1661 pirates razed the city, but it experienced a resurgence over the final third of the seventeenth and the beginning of the eighteenth centuries, on the basis of funds originating in Mexico and invested in the rebuilding of fortifications and in the contraband trade. In the second half of the seventeenth century, ranchers established a patrician oligarchy eager to exhibit its power and autonomy. Eventually, land would prove a source of genuine power and prestige, and the city's population reached 3,000. Santiago was seat of the *cabildo* (municipal council), and its patrician oligarchy ruled the rural economy of the entire jurisdiction.

In 1704 Santiago de Cuba governor Juan Barón de Chávez organized a punitive expedition against the Bahamas. The success of this enterprise earned the city, by a Royal Decree of 1712, the title Very Noble and Very Loyal. At this time autonomous commercial activity in the city led to a hybrid economic model, with a large influx of newly arrived slaves from Africa and the rise of new needs on the part of the rural nobility. A school, the Seminario San Basilio Magno, was founded in 1722.

The mid-eighteenth century brought with it a series of crises. Between June and December 1741 a British expedition of 8,000 men disembarked at Guantánamo Bay in an ultimately failed attempt to take the city. From that point onward, Spain's Bourbon monarchy paid more attention to the eastern region of Cuba. Two decades later, the Bourbon campaign for centralization of royal power, under the model of enlightened despotism, clashed with the autonomous power of Santiago's *criollo* aristocracy. On top of these political conflicts came the devastation wrought by earthquakes in June 1766 and February 1778.

Santiago benefited from the development of plantations in the neighboring French colony of Saint-Domingue (modern Haiti). Sugarcane fields lay on the outskirts of the city. Small tobacco farmers and cattle ranches influenced the adoption of festive traditions and customs by the community at large. The progress of neighboring colonies, together with the reformist impulses of the Bourbon ministers, hastened the thawing of the monopoly on trade. Rebellion broke out among the indigenous population of San Luís del Caney and the copper miners (both slave and free) of Santiago del Prado. These groups were victims of the transformations caused by the growth of sugar mills and the rising demand for livestock (as draft animals and for meat) from St. Domingue, as well as the increase in slaves and land to benefit the great landowners. The continuities of Caribbean life through three centuries were shaken by the slave revolt in Saint-Domingue, which began in 1791 and led to Haiti's independence from France. Under pressure, the Crown granted freedom to the copper miners.

The empire's enlightened rulers of the late eighteenth century paved the way for slaveholding plantations, an enterprise taken up by the waves of immigrants from the neighboring former French colony. These settlers brought slaves with them and possessed the technical knowledge needed to organize a system of forced labor on coffee and sugar plantations. These French-Haitian and French immigrants left a cultural imprint that is one of the distinctive characteristics of the Santiago region. José María Heredia, born in Santiago in 1803 of immigrant parents, furnishes one notable example; he became the romantic poet and singer of "El Niágara." Coffee growing using slave labor expanded throughout the virgin mountains; shipments of this product left through the port of Santiago, destined for the United States and Spain. The number of sugar mills, coffee plantations, and tobacco farms in the jurisdiction increased, as did runaway slaves and *palenques* (the settlements they formed).

Its economy stimulated by free trade, Cuba traveled a dizzying road to progress between 1823 and 1843, and its capital prospered and grew in size. The large slave-based coffee, sugar, and cotton plantations were consolidated, strengthening the alliance between the *criollo* plantation owners and the conservative monarchy. From the 1820s to the 1840s, the slave population was more than 50 percent of the total population. Among free blacks, an awareness of identity emerged that was not acknowledged at the time. The fear of free blacks and slaves was a fundamental reason for the failure of the secessionist campaign—based on the third proclamation of the Cadiz Constitution in Spain—initiated in fall 1836 by Santiago governor Manuel Lorenzo, which extended throughout the Eastern Department. In the course of these events, a previously unknown consciousness of identity arose among the free people of color.

Between 1836 and 1856 new untamed lands were colonized. The mountains were preferred by coffee growers, while sugar production predominated in the plains. The English monopolized the mining industry in the Real de Minas de Cobre region, and the first Chinese settlers arrived in 1858. The port handled commercial operations, spurring urban growth. With the foundation of the Sabanilla-Maroto rail line in Valle Central, villages such as Nueva Numancia sprang up.

The struggle for independence during the Ten Years' War (1868–1878) had devastating effects on the Santiago region. All the coffee wealth disappeared, and other areas of the agrarian economy were adversely affected. When the conflict ended, General Antonio Maceo, a Santiago native (1845–1896) known as El Titán de Bronce (the Bronze Titan), became an example for blacks, mulattoes, and poor whites. The demands for social equality by these groups via the Baraguá Protest of 1878 challenged the Pacto de Zanjón, which declared an end to the fight for independence but did not address the objectives of the rebellion.

Sixteenth-century fortress in Santiago de Cuba. HÉCTOR DELGADO AND ROLANDO PUJOL

For the next seventeen years, little was done to aid economic activity. Slavery was already dying out before its formal abolition in 1886. A new attempt at insurrection, the Little War (1879–1880), originated in the city, with Santiago native Guillermo Moncada as one of its principal organizers. U.S. capital investments were made in the Daiquirí and Firmeza iron mines, which helped make Santiago a mining center. New conspiracy attempts failed during the so-called Manganese Peace.

On 24 February 1895 the War of Independence began again, and the territory suffered several blows. In April 1898 the United States intervened in the conflict, and the landing of troops in June via Daiquirí and Siboney turned Santiago into the primary theater in the conflict with Spain; the city paid the price of the naval blockade. On land, the battles of 1 July took place in the hills of San Juan and El Viso; directly across from the bay, on 3 July a one-sided battle between the navies of both nations took place. Situated near the U.S. army and occupied by the Spanish, Santiago suffered shortages of water and rations, while being bombarded. U.S. troops established a government of occupation on 17 July 1898. Along with advancements, the occupation government also brought with it beliefs in social Darwinism and eugenics, which served to justify the racial and gender inequalities inherited from colonial times. The Bacardí Rum Company industrialist Emilio Bacardí (1844–1922) became the city's first post-independence mayor, and under his leadership the neighborhood council pursued urban development projects, such as asphalt paving of city streets and the Puerto Boniato highway, and improvements in public health. He also founded the Emilio Bacardí Moreau Municipal Museum, which memorializes the wars of independence.

REPUBLICAN PERIOD

Capital first of the province of like name, and after 1905 of the new province of Oriente, Santiago de Cuba did not escape the vicissitudes of a wrenching and transformative new century. This was particularly true given the city's role as sanctuary of Cuban national identity. Modernity strode in with the automobile, the Havana-Santiago rail line, streetcars, public lighting, and movies. The chronicles of city residents Emilio Bacardí and Carlos Forment offer a record of such progress as well as hints as to political differences among Cubans, the interference of the United States, and Santiago natives' enthusiastic patriotism, this latter attested to by the Festival of the Flag and the founding of the Veterans' Column. Another chronicler, an anonymous traveler, shares such piquant details as the profusion of early-morning drinkers of Bacardí rum and the origin of the famous daiquiri cocktail in the old Venus Hotel.

The reinforcement of sugar monoculture spurred the growth of large plantations with lands dedicated to the cultivation of sugarcane. The coffee economy began its revival in the mountains of the Sierra Maestra. Low-wage manual laborers from the Antilles were preferred as cane cutters, while Spanish immigrants took on the harder labor in the iron mines. Foreign capital entered the economy. Struggles between *caudillos* (local strongmen) as well as racial conflict and the reelectionist aspirations of the second Cuban president, José Miguel Gómez, led to a second armed intervention by the United States in 1909. The onerous discrimination against the black veterans of the Ejército Libertador led to the fratricidal Race War of 1912, which was started in the neighboring region by proponents of the Partido de los Independientes de Color (Independent Party of Color). Santiago de Cuba was the setting for the army's operations to put down the uprising, the trials of those implicated in the rebellion, and the burial of the leaders killed in the highly unequal battles. Fear of another armed intervention by the United States was widespread.

The optimism of the first decades of the twentieth century began to pale as residents showed their disgust at the lack of water, poor public hygiene, and neglect of education, among many other problems—to which was added the earthquake of 1932, which made even more precarious the general crisis of capitalism during the Great Depression. During the Gerardo Machado regime (1925–1933), the revolutionary Antonio Guiteras prepared the uprising of Gallinita, near Santiago, but it was aborted.

All the while life continued amid Santiago's staggered rooftops, colorful houses, and inviting entryways, and residents maintained their distinctive culinary habits, drinking *prú* (a local beverage whose base ingredient is a fermented extract from the root of the *bejuco ubí* plant) and enjoying *empanadillas* (small empanadas), *buñuelos* (a donut-like fried bread twisted into a figure eight), and sandwiches in the street. An eclectic array of buildings was erected during the Republican period, and urban infrastructure was improved. The city became the cradle of the *son*, *guaracha*, and *bolero* musical styles, popularized by such figures as Pepe Sánchez, Miguel Matamoros, Compay Segundo, Ñico Saquito, and others.

Three political themes emerged in Santiago after the war: animosity toward the capital, which collected provincial taxes but gave nothing in exchange; the events of the recently ended war; and the rejection of Yankee imperialism. Among the cultured and educated class, new institutional impulses contributed to the progress of Santiago: Acción Ciudadana (Citizen Action), the Sociedad de Geografía e Historia (Geography and History Society), and the Grupo Humboldt, as well as the Universidad de Oriente, all of which signified progress and development in a city constructing new neighborhoods, public buildings, the Circunvalación (ring road) boulevard, and the Charco Mono aqueduct. As in the first years of the Republic, the collaborative activity of civil institutions stimulated the city's development, primarily through the economic growth of a middle class favored by the new circumstances. In politics, the main party of the eastern part of the country, the Partido del Pueblo Cubano (Ortodoxo) (Cuban People's Party, Orthodox), led by Eduardo Chibás, a native of Santiago de Cuba, broke off from the Partido Revolucionario Cubano (Cuban Revolutionary Party). In the capital, Chibás found strong support for his stance against corruption in the higher spheres of government. Citizens' consciousness had been strengthened, and with it their ability to make demands.

REVOLUTIONARY PERIOD

An atmosphere of national self-determination was frustrated by the coup d'état led by Fulgencio Batista. The revolutionary guerrilla war against Batista began with the assault by a group of young rebels of Orthodox origins, led by Fidel Castro, on the Moncada Barracks in 1953. The trial of the rebels that followed was held in the Court of Santiago, where Fidel Castro's manifesto, *La historia me absolverá* (History Will Absolve Me), stirred the public. The terror sowed by the Batista regime in Santiago, led by the paramilitary group Tigres de Masferrer (Tigers of Masferrer), was best evoked by José Soler Puig's novel *Bertillon 166*. As part of the plan to confront the regime, the MR-26-7 revolutionaries, led by the young Santiago native Frank País García, attacked the city's police station and customs house to distract the Batista forces and facilitate the landing of the revolutionary expedition from the *Granma* yacht on the coast of Manzanillo. This group was nonetheless decimated, but those who were able to save themselves organized as guerrilla forces led by Castro; for two long years they confronted the regime's troops, until triumphing on 1 January 1959. Santiago de Cuba, the logistics center of the clandestine operations, supplied men, arms, and medicine to the guerrillas in the mountains; the city feted the first ranks of combatants in the midst of popular jubilation.

In the twenty-first century Santiago de Cuba enjoys a social and economic transformation, with new programs of education, health care, and industrialization, including a refinery, a thermoelectric plant, a cement factory, a flour mill, rum and beer factories, and several sugar processing plants in the region. As of 2011, the province of Santiago de Cuba comprises nine municipalities: II Frente, III Frente, Guamá, Palma Soriano, Contramaestre, Songo–La Maya, San Luís, Mella, and Santiago de Cuba (including the towns of Caney and El Cobre), the capital. In 1997 the Oficina del Conservador de la Ciudad (Office of the City Preservationist) was founded; its essential objective is to restore Santiago de Cuba's historic downtown and to preserve El Morro castle and the industrial complex of the coffee growers in the mountains of the Sierra Maestra as World Heritage Sites.

Of the province's one million residents, half are concentrated in the capital. During the Festival del Caribe (la Fiesta del Fuego, or the Festival of Fire) and Carnaval, city residents and visitors express the Antillean joy of living. Near the Parque Céspedes the Casa de la Trova (House of the Troubadours) is one of the best spots for listening to traditional music. The city's history is essential to defining Cuban identity and culture, preserving the past and the genuine traditions of the nation. Mountainous and mestizo, the city and its province are inexhaustible sources of culture, natural beauty, and human warmth.

BIBLIOGRAPHY

Duharte Jiménez, Rafael, and Elizabet Recio Lobaina, comp. *Santiago de Cuba siglo XX: Cronistas y viajeros miran la ciudad.* Santiago de Cuba: Editorial Oriente, 2005.

Forment Rovira, Carlos E. *Crónicas de Santiago de Cuba, t. II.* Edited by Olga Portuondo Zúñiga. Santiago de Cuba: Ediciones Alqueza, 2006.

Gott, Richard. *Cuba: A New History.* New Haven, CT: Yale University Press, 2004.

Guicharnaud-Tollis, Michèle, and Jean-Louis Joachim. *Cuba: De l'indépendance à nos jours.* Paris: Ellipses Édition Marketing, S.A., 2007.

Junta de Andalucía. *Oriente de Cuba: Guía arquitectura/ An Architectural Guide.* Oriente de Cuba: Andalucía Dirección General de Arquitectura y Vivienda, 2002.

Portuondo Zúñiga, Olga. *Santiago de Cuba, desde la fundación hasta la Guerra de los Diez Años.* Santiago de Cuba: Editorial Oriente, 1996.

■ *See also*

Havana: Architectural Development and City Planning

Health and Health Care: Pre-1959

SCIENCE AND TECHNOLOGY IN CUBA

Rolando García Blanco

Development of science and technology as Cuba forged a national identity.

In order to analyze Cuban history in detail during the last two centuries of Spanish colonial domination, it is important to stress that the colonial system was closely tied to the sugar industry's rampant growth, to the detriment of incipient agricultural diversity and other industrial production. The massive introduction of slaves was a temporary obstacle to the consolidation of the Cuban identity, which ultimately crystallized as a result of the Ten Years' War that began on 10 October 1868. The history of Cuban science and technology dates back to the rudimentary practices of the island's original inhabitants and the subsequent imposition of European culture, which left its mark in such activities as the construction of forts and vessels of various kinds, methods of mineral extraction, and projects to provide the population with water.

SIGNIFICANT ACCOMPLISHMENTS AND DEVELOPMENTS

Initial scientific and technological accomplishments include Cuba's first scientific book, *El arte de navegar* (The Art of Navigation), written in Cuba by Lázaro Flores from 1663 to 1672 and published in Spain in 1673; the introduction of the printing press in 1723; and publication in 1787 of Antonio Parra's *Descripción de las diferentes piezas de historia natural las más del ramo marítimo, representadas en setenta y cinco láminas* (Description of Various Aspects, Mostly Maritime, of Natural History, Illustrated on Seventy-Five Plates). Other significant moments in the development of Cuban science were the founding of the health administration authority, the Protomedicato (1711); the Royal and Pontifical University of San Jerónimo de la Habana (1728); the Royal Seminary College of San Carlos and San Ambrosio (1773); the newspaper *Papel Periódico de la Habana* (1790); and the Royal Economic Society of Friends of the Country (1793). Outstanding representatives of their respective disciplines were José Agustín Caballero (1762–1835) in philosophy; Francisco de Arango y Parreño (1765–1837) in economics; and Tomás Romay y Chacón (1764–1849) in medicine.

In 1797 alone, several significant works were published in Havana. These include: *Discurso sobre las buenas propiedades de la tierra bermeja para el cultivo de la caña de azúcar* (Discussion of the Good Properties of Red Soil for Growing Sugarcane), by Jorge Luis Morejón y Gato; *Disertación sobre algunas plantas cubanas* (Dissertation on Some Cuban Plants), by Baltasar Boldo; *Memoria sobre la cría de las abejas* (Memoir on Beekeeping), by Eugenio de la Plaza; *Memorias sobre el mejor modo de fabricar azúcar* (Memoirs on the Best Way to Produce Sugar), by J. F. Martínez de Campos; *Oración inaugural en elogio de la cirugía* (Inaugural Speech in Praise of Surgery), by Francisco Javier Córdoba; and *Disertación sobre la fiebre maligna llamada vulgarmente vómito negro* (Dissertation on the Malignant Fever Commonly Known as Black Vomit), by Tomás Romay y Chacón.

By the turn of the nineteenth century, members of the Cuban bourgeoisie were promoting new technologies, scientific research, and education. Starting in 1880, technology transfer in the sugar industry intensified in the island's central and eastern regions. In 1837 Cuba became the first Latin American country to have a railroad—Spain itself did not have one at that time—with the laying of the first tracks between Havana and Güines. The track was built by U.S. engineers with British financing and technology, and that same year the United States exported the first two locomotive engines to Cuba. Other technological advances introduced in the nineteenth century include the telegraph, with the first line between Havana and Bejucal (1853) and the first underwater cable between Cuba and Florida (1867); telephone service, installed in Havana in 1881, a few years after it began in the United States; and electric lighting (1889), also just a brief time after it appeared in the United States.

Applied Science In the field of applied science, the Spanish chemist José Luis Casaseca (1800–1869), who founded the Institute of Chemical Research (1848), advocated the use of vacuum evaporation technology in sugar production. His successor was the Cuban chemist Álvaro Reynoso (1829–1888), author of the valuable *Ensayo sobre el cultivo de la caña de azúcar* (Essay on the Cultivation of Sugarcane, 1862).

Applied science was also instrumental in efforts to supply water to the township of San Cristóbal de la Habana, which from its establishment in 1519 until the late nineteenth century depended on the Almendares River, first through the channel called the Zanja Real (1592) and later through the Fernando VII Aqueduct (1835). In 1856, upon request of the Captaincy General, Francisco de Albear y Fernández de Lara (1816–1887), then lieutenant colonel of the Spanish Corps of Engineers, presented the *Proyecto de conducción a La Habana de las aguas de los manantiales de Vento* (Plan for Transporting Water from the Vento Springs to Havana), a proposal for a closed stonework aqueduct system that would deliver water across 11 kilometers from its source. The opening of the Albear Aqueduct in 1893 concluded more than three decades of construction, amid extremely adverse economic and political conditions, and topographic, technical, and sanitation difficulties. Workers building the aqueduct were decimated by what were known as the Vento fevers. The aqueduct, awarded the gold medal at the 1878 Paris Exposition Universelle, was colonial Cuba's most important engineering project and one of the most brilliant of its time anywhere in the world.

Cuban geological research, which had its roots in the *Political Essay on the Island of Cuba*, by the German naturalist and traveler Alexander von Humboldt (1769–1859), was undertaken by Cuban-born Manuel Fernández de Castro (1822–1895). In 1864 Fernández de Castro published *Sobre la formación de la tierra colorada que constituye gran parte de los terrenos de cultivo de la Isla de Cuba* (On the Formation of the Red Soil that Constitutes a Large Part of the Cultivated Land on the Island of Cuba).

With contributions from the distinguished French chemist and bacteriologist Louis Pasteur (1822–1895) and financing from Havana physician

Juan Santos Fernández (1847–1922), the Havana Histology and Bacteriology Laboratory and Institute of Rabies Vaccination was established in 1887. Upon introducing the technology for the production of a rabies vaccine, this institute opened a new scientific field in Latin America and introduced technology for the production of a rabies vaccine. In 1894 Cuba became the first Latin American country to have a diphtheria vaccine, as well as medicine for treating streptococcus and a vaccine against carbuncles.

Natural History Felipe Poey Aloy (1799–1891), a pioneer of Cuban natural history, was the author of *Centuria de los lepidópteros de la Isla de Cuba* (A Century of Lepidoptera on the Island of Cuba, 1832); he published his *Memorias sobre la historia natural de la Isla de Cuba* (Memoirs on the Natural History of the Island of Cuba) from 1851 to 1858. His most important book, which received a gold medal at the International Colonial Exhibition of Amsterdam, was *Ictiología cubana* (Cuban Ichthyology, 1883). In 1877 he was elected president of the Anthropology Society of the Island of Cuba, whose members included Antonio Mestre (1834–1887), Arístides Mestre (1865–1952), Enrique José Varona (1849–1933), and Luis Montané (1849–1936). Montané, considered Cuba's first physical anthropologist, defended his thesis of the "Cuban fossil man" at the International Anthropology and Archaeology Congress (Monaco, 1906) and the Buenos Aires Congress (1911), based on an 1888 find in the Sancti Spíritus region. The resulting controversy diverted attention from his major discovery of the first presumably native simian remains found in Cuba, which the Argentine naturalist Florentino Ameghino (1854–1911) named Montaneia in the discoverer's honor.

Other important figures in natural history were the German-born zoologist Juan Cristóbal Gundlach (1810–1896), the author of *Ornitología cubana*

The Albear Aqueduct in Havana. The opening of the Albear Aqueduct in 1893 concluded more than three decades of construction amid extremely adverse economic and political conditions, as well as topographic, technical, and sanitation difficulties. COURTESY OF THE CUBAN HERITAGE COLLECTION, UNIVERSITY OF MIAMI LIBRARIES, CORAL GABLES, FLORIDA

(Cuban Ornithology, 1893), and Carlos de la Torre y de la Huerta (1858–1950), whose work in the field of malacology established Cuba as a region with one of the largest volumes of endemic species of land mollusks. De la Torre identified marine mollusks from the Jurassic period called ammonites and contributed to the skeletal reconstruction of *Megalocnus rodens*, a North American species of giant sloth.

Physics In physics, of special importance is the creation of the philosophy department at the San Carlos Seminary (1813) and the work of Father Félix Varela (1788–1853). Varela's *Lección preliminar* (Preliminary Lesson, 1818) recognized nature as a field of knowledge. His *Lecciones de filosofía* (Philosophy Lessons, 1818) is the first text written by a Cuban about aspects of physics. In meteorology, the Economic Society of Friends of the Country founded the Havana Physics-Meteorology Observatory (1856), headed until 1869 by Andrés Poey Aguirre (1825–1919). Another outstanding figure was Spanish-born Jesuit priest Benito Viñes (1837–1893), who in 1870 became the director of the Belén College Observatory, founded in 1857. Viñes made valuable contributions to the understanding of tropical hurricanes and to improving relations with institutions in other countries.

MEDICINE

The field of medicine played a fundamental role in Cuba's scientific development. Medical studies, begun when the University of Havana was founded, took on a more practical quality in the late eighteenth century. Tomás Romay (1764–1849) can be credited for the focus on vaccination rather than inoculation against smallpox and the introduction of the smallpox vaccine on the island (1803). Nicolás José Gutiérrez (1800–1890) founded *Repertorio Médico Habanero* (Havana Medical Catalogue, 1840), Cuba's first medical journal. Other advances introduced in Cuba shortly after their discovery were the utilization of inhaled ether as a surgical anesthesia (1847), by Vicente Antonio de Castro (1809–1869), and the use of chloroform for the same purpose (1848), by Dr. Gutiérrez.

The Havana Society for Clinical Studies, established in 1879, sponsored the First Regional Medical Congress of the Island of Cuba (1890), created the Pathology Museum, set up branches in some provinces, and maintained ties with institutions in other countries until its dissolution in 1957. Other scientific organizations included the Hygiene Society (1891–1895), which founded the periodical *La Higiene* (Hygiene), and the Havana Pharmacy College (1880), which published the journal *Repertorio de Farmacia* (Catalogue of Pharmacy).

All this scientific activity culminated in Cuba's most far-reaching contribution to the world of science in the nineteenth century. At the time, the means of transmission of yellow fever (a viral infection known in Cuba as *black vomit*) was unknown. After studying the organs of people who had died of the disease, the Cuban scientist Carlos Juan Finlay (1833–1915) concluded that the pathogenic agent entered the human body through the skin. He developed a hypothesis that yellow fever was transmitted by mosquitoes and presented it in 1881 at the International Sanitary Conference held in Washington, D.C.; the results of his research were subsequently published in "El mosquito hipotéticamente considerado como agente de transmisión de la fiebre amarilla" (The Mosquito Considered Hypothetically as the Vector of Yellow Fever). His discovery came amid controversy between two divergent viewpoints, one hypothesizing that the disease was transmitted through direct interpersonal transmission, the other by way of environmental factors. Scientists searching zealously for a bacterium and its possible pathogenic agents were skeptical of Finlay's hypothesis, and Finlay was unable to design an experiment to prove conclusively to the scientific community that he was correct.

When the United States entered the Spanish-American War in 1898, U.S. troops fell prey to the epidemic. A medical commission headed by Major Walter Reed, a U.S. Army physician, was sent from the United States to investigate how the disease was being spread. The commission proposed to test Finlay's thesis by using disease-bearing mosquitoes, and Finlay immediately supported that initiative. A member of the commission, James Carroll, and a volunteer from the army agreed to allow themselves to be bitten; they came down with the disease but recovered. Another commission member, Jesse Lazear, also became infected, but it remains unclear whether he was bitten by accident or by his own design; within seven days, he was dead. Reed, who had presented preliminary findings in the United States, returned to Cuba determined to design an experiment that would satisfy the scientific community that Finlay's thesis was correct. In this he was ultimately successful. Although Reed and his commission were often credited with stemming yellow fever, Reed credited Finlay for his initial discovery. The World History of Medicine Congresses held in 1935, 1954, and 1956 recognized the Cuban scientist for his enormous contribution to medical science.

The Royal Academy of Medical, Physical, and Natural Sciences of Havana (founded in 1861) was especially important in the development of the scientific movement. Bringing together the island's most distinguished talent, the academy hosted debates on the most advanced theories. Havana physician Nicolás José Gutiérrez was one of its founders and its president for almost thirty years. The only New World organization of its kind that was authorized by Spain, the academy preceded its Mexican counterpart by twenty-three years, the Argentine academy by thirteen years, and the corresponding U.S. academy by two years. Medical matters were among those most debated there, especially those related to smallpox, cholera, and yellow fever; other topics were in the

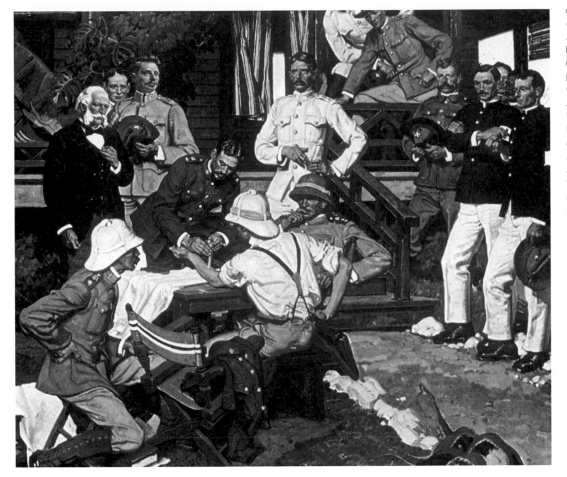

fields of technology, agriculture, pharmacy, hygiene, botany, zoology, and paleontology. Until the end of the colonial period, the academy functioned as an inspection, arbitration, and consulting agency.

DECLINE OF SCIENCE DURING REPUBLICAN PERIOD

By the late nineteenth century, Cuban science reflected a national consciousness in a place not yet a nation and a colonial context in which economic and social backwardness were prevalent. U.S. military intervention (1898–1902) brought to an end Cuba's thirty-year independence struggle against Spanish rule. It also marked the transition to the creation of the Cuban Republic, based on the official establishment of relations with the United States, which had been strengthening during the colonial period. The United States was thus able to assess Cuba's existing natural wealth and resources, as reflected in the 1901 *Report on a Geological Reconnaissance of Cuba*, written by a commission of the U.S. Geological Survey.

Although the Academy of Medical, Physical, and Natural Sciences of Havana lasted throughout the period of the Republic, the moment the word *Royal* was stripped from its name it was also deprived of its previous role as a consulting agency and a scientific

leader, these functions having been reassigned to other government agencies. Headed for the first two decades of the twentieth century by ophthalmologist Juan Santos Fernández Hernández (1847–1922), the academy continued to serve as a forum for discussion, mostly about medicine, even though medical activity in practice was transferred to medical institutions; work in other scientific fields was assumed by new specialized associations. The universalism that the academy was never fully able to achieve was gradually embraced by the University of Havana.

Among the various institutions devoted to dealing with public health problems were the National Laboratory of the Island of Cuba, whose mission was to carry out chemical and bacteriological testing from 1902 to 1944; the Forensic Medical Corps (1903); the National Pharmacy Association (1907); the Cuban Tropical Medicine Society (1908); the Department of Health and Public Welfare (1909), one of the earliest public health ministries in the world; and the National Medical College (1911), whose existence was brief.

At the University of Havana, the island's only center of higher learning at that time, attempts led by Secretary of Education Enrique José Varona (1849–1933) to introduce liberal ideas dominant in the most industrialized countries clashed with Cuba's reality at that time. Indeed, in a speech on 6 August 1900, in which he called for reforms in higher learning, Varona noted that for many years Cuba's general educational level had been declining. He cited the island's extremely deficient elementary education and almost nonexistent secondary education, to the extent that the necessary link between the rudiments of knowledge and higher culture was missing. In addition to the absence of an adequate educational system, Varona argued that learning could not be gained through rote memorization but must be linked to practice. He added that a teacher's role should be to teach students how to learn, how to consult, how to research, and to motivate students; likewise, centers of secondary and higher education should be considered workshops rather than places encouraging mere recitations.

Although many of Varona's proposed reforms, known as the Varona Plan, were implemented, government support for higher education was lacking throughout the Republican period. As a result, there was a shortage of research equipment and lackluster teaching in some fields, leading many Cubans to study abroad. However, when they returned to Cuba they introduced new educational methods and systems into Cuban institutions. The School of Engineers, Electricians, and Architects was established at the University of Havana in October 1900 according to the Plan Varona, but it was not particularly oriented to developing new equipment and technologies.

IMPORTANT ASSOCIATIONS AND SCIENTISTS OF THE REPUBLICAN PERIOD

A group of scientific associations appeared during these years, including the Cuban Society of Engineers (1908); the Felipe Poey Cuban Society of Natural History (1913); the Geography Society of Cuba (1914), which assumed governmental responsibilities in 1930; the History Academy of Cuba (1910), subordinate to the Department of Public Instruction and Fine Arts; and the Cuban International Law Society (1915). Furthermore, several medical associations were formed, specializing in fields such as pharmacy, veterinary medicine, and dentistry. Literary societies, notably the Athenaeum of Havana (1902), undertook scientific research as part of their labors.

Important work in applied research was done during the period of the Republic by the Experimental Agricultural Station in Santiago de las Vegas, created in 1904 (later called the Institute of Fundamental Research in Tropical Agriculture, part of the Cuban Ministry of Agriculture). This agency functioned during the first six decades of the twentieth century with scant resources and a small group of scientists, among them botanists and agronomists Juan Tomás Roig Mesa (1877–1970) and Julián Acuña Galé (1900–1973), along with U.S. naturalist Stephen Cole Bruner (1891–1953). In 1927 the agency introduced, bred, and distributed a sugarcane variety that helped save the Cuban sugar industry from the mosaic virus and demonstrated the station's scientific potential. However, its scientific achievements went unpublished, except for the ones of interest to agribusiness, which profited from an agricultural system based on large landholdings and the exploitation of cheap, temporary labor. Similar fates awaited experimental cane stations of the 1920s, 1930s, and 1940s (such as the Baraguá Sugar Mill in Camagüey, sponsored by the Tropical Plant Research Foundation of Washington, D.C., and the Chaparra Sugar Mill in Las Tunas, directed by Italian engineer Mario Calvino). The Sericulture Station, headed by Italian Mario Tirelli, focused on breeding silkworms; it operated in Santa Clara from 1938 to 1946.

During this period Cuba had a number of outstanding social scientists in various disciplines who raised awareness of the country's political and economic realities. Many distinguished Cuban historians and anthropologists of the time established scientific and methodological guidelines through their work on economics, regional history, and geography.

In regard to technical research, the 1902 and 1934 Reciprocity Treaties formalized the technology transfer from the United States to Cuba that had begun in the nineteenth century. Such transfers were made shortly after a given technology was introduced in the United States, and for that reason, both the equipment and the personnel to operate it were imported. This process was accelerated during the first decades of the twentieth century; one eminent example was the construction of nickel plants in Nicaro and Moa that supplied the New Orleans processing industry with its raw materials.

In 1950 a World Bank mission to Cuba, headed by Francis Adams Truslow, president of the New York Curb Exchange, arrived to study the island's economic situation and to assess the possibility of an International Bank of Reconstruction and Development (IBRD) loan to the government headed by Carlos Prío Socarrás. The result of this visit was the *Report on Cuba*, which confirmed the degree of stagnation affecting the country for the preceding twenty-five years and recommended urgent agricultural and industrial diversification and improvements in transportation and communications. Although the *Report on Cuba* recommended the creation of an institution devoted to technology research, it was not until 1955 that the Cuban Institute of Technology Research (ICIT) was established for the purpose of studying the country's natural resources and recommending ways to use them to the island's economic advantage, and proposing national economic alternatives. Although the ICIT began with limited funding, it was able to attract some alternative financing from the private sector to somewhat mitigate the difficulties it faced. Among the subjects the ICIT researched, on its own or in conjunction with other Cuban government or private agencies, were utilization of sugarcane bagasse and cane juice, improvement of tobacco quality, industrial utilization of Cuban asphalt, development of the castor oil industry, and the nutritional value of Cuban foods. As a complement to its research work, from 1957 to 1962 the institute published the periodical *Boletín Informativo* and its *Serie de Estudios sobre Trabajos de Investigación* (Series of Studies on Research Work).

The National Observatory and the Belén College Observatory carried out only limited meteorological research during the period of the Republic, and the medical research undertaken by the Histology and Bacteriology Laboratory, the Finlay Institute (1927), and the Institute of Tropical Medicine (1937), as part of the University of Havana Medical School, faced similar financial difficulties. A key figure in medical research was Pedro Kourí Esmeja (1900–1964), considered the father of Cuban medical parasitology.

Illustrating the lack of attention paid to science and technology during the first half of the twentieth century is the fact that even the classification of Cuban soils, an effort initiated in 1916, did not progress until 1928, when the sugar boom necessitated the hiring of U.S. specialists to create a map accompanied by a text, *The Soils of Cuba*. This document was released in 1928, but because of the subsequent decline in the sugar market, it was not translated into Spanish until 1962.

RENEWED COMMITMENT TO SCIENCE AFTER THE REVOLUTION

One characteristic of the period beginning with the Revolution in 1959 was the top leaders' understanding of the role that science and technology would play in the country's subsequent development. Fidel Castro stated that Cuba's future would depend on its scientists and thinkers. However, the scientific and technical sector had a shortage of personnel and of institutions necessary to meet the challenges of economic and social development independently. Cuba suffered from a backward agricultural situation, characterized by the predominant sugar monoculture; a high level of illiteracy; and industries with generally outdated equipment. Although the Academy of Sciences was an independent agency, the state subsidy it received was included in the Ministry of Justice's budget; the National Observatory was part of the navy; and the Geographic Society, although autonomous, maintained close ties to the Ministry of State. To a great extent, the work of these institutions depended on meager private financing and above all on the total devotion to research of certain well-known scientists. The 1961 Literacy Campaign succeeded in teaching one million Cubans, out of a total population of barely six million, to read and write. This eradication of illiteracy was followed by an arduous and ongoing effort to improve public instruction, from elementary schools to higher education.

NEW SCIENTIFIC CENTERS

In 1962 the government created the National Commission for the Academy of Sciences of Cuba, under the Council of Ministers. That same year, university reform was undertaken, along with the establishment of scientific research centers. Thus began a phase

characterized by a broad effort by institutions to create opportunities for research, by first bringing together the scant existing scientific personnel and then incorporating groups of young people being trained as professionals. These professionals were soon to become a powerful skilled workforce that could promote the country's scientific and technological development. As part of this process, the Academy of Sciences placed special emphasis on studying the island's natural resources. Socialist countries provided vital assistance by supplying equipment and specialists to train Cuban personnel in its operation.

New research institutions gradually emerged, such as the Institute of Geography (1962), which in coordination with the Soviet Union's Academy of Sciences published the first *Atlas Nacional de Cuba* (National Atlas of Cuba, 1970), winner of the Soviet Union's State Science and Technology Prize (1973). Studies in geology and paleontology began at this institute but were soon transferred to the Institute of Geology and Paleontology, also established in the 1960s. The latter created and published a geological map of Cuba in close collaboration with related academies in the Soviet Union, Hungary, Poland, and Bulgaria.

In 1965 other scientific centers came into being, such as the Soils Institute, whose first major achievement, four years later, was obtaining initial support from the People's Republic of China for publication of a map of Cuban soils; the Institute of Oceanography; and the Institute of Meteorology, which starting with just a few stations created an important material base in collaboration with the Soviet Union, the United Nations Development Program, and the World Meteorological Organization, and which published a climate atlas of Cuba.

The Sugarcane Institute (1964) was established to conduct research related to the country's agricultural development, starting off with three stations that had previously been devoid of material resources. Another important institution, founded in cooperation with the German Democratic Republic, was the Institute of Fundamental Research in Tropical Agriculture, staffed by personnel from the aforementioned Experimental Agricultural Station in Santiago de las Vegas. The Carlos J. Finlay History of Medical Science Museum was created in the 1960s, and in 1963 the Institute of Scientific and Technical Information began to coordinate with a national and international network of information centers. Ernesto Guevara, in his position at that time as minister of industries, played a significant role in promoting research applied to production. In late 1962 he prioritized four lines of development: sugar chemistry, metallurgy, electronics, and shipbuilding. This resulted in the establishment of the Cuban Institute for Research into Sugarcane Derivatives, with a long tradition of research related to sugarcane bagasse, one of whose applications has been the production of newsprint; the Cuban Institute of Mineral Resources, which sponsored mineral prospecting throughout the country; and the Cuban Institute of Mining and Metallurgy, with the objective of promoting mineral processing technologies.

Other important institutions set up in the production sector were the Cuban Institute of Technological Research; the Cuban Institute of Machinery Development, whose mission was the creation of spare parts and agricultural equipment that would replace foreign technologies; the Cuban Institute for Development in the Chemical Industry; and the Industrial Automation Center, which in 1962 took over the work of the Ministry of Industries' Automatic and Electronic Division, playing an outstanding role in training the first Cuban automation specialists.

The universities have played an important part in the establishment of research centers fundamental to the country's strategic development. The National Commission on Scientific Degrees was founded in 1974 as part of the Ministry of Higher Education, but in 1992 it was transferred to the Council of Ministers as an integral system for obtaining those degrees. Another institution directly subordinate to the Council of Ministers is the National Center for Scientific Research, devoted to research on biology, chemistry, medicine, and veterinary medicine; it obtained results related to the elimination of swine fever, which caused considerable losses in 1970. Another such agency was the Institute of Animal Science, which carried out significant work on livestock diseases and nutrition.

THE CHALLENGE OF APPLYING SCIENCE

Research centers were also created in the medical sciences sector under the Ministry of Public Health, in the fields of oncology and radiobiology, neurosurgery, cardiovascular surgery, nephrology, gastroenterology, hematology and immunology, epidemiology and microbiology, endocrinology and metabolic diseases, and sports medicine. In 1974 the National Council of Science and Technology was founded to serve as a guiding body for the various scientific and technical research institutes, in line with a trend promoted by the Council of Mutual Economic Assistance (CMEA) and UNESCO. The National Council was soon superseded by the State Committee on Science and Technology (1976), and subsequently by the Academy of Sciences of Cuba (1980), ushering in what could be considered the second stage of the development of national scientific and technological policy. The new guiding body established priorities for national research under a coordination plan based on scientific problems. Although the network of institutions necessary for scientific and technological research was never completed, the level of development achieved since the 1980s, along with the island's inclusion in the CMEA, confirmed that Cuba had reached a level at which it could begin to achieve a balance between technology transfer and the utilization of scientific and technical knowledge acquired in its many research

centers. However, given the international context in which Cuba functioned as part of a socialist market that provided outdated technology (though under very favorable economic conditions), Cuba was almost completely dependent on technology transfer.

This was the situation for more than a decade, when—despite the scientific advances achieved by the network of research centers—neither the installed capacities nor existing potential were reached. As for the aforementioned coordination plan, the network was unable to subordinate the institutions' specific research interests to national objectives or to commit the utilization of their results to their business elements, linked to industrial entities in the socialist bloc countries. In the early 1980s new elements brought other changes, including the creation of the Biological Front, grouping together various specialized institutions based on the principle of their personnel's devotion to scientific and technological work, with the goal of determining research priorities and a coordinated utilization of existing resources.

Opened in 1986, the Center for Genetic Engineering and Biotechnology quickly became one of the most important institutions of its kind in the Third World. It was initially established for the production of interferon but soon expanded into various lines of research, development, and production. It was the successor to the Center for Biological Research (1982), combining two teams that had been working on leukocyte interferon and recombinant interferon. At that time, other centers were established with facilities for the development of production lines. These included the Immunoassay Center, the Biopreparations Center, the Center for the Production of Laboratory Animals, and the Finlay Institute, whose mission was research on and production of vaccines. In 1986 the category of scientific and technical programs was established, its function to determine the main problems to be tackled by various research sectors, to be engaged with the scientific centers, and to promote the application of results.

Starting in 1994, scientific and technical programs were established in the following realms: integral sugarcane harvesting, medical equipment, biopharmaceuticals, vaccines, biotechnological and sustainable production of animal feed, intensification and improvement of the nickel-cobalt industry, biotechnology applied to tropical crops, development of domestic energy and fuel sources, integral development of mountainous regions, and tourism. That same year, three social science programs were approved: Current Trends in the World Economy and the International Relations System; the Cuban Economy Today: Challenges and Prospects; and Cuban Society and Revolution: Twenty-First-Century Challenges.

The third phase of scientific and technological policy was characterized by a greater interaction with society as a whole. Starting in 1990, it witnessed the introduction of scientific hubs to facilitate the formation of integrated cooperation networks; the introduction of technological management; and the transformation of the Spare Parts Forum into the National Scientific and Technical Forum.

The first scientific hub established, the Western Hub, brought together the work being carried out in the medical-pharmaceutical and biotechnology sectors, based on the creation of major scientific centers on Havana's western edge, subsequently joined by agricultural science institutions in other parts of the city. Likewise, so-called thematic hubs were organized in Havana, centered on industry, biotechnology, and the social sciences, as well as territorial hubs in the other provinces.

The creation of hubs was based on the following prerequisites, among others: the presence of top-priority economic and social objectives; the existence of centers capable of generating scientific knowledge; the possibility of converting that knowledge into social practice; and the availability of groups of scientists willing to devote themselves completely to this work. One constant in these hubs was the involvement of both experts from production and service units and professors and researchers. Hub coordinators were chosen for their ability to integrate systems, their scientific authority, and their administrative backgrounds. Another interesting experience was the periodic convocation of the National Scientific and Technical Forum, a mass movement aimed at promoting popular participation in the practical solution of various problems, by combining efforts for innovation and the systemization of practical applications.

In the development of national scientific policy in the mid-1990s, some of the intervening factors were the important role of scientific and technical programs in the composition of the country's most important research; the progressive influence of environmental problems in the determination of scientific and technical policy; the universities' progressive role within the scientific and technical system; extension of research to the local level and the dissemination of scientific knowledge; technological solutions; and transition from the secure, planned international socialist market to a type of free trade.

In this regard, and taking into account the need for more efficient economic management, the Council of State approved combining the former Academy of Sciences of Cuba, the National Commission on Environmental Protection and the Rational Use of National Resources, and the Executive Secretariat of Nuclear Affairs into the current Ministry of Science, Technology, and the Environment (CITMA). This new organization within the Cuban government's central administration has four fundamental pillars: orientation of scientific and technological activities toward support of the country's socioeconomic development; strengthening Cuba's scientific and technological potential; assimilation of foreign knowledge and technology; and generation of Cuba's own technology.

Major achievements during these years include official acceptance by the World Health Organization of the Cuban hepatitis B vaccine; successful completion of the various clinical trial stages for a group of human and animal vaccines; import substitution; and improvement of the Cuban population's health. Several social and environmental problems have been solved, such as the gradual application of the Esteroflex system, utilized in stereotactic surgery; a study on the causes of droughts in Cuba and their prediction; and the introduction of a new technology for producing currency paper.

Based on cumulative experience and the need to make projections for future research and technological development in line with the country's needs, international scientific and technological progress, and real possibilities, CITMA undertook a preliminary study of Cuba's status quo, compared with the projections of fifteen industrialized countries, seven international agencies, and thirty-seven innovative companies in various countries. This study resulted in a proposal containing seven strategic themes: sustainable energy development; the environment; basic science; food production; social science and humanities studies; manufacture of high-tech products; and new information technologies.

As the first decade of the twenty-first century came to an end, in its "Informe de balance del trienio 2007–2009" (Review of Three-year Period 2007–2009), CITMA reported on the implementation of nineteen national programs, each averaging 290 scientific projects, of which 69 were completed in 2009, and 170 had achieved results. These results were related to vaccines; biotechnological products; renewable energy; new varieties for food production; soil conservation; rescue and preservation of phylogenetic resources; studies on Cuban flora and fauna; pest and disease management; biofertilizers and biopesticides; new Cuban rice varieties and technologies; the Cuban archipelago's fragile and vulnerable ecosystems and risks; and other important scientific and technological achievements. In July 2009, fourteen new periodic journals were accredited and produced 108 hard-copy and electronic scientific publications in the country.

The government provided for the training of new media specialists through the establishment in 2002 of the Informatics University in Havana, belonging to the Ministry of Informatics and Communications, with a student body of ten thousand. Since the start of the revolutionary government, another avenue for the dissemination of scientific knowledge has been attendance by Cuban professionals of all kinds at Cuban and international events. Every year, more than one hundred high-level scientific conferences and meetings are held in Cuba, an expression of an official interest in sharing the country's scientific achievements with colleagues from all over the world.

BIBLIOGRAPHY

Altshuler, José. "La enseñanza tecnológica universitaria y nuestro desarrollo económico." *Cuba Socialista* (April 1962): 13–24.

Altshuler, José, and Miguel González. *Una luz que llegó para quedarse: Comienzos del alumbrado eléctrico y su introducción en Cuba.* Havana: Editorial Científico-Técnica, 1997.

Armas, Ramón de; Eduardo Torres-Cuevas, and Ana Cairo Ballester. *Historia de la Universidad de La Habana.* Havana: Editorial de Ciencias Sociales, 1984.

Bustamante, J. A. *Factores socioeconómicos del desarrollo histórico de la ciencia y la técnica en Cuba.* Moscow: Latin American Institute of the Soviet Union's Academy of Sciences, 1981.

Calvache, Antonio. *Bosquejo histórico del conocimiento de la geología en Cuba.* Havana: Academia de Ciencias de Cuba, 1965.

Castro Díaz-Balart, Fidel. *Cuba: Amanecer del tercer milenio: Ciencia, sociedad y tecnología.* Havana: Editorial Científico-Técnica, 2002.

Castro Ruz, Fidel. "Discurso de resumen en el acto conmemorativo del XX Aniversario de la Sociedad Espeleológica de Cuba." In *Fidel Castro: Ciencia, Tecnología y Sociedad (1959–1989).* Havana: Editora Política, 1990.

Centro de Estudios de Historia y Organización de la Ciencia. *Fidel Castro: Ciencia, Tecnología y Sociedad (1959–1991).* Havana: Editora Política, 1990–1991.

Dathe, Wilfried, and Rosa María González. *Johann Christoph Gundlach (1810–1896): Un naturalista en Cuba.* Marburg an der Lahn, Germany: Basilisken Press, 2002.

Díaz Torre, Alejandro R., Tomás Mallo, and Daniel Pacheco Fernández, eds. *De la ciencia ilustrada a la ciencia romántica.* Madrid: Ediciones Doce Calles, 1995.

Finlay, Carlos J. *Obras completas.* Edited by César Rodríguez Expósito. 6 vols. Havana: Academia de Ciencias de Cuba, 1965–1981.

García Blanco, Rolando. *Cien figuras de la ciencia en Cuba.* Havana: Editorial Científico-Técnica, 2002.

García Blanco, Rolando. *Francisco de Albear: Un genio cubano universal.* Havana: Editorial Científico-Técnica, 2007.

Guerra, Ramiro. *Azúcar y población en Las Antillas.* Havana: Cultural S.A., 1944.

Guevara, Ernesto. "Tareas industriales de la Revolución en los años venideros." *Cuba Socialista* (March 1962): 35–38.

Informe sobre Cuba de la Misión Truslow. Havana: Banco Nacional de Cuba, 1951. (*Report on Cuba.* Baltimore, MD: Johns Hopkins Press, 1951.)

Lafuente, A., A. Elena, and M. L. Ortega. *Mundialización de la ciencia y cultura nacional.* Madrid, Spain: Ediciones Doce Calles, 1993.

Le Riverend, Julio. *Historia económica de Cuba.* 2nd ed. Havana: Editora del Consejo Nacional de Universidades, 1965.

Le Riverend, Julio. "Casaseca, maestro y precursor de Reynoso." *Revista de la Biblioteca Nacional José Martí* (January–April 1971): 5–57.

López, José. "Prólogo." *Índice analítico de los anales de la Academia de Ciencias Médicas, Físicas y Naturales de La Habana.* Havana: Academia de Ciencias de Cuba, 1974.

López Sánchez, José. *Ciencia y medicina: Historia de las ciencias.* Havana: Editorial Científico Técnica, 1986.

Martínez Viera, Rafael. *70 años de la Estación Experimental Agronómica de Santiago de Las Vegas.* Havana: Academia de Ciencias de Cuba, 1977.

Moreno Fraginals, Manuel. *El ingenio: Complejo económico social cubano del azúcar.* 3 vols. Havana: Editorial de Ciencias Sociales, 1978.

Naranjo Orovio, Consuelo, and Armando García González. *Medicina y racismo en Cuba.* Tenerife, Spain: Taller de Historia, Ayuntamiento de la Laguna, Centro de la Cultura Popular Canaria, 1996.

Núñez, Antonio. "Palabras pronunciadas en el acto inaugural de la Conferencia de las Academias de Ciencia Socialistas en La Habana, 2 de diciembre de 1966." In *Academia de Ciencias de Cuba: Nacimiento y forja.* Havana: Departamento de Ediciones de la ACC, 1972.

Ortiz, Fernando. *Cuban Counterpoint, Tobacco and Sugar.* Translated by Harriet de Onís. Durham, NC: Duke University Press, 1995.

Pérez, Diosdado. *Los estudios de ingeniería y arquitectura en La Habana.* Havana: Instituto Superior Politécnico José Antonio Echeverría, 1996.

Poey y Aloy, Felipe. *Ictiología cubana.* Edited by Darío Guitart Manday. Havana: Biblioteca de Clásicos Cubanos, Editorial Imagen Contemporánea, 2000.

Pruna, Pedro M., ed. *Cronología: Hechos históricos relacionados con la ciencia y la tecnología acaecidos en La Habana (1521–1988).* Havana: Editorial Academia, 1994.

Pruna, Pedro M., ed. *Historia de la ciencia y la tecnología en Cuba.* Havana: Editorial Científico-Técnica, 2006.

Sáenz, Tirso W., and Emilio García Capote. *Ciencia y tecnología en Cuba.* Havana: Editorial de Ciencias Sociales, 1989.

Sagra, Ramón de la. *Historia económica-política y estadística de la Isla de Cuba.* Havana: Imprenta de las Viudas de Arazoza y Soler, 1831.

Torres-Cuevas, Eduardo. *Félix Varela: Los orígenes de la ciencia y con-ciencia cubanas.* 3rd ed. Havana: Editorial de Ciencias Sociales, 2002.

Valero, Mercedes. *Catálogo: Instituciones científicas cubanas del siglo XIX.* Havana: Editorial Academia, 1994.

Valle, A. del, and R. Montoro. *Compendio de la historia de la Sociedad Económica de Amigos del País de La Habana.* Havana: Imprenta y Librería "El Universal," 1930.

Varela, Félix. *Lección preliminar dada a sus discípulos por el Presbítero Don Félix Varela al empezar el estudio de la filosofía en el Real Colegio de San Carlos de La Habana, el día 30 de marzo de 1818.* Havana: Imprenta de Don Pedro Nolasco Palmer, 1818.

Varona, Enrique J. *Las reformas en la enseñanza superior.* Havana: Tipografía El Fígaro, 1900.

Zanetti, Oscar, and Alejandro García. *Sugar and Railroads: A Cuban History, 1837–1959.* Translated by Franklin W. Knight and Mary Todd. Chapel Hill: University of North Carolina Press, 1998.

LA SENTENCIA (BELKIS AYÓN)

Flora González Mandri

A pair of collographs by Belkis Ayón, which emphasize the transformative power of women.

Having been trained as an artist at the San Alejandro School of Fine Arts (1982–1986) and the Higher Institute of Art (ISA) in Havana (1986–1991), Belkis Ayón (1967–1999) belonged to a generation of Cuban artists that in the 1980s explored topics outside the mandates imposed during the 1960s and 1970s by Fidel Castro's "Words to the Intellectuals." Like other black artists such as Manuel Mendive (b. 1944) and María Magdalena Campos-Pons (b. 1959), Ayón used African diaspora forms of representation, revisiting cultural content and experimenting with contemporary forms. Ayón excelled in the medium of printmaking, which she transformed from a trade to an art form and promoted fiercely as a teacher and curator. The critic David Mateo is quoted as having summarized her contribution thus: "In Cuban printmaking, there is a before Belkis Ayón and an after Belkis Ayón" (Vives p. 268).

Ayón had many solo exhibitions, principally in Cuba, Japan, the United States, Europe, and South America. She enjoyed a meteoric career, mounting her first solo show in 1988 at the age of twenty, when she first exhibited her large-format prints. In September 2009, the exhibition *Nkame*, held in Havana to commemorate the tenth anniversary of the artist's untimely death, included more than eighty of her works. They appeared in conjunction with the work of six young engravers, attesting to Ayón's influence in the field.

Her large-scale collographs (engravings) in blacks, whites, and grays depict the mythology of the Abakuá, descendants of the Efor and Efik peoples brought as slaves to Cuba in the early 1800s. In the port of Regla, across the bay from the city of Havana, they reconstituted their male-centered secret society (Castellanos and Castellanos pp. 203–237). Through her highly figurative portraits of Sikán—the woman who first heard, then saw the spirit venerated by the Abakuá, and was then sacrificed for divulging the mystery—Ayón vindicates women's right to have a central role in patriarchal societies. But her portraits of Sikán transcend the Abakuá myth. University of Havana professor Lázara Menéndez stressed the transcultural nature of Ayón's work, "with its compositional structure creating the image of a hybrid medium of Byzantine styles, classical typologies, and compositions associated with bourgeois portraiture" (Vives p. 271). Ayón's female figures are highly autobiographical in that their silhouettes are similar to the artist's own body and her highly expressive eyes (Vives p. 267).

La sentencia (The Sentence), the title of a pair of collographs, refers to the sentence imposed on Sikán, who was hanged for having disobeyed her father (Efor king) by divulging to her husband (Efik prince) the sacred mystery of the transformation of the spirit into the sacred fish Tánze. After her sacrifice, the Efor and the Efik united, and Sikán's skin and eyes were used to capture the voice of Tánze in the Ekue drum, later considered sacred (Cabrera 1988, pp. 143, 424; Cabrera 1992, pp. 276–287).

Like her predecessor Wifredo Lam (1902–1982), a modernist artist who honored santería practices, Ayón prized the Abakuá's penchant for transformations. In the Tánze/Sikán myth, spiritual force is translated from spirit to voice to the skin of the fish Tánze, which was captured by Sikán's skin and eyes and later by goatskin to resound again in the Ekue drum. Ayón symbolically reproduced this multiple layering on the Ekue drum in her collages by superimposing multiple cutout paper and cardboard shapes, which were then intaglio-inked and printed.

Ayón mastered the art of symbolic substitution by tracing her own silhouette onto the figure of Sikán. This act of transgression, of placing herself in the place of Sikán, effects an artistic integration of the dismembering that took place when Sikán was initially sacrificed. In the Abakuá symbolic iconography known as *anaforuana*, only Sikán's eyes remain intact and stare out from the past. Ayón's imposing silhouette in both versions of *La Sentencia* traces the black face of the victimized figure bereft of any feature but the eyes, symbols of having witnessed the great mystery. In the Ekue drum, Sikán's eyes look through the skin of the drum to produce sound; in Ayón's representation, the victimized woman's eyes allow the artist to observe critically and to reveal her own human existential pain and anguish (Vives p. 270).

The two versions of *La sentencia* (37 in. x 27 in.) date from 1993 and replicate the actual Abakuá practice of telling a myth in multiple versions, thus validating a communal desire to approach the truth from multiple angles and ensure the complexity of the artistic enterprise. One image depicts Sikán carrying the sacrificial goat; the other shows her clothed in the fish scales. She holds the fish Tánze in her hand, surrounded by the serpent, which haunts her. The crosses on Sikán's chest and hand signify the point at which a tributary joins the sacred river, the site at which Sikán was sacrificed, and marks the spot of confluence between the lands of the Efor and the Efik (Cabrera 1992, p. 278). The cross also ties the spirit of the fish to the spirit of the goat on the surface of the Ekue drum (Castellanos and Castellanos p. 218).

Even though in most Abakuá versions Sikán is sacrificed at the foot of a palm tree, in others it happens at the site of a *ceiba* (silk cotton tree), sacred to African diaspora peoples in Cuba. Ayón emphasized the transcultural nature of Cuban culture when she chose to depict the *ceiba* rather than the palm tree, particularly in the collograph in which multiple leaves

■ *See also*

Faith: Abakuá Society

Gender: Feminism and Masculinity in the Revolutionary Period

Visual Arts: Revolutionary Period

Next page:
Belkis Ayón (1967–1999). Artist Belkis Ayón stands before her collograph *My Vernicle, o tu amor me condena* (My Vernicle, or Your Love Condemns Me), 1998. COURTESY OF KATIA AYÓN AND THE ESTATE OF BELKIS AYÓN

CUBA

serve as a background to the figure of Sikán. The trunk of the tree doubles as Sikán with arms stretched upward, the foundational figure of a culture. In one version of the myth, after she is led blindfolded by her father, her executioner hangs her from the branches of the *ceiba*. As she dies, her eyes bulge out and blood flows from her mouth. With cotton, the executioner draws a cross on the surface of the drum (Castellanos and Castellanos p. 217).

In Ayón's two collographs, Abakuá symbols acquire yet other meanings, with the serpent suggesting a connection between Sikán and the biblical Eve, and the halo that surrounds the head evoking Byzantine Christian icons. In her drawing for Sikán in front of the tree, Ayón recalls the figure of Christ tied to the cross by depicting alternate arms tied to the tree behind her (Vives p. 199). By superimposing Sikán on Christ on the cross, Ayón inverts the prevailing hierarchical order that values European above African culture in Cuban society. In both versions, the ropes used to tie Sikán before her execution have been loosened, reminiscent of the Greek god Prometheus, another rebellious classical figure. In both renditions of Sikán by Ayón, the feminine figure stands triumphant. In the first, she carries the goat on her shoulders as if to transcend the victimized nature of women in Abakuá and modern Cuban society. This image recalls that of Christ as the sacrificial Lamb of God who stands redeemed after his resurrection. In the second version, the figure wears a halo that turns her into a Christ-like figure, both victim and savior. Her white hand, bearing the cross of her victimization, also reaches out in a gesture to stop the abuse of women in patriarchal societies.

By tracing her own silhouette onto her collographs, Ayón appropriates Sikán's figure to represent the artist as seer and transformer of cultural myths. She is quoted as saying: "The image of Sikán is evident in all these works because she, like I, lived and lives through me in restlessness, insistently looking for a way out" (Vives p. 262). By alluding to multiple victimized-then-liberating figures (Sikán, Eve, Christ, and Prometheus), Ayón broke through the barriers that society imposes on women and positioned herself as a major Cuban artist in the second half of the twentieth century.

BIBLIOGRAPHY

Ayón, Belkis. *Nkame.* Curated by Cristina Vives. Havana: Convento San Francisco de Asís, 2009.

Cabrera, Lydia. *Anaforuana: Ritual y símbolos de la iniciación en la sociedad secreta Abakuá (Los de hoy).* Madrid: Ediciones R, 1975.

Cabrera, Lydia. *La lengua sagrada de los ñáñigos.* Miami, FL: Colección del Chicherekú, 1988.

Cabrera, Lydia. *El monte.* Miami, FL: Ediciones Universal, 1992.

Castellanos, Isabel, and Jorge Castellanos. *Cultura afrocubana III: Las religiones y las lenguas.* Miami, FL: Ediciones Universal, 1992.

González Mandri, Flora. *Guarding Cultural Memory: Afro-Cuban Women in Literature and the Arts.* Charlottesville: University of Virginia Press, 2006.

Vives, Cristina, ed. *Belkis Ayón: Nkame.* Text by Cristina Vives, David Mateo, and Lázara Menéndez. Madrid: Editorial Turner, 2010.

Page 863:
La sentencia #1 (1993) by Belkis Ayón. The two versions of *La sentencia,* by Belkis Ayón, replicate the Abakuá practice of telling a myth in multiple versions. One image depicts Sikán carrying a sacrificial goat; the other shows her clothed in fish scales. COURTESY OF KATIA AYÓN AND THE ESTATE OF BELKIS AYÓN. PHOTOGRAPH BY JOSÉ A. FIGUEROA.

Opposite page:
La sentencia #2 (1993) by Belkis Ayón. The crosses on Sikán's chest and hand signify the point at which a tributary joins the sacred river, the site at which Sikán was sacrificed. COURTESY OF KATIA AYÓN AND THE ESTATE OF BELKIS AYÓN. PHOTOGRAPH BY JOSÉ A. FIGUEROA.

℞ SEXUALITY

Cuba's modern emergence from Spanish colonial rule with its slave-based economy and powerful Catholic Church suggests the existence of a complex sexuality combining nationalism, the master-slave relationship, the subordination of women, secrets, the concern for bringing more white people to the island, the concept of sin, and homophobia and machismo—each with its associated myths. During the period of the Republic, there were numerous struggles related to achieving access to full sexuality. These included the fights for women's rights, the social incorporation of people with atypical sexual identities, and the elimination of myths associated with racism. But the colonial and bourgeois societal structures remained in place, continuing to repress sexual freedom.

After 1959, the complex changes experienced in Cuba brought about much greater freedom for women; numerous sexist models were attacked, though others persist to the present day. In the 1960s, homosexuals were sent to Unidades Militares de Ayuda a la Producción (UMAP) work camps. By the end of the twentieth century, a new figure emerged as a result of the economic crisis: the jinetera.

Currently, following the fall of the socialist bloc and Cuba's entrance into the globalized world, views on sexuality have undergone swift transformations. Thinking and writing about gender models have increased and there have been several artistic and literary works denouncing and exploring various aspects of homosexuality.

This entry includes the following articles:

SEXUALITY: COLONIAL PERIOD

Luz M. Mena

The impact of the Catholic Church on sexual behavior and marriage choices in Cuba to the mid-nineteenth century.

The Catholic Church's social influence in colonial Cuba was weaker than in other colonies because of the composition of the Cuban population and the limited colonial administrative presence on the island. The Church tended to have its greatest influence among the upper classes. However, during the eighteenth and nineteenth centuries the Church played a considerable role, alongside secular colonial authorities, in legitimizing and sanctifying royal interpretations of legal criteria, including those that applied to sexual behavior and marriage choices. Thus church authorities in Cuba were at the center of an acute social conflict arising from the social and sexual contact between the races.

Unlike Mexico and Peru, which were viceroyalties, Cuba was not a key site of colonial administration. More important, it did not have a large indigenous population to convert; thus, the central rationale of the Spanish colonial mission of the Americas—which gave the Catholic Church a prominent role in controlling social and labor structures in other colonies—was far less pertinent to Cuba. Because Africans were brought in as enslaved individuals, there was a less urgent need to convert them as a means to extract labor or obedience. Although the conversion of slaves was part of the official colonial agenda, in reality it was given a lesser priority than the conversion of the indigenous population in other colonies.

The shared colonial authority between Church and Crown often involved a negotiation of Christian doctrine, the monarchy's approaches to colonial administration, and the political and economic currents informing Church, Crown, and local authorities at any given time. After the eighteenth century, as the Spanish monarchy moved toward more secular governance and administration of the colonies, church-state relations grew more tense.

SEXUALITY AND MARRIAGE

The Spanish legal code contained elements of Roman law as well as Christian doctrine, both of which were embedded in the thirteenth-century compendium of laws known as the *Siete partidas* (Seven Divisions of Law). The *Siete partidas* established moral and ethical precepts, as well as offering spiritual and philosophical advice, to guide rulers in ideal Christian conduct in the exercise of royal authority. Crown and Church, two paternalistic institutions, largely complemented

each other in sustaining the family under the authority of the father figure as the central organizing principle of the colonies' socioeconomic structure. In this hierarchical structure, organized by race, gender, and social status, elite women's sexuality was closely monitored—morally, spiritually, and legally. Indeed, it was inscribed with a family's honor. Male sexuality was only indirectly influenced by the man's spiritual and legal duty to protect his wife and children. These social demands diminished considerably for nonwhite and poorer individuals.

The Catholic Church held that marriage is a holy sacrament that sanctifies a sexual union and a couple's future offspring; thus, sexuality is a way to abide God's will that humans should reproduce. The Church considered sex within marriage a duty between spouses, known as the conjugal debt and refusal to have sex with one's spouse as a sin. Marital sexual relations were forbidden on certain holy days and during the woman's menstrual period. Sex for pleasure and sex outside of marriage were condemned. Adultery, concubinage, fornication, and masturbation were considered sins. However, Christian doctrine did not prevent concubinage from becoming a well-established practice in the colonies, where marriage was rare—particularly in Cuba, which had some of the lowest marriage rates in the colonies.

Among stable, long-term relationships, informal arrangements and concubinages were the norm. Married men and priests often had concubines, and such relationships often involved interracial mixing. An 1804 legal petition submitted by Don Miguel Joseph Vianes de Salas, a Havana priest, later housed in the Archivo Histórico in Madrid, asked the court to allow him to leave property to his illegitimate son, who was conceived, the priest declared, during his honest love relationship with a mulatto woman before he joined the clergy.

Whereas adultery among upper-class married men was common, an expression of colonial male privilege over women as well as over nonwhites, adultery among elite women was far less common. Husbands held the legal and moral right to punish adulterous wives severely, including physically. From a religious and spiritual perspective, the Catholic Church encouraged women to follow the Virgin Mary's model of virtue and modesty. Overt flirtation, revealing dress, and demonstrations of sensuality were discouraged. Cuba was evidently a challenging place to enforce such modesty. In a 1797 edict by the Bishop of Havana, directed at the "immodest women, who sexually provoke men in the temples," he describes in detail the suggestive way Habaneras walk—with their feet largely uncovered—and their plunging necklines (Archivo General de Indias).

Although the Church discouraged premarital sexual contact by engaged couples, such conduct was not a sin. The effect of this laxity was to diminish the future marriage prospects for elite women after a broken engagement. Those females who lost their virginity with one man had hardly any chance of marrying another. A man who broke a promise to marry could be sued for breach of contract and forced into marriage. The breakup of an engagement could be initiated by one member of the couple (more often the man) or by the parents. Appeals and grievances were often referred to church authorities, who served as mediators.

RACE AND SEXUALITY

Despite little need for the spiritual pacification of Africans in Cuba, the Church did try to indoctrinate them. But enslaved men and women from West Africa, who spoke a variety of languages and practiced a variety of spiritual and social traditions, were not receptive to the moral charge that such indoctrination carried (nor were their freed descendants, blacks and mulattoes). The right to marry the person of one's choice was one of the few individual rights granted by the slave codes, and many took it.

Slave codes consistently encouraged marriage among slaves and prohibited arbitrary sexual encounters, invoking Christian moral principles. But it was not until the late eighteenth and early nineteenth centuries, when the sugar plantation economy was well established, that the sexuality of slaves came to be closely monitored. Maintaining discipline became a factor in the sugar mills, and interracial contact became a concern in the cities. Slave owners punished their slaves' out-of-wedlock pregnancies despite the fact that the newborn would add to their assets. They rationalized this by invoking their duty to discipline slaves according to Christian doctrine as prescribed by the slave codes. A common punishment in the city for an unmarried pregnant slave was to require her to kneel down, beg for forgiveness from God and her owner, change her street clothes for a thick, coarse gown (probably to hide the bodily evidence of her crime), and have her head shaven (to make obvious her moral fault and shame).

Whereas slaves were encouraged and even pressured by their owners to marry, their freed descendants were much less likely to sanctify their union. One reason was the relatively weak influence of the Catholic Church on the majority of Cubans, and another was the competing spiritual beliefs regarding questions of sexual behavior and marriage held by those of African descent. Marriage and its relation to honor and status resonated mostly with the white upper classes. In addition, the courts were unlikely to grant licenses to interracial unions involving free blacks and mulattoes. Until the late eighteenth century, the Catholic Church had the legal authority to grant such licenses on the rare occasions in which an interracial couple sought to sanctify their union despite family disapproval. The Church tended to side with the will of the couple, invoking the Council of Trent's doctrine of free individual will to marry. After the Church lost this authority, interracial sexual relations in Cuba became increasingly restricted.

INTERRACIAL MARRIAGES

During the late 1700s, the Catholic Church played its most meaningful role as an alternative moral and social arbiter to that of the monarchy in questions of interracial relations. This state-church tension held great significance at a time when interracial social and sexual contact had become the central point of conflict among the middle and upper classes regarding sexual attitudes and marriage choices.

Ascendant since 1700, the Bourbons sought to transform the economic and political course of the colonies with liberal reforms that effectively centralized the power of the Crown and increased state revenues. One of these reforms involved the abrogation of the Catholic Church's legal autonomy and its authority to intervene in marriage disputes, including those involving interracial couples. The marginalization of the Church thus effectively centralized the management of interracial marriages in the state. This reform in turn put pressure on the centuries-old tradition of negotiated interracial relations in which the Church played a central role.

In 1776 the Crown promulgated the Royal Pragmatic on Marriage, which was extended to the colonies in 1778. The law gave parents the legal right to forbid the marriage of children under the age of twenty-five in an attempt to prevent unequal unions. One factor determining such inequality was race. The father, or a relative standing in his place, was given the legal duty, formerly a power shared by the Crown and the Church, to sanctify his child's marriage. If the couple objected, they could file a formal appeal with royal authorities. This decree was a key step in the reconfiguration of racial criteria and racial attitudes among the growing upper middle strata in Cuba.

In 1803 a new royal decree was passed setting the age of consent at twenty-three for men and twenty-five for women; the previous age of consent as set by the Catholic Church was fourteen for males and twelve for females. The increase gave parents a longer time in which to intervene. That same year another decree established that only the courts could grant or deny a marriage license. Shortly thereafter, in October 1805, the Cuban colonial courts ruled against three interracial marriage petitions, arguing that marriages between whites and blacks or mulattoes should not be allowed because such marriages degraded the white families. By the 1830s it was generally accepted in Cuba that difference in color was a civil impediment to marriage for which a dispensation was always required.

Several church authorities, in their effort to discourage concubinage and extramarital relations, continued to encourage interracial marriages in Cuba.

Concerned church authorities sought to sanctify these unions as a way of instilling moral and spiritual responsibility. From the late eighteenth to the first half of the nineteenth century, they insisted on blessing such unions despite legal and social strictures against interracial marriage. In the early 1800s Bishop Espada y Landa, a renowned promoter of Enlightenment philosophy in Cuba, stated his belief that the races should be allowed to mix freely. In the 1850s, nearly a decade after the government had formalized racial segregation in Cuban schools, some priests were still playing an active role in blessing interracial unions. In Santiago de Cuba, Archbishop Antonio María Claret (1807–1870), a leading figure in this campaign, instructed his clergy on how to go about collecting necessary documents and holding collective ceremonies to promote marriage among informal interracial couples.

In 1853 colonial authorities in Santiago de Cuba opened a file of complaints against Friar Esteban de Adoain (1808–1880), the most outspoken of the missionaries who followed Claret's leadership. The priest had requested a list from city authorities of all the unmarried couples in the city and had offered to marry them without requesting a license from the government. When asked why he was ignoring the law, Adoain replied that the law mandated that he obtain a marriage license from the government in cases of couples of different races, but it was impossible, he said, to classify people by race in Cuba, a place where hardly anybody could claim to be of pure racial ancestry and at a time when such a mixture was occurring without any dignified, formal blessing. With his response the priest made the point that most Cubans had a racially mixed background (rendering any preoccupation with racial difference meaningless) and also justified his blessing of interracial couples. By collapsing the two problems of interracial unions and unmarried unions into one, the priest demonstrated their inseparability: only by doing his duty in remedying the second was he encouraging the first. He also made a third point: that being moral (by sanctifying one's sexual union) was more relevant to nobility than being considered white.

BIBLIOGRAPHY

Archivo General de Indias. Secretaría General Guerra, 6854, Exp. 40, 1797.

Eljach, Matilde. *La construcción jurídica del negro en la colonia.* Bogotá, Colombia: Ediciones Axis Mundi, 2006.

García Rodríguez, Gloria. *La esclavitud desde la esclavitud: La visión de los siervos.* Havana: Ciencias Sociales, 1996.

Martinez-Alier, Verena. *Marriage, Class, and Colour in Nineteenth-Century Cuba: A Study of Racial Attitudes and Sexual Values in a Slave Society.* 2nd ed. Ann Arbor: University of Michigan Press, 1989.

Ortiz, Fernando. *Los negros esclavos.* Havana: Editorial de Ciencias Sociales, 1976.

Seed, Patricia. *To Love, Honor, and Obey in Colonial Mexico: Conflicts over Marriage Choice, 1574–1821.* Stanford, CA: Stanford University Press, 1988.

Socolow, Susan Migden. *The Women of Colonial Latin America.* Cambridge, U.K.: Cambridge University Press, 2000.

Stoler, Ann Laura. *Race and the Education of Desire: Foucault's History of Sexuality and the Colonial Order of Things.* Durham, NC: Duke University Press, 1995.

Twinam, Ann. *Public Lives, Private Secrets: Gender, Honor, Sexuality, and Illegitimacy in Colonial Spanish America.* Stanford, CA: Stanford University Press, 1999.

Zamora y Coronado, José María. *Biblioteca de legislación ultramarina en forma de diccionario alfabético.* 7 vols. Madrid: Imprenta de Alegría y Charlain, 1844–1849.

SEXUALITY: REPUBLICAN PERIOD

Julio César González Pagés

Sexual roles, prostitution, and pornography in Cuba between 1902 and 1959.

With the advent of Cuba as a nation and a republic, sexual behavior acquired an importance not only as a factor in organizing society and assigning gender roles, but also as an element in the establishment of social norms aimed at bringing about the so-called correct functioning of society, in keeping with the standards of modern life and Western civilization. Inevitably, in a country that had experienced two wars of national liberation, sexuality became highly politicized due to the need for population growth. Citizens' reproductive practices were regulated and moral rules and standards imposed in connection with sexual behavior. The government implemented immigration and ethnic selection policies during the first three decades of the twentieth century to similar ends.

Discrimination on the basis of sex and sexual orientation—including reasons of gender, race, ethnicity, and class, as well as the formation of stereotypes and prejudices—characterized social and cultural relationships during the founding and development of the Cuban nation-state between 1902 and 1958. At the same time, the limits and differences between male and female sexuality emerged in sharp relief, a result of the interaction of such factors as social origins and upbringing. The labeling of sexual behavior as either right or wrong carried implications about the dominant models of maleness and femaleness, and it was naturally linked to a morality based on principles of biological reproduction that held that heterosexuality and married life were the only legitimate avenues of sexual expression for men and women.

From the beginnings of the Republic, the Catholic Church exercised significant power over Cuban society, particularly in matters of morality; this despite the constitution's establishment of a secular state. From the Church's point of view, woman's role was modeled on the Virgin Mary—a devoted mother with no sexual instincts who would faithfully serve men—whereas men were seen as impulsive and dominant in sexual matters. Among the duties religion imposed on women were to accept, forgive, and forget the moral weaknesses of men, that is, their infidelity and constant sexual desire. Men were stereotyped as sexual or carnal; women were spiritual (Smith and Padula pp. 7–8). Platonic friendships between men and women were frowned upon, and friendships between women existed only for women without husbands and children or women who were neglecting their household and marital duties. Moral standards required that all women remain virgins and chaste until marriage.

SEXUALITY AND FEMINISM: WOMEN'S RIGHTS

As the Republican period began, men began to publish theories about women's roles in the new Cuban society, including sexuality. Two complementary types emerged: the cultured woman-citizen, and the woman-housewife whose job it was to raise men to assume positions of power (González Pagés 2005, p. 71).

Marriage, understood as an institution that reduced women to property controlled by their husbands, drew harsh criticism from major Cuban intellectuals of the Republican period, including Miguel de Carrión (1875–1929). His critiques appeared in his well-known novels such as *Las honradas* (The Honest, 1918) and *Las impuras* (The Impure, 1919), and also in the press. A series of his articles were published in the newspaper *Azul y Rojo*, for which he served as editor in chief.

Under the impact of World War I and the modernization of the Cuban society, Congress passed two laws of utmost importance for the feminist movement and women's sexual liberation: Ley de la Patria Potestad (Parental Authority Act, 1917) and Ley de Divorcio (Divorce Act, 1918). This legislation liberated women from the tutelage of their husbands, allowing them to divorce and safeguarding their parental rights.

Ten years later, during the Constitutional Convention of 1928, some of the statements against extending the vote to women were based on arguments about sexuality, class, and morality. Manuel Camps, a conservative politician from Oriente, went so far as to support uxoricide (the murder of a wife by her husband): "men should continue killing adulterous women because they have honor" (González Pagés 2005, p. 114).

Women's right to vote was granted by presidential decree in 1934, and Cuban women voted for the first time in the 1936 elections (González Pagés 2005, pp. 128–130). The 1940 Constitution acknowledged married women's civil rights, according them the power to manage their property and carry out all manner of economic transactions without the need for the husband's permission. It also stipulated the need to safeguard the maternity rights of all women workers, including maids, and recognized women's workplace rights without regard to marital status.

IMMIGRANTS AND SEXUALITY

The adoption of a racist immigration policy in the first three decades of the twentieth century favored the admission of Spaniards on the basis of ethnic and racial selection. In 1906 Federico Córdova, secretary of the Comités Seccionales de Protección al Inmigrante (Local Committees for the Protection of Immigrants), argued on "genetic" grounds for a state policy of preference to immigrant families from the Canary Islands: "The admission of such families would be ideal due to their ability to acclimate and their endurance for hard field labor, and also because they would lead to favorable genetic crosses" (García pp. 56–57).

Ethnic and racial relations of the era were reflected in a type of genre comedy in Cuban theater with three stock characters: the famous trilogy of *negrito*, *mulata*, and *gallego* (the black fellow, the mulatto woman, and the Galician). The Galician character was typically defined by his marked sexual attraction to women of African descent, a preference portrayed in an exaggerated fashion and removed from its social context. Much of the humor in these burlesques rested on the *mulata*'s using the Galician and placing him together with the *negrito* in a position of ridicule. Not without its basis in fact was the stereotype of Galician men's passion for Cuban *mulatas*; many Cuban families in the early 2000s have their origin in relations between members of these two social groups.

Like black Cubans, Chinese immigrants suffered social discrimination, leading them to settle in certain urban areas. The classic such district was Barrio Chino de La Habana (Havana Chinatown), which exists even in the early 2000s. Given the patriarchal nature of Chinese society, Chinese immigrants maintained a strict code of sexual behavior that banned women from holding positions in Chinese ethnic associations and also denied their right to act or even be seen in public. Clan groups, in practice, were exogamous, for the membership shared a common past and, therefore, could not intermarry. The tradition was that when women became wives they integrated into the families and clans of their husbands and adopted their husbands' surnames (Baltar pp. 46–89). Due to the small number of Chinese immigrant women in Cuba (4.09% of total immigrants in 1953), mixed marriages between Chinese men and black, mulatto, and white women were common (Baltar p. 90). Their wives and descendants, who were regarded as mestizos (mixed race), had no right to belong to ethnic associations (Baltar p. 90).

PROSTITUTION

Any discussion of sexuality in a society such as Cuba in the Republican period must prominently address prostitution. During the North American military intervention, the political administration mandated that brothels—known as *casas de tolerancia*—be limited to certain poor districts of cities, as a means of control and marginalization (Barcia pp. 278–279). An example of this ruling was the location of several in Havana's San Isidro neighborhood. At the same time, the military governor Leonard Wood imposed such measures as barring the entry of women into the country for the purpose of engaging in prostitution.

Brothels were frequented by men and also functioned as places of sexual initiation for boys taken there by male relatives or friends. Among the working classes, it was important to reaffirm the myths of masculinity in the Cuban imagination, which demanded as an essential feature of *hombría* (manhood) that men have the greatest possible number of sexual encounters with women.

With the rise of the feminist movement in Cuba during the 1910s and 1920s, women's groups reported the abuses and appalling conditions suffered by so-called sexual workers. The involvement of Galician women in prostitution made them among the most stigmatized groups in Cuba. As ships arrived at the port of Havana, pimps and prostitutes looked to recruit often-illiterate Galician peasant girls. Prostitution was illegal, but the police acted as accomplices, often on orders from above. Neighborhoods and streets in Havana such as San José, the Alley of Dragons (linking Amistad Street to Zanja Street), and Crespo, Colón, and Pajarito Streets became popular spots in the underworld of the sex trade. Five or six young women lived in a typical *casa de tolerancia*, where assignations with clients were held; they were prohibited by law from soliciting customers on the street, so they appeared suggestively at windows to lure in business.

A notorious case in the 1910s involved María Constancia, a woman of Galician descent who worked as a prostitute. Better known by the alias Macorina, she became the subject of a *son* played for years by Cuba's orchestras that exhorted in its chorus, "ponme la mano aquí, Macorina" (put your hand here, Macorina). María Constancia was the owner of three brothels for distinguished and public men, and she was acquainted with President José Miguel Gómez (1909–1913). Before she was bankrupted in the 1930s, she had owned eight brothels and six luxury automobiles, including a red two-seater sports car that, according to Cuban intellectual Renée Méndez Capote, "aroused lust" in onlookers who were put in mind of the racy chorus of "ponme la mano" (González Pagés 2003, p. 23).

Men also worked in the sex trade, mainly for the homosexual market, which was more secretive due to homophobia but still occupied a significant place in the public sphere. In Havana, the neighborhood known as Pajarito (literally little bird; Cuban slang for male homosexual) near Carlos III Avenue was a popular district for such prostitution. The Galician immigrant Manolo, also known as "Manolete" or "Tolete" (in Cuban Spanish a *stick* or *club*), gained renown during the 1910s for his large penis, which he exhibited in theatrical shows and on film.

Many men also participated in this lucrative business as pimps. Alberto Yarini, the best known of these figures, was murdered in the San Isidro neighborhood in 1909 during an argument over control of the trade in French prostitutes.

PORNOGRAPHY

The market for pornographic photographs that developed during the Republic resulted from a fascination with nudity—primarily female—in a society full of restrictions. Pornography depicting women was intended mostly for male consumption. Pictures of male nudes did not abound in the same way, although it did appeal to a more elite, gay audience (García Marrero pp. 92–93).

With the advent of the movie industry, pornography found another avenue of expansion. Scandals were commonplace, such as the one that erupted in 1909 at the Nogueira Theatre in Marianao, where "blue" films with titles such as *La familia modelo* (The Ideal Family) and *Mercados de esclava* (The Slave Girl Market) were shown. The production of movies and running of theatrical shows were so commonplace that Havana's municipal government had to intervene in conflicts between morally outraged local residents and the management of such establishments (González Pagés 2010, p. 25).

The Shanghai, located in Havana's Chinatown from the 1930s to 1950s, was one of the most famous theaters serving the sexual entertainment of *habaneros*. Its theatrical productions and movies labeled "raunchy," in which women were nude and placed in sexually suggestive situations, were intended for a male (particularly young) market. Movies often began with a version of the classic Metro-Goldwyn-Mayer lion, with the lion replaced by an image of a large penis with a shaggy mane. The Shanghai was the first stop on a circuit of sex consumerism, in which patrons would first enjoy a show and then head for houses of prostitution such as those in the nearby Colón neighborhood, which was frequented by American sailors. In many Cuban seaports, bars and brothels catered to that clientele, and when ships came into port in Santiago de Cuba, Guantánamo, and Havana, pimps and prostitutes offered sailors the sexual services of women of all ages.

This environment in which prostitution and pornography flourished, to the chief detriment of women, prompted the Second National Congress on Women (12–18 April 1925) to recommend the "prohibition of any publicity degrading to women, and the suppression of pornography in advertisements, books, newspapers and shows"(González Pagés 2003, p. 27).

SEXUAL DIVERSITY

The prevailing social view that discriminated against all non-heterosexual behavior found in the medical establishment a chief legitimizing institution. Cuban physicians, in their role as guardians of hygiene and correctness in Cuban society, were responsible for many controversies over sexual diversity and negative public opinion toward homosexuals and lesbians.

By the end of the nineteenth century, the Cuban scientific establishment had adopted the view that male homosexuality was a perversion, incompatible with masculinity and linked instead with effeminacy. Their position followed the publication of the influential "Paedophilia in Cuba," a paper on homosexuality by the renowned physician Luis Montané presented at the First Congress on Regional Medicine of the Island of Cuba in January 1890; in the 1930s, Vicente Pardo y Suárez published the text *Lesbianas* (Lesbians). In the 1940s and 1950s, contact with U.S. scientific circles fueled debates in the field of sexology. Sexual orientations such as bisexuality, male homosexuality, and lesbianism received the label of "disorders." This view encouraged the persecution of the non-heterosexual Cuban population, which was subjected to hormonal and psychiatric treatments.

In *Cinco ensayos sobre la vida sexual* (Five Essays on Sexual Life, 1959), the well-known doctor and professor José Chelala questioned Cuban sexology's moralizing tendencies and its failure to determine the boundaries between the normal and the pathological. Following the perspective of American sexologist Alfred Kinsey, Chelala asserted that homosexuality and other types of unconventional sexual behavior did not necessarily coincide with psychotic states or anomalous personality: "It is not true that any deviation from predominant sexual practices implies a neurotic or psychotic disorder" (Chelala pp. 14–16). On the contrary, seeking a new ideal of civilized sexuality more in keeping with the changing times, he affirmed that copulation focused exclusively on the genitalia, "such as occurs in certain types of prostitution and homosexuality," and deviated from the representation of modern sexuality; he labeled the genital obsession as "animal sexuality" (pp. 30–31). At the same time, he stated that homosexuality could be caused by lack of sexual education as well as by adults' negligence in dressing their daughters as boys and vice versa, leading in adulthood, in some cases, to transvestism (wearing clothes of the opposite sex), fantasies of belonging to the opposite sex, and a homosexual way of living (pp. 18–19).

At the same time, many articles by the psychologist Alfonso Bernal linked homosexuality with mental disorders and corruption among Cuban artists. Cuban sexologists, notably Ángel C. Arce, later became famous for their open persecution of homosexuals in 1960s. They opposed Kinsey's theories, which they regarded as licentious. Unfortunately, in the 1960s Arce´s theories prevailed and were extensively disseminated in homophobic speeches with titles such as "Lacras sociales del capitalism" (Capitalism's Social Scourge), "Imposible el cambio del sexo en la especie humana" (Sex Change Is Impossible in Human Beings), and "Bisexualismo? Es un absurdo en la especie humana" (Bisexualism? An Absurdity in the Human Species) (Arce pp. 31–66).

BIBLIOGRAPHY

Arce, Ángel C. *Sexología 1*. Havana: Editorial Pueblo y Educación, 1965.

Baltar Rodríguez, José. *Los chinos de Cuba. Apuntes etnográficos*. Havana: Fundación Fernando Ortiz, 1997.

Barcia, María del Carmen. *Capas populares y modernidad en Cuba (1878–1930)*. Havana: Editorial de Ciencias Sociales, 2009.

Chelala, José. *Cinco ensayos sobre la vida sexual*. Havana: Universidad de La Habana, 1959.

Fowler, Víctor. *La Maldición. Una historia del placer como conquista*. Havana: Letras Cubanas, 1998.

García, A. *Eugenesia, inmigración y "mejoramiento racial" en Cuba, 1900–1940*. Rábida, Spain: Imprenta Provincial, 1998.

García Marrero, Alberto Claudio. "La mujer cubana en la fotografía (1920–1925)." Department of Sociology, Universidad de La Habana, 2002.

González Pagés, Julio César. *Emigración de mujeres gallegas a Cuba: Las hijas de Galicia*. Vigo, Spain: Editorial EcoVigo, 2003.

González Pagés, Julio César. *En busca de un espacio: Historia de mujeres en Cuba*. Havana: Editorial de Ciencias Sociales, 2005.

González Pagés, Julio César. *Macho, varón, masculino. Estudios de Masculinidades en Cuba*. Havana: De la Mujer, 2010.

Montané, Luis. "La pederastia en Cuba." In *Primer Congreso Médico Regional de la Isla de Cuba en enero de 1890*. Havana: A. Álvarez y Compañía, 1890.

Naranjo Orovio, Consuelo. "Blanco sobre negro: Debates en torno a la identidad en Cuba (1898–1920)." In *Relatos de nación: La construcción de las identidades nacionales en el mundo hispánico*, vol. 2, edited by Francisco Colom. Madrid: Iberoamericana-Vervuert, 2005.

Roig de Leuchsenring, Emilio. "El delito de adulterio debe desaparecer de nuestro Código Penal." *Carteles* 28 (February 1926): 14.

Smith, Lois M., and Alfred Padula. *Sex and Revolution: Women in Socialist Cuba*. New York: Oxford University Press, 1996.

SEXUALITY: REVOLUTIONARY PERIOD

Mariela Castro Espín

Isabel Moya Richard

Changing sex and gender roles after 1959 and the development of sex education.

The 1959 Revolution meant the achievement of Cuban national sovereignty, the birth of a project for justice and social equality, and the beginning of the most profound and radical transformation in the history of the nation and its culture. An event of such magnitude could not help but completely change the politics of sexuality and the body.

EROSION OF PATRIARCHY

Women constituted one of the most oppressed groups in Cuba until the triumph of the Revolution. Some statistics illustrate this fact: The illiteracy rate among women was 56 percent in 1961, before the start of the Literacy Campaign (ONE-FMC 2010); according to the 1953 census, fewer than 1 percent of women held university degrees, and only 12 percent were paid or unpaid members of the workforce; and in 1958 the direct maternal mortality rate was 125.3 per 100,000 live births (ONE-FMC).

The Revolution was a process of complex cultural metamorphosis, and women were both beneficiaries and leaders in the confrontations and dialogues among generations, classes, and social strata. The generation that effected this qualitative historical leap already had brought about changes in relationships between men and women, expressed through their sharing of risks and responsibilities during the struggle against the regime of Fulgencio Batista.

This new scenario of broad popular participation was the setting in which the first activities to implement political, economic, and social change unfolded, changes that had an unprecedented impact on the family—especially in its relationships between generations, between genders, between couples— and on sexuality and its bodily expressions. The first Agrarian Reform Law (17 May 1959) made ownership of land possible to both women and men without distinction; equal pay for equal work was implemented in the Fundamental Law of the Republic (7 February 1959).

As part of the process of abolishing all forms of exploitation, brothels were closed and the social reintegration of prostitutes was facilitated. With this measure, the government did away with the custom of young men losing their virginity to prostitutes, a traditional practice hidden within the dominant masculine code. It also liberated more than 100,000 women who, based on their low class and social status, had lacked other options in their lives (see Centro de Información para la Prensa).

The Literacy Campaign of 1961 gave young people from urban areas a legitimate opportunity to leave their homes, with or without the permission of their parents, to undertake a task with great responsibility and social recognition. They traveled to distant, often remote places in rural Cuba and stayed in the homes of families they did not previously know. Only the collective spiritual motivation that the Revolution fostered in the population explains how in a country such as Cuba, 59.5 percent of the literacy trainers were women (Proveyer, Ruiz, Olmedo, et al. p. 21). For their part, teenage girls from the mountainous regions came to Havana for the first time, to the luxurious Hotel Nacional, converted into the Ana Betancourt School for Rural Girls, which graduated 150,000 girls (Castro Ruz 1978, p. 118). This experience inevitably contributed to Cuban women's challenge to the androcentric notion that their sole destiny was to become wives and mothers, as well as their overcoming a sense of fatalism based on geographical origins.

In 1960 the Federación de Mujeres Cubanas (FMC; Federation of Cuban Women) was officially established as an organized mass movement of women in civil society; from that time forward, it developed its own genuine project of empowering women as individuals with legal rights. The FMC has had a deep impact on all of society, politics, and culture, and has become one of the motivating forces of Cuban social development (Castro Ruz 1978, pp. 171–173).

At the same time, other initiatives with broad popular participation were developed, such as military mobilizations to defend the population against attacks from the United States (Sánchez Parodi); women arrived home dressed in their militia uniforms, and this image became familiar both within and outside the country. Norka Menéndez, an internationally famous Cuban model, posed in military uniform as a symbol of the new era, exalting the beauty and dignity women had won (De Armas). The voluntary agricultural work camps and the new teacher and medical training schools located in the mountains (Topes de Collantes, Minas del Frío) brought men and women together in an environment of mutual respect and friendship that encouraged the creation of bonds of solidarity against the traditional subjugation of women.

The broad incorporation of women into the workforce and the public sphere as a whole had a great impact on sexuality (Núñez). The new social condition of women—which, consequently, also changed the condition of men—altered the actual reproductive average from six to less than one child per woman (Alfonso), though a 2010 national study of fertility placed the ideal reproductive rate of women at 2.13, and at 2.31 for men (CEDEM 2009). At the same time, the extension of the new scholarship system (boarding schools), the elimination of private education (mostly by religious orders), and the introduction of free, mandatory secular education contributed to the waning of old racial, class, and gender prejudices.

By 1965 abortion had been institutionalized as a service of the national health system. Abortion was free, performed by experts in hospital conditions, and with the consent of the woman; the goal was to decrease maternal mortality, as well as to promote and guarantee women's right to make decisions about their own bodies. The violation of these requirements was criminalized in 1979 (Espín Guillois 2007; Sosa).

The magazine *Mujeres* (Women), founded by the FMC in 1961, dealt with issues of reproductive health in its very first issues. In the 1970s it added sexual education and later focused on gender. Afterwards, radio, television, and other national print media began to deal with these same subjects. *Muchacha* (Girl), a magazine for teens and young women, was founded in 1980.

As a result of the participatory process led by by the FMC, in 1972 a multidisciplinary group formed to develop a National Sex Education Program. In parallel, the Ministry of Public Health established the Programa Materno Infantil (PAMI; Mothers and Children Program) in 1980, seeking to integrate the health care programs for women, mothers, and children that had been developed since the 1960s. The importance of sex education, which had been recognized in the agreements of the Second Congress of the FMC in 1974, was evidenced in the policies approved by the First Congress of the Cuban Communist Party in 1975, primarily in two of its resolutions: "Regarding Childhood and Youth Education" and "Regarding the Full Exercise of the Equality of Women." The latter declared the need to definitively end discrimination against women and to include sex education as part of a complete education, appropriate for each stage of life, both in school and within the family.

The initiatives of the 1960s were validated in 1975 with the approval of the Family Code, at the time the most advanced legislation of its kind in the Americas, which recognized the rights of men and women to full sexuality and the sharing of domestic and educational responsibilities. As a result, Cuba was the first country to sign, and the second to ratify, government commitments under the Convention on the Elimination of All Forms of Discrimination Against Women (1979).

What is most significant about the 1959–1975 period is the generation of social policies that recognized the specific disadvantages in the historical condition of women and promoted their active participation in change. Priority was given to attending to their needs and interests, principally their rights to education, employment, household services, and health, including reproductive health. Although the home continued to be seen as women's main responsibility, with a conception of women's sexuality focused on reproduction, on the patriarchal pattern, labor legislation nevertheless brought substantial changes in the protection of women's rights. A vision of gender evolved out of a process of participation and social inclusion of women and their families, to include measures for the full exercise of their rights—with a notable impact on political rights. Sex education began to form an element of social policy (Castro Espín). The effect of these measures was demonstrated in the National Fertility Study of 1987, which indicated how far Cuban women had come: 99 percent of the women studied were aware of at least one contraception method, and 93 percent had used contraception (Juan Carlos Alfonso 2006).

Policies for the care of adolescents and youths helped to raise awareness of teenage pregnancy as a problem that had to be addressed from an educational, social, and health care perspective. Women's liberation did not cause teenage pregnancies, which already existed but were largely invisible and had not been a subject of study in the arena of politics. What did change was the social attitude: Now girls were not thrown out of their homes, not obliged to marry the fathers of their babies, not humiliated in the family and school settings. Social and demographic studies provided evidence that "reproductive behavior repeats itself in families where teenage pregnancy was present," and educational projects were developed to legitimize reproductive responsibility in youths of both sexes (Fleitas).

RESPECT FOR FREE SEXUAL ORIENTATION AND GENDER IDENTITY

Cuba is a country with a long tradition of *machismo* and homophobia that was supported for nearly one hundred years by worldwide scientific thought that stigmatized homosexuality, illustrated by the fact that it was not until 1990 that the World Health Organization stopped designating homosexuality as a form of mental illness. From Luis Montané's lecture *La pederastia en Cuba* (Pederasty in Cuba, 1888) to José Chelala's *Cinco ensayos sobre la vida sexual* (Five Studies on Sexual Life, 1959) and Ángel Custodio Arce's *Sexología 1* (Sexology 1, 1965), the Cuban medical science inherited by the Revolution operated as a block against sexual behavior it considered an illness, a prelude to insanity, and a mark of moral decadence.

In addition, Cuba is a Catholic nation, which implied a doctrinal rejection of homosexuality, both in the Church hierarchy and among parishioners. From this perspective, the moral corollaries of the ideological postulate of the Revolution's "New Man"—which the Cuban variant of socialism advocated—coincided with existing cultural traditions, medical discourse, and religious postulates on homosexuality. This rough consensus was a factor favoring practices of discrimination and exclusion against lesbian, gay, bisexual, and transgender (LGBT) individuals for many years.

Within this clash of cultural patterns, the Unidades Militares para la Ayuda de Producción (UMAPs; Military Units to Aid Production) emerged in 1965.

Conceived as a model of mandatory military service in a context of ongoing aggression by the government of the United States, the UMAPs reproduced the homophobic, patriarchal, and anticlerical patterns that prevailed in Cuban society following the Revolution. Separate, stigmatized platoons were formed for homosexuals and religious individuals. Although this form of mandatory mobilization was not at all equivalent to concentration camps for homosexuals (as many academic and media critics charged), there is no doubt that this humiliating differentiation was a harmful and discriminatory practice. The UMAPs were discontinued in 1968. In an interview Fidel Castro assumed responsibility for what occurred there (Lira Saade), but it would be careless to interpret his statement literally. No rigorous study has yet been conducted on the effects of this practice.

The great contradictions of this period are seen in the fact that although some discriminatory practices against homosexuals such as the UMAPs were ended, prejudices and marginalization resurged in other places, such as the First National Congress on Education and Culture (1971). Its final declaration called for barring homosexuals from employment in the fields of education, culture, and the media, because these institutions had a substantial influence on the development of children and youth, at a time when medical science considered homosexuality a mental disorder ("Declaración del Primer Congreso Nacional de Educación y Cultura," 1971). The application of this directive was a salient feature of what later was termed the process of *parametración* (development of parameters) and the *Quinquenio Gris* (Five Grey Years). In 1975 the resolution was declared unconstitutional and abolished by order of the Supreme Court, but the psychological damage to the victims of this arbitrary abuse of power was not undone.

In 1976 cultural policy changed with the creation of the Ministry of Culture, and artists and writers who endured parametración won awards, distinctions, and other forms of public recognition from the state and its institutions. Although efforts have been made to secure legal protection for individuals based on sexual orientation and gender identity, the only achievement as of 2011 has been the decriminalization of homosexuality in the penal code through Decree-Law 175 (1977), from which all references that could be interpreted as discrimination based on sexual orientation were excluded. In 2010 the FMC, together with other institutions and organizations, advocated for a draft bill amending the 1975 Family Code with language regarding respect for freedom of sexual orientation and gender identity, and including legal recognition of same-sex couples.

SEX EDUCATION AS A STATE POLICY

Policy on sex education began to take shape in the early period of the socialist transition in Cuba. The first structures entrusted with developing programs were created in the 1970s, such as the Grupo Nacional de Trabajo de Educación Sexual (GNTES; National Group for Work in Sex Education) headed by the FMC, which since 1976 served as a multidisciplinary advisory group to a permanent working group of the National Assembly of the People's Power (parliament). In 1989 GNTES became the Centro Nacional de Educación Sexual (CENESEX; National Center for Sex Education), an institution funded by the state within the Ministry of Public Health.

As of the early 2000s, the mission of CENESEX was to create and coordinate the national sex education program, with the participation of central government and civil society organizations. The greatest responsibility fell on the Ministries of Health, Education, and Culture, the FMC, and the Unión de Jóvenes Comunistas (UJC; Union of Young Communists). Collaboration takes place through working groups that operated in each province and municipality in the country. Activities focused on developing communication and sex-education strategies; encouraging academic work and scientific studies; providing guidance and therapy services, comprehensive care for transgender individuals, care for victims of gender-based violence and child sexual abuse, and legal counseling in sexual rights with an emphasis on LGBT individuals; developing community programs; and producing publications and audiovisual materials.

Cuba's sex education policy evolved through a process that began with a biological perspective centered on women and their reproductive function and gradually came to incorporate a comprehensive, rights-based vision that focused on gender and diversity. An important milestone was the FMC initiative to stimulate and facilitate the translation of books by foreign authors, including *El hombre y la mujer en la intimidad* (Man and Woman in Intimacy, 1979), by the German sexologist Siegfried Schnabl, which became a bestseller in Cuba. In its pages, Cubans for the first time read the authorized opinion of a scientist affirming that homosexuality is not a disease.

Although the Ministry of Education resisted sex education in the schools in the 1970s and 1980s, topics related to the reproductive function of sexuality were introduced into school textbooks, and in 1996 a sex education program focusing on gender, under the title *Por una educación sexual responsable y feliz* (A Responsible and Joyous Sexual Education) has obtained the support of numerous studies and publications.

As the right to free universal health care was deeply believed by the Cuban population, and as transsexuality is widely considered to be a mental disorder of gender identity by the international scientific community, institutional care for transsexuals began as a free service within the Sistema Nacional de Salud (SNS; National Health System). The first gender reassignment surgery was performed in Cuba in 1988 by Cuban doctors, but the public opposition that this event stirred up led to the suspension of these surgeries for twenty years. In 2008, on the advice of CENESEX, a resolution provided for specialized free health services for transgender persons, including gender reassignment surgery (Castro Espín 2007, 2008, 2011; Alfonso and Rodríguez).

Homophobia is a significant barrier to HIV prevention. To combat this situation, in 2000 the Ministry of Health approved the creation of the project Hombres que tienen Sexo con Hombres (HSH; Men Who Have Sex with Men) within the Centro Nacional de Prevención de Infecciones de Trasmisión Sexual y VIH/SIDA (National Center for the Prevention of Sexually Transmitted Infections and HIV/AIDS), which is charged with developing programs to train sexual health workers in the male homosexual and bisexual population and with creating prevention campaigns directed specifically at this population. In 2004 CENESEX began work on a national strategy for complete care of transgender individuals that included training sexual health workers in HIV prevention among transsexuals, transvestites, and cross-dressers. The strategy was presented in 2005 and 2006 to three permanent commissions of the National Assembly of the People's Power in order to raise awareness of legislative initiatives for protection of rights on gender identity and sexual orientation. To help in the training of sexual rights activists, CENESEX facilitated the development of lesbian and bisexual social networks such as Oremi, Fénix, Las Isabelas, Hombres por la Diversidad (HxD; Men for Diversity), the Family group, and the Youth group. Other activities focused on the development of sex education training for national revolutionary police officers, prosecutors, judges, and attorneys. In addition, initiatives for discussion of sexual diversity in cyberspace included in the sexual diversity section of the CENESEX Web site, the NotiG Electronic Bulletin, and the blog paquitoeldecuba.

The International Day against Homophobia (17 May), which began being celebrated in several Cuban cities in 2008, had a significant impact on the social awareness of the Cuban population. This week-long event included educational activities that promote respect for freedom of sexual orientation and gender identity as an exercise in justice and social equality. Events were coordinated by CENESEX, other state agencies, and civil organizations.

In academia, the development of study and research programs in women's studies departments, in sexology and society (in all medical universities), and in health promotion and sexual education (in teaching universities) made significant contributions to the National Sex Education Program.

The appearance of artistic cultural spaces such as Mejunje, created in 1983 in Santa Clara; the Cine Club Diferente, held monthly since 2008; and numerous shows that include transvestites as artists demonstrated a new, more open view of sexuality, gender, and justice in Cuba. Artistic and literary works of various genres, themes, and authors, some of them award-winning, express the complexities of change in perspectives and policies of social institutions.

REVOLUTIONARY CHANGES

In the early days of the Revolution, in the 1960s, Cuba began a process that deeply transformed the organization of society and individual lives. The interaction of practices and policies meant a profound break in the patriarchal family's control over women, in the reconfiguration of courtship and the couples' relationships, and expressions of heterosexual sexuality. At the same time, many prejudices and traditional ideals were shaken, such as virginity as a precondition for marriage, the idea of marriage for life, the role of the man as provider and head of the family, fidelity for women and infidelity for men, the rejection of interracial relationships, myths surrounding menstruation, and the discrediting of single mothers and unmarried women.

In Cuba, as in the rest of the world, these changes were led by women, but men were compelled by the enormous social pressure exerted by a social revolution to accept this process, which often they did not understand. The FMC was not thought to be a radical organization that advocated attacking or devaluing men; instead, it was seen as an association of women that, together with men, proposed to participate in the process of social transformation (Espín Guillois 1990).

Subsequently, new social figures in the field of sexuality appeared or became more visible in Cuba, including the AIDS patient (male or female, but primarily male); the *jinetera*, a complex and distinctly Cuban type of prostitute (as well as her masculine counterpart, the *pinguero*); the LGBT population, which spontaneously began to gather in public spaces throughout the country; and the presence of transvestites and transsexuals (legitimized in artistic/cultural offerings). Unlike the early decades of this period of Cuban history, these groups receive specific attention from institutions of Cuban society and its policies.

The goal of achieving a full, healthy, responsible, and joyous sexuality—in the complex and contradictory setting of a revolution based on cooperation, social justice, and solidarity among human beings—was beginning to mature in Cuba.

BIBLIOGRAPHY

Alfonso, Ada, and Mayra Rodríguez. "Familia y personas transexuales: Una relación al desnudo." *Sexología y Sociedad* 15, no. 40 (August 2009): 23–29.

Alfonso, Juan Carlos. "El descenso de la fecundidad en Cuba: De la primera a la segunda transición demográfica." *Revisita Cubana de Salud Pública* 32, no. 1 (January–March 2006).

Alfonso, Juan Carlos, Miguel Sosa, and Antonio Farnós. *Cuba: Transición de la fecundidad. Cambio social y conducta reproductiva.* Havana: UNICEF-FNUAP, 1995.

Castro Espín, Mariela. "El programa nacional de educación sexual en la estrategia cubana de desarrollo humano." *Sexología y Sociedad* 8, no. 20 (December 2002): 4–9.

Castro Espín, Mariela. "Aproximación a la transexualidad como noción científica." *Sexología y Sociedad* 13, no. 35 (December 2007): 4–8.

Castro Espín, Mariela. "La atención integral a transexuales en Cuba y su inclusión en las políticas sociales." *Sexología y Sociedad* 14, no. 36 (April 2008).

Castro Espín, Mariela. "La educación sexual como política de estado en Cuba: 1959–2010." *Sexología y Sociedad* 17, no. 44 (April 2011): 4–16.

Castro Ruz, Fidel. *Informe del Comité Central del PCC al Primer Congreso*. Havana: Editorial de Ciencias Sociales, 1978.

Castro Ruz, Fidel. *Mujeres y revolución*. Havana: Editorial de la Mujer, 2006.

Centro de Estudios Demográficos (CEDEM). *Cuba. Población y desarrollo*. Havana: CEDEM–Universidad de La Habana, 2009.

Centro de Información para la Prensa. "Cincuenta años de la Revolución Cubana." Available from http://revolucioncubana.cip.cu/referencias/cronologias/mujer-cubana.

Código de familia (1975). Havana: Gaceta Oficial, 1980.

De Armas, Paquita. "Korda: El hombre que miraba con el corazón." 25 October 2008. Available from http://verbiclara.nireblog.com/.

"Declaración del Primer Congreso Nacional de Educación y Cultura." *Casa de las Américas* 65–66 (March–April 1971): 3–19.

Espín Guillois, Vilma. "Discurso por El XX aniversario de la creación de la FMC." In *La mujer en Cuba*. Havana: Editora Política, 1990.

Espín Guillois, Vilma. "Historia de la educación sexual en Cuba." *Sexología y Sociedad* 13, no. 34 (August 2007): 5–17.

Fleitas, Reina. "Situación de la infancia y la adolescencia en Cuba." 2010. Available from http://www.cenesex.sld.cu/webs/situacion_de_la_infancia_30.htm.

Lira Saade, Carmen. "Entrevista con Fidel Castro." *La Jornada* (31 March 2010): 26.

Núñez, Marta. "Estrategias cubanas para el empleo femenino en los noventa." *Papers de Sociología* 63–64 (2001): 141–170. Available from http://www.raco.cat/.

Oficina Nacional de Estadísticas–Federación de Mujeres Cubanas (ONE–FMC). *Mujeres cubanas. Estadísticas y realidades 1958–2008*. Havana: Author, 2010.

Proveyer Cervantes, Clotilde, Reina Fleitas Ruiz, Graciela González Olmedo, et al. *50 años después: Mujeres en Cuba y cambio social*. Havana: Oxfam Internacional, 2010.

Ramírez, Marta María. *Pedir Perdón sería una hipocresía*. 2010. Available from http://www.cooperacion-suiza.admin.ch/cuba/.

Roque Guerra, Alberto. "Diversidad sexual en las políticas públicas en Cuba. Avances y desafíos." Paper presented at XXV Conferencia Mundial de la Asociación Internacional de Gays, Lesbianas, Bisexuales y Transgéneros (ILGA), São Paulo, December 6, 2010. Available from http://diversidadcenesex.blogcip.cu/.

Sánchez Parodi, Ramón. "CUBA-USA. Diez tiempos de una relación." Havana: Editorial Ocean Sur, 2011.

Sosa, Miguel. *Aborto en Cuba. Breves consideraciones históricas y jurídicas. Situación actual*. Panama City: Publicación FIGO, 2008.

SEXUALITY: JINETERA AND THE SPECIAL PERIOD

Rosa Miriam Elizalde

The resurgence of prostitution in the Special Period.

Jinetera, a colloquial term for a Cuban prostitute, entered the vernacular first in Havana and later in the rest of the island at the beginning of the economic crisis known as the Special Period in the 1990s, after the fall of socialism in Eastern Europe.

There are varying opinions about the origins of the word *jinetera*, and contrary to what one might expect, none points primarily to the sexual act. There is agreement that it is a term of the historical juncture, as were *merolico* (quack doctor) and *candiñas* (ladies of happiness), words derived from popular soap operas broadcast in the 1980s and 1990s, and *fletera*, a nineteenth-century term that according to Miguel Moreno Fraginals referred to a prostitute who walked the streets serving the freighters and flotillas arriving at the Port of Havana: "As Havana was the leading port of both the Americas, steeped in seafaring culture, it is logical that the verbal customs of the sea would be transferred to the ritual language of sex" (Fraginals p. 400).

Some scholars suggested that *jinetera* comes from *ginette*, a French Canadian term for a prostitute. But Rosa Miriam Elizalde's studies of dozens of prostitutes and pimps at the beginning of the 1990s established that *jinetera* is simply a derivation of the Cuban word *jinetero*, which in the 1980s referred to a person linked with foreigners and involved in trafficking goods or selling on the black market when the possession of foreign currency was still a crime in Cuba. *Jinetero* alludes to *jinete*, a person who rides a horse—here it is used figuratively to describe someone who exploits another person.

The term *jinetero* appeared in print for the first time in 1988, in *De lo popular y lo vulgar en el habla cubana* (On the Popular and the Common in Cuban Speech), by the researcher Carlos Paz Pérez. Initially, the word was considered vulgar, but as its use became generalized in the country's new socioeconomic conditions, linguists no longer categorized it as vulgar or colloquial; it penetrated the standard lexicon, and it was used even in official publications.

Jinetera and its derivative *jineterismo*—a term for various, generally illegal, commercial relationships with foreigners, including prostitution—also imply a culture of struggle in an economic crisis that measures social success in terms of obtaining that which is scarce, particularly money. In the Special Period acquiring money meant entering the information economy, the criminal economy, or the emerging economy of business with foreigners. These are the sectors that provided access to currencies with high purchasing value—the U.S. dollar in the 1990s, and any convertible currency, including the Cuban convertible peso, in the 2000s.

The word *jinetera* is a pretense that conceals the practice of prostitution, which is socially stigmatized. For those who work in the sex trade as well as those who benefit from it directly or indirectly, the attempt to disguise the practice of prostitution involves distancing oneself from the historical memory that condemns sex workers to the lowest rung of the social ladder. This distancing is not peculiar to Cuba; it is a characteristic of traditional prostitution in all countries. The sociologist Erving Goffman (1922–1982) explained that a stigmatized individual's personal and social identities are divided (Goffman). In traditional prostitution there is one relationship context in which the prostitute shows herself as she is and another in which she acts in accordance with the social status she invents for herself. The two selves must be differentiated in order to safeguard the personal self from the accusing finger of society.

The majority of women who engage in prostitution in Cuba do so with the complicity of their families and their communities, which at different levels accept the sex trade, benefit from it, and legitimize it as a means of acquiring consumer goods or access to services that cannot be obtained easily through traditional or socially lawful routes. The word *jinetera* helps to maintain the distance from stigma; it draws a veil over the crude face of prostitution.

TRAITS

With the intensive development of tourism in Cuba during the Special Period, the *jinetera* emerged as the first channel for currency entering the country. Initially, the Cuban tourism model was similar to models in other Caribbean countries and in post-Franco Spain: It served primarily single men looking for women, who appreciated that Cuba was an atypical social laboratory with the highest levels of education and safety in the region.

The trigger for the revival of a trade that had all but disappeared in the first years of the Revolution—in 1959 there were 100,000 prostitutes in a population of 6 million—was not just the injection of dollars into the Cuban economy (Cruz Ochoa; Dumont). If this injection had come from sugar exports, for example, the money would have gone directly into business channels rather than circulating in the population. But because the dollars arrived with tourists,

part of the money passed into the state system and part of it circulated freely in the form of tips and payments for services offered by the informal economy.

Yet, the resurgence of prostitution in Cuba was not caused exclusively by the desperate adoption of tourism as the main source of income for the Cuban economy. It was also a reflection of the breakdown of values at the social level—a consequence of the economic crisis and the crisis of paradigms that arose with the fall of socialism in Europe—that made tolerable what was previously unthinkable.

Distorting relationships through the showcase of tourism—in idyllic environments that promote seduction and consumerism—the *jinetera* does not act like a classic prostitute, nor are there brothels in Cuba (though underground economies usually produce them). The Cuban *jinetera* is similar to a paid escort. Typically she is well educated, she displays high self-esteem, and she maintains a relationship with her client that continues after his stay in Cuba. This relationship often includes marriage and travel to his home country. Many *jineteras* are professional women who only occasionally engage in prostitution. Usually they do not carry sexually transmitted diseases, thanks to Cuban health benefits.

Although the sex trade that predominates on the island is nontraditional and small in comparison with global statistics, this commerce is clearly prostitution in that it involves the exchange of sex for cash, payment in kind, or access to luxury services.

The male counterpart to the *jinetera* is the *pinguero*, another vernacular term that refers to a man who, without necessarily considering himself homosexual, prostitutes himself to other men or women, but preferably male tourists. The word *pinguero* alludes to the penis, which in Cuba is known commonly as *pinga*. In contrast to *jineterismo*, the behavior of *pingueros* has been little studied by Cuban social scientists (Hodge; La Fountain-Stokes).

THE *JINETERA* IN THE ARTS AND MEDIA

Since the early 1990s the *jinetera* has been a prevalent theme in the arts and the media, which have attempted to explain this complex social type in contemporary Cuba. The international media have presented stereotypes of the Cuban prostitute, often in attempts to demonstrate that the reappearance of prostitution on the island proves the failure of the Cuban social project.

In addition to many minor, superficial, and opportunist works, the *jinetera* appears in all her complexity in Cuban contemporary art, particularly theater, literature, and film. Among the significant artists who have directly addressed the theme of the *jinetera/pinguero* are the authors Pedro Juan Gutiérrez in *Trilogía sucia de La Habana, novela* (Dirty Trilogy of Havana, a Novel, 1998) and Miguel Mejides in the short story "Rumba-Palace" (1996); the playwrights Nelson Dorr in *Jinetera* (2007) and Abel González

Melo in *Chamaco* (Boyfriend, 2005); the composers Silvio Rodríguez in *Flores desechables* (Throwaway Flowers, 1991) and Nassiry Lugo in *Callejero* (Streetwalker, 2004); the filmmaker Gerardo Chijona in *Perfecto amor equivocado* (Love by Mistake, 2004); and the television director Charlie Medina in *Pompas de jabón* (Soap Bubbles, 2004).

BIBLIOGRAPHY

Causse Cathcart, Mercedes. *Reflexiones en torno a la interpelación entre lengua y cultura.* Santiago de Cuba: Universidad de Oriente, 2009.

Centro de Estudios sobre la Juventud. *Cuba. Jóvenes en los 90.* Havana: Casa Editora Abril, 1999.

Comas, Amparo. *La prostitución femenina en Madrid.* Madrid: Consejería de la Presidencia, 1991.

De la Cruz Ochoa, Ramón. "El delito, la criminología y el derecho penal en Cuba después de 1959." *Revista Electrónica de Ciencia Penal y criminología* 2, no. 2 (2002).

Dumont, René. *Cuba: Intent de critica constructiva.* Barcelona: Nova Terra, 1964.

Elizalde, Rosa Miriam. *Flores desechables. ¿Prostitución en Cuba?* Havana: Editora Abril, 1996.

García Ronda, Denia, et al. "Venturas y desventuras de la narrativa cubana actual." *Temas* 24–25 (2001): 166–192. Available from http://www.temas.cult.cu/revistas/24-25/240201.pdf.

Goffman, Erving. *Estigma. La identidad deteriorada.* Buenos Aires: Editorial Amorrortu, 1970.

Hodge, G. Derrick. "Colonization of the Cuban Body: The Growth of Male Sex Work in Havana." *NACLA Report on the Americas* 34, no. 5 (2001): 20–28.

La Fountain-Stokes, Lawrence M. "Metatextualidades voladoras." *La Habana Elegante* (Spring 2002).

López Sacha, Francisco. "Una aproximación a Pedro Juan Gutiérrez." *Temas* 54 (April–June 2008): 144–150.

Moreno Fraginals, Manuel. "Negros y mulatos: Vida y sobrevida." *Orbita de Manuel Moreno Fraginals.* Havana: Ediciones Unión, 2009.

Paz Pérez, Carlos. *De lo popular y lo vulgar en el habla cubana.* Havana: Editorial de Ciencias Sociales, 1988.

Paz Pérez, Carlos. *Diccionario cubano de términos vulgares y populares.* Havana: Editorial de Ciencias Sociales, 1996.

■ *See also*

Cuban Singers in the United States

The Color of Summer (Reinaldo Arenas)

Fefu and Her Friends (María Irene Fornés)

Life on the Hyphen (Gustavo Pérez-Firmat)

The Mambo Kings Play Songs of Love (Oscar Hijuelos)

Milk of Amnesia (Carmelita Tropicana/ Alina Troyano)

SEXUALITY: DIASPORA AND SEXUALITY

Ricardo L. Ortíz

Survey of sexuality and sexual politics in the U.S.-Cuban diaspora after 1959.

A Cuban diaspora has been emanating from the island from the moment that a recognizably Cuban collective and national culture consolidated and officially recognized itself on the island; such a culture, hence such a diaspora, certainly predates by centuries Cuba's political liberation from Spain in 1898, its eventual emergence as a sovereign republic, and the significant redetermination of its national fate by the Castro Revolution. The experience of the diaspora following the 1959 Revolution had a strong sexual dimension.

The sexual aspects of Cuban cultural and national life have been profoundly shaped by forms of material, collective, and institutional organization, such as the plantation system; the political erotics of slavery and enduring forms of racial hierarchy; the intensely body-focused modalities of Cuban music, Cuban food, and Cuban faith; and the so-called revolutionary constructions of gender (New Men, New Women) after 1959. These systems challenged and complicated prevailing constructions of the sexual and the erotic that insist on private, intimate, and individual conditions. Diasporic experience similarly challenged and complicated these prevailing constructions through a double movement: first, by transferring the difficult conditions of collectivity to the more prominent sites of Cuban diasporic relocation, and, second, by layering over these conditions an additional and transformative mode of collective experience—the condition of diaspora itself.

Cuban-exile and Cuban-diasporic communities in the United States behaved in the decades following 1959 like other large populations displaced from their homelands by the shock of a sudden political crisis: They insisted on maintaining their core cultural values and social practices (an ethic of hard work and social ambition fueled by deep cultural pride, on the one hand, and deeply patriarchal, misogynistic, and homophobic attitudes, on the other) based on the strong assumption of an imminent return to a Cuba liberated from communism. The early exiles arrived in a United States on the brink of profound transformations in sexual attitudes and political values. Cuban-exile and Cuban-diasporic responses to these transformations varied across generations, geographical locations, and social classes, and changed again in the years following the Mariel Boatlift of 1980, which brought additional racial, class, and political diversity to the U.S. Cuban population.

A watershed moment arrived with the production and distribution off-island of *Mauvaise conduite* (*Improper Conduct*, 1984), a documentary film by Néstor Almendros and Orlando Jiménez Leal that claimed to expose the Castro regime's targeting, persecution, and imprisonment of political enemies who were also accused of being gay, a status which in itself was deemed to be detrimental to the Revolution's renewal of Cuban social and political life. Intense reactions to the film provoked criticism of the homophobia common to both the Revolution and conservative Cuban exiles. The film also introduced to a wider audience Reinaldo Arenas (1943–1990), one of its prominent contributors, an openly gay Cuban novelist and poet who had escaped the island as one of the many thousands of *Marielitos*. Arenas's suicide during the late stages of his battle with HIV-AIDS intensified the debate about Cuban and Cuban exile sexual attitudes and sexual politics in the 1990s.

That decade was pivotal in the evolution of sexual attitudes and practices in the U.S.-Cuban diaspora. Arenas's suicide in 1990 opened the decade, and the subsequent publication of his autobiography, *Before Night Falls,* in Spanish and then English brought to light the details of his difficult life in a way unprecedented in Cuban cultural history. Arenas's tragedy was quickly followed by the AIDS activism of another young gay Marielito, Pedro Zamora (1972–1994), who participated in the 1994 edition of MTV's reality show *The Real World*. Zamora succumbed to AIDS only months after his work on MTV, but his willingness to discuss both his sexuality and his HIV-positive status while on the show brought about another profound shift in Cuban exile sexual attitudes. By 1995 the U.S.-based Cuban population had also shifted its political identification, seeing itself more as an immigrant and diasporic community with an increasing stake in U.S. political life and less as an exile outpost waiting for the moment of imminent, redemptive return to the homeland. This newly confident, committed U.S. Cuban immigrant community turned around and, in the course of the 1990s, embraced newly defected and openly gay artists such as the musician Albita Rodríguez (b. 1962), and accepted and claimed as legitimately theirs cultural work dealing with homosexual themes such as the Oscar-nominated film *Strawberry and Chocolate* (1993), by the Cuban, pro-Revolution director Tomás Gutiérrez Alea, and Julian Schnabel's critically acclaimed 2000 film version of Arenas's *Before Night Falls*.

The 1990s also saw the emergence of fully evolved and mature modes of cultural and critical discourse about gender and sexual politics in the U.S. Cuban context. Early work such as Oscar Hijuelos's Pulitzer Prize–winning novel *The Mambo Kings Play Songs of Love* (1989) and Gustavo Pérez-Firmat's field-defining study *Life on the Hyphen* (1994) established the simultaneously intense, conflictual, and playful qualities of sexual life in the U.S. Cuban world. Hijuelos's work was followed by a rich genealogy of literary textual production by a bracing roster of gay and feminist writers, including Cristina García (b. 1958), Achy Obejas (b. 1956), Elías Miguel Muñoz (b. 1954), Eduardo Machado (b. 1953), Rafael Campo (b. 1964), Cecilia Rodríguez-Milanés (b. 1959), Richard Blanco (b. 1968), Nilo Cruz (b. 1960), and Eduardo Santiago (b. 1967). Following Pérez-Firmat's precedent, critical and scholarly work that explored the intersections of gender, sexuality, ethnicity, class, and culture in the diaspora emerged from an impressive group of authors that includes Ruth Behar (b. 1956), María de los Ángeles Torres (b. 1955), José Esteban Muñoz (b. 1967), José Quiroga (b. 1959), Juana María Rodríguez

(b. 1959), Lázaro Lima (b. 1967), and Antonio Viego (b. 1967). In addition to the contributions of these writers and scholars, the understanding of the political erotics of collective Cuban-diasporic life was affected by the work by such figures as the conceptual artist Ana Mendieta (1948–1985), performance artist Carmelita Tropicana (b. 1951), filmmaker Ela Troyano, and art-world impresario Coco Fusco (b. 1960).

Although they cannot capture all the representations of sexual politics and sexual life in the U.S. Cuban diaspora, the rich, varied literary and scholarly discourses testify to the profundity and complexity with which U.S. Cuban sexual life, and certainly its homosexual life, is lived and practiced. In the fiftieth year of a vital, fertile off-island culture, anyone interested or invested in the sexuality of the diaspora must maintain an open disposition toward a future in which meaningful, multiple modes of an erotic *cubanidad* will persist, survive, and proliferate, in any and all spaces claiming to call themselves Cuban.

BIBLIOGRAPHY

Arenas, Reinaldo. *Before Night Falls: A Memoir*. New York: Viking Penguin, 1993.

Hijuelos, Oscar. *The Mambo Kings Play Songs of Love*. New York: Farrar, Straus and Giroux, 1989.

Pérez-Firmat, Gustavo. *Life on the Hyphen*. Austin: University of Texas Press, 1994.

SEXUALITY: GAY AND LESBIAN REPRESENTATION IN CUBAN ART, FILM, AND LITERATURE

Norge Espinosa Mendoza

Cuban artistic and literary works dealing with gay and lesbian themes.

When the Cuban writer Senel Paz was awarded the Juan Rulfo Short Story International Prize (the most important award in the Spanish-speaking world for this genre) for his 1990 story "El bosque, el lobo, y el hombre nuevo" ("The Wolf, the Woods, and the New Man"), his success was not just one more story in Cuban newspapers. This award, won by a story that joins a young Communist and an open homosexual, cleared the way for other public and private fables, recasting the image of the country, its traditions, its cultural roots, and its political life.

The film *Fresa y chocolate* (Strawberry and Chocolate, 1993), directed by the team of Tomás Gutiérrez Alea and Juan Carlos Tabío and based on that story by Paz, exponentially expanded the shock wave set off by a dialogue between voices that, hitherto, would have been considered mutually contradictory. The depth and richness of the story and the film continued in the early 2000s to reverberate in the representation of homoerotic subjects in Cuba. Sometimes these realities are verbalized and celebrated in a roundabout way; at other times, they are discussed explicitly, with demands for literature, the cinema, the stage, and all Cuba to read this groundbreaking story and take yet another step forward.

In 1988, before this story was published, Graciela Sánchez, a Chicana student at the International Film School in San Antonio de los Baños, Cuba, had chosen homosexual themes in order to demystify them in her documentary *No porque lo diga Fidel Castro* (Not Because Fidel Castro Says So). The film recorded the first unmuzzled testimony on a subject that had always been relegated to the back pages of the national agenda. Around this time, other texts also provided signs that Cuban homosexuals were finally coming out of the closet: Among these was a story by Roberto Urías, "¿Por qué llora Leslie Caron?" (Why Does Leslie Caron Cry?), from the book of the same title, which was the winner of the March 13th Prize in 1989. In poetry there was "Vestido de novia" (Bridal Gown) from the 1992 book *Las breves tribulaciones* (Brief Tribulations), by Norge Espinosa, winner of the El Caimán Barbudo prize of the same year. The rapidly changing landscape was also represented by the radio soap opera *Adrián* (1995), by Ernesto Daranas. The inclusive spirit that the culture won by force in the 1980s, through battles large and small, enlarged the Cuban stage so that new characters could emerge from the shadows. In 1988 Marianela Boán unveiled her choreography for *Sin permiso* (Without Permission), showing the first male nude on the Cuban stage as a body freed from garments and atavisms such as those that had ended a riveting spectacle earlier that same year by Víctor Varela, called *La cuarta pared* (The Fourth Wall). These are bodies seeking to win a freedom that allows them to fully express how beautiful and provocative they are, bodies that are no less eloquent than the political billboards that appear on every corner in the country.

The 1990 production *Trilogía de teatro norteamericano* (Trilogy of North American Theater), the debut of theater director Carlos Díaz, shocked many in its audience at the National Theater in Havana. Building on the American plays *The Glass Menagerie*, *Tea and Sympathy*, and *A Streetcar Named Desire*, Díaz reinvented nostalgia and glamour from an obscenely postmodern and neobaroque angle that seduces the viewer with its atmospherics and the male and female bodies that it reveals. He spawned a series of imitators who have followed in his footsteps. From 1992 into the early 2000s Díaz has overseen his own theater company, the Teatro el Público, and his poetics are filtered through a gay lens. Despite these successes, the abrupt shutdown in all avenues of Cuban life imposed by the Special Period in the 1990s, following the loss of the moral and economic support of the socialist world, marked a set of sharp changes in how these characters who had finally been brought onto the national stage would find ways to survive. Gay men and lesbians, who had been silenced for so long, learned that art provides a landscape from which they cannot easily be erased.

Thus language of a new independence overcame the suspicions of the dire days of the forced labor camps of the Unidades Militares para la Ayuda de Producción (UMAP), to which from 1965 to 1968 were sent homosexuals, religious practitioners, and persons accused of living in ways contrary to the new socialist morality. This language was reconstructed by Félix Luis Viera in his 2002 novel *Un ciervo herido* (A Wounded Stag) and illustrated the barriers that kept gays, lesbians, and persons of so-called doubtful morality away from potential leadership for the better part of the 1970s. At the very beginning of the new century literature and the other arts opened a space for new characters such as the sex workers known as *pinguero* (male) and *jinetera* (usually female), protagonists of a new wave of prostitution that rode on the economic hope of tourism. In this cultural environment, the young playwright Raúl Alfonso (b. 1966) wrote and unveiled works such as *El grito* (The Cry, 1990), *Islas solitarias* (Solitary Islands, 1995), and *Bela de noche* (Bela at Night, 1994), whose characters are exiles, persons with AIDS, and transvestites. José Milián unveiled *Las mariposas saltan al vacío* (Butterflies Leap into the Void) in 1995, shortly after José Hevia choreographed lesbian love in *Desnuda* (Naked, 1991). The painter Rocío García portrayed geishas, sailors, and policemen in a splendidly aggressive color series, which in its own way recombined what other big names in the plastic arts (such as Servando Cabrera Moreno and Raúl Martínez) had subliminally worked into the best of their open work. In 1993 the photographer Eduardo Hernández paid tribute to the poet Julián del Casal and then moved on to an exploration of the male body that took him up to the daring edge with *El muro: The Wall*, one of his more impressive works, which appeared as an art book in 2010 under the imprint of Red Trillium Press. By the time Luis Felipe Bernaza and Margaret Gilpin shot *Mariposas en el andamio* (Butterflies on Scaffolding, 1996) and the film *Gay Cuba* (1996), by Sonja de Vries, opened, many of these questions were being addressed in documentaries, because they had not been answered entirely.

By the beginning of the twenty-first century, literature was portraying a different kind of Havana. In the novels of Zoé Valdés and Pedro Juan Gutiérrez one senses a different kind of texture; gays and transvestites enliven these works in the tradition of Grand Guignol. In poetry, a gay sensibility imbues the work of Alberto Acosta-Pérez, Marilín Roque, Arlén Regueiro, Nelson Simón, Damaris Calderón, José Rolando Rivero, Delfín Prats, José Félix León, Juan Carlos Valls, and Francisco Morán, among others, while the narrative genre includes the inventiveness of Abilio Estévez, with *Tuyo es el reino* (Yours Is the Kingdom, 1998), and Leonardo Padura in stories such as "El cazador" (The Hunter, 1994) and his novel *Máscaras* (Masks, 1998), or in texts by Mirta Yáñez and Ana Luz García Calzada. This literary tradition finally allows Virgilio Piñera, Lezama Lima, Calvert Casey, Emilio Ballagas and the uneasy ghost of Reinaldo Arenas to come out of the closet. The tradition reinvents itself with many of these names, which, as in the case of Guillermo Vidal or Ángel Santiesteban, also reformulate the environment of Carlos Montenegro. Youths such as Pedro de Jesús López, Jorge Ángel Pérez, Ena Lucía Portela, Miguel Ángel Fraga, Ana Lidia Vega Serova, and Ernesto Pérez Chang dive deep into narratives where others previously delved only superficially into matters that, once past the initial scandals, begged for better writing. In children's literature, Luis Cabrera Delgado imagines *Ito* (1996) and *¿Dónde está la princesa?* (Where Is the Princess? 2001). The memoirs of Raúl Martínez, called *Yo, Publio* (I, Publius, 2007) were published after Martínez's death and became one of the biggest editorial events of the year. The following year a sample of his homoerotic paintings was displayed in a joint personal exhibition with Rocío García at the Ludwig Foundation of Cuba.

Meanwhile broadcast television was not only behind the curve in covering this issue (it was not until 2007 that *Fresa y chocolate* was rebroadcast), but it was also inconsistent in its approach. The most noteworthy examples are probably more to be appreciated for their generous intentions than for actual artistic achievement, such as the soap operas *The La cara oculta de la luna* (Dark Side of the Moon, 2005) and *Aquí estamos* (Here We Are, 2010). New film projects, such as *Casa vieja* (Old House, 2010), by Lester Hamlet; *Chamaco* (Kid, 2010), by Juan Carlos Cremata; *Boleto al paraíso* (Ticket to Paradise, 2010), by Gerardo Chijona; and *En cuerpo equivocado* (In the Wrong Body, 2010), by Marilyn Solaya, attempted to make up for lost time by acknowledging the homosexual, the male prostitute, the HIV/AIDS patient, and the transsexual, among the multitudes of people. In 2011 a major event transpired when Editorial Letras Cubanas published Cuba's first anthology of homoerotic stories, prepared by Alberto Garrandés under the title *Instrucciones para cruzar el espejo* (Instructions for Crossing the Mirror).

The appearance of books such as *La maldición: Una historia del placer como conquista* (The Curse, A History of Pleasure as Conquest), by Víctor Fowler, and *Del otro lado del espejo: La sexualidad en la construcción de la nación cubana* (On the Other Side of the Mirror: Sexuality in the Construction of the Cuban Nation), by Abel Sierra Madero, started to fill the void of theoretical works and essays on homosexuality. Other critics such as Maggie Mateo, Pedro Pérez, Jesús Jambrina, Andrés Isaac Santana, and Alberto Garrandés contributed a revisionist perspective that confronts a culture weighed down by silence and

encompassing no small number of persons of major public significance in its traditions as well as in modern times. These have yet to be analyzed, based on their intended indexes of sexuality. This is unfortunate, especially in the realm of music, where the sensibility of Bola de Nieve and Ernesto Lecuona and other less well-known figures continues to be an open secret.

In spite of everything, the subject of sexuality in Cuba was going through an entirely new kind of discussion in the early 2000s, very different from that of 1990. Between 1998 and 2000 the writer and activist Norge Espinosa organized the first annual Homoerotic Art Working Days under the auspices of the Saíz Brothers Association of young writers and artists. This event became possible because they discovered new ways to engage in the struggle and break open cultural spaces for the erotic and other edges of people's intemperate reality. In the early 2000s, under the auspices of the Centro Nacional de Educación Sexual (CENESEX), these wishes are claiming an ever larger and more open stage, which they must earn through stronger bonds among internal and external forces. Not just for theater producers such as Tony Díaz, Raúl Martín, and Carlos Celdrán. Not just for the transvestites who gather at El Mejunje of Santa Clara, a truly unique place. Not just for playwrights such as Esther Suárez, Abel González Melo, and Rogelio Orizondo. Not just in order to understand the coded songs of Liuba María Hevia, Amaury Pérez, and Frank Domínguez. Not just for the photographs of René Peña or of the very young Eduardo Rodríguez with his series *17* or of those that Alejandro Ramírez collects under the provocative title *Conducta impropia* (Improper Conduct). Some of them work in Cuba, while others are overseas, where more than a few worthy names continue to redraw the map of people's imagination and desire, including Pedro Monge Rafuls, Nilo Cruz, Jorge Ignacio Cortiñas, and María Irene Fornés; Néstor Díaz de Villegas, Rafael Campo, Chely Lima, Félix Lizárraga, Elías Miguel Muñoz, Odette Alonso, Magaly Alabau, Achy Obejas, and Sonia Rivera-Valdés; Emilio Bejel, Francisco Morán, José Quiroga, Ricardo L. Ortíz, and many others.

IMPORTANT WORKS

Film

Cremata, Juan Carlos, dir. *Chamaco* (2009).

Chijona, Gerardo, dir. *Boleto al paraíso* (2010).

De León, Jorge, dir. *El bosque de Sherwood* (2008).

De Vries, Sonja, dir. *Gay Cuba* (1995).

Farfán, Milagros, dir. *La tarea* (2009).

Gilpin, Margaret, and Luis Felipe Bernaza, dirs. *Mariposas en el andamio* (1996).

Gutiérrez Alea, Tomás, and Juan Carlos Tabío, dirs. *Fresa y chocolate* (1993).

Hernández, Jesús Miguel, dir. *Ella trabaja* (2007).

Padrón, Humberto, dir. *Video de familia* (2001).

Rodríguez, Jessica, dir. *Tacones cercanos* (2008).

Sánchez, Graciela, dir. *No porque lo diga Fidel Castro* (1988).

Solaya, Marilyn, dir. *En cuerpo equivocado* (2010).

Vega, Belkis, dir. *Viviendo al límite* (2004).

Vila, Lizette, dir. *Y hembra es el alma mía* (1994).

Vila, Lizette, dir. *Rasgando velos* (2006).

Zayas, Manuel, dir. *Seres extravagantes* (2004).

Drama

Alfonso, Raúl. *El grito*. Havana: Letras Cubanas, 1994.

González Melo, Abel. *Chamaco*. Havana: Editorial Tablas-Alarcos, 2007.

Milián, José. *Si vas a comer, espera por Virgilio y otras obra*. Havana: Ediciones Unión, 2000.

Orizondo, Rogelio. *Vacas*. Havana: Ediciones Unión, 2008.

Radio and Television Drama

Daranas, Ernesto. *Adrián*. Radio series (1995).

González Figueroa, Rafael "Cheíto," dir. *La cara oculta de la luna*. Television series (2005).

González Figueroa, Rafael "Cheíto," and Hugo Reyes, dirs. *Aquí estamos*. Television series. (2010).

Fiction

Arrufat, Antón. *Ejercicios para hacer de la esterilidad virtud*. Havana: Ediciones Unión, 1997.

Cabrera, Luis. *Ito*. Havana: Editorial Abril, 1996.

De Jesús, Pedro. *Cuentos frígidos*. Madrid: Ediciones Olalla, 1998.

Estévez, Abilio. *Los palacios distantes*. Barcelona: TusQuets, 2002.

Fraga, Miguel Ángel. *No dejes escapar la ira*. Havana: Letras Cubanas, 2001.

Padura, Leonardo. *Máscaras*. Havana: Ediciones Unión, 1998.

Pérez, Jorge Ángel. *El paseante cándido*. Havana: Ediciones Unión, 2001.

Pérez Chang, Ernesto. *Últimas fotos de mamá desnuda*. Havana: Ediciones Unión, 2000.

Portela, Ena Lucía. *El viejo, el asesino, y yo*. Havana: Letras Cubanas, 2000.

Rivera-Valdés, Sonia. *Las historias prohibidas de Marta Veneranda*. Havana: Editorial Casa de las Américas, 1997.

Serova, Ana Lidia. *Anima fatua*. Havana: Letras Cubanas, 2009.

Vidal, Guillermo. *Las manzanas del paraíso*. San Juan, Puerto Rico: Editorial Plaza Mayor, 2002.

Viera, Félix Luis. *Un ciervo herido*. San Juan, Puerto Rico: Editorial Plaza Mayor, 2002.

Poetry

Acosta Pérez, Alberto. *¡Éramos tan puros!* Havana: Letras Cubanas, 1991.

Alonso, Odette. *Palabra del que vuelve*. Havana: Letras Cubanas, 1996.

Calderón, Damaris. *Sílabas/Ecce homo*. Havana: Letras Cubanas, 2001.

Espinosa, Norge. *Las estrategias del páramo*. Havana: Ediciones Unión, 2000.

León, José Félix. *Donde espera la trampa que un día pisó el ciervo*. Havana: Editorial Abril, 1996.

Morán, Francisco. *El cuerpo del delito*. Seville: Ayuntamiento de Sevilla, 2001.

Prats, Delfín. *El esplendor y el caos*. Havana: Ediciones Unión, 2002.

BIBLIOGRAPHY

Abreu, Alberto. *Los juegos de la escritura, o la (re) escritura de la Historia*. Havana: Ediciones Casa de las Américas, 2007.

Béjel, Emilio. *Gay Cuban Nation*. Chicago: University of Chicago Press, 2001.

Espinosa, Carlos, ed. "Literatura homoerótica." *Encuentro de la cultura cubana*, nos. 41–42 (2006).

Espinosa, Norge. *Carlos Díaz, Teatro el Público: La trilogía interminable*. Havana: Editorial Abril, 2001.

Fowler, Víctor. *La maldición, una historia del placer como conquista*. Havana: Letras Cubanas, 1988.

Fowler, Víctor. *Historias del cuerpo*. Havana: Letras Cubanas, 2001.

"Hablemos claro." *Mariel*, no. 5 (1984).

Pérez Rivero, Pedro. *De Sodoma vino un ángel*. Santiago de Cuba: Ediciones Oriente, 2004.

Sierra Madero, Abel. *La nación sexuada*. Havana: Editorial Ciencias Sociales, 2002.

Sierra Madero, Abel. *Del otro lado del espejo: La sexualidad en la construcción de la nación cubana*. Havana: Editorial Casa de las Américas, 2006.

"La voz homoerótica." *Gaceta de Cuba*, no. 5 (2002).

SEXUALITY: THE MULATA FIGURE IN THE CUBAN IMAGINARY

Melissa Blanco Borelli

The association between sexuality and the mulata figure, a classic trope in the Cuban imaginary.

In Cuban culture, the *mulata* (mulatta or mixed-race woman) is an omnipresent fixture. She populates fiction, paintings, musical lyrics, poetry, films, dance, and even religious iconography. Arguably the *sui generis* symbol of the Cuban national and cultural imaginary, the figure of the mulata contends with the many competing narratives of colonialism, race, gender, and sexuality. As a product of the rampant miscegenation that occurred on the island during and after colonial Spanish rule, the mulata is often perceived as a neat embodiment of the different cultures and influences that have shaped the island: European, African,

Chinese, and indigenous. This all-encompassing relationship with everyone renders the mulata a desirable artifact. As a result, sexual desire for the mulata is a recognized and recognizable trope in Cuban culture. Yet, as a living, breathing body, the mulata acts as a benign and aesthetically pleasing buffer against the legacies of racialist discourse in Cuba. In other words, how can there be tension between blackness and whiteness when they merge so well in the figure of the mulata? Historically, she has been celebrated and denigrated, venerated and vilified.

THE MULATA AS RELIGIOUS SYMBOL

The mulata's ties to religiosity begin in 1604 with the Marian apparition to Juan Moreno, ex-captain of the royal slaves of El Cobre, Cuba. He was on a boat with two indigenous brothers Juan and Rodrigo de Hoyos when they witnessed an image of the Virgin floating above the water with an engraved sign that read, "I am the Virgin of Charity." They described this image to the *cobreros*, mostly indigenous and African copper mine workers, who utilized this saintly protector as a form of spiritual leverage against the Spanish.

The idea of community—more specifically, Cuban Creole identity—coalesced onto the Virgin's spiritual female body and persisted into the eighteenth and nineteenth centuries. She became a symbol for Cuba's claim for legitimacy, representation, and acceptance within the colonial system, and her mixed-race appearance represented the different-raced bodies who viewed her as a national symbol. By the end of the nineteenth century, a large majority of the country recognized her as patron of the island.

The continued importation of slave labor through the eighteenth and nineteenth centuries also brought to Cuba the African Lucumí goddess Ochún in the minds and memories of the enslaved. Most of these slaves came from the area of modern Nigeria, where Yoruba cosmology was predominant. They made associations between Ochún and La Virgen, maternal archetypes with similar characteristics: protective, fecund, and strong-willed. Ochún's qualities, such as her relationship to childbirth, her curative powers, and her love of brass, sunflowers, and the color yellow, easily fit with La Virgen's already existing iconography. And, most notably, Ochún was also represented as a lighter-skinned black woman. An avatar of Ochún called Yeyé Kari or Yeyé Moró developed into a Cubanized version of Ochún. This particular Ochún, as described by Miguel Barnet, symbolizes the mulata of the colonial period, the typically Cuban sensual and stylish mulata. According to Lydia Cabrera, Yeyé Kari/Yeyé Moró is "la más alegre, coqueta y disipada de todas. Continuamente está de juerga. Pachanga. Se pinta, se mira en el espejo, se perfuma . . . 'Hasta con los muertos coquetea'" (the happiest, most coquettish and widely known. She is always in a state of revelry. Pachanga. She applies makeup, looks at herself in the mirror, perfumes herself . . . 'she even flirts with the dead') (p. 70).

These characterizations of Ochún by two prominent Cuban anthropologists highlight the confluence of the mulata and Ochún in the nineteenth century. For them, Yeyé Kari is the nineteenth-century *mulata de rumbo* (mulata on the go, or mulata of the party), the vivacious mulata who does not miss a party or a chance to flirt or shake her hips. By the early twentieth century, the mulata de rumbo was a common stereotype in theatrical spectacle, and everyone, whether through live performance or everyday exchanges, was familiar with her specific tropes: tragic, superficial, desirable, yet threatening. A virgin/whore dichotomy appeared and played itself out on the body of the mulata while Cuba struggled to define its national identity outside the confines of Spanish rule.

THE MULATA AND THE LITERARY IMAGINATION

In the nineteenth century, discourses about national identity, *pureza de sangre* (purity of blood), and *cubanidad* (Cubanness) were rampant. Steeped in the racial ideology of the moment, the mulata was pathologized and denigrated by Benjamin Céspedes, author of *La historia de la prostitución en la Habana* (1888; The History of Prostitution in Havana), a scathing and almost voluptuous study of sex, pederasty, prostitution, and so-called unclean mulata or lower-class white women. The mulata threatened the project of *blanqueamiento*, or whitening, that the Cuban national elite undertook to position Cuba outside its legacy of blackness and align it closer to a Spanish one. She was also a racial and economic threat, as most mulatas (and black women) enjoyed a certain degree of autonomy due to their work: laundresses, teachers, nannies, businesswomen, candy sellers. Simultaneously, the circulation of New World products such as sugar, tobacco, and rum increased the desire for this woman, who was often depicted on *marquillas*, or tobacco labels, and cigarette lithographs that traveled across the Atlantic Ocean.

The nineteenth-century lithograph series *Vida y muerte de una mulata* serves as a prescient example of how the mulata was both a consumable yet expendable commodity. In this tale told through fifteen pictures, the life of the mulata is traced from her beginnings as the daughter of an illicit sexual liaison between an Afro-Cuban woman and a white Cuban man. The lithographs depict her, as she grows up, enchanting white upper-class men, trying to move up the strict Cuban social and racial hierarchy. She falls victim to her own hedonism and ambition, eventually meeting her downfall and tragic death. Nevertheless, the series provides ironic hope for its viewers, as the last picture shows both the coffin of the tragic mulata and the living, vibrant body of another, equally nubile one, standing beside the carriage. In other words, there will always be other mulatas available, yet doomed to repeat the same fate.

Anthropologist and author Lydia Cabrera (1900–1991). Cabrera's characterization of Yeyé Kari, an avatar of Ochún, as a sensual, coquettish woman highlights the nineteenth-century conflation of the mulata and Ochún. COURTESY OF THE CUBAN HERITAGE COLLECTION, UNIVERSITY OF MIAMI LIBRARIES, CORAL GABLES, FLORIDA

Arguably, the most popular mulata of the nineteenth century was Cecilia Valdés, the title character in Cirilio Villaverde's novel *Cecilia Valdés, o La loma del Ángel* (Cecilia Valdes or Angel's Hill, 1839; reedited version, 1882). In this quintessential Cuban mulata narrative, the *mulata blanconaza* Cecilia has aspirations to marry up socially and racially. When she meets Leonardo Gamboa, a dandy and the son of a wealthy *criollo*, she has no idea that he is her half-brother. The story ends tragically upon her discovery; she is cloistered in an asylum, never to threaten the social or moral order again.

Cecilia Valdés provided an opportunity for the characters made popular through *costumbrismo*, or Cuban realism, to come alive. Nineteenth-century *costumbrismo* set up the archetypes that circulated in the Cuban cultural imaginary. These were later taken up by the *Afrocubanismo* movement, a historical-cultural trend that emerged during the early decades of the twentieth century. The poetry that came out of this movement continued to assert the sexual value of the mulata, highlighting her hips as a site of desire. Cuban poet Nicolás Guillén, among others, wrote several odes to the physical or aesthetic prowess of the mulata, further establishing the mulata's relationship to sex, body, and desire in the Cuban imaginary.

THE MULATA ON STAGE AND FILM

The popular stages of Cuba were important sites for the dissemination of an early-twentieth-century Cubanidad. In these lavish productions, audiences heard the new rhythms of the *danzón, guaracha,* or *son*, and they saw the representations of the costumbrismo national characters: the *gallego*, (Spanish working-class man) the *calesero* (black coachman or footman), and the mulata de rumbo. It was these archetypes that circulated in the mulata zarzuelas by Ernesto Lecuona, Gonzalo Roig, and Rodrigo Prats.

Cuban audiences were particularly culturally literate in understanding these representations. In 1932, Rita Montaner, a famous mulata singer and musician, played the title role in a production of the zarzuela *Cecilia Valdés*. Here was an opportunity for audiences to witness a genuine mulata body, since most of the actresses playing mulatas on the lyric stages were white. Despite her fame, Montaner often spoke about the difficulties she encountered being mulata in Cuba, highlighting once again the paradoxical relationship the mulata has with the Cuban cultural imaginary. Even in the early 2010s, at the world-famous Tropicana cabaret, mulatas overwhelm its stage, fulfilling the desire of the paying European and Canadian male tourists who come to see the spectacle of flesh and moving hips, while the rise of sex tourism has driven other mulatas to engage in different economic exchanges of the flesh.

Cuban and Mexican films such as *Cecilia Valdés, Lucía, Yamba-O!* and *Mulata* reiterate familiar tropes about the mulata. One notable film, *I Am Cuba* (1964), uses the mulata as metonym for Cuba prior to the Revolution. Here, she is a young, innocent mulata who meets a white American man at a nightclub who subsequently takes sexual advantage of her. Their sexual exchange signifies how Cuba was taken advantage of by the United States. Thus, the complex relationship between imperialism and economic and sexual exploitation is played out on the mulata body in the film.

The conflation of Ochún Yeyé Kari/Yeyé Moro with the clinicalized accounts of Céspedes's mulata, Cecilia Valdés, José María Quintana's *teatro bufo* mulata plays, the mulata zarzuelas, Guillén's *Afrocubanismo* poetry, costumbrismo, and the solidification of nineteenth-century discourses related to racialized female sexuality all contributed to the mulata as icon of sexuality and sexual desire in Cuba. This discursive sensuality in the early twenty-first century gets associated with the contemporary mulatas who populate the cabaret stages, the popular dance floors, and the streets of Cuba. The mulata's body as a national archetype enables a country to represent itself to itself, despite the legacies of colonialism, racism, and sexism that still haunt Cuba's present.

FILMOGRAPHY

Crevenna, Alfredo B., dir. *Yamba-O!*, 1957.

Kalatozov, Mikhail, dir. *Soy Cuba* (*I Am Cuba*, 1964.

Martínez Solares, Gilberto, dir. *Mulata*, 1954.

Solas, Humberto, dir. *Lucía*, 1968.

Solas, Humberto, dir. *Cecilia Valdés*, 1982.

BIBLIOGRAPHY

Blanco Borelli, Melissa. "Hips, Hip-notism, Hip(g)nosis: The Mulata Performances of Ninón Sevilla." In *The Routledge Dance Studies Reader*, 2nd ed., edited by Alexandra Carter and Janet O'Shea. London and New York: Routledge, 2010.

Cabrera, Lydia. *Yemayá y Ochún: Kariocha, Iyalorichas y Olorichas*. Miami: Ediciones Universal, 1996.

Díaz, María Elena. *The Virgin, the King, and the Royal Slaves of El Cobre: Negotiating Freedom in Colonial Cuba, 1670–1780*. Stanford, CA: Stanford University Press, 2000.

Fraunhar, Alison. "Mulata cubana: The Problematics of National Allegory." In *Latin American Cinema: Essays on Modernity, Gender, and National Identity*, edited by Lisa Shaw and Stephanie Dennison. Jefferson, NC: McFarland, 2005.

González, Reynaldo. *Contradanzas y latigazos*, 2nd ed. Havana: Editorial Letras Cubanas, 1992.

Guillén, Nicolás. *Sóngoro cosongo: Poemas mulatos*. Havana: Úcar, García, 1931.

Guillén, Nicolás, ed. "Mulata." In *Motivos de son*, 50th anniversary ed. Havana: Editorial Letras Cubanas, 1980.

Kutzinski, Vera M. *Sugar's Secrets: Race and the Erotics of Cuban Nationalism*. Charlottesville: University Press of Virginia, 1993.

Lane, Jill. *Blackface Cuba, 1840–1895*. Philadelphia: University of Pennsylvania Press, 2005.

Mena, Luz. "Stretching the Limits of Gendered Spaces: Black and Mulatto Women in 1830s Havana." *Cuban Studies* 36 (2005): 87–104.

Núñez Jiménez, Antonio. *Marquillas cigarreras cubanas*. Madrid: Tabapress, 1989.

Portuondo Zúñiga, Olga. *La Virgen de la Caridad del Cobre: Símbolo de cubanía*. Santiago de Cuba: Editorial Oriente, 1995.

Thomas, Susan. *Cuban Zarzuela: Performing Race and Gender on Havana's Lyric Stage*. Chicago: University of Illinois Press, 2008.

Villaverde, Cirilo. *Cecilia Valdés, o La loma del Ángel: Novela de costumbres cubanas*. 1882. Reprint, Havana: Consejo Nacional de Cultura, 1964.

SEXUALITY: THE UMAP CAMPS

Emilio Bejel

The institutionalization of homophobia in the early years of the Cuban Revolution.

The Unidades Militares de Ayuda a la Producción (UMAP; Military Units to Aid Production, 1965–1968) consisted of a group of detainment camps for young people considered antisocial by the Cuban revolutionary government. A large number of young gay men, along with delinquents, youths who refused to work or study, hippies, and Jehovah's Witnesses who declined military service on religious grounds, were among the detainees. Estimates suggest that, at times, the number of detainees in the UMAP camps reached 20,000–25,000 (Werlau p. 149). These camps were located mostly in Camagüey province and served to assist in the planting and harvesting of fruits and other crops. Homophobia was at the center of the UMAP's creation; this situation of forced labor and confinement was characteristic of the Revolution's attitude toward homosexuality, especially from the mid-1960s to the mid-1970s (Bejel pp. 95–106). The work atmosphere in the UMAP camps was undoubtedly abusive, cruel, and sometimes even criminal. Although it is difficult to obtain the documentation necessary to determine precisely what happened in these camps, the activist and author Allen Young states that the detainees were treated so inhumanely that some of the officials responsible for the abuse were later executed (Young 1984, p. 35; 1992, pp. 206–250).

It should be mentioned that, inside Cuba, the Unión de Escritores y Artistas de Cuba (UNEAC; Union of Writers and Artists of Cuba) protested the mistreatment of intellectuals in UMAP. Outside Cuba, in Europe, some prestigious leftist intellectuals such as Graham Greene, Gian Giacomo Feltrinelli, and Jean-Paul Sartre protested energetically against UMAP. Also, the gay American poet and activist Allen Ginsberg, despite his public sympathies in favor of socialism and the Cuban Revolution, protested against the abuses that were being committed against homosexuals in Cuba (Young 1981, p. 20). Fidel Castro himself visited the UMAP camps to see with his own eyes what kind of treatment was being given the detainees. According to the Nicaraguan poet Ernesto Cardenal, around the same time the Cuban government sent 100 members of the Communist Youth—who traveled to the camps without revealing their true identities and intentions—to investigate the situation in UMAP and then inform the highest government officials of their observations (p. 269). Available evidence suggests that the national and international protests, along with the official and unofficial investigative visits, led the Cuban government to close UMAP. It is not known whether the closure occurred in 1967 or 1968, because, given regional economic considerations, some of the camps continued to function for months after the order to dismantle them was given (Hillson).

WHY THE CAMPS WERE ESTABLISHED

One of the explanations given for the creation of the UMAP camps was that, in the rural environment, antisocial youths would be forced to do agricultural work alongside the region's peasants, which would cure them of their bad habits and sexual perversions. This argument implies a perception of the countryside as a place where behaviors such as homosexuality, which were considered urban ills, could be redeemed

■ *See also*

Che Guevara and the New Man

The Color of Summer (Reinaldo Arenas)

Cuban Thought and Cultural Identity: Socialist Thought

Governance and Contestation: The Cuban Revolution

and cleansed (Yglesias p. 275). But it should be noted that at that time in Cuba punishment as a method of education was viewed in a different manner than it is in the early 2010s; for certain forms of offense (such as work-related infractions) punishment was considered an effective and patriotic way to correct a wrong behavior. Here it is important to point out that the Cuban Revolution of 1959 was radically nationalist from its beginnings and aspired to cleanse the country of what its leaders and a great part of the population considered to be national ills, including, in addition to economic, political, and military matters, aspects of sexual morality (Lumsden pp. 55–80). According to this perspective, in order to protect the country from corruption, one had to be increasingly nationalist; and to be more nationalist, it was necessary to revive some of the best and worst traditions, including homophobia.

In terms of homophobia, the worst moments were not seen during the Revolution's first years, but toward the middle of the 1960s, when the revolutionary government began to adopt homophobic policies in its social planning, resulting in serious injustices for many citizens who were homosexual or perceived as such. Such homophobic excesses did not arise only from the personal prejudices of revolutionary leaders but also from national prejudices long a part of Cuban culture (Fowler p.17; Bejel pp. xiii–xix, 3–91). The most noteworthy aspect of the Revolution's homophobic policies did not, however, lie in the prejudices themselves, but rather in their extremism and their institutionalization (Daniels 1984, 1985; Argüelles and Rich 1984, pp. 683–699; 1985, pp. 120–136).

THE "NEW MAN"

Some of the events of 1961 presaged the later intensification and institutionalization of homophobia in the middle of the 1960s. In that year the Revolution declared itself to be Marxist-Leninist, and, therefore, the conflict with the United States worsened. The invasion of the Bay of Pigs (Playa Girón), sponsored by the U.S. government, happened in April of that year, and the great Missile Crisis took place in October 1962. These events highlight the extremely tense atmosphere in which Cubans were living in that period. It was then, in 1961, that a massive dragnet was conducted in the Colón district of Havana to catch pederasts, prostitutes, and pimps. (This event came to be known as the Night of the Three Ps.) However, contemporary observers saw the action as an attempt to clean up Havana's corruption, rather than as a policy change intended to institutionalize a national homophobia (Franqui pp. 138–141; Cabrera Infante pp. 134–135).

The institutionalization of homophobia during the revolutionary era really began in 1965, and UMAP was its best-known expression. Numerous negative ideas about gays and lesbians converged after that year, and some of international communism's intolerance of homosexuality began to reinforce the island's own prejudices, creating a truly systematic and homophobic repression (Epps pp. 237–239). In the last instance, it was a matter of answering the question of how to liberate the so-called "New Man" (and by implication the "New Woman") from the evils of capitalism. The answer to this question always turned out to be that the "New Man" and "New Woman" were fundamentally heterosexual, which left homosexuals excluded from the conceptual nation, or at least from the new nation (Quiroga pp. 168–180). In an atmosphere so socially prejudiced and politically tense, it is unsurprising that the UMAP camps were created to rehabilitate so-called antisocial young people. The process of rehabilitating homosexuals implied an ideology that purported to know, beyond any doubt, the characteristics of that sought-for, universal "New Man."

THE DECLINE OF HOMOPHOBIA

By the mid-1970s, homosexual persecution in Cuba had begun to diminish. Gone were the massive purges of writers and intellectuals, and Resolution Number Three, which had played a major role in the legalization of homophobia, was abolished by order of the Supreme Court in 1975. Legally speaking, from that time in Cuba homosexuality per se was not a crime, but the decrease in homophobia beginning in the mid-1970s should be qualified. The Penal Code of 1979 did not eliminate certain discriminations against homosexuals. It included the Law of Dangerousness, a vague statute that left much to the discretion of often homophobic judges (Leiner pp. 81–95). Also, by the end of the 1970s, the Cuban Communist Party no longer considered homosexual behavior to be in fundamental contradiction with the revolutionary process.

In 1979, the Cuban National Work Group on Sexual Education, created in 1977, published *El hombre y la mujer en la intimidad* (Man and Woman in Their Intimacy), a translation of *Mann und Frau intim*, by East German sexologist Siegfried Schnabl. Schnabl's opinions on male and female sexuality were novel compared with prevailing views in both East Germany and Cuba, and the book caused a sensation. The greatest surprise was the book's final chapter, "Homosexuality in Men and Women." In spite of its brevity (only ten pages), it caused true commotion in Cuban educational and intellectual circles of the day. In this chapter, Schnabl condemns East German society for practicing a homophobia that was emotionally destructive to homosexuals. He states that homosexuality is not a disease but simply a variant of human sexuality. Although published in an edition of only 15,000 copies, Schnabl's book became a best-seller, being passed from one reader to the next (Leiner p. 44).

By the 1980s and especially in the 1990s, it became clear that previous representations of homosexuality in Cuba were being radically questioned. Among the most notable examples in this regard is the critical and popular acclaim of the Cuban film *Fresa y chocolate* (1994; Strawberry and Chocolate, 1995). A later expression of this trajectory is Mariela Castro, Fidel Castro's niece and the director of the Centro Nacional de Educación Sexual (CENESEX; Cuban National Center for Sex Education), who has been active in the cause of gay, lesbian, bisexual, and transgender (GLBT) rights in Cuba. Even Fidel Castro himself, in a 2010 interview with the Mexican journalist Carmen Lira, said that the homophobia of the 1960s and 1970s was simply wrong and that he accepts responsibility for those mistakes, which he attributes not to personal homophobia on his part but to the extreme pressure he and the entire nation were undergoing during those years (Lira Saade p. 26).

BIBLIOGRAPHY

Argüelles, Lourdes, and Ruby Rich. "Homosexuality, Homophobia, and Revolution: Notes toward an Understanding of the Cuban Lesbian and Gay Experience." Part I: *Signs* 9, no. 4 (Summer 1984), 683–699; Part II: *Signs* 11, no. 1 (Winter 1985): 120–136.

Bejel, Emilio. *Gay Cuban Nation.* Chicago: University of Chicago Press, 2001.

Cabrera Infante, Guillermo. "Entrevista." In *Conducta impropia*, edited by Néstor Almendros and Orlando Jiménez-Leal. Madrid: Editorial Playor, 1984.

Cardenal, Ernesto. *En Cuba.* Buenos Aires: Carlos Lohlé, 1972.

Daniels, Ian. "Interview with Ana María Simo." *Torch* (New York), 15 December 1984 and 14 January 1985.

Epps, Brad. "Proper Conduct: Reinaldo Arenas, Fidel Castro, and the Politics of Homosexuality." *Journal of the History of Sexuality* 6, no. 2 (1995): 231–283.

Fowler Calzada, Víctor. *La maldición: Una historia del placer como conquista.* Havana: Editorial Letras Cubanas, 1998.

Franqui, Carlos. *Family Portrait with Fidel: A Memoir.* Translated by Alfred MacAdam. New York: Random House, 1984.

Hillson, Jon. "The Sexual Politics of Reinaldo Arenas: Fact, Fiction, and the Real Record of the Cuban Revolution." *Seeing Red* 4, no. 2 (May 2001). Available from http://www.seeingred.com/Copy/4.2_sexualpolitics.html.

Leiner, Marvin. *Sexual Politics in Cuba: Machismo, Homosexuality, and AIDS.* Boulder, CO: Westview Press, 1994.

Lira Saade, Carmen. "Interview with Fidel Castro." *La Jornada* (Mexico City) 31 (March 2010): 26.

Lumsden, Ian. *Machos, Maricones, and Gays: Cuba and Homosexuality.* Philadelphia: Temple University Press, 1996.

Quiroga, José. "Homosexualities in the Tropic of Revolution." In *Sex and Sexuality in Latin America*, edited by Daniel Balderston and Donna J. Guy. New York: New York University Press, 1997.

Schnabl, Siegfried. *El hombre y la mujer en la intimidad.* Havana: Editorial Científico Técnica, 1979.

Werlau, Maria C. "Political Repression in Castro's Cuba: Policies, Institutions, and Victims." In *Political Violence: Belief, Behavior, and Legitimation*, edited by Paul Hollander. New York: Palgrave Macmillan, 2008.

Yglesias, José. *In the Fist of the Revolution: Life in a Cuban Country Town.* New York: Pantheon, 1968.

Young, Allen. *Gays under the Cuban Revolution.* San Francisco: Grey Fox Press, 1981.

Young, Allen. "Commentary: 'The Cuban Gulag.' Homophobia and the American Left." *The Advocate* 388 (July 10, 1984).

Young, Allen. "Cuba: Gay as the Sun." In *Out of the Closets: Voices of Gay Liberation*, edited by Karla Jay and Allen Young. New York: New York University Press, 1992.

SON INNOVATIONS: ARSENIO RODRÍGUEZ

David F. García

The career of the musician who popularized the Cuban conjunto *and innovated* son montuno.

In the early 1940s Arsenio Rodríguez (1911–1970) popularized the Cuban *conjunto* (small band), transformed the *son* (Cuban sound) musical genre, and, in so doing, contributed to the development of the mambo in the late 1940s and salsa beginning in the 1960s. Rodríguez's *conjunto* consisted of two vocalists (with one doubling on claves and the other on maracas), three trumpets, piano, *tres* (Cuban traditional guitar), guitar (doubling on vocals), bass, bongo, and one conga drum. This instrumental format was an extension of the established *septeto*'s instrumentation, with the addition of two trumpets (totaling three), piano, and conga drum. In applying the musical principles of timbral heterogeneity, musical fullness, and sonic power, Rodríguez crafted a musical style that Cuban dancers valued for its so-called blackness and masculinity. As a result, his *son montuno* rural style not only contributed to the flowering of Cuban *son* music in the early 1940s but also affected the racialization of son that ultimately problematized its status as a symbol of Cuban cultural *mestizaje* (mixture or miscegenation) and national identity.

Ignacio Arsenio Travieso Scull was born on 30 August 1911 in Güira de Macuriges, Matanzas. He would eventually take his maternal grandmother's maiden name Rodríguez as his professional last name. By the time he was four years old, the family had moved to the large agricultural and sugar municipality of Güines on the south coast of the province of La Habana. Several years after moving to Güines, he became blind as a result of receiving a kick to the head

■ *See also*

Music: 1945–1959

Music: Afro-Cuban Religious Influence on Cuban Popular Music

Performing Arts: Cuban Forms of Popular Dance

Radio: Commercial and Cultural Programming in Cuba

from a mule. Around this time he immersed himself in Cuban musical traditions of both Spanish and African heritages, including the sacred drumming repertories of *Palo* and *Santería* (Afro-Cuban folk religions) as well as secular drumming traditions of the Cuban Congolese, *rumba*, and *son*. ("Congo" here refers to the Cuban ethnic group of Congolese of Central African origins.)

In 1926 a devastating hurricane that swept over the western half of the island forced the Rodríguez family to move to Havana. Settling in Marianao, a suburb of the capital, Rodríguez began his professional musical career playing tres. By 1928 he had formed Septeto Bóston, which performed regularly in the rough, working-class *cabarets de tercera* (third-tier cabarets) located along the beaches of Marianao. By 1934 he joined Septeto Bellamar, which played mostly at *academias de baile* (dance academies) in and around downtown Havana. Rodríguez soon took control of the musical direction of the septeto and began to establish the foundations for what would soon become his conjunto and his innovative son montuno style.

On 12 September 1940, Arsenio Rodríguez y Su Conjunto made its first commercial recordings with RCA Victor in Havana. Meanwhile, Rodríguez continued to utilize the septeto format to perform regularly at the Sans Souci, one of Havana's most popular cabarets for tourists and upper-class Cubans. After the onset of World War II, Cuba's tourist industry experienced a significant lull, forcing some black musical groups like Rodríguez's to seek paid engagements with Havana's *sociedades de color* (black social clubs). By May 1942 Rodríguez had completely abandoned the septeto for the conjunto format. Moreover, he had developed his new son montuno style which was distinguished by:

- the use of *contratiempo* (offbeat accentuation);
- the correspondence of sound and dancers' bodily movements;
- the interweaving of rhythmic, melodic, and dance patterns; and
- the steady increase in energy toward a climax.

The son montuno style featured much more contratiempo than earlier styles of commercial son music. Offbeat accenting patterns would also constitute the primary musical feature of the mambo as performed by big bands in Havana, New York City, Mexico City, and elsewhere. What made Rodríguez's style unique, however, was its rhythmic texture, which corresponded directly to and accentuated the son dancers' footwork and bodily movements.

There are three defining characteristics of Rodríguez's son montuno style that distinguished it from earlier styles of son music. The first is his music's consistent accentuation of syncopated beats in both the basic footwork of son dancing and the clave pattern. For example, in "No toque el guao" (Don't Touch the Guao, 1948), the sung refrain and accompanying piano and tres montunos (two- or four-bar ostinato patterns) accent these two syncopated beats and dance steps as the bass *tumbao* (pattern) consistently marks the final three steps of the son footwork. (Regarding the translated name of this song, guao is a poisonous tree in Cuba, and so the title can be translated loosely as "Don't Mess with Me [or Else].")

The second innovative and defining aspect is its melodic and syncopated bass lines. Specifically, these bass lines tend to accentuate the melodic phrasing of the *coros* (sung refrain parts). The bass line heard on "Mi chinita me botó" (My Girl Left Me, 1944), for instance, consists almost entirely of syncopated notes.

The son montuno's third innovative characteristic is the interweaving of rhythmic, melodic, and harmonic patterns involving subtle and intricate sequences of call-and-response figures among the bass, bongo, and conga drums. These patterns in the rhythm section, in turn, interweave with the basic steps executed by son dancers. In the montuno section of "No toque el guao" one such sequence of call-and-response attacks occurs, beginning with the bass's first, second, and third notes in the third bar of the four-bar pattern, followed by the bongo's response of two slaps in bar four. Meanwhile, the conga drum adds an opened-tone attack on the first and third bars' last upbeat (i.e., the "and" of beat four). In short, the interweaving of coros, trumpet riffs, piano and tres montunos, bass lines, and percussion patterns in contratiempo—as best demonstrated in the climactic section of "Kila, Kike y Chocolate" (1950)—constituted Rodríguez's most significant contribution to the music that would become known as mambo.

The popularity of Rodríguez's music and conjunto spread throughout Cuba and the Caribbean as a result of his conjunto's daily radio broadcasts, which began in 1943, on Mil Diez (Radio 1010), owned by the Partido Socialista Popular (PSP, the Cuban Communist Party). After the Cuban government shut down Radio 1010 on 1 May 1948, Radio Salas contracted Rodríguez's conjunto together with the charangas (Cuban-style flute- and violin-based dance bands) Arcaño y Sus Maravillas and Orquesta Melodias del 40 to perform on a daily show during the week titled "Los Tres Grandes" (The Three Giants). The conjunto also recorded with RCA Victor from 1940 to 1956, making 161 recordings, and regularly performed throughout Cuba.

Rodríguez's impact on the local dance music scene in Havana, however, was particularly significant. Situated in the context of self-segregated social club dances, where black dancers constituted his primary audience, dancing and playing son montuno became powerful modes of articulating racial subjectivity. In Havana in the 1940s *sociedades de color* met many

Arsenio Rodríguez (1911–1970). Composer, bandleader, and tres player Arsenio Rodríguez transformed the Cuban son musical genre and contributed to the development of mambo and salsa. He is shown here, at the height of his career, in a recording studio during the 1950s. FRANK DRIGGS COLLECTION/GETTY IMAGES

of the social and cultural needs of their members, including education, athletics, and recreation. These sociedades also imparted an ethos of black pride and unity among their members and communities. What is more, the dances these sociedades organized afforded black dancers and musicians a crucial artistic autonomy in a larger social milieu in which dancing was one of the most segregated cultural activities in Havana.

As a result, for Cuban musicians and dancers of the 1940s, racial in addition to gendered discourses became the predominant rhetorical modes through which they articulated their experience performing and dancing to the music of Cuban conjuntos, including Rodríguez's. It was Rodríguez's style that established the musical criteria—slower tempos, sonic power, contratiempo, and musical fullness—that defined the *estilo negro y macho* (black and masculine style), whereas the styles of conjuntos such as La Sonora Matancera and Conjunto Casino constituted the *estilo blanco y hembra* (white and feminine style). It is important, however, not to attribute the racialization of these styles to the actual skin color of the musicians themselves, for some of the groups to which the category *blanco* was applied were in fact all black or mixed (e.g., La Sonora Matancera) or included black musicians (e.g., Conjunto Casino).

Rather, Cubans used *negro* and *macho* to describe Rodríguez's son montuno style because of these terms' ability to articulate the deep resonance his music had with traditional Afro-Cuban performance practice and aesthetics. For instance, the interplay between his musicians and dancers determined, in large part, the son montuno's rhythmic texture and sonic power. This performative factor was in addition to the dominant race relations at the time, which in fact determined the social setting in which Rodríguez popularized the son montuno performing for *sociedades de color*. The praise of Rodríguez's style as *negro* also signified a shift in the valuation of blackness, which his conjunto and music helped effect in Cuban musical discourse. Rodríguez did this not only by drawing on Afro-Cuban aesthetic principles and procedures but also by directly praising, in turn, the people of Havana's black working-class barrios in songs he called *guaguancós*.

Rodríguez's music was first launched internationally in 1937 by Cuban vocalist Miguelito Valdés and the Orquesta Casino de la Playa, whose recording of Rodríguez's "Bruca maniguá" (Witch from the Bush) was soon after recorded in New York City by several popular Latin orchestras, including Xavier Cugat's, the most popular Latin band at the time. In the following decades mambo and salsa groups from New York and Puerto Rico would record hundreds of Rodríguez's songs, especially his son montunos, making him one of the most recorded composers of Cuban and Latin music. Yet his overall recognition in the United States as well as in South and Central America and Mexico was limited compared to that of his contemporaries such as Pérez Prado and Celia Cruz. His relative obscurity in the transnational Latin music industry can be attributed partially to the industry's preference for more cosmopolitan styles of mambo and the changing musical tastes of the first generation of salsa record buyers and dancers and as well as Rodríguez's own lack of business acumen.

Rodríguez continued his musical career in New York where he had begun to perform and record in 1950. As in Havana, his conjunto performed regularly in working-class neighborhoods in the South Bronx and El Barrio (East Harlem) for Puerto Ricans, Cubans, and other Latinos. His conjunto also performed regularly at the famous Palladium Ballroom in Manhattan through the 1950s. As his recorded output from New York documents, he continued to compose and perform son montunos, though he also composed and recorded other styles of Cuban and Latin music such as *cha-chas* and Afro-Cuban/swing fusion. His performance career waned through the early 1960s; nevertheless, a new generation of Latin musicians, including Johnny Pacheco and Eddie Palmieri, performed and recorded Rodríguez's music, which served early salsa musicians as a reference of stylistic authenticity.

By 1964 Rodríguez had moved to Los Angeles to live with his brothers Kike (sometimes spelled Quique) and Raúl and continued to perform his music with a conjunto. On 28 December 1970 Rodríguez suffered a stroke and was taken to Queen of Angels Hospital in downtown Los Angeles. The stroke was brought on by diabetes, from which he had been suffering since at least the early 1960s. He died on 30 December. On 3 January 1971, his body was flown to New York, where a wake took place on 5 January, followed by burial the next day in Hartsdale, New York. Rodríguez's music continues to be rerecorded and celebrated, as demonstrated by one of the most successful world music endeavors to date, the Buena Vista Social Club and its ongoing solo projects.

DISCOGRAPHY

Rodríguez, Arsenio. *Arsenio Rodríguez: El alma de Cuba* (2008).

BIBLIOGRAPHY

García, David F. *Arsenio Rodríguez and the Transnational Flows of Latin Popular Music.* Philadelphia: Temple University Press, 2006.

SPAIN'S "DISCOVERY" OF CUBA: 1492

Robert C. Nathan

The landing of Christopher Columbus on the shores of Cuba.

In October 1492 Christopher Columbus, in search of riches, a sea route to Asia, and fertile ground for the spread of Christendom, landed at Cuba, a seminal encounter that set in motion the Spanish conquest of the island and its people. Columbus was amazed by the beauty and lushness of the landscape when his ships reached Cuban shores on 28 October 1492. Having departed Spain three months earlier with a commission from the Crown to seek a sea route to the markets of Asia, Columbus quickly took stock of the island's potential value. Although he found none of the trading centers he expected, Columbus saw in Cuba a source of tremendous profit and enrichment for the Catholic monarchs of Spain. The admiral understood his mission to be at once economic and holy, and his journal reveals a singular focus on the identification and exploitation of Cuba's natural and human resources. The uneven process of Spanish exploration and colonization that began with Columbus's landing in 1492 centered on the indigenous Arawak population, first as guides in Columbus's search for gold, cities, and spices; later as targets for Christian evangelization; and ultimately as combatants in the bloody Spanish conquest of the island.

THE VOYAGE AND ITS REWARDS

In the first days of 1492, King Ferdinand and Queen Isabella completed a decade-long campaign to oust Islamic rule from the city of Granada, the last Muslim stronghold in Iberia. This victory excited the Catholic imagination, prompting visions of Spain as carrier of a globally ascendant Christendom. The Columbus expedition emerged from this fertile mix of religious fervor and expansionist zeal. Only months later, the Spanish royals commissioned the Italian sailor from Genoa to seek a route to Asia by sea, which would enable Spain to access the trading centers, resources, and vast populations of the Orient. His contract guaranteed that Columbus would be named viceroy of any new territories, a hereditary appointment to be enjoyed by his descendants. In exchange, the Crown would be entitled to 90 percent of the income from all territories that he governed. Economic and religious objectives coexisted seamlessly in the genesis of the voyage. While Columbus set out to secure trade and resources, the monarchs had sent him as well to determine "the measures to be taken to convert" the peoples of Asia "to our holy faith" (Columbus p. 3).

The expedition made first landfall in the Bahamas on 12 October 1492. Unable to communicate verbally with the people whom he believed to be Indians, Columbus relied on an improvised sign language. Through these exchanges, which usually confirmed his expectations, Columbus learned of a larger island to the south that was "rich in spices" and crowded with "large ships and many seafarers" (pp. 51, 53). He heard them call the island *Colba*, though he believed it to be the island of Cipangu described by Marco Polo, a vibrant trading center from which he would proceed to the Asian mainland.

A strong storm kept Columbus's ships moored just off an unknown coast through the night of 27 October 1492. As dawn broke and the Cuban shoreline came into view, Columbus's anticipation gave way to astonishment. This island, he declared, "is the most beautiful that eyes have ever seen" (p. 59). He drew his ship into the mouth of a deep river "completely surrounded by beautiful green trees, each one with its own kind of flowers and fruit and many birds singing sweetly" (p. 57). At the edge of this inlet, likely near present-day Gibara, Columbus first set foot on Cuban soil. So beautiful was the island, Columbus wrote, that he almost "could not bear to leave it and return" to

his ships (p. 59). Nevertheless, Columbus pursued his mission with speed and purpose. "These lands are very fertile," he reported, and the "people are very gentle and timorous" (p. 69). His journal reads as a catalogue of potential wealth, both economic and spiritual, to be delivered to the Spanish monarchs who sponsored his voyage: The stunning sight of brightly colored birds and flowers gave way to "a thousand other types of fruit," which Columbus ascertained "all must be of great value" (p. 69). He rewarded a boatswain for locating a tree that produced mastic, of which the admiral wrote "there was enough…to collect a thousand quintales every year" (p. 71). Abundant with cotton, the island also possessed "pearls and precious stones and an infinity of spices" that would enrich the Spanish Crown (p. 77). Still expecting to find nearby kingdoms rich with gold and silver, Columbus enumerated a compelling inventory of Cuba's profit potential.

ENCOUNTER WITH ARAWAK SOCIETY

In his ongoing search for gold and silver, Columbus made constant use of Arawak captives as guides. Indeed, much of what is now known about Arawak society and culture in Cuba has come from Columbus's writings. After encountering a small fishing settlement on the coast, he sent members of his expedition further inland, where they reported visiting a village of fifty houses and, they estimated, a thousand people. Arawak houses, Columbus observed, were "built like very large tents," made from thatched palm branches (p. 61). In this village, his men witnessed the fruits of Arawak agriculture in the great quantities of cotton and corn being harvested, as well as tobacco, which the Arawak "are accustomed to smoke" (p. 73).

The admiral also noted the presence of "many statues in the form of a woman and heads like carnival masks," though he did not know if they were for worship (p. 61). Arawak religious practices centered on family and tribal connections, likely involving symbolic totems and idols such as those Columbus encountered. Nevertheless, Columbus was dismissive of Arawak religiosity, believing that they had "no religion that I can see" and would be eager converts to Christianity (p. 101). They were "ready to repeat any prayer" and make the sign of the cross (p. 101). The "end and the beginning" of his mission, Columbus declared, "should be for the promotion and glory of the Christian religion," and "in a short space," the Crown would "succeed in converting to our faith a multitude of peoples and acquiring great kingdoms and riches and all their peoples for Spain" (pp. 77, 101).

CONQUEST: CONSOLIDATING SPANISH CONTROL

For five weeks Columbus and his ships sailed along the northern coast, taking stock of the island's deep, wide harbors and venturing into Arawak towns to pursue rumors of gold, silver, and wealthy cities. By the

end of November, Columbus wrote, the richness of Cuba had compelled him to explore further, toward an island where "the people collect gold by candlelight at night on the beach" (p. 75). His venture through the Caribbean yielded no such scene. Columbus returned to Spain, leaving behind the first European settlement in the Americas at La Navidad, on the island he named La Española (i.e, Hispaniola, embracing the modern

Dominican Republic and Haiti). His second voyage the following year brought him back to Española, where he found La Navidad in ruins. He established a new settlement called Isabella and set out for Cuba, this time spending several months exploring the southern shoreline. Columbus remained confident that he had found a route to Asia and had his notary prepare a document, signed by senior representatives of the crew, affirming that Cuba was indeed a continent.

Maps as early as 1500 showed Cuba as an island, although the issue was not resolved until nearly a decade later when Sebastián de Ocampo sailed from Española to explore the Cuban coast. The 1508 expedition, which circumnavigated the island and gathered detailed information on harbors and coastal terrain, drew renewed attention to the island. The following year the Spanish Crown instructed officials to prepare the settlement of Cuba. In 1511 a party departed Española under the command of Diego Velázquez, a landowner who had distinguished himself in the suppression of indigenous rebellions on that island. Fugitives from that campaign, among them a chief named Hatuey, sought refuge in eastern Cuba. Although Columbus had insisted on the passivity of the indigenous population, tales of the conquest of Española prompted a fierce resistance. The Spanish responded with brutality, capturing Hatuey and pacifying eastern Cuba in a matter of months. As Hatuey was prepared for execution, his captors offered him the chance to accept Christianity and save his soul. According to Bartolomé de Las Casas (1474–1566), the Dominican friar and colonist who would come to oppose Spanish treatment of the Indians, Hatuey responded that if Christians were in heaven, he would prefer to go to hell. As Spanish forces pressed west to pacify and claim new territory, Velázquez established the first permanent European settlement in Cuba at Baracoa. Indigenous resistance quickly collapsed as word of Spanish brutality spread, and by mid-decade the Europeans had established seven settlements on the island, stretching from Santiago de Cuba in the east to Havana in the west. The indigenous population, prized as converts, served as the primary labor source.

It took many decades, even centuries, for Spanish colonists to convert the island that Columbus called "the most beautiful that eyes had ever seen" into the economic centerpiece of an empire (p. 59). The fertile soil that Columbus admired would yield great wealth, but by then the indigenous population had all but vanished from overwork and diseases brought by Europeans and their livestock. Columbus set out from Spain in 1492 in search of new resources, markets, and converts. Although his landfall in Cuba challenged his expectations, Columbus's journal reveals his singular focus on reconciling Cuban realities to his objectives. As he explored the Cuban shoreline, evaluating its resources and potential while assessing the temperament of its peoples, Columbus initiated a process that turned discovery into conquest and colony.

BIBLIOGRAPHY

Columbus, Christopher. *Journal of the First Voyage: 1492.* Translated and edited by B. W. Ife. Warminster, U.K.: Aris & Phillips, 1990.

Kamen, Henry. *Spain's Road to Empire: The Making of a World Power, 1492–1763.* London: Penguin Books, 2003.

Las Casas, Bartolomé de. *The Devastation of the Indies: A Brief Account.* Translated by Herma Briffault. Baltimore: Johns Hopkins University Press, 1992.

Pérez, Louis A., Jr. *Cuba: Between Reform and Revolution.* 4th ed. New York: Oxford University Press, 2011.

Tabío, Ernesto E., and Estrella Rey. *Prehistoria de Cuba.* 2nd ed. Havana: Editorial de Ciencias Sociales,1985.

Wright, Irene A. *The Early History of Cuba, 1492–1586.* [1916.] New York: Octagon Books, 1970.

■

SPANISH-AMERICAN-CUBAN WAR: 1898

David C. Carlson

In the summer of 1898 Spain and the United States went to war over Cuba.

The Cuban War of Independence (1895–1898), the last anticolonial rebellion to achieve separation from Spain, became an international conflict with U.S. intervention during the summer of 1898. The outcome of this international phase, the Spanish-American War, saw Spain stripped of colonies in the Pacific and Caribbean (the Philippines, Guam, Cuba, and Puerto Rico) and led, after the December 1898 Treaty of Paris, to the first U.S. occupation of Cuba (1899–1902), followed by national independence on 20 May 1902 under de facto U.S. protectorate status via the 1901 Platt Amendment written into the Cuban constitution.

THE CUBAN WAR OF INDEPENDENCE (1895–1898) VERSUS THE SPANISH-AMERICAN WAR (1898)

In the United States, the War of 1898 has been long understood as and called the Spanish-American War; histories have minimized the context and role of Cubans in the crucial underlying events. Historians of Cuba have offered a corrective to the emphasis on only the summer of 1898, emphasizing a much longer history of *peninsular* versus *criollo* conflict and noting that the 114-day U.S.-Spanish confrontation was preceded by social and political conditions produced by three years of island-wide anticolonial rebellion and the Spanish counterinsurgency implemented to defeat it. As a result, the more precise term *guerra hispano-cubano-norteamericana* (Spanish-Cuban-North

■ See also

Bayamo

Governance and Contestation: Colonial Period

Guantánamo

José Martí: Political Essays

Platt Amendment

Race: Racial Issues during the Transition to Independence

Ten Years' War: 1868–1878

The World and Cuba: Cuba and Spain in the Colonial Period

The World and Cuba: Cuba and the United States

Opposite page:

Christopher Columbus encounters Arawak society. In October 1492, Christopher Columbus landed in Cuba, a seminal encounter that set in motion the Spanish conquest of the island and its people. This illustration of the encounter, by Benjamin West, appeared in a late-eighteenth-century history of the British colonies in the West Indies. ©SCALA/ WHITE IMAGES/ART RESOURCE, NY

CHRONOLOGY OF EVENTS

1895: Cuban insurrection begins; President Grover Cleveland declares U.S. neutrality.

1896: General Valeriano Weyler adopts *reconcentración* policy in Cuba; insurgent leaders General Antonio Maceo and Captain Panchito Gómez killed.

1897: William Randolph Hearst's *New York Journal* and Joseph Pulitzer's *New York World* promote anti-Spanish sentiment in U.S.; Spanish Prime Minister Antonio Cánovas assassinated; new Liberal government seeks accommodation with Cuba.

1898: January: Spain grants Cuba limited autonomy; U.S. sends battleship *Maine* to Havana harbor.

1898: 15 February: The *Maine* explodes in Havana's harbor.

1898: 29 March: U.S. issues ultimatum to Spain demanding Cuban independence; Spain refuses.

1898: 11 April: President William McKinley asks Congress for a declaration of war against Spain.

1898: 25 April: Congress declares war on Spain; Teller Amendment denies U.S. intention to annex or control Cuba.

1898: 1 May: U.S. Navy sinks Spanish fleet at Manila harbor in the Philippines.

1898: 10 June: American Marines land at Guantánamo.

1898: 15 June: U.S. annexes Hawaii.

1898: 1 & 2 July: Spanish forces defeated at San Juan, Lawton, and El Caney.

1898: 3 July: Spanish fleet destroyed in Santiago harbor.

1898: 15 July: Spanish forces at Santiago surrender

1898: 15 July: Spanish government requests armistice.

1898: 12 August: U.S. and Spain sign a cease-fire; Cuba not included in negotiations.

1898: October: U.S. and Spain conduct Paris peace talks without Cuban or Philippine representatives.

1898: 10 December: U.S. and Spain sign Treaty of Paris, giving Cuba independence and handing over Puerto Rico, the Philippines, and Guam to the United States.

1899: January: U.S. installs provisional military government in Cuba.

1899: 11 April: Spanish-American-Cuban War formally ends.

1901: Cuban Constitution adopted with the Platt Amendment, allowing U.S. to intervene in Cuba's internal affairs.

1902: Tomás Estrada Palma inaugurated as president of Cuban republic.

American War), or *guerra de '95* (the War of '95) for short, is more apt, and the war is typically understood as such in Cuba. Thus, Cubans view the 1898 U.S. entry as only the final phase of a longer war that began three years earlier. That the conflict also came to include the destinies of peoples in Puerto Rico, Micronesia, and the Philippines, laying the basis for a bloody war of occupation—the U.S. Philippine War (1899–1902)—indicates that its name should include those peoples and nations too. The War of 1898 offers a succinct term for the global dimensions in the latter phase of the conflict.

ORIGINS

The Cuban War of Independence began 24 February 1895 with a revolutionary proclamation in eastern Cuba—the *grito de Baire*—issued by separatists unified in the 1892 Partido Revolucionario Cubano (PRC; Cuban Revolutionary Party), which had been founded among patriotic clubs and revolutionary associations by José Martí (1853–1895) to prepare for a renewal of armed anticolonial struggle. PRC members in various parts of eastern Cuba initiated armed actions, but Spanish authorities arrested or dispersed conspirators in western Cuba and Havana. The rebellion of 1895 had several underlying long- and short-term causes. Cuba had undergone various profound social and political changes during the 1880s, while frustrations with Spanish rule continued to mount and promised

post–Ten Years' War (1868–1878) Treaty of Zanjón reforms remained largely unfulfilled.

By the 1880s, Europeans began to consume beet sugar, with the result that U.S. markets became ever more important to Cuban sugarcane producers. North American direct investment in Cuban private railways and sugar mills increased apace. Over 80 percent of Cuban exports—mostly sugar and tobacco—went to U.S. markets. The sugar industry itself underwent considerable consolidation under the *central* system, in which large, capital-intensive, steam-powered sugar mills drew harvested cane from sprawling fields connected by narrow-gauge railway and from sharecropper *colonos,* who cultivated and harvested sugar for the mill in exchange for a portion of their crop. The *colonato* system became a preferred means of labor relations, while many small planters and merchants either joined the system or moved to join the growing urban working and middle class. Large-scale subsidized immigration from Spain brought 417,264 Spaniards to the island between 1868 and 1894, with 224,000 arrivals between 1882 and 1894. Of the latter, 142,000 proved to be sojourners who eventually returned to Spain, but this substantial population of European migrants and settlers transformed western Cuba. Seasonal harvest work and employment on sugar mills coincided with the gradual emancipation of slavery between 1870 and 1880 when *patronato* (apprenticeship) officially replaced slavery

GENERAL WEYLER'S CONCENTRATION CAMPS

General Valeriano Weyler y Nicolau, marquis de Tenerife (1838–1930). During the Cuban War of Independence, General Valeriano Weyler implemented a brutal population-removal policy that led to the deaths of an estimated 10 percent of the island's population. © BETTMANN/CORBIS

From 1896 to 1897, during the Cuban War of Independence (1895–1898), Spanish total-war advocate General Valeriano Weyler (1838–1930) pursued a fight-war-with-war strategy that included *reconcentración* (reconcentration): a removal policy that forcibly relocated the rural populace out of zones where the Liberation army operated into towns and cities under the direct surveillance of the colonial army. This was a nineteenth-century antecedent to twentieth-century counter-insurgencies designed to figuratively drain the sea of popular support in which the elusive rebel fish swam. Conservative estimates suggest that some 10 percent of the island's population lost their lives from disease, malnutrition, and famine caused by forcing rural denizens and refugees into squalid urban areas already severely taxed by depredations of contending armies. Lurid—but not entirely inaccurate—accounts of the humanitarian crisis elicited North American sympathy and earned the Spanish commander the nickname Butcher Weyler. When U.S. forces in the Philippines and the British army in the Boer War later employed a similar population removal strategy, the term *concentration camp* entered the twentieth century's lexicon.

BIBLIOGRAPHY

Pérez Guzmán, Francisco. *Herida profunda*. Havana: Ediciones Unión, 1998.

Ione, John Lawrence. *War and Genocide in Cuba, 1895–1898*. Chapel Hill: University of North Carolina Press, 2006.

Weyler y Nicolau, Valeriano. *Mi mando en Cuba (10 de febrero 1896 a 31 octubre 1897): Historia military y política de la última guerra separatista durante dicho mando*. 5 vols. Madrid: González Rojas, 1910–1911.

David C. Carlson

with token wage payments and opportunities for self-manumission after the payment of thirty to fifty pesos per annum for a specified term of years. A 7 October 1886 royal decree finally ended slavery; the remaining 26,000 slaves were freed and final abolition proclaimed. Free black laborers faced low wages and poor working conditions, but they also tested the limits of their newfound autonomy and constructed a changing sense of *cubanidad* and nationality in countryside and town.

JOSÉ MARTÍ AND THE CUBAN REVOLUTIONARY PARTY

The immediate catalysts of the rebellion included overtaxation, as Cuba underpinned Spain's rising national debt and bore the severe costs of the Ten Years' War; rife corruption by officials securing quick riches prior to a return to Spain; and the effects of the worldwide recession of the 1890s. Exiled from Cuba a second time after 1879, Martí spent the remainder of his life in the United States. By 1892 he organized the PRC among a milieu of younger exiles and immigrants in Florida, New York, and the Antilles, together with key separatist military and political leaders such as Máximo Gómez (1836–1905) and Antonio Maceo (1845–1896). Preparations for resumption of what was hoped to be a short, swift insurrectionary uprising that would eject Spain from Cuba and Puerto Rico accelerated as the global recession hit Cuba particularly hard. The Spanish government levied higher tariffs on North American goods. The United States reciprocated; Cuban tobacco and sugar exports were hard hit, falling by one-half and one-third respectively, with spiraling unemployment and immiseration. Banditry and outlawry, which had smoldered since the Ten Years' War, became commonplace. The 1894 hurricane season produced severe storms that lashed Sagua la Grande and Oriente, increasing privation and desperation.

Martí and separatist plotters hastened their plans. Three schooners carrying weapons and matériel left Fernandina, Florida, to equip rebel forces, but U.S. Revenue Cutters seized them 8 January 1895 for violating U.S. neutrality laws. Nonetheless, separatists decided to resume armed struggle, particularly after legislative efforts to obtain autonomy vis-à-vis Spain and elect officials to the Cortes Generales (the Spanish legislature) went awry due to Spanish colonial wars in Morocco. Only in Oriente Province did the nascent Liberation Army meet with limited success. The relative weakness of the separatist movement and actions by the fourteen-thousand-strong Spanish garrison, along with procolonial and *peninsular* volunteers and police, stamped out manifestations supportive of the insurrection. In Spain, meanwhile, army officers grown accustomed to intervening in politics to get their way forced the Liberal prime minister, Práxedes Sagasta (1825–1903), to dissolve the government in favor of the Conservative Antonio Cánovas del Castillo (1828–1897) on 23 March 1895. In his address on forming a new government, Cánovas declared that Spain was prepared to fight "to the last peseta and the last drop of blood" to preserve Cuba as part of the empire. Cánovas dispatched Arsenio Martínez Campos (1831–1900) to Cuba. It was he who finally brought the Ten Years' War to an end through effective military suppression combined with adroit political negotiations. On 25 March 1895, in Santo Domingo, Martí and Gómez signed the Manifiesto de Montecristi, pledging the unity of whites and blacks and reaffirming Martí's vision of a future democratic republic based on equality and citizenship rights, pledging to respect Spaniards who remained neutral in the conflict. With rebellion in Cuba apparently foundering, the next task lay in having the leadership enter the country to directly organize the campaign.

On 1 April 1895 the brothers Maceo (Antonio and José) and other separatists landed at Duaba beach near Baracoa in eastern Cuba from the schooner *Honor*. They soon came under attack by pro-Spanish militia from Yateras, Guantánamo, who captured or killed several, including the Ten Years' War veteran Flor Crombet (1850–1895). Antonio Maceo spent weeks in the wilderness before he rendezvoused with insurgents. Martí and Gómez landed in southeastern Cuba at Cajobabo beach east of Guantánamo Bay on 11 April and trekked inland. Meanwhile, General Arsenio Martínez Campos arrived in Havana on 15 April as the Spanish captain general, to repress rebellion. On 5 May, Martí, Maceo, and Gómez met at an abandoned sugar mill, La Mejorana, to resolve tensions between military factions and consider the advisability of immediate application of Martí's political and social changes in areas of *Cuba libre* freed from

Spanish control. No satisfactory resolution appeared to have been made between military chiefs and civilian leaders like Martí.

In his last, unfinished letter, written on 18 May to a Mexican friend, Manuel Mercado (1838–1909), Martí wrote of his desire for an independent, sovereign Cuba free of both Spain and the United States:

> Every day now I am in danger of giving my life for my country and my duty—since I understand it and have the spirit to carry it out—in order to prevent, by the timely independence of Cuba, the United States from extending its hold across the Antilles and falling with all the greater force on the lands of our América. All I have done up to now and all I will do is for that … with our blood, we are blocking—to the annexation of the peoples of our América by the turbulent and brutal North that holds them in contempt … I lived in the monster, and I know its entrails—and my sling is the sling of David.

2002, p. 347

The following day, the letter left unfinished, Martí died in action in a skirmish with Spanish troops near Dos Ríos near Bayamo. His body was recovered by Spaniards and taken to Santiago, where he was buried.

With the departure and death of Martí, Tomás Estrada Palma (1836–1908) became head of the PRC in New York; by September, Salvador Cisneros Betancourt (1828–1914)—once president of the Republic in Arms during the Ten Years' War—again became president; Gómez and Maceo again promoted commanding generals of the Liberation Army. Both generals had long planned to carry the insurrection to all parts of the island and to embark on a systematic scorched-earth campaign of economic warfare directed at the fertile, extensive sugar mills to the west of the old Spanish fortified *trocha* defensive line at Júcaro and Morón between Camagüey and Sancti Spíritus. In the Ten Years' War indecision and opposition blocked such a move for almost seven years. Gómez and Maceo would carry it out in 1895 within six months.

WAR AND REBELLION BECOME ISLAND-WIDE

Maceo set about organizing an army of invasion, attracting small farmers and young *orientales* to the cause. Throughout the war, most rebel combatants were men of color, to the degree that almost 60 percent of Liberation Army personnel, and possibly 40 percent of officers, were black or *mulato*. This demographic rekindled standing (antiblack) racist attitudes among many whites during the course of the war. The rebels, whose strength would fluctuate from under 30,000 to 40,000 soldiers at the

Liberation Army's peak, fought an irregular war against the Spanish colonial army, the strength of which would grow to over 180,000 troops—mostly *quintos* (conscripts), shipped across the Atlantic by the second year of the war—and against up to 60,000 pro-Spanish counter-guerrillas, auxiliaries, and volunteers. The outnumbered Liberation Army, therefore, emphasized attacks on property and Spanish-controlled estates and towns and laid ambushes, rather than fighting set-piece battles. Liberation Army combatants received smuggled supplies from separatist supporters abroad and from *pacíficos* (allied civilian supporters) dispersed in rebel-held prefectures. They also looted or expropriated what they needed, including horses and cattle, from noncommittal and pro-Spanish inhabitants. Cuban rebels lived off the land. Modern weapons, ammunition, and other matériel were either scarce or nonexistent. Occasional supply expeditions from abroad or seizure from Spanish adversaries provided rebels with munitions, clothing, and medical supplies; home workshops contrived replacements for worn-out boots, hats, and saddles. The numbers of *mambíses* (the African-derived popular name for Cuban rebels) rose to forty thousand, organized in eighty-six regiments, during the high-water mark of the rebellion, but halved during Spanish offensives, particularly those in 1896 and 1897. The Liberation Army used horses for mobility and speed and largely avoided combat unless it could be fought on terrain and terms of its own choosing.

Just such a battle occurred on 14 July 1895 at Peralejo in eastern Cuba. A force of fifteen hundred Spanish infantry that included Captain-General Martínez Campos himself, led a large supply convoy to Bayamo, which had been the rebel capital briefly in the Ten Years' War. In essence, a portion of the column went on ahead to act as bait. The remainder of the column would pounce on any ambushers. Seeing Cuban cavalry, the Spaniards formed a dated defensive square formation, but in so doing presented a large, compact, massed target that waiting Liberation Army riflemen could not fail to hit. Casualties were about even—130 killed and wounded on each side—but the Spanish retreat boosted Cuban morale and enabled Maceo to draw in more recruits. The Spanish replicated much of their strategy from the Ten Years' War, bringing in a large conscript army of young, typically poor Spaniards performing obligatory military service—and set about fortifying towns and estates within the colonial army's control.

CASUALTIES AND LOSSES

By late 1895 some 120,000 Spanish troops had arrived. Numbers swelled later to 190,000. Casualties among the colonial army over the course of the war included 4,032 combat deaths and 10,956 wounded, but a staggering 22 percent—over 41,000 soldiers—died from tropical diseases such as yellow fever. Estimates for Cuban casualties vary: Combat deaths range from five to six thousand, while deaths from disease range from three thousand to comparable figures for battlefield losses. Tabulating total civilian losses is difficult. Most estimates begin with the postwar 1899 census, which suggests 300,000 people missing due to wartime deaths, emigration, and exile induced by the war, and a reduced birth rate. At least 170,000 civilians in the figure died from the effects of Spanish counterinsurgency policies. Material losses and economic destruction caused by the war were heavy. Fragmentary data from postwar Matanzas indicated that 96 percent of farms and 92 percent of sugar mills suffered disruption or destruction during in the war (On losses and damages, see Pérez 2006, pp. 145–146; Thomas pp. 330, 424; Tone p. 11). Matanzas lost over 90 percent of its horses and cattle. The total acreage under cultivation in the island fell from 1.3 million in 1895 to 900,000 in 1899. Economic losses and damages in just 1896 have been estimated at 40 million dollars.

THE INVASION OF WESTERN CUBA

On 22 October 1895, Gómez and Maceo initiated the invasion of the west, symbolically starting at Baraguá, where in 1878 Maceo had refused surrender. They crossed the old Spanish fortified *trocha* line, often over regionalist objections from *orientales* averse to entering the unfamiliar so-called foreign territory of western Cuba, fighting an important battle at Mal Tiempo near Cienfuegos on 15 December 1895. In January 1896, Maceo's forces reached the westernmost tip of the island at Mantua. Western Cuba's inhabitants faced the prospect of fleeing rebel areas for Spanish-held towns and cities or going over to the insurrection. The rebels carried out prohibitions on harvesting sugar, burning cane fields and plantations in maximal use of scorched-earth tactics. The sugar harvest plummeted from over 1 million tons in 1895 to one-fourth of that total in 1896 and 212,000 tons the year after that.

Without terms for negotiated settlement or means to resolve the rebellion politically, and unprepared to contemplate what an exclusively military resolution to the conflict portended, Martínez Campos tendered his resignation. A June 1895 letter to Prime Minister Cánovas warned that the Spanish colonial army "could concentrate the families of the countryside in the towns," but that this would require considerable force and "misery and hunger would be terrible." He feared the war would "come to this" and "only [General Valeriano] Weyler has the necessary capacity for such a policy," and he concluded that even if Spain should "suppress the rebels ... my loyal and sincere opinion is that, with reforms or without reforms, before twelve years we shall have another war" (quoted in Richard Gott pp. 91–92).

Death of Maceo. Antonio Maceo (1845–1896), a top commander in the Cuban army of independence, was killed by Spanish soldiers near Punta Brava, an event depicted in this illustration from *The Story of Cuba* by Murat Halstead (1898). AMERICAN SCHOOL (19TH CENTURY)/BIBLIOTHÈQUE NATIONALE, PARIS, FRANCE/ARCHIVES CHARMET/THE BRIDGEMAN ART LIBRARY INTERNATIONAL

GENERAL WEYLER AND THE FIGHT-WAR-WITH-WAR POLICY

In 1896 Valeriano Weyler, marquis of Tenerife (1838–1930), a seasoned counterinsurgency commander of long experience, took charge. He extended his predecessor's efforts to rebuild and reinforce *trochas* (fortified lines) in Camagüey and Pinar del Río to prevent rebel movement across the island. He proposed to use mobile columns to drive the rebels against these static positions. He also carried out the *reconcentración* (forcible relocation) of rural inhabitants into towns controlled by pro-Spanish garrisons and razed rural settlements to prevent enemy use. This policy completed the devastation of the countryside. It provoked considerable civilian losses from epidemic disease and malnutrition, estimated at between 155,000 and 170,000, or 10 percent of the island's total population, mostly from epidemic diseases within urban concentration zones. PRC lobbyists in North America, and many U.S. sympathizers eager to aid an anticolonial movement struggling against a European power, decried Spanish counterinsurgency policies, garnering Weyler the nickname "Butcher." Historical controversy persists as to whether Weyler's strategy essentially defeated the Cuban insurrectionary movement only in Pinar del Río and Havana or whether the rebels may have been seriously weakened everywhere except Oriente Province and perhaps parts of Las Villas. Certainly,

Weyler's troops struck heavy blows against the rebels, killing both Maceo and Gómez's son, Francisco "Pancho," at Punta Brava in western Cuba on 7 December 1896. At the same time, however, the strategy's very destructiveness threatened a dire destabilization of the island's society and economy, and the resultant humanitarian crisis generated considerable negative publicity for Spain and the appalling state of affairs in Cuba.

AUTONOMY

In June 1897, an anarchist assassinated Prime Minister Cánovas to avenge the repression of workers in Barcelona. The Conservative government gave way to the formation of a Liberal accession under Práxedes Sagasta, who replaced Weyler with Ramón Blanco y Erenas (1833–1906). By November 1897, offers of autonomy were extended to Cuba, which pleased neither pro-Spanish *integristas* supportive of a colonial status quo ante nor *independentistas* supporting separatism and contemplating no compromise. The announced shift to autonomous status within the Spanish empire by January 1898 led to a much less vigorous prosecution of the war by the Spanish army and its local allies. Insurgents spoke of a "dead war" during the campaign season. For many historians of Cuba, the pronouncement of autonomy signaled that Spain had reached a tipping point or impasse that suggested the separatists were close to

Opposite page: **Cuba's Heroes and Their Flag.** This souvenir lithograph, printed for the Grand Cuban-American Fair held at Madison Square Garden in New York City in 1896, includes portraits of Cuban heroes Máximo Gómez, Antonio Maceo, José Martí, Calixto García, and Salvador Cisneros. THE GRANGER COLLECTION, NEW YORK. REPRODUCED BY PERMISSION.

accomplishing some of their goals. Some U.S. historians and Hispanists insist that the Spanish military had mostly defeated the Liberation Army and that only the recall of Weyler and initiation of autonomy between late 1897 and early 1898 revived it. What is certain, however, is that the extension of autonomy propelled a chain of events that directly led to U.S. intervention and the internationalization of the war.

U.S. INTERVENTION LOOMS

On 12 January 1898 *integristas* rioted against pro-autonomist and U.S. consul Fitzhugh Lee requested action to protect North American citizens and interests. By early 1898, much of the U.S. fleet had been dispatched to Key West and the Dry Tortugas, Florida, and the battleship USS *Maine* steamed into Havana harbor on 25 January, where it remained at anchor. By mid-February 1898, U.S. newspapers—which had recently carried indignant stories of a 9 February letter from the Spanish ambassador Enrique Dupuy de Lôme (1851–1904) deriding President William McKinley as weak-willed—carried banner headlines about the night of 15 February, when the battleship *Maine* exploded, killing 260 of its 354-man crew while many officers were ashore. Subsequently several wounded men succumbed, raising the death toll to 266. Captain Charles D. Sigsbee warned against jumping to hasty conclusions, and some journalists noted the prompt dispatch of help by Spanish and Cuban harbor workers and personnel to the stricken warship, but U.S. military preparations began while a naval court of inquiry traveled to Cuba.

Unable to determine an exact cause for the destruction of the *Maine*, the inquiry nonetheless claimed that the detonation occurred outside the hull. By 29 March 1898 simultaneous congressional resolutions called for recognizing Cuban independence and for a declaration of war against Spain. The Spanish government acceded to virtually every American demand and agreed to arbitration of the *Maine* controversy, but a cease-fire provision to halt hostilities on the island proved impossible to meet, given standing Cuban positions regarding immediate independence. On 11 April 1898, President William McKinley asked Congress for a declaration of war. By 22 April, the U.S. Navy North Atlantic Squadron began blockading the north coast of Cuba, intercepting Spanish vessels on the high seas. Word of these belligerent actions prompted Spain to declare war against the United States; by 25 April 1898, a joint congressional resolution had passed that was in essence a declaration of war: It included the Teller Amendment, whereby the United States government foreswore annexation and overt colonial control over Cuba as an outcome. Officially, then, the U.S. government neither recognized immediate Cuban independence nor accorded belligerency rights; the resolution merely positioned the United States as a neutral intent on ending the armed conflict. Cuban separatists, for the most part, remained guardedly optimistic about the future assurances of independence contained within the Teller Amendment.

U.S. WAR WITH SPAIN—NAVAL ASPECTS

Internationalization of war led to the first major battle between the United States and Spain over Cuba, a battle that took place in the Philippines, on 1 May 1898 at Manila Bay. U.S. Commodore George Dewey (1837–1917) led a powerful squadron of modern warships against a decrepit, obsolete Spanish squadron of unarmored wooden ships southwest of Manila. In an entirely one-sided exchange, the U.S. fleet destroyed the Spanish flotilla.

By 19 May 1898, Spanish Admiral Pascual de Cervera's Caribbean Squadron slipped into Santiago de Cuba, having sailed from Cape Verde. In Santiago, General Arsenio Linares commanded a garrison of nine thousand Spanish troops amid the population of fifty thousand. The U.S. Navy established a blockade of the port, while the Spaniards blocked the entrance to the harbor. With the Spanish squadron bottled up, blockading operations continued, while an expeditionary invasion force was readied in Tampa, Florida. The first U.S. forces to land in Cuba, the First Marine Battalion, landed at Guantánamo Bay between 7 and 10 June 1898 under protection of Captain Bowman H. McCalla of the USS *Marblehead*. The navy intended to use the bay as a coaling station and safe port should the war continue into hurricane season. In skirmishes around the marine positions, Cuban soldiers lent assistance to the Americans. Seven thousand Spanish troops in Guantánamo occupied the region's sugar mills and railway lines and did not move to eject the U.S. position backed by warships.

U.S. ARMY FIFTH CORPS LANDS IN CUBA

Between 20 and 22 June 1898, seventeen thousand U.S. Army troops of the Fifth Corps, commanded by the gouty major general William Rufus "Pecos Bill" Shafter (1835–1906) disembarked from crowded transports at Daiquirí and Siboney east of Santiago after milling in confusion amid lengthy delays in Tampa. Spanish garrisons, facing Cuban rebels to their rear, retreated and did not contest the landings. Ashore, Shafter decided to move against the city garrison of Santiago de Cuba before attempting to eject defending Spaniards from coastal batteries and fortifications at the bay's entrance. Retreating Spaniards fought a sharp skirmish with U.S. Fifth Corps troops and Cubans at Las Guásimas.

Thirty-five hundred out of eight thousand Spanish troops from Manzanillo broke out and began marching overland to join Linares in Santiago de Cuba. Their arrival in early July exacerbated the privations and hunger in the city, but U.S. reactions to

DESTRUCTION OF THE U.S. BATTLESHIP MAINE IN HAVANA HARBOR FEBY 15TH 1898.

Cuban *mambises* (liberation army troops) failing to halt the column exacerbated a growing rift between the erstwhile allies. No Spanish messengers delivered orders to the seven-thousand-soldier garrison at Guantánamo, because the Cuban insurgents prevented communications by land and because U.S. ships and marines occupied the lower portion of Guantánamo Bay. Ahead of the expected arrival of the Spaniards due from Manzanillo, on 1 July, Shafter ordered a three-pronged attack against the town of El Caney on the Santiago-Guantánamo road and against the ridge Loma de San Juan east of Santiago. A day of heavy fighting led to eleven hundred U.S. casualties and Shafter contemplating retreat, but the Spanish defenders, having sustained even greater losses, retired to a secondary line of trenches ringing the city. The press highlighted the colonel of U.S. volunteers, Theodore Roosevelt (1858–1919), and the First U.S. Volunteer Cavalry's role in the fray, which propelled Roosevelt's postwar gubernatorial aspirations for New York, and later the vice presidency, as running mate with McKinley.

Cervera's fleet lay within range of landward bombardment or possible capture if Santiago de Cuba fell, so the admiral followed orders to break out of Santiago harbor into the Windward Passage and make a run along the southern coast to Cienfuegos. At 9:30 a.m. on Sunday, 3 July 1898, the *Infanta María Teresa, Vizcaya, Almirante Oquendo, Cristóbal Colón,* and the destroyers *Furor* and *Plutón* were engaged by the USS *Brooklyn* and USS *Texas* (the sister ship of the *Maine*) before the Spanish flotilla could turn to starboard and head in a westerly direction. The USS *Iowa,* USS *Oregon,* and USS *Indiana* joined other U.S. ships and gave chase. Every Spanish ship was lost, with 323 crew killed, 151 wounded, and 1,700 captured, while only a single American sailor died, and another was wounded. The same evening as this Spanish disaster, 3,500 weary troops from Manzanillo evaded Cuban insurgent patrols and entered the starving city of Santiago. Shafter settled his troops in for a siege, concerned that another frontal attack would result in further heavy losses like at El Caney and San Juan

Destruction of the U.S. battleship *Maine*. The 1898 destruction of the *USS Maine* in Havana Harbor was depicted in this contemporary chromolithograph by the Chicago publisher Kurz and Allison. THE GRANGER COLLECTION, NEW YORK. REPRODUCED BY PERMISSION.

The New York World *a day after*

who had been Populists and those who became Progressives — clamored for the United States to rescue the Cuban people from the Spanish malefactors.

President William McKinley and the conservative Republican leaders in Congress reluctantly gave way before this pressure. Senator Henry Cabot Lodge warned McKinley, "If the war in Cuba drags on through the summer with nothing done we [the Republican party] shall go down in the greatest defeat ever known."

Already, in November 1897, Spain, at the urging of President McKinley, had granted

CUBA

Hill but fearful that delay would lead to outbreaks of yellow fever among his forces.

The Spaniards negotiated the evacuation of half the civilian population, about twenty thousand people, from Santiago. The U.S. Navy and Red Cross delivered additional supplies to Cubans in a similar relief operation near Guantánamo. After several days, General Juan José Toral surrendered the twelve-thousand-man Spanish garrison to the U.S. Fifth Corps and issued orders directing a further twelve thousand, led by subordinates at Guantánamo and other Spanish outposts in eastern Cuba, to also surrender. Some insisted on additional confirmation of the orders before doing so. At each of these locales in Oriente, including Santiago, the North Americans excluded the Cubans from the negotiations, prohibiting them from witnessing the surrender and from entering the cities. After objections from officials in the Cuban Liberation Army, their General Demetrio Castillo temporarily became mayor, only to be replaced days later by the Spanish former mayor Leonardo Ros. North American troops and Spaniards fraternized and commiserated, frequently venting a disdain for Cubans as colonial, mixed-race peoples.

A veteran of all three Cuban wars of independence, General Calixto García (1839–1898) wrote a sharp 17 July 1898 resignation letter to Shafter expressive of Cuban reactions to being sidelined and other U.S. behaviors:

> A rumor, too absurd to be believed, General, describes the reason of your measures and of the orders forbidding my army to enter Santiago for fear of massacres and revenge against the Spaniards. Allow me, sir, to protest against even the shadow of such an idea. We are not savages . . . We are a poor, ragged army as ragged and poor as that of your forefathers in their noble war for independence, but like the heroes of Saratoga and Yorktown, we respect our cause too deeply to disgrace it with barbarism and cowardice.
>
> *Foner p. 370*

The exclusion of Cubans from negotiations and the rehabilitation and restoration of Spanish Crown authorities in several cases prefigured the negotiations that would end the war. This rather

The surrender of Santiago de Cuba. On 13 July 1898, General José Toral, commander of the Spanish garrison at Santiago de Cuba, met with U.S. general William Rufus Shafter to discuss the terms of surrender, an event depicted in this 1899 lithograph. THE GRANGER COLLECTION, NEW YORK. REPRODUCED BY PERMISSION.

Opposite page: **Maine Explosion Caused by Bomb or Torpedo?** The front page of the 17 February 1898 issue of the *New York World* questions the cause of the 15 February explosion that destroyed the *USS Maine* and most of its crew in Havana Harbor. © BETTMANN/CORBIS

high-handed dismissal of Cuban claims suited Spanish sensibilities, which preferred to deal with a victorious rival state than with a former colony whose independence the government and military had never recognized. It also suited occupation authorities and U.S. prerogatives as a great power that preferred to maximize its own freedom of movement without undue complications from consideration of competing demands from a reluctant ally. For a number of Cubans, U.S. actions would be long remembered. The treatment was referenced in January 1959 by a victorious Fidel Castro of the 26th of July Movement, when he derided attempts to exclude the rebel army from Santiago as a prohibition "to those who have liberated the *patria*": "The history of 1895 will not be repeated," he said. "This time the *mambises* will enter Santiago de Cuba."

END OF THE WAR

The War of 1898 came to an end as a result of U.S. intervention, and the United States and Spain alone resolved the standing claims and issues. On 26 July 1898, Spain requested terms from President McKinley, who replied four days later. By 9 August, Madrid relayed acceptance to Washington, and the protocols were signed on 12 August, ending hostilities. Terms agreeing on a formal peace treaty scheduled in Paris excluded Cubans, Filipinos, and other formerly colonized peoples. By 10 December 1898, the Treaty of Paris was signed, stripping Spain of its overseas possessions outside Africa. The United States assumed political control and a protectorate status over the Caribbean and Pacific territories, beginning a three-year occupation of Cuba to supervise installation of a national government, while the Liberation Army was disbanded. By 1901, the United States would agree to departure from Cuba, but with the proviso that Cuba must adopt without modification the Platt Amendment, which placed a de facto protectorate status over an ostensibly independent Cuba, including provisions legitimating future U.S. interventions.

BIBLIOGRAPHY

Acosta Matos, Eliades. *Cien respuestas para un siglo de dudas*. Havana: Editorial Pablo de Torriente, 1999.

Armas Delamarter-Scott, Ramón de. *La revolución pospuesta*. Havana: Centro de Estudios Martianos, 2002.

Boza, Bernabé. *Mi diario de la guerra*. Havana: Editorial de Ciencias Sociales, 1974.

Collazo, Enrique. *Los americanos en Cuba*. 2 vols. Havana: Editorial de Ciencias Sociales, 1972.

Ferrer, Ada. *Insurgent Cuba: Race, Nation, and Revolution, 1868–1898*. Chapel Hill: University of North Carolina Press, 1999.

Foner, Philip S. *The Spanish-Cuban-American War and the Birth of American Imperialism, 1895–1902*. New York: Monthly Review Press, 1972.

García Carranza, Araceli, ed. *Bibliografía de la guerra de independencia, 1895–1898*. Havana: Editorial Orbe, 1976.

Gómez Núñez, Severo. *La guerra hispano-americana*. 5 vols. Madrid: Imprenta del Cuerpo de Artillería, 1899–1902.

Gott, Richard. *Cuba: A New History*. New Haven, CT: Yale University Press, 2004.

Helg, Aline. *Our Rightful Share: The Afro Cuban Struggle for Equality, 1886–1912*. Chapel Hill: University of North Carolina Press, 1995.

Ibarra, Jorge. *Cuba, 1898–1921: Partidos politicos y clases socials*. Havana: Editorial de Ciencias Sociales, 1992.

Instituto de Historia de Cuba. *Las luchas por la independencia nacional y las transformaciones estructurales, 1868–1898*. Havana: Editora Política, 1996.

LaFeber, Walter. *The New Empire: An Interpretation of American Expansionism, 1860–1898*. Ithaca, NY: Cornell University Press, 1963.

Martí, José. *Selected Writings*. Translated by Esther Allen. New York: Penguin Books, 2002.

Martínez Arango, Felipe. *Cronología crítica de la guerra hispano-cubano-americana*. 1950. Havana: Editorial de Ciencias Sociales, 1973.

Miró Argenter, José. *Crónicas de la guerra*. Havana: Editorial Letras Cubanas, 1981.

Musicant, Ivan. *Empire by Default: The Spanish-American War and the Dawn of the American Century*. New York: Henry Holt, 1997.

Offner, John L. *An Unwanted War: The Diplomacy of the United States and Spain over Cuba, 1895–1898*. Chapel Hill: University of North Carolina Press, 1992.

Pérez, Louis A., Jr. *Cuba between Empires, 1878–1902*. Pittsburgh, PA: University of Pittsburgh Press, 1983.

Pérez, Louis A., Jr. *The War of 1898: The United States and Cuba in History and Historiography*. Chapel Hill: University of North Carolina Press, 1998.

Pérez, Louis A., Jr. *Cuba: Between Reform and Revolution* 3rd ed. Oxford: Oxford University Press, 2006.

Pérez Guzmán, Francisco, Rolando Zulueta Zulueta, and Yolanda Díaz Martínez. *Guerra de independencia, 1895–1898*. Havana: Editorial de Ciencias Sociales, 1998.

Pichardo Viñals, Hortensia. *Documentos para la historia de Cuba*. 5 vols. Havana: Editorial Pueblo y Educación, 1984.

Roig de Leuchsenring, Emilio. *Cuba no debe su independencia a los E.U.* Havana: Sociedad Cubana de Estudios Históricos e Internacionales, 1950.

Roig de Leuchsenring, Emilio. *La guerra libertadora cubana de los treinta años, 1868–1898*. Havana: Oficina del Historiador de la Ciudad de La Habana, 1958.

Thomas, Hugh. *Cuba: The Pursuit of Freedom*. New York: Da Capo Press, 1998.

Tone, John Lawrence. *War and Genocide in Cuba, 1895–1898*. Chapel Hill: University of North Carolina Press, 2006.

ⓒ SPORTS

Cubans' passion for baseball and boxing—sports in which the national team is among the best in the world—is well known; however, beyond these two, less is known about the makeup of the Cuban sports movement, its achievements, and the people involved (many of them volunteers).

After 1959, with the creation of the Instituto Nacional de Deportes, Educación Física y la Recreación (INDER; National Institute of Sports, Physical Education, and Recreation) and the group's slogan ("sports, the right of the people"), the elimination of professional sports and the adoption of access to sports for the masses are identifying marks of the Revolution in the field of social rights. Today, hundreds of Cubans associated with sports collaborate with their counterparts in other countries. In addition, in both boxing and baseball, Cuban athletes—including those living in Cuba, those born in the diaspora, and those who have left the island—are considered among the best in their field.

SPORTS: COLONIAL PERIOD

Félix Julio Alfonso López

Principal sports practiced in Cuba during the nineteenth century.

From the sixteenth century to the end of the eighteenth century, non-labor-related physical activity in Cuba was associated mostly with religious and nonreligious festivals, which were enhanced by competitions on horseback such as the *corrida de cinta* and *corrida de sortijas* (ribbon race and ring race), target shooting, greased-pole climbing, sack races, cockfighting, and bullfighting. Traditional Spanish regional sports such as *pelota vasca* (Basque ball) and *lucha canaria* (Canarian wrestling) also were practiced. The most popular games among whites were billiards and bowling, whereas the African slaves played *el juego y baile del maní* (the peanut game and dance), which had elements of combat. Several variants of the African pastime are known: *maní limpio* (clean peanuts), *maní con grasa* (greased peanuts), "with bare fist and wrist" and "with wristbands" (Ortiz pp. 396ff.).

FIRST DISPLAYS OF MODERN SPORTS

The first modern sport regularly practiced in Cuba was fencing. Its first academy and weapons room was founded in Havana in 1836 by the Italian Juan Galletti, and its success with the Cuban upper class led to the establishment of similar schools in Matanzas, Santa Clara, Cienfuegos, Puerto Príncipe, Bayamo, and Santiago de Cuba (Reig Romero pp. 23–24).

On 14 May 1839 the young *criollo* José Rafael de Castro y Bermúdez inaugurated, under the auspices of the Sociedad Económica de Amigos del País (Economic Society of Friends of the Country), the first known gymnasium in Cuba, Gimnasio Normal, which was well received by illustrious academics such as José de la Luz y Caballero and Domingo del Monte

(Reig Romero pp. 25–28). In parallel to the development of the gymnasiums, Cubans began to practice other sports, such as swimming, horse racing, wrestling, French boxing, foot racing, and shooting with pistols and shotguns, whose greatest athlete was Juan Federico Centelles from Matanzas.

CHESS

The first Cuban chess champion, Félix Sicre, was recognized in 1860, and the Havana Chess Circle, founded in 1861, organized tournaments and published a monthly magazine dedicated to the science of the game. In 1862 the U.S. champion Pablo Murphy visited the island and played the first game of blind chess. In 1885, the Havana Chess Club was formed under the presidency of the Spanish chess player Celso Golmayo. Around this time some of the most important chess players in the world visited Cuba, including the Austrian Wilhelm Steinitz (in 1883, 1888, and 1892), the Russian Mikhail Tchigorin (1889), and the German champion Emanuel Lasker (1893).

SPORTS OF THE ELITE

The nineteenth-century criollo bourgeois incorporated into their leisure activities luxury sports such as yachting, lawn tennis, polo, and skating. The Havana Yacht Club was founded in 1886, and in the following year, it hosted Cuba's first nautical championship. Another important nautical sport was rowing, and its most important clubs were created in Havana, Cienfuegos, Matanzas, and Santiago de Cuba.

The first tennis court was built in Havana's Vedado district in 1888, and its first players were women from the upper classes. In 1883 equestrian polo enthusiasts formed the Havana Polo Club, which was made up of upper-class families. The earliest reports of skating in Cuba date to 1877, and in 1879 a skating rink was built in Matanzas, followed quickly by another in the capital. Cycling became popular beginning in the 1880s, and the Cycling Club was formed in 1886. Other sports that gained popularity in the 1880s were walk racing and trapshooting.

BASEBALL

The most important sport practiced in Cuba in the nineteenth century was baseball. All indications are that it was introduced by the brothers Nemesio and Ernesto Guilló with their friend Enrique Porto. The three learned the game while studying in the United States (Mobile, Alabama) and brought a primitive form of baseball (town ball or *fongueo*) to Havana in 1864 (Pi p. 1). The first team, christened the Habana Base Ball Club, was formed in 1868.

During the 1880s baseball spread throughout the western part of the island from Pinar del Río to Las Villas, and numerous teams and small leagues were formed (Pérez 2006, p. 93). Habana, Almendares, and Fe were the main teams of the capital, and Progreso and Matanzas excelled in Matanzas. Until the end of the 1880s, amateur baseball was a gallant social activity that included dinner and dancing after the games. The dance orchestras of Raimundo Valenzuela, Miguel Faílde, and others provided entertainment in the town squares following games (González Echevarría pp. 177–180).

Habana and Almendares, the inspirational clubs of nineteenth-century Cuban baseball, were made up of players from different segments of society and generally were identified with radical nationalism (advocates of independence) or moderate nationalism (autonomists). Habana, managed by the patriarch of Cuban baseball, Emilio Sabourín, won the most tournaments during the period, with nine championships between 1878 and 1892.

In 1889 Wenceslao Gálvez y Delmonte published the first book about baseball in Cuba, *El Base-Ball en Cuba. Historia del base-ball en la isla de Cuba, sin retratos de los principales jugadores y personas más caracterizadas en el juego citado, ni de ninguna otra* (Baseball in Cuba: The History of Baseball on the Island of Cuba, with No Portraits of the Principal Players or the Most Characteristic Figures or Anyone Else in the Game). In it he provides a player's view of events, games, and the baseball environment of the period.

The growing popularity of baseball prompted the establishment of publications devoted to reporting its activities. *Base Ball* (1881), *La Habana Elegante* (Elegant Havana, 1883), *El Fígaro* (1885), and *El Sport* (Sports, 1885), dedicated space in their pages to analyzing baseball as they simultaneously popularized modernist literature.

Between 1895 and 1898 there was no activity on the baseball fields because of the revival of the war of independence, when many players took to the hills or emigrated. Some players joined the fight for independence, including Alfredo Arango, Martín Marrero, Juan Delgado, Leopoldo and Pedro Matos, Ricardo Cabaleiro, the star pitcher Carlos Maciá, and the brothers José Dolores and Manuel Amieva. Emilio Sabourín was imprisoned in Ceuta, where he died in 1897, and the pitcher Juan Manuel Pastoriza was killed by the Spanish in Guanabacoa. Meanwhile, in Tampa and Key West, Florida, Cuban expatriate players were organized into groups to play in fundraisers supporting the cause for independence. The exodus at the start of the war brought many Cuban separatists to neighboring nations such as the Dominican Republic, Venezuela, and Mexico, where they promoted baseball and joined teams as players and managers.

BIBLIOGRAPHY

Alfonso López, Félix Julio. *La esfera y el tiempo.* San Antonio de los Baños, Cuba: Editorial Unicornio, 2007.

Gálvez y Delmonte, Wenceslao. *El base-ball en Cuba. Historia del base-ball en la Isla de Cuba, sin retratos de los principales jugadores y personas más caracterizadas en el juego citado, ni de ninguna otra.* Havana: Imprenta Mercantil de los Herederos de Santiago Spencer, 1889.

González Echevarría, Roberto. *La gloria de Cuba. Historia del beisbol en la Isla.* Madrid: Editorial Colibrí, 2004.

Ortiz, Fernando. *Los bailes y el teatro de los negros en el folklore de Cuba.* Havana: Editorial Letras Cubanas, 1981.

Pérez, Louis A. Jr. "Between Base Ball and Bullfighting: The Quest for Nationality in Cuba, 1868–1898." *Journal of American History* 81 (September 1994): 493–517.

Pérez, Louis A. Jr. *Ser cubanos. Identidad, nacionalidad y cultura.* Havana: Editorial de Ciencias Sociales, 2006.

Pi, Guillermo. "Nemesio Guilló fue quien trajo a Cuba el primer bate y la primera pelota." *Diario de la Marina* (Havana) (January 6, 1924).

Reig Romero, Carlos E. *Historia del deporte cubano. Los inicios.* San Antonio de los Baños, Cuba: Editorial Unicornio, 2007.

SPORTS: REPUBLICAN PERIOD

Carlos Eduardo Reig Romero

The development of amateur and professional sports in Cuba from independence in 1902 to the Revolution in 1959.

The history of sports during the Cuban Republic can be split into two periods, 1902 to 1920 and 1921 to 1958, and those periods are best examined with reference to the emergence of new sports, the rise of associations, school and women's sports, governing bodies, amateurism and professionalism, government interest in sports, and connection with the international Olympic Movement.

1902–1920: THE DEVELOPMENT OF ASSOCIATIONS

During the Republican period, especially in Havana, Cuba introduced reforms and innovations patterned

■ *See also*

Cuban Thought and Cultural Identity: Costumbres in the Republican Period

on American culture that aimed to leave behind the nation's colonial past and form a modern society in which participatory and spectator sports were commonplace. Connected to these trends was the creation of sports associations in numerous cities. The ubiquitous sporting network was made of a heterogeneous array of organizations, formal and informal, amateur and professional, organizers and promoters of sports. Organizations varied substantially according to the social class of their membership and access to financial resources. The extent and the diversity of these associations are demonstrated in the Havana municipal government's register of associations (*Fondo del Registro de Asociaciones del Gobierno de La Habana*), which lists more than 900 sports associations registered from 1902 to 1958 by various social strata, public and private schools, companies, neighborhoods, political organizations and unions, religious institutions, and immigrant groups. The capital's sporting elite was concentrated in the Habana Yacht Club (HYC; 1886), Vedado Tennis Club (VTC; 1902), and the Country Club de La Habana (CCH; 1911), all of which served as models for other organizations (Fariñas Borrego p. 24).

The typical form of sports association was the independent club, reluctant to submit to a governing body with the authority to impose rules and calendars binding on member clubs. In a small number of sports (baseball, cycling, and basketball) this resistance was overcome with the creation of structures such as the Liga Nacional de Basket Ball (1915). Soccer was the only sport to establish its own, relatively stable, national federation (1911).

From 1902 to 1912 in Havana, sports-loving businessmen established associations. In 1908 and 1915 sports leaders attempted to form the Asociación Atlética Amateurs de Cuba (Amateur Athletic Association of Cuba), modeled on the U.S. counterpart, to regulate and organize all amateur sports. Both attempts, however, were frustrated by a lack of consensus (Reig Romero 2001, pp. 145–146; Reig Romero 2007, p. 86).

New Sports Immigrants and tourists introduced and promoted ten U.S. sports (table tennis, automobile racing, handball, water polo, basketball, volleyball, diving, track and field, squash, and motorcycling), two from Europe (soccer and cricket), and one from Japan (jujitsu). These sports, together with the twenty sports already practiced in Cuba, widened leisure-time options, primarily for the middle class, but to some degree for lower-class working people as well. The spread of these sports was uneven and took place in various ways. Some of them were practiced by clubs that took years to join associations and regional groups (track and field, handball, water polo, volleyball, and softball), and others spread more quickly (basketball, soccer, cycling, and boxing). In the capital, the Vedado Tennis Club (1902), the Asociación Cristiana de Jóvenes (Young Men's Christian Association [YMCA];

1905), the Asociación Atlética de la Universidad de La Habana (1906), the Asociación de Dependientes del Comercio de La Habana (Association of Retail Employees of Havana; 1907), and the Club Atlético de Cuba (1909) led the way in promoting sports due to the variety of sports they practiced and their organization of interclub competitions.

Women's Sports and School Sports Tennis was the first sport to establish an official independent competition specifically for women (1904), and it led the way in the women's sports association movement (Lawn Tennis Club, 1913). Gradually, women's sports exhibitions and competitions were introduced, including fencing, rifle shooting, and bowling (*El Mundo Ilustrado* 1907, p. 550; *La Discusión* 1908a, p. 11; *La Discusión* 1908b, p. 11).

During this period, public and private schools (American, secular, Catholic, and Protestant) formed sports teams and sometimes organized inter- or intramural competitions. The University of Havana, Escuelas Normales de Maestros, Institutos de Segunda Enseñanza, Escolapios de Guanabacoa, Belén, La Salle, and La Progresiva were the leaders in this regard.

Sporting Events Spurred by the profit motive, businessmen and corporations organized and controlled the business of producing sporting events. The pillars of spectator sport were baseball, jai alai, and horse and motor racing, with an infrastructure of stadiums, tracks, and other facilities. During the various athletic seasons, sports entrepreneurs competed for the attendance of American tourists and Cuban citizens from diverse social groups. Jai alai and horse racing attracted legal betting. Baseball, which had professional and semiprofessional leagues all over the island, was distinguished by racial inclusion and its exaltation of national pride.

In the 1910s professional boxing matches debuted; the sport was energized by the April 1915 bout between Jack Johnson and Jess Willard that brought 30,000 to Oriental Park (Pérez p. 243). Motor racing did not take long to spread from the capital to the interior of the country, where tourists and Cubans from different social strata attended races. Local theaters offered wrestling, boxing, jujitsu, weightlifting, and gymnastic events. Less frequent were the public amateur events with baseball players, cyclists, track-and-field athletes, soccer players, pelota players, boxers, all-in wrestlers as well as Greco-Roman, yachtsmen, and rowers.

By the end of 1920, Cuban national pride had been lifted by the international success of their sportspersons, including José R. Capablanca, winner of international chess tournaments and world chess champion (1921); Ramón Fonst Segundo, the first Latin American fencing world (1904) and Olympic champion (1900 and 1904); Manuel Dionisio Díaz, saber fencing Olympic (1904) and North American champion; Federico Narganes, the New York Athletic

Club champion in two divisions of Greco-Roman wrestling (1902 and 1905); Enrique Conill, international yacht racing champion; and major league baseball players Armando Marsans, Adolfo Luque, and Miguel Ángel González.

1920–1958

The heterogeneous establishment of sports associations continued in Cuba after 1920, but with some significant changes. First, higher structures for the organization and promotion of amateur sports were created in order to codify rules and regulations, establish procedures and schedules for competitions, recognize the amateur status of athletes, and build relationships with international institutions. The first to appear were the Unión Atlética Amateur de Cuba (UAAC; 1922), the Liga Social de Amateurs de Cuba (1922), the Liga Intersocial de Amateurs de Cuba (1925), Organización Deportiva Amateurs de Cuba (ODAC; 1934), all mainly Afro-Cuban organizations, and the Liga Popular de Cuba (1948). In the school sector—both private and public—athletes could join the pioneering Liga Intercolegial (1924), the Federación Atlética Intercolegial de Cuba (of Catholic schools), Confederación de los Grandes Colegios, Liga Intercolegial y Juvenil de Balompié de La Habana (the Interschool Youth Soccer League of Havana), the Liga Atlética de Escolares Públicos (Athletic League of Public Schoolchildren), and the Liga Intercolegial de Oriente (Interschool League of Oriente Province). During this period school sports flourished in Cuba, from public primary schools to the most distinguished private schools, with both boys and girls competing in beginner, junior, and senior categories. The success of these organizations was reflected in the customarily diverse calendar of local, regional, and national competitions.

In 1935 the Cuban government began to show an interest in the organization and regulation of sports, amateur, professional, school, and social; by Decree-Law No. 409 (13 November 1935) it established the Comisión Nacional de Educación Física y Deportes (National Commission of Physical Education and Sports). Later, the commission's rights, properties, and shares passed to the Bureau of Physical Education and Sports under the Department of Education, pursuant to Decree-Law No. 283 of 1952 (*Gaceta Oficial de Cuba* pp. 14561–14562). The bureau created other bodies: the Federación Atlética Nacional Amateurs Inter-Institutos (FANAI; National Amateur Interinstitutes Athletic Federation) and the Federación Atlética Nacional Amateurs de Secundaria (FANASE; National Amateur Secondary-School Athletic Federations). The Dirección General de Nacional de Deportes (DGND; National Bureau of Sports) was created by Decree-Law No. 1454 of 1938 and abolished by Decree-Law No. 294 of 1952, which then created the Comisión Nacional de Deportes (CND; National Sports Commission). Both of these organizations deserve credit for their contributions to the advancement of Cuban sports.

Women's Sports In the midst of this flurry of organizational activity, another remarkable development of this period was the awakening of women's sports in Cuba, beginning in the 1920s. Women college students, members of social clubs, public and private school students, workers, and freelance athletes emerged suddenly in the competitive arena; their athletic performances, once considered a novelty and only irregularly seen, became daily fare on the sports calendars of several cities. Basketball was the pioneer, and most popular among the girls. Other sports played by women included track and field, table tennis, golf, shooting, soccer, swimming, diving, fencing, volleyball, rowing, sailing, archery, baseball, softball, cycling, skating, equestrian sports, kickball, gymnastics, squash, judo, and synchronized swimming. The first governing body was the Federación Atlética Femenina (Women's Athletic Federation), created in 1931 to organize the swimming competition at the Hotel Nacional. In April 1934 the Asociación Atlética Femenina de Cuba (AAFC; Women's Athletic Association of Cuba) was established, and it endured until the 1950s. Its outstanding work was supported by the UAAC, by school sporting bodies, by the Comisión Deportiva Universitaria (College Sports Commission), and by the DGND.

This intricate network of associations undoubtedly contributed to elevating the quality and organizational strength of Cuban sports, but they were not immune to disagreements, economic, social, and racial exclusions, injustices, favoritism, governmental intrusions, and struggles for control.

International Olympic Movement Another important development during this period was Cuba's joining the International Olympic Movement: Over a thirty-five-year period, the Olympic troika was put in place—representation on the International Olympic Committee (IOC), creation of the National Olympic Committee, and establishment of national federations. The launch of this process came on 19 January 1923 with the lecture of Henry Baillet-Latour, vice president of the International Olympic Committee, at the UAAC. The first contacts with the International Olympic Committee had taken place between 1915 and 1917, when Cuba sought to host the 1920 (Seventh) Games (Reig Romero 2001). The first Cuban delegate to the International Olympic Committee, Porfirio Franca, was selected at the body's twenty-second session, in April 1923. The creation of the National Olympic Committee was a longer process (fourteen years). Although the committee was temporarily named three times (1924, 1929, and 1935), it was not until the publication of Decree-Law No. 1509 of 1937 that the Cuban Olympic Committee became permanent. The International Olympic Committee recognized it on 5 January 1955 (Reig Romero 2007, pp. 86–104).

The Cuban Olympic Committee performed admirably in disseminating the Olympic ideal and overcoming every obstacle and disagreement so as to assure Cuban participation in regional competitions and in the Olympic Games themselves. Moreover, because of the success of those who fought to do away with racial and social-class exclusion of athletes, the soccer team that took part in the Second Central American Games, at Havana in 1930, became the first Afro-Cubans to represent their country in international competition.

The third part of the troika, establishing the national federations, was a difficult task that took almost twenty-five years. In 1958, the great majority of the established national federations were already members of their international counterpart organizations.

Cuba joined the International Olympic Movement with considerable vigor; it participated in almost all of the regional and Olympic competitions (1924, 1948, 1952, and 1956), promoted new ideas, and produced seminal documents at various regional meetings. The first Latin American member of the Executive Committee of the International Olympic Committee was the Cuban Miguel A. Moenck, IOC delegate in Cuba (1938–1969).

New Sports and Competition New sports introduced during this period included kayaking (1930s), archery (1939), modern pentathlon (1940),

kickball (1949), judo (1951), and synchronized swimming (1955). Consequently, by 1958 the roster of sports practiced in Cuba numbered thirty-nine, some of which were highly popular (baseball, boxing, track and field, soccer, basketball, and volleyball), and some with fewer fans (golf, sailing, water polo, equestrian sports, freestyle and Greco-Roman wrestling, and weightlifting). The sports calendar included competitions both amateur and professional, for men and women, social and school. Cuba hosted important international competitions in chess, baseball, boxing, sailing, soccer, shooting, auto racing, and basketball. Meanwhile, Cubans competed in world championship events for chess, basketball, soccer, baseball, professional boxing, tennis (Davis Cup regional qualifying round), shooting, sailing, and volleyball.

Public Events In the world of professional athletes competing against fellow Cubans and foreigners, three particularly important developments marked this period: the rise of boxing, which, like baseball, spread throughout the country; the establishment of professional soccer, operating from the end of the 1940s to the first half of the 1950s; and the boom in motor racing beginning in the 1940s, with the urban circuits, the Marianao speedway, and the circuits of interprovincial highways, and, as a coda, the first and second Cuban Grand Prix (25 February 1957 and 24 February 1958).

Grand Prix of Cuba, 1958. Automobile racers gather at the start of the Grand Prix of Cuba on 24 February 1958. British driver Stirling Moss (front left) was in the lead when the race was halted after one of the cars jumped the track, killing several spectators. © BETTMANN/ CORBIS

In the 1957 Grand Prix the four best drivers in the world competed: the many times world champion Juan Manuel Fangio of Argentina, who won the race in a close finish with Alfonso de Portago of Spain; the English drivers Meter Collins and Stirling Moss; and the Italian racer Eugene Castellotti. The participants in the 1958 Grand Prix included Fangio, Moss (ranked second in the world), the Americans Masten Gregory and Harry Schell (ranked sixth and fifth, respectively), the French driver Jean Behra (ranked eighth), the German Wolfang von Trips, and Porfirio Rubirosa. This competition was marred by two events: the kidnapping of Fangio by members of the 26th of July movement, which prevented his competing and brought to the world's attention the revolution that was taking place in Cuba; and the tragic accident caused by Cuban driver Armando Garcia, who lost control of his vehicle, crashing it into the crowded security area, killing seven people and injuring thirty-five.

The sports boom of the Republican period saw a great increase in associations and marked achievements in organization, number of sports practiced, and the intense and varied calendar of local, national, and international competitions. Nevertheless, racial, economic, social, and territorial exclusions and limitations prevented the full participation of ordinary, working-class Cubans in the sporting life.

■ *See also*

Cuban Thought and Cultural Identity: Socialist Thought

Governance and Contestation: The Cuban Revolution

BIBLIOGRAPHY

Alfonso López, Félix Julio. *La esfera y el tiempo*. San Antonio de los Baños, Cuba: Unicornio, 2007.

Álvarez Guerra, Daisy Anisia, et al. *El deporte universitario: Cuna del deporte cubano*. Havana: Ediciones ENPES, 1991.

Antigas, Juan. "Los precursores del sport en Cuba." In *Escritos políticos y sociales*. Madrid: Talleres Espasa-Calpes, 1931.

Anuario de El País. 1943. Havana: Ediciones El País, 1944.

Barcia, María del Carmen. *Capas populares y modernidad en Cuba (1878–1930)*. Havana: Fundación Fernando Ortiz, Letras Cubanas, 2005.

La Discusión, 15 April 1908.

La Discusión, 18 October 1908.

Fariñas Borrego, Maikel. *Sociabilidad y cultura del ocio. Las élites habaneras y sus clubes de recreo (1902–1930)*. Havana: Fundación Fernando Ortiz, 2009.

Gaceta Oficial de Cuba, 4 August 1952.

González Echevarría, Roberto. *La gloria de Cuba. Historia del béisbol en la isla*. Madrid: Colibrí, 2004.

Havana Yacht Club. *Libro de oro del HYC*. Havana: Author, 1936.

Libro de Cuba. Havana: Talleres litográficos de Artes Gráficas, 1954.

Mandell, Richard D. *Historia cultural del deporte*. Barcelona: Ediciones Bellaterra, 1986.

Méndez Muñiz, Antonio. *La pelota vasca en Cuba. Su evolución hasta 1930*. Havana: Científico-Técnica, 1990.

El Mundo Ilustrado, 20 October 1907.

Pérez, Louis A. Jr. *Ser cubano. Identidad, nacionalidad y cultura*. Havana: Ciencias Sociales, 2006.

Prado Pérez de Peñamil, Santiago. "Balompié: Alternativa simbólica de los españoles en Havana." *Temas* (January–March 2007).

Reig Romero, Carlos E. *VII Juegos Olímpicos: Ilusión cubana*. San Antonio de los Baños, Cuba: Editorial Unicornio, 2001.

Reig Romero, Carlos E. *YMCA de Havana: Memorias deportivas (1905–1910)*. Quito, Ecuador: Latin-American Council of Churches, 2003.

Reig Romero, Carlos E. *Historia del deporte cubano: Los inicios*. San Antonio de los Baños, Cuba: Editorial Unicornio, 2007.

Reig Romero, Carlos E. *Memorias del deporte universitario: Sus inicios*. San Antonio de los Baños, Cuba: Editorial Unicornio, 2009.

Rodríguez Busto, Emilio. *Una inmensa colmena. Historia-informe del Colegio, Presbiteriano La Progresiva*. Havana: Reformed Presbyterian Church of Cuba, 1991.

Sola, José Sixto de. "El deporte como factor patriótico y sociológico. Las grandes figuras deportivas en Cuba." In *Pensando en Cuba*. Havana: Cuba Contemporánea, 1917.

Vedado Tennis Club. *Libro de Oro 1902–1952*. Havana: Tipografía Ponciano, 1952.

SPORTS: REVOLUTIONARY PERIOD

Víctor Joaquín Ortega Izquierdo

Sports in Cuba after 1959.

When the Revolution triumphed in 1959, Cuba was home to champion athletes but did not have a large-scale sports program. Some sports were nearly impossible to engage in, and practicing a sport often required agonizing and heroic efforts. The new government authorities proposed to change this situation.

BUILDING THE BASICS: 1959–FEBRUARY 1961

On 24 January 1959, Fidel Castro declared: "We come here having made the decision to encourage sports and to go quite far with them" (quoted in Torres de Diego p. 19). The young process breathed new life into an old state entity: the Dirección General de Deportes (General Directorate of Sports).

As with other branches, it was impossible to immediately replace existing structures. There were positive steps, however: Twenty free facilities were constructed; various tournaments were initiated; and national teams were encouraged to travel outside the country. In addition, a truly national baseball tournament was organized in 1960, including 240 teams and 5,080 athletes, in which ultimately the University of Havana defeated the Mulos of Nicaro to win the event. Still, less than 1 percent of the population participated in organized sports in 1958, a figure that tripled, to 3 percent, in 1959 (Reig Romero p. 3).

Because of the broad transformations carried out by the Cuban government after 1959, the national sports system needed restructuring. The new system, called the Sistema de Cultura Física y Deportes (Physical Education and Sports System), encompassed four basic subsystems dedicated to the development of the following:

- Physical education, starting at an early age and continuing through university, as well as activities such as therapeutic exercises.
- Organization of sports competitions at a variety of levels among both the school-age and adult populations, the creation of Escuelas de Iniciación Deportiva (Schools for Introduction to Sports, EIDE), regional and municipal sports academies, and Escuelas Superiores de Perfeccionamiento Atlético (School of Higher Learning in Sports Excellence, ESPA), and the preparation of national sports teams.
- Training and improvement of teaching staff.
- Science and technology, especially sports medicine.

In addition, sports specialists in Cuba were provided with information centers, as well as their own lines of scientific research. In hierarchical terms, the structure could be understood as a pyramid whose base represents the spread of practice through physical education; the center involves specialization in different sports schools; and the peak is high-performance athletics.

THE DECISIVE PUSH: 1961–1970

On 23 February 1961, the Instituto Nacional de Deportes, Educación Física, y Recreación (National Institute of Sports, Physical Education, and Recreation, INDER) was born. It instituted, for the first time, a system of sports for the entire country, organized from the base (for the masses) through the peak (high-performance athletes). At the same time that sports for profit were being eliminated, planning began on a rationalized public system that would offer possibilities for all citizens, regardless of sex, income, race, or geographic location. Unknown or unpopular disciplines flourished; these included water polo, rhythmic gymnastics, fencing, weightlifting, and *tablas gimnásticas*, a team sport similar to dance or cheerleading in the United States. The state undertook the purchase or manufacture of equipment and also provided training and the use of facilities at no cost.

The transformation was based on the idea that the fundamental purpose of physical competitions is to forge physically and mentally superior human beings who are more complete and healthy, with physical education as a foundation. Physical education became a mandatory subject at all levels of schooling. Although championships, medals, and scores have encouraged a sense of team spirit, self-esteem, and national identity, the primary function of physical education in Cuba is to build people who are healthy in body and mind. Mass participation and its qualitative improvement guarantee high performance.

Cuba's regions, towns, municipalities, and provinces maintain Consejos Voluntarios Deportivos (Voluntary Sports Councils), organizations that bring together employees, professional trainers, volunteers, and representatives of youth, worker, women's, and neighborhood organizations to promote physical education. The Plan Montaña (Mountain Plan) was established in 1962 to construct playing fields and provide these sites with trainers and equipment.

In 1961, INDER established the Escuela Superior de Educación Física (School of Higher Learning in Physical Education) at the high-school level. It was taken to the university in 1965 and later became known as the Comandante Manuel Fajardo University of the Science of Physical Education and Sports. By 2010, it had granted 43,000 bachelor's degrees in physical education (along with 587 master's degrees and 152 doctorates); in addition, it had produced 82,000 graduates at the high-school level. In 1959, Cuba had one physical education instructor for every 10,000 residents; as of 2010 there was one for every 384. There was also a Department of Physical Education in each province (one for every 11,000 students) and eight high-school-level provincial schools (with 13,333 students).

The National Scholastic Games were launched in 1963. In this competition, qualifying athletes from the base levels compete in age categories. The Escuelas de Iniciación Deportiva (Schools for Introduction to Sports, EIDE) were established to provide initial training and preparation of children and adolescent athletes. These schools prioritized sports disciplines without neglecting academics, since poor grades make students ineligible to compete. Scholarships to these schools are available to those who demonstrate high ability; each province has one such school. In 2009, 370,323 students competed in the base-level elimination rounds; 95,809 in the municipal rounds; 18,916 in the provincial competitions; and 6,524 in the nationals. The pre-EIDE schools occupy a lesser rank, and beneath them are the regional sports associations designed to provide talent to the EIDEs.

Since 1965, the Cuban sports industry has worked to overcome the consequences for sports of the U.S. embargo (referred to as a "blockade" in Cuba) against Cuba. These efforts have been fundamental to the production of sports equipment to replace equipment not sold in Cuba or that comes from far away at high prices, such as bats, balls, gloves, masks, balance beams, vaulting horses, and soccer balls.

The 24 December 1965 founding of the Centro de Documentación e Información Científica y Técnica (Center for Documentation and Scientific and Technical Information, CEDOC) marked the beginning of the qualitative age of sports in Cuba, following the period of popular dissemination of sports and the consolidation of the tripartite revolutionary policy on sports. The Instituto de Medicina Deportiva (Institute for Sports Medicine) was established the following year. In 1970, the Frank País Orthopedic Hospital of Havana, with Dr. Rodrigo Álvarez Cambras at the head, began rehabilitation work with a group of twenty-eight paraplegic patients.

The ESPA, located in the capital, was opened in 1966. It was later renamed the Escuela Superior de Formación de Atletas de Alto Rendimiento Cerro Pelado (School of Higher Learning for the Training of High-Performance Athletes [ESFAAR] Cerro Pelado) and is home to the majority of high-performance athletes who are completing college preparatory and university studies. ESFAAR also runs national schools for gymnastics, volleyball, and boxing. The ESFAAR Córdova Cardín handles track and field and rowing.

In 1966, during the tenth Juegos Centroamericanos y del Caribe (Central American and Caribbean Games) in San Juan, Puerto Rico, the U.S. government prohibited the airplane carrying the Cuban delegation from landing, so the Cubans arrived by ship; even so, there was an attempt to prevent them from disembarking. U.S. airplanes even flew over the ship, anchored across the Bay of San Juan, where the athletes awaited authorization to disembark. Finally, the athletes boarded motorboats that carried them toward the city, where they marched, competed, and finished in second place. Such events defined sports as the new space for ideological battles outside the country.

In the eleventh Juegos Centroamericanos y del Caribe in Panama City in 1970, Cuba took first place, with 210 medals (98 gold, 61 silver, and 51 bronze), followed by Mexico with 124 (38 gold, 46 silver, and 40 bronze). Thereafter, Cuba won the most medals at all the Juegos Centroamericanos y del Caribe, except the 2004 San Salvador and 2010 Mayagüez games, when Cuba did not participate due to poor security conditions.

In the 1963 Pan American Games in São Paulo, Cuba placed fifth (4 gold, 6 silver, and 4 bronze). Cuba took fourth place (8 gold, 14 silver, and 26 bronze) in the 1967 Pan American Games in Winnipeg. In the sixth Pan American Games in Cali in 1971, Cuba placed second with 105 medals (30 gold, 49 silver, and 26 bronze). Between 1971 and 2010, Cuba was only defeated by the U.S. delegation, with the exception of the eleventh games in Havana-Santiago in 1991, when the United States fell to second with fewer gold medals: Cuba: 140 gold, 62 silver, and 63 bronze versus the United States: 130 gold, 125 silver, and 97 bronze. In the eighteenth Olympic Games in Tokyo in 1964, a Cuban athlete won the country's first Olympic medal after the Revolution; Enrique Figuerola won a silver medal in the 100 meters (10.2 seconds). In Mexico in 1968, the Cuban team won four gold medals: in the women's short relay and men's short relay, and in light welterweight and light middleweight boxing.

During this period, the Cuban sports program received multidimensional support from the socialist bloc, with the Soviet Union at its head. This support included trainers, classes, scrimmages overseas or in Cuba, sports equipment, exchange of experiences, and training for sports scientists. This relationship was maintained until the 1989 dissolution of the Eastern Europe socialist bloc and the 1991 disintegration of the Soviet Union.

ADVANCE: 1971–1980

By the 1970s, the demand for teachers and educational technicians had been met. This accomplishment was accompanied by increased participation of students and the number of academic sports centers, as well as a notable rise in the number of international competitions that Cuba attended. In the sixth Pan American Games held in Cali, Colombia, in 1971, triple jumper Pedro Pérez Dueñas achieved the first world record for a Cuban athlete under the revolutionary government. From that time until the 2007 games in Rio de Janeiro, the Cuban team placed second in the Pan American games behind the United States delegation.

In boxing, bantamweight Orlando Martínez became Cuba's first postrevolutionary Olympic champion when he won a gold medal in Munich in 1972. In the Moscow Olympics in 1980, javelin thrower María Caridad Colón became the first Latin American woman to win gold in this type of competition with a throw of 68.40 meters, while heavyweight boxer Teófilo Stevenson won his third Olympic gold, and Cuba took fourth place in the medal tally (8 gold, 7 silver, and 5 bronze). In the Montreal Olympic Games in 1976, Alberto Juantorena became the first runner in history to win both the 400- and 800-meter races.

During this phase, physical education in Cuba developed as a pathway for integrating those with physical or mental disabilities into society. One outcome of this project has been Cuba's participation in the Paralympic Games, the Parapan American Games, and other competitions. Santiago native Yunidis Castillo won the 100- and 200-meter races at the 2008 Paralympic Games in Beijing.

In 1976, the Mártires de Barbados (Barbados Martyrs) EIDE was inaugurated in Havana. The school was named in honor of a group of young Cuban athletes (mostly fencers) who died on 6 October 1976 when their airplane was sabotaged en route home after the fourth Central American and Caribbean Tournament. This crime intensified ideological feelings among Cubans about the country's achievements in sports. In a ceremony on 15 October 1976, Fidel Castro condemned the crime: "Our athletes, sacrificed in the blossoming of their lives and their abilities, will be eternal champions in our hearts. Their medals shall not lie at the bottom of the ocean; they shall be raised as untarnished suns and as symbols on the firmament of Cuba" (quoted in Torres de Diego p. 152).

EXCELLENCE: 1981–1992; RESISTANCE: 1993–1999

The dissolution between 1989 and 1991 of the European socialist bloc, with whose countries Cuba had maintained most of its trade and with whom it coordinated its development plans, caused an economic crisis for the practice of sports in Cuba. Despite this change, no schools closed and no physical education services halted, although there were fewer. Cuba also

National Olympic Games, Havana, 2004. Osniel Tosca competes in the triple jump event in the Cuban National Olympic Games in Havana on 24 April 2004. Tosca placed second with a jump of 17.03 meters. JUAN CARLOS ULATER/REUTERS/LANDOV

maintained its record of achievement in international competitions. However, some traditional competitions, such as the Cycle Tour of Cuba, were suspended, while others, such as the National Series of Baseball, revised their schedules so games could be played during the day to conserve electricity. During this period, Cuba also struggled with the acquisition of sports equipment, participation in high-level international competitions, the nutrition of athletes, and the maintenance and renovation of stadiums, among other challenges.

Important moments during these years include the celebration of the fourteenth Juegos Centroamericanos y del Caribe in Havana in 1982, the eleventh Pan American Games in Havana in 1991, and participation in the Barcelona Olympic Games in 1992, where Cuba finished in fifth place (14 gold, 8 silver, and 11 bronze) out of 169 nations. The best Cuban team of all time, the Cuban women's volleyball team, began its hegemony in Barcelona and later dominated the Olympic Games of 1996 and 2000. The team was led by the best women's volleyball coach in the world, Eugenio George; the best player, Regla Torres; and the most spectacular and popular player, Mireya Luis. George and Torres were selected in October 2000 by a jury of the Fédération Internationale de Volleyball (FIVB) as the best coach and player of the last century.

RECOVERY: 2000–2010

On 13 February 2000, the first Cuban antidoping laboratory was opened. Cuban technicians work in more than fifty countries, primarily in the Third World. On 23 February 2000, the Escuela Internacional de Educación Física y Deporte (International School for Physical Education and Sports) opened its doors. By 2010, this institution had graduated hundreds of young people from seventy-one countries, mostly in Latin America.

In 2006, the Cuban national baseball team placed second after Japan in the World Baseball Classic. In the 2008 Summer Olympic Games in Beijing, the drop in the level of Cuban sports became apparent when Cuba came in twenty-eighth, with only two gold medals: Dayron Robles (110-meter hurdles) and Mijaín López (Greco-Roman wrestling, 120 kilos). In an article in *Granma* on 25 August 2008 titled "Para el honor, medalla de oro" (For Honor, the Gold) Fidel Castro opined: "We have rested on our laurels. Let's be honest and all recognize it.... Let's review each discipline, each human and material resource that we dedicate to sport. We should be deep in our analysis, apply new ideas, concepts, and knowledge."

CONCLUSION

After the revolution in 1959, Cuba joined the elite in two sports, boxing and baseball, although the latter is played in relatively few countries. More than fifty years later, the Cuban sports movement maintains its status in both boxing and baseball, in addition to reaping top-level achievements in track and field, volleyball,

fencing, cycling, weightlifting, tae kwon do, freestyle wrestling, Greco-Roman wrestling, judo, chess, kayaking, rowing, shooting, and diving. Between 1976 and 2004, the country was among the twenty best teams in the Summer Olympic Games, in addition to maintaining second place in the Pan American Games and first place in the Central American and Caribbean Games.

Transformations in the economic life of the Cuban people have promoted numerous private gyms throughout the country and the development of bodybuilding. The legends in this discipline, which is still an exhibition sport, include Cuban athlete Sergio Oliva, who, after leaving the country, built a career in the United States.

Among the problems facing the Cuban sports program, the following are notable: difficulty in acquiring or manufacturing equipment; disproportionate emphasis on body type; decreases in mass participation in sports or lack of a systematic approach; mistakes in the promotion of directives; and a lack of maintenance of sports facilities. In addition, the worldwide growth of professional sports means that more Cuban athletes are tempted to abandon their amateur-only country and join professional teams abroad.

In summary, the policy applied to sports in Cuba yielded the hoped-for results, and in less than thirty years (1964 to 1992) Cuba advanced from thirty-third to fifth in the Olympic Games. At a historic level, the country had accumulated 194 Olympic medals as of 2008 (among the top twenty countries by number of medals), along with 1,793 in the Pan American games, occupying second place over such nations as Canada, Brazil, Mexico, and Argentina.

BIBLIOGRAPHY

Castro Ruiz, Fidel. "Para el honor, medalla de oro," Reflexiones del compañero Fidel. *Granma* 25 August 2008. Available from http://www.granma.cubaweb.cu/secciones/ref-fidel/art40.html

Durántez, Conrado. *Pierre de Coubertin y la filosofía del olimpismo.* Madrid: Spanish Olympic Academy, 1995.

Forbes, Irene, Ana María Luján, and Juan Velázquez. *Famosos y desconocidos: Cubanos en Juegos Olímpicos.* Havana: Editorial Pueblo y Educación. 2003.

Hernández, Armando S. *Deporte cubano: Por un camino de victoria.* Havana: Editorial Deportes, 2006.

Montesinos, Enrique. *Juegos Panamericanos: Desde Buenos Aires–1951 hasta Santo Domingo–2003.* Havana: Editorial Deportes, 2007.

Ortega, Víctor Joaquín. *Desde Atenas, las Olimpiadas.* Havana: Editorial Abril, 1988.

Ortega, Víctor Joaquín. *Cuba en los Panamericanos.* Havana: Editorial Gente Nueva. 1991.

Reig Romero, Carlos E. "Primer inning del béisbol revolucionario." In *Con las bases llenas: Béisbol, historia y revolución,* edited By Félix Julio Alfonso, 1–12. Havana: Editorial Científico-Técnica, 2008.

Torres de Diego, Mario José. *Fidel y el deporte: Selección de pensamientos 1959–2006.* 2nd ed. Havana: Editorial Deportes, 2007.

SPORTS: BASEBALL BEFORE 1959

Félix Julio Alfonso López

The development of Cuban amateur and professional leagues, including interaction with American leagues, prior to the abolition of professional sports in Cuba in 1961.

Beginning in 1900 the Cuban League, founded in 1878, became a fully professional baseball organization comprised of four teams: Havana, Almendares, Fe, and San Francisco. The league changed names and teams several times over the next four decades. In the 1940s it was established as the Cuban Professional Baseball League, with four teams: Havana, Almendares, Marianao, and Cienfuegos.

THE BIG LEAGUES IN CUBA, CUBANS IN THE BIG LEAGUES

The strong influence of the United States on republican Cuban society was seen early in the twentieth century in the frequent visits by Major League teams. Among the most notable is the visit by the Cincinnati Reds in 1908, during the second U.S. military occupation of Cuba (1906–1909). Losing seven of the eleven games played, the visiting team was defeated three times by black pitcher José de la Caridad Méndez, known as "the Black Diamond." In games at Almendares Park between 15 November and 24 December 1908, Méndez tallied forty-five consecutive scoreless innings against the Reds, the independent Key West league, and Havana.

In another great feat of Cuban baseball, on 6 November 1920 outfielder Cristóbal Torriente led the Almendares team to an 11-to-4 victory against the New York Giants, with Babe Ruth added to their barnstorming roster. Torriente scored three home runs, blasted a double against Ruth (who was sent in to pitch in the fifth inning), and batted in six runs. Ruth was able to connect for only one hit in the entire game.

In the first decades of the twentieth century, the prestige achieved by Cuban ballplayers paved the way for a handful of them to sign with Major League teams. Rafael Almeida and Armando Marsans signed with the Cincinnati Reds in 1910, and catcher Miguel Ángel González played for a total of seventeen years with the Boston Braves, the Cincinnati Reds, the Saint Louis Cardinals, the New York Giants, and the Chicago Cubs. Adolfo Luque, known for his feistiness and love of cockfighting, was called the "Pride of Havana" in the United States and "Papá Montero" by Cuban fans. Luque played in the National League for twenty years, with a record of 194 games won and striking out 1,130 rival batters; in the Cuban League, his record was 93 wins and 62 losses.

Afro-Cuban player Martín Dihígo Llanos, considered the greatest Cuban baseball player of all time, had an exceptional career in Cuba, the American Negro Leagues, Mexico, Venezuela, and the Dominican Republic. Known as "El Inmortal" (the immortal) in Cuba and "El Maestro" (the master) in Mexico, Dihígo played all nine positions. As pitcher he accumulated a record of more than 260 wins and as hitter generally batted over .300. Standing 6 feet 1 inch tall, friendly and charismatic, he had a formidable arm and a crushing pitch. He is the only player to be inducted into a Hall of Fame in each of four countries: Cuba, Mexico, Venezuela, and the United States.

Cuban baseball in the 1950s was symbolized by "Minnie" Miñoso (Saturnino Orestes Armas Miñoso Arrieta), who played outfield and infield. From very humble origins, Miñoso debuted on amateur teams and in 1944 was signed by Marianao. That year he was elected Rookie of the Year in Cuba. In 1945 he signed with the Cubans of New York, a Negro League team, which won the championship. In 1949 he began to play for the Cleveland Indians, and after a brief time with the minor league San Diego Padres, in 1951 he became the first black player on the Chicago White Sox, where he played third base, batted .326, scored 112 runs, and was the leader in stolen bases (31) and triples (14) in the American League.

The construction of the Grand Stadium of Cerro in 1946 was a milestone in the history of Cuban baseball. The result of a silent war among the power groups

■ *See also*

Florida

The World and Cuba: U.S. Culture in Cuba

Luis "Mulo" Padrón. Pitcher Luis "Mulo" Padrón of the Havana Lions warms up before a game at Almendares Park in Havana in 1908. MARK RUCKER/TRANSCENDENTAL GRAPHICS/GETTY IMAGES

**Martín Dihígo Llanos
(1906–1971).** Cuban
baseball great Martín
Dihígo is pictured on
a 1946 tobacco card
wearing a Cienfuegos
uniform. MARK RUCKER/
TRANSCENDENTAL
GRAPHICS/GETTY IMAGES

organizations were the Popular Workers Baseball League, Quivicán League, Pedro Betancourt League, Inter-provincial League of Las Villas, Free Amateur Athletic Union of Oriente, and the leagues of the sugar refinery industry, almost all of them providing talent to the profitable winter championship. The World Series of Amateur Baseball, played in Havana beginning in 1939, featured many of the league's biggest talents. In these tournaments the Cuban national team beat out its rivals on multiple occasions. Perhaps the most memorable matchup, however, was a championship playoff game on 22 October 1941 in La Tropical Stadium between Cuba and Venezuela. In a dramatic conclusion, Daniel "El Chino" Canónico led the Venezuelans to a 3-to-1 victory over the powerful local team, which had pulled its pitching star Conrado "Connie" Marrero after only two innings.

THE CARIBBEAN SERIES

In the late 1940s baseball promoters decided to hold a baseball event that would bring together the professional champions of all the Caribbean nations prior to the start of the Major League season. This event, called the Caribbean Series, showcased Latin American players who were playing in Major League Baseball in the United States. Havana hosted the Caribbean Series three times, in 1949, 1953, and 1957, and Cuban teams won in seven of the twelve series in which they participated up to 1960: Almendares (1949), managed by Fermín Guerra; Havana (1952), captained by Miguel Ángel González; Cienfuegos (1956), with victories by Camilo Pascual and Pedro Ramos; Marianao (1957), with Minnie Miñoso, Solly Drake, and star pitcher Jim Bunning; Marianao again (1958), managed by Napoleón Reyes, with Miñoso and José Valdivieso at the head of the offense; Almendares (1959), with an all-star team that included Tony Taylor, Rocky Nelson, Guillermo "Willy" Miranda, Miguel "Mike" Cuéllar, and Camilo Pascual; and Cienfuegos (1960), managed by Tony Castaños, with pitching by Pascual and Orlando Peña and outfielder George Altman leading in hits.

THE 1950s: THE END OF AN ERA

Despite international success and high salaries earned by many players, the 1950s were years of slow decline for Cuban professional ball. As the journalist Eladio Secades, describing the discouraging situation of the island's baseball, observed, "the mystical quality of Havana and Almendares, so much ours, so powerful, with such deep-rooted tradition, is experiencing a crisis, if not of complete inhibition, at least of lethargy, that hopefully will not last a long time" (p. 208).

The connection with organized baseball in the United States was closer in the 1950s than in any other period. The list of Major League players who participated in the Cuban winter league included Brooks Robinson, Carl Erskine, Gene Mauch, Sal Maglie, Billy Herman, Don Zimmer, and Joe Black (for Cienfuegos); Roy Campanella, Jim Bunning,

of baseball on the island, it displaced the dominance that La Tropical had held thus far. The colossus, which boasted a capacity of thirty thousand and a modern, efficient lighting system, was financed by businessman Roberto "Bobby" Maduro, at a cost estimated at around 2 million pesos. The Cienfuegos and Almendares teams played the first game in the stadium on 26 October.

AMATEUR BASEBALL

The 1940s marked the Golden Age of amateur ball. The first league, the Amateur Athletic Union, was founded in 1914 and admitted only white players. Its principal teams throughout its history were Vedado Tennis Club, Atlético de Cuba, Hershey Sport Club, University of Havana, Fortuna, San Antonio de los Baños Artisans Group, Club Atlético de Santiago de las Vegas, Liceo de Regla, Artemisa, Deportivo Matanzas, Telefónicos, and Cubaneleco. Other amateur and semiprofessional

Charlie Lau, and Don Newcombe (for Marianao); Tom Lasorda, Dick Williams, Bob Allison, Roger Craig, Gus Triandos, Jim Grant, Bobby Bragan, Bob Skinner, Billy Hunter, and Willie Mays (for Almendares); and Ken Boyer, Bill Virdon, Hoyt Wilhelm, Dick Sisler, Wally Moon, and Eddie Kasko (for Havana). A Triple-A league based in the eastern United States known as the International League even had a team in Havana known as the Sugar Kings beginning in 1954. The Sugar Kings went on to win the league's Little World Series championship in 1959.

This cooperation between baseball promoters in the United States and Cuba ended shortly after the Cuban Revolution in 1959, as the ideological differences between the two countries led the United States to establish an embargo against Cuba in 1960. American baseball leagues followed suit. Major League Baseball banned Cuban nationals from playing in the league unless they defected and likewise forbade American players from traveling to Cuba to play. Major League Baseball commissioner Ford Frick decided to move the 1961 Caribbean Series, slated to be held in Havana, to Caracas, Venezuela. He also decided to exclude the Cuban national team, which had won the competition the year before. Venezuela refused to organize the event in protest, and the Caribbean Series was suspended until it was revived in 1970.

The January 1959 revolution also had a profound impact on baseball within Cuba's borders. The revolutionary government abolished professional sports leagues in 1961, including professional baseball. The government believed that the value of sports in promoting the health and welfare of the general population needed to be disassociated from the motivation of profit inherent in paying individuals to play. In support of the important new measures enacted by the revolutionary government, on 24 July a symbolic game was played between the Barbudos (the bearded ones, or the revolutionary guerrillas) and the National Revolutionary Police, with Fidel Castro and Camilo Cienfuegos in the lineup for the Barbudos. On 7 February 1961 the last professional baseball game was played in Cuba, between Cienfuegos and Almendares, symbolically the same teams that had inaugurated the Cerro Stadium fifteen years earlier.

BIBLIOGRAPHY

Bjarkman, Peter C. *A History of Cuban Baseball, 1864–2006*. Jefferson, NC: McFarland & Company, 2007.

Casas, Edel, Jorge Alfonso, and Alberto Pestana. *Viva y en juego*. Havana: Editorial Científico Técnica, 1986.

Diez y Muro, Raúl. *El Base Ball en La Habana, Matanzas y Cárdenas: Resumen de los campeonatos celebrados por nuestros clubs de profesionales desde 1878 a 1907*. 1907. 2nd ed. Havana: Imprenta La Prueba, 1949.

Dihígo Castillo, Gilberto. *Mi padre "El Inmortal."* Santo Domingo, Dominican Republic: Impresos El Siglo, 2002.

González Echevarría, Roberto. *The Pride of Havana: A History of Cuban Baseball*. New York: Oxford University Press, 1999.

Nieto Fernández, Severo. *Conrado Marrero: El Premier*. Havana: Editorial Científico Técnica, 2000.

Nieto Fernández, Severo. *José Méndez: El diamante negro*. Havana: Editorial Científico Técnica, 2004.

Pérez, Louis A. Jr. *On Becoming Cuban: Identity, Nationality, and Culture*. Chapel Hill: University of North Carolina Press, 2008.

Rucker, Mark, and Peter C. Bjarkman. *Smoke: The Romance and Lore of Cuban Baseball*. Kingston, NY: Total Sports Illustrated, 1999.

Santana Alonso, Alfredo. *El inmortal del béisbol: Martín Dihígo*. Havana: Editorial Científico Técnica, 2006.

Santana Alonso, Alfredo. *Un astro del montículo: El diamante negro*. Havana: Editorial Científico Técnica, 2009.

Secades, Eladio. "Primeras noticias del Base Ball." *Diario de la Marina* (15 September 1957).

Sola, José Sixto de. "El deporte como factor patriótico y sociológico: Las grandes figuras deportivas de Cuba." *Cuba Contemporánea* 5, no. 2 (1914): 121–167.

Torres, Ángel. *La leyenda del Béisbol Cubano, 1878–1997*. Montebello, CA: Author, 1996.

SPORTS: BASEBALL AFTER 1959

Peter C. Bjarkman

An alternative universe of top-flight baseball featuring homegrown talent.

The popular national sport of baseball maintained and tightened its dominant hold on the island nation of Cuba in the aftermath of the 1959 socialist revolution. In fact, the sport actually expanded in popularity and elevated in talent level during several decades immediately following Fidel Castro's mid-century rise to power. Once the four-team professional winter league affiliated with North American Major League baseball was shut down after the 1961 season due to political tension between the United States and Cuba, the door was finally thrown open for establishing a truly island-wide baseball circuit that would feature homegrown talent rather than imported foreign professionals.

This new version of Cuban baseball launched a five-decade domination of international tournament competitions that as of 2011 stands as the centerpiece of nearly a century and a half of island baseball history. With its novel brand of postrevolutionary amateur baseball, Cuba also developed during the second half of the twentieth century a genuine alternative universe to better publicized professional circuits represented by the North American and Japanese professional leagues.

■ *See also*

Cuban Thought and Cultural Identity: Costumbres in the Revolutionary Period

Governance and Contestation: The Cuban Revolution

THE MYSTERY AND MYTHS OF CUBAN BASEBALL

The political estrangement between Cuba and the United States after 1962 not only largely ended the earlier moderate flow of Cuban ballplayers to North American major and minor league teams but also cast an aura of mystery over baseball development on the island. North American fans knew little about island baseball developments between the early 1960s and the early 2000s. Island league stars played in the same virtual obscurity as did the North American Negro Leaguers of the first half of the twentieth century. One result of this isolation from the mainstream North American sporting press is the persistence of several widespread myths concerning Cuba's postrevolutionary baseball era. First and most damaging has been a notion that the level of Cuban baseball diminished dramatically once the professional winter league was scrapped for a new form of amateur baseball competition. A related and equally false notion is one suggesting that inferior amateur play replaced superior professional competitions as the central focus of the Cuban national sport.

Those maintaining this latter view overlook the fact that widespread pre-1950 amateur leagues across the island drew far more interest and produced more native island talent than did the Havana-based pro circuit of the pre-Castro era. The Cuban winter league of the earlier epoch attracted most of its star players from among imported North American Negro Leaguers, drew a fan following among few Cubans living outside the capital city, and produced only a tiny handful of native big leaguers of true all-star stature, namely Adolfo Luque (1920s), Orestes Miñoso (1950s), and Camilo Pascual (1960s). Greater impact on Major League Baseball came from an equally small group of Cuban-born athletes who chose to play professionally in the United States after the Revolution (Sandy Amorós, Zoilo Versalles, Tony Oliva, and Luis Tiant Jr.), along with Florida-raised Cuban Americans such as José Canseco and Rafael Palmeiro. It is also indisputable that a half-dozen Cuban Leaguers who abandoned the island during the late 1990s and early twenty-first century for big league careers in the United States far outstripped the achievements of the small cadre of pre-Revolution Cuban big leaguers. Among the new generation of superior Cuban major leaguers originally trained in the post-1962 Cuban circuit are slugger Kendry Morales of the Los Angeles Angels of Anaheim, flashy infielder Alexei Ramírez of the Chicago White Sox, and pitchers Orlando "El Duque" Hernández, José Contreras, and Liván Hernández, as well as fastball phenomenon Aroldis Chapman.

THE CUBAN NATIONAL SERIES

The Cuban League—known as the Cuban National Series—celebrated its fiftieth season with the campaign that began in November 2010. This National Series competition slowly evolved since the early 1960s through several manifestations. While geographically based league teams have always represented provinces (states) or groups of provinces, these clubs have often changed names from year to year, and only beginning in the first decade of the twenty-first century have the teams been consistently named for the home province, with a team nickname attached (e.g., Cienfuegos Elephants, Villa Clara Orangemen, Camagüey Potters). The league structure for the 2010–2011 season involved fourteen provincial teams and two ball clubs (Industriales Blue Lions and Metropolitanos Warriors) representing the capital city of Havana. There were also several manifestations along the way of a second (usually shorter) Cuban league season. A Selective Series (often with the fourteen provincial clubs combined into eight regional all-star squads) operated in late spring and summer between 1975 and 1995. In addition, a short four- or five-team Super League was staged in June during the early years of the twenty-first century (2002–2005).

National Series play was inaugurated in mid-January 1962 and involved only a handful of teams during its earliest campaigns. Players were drawn from all areas of the island, and the initial teams—known as Occidentales, Azucareros, Orientales, and Habana—played the bulk of the opening-season twenty-seven-game schedule in Havana's Cerro Stadium (renamed Latinoamericano Stadium in 1971 and still in use in the early twenty-first century). Over the course of its opening decade, the National Series expanded to first six teams (1966) and eventually twelve ball clubs (1968). The number of games for each club expanded to sixty-five by mid-decade (1966) and eventually to ninety-nine (1968). The league reached its full stride once all provinces were represented by the mid-1970s and once postseason playoffs were introduced for the 1985–1986 season as a means of determining an eventual league champion. As the ever-changing league evolved in size, it also regularly changed in shape, with a division into two groups or zones after 1988, and then four groups after 1993. A two-division structure—with a western league (Occidental) and eastern league (Oriental)—was once again adopted with the 2007–2008 season, and a ninety-game schedule has been the standard since National Series #37 (1997–1998).

The National Series structure of the early 1960s not only expanded organized league baseball island-wide for the first time, it also extended and expanded a tradition of popular amateur leagues that had been at the center of the nation's baseball since its origins in the late nineteenth and early twentieth centuries. Amateur baseball had always been the island's most popular sport, and it did not appear—as some accounts have it—only with the Castro-led revolutionary government of the early 1960s. Throughout the century's first five decades, it was not the racially integrated Havana pro circuit but rather the more geographically diverse and all-white amateur league that drew both the largest fan followings and the island's top athletic talent. Many skilled players chose to remain amateurs because amateur teams offered greater financial

rewards (lucrative jobs with sponsoring companies) and easier playing conditions (games played only on weekends). The Cuban League of the early twenty-first century, however, is no longer amateur in the strict sense because players are salaried and devote their entire energies to their baseball profession. It is the lack of any corporate team ownership or ballplayer free agency that sustains a largely amateur flavor for the government-run Cuban baseball enterprise.

DEFINING CHARACTERISTICS OF CUBAN BASEBALL

Cuban baseball of the modern post-Revolution era is characterized by two unique features—the league's geographical rather than corporate structure and the fact that ballplayers perform for regional teams during the entire duration of their careers. Having ball clubs represent provinces and not private businesses results in intense fan loyalties because one's local team is comprised of strictly hometown athletes. This feature of fan loyalty is intensified by the fact that Cuban ballplayers are never sold or traded from one club to another, thus remaining with the hometown squad for their entire career. One consequence of such a regional structure is imbalanced competition because more populous regions have greater access to ball-playing talent; another result is the added attraction of true regional competitions. Havana's Industriales Blue Lions remain the island's most popular club, which is not surprising given that this team represents the capital city region, home to one-third of the nation's population. The Industriales team (as documented in Ian Padrón's award-winning 2007 documentary film, *Fuera de la liga*) has also enjoyed the greatest championship success: The Lions have claimed a dozen title banners, four more than the Santiago de Cuba Wasps ball club, which represents the island's second most populous region.

The second defining characteristic of Cuban League baseball is that a championship season exists with the primary purpose of training and selecting national team rosters for top-level international competitions. Since the 1960s, the focus of Cuban baseball has been on capturing international championships and thus fostering the nation's celebrated socialist-style sporting image. Cuba's national teams have as a result dominated international baseball since the early 1960s and established a winning ledger that is one of the most remarkable in the history of the sport at any level. During this half-century, Cuba's national teams either won or reached the championship game of more than fifty straight major international tournaments. This unparalleled streak finally came to an end with a second-round ouster of Team Cuba at the 2009 World Baseball Classic. Cuban teams during that half-century maintained their dominance by capturing three gold and two silver medals in the five official Olympic baseball tournaments, as well as winning eighteen of the twenty-two championship banners contested in the Baseball World Cup matches governed by the International Baseball Federation (IBAF). Team Cuba's overall individual-game winning percentage also stands well above 90 percent.

TOP INDIVIDUAL PERFORMANCES AND STARS

The Cuban League has been especially noted for numerous unusual individual performances, some rarely if

World Cup champions. The Cuban team poses after defeating Panama to win the 2003 Baseball World Cup. PETER C. BJARKMAN

ever duplicated in the world's other top professional circuits. One of the most noteworthy was the home-run-hitting feats of Santiago outfielder Alexei Bell, who during the 2009–2010 season blasted a record seven bases-loaded home runs in the league's short ninety-game schedule. Bell began the 2009–2010 season with consecutive grand slam home runs in the initial inning of the season's opening game. Also noteworthy is the long-ball-hitting of Granma star Alfredo Despaigne, who established a new single-season mark for thirty-two home runs during the 2008–2009 season and then slugged another thirty-one a season later. Perhaps more remarkable still were the five consecutive batting titles of Las Tunas star Osmani Urrutia. Between 2000 and 2005, Urrutia compiled a five-season composite batting average above .400 (.422), a feat never equaled in North American major league competition.

Many top Cuban stars of the late twentieth and early twenty-first centuries have ranked among the world's best ballplayers, despite having never showcased their talents in the professional North American major leagues. Pinar del Río mainstay Omar Linares—the Cuban League career batting leader with a lifetime .368 average compiled over twenty National Series and Selective Series seasons—was for two decades considered the world's best amateur player and the greatest third baseman never to appear in the major leagues. In addition, the two stagings of the World Baseball Classic sponsored by Major League Baseball in 2006 and 2009 demonstrated that Cuban League all-stars can easily match major leaguers in top-level tournament competitions. Cuba surprised the professional baseball world by reaching the finals of the initial MLB event, while outfielder Freddie

Cepeda was the only unanimous all-star selection at the 2009 World Baseball Classic. Also noteworthy is that the aforementioned Despaigne established an all-time home run mark—eleven in fifteen games—while leading the Cuban national squad to the finals of the 2009 Baseball World Cup, which was held in Europe.

BIBLIOGRAPHY

Alfonso López, Félix Julio. *Con las bases llenas: Béisbol, historia y revolución.* Havana: Editorial Científico-Técnica, 2008.

Bjarkman, Peter C. *A History of Cuban Baseball, 1864–2006.* Jefferson, NC: McFarland, 2007.

Bjarkman, Peter C. *Baseball's Other Big Red Machine: The History of the Cuban National Team.* Jefferson, NC: McFarland, 2011.

Jamail, Milton H. *Full Count: Inside Cuban Baseball.* Carbondale: Southern Illinois University Press, 2000.

SPORTS: BOXING BEFORE 1959

Enver M. Casimir

The history of boxing in Cuba before 1959, tracing it from an activity that was banned by authorities to a sport that produced many of Cuba's most famous athletes.

Between 1910 and 1959 Cuba evolved from a country in which boxing was virtually nonexistent to the

■ *See also*

Cuban Thought and Cultural Identity: Costumbres in the Republican Period

Kid Chocolate

home of dozens of world-class boxers. Encouragement by the state, the activities of promoters, and the aspirations of young athletes combined to create a vibrant boxing culture on the island. Details about the first boxing match to take place in Cuba are most likely lost to history, but the Chilean John Budinich has been credited with having opened the first boxing gym in Havana in 1910. Hoping to earn a living as a boxing instructor, Budinich also staged exhibition matches in order to generate interest in his services, and there was enough interest to make his gym a moderate success. Many of the fighters Budinich trained went on to become trainers, further spreading knowledge of the sport within Cuba. During the 1910s fights often were staged in the homes of either boxers themselves or their close friends, but Budinich and other promoters also managed to stage fights in public venues in Havana and some provincial cities.

During the 1910s Cuban authorities made a number of attempts to suppress the sport. In 1912 the Interior Ministry issued a directive banning boxing matches on the island in the wake of violence and racial conflict related to the suppression of the Partido Independiente de Color that occurred in spring of that year. The purpose of the decree was to prevent public disturbances that might occur during matches between white and black boxers. The prohibition notwithstanding, fights continued clandestinely for a number of years. It is unclear how long the decree remained in effect, but early in 1915 the American businessman George Brandt, owner of the *Havana Post*, opened the first venue in Havana dedicated solely to boxing. Known as the Stadium, the venue hosted a number of fights between American boxers and met with limited commercial success before Brandt closed it due to lack of fan interest.

JOHNSON-WILLARD HEAVYWEIGHT TITLE FIGHT

The interest of Cuban fans was reenergized when Jack Johnson (1878–1946), the first African American world heavyweight champion, came to Havana to defend his title against challenger Jess Willard (1891–1968) in April 1915. Because Johnson was wanted in the United States after having been convicted of violating the Mann Act, Havana was chosen as a venue; it was outside U.S. jurisdiction but close enough to attract American fans. The fight drew tremendous interest, attracting a crowd of 32,000 spectators. The *New York Tribune* declared that Havana was "fight mad" in the days leading up to the bout. The Cuban Congress canceled activities on the day of the fight so that its members could attend, and President Mario García Menocal also came and watched Johnson lose his title to Willard via a knockout in the twenty-sixth round. Whether Johnson deliberately lost the fight has been the subject of considerable debate. In Cuba most people believe that Johnson deliberately threw the fight in

what was described as "the farce of the century"; in the United States, the loss was generally considered genuine.

The legitimacy of the results notwithstanding, the fight had the effect of generating lasting Cuban interest in the sport. Increasingly, foreign boxers were brought to the island to headline programs; Cuban boxers fought in preliminary bouts. When Varona Suárez, the mayor of Havana, issued decrees prohibiting boxing in the city in 1916 and again in 1919, promoters organized tours in the provinces. In addition, private social and athletic clubs began organizing tournaments for amateurs. Although Suárez's ban inhibited matches in the capital, it also had the effect of promoting the popularity of the sport elsewhere on the island. The 1910s saw a steady growth of the sport in Cuba despite state suppression.

OFFICIAL SANCTION AND CONTINUED GROWTH

In the 1920s state suppression became official sanction. In 1921 the Ministry of the Interior created the National Boxing and Wrestling Commission, granting full legitimacy to the sport. The commission was charged with the tasks of licensing professional boxers, authorizing programs, and determining national champions. One year later the ban on boxing in Havana was lifted, and the Amateur Athletic Union established a boxing commission to oversee competition and hold national tournaments. By summer 1922 even boxing tournaments for boys were being staged in Havana. The performance of the National Boxing Commission was mixed at best, and contemporary observers often complained about its inability to prevent the staging of fixed bouts and to adequately oversee the licensing of boxers. Nonetheless, during the 1920s engagements in Havana proliferated. Venues such as Arena Polar, the Miramar Garden, and Arena Colón staged boxing programs on a regular basis. Young Cuban athletes increasingly dedicated themselves to becoming accomplished pugilists.

Many of these aspiring young boxers became skillful enough to pursue successful professional careers abroad. Among the most famous of these were Kid Charol (Esteban Gallard, 1901–1929), who boxed professionally in Argentina from 1926 to 1929, and Black Bill (Eladio Valdes, 1905–1933), who became the first Cuban to fight for a world title, achieving moderate success in the United States before succumbing to blindness and later committing suicide. The most successful Cuban boxer to seek fame and fortune abroad during this period was Kid Chocolate (Eligio Sardiñas Montalvo, 1910–1988). Chocolate achieved tremendous success in the boxing mecca of New York, becoming a fan favorite. He drew tens of thousands of fans to venues such as Madison Square Garden and the Polo Grounds and garnered acclaim from critics as one the best boxers of the day. In July 1931 he became the first

Kid Gavilán (1926–2003). Cuban boxer Gerardo González, better known as Kid Gavilán (left), won the world welterweight championship in 1951 and held it for more than three years. He is shown here in a bout against French boxer Laurent Dautheuille in Montreal on 21 November 1949. © BETTMANN/CORBIS

■ *See also*

Cuban Thought and Cultural Identity: Costumbres in the Revolutionary Period

Governance and Contestation: The Cuban Revolution

Cuban to win a world boxing championship by winning the junior lightweight title. At home in Cuba sportswriters hailed him as a national hero, and immense crowds came out to greet him when he returned to Cuba after successful campaigns in New York. He received official accolades from government officials, including personal congratulations via telegram from President Gerardo Machado after winning his first world title. Even in the early 2010s, he was still considered by many to be the best Cuban boxer of all time.

EXPANDED DEVELOPMENT EFFORTS

The success that Kid Chocolate enjoyed in the United States further stimulated Cuban interest in boxing. Young Cuban boxers strove to become the next Kid Chocolate, assuming ring names such as Chocolatico Habanero, Chocolate Reglano, Chocolate de Marianao, and Chocolate Pinareño. Likewise, toward the end of Chocolate's career, Cuban officials began to take measures to encourage the development and emergence of the next great Cuban champion. In July 1938 the Dirección General de Deportes was created by executive decree and charged with the oversight of all sports in Cuba as well as the execution of measures to promote sport on the island. The agency established the National Boxing Academy as a center for instruction, and also oversaw the creation of the Cuban Golden Gloves, a boxing tournament for aspiring amateurs modeled on the event of the same name established in Chicago in 1926.

Soon after his retirement from boxing in December 1938, Chocolate himself became an instructor at the National Boxing Academy, and his former manager, Luis "Pincho" Gutiérrez, became the head boxing adviser for the agency. In 1940 Gutiérrez claimed that there were more than 2,500 boxers registered with the National Boxing Commission. Both officials and sportswriters saw potential social, ideological, and economic benefits

accruing from the development of young Cuban boxers. Boxing programs provided an avenue for the development of Cuban boys and young men. In addition, athletes who were successful in international competition could generate international prestige for Cuba, as Kid Chocolate had done so effectively. Lastly, the development of Cuba as a prominent venue for boxing competitions could stimulate the tourism industry on the island.

Official initiatives contributed to the development of quality Cuban boxers. Outstanding among those who emerged in the 1940s and 1950s was Kid Gavilán (1926–2003). Born Gerardo González in the province of Camagüey, Gavilán won the world welterweight championship in 1951 and held it for more than three years. Although the post-1959 government granted Gavilán a pension in 1959, he eventually became a Jehovah's Witness and left Cuba for Miami in 1968. Like Kid Chocolate, Gavilán is considered to be one of the best fighters of all time in his weight class. Both are members of the International Boxing Hall of Fame. Although the postrevolutionary government outlawed professional boxing in 1962, Cuba maintained its status as the home of world-class boxers. Five of the boxers who left Cuba in the 1960s to box professionally went on to become world champions: Luis Manuel Rodríguez (1937–1996), Ultiminio "Sugar" Ramos (1941–), José Ángel "Mantequilla" Nápoles (1940–), José Legra Utria (1943–), and Bernardo "Benny Kid" Paret (1937–1962). In the meantime, Cuba developed a dominant amateur program by the 1970s.

BIBLIOGRAPHY

Alfonso, Jorge. *Puños dorados: Apuntes para la historia del boxeo en Cuba.* Santiago de Cuba: Editorial Oriente, 1988.

Del Pino, Willy, ed. *Enciclopedia del boxeo cubano.* Miami: Manolo de la Tejera and Willy del Pino, 1988.

Encinosa, Enrique. *Azúcar y chocolate: Historia del boxeo cubano.* Miami: Ediciones Universal, 2004.

Menéndez, Elio, and Víctor Joaquín Ortega. *Kid Chocolate: El boxeo soy yo.* 2nd ed. Havana: Editorial Pablo de la Torriente, 1990.

Roberts, Randy. *Papa Jack: Jack Johnson and the Era of White Hopes.* New York: Free Press, 1983.

Ward, Geoffrey C. *Unforgivable Blackness: The Rise and Fall of Jack Johnson.* New York: Alfred A. Knopf, 2004.

SPORTS: BOXING AFTER 1959

Elio Menéndez

The strong tradition of boxing in Cuba during the Revolutionary Period.

In the first half of the twentieth century, Cuba astonished the world with the quality of its boxers, several of whom, "Kid Chocolate" (Eligio Sardiñas Montalvo, 1910–1988) being the first, had become world champions at the professional level. After the triumph of the Revolution in 1959, professionalism was banned in sports by Resolution 83-A, passed by the Instituto Nacional de Deportes, Educación Física y Recreación (INDER; National Institute of Sports, Physical Education and Recreation).

In October 1961 the first Playa Girón National Boxing Championship was held. At this annual competition with rotating venues, boxers from all over the island came together in an event that served as the farm system from which the majority of Cuba's Olympic and world champions emerged. In addition to Playa Girón, from 1964 the annual Giraldo Córdova Cardín international tournament provided experience for boxers from the provinces who aspired to join the first-class national team.

With professional boxing banned on the island, several boxers emigrated to the United States to pursue professional careers. Of them, Bernardo "Kid" Paret (reigned 1960–1962), Luis Manuel Rodríguez (1963), and José "Mantequilla" Nápoles (1969–1975), all became welterweight world champions, and Ultiminio Ramos (1963–1964) and José Legrá (1968–1973) became featherweight world champions. Subsequently, Joel Casamayor and Yuriolkis Gamboa, who had won gold medals for Cuba in the Olympic Games in Barcelona in 1992 and Athens in 2004, respectively, also won titles in their divisions. Juan Carlos Gómez, a member of the Cuban national team in the 1980s, also won a world title belt, in the cruiserweight division.

Of these champions, several were named to the International Boxing Hall of Fame in Canastota, New York, including "Mantequilla" Nápoles in 1990, Luis Manuel Rodríguez in 1997, and Ultiminio Ramos in 2001. "Kid" Gavilán, who dominated the welterweights from 1950 to 1954, was named to the Hall of Fame in 1990, and the legendary "Kid Chocolate" was honored in 1994.

THE OLYMPIC GAMES

Boxing debuted in the Third Olympic Games, in St. Louis in 1904, but it was another fifty-six years before Cuban boxers entered the fray, at the Rome Olympics in 1960, when the lone Cuban fighter, the lightweight Esteban Aguilera, was eliminated in his first match.

In Tokyo in 1964 the featherweight Fermín Espinosa and the welterweight Félix Betancourt won two matches each but were ruled out of the quarterfinals by injuries they suffered in the previous fights. In the 1968 Mexico City games, Cuba won its first two medals, both silver, earned by light welterweight Enrique Regüeiferos and the light middleweight Rolando Garbey. Cuba's first gold medals were won in the 1972 Munich games by the flyweight Orlando

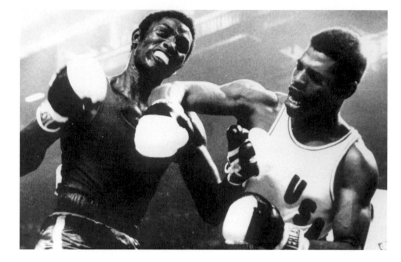

Leon Spinks and Sixto Soria (b. 1954) at the 1976 Olympics. American boxer Leon Spinks (right) fights Cuba's Sixto Soria in the light-heavyweight boxing final of the 1976 Summer Olympics in Montreal. Spinks won the match for the gold medal, with Soria taking the silver. POPPERFOTO/GETTY IMAGES

Martínez, the welterweight Emilio Correa, and the heavyweight Teófilo Stevenson, whose victory over Duane Bobick of the United States in the quarterfinals started him on the road to glory.

The Cubans continued with win after win, though in the 1976 Montreal games they fell short by a single point to the United States, which brought the finest team it had ever assembled in amateur competition. Between 1976 and the 2008 Beijing games, Cuba's Olympic pugilists won thirty-two gold medals, nineteen silver, and twelve bronze medals.

Having reclaimed their dominance in the 1980 Moscow games, the Cuban boxing squads prevailed in all other Olympics in which they participated (they boycotted the games in 1984 and 1988) until 2008. In that year at Beijing, the decline in quality was palpable, owing in large part to the absence of the 2004 Athens Olympic champions Guillermo Rigondeaux, Odlaniel Solís, Yuriolski Gamboa, and Yan Barthelemi, and the titleholder from the Bangkok 2007 World Championship, Erislandi Lara. All of these fighters made the jump to professional boxing around the time of the Beijing games, leaving the team with gaps nearly impossible to fill on such short notice. These challenges were compounded by weaknesses in the recruitment and training of young talent, as well as poor morale among the ground-level trainers and the athletes themselves due to dwindling resources that made training difficult and even forced cancellation of national tournaments, which had been vital to young boxers' development.

Half of the thirty-two Olympic gold medals won by Cubans were won by seven athletes: Two-time gold winners are Ángel Herrera (featherweight, Montreal 1976; lightweight, Moscow 1980); Héctor Vinent (light welterweight, Barcelona 1992 and

2000 and Athens 2004). Teófilo Stevenson (heavyweight, Munich 1972, Montreal 1976, and Moscow 1980) and Félix Savón (heavyweight, Barcelona 1992, Athens 1996, and Sydney 2000) each won three Olympic gold medals. Besides the Olympic titles, Stevenson won three world titles, and Savón won six.

Savón could have won gold in four Olympics had he competed at Seoul in 1988, considering that he had recently won his first major title two years earlier in the World Championship at Reno in 1986. Cuba's absence from the 1984 Los Angeles and 1988 Seoul games likewise deprived Stevenson of the opportunity to compete for two more Olympic titles. In 1984, while the Olympic Games went on in Los Angeles, Cuba held a special Torneo Amistad (Friendship Tournament) in Havana; the level of competition compared favorably with that in the Olympics. In Los Angeles, the heavyweight boxing gold medal was won by Tyrrell Biggs, whom Stevenson had defeated twice.

WORLD CHAMPIONSHIPS

Cuban boxers dominated not only the Olympic Games; they also reigned supreme in world titles in both the adult and junior categories. Between the world championship competitions in Havana in 1974 and Milan in 2009, Cuba won 63 gold medals, 27 silver medals, and 23 bronze medals, enough to win 13 of the 16 world championship competitions held. The world championship was held every four years until 1989, when it was changed to every two years, which allowed Félix Savón to compete in seven world championships.

The most successful boxer in world competitions was the cruiserweight Félix Savón, the winner of six consecutive titles from Reno 1986 to Budapest 1997. In Houston in 1999 he finished with the silver medal after the Cuban delegation withdrew from the competition amid a disagreement over the refereeing.

In the junior (under-eighteen) category, Cubans have won 66 gold medals, 24 silver medals, and 21 bronze medals, enough to come out on top in 10 of the 15 junior world championships in which they have competed. Absent from the first junior championship, at Yokohama, Japan, in 1981, the young Cubans debuted in the second, in the Dominican Republic in 1983, where their first title was won by the flyweight Julio González.

Because the junior category is limited to competitors under eighteen years of age, it requires the development of new talent for each competition, for with a single historic exception, no athlete can compete in consecutive championships. Cuba is the only country to repeat a junior title with the same athlete—Ariel Hernández, winner of the featherweight division in Bayamón, Puerto Rico, in

Carlos Banteaux Suárez (b. 1986) at the 2008 Olympics. Cuban boxer Carlos Banteaux Suárez (left) won the silver medal in the men's welterweight division of the 2008 Beijing Olympics. He is shown here after the medal ceremony with gold medalist Bakhyt Sarsekbayev (center) of Kazakhstan and bronze medalists Hanati Silamu (right) of China and Kim Jungjoo of South Korea. AL BELLO/GETTY IMAGES

Boxing medals won in the Olympic Games

Olympics	Gold	Silver	Bronze	Total
Rome, 1960	-	-	-	0
Tokyo, 1964	-	-	-	0
Mexico, 1968	-	2	-	2
Munich, 1972	3	1	1	5
Montreal, 1976	3	3	2	8
Moscow, 1980	6	2	2	10
Los Angeles, 1984*				
Seoul, 1988*				
Barcelona, 1992	7	2	-	9
Atlanta, 1996	4	3	-	7
Sydney, 2000	4	-	2	6
Athens, 2004	5	2	1	8
Beijing, 2008	-	4	4	8
Totals	32	19	12	63

SOURCE: Centro de Estadísticas y Matematicas Aplicadas (CEMA), Instituto Nacional de Deportes, Educación Física y Recreación, (INDEF). www.inder.cu

Table 1   * Cuba did not attend.

Atlanta 1996); Ariel Hernández (middleweight, Barcelona 1992 and Atlanta 1996); Mario Kindelán (lightweight, Sydney 2000 and Athens 2004); and Guillermo Rigondeaux (bantamweight, Sydney

1989, and the welterweight division in Lima, Peru, in 1990. The Lima World Championship, which should have taken place in 1991, had to be moved up a year because it conflicted with another high-level competition.

THE CENTRAL AMERICAN GAMES AND THE PANAMERICAN GAMES

The Central American Games (later renamed the Central American and Caribbean Games) began in El Salvador in 1935, but it was not until the Kingston, Jamaica, games in 1962 that Cuba won first place in the team division by winning 4 gold, 2 silver, and 2 bronze medals. Cuba maintained that dominance from then on. In the Cartagena, Colombia, games in 2010 (Cuba did not compete in El Salvador in 2002 or Mayagüez, Puerto Rico, in 2010), Cuba earned 87 golds, 12 silvers, and 13 bronzes.

Buenos Aires was the venue of the First Pan American Games in 1951, but Cuba had to wait until the São Paulo games in 1963 to win its first continental title, at the hands of Roberto "Chocolatico" Pérez (1945–2010). The conquest of gold medals grew to three in 1967 in Winnipeg, Canada, and to four in 1971 in Cali, Colombia, where Cuba took the lead in the gold medal count. It lengthened this lead in the Rio de Janeiro games of 2007, where it won 5 gold, 1 silver, and 2 bronze medals, bringing its total to 76 gold, 15 silver, and 14 bronze.

FOUNDATION OF THE TRIUMPHS

The success of Cuban boxers in particular and Cuban athletes in general is due to a system of mass participation. This extends from the beginning, recreational level up through a structure of development of talent, including special schools for sporting excellence where promising athletes are trained by qualified teachers. Young boxers ascend the steps to higher and higher levels until they get to the farm system for the national teams and—without interrupting their schoolwork—become members of the national youth and adult squads. Also essential to success are the trainers who work with the athletes, the painstaking attention of sports medicine specialists, and, above all, the strong discipline required of all the athletes, from the youngest fighter new to the team all the way up to the most accomplished gold medalist.

Considerable credit is due to Alcides Sagarra Carón (b. 1936), the main architect of Cuban boxing victories since the 1960s, who was supported by skilled, internationally respected coaches. Also crucial was the early assistance of coaches from the former socialist bloc countries who introduced the basic principles of Olympic boxing, markedly different from the style previously practiced in Cuba by amateur boxers heavily influenced by the professional game.

Medals won in world championships

Location	Gold	Silver	Bronze	Total
Havana, 1974	5	1	2	8
Belgrade, 1987	5	3	-	8
Munich, 1982	5	1	1	7
Reno, 1986	7	2	2	11
Moscow, 1989	4	4	1	9
Sydney, 1991	4	2	3	9
Tampere, 1993	8	3	-	11
Berlin, 1995	4	2	3	9
Budapest, 1997	4	3	3	10
Houston, 1999*	2	3	-	5
Belfast, 2001	7	-	2	9
Chicago, 2003**				
Pyong Yang, 2005	4	1	3	8
Bangkok, 2007	3	1	1	5
Milan, 2009	1	1	2	4
Totals	63	27	23	113

SOURCE: Centro de Estadísticas y Matematicas Aplicadas (CEMA), Instituto Nacional de Deportes, Educación Física y Recreación, (INDEF). www.inder.cu

* Cuba left the competition in semi-finals.
** Cuba did not attend.

Table 2

BIBLIOGRAPHY

Crespo, Rolando. *Cuba en el boxeo olímpico*. Havana: Editorial Científico-Técnica, 1999.

Instituto Nacional de Deportes, Educación Física y la Recreación (INDER) Web site. Available from http://www.inder.cu/.

Odd, Gilbert. *The Encyclopedia of Boxing*. Secaucus, NJ: Chartwell Books, 1989.

SPORTS: SOCCER IN THE CUBAN REPUBLIC

Santiago Prado Pérez de Peñamil

The progression of the sport of soccer in Cuba since the first game was played in 1911.

Soccer, which emerged as a sport on the island toward the end of the 1910s, was brought back by Cubans

The Cuban National Soccer Team at the World Cup, 1938. The Cuban team faced Romania in the first round of the World Cup in Toulouse, France, on 5 June 1938. Cuba's team captain, Manuel Chorens (left), is shown here exchanging pennants with his Romanian counterpart, Gheorghe Rasinaru, before the game. The match ended in a 3–3 tie, with Cuba winning the rematch (2–1) four days later. Cuba lost to Sweden in the next round. AFP/GETTY IMAGES

in from Spain or sometimes with other European players. Cuba's first decade of soccer saw the formation of the Euskeria club, made up of Basques; Deportivo Hispano-America, with a certain pan-Spanish influence; Iberia, one of the most rabid defenders of Spanishness; the Fortuna Sport Club, the most cosmopolitan team from its beginning; and Cataluña, Olimpia, Vigo, and Canarias. By the 1920s other teams had emerged that consolidated the Spanish position: Baleares, Tenerife, Juventud Asturiana, and Centro Gallego, the latter two teams remaining active throughout the republican period. The tens of thousands of Spaniards living in Havana regularly attended soccer games.

In the early 1920s Hatuey and the Rovers fell into decline. All that remained was the pride of their having been the pioneers of Cuban soccer and of having alternated in holding the Copa Orr trophy until 1921, when the Hispano-America club won it. Throughout the 1910s Spanish societies and individuals from that community had donated other cups, such as the Orensana, Santander, Cataluña, Segoviana, Zamorana, Beneficencia Gallega, España, Omega, and Reina Victoria, among many others. One representative of the English, the wealthy Scotsman William Campbell, managed to impose himself even in situations in which the Spanish maintained absolute control, at times serving as president or director of the various federations. He had the advantage of maintaining ties to the Fédération Internationale de Football Association (FIFA), and this connection gave him clear influence. In fact, his personal intervention was essential to Cuba's obtaining membership in that organization. However, the Spanish leadership in the federation controlled everything related to the importing of players, championships, and the press. The Spanish team's silver medal in the 1920 Summer Olympics held in Antwerp, Belgium, further encouraged the Spanish obsession with the sport.

Several organizations presided over the structure of the sport, including the Federación Occidental de Foot Ball Amateur (FOFA; Western Amateur Soccer Federation) and the Federación de Fútbol de La Habana (Havana Soccer Federation), created in 1928, which governed soccer activity in the city. That same year, a new macro-level social institution, the Asociación Nacional de Fútbol de la República de Cuba (National Soccer Association of the Republic of Cuba), was created. In addition, the Colegio de Árbitros (Referees' Association) was founded by the eminent Catalan José Lloveras. These organizations held discussions with municipal and national institutions, contracted all the players, and negotiated visits and international matches.

The fact that Cubans rejected soccer had a direct influence on the clubs' need to acquire foreign players. They continued creating networks to attract players from various regions of Spain. Individuals living in Havana who were connected with sports clubs

who had studied in England or Spain. Regarded as the universal sport of Europe, soccer took hold gradually in Cuba. It gained in popularity when members of the Sport Club Hatuey began to practice on the fields of Palatino in Havana in 1907, and the sizable English presence in the city contributed to its initial take-off. The English formed an official team, the Rovers Athletic Club, which faced off against Hatuey on 11 December 1911, recognized as the date of the first official soccer game in Cuba.

Massive immigration to the island at the beginning of the twentieth century resulted in large numbers of non-Spanish Europeans who actively participated in soccer. The first soccer organization, the Federación de Foot Ball Association de Cuba (Soccer Associations of Cuba), was founded by Cubans Manolo Rodríguez and Raúl Lombardo on 11 November 1911, with a minority of Cubans on the Hatuey roster. The squad included seven Spaniards, one German, one Belgian, one Frenchman, and five Cubans. Nevertheless, when the Rovers and Hatuey vied for Cuba's first soccer championship on the baseball field in Almendares Park, the press created exaggerated hopes for the Cuban team and wildly praised its victory over the English. From that moment on, soccer clubs began to form in Havana as well as in Oriente, Camagüey, Cienfuegos, Matanzas, and other places, as new players and an avid fan base emerged.

THE SPANISH ELEMENT

Commonly, the soccer clubs that formed had nothing to do with Cubans. Many promoted Spanish activities and served as standard-bearers of a national conscience far removed from the interests of Cuba. Indeed, these clubs inundated the city with a sport that Cubans began to detest. Typically, new teams would be organized, almost on principle, by Spanish players. All the teams expanded their rosters with players brought

Fidel Castro plays soccer. Fidel Castro, wearing the jersey of Cuba's national soccer team, kicks the ball to open the Central American soccer championships on 14 February 1960. © BETTMANN/CORBIS

emerged as representatives. When they visited their homelands, they were responsible for contracting one or more players. In other cases, permanent delegates were maintained in Spanish towns for this purpose. The word *importation* became the most common expression in the press to designate the arriving players, especially those from Spain but also from other countries. Players from other countries were in the minority but did join top-level teams. The most well-known case was that of the Fortuna Sport Club, which between 1925 and 1928 contracted five Hungarian players. Some Costa Ricans also arrived.

In 1925 the Fortuna team became the first to travel outside of Cuba, winning the Robert Cup in Costa Rica. Clubs traveled more frequently after that. In 1926 the Galicia Sporting Club became the first foreign team to visit Cuba. Many others soon followed, among them Barcelona's Club Español, Real Madrid, Colo Colo, Vélez Sarsfield, Sabaria, and especially the Club Nacional of Montevideo, Uruguay, the reigning Olympic champion. The visiting teams became a uniting force for followers of soccer in Cuba. The presence of the Spanish goalkeeper Ricardo Zamora, known as El Divino (the divine), brought on paroxysms of hope and moments of exaltation among Spanish fans. The press whipped up emotions, publishing photographs of the teams and reports of their heroic histories. Soccer was incorporated into *romerías* (processions of

Spanish origin to a local shrine followed by festivities) and tours as a unifying element and an essential component of the Spanish community. Through soccer, the community strengthened its command of urban public spaces and exercised the social autonomy pursued by the most eminent Spanish ideologues in the city. The experiences were extended to the permanent discussions and commentaries in workshops, factories, stores, and businesses, where the mystique of the sports fantasy was reproduced. A closed world was formed, shaped by their particular interests.

THE CUBAN ELEMENT

Toward the end of the 1920s, Cubans began to show a greater interest in soccer. Here and there, schoolyard players were introduced into second-tier teams, though only very rarely did they earn positions on the elite teams. In addition, some children of Spaniards, influenced by their family environment, accepted soccer. The country's economic crisis in the late 1920s began to have financial repercussions for the teams, and they were forced to adjust their rosters. Coming from Havana, as well as from Camagüey and Oriente, Cubans joined the major clubs. In addition to Iberia, which had three Cubans, Olimpia began to fill its roster primarily with players from the America club, the only second-tier team to be composed entirely of Cubans. The Puentes Grandes club also emerged in the second tier as an example of the Cuban presence. Soccer in Cuba was never racially divided, and blacks and whites mingled on the teams. Despite the reigning skepticism and some clear obstacles, Cuba managed to field a team to participate in the Central American Games of 1930. Cuba won every one of its matches.

In the early 1930s the trend of Spanish players leaving Cuba accelerated, and many teams broke up. By the middle of the decade, some clubs had disappeared, but others rebuilt their rosters with Cuban players. Whereas only a few Spanish athletes remained, a large number of referees and coaches from Spain stayed on and continued to teach the sport in Cuba. In 1938 Cuba attended the World Cup in France and performed well. Eleven of its fifteen players were Cuban by birth.

With Cubans now playing the leading role in soccer on the island, new teams were created with Cuban-born players. The Federación Nacional de Amateur de Foot Ball Intercolegial de Cuba (Cuban National Federation of Interscholastic Amateur Soccer) was founded, which gave continuity to *criollo* efforts by encouraging younger players to play the sport. In addition, the operation of provincial federations was integrated so as to nationalize the sport. During the 1940s and 1950s, ten top-level amateur teams formed in Havana. Between 1948 and 1953, one sector of soccer turned professional with the help of a new wave of arriving foreigners, this time Latin Americans, creating new hope among largely Cuban fans. But Cuba never achieved the boom that existed in other countries where soccer was the national sport. The omnipresence of baseball, its connection to the United States, and the support of television for that sport beginning in 1950 kept soccer from becoming more deeply rooted in Cuban society.

In the 1960s, soccer extended to all social spheres, but since baseball monopolized the public's attention, it was not until 1976 that Cuban soccer had a major achievement: At the Summer Olympics in Montreal, Canada, the Cuban team tied with Poland 0-0. Since then the national teams have been relatively lacking in power. Nevertheless, the passion for soccer again took hold in the country, stoked by the televising of regular top-level matches and the World Cup in South Africa in summer 2010. In fact, the 2010 World Cup translated into soccer fever: Fans filled Havana movie theaters, whose screens were dedicated to showing the games. FIFA's published rankings for 2010 placed Cuba at number sixty-two in the world, and number five in the Confederation of North, Central America, and Caribbean Association Football (CONCACAF). Despite the numerous difficulties Cuban soccer has faced (equipment problems, shortage of match-ups with top-level teams, shortage of first-class coaches), the support of FIFA and the administrative organs of the sport in Cuba may enable Cuban soccer, which marked its hundredth anniversary in 2011, to recall its former glories and look forward to new aspirations.

BIBLIOGRAPHY

Fariñas Borregas, Maikel. *Sociabilidad y cultura del ocio: Las élites habaneras y sus clubes de recreo (1902–1930)*. Havana: Fundación Fernando Ortiz, 2009.

Fernández Alonso, Pedro. *Algo de la historia del balompié en Cuba*. Havana: Editorial Atalaya S.A., 1949.

Ibarra Cuesta, Jorge. "Herencia española, influencia estadounidense." In *Nuestra común historia: Cultura y sociedad*. Havana: Editorial Ciencias Sociales, 1995.

Llordén Miñambres, Moisés. "Las asociaciones españolas de emigrantes." In *Arte, cultura y sociedad en la emigración española a América*, edited by María Cruz Morales Faro and Moisés Llordén Miñambres. Oviedo, Spain: Universidad de Oviedo, Servicio de Publicaciones, 1992.

Martínez Perugorría, Rafael Luis. *Cuba, 62 en el Ranking Mundial FIFA y 5 en CONCACAF*. 19 December 2010. Available from http://www.telepinar.

Pascual, Miguel. *Los ases del futbolismo cubano: Como viven y como juegan*. Havana: Imprenta P. Fernández C.A., 1930.

Pérez, Louis A. Jr. *On Becoming Cuban: Identity, Nationality, and Culture*. Chapel Hill: University of North Carolina Press, 2008.

Prado Pérez de Peñamil, Santiago. "Balompié: Alternativa simbólica de los españoles en La Habana, (1898–1935)." *Temas* 49 (January–March 2007): 46–54.

Reig Romero, Carlos E. *Historia del deporte cubano: Los inicios*. Havana: Editorial Unicornio, 2007.

■

THE STILL LIFES OF AMELIA PELÁEZ

Roberto Cobas Amate

One of Cuba's foremost modern still-life artists and her important painting.

In the 1930s a new generation of painters and sculptors burst onto the Cuban visual art scene, bringing with it artistic concerns previously unknown on the island. Outstanding among these artists was Amelia Peláez del Casal (1896–1968), who established a new way of perceiving reality, with the principles of modernity as her guide.

An artist with a firm mastery of academic language, Peláez gained recognition with her first works, produced in the early 1920s when she was a follower of Leopoldo Romañach (1862–1951). In 1927 she went to Paris and came into contact with the avant-garde artists of the School of Paris and, consequently, with the modernist style that she fully adopted as her own. Eager for knowledge, she enrolled in a number of

■ *See also*

The Orígenes Group and Journal

Visual Arts: Republican Period

Opposite page:
Peces **(1943)**. An oil painting on canvas by Amelia Peláez del Casal (1896–1968). DIGITAL IMAGE © THE MUSEUM OF MODERN ART/LICENSED BY SCALA/ART RESOURCE, NY

free classes. It was a stimulating environment for learning, and the works of Cézanne, Braque, and Matisse influenced her, but the decisive effect on her artistic education was her acquaintance with Alexandra Exter (1882–1949), a painter from Russia with whom she studied avant-garde painting, in particular the dynamics of color, abstract art, and stage design.

Her first exhibition in Paris, at the Zak Gallery in 1933, was a success. The quality of her painting stood out, and the rigorous structure of her compositions was noticed. The variety of the pieces in her show suggested that the young Peláez, though still in the process of defining her aesthetic, was already exhibiting mature work. Included in the group of works exhibited were still lifes that emerged as a sudden source of inspiration; from the 1940s they took a central place in her work.

When she returned to Cuba in January 1934, Peláez brought with her the work she had produced in Europe and the education of an accomplished modern painter. She had fully developed as an artist in Paris, returning home with a powerful, creative maturity. However, she did not rush to exhibit on the island: Faced with the exuberant reality that surrounded her, she decided to continue to develop her artistic sensibility by drawing.

A year after her return from Paris, in 1935, she put on an individual exhibition at the Lyceum in Havana, in which she showed a selection of works from her European tour. This show positioned her as a top-ranking force in the modern visual art scene of Cuba. Peláez explored new content as she reconnected with the land of her birth.

The experimental quality of her painting manifests itself in the magnificent sketches *Naturaleza muerta con frutabomba* (Still Life with Papaya) and *Naturaleza muerta con frutas y vitrales* (Still Life with Fruits and Stained-glass Windows), which show how Peláez had surmounted European style to immerse herself in a morphology, luminosity, and palette particular to the island world of Cuba. These works indicate the form that became her chief interest: the still life.

In her exploration of the still life, Amelia Peláez achieved the center of gravity that best defines her artwork. This became evident from early on in her iron-willed discipline of the 1930s, still far from the sensuality and baroque style she achieved later, in her work of the 1940s. Her painting aligned with the poetic and intellectual thought of José Lezama Lima and the generation of artists and writers that gathered around the magazine *Orígenes* (1944–1956). Linked closely with Lezama since 1939, when he published the magazine *Espuela de Plata*, thanks to Lezamian ideology, Peláez joined a group of younger painters, including Mariano Rodríguez and René Portocarrero, who attempted to recover the the Hispanic roots of Cuban culture.

The nature of this reclamation of the past is dynamic and creative, the keystone of a modern image that feeds back into a strengthened identity and is projected as a paradigm of the Cuban character. In this regard, the Peláez still lifes play a leading role beside the domestic interiors of Portocarrero and Mariano. And while Mariano went out into the street to capture colorful reality in such works as *La catedral de La Habana* (The Cathedral of Havana) and *El parque* (The Park), Peláez delighted in a closed and intimate interior space where Cuban fruit occupies the center of attention and in the innumerable expressive possibilities presented by the still-life genre in an environment that appreciates the embellishments of colonial architecture. Out of this subject matter emerges her handling of the fan-shaped stained-glass windows known as *medios puntos* that decisively shape how she structures her compositions. With exquisite delicacy she filtered colors that contribute an essential mystery to her works.

When Alfred Barr Jr., director of the Museum of Modern Art (MOMA) in New York, decided to present an exhibition of Cuban painting in 1944, he rightly assessed the great potential of the art that was being produced at the time on the small Caribbean island. He consulted with the curator and critic José Gómez Sicre and got enthusiastic support from María Luisa Gómez Mena, a patron of the arts and one of the most interesting personalities in Cuban society of the era. Barr and Gómez Sicre selected the pieces. Among the artists with the largest representation was Amelia Peláez with eleven pieces—oils, watercolors, drawings, and a gouache—confirming her as one of the foremost artists of the island. Among the oil paintings chosen was *Peces* (Fishes, 1943), later in MOMA's permanent collection. In this painting Peláez incorporates her most personal morphology, which can be appreciated as the totality of the brilliantly colored stained-glass windows, the ironwork grill, and the astonishing ornamented border at the center of the table with the fish providing the focal point. The intense light that passes through the stained-glass windows produces brilliant and cheerful colors in the space, separated into saturated shades of reds, greens, and yellows. The black line divides the composition into sections and gives structure to the color. *Peces* is a synthesis of the process of creolization that occurred in the Cuban art from the first half of the 1940s, impacting the most important painters of the period. Mariano, Portocarrero, and Cundo Bermúdez, among others, participated in the generational effort to recover the past through modern eyes. Amelia Peláez, in capturing this reality, produced an unparalleled formal display in which figuration and abstraction are combined in a harmonic balance to create an intimate, sublimated universe.

Amelia Peláez's work represents a monument to the defense of the value of identity in Cuban culture. From deep Cuban roots it creates a universal language of striking unity. It evolves without sudden leaps, in a continuity sustained by a will to be true to itself without detours or repetitions. Peláez found something different without losing the essence of her Cubanness.

For this reason she occupies a place of honor in the island's art world and has attained well-deserved recognition throughout Latin America and beyond.

BIBLIOGRAPHY

Alonso, Alejandro G. *Amelia Peláez*. Havana: Editorial Letras Cubanas, 1990.

Gómez Sicre, José. *Pintura cubana de hoy*. Havana: María Luisa Gómez Mena, 1944.

Jubrías, María Elena. *Amelia Peláez: Cerámica*. Seville: Ediciones Vanguardia Cubana, 2008.

Vázquez Díaz, Ramón. "Encuentro con Amelia Peláez." In *Amelia Peláez: Óleos, temperas y dibujos [1929–1964]*. Salamanca: Gráfica Varona, 1998.

STRAWBERRY AND CHOCOLATE (TOMÁS GUTIÉRREZ ALEA AND JUAN CARLOS TABÍO)

Frank Padrón

Internationally acclaimed Cuban film exploring the social transformations of the Special Period.

Cuban society in the early 1990s almost seemed to be waiting for *Fresa y chocolate* (*Strawberry and Chocolate*, 1993), a Cuban film that documented and commented on the social transformations roiling the country during the economic crisis known as the Special Period. The film is largely based on the short story "El lobo, el bosque y el hombre nuevo" (The Wolf, the Forest, and the New Man, 1990), by Senel Paz (b. 1950), who also wrote the screenplay for *Strawberry and Chocolate*, directed by Tomás "Titón" Gutiérrez Alea (1928–1996) and Juan Carlos Tabío (b. 1942).

For Cuban film, the 1990s began with a bang set off by the scandalous film *Alicia en el pueblo de Maravillas* (Alice in Wondertown, 1990), by Daniel Díaz Tórres (b. 1948), which used the language of satire to deliver an acid critique of the deep-rooted maladies of Cuban society. The government took a hard-line approach, banning the film. The new social and economic circumstances in Cuba had created a rich cultural climate for acceptance (even official acceptance) of a film that broached the issue of equality among those who are different. Thus *Strawberry and Chocolate* was released at the best possible moment; it was indeed a timely work. The increasing international gains made by lesbian, gay, bisexual, and transgendered (LGBT) minorities, the fall of the socialist bloc, and the internal crisis that it precipitated, facilitated a climate of tolerance and national unity along the lines of *todos ante la adversidad* (all in the face of adversity). A film such as *Strawberry and Chocolate* became an efficient aesthetic weapon to undertake this resistance.

POLITICS OF THE REVOLUTION

Critics and other viewers have insisted that *Strawberry and Chocolate* is not a homoerotic film, but instead a tale of tolerance and a call for communication between diverse peoples and respect for the Other. This is certainly true, but it was also the first Cuban film to feature a gay character as the dramatic and narrative subject.

Diego (Jorge Perugorría) is a gay artist who has a pursuit to which he devotes his life and work: Cuban culture. In his personal life he values friendship over sex, so although he is unable to seduce the young militant Communist David (Vladimir Cruz), he allows him to pay visits and even embarks on a plan to give his young comrade an artistic and moral makeover that will turn him into a genuinely new man. For Diego, it is an understanding of ethical and humanistic values that will allow the generation of the Revolution to develop in terms of its own culture and humanity. In accordance with Diego's teachings, David will become a man without prejudices who not only tolerates those who think and feel differently but also can accept them as friends and comrades working together to build a better society—a society that is fairer because it is more inclusive, achieving José Martí's dream of a nation "with all and for the good of all." Diego suggests this in one of his first verbal skirmishes with David:

> I know there are good things about the Revolution, but I've had some very bad things happen to me, and anyways, I have my own ideas about some of them. . . . I'm willing to reason, to change my opinion, but I have never been able to have a conversation with a revolutionary. You only talk to yourselves. You could care less about what the rest of us think.

The majority's failure to include those who are different because it perceives them without nuances, as somehow wrong or dissident is a familiar theme in Gutiérrez Alea's work. In his groundbreaking *Memorias del subdesarrollo* (Memoirs of Underdevelopment, 1968) Gutiérrez Alea subtly censures social mechanisms that exclude the Other—in this case a skeptical and dilettantish bourgeois who despite his shortcomings maintains an unassailable virtue: his love for his city (Havana) and for Cuba. In *Strawberry and Chocolate* Diego's aspirations for what might be called an alternative nation clash with ignorance and intolerance, and if official hostility toward the Other continues, then he will be left with no choice except exile.

But if Diego demurs, there is another gay character in *Strawberry and Chocolate* with a different attitude—the sculptor Germán (Joel Angelino), Diego's friend. This ostensibly irrational and frivolous

■ *See also*

Che Guevara and the New Man

Cuban Thought and Cultural Identity: Socialist Thought

Economy: Special Period

Sexuality: Gay and Lesbian Representation in Cuban Art, Film, and Literature

Jorge Perugorría (left) and Vladimir Cruz in *Strawberry and Chocolate*. Tomás Gutiérrez Alea's 1993 film commented on the social transformations coursing through Cuba as the result of worldwide events. MARY EVANS/RONALD GRANT/EVERETT COLLECTION

Movie poster for *Fresa y chocolate* (1993). The movie was the first Cuban film to feature a gay character as the narrative subject. ICAIC/IMCINE/TELEMADRID/THE KOBAL COLLECTION/THE PICTURE DESK, INC.

loca (queer), as Diego calls him, decides to stay in Cuba, refusing to surrender or retreat into exile, though he is forced to temporarily give up exhibiting his sculptures. He brings to mind Galileo, playfully mocking the powers that be, certain that all will eventually change. In the words of Miguel Barnet, "Germán knows that over time the beheaded statues will get their heads back," which may be read as a metaphor for Germán's belief in the struggle for that national project; in contrast, Diego enters the fray but does not fight on, defeated by the loss of the first few battles.

Although the character Diego represents an advance in the depiction of homosexuals in Cuban cinema, he is still a loser. He does not die in the story, like the protagonist of Enrique P. Barnet's *La bella del Alambra* (The Beauty of the Alhambra, 1989), but he becomes a sad shield on which the hetero-aggressor keeps beating; in any case, he does not win his battle, and he admits as much once he has decided to leave Cuba. His defeat lies in his incapacity to transform his environment—an environment that refuses to assimilate, understand, or even listen to him:

> What can I do about it? Fight? No, I'm weak, and your world is not for the weak. . . . You can also be a *maricón* [queer] and strong. There are plenty of examples. . . . I'm weak, I'm terrified by age, I can't wait ten or fifteen years for you to rethink things, no matter how much confidence you have that the Revolution will end up fixing its own blunders.

Diego's words are prophetic. By the time Paz was writing the screenplay and Gutiérrez Alea and Tabío were shooting the film, the Revolution had already fixed its "blunders" in regard to its attitude toward homosexuals. But the present of the film is 1979, and although the plot is steeped in allusions to events from the 1980s right up to its release in the beginning of the 1990s, the action takes place primarily within the 1960s, when gays

generally were handed over to the Unidades Militares para la Ayuda de Producción (UMAPs; Military Units for Support of Production) or marginalized, and languished in a twilight zone with no role in society. Accordingly, the supporting character Germán is the true hero of the movie: He is sufficiently respected and he has a satisfactory social life, but most importantly, he does not give up.

Another important contribution of the film is its shattering of a cliché: In *Strawberry and Chocolate* the bad guy is a young man from the Unión de Jóvenes Comunistas (UJC; Young Communist Union). Miguel, a friend of David's, is mass-produced, programmed, and dogmatic, reflecting a sad reality prevalent in Cuba in the 1960s and 1970s. These decades frame the film and point to another of its virtues: its treatment of time. *Strawberry and Chocolate* mixes eras, thrusting the narrative backward and forward in time with a masterful touch that is written into the screenplay.

ARTISTRY

Strawberry and Chocolate joins the repertoire of Cuban cinema's love songs to Havana, which is not merely a physical location, but also a cultural and philosophical ideal. As in *Memorias del subdesarrollo*, Enrique Álvarez's *La ola* (The Wave, 1995), and Fernando Pérez's *Suite Habana* (2003), the characters of *Strawberry and Chocolate* wander the city's old streets, re-acquainting themselves with all its wonders and ugliness. The fine score by José María Vitier (b. 1954), the cinematography by Mario García Joya that captures the "young light" described by the poet Eliseo Diego, the intelligent editing by Talavera/Donatien, the exquisite production design of Fernando O'Reilly, and the crisp sound by Germinal Hernández all contribute to the success of the film, which is shot in a fairly conventional manner, in keeping with the story and its implications and subtext. The references to the esoteric and to Santería are not as successful; in contrast to the Catholicism in the original story, the film follows the syncretistic trend of replacing religion with superstition in a treatment that amounts to a mere sideshow rather than an essential statement. Other collateral aspects the film such as the political sloganeering and the references to double standards and diverse discriminations are seamlessly woven into the dialogue.

Much has been written about the excellent performances of the actors, particularly Jorge Perugorría, who was launched into an international career. Although at first his portrayal of Diego seems a little affected, Perugorría struggles indefatigably against the caricatures and stereotypes of gay men to reveal the sympathies and tensions that make Diego the man he is, a typical Cuban gay man. Vladimir Cruz also has a difficult role role as David, the timid young man who is evolving, maturing, and enriching his life, humanely, through his friendship with

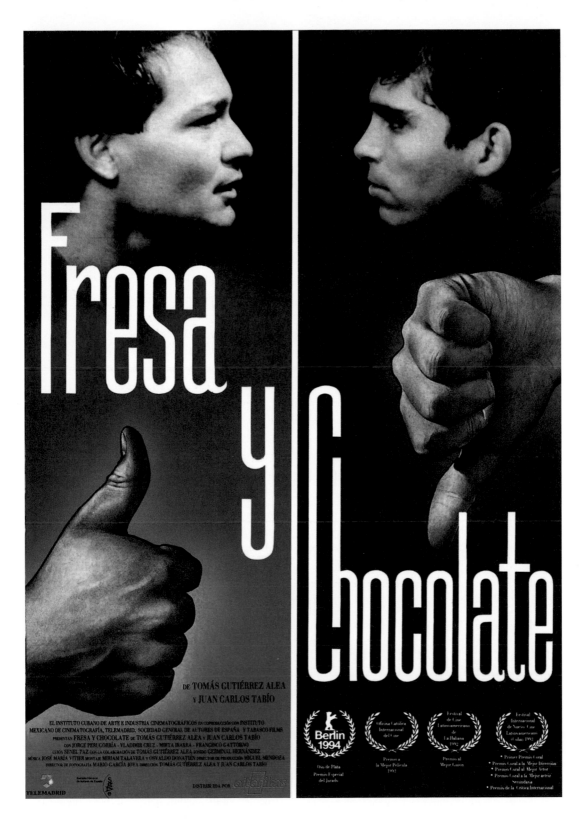

the Other. The performances of the supporting actors Mirta Ybarra and Joel Angelino complete the brilliant ensemble. *Strawberry and Chocolate* gained a great deal of international attention, winning prizes at film festivals in Mexico, Brazil, and Berlin, as well as an Oscar nomination (1994) for best foreign film.

BIBLIOGRAPHY

Béjel, Emilio. "Fresa y chocolate, o La salida de la guarida." *Casa de las Américas* 196 (1994): 10–22.

Jambrina, Jesús. "Sujeto homosexual y disloque nacional." *La Gaceta de Cuba* 5 (September–October 2003): 20.

Paz, Senel. *El bosque, el lobo y el hombre nuevo*. Havana: Editorial Letras Cubanas, 1991.

Santana, Andrés Isaac. "La voz homoerótica." *La Gaceta de Cuba* 5 (September–October 2003): 3–7.

West, Cornel. "Las nuevas políticas culturales de la diferencia." *Temas* 28 (January–March 2002): 4–14.

Woods, Gregory. *Historia de la literatura gay*. Madrid: Ediciones Akal, 2001.

SUGAR

"Without sugar there is no country," proclaimed the old adage by which the conventional wisdom of Cuban dependency on sugar was conveyed. The impact of sugar on Cuban national development was pervasive. There was indeed much truth to the observation by the anthropologist Fernando Ortiz that the history of Cuba is the history of sugar. Beginning in the late eighteenth century, and continuing through the early years of the twenty-first century, sugar production shaped the broad contours along which Cuban history developed. Sugar summoned into existence a plantation economy and the attending banes of monoculture, chattel slavery, and large-scale commercial production for export. The social composition of the population was permanently changed, as the labor requirements necessitated by sugar production resulted in the introduction onto the island of hundreds of thousands of enslaved Africans. Sugar shaped property relations, class structure, land tenure forms, labor systems, the process of capital accumulation, patterns of trade and commerce, the priorities of domestic policies, and the politics of international relations.

The essays address the multiple and complex facets of sugar, both as a matter of historical process and national development: those elements that contributed to making Cubans the people who they have become. These essays bear on distinct historical periods, of course, including the colonial period, the early republic, and the revolutionary period. But it is also true that the meaning of sugar insinuated itself into larger realms of Cuban aesthetic sensibilities and popular culture, in poetry and landscape paintings, in music and fiction, in the very language by which the experience of daily life was lived. The essays serve to set in relief the ubiquity of sugar as the context in which to take measure of the Cuban experience.

SUGAR: COLONIAL PERIOD

Alejandro García Álvarez

The rise of sugar as Cuba's most important industry in the eighteenth and nineteenth centuries.

The origin of Cuban sugar mills can be traced to a few cane shoots brought to the Americas by Christopher Columbus on his second transatlantic voyage. Along with the plant itself, Columbus brought with him to the New World the artisanal procedures for turning cane juice into sugar, molasses, and alcohol. Sugar cane planting previously had been undertaken in Andalusia and the Atlantic islands of Madeira, the Azores, and the Fortunate Isles (Canaries), and the crop proved perfectly adaptable to the climate and soils of most of the European possessions in the Caribbean and many others on the American mainland (Moreno Fraginals pp. 432–429). During the sixteenth and seventeenth centuries sugar was regarded in Cuba as a less attractive product than livestock, tobacco, lumber, and fruit. Beginning in the second half of the eighteenth century, however, production and export of the sweetener acquired a new dynamism that made it an industry of special importance for the country. Sugar's growing influence changed the agro-industrial and foreign trade structures of the colony, putting in place the society's defining characteristics in the centuries to follow.

CHARACTERISTICS OF THE PROCESS

In contrast to other production lines such as raising livestock or growing tobacco, founding a sugar mill required significant resources. Whereas the other

CHRONOLOGY OF EVENTS

1573: Ordenanzas de Cáceres establish land-use regulations.

1595: Law on Privileges of Sugar Mills aids expansion of sugar production.

1797: Failed effort to use steam engine at Seybabo plantation mill.

1817: First successful use of steam power in sugar production at Limonar mill.

1841: Introduction of vacuum evaporators at La Mella mill, Matanzas.

1849: Centrifuge first applied to sugar production at La Amistad mill, Havana province.

1865: Protections of sugar mills established by 1595 Law on Privileges overturned.

1873: Juan Poey establishes laboratory at Las Cañas mill, promotes use of fertilizer.

1890: U.S. Congress passes McKinley Tariff removing duties on sugar.

1894: Cuban sugar harvest exceeds 1 million tons for first time.

1922: U.S. Congress passes Fordney-McCumber Tariff, raising duties on Cuban sugar.

1926: The Verdeja Act attempts to limit sugar production.

1931: Chadbourne Plan attempts to bring stability to the sugar market.

1937: London Convention on international trade; Cuba enacts Sugar Production Coordination Law.

1950: Cuban sugar production exceeds 6 million tons.

1959: Castro's revolutionary government passes Agrarian Reform Act.

1960: U.S. Congress passes the Sugar Act, eliminating Cuba's sugar quota; Cuban government nationalizes all U.S. businesses.

1961: Cuban sugar production peaks at 7.5 million tons.

1963: New Agrarian Reform Act sets 165-acre maximum on private ownership; sugar production declines to 4.2 million tons.

1964: Cuba and Soviet Union sign trade agreement that stabilizes price of sugar.

1970: Government attempts 10-million ton harvest; attains 8.5 million tons at cost of major disruption to Cuban economy.

1972: Cuba joins Soviet-dominated Council for Mutual Economic Assistance (CMEA).

1984: International Sugar Agreement ends.

1991: Collapse of Soviet Union and CMEA deprives Cuba of primary market for its sugar.

2005: Sugar harvest reaches lowest point in a century, 1.3 million tons.

The sugarcane plant. On his second transatlantic voyage, Christopher Columbus brought to the New World a few shoots of sugarcane, a tall perennial grass native to tropical southeast Asia. The sugarcane plant proved highly adaptable to the climate and soils of the Caribbean. © JIMMY DURANTES/LATIN FOCUS. COM

activities needed only land of the proper type, a minimal number of workers, and the purchase of relatively simple and cheap equipment, transformation of cane juice into sugar, molasses, or alcohol required investment in relatively expensive means of production. These included buildings to house the operation, mechanical devices to extract the juice, kettles in which to concentrate the liquid, the equipment needed to separate the crystals, and hired technicians well trained in sugar making. Also indispensable, from the viewpoint of producers, were enough slave workers to guarantee successful cultivation, harvesting, and

STAGES OF SUGAR PRODUCTION (COLONIAL ERA)

AGRICULTURAL STAGE

Planting took place from September to December (cold weather planting) and from April to June (spring planting). The maturation period was ten months. In Cuba the roots generally remained active for several consecutive harvests. Cutting began in December and generally lasted until May of the following year. The stalk was cut at ground level and then divided into three or four sections, according to the length of the cane.

RAW MATERIAL TRANSPORTATION STAGE

Harvested cane had to be transported to the mill within less than twenty-four hours after cutting. Direct carriage was in ox-drawn carts or by railway, linking the agricultural stage with the industrial one. This transport was an important element in coordinating the flow of production.

INDUSTRIAL STAGE

The grinding of the cane was the focus of innovations introduced in several eras: (1) by wooden or iron rollers, arranged vertically or horizontally; (2) by animal power, wind power, or steam power, in accordance with each mill's resources; (3) by shredders and processes of pounding and soaking, all with the goal of increasing sucrose yield.

Concentration of the cane juice was effected by a process of cooking and evaporating in pans and kettles, through direct application of heat produced by burning wood or bagasse (cane waste). Carbon filters were used. Later, double- and triple-action vacuum evaporators were introduced, and filters and defecators to remove impurities; all of these replaced the old so-called trains of successive kettles and pans.

In the curing and draining stage, sugar crystals were separated from molasses. The process evolved from the primitive use of clay or tin molds that filtered the molasses by gravity, to the introduction of steam turbines as centrifuges.

Methods of packing the sugar also evolved during the colonial era. Wooden boxes were replaced by *bocoyes* (large barrels). Then, from the 1860s on, jute-fiber sacks replaced older and more costly packing materials as the best method for transporting an industrial product with lower molasses content.

carting of the cane, as well as its subsequent transformation into sugar. At the same time, the nature of the system of colonial domination obstructed the first phase of developing a sugar production and export industry because of the colonial power's rigid control over international trade and because of the lack of sufficient markets in Spain itself, given the existence of sugar mills on the peninsula (Guerra p. 54). As a result of this situation, manufacture of the sweetener grew only slowly during the first two centuries of the colony.

The eighteenth century brought more favorable conditions, thanks to changes adopted by the new Bourbon royal dynasty enthroned in Spain in 1701. The excessive centralization of administration, the absolute monopoly over trade transactions enforced through restrictions and prohibitions, and the anachronistic treasury system that had characterized colonial administration over the previous centuries were gradually rendered more flexible or replaced by more modern and efficient means of extracting profit from the colonies (Santamaría García and García Álvarez pp. 55–59). The trading monopoly passed from the hands of the state to commercial entities—still monopolies, but made up of private interests. The Crown also took the first steps toward gradual authorization of commerce with third countries and modernization of the system for taxing international trade. Moreover, the old system that required specific authorizations for importing slaves was replaced by unregulated importation of a captive labor force. In parallel with these developments, the activities that had dominated the island's economy over more than two centuries had favored the emergence of very powerful oligarchic groups; now, for several decades, the capital accumulated by these oligarchs, by certain religious orders, and also by some merchants was invested and reinvested in the creation of sugar mills (García Rodríguez pp. 64–73). Historians have argued that by the eighteenth century, Cuba had all the objective conditions necessary for the emergence of large-scale sugar production (Moreno Fraginals, vol. 1, pp. 15–19). As a result of this process, the great Cuban sugar mills of the nineteenth century became industrial models by virtue of their productive capacity and the large numbers of slave and wage workers they employed, and by virtue of the modernity of their equipment.

From the beginning, Cuban sugar was regarded as an export product. Thus, it had a high susceptibility to price fluctuations in foreign markets and to competition from other producers. In the midst of changes in competitive international trade in the nineteenth century, the destination of Cuban sugar output shifted gradually from the European market to the United States. As a result of the need to produce sugar that met the quality standards of this market and the simultaneous need to reduce production costs, the less efficient mills were gradually eliminated, and production became concentrated in the more modern and competitive ones. This set of circumstances led the Cuban

F. 10128   CUBA.—THE GREAT SUGAR INDUSTRY—CUTTING AND LOADING THE CANE ON THE PLANTATION OF LAS CAÑAS.—FROM SKETCHES BY WALTER YEAGER.—SEE PAGE 459.

Sugarcane harvest. During most of the colonial period, sugar plantations depended on an enslaved workforce assigned to harvest the crop and transport it to the mills. © BETTMANN/ CORBIS

industry to undergo an intense process of centralization and technological and organizational modernization, in search of maximum improvement in continuous production techniques. Thus emerged a new phenomenon, the giant mill of the late nineteenth century, and a new term to identify it: the *central* (Iglesias García 1998, pp. 43–55; Dye p. 73). Yet the country's political situation caused this process to be interrupted by an important event: the War of Independence waged by the Cubans between 1895 and 1898. Unlike the Ten Years' War (1868–1878), this new conflict saw the fighting spread throughout the island. Many mills were destroyed or put out of action, causing a considerable drop in sugar output, from more than 22 million *quintales* (1.1 million tons) in 1894 to only one-fifth that amount in 1897. The disasters brought on by the war and the country's overall impoverishment in its aftermath helped make way for the opening of a new era in Cuban sugar production.

LAND

The starting point for the creation of sugar mills in Cuba was land. In the process that created local oligarchies, possession of this basic resource constituted the major material and symbolic pillar of power. During the earliest centuries of the colony, all land on the island was formally owned by the Spanish Crown. In turn, the king or queen granted usufruct rights over parcels of this land to many officials, military officers, clergy, merchants, adventurers, and favorites within the colonial bureaucracy. These *mercedes* (land grants) were circular parcels that tended to encompass between 5.3 and 10.6 square miles. Given their rights to these lands, the above-mentioned groups came to dominate the municipal governments or *cabildos* (councils), accumulating positions, functions, and titles (Sorhegui and de la Fuente 1994, pp. 123–124). As of the year 1573, the workings of the cabildos were codified in a series of regulations called the Ordenanzas de Cáceres, which designated lands farther from population centers for extensive cattle grazing and reserved the land closer to towns and cities for communal uses and the creation of small farms and work sites (Pichardo pp. 124–127). Nonetheless, the outskirts of cities and other areas close to the coasts became zones where, alongside livestock raising, commercial agriculture grew up. This pattern seems to be confirmed by the example of Havana at the close of the sixteenth century, when a group of primitive sugar mills surrounded the capital. As might be imagined, their proprietors included several of the most prominent members of the local cabildo (De la Torre pp. 139–140; García Rodríguez pp. 55–56).

Table 1

Annual production of sugar in Cuba between 1550 and 1899

Years	Annual Production (in metric tons)	Years	Annual Production (in metric tons)	Years	Annual Production (in metric tons)
1550–1599	239	1801–1805	35,243	1850–1854	355,932
1600–1699	460	1806–1810	34,877	1855–1859	442,135
1700–1753	1,340	1811–1815	35,640	1860–1864	477,678
1761–1765	1,457	1816–1820	41,237	1865–1869	561,562
1766–1770	4,416	1820–1824	62,892	1870–1874	719,243
1771–1775	6,982	1825–1829	74,373	1875–1879	644,229
1776–1780	14,000	1830–1834	99,148	1880–1884	609,603
1781–1785	14,000	1835–1839	120,729	1885–1889	645,169
1786–1790	12,541	1840–1844	182,898	1890–1894	900,160
1791–1795	19,211	1845–1849	214,220	1895–1899	426,573
1796–1800	26,023				

SOURCES: Pedrosa Puertas, R. *Cinco Siglos de Industria Azucarera Cubana*. Havana, MINAZ, (n.d.), Table 1-A, "Producción de Azúcar Crudo. Años 1550-1856," p. 13; Moreno Fraginals, Manuel. *El ingenio. Complejo económico social cubano del azúcar*. Havana: Editorial de Ciencias Sociales, 1978, Chart I, "Producción azucarera mundial y cubana, caña y remolacha 1820–1967," Table III, Appendix I, pp. 35–38.

LIBERALIZING MEASURES

When in 1729 the cabildos were deprived of the authority to assign land, almost the entire area of the island had already been distributed. Despite this apparent spatial limitation and the obligation to preserve some forest areas as a reserve for lumber to be used in ship production (Funes pp. 110–119), certain commercial crops such as sugarcane continued to spread. As a result of land use diversification, the great *latifundios* (estates) originally used for ranching became part of a process of division or elimination. Economic necessity finally triumphed, and in 1754 procedures for transfer and registration of property in land were formalized (Portuondo p. 184). This process made room for reconfiguration of the old ranches and corrals, especially in the western part of the country. Free disposition of land use accelerated the process of land transfer and, as a result, accelerated the movement of capital into sugar and coffee production. The conversion of land into an object of commerce eased the adoption of strategies designed to promote the physical growth of existing plantations and the creation of new mills. Large slave-based plantations absorbed new expanses of land for cane planting as a way to guarantee progressive increases in production. The problem of declining yields caused by repeated use of the same soil also brought a demand for more land, which caused the movement of many mills from coastal areas to new and more fertile zones (Fernández Prieto pp. 145; Funes pp. 67–68; García Rodríguez pp. 100–101).

The trend toward free disposition of land use reached a new height in 1819, when a royal decree legalized full-fledged ownership of this basic means of production. However, property rights over rural areas were not awarded to those who were actually working the land at that moment, but rather to those formally registered as possessing the usufruct rights. The effect was to reinforce the power of the old municipal oligarchies. The final liberalizing measure was taken in 1865, with the total elimination of the *privilegio de ingenios* that, since 1595, had protected mills from being foreclosed by creditors. Ownership of land as full-fledged private property made transactions easier. It allowed for still greater increases in the size of slave-based plantations until nearly the end of the nineteenth century, when the slave trade had finally ended, slavery showed signs of exhaustion as a system, and plantation owners' financial resources for modernizing mills and buying more land seemed to have run out.

As soon as slavery ended, a countervailing trend in the vertical organization of sugar production appeared. After some years of discussion about the advisability of separating the agricultural and industrial sectors of the sugar complex, the proposed new model consisted of the mill owners dividing the cane growing areas they owned and renting them out to independent producers who were in charge of supplying the raw material to the mill. In many cases, cane fields belonging to the least industrially efficient mills became cane providers to the larger mills that remained in operation. The new formula replaced the old pattern in which the two sectors were administered jointly, under the sole direction of the plantation owner who owned both land and mill (Iglesias García 1998, pp. 115–118). The new formula involved individual contracts between the mill and independent producers making use of the mill's lands or their own to supply the agricultural raw material to the industrial plant. That practice was gradually adopted in most Cuban sugar mills over the last part of the nineteenth century.

TECHNOLOGY

The technology used to produce sugar in Cuba remained practically unchanged until the mid-eighteenth century. The mill complexes were made up of three basic sectors: agricultural, factory, and living quarters. The nucleus of sugar manufacturing, the mill itself, was situated in the center of the *batey* (mill village). This factory area of the old mills was in turn made up of four buildings. The manufacturing process began with the *trapiche*, the mechanical press that ground the cane, powered by animal traction, wind, or water. This grinding mill was usually protected by an open-sided circular structure, in which wooden columns supported a palm-thatch or clay-tile roof. Not far off lay a rectangular, single-story building where a series of copper pans or kettles were mounted over a fire and organized by size from largest to smallest. In this construction, known as a *train*, the *guarapo* (cane juice) was cooked over direct heat until the proper degree of concentration was reached. Another building was called by two interchangeable names: the mold room or draining room. There, sugar crystals were separated from the syrup or molasses. The technique was based on allowing the fluids to drain and then washing the sugar crystals deposited in conical molds made of metal or clay. Finally, the sugar was removed from these cones and placed in the sun to dry. During this era, technical advances were few. Among them were the *returners*, whose function was to reinsert the cane stalks between the grinding rollers of the mill. Other changes seen as advances were a change from vertical to horizontal grinding and the use of iron rollers in place of wooden ones (García Rodríguez pp. 169–171).

Modernization of the Mill With some delay, the results of the so-called first industrial revolution reached the Cuban sugar industry. In 1784 the double-acting steam engine emerged as a technology useful in any type of industry. By this time, there was already clear awareness of the need to incorporate such advances into the development of Cuban sugar making. Between 1784 and 1785, in order to realize that potential, two important figures in the Havana oligarchy, Francisco de Arango (1765–1837) and Ignacio Montalvo Ambulodi (1748–1795), traveled to Europe and the colonial sugar islands of the Caribbean to seek first-hand information about the latest technological advances applicable to sugar production and, especially, about the use of steam power in grinding cane. These efforts led to a pioneering attempt to put a steam engine to work in Cuba. The design of a steam-driven grinding mill was entrusted

to the Canaries-born engineer Agustín de Betancourt (1758–1824), who worked closely with the two Cuban travelers during their European journey. The first trial of Betancourt's machine took place in 1797 in the Seybabo mill owned by the Count of Jaruco y Mopox, but this attempt failed. Still, the voyage led to a valuable conclusion: that Cuba should follow a strategy of producing refined sugar (sugar for direct consumption) rather than follow the practice of the rest of the Caribbean colonies, which was to produce *mascabado*, a raw material exported to Europe for refining (González-Ripoll Navarro 2002, pp. 90–91). From then on, scientific-technical knowledge about sugar production was disseminated by way of pamphlets, recommendations, manuals, reports, and essays about the best methods for growing cane and producing sugar. Among the authors were José Ricardo O'Farrill, José Luis de Casaseca, Álvaro Reynoso, and Alejandro Oliván, followed in a later period by José María Dau, Eugenio Pimienta, and other scientists, technicians, and planters (Fernández Prieto pp. 81–82, 99; Ely pp. 579–581).

The application of technology from the first industrial revolution to the making of sugar from beets influenced the Cuban sweetener industry in several ways. The beet sugar industry's initial success in France prompted its spread to other nearby countries, creating a dangerous competitor to Cuban sugar in European markets. This situation obliged the island's producers to work not only to continually increase output but also to lower production costs. Therefore, Cuban planters looked for ways to introduce the scientific-technical advances of the competing industry into their own mills.

At first, the use of steam power in cane grinding was the sole innovation. This use of steam only partly mechanized the factory, though it did speed up its work rhythm, thus increasing productivity and forcing the rest of the factory's operations to increase their processing capacity. Steam power was first applied successfully in 1817, in a mill located in Limonar, Matanzas, using a machine manufactured in England and imported by the planter Juan Madrazo (Moreno Fraginals 1978, vol. 1, p. 207). The introduction of steam power improved the technical conditions of the grinding itself, which in turn required adoption of other measures to increase output. These included expanding the cane-growing area and increasing the number of slave workers assigned to cutting, carrying, and carting the raw material, all of which also required more draft animals. In such conditions, greater production and efficiency on the plantation depended on incorporating equipment similar to that being used in the mill's production chain. Within a few decades, steam was also applied to other stages downstream from the grinding, turning the mill into a completely mechanized entity.

Modernization was introduced in the heating of the cane juice through the use of double- or triple-action vacuum evaporators, a state-of-the-art technology first adopted in 1841 by the La Mella

INFORME

Á

LA JUNTA DE GOBIERNO

DEL REAL CONSULADO

SOBRE EL ENSAYO DEL NUEVO TREN DE ELABORAR AZÚCAR,

SENTADO EN EL INGENIO DE SAN JOSÉ

POR

LA COMISION ENCARGADA DE PRESENCIARLO, SEGUIDO DE UN OFICIO DE D. ALEJANDRO OLIVAN, REFERENTE AL PROPIO OBGETO: IMPRESOS POR ACUERDO DE LA MISMA JUNTA DE GOBIERNO.

HABANA: 1831.

IMPRENTA FRATERNAL, CALLE DE LA OBRA PIA.

mill near the city of Matanzas. In that same decade, a machine that would replace the draining room arrived in Cuba: the centrifuge, a turbine designed to improve and speed up the final stage of production by rapidly separating out the sugar crystals. This invention premiered in Cuba in 1849 in La Amistad, a mill in the valley of Guines in Havana province (Moreno Fraginals vol. 1, p. 232).

Other, later innovations made milling more efficient. These included the introduction of shredders and choppers and of belts to move the cane. Also, soaking and pounding of the raw material were employed in attempts to improve the sucrose yield. Further, in the mid-nineteenth century planters began to introduce a variety of instruments to control product quality through chemical analysis. The first known laboratory was set up in Juan Poey's paradigmatic Las Cañas mill in 1873 (Perret Ballester p. 45). This illustrious planter's efforts also led to the first use of fertilizers in cane growing. His steps in this direction began in 1860 and continued as other planters joined him in applying fertilizers and also manufacturing or importing them (Fernández Prieto pp. 156–157; Ely pp. 574–579). However, these advanced techniques introduced in some mills were not extended to all, mainly because of the unequal distribution of financial resources among the owners. Thus, in the different sugar-producing regions of the country there were units with quite different productive capacities and varying degrees of application of science and technology. That remained so throughout the rest of the nineteenth century.

Railroads The modernizing features of the first industrial revolution that reached Cuba were soon joined, in 1837, by the iron horse. Railroads lowered the cost of transporting sugar to the ports, and they provided crucial support for the spread of sugar planting into new lands much further from the coasts. Indeed, the first steam railway in Cuba was conceived for the purpose of facilitating the transportation of sugar and other products to the port of Havana from the plains to its south and of lessening the cost. The planters in other sugar-industry areas followed suit. Railroad transportation soon reached the pioneer sugar lands of Cárdenas (1840), Matanzas (1843), Cienfuegos (1851), and Sagua la Grande (1858). A few decades later, steam locomotives likewise became an internal component of Cuban sugar plantations, being used to move the cane from the fields to the industrial plants (Zanetti and García pp. 146–155).

IMAGES OF COLONIAL MILLS

As technological improvements were introduced, the various parts of the sugar-making process moved closer together and came to be housed under a single roof or in buildings attached to the grinding house. The modern, mid-nineteenth-century mill was lit by gas lanterns, but before the century was out the mill would incorporate one of the fundamental achievements of the second industrial revolution—electricity. The first recorded use of a generator or dynamo to light an industrial plant

Lithograph of sugar plantation by Eduardo Laplante. The French artist Eduardo Laplante created a series of prints that appeared in Justo G. Cantero's *Los ingenios de Cuba* (The Mills of Cuba), published in 1857. Laplante's pictures show exterior and interior views of Cuba's sugar mills, along with the technology of the era, including railroads, a central component of the sugar industry. LITHOGRAPH BY EDUARDO LAPLANTE.

THE BACARDÍ FAMILY: CUBA'S RUM KINGS

After emigrating from Spain in the early nineteenth century, the Bacardí family became one of the most important and influential families in Cuba. Facundo Bacardí began producing rum from Cuban sugar in 1862, and his brand quickly became popular. His eldest son, Emilio, the first Bacardí born in Cuba, distinguished himself both as a businessman and as a patriot, aiding the nationalist uprising in 1868 as he ascended to the presidency of Bacardí y compañía. After his son and namesake Emilito left Santiago to join the new rebellion in 1895, Emilio funneled money and supplies to the insurgents. Emilio Bacardí became mayor of Santiago after the end of Spanish rule, and he later ascended to the Senate. The fortunes of the family and brand continued to rise through trade and tourism from the United States. The company aided Fidel Castro's insurrection in the 1950s, but the relationship between the distiller and the revolutionaries quickly deteriorated. The revolutionary government nationalized Bacardí in 1960, prompting both the family and company to flee the island. Bacardí reconstituted itself abroad under its familiar name and logo. From exile, the Bacardí family remained active in Cuban affairs, organizing opposition to the Castro government and planning the company's return to the island.

BIBLIOGRAPHY

Aixalá Dawson, Mari, and Pepín R. Argamasilla. *Bacardí: A Tale of Merchants, Family, and Company.* Miami: Facundo and Amalia Bacardi Foundation, 2006.

Calvo Ospina, Hernando. *Bacardí: The Hidden War.* Translated by Stephen Wilkinson and Alasdair Holden. London: Pluto Press, 2002.

Foster, Peter. *Family Spirits: The Bacardí Saga.* Toronto: Macfarlane Walter and Ross, 1990.

Gjelten, Tom. *Bacardí and the Long Fight for Cuba: The Biography of a Cause.* New York: Viking, 2008.

Voss, Ursula L. *Los Bacardí: Una familia entre el ron y la revolución cubana.* Mexico City: Plaza and Janés, 2006.

Robert C. Nathan

in Cuba dates from 1879 (Perret Ballester p. 43) in the San Joaquín, a sugar mill on the Matanzas plain. By the end of the nineteenth century this type of illumination began to replace gas in other mills, though the direct application of electricity to the process of producing sugar took longer to occur. As mills grew larger and more technologically modern and began to acquire the status of *central*, they required new elements of construction and technique. Tilt cradles for transferring loads of cane, rail yards and repair shops, fuel tanks, and warehouses were added to the equipment and structures of the original factories. These changes did more than technically modernize the different stages of production: They also changed the image of the old colonial mill.

In images of the interiors of some of the most emblematic mid-nineteenth-century Cuban mills, viewers observe the coexistence of traditional procedures for extracting sugar from cane with modern technical innovations of the era, all within the same factory. The prints made by the Cuban lithographer Eduardo Laplante (1818–1860) and the texts by Cuban planter Justo G. Cantero of Trinidad are particularly valuable. They appear together in *Los ingenios de Cuba*, originally published in 1857, which shows exterior and interior views of sugar mills that portray the technology of the era, as well as showing railroads as a component of the industry. The book also contains plans for the layout of *bateyes* (mill villages) such as those of the Armonía, San Martín, and Flor de Cuba mills (García Mora and Santamaría García 2002, pp. 181, 199, 252).

LABOR FORCE

For nearly four centuries the supply of workers to Cuban sugar mills depended on the importation of slaves. The immigration of free men destined to the same end is a phenomenon of the late decades of the nineteenth century. The causes of this phenomenon lie in the island's history. The population density of the Cuban archipelago was originally quite low. Its indigenous population was decimated by the Spanish conquest, and European immigration during the early colonial centuries was small. Because sugar exports to Spain faced heavy taxation and other controls, the sector created no effective demand for the purchase of captive laborers. In the mid-seventeenth century there were said to be barely 1,000 slaves. Five thousand more apparently were brought in legally during the next century, plus an unknown additional number brought in by smugglers (Ortiz pp. 446–447; Marrero p. 40).

African Slaves Official authorizations to import slaves during the early centuries of the colony were almost always issued to Portuguese, Genovese, or other traders who were also engaged in additional sorts of trade with Europe or other Caribbean colonies. The first important authorization to bring captives to Cuba was issued in 1595. During the next century, additional authorizations and probable contraband traffic supplied an enslaved labor force to work in copper mines, construction of fortifications, and sugar mills. This made possible a slow and gradual increase in sugar production during a period when the primitive mills required only small numbers of slaves. In that era, small mills had only two or three slaves, and a maximum of thirty made up the crews of large producers.

In the course of the eighteenth century, sugar production increased notably, reaching an annual total of more than 500,000 *quintales* (25,000 tons) (Pedrosa Puertas p. 13). Because the industry's growth depended entirely on importation of a captive labor force, the slave trade was spurred on decisively by concessions granted to experienced English traffickers and to a few companies formed by local capitalists. In the second half of the eighteenth century the demand for sugar made conditions favorable to further development of Cuban production. Prospects grew more favorable during the English occupation of Havana in 1763, and later when

Importation of slaves to Cuba between 1763 and 1873

Table 2

Year	Median Number of Slaves Imported Annually	Year	Median Number of Slaves Imported Annually	Year	Median Number of Slaves Imported Annually
1763–1764	3,899	1800–1804	8,130	1840–1844	20,000
1765–1769	1,363	1805–1809	3,343	1845–1849	2,000
1770–1774	985	1810–1814	6,261	1850–1854	8,000
1775–1779	2,394	1815–1819	21,681	1855–1859	10,800
1780–1784	1,969	1820–1824	20,200	1860–1864	10,400
1785–1789	2,413	1825–1829	32,200	1865–1869	6,500
1790–1794	6,542	1830–1834	29,600	1870–1873	2,800
1795–1799	4,847	1835–1839	32,000		

SOURCES: Instituto de Historia de Cuba. *La colonia, evolución socioeconómica y formación nacional, de los orígenes hasta 1867*. Havana: Editora Política, 1994, Table No. 11, "Importación de esclavos de ambos sexos por varios puertos de Cuba, 1763–1820," pp. 471–472; Barcia, María del Carmen. *Burguesía esclavista y abolición*. Havana: Editorial de Ciencias Sociales, 1987, Appendix No. 1, pp. 161–162.

markets opened in the former British colonies of North America. The position of Cuban sugar improved still further after 1790, when Haiti disappeared as a supplier of the world market because of the slave revolt in the French colony. This event spurred the growth of both exports. Because it was impossible to produce sugar in Cuba without slaves, the colonial power responded to requests from the island's planters with regulations issued between 1789 and 1798 that liberalized trade in Africans. The results were reflected in an immediate increase in imports of slaves, from an annual average of about 2,000 slaves between 1775 and 1788 to an annual average of 5,000 between 1789 and 1800 (Instituto de Historia de Cuba, Table 11, pp. 472–473).

In the nineteenth century the sugar industry added technological innovations that intensified the rhythm of production and increased the efficiency of the factories. As a result of unequal implementation of these techniques, the slave-based sugar plantation took shape in the midst of great technological diversity. The large units might employ a labor force of nearly 500 slaves. Thus the annual number of captives imported continued to multiply, reaching totals of more than 25,000 or 30,000 a year in the decades from 1820 to 1840 (Barcia pp. 161–162). Imports of an African labor force remained high through the mid-1840s. Thereafter, the numbers dropped for nearly ten years because of a temporary drop in sugar prices and because of the negative implications of slave revolts in western Cuba in 1843 and 1844. At this point, planters, for the first time, went in search of new sources of cheap laborers who could be forced into sugar work. The result was the hiring of indentured Asians and Yucatecans, as well as free farm workers from various regions of Spain.

Contract Laborers The first non-African workers were imported in 1847, when two shipments of so-called coolies, also called simply Asians, arrived in Havana. This traffic was temporarily interrupted and then revived in 1851 when sugar prices began to rise. The revival of the market also stimulated new imports of Africans, though the price of these bondmen had increased as well. The combination of high sugar prices and high prices for African slaves led to the arrival of more shiploads of Asian contract laborers, who in the year 1858 alone totaled a record 16,414 individuals. In the 1860s imports of African slaves again began to drop, as arrivals of Asians grew (Barcia pp. 102–105, 161–162; Pérez de la Riva pp. 65–78, Piqueras, ch. 2, pp. 3, 4, 7). During that decade the demand for workers on the Matanzas plains was met largely by incorporating Chinese workers into the crews of the region's countless mills.

Although the Asian contract laborer's status was formally distinct from that of the African slave, essentially the same system of exploitation was applied to both. The only difference was that the Asians' contracts had an expiration date, whereas slavery was still a lifelong condition. Traffic in Chinese laborers ended in 1874, barely a year after the traffic in Africans. Mutinies on board the ships, frequent enlistment of the Asians on the Cuban side in the Ten Years' War, and intervention by the Chinese government put an end to this shameful activity. During the twenty-seven years that it had continued, approximately 125,000 Asian contract laborers entered the country (Pérez de la Riva p. 81; Balboa p. 56).

Another effort to supply workers to plantations and services was the importation of Mayans from the Yucatán. This proceeding involved the authorities of neighboring Mexico, who were immersed in a local conflict with the indigenous people of that region.

Human trafficking with Mexico was cheaper than with China, both because of geography and because it made use of the ships belonging to an unscrupulous Havana entrepreneur involved in fishing operations in the Gulf of Mexico. Intervention by the British government and the departure of the governor of the Yucatán put an end to the transport of Yucatecans to Havana, but a total of between 2,000 and 3,000 such contract laborers arrived during the years the practice endured. As time passed, the Yucatecans made their way to cities and towns in western Cuba, where they found different kinds of work. Only a few remained on sugar plantations (García Álvarez pp. 33–46; Strade pp. 93–109; Pérez de la Riva pp. 51–54).

Importation of free workers from Spain and the Canaries began in the 1850s, when some 2,000 individuals were brought to Cuba from Galicia. Entrepreneurs' attempts to force legally free men into labor and to limit their movements, based on rights supposedly acquired by the importing company, ended in rebellions wherever the workers were employed. Coercion, bad food, and lodgings similar to slave quarters caused the failure of this approach (Pérez de la Riva pp. 45–48; Zanetti and García pp. 120–121).

Free Workers For centuries, the supply of cane on sugar plantations depended on a slave workforce assigned to harvest the crop and transport it to the mills. At the height of the plantation system, the captives tended to share the work with a small number of paid workers who specialized in specific production tasks. The mill was an agro-manufacturing complex organized and run as a single property, including all the basic factors of production: land, means of production, and workforce. However, although slaves continued to be imported as late as the 1860s, the most advanced mill owners began to consider replacing slave labor with more modern and economical labor systems. At the same time, attitudes opposed to the African slave trade had emerged within the Spanish government, as had demands for the relatively rapid abolition of slavery. In Cuba's first war for independence, begun in 1868, the Cuban side also adopted the principle of total suppression of this system of exploitation. As a result of this confluence of factors, the Spanish government issued the Moret Law, also called the Law of Free Wombs, according to which all children of slaves born from 1870 on would be free. Thus began a lengthy process that included the Patronato law of 1880, which offered a delay in the suppression of the system and culminated in the definitive abolition of slavery in Cuba in 1886 (Barcia pp. 139–145, 149–153).

With slavery abolished, the workforce carrying out agricultural and industrial work in the sugar mills became free. Cane production began to be administratively decentralized under an approach that distributed cane lands among independent farmers by way of leases or other forms of temporary transfer. Under this system the harvesters were committed to turning quantities of cut cane over to the mill according to a schedule and conditions set by individual agreements. This relationship led to the emergence of *colonias* (cane farms), a new agricultural, territorial, and labor entity that played a key role in the Cuban sugar industry in the following decades. The colonias were worked not only by their owners or renters and their families, but also by some 25,000 ex-slaves still attached to the land by the patronato system, who became part of a reserve army of labor for the temporary work of the sugar harvest. Nonetheless, the main source of new workers to produce the growing sugar output of the island continued to come from massive immigration. Measures taken by planters and sugar merchants led to movements in favor of establishing public entities (such as the Protective Society for Spanish Labor in the Overseas Territories) that sponsored seasonal immigration by Spaniards and Canary Islanders into Cuba during the final decades of the nineteenth century (Balboa pp. 73–75; García 2002, pp. 99–111).

EARLY PRODUCTION AND TRADE STRATEGIES

To achieve their goals of widespread production and export to foreign markets, colonial-era Cuban sugar producers had to diversify their strategy in order to solve problems related to occupation and use of land, introduction of new technology, and limits on their access to a labor force. The planters' efforts also sought to resolve other issues of similar strategic importance, such as the employment of capital in sugar production, competition from beet sugar, the introduction of techniques of continuous processing, and vertical decentralization.

During the early colonial centuries, lack of capital prevented fuller exploitation of the island's capacity to produce sugar. This limitation stemmed largely from Spain's view on how to extract profit from its colonies, which centered on a rigid monopoly over sugar commerce and maritime transport, as well as ferocious taxation of colonial products. The port of Havana was designated as the only port that could engage in foreign commerce and the Spanish fleet system as the only means of shipping. These limits, alongside a complex international situation, led the residents of the rest of the country to opt for black-market trading or smuggling, known in Spanish as *rescate* (ransom) (Ely p. 38). As production and trade in sugar grew, however, the growers' pressure on Spanish authorities led to some relaxation of this system. Still, its exploitative essence remained unchanged until the end of Spanish colonial control in 1898.

When Cuba's sugar industry first emerged, the same methods of stimulation that had already been used on the island of Hispaniola were applied. Local actions to promote the industry took the form of petitions for royal treasury loans to support the creation of sugar mills and exemptions or discounts from taxes on sugar production and trade. Alongside these came requests to import workers and equipment as exceptions to the controls imposed by the Casa de Contratación in Seville on commerce with the Americas. The strategy of seeking

Ship-bound passengers arriving in Cuba, 1882–1894

Figure 1

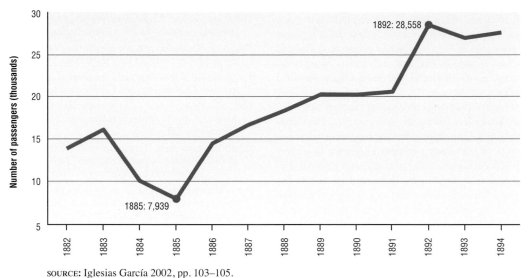

SOURCE: Iglesias García 2002, pp. 103–105.

these types of aid from the Spanish monarchs, and the arguments wielded to this effect, were based on a reality that could not be hidden: lack of sufficient local funds to create sugar mills. In the final decade of the sixteenth century some such concessions were won. The most important was the promulgation in December 1595 of a royal decree exempting Cuban sugar mills from seizures and attachments. This decree was known as the *privilegio de ingenios* (sugar mill privilege). It exempted land, animals, and slaves devoted to sugar production from attachment for unpaid debts, so that their operations would be protected from interruptions due to lawsuits over debts or disputed inheritances (Ortiz pp. 446–449).

As the seventeenth century progressed, conditions in Cuba changed because pirates and corsairs of various nationalities who preyed on ships and settlements in Spanish America threatened the stability of the fleet system. In response, the sugar trade sought other ways of shipping the product to other parts of the Americas, both legally and as contraband. The shift to a strategy of illegal trade via foreign ships favored a diversification of the island's commerce and production. As a result of gains achieved in both legal and illegal commerce, by the mid-seventeenth century seventy sugar mills were operating in Havana, and there were others around Santiago and Bayamo. By the end of the century Havana was exporting many times the sugar that had been sent abroad at the beginning of the century (Fuente pp. 66–67).

Later Strategies By the late decades of the eighteenth century, the island's local oligarchies had become the most powerful and experienced sector of Cuban society. This situation was the result of a long process of generational turnover during which these groups had applied themselves to all sorts of production and trade, both legitimate and clandestine, as well as holding and wielding administrative posts, founding estates, and

creating important family fortunes. Advances in sugar production strengthened the position of the members of this class, identified as sugar producers or plantation owners. Their growing influence in official circles was reflected in the founding of institutions to represent their interests. Among these were the Real Consulado de Agricultura y Comercio (Royal Chamber of Agriculture and Commerce); the Sociedad Económica de Amigos del País (Economic Society of Friends of the Land of Cuba); and other scientific, beneficial, or cultural councils and societies. These entities were created and maintained for the purpose of channeling the needs, requests, and demands of the social sector most tightly tied to sugar production. Among their most illustrious members was Francisco de Arango y Parreño (1765–1837), the ideological spearhead of a program for promotion, protection, and stimulation of the sugar industry at a historical moment especially propitious for achieving the great leap in Cuban production that occurred. With the creation of these institutions, the sugar producers' general strategy cohered and reached a new level of sophistication and self-expression. At the center of this strategy lay demands for reforms in the commercial and tax system and demands for means of importing more slave labor (González-Ripoll Navarro 1999, pp. 156–159, 165). With the issue of freedom to buy and sell land partially resolved, sugar producers of the late eighteenth century also turned their attention to raising the quality of their product, so as to give Cuban refined sugar a competitive advantage in the international market.

The nineteenth century offered a promising context for both production and international trade in sugar. Nonetheless, although Cuban output and exports showed sustained growth during nearly seven decades, competition from beet sugar finally brought a downward trend in prices, dislodging Cuba from much of the European market (Zanetti Lecuona pp. 21–22). This situation forced the planters to develop a new strategy, aimed at maintaining output while improving the industrial efficiency of the mills to reduce production costs. Thus, technological innovation became an indispensable condition of keeping the mills in operation. The old practices of semi-mechanized mills had to be replaced. In semi-mechanized mills, the steam engine was used only to grind the cane; the means of increasing capacity were limited to adding more acres of cane-growing land, more kettles for cooking the cane juice, and more dripping molds. The replacement strategy involved a new concept of introducing modern machinery into every step of production in order to achieve continuous industrial production with totally mechanized operations. The impossibility of implementing such changes in many of the old semi-mechanized mills turned them into producers of low-quality sugar or suppliers of raw materials to the more modern and efficient centrales.

In the final decades of the nineteenth century the majority of the sugar and molasses produced in Cuba was destined for the U.S. market; shipments fell to European countries that had increased their output of beet sugar (Moreno Fraginals, vol. 3, table 7). The North American market demanded a quality product that could serve as raw material for a powerful refining industry that had emerged there. Cuba thus became part of the first link in a capitalist agro-industrial and commercial chain whose goal was mass production of refined sugar. Between 80 and 90 percent of Cuban sugar production went to the United States. For more than a decade, Spain turned the advantage of having such a huge market for the island's sugar into a prop for its own balance of trade (Piqueras pp. 113–115). This cross-purpose led to serious conflict between the colonial government and Cuban sugar producers, who wanted to defend their preferential access to the North American market. Thus the planters were constantly pressuring Spain to open the doors to negotiations with the United States. This occurred on two occasions, in 1884 and 1892, but came to a definitive end in 1894 (Zanetti Lecuona pp. 125, 193, 205; Piqueras pp. 163–184). U.S. intervention in the Cuban War of Independence in 1898 ended the conflict between local sugar producers and the Spanish commercial, treasury, and bureaucratic interests on the island. It gave rise to a new era of relations between sugar producers in Cuba and foreign capital interests who wanted to promote production and commercialization of the sweetener on a global scale.

BIBLIOGRAPHY

Balboa Navarro, Imilcy. *Los brazos necesarios*. Valencia, Spain: Biblioteca Historia Social, 2000.

Balboa, Navarro, Imilcy. "Brazos para el azúcar: Cuba, 1820–1866." In *Azúcar y esclavitud en el final del trabajo forzado*, edited by José A. Piqueras. Madrid: Fondo de Cultura Económica, 2002.

Barcia, María del Carmen. *Burguesía esclavista y abolición*. Havana: Editorial de Ciencias Sociales, 1987.

Bergard, Laird W. *Cuban Rural Society in the Nineteenth Century: The Social and Economic History of*

Monoculture in Matanzas. Princeton, NJ: Princeton University Press, 1990.

De la Torre, José M. *Lo que fuimos y lo que somos: La Habana antigua y moderna*. Havana: Librería Cervantes, 1913.

Dye, Alan. *Cuban Sugar in the Age of Mass Production*. Stanford, CA: Stanford University Press, 1998.

Ely, Roland T. *Cuando reinaba su majestad el azúcar*. Havana: Ediciones Imagen Contemporánea, 2000.

Fernández Prieto, Leida. *Cuba agrícola: Mito y tradición*. Madrid: Consejo Superior de Investigaciones Científicas, 2005.

Fuente, Alejandro de la. "Economía, 1500–1700." In *Historia de Cuba*, edited by Consuelo Naranjo Orovio. Madrid: Consejo Superior de Investigaciones Científicas, 2009.

Funes Monzote, Reinaldo. *De los bosques a los cañaverales: Una historia ambiental de Cuba 1492–1926*. Havana: Editorial de Ciencias Sociales, 2008.

García, Gloria, "Tecnología y abolición." In *Azúcar y esclavitud en el final del trabajo forzado*, edited by José A. Piqueras. Madrid: Fondo de Cultura Económica, 2002.

García Álvarez, Alejandro. "Traficantes en el Golfo." *Revista Historia Social* 17 (Autumn 1993): 33–46.

García Mora, Luis Miguel, and Antonio Santamaría García. "Esclavos por centrales: Mano de obra y tecnología en la industria azucarera. Un ensayo cuantitativo, 1860–1877." In *Azúcar y esclavitud en el final del trabajo forzado*, edited by José A. Piqueras. Madrid: Fondo de Cultura Económica, 2002.

García Mora, Luis Miguel, and Antonio Santamaría García, eds. *Los ingenios de la Isla de Cuba*. Madrid: Ediciones Doce Calles, 2005.

García Rodríguez, Mercedes. *Entre haciendas y plantaciones: Orígenes de la manufactura azucarera en La Habana*. Havana: Editorial de Ciencias sociales, 2007.

González-Ripoll Navarro, María Dolores. *Cuba, la isla de los ensayos cultura y sociedad (1790–1815)*. Madrid: Consejo Superior de Investigaciones Científicas, 1999.

González-Ripoll Navarro, María Dolores. "Dos viajes, una intención: Francisco Arango y Alejandro Oliván en Europa y las Antillas Azucareras (1794 y 1829)." *Revista de Indias* 62, no. 224 (January–April 2002): 85–102.

Guerra Sánchez, Ramiro. *Azúcar y población de las Antillas*. Havana: Editorial Lex, 1961.

Iglesias García, Fé. *Del ingenio al central*. San Juan: Editorial de la Universidad de Puerto Rico, 1998.

Iglesias García, Fé. "Cuba: La abolición de la esclavitud y el canal de la inmigración jornalera (1880–1895)." In *Azúcar y esclavitud en el final del trabajo forzado*, edited by José A. Piqueras. Madrid: Fondo de Cultura Económica, 2002.

Instituto de Historia de Cuba. *La colonia: Evolución socio-económica y formación nacional. De los orígenes hasta 1867*. Havana: Editora Política, 1994.

Knight, Franklin. *Slave Society in Cuba during the Nineteenth Century*. Madison: University of Wisconsin Press, 1974.

Marrero, Leví. *Cuba, economía y sociedad*. Vol. 3. Madrid: Editorial Playal, 1978.

Moreno Fraginals, Manuel. *El ingenio: Complejo económico social cubano del azúcar*. 3 vols. Havana: Editorial de Ciencias Sociales, 1978.

Moreno Fraginals, Manuel. "La introducción de la caña de azúcar y las técnicas árabes de producción azucarera en América." In *Órbita de Manuel Moreno Fraginals*, edited by Alfredo Prieto and Oscar Zanetti. Havana: Ediciones Unión, 2009.

Ortiz, Fernando. *Contrapunteo cubano del tabaco y el azúcar*. Havana: Consejo Nacional de Cultura, 1963.

Pedrosa Puertas, Rafael. *Cinco siglos de industria azucarera cubana*. Havana: Ministerio del Azúcar, n.d.

Pérez, Louis A. *Cuba between Empires, 1878–1902*. Pittsburgh, PA: University of Pittsburgh Press, 1983.

Pérez de la Riva, Juan. *Los culíes chinos en Cuba*. Havana: Editorial de Ciencias Sociales, 2000.

Perret Ballester, Alberto. *El azúcar en Matanzas y sus dueños en La Habana: Apuntes e iconografía*. Havana: Editorial de Ciencias Sociales, 2007.

Pichardo, Hortensia. *Documentos para la historia de Cuba*. Havana: Editora del Consejo Nacional de Universidades, 1965.

Piqueras, José A. *Cuba, emporio y colonia: La disputa por un mercado interferido (1878–1895)*. Madrid: Fondo de Cultura Económica, 2003.

Portuondo Zúñiga, Olga. "La consolidación de la sociedad criolla (1700–1765)." In *La colonia: Evolución socioeconómica y formación nacional. De los orígenes hasta 1867*, edited by Instituto de Historia de Cuba. Havana: Editora Política, 1994.

Santamaría García, Antonio, and Alejandro García Álvarez. *Economía y colonia: La economía cubana y la relación con España, 1765–1902*. Madrid: Consejo Superior de Investigaciones Científicas, 2004.

Santamaría García, Antonio, and Luis Miguel García Mora. "Colonos. Agricultores cañeros, ¿clase media rural en Cuba? 1880–1898." *Revista de Indias* 63, no. 212 (January–April 1998): 131–161.

Scott, Rebecca. *Slave Emancipation in Cuba: The Transition to Free Labor, 1860–1899*. Princeton, NJ: Princeton University Press, 1985.

Sorhegui, Arturo, and Alejandro de la Fuente. "El surgimiento de la sociedad criolla en Cuba (1553–1608)." In *La colonia: Evolución socioeconómica y formación nacional. De los orígenes hasta 1867*, edited by Instituto de Historia de Cuba. Havana: Editora Política, 1994.

Strade, Paul. "Los colonos yucatecos como sustitutos de los esclavos negros." In *Cuba, la perla de las Antillas*, edited by Consuelo Naranjo Orovio and Tomás Mallo Gutiérrez. Madrid: Ediciones Doce Calles, 1994.

Zanetti, Oscar, and Alejandro García. *Sugar and Railroads: A Cuban History, 1837–1959*. Chapel Hill: North Carolina University Press, 1998.

Zanetti Lecuona, Oscar. *Comercio y poder: Relaciones cubano-hispano-norteamericanas en torno a 1898*. Havana: Premio Casa de las Américas, 1998.

SUGAR: REPUBLICAN PERIOD

Oscar Zanetti

The rapid expansion and subsequent stagnation of Cuba's sugar industry between 1902 and 1959.

The modern sugar industry in Cuba has very old roots, but its recent history started in the 1880s when, facing growing competition from beet sugar and the inevitable abolition of slavery, sugar production on the island underwent a profound transformation. Forced to reduce costs as prices fell and the cost of labor rose, sugar producers used new technology to boost production levels and increase profits. The new plants, with production capabilities ten or even twenty times greater than the old mills, could produce between 4,000 and 10,000 metric tons of sugar per harvest and extract twice as much sucrose from the canes. Changes were not limited to assimilating a complex, continuous processing technology; they also involved a complete reordering of the production system. The substantial investments required for large-scale industrial equipment, the expense of developing extensive sugarcane plantations to satisfy the growing demand for raw material, and the difficulties of managing a large number of free workers, meant that sugarcane agriculture moved into the hands of the more or less independent *colonos* (farmers) who had been recruited from among financially ruined landowners, the smaller peasant farmers who lived close to the plants, and the tenant farmers living on sugar mill property. Because the new factory was the destination for the product harvested from many large plantations, the mill came to be called a *central*.

Centralization was achieved around 1894, when Cuba produced a sugar harvest of more than 1 million tons for the first time; in little more than a decade, the island had doubled its sugar production and had reduced by two-thirds—to about 400—the number of mills that produced it. The main driving forces of this process were local sugar mill proprietors and large landowners, both Cuban and Spanish. For many of them, their conversion to industrial entrepreneurs involved a burdensome debt, mainly to banks and U.S. suppliers. Having lost their European market due to the sugar beet competition, Cuban sugar producers had become more and more dependent on the U.S. market, to which they exported 90 percent of their product during the last decade of the nineteenth century. The formation of the powerful American Sugar Refining Company reinforced this dependency because essentially it could dictate the characteristics of the sugar it imported. The McKinley Tariff in 1890 made this clear, as did the reciprocal trade agreement between Spain and the United States that followed, which was meant to ensure access for Cuban sugar to that vital market.

The outbreak of the War of Independence in 1895 accelerated the structural transformations the Cuban economy had been undergoing for many years. The hostilities were especially devastating to sugar production because the burning of sugarcane plantations and the destruction of plants (which began in the first year of the war) reduced production by 70 percent. Exactly how many sugar mills were destroyed is unknown. When the United States took over the island's government after the brief war of 1898, the supervising authorities inspected 217 plants that had the capacity for milling in the short term; the fact that the total production capacity of these units was estimated at 1,052,691 tons—a capacity very

■ *See also*

Ecology and Environment: Republican Period

Economy: Republican Period

Governance and Contestation: The Cuban Revolution

Mario Carreño: His Art and World

The Sugarmill (Manuel Moreno Fraginals)

Cuban-American Sugar Company, common stock certificate. During the early twentieth century, American economic hegemony in Cuba lured U.S. capital to the island. By the 1920s, U.S. firms controlled 60 percent of Cuba's sugar industry. The Cuban-American Sugar Company was one of the largest conglomerates. IMAGE COURTESY OF HERITAGE AUCTION GALLERIES/ WWW.HA.COM.

close to 1894's record production—indicates that the centrales that survived were for the most part those in which the industry's processing capacities were concentrated. Sugar production again exceeded 1 million tons in 1903, a year in which only 171 centrales were milling. The war, by dealing the coup de grâce to small and insolvent mills, had contributed to the completion of the centralization process.

The sugar economy's transformation was completed within the context of the institutional changes that Cuba underwent during U.S. intervention (1899–1902). The Platt Amendment, which reduced Cuba to a protectorate, came after measures for economic restructuring were dictated by the U.S. authorities on the island. In the same year that the Cuban republic was created (1902), a new reciprocal trade treaty with the United States was established, and for once and for all, the island's sugar was tied to a preferential market. The 20-percent tariff margin on sugar was an indisputable advantage for producers, but it was won at the price of granting U.S. goods privileged access to Cuba. The U.S. political and economic hegemony in Cuba was a powerful lure for more U.S. capital, which had begun to flow into the Cuban sugar industry years earlier. During the intervention stage and immediately thereafter, U.S. firms acquired seven centrales and developed another four, demonstrating a clear trend toward control of Cuban production.

GROWTH IN PRODUCTION

Sugar production grew quickly, quintupling over a period of just two decades. This change developed over three different stages. During the first period, from 1904 to 1913, growth was in response to the expanded access to the U.S. market made possible by the reciprocal trade agreement. By 1913, with the sale of 2.1 million tons of sugar (87% of its total production), Cuba had displaced the other foreign suppliers to the United States. After that, the Cuban sugar production might have been expected to slow down, but the outbreak of World War I opened a second stage of growth

that stimulated production to fill the shortage in the world sugar supply that resulted from the destruction of the European sugar beet industry.

Cuban production reached 4.6 million short tons during 1919. During the third and last stage, from 1920 to 1925, there was no stimulus from demand; in fact, the market was uncertain. Nevertheless, the U.S. sugar firms, which had come to control 60 percent of the Cuban industry following heavy investment during the war, raised the amount of the sugar harvest by an additional 1 million tons in order to secure an unbeatable competitive position. In 1925 the unstoppable decline in price ended this period of expansion.

These three decades of almost uninterrupted growth fundamentally changed the Cuban sugar economy. One obvious change was in its geographic distribution, as the development of plants and sugarcane plantations in the eastern regions brought an end to the traditional western dominance. During 1925 more than one-half of all sugar production came from the eastern part of the island. Expansion was not just geographic; the average production for each sugar mill grew at a rate similar to the rate of total production. Although production quintupled, the number of plants only increased by little more than 10 percent. Hence the process of concentrating production that had begun with centralization forged ahead during the boom decades.

A related effect of the prolonged period of expansion was a change in the typical size of the mill. In 1925 the Cuban centrales were among the biggest sugarcane plants in the world. The trend toward large industry that had begun at the end of the nineteenth century crystallized during the first decades of the twentieth century as companies capitalized on sugar production technology's principal innovations, particularly the tandems, or multiple-mill systems. Most investors increased production by expanding milling capacity, a technical option based on Cuba's unusual production factors—an abundance of fertile land and a comparative scarcity of manpower. Although the massive employment of immigrants (including farm laborers from the West Indies and Haiti who were hired from 1913 on) counteracted the labor shortage, the hiring of workers continued to be costly because there was a growing demand for them. But available land seemed almost unlimited, particularly in the eastern provinces where extended territories were still virgin at the beginning of the twentieth century. In line with this situation and favorable natural conditions, sugarcane cultivation used rather rudimentary extensive techniques rather than intensive ones. Cuban sugarcane agriculture thus was characterized by a yield (amount of sugarcane per cultivated area) that was relatively low, and the result of prolonged exploitation of shoots, scant fertilization, and minimal irrigation on the plantations. This situation was offset by a greater yield of sugar from the canes, which was achieved because of the great pains taken to organize the harvest.

The sugar companies called on different resources to ensure that there was enough raw material. They appropriated all the available land in the zones where they installed their centrales, which led to the creation of enormous estates, in some cases containing more than 170,000 acres. Generally speaking, the amount of land exceeded what was actually needed, but this allowed for complete control over the planters who, for the most part, were established as tenant farmers on the sugar mill properties. No less important as a means of control were the centrales' railroads, whose extensive network of tracks covered the entire cultivation zone, guaranteeing not only the prompt receipt of raw materials but also domination over the colonos for whom the railroads were the only means to transport their sugarcane. This arrangement was particularly typical of the east-central provinces where the big North American–owned centrales were concentrated, but owners' monopolizing of lands and control of the infrastructure was also the generalized consequence of the period of growth in sugar production. Equally significant was the transfer of properties into U.S. hands; by 1924, Americans already owned seventy-four centrales that produced most of Cuba's sugar. That transformation involved a significant transfer of control over the country's production machine and also a change from a system based on private ownership (the small family-run business, the traditional landowner) to a system dominated by large corporations that often controlled a large number of plants.

The effects of the sugar boom on the national economy are difficult to assess. On one hand, there was indisputable, spectacular growth, summarized by the annual average growth rate of 9.6 percent for exports. On the other hand, although the export value of sugar and its byproducts grew almost tenfold, other exportable products did not even double in sales. This obvious distortion was not alleviated by the performance of the product lines destined for domestic consumption because, except for cattle farming and coffee bean cultivation in the agricultural sector and certain food products and building materials in the industrial one, recorded increases for the remaining areas were insignificant. Without a doubt, the expansion of the sugar industry contributed to the modernization of Cuban society through the enlargement of infrastructure, the broadening of the domestic market, the articulation of business and financial networks, and the introduction of new services.

Cuba: number of plants and sugar production
(SHORT TONS)

Year	Active Centrales	Production	Production per Central
1903	171	1,133,081	6,625
1910	171	2,771,643	16,208
1919	196	4,607,044	23,504
1925	183	5,935,705	32,435

SOURCE: Moreno Fraginals, Manuel. *El ingenio. Complejo económico social cubano del azúcar*. Havana: Editorial de Ciencias Sociales, 1978, vol. 3, Table 3; *Anuario azucarero de Cuba, 1959*. Havana: Cuba Económica y Financiera, p. 92.

Figure 1

Table 1

Cuba: sugar production, 1900–1929

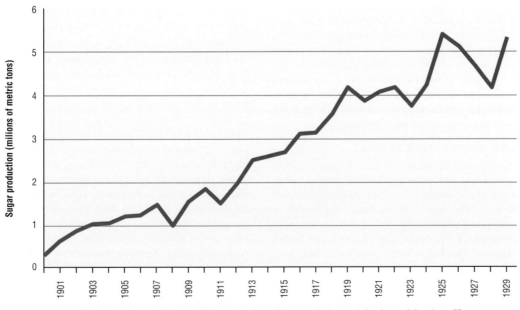

SOURCE: Moreno Fraginals, Manuel. *El ingenio. Complejo económico social cubano del azúcar*. Havana: Editorial de Ciencias Sociales, 1978, vol. 3, Table 1.

Laborers in a Cuban sugar field, c. 1910. The expansion of the sugar industry in the first quarter of the twentieth century led to a high demand for labor. GENERAL RESEARCH & REFERENCE DIVISION, SCHOMBURG CENTER FOR RESEARCH IN BLACK CULTURE, THE NEW YORK PUBLIC LIBRARY, ASTOR, LENOX AND TILDEN FOUNDATIONS

All this could have favored development, and, certainly, some specific industries did succeed in making the most of increased demand and improved transport, but gains were limited. The structural framework created through and for sugar production growth greatly reduced the benefits that might have been derived. The same trade mechanisms that favored the export of sugar turned consumption in the direction of imports, thus supporting dependency. The superior profitability of sugarcane cultivation gave rise to land monopolies and a concentration of material and human resources to the detriment of other agricultural goods. Remittances by immigrant workers, capital repaid to foreign investors, and other factors meant that much of the surplus generated by the sugar industry went to other countries. The extreme specialization of the Cuban economy during those years emphasized the island's already well-defined reputation as a single-commodity producer.

CRISIS AND RESTRUCTURING

The fragility of the economic base that sugar industry expansion had generated became obvious before the end of the 1920s, when the world sugar market took a negative turn. On one hand, the growth of consumption was slowing, particularly in industrial nations, which was due to their demographics as well as saturated demand. On the other hand, large consumer countries were tending toward self-sufficiency by implementing strict protectionist measures. As a clear example of both trends, the United States took its tariffs to prohibitive extremes in 1929, coinciding with the start of the worldwide Great Depression.

Cuban sugar interests had reached a difficult crossroads. Trying to compete in the realm of prices by relying on the island's comparatively low production costs was a nonviable strategy given the effectiveness of protectionist barriers. The alternative, which was to try to put a floor under prices by reducing the supply, risked a loss of markets unless it was achieved through an international producers' agreement. In 1925, when prices averaged a mere 2 cents per pound, the Cuban sugar industry's majority interests—U.S. companies that produced raw sugar and native sugar mill owners—mobilized to introduce restrictions on production. But attaining an international agreement to stabilize the markets and organizing production based on contracted commitments were both measures beyond the control of the entrepreneurs' individual initiatives. Those measures required intervention from the state, which had so far stayed on the fringe of the sugar business.

In 1926, with the enactment of a law that restricted sugar production by 10 percent, the Cuban government launched a reorganization of the industry that lasted more than a decade. Increasing intervention by the state was the decisive component in the industry's transformation. The entire production process from setting the start date of the harvest to determining destinations, the quantities, and forms of sugar shipments, including production quotas, prices, wages, and so on—all of the sector's activities were regulated by detailed, far-reaching laws. At the same time, Cuba's attempts to regulate the world sugar market through international agreements were largely unsuccessful until 1937, when a process involving representatives from the largest consumer countries led to the signing of an agreement in London. Yet, the quota regulations implemented by the U.S. government in 1934—which made the United States a preferential market with a pre-established, proportional supply and differentiated prices—had quicker and more substantial effects.

The protectionist U.S. policy was disastrous for Cuba. Its share in the U.S. market was reduced from over 50 percent of total consumption during the 1920s to only 24.9 percent in 1934, which meant losses of close to 2 million tons in sugar exports. The Franklin D. Roosevelt administration, which had come to power in 1933, believed such existing policies had not produced the advantage that had been anticipated for domestic sugar production, so it adopted a new system using quotas that were proportionally distributed among its customary suppliers. Although the share assigned to Cuba (29.4%) was much smaller than its historical share, it represented longed-for stability with Cuba's most important customer, as well as the possibility of getting a somewhat higher price than the prevailing world market price because the new system included a mechanism that was meant to offset the U.S. producers' higher costs. The U.S. quota remained in force for almost three decades (except for a brief lapse during World War II), operating as the

Cuban industry's primary functional determining factor throughout the entire period.

In most years from 1926 to 1959, Cuban sugar harvests had to be adjusted and domestic distribution of production quotas was one of the prerogatives of state intervention. If the system of free competition had stayed in force during this time of fallen prices and decreased production, the centralization process would have continued its inexorable march and scores of centrales would have disappeared. In such a situation, those who would be most damaged would have been the Cuban sugar mill owners, who were less competitive, and, of course, the thousands of cane growers and tens of thousands of laborers who would have lost their source of income. The grave consequences of the contraction of the sugar industry for a single staple producer such as Cuba were felt during the profound sociopolitical crisis that hit the island between 1930 and 1935.

The Cuban state's regulation of the sugar sector pursued goals that were social as well as economic. When the system was formulated in 1930 it became evident that the state meant to ensure a place for all participants in sugar production. The total amount of the sugar harvest, which was determined by the government, was distributed among all active centrales (construction of new sugar mills had been prohibited since 1926) using a complicated procedure that ultimately privileged the smaller, least efficient plants. A similar trend occurred in

agriculture, first as sugar centrales were prevented from favoring their own cane fields to the detriment of the colonos and later through the Sugar Production Coordination Law, which more fully regulated the relationship between the farmers and the centrales. This legal instrument, enacted in 1937, supported cane growers by allowing them to stay on the land as long as the land produced the assigned quota and they paid the rent, and it introduced a payment procedure that increased the colono's share in the final product made from his cane. In addition, the law established a payment and wages scale that reflected the price of sugar.

LIMITED RECOVERY

During the three decades from 1930 to 1959, Cuba's sugar production reflected the influence of market situations and state regulation. First, the combined effects of U.S. protectionism and the fall in prices caused by the Great Depression effected a drastic drop in production between 1929 and 1933; sugar production in 1933 was barely 40 percent what it had been in 1929. Beginning in 1934, the U.S. quota system and a slight improvement in the international market gave rise to some degree of recovery, but production levels were still clearly depressed when compared to the previous decade's average. The outbreak of World War II made possible the revival of the Cuban industry, which in the postwar years—extended by

Sugarcane grinder, Havana, 1942 The outbreak of World War II brought about a revival of the Cuban sugar industry, as mill owners ground more sugarcane to meet the war needs of the Allied nations. The cane was ground into a pulp from which a byproduct, molasses, could be used for the manufacturing of alcohol to be used in explosives. AP IMAGES

Figure 2

Cuba: sugar production, 1929–1960

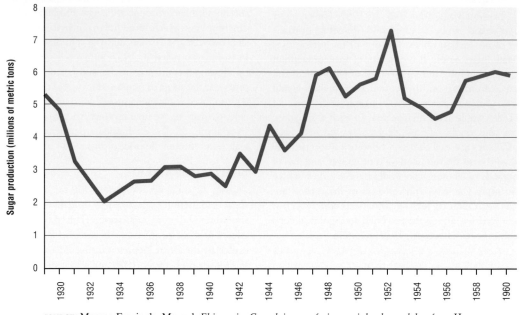

SOURCE: Moreno Fraginals, Manuel. *El ingenio. Complejo económico social cubano del azúcar*. Havana: Editorial de Ciencias Sociales, 1978, vol. 3, Table 1.

Cuban population employed in the production of sugar

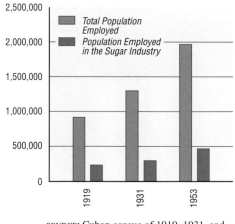

SOURCE: Cuban census of 1919, 1931, and 1953; Santamaria Garcia, Antonio. *Sin azúcar no hay país. La industria azucarera y la economía cubana (1919-1939)*. Seville: Universidad de Sevilla, 2001, Chart IX.6.

Figure 3

the Korean conflict—exceeded the record sugar yields of 1925 and 1929. This was an ephemeral boom, however: Starting in 1953 yearly production fluctuated widely, barely surpassing the average for the five-year period from 1925 through 1929. These years of sugar production have been characterized as a period of stagnation, though the stagnation was relative.

The relatively low profits meant that the sugar industry no longer had abundant capital at its disposal. Moreover, state intervention had put cost pressures on the industry with its regulation of sugarcane payments that favored cane growers and with successive wage increases won by workers during World War II and the postwar period. The strong labor union movement also obtained labor laws that counteracted the depressive effect on wages of growing unemployment. The availability of land was the only factor that did not change. Because of social pressure, large estates were outlawed by the 1940 Constitution, but in practice the extensive lands that the centrales controlled remained untouchable.

Because substantial increases in production volume had been ruled out by the state, sugar businesses designed a strategy aimed at controlling costs based on the seasonal nature of the industry. Though they cut the number of milling days by about thirty, sugar production levels during the 1950s were similar to or better than levels from 1925 to 1929. Through some timely investments—the introduction of new filters and clarifiers, for example—the industry was able to adapt to new operating conditions and thus increase the amount of daily milling, thereby improving production rates.

Those meticulous adjustment measures balanced the situation of the sugar industry so that it had a moderate margin of profit but made it hard for the industry to exercise its traditional role as the driving force of the national economy. Sugar production was still Cuban society's main source of employment, but there was no growth. In order to sustain employment, official measures hindered the introduction of technologies that would have saved on manpower and eliminated obsolete installations that had an adverse effect on productivity. The country had to revive its economy. Options for the sugar industry had been exhausted, so diversification in production—either substituting for imports or developing new product lines—was introduced as the most appropriate formula. But the structural ties that existed with single-commodity production turned out to be difficult to break: The U.S. quota regulations that offered market security and higher prices for the sugar industry were offset by tariffs advantageous to goods imported from the north. This made competition difficult for any local product intended to replace them.

Due more to the structures that had been established in years past than to natural conditions, sugar production retained an overwhelming advantage within the Cuban economy, even when its profitability declined. Because of that, domestic investors considered the acquisition of sugar mills to be an excellent business venture when, in the 1940s and 1950s, U.S. corporations disposed of their less efficient plants. These investments brought majority control of production back into Cuban hands. The same factors explain the continued existence of the large sugar plantations, despite the fact that a large number of their fields had been left idle. Market forces exerted only a weak pressure to put that land to another purpose. Although its possibilities for expansion were practically void, the requirements of Cuba's so-called first industry continued to control the Cuban economy, and they contributed to the deterioration of social conditions. This was especially felt in soaring unemployment, a phenomenon in the late 1950s that affected about one-third of the country's workforce.

BIBLIOGRAPHY

Abad, Luis V. de. *Azúcar y caña de azúcar. Ensayo de orientación cubana*. Havana: Editora Mercantil, 1945.

Anuario azucarero de Cuba, 1959. Havana: Cuba Económica y Financiera, 1959.

Dye, Alan D. *Cuban Sugar in the Age of Mass Production: Technology and the Economy of the Sugar Central, 1899–1929*. Stanford, CA: Stanford University Press, 1998.

Guerra, Ramiro. *La industria azucarera de Cuba*. Havana: Cultural S.A., 1940.

Iglesias, Fe. *Del ingenio al central*. San Juan: Universidad de Puerto Rico, 1998.

Moreno Fraginals, Manuel. *El ingenio: Complejo económico social cubano del azúcar*. 3 vols. Havana: Editorial Ciencias Sociales, 1978.

Santamaría, Antonio. *Sin azúcar no hay país. La industria azucarera y la economía cubana (1919–1939)*. Seville: Consejo Superior de Investigaciones Científicas, Universidad de Sevilla y Diputación de Sevilla, 2001.

Zanetti, Oscar. *Las manos en el dulce. Estado e intereses en la regulación de la industria azucarera cubana*. Havana: Ciencias Sociales, 2004.

Zanetti, Oscar. *Economía azucarera cubana. Estudios históricos*. Havana: Ciencias Sociales, 2009.

SUGAR: REVOLUTIONARY PERIOD

Oscar Zanetti

The peak of the Cuban sugar industry and its decline.

The triumph of the Cuban Revolution in 1959 sparked a process of enormous significance in the history of the island's sugar industry. First came the elimination of large landholdings and the nationalization of sugar mills, a radical transformation that turned the government into the sugar economy's main actor. In addition, when Cuba lost the U.S. market, on which it had long depended, and opened up preferential trade with the Soviet Union and other socialist countries, it was able to cater to a growing demand that engendered a new cycle of expanding production. Finally, the collapse of the Soviet Union and the preferential socialist market in 1990 resulted in a profound restructuring, accompanied by a sharp decline in the Cuban sugar industry.

TRANSFORMATIONS

After three decades of virtual stagnation and extensive state regulation, Cuba's number-one industry had in a sense achieved by 1959 a state of equilibrium, based in large measure on most of the sugar mills' meticulous technological and organizational adjustment to the conditions of restricted production. This delicate stability was inevitably disturbed by a revolution that aimed to overcome the traditional obstacles to development by implementing profound structural changes and broad social mobilization. The Agrarian Reform Act passed in May 1959—which gave tenant farmers ownership of the land they worked and simultaneously expropriated large landholdings—shattered the foundations of sugarcane agriculture that had existed in the country for hundreds of years. Although the legislation permitted plantations of up to 3,300 acres to remain in private hands if they were worked to their fullest, almost no property met that requirement. Thus, the mill-owning sugar plantations, as well as the large plantations that sold their cane to outside mills, were taken over within a year by the Instituto Nacional de Reforma Agraria (INRA; National Institute of Agrarian Reform) and turned into sugarcane cooperatives. More radical in its application than in concept, the agrarian reform law intensified confrontation with the U.S. government and the old ruling class, which in turn rapidly transformed the national reality. The United States broke economic ties with Cuba within just two years, suspending all trade and its sugar import quota; meanwhile, the revolutionary government nationalized industry, banks, and major commercial networks and services. After decades of increasing involvement in the sugar industry, the state became both a manager and a decision-maker of the industry's future.

■ *See also*

Ecology and Environment: Revolutionary Period

Economy: Revolutionary Period

Economy: Special Period

Cutting cane. Sugarcane is allowed to mature for 12-18 months, after which it is cut at the ground level using a cane knife and cane harvesters. © RAFAEL/LATIN FOCUS. COM

In its efforts to eliminate social inequalities and accelerate economic growth, the Cuban government created agricultural diversification and industrial development programs aimed at replacing imports with domestic goods. The sugar sector's initial reorganization took place within this framework. The administration of sugar mills was put in the hands of the Empresa Consolidada del Azúcar (Consolidated Sugar Enterprise), part of the Ministerio de Industria (Ministry of Industry), while large plantations, originally organized into cooperatives, were changed in 1962 into state farms under the aegis of INRA.

The following year, a new agrarian law reducing maximum private land ownership to 165 acres completed the organizational foundation of the sugar agribusiness. Production had to adapt to the new circumstances; sugarcane farms were authorized to grow other crops on fallow land, and about ten small and inefficient sugar mills were closed down in order to take advantage of new sources of employment.

Nonetheless, the proposed reorganization of the sugar sector very soon devolved into disorganized demolition of plantations. Given that the sugar industry had been associated for centuries with colonialism and brutal forms of exploitation, it is not surprising that the social movement unleashed by the revolution should take an anti-sugar bent. In just two years

(1961–1963), five hundred thousand acres of cane fields were eliminated, and domestic sugar production dropped from 7.5 million to 4.2 million tons without an improvement in other areas of production that could compensate for this loss in income.

Such a decline in production, along with the damaging consequences of the U.S. trade embargo, threatened to leave the state without financial resources for its development programs. The Cuban Revolution's orientation and its confrontation with the United States within the context of the Cold War had strengthened Cuba's trade ties with the Soviet Union and the other socialist countries. Agreements signed by Cuba with most of the socialist countries in 1960 and 1961 offset the negative effects of the suspension by the United States of its sugar import quota; as a result, sugar sales continued to be a key source of the country's income. Apart from the political support, these relations were possible because the socialist community constituted a unique sector within the international sugar market in that socialist countries had the ability to afford their increasing demand for sugar. In early 1964, Cuba signed a medium-term agreement with the Soviet Union for the sale of large amounts of sugar at the stable price of 6.11 cents per pound. This and similar mechanisms with various socialist countries represented the articulation between Cuban sugar

Sugar harvest, 1961. Workers use a military truck to transport newly harvested cane on a formerly private sugar plantation that became a cooperative under Cuba's land-reform program. ALAN OXLEY/ GETTY IMAGES

and a new preferential market for it, offering security for increased exports at rewarding prices. These conditions made it possible for Cuba to renew its development strategy, with sugar as the driving force of the economy. Under a socialist planning system, sugar would generate the income needed for economic autonomy and diversified development.

THE NEW CYCLE OF EXPANSION

In the mid-1960s Cuba began a new cycle of growth in the sugar industry at a time when sugar production had begun to stagnate or diminish in other Caribbean countries. But achieving the production levels required to meet trade commitments was not a simple task for Cuba's top industry, especially when the revolution had profoundly altered its operating conditions. The creation of a centralized, state-owned economy wrought radical changes in property ownership and management systems; it also altered the combination of productive forces. New sources of employment in the cities and the countryside almost immediately generated a severe labor deficit in the sugar sector, among agricultural workers and in the technical workforce.

Of course the land—traditionally abundant—did not disappear; in the new period of expansion, some of the demolished plantations were recovered, and sugarcane cultivation once again occupied 3.5 million acres. But the population's growing and generally unsatisfied demand for food exerted pressure on land resources.

Because other factors of production had little ability to expand, production growth depended on greater capitalization; during the 1965–1969 period,

Cuba: distribution of sugar exports

Year	United States %	Socialist Countries %	Other Countries %	Total Exports (tons)
1959	60	6	34	5,367,000
1965	0	65	35	5,857,000
1975	0	71	29	6,328,000
1985	0	76	24	7,951,000

SOURCE: Fernandez, Marcelo. *Cuba y la economía azucarera mundial*. Havana: Pueblo y Educación, 1989, tables 70 and 87.

Table 1

investments totaled about one billion pesos. Credits and financing coming from socialist countries provided broad support for the planned expansion, even though these resources often took the shape of outdated technology that was expensive to maintain. New plantations were established in order to produce more sugarcane, the use of chemical fertilizers became commonplace, and irrigation was more widely utilized.

There were efforts to offset labor shortages through the mechanization of sugarcane planting, cultivation, and harvesting. However, available technology facilitated great advances in cane loading operations, but not in cane cutting, which required the mobilization of tens of thousands of volunteers who generally had little experience in such work.

The goal of the sugar program was to produce 10 million metric tons of sugarcane—equal to 11 million short tons— in the 1970 harvest, which required considerable expansion and renovation of industrial equipment. But most investments could not be applied in time or with the necessary quality. When combined with other shortages and difficulties, these factors caused the 1965–1970 plan to fall far short of its goal. Sugarcane harvests in those years experienced considerable ups and downs and did not surpass 6.5 million tons. The only exception was the target year 1970, when production was 9.4 million short tons—more than 1.5 million less than the expected amount—after almost a whole year of uninterrupted harvesting.

The development of the sugar economy required more than mere expansion or a quantitative increase; it necessitated a complete and complex restructuring of the agribusiness industry, a process that did not come to fruition until the late 1970s. In 1972 Cuba joined the socialist bloc's Council for Mutual Economic Assistance, known as the CMEA or COMECON, thereby consolidating the preferential sugar market at highly advantageous prices and assuring the supply of goods and financial backing. Along with that move came the adoption of Soviet-style economic management formulas to sustain a plan of continuous production increases.

Annual investments of more than 300 million pesos in subsequent years were used to modernize the equipment in sugar mills to greater or lesser degrees and to increase the capacities of forty mills. Six relatively large mills were built in the 1980s, the industry's first new facilities in more than fifty years. Thus, the country attained a significant increase in production per active sugar mill, continuing the age-old tendency toward a concentration of production, as seen in Table 2.

As a result of these investments, the industry's milling capacity reached 700,000 tons of cane a day, more than 15 percent higher than in 1958. In cane cultivation, efforts were concentrated on raising yields; obtaining new commercial cane varieties; and, above all, mechanizing the harvest.

After developing different prototypes of harvesters and importing some of them from Australia and other countries, Cuba and the Soviet Union cooperated to produce a combine model that made it possible to mechanize two-thirds of the cane cutting in the late 1980s. Consequently, sugar production witnessed the end of the fluctuations characteristic of the 1965–1974 period, achieving between 8 and 9 million tons during the 1980s, a 35 percent increase over the average in the 1950s.

There was also considerable progress in sugarcane yields, which reached a high of 29 tons per acre in 1988. Sales of sugar, mainly raw, constituted three-fourths of Cuba's exports and produced an average annual income of 4 billion pesos. Sugar, still a raw material, remained at the center of the country's economic activity.

Cuba: average annual production by sugar mill and industrial yield
(SHORT TONS)

Year	Average Production (short tons)	Industrial Yield
1958	40,374	12.8
1965	43,753	12.5
1975	47,133	12.4
1990	57,388	9.9

SOURCE: Nova González, Armando. *La agricultura en Cuba*. Havana: Editorial Ciencias Sociales, 2006, pp. 236, 239.

Table 2

Chart 1

Cuba: sugar production, 1959–1990
(SHORT TONS)

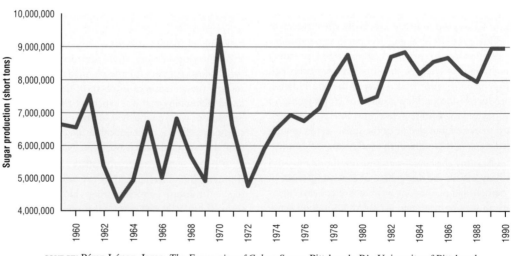

SOURCE: Pérez-López, Jorge. *The Economics of Cuban Sugar*. Pittsburgh, PA: University of Pittsburgh Press, 1991, Table 8; Nova González, Armando. *La agricultura en Cuba: Evolución y trayectoria (1959–2005)*. Havana: Editorial Ciencias Sociales, 2006, chart 11.

By the late 1980s Cuba possessed a total of 156 sugar mills, 13 refineries, and 13 bulk sugar-loading port facilities and had considerably broadened its linkage within the national economy. More than a dozen factories made equipment and parts for the sugar industry, in addition to a factory that manufactured steam boilers and another that repaired turbines and engines. These, plus the construction of the first Cuban milling systems, satisfied as much as 75 percent of the industry's mechanical needs. There were similar results in the manufacture of agricultural implements, thanks in particular to a factory that could turn out 600 harvesters a year, assembled from Soviet and Cuban components.

There was also a much greater focus on sugar byproducts and derivatives. Traditionally limited to the production of alcohol and rum, the derivatives industry had begun its development in the late 1950s with the creation of factories that produced paper and composite board from cane bagasse—the fibrous leftovers from cane processing. In the 1980s these product lines were expanded, and Cuba also began manufacturing yeast for animal feed, sorbitol, dextran, and other chemical derivatives.

Although this model seems like a successful one, it is in no way complete. The increase in agricultural yield was accompanied by a drop of almost 15 percent in industrial yield, which virtually nullified advances in terms of the sugar obtained per area of cultivated sugarcane. Increased productivity was hampered by a twenty-day extension of the sugar harvest; in fact, with an average production of 16.5 pounds per worker-hour in the 1990 harvest—the revolutionary period's largest—Cuba ranked slightly under the world productivity average and far below the countries with the most efficient production, which generated double that figure.

The decrease in Cuba's efficiency indices can be attributed in some measure to the mechanization of cane cutting, which significantly raised the proportion of extraneous matter in milled cane and made coordination of operations more complex. But the deterioration of indices such as lost industrial time—almost double the statistic in the 1950s—and large losses of cane during the harvest revealed indisputable operational and functional management problems. Cane agriculture in particular suffered from excessive centralization, incongruous price setting, an imbalance between production and income, and lack of incentive for workers, among other deficiencies, some of which were also present in industrial management. The situation was aggravated by the tendency to escape those problems by increasing capitalization—excess machinery, land levelling, complex irrigation systems, and so on—with the subsequent squandering of resources.

Although there is a universal tendency toward increased costs among sugar producers, everything seems to indicate that in the case of Cuba, this variable grew more steeply than the average. Various estimates

Prices obtained for sugar (1986–1990)

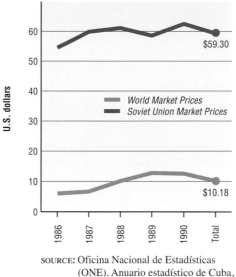

SOURCE: Oficina Nacional de Estadísticas (ONE). Anuario estadístico de Cuba, 1985, 2000, and 2006.

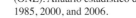
Chart 2

and data seem to place Cuba, with an approximate production cost of ten cents per pound in the late 1980s, at an intermediate level within world parameters but at a clear disadvantage compared to the main exporters of sugarcane. Cuba's special trade relationship with the Soviet Union, resulting in prices in the 1980s that were much higher than those on the world market (shown in Chart 2) as well as the acquisition of supplies at lower costs, made it possible to evade threats of unprofitability. But this dangerous tendency, inseparable from subsidized production, could already be seen.

RESTRUCTURING AND DECLINE

Cuba's special relationship with socialist countries afforded its sugar industry protection similar to that offered by the European Community, Japan, and other countries to their own producers. This relationship insulated Cuba from the international economic context, allowing the country to develop in some innovative agricultural and industrial fields—such as metalwork—at the same time that it achieved noteworthy social progress. However, in addition to bringing Cuba advantageous prices that were much higher than market prices, integration into the socialist bloc meant the assimilation of relatively outdated technology, the adoption of slow and costly investment systems, a marked dependence on external financing—and the accumulation of considerable debt—and a demand for many imported goods for the poorly integrated domestic economy, whose products did not generally meet international competitive standards. These risks, already visible in the 1980s, became dramatically evident in the early 1990s, following the collapse of the Soviet Union.

When its principal economic ties were cut, Cuba's foreign trade dropped from 13.5 billion pesos in 1989

Cuba: evolution of sugarcane production

Year	Cane produced (millions of tons)	Harvested Area (thousands of acres)	Yields (tons/acre)
1991	78.2	3,334	23.4
1994	35.7	2,477	14.5
1997	31.0	2,287	13.5
2000	29.6	1,934	15.3
2003	18.6	1,190	15.6

SOURCE: Economic Commission for Latin America and the Caribbean (ECLAC): *La economía cubana. Reformas estructurales y desempeño en los noventa*. Mexico City: Fund for Economic Culture, 1997, Table IV.15; Sulrocas, F. "El redimensionamiento de la industria azucarera cubana y sus perspectivas en el nuevo siglo." (unpublished), Table 6.

Table 3

to just over 3 billion in 1994, while GDP contracted by 35 percent and social conditions deteriorated severely. The country had to restructure its international economic relations amid very serious difficulties, created in part by an unrelenting economic blockade that the United States was quick to intensify.

Deprived of preferential markets for the first time in the twentieth century, the Cuban sugar industry had to adjust to international market rules. However, during the prolonged interlude in which Cuba belonged to the socialist system, those rules had become much harsher. In the mid-twentieth century, more than half of all the sugar produced in the world was sold on the so-called free market, but forty years later only 30 percent was traded that way, due to the sustained tendency toward self-sufficiency and protectionist practices. The European Community was a prime example of this trend: Thanks to the subsidies of the Common Agricultural Policy, it no longer imported sugar and became the world's greatest sugar exporter. The International Sugar Agreement, renegotiated with difficulty over three decades, had been terminated in 1984, given the impossibility of bringing together such diverse interests.

Meanwhile, per capita sugar consumption in the large industrialized countries stagnated or declined, and worse still, high-fructose corn syrup and artificial sweeteners—such as aspartame, whose sweetening strength is much greater than cane or beet sugar—were capturing an increasingly greater market share. The most dynamic demand on the international sugar market during the early twenty-first century came from underdeveloped countries, whose lower purchasing power augured the predominance of low prices; consequently, selling was only feasible for countries that could subsidize their exports or that—like Brazil and Australia—could rely on large domestic markets or technological advances consistently capable of reducing or offsetting production costs.

The critical conditions of the 1990s not only brought to light the Cuban sugar industry's rising costs, but even tended to aggravate them. Lacking essential supplies—especially fertilizers and fuels—sugarcane agriculture's yields were reduced by half, creating a chronic shortage of raw materials, as Table 3 demonstrates.

Facing the same financial restrictions, the industrial sector experienced serious supply difficulties that generated major gaps in machinery maintenance and replacement. From a high of 8.4 million metric tons in 1990, production plunged to half that amount in 1994 and, following minor oscillations, reached a low of 3.5 million tons in 1998.

Weighed down by the dearth of financing, the government tried to get the most out of the sugar sector's declining potential: The 1996 and 1997 sugar harvests were extended so that all the available cane could be cut, thereby lowering efficiency rates even more and increasing the raw material shortage because much of the milled cane had not completed its maturation cycle. The state had to assume the major losses resulting from these factors, because it could not do without a sector that was the country's principal source of employment and income.

For the Cuban sugar industry, the economic cataclysm of the early 1990s ushered in a new phase of reorganization, the fourth in slightly more than a century. The combination of factors of production had shifted once again, especially the severe—and by all estimates prolonged—restriction of capital. Land and labor availability also presented certain limitations, the former because of the need to increase cultivation of subsistence crops and the latter because certain jobs in the sugar industry were not attractive to the available workforce.

The new period of adjustment began in 1993, when 73 percent of the land used to grow sugarcane was shifted to Unidades Básicas de Producción Cooperativa (UBPC; Basic Units of Cooperative Production), leaving only 10 percent of the cane-growing areas under the direct administration of government entities. Next came the promotion of external financing of production, new labor incentive systems, the modification of technological processes, the modernization of harvesters, and other steps aimed at putting the brakes on falling production and efficiency. The results were not encouraging; most of the UBPCs, for example, operated at a loss, demonstrating the complexities of changing the attitudes of economic actors.

In 1998 studies were undertaken concerning what was called the resizing of the sugar sector. In addition to shutting down some sugar mills, enterprises were reorganized and the number of UBPCs was reduced, while the remaining ones increased their cane acreage to counteract the drop in cane yields. This change brought a momentary stabilization at the end of the century, but in 2002, with the price of sugar at six cents a pound and a severe fuel shortage, the industry's reorganization was intensified. With the goal of cutting costs and promoting product

Cuba: sugar production, 1991–2005
(SHORT TONS)

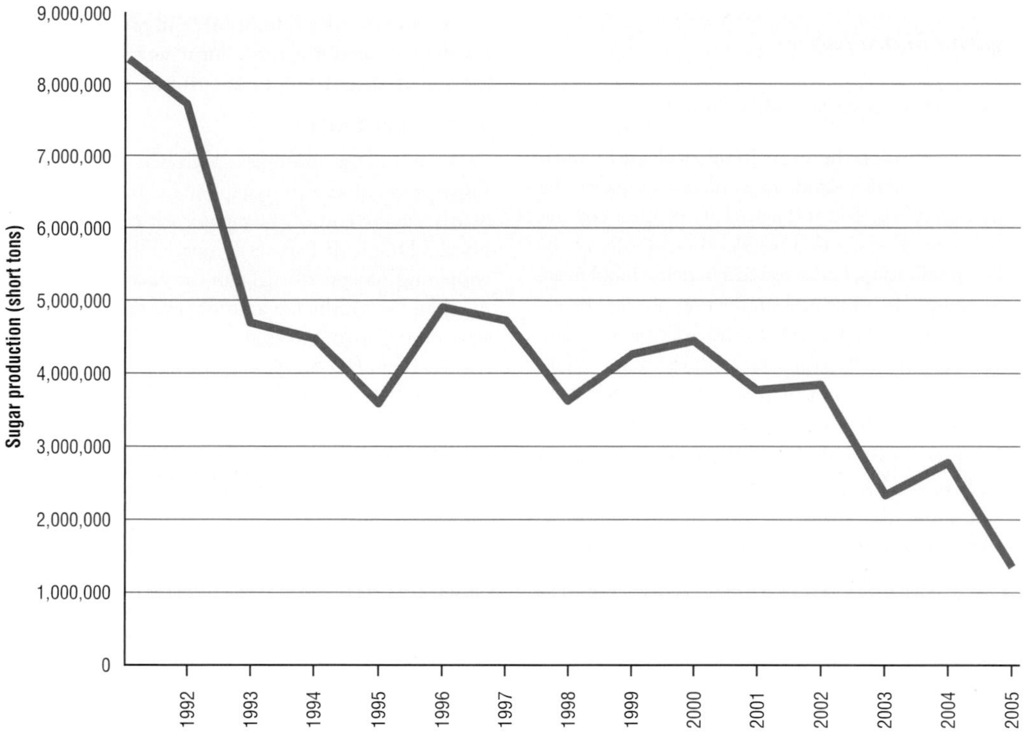

Chart 3

SOURCE: Pérez-López, Jorge. *The Economics of Cuban Sugar*. Pittsburgh, PA: University of Pittsburgh Press, 1991, table 32.

diversification, especially in agriculture, seventy sugar mills were dismantled and converted into diversified agricultural enterprises, and 1.7 million acres of cane-growing land were designated for other uses. The agricultural and industrial resources still devoted to sugar were considered adequate to sustain a yield of 4 million tons and to achieve a product diversification that would offset the low price of raw sugar.

In 2005 the sugar harvest was the lowest in a century: 1.3 million tons. Persistently low prices and financial restrictions, along with severe drought, took the industry's restructuring into a second phase, with the closure of another twenty-four sugar mills and the reassignment of 700,000 additional acres to other purposes. Even taking the unfavorable weather conditions into account, the factor that most influenced the drop in production was the lack of sugarcane (see Chart 3), resulting from excessive centralization of cane agriculture, inadequate attention to planting, and lack of incentives for workers. Even more significantly, the results of the restructuring seemed to reflect the extensive nature of the sugar economy, because savings—certainly considerable—were accompanied by a corresponding decrease in production indices.

In 2009, with prices on the rise, the sugar sector's objectives were reaffirmed when forty-six agricultural enterprises operated by the Ministry of the Sugar Industry were transferred to the Ministry of Agriculture and greater resources were designated to the sugar industry for revitalization of its production. The results of this effort remained uncertain as of early 2011, but the resources still devoted to sugar production—including 1.8 million acres and sixty sugar mills—along with adequate financing and efficient management, were anticipated to make a significant contribution to the development of the Cuban economy.

BIBLIOGRAPHY

Álvarez, José, and Lázaro Peña. *Cuba's Sugar Industry*. Gainesville: University Press of Florida, 2001.

Brunner, Heinrich. *Cuban Sugar Policy from 1963 to 1970*. Pittsburgh, PA: University of Pittsburgh Press, 1977.

Charadán, Fernando. *La industria azucarera en Cuba*. Havana: Editorial de Ciencias Sociales, 1982.

Fernández, Marcelo. *Cuba y la economía azucarera mundial*. Havana: Editorial Pueblo y Educación, 1989.

Nova, Armando. *La agricultura en Cuba: Evolución y trayectoria (1959–2005)*. Havana: Editorial Ciencias Sociales, 2006.

Pérez-López, Jorge. *The Economics of Cuban Sugar*. Pittsburgh, PA: University of Pittsburgh Press, 1991.

Zanetti, Oscar. *Economía azucarera cubana: Estudios históricos*. Havana: Editorial Ciencias Sociales, 2009.

CUBA

SUGAR: REPRESENTATION IN CUBAN CULTURE

Margarita Mateo Palmer

The symbolism of sugar in Cuban culture.

Across the centuries, the sugar industry shaped Cuban culture. It defined the island's racial hierarchy, shaped the country's economy, and influenced its people's cultural mix. Its stages of production paralleled racial values associated with skin color, and it served as a rich symbol in art and literature. The value and production of sugar determined international relationships and political structure. The vast sugar plantations and mills recreated the Cuban landscape ecologically and shaped its people, their lives, their standard of living, and their modes of creativity.

With surprising accuracy, the stages in making sugar mirror the hierarchy of races that predominated for centuries on the island of Cuba. The best and most desired sugar is white; the darker shades of sugar are less valued; and black burned sugar is useless even as fodder for livestock. These grades of sugar parallel the racial hierarchy in Cuba, which designates or ranks individuals by their skin tone: pure whites, mulattoes, quadroons, octoroons, and less exact designations such as *jabado* and *capirro* (light-skinned mulatto), *Russian mulatto*, *saltoatrás* (literally, a throwback to a colored ancestor), *mulato blanconazo* (son of a quadroon woman and a European), and *mulato de la tierra* (earthen-colored mulatto). Sugar seemed to symbolize the Cuban disposition to discrimination.

THE SUGAR MILL

There are several examples in Cuban culture that use sugar production as a metaphor for moral or spiritual worth. At the end of the eighteenth century the cleric Nicolás Duque de Estrada compared the purification or whitening process of sugar in the *casa de purga* (purging house) with the metamorphosis that the soul of the slave must undergo to attain the purity required to enter the Christian heaven. Similarly, in *Cecilia Valdés* (1839, 1882), the most significant Cuban novel of the nineteenth century, author Cirilo Villaverde (1812–1894) described the boiler house, the area of the sugar mill that houses the sugar kettles, in terms of Hell. In the area of the Tinaja sugar mill factory where juice was extracted from the sugarcane, the blacks were outlined by the red flames of the fires that "just like a sinister flash of lightning on a stormy night, illuminated them from head to toe, so that one could see they were human beings carrying out vigorous labors, not phantoms risen from some infernal underworld" (p. 383).

Corte de caña (Cutting Cane) by Víctor Patricio Landaluze, 1874. The sugar plantation has been a central motif in Cuban art and culture. During the nineteenth century, this theme was often romanticized, as in this scene of workers harvesting cane by the Spanish-born artist Víctor Patricio Landaluze. AKG-IMAGES/NEWSCOM

Nineteenth-century sugar factory. This mid-nineteenth-century engraving shows the spacious interior of a Cuban sugar factory. MADRID, NATIONAL FINE ARTS

Language also reflected metaphoric appropriations of sugar production. The sound of the *cuero* (whip) was often heard in the diabolic clamor of the sugar mill. The word *cuero* is used in various ways in the contemporary lexicon: *Dar cuero* or *arrimar el cuero* (apply the leather) means to beat or spank, give a thrashing, and in modern usage, to put a person in an uncomfortable position during an argument. *Tocar el cuero* or *sonar el cuero* means to crack the whip when giving an order. As a symbol of control and authority it has phallic overtones because of the shape of the handle, and *cuerazo* suggests sexual intercourse. The image of the overseer as a sinister figure cracking the whip appeared often in the political cartoons of Rafael Blanco (1885–1955) that were printed in *El Mundo* during the 1920s.

The bell located in the highest tower of the sugar mill had nothing to do with morning prayers and hymns of praise; it served as an echo of the overseer's voice, a language of command and authority that ruled the lives of the workers. Like a nightmare, a succession of bells sounded throughout the day in different locations in the factory: There was a bell in the house where the juice from the sugarcane was extracted, a bell in the boiler house, and one in the purifying house. In *Tam-Tam* (1941), a novel by Federico de Ibarzábal (1894–1955), the ringing of the bronze bell sounded "like a death rattle buried in the throat of a dying person," reminding the slaves of their human condition (p. 91). In the twentieth century the industrial factory whistle supplanted the bells of the sugar mill.

A curious sight in the Valle de los Ingenios near Trinidad is the tower of the Manacas sugar mill, constructed around 1848 by the Iznaga family. This solitary stone structure in the middle of the plain housed a bell that tolled to get the slaves lined up in the morning. The popular imagination produced several legends about the unusual structure—that it was a lookout tower used to spot pirate ships and that it had a counterpart in a well somewhere that matched in depth the tower's height. In the first half of the film *Lucía* (1968), by Humberto Solás (1941–2008), the tower appears in the background when the lovers are talking after their amorous tryst in the ruins of the sugar mill.

Eventually the bell became a symbol of the struggle for freedom, when it sounded the alarm at the Demajagua sugar mill to announce not the flight of a slave but the call to emancipation. After that, the machete, the basic tool for harvesting sugarcane, became the weapon of the *mambises* (Cuban insurgents) during the wars of independence. In *La primera carga al machete* (The First Charge of the Machete, 1969), a film by Manuel Octavio Gómez (1934–1988), the machete—popularly known as *el garantizado* (the guaranteed one) when it bore the Collin brand—is a weapon feared by the Spanish soldiers. Images of the machete being sharpened on the whetstone and of laborers wielding it during harvesting are repeated motifs in Cuban visual arts. In the well-known mural *Isla 70* (Island 70, 1970), by Raúl Martínez (1927–1955), a harvester wearing a straw sombrero stands in the foreground with his machete held high; in the background are sugarcane and a sugar mill. The symbol also is prominent in a painting by Esterio Segura (b. 1970), *Santo de paseo por el trópico* (Saint Passing through Hardships, 1991).

The soft perfume of the sugarcane plantation and the strong odor that pervaded the fields during the milling season are scents evoked in one of the great poems about sugar, "La zafra" (The Sugarcane Crop, 1926), by the Matanzas writer Agustín Acosta (1886–1979):

There is a smell of sugarcane wafting
Over the green
cacophony of the plantations,
a trembling, a twitching,
an impalpable vibration
that livens up the fields and covers them
with a marvel of transparent shawls . . .

The greatest effect of this poem, according to the critic Cintio Vitier, lies in its sensual polarization of the island, expressed through the irrepressible odor "with its mixture of delight and anguish, silently charged with longings, threats, resentment, repressed violence" (p. 253). Another sense—taste—expresses the paradox of sugar's sweetness and bitterness. For black slaves, Chinese coolies, paid workers, poor farmers, and Caribbean immigrants, the sweet crystal could be transformed into sharp bile; this is expressed in the verses of the poets and in the colloquial language as *azúcar amarga* (bitter sugar).

The *tiempo muerto* (down time between milling seasons), when the poverty of the harvesters and mill workers increased, stood in stark contrast to the milling season, which had an intense rhythm dictated by the relentless speed of the machinery during harvest. Time standing still, unproductive, feared by the workers, the *tiempo muerto* was described in the poem "Tiempo muerto (Cañaveral)" (1936), by Angel Augier (1910–2010), and the short story "El cuentero" (The Storyteller, 1958), by Onelio Jorge Cardoso (1914–1986).

From the old sugar mill of long ago heralded by poet Francisco Javier Pichardo (1873–1941) to the twentieth century's great sugar factory, the refinery has been a leitmotiv in Cuban culture. *Los ingenios de Cuba* (The Sugar Mills of Cuba, 1857), by Justo Germán Cantero (1815–1871) and Eduardo Laplante (1818–c.1860), with Laplante's fabulous lithographs, is one of the most valuable guides to the sugar culture. Celebrated artistic renditions of the Cuban world of sugar are found in paintings of Víctor Patricio Landaluze (1828–1889); Esteban Chartrand (1840–1884)—particularly *Un ingenio en Bolondrón* and *Vista del ingenio Tinguaro*; Leopoldo Romañach (1862–1951)—particularly his disturbing *La niña de las cañas*; and the work of Guantánamo's Gonzalo Escalante (1865–1939).

THE LIVES OF THE SLAVES

The hardship caused by sugar production notwithstanding, the slaves still found some sweetness in their lives. In the mill's *barracón* (slave barracks) during festival days, the slaves washed and dressed and participated in games, played the drums, and danced to the tunes and rhythms brought from different African lands. Various traditions melded in an incessant process of transculturalization that became the basis of a national culture. The Cuban antislavery literature of the nineteenth century recounts these rare moments of black creative expression, particularly as depicted in the work of Anselmo Suárez y Romero (1818–1878), who described in detail the gyrations of the dancers in *Colección de artículos* (Collection of Articles, 1859). In Miguel Barnet's *Biografía de un cimarrón* (Biography of a Runaway Slave, 1966), the old slave Esteban Montejo recalls life in the barracónes, how on Sundays the women got fixed up, styling their hair in traditional fashion and putting on necklaces and bracelets and colorful kerchiefs, all in preparation to enjoy the general gaiety: "At sunrise the noise began, and the games, and the children began to spin around. The barracón came to life in a flash. It seemed like the world would come to an end. And even with all the work, everybody got up happy" (Barnet p. 30).

In the barracón, considered by the historian Juan Pérez de la Riva to be one of the most ignominious symbols in Cuban slavery, slaves of different national origins and ethnic groups lived together, mixing their traditions and customs. Over time *criollo* culture was integrated with Asian traditions too, given that from about the middle of the nineteenth century there was a massive influx of Chinese indentured laborers. In the twentieth century the need for cheap manual labor to operate the colossal sugar production brought more immigrants, and their traditions were integrated too. In *Batey* (1930), by Pablo de la Torriente Brau (1901–1936), reference is made to "the international polyglot camp of Dutch from Aruba, English from Barbados, Jamaicans, Haitians, Colombians, Galicians, Venezuelans, and criollos" that fills the dusk "with sad songs from all the countries" (p. 55). In *Ecue-Yamba-O!* (Praised be God! 1933), the first work of Alejo Carpentier (1904–1980), the mixture of cultures in the *batey* (sugar company town) is vividly depicted: "The wailing of religious hymns by the Jamaicans alternates with *punto guajiro* verses keeping time to the rhythm of the *claves* [rhythm sticks]. From the Chinese shop the phonograph blares out Cantonese love songs. A Galician's fat bagpipes challenge the Haitian's asthmatic accordions" (p. 20).

Life in the sugar mill generated a great many sexual expressions that survive to modern times. As Manuel Moreno Fraginals wrote in his fundamental history *El ingenio* (The Sugar Mill, 1966), the common slang term for the sexual act *echar un palo* (to toss a log) has its origin in the slaves' practice of stealing a moment to go out to the *tumbadero* (the large woodpile on the outskirts of the sugar mill) to engage in sex. It followed that tumbadero came to signify the place where one engages in sexual contact. The identification of *paila* with buttocks, *pailero* with homosexual, *bollo* with vulva, *manjarría* with penis, *bocabajo* and *cuerazo* with coitus, and *botar paja* with masturbation all derive from terms associated with the sugar mills. Similarly, the association of *papaya* with vulva in the western region of Cuba comes from the female slaves' contraceptive use of the plant.

A film by Sergio Giral (b. 1937), *El otro Francisco* (The Other Francisco, 1974), contrasts the dreadful real conditions of the sexual life of the slaves with the idyllic vision in the romantic antislavery literature of the nineteenth century. The link between sugar and eroticism has been treated in various ways, from the association of the beloved with the sugarcane flower in "La flor de la caña," the well-known poem of Plácido (Gabriel de la Concepción Valdés, 1809–1844) to the intense sensuality in these verses by Nicolás Guillén (1902–1989):

> Your body moves slowly forward
> Your hands reach out in their realm
> Of intoxication;
> Your feet of lingering sugar burnt by the dance
> [...] and your waist
> of rich caramel
> [...]
> A river of promises under
> your hair,
> rests upon your breasts,
> settles at last into a tiny pool of honey in your
> womb
> in the stealth of the night, violates your firm
> flesh.

THE SUGAR ARISTOCRACY

When the Cuban millionaire Miguel Aldama (1821–1888) described in a letter to his brother-in-law in Paris how the indoor toilet in his Havana residence worked, this device was still unknown in Europe. The sugar barons of the provinces adopted modern technology not only to enjoy a more refined standard of living but also, of course, to increase production at the mills. In order to transport sugar, they built a railroad in Cuba in 1837, long before Spain and the rest of Latin America had railroads. Some of the great technological contributions of industrialization—the steam engine, gas, electricity, the telegraph, and the telephone—were adopted early on to make the sugar industry more productive.

The development of the economy was an indigenous Cuban phenomenon, not an enterprise of the Spanish Crown. The criollo landowners were especially enterprising, founding the extremely influential *Papel periódico de la Havana* (The Havana Newspaper) and other publications of the colonial era. *Ensayo sobre el cultivo de la caña de azúcar* (An Essay on the Cultivation of Sugarcane, 1862), by Alvaro Reynoso (1829–1888), a scientific text of extraordinary value during its time, was translated into other languages and widely used outside of Cuba. Very early on, the criollo landowners became interested in establishing schools of chemistry (the science involved in the so-called art of producing sugar), physics, botany, and political economy. The use of statistics, essential for the control of sugar production, reached a higher level

at the beginning of the nineteenth century in Cuba than in any other colony in the world.

Concern about the length of a slave's working life—given that slaves were relatively expensive—stimulated an interest in keeping slaves healthy. When a royal expedition reached Havana in 1804 to spread awareness of vaccination against smallpox in the Americas, its members found the technique already being used in Cuba; recently arrived slaves from Africa were vaccinated before being transferred to the plantations. Moreno Fraginals had good reason to refer to the sugar mill as an intellectual adventure and to the Cuban sugar aristocracy as "the social class of the highest cultural level and the most conscientious, aggressive and 'modern' (in the bourgeois sense of the word) known to Latin America in the first half of the nineteenth century" (vol. 2, p. 76).

The wealth that was accumulated in Cuba from the nineteenth century rivaled any other in the world. There are many accounts by travelers to Cuba who admired the lifestyle of the wealthy, including the writings of the German scientist Alexander von Humboldt (1769–1859) and the observations of North Americans mentioned in *Cuando reinba su majestad el azúcar* (When Sugar Was King, 2001), by Roland T. Ely. Lavish hospitality, luxury, ostentation, waste, and the acquisition of noble titles typified the criollo landowners. The family of millionaire Tomás Terry (who left one of the world's greatest fortunes when he died in 1886) was among the principal investors in the Suez Canal. This family also donated the magnificent Teatro Terry to the city of Cienfuegos. Built in 1837, this theater served as the headquarters of the National Ballet of Cuba and was the site of brilliant opera productions. Some urban improvements, such as paving roads and constructing large warehouses next to the docks, were made originally to facilitate the sugar industry.

Some of this great wealth spilled over into the twentieth century. Even though many sugar factories were U.S. owned, certain Cubans profited greatly from the industry. Before the 1959 Revolution, there were Cuban sugar magnates such as the Sugar King, Julio Lobo (1898–1983), one of the most famous millionaires of modern Cuba. Many of the great mansions of Vedado, including the home of the Falla Gutiérrez family and the residence of Catalina Laza, were built by the big Cuban sugar producers. Sugar magnates were also responsible for starting important magazines during the twentieth century, including *Cúspide* from the Mercedita mill, and *Orígenes* and *Ciclón*, under the patronage of José Rodríguez Feo, the nephew of a sugar magnate.

CONSEQUENCES OF SUGAR DOMINATION

Lamentably, much of the wealth gained from sugar production did nothing for the nation's development. Indeed, Cuba's underdevelopment was in part attributed to the practices of the sugar industry itself, which was dependent first on slave labor and later on poorly paid farmers and workers. Deforestation, impoverished soil, single-crop planting, the *latifundio* (large estates), and foreign penetration (mainly from the United States) resulted from sugar's domination of the economy. In his *Contrapunteo cubano del tabaco y el azúcar* (Cuban Counterpoint: Tobacco and Sugar, 1940) the social scientist Fernando Ortiz saw in Cuba's crop production a force that would undermine the nation's future. Ortiz wrote: "When the Cuban people are not so enslaved to sugar, their food will taste sweeter and their lives will be more savory" (p. 256).

Both historians and literary authors addressed the dark side of sugar during the first half of the twentieth century, when big sugar mill factories were expanded and U.S. companies arrived on the island. *Tembladera* (*Quaking Earth*, 1918), a play by José Antonio Ramos (1885–1946), revolves around the loss of economic independence caused by North Americans taking over Cuban land and mills. Ramos explored that theme again in his novel *Coaybay* (1926). "El poema of los cañaverales" (Poem of the Sugarcane Plantations, 1926), by Felipe Pichardo Moya (1892–1957), similarly warned of the danger to national sovereignty represented by the U.S.-owned penetration of the Cuban sugar industry. Artists and musicians also sounded warnings. In his famous oil painting *Paisaje cubano* (Cuban Landscape, 1933), Marcelo Pogolotti (1902–1988) juxtaposed elements of sugar mill production that pillaged the nation: workers and sugarcane harvesters watched by soldiers, the sugar mill, the ship that transported the wealth to the United States, and, in the background, threatening North American gunboats. A popular Cuban *son*, "Caña quemá" (Burnt Sugarcane), written by Lorenzo Hierrezuelo and performed by Trío Matamoros and Los Compadres, tells of at least fifteen sugar mills where the owners, pressured by U.S. interests, burned the sugarcane in order to manipulate the price of sugar.

The sugar industry produced a culture of its own. U.S.-owned sugar mills were surrounded by bungalows of a certain type. *Marcos Antilla, Relatos del cañaveral* (Stories from the Sugarcane Plantation, 1932), Luis Felipe Rodríguez's short story collection set in the Cubanacán Sugar Company, describes the cultural life of the batey, with its itinerant preachers and its tennis matches and baseball games. *Los niños se despiden* (The Children Say Goodbye, 1963), by Pablo Armando Fernández (b. 1930), who grew up on the Delicias sugar mill, is an account of life in a U.S.-owned sugar mill, seen through the eyes of the main character's family. Some companies exploited their workers by paying them in company tokens, which obligated them to buy their goods at the company store that charged inflated prices. *El token* (1976), a film documentary by Melchor Casals (b. 1939), deals with this form of exploitation.

The struggle of the sugar workers through the union movement was intense during the Republican period. Nicolás Guillén's "Elegía a Jesús Menéndez" (Elegy to Jesús Menéndez, 1951) pays homage to one of the union leaders—the Sugarcane General—assassinated by the army in Manzanillo. After the Revolution of 1959 the factories and the sugarcane latifundios were nationalized, radically changing worker relations. The *zafras del pueblo* (people's harvests) established in 1960 in response to the demand for manual labor, mobilized different sectors of the population to harvest sugarcane on a voluntary basis. This new situation was described in works such as the short story "No hay Dios que aguante esto" (There Is No God Who Will Put Up with This, 1966), by Jesús Díaz, and the unusual play *La tierra permanente* (The Permanent Land, 1987), by Antón Arrufat (b. 1935). Reinaldo Arenas (1943–1990) offered a different vision in his lengthy poem "El central" (The Sugar Mill, 1984).

SUGAR CULTURE IN THE LATE TWENTIETH CENTURY

In the late 1960s the sports announcer Bobby Salamanca (1934–1989) created an original style for announcing baseball games based on comparisons of the game and harvesting sugarcane. When a batter struck out, he would say: "Tres golpes de mocha y lo tiró pa la tonga!" (Three strikes of the machete and he tossed the cane onto the pile!). If a fielder was chasing a foul ball and could not catch it, he would shout: "No, no, no! No deje la caña regada fuera del surco, que es azúcar que se pierde!" (No, no, no! Don't leave the sugarcane in the field, that's wasted sugar!). A foul ball behind the plate was a "caguazo a las mallas," an allusion to the dry grass used as fodder for mules, and when there were no men on base, "las guardarrayas estaban limpias" (the paths between the cane fields were clean). Only a nation so intimately familiar with sugarcane harvesting and its industrial production could fully appreciate his style of announcing rooted in these allusions.

Novels such as *Sacchario* (1971), by Miguel Cossio, and *Las iniciales de la tierra* (The Initials of the Earth, 1988), by Jesús Díaz, and essays such as "Contradanzas y latigazos" (Folk Dances and Lashes, 1983), by Reynaldo González (b. 1940), illustrate how the theme of sugar is addressed in Cuban literature from the second half of the twentieth century. Even the novel *Paradiso* (1966), by José Lezama Lima (1910–1976), placed in an urban setting, tackled this theme via retelling a family history in the Resolución sugar mill and the protagonist's excursion into the world of the Tres Suertes factory.

For most of Cuba's modern history, sugar determined the rhythm of the national economy, and it had an enormous influence on the social psychology of Cubans. Although its physical signs may be difficult to detect in urban settings, contemporary language bears the mark of the sugar culture. Phrases such as *meter caña* (to drive someone hard) or *estar la caña a tres trozos* (the situation is difficult) are examples of this impress. Likewise, the sayings *Quien tiene un amigo tiene un central*

(He who has a friend has a sugar refinery) and *Año de poco güin, caña ruin* (A year of poor sugarcane crops, a year of bad rum) and simple phrases such as *estar la caña a tres trozos* or *no cojas lucha, que la caña es mucha* (Don't worry because you can't win the fight anyway) demonstrate the omnipresence of sugar in the Cuban culture.

From the 1980s into the early 2000s Cuba witnessed the demolition of several sugar mills and the dismantling of the enormous machinery that was so closely tied to the nation's history. The documentary *deMOLER* (Demolish, 2004), by Alejandro Ramírez Anderson (b. 1973), described the sense of loss and confusion of the sugar mill workers who identify their new situation as an interminable *tiempo muerto*. The lament of Cuban sugar industry workers, the requiem for the noise of the machinery and the whistles that no longer herald the beginning of harvest season, the conversion of colossal sugar mills into museums, all of these are new effects caused by sugar, both enemy and friend, both bitter and sweet.

BIBLIOGRAPHY

Acosta, Agustín. *La zafra. Poema de combate*. Havana: Sociedad Económica de Amigos del País, 2004.

Arrufat, Antón. *La tierra permanente*. Havana: Editorial Letras Cubanas, 1987.

Barnet, Miguel. *Biography of a Runaway Slave*. Translated by Nick Hill. Willimantic, CT: Curbstone Press, 1994.

Carpentier, Alejo. *¡Écue-Yamba-O!*. Havana: Editorial Letras Cubanas, 1975.

De la Torriente Brau, Pablo. *Narrativa*. Havana: Ediciones La Memoria, 2003.

Duque de Estrada, Nicolás. *Explicación de la doctrina cristiana acomodada a la capacidad de los negros bozales*. Havana: Boloña, 1823.

Ely, Roland T. *Cuando reinaba su majestad el azúcar*. Havana: Ediciones Imagen Contemporánea, 2001.

García Ronda, Denia. "Agustín Acosta, el poeta de la zafra." In *La zafra. Poema de combate*. Havana: Sociedad Económica de Amigos del País, 2004.

Guerra, Ramiro. *Azúcar y población en las Antillas*. Havana: Editorial Ciencias Sociales, 1970.

Guillén, Nicolás. *Poesía completa*. Havana: Editorial Letras Cubanas, 1973.

Ibarzábal de, Federico. *Tam-Tam*. Havana: Editorial Alpha, 1941.

Moreno Fraginals, Manuel. *El ingenio. Complejo economico-social cubano del azúcar*. 2nd ed. 3 vols. Havana: Editorial de Ciencias Sociales, 1978.

Ortiz, Fernando. *Contrapunteo cubano del tabaco y el azúcar*. Havana: Consejo Nacional de Cultura, 1963.

Pérez de la Riva, Juan. *El barracón y otros ensayos*. Havana: Editorial de Ciencias Sociales, 1975.

Rodríguez, Luis Felipe. *Marcos Antilla, relatos del cañaveral*. Havana: Instituto Cubano del Libro, 1971.

Villaverde, Cirilo. *Cecilia Valdés*. Havana: Editorial Letras Cubanas, 2001.

Vitier, Cintio. *Lo cubano en la poesía*. Havana: Editorial Letras Cubanas, 1998.

THE SUGARMILL (MANUEL MORENO FRAGINALS)

Oscar Zanetti

A milestone in world literature about slavery and plantations.

Manuel R. Moreno Fraginals's *El ingenio: Complejo economic social cubano del azúcar* (1964; best known in its English translation, *The Sugarmill: The Socioeconomic Complex of Sugar in Cuba*, 1976) is one of the most important works published about Cuba during the second half of the twentieth century. This historical study about the so-called golden age of the slave-labor sugar plantations is a classic of Cuban historical writing. The first edition of *El ingenio* appeared in 1964; the second, three-volume edition appeared in 1978.

ABOUT MANUEL MORENO FRAGINALS

Manuel R. Moreno Fraginals (1920–2001) was born in Havana to Elpidio Moreno Uría and Juana Fraginals Collazo. He attended primary school at Escuela Zapata, part of the Sociedad Económica de Amigos del País (Economic Society of Friends of the Country). After graduating from high school in 1940, he enrolled in Havana University's School of Law. His unpublished monograph "Viajes de Colón en aguas de Cuba" (Columbus's Travels in Cuban Waters), which was awarded a prize in 1942 by the Sociedad Colombista Panamericana (Pan American Colombus Society), is evidence of his early vocation for history. Moreno Fraginals was one of the first Cubans to pursue history studies at Colegio de México (College of Mexico). In 1947 a scholarship awarded by the Instituto de Cultura Hispánica (Institute of Hispanic Culture) allowed him to work for more than a year in Spanish archives and libraries and become familiar with the Hispanic intellectual environment.

After returning to Cuba he began to work in 1949 at the Biblioteca Nacional (the National Library) and ended up as its acting deputy director in 1950. At the end of the same year, he obtained a post as professor at Universidad de Oriente (Eastern University) in Santiago de Cuba, but he served in that position only briefly. Back in the capital once again, he worked with the University of Havana Extension Office on organizing summer courses and other activities. His first published works came out of this period: a short study on the writer Anselmo Suárez Romero (1818–1878) and another article, "Agustín Iturbide: El caudillo," which was a revised version of a text that he prepared for the history seminar offered at the Colegio de México. A monograph he also started at the Colegio, *José Antonio Saco. Estudio y bibliografía* (1962), won the

▪ *See also*

Ecology and Environment: Colonial Period

Economy: Colonial Period

Race: Slavery in Cuba

Sugar: Colonial Period

Sugar: Representation in Cuban Culture

prize awarded by Cuba's Librarians Society, though it was not published until ten years later. In 1951, the Pan American Institute of Geography and History published his pamphlet *Misiones cubanas en los archivos europeos* (Cuban Missions in European Archives).

In 1954 Moreno emigrated to Venezuela, where he worked as an advertising manager for the Cervecería Caracas brewery and entered the radio broadcasting business. Returning to Cuba after the 1959 revolution, he taught history at the Universidad Central in Las Villas and did research on the sugar economy. Named secretary of the Cuban Republic's Chamber of Commerce in 1963, he returned to Havana and in the following year published, under the title *El ingenio: Complejo económico social cubano del azúcar* (1964; *The Sugarmill: The Socioeconomic Complex of Sugar in Cuba*, 1976), what was announced as the first part of an ambitious historical and economic monograph. During the rest of the 1960s the author split his time between his work as director in the Ministry of Foreign Trade and writing history.

In the mid-1970s he worked for UNESCO, coordinating the book *África en América Latina*, to which he contributed his penetrating essay "Aportes culturales y deculturación" (Cultural Contributions and Deculturization). During those years he finished his greatest work, the final version of *El ingenio*, which was published in 1978. At the newly created Havana Instituto Superior de Arte (Havana Arts University), where he had been named senior professor of Cuban cultural history, he directed an ambitious project on the same theme that he was to leave unfinished but from which important partial studies were derived. In later years, Moreno Fraginals also worked as a guest lecturer at several U.S. and European universities, coordinated works projects for Cuban and foreign cultural institutions, organized conferences, and published more books, including *Guerra, migración y muerte (el ejército español en Cuba como vía migratoria)* (War, Migration, and Death: The Spanish Army in Cuba as a Migratory Pathway, 1993), written in collaboration with his son, José Joaquín Moreno Masó, and *Cuba/España, España/Cuba: Historia común* (Cuba/Spain, Spain/Cuba: A Common History), published in Barcelona in 1995. The year before that work was published, the author left Cuba to settle in the United States. That country, along with Spain, was the stage for his last professional activities. He died 9 May 2001 in Miami.

RECEPTION OF *EL INGENIO*

The 1964 publication of the first version of *El ingenio: Complejo económico social cubano del azúcar*, by Cuba's National Commission for UNESCO, was a cultural event in Cuba. After the Revolution in 1959, the new writing of the island's history—faithful to the nationalist tradition and laden with Marxist intentionality—aimed to reinterpret the country's past by means of texts of highly differing value. Almost always written

with an educational objective, the so-called emergency historical literature revealed some glaring limitations, and Moreno's penetrating monograph took care to make this obvious.

The Sugarmill demonstrated that although the first sixty years of the nineteenth century constituted one of the most highly documented periods in the island's development, the maturation of Cuban society could not be explained properly with a simple critical rewriting of earlier history texts. Moreno's innovative monograph delved deeper into one of the most complex processes in Cuban history and analyzed it, starting with the development of the institution that best represented its material foundation: the sugarcane plantation. In support of its thesis, the monograph made use of documents that had been ignored and literature that was out of the ordinary. Moreno examined this data with an agile, fresh Marxist approach that revealed several of the essential threads in the island's history. Because of his fine prose style, the book captivated a diverse group of readers, yet Moreno also had his detractors. For some supporters of the traditional historical discourse, Moreno's work suffered from constructions that were too fanciful, and that, above all, gave flight to an iconoclasm that was overly passionate. Thus, the publication of *The Sugarmill* gave rise to a debate—both public and private—among the most distinguished Cuban historians on the eve of the centenary of the 1868 revolution.

THE NEW *INGENIO*

At the end of another fifteen years of research, Moreno Fraginals finished the definitive version of *El ingenio*, which was published in Havana by Editorial de Ciencias Sociales in 1978. In the interim his project had changed; what was first announced as a general history of the Cuban sugar industry ended up concentrating on one of the basic phases of its evolution—still slave-based but introducing industrial techniques. What the original plan lost in breadth, the work more than gained in depth. The idea in the monograph's subtitle (Socioeconomic Complex of the Sugar Industry) now was fully evidenced in an analysis that not only defined the structure, functioning, and problems encountered with a slave-based sugar economy and made clear its relationship to the social phenomena and political events of the time but also followed the threads leading from the sugar industry to phenomena like the creation of a university chair or the spread of certain religious practices. In its final version, *The Sugarmill* offered a vivid portrait of an entire civilization's social, political, and cultural manifestations, tracing them back to their most hidden sources.

The "new *Ingenio*," in its splendid three-volume edition, included the original monograph from 1964—which constitutes the basic content of volume 1—now preceded by an introductory chapter devoted to examining the conditions under which the Cuban sugar boom had to be forged, particularly during the first half of the eighteenth century. The slow, progressive growth in sugar production around Havana between 1701 and 1758 revealed in those pages explains why its history did not start with the taking of Havana by the British in 1762, as so many writers (beginning with Francisco de Arango y Parreño) maintained. After that preamble, the sequence established in the first version of *The Sugarmill* continues: a consideration of the determining factors in the rise of Cuba's sugar industry, through the Spanish Crown's land grants (*mercedes*), the relaxation of strictures on the slave trade, and the accumulation of real capital, without neglecting other manifestations of the process in the colonial institutions and culture. An analysis of the impact that plantation expansion had on the island's landscape concludes with a long chapter (described as a "technical and economic digression") devoted to characterizing the slave-based sugar industry, in which the author provides abundant data related to production practices and the progress of sugar-manufacturing technology. An old epigraph, *el mercado de brazos* (the slave labor market), expanded into an entire chapter, closes the first volume of the 1978 edition with a broad, precise consideration of the workforce problem on the slave plantation, especially as regards the black slave trade.

VOLUME 2

The social aspects of the sugar complex are examined in the second volume in a long chapter titled "Labor and Society," in which Moreno carries out a broad, systematic analysis of the phenomenon of slavery in terms that are previously found in Cuban historiography only in *Los negros esclavos* (The Black Slaves), the extensive monograph that Don Fernando Ortiz published in 1916. The author has an evident interest in examining the slave system from different angles. He first addresses the economic significance of this form of labor that conceives of man as a machine, which is the premise for a subsequent functional analysis of the slave system of production. Moreno emphasizes the system's tenacious enthusiasm for assimilating the most dissimilar formulas of nineteenth-century capitalism and its well-known difficulties in utilizing technical progress as the basis for his controversial opinion about the technological limitations of the slave economy.

This thesis, maintained even more frankly by the author in his other works such as "Desgarramiento azucarero e integración nacional" (Sugar Industry Upheaval and National Integration), was a somewhat schematic application of a well-known Marxist theory regarding the dialectical relationship between the forces of production and the relationship of production to the problem of the historical limitations of plantation slavery. This approach has given rise to disagreements, sometimes argued with research demonstrating the ongoing profitability of the plantations and sometimes by analysis of other factors such as slave resistance that contributed to the breakdown of the odious institution.

But the problem of slavery in such a system was rooted in the fact that not only could it not develop, but also, as Moreno explains, it did not lead to a sustainable model for the exploitation of labor, eroded as it was by the impossibility of reproducing its labor force. This was well documented in *The Sugarmill* by a series of anthropological, demographic, sociological, and medical resources—as well as a very clever analysis of sexuality within the sugar refinery workforce—through which this work provides a uniquely vivid and harsh picture of the life of a plantation slave.

The work's last section, "Un paréntesis comercial" (A Digression on Commerce), is devoted to the study of how commercial factors set the conditions for the development of slave-based sugar plantations. After looking into the dynamics of the Cuban economy and its connections to the world market, this long chapter divides the country's economic history into periods, through the analysis of extensive statistics, whose indicators were selected using criteria that the historian makes explicit to facilitate his discussion. Moreno centers his review on the cycle that he characterizes as "manufacturing predominance" (1788–1873)—the basic subject of his investigation—and he analyzes it in phases, giving particular attention to the principal markets for Cuban sugar (the United States, England, and Spain) in order to clarify the circumstances under which the island's economic dependence was nurtured and supported. Of special importance in that context were Cuban-Spanish relations, characterized by the author as an anomaly in colonial models because Spain's economic backwardness made complementarity with its valuable Antilles possession difficult, preventing it from forming a modern, British-style connection in which the mother country fully participated. Beyond that theory (developed by Moreno in later works, giving rise to more than one critique), a detailed analysis of the economic relations between Cuba and Spain and the interests linked to them is set out in pages bursting with valuable information and thought-provoking theories.

VOLUME 3

Although the basic text of the work is in the first two volumes of its Cuban edition (1978), the importance of the third volume cannot be overlooked. The last volume contains a large, chronologically organized statistical appendix that coherently presents data analyzed in different sections of the book; its preparation required research with its own inherent value. This volume also includes a useful glossary of sugar-industry terms found in the literature of the period (and in many cases still used by workers in the industry) as well as an extensive, detailed critical bibliography that contains some unusual items. To all this is added a small, relatively autonomous study, *La brecha informativa* (The Information Gap), which in an unusual manner establishes the criteria for the evaluation of statistical sources related to the sugar industry, starting with consideration of the mechanisms of sugar commercialization throughout the nineteenth century, and discusses the self-serving way in which information about this lucrative trade was handled. Equally important as this supplementary information, this complete first edition of *The Sugarmill* provided in its three volumes a great diversity of enormously valuable pictures, diagrams, and other illustrative resources, though some necessary cartographical representations are lacking.

The Sugarmill is an indispensable reference for anyone studying slavery and the plantation economy in the Caribbean as well as other geographic regions. *El ingenio: Complejo económico social cubano del azúcar* became one of the pillars of what was then described in Latin America as the New History, with a highly defined social commitment. This classic of Cuban historiography has been published in various editions and translated into English and Portuguese, with more or less extensive excerpts in other languages as well. In the United States, where the work was published in 1976—in the midst of debates about the new economic history—under the title *The Sugarmill*, Manuel Moreno Fraginals's masterpiece won the Clarence H. Haring Prize for the best book in Latin American history, awarded by the American Historical Association in 1982.

BIBLIOGRAPHY

Márquez, Robert. "*El ingenio*." *Unión* 16, no. 3 (September 1977): 159–162.

Rodríguez, Pedro Pablo. "El hombre de el ingenio." *Gaceta de Cuba* 4 (July–August 2001): 27.

Schmidt-Nowara, Christopher. "Manuel Moreno Fraginals: An Appreciation." *Hispanic American Historical Review* 82, no. 1 (2002): 125–127.

Zanetti Lecuona, Oscar. "El nuevo ingenio." *Revista de la Biblioteca Nacional José Martí* 21, no. 1 (January–April 1979): 177–187.

Zanetti Lecuona, Oscar, ed. *Órbita de Manuel Moreno Fraginals*. Havana: Ediciones Unión, 2009.

■ *See also*

Economy: Special Period

Film: 1989–2010

Havana: Urban and Social History in the Twentieth Century

SUITE HABANA (FERNANDO PÉREZ)

Jorge Ruffinelli

Fernando Pérez's poetic film portrait of a day in the life of Havana.

Suite Habana (2003), a documentary film by the Cuban director Fernando Pérez, is a cinematic anomaly. In it Pérez breaks from the oral tradition of film and even from the tradition of apparent objectivity that had become a dogma in the documentary genre. This sets his film halfway between a documentary and fiction, since Pérez undermines what might have been

a conventional documentary portrayal by using neither dialogue nor voiceover narration, yet neutralizes a fictional approach by using real characters—nonactors who star in their own lives, their own habitats, their own affairs, in their own individual rhythms. It is difficult to compare the film even to the cinematic experiments in silence of Paul Leduc (such as *Latino Bar*, 1991), because Leduc is, in part, filming a theatrical production. Pérez's characters' not speaking is the formal means by which the director shows that they focus their lives elsewhere than in the everyday chit-chat and conversational give-and-take that a conventional documentary, with its built-in bias toward recording everything, would so readily exploit.

In *Suite Habana* Pérez selects twelve characters and follows their individual paths through a day. We could say there are actually thirteen characters, although one of them, John Lennon, is no more than a statue in the park that bears his name. Twelve Cubans, between ten and seventy-nine years of age, men and women, are characterized by their modest lives, by their lightly borne poverty, and by an almost generic air of melancholy. (There are three other characters presented in the course of the film—Caridad, age seventy; Natividad, age ninety-seven; and Inés, age sixty-nine—but they are not mentioned at the end as characters in the summary of dreams.) The time frame of the movie is one full day.

PORTRAIT OF A CITY

Suite Habana was originally part of a project that was intended to include other cities in other countries. As the filmmaker himself has said, the head of the Spanish production company Wanda Visión, José María Morales, arrived in Cuba one December day and proposed shooting a film about Havana, with two characteristics: it should be no longer than 55 minutes, and it had to be digitally recorded. In light of his reluctance to make documentaries, and because he wanted to work on other projects, Pérez hesitated, but finally took on the job, which ended up being one of his most personal films.

The great precedent for a film portrait of a city is *Berlin: Symphony of a Great City* (1917), by the German Walter Ruttman. Nevertheless, Morales's intent was neither to imitate that model nor to create a new one. The directors who were to film their respective cities would work freely, based on their own ideas. The overall project came to grief when *Suite Habana* was in preproduction, but Wanda Visión allowed the Cuban film, whose planning was already quite advanced, to move ahead. Its planned length was increased from 55 to 80 minutes and it became an authentic full-length production.

Suite Habana has a sensibility clearly derived from the late decades of the twentieth century, that is to say, a feeling of crisis. Following Pérez's 1994 film *Madagascar* (about a Cuban female adolescent who, in the midst of a personal crisis, seeks a personal utopia symbolized by the far away island of Madagascar), it was a logical development, clearly the product of a filmmaker who had lived through the revolutionary utopia of the 1960s, the gray decade of the 1970s, and the Special Period of the 1990s: an arc of experience reflected in the wrinkled and lined faces and the peeling walls of Havana.

Indeed, *Suite Habana* is undoubtedly not only about a place, but also about the passage of time. It is about how the people of a place live in the time that belongs to them. It reveals a biological arc that encompasses the lives of the boy Francisquito and the elderly peanut vendor Amanda; the twenty-something ballet dancer Ernesto, the thirty-something hospital worker/transvestite Iván, the physician and occasional clown Juan Carlos, and the other middle-aged characters, whom the movie brings together in a single day in Havana in the year 2003. It is about people who have their lives ahead of them, and others who are close to taking their leave. Perhaps the melancholy tone of the film derives from the awareness it gradually communicates that to live is to survive in difficult circumstances and to learn the fragility of dreams.

BIBLIOGRAPHY

Armas Fonseca, Paquita. "Suite Habana: La película anormal de Fernando Pérez." *El Caimán Barbudo* 338 (March–April 2003). Available online at http://www.caimanbarbudo.cu/html_total/simpresas/articulos/338/index_articulo_20a.htm.

Cruz Carvajal, Isieni. "A través de la imagen silenciosa." *Kinetoscopio* 11, no. 55 (2000).

Del Río, Joel. "La *Suite* del sueño inveterado." *La Jiribilla* 115 (18 July 2003). Available online at http://www.lajiribilla.co.cu/2003/n115_07.html.

Díaz Torres, Daniel. "Redención de la melancolía (sobre *Suite Habana*, una película de Fernando Pérez)." *Cine Cubano* 156 (primer trimestre 2003).

García Borrero, Juan Antonio. "Las iniciales de la ciudad: La libertad expresiva en el cine de Fernando Pérez." *Cinémas d'Amerique Latine* 12 (2004), 75–91.

Mayán, Shelly P. "*Suite Habana*: The Sound of Silence." *La Jiribilla* 117 (2 August 2003). Available online at http://www.lajiribilla.co.cu/2003/n117_08/117_11.html.

Nórido, Yuris. "*Suite de La Habana*." *Trabajadores* August 2003.

Oramas, Ada: "Consagración de una estética." *Tribuna de La Habana*, 20 July 2003. Available online at http://www.cubarte.cult.cu/periodico/print/articulo/11667.html.

Padrón Nodarse, Frank. "Una Habana que llora (y que sueña)." *Cine Cubano* 157 (2003).

Pérez Betancourt, Rolando. "*Suite Habana*." *Granma*, 28 June 2003. Available online at http://www.granma.cu/espanol/2003/junio/lun30/suite.html.

Plasencia, Azucena. "*Suite Habana*." *Bohemia*. 23 July 2003. Available online at http://www.bohemia.cu/2003/07/02semana/sumarios/cultura/articulo3.html.

Ramos, Alberto. "El entramado de un tapiz." *Kinetoscopio* 14, no. 68 June–September 2004).

Santos Moray, Mercedes. "*Suite Habana*: Una obra maestra del cine cubano." *Trabajadores*, March 2003.

Ubieta Gómez, Enrique, ed. *El valor de las pequeñas cosas: Primeras aproximaciones críticas de la prensa cubana a* Suite Habana. Havana: Ediciones ICAIC, n.d.

Ubieta Gómez, Enrique. "*Suite Habana*: Subir más alto." *Juventud Rebelde*, 30 March 2003.

Vázquez Muñoz, Luis Raúl. "Las claves de *Suite Habana*." *Juventud Rebelde*, 28 June 2003.

EL SUPER (LEÓN ICHASO)

Ana M. López

The quintessential Cuban exile film.

On a frigid New York City morning during the notoriously snowy winter of 1978, the protagonist of *El Super*, Roberto, harshly awakens to the sound of the pipes clanging and tenants clamoring for the boiler to be turned on. Roberto (Raymundo Hidalgo-Gato) is the Cuban exile superintendent ("el super") of a building in Washington Heights, where he lives with wife Aurelia (soap-opera star Zully Montero) and teenage daughter Aurelita (Elizabeth Peña in her first movie role). After ten years in exile, Roberto has trouble believing in the possibility of a mythical return to the island and even more difficulty dealing with the dreariness of the tenants' unending demands and the harshness of winter. His wife is still psychologically in Cuba, bemoaning that all she sees through their basement windows is feet, while daughter Aurelita has moved away from the Cuban way and seems to be fully embracing the American teen

Suite Habana
(2003). Fernando Pérez's lyrical documentary *Suite Habana* (Havana Suite) examines the everyday lives of a diverse group of Cubans, including this railroad worker. CINEMA TROPICAL, COURTESY EVERETT COLLECTION

■ *See also*

Diasporas: Waves of Immigration Since 1959

Film: Cuban Cinema of the Diaspora

New York City

life of late 1970s New York (marijuana, sex, and disco dancing).

Produced on a shoestring ($20,000) with a mostly volunteer cast and crew, *El Super* remains, more than thirty years after its release in 1979, the most poignant filmic articulation of the Cuban exile life as it became a permanent state. Based on a 1977 play by Iván Acosta that premiered to acclaim at the Centro Cultural Cubano de Nueva York—a vital promoter of Cuban American theater in New York in the 1970s—*El Super* was a labor of love for director León Ichaso (his brother-in law, filmmaker Orlando Jiménez Leal, is credited as co-director but has conceded that he worked primarily as cinematographer on the film). The son of well-known poet and radio-TV personality Justo Rodríguez Santos and Antonia Ichaso (who also had her own radio show in 1940s Cuba), Ichaso and his mother and sister went into exile in 1963, leaving his father, who believed in the Revolution, behind (Justo joined the family in New York five years later). Ichaso grew up in New York City, drifting through the radical youth culture of the period. By the late 1970s, he was working in advertising, and he made *El Super*, his first feature film, with money earned from making Goya commercials. He went on to have a very interesting, albeit unusual, career as a filmmaker, moving from big-budget Hollywood films such as *Sugar Hill* (1994) to mainstream TV productions (*Miami Vice*) and, notably, completing a Cuban American trilogy that encompasses *El Super*, *Azúcar amarga* (1996), and *Paraiso* (2009). Ichaso is, without doubt, the most successful Cuban American filmmaker and also the one who has most vividly captured the Cuban exile experience on film.

THE FILM

Stylistically as deceptively simple as the Cuban American lives it chronicles, *El Super* is deeply indebted to its theatrical precursor: All but two of the actors in the film had also been in the cast of the original play, and most of the action is set in the closed and claustrophobic world of a real basement in Washington Heights (192nd Street and Broadway). Yet, *El Super* is never simply theatrical. Carefully deploying a very classic and transparent style of editing, the film evidences a tremendous visual sensibility via its careful use of framing, a realistic but symbolically charged mise-en-scène (the close-ups of the flaming boiler, the calendar with the Virgen de la Caridad on the wall, and the small altar to Santa Barbara, for example), and its measured cinematography. After the claustrophobia and humor of the action set in the basement apartment, Roberto's forays into the frigid streets of New York, replete with plowed snowbanks at every corner and mounds of garbage in front of every building, are carefully framed and filmed. Rather than represent moments of openness or freedom, the figure of Roberto in his tightly buttoned heavy coat and ear-flapped cap surrounded

by snow and the oppressively gray skies remains visually as downtrodden as when he is inside.

What makes *El Super* unusual, especially for 1979, is the way it frames the Cuban American experience. Most of the films produced by first-generation Cuban exile filmmakers such as Orlando Jiménez Leal and Néstor Almendros (for example, *The Other Cuba* [1983] and *Improper Conduct* [1984]) used the documentary genre to articulate a contradictory tragic discourse that mythologizes pre-revolutionary Cuba in order to radically differentiate it from the revolutionary present of the island and link it to justify and make sense of their exile. *El Super* avoids the self-justificatory work of denunciation found in the later documentaries. It is a film of exile, longing, and displacement. As Juan Antonio García Borrero argues, Roberto and his family are perhaps the very same characters that Sergio had said goodbye to at the airport a decade earlier in *Memories of Underdevelopment* (1968; directed by Tomás Gutiérrez Alea). In this decade spent "cleaning stairs, picking up garbage, and shoveling snow," Roberto has come to recognize that the reality of exile is far more tragic than the simple act of leaving to escape an allegedly impossible and frustrating situation and/or to make a political statement (as his friend Pancho wants to argue). Leaving means losing a way of life and one's moorings and passions, and the exile's life is one of loss and anxiety. No matter how hard he tries to invoke Cuba as he asks Aurelia whether she remembers the first time they ever danced together or what Sundays were like back home, Roberto's home is now the dreary basement, the grim reality of a blustery New York winter, and his increasingly Americanized daughter who blasts the radio even though he "can't stand English first thing in the morning."

The genius of *El Super*, however, is that it presents this pathos without melodramatic grandiosity. Rather, its gently humorous rendering of Cuban American angst operates to demystify a community that all too often had been characterized exclusively by its sociopolitical positions. In *El Super*, Pancho is the epitome of that rabidly antirevolutionary figure who claims, with visible hyperbole, to have played a crucial role in the Bay of Pigs invasion and who insists that those who refuse to leave must be left to suffer. But Roberto and Aurelia stand in sharp contrast to this stereotype: Not particularly political back in Cuba or now, they participate in a structure of feeling of loss, anxiety, and guilt that the film is at pains to capture. As Roberto poignantly exclaims, "If I had known this I would have stayed in Cuba. In Cuba you have to cut cane but at least it's our cane."

The film ends with Roberto's decision to accept a job in a factory in Miami and to move the family. Framed by the dream of palm trees, warm weather, and Spanish, the viewer leaves Roberto precisely as he and the family (against Aurelita's wishes, of course) plan to undertake what will become yet another exile, this time to the land of enervating nostalgia and, possibly, the assumption of the stereotypical role of the Cuban exile as historical victim. This solution to Roberto's angst ends the story on a somewhat hollow note, for Roberto can never have that which he longs for most: not to have left Cuba.

LEGACY

El Super's impact upon its release (it was shown as part of the Museum of Modern Art's New Directors series and distributed by New Yorker Films) had two layers. It was very well received as an art film by the critical intelligentsia and favorably reviewed. Vincent Canby, writing in the *New York Times* in 1979, for example, appropriately argued that it was "less about politics than the disorientation of exiles who become living metaphors for the human condition" (p. 58). It also went on to win several international awards, including the Grand Prize at the Mannheim-Heidelberg International Film Festival. Thus, it served Ichaso well as a calling card that facilitated his subsequent entry into Hollywood.

At another level, however, the film has become a cult film for Cuban Americans everywhere. It is frequently screened and is widely available in video/DVD stores in Cuban American areas such as Miami. Its anniversaries have also been celebrated with gala screenings, including for its twentieth anniversary in Miami and for its thirtieth at the Bronx Museum in New York. As recounted in a piece by Ian Frazier in the *New Yorker*, the thirtieth anniversary screening was standing-room only, and the crowd "turned upward to the screen with the expectant, half-smiling expressions of those waiting to be shown a favorite magic trick" (p. 50). *El Super* has become the film that has helped Cuban Americans understand their lives. It functioned as a kind of coming-out movie for the hyphenated existence of a Cuban American community and way of life. After *El Super*, there can no longer be any pretense that a return to the island is either immediate (the "next year in Havana" syndrome) or even a distant reality. This is now a community that is in the United States to stay—and that can begin to laugh at itself. As Ichaso himself argued in 1999, "*El Super* was a catharsis. It said we were here, we weren't going back to Cuba tomorrow, and we could laugh at what we had become" (quoted in Fernández).

BIBLIOGRAPHY

Canby, Vincent. "*El Super*: A Cuban American Tale." *New York Times* April 29, 1979, p. 58.

Fernández, Enrique. "Exile Cinema Never as Super as Once Hoped," *Sun Sentinel* September 26, 1999. Available from http://articles.sun-sentinel.com/1999-09-26/entertainment/9909240893_1_cuban-americans-cuban-exile-cuban-women.

Frazier, Ian. "*El Super*," *New Yorker* December 21, 2009, p. 50.

García Borrero, Juan Antonio. "*El Super* (1978) de León Ichaso y Orlando Jiménez Leal." *Cine cubano, la pupila insomne* (blog). Available from http://cine-cubano-la-pupila-insomne.nireblog.com/post/2007/06/20/el-super-1978-de-leon-ichaso-y-orlando-jimenez-leal.

Geller, Lynn. "Leon Ichaso." *BOMB* 78 (Winter 2002). Available from http://bombsite.com/issues/78/articles/2447.

López, Ana M. "Cuban Cinema in Exile: The 'Other' Island." *Jump Cut: A Review of Contemporary Media* 38 (June 1993): 51–59.

Santiago, Fabiola. "That Old Feeling." *Miami Herald* September 29, 1999. Available from http://www.cubanet.org/CNews/y99/oct99/01e8.htm.

T

TELEVISION

In a bold commercial venture, Cuba was one of the first countries in the world to have television broadcasts. In the short period between 1950 and 1959, Cuban television produced several programs that are still remembered fondly. Soap operas, especially, were popular and are still favorites among Cuban audiences. Cuban baseball games were also telecast.

During the 1970s and 1980s, television programs from socialist countries filled Cuban airwaves, both for ideological reasons and because of the U.S. embargo on programming and equipment. Generations of Cuban children grew up watching what they called Russian cartoons rather than Disney programming. Today, Cuban television is an important vehicle for cultural diversification, and the broadcast week is filled with musical programs, soap operas, serials, and cartoons.

TELEVISION: BEGINNINGS AND DEVELOPMENT

Mayra Cué Sierra

The first ten years of television in Cuba, from 1950 to the Revolution in 1959.

In Havana in December 1946 the renowned actress and singer María de los Ángeles Santana (1914–2011) and her husband Julio Vega organized Cuba's first demonstration of closed-circuit television. Television operations were officially inaugurated in October 1950 by Unión Radio-TV, channel 4. That company, headed by the Spaniard Gaspar Pumarejo, included among its major shareholders the Mestre brothers, José Antonio and Alberto, as well as Miguel Lastra and Carlos Humara, Cuban representatives for RCA Victor.

In December 1950 the brothers Mestre Espinosa (Goar, Luís Augusto, and Abel—no relation to the Mestre brothers) launched CMQ-TV, the most important communications group in the country and the first television network with headquarters outside Havana. The broadcasting station started operation in 1951 and was progressively expanded. It had its own signal transmitters. In 1951 Manuel Alonso, the owner of Telenews and director and editor for newsreels such as *América*, *El País*, and *Royal News*, acquired Unión Radio-TV and renamed it Televisión Nacional.

The system became more diversified in 1953. Alberto Hernández Catá, who presided over CMBF-TV (owned by the Mestre Espinosas' Radio Universal), began to broadcast U.S. films and various TV series. Telemundo debuted, owned by Radio Televisión El Mundo, whose partners were the Italian Amadeo Barletta (owner of the daily newspaper *El Mundo*), Ángel Cambó (former owner of CMQ Radio and TV), Miguel Lastra, and Carlos Humara. Telemundo then acquired Unión Radio and channel 4 and incorporated TV Caribe (1953), run by J. L. Meneses and Manuel Autran, a former owner of Cuban radio stations.

In 1954 TV Habanera, whose president was Reuben Moulds, the representative of the North American network NBC, ended its broadcasts after only six months. In 1957 Telecolor inaugurated the first commercial operation in color technology outside the United States and introduced specialized information in news services. The company's shareholders included its CEO, Gaspar Pumarejo, the American Edmund Chester, and Martha Fernández de Batista.

Thus, the Cuban radio industry financed the first television broadcasting companies when the nation still lacked television sets, sponsors, and audiences. Radio and television industries shared practices, formats, resources, methods, and an experienced human capital, already successful in the national and regional media, communications, and cultural arenas.

The developing system focused its broadcasts within the reduced perimeter of the original stations; it was up against television stations with large capital, organizational systems, influence, and powerful independent audiovisual production companies—soap companies such as Crusellas and Sabaté, and national and North American transnational affiliates such as Gaspar Pumarejo's and Otto Sirgo's Escuela de Televisión (School of Television).

Havana was the forerunner in the number of Spanish-language television channels, latest technical equipment, and the television advertising market. Its influence and prestige were sustained by the following:

- advanced technology;
- artistic, technical, and acting excellence;
- live and pre-recorded broadcasting;
- conversion of genres, formats, and plot lines;
- the interconnectedness of entertainment, popular culture, and commercial media;
- projects that fully integrated activities, agents, actors, products, and companies;
- an internal and external continuous improvement process, research-based and utilizing communications tools for adapting content and method to different audiences.

Havana became the center of commercial, technological, media, and symbolic exchange and the intermediary connecting the United States with the rest of Latin America. Cuba created the Latin American models for programming formats and genres, enhancing its leadership in the field of Spanish-language television. Cuban television executives, specialists, and artists promoted the regional development of the industry by participating in the creation and initial operations management of the first television stations in several countries, notably Venezuela and Colombia, and they were majority shareholders in WAPA-TV (Puerto Rico).

When private ownership and commercial activities were suspended in Cuba in 1960, Cuban television executives and many television artists and specialists emigrated to other countries in the Americas. A noteworthy example is Goar Mestre Espinosa, who established important television stations and audiovisual production companies in Argentina and contributed to other Latin American media projects as well.

CULTURAL VALUE

Cuban television exalted youth, beauty, talent, theatricality, and entertainment through a star system. It appropriated foreign and national cultural models and transformed them, adding new expressive language resources and perspectives for commercial products that were shown to Cuban society. It made headway in developing innovations in cinematography, production, painting, set design, sound effects, wardrobe, dance, music, sports, and nonverbal communication practices.

This medium combined experienced artists with new, promising talent who learned acting and the use of cameras through hands-on experience. Television created audiences out of diverse social sectors, even outsiders to the world of art and communications, and it positioned the productive, creative, financial, and symbolic management of its social actors.

In spite of the inevitable imitation of U.S. models, patterns, and concepts, Cuban television programming shaped contexts and aesthetics using Latin American traditions and sensibilities, fusing the classical with the popular. It brought products face-to-face with audiences and sought its average viewer through an impressive thematic, temporal, visual, and spatial adjustment dependent on editing, the language of the camera, audiovisual rhythms, set dimensions, and viewer preferences. Television's creative, financial, and communications leadership was expressed in the synthesis of its rhythm, modernity, and the Cuban national character. It fostered news, sports, the dramatic arts, and music, along with competitions and commercial messages and interaction with viewers.

The most significant programs—whether they were original scripts or literary, theatrical, or cinematographic adaptations, single-episode, series, or vignettes inserted into participatory, educational, historical, sports, and musical projects—set the bar for thematic and theatrical selectivity in drama and comedies. Some of television's themes and formats inspired practices that were reproduced in other Latin American countries. Unión Radio-TV and Televisión Nacional led the region with the following shows:

- the first televised baseball games (October 1950);
- cooking shows such as *Teleclub del hogar* (Teleclub at Home, October 1950);
- puppet shows (November 1950);
- boxing matches (November 1950);
- *costumbrista* humor in shows such as *Los cuatro grandes* (The Four Big Men, November 1950);
- carnival parades (February 1951);
- *Teatro del lunes* (Monday Theater, shown in Cuba and internationally in March 1951);
- classical ballet and contemporary dance in *Variedades musicales* (Musical Varieties, April 1951);

- jai alai and freestyle wrestling matches (January 1951);
- bullfights in Cuba and other countries (November 1951 and January 1953);
- *Periódico El Mundo en televisión* (*El Mundo* newspaper on television, August 1952);
- situation comedies such as *Las aventuras de Paco, Pepe y Pipo* (The Adventures of Paco, Pepe, and Pipo, 1954); and
- charity telethons (1953).

In December 1951, channel 6 (CMQ-TV) broadcast *Tensión*, the first original detective series of its kind, on the day the station premiered. In October 1952 it launched *La novela en televisión* (The Novel on Television) in a series of episodes that ran for six consecutive days, which would become the model for media drama in Latin America. CMQ-TV also led the way with *Zarzuelas en gran teatro lírico ESSO* (*Zarzuelas* on ESSO's Great Musical Theater, October 1951) and with classical theater and excerpts from operas on *Gran teatro del sábado* (Saturday's Grand Theater, November 1955). One month later, Telemundo showed *La Bohème* in its entirety on *Noches de Ambar Motors* (Ambar Motors Nights).

Television and its moving images and audiovisual culture, vital in its immediacy, intense weekly frequency, and programming schedules of more than eight continuous hours each day, had a daily impact, which resulted in successive and varied projects aimed at different audiences. It generated appropriations, set precedents, and originated artistic and media-related products and expressions of Latin America's popular culture, which spread throughout Latin America. In cases such as the *telenovela*, Cuban television penetrated even the North American market. In the Spanish-speaking world, the contributions and legacy of Cuban commercial television turned it into a vast reservoir of the media, communication, and cultural historiography of Ibero-America.

BIBLIOGRAPHY

Bracero Torres, Josefa. *Silencio ... se habla*. Havana: Editorial Pablo de la Torriente Brau, 2007.

Cué Sierra, Mayra. "Senderos de amor. La génesis del modelo latino de la telenovela." Ph.D. diss., Department of Communication, University of Havana, 2007.

Dávila Mune, Iris. *El melodrama. Un caso en tela de juicio y En torno al serial en Delirio de periodista*. Havana: Ediciones Unión, 2007.

González Martínez, Víctor J. "La industria cultural cubana y la gestión del grupo Mestre Espinosa." Ph.D. diss., Department of Communication, University of Havana, 2009.

López Fernández, Oscar Luís. *La radio en Cuba*. 3rd ed. Havana: Editorial Letras Cubanas, 2002.

Salwen, Michael B. *Radio and Television in Cuba: The Pre-Castro Era*. Ames: Iowa State University Press, 1994.

TELEVISION: TELEVISION SINCE 1959

Paquita Armas Fonseca

Television programming in Cuba under the Instituto Cubano de Radio y Televisión during the revolutionary period.

The triumph of the Cuban Revolution in 1959 set in motion a process of change that affected the structure as well as the content of television programming. Fidel Castro, at the time a young, charismatic speaker, used television in a manner that until then very few government leaders had tried. In his television appearances, which sometimes lasted several hours, he enumerated and explained every measure the new government adopted. During the early years of the new regime, the nationalization of U.S. companies operating in Cuba (ultimately the total reached 383) led to the disappearance of TV commercials and thus the means of financing operations and generating a profit. The state was obliged to assume the entire cost of production, including payroll, in a notably expensive medium.

The U.S. economic embargo of Cuba, initiated in 1960 by President Dwight Eisenhower and reinforced in 1962 by President John F. Kennedy, worsened the situation. The television industry did not escape the effects of this policy. All equipment, from basic parts to state-of-the-art cameras, came from the United States; producers of such equipment could no longer sell new or second-hand technology to Cuba without paying large fines. It thus became impossible, beginning in the 1960s, to acquire equipment of U.S. origin. Before the Revolution there had been seven channels, two of which broadcast nationwide, though they reached only one-fourth of the population; after it, Cuban technicians had to use their ingenuity to keep just two channels on the air: Channel 6 (the old CMQ) and Channel 2. In addition to the embargo on U.S. equipment, Cuba could not obtain TV programs made or distributed in the United States. In the late 1960s and early 1970s, several types of programs then being produced in the Soviet Union and the Eastern Bloc nations started being aired in Cuba.

ICRT: CREATION AND DEVELOPMENT

In order to create an adequate programming policy and carry out public television operations, on 24 May 1962 the government created the Instituto Cubano de Radiodifusión (ICR; Cuban Radio Broadcasting Institute), with the same powers as a government ministry. Although not reflected in the agency's name, television was included in its scope; in 1976, with the status of a cabinet ministry, it became known as the Instituto Cubano de Radio y Televisión (ICRT; Cuban Institute of Radio and Television). The ICRT was responsible for production, broadcasting policies, and hiring personnel. It governed international agreements and, with government funding, managed investments in equipment and real estate. Over the years, the ICRT went through various structural changes. At first divided into independently managed channels, the ICRT was later reorganized to meet all of the production and broadcasting needs by programming areas: dramas, children's shows, news, and so on. Later, planning was undertaken for a new organizational structure that would decentralize program production and provide each channel with its own technological and human resources. The introduction of color television was a major endeavor from the mid-1970s through the 1980s. In some instances, the same channel would broadcast some programs in color and others in black and white. The public did not have widespread access to color television sets until the mid-1980s, when the government made a large investment in thousands of Soviet-made television sets to replace black-and-white ones.

As a means to enrich popular culture and improve instruction at various grade levels, the ICRT launched the Educational Channel in May 2002 and Educational Channel Two in April 2004. A previous attempt in the mid-1960s to establish instruction through television programming had failed. The newer educational channels were intended to develop, produce, and broadcast programs with cultural, educational, and social content, including televised classes for secondary students, broadcast during the school year and prepared by academically trained specialists. To enable high school students throughout the country to view these programs, the government provided televisions and VCRs to every school in the nation. By so doing, educational television reached 82 percent of the population. In addition to the educational channels, after October 2000 Cubavisión (the former CMQ) broadcast *Universidad para todos* (University for All) to encourage reading and the study of history, geography, and English and even instruction in art appreciation, chess, and cooking, among other subjects. Another option on Cuban television was Channel Multivisión, which began broadcasting twenty-four hours a day in July 2008 and aired foreign productions such as films, musicals, historic and scientific documentaries, and dramatic series.

Some of the more memorable Cuban television programs after 1959 are *Palmas y cañas* (Palms and Sugarcane), which was aimed at farmers and remained as of 2011 on the air; *San Nicolás del Peladero*, a period comedy satirizing the Republic's mayors; and *Álbum de Cuba*, a showcase for singers. In the 1980s, *Para bailar* (Let's Dance) was created to preserve popular dances and promote Cuban music. The whole nation tuned in to the show every Sunday afternoon, and young people learned the dances of earlier generations. Several singers popular in Cuba got their start on the talent show *Todo el mundo canta* (Everybody Sings). On 18 September 1980 the voyage into space

by Cuban Arnaldo Tamayo, the first black and first Latino cosmonaut, aired on Cuban television via satellite from the former Soviet Union. This broadcast was a landmark event in the history of Cuban television, given the time difference, the use of color, and the excitement it generated among Cubans.

TELECENTERS

Television broadcasting beyond Havana began in 1959 with a small television studio in Camagüey, which operated for only a short time. In 1968 the first provincial channel, Telerebelde, in Santiago de Cuba, broadcast its signal to the entire former Oriente Province. In 1976 the Oriente region was divided into five provinces, and the Santiago studio started receiving tax revenues from as far away as Holguín Province. In the early 1980s Telerebelde went national, broadcasting over Channel 2 and transmitting provincial programming for two hours a day.

The introduction of videotape in the late 1970s marked the beginning of a technological revolution, causing television news bureaus to be organized in every province. Regional information centers appeared in Camagüey, Villa Clara, and Pinar de Río; in 1986, with some restructuring, those centers were transformed into five provincial channels or *telecentros,* as they were commonly referred to in Cuba: Tele Turquino (covering Santiago de Cuba, Guantánamo, and Granma), Tele Cristal (Holguín and Las Tunas), TV Camagüey (Camagüey and Ciego de Ávila), Tele Cubanacán (Sancti Spíritus, Villa Clara, and Cienfuegos), and Tele Pinar (Pinar del Río). Ten more telecenters were subsequently created, one for each province and another in the special municipality of Isla de la Juventud (Island of Youth). The establishment of municipal telecenters began in 2004. With the organization of these units, the number of local news bureaus reached seventy. In combination with the provincial television stations, this made it possible to broadcast from 101 different parts of the country. The telecenters were based on the principles of community television: In each province or municipality, broadcasting reflected local and regional issues so that viewers were not a mere passive audience. Much of the programming thus created and notable for its high production standards was subsequently broadcast by the national channels. Each telecenter now had its own Web site as well.

CANAL HABANA AND TELEVISIÓN SERRANA

Canal Habana, which broadcast for the jurisdictions of Havana, Mayabeque, and Artemisa, stood out on the landscape of Cuban television. The station was created in 2006, splitting off from CHTV (the telecenter for Havana City and the Havana region, launched in 1990). Broadcasting on Channel 27 on the newly inaugurated UHF spectrum for the capital area, the station reached some three million residents. It operated at Mazón and San Miguel, where the first Cuban television station broadcast, Union Radio Television, was launched on 24 October 1950. With its strong design sense and fresh content, Canal Habana had an artistic appeal that distinguished it from other stations in Cuba. It presented information and news in a vivid and timely manner and reflected the concerns of its viewers. Camera in hand, the channel's young journalists covered a wide range of citizens' everyday problems, varied and in some cases thorny. Many shows featured well-known specialists in various fields and took phoned-in questions from viewers on the air. The directors and screenwriters relied on help from the ICRT's Centro de Investigaciones Sociales (Center for Social Research), which provided guidance from researchers based on surveys and studies. They also gathered viewer comments, which they considered valuable feedback on the programming. Canal Habana earned many awards in the first few years it was on the air, and a great number of the programs it produced were rebroadcast nationwide. An unpublished survey conducted by the Centro de Investigaciones Sociales del Instituto Cubano de Radio y Televisión in 2009 found that six out of every ten residents of Havana named it as their favorite channel—a considerable achievement for such a new operation.

Televisión Serrana, another remarkable telecenter, was the brainchild of the documentarian Daniel Diez Castillo, who in the early 1990s started looking for support to commence broadcasting from the rugged interior of the Sierra Maestra, Cuba's largest mountain range. Diez Castillo returned to the documentary heritage of renowned Cuban filmmaker Santiago Álvarez. Initially, he relied on funds provided by UNESCO, while the ICRT provided personnel and training. The Asociación Nacional de Agricultores Pequeños (ANAP; National Association of Small Farmers), a nongovernmental organization, also supported the creation of this media resource, which though it is considered a telecenter did not operate as such.

Televisión Serrana filmmakers arrived in the village of San Pablo de Yao, Buey Arriba municipality, in the heart of Sierra Maestra, with inexpensive video equipment and created a continuing plotline: They filmed local people talking about their lives, their dreams, and troubles, transforming the footage into programs subsequently viewed by other inhabitants of the region. Thus Televisión Serrana was a community channel in the purest sense. Many local young people fell in love with the idea of sharing their customs, their tastes, and their hopes through video. Local children made video letters to be seen by other children in Cuba and abroad; their sincere and authentic messages became famous. Televisión Serrana continued as of 2011 to exist as the voice of the community. Buey Arriba was unique in Cuba, a place where the cameras and the locals coexisted in harmony. Rural people became participants in video creation, and directors, who used to come from Havana, later mostly came from nearby rural areas. This unique project launched

an exchange program in 2001 with students from a similar center in Harlem, New York, and several videographers and television directors from various places visited Buey Arriba, spreading the concept to other mountain villages in Granma Province where a kindred project was underway.

FROM CUBA TO THE WORLD

Cubavisión Internacional, created in 1986, was in charge of broadcasting Cuba's image to the world. It began broadcasting around the clock in 2003 and had approximately 18 million viewers worldwide. Cubavisión also provided services to news agencies and television networks from abroad that broadcast coverage from Cuba. Its signal was used either continuously or occasionally by one hundred stations around the world; twenty Latin American countries received its frequency through close to three hundred cable systems. In addition, it had three satellite transmitters that covered Europe and Latin America. In 2000 the Centro de Operaciones Internacionales (Center for International Operations), which was created within the ICRT in 1978 and equipped with modern technology, started presenting Cubavisión Internacional via the Internet. This feed, in both Spanish and English, offered a diverse selection of news and other kinds of programming and could be viewed worldwide.

Cuban technicians and artists distinguished for their work in television provided services to Venezuela, Angola, Guinea, Vietnam, and Nicaragua. A member of Telesur, a pan–Latin American television network, Cuba had sixteen accredited international affiliates, including CNN (USA), Televisión Española (Spain), NHK (Japan), ZDF (Germany), and XINJUA (China). The international signal covered a large territory that started with the Simón Bolívar satellite. The use of different satellites presented difficulties whose resolution awaited the country's access to fiber-optic cable, which was expected to be installed from Venezuela to Santiago de Cuba, in the eastern part of the country. This arrangement was considered necessary due to provisions of the economic embargo which barred Cuban access to the U.S. fiber optic network, despite the fact that it runs very close to the Cuban coast. Television, Internet, and telephone transmission were anticipated to be greatly improved with the forthcoming connection.

CUBAN TELEVISION SINCE THE 1990s

By the late twentieth century Cuban television had a total of five national channels, one international channel, and 101 local stations throughout the country that included both provincial and municipal telecenters and local news bureaus. The system included production departments, research and training centers, commercial entities, and other departments needed for public television, especially given that Cuban television remained unique in the world with respect to its funding mechanisms and production methods.

Despite the complete absence of commercials, Cuban channels broadcast films, including notable recent releases, drama series from various countries, documentaries, musical programs, and sports. Between 65 and 70 percent of all programming, as of 2011, was Cuban. Cubavisión and Multivisión each broadcast around the clock, with Telerebelde offering seventeen hours of programming, and two educational channels sixteen hours. The signal frequencies covered 95 percent of the country. In the early 2000s, it was estimated that there were three million television sets in the country. Research showed that the average Cuban watched between four and six hours of television a day.

Several festivals and awards recognize the best in Cuban television and encourage further creativity. The Festival Nacional de Telecentros (National Telecenter Festival), which has been held regularly since the early 1990s, recognized the best Cuban community productions. Programming from the most remote places participated. Likewise, the Festival Nacional de la Televisión (National Festival of Television) has been held annually since 2004; this forum has encouraged a healthy competition among all channels, national, provincial, and municipal. The National Television Award for lifetime achievement has been given annually since 2003 to directors, commentators, actors, and technicians who excelled in this medium. Another yearly honor is the Caracol Prize, given by the Asociación de Medios Audiovisuales y Radio (Association of Audiovisual Media and Radio), part of the Unión de Escritores y Artistas de Cuba (UNEAC; Union of Writers and Artists of Cuba). The association comprises the leading figures of Cuban television, radio, and film. Artists from all over the country make up both the jury and the nominees for the prize. In addition to the awarding of the prize, the Caracol workshops bring together those working in the field to discuss the most critical problems faced by Cuban media, especially television.

BIBLIOGRAPHY

González Castro, Vicente. *Para entender la televisión.* Havana: Editorial Pablo de la Torriente, 1995.

González, Reinaldo. *Llorar es un placer.* Havana: Editorial Letras Cubanas, 1988.

Gutiérrez Alea, Tomás. *Dialéctica del espectador.* Havana: Unión, 1982. English edition: *The Viewer's Dialectic.* Edited by Iraida Sánchez Oliva. Translated by Julia Lesage. Havana: Editorial José Martí, 1988.

Kornhauser, William. *The Politics of Mass Society.* New Brunswick, NJ: Transaction, 2008.

Kraus, Sidney, ed. *Mass Communication and Political Information Processing.* Hillsdale, NJ: L. Erlbaum Associates, 1990.

Kraus, Sidney, and Dennis Davis. *The Effects of Mass Communication on Political Behavior.* University Park: Pennsylvania State University Press, 1976.

Meyrowitz, Joshua. *No Sense of Place: The Impact of Electronic Media on Social Behavior.* New York: Oxford University Press, 1985.

Muñiz Egea, Mirta. *La publicidad en Cuba mito y realidad.* Havana: Ediciones Logos, 2003.

Rothman, Stanley, ed. *The Mass Media in Liberal Democratic Societies.* New York: Paragon House, 1992.

Segura Jiménez, Rolando. *En torno a la televisión.* Havana: Editorial Félix Varela, 2004.

Vilches, Lorenzo. *La televisión: Los efectos del bien y del mal.* Barcelona, Spain: Edicioines Paidós, 1993.

Wolf, Mauro. *La investigación de la comunicación de masas.* Havana: Editorial Pablo de la Torriente, 2004.

Zaldivar Diéguez, Andrés. *Bloqueo: El asedio económico más prolongado de la historia.* San Luis: Editorial Capitán, 2003.

TELEVISION: RUSSIAN CARTOONS

Jacqueline Loss

Muñequitos rusos *(Russian cartoons) on Cuba television at 6:00 p.m. throughout the 1960s, 1970s, and 1980s.*

Not all the cartoons were Russian; the inexact term *muñequitos rusos* corresponds to the tendency among Cubans to refer to all people and things from the Soviet bloc nations as *rusos* (Russians). These cartoons demonstrate that the Cuba–Soviet Union alliance meant more than the importation of goods such as oil, machinery, and other everyday items; it also meant the importation of culture.

Although Russian meat, Lada and Moscovich automobiles, and Krim, Electron, and Caribe (the island brand) televisions may be the most memorable dimensions of material culture of the era, in the aftermath of disintegration of the Soviet bloc muñequitos rusos have become the glue that symbolically holds together a generation of Cubans born in the 1960s, 1970s, and 1980s. The cartoons' moral lessons, rhythm, and appearance are difficult to assimilate for some who grew up on faster and more aggressive U.S. animation. At the same time, the remarkable aesthetic richness of many of these cartoons earned them a place in the archives of animation aficionados across the globe. Yuri Norstein's *The Hedgehog in the Fog* (1975) and particularly his *Tale of Tales* (1979), which was chosen by international juries as the greatest animation film of all time, are examples of astounding innovation for their implementation of multiple glass planes and lyrical cut-out animation.

One of the most beloved characters was the anthropomorphic, furry and big-eared Cheburashka who, having accidentally tumbled into an orange crate, was shipped to the Soviet Union. He often is accompanied by his crocodile friend Gena. The cartoon was based on a 1966 story by the famous Soviet children's writer Eduard Uspensky (b. 1937)

and was first adapted for the Soviet stop-motion film *El cocodrilo Gena* (Gena the Crocodile), directed by Roman Kachanov, in 1969. Another well-known Soviet cartoon in Cuba, based on a Brothers Grimm fairytale, was *La liebre y el erizo* (The Hare and the Hedgehog), produced by Kiev Science Film in 1963 and directed by Irina Gurvich. Its transparent moral was recognizable to anyone familiar with Aesop's fable "The Tortoise and the Hare": Don't ridicule and underestimate those weaker than you. The protagonist of *Uncle Stiopa* (1964, Soyuzmultfilm), which was based on a series of poems by Sergey Mikhalkov (1913–2009), is a tall policeman who regularly performs good deeds and serves as a model for children in civic duties. *Bolek and Lolek*, a popular Polish series about two young boys who travel the world, introduced Cuban children to exotic lands. Other memorable cartoons include *Deja que te coja* (Just You Wait, Soyuzmultfilm), *Los músicos de Bremen* (Bremen-Town Musicians, Soyuzmultfilm), *Los chapuceros* (Pat & Mat, Czechoslovakia), *El cartero fogón* (The Mailman Pechkin, Soyuzmultfilm), *La hija del sol* (The Daughter of the Sun, Soyuzmultfilm), and *Las aventuras de Aladar Mezga* (The Adventures of Aladar Mezga, Hungary). There were also series geared for adults, such as *Gustavus* (Hungary).

VIRTUAL AND REAL COMMUNITIES

With the launch in 2005 of the Internet blog "Russian Cartoons and Others: For Cubans like myself who keep remembering them with longing," Aurora Jácome, a Cuban born in 1976, brought international attention to the nostalgia that is usually expressed privately among peers. In the first entry of her blog, Jácome affirmed that as a Cuban émigré to Spain at age sixteen, she has more in common with Eastern Europeans of her generation than with Spaniards because she was raised within a Soviet television community. Those who blame the Soviets for Cubans' failures under Fidel Castro are less likely to feel affection for such symbols of the Eastern bloc. An example of the use of muñequitos rusos as a tool in ideological debate occurred in the 1970s, when the comedian Enrique Arredondo was suspended from his role as Bernabé on the television program *Detrás de la fachada* for warning his grandson, "if you don't behave, I'll punish you by forcing you to watch the muñequitos rusos," a message that expressed people's bitterness toward the Soviet Union.

Cubans' feelings about Soviet animation were not determined by where they lived. For example, in Miami, a city traditionally known as an anti-Castro stronghold, Cuban cartoons became available and sought after at video stores, because for many post-1991 immigrants, cartoons from the Soviet bloc represent their relationship to their homeland. Although not all are as enthusiastic as Jácome, there are many Cuban consumers of muñequitos rusos on the Internet. The famous Cuban blogger Yoani

■ *See also*

Cuban Thought and Cultural Identity: Costumbres in the Revolutionary Period

Cuban Thought and Cultural Identity: Socialist Thought

The World and Cuba: Cuba and Socialist Countries

The Story of One Crime. The Russian animated film *The Story of One Crime* (1962), directed by Fyodor Khitruk, concerns an ordinary man driven by rude neighbors to commit a crime. © RIA NOVOSTI/ALAMY

Sánchez has defined her blog and her own generation ("Generation Y") by, among other things, their relationship to this foreign import.

One piece left out of this puzzle is the discrepancy between virtual and real space. In Cuba, entries from blogs, including Jácome's, are regularly cut and pasted into e-mails in order to reach those with restricted access to the Internet. In addition, even prior to the rise of blogging, in the first decade of the twenty-first century, a small group of the adult children of mixed marriages between Cubans and citizens of the former Soviet bloc, led by Polina Martínez Shvietsova and Dmitri Prieto Samsonov, sought access to the cartoon archives. Of the many events they organized was *Koniec*, which featured screenings of the cartoons. *Koniec* (end)—which flashed on screen at the conclusion of every cartoon—is, along with *tovarich* (comrade), the Russian word with which Cubans are most familiar. But the recovery of these cartoons on the island extends beyond the efforts of Generation Y'ers and Russian cartoon fans; in keeping with the theme of Cuba's 2010 International Book Fair, which honored Russia, muñequitos rusos of different decades reappeared on Cuban national television.

DOCUMENTING THE MEMORIES

Consideration of Cubans' feelings toward muñequitos rusos brings to mind the phenomenon in Germany known as *Ostalgie* (nostalgia for East Germany). That parallel is brought home by the short documentary *Goodbye, Lolek!* (2005), directed by Asori Soto, in which interviewees assess the impact of the cartoons. Interspersed throughout the documentary are clips from the cartoons, and the theme song from the popular muñequito ruso *The Town Musicans of Bremen*, which first appeared in Cuba in 1969, is featured in a punk rock version by the controversial band Porno para Ricardo. The band also released a video,

directed by Ernesto René Rodríguez, which refers to the original Brothers Grimm fairytale and fictionalizes Cubans' complex memories of the Soviet period. Two other documentaries that deal with the impact of the Soviet-Cuban solidarity, *9550* (2006, directed by Ernesto René Rodríguez and Jorge E. Betancourt) and *Los rusos en Cuba* (2008, directed by Enrique Colina), also contain interpretations of muñequitos rusos.

The significance of the memorialization of muñequitos rusos within a global Cuba ought to be considered as emblematic of a wider phenomenon of Cubans' complicated recollections of their country's solidarity with the Eastern bloc. Although the collective filter to the world that the Soviet Union provided Cuba disappeared, it has not departed from the imagination of Cubans, because not only was some Soviet bloc art entertaining, it was also aesthetically first-rate and distinct from animation styles that followed it. Along with the fact that, in the aftermath of the demise of the Soviet bloc, some Cubans re-evaluated their own relationship to the material and cultural products from the Soviet Union on which they previously depended, this combination of aesthetic and ethical entertainment means that muñequitos rusos persist as a crucial dimension of an elaborate audiovisual imaginary from the Soviet bloc in Cuba.

BIBLIOGRAPHY

Barash, Zoia. "Notas sobre los dibujos animados en Rusia." *Miradas: Revista del audiovisual.* Available from http://www.eictv.co.cu/miradas/.

Betancourt, Jorge E., and Ernesto René Rodríguez. *9550.* Film documentary. Producciones por la Izquierda. 2006.

Colina, Enrique. *Los rusos en Cuba.* Film documentary. 2008.

Díaz, Duanel. "Muñequitos rusos, nostalgia cubiche." *Cuba: La memoria inconsolable: Apuntes sobre cultura, historia e ideología.* April 6, 2007. Available from http://www.duaneldiaz.blogspot.com/2007/04/muequitos-rusos-nostalgia-cubiche.html.

Instituto Cubano de Radio y Televisión. Memorias TVC. Available from http://www.uncleernest.com/tvc/munequitosrusos.html.

Jácome, Aurora. "Muñequitos Rusos y otros: Para los cubanos que como yo, los siguen recordando con añoranza." Available from http://www.munequitosrusos.blogspot.com.

Kitson, Clare. *Yuri Norstein and Tale of Tales: An Animator's Journey.* Bloomington: Indiana University Press, 2005.

Loss, Jacqueline. "Vintage Soviets in Post-Cold War Cuba." *Mandorla: Nueva Escritura de las Américas* 7 (2003): 79–84.

Loss, Jacqueline. "Wandering in Russian." In *Cuba in the Special Period: Culture and Ideology in the 1990s,* edited by Ariana Hernández-Reguant. New York: Palgrave, 2009.

Martínez Shvietsova, Polina, and Dmitri Prieto Samsonov. "Acercamiento a la diáspora post-soviética en Cuba." *Cahiers des amériques latines* 57–58 (2008): 113–123.

MacFadyen, David. *Yellow Crocodiles and Blue Oranges: Russian Animated Film since World War Two.* Montreal: McGill–Queen's University Press, 2005.

Reyes, Dean Luis. "Arqueología de la nostalgia o de cómo aprendí a amar a Tío Stíopa." *Gaceta de Cuba* 1 (2010): 6–10.

Sánchez, Yoani. "Generation Y." Web blog. Available from http://www.desdecuba.com/generaciony/.

Soto, Asori. "Good bye, Lolek!" Film documentary. Producciones Aguaje. 2005.

Yoss. "Lo que dejaron los rusos." *Temas* 37–38 (April–September 2004): 138–144.

TELEVISION: SOAP OPERAS

Magda González Grau

The enduring popularity of televised soap operas among Cubans.

Since the end of the 1940s Félix B. Caignet's legendary radio soap opera *El derecho de nacer* (The Right to Be Born) has captivated the Cuban public with its romantic Dr. Albertico Limonta and the cataleptic muteness of Don Rafael del Junco. Its popularity helped maintain the Cuban television audience's preference for melodrama. Soap operas continued to captivate the country in the first decade of the twenty-first century, and the adventures they portray inspire heated discussions in homes, on public buses, and in the pages of the nation's leading newspapers.

HISTORY

Since the introduction of television in Cuba in 1950, soap operas have occupied a privileged space in prime-time slots. The producers of merchandise for housewives invested millions in television commercials during these serials. With the triumph of the Revolution in 1959 attitudes toward these programs changed substantially. The genre was stigmatized because of its links to bourgeois commercialism. Soap operas should have disappeared in a social system in which the laws of the market were viewed negatively as a holdover from the past, but against all official dictates, including those of the cultural elite, the genre survived. Yet, as Cuban social psychology changed and the media were transferred to state control, there were important modifications in the themes of these shows and the make-up of their characters. The Revolution created new realities that the serials could not ignore.

Aleida Amaya, a scriptwriter who worked in commercial radio and television, wrote for *Horizontes* (Horizons, 1967), which aired in an evening time slot. In this serial a *guajirita* (peasant woman) deceived by a wealthy landowner had her revenge when her bastard son, dressed as a revolutionary militiaman, confiscated the lands of the father who never recognized him.

In the 1960s the screenwriter Mayté Vera launched a phenomenon known as *novelas de los sindicatos* (soap operas of the unions), in which the social struggles of the laboring classes served as the backdrop for stories of love and hate, following the formula of "Before the Revolution, suffering; after the Revolution, joy." This genre enjoyed several years of popularity. *Oro verde* (Green Gold, 1982) centered on the struggles of the sugar sector; *El viejo espigón* (The Old Pier, 1981) was set in the port sector; and *La Peña del León* (Lion's Rock, 1976) focused on the organization of small farmers into cooperatives. One indication of the popularity of these shows was the following that developed for Melesio, a character from *La Peña del León* portrayed by the actor Reynaldo Miravalles (b. 1923), who was typecast as the stereotypical *guajiro* for the rest of his acting career.

In the 1980s Channel 2 purchased the Brazilian soap opera *La esclava* (The Slave, 1976) from the Brazilian network O'Globo. *La esclava* dazzled Cuban viewers by its superior production values. To compete, Channel 6 purchased from the Mexican network Televisa *El Árabe* (The Arab, 1980), whose plot was reminiscent of the films of Rudolph Valentino. The ensuing ratings war inspired a theatrical production called *La esclava contra el Árabe* (The Slave against the Arab, 1983), which was written by and starred the singer-songwriter and comedian Alejandro García Villalón, also known as Virulo (b. 1955). It satirized both soap operas and in weeks broke ticket sales records in the largest theater in the country.

Fidel Castro, surprised by the scope of this phenomenon, asked producers to create a similar Cuban soap opera. Cuban television responded with *Sol de batey* (Sun in the Sugar Town, 1985), a melodrama set in colonial Cuba focusing on a young abused slave girl and an evil, wealthy, and controlling couple. The success of *Sol de batey* demonstrated that professionals such as Roberto Garriga (1926–1988), a director from the days of commercial television, stood ready to revive the genre.

Another show in the 1980s was the Mexican soap opera *Gotita de gente* (Droplets of People, 1978) from the Televisa network, which was broadcast in midday. The story of the tribulations of a little orphan girl had such surprising success that it had to be rebroadcast in an evening time slot in order to avoid bringing the workday to a halt. Even in the early 2000s, traveling salesmen in Cuba are called *merolicos* after a character in the series.

In the 1990s production quality took a leap forward with O'Globo's hit *Vale todo* (It's All Worth

■ *See also*

Cuban Thought and Cultural Identity: Costumbres in the Revolutionary Period

Radio: Soap Operas

Sexuality: Revolutionary Period

The World and Cuba: U.S. Culture in Cuba

It, 1988), considered by experts to be one of the best productions of the genre. Private food service businesses are still called *paladares* in Cuba, after the name of the fictional company that pulled the character Regina Duarte out of poverty. *Vale todo* demonstrated to Cuban producers that they could make an interesting show in a contemporary setting, with a strong social aspect and staging appropriate for modern television. Thus, silhouetted scenes, strong lighting contrasts, sets with roofs, and other elements of high-budget productions appeared, revitalizing the antiquated style of Cuban soap operas.

THE PRESENT AND FUTURE

The growth of the Internet, satellite dishes, and digital reproduction since 2000 means that Cuban viewers have points of reference from all latitudes, a fact which producers must consider when planning to make or broadcast soap operas. Cuban television broadcasts the best series from the United States, along with less impressive U.S. shows that offer trivial stories dressed up with dazzling special effects. The vast amount of resources invested in these productions—money and also expertise—sets a standard that is difficult to meet, because Cuban productions cannot dream of having the resources available to foreign programs.

Faced with this complex reality, Cuban television offers viewers what they seem to want: a faithful reflection of their own reality. No foreign broadcaster is going to produce dramas about the reality of a social process as atypical as the Cuban revolutionary one. Thus the trump card of Cuban television is in creating series and soap operas that reflect the everyday lives of Cubans, with characters viewers can identify with. The first attempt at this was *La séptima familia* (The Seventh Family, 1987), by Rubén Geller and Juan Vilar. More a series than a soap opera, *La séptima familia* examined the conflicts of dysfunctional families in a society undergoing fundamental social changes.

Exceptions to this trend were Eduardo Macías's *Pasión y prejuicio* (Passion and Prejudice, 1994), a show set in the republican period and noted for its meticulous production values; *Tierra brava* (Wild Land, 1996), by Xiomara Blanco, a decontextualized story rich in subplots and memorable performances; and *Al compás del son* (To the Beat of the *Son*, 2005), by Mayté Vera and Rolando Chiong, which introduced the younger generations to the music of the 1920s and 1930s.

Not all viewers are satisfied with the real-life dramas broadcast on Cuban television. One segment of the viewing public wants soap operas to serve as an escape from the reality they suffer in their daily lives; they consume the typical melodramatic kitschy soap operas known as *culebrón* via videotapes or DVDs rented illegally from private dealers.

Yet, if Cuban television were to broadcast this type of production, a large part of their audience would protest at such an affront to their intelligence. The dilemma persists, and when new projects are introduced there are heated discussions about whether fiction should depict everyday life; even the viewers who reject this notion tune in to the programs so they can participate in debate the next day at work or in public places.

Cuban television has wavered between these positions. On the one hand, it draws criticism from progressive sectors when it lightens up, as it did with *Si me pudieras querer* (If You Could Love Me, 1998), by Nelson Flores, Amado del Pino, and Rafael González. On the other hand, it provokes a visceral rejection from conservative sectors if it uses themes of HIV, homosexuality, drug addiction, and marginality, as in *La cara oculta de la luna* (The Moon's Hidden Face, 2006), by Freddy Domínguez and Rafael González; themes of the loss of values, machismo, and teen pregnancy, as in *Oh, la Habana* (Oh, Havana, 2007), by Abraham Rodríguez and Charlie Medina; and stories of existential crises of young people (whose conflicts allow them to address themes involving drug addiction, emigration, marginality, internal migration, and other issues), as in *Aquí estamos* (Here We Are, 2010), by Hugo Reyes, Alfredo Pérez, and Rafael González.

Cuban television viewers in the early 2000s have much in common with the Cuban radio listeners of the 1940s who tuned in to find out whether Don Rafael del Junco would recover the ability to speak after his trauma. They are still emotionally susceptible to themes such as the search for happiness, the triumph of love, and the drama of death. Where they are different is that after living for fifty years immersed in a social process unlike any other in the world, after growing up instructed in doctrines that have shaped their way of thinking, and after living lives very different from those of other latitudes, they need to see themselves on the screen, as a mirror where they can find an explanation for their weaknesses, their shortcomings, and their suffering, but also support for their everyday sacrifices.

BIBLIOGRAPHY

Casado, Nelia. *La producción actual de dramatizados en la cuban televisión. Algunas problemáticas desde la óptica de la investigación social.* Havana: Centro de Investigaciones Sociales (CIS), Instituto Cubano de Radio y Televisión, 2009.

Cueva, Alvaro. *Sangre de mi sangre.* Madrid: Plaza & Janés, 2001.

Dávila, Iris. *Delirio de periodista.* Havana: Ediciones Unión, 2007.

González, Reynaldo. *Llorar es un placer.* Havana: Editorial Letras Cubanas, 1988.

González, Reynaldo. *El más humano de los autores.* Havana: Ediciones Unión, 2009.

López Sacha, Francisco. "Tres fuentes y tres partes inte-grantes de la telenovela." In *Pastel flameante*. Havana: Editorial Letras Cubanas, 2006.

TEN YEARS' WAR: 1868–1878

David C. Carlson

The first of three late-nineteenth-century wars fought by Cuba in an attempt to gain independence from Spain.

The Ten Years' War (1868–1878), the first of three late-nineteenth-century wars of independence from Spanish colonial rule waged by Cuban separatists, failed to accomplish the objectives of its leadership. Nevertheless, it inaugurated a sustained pro-independence movement, defined aspects of Cuban nationality and national symbols, and gave rise to an influential cohort of nationalist figures who proved instrumental in the War of Independence, including the military commanders Máximo Gómez (1836–1905), Antonio Maceo (1845–1896), and the so-called apostle of Cuban independence, José Martí (1853–1895)—first jailed and exiled at age sixteen during the war—who claimed the conflict was "our sacred mother."

BACKGROUND TO THE WAR

Cuba's first war of independence began 10 October 1868 with an uprising in eastern Cuba, led by the wealthy Bayamo lawyer and landowner Carlos Manuel de Céspedes (1819–1874) at his sugar estate La Demajagua near Manzanillo. A conspirator within Masonic lodges with other eastern planters and ranchers, Céspedes had been detained periodically by authorities for his oppositional politics. In the early nineteenth century, Cuba and Puerto Rico remained colonies while the rest of Spanish America gained independence. There had been conspiracies to join mainland struggles against colonial rule, an 1812 rebellion among people of color led by a black carpenter, José Antonio Aponte (d. 1812), and many slave rebellions, particularly in those parts of the island where sugar cultivation—based on African slave labor—transformed the island's development, economy, society, and demographics.

Western Cuba's plantation colony emphasis—principally, sugar and coffee—generated considerable economic growth and made many planters wealthy but also political targets. Antagonism between Spanish-born *peninsulares* and native *criollos* deepened. A reform commission—the Junta de Información de Ultramar—to secure from Madrid parliamentary representation and measures of home rule failed, while Spanish reversals revealed the declining power of the metropolis. During the U.S. Civil War, with the Monroe Doctrine in abeyance, the Spanish government's attempt to reannex the Dominican Republic culminated in the War of the Restoration (1863–1865) and Spanish failure. Ventures in Africa and defeat in an 1865–1866 naval war with Peru and Chile increased a national debt borne by new direct taxes and tariffs levied on the colonies, which pushed eastern Cuban planters to plot rebellion. In September 1868, a liberal revolution in Spain overthrew the Bourbon queen Isabel II (1830–1904). From 1868 to 1874, the metropolitan political scene was fraught with instability, two civil wars, and brief attempts to establish a constitutional monarchy under Amadeo I of Savoy (1845–1901), followed by a stillborn republic.

UPRISING IN 1868

For separatists, including Céspedes and the prominent landowner Vicente Aguilera (1821–1877), the year 1868 seemed propitious for initiating rebellion. On 23 September plotters in Puerto Rico proclaimed a *grito* (cry) at Lares, but authorities rapidly suppressed it. Cuban conspirators had initiated their declaration ahead of pre-emptive arrests on 10 October in the eastern town Yara, an event known as the *Grito de Yara*. Many leaders opposed slavery but sought a gradual emancipation that would minimize economic losses, with compensation paid to offset capital invested in slave labor. Many people favored independence, which was declared, but some sought annexation or some form of union with the United States, given the elite's concerns about extreme inequality and slavery-derived racial animus permeating colonial society.

Postponing abolition until after independence would prove impossible, but some eastern separatists hoped that such policies would appeal to the far wealthier and more influential reformist sugar barons in western Cuba, some of whom sought to exert influence abroad. In the east, many rural whites, free people of color, and slaves joined the rebellion, creating a liberation army nicknamed *mambises* by supporters and enemies alike, after the Angolan or possibly Dominican word *mambí* (bad man). The army grew to some 10,000 or 12,000 combatants, and many more civilian supporters dispersed in countryside camps known as prefectures. By 22 October 1868, the insurrection had captured Bayamo, which became briefly the capital city of *Cuba libre*. (Cuba's national anthem, written by Pedro Figueredo (1819–1870), who was captured and shot in 1870, begins by invoking the valor of the *bayameses*.) In November, Separatists revolted in Camagüey under Salvador Cisneros Betancourt (1824–1914) and Ignacio Agramonte (1841–1873). Rebels took several small towns in the east

CHRONOLOGY OF EVENTS

1866: Junta de Información founded, seeking reforms in Cuba.

1868: August: Revolutionary committees formed in Las Tunas and Santiago.

1868: September: Queen Isabella II of Spain dethroned; a revolutionary junta proclaims the Puerto Rican Republic.

1868: 10 October: Carlos Manuel de Céspedes proclaims Cuban independence, launching Ten Years' War.

1868: 28 October: Revolutionary Council seizes control of Bayamo, calls for abolition of slavery.

1868: November: Rebels win several minor victories; Spain sends 35,000 reinforcements; rebellion spreads to Camagüey.

1869: January: Spanish troops defeat the rebels at El Saladillo; the people of Bayamo torch their city before it falls into Spanish hands.

1869: April: Rebel Constitutional Convention at Guaimaro declares a republic, outlaws slavery, and appoints Manuel de Quesada military commander.

1869: June: Charged with being too lenient, Captain General Domingo Dulce replaced by Antonio Caballero de Rodas.

1870: June and July: Máximo Gómez, Calixto García, and Antonio Maceo rise to leadership of rebel army, emphasizing guerrilla warfare.

1870: August: Pedro Figueredo, author of national anthem "Cuba Libre," captured and executed.

1870: November: Amadeo I becomes king of Spain.

1870: December: Spain's Prime Minister Juan Prim y Pratas assassinated in Madrid.

1871: November: A Spanish firing squad kills eight medical students suspected of disloyalty.

1872: 27 March: Maceo wins the Battle of Loma del Burro.

1872: July: Rebel forces win a series of victories in the Guantánamo district.

1872: December: A new captain general, Cándido Pieltán, arrives with an additional 54,000 troops.

1873: October: Rebel legislature removes Céspedes, replacing him with Salvador Cisneros Betancourt.

1873: November: The *Virginius* Affair draws international condemnation.

1874: February: Rebel forces win Battle of Naranjo; Céspedes killed in battle.

1874: March: Rebels victorious at Battle of Las Guásimas.

1874: July: Cisneros resigns as president, replaced by Juan B. Spotorno.

1874: December: Alfonso XII becomes king of Spain.

1876: January: Alfonso appoints Joaquín Jovellar captain general of Cuba.

1876: March: Tomás Estrada Palma replaces Spotorno as president of the Republic.

1876: November: Spanish troops capture Estrada Palma; General Vicente García named his successor.

1876: December: García's government discusses peace terms with General Martínez Campos.

1878: February: García's government resigns, appointing a committee to negotiate peace.

1878: March: Maceo refuses to surrender, issuing "The Protest of Baraguá."

1878: May: Maceo leaves Cuba for Jamaica; rebels accept Spanish peace terms, ending Ten Years' War.

1879: August: Maceo and García launch another rebellion, known as "The Little War."

1880: June: Rebel leaders José Maceo, Rafael Maceo, and Guillermo Moncada surrender; Antonio Maceo goes to New York.

1880: August: García surrenders.

and laid siege to a pro-Spanish garrison in Holguín in December 1868.

Initial opposition to the insurrection included some 20,000 Spanish colonial troops and 30,000 volunteers made up of peninsular Spaniards and those favoring colonial rule—*integridad nacional* (national integrity)—of Cuba, which they called Overseas Spain. Captain General Francisco Lersundi (1817–1874), powerful merchants, and the *casino español* (Spanish interest groups) supported the volunteers, who vehemently opposed separatism, reform, and abolition. Volunteers fanned the flames of peninsular conflicts with criollos and even deposed Captain General Domingo Dulce (1808–1869), whom they viewed as excessively lenient and predisposed to negotiate abolition and favorable peace terms with the insurrectionists. These volunteers in urban locales attacked separatists and freed Spanish forces to pursue rebels in the countryside. They exercised a forbidding counterinsurgent role, assailing manifestations of disloyalty, perpetrating notorious acts of counterrevolutionary terror, carrying out summary executions, and forcing opponents into exile. On 27 November 1871, eight medical students thought to have profaned the tomb of a pro-Spanish editor were shot by volunteers, horrifying criollos and some Spaniards. Volunteers imprisoned the young José Martí for sedition, a crime for which he was eventually exiled, joining the many other Cubans subject to expulsion, jail, or deportation. Intransigent volunteers exerted considerable influence in island politics and forced underground any manifestation of separatism.

THE WAR INTENSIFIES AND SPREADS

The bulk of fighting and resultant destruction occurred in the eastern and central parts of the island. In early 1869, Captain General Dulce in Havana intended reforms and an offered amnesty to woo separatists, but in Oriente Province a column of Spanish troops under Blas de Villate, Count of Valmaseda (1824–1882) that included Valeriano Weyler (1838–1930) and Arsenio Martínez Campos (1831–1900) relieved their compatriots in Holguín and then defeated some 4,000 poorly armed rebels attempting to impede their path to Bayamo. On 12 January 1869 citizens razed Bayamo as Valmaseda's troops closed in. Battlefield success convinced many Spaniards that military suppression of the insurgency was nigh and that minimal political overtures would be necessary. Reprisals intended to instill terror among that portion of the populace supporting the Liberation army fed resistance and convinced many there was little recourse but to fight on.

On 10 April 1869, separatists from Camagüey and Oriente met in a constitutional assembly at Guáimaro (Camagüey) to establish a federalist legislature; propose the immediate abolition of slavery, with a future indemnity to be paid to owners and with the proviso that *libertos* (freed people) remain working for former masters for the duration of the conflict; ratify Céspedes as president; and appoint Manuel de Quesada (1830–1886) military commander. Quesada was a veteran of the wars of the liberal Mexican president Benito Juárez (1806–1872). The assembly adopted the flag first flown by Narciso López (1797–1851) in 1850, thereby transforming the meaning of the banner into the Cuban national symbol still in use in the early 2000s.

Exile communities in the United States lobbied politicians and, in some cases, purchased arms to be smuggled into their homeland. A number of such supply expeditions landed clandestinely, and the coastline proved difficult for Spanish navy ships to patrol. In 1869, the *Perritt* delivered munitions and an ex-Confederate cavalry general, Thomas Jordan (1819–1895), who briefly commanded Cuban forces. U.S. customs officials interdicted other expeditions as violating the Neutrality Act. Spain, as a recognized state, was free to purchase arms from U.S. firms. Wealthy planters favoring reform or separatism sought to use their positions in the United States to support independence, and several times the war's scope threatened to become international.

On 31 October 1873, the Spanish corvette *Tornado* captured the ex-Confederate blockade-runner *Virginius* laden with materiel for the Liberation army off Santiago. Officials summarily tried as pirates fifty-three passengers and crew, including U.S. citizens and British subjects, and began to execute them. British consuls summoned Commodore Lambton Lorraine (1838–1917) and the Royal Navy sloop-of-war HMS *Niobe* from Jamaica. He halted the executions by threatening to bombard the city. This incident nearly provoked a Spanish-American war, but the nascent Spanish republic and the United States resolved tensions diplomatically. U.S. officials withheld recognition of the Cuban Republic in Arms and its belligerency rights; in contrast, in Peru, Colombia, and Mexico some political figures advocated armed

intervention to assist Cuban separatists in ejecting Spain from its last Antillean colonies, but these plans were never realized.

IRREGULAR WARFARE

The situation of the insurrection grew increasingly dire. By October 1869, with supporters dispersed throughout the countryside fighting only under favorable circumstances or in self-defense from Spanish patrols, Cuban leaders convinced the Liberation army of the imperative for irregular warfare and sabotage, principally in the form of burning coffee and sugar estates. As civil conflicts in Spain eased, conscripts from Spain—possibly more than 200,000 by the end of the war—reinforced Spanish garrisons. Tropical diseases ravaged these newcomers, and the ranks constantly thinned from high mortality rates. In response to rebel tactics, the Spaniards directed forces to preserve the plantations, fortifying towns and estates in their control. In addition, to restrict the insurgency to the poorer, less-developed, economically marginal eastern zones of the island, Spanish forces erected a *trocha militar* (fortified barrier) across the narrowest portion of the island, from Júcaro through Ciego de Ávila to Morón. This network of forts and outposts connected by rail and communication towers hindered insurgents from crossing into the much more valuable and extensively cultivated western portion of the island. It was the largest Spanish fortification ever built in the Americas.

Liberation army chiefs skilled in irregular warfare rose to prominence, including Máximo Gómez

Carlos Manuel de Céspedes (1819–1874) Carlos Manuel de Céspedes, a plantation owner, lawyer, and revolutionary leader, was proclaimed president of the Republic of Cuba in 1869. © CORBIS

(1836–1906), a Dominican veteran of the Spanish army, and Antonio Maceo (1845–1896), a *mulato* who joined up with his brothers and rose through the ranks through valor and redoubtable tactical acumen. Another leader, the *holguinero* Calixto García (1839–1898), took command of a force after a superior officer's death from disease; in 1874, facing capture, he shot himself through the head, but survived. The Ten Years' War thus produced enduring nationalist archetypes based on self-sacrifice and armed struggle, as well as a cohort that would lead future wars of independence. The war also convinced leaders such as Gómez and Maceo that the insurgency stood little chance of success unless it assailed the colonial economy directly by burning the cane fields and including slaves in insurrection. Others refused to contemplate such tactics. They undermined Gómez and Maceo's position by asserting their unsuitability to command, depicting them as a Dominican foreigner and a black would-be *caudillo* (military leader) bent on fomenting race war, a fear that had preoccupied the imaginations of the elites since the Haitian Revolution (1791–1804).

THE ISSUE OF SLAVERY

In Spain, the search for a monarch to replace Isabella II led to the ascension of Amadeo I (1845–1890) in late 1870 (he reigned for only three years). In the same year, Spain passed a law that allowed for the gradual abolition of slavery in Cuba, the Moret Law, referred to as the Law of the Free Womb because children born into slavery after 17 September 1868, would not inherit the slave status of their mothers. The law also freed slaves over sixty years of age and slaves who had served in the Spanish army. Slavery was abolished in Puerto Rico in March 1873, but not in Cuba until an 1880 apprenticeship law curtailed it and an 1886 law finally emancipated the slaves. In the Americas, only Brazil enacted abolition later, in 1888.

Differences over the issue of slavery were symptomatic of insurmountable divisions among the leadership of the insurrection. An elitist and racist hostility to the rise of Cubans of humble social origins (who were typically of African descent), the changing roles of free people of color and former slaves, and abiding regional distinctions all militated against a unity of purpose and common aims. On 1 October 1873, the rebel legislature divested Céspedes of the presidency, ostensibly for authoritarianism and incompetence. His replacement by Cisneros, however, suggested an enduring regionalism among *orientales* and *camagüey-anos* and *villareños* that rent the separatist movement. At one point Céspedes was warned that his son Oscar, held hostage by volunteers, would be executed unless he surrendered. Céspedes famously replied that all Cubans who perished fighting for independence were his children and refused to capitulate. Oscar was shot. This incident, and Céspedes's role in the *Grito de Yara*,

prompted his postwar nickname *padre de la patria* (father of the nation). Céspedes did not survive the war. On 27 February 1874, a Spanish patrol killed him at San Lorenzo in the Sierra Maestra. His body is buried in Santa Ifigenia cemetery in Santiago de Cuba, as is that of Martí.

THE END OF THE WAR AND ITS AFTERMATH

In late 1874, Martínez Campos overthrew the first republic in Spain, restoring the Bourbon dynasty. After the consolidation of the monarchy, larger numbers of Spanish troops could be dispatched overseas. In 1875, Gómez and Maceo finally carried out an abortive invasion of Las Villas west of the *trocha*, burning almost 100 sugar estates and defeating or eluding Spanish forces, but opposition to their military authority and strategy undercut the belated offensive. Eventually they were driven back across the fortified barrier. In 1876, Martínez Campos, placed in command of the reinvigorated counterinsurgency against rebel-held zones, recognized that a political settlement could end the war. Several insurgent leaders were captured or killed, including a North American, Henry Reeve (1850–1876).

Offers of amnesty, freedom for former slaves and Chinese indentured workers in the Liberation army ranks, and promises of future negotiations on reform issues and semi-autonomy convinced many separatists to surrender. On 12 February 1878, the Pact of Zanjón ended the Ten Years' War in Cuba, conceding neither independence—proposing instead administrative reforms whereby representatives could be sent to the Cortés—nor an immediate end to slavery.

The failure to secure independence and abolition after a decade of war was unacceptable to Maceo and his radical supporters. They broke with insurgent leaders who advocated surrender, and at a meeting between Maceo and Martínez Campos in a mango thicket at Baraguá north of Santiago on 15 March 1878, Cubans refused to hand in arms without accomplishing those two objectives. This event, the Protest of Baraguá, symbolized separatist intransigence and refusal to compromise on core principles. Maceo was forced into exile, and with the full weight of Spanish forces brought to bear on the holdouts, the Ten Years' War came to an end.

In the war, the Spanish colonial army sustained 145,884 fatalities—133,555 from disease and 12,329 combat deaths. Estimates of Cuban losses among combatants and civilians vary widely but are thought to be comparable; there were also a great number who fled during the conflict. Eastern and central Cuba lay devastated by contending armies. Damages estimated at $300 million and the destruction of farms, cattle, towns, and plantations in the east and center of the island prostrated the society and economy. Almost every sugar mill in Camagüey, Manzanillo, Holgín, and Bayamo had been destroyed. Particularly hard hit, coffee production in the mountainous regions of Oriente did not recover until the twentieth century. Banditry and internecine rebellion persisted, underscored by periodic renewals of anticolonial violence such as the *Guerra Chiquita* (Little War) of 24 August 1879, to 10 June 1880, which was repressed with a heavy hand.

Crown officials deported many separatists to African penal colonies and prisons. The first war of independence gave rise to autonomism in Cuba, overturned many of the unfair strictures confining Cubans of salient African ancestry, and augured a rupture between Spain and Cuba. Spain's failure to substantively carry out proposed reforms after the war, combined with a more sophisticated and determined independence movement in Cuba, unified by veterans of the earlier war and figures such as Martí—who voiced a compelling and racially egalitarian vision of nationhood that posited a unified, free, independent, and sovereign Cuba—led to the War of Independence in early 1895.

BIBLIOGRAPHY

Abreu Cardet, José Miguel. *Introducción a las armas: La guerra de 1868 en Cuba.* Havana: Editorial de Ciencias Sociales, 2005.

Abreu Cardet, José Miguel. *Las fronteras de la guerra: Mujeres, soldados y regionalismo en el '68.* Santiago de Cuba: Editorial Oriente, 2007.

Barcia, María del Carmen, Gloria García, and Eduardo Torres-Cuevas, eds. *Las luchas por la independencia nacional y las transformaciones estructurales, 1868–1898.* Havana: Editora Política, 1996.

Bradford, Richard H. *The Virginius Affair.* Boulder: Colorado Associated University Press, 1980.

Cepero Bonilla, Raúl. *Azúcar y abolición.* Havana: Editorial de Ciencias Sociales, 1971.

Collazo, Enrique. *Desde Yara hasta el Zanjón.* Havana: Instituto del Libro, 1967.

Ferrer, Ada. *Insurgent Cuba: Race, Nation, and Revolution, 1868–1898.* Chapel Hill: University of North Carolina Press, 1999.

Ferrer, Ada. "Armed Slaves and Anticolonial Insurgency in Late Nineteenth-Century Cuba." In *Arming Slaves: From Classical Times to the Modern Age,* edited by Christopher Leslie Brown and Philip D. Morgan. New Haven, CT: Yale University Press, 2006.

Figueredo Socarrás, Fernando. *La Revolución de Yara, 1868–1878.* Havana: Editorial de Ciencias Sociales, 2000.

Guerra y Sánchez, Ramiro. *Guerra de los Diez Años, 1868–1878.* 2 vols. Havana: Editorial de Ciencias Sociales, 1972.

Ibarra Cuesta, Jorge. *Ideología mambisa.* Havana: Instituto Cubano del Libro, 1972.

Ibarra Cuesta, Jorge. *Encrucijadas de la guerra prolongada.* Santiago de Cuba: Editorial Oriente, 2008.

Mollin, Volker. *Guerra pequeña, guerra olvidada.* Santiago de Cuba: Editorial Oriente, 2003.

O'Kelly, James. *The Mambi-Land; or, Adventures of a Herald Correspondent in Cuba.* 1874. Reprint, Ann Arbor: University of Michigan Library Scholarly Publishing Office, 2001.

Pérez Guzmán, Francisco, and Rodolfo Sarracino. *La Guerra Chiquita: Una experiencia necesaria.* Havana: Editorial Letras Cubanas, 1982.

Pirala y Criado, Antonio. *Anales de la guerra de Cuba.* 3 vols. Madrid: F. González Rojas, 1895–1898.

Plasencia Moro, Aleida. *Bibliografía de la Guerra de los Diez Años.* Havana: Biblioteca Nacional José Martí, 1968.

Portuondo del Prado, Fernando, and Hortensia Pichardo Viñals, eds. *Carlos Manuel de Céspedes: Escritos.* 2 vols. Havana: Instituto Cubano del Libro, 1974.

Quiroz, Alonso W. "Loyalist Overkill: The Socioeconomic Costs of 'Repressing' the Separatist Insurrection in Cuba, 1868–1878." *Hispanic American Historical Review* 78 (1998): 261–305.

Robert, Karen. "Slavery and Freedom in the Ten Years' War, Cuba, 1868–1878." *Slavery and Abolition* 13, no. 3 (December 1992): 181–200.

Thomas, Hugh. *Cuba: The Pursuit of Freedom.* New York: Da Capo Press, 1998.

THREE TRAPPED TIGERS (GUILLERMO CABRERA INFANTE)

Nivia Montenegro

An experimental novel of the so-called Latin American Boom of the 1960s.

Three Trapped Tigers (1971), originally published as *Tres tristes tigres* (1967), by Guillermo Cabrera Infante (1929–2005), is one of the most experimental novels of the so-called Latin American Boom of the 1960s and marks a key moment in the development of Hispanic narrative. Published for the first time in 1967, the novel, or the book, as its author always referred to it, represents, both for its linguistic experimentation and for its playful imagination, a rejection of the realist tradition and an integration of diverse forms from popular culture. The text is characterized by its light-hearted sense of humor and its fondness for Cuban manners of speaking, specifically the Havana style. There is no doubt that *Three Trapped Tigers* (*TTT*) is an example—almost a compendium—of the derisive Cuban humor, or *choteo*, of the time. This choteo, defined by the writer Jorge Mañach in 1928 as an aggressive challenge to any type of authority or dominance, is the backbone of the book in different registers, since both the writing and the publication took place during the turbulent

■ *See also*

Havana: Urban and Social History in the Twentieth Century

Literature: Fiction in the Revolutionary Period

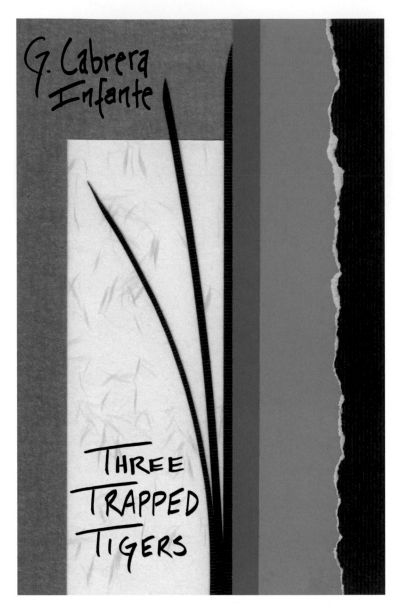

Three Trapped Tigers (1967). The experimental novel *Three Trapped Tigers* marked a key moment in the development of Hispanic narrative. This edition of the 1971 translation by Donald Gardner and Suzanne Jill Levine was published in 2004. COVER OF *THREE TRAPPED TIGERS* BY GUILLERMO CABRERA INFANTE. USED WITH PERMISSION OF DALKEY ARCHIVE PRESS

film, *TTT* recreates Havana: the streets, the manners of speaking, the scents and sounds of the capital, the fluid rhythm of life in the city by the sea. But *TTT* is at the same time heir to the great Hispanic tradition of the Baroque, which includes Cervantes, Quevedo, and Góngora. Under the watchful eye of Cabrera Infante, 1958 nighttime Havana—on the cusp of the great political and social change that was approaching—appears to be almost a cultural recovery project by the author. The epigraph, taken from *Alice's Adventures in Wonderland*, signals this intent: "And she tried to fancy what the flame of a candle looks like after the candle is blown out."

THE PRIZE-WINNING MANUSCRIPT

The history of the book published in 1967 under the title *Tres tristes tigres* includes political and autobiographical twists that merit separate mention. In 1964, a manuscript entitled *Vista del amanecer en el tropico* (View of Dawn in the Tropics), written by Cabrera Infante almost entirely in Brussels while he worked there as a cultural attaché to the Cuban embassy, won the Biblioteca Breve Prize awarded by the Barcelona publishing house Seix Barral, at that time the most prestigious prize in the Spanish language. This manuscript is a narrative of the last months of the Batista government, which counterpoints the amusing story of the nightlife of a group of characters in Havana and a series of vignettes capturing the violence of the struggle against the regime. But publication of the work was delayed for several reasons. The censors of the Franco government in Spain, whose approval was necessary for publication, rejected it three times because of its allusions to revolutionary struggle and what qualified, for them, as obscenity. And Cabrera Infante himself, first a journalist and later editor of the cultural supplement *Lunes de Revolución* (Revolution Monday) between 1959 and 1961, was becoming progressively distanced from the new Cuban regime. One significant event in Cabrera Infante's career was the censorship of the short documentary film *PM*, produced in Havana in 1961 by his brother Alberto "Sabá" Cabrera Infante and Orlando Jiménez Leal. The film, produced in the free-cinema style, centered on the nightlife of the bars and cafés around the port of Havana. Its prohibition and the later controversy gave rise to a series of conversations between Fidel Castro and writers and artists in the National Library, which culminated with the well-known words of Castro, "Inside the Revolution, everything; against the Revolution, nothing." These events resulted in the closing of *Lunes de Revolución* in August 1961 and marked the beginning of a policy of strict control of the country's cultural production.

In 1962, Cabrera Infante was named cultural attaché to the Cuban embassy in Brussels, a post he held until 1965. The censorship of *PM* and the closing of *Lunes de Revolución* inspired him to modify

first decade of the Cuban Revolution of 1959. The title of the book literally translates as "three sad tigers"; in English it was rendered as *Three Trapped Tigers* to preserve the alliteration. It is based on a Spanish tongue twister: *Tres tristes tigres en un trigal / traen trigo de tigre tras trillar* (Literal translation: Three sad tigers in a wheat field bring tiger wheat after threshing). It serves as a preview of the novel's marked interest in spoken language, with its fragmentation of content and apprehension of meaning based on sound and form.

Because of this interest in the primacy of sound for the formation of meaning, *TTT* can be compared to Lewis Carroll's *Alice's Adventures in Wonderland* (1865) and James Joyce's *Ulysses* (1922). Venturing into the popular culture, particularly music and

the original manuscript recognized by Seix Barral. These two events occurred around the same time as the death in Puerto Rico of the young Afro-Cuban bolero singer, Fredesvinda García Valdés (1939–1961), known by her stage name, Fredy. While the censorship of the film and the closing of the cultural supplement led him to produce *PM* "by other means," as he stated repeatedly in interviews years later, the death of the singer, who appears in *TTT* as La Estrella (the Star), provided a mournful musical framework for the new work written far from Havana.

COMPLETION, PUBLICATION, AND INITIAL RECEPTION

In 1965, the illness and death of his mother, Zoila Infante, brought Cabrera Infante back to Havana in August; afterward permission to leave the country again was agonizingly delayed until October, when, now with two daughters from his first marriage, he left Cuba permanently, at first for Spain. He devoted himself to rewriting and completing the award-winning manuscript. But he was no longer dealing with a counterpoint between day and night, the light-hearted and the epic; the new work deleted the epic vignettes about the revolutionary struggle and concentrated on the Havana nightlife that the author had known and enjoyed before 1959. His view, at once nostalgic and playful, was a re-creation of bohemian Havana and its way of life, which alludes to the struggle of peasants, poor, blacks, and mulattoes to succeed within a social order that at best ignored them. From this perspective, one must take note of Cabrera Infante's careful examination of those fighting to achieve success and, therefore, disposed to erase or diminish their accents, hide their origins, or transform their identifying features.

Unable to secure legal residency in Franco's Spain—the political affiliations of his family (his parents were founders of the Communist Party in Gibara) and the writer's position in the Castro government made it impossible—Cabrera Infante completed his work in London, where he was to live with his family in exile until his death in 2005. The publication of *Tres tristes tigres* in 1967, a key year in the Boom—in which *Cien años de soledad* (*One Hundred Years of Solitude*), by Gabriel García Márquez, and *De donde son los cantantes* (Where the Singers Come From), by Severo Sarduy, also appeared—was jubilantly received by readers and critics.

TTT, both for its fragmented structure and its literary exploration of the Cuban language, established benchmarks in the fiction of the time and charted new paths in exploring the concept of Cubanness. *TTT* examines the idea of what it means to be Cuban, including the varied cultural influences experienced by the island throughout its long colonial history and its brief republican existence.

It forged a transnational cultural model long before such ideas became as widespread as they are in the last thirty years. The work also pioneered the use of forms of popular culture, particularly film, music, and advertising.

In 1968, in an interview with the Argentine magazine *Primera plana* (Front Page), Cabrera Infante publicly broke with the Cuban government, then at the height of its international prestige, an act that was to mark his life and literary career. The same year he was expelled from the Unión de Escritores y Artistas de Cuba (UNEAC; Union of Writers and Artists of Cuba), the largest cultural organization on the island, and was denounced by the Cuban regime and its official intellectuals as "a traitor to the revolutionary cause." The sequels of this rejection include the writer's subsequent illness—he suffered a breakdown in 1971 for which he was hospitalized and treated with electroshocks—and the manifest hostility toward and shunning of the author by leftist intellectuals, particularly in Latin America. The importance of his work was recognized in Spain in 1998 with the Cervantes Prize, the highest honor awarded for literature in the Hispanic world. By contrast, his name is not included in the *Diccionario de literatura cubana* (1980–1984; Dictionary of Cuban Literature), published in Havana by the government-sponsored Letras Cubanas publishing house.

Perhaps due to its complex narrative structure and entertaining allusions, the initial reception of *Tres tristes tigres* was almost always focused on its experimental character and linguistic creativity. The book's puns, plays on words, multilingual jokes, and parody captured the attention of most critics. The plot was interpreted either as a series of stories or as fragments of stories woven around the main characters without much connection between them. The cosmopolitan dimension of the work—its numerous references to foreign literature, cinematography, philosophy, and music—also received much comment. The Cuban dimension of the novel and its place in the national literary canon received less. The remainder of this article addresses the construction of this locus of imagery.

THE STRUCTURE OF THE WORK

The narration of *TTT* takes on a choral form: a series of voices alternating and competing among themselves to take up the thread of the narrative, which gives the novel a fragmented quality. In addition, eleven monologues are inserted, between an anonymous woman and her psychiatrist, spaced out through the book. In the central part of the text, the well-known parodies of Trotsky's death tell of the assassination of the Russian revolutionary in the styles of seven Cuban writers. There is also a note in the text, written by a character, GCI, who asks the character Silvestre for a new translation of the section titled "Los visitantes" (Vae Visitors).

The work opens with a prologue constructed as a presentation preceding a show at the famous Tropicana cabaret. Following this is the section "Los debutantes" (The Debutantes), a series of presentations in the first person of the principal characters, before their entry into the world of bohemian nightlife. The presentations are a sort of visit to the dressing room; we see the characters at an earlier time, either as children or provincials recently arrived in the capital. Appearing anonymously and in a very different environment, the presentations emphasize, on one hand, the modern fragmentation of the self and, on the other, the constructed nature of the social world. *TTT* gives primacy to this method of narration—in the form of debate or counterpoint—throughout the text, although it is particularly emphasized in "Los visitantes" and "La muerte de Trotsky referida por varios escritores cubanos, años después—o antes" (The Death of Trotsky as Described by Various Cuban Writers Several Years after the Event—Or Before).

The character of Silvestre Isla, the fictional author of the novel, is profiled throughout the narrative, very specifically in "Los visitantes" (Cabrera Infante 2010, pp. 333–366) and particularly in "Bachata" (pp. 467–654). As readers approach the end of the book, allusions to the verbal duel between the actor Arsenio Cué and the writer Silvestre intensify, and allusions are made to the work that Silvestre may write (the very book readers are reading). This marked self-awareness is complemented by the presence of Guillermo Cabrera Infante, who appears under the initials GCI as the writer of the note to Silvestre requesting a new translation of Mr. Campbell's story (p. 644). It is not, however, a simple experimental or narrative gesture. Both translation (literal or literary) and the transfer of spoken language to literary writing involve a theatrical presentation of the Baroque nature of Cuban culture; the story moves from the ostentatious presentation of the Master of Ceremonies on the night of the Tropicana cabaret to the obsessive monologue of a madwoman in a park, who appears to resist any type of limitation or restriction. Both types of speech circulate throughout the book, the first as a starting point of linguistic and cultural games, the second as a limit, but also resistance, to that very possibility. By completing the account of the night with the madwoman's speech in full daylight, *TTT* becomes complicit in the resistance to hierarchies and judgments that characterizes choteo, the derisive Cuban humor, and points to a new day to come in Cuba's history, which the author would later explore in *Vista del amanecer en el trópico* (1974).

THE MYTHIFICATION OF CUBAN CULTURE

The mythification of Havana that the novel attempts through its rhetorical and narrative games has a counterpart in the portrayal of different versions of the nation through three female characters: Cuba Venegas, Estrella Rodríguez, and Laura Díaz.

Through the three, a range of colorings and personal characteristics is revealed that gives them symbolic value. The book also includes, in "Los visitantes," a satirical jab at colonial culture, to which the author alludes using carnivalization and choteo humor.

The parody structure of the section about Trotsky's murder suggests an interpretation of the canon of Cuban literature, in which *TTT* is inserted and which highlights two aspects: popular spoken language versus cosmopolitan-style written language. Placing Lydia Cabrera, cofounder with Fernando Ortiz of Afro-Cuban studies, at the center, highlights these two registers. On one hand, Lydia Cabrera is engaged in collecting and transcribing an Afro-Cuban legacy and incorporating it into the cultural archive of the nation. On the other, her work attempts to capture Cuban ways of speaking (and thinking) and to transcribe them—put them into writing—as faithfully as possible. These propositions also characterize the intent of *TTT* as a recovery of a particular culture in a particular time and place.

Three Trapped Tigers is an innovation in Hispanic narrative, both for its formal experimentation and for its interest in popular culture. But its exploration of history and the nation's cultural transformation are also decisive contributions to Cuba's cultural canon. *TTT* recollects not just Havana's nightlife and the various lifestyles and customs of its inhabitants but also the importance of the sea and of commerce in its history and the continuous flow of foreign cultures arriving on the island from Africa, Europe, and the United States that has been changed, adapted, and implanted by Cubans. From this perspective, *Three Trapped Tigers* represents a successful effort to recreate, in the rhythms of its speech and its sense of humor, that maritime influx that makes Havana a city of confluences, full of light and secrets; it is perhaps that wet nymph that appears in the novel and becomes an obsession for Guillermo Cabrera Infante.

BIBLIOGRAPHY

Álvarez-Borland, Isabel. *Discontinuidad y ruptura en Guillermo Cabrera Infante*. Gaithersburg, MD: Hispamérica, 1982.

Bakhtin, Mikhail. *The Dialogic Imagination: Four Essays*, edited by Michael Holquist. Translated by Caryl Emerson and Michael Holquist. Austin: University of Texas Press, 1981.

Benítez Rojo, Antonio. *La isla que se repite: El Caribe y la perspectiva posmoderna*. Hanover, NH: Ediciones del Norte, 1989.

Cabrera Infante, Guillermo. *Three Trapped Tigers*, translated by Donald Gardner and Suzanne Jill Levine in collaboration with the author. Champaign, IL and London: Dalkey Archive, 2004.

Cabrera Infante, Guillermo. *Tres tristes tigres*, ed. Nivia Montenegro and Enrico Mario Santí. Madrid: Cátedra, 2010.

Cuervo Hewitt, Julia. "In(ter)vención y (sub)versión de Ecué en *Tres tristes tigres*." *La Chispa '95: Selected Proceedings.* Selected Proceedings of the Sixteenth Louisiana Conference on Hispanic Languages and Literatures. March 2–4, 1995. New Orleans: Tulane University, 1995.

Fuentes, Carlos. *La nueva novela hispanoamericana.* Mexico City: Joaquín Mortiz, 1969.

Guibert, Rita. *Seven Voices: Seven Latin American Writers Talk to Rita Guibert.* New York: Knopf, 1973.

Hall, Kenneth. *GCI and the Cinema.* Newark, DE: Juan de la Cuesta, 1989.

Hammerschmidt, Claudia. *"Mi genio es un enano llamado Walter Ego": Strategien von Autorschaft bei Guillermo Cabrera Infante.* Frankfurt am Main: Vervuert, 2002.

Hartman, Carmen Teresa. *Cabrera Infante's "Tres Tristes Tigres": The Trapping Effect of the Signifier over Subject and Text.* New York: Peter Lang, 2003.

Levine, Suzanne Jill. "Ingenios y trucos con Guillermo Cabrera Infante." *Américas* 47, no. 4 (1995): 25–29.

Luis, William. *Lunes de revolución: Literatura y cultura en los primeros años de la Revolución Cubana.* Madrid: Verbum, 2003.

MacAdam, Alfred J. *Modern Latin American Narratives: The Dreams of Reason.* Chicago: University of Chicago Press, 1977.

Malcuzynski, M. Pierrette. "*Tres tristes tigres*, or The Treacherous Play on Carnival." *Ideologies & Literature* 3 (1981): 33–56.

Mañach, Jorge. *Indagación del choteo*, 2nd ed. Havana: La Verónica, 1940.

Merrim, Stephanie. *Logos and the Word: The Novel of Language and Linguistic Motivation in "Gran Sertão: Veredas" and "Tres tristes tigres."* Berne and New York: Peter Lang, 1983.

Montenegro, Nivia. "Tropologías de la cultura cubana en *Tres tristes tigres*." In *Le néo-baroque cubain: "De donde son los cantantes" et Tres tristes tigres,"* edited by Néstor Ponce. Paris: Éditions du Temps, 1997.

Montenegro, Nivia. "¿Qué dise/mi/nación?: Island Vision in Guillermo Cabrera Infante's *Vista del amanecer en el trópico*." *Cuban Studies* 28 (1998): 125–153.

Montenegro, Nivia. "Cuerpos de Cuba: Mujer y nación en *Tres tristes tigres*." *Encuentro de la Cultura Cubana* 37–38 (2005): 276–283.

Nelson, Ardis. *Guillermo Cabrera Infante in the Menippean Tradition.* Newark, DE: Juan de la Cuesta, 1983.

Orr, Leonard. "Joyce and the Contemporary Cuban Novel: Lezama Lima and Cabrera Infante." *Neohelicon: Acta Comparationis Litterarum Universarum* 19, no. 2 (1992): 17–25.

Pereda, Rosa María. *Guillermo Cabrera Infante.* Madrid: EDAF, 1979.

Rodríguez Monegal, Emir. "Las fuentes de la narración." *Mundo Nuevo* 25 (1968): 41–58.

Santí, Enrico Mario. "Digresiones torpes sobre Guillermo." *Encuentro de la Cultura Cubana* 37–38 (2005): 256–260.

Sarduy, Severo. "El barroco y el neobarroco." In *América Latina en su literatura*, edited by César Moreno. Mexico City: Siglo XXI, 1972.

Siemens, William L. "Rayas extravagantes: *Tres tristes tigres* y el neobarroco cubano." *Revista Iberoamericana* 57, no. 154 (1991): 235–243.

Souza, Raymond D. *Guillermo Cabrera Infante: Two Islands, Many Worlds.* Austin: University of Texas Press, 1996.

Torres Fierro, Danubio. "Memoria plural: Entrevista con Danubio Torres Fierro." In *Infantería: Guillermo Cabrera Infante*, edited by Nivia Montenegro and Enrico Mario Santí. Mexico City: Fondo de Cultura Económica, 1998.

Volek, Emil. *Cuatro claves para la modernidad: Análisis semiótico de textos hispánicos: Aleixandre, Borges, Carpentier, Cabrera Infante.* Madrid: Gredos, 1984.

℞ TOBACCO

The species Nicotiana tabacum *L, native to the Peruvian and Bolivian Andes, arrived in Cuba 2,000 to 3,000 years ago and, after a long period of adaptation, became Cuban black tobacco.*

The essays that follow address the history and culture of tobacco in a wide range of forms, examining its origin, variety, and cultivation; its chemical processing, aging, and result as a final product; cigar labels and their presence in art and popular culture and their importance in the development of the tobacco industry; and the tobacco readers, people who read to employees as they rolled tobacco.

Present in the life of the original indigenous Cubans, tobacco has become part of their mythology, magic, religion, fishing, medicine, and customs. Cubans gave gifts of tobacco leaves or plants as gestures of peace and friendship.

Commercial cultivation of tobacco began in 1520. In the late nineteenth century, other countries introduced seeds, bringing about the mixing of varieties with the original Cuban tobacco. Beginning in 1840, the labels and wrappers of Cuban cigars have portrayed social, political, and cultural events of the time.

This entry includes the following articles:

TOBACCO: IN ART AND CULTURE

TOBACCO: ART OF TOBACCO LABELS

TOBACCO: CULTIVATION: BOTANY

TOBACCO: CULTIVATION: CHEMISTRY

In Cuba, cigarettes, machine-made cigars, and Habano cigars are produced for domestic and export markets. The Habano cigar is made in different strengths and flavors.

The historiography presented by the authors focuses on such diverse areas as anthropology, history, culture, and gender.

■ *See also*

Cuban Counterpoint: Tobacco and Sugar (Fernando Ortiz)

TOBACCO: IN ART AND CULTURE

Zoila Mercedes Lapique Becali

Tobacco and the joys of smoking as themes of Cuban poetry, art, handicrafts, and music.

Tobacco was ever-present in indigenous life. As the noted Cuban scholar Fernando Ortiz stated in his famous work, *Contrapunteo cubano del tabaco y el azúcar,* "It was part of their mythology, their religion, their magic, their medicine, their agriculture, their fishing, their collective effort, their customs both public and private" (p. 216). It is known that the indigenous people of Cuba would offer tobacco leaves or a tobacco plant as a gesture of peace and friendship, and the essence of this custom endures even in the early 2000s in Cuba and indeed around the world. But in modern times one invites friends or acquaintances to serve themselves tobacco out of the same box or pouch to smoke in their pipes, or offers a prepared cigar or cigarette, so as to share the pleasure of smoking while chatting and exchanging opinions.

Known for producing the world's best tobacco, Cuba is also noted for the quality of its manufactured products. Cuban cigars, prized for their aroma and craftsmanship, have long been in demand on the foreign market. Over the centuries, countless scientists, musicians, artists, and writers of stature have been drawn to smoking, and the cigars, cigarettes, and pipe tobacco produced by Cuban workshops and factories since the end of the eighteenth century have earned pride of place worldwide for the quality of the leaf, its aroma, the high standard of craftsmanship, and the aesthetic presentation of its products. In the happy phrase of British statesman Winston Churchill, inveterate smoker of genuine Cuban cigars, the experience was "almost like having Cuba on your lips."

MUSIC AND LITERATURE

Tobacco appears as a thematic element in many works of Cuban art and popular culture. Oddly though, given the predominance of Cuban tobacco, it has been the subject of relatively little popular music. The song "Tabaco Verde" (Green Tobacco), by the Cuban composer Eliseo Grenet (1893–1950), is a beautifully wrought musical homage to tobacco. Music of the countryside—*punto* songs and their regional variants from across Cuba—celebrate the pleasures of smoking good cigars and the exquisite aroma that pervades the air around a smoker. Later, singer-songwriter Gerardo Alfonso (b. 1958), in a song dedicated to Havana, describes its aroma of "coffee, tobacco, and rum."

Tobacco has figured in the lives of numerous writers and artists. One of the oldest examples from literature occurs from a play by Spanish writer Lope de Vega (1562–1635) in which a character states, "Take a bit of tobacco and your anger will pass." A poem by Frenchman Charles Perrault (1626–1703) entitled "Elogio de tabaco en humo" (In Praise of Smoked Tobacco) states, "Tobacco, enemy of sorrow/ The plant that Bacchus has sown/The friend of wine/ That makes the party lively/And which serves as an antidote/To life's troubles, which cheers us on." The French writer George Sand (1804–1876) said that "cigars soothe pain and fill solitude with a thousand pleasant images." Victor Hugo (1802–1885) claimed that "tobacco changes thoughts into dreams."

Tobacco appears repeatedly in works by Cuban poets of the nineteenth century. Narciso Foxá (1822–1863) sings tobacco's praises as "a special gift granted to Cuba." In the words of Francisco Poveda (1796–1888), "There in the fertile source / It goes from the river to the shore. / We see the indefatigable tobacco farmer / Transplanting the seed / Of great

Cigar aficionado Winston Churchill (1874–1965). British statesman Winston Churchill was a well-known smoker of genuine habanas. The preference on the part of foreign consumers for Cuban cigars stemmed from the consistent quality of the tobacco, as well as their careful manufacture and finish. © BETTMANN/ CORBIS

cigar tobacco." Among the many verses written about indigenous Cubans by Juan Cristóbal Nápoles Fajardo, better known by his pen name, El Cucalambé (1829–1862), one image stands out: "With firefly in hand, / And great cigar in his mouth, / An Indian from a rock / surveyed the Cuban sky." The poet known as Plácido, Gabriel de la Concepción Valdés (1809–1844), who was executed by firing squad for his alleged involvement in a slave revolt, wrote a rondeau, "La flor de la caña" (Sugarcane Blossom). In this poem of love for a beautiful girl who works in the tobacco fields, and to whom he has declared his love in a passionate letter, the narrator learns that his love is requited when she gives him a small cigar case in which he finds

> Un tabaco puro
> De Manicaragua,
> Con una sortija
> Que ajusta la Capa,
> Y en lugar de Tripa,
> Le encontré una carta,
> Para mí más bella
> Que la flor de la caña.

> [A genuine Cuban cigar
> From Manicaragua,
> A ring tightly embracing
> The wrapper leaf,
> And within, in place of the filler,
> I found a letter,
> More beautiful to me
> Than a sugarcane blossom.]

José Jacinto Milanés (1814–1863) extols "The aromatic leaf, / Which cures man's tedium and disgust, / Dissolving it into gentle smoke." Manuel González del Valle (1802–1884), in his "Canción del tabaco" (Song of Tobacco), longs for tobacco: "Return to my lips, savory tobacco / Cherished gift of my country." Another poet, Ignacio Valdés Machuca (1800–1850), sings the praises of tobacco and its amorous effect on the country girl who smokes it. Domingo del Monte (1804–1853), the host of a famous literary salon, paid poetic homage in "El veguero" (The Tobacco Farmer) to the skill of the men who cultivate the plant. Cuban patriot and writer Miguel Teurbe Tolón (1820–1858) stated "From one sip to the next / Pure aroma rises / From the steaming cup / And from puff to puff / Of the delicious cigar / Both are enjoyed." In the delirious fantasy of his "Oda al tabaco cubano" (Ode to Cuban Tobacco), Ricardo del Monte (1828–1909) imagines Cuban tobacco uniting mankind, "wrapped in fragrant clouds / of bluish vapor rising in waves, / the whole world gives its grateful blessing to Cuba." Tobacco also appears in Cuban fiction. In one scene in Cirilo Villaverde's legendary novel *Cecilia Valdés*, published in New York in 1882, a priest, a captain, and a plantation administrator smoke fragrant cigars after an opulent meal.

The praise of tobacco continued in the literature of the twentieth century. Poet Guillermo Villarronda declares that "Cuba stands tall and noble for its fragrant leaf / and in that leaf has its second flag! /. . . Tobacco, the blood of the Cuban heart, its heartbeat felt the world over." Emilio Ballagas (1908–1954), in "Cuba, poesía" (Cuba, Poetry), draws on an Afro-Cuban song in praise of the island's natural wonders: "This palpitating and undulating music stirs me, like a snake / Vibrating and voluptuous as the surf on your coasts. / This fragrance of fresh tobacco will pull my eyes closed / And my blood stirs inside like the red scarf of the rumba." Eduardo Abela (1891–1964), writer, painter, and cartoonist, created the character El Bobo (The Fool) through which he criticized, on a daily basis, Gerardo Machado's regime (1925–1933). The eminent Cuban writer José Lezama Lima (1910–1976), recalling a photograph showing the French poets Paul Valéry and Stephane Mallarmé smoking cigarettes together, declares his love for smoking cigars, a pleasure that has accompanied him since he took up the habit at age nineteen. The poem "Blacks Dancing to Cuban Rhythms," from the collection *Poeta en Nueva York* (Poet in New York, 1942), by the Spanish poet Federico García Lorca (1898–1936), recalls the beautiful, full-color lithographic labels on two famous brands of Cuban cigars, Romeo y Julieta and Fonseca: "When the full moon appears / I will go to Santiago /...with Fonseca's blond head / I will go to Santiago / And with Romeo and Juliet's rose / I will go to Santiago / On a paper sea, and with silver coins/ I will go to Santiago."

VISUAL ARTS

Indeed, the lithographic labels on the containers of cigars and other tobacco products are a distinctive Cuban art form. During the first half of the nineteenth century, labels displayed simple designs in black ink on pale, colored paper to enhance the legibility of their text. Over time, the designs became more complicated, so as to make it more difficult to produce fakes and imitations abroad. Starting in 1860 the cigarette factory known as La Honradez (Honor), owned by the Susini family, introduced chromolithography on its labels and wrappers, revolutionizing the presentation of cigarettes in Cuba and influencing other manufacturers through the pressure of competition. Nevertheless, chromolithography would not be used for the presentation and decoration of cigar containers and packages of pipe tobacco until the 1880s. The use of trimmings began in 1884, consisting of labels of various shapes and sizes that not only decorated containers and wrappers but also protected them. Such wrappers are still in use.

Cuban artists have often depicted people both at work and play enjoying a good smoke. In *La curandera* (The Folk Healer), an illustration by the Basque-Cuban artist Víctor Patricio de Landaluze (1828–1889) included in *Tipos y costumbres de la isla de Cuba* (Characters and Customs of the Island of Cuba, 1881), an old woman

is seen selecting herbs, a cigar in her mouth. This book also contains an illustration showing two tobacco growers picking leaves for hand-rolled cigars. In the oil painting *Las despalilladoras* (The Tobacco Strippers), by Armando Menocal (1863–1942), the artist pays homage to a group of women performing that task. Beginning with the Revolution, artists and craftsmen worked with a variety of materials to make images and objects associated with the world of tobacco and the art of smoking. These works are closely linked to Cuban popular traditions, depicting everyday life and capturing customs and values among the most dearly held by the Cuban people. The tobacco theme also appears in works by contemporary painters such as Flora Fong (b. 1941), Nelson Domínguez (b. 1947), Zaida del Río (b. 1954), Ileana Mulet (b. 1952), and Eduardo Roca, known as Choco (b. 1949). These artists use a variety of media—oils, watercolors, and drawings on manufactured paper—as well as overlaid tobacco leaves of different shades (from green to dark brown, depending on the ripeness of the leaf).

CIGAR PARAPHERNALIA AND CRAFTS

Many fairs and exhibits are devoted to a vast array of smoking paraphernalia in materials such as hardwoods, metals, textiles, papier-mâché, shells, ceramics, and overlays of animal or plant products. Among pieces noted for their originality are hardwood pipes, many

of them in miniature; handmade decorated humidors whose embossed, engraved, and patinated metal recreates a feeling of days gone by; and humidors of various sizes fashioned to resemble steamer trunks made from interwoven and pyrographed leather) and lined with cedar to retain the aroma of the cigars. Also fashioned of leather are cigar boxes that fit from twenty-five to fifty cigars, and pocket-sized cigar cases for a day's worth of smoking. It is also worth noting that, before the middle of the nineteenth century, Cuba imported various types of cigar cases and boxes of materials ranging from tumbaga to leather. Other artifacts associated with tobacco make use of shells and fabric. Shell etchings reproduce the lithograph designs of famous Cuban cigar brands, landscapes of tobacco plantations, tobacco curing sheds, and tobacco farmers at their daily tasks. The fabric used to cover the tobacco on the plantations is used to make costumes, such as dresses decorated with tobacco leaves and overlaid with other materials dyed in tobacco colors. Artisans also create patchwork tapestries depicting cigar labels, urban landscapes with tobacco factories and warehouses, and rural plantation landscapes. Fabric items for the home, such as cushions, lampshades, bedding, and tablecloths, as well as carpets, reproduce the labels of famous cigar brands in embroidery, beadwork, and sequins. Other

READERS FOR TOBACCO WORKERS

Cigar factory reader (c. 1900–1910). A paid reader helps alleviate the monotony of cigar-rolling by reading the news to workers in a Cuban cigar factory. © HULTON-DEUTSCH COLLECTION/CORBIS

A *lector* (reader) in a cigar factory is someone who reads newspapers, magazines, and books to the cigar workers while they are working. The only requirement in rolling a cigar is manual dexterity and artistic ability; the worker's mind is free to think and to absorb information. The lack of noise in cigar workshops makes it possible to hear the voice of the lector. Reading in cigar factories traces its origins to Cuba in 1865, and the practice continues there in the early 2010s. Although meant to entertain, the *lectores* have also been educators and sometimes advocates for causes, as they read from great works of literature such as *Les miserables*, works of philosophical or scientific interest, or about current events affecting working-class lives.

Because of the wars for Cuban independence at the end of the nineteenth century, thousands of cigar workers fled Cuba. In exile, they established or found work in cigar factories in Spain, the United States, Puerto Rico, Mexico, and the Dominican Republic, where the practice of reading to the workers resumed. As of 2010 there were lectors employed in both Cuba and the Dominican Republic. In Cuba, 140 of the 238 readers were women.

Araceli Tinajero

handicrafts with tobacco themes include hardwood partition screens with intricate pyroengravings, wood carvings, and busts and sculptures depicting Cubans and foreigners famed for their achievements, social position, style, or simply for their proclaimed pursuit of the art of smoking.

Every year the Havana Tobacco Museum hosts some dozen tobacco-related exhibitions featuring artists, craftspeople, and collectors. In addition, presentations of creative work are held, as well as lectures by specialists in the field of tobacco production, tobacco handicrafts, and tobacco history. In Matanzas, 60 percent of arts and crafts production is devoted to tobacco. The Asociación Cubana de Artesanos y Artistas (ACAA; Cuban Association of Craftsmen and Artists) holds yearly fairs and expositions, where the visiting public has the opportunity to admire and purchase handicrafts.

BIBLIOGRAPHY

García Galló, Gaspar Jorge. *Biografía del tabaco habano.* Santa Clara, Cuba: Universidad Central de Las Villas, 1959.

González, Reynaldo. *El bello habano: Biografía íntima del tabaco.* Havana: Letras Cubanas, 2004.

Gordon y de Acosta, Antonio María de. *El tabaco en Cuba: Apuntes para su historia.* Havana, 1897.

Hazard, Samuel. *Cuba a pluma y lápiz.* 3 vols. Havana, 1928.

Juan, Adelaida de. *Pintura y grabados coloniales cubanos.* Havana: Editorial Pueblo y Educación, 1974.

Lapique Becali, Zoila. *La memoria en las piedras.* Havana: Ediciones Boloña, 2002.

Lapique Becali, Zoila, et al. "La primera imprenta litográfica en Cuba." *Revista de la Biblioteca Nacional José Martí* 12, no. 3 (1970): 35–47.

Lezama Lima, José, ed. *Antología de la poesía cubana.* 3 vols. Havana: Consejo Nacional de Cultura, 1965.

López Lemus, Virgilio, ed. *Doscientos años de poesía cubana (1790–1990).* Havana: Casa Editora Abril, 1999.

Núñez Jiménez, Antonio. "Descubrimiento del tabaco." *Revista Habano* 11, no. 12 (December 1945).

Núñez Jiménez, Antonio. *El libro del tabaco.* Nuevo León, Mexico: Pulsar, 1996.

Ortiz, Fernando. *Contrapunteo cubano del tabaco y el azúcar.* Havana: Consejo Nacional de Cultura, 1963.

English edition: *Cuban Counterpoint: Tobacco and Sugar*. Translated by Harriet de Onís. Durham, NC: Duke University Press, 1995.

Perdomo, José E. *Léxico tabacalero cubano*. Havana: Impr. "El Siglo XX," 1940.

Rivero Muñiz, José. *Tabaco, su historia en Cuba*. 2 vols. Havana: Academia de Ciencias, 1964.

Rivero Muñiz, José, and Andrés de Piedra-Bueno. *Pequeña antología del tabaco*. Havana: Editorial "Revista Tobaco," 1946.

■ *See also*

Economy: Colonial Period

Economy: Republican Period

Havana: Havana as Cultural Center

TOBACCO: ART OF TOBACCO LABELS

Zoila Lapique Becali

The tobacco industry and the growth of lithography in Cuba.

The polychromic beauty of the lithographed labels adorning Cuban cigar boxes has led to the exclusive association of that technical process in Cuba with the growth of its tobacco industry. But this association was not always the case, as lithography was brought to Havana in 1822 in order to reproduce musical works. The capital city was, at the time, a center of high quality musical activity.

In addition, Cuban cigars were restricted for a century during a period known as the *Estanco del Tabaco* (1717–1817), when the Spanish Crown imposed a monopoly on tobacco production in Cuba. This monopoly was abolished by royal decree on 23 June 1817, when King Charles IV lifted all restrictions on the cultivation, manufacturing, and sale of tobacco on the island. This decree allowed the exportation of tobacco leaf and manufactured tobacco for the old Spanish factories in Cádiz and Seville.

The growing demand around the world among fashionable society and military officers, inspired by romanticism, to smoke *tabaco torcido* (rolled tobacco) in the Cuban style, led to the development of Cuban *vitolas* and the lithographic art employed to present them in the national and international markets. *Vitola* is the term used to describe the individual and specific measurement that defines each cigar by shape, length, and thickness. Cigars also bear the name of *tabaco elaborado*, *puro*, or *habano*—the last term referring to the port of Havana from which they left for foreign markets.

This ascent of Habanos on the market coincided with the near-simultaneous establishment in Havana of two high-quality, European lithographic print shops in the first weeks of January 1839. But these were not the first craftsmen to work on the presentation of cigars and packages for *cigarillos* (machine-made cigars, approximately the size of a cigarette made of shredded tobacco wrapped in a tobacco leaf) using other printing methods. In Europe, starting in the early eighteenth century, engraved labels were used with titles and/or scenes to identify the different products being manufactured from tobacco, originating in the New World. These small European labels from the eighteenth and nineteenth centuries, with their graphic representations, are highly sought after by collectors because of their historical and artistic value, despite being seen as allegorical, repetitive, and clichéd.

Nevertheless, in Cuba, the Caribbean island where the best tobacco in the world was produced, this sort of graphics was unknown for identification, advertising, or commercial promotion. Cuban production was exported directly to Spain, and when it was sold at retail on the local island market, identification was not yet necessary. In addition, the tobacco smuggled from Cuban coasts lacked such commercial subtleties.

By the middle of the nineteenth century, tobacco had become the most important industry in Cuba, after sugarcane, and the value of certain brands of cigars was incalculable given the international demand for them. That preference on the part of the foreign consumer stemmed from the prestige attained by Habanos, not just because of the consistent quality of the tobacco leaf used but also because of their manufacture and finish in the form of *vitolas*, in contrast to cigars manufactured abroad, which were made from a less aromatic raw material and assembled in a cruder manner. This is why manufacturers sought not only protection of the merchandise from fraud and imitation but also a more attractive presentation to the consuming public in Cuba and, above all, abroad.

EARLY DEVELOPMENT OF TOBACCO LABELS

The art of labels for tobacco and its manufactured products developed in Cuba well into the nineteenth century, long after the country received the decree to abolish the Estanco in 1817. The king had fixed his royal "attention on the promotion and cultivation of the precious tobacco plant, of such importance due to the exclusive privilege Nature has bestowed on the soil of the Island of Cuba to produce that leaf whose quality is the most exquisite in the world" (De la Pezuela p. 559).

From Spain the hand-rolled cigar, or Habano, quickly spread to France, England, and other parts of Europe, disseminated primarily during the 1830s and 1840s. It acquired an equally strong popularity in the United States and Latin America. Consequently, *chinchales* (small cigar-rolling factories) sprouted up in Havana and in certain spots in the interior of the island. Over time, some of them developed into major factories.

A brief, historical overview yields the pioneering name of Francisco Javier Báez y Pérez (1746–1828) of Havana, an engraver on metal and wood. While almost all of his work is religious, he also illustrated publications and the vignettes on the wrappers of Díaz cigarettes. Years later, in the 12 July 1835 issue of *Noticioso y Lucero de La Habana*, an advertisement was posted by an engraver who manufactured metal stencils used to produce labels: "Attention cigar makers. At 88 Calle de la Lamparilla metal templates are made to order for cigar boxes of every kind, with letters and numbers, with the greatest perfection, sturdiness and consistency." In the 11 June 1836 issue of the same newspaper, a notice stated that in Juan de Rozán's silversmith shop, located at 17 Calle de Santa Teresa (later Teniente Rey), "all types of templates are cut for printing by brush, including letters, numbers, labels, inscriptions, vignettes, flowers for cigar boxes."

In the 1830s, not only were the boxes printed on and covered with paper decorated with flowers and vignettes, but additional ornamentation called *precintas* or *filetes* was used to seal the edges of the boxes, keeping the aroma of the cigars in, and serving as adornment. So it is that in the *Noticioso y Lucero de La Habana* on 31 July 1835, an advertisement appeared for "a Carabalí Negro, 15 or 16 years old, with two months as an apprentice to a carriage driver and an excellent *precintador* [applier of *precintas*] of cigar boxes."

Before 1839, there is documentary but no graphic evidence of labels for brands of cigars and cigarillos made by methods other than lithography. The design and printing of these labels was quite simple: A xylographic (engraving with wood) drawing was made and stamped on a sheet of paper or the ink was pressed directly onto the box using a heated iron plate. In this way the factory name and address, the name of the owner, and the key word *Habana* were applied to the box. Otherwise, templates made of metal were used to produce labels that were painted in the middle by hand, using various types of paintbrushes.

Not all of the small and midsize cigar factories could afford to take on this expense. Nor was there any way to produce such labels in Havana. The engravers working in metal and wood, most of them foreigners visiting or residing in Havana, were able to meet the printing and label-making needs of the local businesses and industry. But with the new international popularity of the Cuban cigar, it became necessary to show its best face and, at the same time, prevent fraud.

Two lithographic print shops were established in Havana in 1839. One was the print shop of the Frenchmen, François Michel Cosnier and Alexandre Moreau de Jonnes, which later operated under the aegis of the Real Sociedad Patriótica (Royal Patriotic Society). The other was the print shop of the Spaniards, run by Fernando de la Costa

y Hermano, which was also known as Litografía del Gobierno (Government Lithographic Studio). Both businesses published picturesque albums in the romantic vein that presented the country, its landscapes, scenes of society, and traditions. They also took on printing illustrations for serial publications, plates for books and pamphlets, and other printed matter.

Soon the makers of cigars or cigarettes were using the services of these two print shops to print the labels that identified their products. This line of business, more commercial and less artistic, though no less beautiful despite its primitivism, produced a more reliable and profitable source of income.

At this early stage, extending from 1839 to 1860 (concluding in this last year with the introduction to Cuba of chromolithography), printed impressions were quite poorly designed and executed. The images are out of proportion, oversimplified, and flat, because of the limited experience of Cuban craftsmen, who were training beside the Europeans who had brought this method of reproduction to Cuba. In time, the Cubans would reach the heights of craftsmanship; around the 1880s, *habilitación* (a collection of labels of various shapes and sizes) was used to decorate the various types of cigar boxes, packs of cigarettes, and packages of shredded tobacco.

Until 1860, the printing of lithographed labels and wrappers was done on hand-operated presses, using a single ink color on paper of different colors: green, blue, yellow, pink, gray, white, or lilac—all in pale shades so that the printed texts and pictures would be more legible. The texts on many of these labels were printed in English, French, or German, as well as Spanish, depending on the markets and the interest of the cigar makers. Using this system,

Cigar rings. A thin band of lithographed paper known as the anilla, anillo, or sortija is wrapped around the upper part of the cigar to keep the leaves from unwrapping and to identify the cigar's type or maker. © VLADIMIR WRANGEL/ALAMY

print shops could produce up to one hundred impressions an hour.

DEVELOPMENTS IN THE 1840s AND 1850s

In the 1840s, before the art of lithographed labels used to identify the different brands belonging to each cigar maker had been developed, the containers were still being decorated with colored paper imported from France for this purpose. One announcement from the press advertised "paper specifically for manufacturers of cigars, for covering cigar boxes . . . for sale at 10 *reales fuertes* per ream . . . at B May and Co. booksellers and printers, 6 Calle de la Obrapía, between Mercaderes and San Ignacio" (*Diario de la Marina*, 31 January 1847). A few months later, on 21 March, another such announcement appeared in the same newspaper: "Colored paper. For cigar manufacturers. At 14 Calle del Obispo, a parcel of reams has just arrived specifically for decorating and embellishing cigar boxes. For sale wholesale and retail at exceedingly low prices."

The lithographic press Litografía del Comercio was established in 1845. It was here that Gustavo Muguet distinguished himself as an outstanding draftsman. This print shop also did work for the cigar and cigarette factories, according to an announcement that appeared in the *Diario de la Habana* on 16 May 1845: "those cigar-making gentlemen whose brands are housed at said establishment will not be charged for plates, and an imitation of any original presented will be rendered." In Matanzas, the Catalan Pablo Fonoll established the Litografía Matancera in 1846. Not by chance, Fonoll was also the owner of a tobacco and cigar shop in that same city.

Alongside the high quality of Cuban cigars, the fame of their packaging and presentation also grew abroad. Proof of this is Queen Isabella II's royal order of January 1858, conveying a request by the treasurer-general of the Philippine Islands, asking his counterpart in Cuba to send samples of the various types of containers being made for cigars and the manner in which they were decorated. Colonists in the Philippines, said the queen, wanted information about the wood Cubans used to produce the containers and also how they covered "the boxes with colored paper that imitated lace and with friezes that embellished the edges." To that end, she asked that the Cuban treasurer-general send "as a model, the various boxes of all the types used in Cuba along with a machine used to cut paper to resemble lace and plates used to cut and emboss the sheets of paper that cover the cigars inside the box and to make borders and ornaments that are used to decorate and seal the edges" (Rodríguez San Pedro p. 626). The queen stipulated that the treasurer-general in Havana collect all the requested tools and inquire in France about the cost of the machines used to carry out all those tasks and that they all be sent to the Philippine official. No record exists of the response of the Cuban treasurer-general, but the document certainly points to the prestige and beautiful presentation that characterized Cuban cigar boxes abroad.

COLLECTING AND LATER LITHOGRAPHIC DEVELOPMENTS

In the middle of the nineteenth century, the variety of labels with their range of illustrations made for the cigar and cigarette factories led to the habit among children and youth in Havana of collecting labels or parts of the wrappings, cutting out the vignettes or pictures from the scenes, and pasting them onto album pages, just as they did with portraits. This enthusiasm for collecting was common in Europe of the day, above all in France, Belgium, and other industrial countries. Sought after in those countries were postcards, wrappers, and labels from a variety of products—including raisins, almonds, and chocolate—that were sold to the consumer at an elevated price because of the value that collectors put on the image on the wrapper. Products sold in plain, standard containers cost far less. The Havana press promoted interest among children and youth for collecting these images. But collectors were most passionate about the labels from Cuban cigars and cigarettes.

Lithographic prints became truly magnificent after 1860, when the Susini family—Luis and José Susini, father and son, and their respective wives—imported a machine from France to chromolithograph labels and wrappers for their large cigarette factory, La Honradez, located in the square of the Convent of Santa Clara. Other manufacturers were soon using color for their own brands. Several years passed, however, before color was introduced into the designs of cigar labels, along with other later innovations such as embossing (1890).

In 1884 legal regulations were established regarding the creation of new brands of cigars, cigarettes, and packages of shredded tobacco. But despite the presentation and colorful adornment of cigar containers, Cuban cigar makers were still haunted by the specter of foreign forgeries. Each manufacturer, when it created a new brand, had to register it with the ministry of the Sociedad Económica de Amigos del País (Economic Society of Friends of the Country), which catalogued and controlled the various brands established in Cuba along with their respective designs. Further, manufacturers were expected to abide by the stipulations of this legislation.

The *habilitación* and its component labels were:

- *Hierro*: image printed on paper or engraved directly with a hot iron on the wood of the container, on its outside face, thereby breaking the wood.
- *Vista*: label placed on the inside of the cover, so it was visible when the cigar box was opened, and at times on the outside as well. Generally very elaborate, with varnish, gilt, and reliefs.

- *Bofetón*: label placed on the inside of the cigar boxes, covering the top layer of cigars. Such labels generally reproduced the picture on the *vista*, though without varnish or reliefs that might damage or alter the taste of the cigars.

- *Papeleta*: label affixed to the sides of the cigar box and part of the top in such a way that, when the box is opened, the label is broken. At other times, these labels were placed on the side as a simple decoration. In the early 2000s such a label is called a *costero*. Its size and shape varies. An alternate name was *testero*.

- *Tapaclavo*: label or seal placed over the small nail fastening the cigar box lid, adhered at the center, to the box,

guaranteeing the product's integrity; when the box is opened, this seal is broken. The seal had a round or oval shape and was also called a *contraseña*.

- *Filete*: thin band of attractive lithographic paper used to cover the outer edges of the cigar box. It helps seal the box hermetically, guaranteeing the quality and persistence of the aroma of the genuine Cuban cigar as well as contributing to its decoration. The worker in charge of decorating the cigar boxes with labels and *filetes* came to be called a *fileteador*. After 1835, the *filete* was called a *precinta*, and the worker, a *precintador*.

- *Anilla*: thin band of lithographed paper, generally of the same color and design as the brand. The *anilla* is wrapped around the upper part of the cigar. In the nineteenth century it was called an *anillo* or *sortija* (both meaning *ring*), and its initial function was to keep the layers of the cigar from unwrapping.

The following lines from the short lyric *letrilla*, by Gabriel de la Concepción Valdés (Plácido; 1809–1844), titled "La flor de la caña" describes the cigar ring's purpose:

...Un tabaco puro
de Manicaragua,
con una sortija
que ajusta la capa ...

Vol. 2, p. 281

[...A genuine Cuban cigar
from Manicaragua,
with a ring
that holds the wrapper leaf tight ...]

In these lines, the poet indicates that initially the use of the anillo, anilla, or sortija was to hold tight the leaves of the cigar. Subsequently, the narrow band of paper that was the anilla served as an identification for each individual cigar.

If the artists and artisans came to Cuba from Europe, the young Cuban *criollos* who entered those workshops as apprentices watched carefully and learned the secrets of that art from the foreigners. Later, as master lithographers, they were able to draw out of the stone new and distinct graphic expressions more faithful to the country's true character. With this novel, deeply Cuban iconography, they illustrated magazines, books, pamphlets, and offprints from romantic picture albums, in addition to creating the labels and wrappers that decorated boxes for cigars and cigarettes, both of which were made from a product that came from Cuban land: tobacco.

By the end of the nineteenth century, important lithographic workshops existed in Havana that essentially derived their income from printing labels and wrappers for the various factories of chocolates, preserved sweets, pharmaceutical products, drinks and liqueurs, perfumes and soaps, matches, and other industrial and commercial products. But above all they served the various cigar and cigarette factories. The lithographers who produced this whole range of labels not only had to fight against the importation of labels fraudulently printed abroad and brought into the country under the noses of the treasury authorities by falsely labeling them as photographs; they had to contend, too, with the high cost of the ink they had to import from France and Germany, which pushed up the price of the printing process that required as many as fourteen to twenty-two colors. This is why the most important

lithographic print shops joined together at the end of the nineteenth century to form La Compañía Litográfica de la Habana. In 1927 this company abandoned its use of lithographic stones in favor of metal plates for printing, using the offset system. Of course this system could never compete with the beauty of the lithographic stone. The rich and polychromatic *habilitación* of the cigar boxes brought about the exclusive association of the tobacco industry with the birth and growth of the art of lithography in Cuba.

BIBLIOGRAPHY

De la Concepción Valdés, Gabriel. "La flor de la caña," In *Antología de la poesía cubana*, ed. by José Lezama Lima. Vol. 2. Havana: Consejo Nacional de Cultura, 1965.

De la Pezuela, Jacobo. *Diccionario geográfico, estadístico, histórico de la Isla de Cuba*. Vol. 4. Madrid: Banco Industrial y Mercantil, 1866.

García Galló, Gaspar M. Jorge. *Biografía del tabaco habano*. Santa Clara, Cuba: Universidad Central de Las Villas, Departamento de Relaciones Culturales, 1959.

Infante, Enzo A. *Havana Cigars, 1817–1960*. Neptune City, NJ: TFH Publications, 1997.

Lapique Becali, Zoila. *La mujer en los habanos*. Havana, Cuba: Visual América Ediciones, 1996.

Lapique Becali, Zoila. *La memoria en las piedras*. Havana, Cuba: Ediciones Boloña, 2002.

Lapique Becali, Zoila. "La litografía cubana en el siglo XIX." *Catauro: Revista cubana de antropología* (Havana), no. 12 (July–December 2005): 18–24.

Lapique Becali, Zoila, and Juana Zurbarán. "La temática internacional en las marquillas de tabaco." *Cuba Comercio Exterior* (Havana), nos. 1–2 (1968): 8–13.

Martínez Rius, Adriano. *Habano, el rey*. Barcelona, Spain: Epicur Publicaciones, 1999.

Menocal, Narciso. *Cuban Cigar Labels: The Tobacco Industry in Cuba and Florida; Its Golden Age in Lithography and Architecture*. Coral Gables, FL: Cuban National Heritage, 1995.

Núñez Jiménez, Antonio. *El libro del tabaco*. Nuevo León, Mexico: Pulsar, 1994.

Ortiz, Fernando. *Cuban Counterpoint: Tobacco and Sugar*. Translated by Harriet de Onís. New York: Knopf, 1947. Reprint, Durham, NC: Duke University Press, 1995.

Perdomo, José E. *Léxico tabacalero cubano*. 2nd ed. Miami: Ediciones Universal, 1998.

Rivero Muñiz, José. *Tabaco: Su historia en Cuba*. 2 vols. Havana: Instituto de Historia, Comisión Nacional de la Academia de Ciencias de la República de Cuba, 1964–1965.

Rodríguez San Pedro, Joaquin. *Legislación ultramarina: Concordada y anotada*. Vol. 8. Madrid: Imprenta de Manuel Minuesa, 1867.

Stubbs, Jean. *Tobacco on the Periphery: A Case Study in Cuban Labour History, 1860–1958*. Cambridge, U.K.: Cambridge University Press, 1985.

TOBACCO: CULTIVATION: BOTANY

Eumelio M. Espino Marrero

The cultivation of Cuban tobacco seeds from 1520 to the early 2000s.

Nicotiana tabacum L. is a natural amphidiploid of the species *Nicotiana tomentosiformis* and *Nicotiana sylvestris*. It came from the Peruvian-Bolivian Andes area (Goodspeed). It arrived in Cuba around 3000 to 2000 BCE and underwent a long period of adaptation until it finally became the agroecotype known in modern times as Cuban black tobacco (Espino).

Tobacco was first cultivated in Cuba for commercial purposes in 1520. At that time it was limited to the areas around cities with ports, through which it was illegally traded. It was not until 1659 that the cultivation of tobacco was officially authorized and the first plantations arose on the banks of the Caracusey, Agabama, and Arimao rivers, in the center of the island. In 1719 tobacco came to Pinar del Río, where it achieved the organoleptic quality that brought Cuban tobacco its reputation as the best black tobacco in the world.

At the end of the nineteenth century, as a consequence of the wars for independence, the seeds of what had become the basic Cuban black tobacco were nearly completely lost. Seeds were brought from other countries, and that, added to a lack of technical methods for seed production, resulted in the mixing of those new varieties with the original Cuban tobacco. In 1937 the first experimental tobacco station was set up in the city of San Juan y Martínez in Pinar del Río province. It embarked on a project to restore the original tobacco variety by means of a rigorous selection program, and it achieved its goal in 1940 with the creation of the Criollo variety, a genuine Cuban black tobacco. For more than fifty years, the Criollo variety was the only commercial type used in the production of Habanos (Cuban cigars). This tobacco is no longer cultivated because of its high susceptibility to the adverse effects of blue mold, but it is a basic material that must be used in all the genetic improvement programs that have been developed in Cuba.

In 1947 the owner of the El Corojo farm developed the exceptional Corojo variety, and ever since, it has been the only one used to produce the layer that wraps around Habanos, giving them the signature look that distinguishes them from cigars from other parts of the world. For many years the traditional Corojo and Criollo Cuban varieties produced the world's best black tobacco.

The resurgence of blue mold (*Peronospora tabacina*) in Cuba during the 1979–1980 season caused the loss

GLOSSARY OF TERMS

capote (binder) Tobacco leaf that covers the filler.

fitotecnia Methods of cultivation and harvesting.

necrosis ambiental Weather fleck; brought on by high concentrations of ozone in the air.

organoleptic Characteristics that can be appreciated by the senses, for example, taste, aroma, and strength.

pata prieta Black shank disease caused by the fungus *Phytophthora parasitica var. nicotianae;* known in Cuba as Pata Prieta.

tripa Filler; leaf that constitutes the inside part of the cigar.

■ *See also*

Economy: Colonial Period

Governance and Contestation: Colonial Period

Spain's "Discovery" of Cuba: 1492

of 95 percent of the tobacco crop because the Criollo and Corojo varieties, as well as the Pelo de Oro variety, which was cultivated in the country's middle and eastern regions for the export of leaves and for domestic consumption, all were highly susceptible to the disease. The Cuban Institute for Tobacco Research began a program to develop new Cuban black tobacco varieties that preserved the organoleptic quality of the traditional varieties and also were resistant to blue mold and other diseases such as black shank (*Phytophthora nicotianae*) and environmental necrosis (ozone-induced), all of which could have a significant economic impact on the Cuban tobacco industry.

Eumelio Espino and Xiomara Rey achieved the first results with the new Habana-92 and Habana-2000 varieties. The Habana-92 variety was developed for cultivation in sun on the select tobacco plantations of Vuelta Abajo to produce the inner and outer layers of Habanos and for cultivation in the middle and eastern regions of the country to replace the Pelo de Oro variety. The Havana-2000 variety, which replaced the Corojo variety, was to be grown under netting for the production of cigar layers. Both varieties are resistant to blue mold, blank shank, and environmental necrosis (weather fleck), with high production potential and smoking quality that corresponds to the organoleptic standards of Cuban black tobacco. In a second program aimed at genetic improvement, V. Emis Mena García, Nancy Ferrer, and Betty Hernández developed the Criollo-98 and Corojo-99 varieties, which are

Tobacco field, Pinar del Río Province. Farmers began to cultivate tobacco in Pinar del Río in 1719. There, tobacco found its natural habitat and achieved the organoleptic quality that brought it the fairly won reputation of being the best black tobacco in the world. HÉCTOR DELGADO AND ROLANDO PUJOL

resistant to blue mold, black shank, environmental necrosis, and mosaic virus. Both have high productive potential and good organoleptic quality that can been adapted to the different forms of cultivation used in the production of Cuban black tobacco.

The plant science used for each variety and the cultivation methods employed respond to industry demands (Espino and Torrecilla). For the production of the raw materials that make up the inner and outer layers of Habanos, the tobacco is cultivated on the select plantations of Vuelta Abajo in broad sunlight, and it is gathered, leaf by leaf, over five different harvests. Tobacco destined for the production of layers is cultivated under netting. The goal is to lower the intensity of the sun's light by about 30 percent so that the plant develops finer leaves with veins that are just slightly pronounced, uniform in color, and with an adequate amount of plant oil and good elasticity. This tobacco is gathered, leaf by leaf, over eight harvests and positions on the stalk. Lastly, the tobacco that is produced for leaf export and domestic consumption is cultivated in broad sunlight and gathered using the *mancuerna* (two- or three-stalk cutting method).

To apply this system, the variety should be uniformly ripe, technically speaking, because it is harvested all at once. The leaves on the lower part of the plant, as well as those in the middle and at the top, should exhibit an adequate level of ripeness.

Improving harvesting methods is an ongoing effort. New technologies have been introduced, such as the production of plants in raised beds, on floating trays, and via double-row planting, all of which are aimed at increasing yield and work efficiency. This important aspect of production is overseen by the Agricultural Extension Service through the Tobacco Research Institute, which also guarantees compliance with technological requirements on the part of all of the country's tobacco growers by means of an inspection program.

BIBLIOGRAPHY

Espino, Eumelio. *Cuban Cigar Tobacco: Why Cuban Cigars Are the World's Best.* Neptune, NJ: TFH Publications, 1996.

Espino, Eumelio, and Gilberto Torrecilla. *El tabaco cubano. Recursos Fitogenéticos.* Havana: Editorial Científico-Técnica, 1999.

Espino, Eumelio, and Xiomara Rey. "Habana-92 y Habana-2000: Dos variedades cubanas de tabaco negro resistentes al moho azul (Peronospora tabacina)." *Revista Cubana de Ciencia Agricola* 1 (2000): 15–24.

García, V. Emis Mena, Nancy Ferrer, and Betty Hernández. "Nuevas variedades de tabaco negro productoras de capas y capotes, resistentes a las principales enfermedades." *Cubatabaco* 3, no. 2 (2002): 48–53.

Goodspeed, Thomas H. "The Genus Nicotiana: Origins, Relationships and Evolution of Its Species in the Light of Their Distribution, Morphology and Cytogenetics." *Chronica Botánica* 16 (1954): i–xxii, 1–536.

TOBACCO: CULTIVATION: CHEMISTRY

Norma del Castillo Alonso

Black tobacco from fermentation to final product.

Due to its high organoleptic quality, black tobacco (dark tobacco) has become the most economically important strain of tobacco cultivated in Cuba. The processes of curing, fermentation, and aging contribute to its increased smoke, aroma, and flavor, as well as the darkening of the leaf color. The bulk of black tobacco leaves grown in various zones of the country are exported as raw material or used in machine-made cigars and cigarettes. However, the best products from Vuelta Abajo in Pinar del Río and from Partido are reserved for the wrapping, filling, and binding of the world-famous Habano cigars.

FERMENTATION AND AGING PROCESS

Fermentation is a complex chemical, biochemical, and microbiological process to which black tobacco is subjected after natural curing has taken place. Fermentation transforms the chemical composition of the leaves, making them thinner and darker, as well as developing their aroma, smoothing their harshness, and making them easier to burn. The first fermentation occurs in the curing house after the leaves have been dried. They are heaped in *pilones* (stacks of tobacco with specific dimensions). The fermentation process then continues in sorting and stripping houses. This is also done in stacks under regulated humidity and with a noticeable, yet regulated, increase in temperature. This severe fermentation process is a standard practice only in the processing of cigar tobacco.

The aging process for black tobacco consists of a very slow fermentation that does not result in an increase in temperature. It is carried out in barrels, bundles wrapped in royal palm leaf sheaths, or burlap sacks, at a humidity of 12–13 percent. The process, which can take years in warehouses, promotes the balance of the tobacco's sensory properties (aroma, flavor, and strength). After the cigar is made, this aging process continues in distributors' and importers' warehouses or private humidors. The aging of the final product is a distinct aspect of cigar manufacturing.

CHEMICAL COMPOSITION OF TOBACCO AND SMOKE

The chemical composition of tobacco and tobacco smoke are influenced by the plant variety, the weather, the soil, the agricultural and processing practices, and the position of the leaf on the stalk, among other factors. Curing and fermentation remove almost all of the sugar and starch, and proteins are transformed into amino acids. Other reactions include the reduction of nitrogenated compounds and the oxidation of pigments and polyphenols. Black tobacco (dark tobacco) is known to have a greater proportion of nitrogenated compounds than flue-cured or Oriental tobacco. Its pH is closer to neutral, its reducing sugars are extremely low, and its ash percentage is elevated. The lower leaves have a higher concentration of minerals and, therefore, burn more easily; whereas the upper leaves are richer in organic compounds. Tobacco's nitrogenated compounds include alkaloids, of which nicotine is most important due to its effects on physiological strength.

A classification of cigars based on the analysis of its non-volatile organic acids was done in Canada (Ng et al. pp. 1132–1138).

During combustion, some of the leaf's chemical compounds, such as nicotine, transfer to the smoke relatively intact. Others are pyrolized, and new compounds are formed. About four thousand compounds have been detected in tobacco smoke, either in solid-liquid or gas phases, or in both. Smoke is composed mainly of oxygen and nitrogen (73–76%); the gas phase constitutes about 19 percent. Although the solid-liquid phase represents only 4.5–8 percent of the smoke, it is here that are found phenols, resins, alcohols, esters, alkaloids, and so on, many of which influence the sensory properties of the product. The solid-liquid phase, minus water and nicotine, is known as TAR or nicotine-free dry particulate matter (NFDPM).

The mainstream smoke (smoke which leaves the butt end of a cigar or cigarette during the smoking process) is collected for analysis using smoking machines with fixed parameters (butt length, puff volume, puff duration, puff frequency, and puff profile). Its solid-liquid phase is collected in traps with fiberglass filters (such as the Cambridge filter pad), and the gas phase is collected in special bags. The sidestream smoke (smoke which leaves a cigar or cigarette during the smoking process other than from the butt end) is collected for analysis with a specific additive (fish tail).

■ *See also*

Ecology and Environment: Colonial Period

Economy: Colonial Period

GLOSSARY OF TERMS

agresividad (**aggressiveness**) The penetrating, unpleasant, harsh sensation of smoke in one's throat.

bonche (**bunch**) A cylinder of leaves containing the corresponding *ligada*, or bundle of leaves, for a cigar wrapped in an outer wrapper.

capa (**coat/cape**) A leaf from a plant grown under cloth. It is elastic, thin, and uniform in color and is used for a cigar's outer wrapper.

capote (**cape**) A leaf used for the binder that wraps the filler that forms the bulk of a cigar.

CO Carbon monoxide, a toxic compound found in the gas phase of smoke. It represents 4 percent of the gas phase.

gas phase The smoke that passes through the particulate matter trap during smoking.

Cambridge filter A filter that collects particulate matter from the smoke that reaches the trap.

fish tail An attachment shaped like the tail of a fish that is placed on a smoking machine to collect the secondary stream during smoking.

humidor A storeroom with regulated humidity and temperature for cigar storage.

ligada (**blend**) A bundle of leaves with different characteristics or *tiempos* that make up a predetermined sensorial profile.

ligero A grouping of leaves with a medium to thick texture which contribute to the cigar's strength and are used for filler.

mainstream smoke The air that goes through the combustion zone and exits through the smoker's end of the cigarette or cigar during puffing.

mano molde (**hand molding**) The technology of utilizing molds for the *bonches* to make wrapping the *capas* easier.

medio tiempo The plant's higher leaves, which have a thicker texture, more strength, and are used for cigar fillers

physiological strength The sensation or impact of the smoke when it reaches one's throat.

puff profile The measurable volume directly behind the cigarette's or cigar's mouthpiece, represented graphically over time.

pyrolysis The thermal decomposing of the cigarette's or cigar's components during smoking.

seco A leaf of medium texture that contributes to the aroma and flavor of a cigar's filler.

sidestream smoke During machine smoking, the smoke that exits a cigarette or cigar, through some point other than the end that is attached to the machine.

smoke trap A device to collect smoke from a cigarette or cigar sample.

solid-liquid phase The smoke that is retained in the particulate matter trap during smoking.

TAR or NFDPM Nicotine-free dry particulate matter; the condensed dry smoke after the nicotine has been removed.

tercio A container to transport and store tobacco leaves, which is covered by *yaguas* (royal palm fronds) and tied with cords. It is mostly used for *capa* leaves.

tiempo (**class**) A term (such as *seco, ligero, medio tiempo*) used to designate a leaf's texture, color, and oiliness. It is based on the strength and the position of the leaves on the plant.

tripa (**filler**) Leaves with various characteristics that make up the bulk of the cigar.

vitola A term used to designate the type of a cigar based on its diameter, length, and shape. The same *vitola* may be made from different *ligadas*, depending on its brand.

volado A leaf from the lower parts of a plant; it has a thin texture, is combustible, and is used for cigar fillers.

yagua (**royal palm**) A dry, fibrous fabric made from royal palm fronds and used to make *tercios*.

Certain compounds in cigarette smoke are subject to international regulation; in the solid-liquid phase: TAR (10 Mg/cigarette) and nicotine (1 Mg/cigarette); in the gas phase: CO (carbon monoxide), (10 Mg/cigarette). These or similar regulations will be applied to all smoking products as countries continue researching the effects of smoking.

Setting parameters for smoking cigars is more difficult due to their variety of dimensions, shapes, and weight. After much research, the Centre de Coopération

Cutting tobacco. Cuban cigars are rolled by hand after tobacco leaves are carefully cut with a knife called a chaveta. PHOTO BY BARRY LEWIS/REX USA, COURTESY EVERETT COLLECTION

pour les Recherches Scientifiques Relatives au Tabac (CORESTA; the Cooperation Center for Scientific Research Relative to Tobacco, a private international organization headquartered in Paris) recommended six methods: conditioning, sampling, machine smoking, NFDPM, nicotine, and water determinations.

TOBACCO PRODUCTS: THEIR PRODUCTION AND SENSORY QUALITIES

Cuba produces cigarettes, machine-made cigars, and Habano (handmade) cigars—the famous Cuban cigars—all for domestic consumption and for export. There are ten brands of machine-made cigars, each with different trade dress (labeling and dimensions). The Habano cigar is made using tobacco from plantations in Pinar del Río with wrappers sometimes coming from plantations in Partido. It consists of filler, an inner wrapper or binder, and an outer wrapper. There are about twenty-seven brands of Habanos and over eighty-nine *vitolas* (dimensions or formats), with different strengths and flavors.

Many Habano brands appeared in the nineteenth century, such as Partagás (1845) and Romeo y Julieta (1875). Others surfaced in the twentieth century, including Montecristo (1935), Cohiba (1966), and Trinidad (1998). The older brands are updated with the release of cigars in new vitolas, such as the Montecristo Edmundo and Cohiba Maduro, manufactured by Tabacuba.

The sensory properties and the concentration of nicotine, and therefore the cigar's physiological strength, vary according to the *tiempo* (class), which is determined by the position of the leaf on the plant.

Some chemical compounds in black tobacco

Compound	Content (%)
Nicotine	1.00–3.94
Total Nitrogen	3.32–4.58
Ash	15.30–22.80
Resins	2.06–5.32
Calcium (CaO)	2.31–4.98
Potassium (K₂O)	3.82–6.34
Magnesium (MgO)	0.85–1.88

SOURCE: Del Castillo, Norma, and J. J. López. *Caracterización del tabaco de diferentes zonas*. Havana: Instituto de Investigaciones del Tabaco, 2004.

Table 1

The leaves are combined into *ligadas* (blends) that are evaluated by expert judges who select the one that best matches the pre-established profile.

Because smoking products are consumed in the form of smoke, they are difficult to evaluate. Judges are selected by specialists who evaluate their skillfulness in recognizing cigars with different blends and flavors using their basic senses. They are then trained to evaluate attributes and are taught the specific terminology and the most widely used tests (*pareada* or two-way comparison, *triangular* or three-way comparison) and

Table 2

The relation between TAR and smoke nicotine with organoleptic properties

Property Compound	Aroma	Flavor	Strength	General Quality
Nicotine smoke	0.0681	0.5202	0.7934	0.2649
TAR	0.5590	0.6257	0.5354	0.6758

SOURCE: Del Castillo, Norma, J. J. López, and G. Betancourt. "Relación entre la composición del humo y sus características organolépticas." Presentation at Seminario Científico de la Subdirección Industrial. Havana: Instituto de Investigaciones del Tabaco, 2003.

Sensory properties of the tiempo (from top to bottom of plant)

Tiempo	Physiological Strength	Main Characteristic
Volado	Mild	Combustibility
Seco	Medium	Aroma
Ligero	Strong	Aroma and Flavor
Medio Tiempo	Very Strong	Flavor

Table 3   SOURCE: Norma del Castillo Alonso.

characterization. When evaluating, they consider elements such as aroma, flavor, strength, combustibility, and general quality, among others.

MAKING AND MARKETING HABANO CIGARS

The making of Habano cigars starts with the purchase, receiving, storage, and preparation of the tobacco for the inner wrappers, outer wrappers, and fillers. The cigars are molded by hand: The roller forms a cylinder of leaves from each tiempo, with quantities varying depending on the blend, wraps it in the binder, then wraps the outer wrapper around it, locates the smoking end, and cuts the final product. The fumigated cigars are then placed in a facility maintaining a relative humidity of 65–70 percent and a temperature of 60.8° Fahrenheit (16–18°C) for five days to establish their humidity.

Cigars are classified by colors and packed in the sorting room. Wooden boxes are first lined inside and out with lithographed labels. Each cigar is then adorned with a ring. After that, the containers are nailed shut, sealed, and identified with stickers and labels. The product is kept in climate-controlled storage. There is rigorous quality control throughout the entire process and a final inspection. The smoking quality is controlled through daily sensory evaluations of the rollers' work. Habanos are marketed through exclusive distributors or established Habano cigar shops.

BIBLIOGRAPHY

Centre de Coopération pour les Recherches Scientifiques Relatives au Tabac (CORESTA). "CORESTA Recommended Methods": No. 46: "Atmosphere for Conditioning and Testing Cigars." May 1998. Available from http://www.coresta.org.

Centre de Coopération pour les Recherches Scientifiques Relatives au Tabac (CORESTA). "CORESTA Recommended Methods": No. 47: "Cigars–Sampling." January 2000. Available from http://www.coresta.org.

Centre de Coopération pour les Recherches Scientifiques Relatives au Tabac (CORESTA). "CORESTA Recommended Methods": No. 64: "Routine Analytical Cigar-Smoking Machine—Specifications, Definitions and Standard Conditions." November 2005. Available from http://www.coresta.org.

Centre de Coopération pour les Recherches Scientifiques Relatives au Tabac (CORESTA). "CORESTA Recommended Methods": No. 65: "Determination of Total and Nicotine-Free Dry Particulate Matter Using a Routine Analytical Cigar-Smoking Machine—Determination of Total Particulate Matter and Preparation for Water and Nicotine Measurements." 4th ed. June 2010. Available from http://www.coresta.org.

Centre de Coopération pour les Recherches Scientifiques Relatives au Tabac (CORESTA). "CORESTA Recommended Methods": No. 66: "Determination of Nicotine in the Mainstream Smoke of Cigars by Gas Chromatographic Analysis." November 2005. Available from http://www.coresta.org.

Centre de Coopération pour les Recherches Scientifiques Relatives au Tabac CORESTA). "CORESTA Recommended Methods": No. 67: "Determination of Water in the Mainstream Smoke of Cigars by Gas Chromatographic Analysis." November 2005. Available from http://www.coresta.org.

Ng, Lay-Keow, Michel Hupé, Micheline Vanier, and Dennis Moccia. "Characterization of Cigar Tobaccos by GC/MS Analysis of Nonvolatile Organic Acids: Application to the Authentication of Cuban Cigars." *Journal of Agricultural and Food Chemistry* 49, no. 3 (2001): 1132–1138.

Cuban Cigar Website. http//www.cubancigarwebsite.com.

TRINIDAD

Carlos Venegas Fornias

A city of colonial architecture in Cuba.

The city of Trinidad pays tribute to its past with some of the best-maintained colonial buildings in the Antilles and the Caribbean. The development of the town of Santísima Trinidad, the third of the seven original Spanish settlements on the island, began in 1514, but it came to a halt with the sudden decline of the sugar industry in the middle of the nineteenth century. The town was deserted, along with other cities in the Americas that had also counted on a single product and on an unpredictable market.

Trinidad is highly valued for its scenic views. It is located on the central southern coast of the island, on a stretch of rocky coastline. The Spanish found it accessible and especially attractive because of its large indigenous population and its short river that descends from the mountains of Escambray into the Caribbean Sea, carrying alluvial gold in its sand. After a brief period when it was positioned near the Bay of Jagua (later Cienfuegos), the town was established at its modern location on the slope of a hill at about twenty-three feet above sea level and about three miles from the sea, next to the Táyaba River and its lush valley.

Because of its ideal location for observing the movement of ships, Trinidad supported the first colonization efforts and the conquest of continental land. In 1515 Ferdinand V (1452–1516) promoted it to the status of city, and it became associated with well-known figures in the chronicles of the Indies. Hernán Cortés (1485–1547) recruited his soldiers for the conquest of Mexico there; Bartolomé de Las Casas (1484–1566) took up the cause of its indigenous people after living near them; Alvar Núñez Cabeza de Vaca (c. 1488–c. 1557) described the fury of the hurricane at its port before he departed to conquer Florida; and Bernal Díaz del Castillo (1492–1585), Pedro de Alvarado (c. 1485–1541), and others visited the city.

After the time of the great discoveries, navigation routes to Mexico and Peru no longer passed through Trinidad's coastal waters; by 1536 the city had only a dozen inhabitants, and soon after it had no Spanish residents at all. With the abolition of the *encomienda* system of distributing land to Spanish settlers, Trinidad became a settlement for the few remaining indigenous people. In 1573 the Spanish *cabildo* (town council) was reinstated, and the city grew slowly throughout the following century, but it remained a sparsely populated city.

GEOGRAPHIC LOCATION AND ECONOMY

Trinidad's economy relied on cattle products and tobacco, which were sold to other Spanish colonies and to the colonies of other foreign powers, avoiding the Spanish monopoly and its fleets. Its proximity to the sea made it vulnerable to frequent pirate attacks, weakened its residential character, and decreased the value of its buildings. The city's residents abandoned it to find security on inland estates. Because urban development was constricted by nature at the time, during its first two centuries Trinidad had to adjust to the roughness of its terrain, which resulted in the whimsical layout of the upper part of the city. Its many outlooks, unexpected intersections, and the intricate weave of streets and alleys make it picturesque. The city hall's coat of arms depicts an old *jigüe* (acacia) tree, a symbol the conquistadores chose as an emblem of their rule over the territory and after which Trinidad's main street was named. The houses were made of board, mud, and poles, with palm-thatched roofs.

Trinidadians' sense of identity was linked to the preservation of this site, which guaranteed its inhabitants land ownership and a favorable location for contraband trade. The Spanish Crown tried to eradicate the residents or relocate them to the nearby Bay of Jagua, next to a new fortress, but during the eighteenth century, the city played an important role in defending Spain's interests in the Caribbean. Its residents built privateer ships that were used against the English, and they expanded their local militias.

The port's strategic position on the Caribbean coast of Cuba, across from the non-Spanish Antilles, made it extremely valuable and assured its longevity. Trinidad was able to secure concessions and privileges that stimulated its economy and helped it become the wealthiest city in the area. In 1731 it was the designated headquarters for the government of the central region of the island, and from 1778 until 1792, its port was authorized successively to trade with Spanish ports, to trade slaves, and to trade with neutral nations and with nations that were Spain's allies in repeated wars. The old privateers became the landowner elite who owned slave-labor plantations. In a gathering to welcome the geographer Alexander von Humboldt (1769–1859) in 1801, members of this new elite expressed their rivalry with Havana and their desire to reach an urban growth more on par with other centers throughout the country.

SLAVERY AND THE SUGAR PLANTATION BOOM

In 1811 local authorities confirmed that in the previous twenty years Trinidad's population had grown and new buildings had been built at an unprecedented rate. Between 1827 and 1845 the Cuban census placed Trinidad among the largest cities, with just over 12,000 inhabitants, 50 sugar plantations, 50 coffee plantations, and 50 other rural establishments where about 10,000 slaves worked. Its cobblestone streets extended to the lower lands to the south. They were more uniformly laid out

■ *See also*

Economy: Colonial Period

Governance and Contestation: Colonial Period

Governance and Contestation: Insurrection, 1952–1959

Lucía (Humberto Solás)

and covered about 158 hectares, with nearly 1,000 buildings made of stone with tile roofs, and a similar number constructed from less expensive materials (Venegas Fornias p. 122).

The urban area contained many private homes. Most of the dwellings, like those in every old Cuban town, were one-story terraced homes that enclosed interior patios behind their uninterrupted facades. Spacious front doors were flanked by windows opening onto the street and covered with cast-iron or wooden grills. All the buildings were crowned with prominent eaves that protected the broad stone walls from rain erosion. The buildings were painted in different colors so that the intense brightness would not disturb passers-by.

The interiors of the homes were exposed to the public spaces. The floor plans consisted of large parlors surrounded by rooms topped with roof frames made of hardwoods. This typical Mudejar (Spanish-Muslim) architecture was established early on in Caribbean settlements, where it became less introverted as it adapted to the needs of a new climate and society. Later, when more refined expressions were in demand, the carpentry and wall painting were updated with baroque and neoclassical motifs. The combination of global influences made Trinidad's buildings a classic example of Caribbean architecture that enriched and reinvented tradition by applying its own solutions.

A well-known handbook published in 1852, acknowledged Trinidad's uniqueness:

> The homes in Trinidad are different from the homes in Havana in view of the fact that they do not have a divider wall between the living room and the dining room. These areas are divided by one or more open arches. The living room and the dining room make up a square parlor with columns in the middle. This gives the homes a sense of magnificence, freedom and ampleness. The living room has a door to the street, even when there is an entrance hall, and when the door is opened wide in the evening onto the drawing room, the abundance of fine furniture, the lighting and most of all, the beauty of the Trinidadian ladies are striking to foreigners.

> *García de Arboleya p. 341*

One of the indications of the wealth the city acquired through the sugar trade was the ornaments displayed in the drawing rooms where guests were received, for example, marble and alabaster objects, porcelains, Viennese mirrors, and lamps. The exquisite furniture was made by the dozens of carpenters, mostly black or mulatto, who provided their services to the city. In 1842 the French traveler Rosemond de Beauvallon, mesmerized by the furnishings in these houses, affirmed:

> These are not the vast Italian mansions that the splendid Middle Ages endowed to disinherited children, in which no gold, magnificence, wealth or life circulate. . . . Here, family names count too, but the fortunes are young and vigorous; and the gold on the surfaces of the furniture and innumerable sculptures that time and use tarnishes, soon reappears even brilliant, because behind this luxury are the vast lands that sustain it.

> *Beauvallon p. 216*

THE QUICK DECLINE

At the height of Trinidad's splendor, the exportation of sugar, that in 1841 had surpassed one million arrobas, was reduced in four years by one-third, and the city began its decline. The landowners and business owners migrated to the nearby port of Cienfuegos, which was surrounded by rich plains. There, sugar was manufactured in brand new refineries at a lower cost than in the mills of Trinidad, where the exhausted soil was surrounded by mountains, complicating the expansion of the railroad system. In 1861 a bystander wondered:

> Could that really be Trinidad? The prosperous city that was nourished by the products of its fertile valley? The one we had grown to see as an emporium of abundance and a home to opulence? Its streets with weeds invading the spaces left by missing cobblestones; its ruined homes, seen here and there, with parasitic vines thriving on their crumbling walls. The solitude and absence of activity that make her gloomy are those of a different city.

> *Auber p. 216*

The wars of independence and the abolition of slavery accelerated Trinidad's ruin, and in the next century most of its population relied upon craft industries from the past, producing palm hats, homemade sweets, pottery, roof tiles, and embroideries to earn a living. Trinidad became a symbol of the dangers of the growth without development that plantation-based economies generated.

As Trinidad became impoverished and was abandoned, its families saw their estates shrink, and historic memory was replaced with legendary tales about a splendid past that could still be detected in Trinidad's architecture. In a country that was quickly modernizing, the city was living in the past: It had no cars, no paved streets, and no reinforced concrete constructions. Trinidad became attractive because of its peaceful charm and the nostalgia it aroused. The potential for tourism was identified early on, and its development provided the resources to keep the city alive.

PATRIMONY AS A SOURCE OF SURVIVAL

In 1929, Cuba's first government decree to protect historic buildings focused enforcement efforts on Trinidad. In 1942, when the city's urban population had revived to nineteenth-century numbers of about 15,000, a local institution to recover and utilize estates, the Sociedad Protrinidad (Pro-Trinidad Society), was established and opened its first museum. The city came to be seen as a symbol of colonial times. Its Holy Week processions that were promoted nationwide and its hosting of the first national history conferences were especially helpful. Cuban writers such as José Antonio Ramos, Lydia Cabrera, and Enrique Serpa wrote about Trinidad. Most importantly, photos, paintings, and engravings that appeared in the press promoted its architectural landmarks, especially the bell towers of the Convent of San Francisco (1812) and of the Manaca-Iznaga sugar refinery (1828).

In the mid-twentieth century, plans were drawn up for tourism development, but they were interrupted in 1957 by a long insurrection in the Escambray mountains that festered for more than a decade and turned the city into a center of military operations. Changes brought on by the Cuban Revolution affected Trinidad's economy and the composition of the population, but the appeal of its character and its designation as a historical monument went unaltered. In 1965, a local commission for monuments was established, and in 1969 a group dedicated to the restoration and maintenance of monuments was set up. The Cuban film industry chose Trinidad as its favorite setting for historical films.

In the 1980s cultural heritage property throughout Cuba was handed over to institutions. New museums were established, recovering a good deal of the most valuable real estate for their collections, and local construction techniques for architectural preservation and restoration were recovered. These efforts culminated in 1988 with the city and the valley of the sugar plantations being listed as a UNESCO World Heritage site.

The delayed impact of international tourism transformed the city's fortunes in the middle of Cuba's economic crisis of the 1990s. After that, aside from generating income for government enterprises as well as high tax revenues, tourism ensured a steady income for much of the population through room rentals in homes, food services, and the sale of arts and crafts.

The usual tension between tourism and historic preservation is evident when urban homeowners alter their dwellings to accommodate more guests

Valley of the Sugar Mills. The Valley of the Sugar Mills near Trinidad was a center of the Cuban sugar industry during the eighteenth and nineteenth centuries. The ruins of numerous sugar mills and other buildings related to sugar production still stand in the valley. HÉCTOR DELGADO AND ROLANDO PUJOL

at the cost of damaging the properties' historic value, and also when old buildings in areas outside the city and less protected are renovated with poor quality architecture and poor design. Trinidad aims to establish a sustainable tourism economy that promotes the preservation of a valuable city while avoiding the type of progress that can fragment it.

BIBLIOGRAPHY

Auber, Emilio. "Entre la Habana y Trinidad." *Cuba Literaria* 1 (1861): 216.

Beauvallon, Rosemond de. *La isla de Cuba*. Santiago de Cuba: Editorial Oriente, 2002.

García de Arboleya, José. *Manual de la isla de Cuba*. Havana: Imprenta del Gobierno, 1852.

García Santana, Alicia. *Trinidad de Cuba: Ciudad, plazas, casas y valle*. Havana: Consejo Nacional de Patrimonio Cultural, 2004.

Venegas Arbolaez, Bárbara, and Silvia Teresita Angelbello Izquierdo. *Trinidad precolombina y colonial*. Sancti Spíritus, Cuba: Ediciones Luminaria, 2008.

Venegas Delgado, Hernán. *Trinidad de Cuba: Corsarios, azúcar y revolución en el Caribe*. Havana: Oficina del Conservador de la ciudad de Trinidad and Centro de Investigación y Desarrollo de la Cultura Cubana Juan Marinello, 2006.

Venegas Fornias, Carlos. "Trinidad." In *La Habana Vieja, Trinidad: Patrimonio mundial de la humanidad*, edited by Enrique Capablanca and Carlos Venegas Fornias. Havana: Editorial Letras Cubanas, 1998.

■ *See also*

Cuban Thought and Cultural Identity: Costumbres in the Republican Period

La gitana tropical and the Artistic Influence of Víctor Manuel

Visual Arts: Republican Period

EL TRIUNFO DE LA RUMBA (EDUARDO ABELA)

Juan A. Martínez

A groundbreaking painting in Cuban modern art and culture.

Opposite page:
El triunfo de la rumba (c. 1928) by Eduardo Abela (1889–1965). This pioneering modernist painting by Eduardo Abela depicts figures playing music and dancing a rhumba through the dynamic use of lines and vibrant colors. COLECCIÓN MUSEO NACIONAL DE BELLAS ARTES, LA HABANA, CUBA

Eduardo Abela (1889–1965) was a pioneer of the modernist movement in Cuban art and one of its foremost caricaturists. He graduated from Havana's San Alejandro Academy of Fine Arts in 1921 and continued his artistic development in Madrid from 1921 to 1924 and in Paris from 1927 to 1929. His Parisian stay culminated with a 1928 exhibition at the exclusive Galerie Zak, where he showed six drawings and fourteen oils, including *El triunfo de la rumba* (c. 1928; The Triumph of the Rhumba). In a chronicle from Paris, the Cuban writer and cultural critic Alejo Carpentier wrote: "I doubt that Cuban painting—the one inspired by *criollo* culture—has ever produced such a vigorous result as Abela's current style" (p. 165). This exhibition was at the vanguard of the Cuban modernist art movement as Abela's paintings and drawings combined modern artistic language and national cultural themes. Interestingly, the earliest and best-known examples of Cuban modern art, *El triunfo de la rumba* and Víctor Manuel's *La gitana tropical* (1929), were done in Paris. One of the early chapters of the Cuban modernist art movement took place in Paris and Madrid as seen in the paintings of Abela, Víctor Manuel, Amelia Peláez, Carlos Enríquez, and Marcelo Pogolotti from the late 1920s and early 1930s. Distance, nostalgia, and the awareness of cultural differences seem to have been important factors in this movement. In his Parisian production, Abela developed a highly personal and, in the case of Cuba, highly inventive modernist style, tending in the direction of figurative expressionism.

THE PAINTING'S RHYTHMS AND INNOVATIVE STYLE

The title of *El triunfo de la rumba* alludes to a family of percussive rhythms, song, and dance that originated in Cuba and was popular in Havana, Paris, and New York at the time—thus its "triumph." The painting expresses more than depicts figures playing music and dancing a rhumba through the dynamic use of lines and vibrant colors. The strong emphasis on rhythm is designed to express one of the essential elements of the music it represents. As is the case with the works of contemporary Cuban poets, such as Nicolás Guillén, José Z. Tallet, and Emilio Ballagas, or such musicians as Amadeo Roldán and Alejandro García Caturla, who also introduced Afro-Cuban popular themes into their work, the emphasis in *El triunfo de la rumba* is on the element of rhythm. Artists and intellectuals associated with the loose *Afrocubanismo* movement of the 1920s and 1930s in Havana, which first acknowledged the validity of Cuba's African traditions and culture as part of that which is Cuban, saw rhythm as a key aspect not only of Afro-Cuban music but also the culture in general. Stereotypes aside, Afro-Cuban music preserved numerous types of African rhythms, which are widely acknowledged as enriching many forms of contemporary music.

El triunfo de la rumba was innovative not only in style but also in its subject matter: Afro-Cuban myth and music in the context of secular popular culture, specifically the Havana carnival. The female dancer dressed in white, the musicians and dancers in the second plane, and the banana tree in the background seem to be part of a parade float (notice the wheel-like forms) moving through a narrow landscape near a shoreline, suggesting an island. The central female figure's white dress ends in a mermaid-like tail,

which along with the seascape, alludes to the popular Santería deity of Yoruba descent Yemayá, owner of all water. Afro-Cuban mythological figures became subjects in the Cuban music, literature, and art of the late 1920s and 1930s. In this respect, Abela's *El triunfo de la rumba,* with its reference to Afro-Cuban music, myth, and the Havana carnival, is a seminal work. Later artists such as Wifredo Lam, Manuel Mendive, and José Bedia expanded and deepened the expression of Cuba's African heritage in its high art. In the early twenty-first century, Afro-Cuban themes and perspectives abound in Cuban art on and off the island.

ABELA'S LATER ARTISTIC DEVELOPMENT

From this early bright moment in his artistic development, the Parisian period of 1927–1929, Abela went on to become a major figure in Cuban caricature and painting. On his return to Cuba in 1929, he turned to caricature, which he published in *El Diario de la Marina, La Semana, Información,* and *El País.* He developed a character named "El Bobo" (Idiot), which suggested criticism of the repressive regime of then president Gerardo Machado and Cuba's social ills. After Machado's downfall in 1933, Abela did not see the relevance of continuing El Bobo," ending a brief but influential career as a caricaturist. Finding it hard to make a living as an artist, he entered the foreign service and served as Cuba's cultural ambassador to Milan. In Italy, he was impressed by early Renaissance painting, which influenced his work in the late 1930s. During this period he produced *Los guajiros* (1938; The peasants). In this iconic painting, he monumentalizes the Cuban peasant, showing a group of them at rest in the outskirts of a rural town. The peasantry's legendary love of horses, roosters, and women is suggested by the inclusion of these subjects in the composition.

In the 1940s, Abela continued to balance his work as a diplomat, during most of that decade performed in Guatemala, with his painting. In 1955, he retired from the diplomatic corps and dedicated the last decade of his life to painting, developing his most personal style and a significant body of paintings. Influenced to some extent by the work of Paul Klee, his last period shows a tendency toward fantasy. He painted in a childlike manner of simplified lines, visible brushstrokes often creating a thick texture, and brilliant colors. The subjects are for the most part children, animals, and cityscapes. Among the most recognized works of the time are *La vaca* (1956) and *José Martí* (1960).

In 1964, the year before his death, Abela had a major retrospective exhibition at the Galería de La Habana, where the Consejo Nacional de Cultura, Cuba's highest cultural institution at the time, bought almost the entire exhibition (Veigas and Rodríguez). Some of these paintings, such as *El triunfo de la rumba* and *Los guajiros,* are on permanent display at the Museo Nacional de Bellas Artes in Havana. In the early 2000s, Abela is considered one of Cuba's foremost pioneers of Cuban modern art and caricature.

BIBLIOGRAPHY

Carpentier, Alejo. "Abela en la Galería Zak." In *Obras completas de Alejo Carpentier,* Vol. 9: 165–169. Mexico City: Siglo, 1986. Originally published in *Social* 14, no. 1 (1929): 51, 60.

Seoane Gallo, José. *Eduardo Abela, cerca del cerco.* Havana: Editorial Letras Cubanas, 1986.

Veigas Zamora, José, and Beatriz Gago Rodríguez, eds. *Abela: De lo real a lo imaginario.* Madrid: Fundación Arte Cubano, 2010.

U–V

ÚLTIMOS DÍAS DE UNA CASA (DULCE MARÍA LOYNAZ)

Zaida Capote Cruz

An important poem in the oeuvre of Dulce María Loynaz (1902–1997).

First published in Spain, like most of her work, Dulce María Loynaz's *Últimos días de una casa* (Last Days of a House, 1958) gives voice to an old house, abandoned by the family that had always occupied it. Its soliloquy begins in the midst of a tremendous silence, a profound lethargy that portends death: The house feels penetrated "by mute water," submerged in the viscous slime of solitude. It recounts stories of its former inhabitants: nights of celebration, days of wakes or sickness—in a word, life. All has now ended, like the view of the sea that could be glimpsed in the past. In the present the sea cannot be seen; the horizon is blocked by the towers of new buildings, and the house can no longer see its peers, since each day there are fewer by its side. Other old houses like this one have been disappearing, little by little, leaving it drowned in a sea of new construction without history. So this one suspects with sorrow:

> Tal vez el mar no exista ya tampoco.
> O lo hayan cambiado de lugar.
> O de sustancia. Y todo: el mar, el aire,
> los jardines, los pájaros,
> se haya vuelto también de piedra gris,
> de cemento sin nombre.

> [Perhaps the sea doesn't exist now either.
> Or it has moved to a new place.
> Or changed substance. And everything: the sea,
>   the air
> the gardens, the birds

have turned back into grey stone,
into nameless cement.]

It is all a world that is dying, the habits of a recent past that the present endeavors to forget, and to erase.

With the last moving of furniture the house appears to have driven out all trace of life, recorded in everyday objects; the move itself is already a painful awakening to death: "Me siento ya una casa enferma, / una casa leprosa" (I already feel like a sick house, / a leper house), it says, for the moment recovering and rejecting death. "No he de caerme, no, que yo soy fuerte" (I don't have to fall, no, I am strong). Old and alone, the house tries to recount its memories; it sometimes forgets what it is talking about and then recovers, emerging proudly as a space with its own soul, owner of itself, still able to accommodate many people. Soon, however, its faith grows weaker: a new day arrives and with it life is reborn—there is the smell of coffee, the sound of work—the workers have arrived at its garden and come toward the house with "sus picas en alto" (their spades held high). In the drowsiness of the unconsciousness before death, the house is still able to record its sensations: the blows, the pain, the wounds inflicted by these men, similar to those it had sheltered, those whose ambition has condemned it. From the happy memories, it passes without transition to a diatribe against the people who abandoned it.

A RECURRENT THEME

Similar in tone and length to some of Loynaz's other poems in which marginal subjects also appear—"Canto a la mujer estéril" (Song to a Barren Woman, 1937) or "La novia de Lázaro" (Lázaro's Bride, 1991)—*Últimos días de una casa* masterfully condenses a recurrent theme in Loynaz's work, where the advent of progress brings with it the end of a world, a friendly and idealized world where money does not exist and life takes place in closed, autonomous spaces, as occurs in *Jardín: Novela lírica* (Garden: A Lyric Novel, 1951).

Published in 1958, on the eve of the Revolution, the poem has been read as a metaphor for the end of

■ *See also*

Cuban Thought and Cultural Identity: Costumbres in the Republican Period

Literature: Poetry in the Republican Period

an era, as a kind of farewell to the protected space in which its life has unfolded; however, Loynaz herself once declared, "If you believe in premonitions, you might think this was one, because I was destined to attend the painful destruction of a house. But when I wrote the poem I couldn't have known that. It could also have been a coincidence" (quoted in Simón p. 61). Conceptually, the poem is much like her other works, which contain a certain modernist hint of the past and a certain rejection of progress and modernity. The house in *Últimos días* is witness to an older time, of a patriarchal and slow-paced life that modernity inevitably brings to an end. Because it is located close to the sea, the house in the poem is often identified with the Loynaz family home—located on the corner of Línea Street and Fourteenth, in the Vedado section (downtown) of Havana, still precariously standing—where the young Loynaz siblings—Dulce María and her brothers—held their social gatherings every Thursday.

Loynaz's dying house has also been compared to the Cuban nation, victim of a tremendous crisis of values that would lead, historically, to the 1959 Revolution, and literarily, to many similar gestures from the authors of the day, such as the *Orígenes* group. Such disenchantment is, in the "cosmic heroism" of Loynaz's house, an example for all Cubans, since the house here is a reservoir of identity and witness to a time before the dispersion (Barquet pp. 23–54). By adopting the voice and perspective of the house, Loynaz humanizes it, while its former residents are progressively dehumanizing themselves. They are the ones who, upon abandoning it, reject their memories, the intimate link with this space where they were born, loved, and saw their family members die.

Dulce María Loynaz (1902–1997). Cuban poet Dulce María Loynaz receives the 1992 Cervantes Prize for literature from King Juan Carlos of Spain, 23 April 1993. NEWSCOM

SYMBOLIC SPACES

The family space as reservoir of identity is a subject dear to Loynaz: Bárbara, the young protagonist of *Jardín*, reconstructs her own being on old photographs and the sinister legacy of the anonymous love letters of another woman, an ancestor of hers with a similar name. Another symbolic space frequently found in Loynaz's writing is the sea. Its loss, the horizon erased by the new cement buildings, confronts the possibility of movement, of spaciousness, with the static grayness of the recent constructions. The opposition between movement/freedom and stillness/enclosure evolves from her attempt to portray the past as better than the present particularly in regard to how progress and technology disrupt the memory of the former self-sufficient time, in which life was happy, a past that, in terms of the house/nation metaphor, can also be understood as a time before the U.S. intervention, at the very beginning of the twentieth century in Cuba.

For a person with strong Spanish roots such as Dulce María Loynaz—whose deep commitment is also expressed in her dedication to the Academia Cubana de la Lengua (Cuban Academy of the Spanish Language), which she directed until her death—modernization (often perceived as Americanization) can be considered a pernicious influence on the Cuban nation. Raúl Hernández Novás compared the poetic work of Loynaz with the participation of her father, General Enrique Loynaz del Castillo (1871–1963), in the Cuban war of independence: "To raise a literary work of resistance in solitude, in the void, without echo, in a struggle against more than conventionalism—often against oneself—can also be an act of heroism" (quoted in Simón p. 227). The many possible readings of *Últimos días de una casa* are testimony to the richness of this poem, which reads like a performed theatrical monologue. Scholarly analyses of the poem show that it may be read fruitfully not only in comparison with the work of the poet's contemporaries but for insight into the entire body of her work.

CONTEMPORARY CONCERNS AND INFLUENCES

In one poem Loynaz states, "I will care for the house and the garden," spaces conceived as strongholds where the *I* is maintained intact and protected from the outside world and a future that is almost always unpredictable or simply unnecessary. Her focus on the past and the intimate undoubtedly influenced the perception of her work as frozen in time —"I stayed outside of time," she wrote—a unique plot of modernist stamp and intimist tone. Critics have often referred to the secret, the mysterious, the ungraspable in her poetry and to the lack of sustained development in her writing (Arcos p. xxviii), but those who read her work carefully, from beginning to end, understand that she responded (albeit discreetly) to the same concerns and influences as her contemporaries. The mark of García Lorca's musicality can be found in her work, even in some of the austere verses in *Poemas sin nombre* (Unnamed Poems, 1953). In her novel *Jardín* readers observe gestures of the avant-garde and themes beloved by the precursors of the Latin American Boom of the 1960s. In this, the novel is similar to Alejo Carpentier's *Los pasos perdidos* (The Lost Steps, 1953), which also expresses the urge to rewrite—as Cinto Vitier and Fina García Marruz (Simón pp. 160, 549) noted at their time—the traditional so-called novel of the land. The same can be said for her preoccupation with the social status of women and the consequences of infertility, divorce, and motherhood on their everyday lives.

Some of her other texts were autobiographical: *Un verano en Tenerife* (One Summer in Tenerife, 1958), a stylized chronicle of a trip to the Canary Islands homeland of her second husband, Pablo Álvarez de Cañas; and the exceptional testimonial *Fe de vida* (Proof of Life, 1993), in which she bitterly relates the final years of her life—a text without grand stylistic pretensions, but one that provides valuable insight into her motives.

Loynaz's decision to publish nearly all of her works in Spain and to remain outside of literary circles fueled the misconception that her work is detached from that of her contemporaries, as if hers is an exception to the national literary tradition. Her works were kept from Cuban readers for many years, above all when, after the revolution, the critical debate privileged historical and social realism in literature. However, with the publication of Loynaz's *Poesías escogidas* (Selected Poems) in 1985, the work of Dulce María Loynaz once again circulated among Cuban readers and captured the attention of critics. In 1987, Loynaz received the Premio Nacional de Literatura (National Award for Literature). The magazines *Vitral* (Pinar del Río), *Anthropos* (Barcelona), *Iztapalapa* (Mexico City), and *La Gaceta de Cuba* (Havana), among others, have dedicated special issues to her. She received the Cervantes Prize in 1992, which revived interest in her early works and led to numerous republications. By the early 2000s, the literary legacy of Loynaz, and her place in the Cuban canon, seemed assured.

BIBLIOGRAPHY

Selected Works by Dulce María Loynaz

Ensayos literarios. Salamanca, Spain: Universidad de Salamanca, 1993.

Poesía completa. Havana: Letras Cubanas, 1993.

Un verano en Tenerife. Havana: Letras Cubanas, 1994.

Fe de vida: Evocación de Pablo Álvarez de Cañas y el mundo en que vivió: Memorias. Havana: Letras Cubanas, 1995.

Cartas que no se extraviaron. Valladolid, Spain: Fundación Jorge Guillén; Pinar del Río, Cuba: Fundación Hermanos Loynaz, 1997.

Jardín: Novela lírica. Havana: Letras Cubanas, 2002.

Against Heaven: Selected Poems, translated by James O'Connor. Manchester, U.K.: Carcanet, 2007.

Secondary Sources

Álvarez González, Ileana, and Francis Sánchez Rodríguez. *Dulce María Loynaz: La agonía de un mito*. Havana: Centro Juan Marinello, 2001.

Arcos, Jorge Luis, ed. *Las palabras son islas: Panorama de la poesía cubana siglo XX (1900–1998)*. Havana: Letras Cubanas, 1999.

Barquet, Jesús J. *Escrituras poéticas de una nación: Dulce María Loynaz, Juana Rosa Pita y Carlota Caulfield*. Havana: Ediciones Unión, 1999.

Capote Cruz, Zaida. *Contra el silencio: Otra lectura de la obra de Dulce María Loynaz*. Havana: Letras Cubanas, 2005.

Davies, Catherine. *A Place in the Sun? Women Writers in Twentieth Century Cuba*. London: Zed Books, 1997.

Garrandés, Alberto. *Silencio y destino: Anatomía de una novela lírica*. Havana: Letras Cubanas, 1996.

Martínez Malo, Aldo. *Confesiones de Dulce María Loynaz*. Havana: José Martí, 1999.

Simón, Pedro, ed. *Dulce María Loynaz*. Havana: Centro de Investigaciones Literarias, Casa de las Américas, 1991.

VALLE DE VIÑALES

Reinaldo Estrada

Viñales, a heritage site for Cuba and the world.

Valle de Viñales, one of the most spectacular, important, and well-known sites in Cuba, was declared a cultural World Heritage Site by the United Nations Educational, Scientific and Cultural Organization (UNESCO) in 1999. The valley and its surrounding mountains boast superlative natural, historical, and cultural assets, which leads to Viñales being spoken of as more than just the valley itself—but as a diverse part of world heritage, both natural and cultural.

COUNTERPOINT OF TITLES AND TERRAIN

Prior to its designation as a World Heritage Site (one of nine such sites in Cuba), Valle de Viñales was declared a National Monument in 1978. The site encompasses twenty-three square miles, covering the entire valley and nearby *mogotes* (limestone outcroppings). These mogotes, resembling gigantic elephants or the organ pipes suitable for a large cathedral, serve as a backdrop for the mosaic of red soils, verdant traditional crops, palm-thatched peasants' huts and tobacco sheds with guano roofs, pines, and palms—together comprising a conceptual landscape that strikes wonder in the visitor at first sight. Yet, Viñales clearly encompasses much more than its spectacular traditional valley landscape.

The mountainous limestone outcroppings—running from San Vicente and Guasasa to Pan de Azúcar and Infierno, which are part of the Sierra de los Órganos, together with some isolated mogotes, small portions of Valle de Viñales, and other valleys and

■ *See also*

Ecology and Environment: Revolutionary Period

Spain's "Discovery" of Cuba: 1492

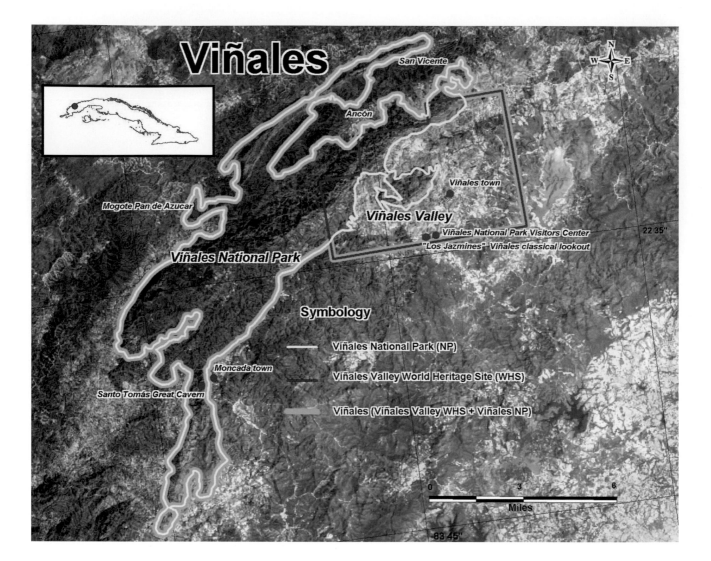

Figure 1. Viñales Valley World Heritage Site, Viñales National Park, and the surrounding area in Pinar del Río Province. LIC REINALDO ESTRADA, FUNDACIÓN ANTONIO NÚÑEZ JIMÉNEZ DE LA NATURALEZA Y EL HOMBRE

lesser mountains—were declared Viñales National Park in 2001 because of their natural assets, which meet the requirements for this category established by the International Union for Conservation of Nature (IUCN). In addition, the region has been considered for nomination as a Biosphere Reserve. Extending 42.93 square miles, this national park, together with the Valle de Viñales World Heritage Site and surrounding areas (see Figure 1), are all referred to below as Viñales. Within the inseparable dichotomy of valleys and mountains, the former cannot be grandiose without the peaks arising from the same bedrock, to which they owe their noble lineage. The sum total of this region's great natural, historic, and cultural value make it a World Heritage Site.

AMONG THE WONDERS OF THE WORLD: ORIGINS, GEOLOGY, AND TERRAIN

Viñales, centered in the municipality of the same name in the westernmost province of Cuba, Pinar del Río, is situated in the Cordillera de Guaniguanico, in the limestone ridges of the Sierra de los Órganos and the Alturas de Pizarras. The mogotes (the Cuban term that has worldwide recognition) are the distinguishing feature of the Sierra de los Órganos. Similar to what is known in English as *tower karst* or *cone karst*, or in Chinese as *fenglin* or *fengcong*, the mogotes of Viñales are among the largest in the world, with heights of up to 1,600 feet, vertical walls that reach over 660 feet, and rounded peaks. Only a very few sites in the world—such as Guilin-Yangshuo, Wulong, and Libo (China); Ha Long Bay (Vietnam); Phang Nga Bay (Thailand); and Sangkulirang (Indonesia)—reach this magnitude with similarly spectacular topography, while other Caribbean sites in Puerto Rico and Jamaica are of a lesser scale.

The mogotes were formed from dark massive or stratified limestone dating from the Late Jurassic to the Late Cretaceous periods (161 million to 65 million years ago). Their nonporous limestone composition, massiveness, and cracking allow runoff from rainfall and rivers to flow through crevices and faults, where it

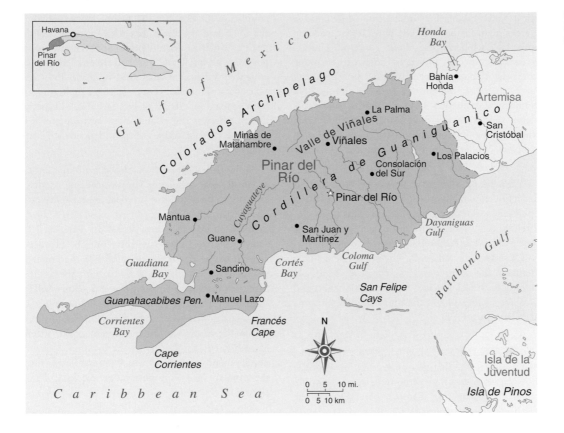

has worked together with the processes of dissolution and erosion to gradually carve away the biggest of the Cuban cave systems.

The system of caves, caverns, and pits found in Viñales comprises an entire underground network, with between five and fourteen levels of caverns, making this area the capital of Cuban subterranean cave systems. Notable systems include the Gran Caverna de Santo Tomás, a national monument that spans more than 28 miles and that because of its extensive development and beauty is considered "the Princess of Cuban Caves," and the Palmarito–Novillo–Pan de Azúcar cave system, the largest in the country, covering more than 31 miles.

Surrounding the mogote-filled mountain ranges are the Northern and Southern Alturas de Pizarras, chains of mountainous peaks formed of quartz, slate, and sandstone dating to the Early through Late Jurassic—the oldest rocks in the region are some 200 million years old. These ranges, completely unlike the mogotes, are mountains with gentle slopes and rich networks of waterways. Running toward the limestone mountains and under the influence of past up-and-down fluctuations of terrain and sea level, they have played a fundamental role in the origin of the cave systems in this area. In the zone of contact between the Alturas de Pizarras and the mogotes, the differential erosion between the former—soft and easily eroded—and the hard limestone that makes up the mogotes,

together with the mogotes' processes of dissolving, collapsing, and retreating under the influence of the tropical climate, have given rise to fertile intermountain karst valleys, of which the Valle de Viñales is the best example.

Fossils of fauna and flora dating back to the Jurassic period are relatively abundant in the region's rocks and caves and include ammonites, dinosaurs, and ichthyosaurs, as well as more modern Pleistocene fauna such as sloths, Cuban solenodons, and monkeys. This makes Viñales one of the most important paleontological sites in the Caribbean.

A curiosity in and of itself is the existence in the Moncada region of rocks offering evidence of one of the most important events in the history of the world: the impact of a gigantic meteorite in Chicxulub, Yucatan Peninsula, 65 million years ago. This event is considered to be the primary cause of the extinction of the dinosaurs.

FLORA AND FAUNA

Like the mogotes, the flora and fauna of Viñales are the result of the area's evolutionary history, climate, and geology. They have a unique international value owing to their characteristics, level of conservation, and endemism.

The Alturas de Pizarras, covered with pine groves, and the mogotes with their mesophytic-forested slopes, xerophytic-capped summits, and nearly naked vertical walls, establish a fundamental difference in the area's plant formations. The pine groves, made up mainly of Caribbean pine (*Pinus caribaea*), contain few endemic species, but most noteworthy among them is the island's only endemic oak, the Cuban oak (*Quercus cubana*). The greatest degree of unique flora is found in the mogotes, home to approximately 232 endemic species, twenty-three of them local, including a true jewel—a living fossil in danger of extinction—*Microcycas calocoma* (cork palm), the only endemic species in the genus *Microcycas*.

The area's fauna, both above and below ground, is also highly endemic, particularly within the mollusk, amphibian, and reptile groups, where Cuba holds global relevance. Viñales continues to have the greatest richness of land mollusks in Cuba, with some 136 species (Oliva-Olivera and Real), of which 90 percent are endemic to the country and 33 percent are regionally or locally endemic. Notable for their uniqueness and beauty are such species as the land snails *Viana regina* and *Blaesospira echinus*.

There are thirty-three species of amphibians and reptiles in this area, of which thirty are endemic. Notable among the first group are amphibians of the genus *Eleutherodactylus*, while noteworthy reptiles include the Cuban boa (*Epicrates angulifer*) and the River lizard *Anolis vermiculatus*.

Birds are well represented by species that stand out for their uniqueness, coloring, song, or size. Noteworthy species include the Cuban solitaire (*Myadestes elisabeth*), the Cuban trogon or *tocororo* (the island's national bird, *Priotelus temnurus*), the Cuban tody (*Todus multicolor*), and the bee hummingbird or *zunzuncito* (*Mellisuga helenae*), which is the smallest bird in the world.

HISTORY, CULTURE, AND TRADITIONS

The first residents of Viñales were indigenous hunter-gatherers who were rapidly exterminated during the period of Spanish colonization. Evidence of these people exists through archaeological remains and pictographs and petroglyphs found at some sixty sites, almost all in caves.

The first historical reports of the area were made in 1607, when the San Francisco de Viñales livestock ranch was granted to Bernardo Bernabé Sánchez. There are few subsequent references to the area, which remained relatively unpopulated and unknown. This, together with the rugged character of the mogote-studded ranges, the abundance of water, and the mountain pits and caves, made the area a haven for runaway slaves, or *cimarrones*, of whom evidence has been found at more than forty sites.

The traditionally low population level in the Vuelta Abajo, as Pinar del Río was called, is partly related to the fact that the town of Viñales was not founded until 1868, with its main activity concentrated on the cultivation of tobacco. The planned development of the town and the main axis road encouraged urban features (such as alignment, masonry houses; broad porches with brick columns; and *criollo* tiles) that have enhanced Viñales' architectural value. In the Cuban War of Independence (1895–1898), people who were born or lived in Viñales played a vital role. Especially noteworthy was the valiant nurse and captain of the *mambisas* (female soldiers of the independence), Adela Azcuy.

The recognition of Viñales as a unique location began in 1909, when the Cuban academic Carlos de la Torre, in his search for proof of the existence of the Jurassic period in the Caribbean, discovered the first ammonite fossils in Puerta de Ancón. Later, in 1916, the North American naturalist John B. Henderson referred to the area when he published the important results of his expedition to Cuba with the Smithsonian Institution, describing the marvelous Valle de Viñales and comparing it with Yosemite Valley and the Colorado River's Grand Canyon. Beginning in the 1920s, the medicinal mineral waters in San Vicente, in addition to the beauty of the location, fueled the development of tourism, which spread knowledge of the zone to various important people in Cuba and elsewhere.

Two key figures in the national and international popularization of the area were Dr. Pedro García Valdés, "The Best Singer of Viñales Valley," and Domingo Ramos, "The Valley Painter," both later immortalized in commemorative busts there. In 1936 García Valdés published *El valle de Viñales*, which was republished eighteen times by 1953. This text describes Viñales in beautiful poetic prose. Ramos, a landscape painter, exhibited his paintings of the area in 1939, during the Century of Progress Exposition in New York City, where the beauty he depicted was so great that a visiting artist even questioned whether the place was real. A phenomenon that brought national attention arose around that same time: the appearance of the cult (later a legend, tradition, and local myth) of the Acuáticos who "healed" using water. The cult began in 1936 when a peasant woman, Antoñica Izquierdo, supposedly cured her child with nothing more than this liquid.

Other prominent Cuban figures have made Viñales the subject of their work. Notably, the writer Dora Alonso located her work *El valle de la Pájara Pinta* (Valley of the Painted Bird, 1984) there, while her poem "Testamento" (Testament, 1987) reflects her desire to be buried in Viñales. The geographer, explorer, spelunker, and revolutionary army captain Antonio Núñez Jiménez, the so-called Fourth Discoverer of Cuba, merits special mention. From 1943 until his death in 1998, Jiménez conducted numerous expeditions to study the area and its caves, including the Gran Caverna de Santo Tomás, founding the National School of Spelunking at the mount to this important cave.

REVOLUTIONARY PERIOD AND VIÑALES IN THE EARLY 2000s

In 1959, the year the Cuban Revolution triumphed, Fidel Castro, Núñez Jiménez, and others created the first revolutionary militia in this zone. Known as the Malagones, these twelve peasants were organized to capture Cabo Lara, leader of a criminal rebel gang in the region. With their success the Malagones demonstrated the feasibility of this type of militia for combating insurgents.

In Viñales, as in all of Cuba, the revolution brought great social and economic change, including a forward push in the development of tourism and the conservation of the area. These changes were not without problems, but they did not alter the area's traditional essence. During this period, facilities for tourist services were built (and many existing facilities were rebuilt, respecting their significance), including the Antonio Núñez Jiménez National School of Spelunking, the Monument to the Malagones, the Viñales National Park visitor center, along with various museums, cultural centers, and other buildings.

The construction of the community of Moncada, following an original system of planning and architectural style that was integrated with the landscape, deserves particular mention. So too does the *Mural de la Prehistoria*, painted in 1959 by Leovigildo González (disciple of the Mexican muralist Diego Rivera), a monumental work 393 feet high painted on the wall of a mogote.

Alongside the traditional cultivation of tobacco and other crops, tourism has become one of the principal economic activities in Viñales, due to the region's natural assets and beauty. To the development of these natural assets can be added the hospitality, customs, and rural traditions of the local people, which can be appreciated in the area's houses and rustic huts, especially in sites such as the Jardín de Caridad y Carmen (Caridad and Carmen's Garden), created over many years as an example of love of nature.

BIBLIOGRAPHY

Conseil National du Patrimoine Culturel. "Le Vallée de Viñales, Pinar del Río." Havana: 1998.

Corvea, Jose Luis, Martín Luis López, Roberto Novo, et al. *Plan de Manejo Parque Nacional Viñales, 2004–2008.* Centro de Investigaciones y Servicios Ambientales ECOVIDA. Ministerio de Ciencia, Tecnología y Medio Ambiente. Unpublished manuscript, last modified 2003.

Gaiga, Joaquín. *La Cruz al pie de los Mogotes: Apuntes para la historia de Viñales.* Pinar del Río, Cuba: Ediciones Vitral, 2008.

Hamilton-Smith, Elery. "Thinking about Karst and World Heritage." *Helictite* 39, no. 2 (2006): 51–54.

Hernández, Pedro Luis, and Rosa Pablos de la Rosa, eds. "Arqueología." Special issue, *El Explorador: Periódico digital espeleológico.* 7 August 2007. Available from http://www.geda.pinarte.cult.cu

Iturralde-Vinent, Manuel A. "Los mogotes de la Sierra de los Órganos, Pinar del Río: Su origen, desarrollo y desaparición." *Boletín informativo de la Comisión de Geoespeleología* (Federación Espeleológica de América Latina y el Caribe), no. 63 (September 2005): 2–8. Available from http://www.fealc.org/boletines/.

Larramendi, Julio, Jorge Freddy Ramírez Pérez, Pedro Luis Hernández Pérez, and Jorge Luis Zamora Martín. *Viñales de Cuba.* Havana: Editorial José Martí, 2005.

Luis López, Martín. "En Viñales I." *Viajes Cuba Blog,* 12 January 2008. Available from http://www.umbrellatravel.com/cubablog/es/?p=10.

Molerio León, Leslie F. "Los mogotes del valle de Viñales, Monumento Nacional, Pinar del Río, Cuba." *Mapping interactivo: Revista internacional de ciencias de la tierra,* no. 98 (November–December 2004). Available from http://www.mappinginteractivo.com/plantilla-ante.asp?id_articulo=815.

Núñez Jiménez, Antonio. "Cuba: Joya del Caribe; El valle de Viñales." Fundación Antonio Núñez Jiménez de la Naturaleza y el Hombre. Unpublished.

Oliva-Olivera, Wilfredo, and Raimundo Real. "Moluscos terrestres de las elevaciones cársticas de Viñales, Pinar del Río, Cuba." *Revista de Biología Tropical* 57, no. 3 (2009): 589–604.

United Nations Educational, Scientific and Cultural Organization (UNESCO). "World Heritage List: Viñales Valley." Available from http://whc.unesco.org/en/list/840.

VARADERO

María Eugenia Alegría Núñez

The history of Cuba's tourism capital.

The short history of Varadero includes some of the most important moments of Cuba's national life. A small town at the turn of the twentieth century, it became a popular destination for tourists.

Varadero is located in the province of Matanzas, on the narrow Hicacos Peninsula that juts at an angle into the Straits of Florida from the northern coast of Cuba, north of the city of Cárdenas. After briefly being its own municipality, it once more became administratively a part of Cárdenas in 2010. Varadero's northern shore consists of fourteen miles of fine white sand on the clear blue waters of the Straits; to its south lies the Bay of Cárdenas, its grayish-green water dotted with rocks and reefs against low, swampy terrain.

The region was originally inhabited by pre-agricultural and pre-ceramic communities as early as 3,000 years ago. During the sixteenth, seventeenth, and eighteenth centuries Varadero was the site of significant economic activity, especially generated by its famous salt mines. The city's role in tourism dates from

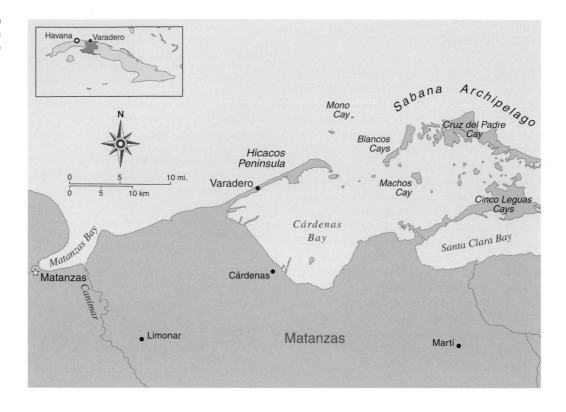

1883, when a group of ten landowners and businessmen from the city of Cárdenas, known as the Decenviros, formed a corporation to promote Varadero as an idyllic summer vacation spot for the wealthy, who enjoyed its beaches, large dunes, and sandy paths lined with oleander and periwinkle.

THE ERA OF THE CUBAN REPUBLIC (1902–1959)

The advent of the Cuban Republic in 1898 was linked to the birth of Varadero as a tourist destination, and a sporting event was the spark that signaled its development. In 1910 a group of college students from Cárdenas and Havana decided to hold a rowing competition that soon received the support of Havana sports clubs and the founding members in Cárdenas of the Club Náutico de Varadero boating club. The extraordinary popularity of these regattas brought the Playa Azul (Blue Beach), as Varadero is also called, national and international attention. The regattas became a tradition of Varadero, and though they maintained great popular support and were, in truth, a festivity for all Cubans, they were exclusive events for wealthy members of sporting clubs. The revolutionary government proposed to change this elitist image of sports: It created schools and sport centers all over the country for ordinary people and established a new National Rowing School in Varadero. Although the city continued hosting regattas, Varadero lost its traditional role as having a hometown team that faced rival regional challengers,

because teams were now made up of athletes from all over the country selected for their competitive ability and not for their place of origin. However, these competitions received scarce official promotion. The once famous regatta of Varadero lost its fascination and became, simply, just another sporting event. At the same time, the number of U.S. tourists visiting Varadero, especially as a winter vacation spot, increased significantly in response to a real estate company's promotion of the resort in 1910.

The year 1926 marked the arrival of U.S. millionaire Irenée Dupont (1876–1963), a particularly controversial figure in Varadero's history. Many consider Dupont a philanthropist, others a predatory colonialist, but there is no doubt that he did wonders for the resort. The construction and sanitation work he subsidized for his own benefit boosted the town's prosperity and tourism development, resulting in considerable urbanization and the construction of large houses, small hotels, and guest houses that offered a less expensive alternative for vacationers. Then in the 1950s the peninsula attracted the attention of large investors. On 24 December 1950, the Hotel Internacional opened its doors. Built in the style of major U.S. hotels, it was the most important structure built in all of Matanzas until the building boom of the 1990s. In the residential sector, Cuba's wealthiest families and many foreigners, especially from the United States, built mansions of considerable architectural interest. More and more middle-class families and professionals took up residence in Varadero; however, fishermen

A luxury hotel in the resort town of Varadero. In the mid-1970s, the Cuban government opened the country to foreign tourists, and Varadero, with its beach, white sands, and blue waters, became the country's top tourist destination.
© MARKA/ALAMY

on the southern coast living in poverty and unhealthy conditions could not benefit from the peninsula's growing prosperity.

In 1955, as part of an effort to promote Varadero's role in international tourism, Fulgencio Batista's government undertook projects such as a drawbridge fascilitating access to the peninsula; an aqueduct; the southern highway, the Vía Blanca highway; and the international airport. These advances greatly increased Cuban and U.S. tourism to the beach resort, so much so that in 1958, despite political unrest and the imminent triumph of the Revolution, Varadero broke all records for the number of visitors. At that time, a social commentator dubbed Varadero "Cuba's tourism capital," a name by which it was known thereafter (Álvarez Blanco and Iglesias Oduardo p. 126).

AFTER THE REVOLUTION

The Revolution succeeded on 1 January 1959. The revolutionary government undertook profound social reforms that lasted until the late 1980s, when the collapse of the Soviet bloc set off an enormous crisis within Cuban society that fractured its earlier idealism.

One of the first laws passed by the revolutionary government decreed that all Cubans should have total access to the island's beaches. The first year the government initiated a large public works program; in Varadero, the Granma residential district was built, as was the Parque de las 8000 Taquillas (Park of the 8,000 Lockers), providing day lockers for thousands of beachgoers. The following year the 1ro de enero (1st of January) neighborhood was built for fishing families living in the slum known as Tibores.

In those early years of the Revolution, Varadero witnessed heavy class antagonism, given its characteristics as a beach resort and its extreme social contrasts. The region's new authorities committed willful acts of destruction, such as the demolition of the Club Náutico in 1962, and of many beautiful beachfront houses. An urban legend offers a curious explanation for these actions: On a trip to Varadero, revolutionary leader Fidel Castro (b. 1926) made a casual comment about how lovely the beach would look if it were lined with large pine trees, so a functionary ordered that the houses along the beach be torn down so that thousands of seedlings could be planted. Whatever the reasons for it, the results were horrible. Coastal vegetation on the dune was destroyed and organic debris from the trees sullied the sands. It was not until the early 1970s, when more capable authorities issued orders to cut down the pine trees, that the sands turned white again.

Starting in the mid-1960s, Varadero was the home of so-called revolutionary tourism, in which rooms in the major hotels and buildings in the Granma district were booked for outstanding small farmers and workers from all over the country, in a process known as Emulation Socialista (socialist competitiveness).

Given the country's higher standard of living, fueled by wage increases and social reforms, Varadero became the most popular destination for Cuban tourists. Until the late 1970s there was virtually no international tourism in Cuba, and government investment in that field was minimal. The beautiful mansions in the Kawama neighborhood along the canal were turned into schools, and the elegant residences in Reparto de la Torre became guest houses for government agencies.

In the mid-1970s the government decided to open Cuba to foreign tourists, and Varadero became the country's top tourist destination. In 1972 the first Canadian tourists arrived. Houses that had been used as schools or government guest houses were converted into tourist villages. In 1980 the Hotel Siboney, the first hotel built since 1958, was inaugurated. The following year the Atabey opened, and remodeling began on buildings that would soon be the Hotel Bellamar.

During this period, the country's economic and social recovery was reflected in the population's prosperity; Cubans frequented restaurants and discotheques, took excursions and stayed in hotels that still accepted Cubans and foreigners on an almost equal basis. All the streets of Varadero were paved, and much of the city was painted and fixed up. Varadero was extremely attractive to tourists, and the interaction among Cubans and foreigners was quite comfortable, despite the large economic gap between the two groups.

CRISIS IN THE 1990s AND BEYOND

With the fall of the Berlin Wall and the later dissolution of the Soviet Union and its Comecon trading bloc, Cuba fell into a major economic and social crisis due to its heavy dependence on those countries. When the Special Period—the official name for this unprecedented crisis—was declared, international tourism became a survival strategy at a time when the U.S. trade embargo intensified Cuba's economic problems. Varadero was abuzz with hotel construction as joint ventures injected much-needed foreign capital.

The Playa Azul became absurdly and unnaturally polarized. Segregation by nationality was implemented, and Cubans were prohibited from entering hotels. In a very short time, as a consequence of the country's impoverishment, Varadero turned into a center for prostitution, corruption, and drugs. The territory was burdened with the stigma of sexual tourism. Prostitutes of both sexes abounded, the most evident being very young females, most of them from the impoverished provinces of eastern Cuba. Faced with this scandalous state of affairs, the highest levels of government finally instituted measures to end the situation or at least reduce it substantially. Hundreds of females were sent back to their hometowns or to jail, depending on the gravity of their activities, and the full weight of the law was brought to bear on pimps and other offenders.

In that period, other steps taken to improve Cuba's financial situation were, in a sense, signs of the times. In 1994 it became legal for Cubans to possess foreign currency, and this was quite a boon for the residents of Varadero, who began to remodel and even rebuild their homes with high-quality materials, often purchased from hotel construction workers.

In the early 1990s large hotels were built in an unpopulated area of the peninsula. With the establishment of all-inclusive resorts, Varadero became an isolated tourism enclave. Nightlife was limited to hotel discotheques and a few uncrowded bars. The city, saved from its former scourge, languished at nightfall, its deserted avenues often only partially lighted. By day it was a typical Cuban city, with a working population that went to bed early. Nonetheless, in the three years preceding 2010, it maintained the miraculous total of one million visitors annually, according to Ventura De Jesús in a 2010 article for *Granma*.

Varadero's beach is a tropical paradise to some, with its mild climate, white sands, and blue waters, but an austere disappointment to others who, disgusted by the uniformity of the hotels, long for cultural contact and social integration between Cubans and foreigners. Yet Varadero, that gift of nature, has been made what it is by history.

BIBLIOGRAPHY

Abad, Ángel. *Historia de las Parroquias de Cárdenas y Varadero*. Havana: Guerrero, 1954.

Álvarez Blanco, Ernesto, and Teresa Iglesias Oduardo. *Varadero, de caserío a centro turístico, 1883–1958*. Matanzas, Cuba: Ediciones Matanzas, 2008.

Comisión de Historia del Comité Municipal del Partido Comunista de Cuba. *Apuntes para la Historia de Varadero*. Available at the José Smith Comas Library, Varadero, Cuba.

De Jesús, Ventura. "Varadero alista sus playas." *Granma* (Havana) (November 10, 2010): 2.

Fernández, Olga. *Varadero, la gran playa azul*. Havana: Ediciones Turisticas, 1983.

Roig de Leuchsenring, Emilio. "Varadero." *Revista Social* 1, no. 8 (1916).

Sainsbury, Brendan. *Cuba*, 5th ed. Footscray, Victoria, Australia: Lonely Planet, 2009.

VERSOS SENCILLOS (JOSÉ MARTÍ)

Caridad Atencio

The most important and best-known book of poetry written by Cuba's national hero.

Versos sencillos (Simple Verses, 1891) is the most important and best-known book of poetry written by José Martí (1853–1895); it is his "poetic testament" (García Marruz 1995, p. 87). These verses represent not only the most refined of Martí's art, but also the

■ *See also*

"La Guantanamera"

José Martí: Exile in New York

José Martí: Political Essays

José Martí: Writings for and about Children

Spanish-American-Cuban War: 1898

culmination of his thought. Published in October 1891 in New York City, the book was the result of Martí's involvement in social and political work aimed at organizing Cuba's Necessary War (1895–1898) to obtain independence from Spain. It was written on the occasion of the Pan American Conference of 1889:

> where, as he said, "under the frightful eagle" of Washington our American peoples met, and it was the fruit of anguish, as Martí states in the prologue, of knowing that one of the underlying purposes of the Conference was Palmer's proposition to Spain that the U.S. purchase Cuba, which is stated in a letter to his friend Enrique Estrázulas [...] and which, fortunately, Spain did not accept.
>
> *García Marruz 1995, p. 84*

In the book's prologue Martí alludes to this event and more broadly to U.S. ambitions. These issues are essential to the poetry, though they are not repeated throughout the work. On 13 December 1890 he gave a public reading of his verses in his home, and on that evening the idea to publish them was born, despite Martí's earlier opposition to making poetry a commercial object.

FORM AND CONTENT

Between 1889 and 1891 several fundamental events occurred in Martí's life. He separated permanently from his wife, and he was appointed consul of Argentina and Paraguay, then resigned those positions, as well as his position as consul of Uruguay. He resigned as correspondent with *La Nación* (The Nation) of Buenos Aires and formed the Partido Revolucionario Cubano (Cuban Revolutionary Party). He attended the First International Conference of American States in Washington, D.C., which prompted his Americanist discourse and the essay "Nuestra América" (Our America). He was also a delegate in the International Monetary Conference. Martí left *La Edad de Oro* (The Golden Age) because he disagreed with the editor on religious education, and he published *Versos sencillos* (Rama pp. 353–354). All these events—personal, political, philosophical, religious, and literary—influenced the hybrid text *Versos sencillos*. Reading the poems requires identifying the heterogeneous nuances that reveal how form and content combine—in other words, how the poet displays stylistic simplicity and complexity at the same time.

The poems are composed in octosyllabic lines that at times make up couplets, quartets, or roundelays—stanzas that are part of European literary tradition. But while Martí restores the medieval metric form of the *copla de arte menor* (verse of lesser art), he exploits its possibilities and peculiarities, creating tension between related and unrelated elements in the poems. Many academics assert that *Versos sencillos* is a compendium of the critical moments of Martí's life. Both bare and mysterious, the work reveals the multiplicity of expressive resources at work in these extremely polished poems. Hyperbaton and ellipsis play a central role; alliteration and repetition convey what Martí called "a consonant of intention." Indeed, repetitions of words and even verses serve as a sort of semantic game. In addition, a metric process uses graphic rhyme, contrasting rhyme that puts together words of dissimilar semantic types (such as *palma* and *alma* in the first stanza of Poem I). Other stylistic features include plasticity and coloring, a variety of rhythmic effects, and the absence of rhyme. All of these techniques give the poetry a richness and diversity that contributes to its metric form (where the poems are numbered rather than titled) and the contemplation it prompts. These poems are unique in their use of thematic elements that encapsulate ethical, philosophical, aesthetic, and other ideas; they express a worldview at an artistic level by drawing on the influences of other writers, styles, and literary traditions.

All the poems share a single subject, according to the critic Cintio Vitier: the contradictory, painful unity of life (p. 163). In *Versos sencillos*, Martí evokes those moments that create song, because the history that remains untouched by time in memory is the essence of song. This movement from story to song is what gives air and light to the verses; the fair and tranquil condition in the midst of suffering is reflected in the vocal structure of the verse and in the opening to another order of reality or law of harmonious similarity (García Marruz 1969, p. 253). Upon examination it becomes clear that Martí's simple poetry is also about content, not just structural force, but not so much for its intellectual discourse as for its meaning (Rama). These are ways of thinking, using the specific and the particular details of the reality they address; they are materials submitted to a rationality that was central to the poet who rejected rhetoric and ornamentation as nonessential elements (Rama p. 369).

The artistic innovations that Martí used in *Versos sencillos* and in his other writings, complemented by a number of original theories equally well formulated, arose as a consequence of Martí's wish to renew the rhetorical and academic style that predominated during the second half of the nineteenth century. Modernism is found in the open and multifaceted text of *Versos sencillos*, combating verbosity and defending the vigorous, sober style that is elegant and deep in sentiment. The style is enriched with techniques from the classic Spanish golden age and from foreign contemporary literature. In these poems, Martí discovered color, plasticity, the exacting workmanship of nineteenth-century Parnassianism, music, nuance, and the vagueness of the French symbolists (González and Schulman p. 115). In sum, it is an emancipating text, playfully educational with innovative text and lexicon that adapts the cultural stores of the west and the east in an attempt to define its identity in terms of otherness (Schulman p. 98).

RECOVERING THE U. S. HISPANIC LITERARY HERITAGE

Versos sencillos/Simple Verses

José Martí

Translated, with an Introduction, by Manuel A. Tellechea

Versos sencillos is modernist in its attempts to annul the historical process that undermined the objective value of human perceptions and to validate and recollect the historical quality of experience through the narration of subjective visions. Martí records his memories and visions to create a political text that authorizes the individual who makes sense of what would otherwise be a senseless world, and he broadens the field of poetic discourse to include struggle and subversion, signs of the universal remolding and transfiguration of modernity (Schulman pp. 98–99).

HISTORY AND NATURE

In *Versos sencillos*, story portrays itself. The poet enters an event directly, without saying he is going to tell a story, although he does just that. He portrays (narrates, evokes) the experience of the lyrical self, showing nature in terms of experiences. This reflection of the historical makes use of various resources. In Verse XLV, for example, the lyric self assumes the duties of a hero called to account by earlier generations of heroes: "Mute, I kiss your hand." Verse XXVII refers to the bloody fracas at the Villanueva Theater on 22 January 1869 that pitted Spanish volunteers against the *criollo* sympathizers of independence, indistinctly moving from past to present from one stanza to the next. The stanzas written in the past tense recount less dramatic events; the more harrowing events are related in the present: "El enemigo brutal / Nos pone fuego a la casa / El sable la calle arrasa, / A la luna tropical" (The brutal enemy / Sets fire to the house / The saber destroys the street / Under the tropical moon). In Verse XXX, nature increases the horror of slavery in strokes both contained and harrowing: "Salió el sol al horizonte; / Y alumbró un esclavo muerto / Colgado a un seibo del monte" (The sun rose on the horizon; / And lit upon a dead slave / Hanged from a mountain ceibo tree). In Verse XXXIV, personal pain is renounced for the fight against the world's pain: "Yo sé de un pesar profundo / Entre las penas sin nombres: / ¡La esclavitud de los hombres / Es la gran pena del mundo!" (I know a deep sorrow / Among sorrows unspeakable / The enslavement of men / Is the great sorrow of the world!).

Nature functions as the support and foundation of projection and return. In his vision Martí prioritizes the cycle of nature: The poetry in *Versos sencillos* alludes to the maxim of Ralph Waldo Emerson (1803–1882) that nature is the symbol of spirit. It is not the "objective nature of Bello's Neoclassical Ode, nor the subjective nature of Heredia's Romantic Ode, nor the nature suggested by the country-city dichotomy of the Modernists" (García Marruz 1995, p. 84); what differentiates Martí's vision of nature from Emerson's is the role that Martí assigns to sacrifice as an essential condition for transforming and bringing balance to nature. This becomes the historical commitment of the Cuban national hero. Although North American transcendentalists, particularly Emerson, influenced Martí's conception of the harmonic balance of nature, the neutralizing ennoblement of *feismo* (ugliness) can be traced to Walt Whitman (1819–1892) and the realist school of literature and art. Beyond these artistic sources, this praise is derived from Martí's own experience tirelessly working in New York City to help the masses of poor immigrants (Rama p. 372). Vitier wrote that the lines—"Todo es hermoso y constante / Todo es música y razón / Y todo como el diamante, / Antes de luz es carbón" (All is beautiful and constant / All is music and reason / And all, like a diamond, / Is coal before becoming light)—establish the philosophy of *Versos sencillos*, in which there is total accord between man and nature.

MUSIC OF *VERSOS SENCILLOS*

Based on this accord that he calls the foundation of form, Martí divides his poetry into specific themes, but that does not break the fundamental rhythm, the constant flow of cosmic harmony that, according to Vitier, is the unyielding discovery of these verses. Vitier wrote:

> in *Versos sencillos*, Martí assumes the voice of the people without local color, as substance and essence, in absolutely oral verses that call from their heart for the guitar, the *guajira*, the eternal melody. This was the intuitive answer of Julián Orbón in the 1950s when he discovered the possibility and marvel of singing these verses to the music of "Guantanamera."
>
> *p. 167*

"Guantanamera" is a melody of humble popular origin that, in its metamorphosis, was primarily epic and characterized a good part of Cuban identity. Though the song was originally about a woman from Guantánamo, the addition of Martí's verses gave it a timelessness that connected Cuba's colonial past with its revolutionary present. According to Manuel Villar,

> it had been sung by Joseíto Fernández, its writer, since the 1930s. The success of this work peaked when it began to be used, in interspersed decimes, in radio reports on events that had occurred, especially violent events. In 1962, Pete Seeger, known for singing protest songs, heard it sung by a choir directed by the young Héctor Angulo, with the decimes changed to quartets: the *Versos sencillos* of José Martí and with the musical structure created by the master Julián Orbón.
>
> *Iraida and Santiago pp. 105–106*

These verses to the tune of "Guantanamera" appeared in the album *We Shall Overcome*, recorded live by Pete Seeger in concert at Carnegie Hall on 8 June 1963.

The stanzas chosen for the song authenticate some of the functions of the book, offering ethical or historical-patriotic lessons and allowing an appreciation of the taste and enjoyment of the poetic text and the innate rhythm of the language. After the marriage of verses and tune, "Guantanamera" became a protest song, an anthem of battle and eternal solidarity with Martí, sung in the most important venues by some of the world's most notable singers.

The verses also were set to music by important Cuban and foreign musicians. Notable recordings include Pablo Milanés's *Versos de José Martí* (Verses of José Martí, 1978), Sara González's *José Martí. Versos cantados por Sara González* (José Martí: Verses Sung by Sara González, 1994), Amaury Pérez's *Poemas de José Martí cantados por Amaury Pérez* (Poems of José Martí Sung by Amaury Pérez, 1978), selections from Muslim Magomaev's *Canta Muslim Magomaev* (Muslim Magomaev Sings, 1986), and Oscar Chávez's *Versos sencillos cantados por Oscar Chávez* (*Versos sencillos* Sung by Oscar Chávez, 1972).

Versos sencillos has been translated in its entirety into English, French, Chinese, Romanian, Czech, Italian, Ukrainian, and Guaraní; selections have been translated into German, Russian, Polish, Hungarian, Japanese, and Moldavian. This important work is the synthesis of Martí's thinking, an outstanding book of lyrics in the Spanish language and a modern text.

BIBLIOGRAPHY
Primary Works by José Martí

Obras Completas. Havana: Editorial de Ciencias Sociales, 1975.

Versos sencillos en Obras Completas. Edición Crítica. Havana: Centro de Estudios Martianos, 2007.

Secondary Works

Atencio, Caridad. *Recepción de* Versos sencillos: *Poesía del metatexto*. Havana: Editorial Abril, 2001.

García Marruz, Fina. "Los versos de Martí." In *Temas Martianos*. Series 1. Havana: Biblioteca Nacional José Martí and Instituto Cubano del Libro, 1969.

García Marruz, Fina. "Los versos sencillos." *Casa de las Américas* 200 (July–September 1995): 83–96.

González, Manuel Pedro, and Ivan Schulman. *José Martí, Esquema Ideológico*. Mexico City: Editorial Cultura T.G. S. A, 1961.

Iraida, Sánchez Oliva, and Moreaux Jardines Santiago. *La Guantanamera*. Havana: Editorial José Martí, 1999.

Mistral, Gabriela. "Los *Versos sencillos* de José Martí." In *José Martí. Valoración múltiple*. Havana: Fondo Editorial Casa de las Américas, 2007.

Rama, Ángel. "Indagación de la ideología en la poesía. (Los dípticos seriados de Versos sencillos)." *Revista Iberoamericana* 112–113 (July–December 1980): 353–500.

Schulman, Iván. "(Re)visionando la ordenación poética de *los Versos sencillos* de José Martí." In *Vigencias:*

Martí y el modernismo. Havana: Centro de Estudios Martianos, 2005.

Vitier, Cintio. "Los *Versos sencillos*." In *Temas Martianos*. Series 1. Havana: Biblioteca Nacional José Martí e Instituto Cubano del Libro, 1969.

■ *See also*

Faith: Catholicism

Faith: Regla de Ocha and Ifá

LA VIRGEN DE LA CARIDAD DEL COBRE
Olga Sarina Portuondo Zúñiga

La Virgen del Cobre nurtures the Cuban religious soul.

La Virgen de la Caridad del Cobre—the Virgin (or Our Lady) of Charity of El Cobre—is the patron saint of Cuba. Her olive complexion evokes the mestizo identity and the unity of all Cubans, including nonbelievers. One of her most common iconographies depicts her with a small boat containing a black man, a white man, and a mixed-race (white and black or white and indigenous) man. These three sailors are known as the *tres Juanes* (three Juans). Together they represent the ethnic and cultural composition of the Cuban people.

THE INDIGENOUS, THE COLONIZER, AND THE BLESSED VIRGIN

The conquest of the Americas was envisioned as a crusade with the Catholic monarchs and the Roman Church marching together in alliance. In the conquered lands the *encomenderos*—Spaniards entrusted with control over parcels of land and their inhabitants—were required to evangelize the Indians, but the religious education imparted to the Indians was very shallow, rarely extending beyond memorizing the Lord's Prayer, the Apostles' Creed, and the Hail Mary. Africans also were superficially indoctrinated in the Catholic faith.

As Fernando Ortiz noted in *Historia de una pelea cubana contra los demonios* (History of a Cuban Battle Against the Demons, 1975), Spanish-born friars who served in local town parishes during the first centuries of the colonization of the Americas were not armed with strict orthodox doctrine; local priests, even less so. In Cuba the convictions of the indigenous population changed very little, and in spite of the priests' work, a centuries-old legacy concealed since pre-Christian times continued to be passed down from indigenous mothers to mestizo children (who proliferated in the sixteenth century). Faith in Our Lady of El Cobre symbolizes the efforts of the mestizo—a man of mixed Indian, European, and African heritage—to take control of the island. Men from three different continents, brought together on Cuban soil and working together, gave rise to a religious concept that, in its essence, represents the birth of a new culture.

THE *TRES JUANES*: A *CRIOLLO* CULTURE

Historic documents about the Crown's copper mining industry, which began in Santiago del Prado in 1599 under the charge of Captain Francisco Sánchez de Moya, confirm the identity of the three men who claimed to witness the apparition of the Virgin on the waters of Nipe Bay: the two indigenous brothers Rodrigo and Juan de Hoyos, who were laborers in the mines, and Juan Moreno, a *criollo* boy born to Angolan slave parents. Over time, the iconography varied with regard to the men's ethnicities and occupations, depending on the vicissitudes of Cuban society.

Seville's Archivo General de Indias (General Archive of the Indies) contains manuscripts from 1687 to 1688 in which the eighty-five-year-old Juan Moreno tells the story of what he experienced more than half a century before, in 1612 (which was reported originally by Onofre de Fonseca, the first chaplain of the sanctuary dedicated to the Virgin). Moreno relates that as he and the Hoyos brothers sailed on calm waters one morning, looking for salt for smelting copper and curing hides, they saw something floating on the surf. At first they thought it was a bird, then a girl, and finally they realized it was a statue of the Virgin Mary fastened to a small board with the message "I am the Virgin of Charity." They were surprised because the clothes on the statue were not wet. They picked it out of the water and took it to the cattle ranch of Barajagua, where the foreman reported the event to the mine manager, Sánchez de Moya, who approved the construction of a hut where the statue was placed on a rustic wooden altar. During the first ten years of the seventeenth century Sánchez de Moya had previously built a shrine on a mountain so that he could better oversee the religious education of the enslaved black copper miners.

In was in this milieu of extensive racial mixing that devotion to Our Lady of El Cobre arose at the beginning of the seventeenth century. The Marian confraternity, with its universal values of motherhood, maternal love, and devotion to Mother Earth, touched a chord with Indians and Africans, whose cultural contributions and evolving relations were crucial to its growth. Marianism flourished among the slaves of the mines in Santiago del Prado (El Cobre) for more than a century. The mestizo copper mining community (freemen and slaves) instituted Our Lady of Charity of El Cobre as the symbol of their unity.

This Marian confraternity became politicized when it was used to exemplify the *criollo* social condition. At the end of the seventeenth century, the copper miners used their own funds to build a large sanctuary for Our Lady of Charity of El Cobre. Recognizing the power of the miners' devotion, the Catholic Church organized and took control of its practice,

The Virgin of Charity (La Virgen de la Caridad) in El Cobre. The Virgin of Charity of El Cobre is the religious patroness of Cuba and a powerful symbol of Cuban identity. HÉCTOR DELGADO AND ROLANDO PUJOL

especially among the rebellious copper miners. Juan Moreno became the link between the indigenous and the *criollo*. For their part, the copper miners' dedication to the Virgin of Charity of El Cobre became the best defense of their status as *criollos*: Devotion to the Virgin injected Catholic faith into the community and underpinned their claim to the land as the rightful heirs of the indigenous people. Building the sanctuary proved that the community was able to organize and govern itself.

Copper miners fled slavery to hide in the mountains during several periods, particularly in 1780 when a royal decree authorized the recapture of runaway slaves. In 1997, in the steepest part of the remains of Cardenillo hill, a bronze monument to fugitive slaves by the sculptor Alberto Lescay (b. 1950) was inaugurated in commemoration of the miners' forging of a *criollo* identity that had given rise to an embryonic seed of patriotism. The copper miners demanded that their natural rights be set above the privileges of conquest. In 1800 a royal decree granted them their freedom, but it did not acknowledge them as natural inheritors of the land, and the colonial administration stripped them of their lands.

These principles of natural sovereignty and individual and collective rights were transmitted to the descendants of the copper miners and their neighbors, along with their devotion to Our Lady of El Cobre. Indeed, their convictions grew and expanded among the humble peasantry around El Cobre. In 1795 the mestizo peasants who participated in a revolt in Bayamo led by the mulatto Nicolás Morales (d. 1795) demanded equality with whites in agrarian legislation. Their shared devotion to Our Lady of El Cobre gave them a sense of identity derived from the myth of her origins. Similarly, during the Wars of Independence (1868–1898) devotion to Our Lady of Charity of El Cobre united the *mambí* troops and drew people to a fight framed as a struggle for ethnic and cultural unity. When the Father of the Nation Carlos Manuel de Céspedes (1819–1874) visited El Cobre in 1868, the mestizo community welcomed him warmly. Céspedes knelt in front of the statue of the Virgin in a gesture more political than religious and thus accepted the mission of creating a Cuban identity.

OUR LADY OF EL COBRE AND THE HISTORY OF THE CUBAN NATION

Marianism, fueled by separatist sentiment, spread throughout the island during the U.S. intervention (1868–1902). The Virgin of Charity of El Cobre came to be seen as a religious symbol of Cuban identity, and as devotion to the Virgin grew, the Catholic Church recognized its potential in helping the Church regain the loyalty of the Cuban people that it had lost by supporting Spain. In the last quarter of the nineteenth century nationalism in the worship of Our Lady of El Cobre was nourished by its relationship with the social demands of the *mambís* from the remote countryside and by the ideal of a nation forged through struggle. Eventually it became impossible to separate the cult of Our Lady of El Cobre from Cuban national identity.

Once again, Our Lady of Charity of El Cobre protected the Cuban priests as they attempted to break the Spanish clergy's domination of the Cuban Catholic community. Father Guillermo González Arocha (1868–1939), who had participated in the Wars of Independence, defended the popular nature of her devotion on account of its *criollo* roots and its connections to national history, over and against the other Marian confraternities favored by the Spanish clergy (Our Lady of Lourdes, Saint Teresita, and others). In 1901 the prelates of Santiago de Cuba and Havana requested her official sanctification. This deliberate act cemented the relationship between Our Lady of El Cobre, Patroness of Cuba, and the quest for supremacy by a Cuban Catholic Church that would reflect the needs of its followers.

The bloodshed of the uprising known as the *Guerrita de raza* (Little Race War, 1912) fostered bitterness and unfounded mistrust of the entire black population of the eastern province of Oriente. It also prompted a change in the Catholic Church's missionary strategy: In order to smooth things over, the Church sided with the government over the people, relying on propagation of the devotion to Our Lady of Charity of El Cobre among poor mestizos to emphasize the message of its new evangelization efforts.

On 24 September 1915 a group of former officers of the Liberation army led by generals Jesús Rabí (1845–1915) and Agustín Cebreco (1855–1924) and accompanied by two thousand soldiers left Santiago de Cuba on horseback for El Cobre to entreat the Holy See to recognize Our Lady of Charity of El Cobre as patroness of Cuba. The petitioners were white, black, and mulatto, and they belonged to the Conservative, Liberal, and the Socialist parties, but they were united in their goal to establish a symbol of national unity and to focus the people's attention on ethnic and cultural integration. In response, on 10 May 1916, Pope Benedict XV declared Our Lady of Charity and Remedy, worshiped in El Cobre, the patroness of the Republic of Cuba. Later the pope turned the old Havana parish of La Guadalupe into the western center of worship for Our Lady of El Cobre. A new basilica to house her was built between 1927 and 1931.

Throughout the twentieth century Our Lady of Charity was linked to historical and political events by her followers, by the church hierarchy, or by national authorities. She was crowned on Alameda Michaelsen in Santiago de Cuba before an immense crowd in 1937, as the nation suffered the aftermath of a failed revolution. In commemoration of the fiftieth anniversary of the Republic in 1952, the Mambísa Virgin, one of the oldest images of Our Lady of El Cobre, was carried throughout the country, visiting every town, and then brought to Havana to rally Cuban consciousness after the coup that brought Fulgencio Batista (1901–1973) to power. After the insurrection against Batista's regime in December 1959, a large crowd gathered at the Plaza Cívica (Civic Plaza) in Havana to attend a solemn mass before the icon to pray for peace and national harmony.

When Cuban artists want to emphasize the authentic Cubanness of a character or to lend a patriotic tone to their work, they refer to Our Lady of El Cobre or the *tres Juanes*. There are many musical pieces, works of literature, and films inspired by her, including "A la Virgen del Cobre" (To the Virgin of El Cobre), a bolero by the singer María Teresa Vera (1895–1965); "Virgen del Cobre," a prayer by Pedro

Flores (1894–1979) famously recorded by Daniel Santos (1916–1992); "Balcón de Oriente" by the singer Compay Segundo (Francisco Repilado, 1907–2003); the silent movie *La Virgen de la Caridad* (1930); the light opera *Manita en el suelo* (Manita on the Ground), by Alejandro García Caturla (1906–1940) and Alejo Carpentier (1904–1980); and the poem "Septiembre" (September), by the Matanzas native Hilarión Cabrisas (1883–1939), which affirms: "she leads to safe shores / the paltry, frail vessel / in which the Cuban people travel" (pp. 78–81).

In the mid-twentieth century fervor for the patroness of Cuba grew alongside Cuban anguish. In the 1940s radio serial *El derecho de nacer* (The Right to Be Born), Mamá Dolores often invoked the Virgin, calling out, "Oh! Dear Lady of El Cobre!" In the political comedies of the 1950s, Liborio (a fictional representation of Cuba, the equivalent to Uncle Sam in the United States) advised political authorities to ask her to solve their problems. The post-Revolution film *Fresa y chocolate* (Strawberry and Chocolate, 1994), by Tomás Gutiérrez Alea (1928–1996) and Juan Carlos Tabío (b. 1942), alludes to the popular devotion to Our Lady of El Cobre. She appears in the fiction of José Lezama Lima (1910–1976), Lisandro Otero (1932–2008), Leonardo Padura (b. 1955), Senel Paz (b. 1950), and Onelio Jorge Cardoso (1914–1986), among others. She is the subject of *Misa cubana a la virgen de la Caridad del Cobre* (Cuban Mass to Our Lady of Charity of Cobre), by José María Vitier (b. 1954), which premiered at the Havana cathedral in 1996.

Cubans carried the cult with them when they emigrated to Miami, where they inaugurated a shrine to Our Lady of Charity of Cobre on 2 December 1973. A palm-flanked road leads to the shrine, which is shaped like a stylized version of the Virgin's cone-shaped garments. She is supported by six columns that represent Cuba's six former provinces, and over the entrance hangs a painting of the *tres Juanes* in their boat. The shrine is filled with symbols that demonstrate the exiles' nostalgia for the land they left but still love, as well as their desire to reaffirm and preserve their Cuban identity in a foreign country.

VENERATION OF OUR LADY OF CHARITY

In 1982 the statue of Our Lady of Charity at the El Cobre sanctuary was restored by the specialist Francisco Figueroa, who uncovered a more refined facial expression. In 1982 she was dressed in garments that displayed Cuba's national coat of arms and the arms of the country's six former provinces. After the commemoration of the fiftieth anniversary of the canonical coronation on 10 June 1984, she was dressed in an outfit embroidered by cloister nuns at Cristo Sacerdote near Madrid. Woven of gold thread embroidered over gold, the coat of arms was embroidered on the front of her robe using jewels and gemstones of different colors; its design was inspired by her traditional dress.

When Pope John Paul II visited Cuba in January 1998, he stopped in Santiago to personally crown the Infant Jesus and the patroness of Cuba before a crowd of hundreds of thousands. The statue of Our Lady of El Cobre was transported from her sanctuary to the plaza presided over by the sculpture of General Antonio Maceo, and on the esplanade an altar and a small throne were built for her. Over his cassock John Paul II wore a white gown and stole, as well as a chasuble decorated with Cuban and Our Lady of El Cobre motifs. In the right hand of the statue he placed a rosary made of gold and pearls.

Our Lady of El Cobre continues to draw visitors who view the statue standing on her eighteenth-century silver pedestal displaying the crown, the radiance of her 1937 investiture, her robe made of silver and gold, and the rosary, a gift from the pope. On her feast day, 8 September, despite a prohibition, fervent worshippers cover the antique silver altar with their candles. Votive offerings are placed on two large tables by thankful pilgrims; in addition to traditional offerings are improbable modern ones—ceramic objects, dolls, balls, baseball caps, medals, soil once carried into outer space—as well as others of African religious origin. Ernest Hemingway presented to her the Nobel Prize medal he was awarded for *The Old Man and the Sea* (1951), set in Cuba.

After the homily, the crowd in the sanctuary sings the Cuban national anthem and a song to La Virgen by Miguel Matamoros:

> And if you go to El Cobre
> I want you to bring me
> a figurine of Our Lady of Charity
> I don't want flowers
> I don't want engravings
> what I want is Our Lady of Charity.
>   ("Veneración")

BIBLIOGRAPHY

Arrom, José Juan. *Certidumbre de América, estudios de letras, folklore y cultura.* Havana: Editorial Letras Cubanas, 1980.

Cabrisas, Hilarión. "Los motivos del amor doliente." In *Breviarios de mi vida inútil.* Havana: Talleres Tipográficos de Carasa, 1932.

Fonseca, P. Onofre de, Bernardino Ramírez, and J. Antonio Veyrunes Dubois. *Historia de la milagrosa aparición de nuestra señora de la Caridad, Patrona de Cuba, y de su Santuario en la villa del Cobre.* Santiago de Cuba: Escuela Tipográfica Don Bosco, 1935.

Marrero, Leví. *Cuba: Economía y sociedad.* Vol. 1. Rio Piedras, Puerto Rico: Editorial San Juan, 1972; vols. 2–9, Madrid: Editorial Playor, 1974–1983.

Ortiz, Fernando. *Historia de una pelea cubana contra los demonios*. Havana: Editorial Ciencias Sociales, 1975.

Ortiz, Fernando. *La Virgen de la Caridad del Cobre. Historia y etnografía*. Edited by José Antonio Matos Arévalos. Havana: Fundación Fernando Ortiz, 2008.

Portuondo Zúñiga, Olga. *El Cobre, santuário nacional*. Madrid: Editorial Pablo de la Torriente, 1997.

Portuondo Zúñiga, Olga. *La Virgen de la Caridad del Cobre, símbolo de cubanía*. Santiago de Cuba: Editorial Oriente, 2008.

Tweed, Thomas A. *Our Lady of the Exile: Diasporic Religion at a Cuban Catholic Shrine in Miami*. New York: Oxford University Press, 1997.

Villaverde, Alberto J. *Santa María. Virgen de la Caridad del Cobre; Origen de la imagen y de la devoción de los cubanos*. San Juan, Puerto Rico: Publirin, 1994.

VISUAL ARTS

The visual arts in Cuba since independence have been technically advanced, obstinately contemporary, attentive to every new international trend, yet stubbornly concerned with the expression of national identity. If in the Spanish colonial period the establishment of the Academia San Alejandro in 1818 helped train professional criollo artists in traditional easel portraiture and landscape, discontent with Gerardo Machado's dictatorship and the neocolonial order drove Cuban artists to seek new terms for esthetical renewal in the iconoclastic European avant-garde. From the 1927 Exposición de Arte Nuevo in Havana of 1927 to the 1944 Modern Cuban Painters exhibit at New York's Museum of Modern Art and beyond, Cuban artists carefully mastered the vocabularies of cubism, surrealism, abstraction, abstract expressionism, concrete art, and conceptualism. They produced astonishingly modern works while fashioning their own vernacular idioms, styles, and motifs. Afro-Cuban orishas inhabited cubist/surrealist jungles, Dyonisian forces pulsated in peasant landscapes, and Cuban vitral designs reshaped color and light in abstract canvases.

The Cuban Revolution of 1959 did not dampen Cuba's romance with vanguard contrarianism in the visual arts. Even at the height of utopian patriotism in the 1960s, New Figuration painters and Cuban Pop artists buckled socialist realism with grotesque tableaus and Warhol-inspired iconizations. The founding of the experimental Instituto Superior de Arte (ISA) in 1976 counteracted the official strictures of the quinquenio gris and unleashed a storm of powerful innovators conversant with the latest international trends in performance, conceptual, installation, video, and body art. Many ISA alumni now continue their work in exile as part of a rich diasporic network of Cuban artists while others still work in Cuba. These essays, by key experts in the field, trace the top names, works, trends, and exhibits in the history of Cuban visual arts during the Republican, the Revolutionary, and the post-1989 periods.

■ *See also*

The Art of René Portocarrero

Faith: Regla de Ocha and Ifá

Gallo amarillo (Mariano Rodríguez)

La gitana tropical and the Artistic Influence of Víctor Manuel

Mario Carreño: His Art and World

The Still Lifes of Amelia Peláez

El triunfo de la rumba (Eduardo Abela)

VISUAL ARTS: REPUBLICAN PERIOD

Juan A. Martínez

Major developments, artists, art critics, and institutions related to Cuban modern painting during the Republican period.

Easel painting was officially established in Cuba with the opening of a free national school of drawing and painting in 1818, the Academia de San Alejandro. This academy was instituted by the Spanish authorities in Cuba, a colony with a rapidly growing economy and strategic value, in order to elevate the practice of drawing and painting from a craft to a fine art, thus making it possible for whites to enter what up to then had been considered the craft of blacks and mulattoes. From the mid-nineteenth century on, some of Cuba's most important artists received part of their training there. By late century, there were a number of painters among the *criollos*, mostly upper class, who had mastered the medium of easel painting and used it to represent their social class through portraiture and their motherland through landscape. Outstanding among them were Federico Martínez (1828–1912?), Guillermo Collazo (1850–1896), José Arburu Morell (1864–1889), Esteban Chartrand (1824–1884), Armando Menocal (1863–1942), and Juana Borrero (1877–1896).

THE 1930s

Painting in Cuba came into its own in the late 1920s, when academic painters such as Leopoldo Romañach (1862–1951) and Domingo Ramos (1894–1967) were at the top of their game, and a new generation of painters, known as moderns, appeared on the scene. As in the rest of Latin America in the 1920s, Cuban artists and intellectuals inspired by the ideals of European modernism (science, industry, democracy, universal literacy, artistic license, and so on) aimed to change their society. At the top of their agenda was cultural renovation. Two related elite groups responsible for reforming Cuba's high culture in the 1920s were the Grupo Minorista and the cultural magazine *Revista de Avance* (1927–1930). The writers, caricaturists, painters, and composers associated with these overlapping groups broke with the norms in their respective arts, introducing the ideas and forms of European modernism to better articulate personal and collective visions of personal and national identities. *Revista de Avance* in particular played an important role in the emergence of modern painting in Cuba. This magazine sponsored the landmark Exposición de Arte Nuevo (Exhibition of New Art) in 1927, where the majority of the emerging modernist artists first exhibited together. Moreover, it contained in its pages discourses on the nascent modern movement in Havana and reproductions of drawings and paintings by its participants. The major themes of this movement in the 1930s—the peasant, the Afro-Cuban, and social protest—first appeared in the drawings published by *Revista de Avance*.

This first phase of Cuban modern painting went into high gear in the early 1930s, when many of the painters of this generation returned to Cuba from their artistic pilgrimages to Paris and in some cases also Madrid. In Europe, they had acquired the conceptual and formal tools to develop their personal artistic languages and interpretations of their natural and social environment. The salient painters of this movement were Eduardo Abela (1889–1965), Jorge Arche (1905–1957), Carlos Enriquez (1900–1957), Aristides Fernandez (1904–1934), Antonio Gattorno (1904–1980), Víctor Manuel (1897–1969), Amelia Peláez (1896–1968), Marcelo Pogolotti (1902–1988), and Fidelio Ponce (1895–1949). Using a combination of narrative and symbolism, these painters reformed traditional vernacular themes to imagine and visualize the nation. For the most part they associated the nation with the countryside and with the most humble and exploited sectors of rural and urban society.

In its initial stage, modernism in Cuban art received a measure of support from new institutions. In 1929, a group of civic-minded women founded Lyceum, a nonprofit organization to promote Havana's high culture through art exhibitions, concerts, recitals, conferences, and a circulating library. The Lyceum immediately became the main exhibition venue for modern painting in the 1930s. Modern painting also benefited from the government's creation of the Directory of Culture as a branch of the Ministry of Education. For a brief period in 1937, the Directory funded a free studio of art, where students from Havana's working class were directed and taught by modernist artists. More lasting in its impact was the Directory's organization of the first and second National Salons of Painting and Sculpture in 1935 and 1938, respectively. These salons convened a large number of academic and modernist artists and provided purchase awards for works of art that in the early 2010s are considered among the most important paintings in the collection of the Museo Nacional de Bellas Artes (National Museum of Fine Arts) in Havana.

THE 1940s

The political turbulence and depressed economy of the 1930s gave way to a more hopeful decade, which began in 1940 with a new constitution and elected president. While World War II was ravaging large parts of the globe, Cuba was living a period of relative political stability and economic prosperity. In contrast to the previous decade, when modernist painting came into its own against all odds, the visual arts in the 1940s thrived with the help of increased institutional support and the benefit of a previous generation of artists who had made modernism mainstream among an educated elite within a growing middle class.

The 1940s generation included Wifredo Lam (1902–1982), Mario Carreño (1913–1999), René Portocarrero (1912–1985), Mariano Rodríguez (1912–1990), Cundo Bermúdez (1914–2008), Mirta Cerra (1904–1986), and Roberto Diago (1920–1955), among others. These artists had a more Dionysian and symbolic vision of self and nation than their predecessors. Visually, they developed a monumental and volumetric approach to form, and they also brightened their palette considerably. Monumentality of form gave a certain transcendental quality to their vernacular subject matter, and their bright palette aimed to parallel the intensity of tropical colors. Like their predecessors, these artists continued to favor an expressive content in art imagining and visualizing aspects of personal and collective identity. However, these two groups of artists, given their different historical contexts, privileged different concepts and images of national identity. In general, the 1930s generation favored a popular and leftist-oriented art of social commentary with emphasis on the working class, whereas the 1940s generation aimed for an elitist and transcendental art with emphasis on Ibero-Cuban or white *criollo* traditions (with the notable exception of Lam). The different locations of *lo cubano* (the countryside versus the capital, the African versus the Spanish heritage, popular versus elitist) and their shifting importance over time (the countryside and Afrocuban themes dominated the 1930s; the city of Havana and white *criollo* themes prevailed in the 1940s) suggest that Cuban modernist painters' symbolization of a national cultural identity (or identities) was a subjective and selective process of construction and reconstruction.

As *Revista de Avance* promoted the initial stages of modern art in Cuba, the group-magazine *Orígenes* (1944–1956) advanced the cause of the modern movement in the 1940s. Its editor, the poet José Lezama Lima (1910–1976), was one of the major ideologists of that generation, and in the magazine, he published articles on specific artists and artistic issues and printed original drawings on the cover and inside. A friend of Lezama Lima, the art historian Guy Pérez Cisneros (1915–1953) became the leading critic of the 1940s generation of artists. At the state level, the Instituto Nacional de Bellas Artes (National Institute of Fine Arts), founded in 1939, sponsored major exhibitions of historical and contemporary Cuban art as well as national salons of fine art during the 1940s and 1950s. Of these exhibitions, *300 Años de Arte en Cuba* (300 Years of Art in Cuba, 1940) stands out for offering the first survey of Cuban art, opening the eyes of contemporary artists to the fact that they had an artistic past. Organizations such as the Cuban Commission of Intellectual Cooperation also organized important exhibitions of contemporary art, with accompanying catalogs. The 1940s also saw the first attempt to open a professional private art gallery specializing in modern art, Galería del Prado (1943–1944). Its owner, Maria Luisa Gómez Mena, and its director, José Gómez Sicre, a major promoter of Cuban modern art in the 1940s and later, were instrumental in the organization of the renowned *Modern Cuban Painters* exhibition at the Museum of Modern Art in New York and were responsible for one of the classic books on Cuban modern art, *Pintura cubana de hoy* (Cuban Painting Today, 1944).

THE 1950s

The end of the 1940s closed a chapter in Cuban art. In the following decade, Cuban painters in tune with international artistic trends and their own personal and national circumstances took a turn toward greater subjectivity and abstraction. The 1950s generation of artists reacted against the representational and narrative or symbolic art of their predecessors with its strong nationalist bend. Armed with the knowledge of the latest vanguard art movements in New York and Paris after World War II—abstract expressionism and informalism—the 1950s generation of Cuban abstract artists aimed for a more universal expression in art. The trend toward abstraction was also connected to developments in Cuba. Twenty years of nationalist discourse in art was wearing thin, and political turbulence, which began with a military coup by the Right in 1952 and ended with a full-fledged leftist revolution in 1959, seems to have encouraged artists during that decade to look within and explore the territory of the self rather than imagine the nation.

These modernist artists were quite varied in their approaches to abstraction. Some adopted the vocabulary of cubism, many followed abstract expressionism, and still others practiced concrete art. Probably the most important artistic development of the 1950s was the formation of the group Los Once (The Eleven, 1953–1955). Its leading members, the painters Guido Llinás (1923–2005), Hugo Consuegra (1929–2003), Raúl Martínez (1927–1995), Antonio Vidal (b. 1928), Fayad Jamis (1930–1988), and the sculptors Tomás Oliva (1931–1996) and Agustín Cárdenas (1927–2001), introduced in Cuba the practice of art as an autonomous aesthetic object, beyond narration and symbolism, but with a strong emotional content.

The different generations and groups of Cuban artists working in Havana in the 1950s were supported by a growing but still fragile infrastructure. The Academia de San Alejandro was still Cuba's only official art school, and the Círculo de Bellas Artes the forum for academic art. At last, the Museo Nacional de Bellas Artes (established in 1913) was given an adequate and permanent building in the center of Havana, and it became the seat of the national salons of art and permanent exhibitions of Cuban art from pre-Colombian times to the 1950s. In the early 2010s, its permanent exhibitions feature art from the colonial period to the present. Nonprofit cultural organizations such as Lyceum and Sociedad Cultural Nuestro Tiempo (founded in 1950) continued to play an important role in Havana's cultural life and specifically the development of the visual arts.

During the decade a few commercial galleries— La Habana, La Rampa, and Color Azul—emerged in Havana, yet most were short-lived. Collecting was still dominated by an elite within the Cuban middle class and by North Americans who came into contact with Cuban art as tourists in Havana or through exhibitions in the United States. This generation of artists had their share of literary friends and journalists who interpreted and supported their art, such as Joaquín Texidor, Luis Dulzaides Noda, Edmundo Desnoes (b. 1930), and José Alvarez Baragaño (1932–1962).

Easel painting in Cuba reached its highest manifestation between the 1920s and the 1960s. Up until 1927 painting in Cuba remained far behind literature and music in achievements, and after the 1960s it lost ground to photography, mixed media, video, and installation art. During the Republican period three generations of modernist artists drew knowledge and inspiration from movements of international modern art and from their own historical and social circumstances. The overall development was characterized by a progression from academic to abstract art, from the adaptation of European artistic models to North American ones, and from the emphasis on the representation of a collective cultural identity to the making of introspective signs. The outstanding contribution of modern painting to Cuban high culture during the Republican period, besides its unique aesthetic value, was its visualization of collective narratives and symbols, which, along with the other arts, helped a progressive sector within the educated middle class to imagine and construct an evolving and influential concept of the nation.

BIBLIOGRAPHY

Barr, Alfred H. "Modern Cuban Painters." *Bulletin of the Museum of Modern Art* 11 (April 1944): 2–14.

Bondil, Nathalie, ed. *Cuba: Art and History from 1868 to Today*. New York: Prestel, 2008.

Cisneros, Guy Pérez. "Pintura y escultura en 1943." In *Anuario Cultural de Cuba*. Havana: Dirección General de Relaciones Culturales, 1943.

De la Torriente, Loló. *Estudio de las artes plásticas en Cuba*. Havana: Ucar García SA, 1954.

Desnoes, Edmundo. "1952–1962 en la pintura cubana." In *Pintores cubanos*. Havana: Ediciones R, 1962.

Gómez Sicre, José. *Pintura cubana de hoy*. Havana: Maria Luisa Gómez Mena, 1944.

Martínez, Juan A. *Cuban Art and National Identity: The Vanguardia Painters, 1927–1950*. Gainesville: University Press of Florida, 1994.

VISUAL ARTS: REVOLUTIONARY PERIOD

Rachel Weiss

The major trends and artists in Cuban art from the revolutionary idealism of the 1960s to the repression of the 1970s to the renewed creativity of the 1980s.

A schematic version of the history of Cuban cultural policy during the three decades following the revolution in 1959 would classify the 1960s as a time of revolutionary enthusiasm, experimentation, and creative efflorescence; the 1970s as the dark years, when sectarian and Soviet-inflected forces, together with revolutionary morals (entailing homophobia, xenophobia, and an abhorrence of extravagance) curtailed creative expression and penalized deviations from a prescribed norm, leading to conformist and inertly patriotic imagery; and the 1980s as a time when a more liberal current of thinking led to renewed creativity and protected it with an enhanced institutional framework, allowing for an explosively new, youthful art. (A more accurate periodization would place the first phase from 1959 to 1968, the second from 1968 to 1976, and the third from 1976 to 1989.) There is some truth to this scheme, but its neatness misses the broad stylistic, aesthetic, and conceptual diversity at each point along the way. Despite strong tendencies in cultural policy during each period, artistic production always overflowed any channels prepared for it by the state.

Cuban artists have pursued multiple paths, often sympathetic to the political changes in their country but not necessarily convinced that political affiliation should guide artistic experimentation and choices. In any case, there has never been consensus about what attributes a revolutionary culture should have. Debate has centered on key questions: To what extent are bourgeois (experimental) and proletarian (massified/politicized) culture mutually exclusive and antagonistic? Should art align itself with vernacular culture or the other way around? Should Cuban culture be part of a broad international cultural community or primarily a tool for nation building? Should limits be placed on what art should address, and if so, who should determine them?

THE 1960s

Artistic production during the 1960s ranged from effusively patriotic imagery, to expressionist and angst-ridden monsters, to luridly colorful pop-art paintings of subjects both high (revolutionary heroes) and low (cows and plumbing), along with the voluminous works produced through the state-sponsored Movimiento de Aficionados (Amateurs' Movement), begun in 1960. According to a 1996 essay by the critic Iván de la Nuez, several currents in Cuban visual art were active at the time of the revolution, including abstraction (especially expressionist and geometric or concrete imagery), baroque pictorialism, and narrative painting based on social themes, in addition to the popular peasant art championed by the influential artist and writer Samuel Feijóo (Borràs and Zaya). All these streams continued into the 1960s. However, with the new imperative revolutionary present, the languages of a "new figuration" (exemplified by Antonia Eiriz) and of Pop art (Raúl Martínez) arose (Fornet p. 256). The new figuration was a revival of figurative painting in place of the abstraction that had previously been dominant. These were in some cases a straightforward effort to depict the new reality, especially in terms of the new revolutionary subjectivity being formed, whereas in other cases they were a refusal of that identification. Throughout the decade an energetic and highly accomplished design sector also produced posters, graphics, books, and other publications. In the midst of the artistic diversity that followed political upheaval, it is perhaps telling that many creators turned to images of the grotesque; furthermore, it is significant that, by the end of the decade, two of the most important artists (Eiriz and Umberto Peña) had stopped working in protest while two others (Martínez and Santiago Armada, known as Chago) had moved into a softer form of artistic retirement.

Raúl Martínez is emblematic of the approaches and pressures of the period. During the 1960s, he moved from abstract expressionism to a collaged painting that included references to the social-political environment and reflected a growing sense that the new society demanded a different kind of art. Later

■ *See also*

La anunciación
(Antonia Eiriz)

Cuban Thought and Cultural Identity: Socialist Thought

Dreaming of an Island
(María Magdalena Campos-Pons)

La sentencia
(Belkis Ayón)

MAJOR EXHIBITIONS

1959: Enormous shows organized as "cultural mobilizations" included *Arte para Oriente* and *Arte y artesanías Cubanas* (Lyceum Lawn Tennis Club, Havana). Most artists active in the country participated.

1959: *Diez Pintores Concretos* (Galería de Arte, Color-Luz) along with the 1963 *Expresionismo Abstracto* (Galería de La Habana) proved that the revolutionary triumph in 1959 did not radically shear off prerevolutionary culture from the new society.

1959: The *Salón Anual* was dominated by abstract works, which were already being criticized as excessively individualistic and introspective, unable to reflect the new collective reality.

1967: An exhibition of the Salon de Mai was brought from Paris, presenting the Cuban public with 200 works from the European avant-garde, including examples of surrealism, lettrism, situ-ationism, neorealism, and pop and op art. There was, however, no socialist realism.

1968: *Panorama del Arte en Cuba* (Museo Nacional de Bellas Artes) was important because it codified the practice of excluding all artists who had emigrated from the category of Cuban art.

1970: *Salón 70* was to have been a celebration of the ten-million-ton sugar harvest (although the harvest fell far short of ten-million tons). The exhibit included a diverse array of production, graphic design elements (from magazine covers to cookie tins), posters, and a special gallery for popular (primitive) painters, which heralded an important policy direction in subsequent years. The 1970 Salón is generally regarded as the line dividing one era from the next.

1971: *Salón 71*, unlike preceding years in which the national salon was mostly dedicated to the work of professional artists, was an exhibition of *participación masiva* (mass participation), bringing together works by amateur artists, workers, and students under the age of thirty-five, all selected through a series of provincial salons, as well as that of formally trained artists.

1973: *Concurso '26 de Julio* (Museo Nacional de Bellas Artes), organized by the Ministry of Armed Forces, announced a new direction for art as a means to transmit official ideology. Many of the 520 exhibited works depicted revolutionary heroes or martyrs or made reference to patriotic themes. The show established a template for exhibitions in the ensuing years, most of which were likewise organized under the rubric of commemorations or tributes by which revolutionary history was exalted.

1981: *Volumen Uno* (Centro Internacional de Arte) included works by Flavio Garciandía, Tomás Sánchez, José Manuel Fors, José Bedia, Gustavo Pérez Monzón, Ricardo Rodríguez Brey, Leandro Soto, Israel León, Juan Francisco Elso, Rubén Torres Llorca, and Rogelio López Marín (Gory).

---

in the decade, Martínez developed a Cuban pop art, equidistant from socialist realism and Andy Warhol–style irony, with which he portrayed national heroes. Some critics at the time opposed this work on the grounds that it was a foreign aesthetic imported from the capitalist North and, therefore, unsuitable in the revolutionary context. Martínez's trajectory, and the critical response to it, points to the complexities for both artists and the political class of defining the parameters of a revolutionary artistic practice.

Antonia Eiriz, a major proponent of the new figuration, was known for her dark, pained works, such as the well-known *Christ Departing from Juanelo*, in which she expressed her sympathies for the downtrodden as well as her mistrust of demagoguery. Her characteristically grotesque images depicted malevolent spirits, faceless hordes, and corpses rotting in the sun. The work of Servando Cabrera Moreno also stands out among the new figuration artists. Although previously a cubist-inspired figurative painter, after 1959 he began to work with revolutionary themes in eroticized images of *milicianos* (militiamen) and other new popular heroes. A parallel stream of work comprised explicitly homoerotic figures, presumably tolerated because of his more politically affirmative work.

Umberto Peña's paintings display a kind of genial aggression, with images of teeth, viscera, and plumbing and consonant-drenched exclamations spewing out across the canvas. His sharply composed canvases, combining elements of expressionistic pop, new figuration, and comics, reflected his background in design. Scatological images, which were common in Peña's work between about 1965 and 1971, appear also in the work of his friend Chago, who started out as a political cartoonist for the guerrillas during the armed insurrection. In the mid-1960s, Chago switched to darkly expressionist graphics that sounded skeptical and even fearful notes about the nature of life in the new society. Ángel Acosta León executed works of intense isolation and loneliness, suggesting that the identification of national traits was not so simple and sunny a matter. His large canvases transformed common objects such as coffee pots into fevered images.

As de la Nuez notes with reference especially to Chago, Peña, Eiriz, and Martínez, these artists "experimented in different ways with Cuba's aesthetic identity," searching "for something different from the cultural massification of the country" (quoted in Borràs and Zaya p. 375). By the end of the 1960s, the critical establishment came to see the trends in pop and new figuration as problematic. Under the pressures of the misunderstanding of their work, Chago, Martínez, and Peña turned to graphic design and Eiriz to neighborhood papier-mâché workshops. Notably, the new artists of the 1980s would cite these four artists as crucial antecedents and mentors.

Visually forceful, embracing a wide range of formal approaches and artistic concerns, these artists demonstrate that the 1960s were a time of great creative energy that paralleled profound social-political changes. Their eventual exclusion or self-exclusion

The exhibition was the first public display of what came to be called the new Cuban art, which reflected young artists' dissatisfaction with and rejection of the formerly subservient position of many artists.

1981: The *Salón Nacional de Pequeño Formato* (Salón Lalo Carrasco, Habana Libre Hotel) was noteworthy for being the first exhibit on the island since 1959 to include the work of a Cuban artist living in the United States (Ana Mendieta).

1981: *Artistas Populares de Cuba* (Museo Nacional de Bellas Artes) was the first major scholarly exhibition to showcase the work of popular artists across the island, as advocated in the 1960s by the artist Samuel Feijóo. Although it had already been a decade since such work was lionized by the cultural apparatus, it had never before been given a full scholarly treatment.

1983: *La Generación de Miami: Nueve Artistas Cubano-Americanos* (*The Miami Generation:* *Nine Cuban-American Artists*; Museo Cubano de Arte y Cultura, Miami, Florida) was regarded as the Miami version of *Volumen Uno*, both as an effort to consolidate a group of artists as a new generation and as evidence of a break with the work that preceded it.

1986: *Puré Expone* (Galería L.), which came five years after *Volumen Uno*, showed work by very young artists, many of them the students of the artists participating in the earlier exhibit. It signaled the rapid pace of development and the high energy level of the new art. *Puré* was widely understood to have taken up the proposals of *Volumen Uno*, especially in the artists' interest in and attachment to the vernacular, and pushed them to a new level of action against complacency. The show stands as a hinge between the 1981 artistic efflorescence and the torrent of performance art and interventions (art happenings) that started up shortly thereafter.

1989: The Castillo de la Fuerza project was a cycle of exhibitions originally intended to serve as a forum for the discussion of the contestatory works produced at the end of the decade; many of these shows were either curtailed or closed outright. Shortly thereafter the facility was converted into the Museum of Ceramics.

1990: *Kuba O.K. Aktuelle Kunst aus Kuba/ Arte Actual de Cuba* (Städtische Kunsthalle Düsseldorf, Dusseldorf, Germany) was one in a series of exhibitions of new art organized in museums abroad beginning around 1988. This particular exhibition was significant because most of the work was subsequently sold to the art collector Peter Ludwig, setting off a period of rapid marketization of new art at the same time that artists were being encouraged to work abroad by cultural officials.

shows the sharp contradictions and tensions that were always present in the Cuban utopian scenario.

THE 1970s

The process of consolidation and institutionalization, much of it along Soviet lines, that replaced the radical experimentation of previous years entailed cultural ramifications. The new emphasis was on mass participation, with an operative definition of art as propaganda designed to facilitate compliance and social control. The 1971 Congress on Education and Culture set out new parameters for art that was to be "a weapon of the struggle." Also that year, Armed Forces commissar Luis Pavón was appointed director of the Consejo Nacional de Cultura (National Council of Culture), signaling a broader campaign to purge culture of its more liberal advocates and realign the sector with political objectives.

Early in the decade a torrent of official exhibitions and competitions hewed to patriotic themes. During the so-called *quinquenio gris*, the "gray five years" from 1971 to 1976, in addition to patriotic images, Cuban artists produced portraits, vernacular landscapes, and works related to sociohistorical topics and rural traditions. These subjects were taken up, with varying degrees of sincerity, servility, independence, and innovation, by artists such as Nelson Domínguez and Roberto Fabelo, both of whom were expressionists strongly influenced by Eiriz. As Amate Roberto Cobas notes in his 2001 book, the official promotion of work by the untrained artists Ruperto Jay Matamoros,

Gilberto de la Nuez, Benjamín Duarte, Mario Bermúdez, and Benito Ortiz, which constituted a *pintura popular* (popular painting), reflected the cultural politics at the time.

The founding of the Ministry of Culture and the Instituto Superior de Arte (ISA) in 1976 had signaled either the presence of (in the first case) or the possibility for a significant change in direction. The shift was clearly manifest in the personnel appointed to cultural leadership: The civilian and relatively liberal Armando Hart was named to lead the new Ministry in 1976. At the same time, and not incidentally, Hart's appointment replaced what had been a string of Castro opponents with a confidant, and so his appointment may have actually placed culture even more directly under state control. In other words, while there was some shift in the ostensible direction of policy, the mechanisms remained firmly within the system of centralized, top-down control, indicating that the new policy direction would always have a relatively contingent status.

Hart took several steps to repair the damage that had been done to creativity and morale by institutionalized intolerance. He discouraged the old provincialism—in the next decade, the establishment of the Havana Biennial was a major initiative in this regard—and rehabilitated important figures who had been marginalized. He also advanced the populist planks of revolutionary cultural policy, establishing a system of *instructores de arte* (art instructors) and creating Casas de Cultura (official houses of culture) in

municipalities across the island, and initiated a series of projects that engaged artists in public spaces and industrial production.

Despite official policy, artistic production remained diverse, with new currents and alternative strategies emerging. Photorealism had proved a useful method for the depiction of heroes and martyrs, but from about 1973 to 1979 a loose group of younger artists, borrowing from the photorealism in vogue among New York artists, began to employ hyperrealism to undermine the conventions of representation. Like the abstractionism of the 1950s, hyperrealism was an anti-dogmatic gesture against prevailing currents. These artists played with the idea of a strictly national art as they fashioned images of banal or odd subjects in a technique that emphasized fidelity to reality. Hyperrealism thus served as an antidote to the stultified passivity of obligatory realism, yet it reignited a debate as to the westernization of Cuban art. Since the beginning of the revolutionary period there had been a polemical rejection of such *foreign* importations in favor of *authentic* Cuban expression; consequently, hyperrealism was attacked on ideological grounds much as pop art had been.

Relatively few artists took up the hyperrealist style of painting, but even among them there was a range of approaches: Some, like Flavio Garciandía or Rogelio López Marin (Gory), attended to the banalities of everyday life. Garciandía's 1975 *All You Need Is Love* stands as a high point of Cuban hyperrealism.

The painting, a fatuous, soft-focus portrait of a pretty young girl lying in the grass, can be taken as (though this was never made explicit) a parody of socialist realism's pearly optimism. (It was no great leap when in the 1980s Garciandía began to toy with the Cuban taste for kitsch, producing paintings and installations based on so-called bad forms, resplendent with swans and glitter.) César Leal, fundamentally a realist, had already taken up expressionism and pop art as vehicles and then added hyperrealism to his evolving vocabulary.

Around 1974, coinciding with a decline in the estimation of expressionism in Cuba, Tomás Sánchez shifted from a neo-expressionist style and monstrous figurative subjects to landscapes in a more naturalistic style. Painted with a meditative attention to detail, these landscapes are unlike the works of other hyperrealist painters in that Sánchez did not paint from photographs since the point was not to be found in the act of reproduction of an image, a choice that seems linked to the artist's interests in meditation and yoga, with their inward focus. Nélida López and Aldo Menéndez came closest to a programmatic use of the style, though even their work showed little hint of the realist orthodoxies expounded in the Soviet Union.

The quasi-primitivist idiom of Manuel Mendive's early work, together with a focus on the mythical world of Santería belief and practice, caused critics to pigeonhole him within popular art. In the 1970s, he began to incorporate topical imagery related to history, politics, and current events. His works thus form a link between high art and the anonymous popular traditions of Afro-Cuban vernacular culture.

THE 1980s

In the late 1970s a new generation of young artists, fed up with the complacency of the art that was being promoted in the name of the nation, determined to reset the terms of the debate. Their work first became visible in the 1981 exhibition *Volumen Uno* (which also included work by Garciandía, Sánchez, and Gory), and which the artists themselves organized. The participating artists, most of them still in school, offered up a fresh, eclectic mix of pop, minimalism, conceptualism, performance, graffiti, and arte povera, reconfigured and reactivated in the name of an art that strove to be, as the critic Osvaldo Sánchez put it, "critically, ethically, and organically Cuban" (p. 23). *Volumen Uno* had no overall theme or unifying stylistic tendency; rather, the works followed the interests, aesthetics, and talents of eleven individual young people. The show was not just a break in formal terms but also in content: The works' substitution of Indians, popular religions, and the kitsch aesthetic of popular home decoration for the revolutionary dramatis personae was as significant as its refusal of the tonalities and compositions of that patriotic imagery. *Volumen Uno* was a turning point not only because of the works themselves but because it presented a spectrum of works that deviated from what was being officially promoted. After the repression of artistic expression during the 1970s, the very fact that such nonconformity existed was significant.

The show was as controversial as it was popular (some 10,000 people visited the gallery in two weeks), with some critics celebrating the freshness of the works and others denouncing it for aesthetic or political defects. In a review Ángel Tomás González attacked the exhibit as "a kind of cosmopolitan art that feigns ignorance of all geographical or ideological borders and thus leans toward an abandonment of any identification with the values that define our national identity. ... This aesthetic attitude can imply the dangers of ... the 'vanguards' promoted and manipulated by the metropolitan powers" (pp. 7, 27).

In the mid-1980s, a still younger cohort of artists, often working in small, informal collectives, began to produce and exhibit works that pushed even farther into an explicitly critical language, raising for public discussion the taboo subjects of corruption, dogmatism, cult of personality, and lack of democracy. These artists shared a determination to stretch the limits of art so as to stretch what was permissible in political terms. Their work coincided with Fidel Castro's announcement of a process of *rectification*, intended to return the country to the original revolutionary ideals and ethics. By the end of the decade, the government would no longer tolerate the young artists' criticism, and a cycle of censorship and reprisals began. The decade came to a close with a symbolic baseball game staged by artists in September 1989: Most of the artists active during the decade participated under the motto, "If we can't make art, we'll play ball."

The young artists' conceptualist approach allowed them to incorporate an eclectic range of styles and to work in a range of media, including painting, installations, land art, photography (wresting it from the documentary assignment it had been given), and performance. Although the work was initially attacked as formalist, it had a clear social basis and content— though not the social vocation previously assigned to art. General tendencies included a reengagement with avant-garde art from North America, an interest in African and Indo-American roots and spiritual practices, and in vernacular aesthetics and kitsch; overall, these artists insisted on an ethical role for art and on an artistic process not predetermined by government-decreed ideology. A group of sympathetic and influential critics argued persuasively on behalf of the new work, and a few sympathetic administrators saw in the new art an opportunity to reestablish the country's prestige in the international arena. In addition to the support provided by these individuals, it is worth noting that, in spite of the restrictions that had been imposed on artists by official policies throughout the period under consideration here, there were always gaps and variances that provided fertile spaces and moments for expression.

In 1984, the Havana Biennial established the city as a center of art of the developing world and provided an international audience for the young artists. A market for their works sprang up, especially in Europe and the United States. Significant works of the early 1980s include Juan Francisco Elso's *Por América*, an effigy of José Martí wrought as a humble, barefoot figure; Garciandía's series exploring kitsch; José Bedia's drawings, paintings, and installations delving into Afro-Cuban spiritual beliefs; Marta María Pérez's photographic series exploring popular beliefs in relation to her own pregnancy; Leandro Soto's experiments with performance art and his landmark installation about his family's history as revolutionary militants; Consuelo Castañeda's postmodernist appropriations; and Antonio Eligio's (Tonel) installation *Bloqueo*, making ironic commentary on the self-imposed aspects of the island's isolation.

Key works of the second half of the 1980s include Glexis Novoa's *Etapa Práctica*, installations that ironically adopt and mutate a Soviet-style monumentality; Carlos Rodríguez Cárdenas's often scatological series of paintings mocking the sloganeering of Cuban political discourse; Tomás Esson's infamous painting of monsters copulating in front of a portrait of a mulatto Che Guevara; Ciro Quintana's elaborate collages in comic-book style, which make jokes about the adoption of postmodernist rhetoric and idioms in Cuba; Eduardo Ponjuán and René Francisco Rodríguez's collaborative

■ *See also*

Economy: Special Period

Palo Monte and
Ancestral Spirits: The Art
of José Bedia

works critical of the nascent art market; Lázaro Saavedra's works in various media that examine artists' complicity with the very systems they were critical of; Aldito Menéndez's "Reviva la revolu..." installation requesting donations to complete the artistic (and, by extension, revolutionary) project, and Segundo Planes's baroque and surreal paintings and drawings. Among the collectives, Arte Calle was known for street murals, sometimes executed with neighborhood participation; Grupo Provisional for its anarchic and improvisatory happenings, which often sprang up in public spaces; ABTV for its projects deconstructing Cuban cultural politics; and Art-De for works staged in parks that directly, and provocatively, engaged with passersby.

BIBLIOGRAPHY

Bondil, Nathalie, ed. *Cuba: Art and History, from 1868 to Today.* Translated by Timothy Bernard et al. Montreal: Montreal Museum of Fine Arts, 2008.

Borràs, Maria Lluïsa, and Antonio Zaya, eds. *Cuba siglo XX: Modernidad y sincretismo.* Exhibition catalog. Las Palmas de Gran Canaria, Spain: Centro Atlántico de Arte Moderno; Palma, Spain: Fundació "La Caixa"; Barcelona, Spain: Centre d'Art Santa Mónica, 1996.

Camnitzer, Luis. *New Art of Cuba.* Rev. ed. Austin: University of Texas Press, 2003.

Cobas Amate, Roberto, coordinator. *Museo Nacional de Bellas Artes: Colección de arte Cubano.* Old Havana: Museo Nacional de Bellas Artes; Barcelona: Ambit, 2001.

Espinosa, Magaly, and Kevin Power. *Antología de textos críticos: El nuevo arte Cubano.* Santa Monica, CA: Perceval, 2006.

González, Ángel Tomás. "Desafío en San Rafael." *El Caimán Barbudo* 159 (Havana) (March 1981): 7, 27.

Hurtado, Oscar, and Edmundo Desnoes. *Pintores Cubanos.* Havana: Ediciones Revolución, 1962.

Marinello, Juan. *Conversación con nuestros pintores abstractos.* Santiago de Cuba: Universidad de Oriente, Departamento de Extensión y Relaciones Culturales, 1960.

Mosquera, Gerardo. *Trece artistas jóvenes.* Havana: Universidad de la Habana, 1980.

Mosquera, Gerardo. *Exploraciones en la plástica Cubana.* Havana: Editorial Letras Cubanas, 1983.

Mosquera, Gerardo. Untitled essay in catalog for *Nosotros* exhibition. Havana: Museo Nacional Palacio de Bellas Artes, 1988, n.p.

Portuondo, José Antonio. *Estética y revolución.* Havana: Unión ee Escritores y Artistas de Cuba, 1963.

Portuondo, José Antonio. *Itinerario estético de la revolución Cubana.* Havana: Editorial Letras Cubanas, 1979.

Rodríguez, Carlos Rafael. *Problemas del arte en la Revolución.* Havana: Editorial Letras Cubanas, 1979.

Veigas, José, Cristina Vives, Adolfo V. Nodal, et al. *Memoria: Cuban Art of the 20th Century.* Los Angeles: California/International Arts Foundation, 2002.

Weiss, Rachel. *To and from Utopia in the New Cuban Art.* Minneapolis: University of Minnesota Press, 2011.

VISUAL ARTS: SPECIAL PERIOD

Antonio Eligio Fernández

Transformations affecting Cuban artists and the art world since a time of national crisis.

The world of the visual arts, embodying a variety of aesthetic and ideological standpoints, sheds light on Cuba's transition from the 1980s to a period of national crisis in the 1990s. Cuba's active artists, like other people living there, have been affected by economic hardship and migration. In a process of renewal, art school faculties have revised their ideas and curricula. Although the aftermath of the Special Period of the 1990s was still very much evident in Cuban art at the beginning of the twenty-first century, the limited opening of the economy to private enterprise, foreign investment, and the free circulation of hard currencies has created new opportunities for the marketing of art and stimulated connection with the global marketplace.

IN THE WORLD AND AT HOME: INSIDE AND OUTSIDE ARTISTS

For Cuban society the 1990s, as Haroldo Dilla has noted, meant "the extremely rapid colonization of social relations and everyday life by the market" (Dilla p. 65). Just as quickly, this process helped broaden the presence of Cuban work in galleries and exhibitions around the world. This expansion was inescapable given the new circumstances on the island, with its small, unstable national market dependent on foreign buyers. Between 1990 and 2010 (and for the first time after 1959), establishing professional relationships outside Cuba became a key objective for most artists who seek an active career.

A number of figures who appeared on the scene during the 1990s acquired high profiles outside Cuba. Kcho, Tania Bruguera, Carlos Garaicoa, José Toirac, Los Carpinteros, and Diango Hernández gained entry into the circuit defined by global investment and institutions in New York and European art centers, as well as biennials (such as those in Venice, São Paulo, Istanbul, Shanghai, and Gwangju) that have a decisive say in the rankings of artists and their works. At the same time, the number and importance of collections wholly or partially focused on Cuba's artistic output has grown. The exhibition *Kuba OK* (Städtische Kunsthalle, Düsseldorf, Germany, 1990) stirred the interest of the German collectors Peter and Irene Ludwig, who purchased most of the works and installed them in the newly created Ludwig Museum for International Art in Aachen, Germany. The collection of Howard and Patricia Farber, dedicated to Cuban art after 1980, started to take shape in 2001; portions of the Farber collection have been widely shown in the United States. Other private and public collections on several continents are curating and strengthening major collections of recent Cuban art.

Inside Cuba, the Havana Biennial continues to be the most important event for the visual arts, although its international scope and influence has shrunk in a world where new biennials compete relentlessly for globalized investment and cultural tourism. The Contemporary Art Salon, inaugurated in 1995, is held in the biennial's off-year and provides a regular reappraisal of the art scene in Cuba.

After 1990 small private galleries and street studios in Cuba appeared, as well as shows improvised on crowded sidewalks, works displayed in hotels and open-air markets, and stalls designed to catch the attention of foreign tourists. The works thus marketed tended to fall into the category of souvenirs. With a drive that was quite different from this sort of marketing, the artists Ezequiel Suárez and Sandra Ceballos founded the Espacio Aglutinador in 1994, at their joint residence in El Vedado. During a later period Ceballos worked with René Quintana as her closest collaborator. This private, alternative site, part gallery and part studio, developed a coherent program of events and exhibitions that promoted the work of young artists, such as Grethell Rasúa, Celia González, Yunior Aguilar, Javier Castro, and Hamlet Lavastida, among others, and launched their careers in the early 2000s. Aglutinador's vision is an inclusive one; it has exhibited a diverse roster of artists, including the work of Cuban artists who live overseas, such as Ernesto Pujol, Eduardo Aparicio, Arturo Cuenca, Glexis Novoa, and the late Ana Mendieta.

The work of Cuban artists living outside Cuba is increasingly exhibited on the island. Along with those mentioned above, Havana shows have exhibited the work of Rosa Irigoyen, Tony Labat, Felipe Dulzaides, Gertrudis Rivalta, Osvaldo Yero, Carlos García, Ángel Ricardo Ríos, José Bedia, and others. By the same token, artists living in Cuba face a less rigid migration policy. This increased flexibility, coupled with the changes in the economy and more favorable external circumstances, has allowed many artists whose careers have already taken off in Cuba to keep a residence in their homeland while moving freely on the international stage.

A CULTURE OF CYNICISM

The 1990 opening of *El objeto esculturado* (The Sculptured Object), at the Centro de Desarrollo de las Artes Visuales (CDAV; Center for Development of the Visual Arts), staged a spectacular work of performance art called *La esperanza es lo último que se está perdiendo* (Hope Is the Last Thing Being Lost), by the artist Ángel Delgado. By defecating on the gallery floor as he squatted over the newspaper *Granma*, an official publication of the Communist Party of Cuba, Delgado made a scatological statement about that moment in time: for society, for culture, and for the arts of his country. Tried and convicted, Delgado was sentenced to six months in prison. His action, in visceral fashion, said farewell to the 1980s and ushered in the 1990s.

The Special Period encouraged broadening the range of subject matter open to art through new approaches and more intense examination but doing so from previously established perspectives. New topics that were increasingly important included the conflicted relationship between Cuba and the Soviet Union, the final implosion of the utopia and the ensuing ideological crisis, emigration and the Rafter Crisis of 1994, changes in material culture, the rising social importance of money, the presence of foreign investment in the national economy, rising racism and poverty, the enhanced visibility of religions in general and of Afro-Cuban religions in particular, *jineterismo* and the rise of other forms of prostitution, and a focus on the body with a gaze that dwelled on the grotesque.

Critics such as Magaly Espinosa (2003) have identified a "culture of cynicism" in the art of the Special Period. In an essay, Cuban writer and art critic Orlando Hernández views it as "becoming ever more happy-go-lucky and hedonistic, and ever more concerned with its own appearance, and with potential successes and rewards" (p. 19). Cynicism and hedonism seem to be inseparable from the rising importance of the art market in Cuba. Others have detected less irony and sarcasm and a greater focus on formal elements and aesthetics than was seen among artists of the 1980s.

EDUCATION

Several vital educational projects, mostly originated by the Instituto Superior de Arte (ISA), took shape during the 1990s and 2000s. The most important is Desde una Pragmática Pedagógica (DUPP; From an Educational Practice), a space started by René Francisco Rodríguez in 1989 and 1990. DUPP encourages engagement in the public arena and works that are defined by the needs of individuals or specific communities. This open, flexible workshop is a platform that has launched many careers in art. Ruslán Torres, a professor in the ISA painting department who was trained by DUPP, in 2001 created workshops stressing artists' interaction with the public. Lázaro Saavedra organized several workshops at ISA that led to the founding of the Colectivo Enema (Enema Collective, 1999), a group characterized by its exploration of the concept of the collective body through performance art documented in video and photographs. Enema was a highlight of the Eighth Biennial in Havana (2003) with its installation of *Morcilla* (Blood Sausage), which focused on the manufacture and cooking of a sausage made out of the participants' own blood.

Tania Bruguera founded the Department of Art and Behavior in 2003, in coordination with although independent of ISA. Art and Behavior has gathered many young people from diverse backgrounds to

MAJOR EXHIBITIONS

1990: *El objeto esculturado* (The sculptured object). Centro de Desarrollo de las Artes Visuales of Havana. Organized by Félix Suazo and Alexis Somoza. During the opening Ángel Delgado did the performance *La esperanza es lo único que se está perdiendo* (Hope Is the Only Thing Being Lost).

1990: *Kuba OK.* Städtische Kunsthalle, Dusseldorf, Germany, in collaboration with Centro de Desarrollo de las Artes Visuales of Havana. Curated by Jürgen Harten and Antonio Eligio (Tonel).

1991: Fourth Havana Biennial, Centro Wifredo Lam.

1991: *Lam desconocido* (The Unknown Lam). Works of Wifredo Lam from private collections, on the occasion of the Fourth Havana Biennial. Casa de las Américas, Havana.

1991: *The Nearest Edge of the World: Art in Cuba Now*, Massachusetts College of Art, Boston, Massachusetts, and Bronx Museum, Bronx, New York. Curated by Rachel Weiss and Gerardo Mosquera.

1991: *Los hijos de Guillermo Tell* (The Children of William Tell). Alejandro Otero Museum of the Visual Arts, Caracas, Venezuela, and the Ángel Arango Library, Banco de la República, Bogotá, Colombia. Curated by Gerardo Mosquera and Graciela Pantín.

1992: *Arte cubano contemporáneo* (Contemporary Cuban Art). Kcho, Ibrahim Miranda, Eduardo Ponjuán, José Bedia, and Juan Francisco Elso. Cultural Center for Contemporary Art, Mexico City.

1993: First Video Art Encounter, Museo Nacional de Bellas Artes de La Habana, Havana. Organized by David Mateo and Luisa Marisy.

1993: *Las metáforas del templo* (The Metaphors of the Temple). Centro de Desarrollo de las Artes Visuales, Havana. Curated by Carlos Garaicoa and Esterio Segura.

1994: Fifth Havana Biennial, Centro Wifredo Lam, Havana.

1994: *Art cubain actuel* (Current Art of Cuba). Organized by the Ludwig Foundation of Cuba. Galerie de L'UQAM. Universidad de Québec, Montreal, Canada.

1995: *Primer salón de arte cubano contemporáneo* (First Salon of Cuban Contemporary Art). Organized at various venues by the Centro de Desarrollo de las Artes Visuales, Havana.

1995: *Una de cada clase* (One from Each Class). Set of twelve exhibitions presented by the Ludwig Foundation of Cuba. Venues: National Center for Preservation, Restoration, and Museum Science; Museo Nacional de Bellas Artes de La Habana; Luis de Soto Gallery of the Faculty of Arts and Letters; Provincial Center for

Plastic Arts and Design; and Wifredo Lam Center, all in Havana.

1995: *Cuba: La isla posible* (Cuba: The Possible Island). Center for Contemporary Culture, Barcelona, Spain. Curated by Juan Pablo Ballester, María Elena Escalona, and Iván de la Nuez.

1995: *New Art from Cuba.* Whitechapel Art Gallery, London. Curated by James Peto and Laurie Short.

1996: *La huella múltiple* (The Multiple Trace). Organized by the artists Belkis Ayón, Sandra Ramos, and Abel Barroso.

1996: *Mundo soñado: Joven plástica cubana* (Dream World: Young Cuban Plastic Arts). House of the Americas, Madrid, Spain, in collaboration with the Ludwig Foundation of Cuba. Curated by Helmo Hernández.

1996: *Cuba siglo XX: Modernidad y sincretismo* (Twentieth-century Cuba: Modernism and Syncretism). Atlantic Center for Modern Art, Las Palmas, Grand Canary Island; La Caixa Foundation, Palma; Santa Monica Art Center, Barcelona, Spain. Curated by Maria Lluïsa Borrás and Antonio Zaya.

1996: *Right Now: Contemporary Art of Cuba.* University of Gainesville, Florida. Curated by Cynthia Berman.

1997: Sixth Havana Biennial.

1997: *Utopian Territories: New Art from Cuba.* Morris and Helen Belkin Gallery and other

---

contribute to installations, performances, and videos, along with learning based on exchanges with academics and Cuban and foreign artists. The work to date has featured passionate opinions on the phenomena shaping the day-to-day political, economic, ethical, and cultural life of Cubans. Bruguera, along with other members of the department, has participated in several international biennials.

In 2008 Rocío García founded the Nuevos Fieras (New Beasts) workshop at the academy of San Alejandro as a haven for students of painting. The name underscores its key objective: for participants to be able to assimilate and become familiar with the principles of color and form explored at the beginning of the twentieth century by the Fauvist painters.

ENGRAVING, PHOTOGRAPHY, AND VIDEO

The stature achieved by engraving, which expanded into three-dimensional work and installations, is one of the highlights of the 1990s. A large new cohort of

ambitious and highly skilled creators has propelled this genre to new heights. For example, Belkis Ayón, Abel Barroso, and Sandra Ramos founded La Huella Múltiple (The Multiple Trace) in 1996, a serial event offering exhibitions, workshops, and conferences. These gatherings steer clear of the limits set by conventional technical criteria while accommodating works based on traditional forms, such as wood engraving, silk screen printing, and chalcography, as well as multimedia experiments. The Joven Estampa (Young Print) prize, sponsored by the Casa de las Américas in Havana since 1987 and open to young artists in Latin America, provides visibility and momentum to the field of engraving.

Extraordinary changes have taken place in photography since 1990. A movement has gathered around the Fototeca de Cuba, which includes experienced figures such as Marta María Pérez Bravo and José M. Fors as well as many new arrivals. The critic José Antonio Molina observes that the photography movement of the 1990s managed "to stop being strictly informative

venues, Vancouver, Canada. Curated by Scott Watson, Keith Wallace, Juan A. Molina, and Eugenio Valdés.

1998: *Festival de performance Ana Mendieta* (Ana Mendieta Performance Art Festival). Unión de Escritores y Artistas de Cuba (UNEAC), Havana.

1998: *Contemporary Art from Cuba: Irony and Survival in the Utopian Island.* Arizona State University Museum, Tempe, Arizona. Curated by Marilyn Zeitlin.

1998: *La dirección de la mirada: Arte cubano contemporáneo* (The Direction of the Gaze: Contemporary Cuban Art). Stadthaus Zürich, Switzerland. Curated by Eugenio Valdés.

1999: *While Cuba Waits: Art from the Nineties.* Track 16 Gallery, Santa Monica, California. Curated by Kevin Power and Pilar Pérez.

2000: Seventh Havana Biennial.

2000: *From the Negative: Conceptual Photography from Cuba.* North Dakota Museum of Art. Organized by pARTs Photographics Arts, Minneapolis, Minnesota. Curated by Cristina Vives.

2001: Museo Nacional de Bellas Artes de La Habana reopens after four years of renovations and inaugurates new buildings and galleries.

2002: *Copyright.* Spanish Cultural Center in Havana. Curated by Suset Sánchez and Giselle Gómez.

2002: *El arte no es para entenderlo* (Art Is Not to Be Understood). Centro de Desarrollo de las Artes Visuales, Havana. Curated by Mabel Llevat.

2002: The first *Havana Auction* is organized and held by the National Council for the Plastic Arts, Havana.

2003: Eighth Havana Biennial.

2003: *Labores Domésticas: Lecciones para otra historia de la visualidad en Cuba: Género, raza y grupos sociales* (Household Chores: Lessons for Another History of the Visual in Cuba: Gender, Race, and Social Groups). Provincial Center for the Visual Arts, Telepinar Gallery, and UNEAC Gallery, Pinar del Río. Curated by Dannys Montes de Oca.

2004: *Mirar a los 60: Antología cultural de una década* (Looking at the 1960s: Cultural Anthology of a Decade). Museo Nacional de Bellas Artes de La Habana.

2005: *Fast Forward I.* Collective exhibition of video art. ICAIC Cinematographic Cultural Center, Havana. Curated by Luisa Marisy.

2005: *Afrocuba: Works on Paper, 1968–2003.* Fine Art Gallery, San Francisco State University, California. Curated by Judith Bettelheim.

2006: Ninth Havana Biennial.

2007: The Servando Cabrera Moreno Museum of Havana is inaugurated, dedicated to preserving

and promoting the personal collection and documentary memory of this Cuban artist.

2008: *Cuba: Art and History from 1868 to Today.* Musée des Beaux Arts de Montreal, Canada. Cosponsored by the Museo Nacional de Bellas Artes de La Habana. Curated by Natalie Bondil.

2008: *States of Exchange: Artists from Cuba.* Institute of International Visual Arts, London. Curated by Gerardo Mosquera and Cylena Simons.

2009: *Exposición y evento teórico: Género (trans) género y los (des) generados* (Exposition and Theoretical Event: Gender [trans] gender and the [de]generated). Bertolt Brecht Cultural Center, Havana. Curated by Andrés Abreu.

2009: *Resistencia y libertad* (Resistance and Liberty). Works by Wifredo Lam, José Bedia, and Raúl Martínez. Museo Nacional de Bellas Artes de La Habana. Curated by Corina Matamoros.

2010: *Without Masks: Contemporary Afrocuban Art.* Johannesburg Art Gallery, South Africa. Curated by Orlando Hernández.

2010: *Queloides: Raza y racismo en el arte cubano contemporáneo* (Keloids: Race and Racism in Cuban Contemporary Art). Centro Wifredo Lam, Havana, and The Mattress Factory, Pittsburgh, Pennsylvania.

This chronology is based primarily on research done in Havana by the specialist Beatriz Gago, with the advisory assistance of José Veigas.

and propagandistic, and moved forward to claim an artistic space" (p. 156).

Many contemporary Cuban photographers focus on the body as a way to stress the fragility of human beings in times of crisis, while simultaneously highlighting the pressing issues of contemporary Cuban society. Women are recognized as a symbol of maternal strength, as the mainstay of cultural traditions, and as objects of desire, vulnerable and sometimes prostituted. Other work explores black and mestizo identity; sexualities in counterpoint to the heterosexual canon; the gay body; memory and records (which can be fictitious) as tools for reconstructing history and identity; poverty and the varieties of marginalization, which are inseparable from class, race, and gender identities, and the relative isolation of specific communities; and a history that is trapped in the ruins of an urban and architectural context, especially Havana.

As a tool available to plastic artists, video was a relatively late arrival on the Cuban art scene, having spread throughout America, Europe, and Asia by the late 1960s. It was not till the mid-1990s that video became a notable presence on the island, but it quickly became one of the most frequently used media formats. The exhibition *Proyecto circo: Performances y audiovisuales* (Circus Project: Performances and Audiovisuals, 2003), organized by Ada Azor and Juan Rivero and presented in tandem with the Havana Biennial, was one of the first to include an array of audiovisual art within a context that gave equal billing to music, dance, theater, and the circus arts. *Play video cubano,* a sampling of contemporary Cuban audiovisuals (2006) curated by Maylin Machado, was one of the first anthological exhibitions of the new media. The international recognition it received made it possible to promote videos both inside and outside Cuba. Machado also curated *Tanda corrida* (Double Feature, 2008), a summation of the achievements in Cuban video between 2005 and 2008. Between 2005 and 2008, the specialist Luisa Marisy organized yearly shows of video and experimental film under the title

Gone with the Macho **(2006), by Elio Rodríguez.** This parody of the movie poster for the American movie *Gone with the Wind* suggests the engagement of Cuban artists with a globalized reality and their fascination with both vernacular sources and the art and culture happening beyond Cuba. © (2006) BY ELIO RODRÍGUEZ

Opposite page: La expresión psicógena **(1996) by Sandra Ceballos.** Multimedia and performance artist Sandra Ceballos (b. 1961) worked with other artists to develop a coherent program of events and exhibitions that promoted the work of young artists. © SANDRA CEBALLOS

Fast-Forward. Since 2008 the city of Camagüey has hosted the International Video Art Festival, the only event of its kind in the country. Other spaces whose exhibition and promotion of video art has been outstanding include the Salón de Arte Digital (Digital Art Salon, since 1990) and the Muestra de Jóvenes Realizadores (Sample of Young Producers, since 2003). In Cuba the development of new media has been retarded by technological constraints and lack of Internet access. ISA's creation of a chair specializing in New Media (directed by Luis Gómez) was expected to hasten development in this field, which was being

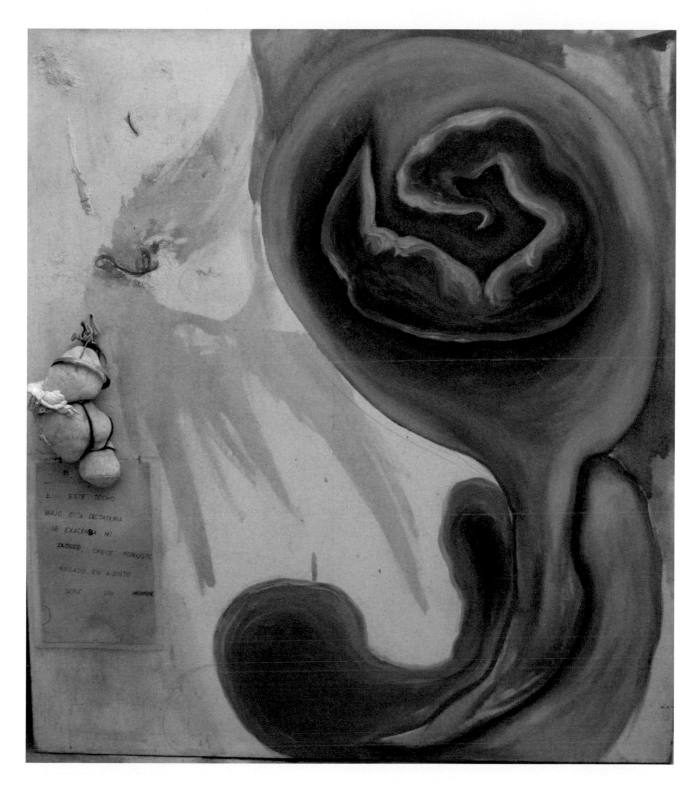

enriched by contributions from Gómez himself, Raúl Cordero, José Fidel García, and Glenda León among others.

Contemporary visual arts in Cuba are engaged in a globalized reality: they are moving on cultural currents that flow over national boundaries, in a world that is increasingly interdependent thanks to patterns of investment and new technology. This transformation builds on a historical foundation of Cuban artists' intense attraction to vernacular sources and their fascination with the art and culture beyond Cuba's shores.

BIBLIOGRAPHY

Dilla Alfonso, Haroldo. "Cuba: The Changing Scenarios
of Governability." *Boundary 2* (special issue from
Cuba edited by John Beverley) 29, no. 3 (Fall 2002):
55–75.

Espinosa, Magaly. *Indagaciones: El nuevo arte cubano y su
estética.* Pinar del Río: Ediciones Almargen, 2003.

Espinosa, Magaly, and Kevin Power, eds. *Antologia de tex-
tos criticos: ElnNuevo arte cubano.* Santa Monica, CA:
Perceval Press, and Torrevieja, Spain: Excelentísimo
Ayuntamiento de Torrevieja, 2006.

Hernández, Orlando. "The Importance of Being Local."
In *Alberto Casado: Todo clandestine, todo popular.*
(Exhibition catalog.) New York: Art in General,
2005.

Hernández, Rafael. *Mirar a Cuba: Ensayos sobre cultura
y sociedad civil.* Havana: Editorial Letras Cubanas,
1999.

Hernández-Reguant, Ariana. "Writing the Special Period."
In *Cuba in the Special Period: Culture and Ideology in
the 1990s,* edited by Ariana Hernández-Reguant.
New York: Palgrave Macmillan, 2009.

Molina, Juan A. "Cuban Art: The Desire to Keep on
Playing." In *Utopian Territories: New Art from Cuba.*
(Exhibition catalog.) Vancouver, Canada: Morris
and Helen Belkin Art Gallery, University of British
Columbia, 1997.

Santana, Andres Isaac, ed. *Nosotros, los más infieles:
Narraciones criticas sobre el arte cubano (1993 – 2005).*
Murcia, Spain: CENDEAC, 2008.

VISUAL ARTS: PHOTOGRAPHY

Rolando Pujol

Héctor Delgado

*Cuban photography and its role in providing a
journalistic record of events and cultural life.*

Photography, one of Cuba's national passions since
it was first introduced, has played an important role
both in the recording of historical events and the artistic life of the country. On 19 March 1839 *Diario de La
Habana* introduced the daguerreotype to Cuba in an
article translated from the *Gazette de France*, explain-
ing that Louis Daguerre had found a way to fix images
obtained from a *camera obscura*. Soon after, Pedro
Téllez Girón, the son of the captain general of the
island, took what is considered the first daguerreotype
made in Cuba, an image of the Plaza de Armas taken
from the Palacio de los Capitanes Generales across
the street. A report in *Noticioso y Lucero* on 5 April
1840 first described this photographic in great detail.
The American George Washington Halsey, who had
previously taught classes in drawing and calligraphy
in Havana, returned to Cuba at the end of 1840 and
asked the colonial authorities for permission to open

a daguerreotype portrait studio. Opening in January 1841, this was the first photography studio in Cuba and the second, after that in the United States, in the world; it preceded those in France and England by several months.

Federico Miahle, a French artist and lithographer who had attended presentations of Daguerre's invention before members of the Academy of Sciences, also arrived in Havana and obtained permission to work as a daguerreotypist. Miahle made Cuba's first lithographic prints of landscapes taken with daguerreotypes. These consisted of a view of the Fuente de India and another of the Santo Cristo del Buen Viaje church, captured by the Italian daguerreotypist Antonio Rezzonico during his stay in Havana. The engravings were included in the fourth edition of *Isla de Cuba Pintoresca* (Picturesque Island of Cuba), published in July 1841, which brought photography and printing together for the first time in Cuba.

COLONIAL PERIOD: GROWING POPULARITY

As the daguerreotype became more popular, the granting of licenses to proprietors of galleries and camera shops became more flexible. A group of foreign daguerreotypists, with varying levels of success, attempted to establish themselves in Havana. Halsey sold his equipment to the American Randall W. Hoit, who thus acquired the excellent camera patented by Alexander Simon Wolcott in New York. Its optical system was different from that of Daguerre, offering a noticeably reduced exposure time of between three and thirty seconds, depending on whether it was sunny or cloudy. In November 1843, Esteban Arteaga became the first Cuban to open a daguerreotype gallery in Havana. In addition to traditional portraits, Arteaga offered colorized daguerreotype images, sold cameras and chemicals, and gave classes that he claimed would allow anyone to master the technique in four days. The 1859 *Anuario y Directorio de La Habana* (Havana Yearbook and Directory) ran a story about other daguerreotype portraitists, including Encarnación Iróstegui, Cuba's first female photographer, and listed nearly twenty galleries and luxurious photography studios.

The daguerreotype was used in Cuba until the mid-1850s, when it began to be replaced by a process known as paper daguerreotype. Gradually, other techniques became known and used in Cuba, such as the collodion process, which despite its complicated handling requirements replaced the daguerreotype and predominated in photography studios until the dry plate appeared in 1880. Images were presented in a variety of styles and formats, reflecting the fashions of the moment. Important galleries also had their own formats, such as the Molinatype of José López Molina, the Bellotype of Adolfo Bello, and the Mestreotype of Esteban Mestre. Mestre, of Catalan origin, ran one of the most renowned and prestigious galleries in Havana

for thirty years; innumerable subjects, both famous and anonymous, were photographed there. Mestre took a portrait of the young José Martí, leaving for posterity one of the few existing childhood photographs of the national hero. Mestre was also well-known as a landscape photographer. His great control over light and the grayscale produced images with an intense romantic atmosphere. Among his most notable and historically valuable photos is the image of Captain General Domingo Dulce and his retinue during the ceremony initiating the demolition of the old walls of Havana on 8 August 1863, which is considered the first news photograph taken in Cuba.

The Rise of Photojournalism The Ten Years' War (1868–1878) gave rise to the first journalistic photographs taken in Cuba. The images from this conflict are compiled in *Album Histórico Fotográfico de la Guerra de Cuba* (Historical Photograph Album of the War of Cuba), with twenty-four large-format images by Galician photographer Leopoldo Varela, and *Album de la Paz* (Album of the Peace Accord), with seventeen photos, completed at the end of the war, by Elías Ibañez. After the war, photography flourished in Cuba as a wave of photographers spread throughout the island. In 1882 a Cuban photographic film, *Tropical Cubana*, was introduced using emulsions specially prepared for the tropics. The opening in 1881 of the first photogravure workshop in Cuba, owned by the Portuguese Alfredo Pereira y Taveira, allowed halftone photography to take the lead in the major illustrated periodicals of the time, such as *La Habana Elegante* and *El Fígaro*. The visit of Spanish princess Eulalia de Borbón to Cuba in 1892 was reported in a grand photographic display in these publications.

The new era of illustrated press relied on photographers working exclusively as photojournalists. José Gómez de la Carrera and Rafael Blanco Santa Coloma were the first to relay important reports from the War of Independence from 1895 through 1898; they were able to visit both the Spanish encampments and those of the Cuban *mambises* (liberation fighters). Other noteworthy war correspondents were Mestre, Antonio Desquirón, Elias Ibañez, Gregorio Casañas, Ramón Carreras, Pérez Argení, Miguel Reyna, Luis V. López, Trelles y Otero, and Colominas. Some of these photographers attempted to reproduce scenes of the battles through posed reenactments; but most of their work consisted of group portraits of the officer corps or soldiers or scenes of troops in encampments or in battle formations. There were, however, particularly brutal photographs taken during the so-called reconcentration decreed by Captain General Valeriano Weyler, when thousands of peasants were confined in villages controlled by the Spanish army, without the most basic resources for subsistence, resulting in more than 200,000 deaths. Dantesque scenes of hunger and desolation were captured by the cameras.

The events related to the explosion on 15 February 1898 of the battleship *U.S.S. Maine* in Havana Bay, which accelerated the end of the war, were recorded by photographer Gómez de la Carrera, who worked as a reporter and official photographer. Images of this event were also captured by Armando Mestri and the Agencia American Photo Studio. With the end of Spanish colonial domination and the transfer of power to U.S. occupying troops on 1 January 1899, the Spanish flag was lowered on the Castillo de los Tres Reyes Magos del Morro (Morro Castle). The ceremony, attended by Spanish general Adolfo Jiménez de Castellanos and U.S. occupation governor John R. Brooke, was photographed by Luis Mestre from the shore across the bay and by Gómez de la Carrera on the Morro Castle esplanade. When the occupation ended two years later, on 20 May 1902, the act of lowering the U.S. flag and raising the Cuban flag was photographically recorded by Gómez de la Carrera and Adolfo Roqueñí.

PHOTOGRAPHY IN THE REPUBLIC

At the start of the Republic, the population continued to be mired in poverty as a consequence of the war. The Platt Amendment, which granted the United States the right to intervene on the island when it considered it necessary, sparked a fierce debate among Cuban politicians and intellectuals. Cuban elites placed a priority on recuperating their wealth. Journalism flourished in this milieu, and publications devoted more and more space to photography. Photojournalists became highly

esteemed, and their work was recognized for its artistry. Gómez de la Carrera and Rafael Santa Coloma, who worked with tripods and magnesium, are the two most important photographers of this period. Agile as squirrels, fast-talking, and likable, the bohemian photographers strolled around Havana hunting for photographable moments to offset the unpredictable nature of their fees.

For the public, photography became more and more accessible. At a price of 1 to 35 pesos, Cubans could buy a Kodak camera and learn to develop the film. Collections of postcards with landscapes and folkloric scenes could be found for sale at American photography shops everywhere. Stereoscopic photos, which for a few cents could take customers on a trip around the world, became popular. Photo aficionados appeared in droves, along with family albums of trips, celebrations, and religious events, among other subjects. The illustrated press dedicated ample space to reflecting high society, with photos of parties and debutante balls, posh weddings, meetings and banquets, laudatory portraits of upstanding citizens, artists, and so on.

Around 1920 magazines such as *Social*, founded by a group of avant-garde intellectuals, developed an editorial philosophy of discovery that granted equal consideration to fine arts and photography. Such magazines published the major photographers of the day, of whom Joaquín Blez (1886–1974) was the most important. His first photos, unlike any that had been seen in Cuba, had a strong impact. His style bore the influences of art nouveau, an internationally popular decorative arts movement at the turn of the century; his photos were delicately retouched, and many, particularly his female nudes, bore his characteristic seal.

The 1930s marked a memorable period for photography in Cuba. During this decade the magazine *Grafos* set standards among artists of the lens. Noteworthy photographers of this period were Van Dyck and Rembrandt, pseudonyms for, respectively, the photographer Lobo, of Spanish origin, and Aladar Hajdú, of Hungarian origin; the painterly sensibility of their images recalled their Flemish and Dutch namesakes. The Photography Cooperative, founded in 1933, provided round-the-clock photographic services and brought together a diverse group of photographers, who competed ferociously for work. They were famous for the bizarre paparazzi style of their pranks and professional trickery. Members of the cooperative were known for their grand photos set in bank lobbies and public buildings in Havana. The 1930s were also memorable for technical innovations undertaken by José Agraz Solans (1909–1982), together with his brother Lorenzo. Agraz, who had an affinity for action shots, took the first photographic sequence published in Cuba—at a bullfight—using one of his photomechanical inventions. He also photographed sports scenes with ambient light, dispensing with the magnesium flash. In 1933 the photographer Rafael Pegudo recorded the general strike and popular uprising that precipitated the fall of the Gerardo Machado regime. One of the most memorable is his photo of a soldier, rifle raised in salute, celebrating the victory along with the people.

During the 1940s and 1950s, photography clubs contributed to the art of photography. Work emerging from the Club Fotográfico de Cuba (Photography Club of Cuba), founded by a group of aficionados, strove to achieve impeccable images through formal and academic means. The club fostered artists such as Rogelio Moré, Tito Álvarez, and Roberto Rodríguez, who would leave a profound mark on Cuban photography through their work and teaching. Another notable name from that period, Alberto Díaz Gutiérrez (1928–2001), known as Alberto Korda, came from the world of advertising. He would later become the photographer behind the famous photo of Che Guevara taken in 1960. Because of his technical and artistic mastery, he was coveted by the most demanding of clients. He was the first to introduce the small format in commercial photography, and he brought sophistication to the image of Cuban models, achieving noteworthy photos in this vein of his wife Natalia Menendez, the fashion model known as Norka.

The social, political, and economic problems that marked this era were not without effect on photography. Images by photographers such as Constantino Arias Miranda (1920–1991), Raúl Corrales (1925–2006), and José Tabío (1915–1975) attest to the profound contradictions that governed the country's destiny. Arias worked for the *Diario Nacional*, *La Calle*, and the magazines *Bohemia* and *Alma Mater*. From humble origins, he captured the everyday life of Havana in his photographs, which depicted political lampooning, prostitutes, gambling, the poor, and picturesque characters. He also covered all types of political events. At the same time, he worked in the Hotel Nacional, where he could record the opulent lifestyle of Havana's high society, giving invaluable testimony to the two extremes of society. Corrales worked for *Prensa Obrera* and the magazines *Bohemia*, *Carteles*, and *Vanidades*, among others. His work during the 1940s and 1950s demonstrated the precarious situation in which the peasants lived. His images broke with the established practice by getting closer to the photographic subject and awarding a leading role to details and objects in the foreground. Tabío framed his photographic work within the themes of social criticism. His photos appear in *Gente de pueblo* (*Village People*), a 1962 book by Onelio Jorge Cardoso. He also published frequently in *Bohemia* and *Carteles* and participated in the filming of several documentaries.

Marking a memorable moment in Republican photography, on 10 March 1949 Fernando Chaviano captured the instant in which several U.S. Marines desecrated the statue of José Martí in Havana's Parque Central. Other photos that had a great journalistic impact were those taken by Panchito Cano and Ernesto Ocaña in the Moncada Barracks on 26 July 1953,

showing the army's execution of prisoners following the attack directed by Fidel Castro. The armed insurrection that this attack initiated would culminate in the Cuban Revolution on 1 January 1959. Powerful images remain from the five-year period of guerilla warfare, taken by foreign correspondents able to reach the war front in the mountains as well as by professional and amateur photographers who witnessed the 1958 final offensive of the Rebel Army.

THE REVOLUTIONARY ERA

The photographic image continued to be the fundamental medium to illustrate any newsworthy event. Because of its availability, photography would also be the most significant form of artistic expression during the first years of the Revolution, reflecting the aesthetic and political imperatives of the moment and demonstrating like never before the social value of the photographer and photography in Cuba. The staggering events taking place made it clear that technical and conceptual changes were needed, thus ushering in the use of 35mm cameras and ambient light as creative tools; the resulting style yielded notable expressive results. Giving dignity to the common man, the peasant, the worker, the soldier, the Afro-Cuban—this was established as a paradigm in revolutionary political discourse and was also incorporated into photography. Such subjects occupied grand spaces in the press as the new heroes of everyday life, exalting human dignity and national pride. Among the most important photojournalists of the 1960s were Osvaldo Salas Freire, Roberto Salas, Alberto Korda, Jorge Oller, José Agraz Solans, Raúl Corrales, Tito Álvarez, Constantino Arias Miranda, Perfecto Romero Ramírez, Mario Collado, Liborio Noval, and Ernesto Fernández Nogueras.

Facing difficult moments and the activities of both internal and foreign enemies, the Revolution made use of photography to call out to and raise the awareness of the masses. Printed photographs on posters and billboards bore such captions as "To Arms! Everyone to the Plaza!" and "Commander in Chief, At Your Orders!" Confrontation with the United States and various counterrevolutionary actions led to bloody events, such as the explosion in Havana harbor of the French freighter *La Coubre* on 4 August 1960. There, José Agraz and Generoso Funcasta took impressive photographs of the first moments of the tragedy. During the burial of the victims, Alberto Korda took the famous photograph of Ernesto Che Guevara, considered the most reproduced photograph in the world. When the Bay of Pigs invasion took place on 17 April 1961, Raúl Corrales, Ernesto Fernández, Sergio Canales, and Tirso Martínez were present as photojournalist war correspondents. Martínez took the iconic photograph of this event, capturing the moment when Castro descended from a T-34 tank. Cuban photojournalists also created graphic testimony

***Zoo-logos* (1991–1992), by Eduardo Muñoz Ordoqui.** This photograph was part of a series titled *Zoo-logos,* produced in 1991 and 1992 by Cuban photographer Eduardo Muñoz Ordoqui (b. 1964). © EDUARDO MUÑOZ ORDOQUI

to the mobilization of the people during the dangerous crises of the Cuban Missile Crisis and the War against the Bandits in the mountains of Escambray, which cast a shadow over relations between Cuba and the United States during the 1960s.

At the same time, great emphasis was placed on publications like *Bohemia, INRA, Verde Olivo, Revolución, Hoy,* and many others, which published images of economic and social development, with extensive photo features about education, agriculture and industry, mobilization of the sugar harvests, defense preparations, development of children and women, and health and culture. The structural changes occurring in Cuban society were reflected among intellectuals and artists, with photographers demonstrating a marked inclination toward more sensitive and reflexive photography. During this period, called the Transition, which lasted approximately from the late 1960s to the early 1980s, the majority of photographers of the preceding period continued to work, along with other notables such as Ivan Cañas, Mario Ferrer, Maria Eugenia Haya, Mario García Joya, Félix Arencibia, Adalberto Roque, and Fernando Guillermo López (Chinolope).

The so-called contemporary transformative movement, which began in the mid-1980s, witnessed the rise of a generation of new photographers who, without distancing themselves from documentary, assume an intimist vision, more aesthetic and conceptual. Many of these artists reexamined images of the body, psychological portraiture, expressionist landscapes, self-portraiture, abstract photography,

and surrealism. Large-scale personal exhibitions returned, and Cuban photography began to be seen in important cultural venues such as Paris and New York. Fototeca de Cuba, as an official institution, took on an important promotional role and was responsible for producing numerous projects. In the twenty-first century, the most notable photographers include, among many others, Raúl Cañibano, Pedro Abascal, René Peña, Gonzo González, Cirenaica Moreira, José Manuel Fors, and Abigail González. The development of digital photographic techniques has opened new areas of experimentation to those who have absorbed the legacy of several generations of photographers—a legacy they are extending through their own creativity and skill.

BIBLIOGRAPHY

Cardoso, Onelio Jorge. *Gente de un nuevo pueblo.* Giron, 1981.

Cuba: 100 años de fotografía. Curated by Juan M. Díaz Burgos, Mario Díaz, and Paco Salinas, with texts by Miguel Castro Muñiz and Jorge Oller Oller. Spain: Librería Mestizo, in collaboration with Fototeca de Cuba, 1998.

Lagomasino, Julio. *Historia del Fotorreporterismo en Cuba.* [Album of the Fiftieth Anniversary of the Reporters Association of Havana.] 1952.

Martínez, Mayra. "Historia de la Fotografía Cubana." *Revolución y Cultura* (May 1980).

Valle, Rufino del. "Historia de la Fotografía Cubana en el siglo XIX." *Opus Habana* 8, no. 3 (2004–2005).

VISUAL ARTS: POSTER ART

Sara Vega Miche

Visually striking politics, art, and culture in posters.

The stature that political and cultural posters have attained in Cuba and abroad since the Revolution of 1959 is undeniable. Much has been written and remarked about this unique phenomenon in the visual arts of the island.

POLITICAL POSTERS OF THE REVOLUTION

During the 1960s and 1970s a new visual idiom was established within Cuban culture, especially in the urban context. As a bearer of all types of fascinating images and messages, posters became an ideal medium to convey the values of the newborn revolution. Posters in a diverse array of formats appeared all over Havana and its buildings, attracting a public in search of new and different ideas. The target audience was transformed—better informed and more highly cultured, with a heightened aesthetic sensibility.

Before the triumph of the Revolution, the occasional and sporadic nature of the national movie industry did not encourage the growth of high-quality graphics. Posters that advertised the showings of local and foreign films complied with the visual standards of the age where American graphics reigned supreme thanks to the worldwide reach of U.S. films. The elements most frequently used by Cuban designers of the day included the faces of the movie stars, the exaltation of a certain so-called tropical feeling—royal palms, thatched huts, horse carts, dance, eroticism, landscapes—and a large area to insert the names of musicians, dancers, and song titles if the film happened to be a musical.

There was a noticeable abuse of typographic information in order to fill up the leftover space on the poster. In order to hook the viewer, certain features deemed essential were exaggerated. The heroes were depicted as tougher than they were on screen and the women as more sensual; the violence and the love scenes were quite explicit on the posters. In the 1950s certain Cuban designers redesigned foreign posters, particularly those from Europe, in order to adapt them to the preferences of a Cuban public whose tastes had already been shaped by American styles. During this period advertising was gaining importance in the Cuban media, and it undoubtedly prepared the ground for future changes in the promotion of cultural and political messages. Indeed, next to the United States, Cuba became the country with the greatest amount and the most effective marketing propaganda in Latin America. After the triumph of the Revolution in 1959, the Cuban advertising agencies were immediately nationalized. Accordingly, many commercial illustrators with enormous experience looked toward new fields that were opening up, especially that of revolutionary propaganda, where posters began to play a key role.

The new messages appeared on posters, flyers, print ads, television spots, urban billboards, newspapers, and magazines and were created by designers and public relations personnel from advertising agencies. Raúl Martínez, Jesús Forjans, Tony Évora, Olivio Martínez, Mario Sandoval, and Rolando de Oráa, among others, emerged as the leaders of a rising visual language as they transformed the public and private atmosphere of Havana and other cities in Cuba.

During those first few years, illustrators experienced in advertising were recruited to convey the new messages. The reality of the Revolution imposed new codes, both for movie posters and for economic, educational, political, and health campaigns. In order to foster change throughout Cuba, there was a new requirement to explain, exhort, and convince, and graphic design became a key instrument in that social process. Insofar as the promotion and sale of articles and goods were no longer of interest to managers and the general public, advertising was thus drained of content.

The nationalization of the advertising agencies encouraged the rise of the Comisión de Orientación Revolucionaria (COR; Revolutionary Orientation Commission), which was attached to the party of the Revolution and took over responsibility for all political propaganda in an effort to control the message. Political posters, for example, increasingly showed images of the leaders of the Revolution along with slogans and quotations from their speeches. At the same time, the use of graphic images of tools, weapons, rotary gears, and the sinewy arms of the workers demonstrated a certain influence of socialist realism as an aesthetic current. Photography, too, was convenient, given the speed with which certain messages had to be designed. It provided the figure to complement the text, reinforcing the general image underlying the ideological message.

Over time, COR's posters improved from an aesthetic point of view. Notable examples include *A las armas* (To Arms, 1962), by Roberto Quintana; *Clik* (Click, 1969) and *Devuelve el aceite usado* (Give Used Oil Back, 1969), by Felix Beltrán; and *Ahórrala* (Save It, 1969), by Faustino Pérez, which were designed for the electricity, oil, and water conservation campaigns. Others that were effective include *Hasta la victoria siempre* (Ever Onward to Victory, 1968), by Antonio Pérez (Ñiko), commemorating Che Guevara after his death; and *XIV Aniversario del Asalto al Cuartel Moncada* (Fourteenth Anniversary of the Assault on the Moncada Barracks, 1967), by Olivio Martínez.

A key factor in the appearance of better and more effective political posters was the establishment in 1966 of the Organización de Solidaridad con los Pueblos de África, Asia, y América Latina (OPSAAAL; Organization for Solidarity with the Peoples of Africa,

■ *See also*

Cuban Thought and Cultural Identity: Socialist Thought

Education: Literacy Campaign of 1961

Film: 1959–1989

La paz de Nixon (1972) by Lazaro Abreu. Toward the end of the 1960s, political posters came to be perceived as a vanguard in the panorama of Cuba's visual language. This poster, *La paz de Nixon* (Nixon's Peace), comments on the U.S. bombing campaign over Southeast Asia during the Vietnam War. THE ART ARCHIVE/ THE PICTURE DESK, INC.

by Alfredo Rostgaard, both from 1969; *Jornada de solidaridad con América Latina* (Latin America Solidarity Day, 1970), by Asela Pérez; and *Todos con Viet Nam* (Everyone with Vietnam, 1971), by Ernesto Padrón.

CULTURAL POSTERS

Toward the end of the 1960s and throughout the next decade, political posters underwent a major evolution in their use of photographs (whether in outline, solarized, or high contrast), in the integration of image and text, and in their economy of expressive resources. In this new phase, the political poster was perceived as a vanguard in the panorama of Cuba's visual language. However, the history of cultural posters after the triumph of the Revolution followed a different path than that of political posters. Almost from the very beginning, graphic design in the vast domain of culture had greater thematic diversity and creative freedom because it was not bound by the limitations of messages determined by an ideology.

Among the cultural institutions that broke new ground in the visual arts were the Instituto Cubano del Arte e Industria Cinematográficos (ICAIC; Cuban Institute of the Cinematographic Arts and Industry), the Unión de Escritores y Artistas de Cuba (UNEAC; Union of Writers and Artists of Cuba), the Casa de las Américas (House of the Americas), and the Consejo Nacional de Cultura (CNC; National Culture Council).

During the early 1960s the CNC focused on elevating the culture of the citizenry by sponsoring art shows, theater productions, ballet, and festivals. Rolando de Oráa and José M. Villa worked for the CNC; subsequently, due to the increasing number of cultural promotions, they were joined by Héctor Villaverde, César Mazola, Roger Aguilar, Ricardo Reymena, Rafael Zarza, and Juan Boza. When José Gómez Fresquet (Frémez) took over the leadership of the design team in 1967, he introduced major changes such as increased experimentation with abstract symbols as well as figurative elements using collages and photomontage. Remarkable posters from the CNC include *El robo del cochino* (The Pig Robbery, 1961), by Raúl Martínez; *La ópera de los tres centavos* (The Three-Penny Opera), by Héctor Villaverde and *Quién le teme a Virginia Woolf* (Who's Afraid of Virginia Woolf), by Rolando de Oráa, both from 1967; and *Vade Retro* (1968), by Umberto Peña.

Casa de las Américas and UNEAC sponsored all sorts of events, including some of the country's political anniversaries. In 1967 Rostgaard designed the emblematic *Canción Protesta* (Protest Song) for Casa de las Américas, which became an icon among Cuban posters. The work of Umberto Peña was also widely recognized at this institution, no less for his editorial design than for his poster work.

ICAIC, which was founded in March 1959 and led by Alfredo Guevara, immediately established the standard for graphic design for the new Cuban film,

Asia, and Latin America), whose purpose was to unite all the progressive forces of the so-called Third World nations, and, subsequently, the founding of its magazine *Tricontinental*, whose artistic director from 1967 to 1969 was the remarkable designer Alfredo Rostgaard. The magazine was designed for readers on three continents and published in several languages; inserted in each copy was a small-format, offset-printed poster. Many of these posters were noteworthy for their trend toward synthesis and the use of flat color fields, a veiled graphical influence of posters designed for the movies. Among the many important and effective works by OSPAAAL are *Semana de solidaridad con Viet Nam* (Vietnam Solidarity Week, 1968), by René Mederos; *Cristo Guerrillero* (Guerrilla Christ) and *Black Power*,

and it became a leading influence in the country. Saúl Yelín, the promoter of this poster art movement, developed a major aesthetic movement that included designers with enormous advertising experience as well as young artists who already had some training. The posters of Eduardo Muñoz Bachs, Antonio Fernández Reboiro, Alfredo Rostgaard, Rafael Morante, Julio Eloy Mesa, and Antonio Pérez (Ñiko), among others, quickly made their mark with the public. These designers tapped into the aesthetic currents that dominated the visual arts around the world at that time: pop art, op art, psychedelics, kinetic art, and others less known.

The rejection of all that had come before, as well as the shortages of certain resources after 1964, presented a challenge to these designers. They resorted to the wide variety of resources that actually were available to them: drawing, painting, and collage, along with clippings of images and texts from a variety of magazines. Given the impossibility of using catalogued and printable typographics, they suggested to the silkscreen printers the locations, font sizes, and styles that the typography of film credits would have had. Their design mock-ups were based on photographs, *trouvé* color paper, vignettes, and images printed on any underlying medium. Movie posters, which up until then had been unappreciated and undervalued in the universe of Cuban visual arts, acquired such importance that ICAIC became the flagship for silkscreen printing in the country.

The silkscreen printers in charge of producing the posters faced shortages of ink, paper, squeegees, and silk even as they discovered new ways to mix paints, bases, and alcohols from a variety of sources. When faced with emergencies (which happened regularly) they came up with timely solutions, adapting their design sketches to the real technical possibilities of the workshop and the availability of colors.

Under the aegis of encouragement of all things artistic, innovative, and transcendent, ICAIC's designers defied all obstacles, transforming the existing visual communication codes and asking the viewer for a heightened, more complex decoding. They limited typographic information to the film title and its main credits to avoid interfering with the general design of the poster, or else they integrated it naturally. They worked within an economy of means and incorporated anything they found to be useful. Often they conceived designs with a starkly restricted chromatic spectrum over backgrounds that were primarily black and white. The movie posters were not based on ideological conditioning or marketing principles; instead, they aimed to enrich the visual education of the viewer to promote the broadest cultural values.

POSTERS IN THE COMMUNITY

The 1960s ushered in changes in the political and cultural realms all around the world, and the ambition to change the world remained alive in Cuba during the following decade. From the early 2000s, this period

is looked back on with nostalgia for its idealistic faith that political and social goals—particularly those of the left and the progressive forces—were not only right, but reachable.

ICAIC's period of cinematographic splendor produced some of the most valuable films in the nation's history. Cuban film came into its own and gained international recognition as a different aesthetic, with new trends and new creators who delved deeply into the essential aspects of Cuban identity. These also were transformative years for the visual cosmos of graphic design, which became an effective instrument of revolutionary propaganda. Posters ushered in the magnificence of that decade and sustained it, contributing to a gradual elevation of the viewer's intelligent gaze. Posters were freed from commonplace locations—building facades and windows—to take over streets so that passersby could see how they changed the city virtually overnight. City billboards, which hitherto had been

Canción protesta (1967) by Alfredo Rostgaard. The posters of Alfredo Rostgaard (b. 1943) and other designers tapped into the aesthetic currents that dominated the visual arts around the world during the 1960s, including pop art, op art, psychedelics, and kinetic art. DIGITAL IMAGE © THE MUSEUM OF MODERN ART/LICENSED BY SCALA/ART RESOURCE, NY

reserved for commercial advertising, were utilized for political and cultural propaganda that reached every sector of the community. Public spaces became the ideal stage for the expression and promotion of political, economic, and cultural themes. Starting with their sharp break with the old visual language, posters, billboards and murals made it possible for interest and reflection to become an essential part of social life. Graphic design went even further and attained a vital space in the visual arts of Cuba.

BIBLIOGRAPHY

Alonso, Luis. *10 dibujantes cubanos: Sus influencias y participación en el desarrollo del anuncio ilustrado*. Cuba: n.p., 1958.

Bermúdez, Jorge R. *La imagen constante: El cartel cubano del siglo XX*. Havana: Editorial Letras Cubanas, 2000.

Carpentier, Alejo. "Una siempre renovada muestra de artes sugerentes." *Cine Cubano* 54–55 (1969): 90–91.

Juan, Adelaida de. *Pintura cubana: Temas y variaciones*. Havana: Ediciones UNEAC, 1978.

López Oliva, Manuel. "Carteles cubanos de cine, impresos de veinte años." *Cine Cubano* 95 (1979): 95–107.

Pogolotti, Graziella. Introduction to *1000 Carteles cubanos de cine*. Havana: Museo Nacional de Bellas Artes de La Habana, 1979.

Pogolotti, Marcelo. *La república al través de sus escritores*. Havana: Editorial Letras Cubanas, 2002.

Rodríguez González, Marina. *El cartel cubano: Conversando con Rostgaard*. Havana: Editora Política, 1999.

Stermer, Dugald, and Susan Sontag. *The Art of the Revolution*. London: Pall Mall, 1970.

Vega, Jesús. *El cartel cubano de cine*. Havana: Editorial Letras Cubanas, 1996.

W–Z

THE WORKS OF TANIA BRUGUERA

Carrie Lambert-Beatty

Political and performance artist Tania Bruguera's risk-taking as a form of art.

The work of Cuban artist Tania Bruguera, born in Havana in 1968, both maps the field of performance in contemporary art and exceeds it. In an ongoing exploration of power and politics, engagement and expression, she has moved through several distinct modes of performance, producing a series of remarkable experiences for audiences, which are also complex tools for thinking about the political present in Cuba and beyond.

Bruguera was born in Cuba, but because her father was a Cuban diplomat, she spent many years of her childhood abroad, in France, Lebanon, and Panama. She attended the Instituto Superior de Arte in Havana, where she began her career with a project reenacting and interpreting the oeuvre of Cuban American artist Ana Mendieta (anticipating by many years the interest in re-performance that characterized contemporary art in the early 2000s). Bruguera came to international attention with powerfully symbolic actions in the tradition of performance art pioneers such as Mendieta, Joseph Beuys, or Marina Abramovic.

Like the best of this historical performance, Bruguera's *El peso de la culpa* (The Burden of Guilt, 1997) is a deftly managed balancing act. On the one hand, her action is abject and shocking: While wearing a gutted lamb draped over the front of her naked body, she mixes a paste of salt water and Cuban soil and eats it. When she stands to eat, the animal's vertical axis aligns with hers, creating the impression that it is her body opening, martyr-like, before the viewer. This powerful image had specific meanings in its original context.

In Cuban Spanish, *eating dirt* is a reference to poverty and a metaphor of hard times; in English, it is an idiom for shame. It also invokes a legend which holds that rather than submit to their colonial occupiers, indigenous Cubans committed collective suicide by ingesting the soil of their island, making her performance an image of national guilt and unsettled debts, submission and sacrifice that was highly suggestive in the context of 1990s Cuba.

ARTISTIC COMING-OF-AGE

Bruguera's artistic coming-of-age in the 1990s coincided with seismic shifts in Cuban history—the collapse of the Soviet Union, the Special Economic Period—and in the nation's art world as well. Most notably, at the beginning of the decade, many of the politically inclined artists who had shaped Cuban art in the 1980s left the country. *El peso de la culpa* may register these changed conditions. The most notorious artwork of the 1980s was Angel Delgado's performance *La esperanza es lo único que se está perdiendo* (Hope Is the Only Thing We Are Losing), in which the artist defecated near a prepared copy of the official government newspaper. Bruguera, ingesting a base, almost fecal material, might be figuratively cleaning up after Delgado, taking in what had been expelled and replacing the outward-directed gesture of defiance with the inwardness of guilt.

ART AND POLITICS

However, Bruguera soon began to question the mode of body-based art represented by *El peso de la culpa.* Shifting the emphasis from the artist's body to the experience of the viewer, in *Untitled (Havana, 2000)* Bruguera created a sort of lived metaphor for the contradictions of political life in Cuba. Viewers walking into the infamous Fortaleza de la Cabaña entered a long hall that was almost completely dark, stumbling and picking their way over a floor covered with rotting sugarcane. At the end of the hall was a television monitor showing historical images of Fidel Castro. Finally, as viewers' eyes adjusted to the dark, they perceived naked figures in the shadows, making repeated,

Tania Bruguera in Havana, 2000. Cuban artists of the 1990s recast the exodus of friends, family members, and teachers as both a personal loss and a political statement. Rafts, like this one by Tania Bruguera (b. 1968), became a central motif in their works. AP IMAGES/ CRISTOBAL HERRERA

obsessive gestures, such as wiping their faces or bodies. Outside of Cuba, Bruguera made a number of works that subjected viewers to operations of power. At one exhibition, for instance, viewers gradually noticed an increasing number of uniformed officers walking guard dogs through the space. In another, museumgoers submitted to pat downs and bag searches.

No Safe Haven Most dramatically, in 2008, museumgoers at London's Tate Modern found themselves being herded about the huge Turbine Hall by police on horseback who used their accustomed crowd-control techniques on the audience. In this set of works, Bruguera questioned the illusion that art is a safe haven, removed from the operations of power. Her tactic was characteristically discomforting as well as ambiguous. She herself subjected viewers to operations of repressive power on the one hand. On the other, by treating the viewers *as if they were dangerous*, she made a proposition about the potential potency of the audience—and of art.

Tatlin's Whisper #6 In modernity, art is a space of special freedoms but also of circumscribed effects. Bruguera's work pushes at both sides of the paradox of art's power, perhaps nowhere more dramatically than in *El susurro de Tatlin #6 (versión para La Habana)*, (Tatlin's Whisper #6 [Havana Version]) Bruguera set up an empty stage at the official exhibition venue of the 2008 Havana Biennial, wiring a microphone to speakers on the street outside the building. She then simply invited members of the audience to speak about whatever they wanted, for one minute each. Since the mid-1990s, the Cuban government has censored visual art less severely than the media or other forums. Bruguera was putting this censorship to the test, essentially making her artwork a loophole for free speech. Among the viewers who took the stage were several who had experienced censure by the state, such as the dissident blogger Yoani Sanchez and the Cuban critic Guadalupe Alvarez, who lives in exile in Ecuador and who stood at the microphone for her full minute, silently crying. In some ways the artwork became what Hakim Bey calls a "temporary autonomous zone," but it was a very limited one. A man and a woman wearing army fatigues perched a live dove on the shoulder of each speaker who took the stage—referring to the dove that landed on Castro's shoulder during his famous 1959 speech. When the minute of allotted time ran out, the military figures summarily removed each speaker from the stage.

Arte de Conducta *El susurro de Tatlin #6 (versión para La Habana)* was a work of art, a touching and provocative image of hopes and constraints in contemporary Cuba, but it was also a political event; not only a representation of dissident speech, but actually a forum for it. Of course, this begs a question. What is speech if not representation? Like much of Bruguera's work, *El susurro de Tatlin #6* gives the lie to the diametrical opposition of art and real life. The refusal of that binarism is at the center of what Bruguera has termed Arte de Conducta (art of behavior). Examples from her own work include teaching gallerygoers how to make Molotov cocktails; playing Russian roulette during a speech about art's role in politics; and starting a political party for immigrants, based in Queens, New York. But perhaps her most influential work in this vein is the *Cátedra de Arte de Conducta*, a study program in behavior art that Bruguera ran in Havana from 2002 to 2009, exploring critical and political art. This is performance, not as theatrical event, but as pedagogical experiment. At the opposite end of the spectrum from choreographed rituals such as *El peso de la culpa*, the *Cátedra de Arte de Conducta* was less a performance than an intervention, one whose effects on Cuban art—and politics—might play out for years to come.

BIBLIOGRAPHY

Bey, Hakim. *T.A.Z.: The Temporary Autonomous Zone, Ontological Anarchy, Poetic Terrorism*. 2nd ed. New York: Autonomedia, 2003.

Bishop, Claire. "Speech Disorder." *Artforum* (Summer 2009): 121–122.

Camnitzer, Luis. *New Art of Cuba*. 2nd ed. Austin: University of Texas Press, 2003.

Goldberg, Roselee. "Regarding Ana," interview with Tania Bruguera. In *Tania Bruguera*. Chicago, and Venice, Italy: Lowitz & Sons for the 51 Biennale di Venezia Art Exhibition, 2005, pp. 8–21.

Matt, Gerald. Interview with Tania Bruguera. In *Interviews*. Cologne, Germany: Walther König, 2007.

Mosquera, Gerardo. "Cuba in Tania Bruguera's Work: The Body Is the Social Body." In *Tania Bruguera: On the Political Imaginary*, edited by Helene Posner. Milan, Italy, and New York: Charta/Neuberger Museum of Art, 2010.

Muñoz, José. "Performing Greater Cuba: Tania Bruguera and the Burden of Guilt. In *Holy Terrors: Latin American Women Perform*, edited by Diana Taylor and Roselyn Constantino. Durham, NC: Duke University Press, 2003.

Perez-Rementeria, Dinorah. "Performance: An Open-Heart Operation on Selected Works by Tania Bruguera." *Art Nexus* 7, no. 70 (September–October 2008): 94–99.

Sanchez, Yoani. "And They Gave Us the Microphones . . . ," *Generation Y*. 30 March 2009. Available from http://www.desdecuba.com/generationy/?p=472.

☟ THE WORLD AND CUBA

Historically, ports have represented gateways to other worlds, as ships entered and exited through them. Ports are the entry point onto an island, and through them products and cultures absorb the world that touches them. Over the course of its history, the island nation of Cuba has been influenced by many foreign cultures through its ports, beginning with the colonial power of Spain. In addition, the African cultures of Cuba's slave population had an impact on Cuba's music and culture.

Following Cuba's independence from Spain in 1898, Cuba's northern neighbor, the United States, had a powerful effect on the island. The United States intervened militarily and politically in Cuba, while its culture influenced Cuba's language, customs, and even holidays.

Cuba was not only an importer of other cultures; it also was an exporter of its own unique culture throughout the twentieth century. Cuban music, dance, and literature were found throughout the world. The mambo craze, begun by Cuban musicians, influenced the music of a generation of Americans and Mexicans.

The Cuban Revolution in 1959 captured the imagination of the international New Left, and groups throughout the world, including the United States, modeled their struggles on that of Cuba. In Latin America, in particular, the revolution had a profound impact as armed movements challenged military regimes backed by the United States. That Cuba could be an inspiration in bringing together the disparate nations of the hemisphere had long been a dream of the Cuban writer José Martí, whose essay "Our America" had foreshadowed some of the issues that Latin America grappled with in the twentieth century.

THE WORLD AND CUBA: CUBA AND SPAIN IN THE COLONIAL PERIOD

Consuelo Naranjo Orovio

Cuba in the Spanish imagination.

Cuba has occupied a special place in Spanish literature and art ever since explorer Christopher Columbus wrote letters to his sponsors King Ferdinand and Queen Isabella of Spain describing the beauty of the island during his first visit there in 1492.

Authors of books about Cuba such as José María de Andueza (*Isla de Cuba pintoresca* [1841; Picturesque Island of Cuba]) and Frédéric Mialhe (*Álbum pintoresco de la isla de Cuba* [1848; Picturesque Album of the Island of Cuba]) described it as exotic and picturesque and that description took root. Cuban faces and ways of life, captured in images ranging from Landaluce's engravings to cigar bands and labels, have left an illustrated history of Cuba and Spain, creating impressions that endure to modern times.

THE CREATION OF A MYTH: TRAVELERS AND WRITERS

Descriptions by Columbus and later chroniclers created the aura of an exuberant, lush, and exotic Cuba that has never faded. Its geography, climate, rich vegetation, and colors, with inhabitants so different

CHRONOLOGY OF EVENTS

1492: Columbus's letters to Spanish monarchs offer first written description of Cuba.

1608: Publication of "Espejo de paciencia" ("Mirror of Patience") by Silvestre de Balboa.

1733: Don Santiago de Pita writes the first theatrical work by a Cuban, "El Principe Jardinero" ("The Gardener Prince").

1761: José Martín Félix celebrates Cuban identity in *Llave del Nuevo Mundo* (*Key to the New World*).

1790: *Papel Periódico de la Havana*, the first Cuban newspaper, begins publication.

1819: At the request of Governor-General José Cienfuegos, the Spanish king names Cuba "La Siempre Fidelísima Isla" ("The Always Most Faithful Island").

1831: The magazine *Revista bimestre de la Isla de Cuba* begins publication in Havana.

1833: The Cuban Academy of Literature founded.

1841: *Isla de Cuba pintoresca* (*The Picturesque Island of Cuba*) by José María de Andueza sets the tone for romantic portrayals of Cuba.

1882: José Martí publishes his first book of poetry, *Ismaelillo*, considered the first major work of *Modernismo*, an effort to craft a uniquely Latin American literature.

1890: José Julián del Casal seeks an authentic Cuban voice in his *Hojas al Viento* (*Leaves in the Wind*).

1898: Cuba gains independence from Spain under the Treaty of Paris.

from Europeans, led some of those arriving in the New World to feel they were in a tropical paradise. On his first trip, Columbus described Cuba in a letter to his royal sponsors as "the most beautiful land that eyes have seen": "And I assure your highnesses it seems to me that under the sun there couldn't be found better in fertility, in temperature, in abundance of good and healthy water, unlike the rivers of Guinea, which are all pestilent" (Colon p. 150).

At another time, Columbus noted:

The island of Juana [Cuba] has mountains that seem to touch the sky: many abundant and healthy rivers bathe them everywhere. . . . All the land presents various perspectives full of much diversity of immensely high trees, with leaves as green and shiny as those in Spain in the month of May. . . . There are seven or eight varieties of palm trees, superior to ours in their beauty and height; there are admirable pine trees, vast fields and meadows.

Humboldt p. 405

Columbus's descriptions helped create an image that gave birth to the myth of the Americas as the land of wealth and promise. Added to this idea of paradise, which emanated directly from the geography, were new visions of the island and the Americas in general, influenced by the goals of those who attempted to conquer and colonize this New World. Whether driven by a thirst for knowledge, the thrill of adventure, or by hunger, all of them—conquerors, sailors, fugitives, immigrants—came to view paradise as a place where it was easy to get rich on an abundance of gold and precious metals. The dream of "making America," the idea that led millions of Spaniards to immigrate to the New World, was based in large measure on this fascination, dating from the conquest of the Americas.

Cuba's lack of precious metals pushed the Spaniards to conquer other lands. In their campaign of conquest and colonization, the islands of the Caribbean, and especially Cuba, were springboards for expeditions to the continent headed by Hernández de Córdova, Juan de Grijalva, Hernán Cortés, Hernando de Soto, Pedro Menéndez de Avilés, and others. With the establishment of new maritime routes, Cuba became a strategic transit and supply point for troops and fleets. At first a colonial trading post, the island came to have a specific weight in the Spanish monarchy's policies, and for centuries it was the only place offering access to the American continent. Furthermore, in the seventeenth and eighteenth centuries, the Caribbean was a theater of confrontation among empires; Cuba and the Antilles became simultaneously strongholds of Spanish power and centers of resistance to that power. The fortification and walling of Cuban cities, along with the dispatch of additional troops, made Cuba vital to the maintenance of the Spanish empire.

CRIOLLO CUBA

It is impossible to understand how the idea of Cuba was formed and transformed, and how it was perceived in Spain, without considering what was taking place on the island. In this context, it is important to note that Cuba's criollos—naturalized descendants of the Spanish—were the first to value and acknowledge their land. This recognition of their own terrain, while extolling its riches, geography, people, natural bounty, and plants, defined some features of Cuba's identity as well as its place in the world. The island's strategic position was highlighted by historian José Martín Félix de Arrate in his history of Havana, *Llave del Nuevo Mundo Antemural de las Indias Occidentales* (Key to the New World, Bulwark of the Indies), written in 1761 and published in 1830 by the Economic Society of Friends of the Country. (Its title was the official name given to Havana by royal charter in May 1634.) In the second half of the eighteenth century, histories written by Bernardo Joseph de Urrutia y Matos, Ignacio José Urrutia y Montoya, Pedro Agustín Morell de Santa Cruz, and Nicolás Joseph Ribera, among others, also promoted the image of Cuba as a bucolic paradise and demonstrated its riches and the means to develop them, showing the world that they, the criollos, were the true inhabitants and owners of a territory they recognized as their own. Criollos, travelers, governing authorities, and the wealth generated by the escalating production of sugar all contributed to the concept of Cuba as "the Albion of the Americas" (Abate Raynal 1759) and the "Pearl of the Antilles." Thus, Cuba played a leading role in the international context, indirectly instilling in its inhabitants the pride of living in that country.

Travelers' accounts and *costumbrista* novels about local life and customs helped popularize the slowly developing view of a colonial Cuba in which rhythm and music, the color of its men and women, and bucolic landscapes concealed other realities. Alexander Humboldt, the Countess of Merlín Gertrúdis Gómez de Avellaneda, Samuel Hazard, Frederika Bremer, and Abiel Abbot are some of the nineteenth-century authors who depicted a benevolent and pleasant image of Cuba and its inhabitants. Some of Samuel Hazard's commentaries on his visit to Cuba in 1868 reflect his fascination:

> Good heavens, what a sight greets us there! Lights blaze in such profusion that it seems more than day; music and dancing are everywhere; songs, deviltry, and mirth have taken complete possession of the place; while people of all ages, sexes, and colors are mixed up together, in what seems inextricable confusion, intent upon having a good time in the open air, while their masters and betters are doing the same thing under cover.

pp. 122–123

COLONIAL CUBA AFTER THE AMERICAS' INDEPENDENCE, 1824–1898

Cuba and Puerto Rico were the territories that remained faithful to Spain following the independence of the continental Latin America territories. After 1824, several factors made it possible for Cuba to remain under Spanish rule. Spokesman of the Cuban planters, Francisco de Arango y Parreño (1765–1837), and other illustrious men quickly declared their support for the mother country. The existence of slavery and, fundamentally, convergent interests among the Cuban and Spanish elites and the Spanish government established a new framework for relations, in which agreement and continual negotiation were key to maintaining the status quo. Economic interests were more important than the desire for independence; instead, throughout the nineteenth century, ever-stronger voices demanded administrative and commercial reforms that would give Cuba rights similar to those enjoyed in peninsular Spain. The Criollo elite navigated between profits and various fears: fear of the blacks, fear that at any moment a revolution spearheaded by slaves could erupt, and fear of the Africanization of its people and culture resulting from the massive influx of African slaves. In 1819, when his position as captain general came to an end, José Cienfuegos requested that the king grant Cuba the title of "The Always Faithful Island of Cuba," a name repeated over and over and printed on numerous documents, currency, and other objects.

In some Spanish political circles during the last quarter of the nineteenth century, Cuba acquired a decisive role as guarantor of the Restoration's political regime. Many felt that it was necessary to retain Cuba at any price—"to the last man, to the last peseta," as Spanish prime minister Antonio Cánovas del Castillo insisted in 1897—and this attitude prolonged Cuba's independence struggle (in two wars, 1868–1878 and 1895–1898), as well as prevented the adoption of measures that would have established a new framework of Spanish-Cuban relations. When the island finally achieved its independence, Spaniards considered it a tragedy. The loss of the overseas empire in 1898 was the so-called Spanish disaster. The well-known phrase "more was lost in Cuba" is part of the collective memory of the disaster of 1898, also viewed as the result of a degeneration of the Spanish people, a degeneration that was cultural, social, and moral as well as political.

The island's bucolic and gentle image returned to the Spanish imagination with the passage of time despite the negative associations of the loss of Cuba. This theme is recurrent in emigrants' accounts and in songs of comings and goings called *habaneras*, recalling the land left behind and, in many cases, the love also left behind. Brimming with nostalgia, these songs embody the sensation of those lands and people so different from Spaniards, intertwining common history into their short verses. The titles speak for themselves: "Mi madre fue una mulata" (My Mother Was Mulatta), with the lyrics, "My mother was dark-skinned and my father a general/I'm the lieutenant of a frigate that sails the high seas"; "Allá en La Habana" (Over There in Havana); "La Península," whose lyrics include, "Farewell to my lovely Peninsula, farewell for duty calls, farewell, farewell, farewell/for I'm bound for Havana, to fight, to fight for the nation"; "La caña dulce" (Sweet Sugarcane); "La cotorrita" (The Little Parrot); "La hamaca" (The Hammock); and many others. In the early 2000s, Spain continued to hold habanera festivals that exploit the nostalgia of that music from another era. In addition to the old habaneras, they featured new compositions in which love, the loss of Cuba, the soldiers who fought in that last war of independence, and nature continued to be themes.

AFTER CUBA'S INDEPENDENCE

Following the loss of Cuba, the continual flow of immigrants between the two countries favored remembrance, reinforced old images, and contributed new ones to the collective Spanish imagination. Travelers to Cuba renewed former perceptions, reviving the memory of Cuba that had been obscured after 1898, as if that page of Spain's history could be forgotten or wiped away. Former struggles for power and advantageous concessions dissipated in the face of new ties forged by immigration, and along with the old business deals that managed to survive through commercial networks, new links based on kinship emerged. Legends of Spanish emigrants and letters and photos sent from the island fed the Spanish imagination and led people all over Spain to feel that Cuba was a close and familiar land. Meanwhile, Cuban families often included a *gallego*, a term meaning, literally, *Galician*, but used to describe immigrants from any Spanish region (except those from the Canary Islands, who were known as *isleños*, or islanders). A direct descendent of one of these immigrants was called a *pichón* (young pigeon), as in *pichón de gallego* (a Galician's pigeon), *pichón de asturiano* (an Asturian's pigeon), *pichón de canario* (a Canary Islander's pigeon). The closeness of these two peoples, transcending any specific moment in history, was captured by Fernando Ortiz: "Really Cuba, in more than a few ways, is more Spanish than Spain itself" (p. 13). Emigration helped reestablish relations and contributed to the creation of a Spanish Cuban identity in both Cuba and Spain, opening a space in the social imaginary in which Spain and Cuba figure closely to each other.

BIBLIOGRAPHY

Arrate, José Martín Félix de. *Llave del Nuevo Mundo, Antemural de las Indias Occidentales. La Habana descripta: Noticia de su fundación, aumento y estado*. Mexico City: Fondo de Cultura Económica, 1949.

Colón, Cristobal. *Diario de a bordo*. Edited by Luis Arranz. Madrid: Editorial EDAF, 2006.

Hazard, Samuel. *Cuba with Pen and Pencil*. Hartford, CT: Hartford Publishing Company, 1871.

Humboldt, Alejandro de. *Cristobal Colón y el descubrimiento de América*. Buenos Aires: Centro Difusor del Libro, 1946.

Ortiz, Fernando. *Entre cubanos. Psicología tropical*. Havana: Editorial Ciencias Sociales, 1986.

Urrutia y Matos, Bernardo Joseph de. *Cuba, fomento de la isla 1749: Primer estudio geo-económico de la isla*. San Juan, PR: Ediciones Capiro, 1993.

Urrutia y Montoya, Ignacio José de. *Obras de Ignacio José de Urrutia*. 2 vols. Havana: Siglo XX, 1931.

Urrutia y Montoya, Ignacio José de. *Teatro histórico, jurídico y político militar de la Isla Fernandina de Cuba y principalmente de su capital, La Habana*. Havana: Cuba National Commission for UNESCO, 1963.

THE WORLD AND CUBA: CUBA AND SPAIN IN THE POST-COLONIAL PERIOD

Consuelo Naranjo Orovio

Relations between Cuba and Spain from the nineteenth century through end of the Spanish Civil War in 1939 that transcended economics, trade, and politics.

During the first decades of the nineteenth century the Spanish government prioritized the colonization of Cuban territory. For the purposes of the island's defense, development, and integration, it designed a plan for Spaniards to settle near the coast or in areas far from existing production centers. This plan was aimed at promoting the accumulation of wealth, developing agriculture, protecting the country from smuggling, and maintaining order in the event of invasions by foreigners, or by ideas that could spur political destabilization. Two ideas drove the plan: the need to develop new areas of production and fears that the revolutionary flame lit in Haiti could spread to Cuba. The Spanish government wielded the specter of slave rebellion to convince Cuban landowners to maintain their colonial pact. To that end, the government backed both the massive importation of slave labor from Africa as well as a migratory policy aimed at making the island whiter. These two programs arose from different needs and were manipulated according to the demands and advantages they yielded. This dual policy, which lasted with varying degrees of success throughout the nineteenth century, experienced shifting scope and content depending on the elite's economic and, more importantly, political interests. The political ups and downs of the mid-nineteenth century and the conflicts between reformers and Spain were reflected in a colonization policy that, though clearly set down on paper, never really gained momentum. In response to the continued importation of new slaves and the maintenance of the slave labor system, criollo reformers argued for the influx of new white settlers as a way of whitening the population and civilizing the country. It was no longer only a question of accumulating wealth but of promoting progress and therefore it was necessary to bring in free white workers and stop the entry of more slaves.

SPANISH MIGRATION TO CUBA

But any hint of change or reform sparked renewed fear; suspicions led to shifting views of future colonization. Thus, by the mid-1830s, the notion grew that if slavery was one of the pillars of the Spanish colonial system, any weakening of its influence would lead to changes in the status quo, particularly because the descendants of the settlers might push for short-term reforms that would eventually lead to independence.

But following the Ten Years' War (1868–1878), Spain again viewed the settlers as a bastion of Spanish power on the island. In this atmosphere of uncertainty and conflicting interests, a large number of colonization projects were undertaken, through which the island was gradually populated with people largely from peninsular Spain and the Canary Islands. The generous terms of these colonization plans convinced many Spanish farming families to go to Cuba. The payment of passage by the promoter of colonization (government, landowner, company, or merchant); grants and subsequent sales of a *caballería* (13.41 hectares) of land; free farming implements and tools for clearing and cultivation; and exemption from paying taxes for several years favored the continual arrival and settlement of families (Naranjo Orovio 2009).

Following the post-1878 restructuring of the sugar industry and the abolition of slavery in 1886, more and more Spanish immigrants settled in Cuba. They were attracted by economic growth in the 1880s that stemmed from expansion of the sugar industry and resulted in a larger domestic market and an increase in the service sector, especially in urban areas, and a greater demand for day laborers in the rural areas. La Sociedad de Colonización (The Colonization Society, 1872), the Comisión Central de Colonización (Central Colonization Commission, 1873), the Círculo de Hacendados de la isla de Cuba (Cuban Landowners' Circle, 1878), and the Junta de Colonización (Colonization Board, 1890) were the institutions that promoted the influx of laborers and immigrants. In the countryside, the sugar plantations' demand for a labor force during the harvest season led to the temporary hiring of thousands of Spanish workers, especially from the Canary Islands. The so-called birds-of-passage emigration saw Spanish laborers flock year after year to Cuba and other countries, to do agricultural work and then return home (Naranjo Orovio 1992). From 1882 to 1894, some 300,000 Spanish immigrants entered Cuba, of whom about 100,000 settled there permanently (Maluquer).

Instead of stagnating, Spanish immigration increased after Cuba gained its independence in 1898. The continued Spanish immigrant presence helped maintain and strengthen Hispanic-Cuban culture and relations between the two countries. Although Galicia (37%) and Asturias (33%) were the dominant source regions for Spanish migration to Cuba, it is important to realize that every region of Spain sent emigrants. Between 1898 and 1933 (after which year the emigration virtually ceased), the largest volume of immigrants arrived between 1912 and 1921, given Cuba's status during World War I as the principal sugar supplier. Compared to other immigrant groups, Spaniards were the most numerous: From 1900 to 1916 they made up over 75 percent of all immigrants to Cuba, and in 1931 they represented 59 percent of the foreign-born population (Naranjo Orovio 1992; *Censo de Población de la República de Cuba, 1931*).

Because of their numerical strength and their social, economic, and cultural importance in Cuba, Spaniards did not have to compete with other groups the way they did in other countries of the Americas. Recognition of the Spanish presence made it possible to distinguish local Spanish identities, which functioned parallel to and on different levels from that of the Spanish. These identities proved compatible with one another and not conflicting, because there was no need to defend Spanish culture against other foreign groups. The profusion of centers and associations pertaining to various scales of origin (regional, district, local), as well as mutual-aid and recreational societies, each with its own publications and means of publicity, undoubtedly contributed to the strengthening of the image of Spain, its culture, and its traditions. Spanish social institutions promoted intra-ethnic and inter-ethnic contact. They served as meeting places for the Spanish community and its associates who were now Cuban, including the children and grandchildren of immigrants, as well as other Cubans who found in these societies a source of educational and, above all, health assistance otherwise lacking in Cuba. Moreover, these associations were places where memories of Spain were preserved and identities both specific and broad were created through the celebration of Spanish national holidays, saints' days, pilgrimages, and processions. They formed a womb within which a Hispanic-Cuban identity matured, one based on a set of values, symbols, and traditions shared by Cubans and Spaniards.

This was an important political moment for Cuba, a young country that was building its state structure and defining its societal model and identity. In the face of powerful others, Spain and the United States, a necessary step in defining and presenting itself as a sovereign country was to seek the cultural roots that shaped and united society. Doing so helped to define the nation's boundaries, commonalities, and differences with Spain and to create a national imaginary in which the white Cuban elite identified with many of Spain's traditional elements, reinforced by the size and dynamism of the Spanish presence.

TRADE AND THE SPANISH MERCHANT CLASS

In addition to their visibility and influence, given their involvement in the country's social, cultural, and political life, the Spanish participated actively in Cuba's economy. Meanwhile, Spanish culture became more and more prevalent with the arrival of new immigrants and the large volume of Spanish imports that emerged, especially of foodstuffs and shoes. Although Spain's position in the Cuban market diminished in the twentieth century, the demand for Spanish products was sustained by the large number of Spaniards living on the island, and imports remained strong until the 1930s (Zanetti). The marketing of Spanish goods was facilitated by the persistence of commercial networks and the fact that many trading companies were owned by Spaniards or by Cubans of Spanish heritage. According to the 1907 and 1919 censuses, the percentages of Spaniards involved in commercial activities in Cuba were 52.6 percent and 44.6 percent, respectively (Naranjo Orovio 1992; *Censo de la República de Cuba, 1907; Censo de la República de Cuba, 1919*).

The Spaniards' inclination toward the merchant trade often was passed on to their offspring. Anecdotal evidence and academic studies of the commercial houses indicate the existence of a sort of merchant culture that, through the advantage of buying on credit, allowed Spaniards and their descendants to undergo a transformation from shop-keepers to diversified entrepreneurs (García Álvarez; Marqués). Likewise, company structures were passed down from one generation to the next, and they defined the Cuban business and commercial world for many decades. During the first decades of the twentieth century, a pattern prevailed wherein newly arrived Spanish immigrants were put to work at entry-level jobs in exchange for food and lodging, plus a few pesos to pay dues to a regional center.

The Spanish immigrants' concentration in port cities resulted in the expansion of the sugar industry and the economic niches favored by Spaniards (import-export, retail, and wholesale trade), as well as the growth of Spanish influence in urban areas. In some municipalities such as Santiago de Cuba and Camagüey the Spanish population doubled and even tripled its share of the overall population (García Álvarez).

These comings and goings of people and goods created ties between Spain and Cuba that survived the end of Spanish political domination and the gradual decrease in trade. Spanish poetry and the lyrics of some *habaneras* (Cuban dance music) articulated the sentiment of this new world. In "Cuba dentro de un piano" (Cuba Inside a Piano), the poet Rafael Alberti (1902–1999) wrote:

> When my mother wore a strawberry sorbet on
> her head
> and the ships' steam was still Havana smoke.
> Mulatto woman of Vueltabajo.
> Cadiz slept among fandangos and habaneras
> and a little bird at the piano wanted to sing
> tenor.
> ... tell me where is the flower that man so
> adores.
> My Uncle Antonio returned with his air of
> insurrection.
> La Cabaña and El Príncipe loomed over the
> Port's yards.
> (The blue Pearl of the Antilles no longer shines.
> It is extinguished, it has died.)
> I found my lovely Trinidad ...

> Cuba had been lost and now it was real.
> It was real,
> it wasn't a lie.
> A stray gunship arrived singing guajiras.
> Havana was lost.
> Money was to blame ...
> The gunship fell silent,
> it fell.
> But after, oh! but after ...
> was when SÍ
> became YES.

On 7 March 1930 Federico García Lorca (1898–1936) arrived in Havana. Like so many others, the Spanish poet was fascinated by the island's beauty and its similarity to his native land. Out of his visit came verses, as quoted by Bianchi Ross, that illuminate the ties of a shared history:

> the boat gets closer and closer, and the scent of palm trees starts to fill the space, the perfume of the Americas, with its roots, God's Americas. But what do I find here? Spain again? Again, everyone's Andalusia? It is the yellowish color of Cadiz, even brighter here, the pink of Seville, almost red, and the green of Granada mixed with a dazzling clear blue light

p. 19

CULTURAL AND SCIENTIFIC RELATIONS

Just as with Spanish immigration, after Cuba's independence in 1898 cultural relations between the two countries did not diminish, although they did change in content, scope, and significance within a new context. But it was not until the 1920s that the Cuban anthropologist and jurist Fernando Ortiz (1881–1969) officially opened cultural exchange between Spain and Cuba. Avoiding the topics that many New World and Old World intellectuals had advocated as the elements that united Latin American countries with Spain, Ortiz insisted that only understanding and mutual respect for each country's characteristics could lead to balanced relations. On several occasions Ortiz attacked those who, like Rafael Altamira during his visit to Cuba in 1910, maintained that the spiritual union between Spain and Latin America was based on a "common race," a "shared race," a "race culture," a "common fatherland," and "indestructible ties." Beneath these terms lay the pan-Hispanism that Ortiz criticized so scathingly in *La reconquista de América* (The Reconquest of the Americas, 1910). Science, rather than religion, history, and language, would be the foundation for those relations.

Fernando Ortiz's Spanish past, via his direct descent from Spaniards and his doctoral studies in Spain, helped in establishing relations in 1926 between the Institución Hispano-Cubana de

Cultura (IHCC; Hispanic-Cuban Cultural Institution), founded by Ortiz that year, and the Junta para Ampliación de Estudios (JAE; Board for Expanded Scholarship), headed by Santiago Ramón y Cajal and founded in 1907, which sponsored a major project for the renewal and modernization of Spain's educational and scientific life. The IHCC also supported modernization, renewal, and broader perspectives, and for that reason Ortiz chose the JAE as its counterpart in Spain and José María Chacón y Calvo as its representative. This was the start of the productive academic collaboration of professors and students of the two countries. The publications *Surco, Mensajes de la Institución Hispanocubana de Cultura,* and *Ultra* reported on lectures and research trips by Spanish and Cuban professors Federico García Lorca, Luis de Zulueta, Pío del Río-Hortega, Ramón Menéndez Pidal, Juan Ramón Jiménez, Joaquín Turina, José Pijoán, Camilo Barcia Trelles, Francisco Durán Reynals, Gustavo Pittaluga, Claudio Sánchez Albornoz, María Zambrano, Rita Shelton, and others. A few years later, when the Spanish Civil War broke out in 1936, many of the Spanish intellectuals and academics who since 1927 had frequented the university classrooms, laboratories, and lecture halls across the island found their way back to Cuba.

During their time in Cuba in the 1930s, many of these Spanish intellectuals came into contact with Cuban writers and artists. The poet Dulce María Loynaz (1902–1997), who knew great writers from both countries, hosted many gatherings, and her work reflects the influence of these Cuban and Spanish intellectuals. The Thursday-night soirees at her home were frequented by García Lorca, Juan Ramón Jiménez, Alejo Carpentier, Rafael Marquina, and many others. Loynaz's marriage to the Spaniard Pablo Álvarez de Cañas and her stays in the Canary Islands contributed to the great popularity of her poetry in Spain; several of her books were published in that country in the 1940s and 1950s, and she was honored many times. The poet Carmen Conde paid tribute to Loynaz in "Del lírico epistolario dormido. Carta a la poetisa cubana Dulce María Loynaz" (Sleeping Lyric Epistolary: Letter to Cuban Poet Dulce María Loynaz); Juan Ramón Jiménez lauded her work; and she was awarded the Miguel de Cervantes Prize for literature in 1992.

RELATIONS OF SOLIDARITY: CUBA AND THE SPANISH CIVIL WAR

Far from being limited to academic exchanges, the efforts that Fernando Ortiz initiated in 1926 became the very model of the sort of cultural and scientific relations that Spain had enjoyed with other Latin American countries in previous years. Thanks to these relations, many Republicans forced to flee Spain found refuge in the Americas and particularly in Cuba. When the Spanish Civil War broke out, Ortiz urged

friends such as the Columbia University professor Federico de Onís and the Society for the Protection of Science and Learning to support the Spanish Republicans, and he encouraged Spanish professors to take refuge in Cuba. Ortiz convinced the rector of the University of Havana to authorize the meeting of the Reunión de Profesores Universitarios Españoles en el Extranjero (Association of Spanish University Professors Abroad), held in Havana in 1943 and attended by more than forty Spaniards exiled in various countries who specialized in science, politics, and culture. Participants approved important resolutions about the need to join forces and continue to struggle for recognition of the Republic's government. The two most important resolutions were the *Declaración de La Habana* (Declaration of Havana) and the proposal to create the *Junta Española de Liberación* (Spanish Liberation Committee), which began operating two months later in Mexico.

In addition to influencing the cultural realm, the Spanish Civil War caused repercussions in Cuban politics, trade unions, intellectuals, newspapers, and radio. The war's significance touched all aspects of Cuban society; associations, committees, and magazines were created for the single purpose of fundraising for the republican cause. The Asociación de Ayuda al Niño del Pueblo Español (AANPE, Association for Aid to Spanish Children) and the magazine *¡Ayuda!* are examples of activities undertaken in Cuba in support of the Spanish Republic (Naranjo Orovio 1988).

Certainly the size of the Spanish community on the island played a large part in this support, but also the very internationalization of the conflict made the Cuban public, the intellectual community, trade unions, political parties, and regional centers more aware of the drama being played out in Spain. Many Cuban intellectuals viewed the war as a battle of freedom and democracy versus fascism; among the most distinguished to lend their support to the Republican cause were the educator Rosa Pastora Leclerc (1888–1966) and the writer Pablo de la Torriente Brau (1901–1936). In 1938 the magazine *Mediodía* published a long list of material aid and demonstrations of moral support offered by Cubans, along with a statement of solidarity. The long list of signers included Rafael Suárez Solís, Emilio Ballagas, Juan Marinello, Roberto Agramonte, Raimundo Lazo, Luis G. Wagermert, Fernando G. Campoamor, Leclerc, Inés Segura Bustamante, José Luciano Franco, and Alberto Peña. The aid included the foundation in May 1938 of the Casa-Escuela Pueblo de Cuba (People of Cuba House-School), a refuge for Spanish children center in Sitges under the direction of Rosa Pastora Leclerc. In December 1938 the AANPE, cofounded by Leclerc, who also served as its vice president and representative at meetings of the Bureau International Pour L'Enfance (International Office for Children), sent CUP$1,572.60 to support the school. Leclerc also participated in the International Conference to Aid Spanish Children, where she discussed the initial achievements of the House-School.

When war broke out Torriente Brau quickly arranged to be sent as a war correspondent from New York, where he was in exile, to Spain. He joined the "El Campesino" Battalion, Fifth Regiment, First Mobile Brigade, and became its quartermaster, participating in the political rallies of the Alianza de Intelectuales Antifascistas (Alliance of Intellectuals against Fascism) (Torriente Brau). Shortly after arriving in Spain in December 1936, he died in battle in Majadahonda, outside Madrid. His friend the poet Miguel Hernández (1910–1942) eulogized him in "Elegía segunda" (Second Elegy):

> Me quedaré en España compañero
> me dijiste con gesto enamorado.
> Y al fin sin tu edificio tronante de guerrero
> en la hierba de España te has quedado.
>
> *p. 100*

> [I'll stay in Spain, comrade,
> you told me with a loving gesture.
> And finally, without your thundering warrior's
> edifice,
> you have stayed in the meadows of Spain.]

In addition to Torriente Brau, seven hundred Cubans belonging to different political parties and organizations such as the Comité de Revolucionarios Antiimperialistas Cubanos (Committee of Anti-imperialist Cuban Revolutionaries), Joven Cuba (Young Cuba), el Partido Comunista Cubano (the Communist Party of Cuba), and the Partido Auténtico fought in Spain; 638 of them joined the International Brigades. The Communists were assigned the task of recruiting and transporting the Voluntarios Internacionales de la Libertad (International Freedom Volunteers); this effort was led by Ramón Nicolau. They traveled from Havana directly to France or first to New York, where they sailed to France and then made their way to Spain.

At the end of the war, a portion of Cuban society continued to assist Spanish exiles. The IHCC and other organizations supported the arrival of refugees and the continuing struggle against the Franco dictatorship through the Asociación de Ayuda a las Víctimas de la Guerra de España (Association for Aid to Victims of the Spanish War), created in 1939; the Alianza de Intelectuales Antifranquistas, founded in 1944; *España Errante* newspaper; the Sociedad de Amistad Cubano-Española (Cuban-Spanish Friendship Association); and *Hoy* newspaper. Cuban writer Cintio Vitier recalled the time the poet Juan Ramón Jiménez (1936–1937), among other Spanish exiles, spent in Cuba: "A climate of poetic fervor arose around him. . . . A fertile moment in our cultural, and especially poetic, process, filled with enchantment, lessons and hope for those of us who were younger then, a moment that left an indelible mark on the history of Cuban sensibility" (quoted in Leante p. 208).

BIBLIOGRAPHY

Alberti, Rafael. "Cuba dentro de un piano." In *Poesía escogida, 1924–1982*. Havana: Editorial Arte y Literatura, 1990.

Bianchi Ross, Ciro. *García Lorca: pasaje a la Habana*. Barcelona: Puvill Libros, 1997.

Censo de la República de Cuba, 1907. Washington, DC: Office of the Census of the U.S. Government, 1908.

Censo de la República de Cuba, 1919. Havana: Maza, Arroyo y Caso S. en C. (printers), 1919.

Censo de Población de la República de Cuba, 1931. Havana: Editorial de Ciencias Sociales, 1978.

García Álvarez, Alejandro. *La gran burguesía comercial en Cuba 1899–1920*. Havana: Editorial de Ciencias Sociales, 1990.

Hernández, Miguel. "Elegía segunda." In *Viento del pueblo*. Valencia, Spain: Socorro Rojo, 1937.

Leante, César. "El exilio en Cuba." *Cuadernos Hispanoamericanos* 473–474 (1989): 201–210.

Maluquer, Jordi. *Nación e inmigración: los españoles en Cuba (ss. XIX y XX)*. Oviedo, Spain: Fundación Archivo de Indianos, 1992.

Marqués, Maria Antonia. *Las industrias menores: empresarios y empresas en Cuba (1880–1920)*. Havana: Política, 2002.

Naranjo Orovio, Consuelo. *Cuba, otro escenario de lucha. La Guerra Civil y el exilio republicano español*. Madrid: CSIC, 1988.

Naranjo Orovio, Consuelo. "Trabajo libre e inmigración española en Cuba, 1880–1930." *Revista de Indias* 195–196 (May–December 1992): 749–794.

Naranjo Orovio, Consuelo. "Cara y cruz de una política colonial: azúcar y población en Cuba." In *Más allá del azúcar: política, diversificación y prácticas económicas en Cuba, 1878–1930*, edited by Antonio Santamaría and Consuelo Naranjo Orovio. Aranjuez, Spain: Doce Calles: 2009.

Nicolau, Ramón, dir. *Cuba y la defensa de la República Española*. Havana: Instituto de Historia del Movimiento Comunista, Editorial Política, 1981.

Ortiz, Fernando. *La reconquista de América. Reflexiones sobre el panhispanismo*. Paris: Librería de Paul Ollendorf, 1910.

Torriente Brau, Pablo de la. *Cartas y crónicas de España*. Edited by Víctor Casaus. Havana: Centro Cultural Pablo de la Torriente Brau, 1999.

Zanetti, Oscar. "Comercio en transición. Presencia española en el mercado cubano, 1885–1913." In *Más allá del azúcar: política, diversificación y prácticas económicas en Cuba, 1878–1930*, edited by Antonio Santamaría and Consuelo Naranjo Orovio. Aranjuez, Spain: Doce Calles, 2009.

THE WORLD AND CUBA: CUBA AND THE UNITED STATES

Philip Brenner

U.S. perceptions of Cuba that reveal how the United States has viewed its own role—and Cuba's—in the world.

Cuba has fascinated, frustrated, and enticed Americans for more than two hundred years. As early as 1809, one year after the United States ended the legal importation of slaves, former president Thomas Jefferson wrote that he had long viewed Cuba—which had become the main transit hub for the slave trade—as "the most interesting addition that could be made to our system of States." By the end of the century, President William McKinley, in his 1899 State of the Union message, described the U.S.-Cuban relationship as "ties of singular intimacy." Those ties are reflected in the ways U.S. officials and elites have perceived Cuba over two centuries and in the images they have used to describe the relationship between the two countries. The images reinforced U.S. prejudices with respect to Cuba and provided ready justifications for U.S. policy. The U.S.–Cuban relationship, and the images of Cuba that emerged from it, are evident in three periods examined here: 1823–1868, 1868–1934, and 1959–1991.

1823–1868: RIPE FRUIT (*FRUTA MADURA*)

In 1823, Secretary of State John Quincy Adams, in a letter to Hugh Nelson, the new U.S. ambassador in Madrid, explained:

> there are laws of political as well as of physical gravitation; and if an apple severed by the tempest from its native tree cannot choose but fall to the ground, Cuba, forcibly disjoined from its own unnatural connection with Spain, and incapable of self support, can gravitate only towards the North American Union, which by the same law of nature cannot cast her off from its bosom.
>
> *Holden and Zolov p. 11*

In Cuba this metaphor is known as the ripe fruit (*la fruta madura*) syndrome, an ongoing U.S. self-justification for an imperial approach toward the island. Adams made clear in his letter that ultimate control of Cuba would be essential for realizing his vision of the United States as a great power. Cuba's "commanding position with reference to the Gulf of Mexico," he asserted, along with its location halfway to the Dominican Republic, Havana's "capacious harbor," and Cuba's possibilities for "immensely profitable" commerce, "give it an importance in the sum of our national interests, with which that of no other foreign territory can be compared" (pp. 10–11).

But Adams did not dream of the United States as a traditional empire. Cuba would be incorporated into the United States as a full-fledged participant. He could not imagine that properly educated Cubans might not want to be annexed by their northern neighbor. In his view the exceptional nature of the United States precluded such a possibility. Moreover, the United States needed Cuba, and U.S. interests would take priority because of its special providence. Within a half-century, he predicted, "the annexation of Cuba to our federal republic will be indispensable to the continuance and integrity of the Union itself" (p. 11).

As the historian Richard Immerman explains in his 2010 study *Empire for Liberty*, Adams was confronted with a dilemma that repeatedly haunted U.S. leaders. On the one hand, they believed the United States was distinctive and better than other nations because its founding principle was liberty; thus, the United States accepted a divinely inspired responsibility to expand and promote liberty. On the other hand, American leaders believed that expansion involving colonization would necessarily deny liberty to those whom the United States colonized. The ripe fruit metaphor helped to obscure the seeming contradiction. The U.S. intention toward Cuba would be annexation, not colonization. Yet Cuba was not yet mature enough, that is, sufficiently ripe, to warrant inclusion in the federal republic. As Adams told Nelson, "Were the population of the island of one blood and color, there could be no doubt or hesitation with regard to the course which they would pursue." But Cubans, he concluded, "are not competent to a system of permanent self-dependence" (p. 12).

Adams was not alone in seeking to delay Cuban annexation. Spain's continued presence there, at least for the moment, meant that U.S. troops were not needed to curb instability on the island. The 1812 Aponte slave rebellion provided an example of what might happen if Cubans gained their freedom from Spain. The still-fledgling United States did not have the military capacity both to station soldiers on the frontier and to quell uprisings in Cuba. Alternately, if it allowed instability to mount in an independent Cuba, that situation might encourage a European power to occupy the island in place of Spain. At the same time, had Cuba been admitted to the Union, it undoubtedly would have sided with the Southern slave states. For Northerners wary of increasing Southern influence in Congress, that possibility was reason enough to hold off Cuban annexation. In this way, domestic and international U.S. interests coincided to promote the ripe fruit metaphor.

1868–1934: PROTECTORATE, OR THE HELPLESS CHILD

Cuba's proximity to the United States also fostered the image of the island as neighbor, which, as Louis A. Pérez notes, "evoked a complex ensemble of moral meanings in the service of North American interests" (2008, p. 31). Neighborliness required adherence to a set of rules and responsibilities that the United States established, including the responsibility of the stronger, more mature neighbor to guide the weaker, less developed neighbor.

By the mid-nineteenth century, as U.S. trade with Cuba expanded, the neighbor image evolved into another image that conveyed an even closer relationship between Cuba and the United States. In 1859, Senator William Seward enunciated the view that "every rock and every grain of sand in the island were drifted and washed out from American soil by the floods of the Mississippi, and other estuaries of the Gulf of Mexico" (quoted in Pérez 2008, p. 29). Thus Cuba was cast as having emerged from the United States, a kind of lost child that Spain abused as a "cruel stepmother" (U.S. Senate Committee 1896, p. 26). The image of Cubans as children merged easily with Americans' impression of Latin Americans as people lacking in discipline, reason, and morals who did not appreciate that the rule of law is the foundation for democratic governance. Like all children, they needed adult guidance and authority.

In 1885, the Statue of Liberty was erected in New York Harbor, bearing on its base an excerpt from Emma Lazarus's poem "The New Colossus": "Give me your tired, your poor, / Your huddled masses yearning to breathe free." Lady Liberty conveyed the emerging U.S. self-image as the protector of the downtrodden and oppressed—an image that meshed with the depiction of Cuba as a child or woman in distress. (For a short time during the late nineteenth century, political cartoons and discourse portrayed Cuba as a woman in need of protection, a dignified but fragile supplicant dressed in rags or shackled by the Spaniards, beseeching the United States to come to her rescue.) Cuba's need for protection offered justification for the 1898 U.S. intervention in the Cuban War of Independence: The United States entered the war with an apparent abundance of altruism. Wary of following in the footsteps of European imperialists, the U.S. Congress added the Teller Amendment to its declaration of war against Spain, thus disclaiming "any disposition or intention to exercise sovereignty, jurisdiction, or control over said Island except for the pacification thereof, and asserts its determination, when that is accomplished, to leave the government and control of the Island to its people."

But pacification of those childlike Cubans could not be accomplished easily. Their disobedience was not so much a threat as a nuisance, as President Theodore Roosevelt suggested in a 1905 letter: "I am so angry with that infernal little Cuban republic that I would like to wipe its people off the face of the earth" (quoted in Schoultz p. 25). Even at the moment of victory, the *Washington Post* in 1898 quoted Major General S. B. M. Young complaining that "the insurgents are a lot of degenerates, absolutely devoid of honor or gratitude" and adding that "the Cubans are no more capable of self-government than the savages of Africa" ("Cannot Trust the Cubans"). By the start of the twentieth century, as a front page cartoon in the *Minneapolis Journal* (23 February 1901) showed, protecting these "children" meant forcing them to take U.S. medicine for their own good. The cartoon depicts a kindly Uncle Sam trying to spoon feed his "Oversight Tonic" to an unkempt, wallowing boy who is sitting on his knee. "Take it, sonny," Uncle Sam declares in the caption, "it's good for your constitution."

One form of Cuba's medicine was the 1901 Platt Amendment, under which the Cuban constitution granted the United States the right to intervene in Cuba's internal affairs. In "The Pacification of Cuba," Senator Orville Platt proclaimed that by virtue of this amendment "the United States set a high and new example to the nations of the world and gave a mighty impetus to the cause of free government." The United States, in his estimation, became the first conquering nation in history to relinquish territory without giving up responsibility for those whom it had conquered.

Even the U.S. State Department acknowledged a century later that U.S. motives for the Platt Amendment were in fact less noble than Platt claimed:

> The rationale behind the Platt Amendment was straightforward. The United States Government had intervened in Cuba in order to safeguard its significant commercial interests on the island in the wake of Spain's inability to preserve law and order. As U.S. military occupation of the island was to end, the United States needed some method of maintaining a permanent presence and order.... By directly incorporating the requirements of the Platt Amendment into the Cuban constitution, the McKinley Administration was able to shape Cuban affairs without violating the Teller Amendment.
>
> *"The United States, Cuba, and the Platt Amendment, 1901"*

To President Roosevelt and Senator Henry Cabot Lodge, both ardent proponents of an American empire, control over Cuba seemed to serve several newly acquired imperial interests in addition to the direct protection of U.S. investments on the island and the extraction of profits. It would establish the U.S. stake in the Caribbean, provide a way to increase protection for the planned Panama Canal, and flaunt U.S. power. Lodge argued that wherever "the flag once goes up it must never come down" (quoted in Immerman, p. 150). Thus, under the guise of benevolence, the conquest of Cuba opened the door to the U.S. aspiration of establishing an American century.

The image of Cuba as child lasted well into the twentieth century. As Pérez observes, "the metaphor of Cubans as children drew upon the dense web of reciprocities commonly understood to regulate the parent-child relationship as model for governance: the parent to supervise, the child to submit; the parent to discipline, the child to obey.... The Cubans as children were expected...to be heedful and compliant and always properly appreciative and grateful" (2008, pp. 122–124).

1959–1991: ENEMY

The initial U.S. reaction to the 1959 Cuban revolution was rooted in the dominant metaphor of parent and child. U.S. officials indicated privately that they viewed Cuban leader Fidel Castro as an irascible child with whom they could live but who needed a stern lecture from an adult. Vice President Richard Nixon boasted that during his meeting with Castro in April 1959, "I talked to him like a Dutch uncle" (quoted in Paterson, p. 257). Acting Secretary of State Christian Herter had met with Castro the day before and reported to President Dwight D. Eisenhower that the Cuban leader was "very much like a child in many ways, quite immature regarding problems of government" ("Memorandum of a Conference" p. 475).

U.S. cartoonists followed suit, mocking Castro as a childlike buffoon. However, soon afterward the official image changed, and the U.S. press quickly picked up the new line. For example, "Chain Reaction," a November 1960 cartoon in the *Memphis Commercial Appeal*, depicted Castro holding the chain of a subdued Cuban in irons, while a menacing Communist hand across the ocean held a chain attached to Castro's neck. Similarly, a November 1960 cartoon in the *Indianapolis Star* depicted Soviet premier Nikita Khrushchev with his arm around Castro, bellowing, "Don't mess around with us Cubans." This was five months before Castro even asserted that the Cuban revolution had a "socialist character." Cuba's governing party was dominated by the July 26th Movement, not the Popular Socialist Party that had been close to Moscow. It was an easy jump from this image to ones conveying the official U.S. position, that Cuba under Castro's leadership was a mortal U.S. enemy.

The expression of Cuba as U.S. enemy remained dominant throughout the Cold War. At times, as Jorge I. Domínguez notes in his 1989 book *To Make a World Safe for Revolution*, the Cuban threat was viewed as emanating directly from Cuba or Castro's own ambitions, which were described as fundamentally antagonistic to U.S. interests. For example, in a 17 November 1977 background interview with Hedrick Smith of the *New York Times*, U.S. national security adviser Zbigniew Brzezinski voiced the view that Cuba's military presence in Africa was part of a strategy to foment revolution there, as it had been a decade earlier in Latin America. But he also expressed concern "that Cuba's involvement in Angola and elsewhere may be at the encouragement of Moscow." Indeed, Cuba was most commonly characterized as an enemy because of its ties to the Soviet Union and its alleged subservience to Soviet interests. This was especially true during the Ronald Reagan administration. In March 1985, the departments of State and Defense jointly issued a booklet on U.S. policy in Central America, which asserted: "Working through its key proxy in the region, Cuba, the Soviet Union hopes to force the United States to divert attention and military resources to an area that has not been a serious security concern to the United States in the past" ("The Soviet-Cuban Connection," p. 2).

Because of the threat of nuclear conflagration, the United States did not want to engage the Soviet Union directly. But it did want to promote Western-style liberty throughout the world. Indeed, U.S. leaders acted on the premise, established in the 1950 policy directive *NSC-68*, that U.S. vital interests were not confined to the defense of its sovereignty—the traditional definition of a state's vital interest—but were global. To confront Soviet interests without risking a nuclear war, the United States needed to pose a credible threat as a deterrent. Maintaining that credible threat required an image of the United States as a powerful force that would not shrink from destroying any opposition. Thus conveying and protecting this image became a foremost goal of U.S. foreign policy.

W. H. S.—" *Look, Uncle—there's a bully pear ! let me pluck it for you.*"
UNCLE SAM—" *Wait a bit, Willy—when it's ripe I will pull into our grounds.*"

The question of the U.S. annexation of Cuba. This political cartoon, published in the United States in 1868, depicts Uncle Sam and Secretary of State William H. Seward discussing the possibility of annexing Cuba. Seward favors cutting the pear; Uncle Sam advises patience. © CORBIS

In this way, Cuba's unwillingness to bend to U.S. wishes threatened the credibility of U.S. vows to back up its rhetoric with muscle, which U.S. leaders perceived as a vital interest. Secretary of State Herter expressed this view succinctly in a November 1959 review of U.S. policy toward Cuba, stating that Castro "has veered towards a 'neutralist' anti-American foreign policy for Cuba which, if emulated by other Latin American countries, would have serious adverse effects on Free World support of our leadership" ("Memorandum from the Secretary of State" p. 657).

To be sure, Cuban willfulness also seemed to conflict with other aspects of the U.S. self-image. Mendel Rivers, Democratic U.S. representative from South Carolina and the chair of the House Armed Services Committee, declared that Cuba "stands as an insult to American prestige, a challenge to American dignity" (quoted in Pérez 2002, p. 240). As Domínguez observed, "Cuba is a small country, but it has the foreign policy of a big power" (p. 6). Its behavior seemed to defy the natural order, in which the United States was supposed to be at the top.

Successive U.S. governments have also maintained an image of the United States as a gentle, benevolent giant, akin to Gulliver as he confronted the Lilliputians. Gulliver was well-aware that the Lilliputians were no match for him: "while I had my liberty," he recounted, "the whole strength of that empire could hardly subdue me, and I might easily with stones pelt the metropolis to pieces" (Swift p. 85). But he restrained himself, out of a sense of "honor." His intention was to help, not harm them. Likewise, despite a fifty-year campaign to subvert the Cuban government, which included an embargo that restricts even the sale of medicine and food to Cuba, as well as numerous efforts to assassinate Cuban leaders, the United States has presented itself as acting with noble restraint. In August 2006 Secretary of State Condoleezza Rice stated that "the notion that somehow the United States is going to invade Cuba because there are troubles in Cuba is simply far-fetched and it's simply not true. The United States wants to be a partner and a friend for the Cuban people." (quoted in Brenner and Castro p. 237).

METAPHORS AND POLICY

After the collapse of the Soviet Union in 1991 and thus the end of the Cold War, the George H. W. Bush administration essentially relinquished control of Cuba policy to the U.S. Congress. For the president, Cuba had become a domestic policy issue because the factors that had made Cuba an enemy disappeared. Russian troops were out of the Caribbean, Cuba had ended its presence in Africa, and Castro publicly disavowed any further support for revolutionary movements. In turn, Cuban Americans in Congress and some of their colleagues relied on a panoply of negative images to justify legislation tightening the U.S. economic embargo on Cuba. But the images had little staying power,

as the Congress voted in 2000 to permit some trade with Cuba and later the House and Senate separately supported bills to lift travel restrictions.

When the executive branch did weigh in on Cuba policy after 1992, it tended to brand Cuba as a pariah. Officials described Cuba as out of step with the hemisphere on democracy and human rights because Cuba was the only country in the region not to sign the Inter-American Democratic Charter. But the image had little potency outside the United States. By 2010, every country in the Western Hemisphere except the United States established diplomatic relations with Cuba. Similarly, from 1992 on an ever-increasing majority of the U.N. General Assembly voted in favor of an annual resolution condemning the U.S. embargo against Cuba. The vote in 2010 was 187 to 2, with 3 abstentions. Still, the image of Cuba as a child lurks in the background. Shortly after leaving her post, Vicki Huddleston, chief of the U.S. Interests Section in Havana from 1999 to 2002, commented that "it is fundamental that Cubans begin to learn how to govern themselves" (quoted in Wylie p. 24).

The implication of the parent-child metaphor, as George Lakoff explains, is that "when children disobey, the father is obligated to punish" (Lakoff p. 58). Cuba is neither grateful to the United States nor willing to be obedient. This attitude may, in fact, be the main reason for continued hostility toward the Cuban government. The State Department's primary justification for maintaining Cuba on its State Sponsors of Terrorism list is that Cuba has remained "critical of the U.S. approach to combating international terrorism" (*Country Reports on Terrorism 2009* p. 191). U.S. officials often link country metaphors to particular leaders, and they have associated Cuba's disobedience with Fidel and Raúl Castro. If new U.S. images of Cuba arise when the two revolutionary leaders are gone, then perhaps U.S. leaders will be able to consider U.S. interests without the distortion imparted by old metaphors.

BIBLIOGRAPHY

Adams, John Quincy. Letter to Hugh Nelson, April 28, 1823. Reprinted in *Latin America and the United States: A Documentary History*, 2nd ed. Edited by Robert H. Holden and Eric Zolov. New York: Oxford University Press, 2011.

Alzugaray Treto, Carlos. *De la Fruta Madura a la Ley Helms-Burton: Auge, Decadencia y Fracaso de la Política Imperialista de Estados Unidos hacia Cuba*. Panama: Editorial Universitaria, 1997.

Brenner, Philip, and Soraya M. Castro Mariño. "David and Gulliver: Fifty Years of Competing Metaphors in the Cuban–United States Relationship." *Diplomacy and Statecraft* 20, no. 2 (2009): 236–257.

"Cannot Trust the Cubans." *Washington Post*, August 6, 1898, p. 4.

Domínguez, Jorge I. *To Make a World Safe for Revolution: Cuba's Foreign Policy*. Cambridge, MA: Harvard University Press, 1989.

Immerman, Richard H. *Empire for Liberty: A History of American Imperialism from Benjamin Franklin to Paul Wolfowitz.* Princeton, NJ: Princeton University Press, 2010.

Lakoff, George, and the Rockridge Institute. *Thinking Points: Communicating Our American Values and Vision: A Progressive's Handbook.* New York: Farrar, Straus and Giroux, 2006.

"Must Take His Medicine." *Minneapolis Journal* (23 February 1901): p. 1.

NSC 68: United States Objectives and Programs for National Security. 14 April 1950. Available from http://www.fas.org/irp/offdocs/nsc-hst/nsc-68.htm.

Paterson, Thomas G. *Contesting Castro: The United States and the Triumph of the Cuban Revolution.* New York: Oxford University Press, 1994.

Pérez, Louis A., Jr. "Fear and Loathing of Fidel Castro: Sources of U.S. Policy toward Cuba." *Journal of Latin American Studies* 34, no. 2 (May 2002): 227–254.

Pérez, Louis A., Jr. *Cuba and the United States: Ties of Singular Intimacy.* 3rd edition. Athens: University of Georgia Press, 2003.

Pérez, Louis A., Jr. *Cuba in the American Imagination: Metaphor and the Imperial Ethos.* Chapel Hill: University of North Carolina Press, 2008.

Platt, Orville H. "The Pacification of Cuba." *The Independent* (27 June 1901).

Schoultz, Lars. *That Infernal Little Republic: The United States and the Cuban Revolution.* Chapel Hill: University of North Carolina Press, 2009.

Smith, Hedrick. "U.S. Says Castro Has Transferred 60's Policy of Intervention to Africa." *New York Times* (17 November 1977).

Swift, Jonathon. *Gulliver's Travels.* London: Jones and Company, 1826.

U.S. Congress, Senate, Committee on Foreign Relations, *Recognition of Cuba Independence.* 54th Cong., 2d sess., 21 December 1896. S. Rep. 1160. p. 26.

U.S. Department of State. "Memorandum from the Secretary of State to the President: Current Basic United States Policy toward Cuba." In *Foreign Relations of the United States, 1958–1960*, edited by John P. Glennon. Vol. VI: Cuba , no. 387. Washington, DC: U.S. Government Printing Office, 1958–1960. Available from http://digital.library.wisc.edu/1711.dl/FRUS.FRUS195860v06.

U.S. Department of State. "Memorandum of a Conference between the President and the Acting Secretary of State, Augusta, Georgia, April 18, 1959." In *Foreign Relations of the United States, 1958–1960*, edited by John P. Glennon. Vol. VI: Cuba, no. 286. Washington, DC: U.S. Government Printing Office, 1958–1960. Available from http://digital.library.wisc.edu/1711.dl/FRUS.FRUS195860v06.

U.S. Department of State, Office of the Coordinator for Counterterrorism. *Country Reports on Terrorism 2009.* "Chapter 3: State Sponsors of Terrorism." 5 August 2010.

U.S. Department of State, Office of the Historian. "The United States, Cuba, and the Platt Amendment, 1901." Available from http://history.state.gov/milestones/1899-1913/Platt.

U.S. Department of State and U.S. Department of Defense. "The Soviet-Cuban Connection in Central America and the Caribbean." Booklet. Washington, DC: U.S. Government Printing Office, 1985.

Wylie, Lana. *Perceptions of Cuba: Canadian and American Policies in Comparative Perspective.* Toronto: University of Toronto Press, 2010.

THE WORLD AND CUBA: U.S. CULTURE IN CUBA

Víctor Fowler Calzada

The persistence of U.S. cultural influence in Cuba.

During the Republican Period (1902–1959) the average Cuban was surrounded by objects imported from the United States. In addition, Cubans adopted many habits of everyday life from their American neighbors, and art and literature also reflected North American influences. Although the embargo imposed on Cuba by the United States in 1962 resulted in acrimonious relations between the two countries supported by daily political discourse, education, and anti-imperialist propaganda within Cuba, the presence and cultural influence of the United States endured in Cuba even into the twenty-first century.

COORDINATES OF A CULTURAL CONTRADICTION

On 24 October 1823, Thomas Jefferson wrote to James Monroe, president of the United States, saying "I candidly confess that I have ever looked on Cuba as the most interesting addition that could ever be made to our system of States." Although the letter is not so much an expression of the intention to annex as it is evidence of a desire to preserve the United States in the face of British efforts at reconquest, it speaks only of the territory, without any consideration of its inhabitants. The political weight of this declaration (together with the famous premonition of John Quincy Adams, for whom the island was a "ripe fruit" that, by nature, would necessarily gravitate toward the great nation to the north) is fundamental to Cuba's claims of being an independent country. These claims reached their greatest intensity after Fidel Castro overthrew the regime of Fulgencio Batista in 1959, ushering in the revolutionary period and obscuring the enormous influence the United States has exercised over the whole of Cuban culture.

THE DISPUTED U.S. PRESENCE

The cultural significance of U.S. presence in the country became a topic of discussion among intellectuals (Cubans and Spanish) by the middle of the nineteenth century. One political current favored annexation by the United States, placing its hopes on abandoning the Spanish colonial status with being incorporated by the young northern power. Ideologues in Spain

EVIDENCE OF U.S. CULTURE IN CUBA

U.S. influence has been pervasive, as exemplified in the following categories:

- **Architecture:** art deco buildings; housing at U.S.-owned sugar mills or in towns founded by American settlers (in the first decades of the twentieth century, fifteen thousand settled in Cuba); upper-middle-class Havana homes with "bars, dining rooms, halls, pantries, garden palms, together with other rooms for cocktail parties and other social events" (Morillas Valdés and del Valle Torres 2005).

- **Celebrations:** Christmas (Santa Claus), Valentine's Day.

- **Film:** 56 percent of movies that premiered in 1958 (256 out of 458) were from the United States.

- **Fine arts:** influence of pop art on painters such as Raúl Martínez and Umberto Peña, as well as on poster art, after 1959.

- **Food:** chewing gum, canned goods, soft drinks, powdered soups, hot dogs, sandwiches, cake at festive occasions.

- **Household products:** electrical appliances such as blenders, washers, air conditioning, electric stoves, pressure cookers, and refrigerators.

- **Housing:** use of the indoor toilet.

- **Hygiene, public health, and social order:** street paving, organized trash collection, extension of the water and electric streetcar networks, hygiene and public health campaigns that greatly reduced yellow fever and—paired with the development of commercial aviation in the 1930s—helped make possible the first great wave of tourism to the island.

- **Language:** use of semantic Anglicisms (borrowed), lexicon (copied), syntax, and morphology

- **Leisure:** bridge, bingo, and canasta.

- **Literature:** stylistic stamp of American writers Damon Ruyon and Ernest Hemingway on Cuban writers such as Guillermo Cabrera Infante and Lisandro Otero Jr. in the 1950s; of American authors such as Truman Capote, Erskine Caldwell, John Steinbeck, and Norman Mailer on what was called the Cuban "narrative of violence" in the 1960s; of Beat poetry on Cuban "conversational" poetry, also in the 1960s; of science-fiction authors (Isaac Asimov, Ray Bradbury) and the classical crime novel or the noir novel (Edgar Allan Poe, the Queen brothers, J. D. Carr, Dashiell

resisted fiercely the annexation idea. Generally, they advised Cubans—with little or no acknowledgement of the violence caused by colonialism—that they would lose all identity in the event of a U.S. occupation and would no longer be a people but instead be transformed into a despised and decadent mass.

In Cuba at the end of the nineteenth century, this array of views evolved into four trends that contradicted each other in terms of politics, economics, culture, and vision of the ideal society: annexationism (a weak tendency after 1880), integrationism, autonomism, and independence advocacy. During the war with Spain—at a time when most commerce was carried out with the United States—thousands of Cubans, many from the upper classes, fled into exile, primarily to New York and Florida. Thus, although the war affirmed Cubans' will for independence, their ideals of modern society and of comfort remained intimately connected to the United States. Such intimacy, however, carried a radical cultural contradiction

that would structure Cuban life into the twenty-first century. The most significant example is that of José Martí, who lived in the United States during his fifteen years of exile and whose work demonstrated both admiration for and rejection of various aspects of the U.S. culture of his day (Ramos).

The significant hiatus in Cuban political traditions toward the end of the war with Spain explains why the U.S. Army's occupation of the country (1898–1902), the First Intervention, was experienced as traumatic. Many Cubans who viewed U.S. intervention as a positive aid to their struggle for freedom were quickly disappointed when they were left out of the occupying forces' government. For Marial Iglesias, "Precisely in this historical enclave, the United States began to represent the 'other' against which the new national identity was constructed" (Lorini). The readjustment of life that then took place occurred in the midst of much debate and factionalism with respect to increased foreign presence (physical, political,

Hammett, Raymond Chandler) on Cuban genre fiction after the Revolution; and of "dirty realism" on more subsequent fiction.

- **Music:** jazz affects modes of orchestration and the format of musical groups, along with instrumental techniques; appearance and extension of Afro-Cuban Jazz; influence of the blues on the appearance and consolidation of *filín* (from the English "feeling"), a jazz-influenced crooner style of song popular in the 1940s and 1950s. American rock and rap likewise influence Cuban music beginning in the late 1980s and early 1990s.

- **Religious structure:** introduction and expansion—in a Catholic country—of Protestant missionaries from the United States; more than twenty-four missions came immediately after 1898.

- **Sports and recreational associations:** proliferation and strength of athletic clubs.

- **Tourism industry:** American tourists to Havana results in the development of an enormous service industry in response to U.S. tourists; in the late 1920s there were more than 7,500 bars in the city and in 1957 some 370,000 tourists.

- **Urban development:** design of the Country Club neighborhood, a wealthy suburb west of Havana that took its name from the social club of the same name whose main activity was golf, a foreign sport (Hernández 2001).

- **Women:** incorporation of women into the world of work and the adoption of many American feminist ideas.

Cubans take from the United States their main sports (baseball, boxing, volleyball), fashion trends such as the short skirt, the *garcon* (the pageboy, a short, cropped hairstyle) for women and center-parted hair for men, sneakers, blue jeans, overalls, and sunglasses. The case of baseball is unique, since it has become the national sport of Cuba. The high quality of the players on the island has allowed many of them to enjoy careers in the North American major leagues and has made Cuba the most consistent winner in international competitions except for the United States. Particularly since the Revolution, baseball has been one of the main vehicles of nationalism in the country.

Average, middle-class Cubans lived in surroundings saturated with such North American products as Admiral televisions, Singer sewing machines, Osterizer blenders, Ford or Chevrolet automobiles, RCA Victor radios or record players, Firestone or Goodrich tires, Alka-Seltzer antacid tablets, Coca-Cola or Pepsi soft drinks, Underwood or Remington typewriters. These material objects were symbols of comfort and normalcy or represented immediate aspirations.

and cultural). The two points of greatest friction in this regard were the Platt Amendment (1901) and the growing weight of U.S.-owned estates in Cuban economic life. These points of friction had substantive and symbolic significance. The Platt Amendment had three features: "[an] *Amendment* of the Tax Credit Law for the United States Army, an *appendix* imposed on the Cuban Constitution of 1901, and [a] permanent *Treaty* of Relations between Cuba and the United States of 1903, [that] complemented the appetite for covert annexation" (Miranda Bravo). The second major friction point, U.S. ownership of Cuban estates, was heightened by the enactment of Order No. 62 by the intervening military authority in May 1902 (Pichardo). This act promoted the privatization of land in Cuba and had profound consequences on the U.S. presence in the country.

During the 1950s tourists came to Cuba, along with heavy investment by Mafia leaders (Santo Traficante Sr., Meyer Lansky, Vito Genovese, and Sam Giancana, among others) in Havana's luxury hotels and casinos. These investments were encouraged and protected by Fulgencio Batista, who sought an alternative to sugar in order to increase national income. Cuba's political "marriage to the Mob," along with the expansion of prostitution, had a profound effect on Cuban political culture (Schwartz).

Throughout the republican period, an enormous range of intellectual perspectives emerged concerning relations between Cuba and the United States, alternatively expressing distress or acceptance in the face of what Lars Schoultz called a "benevolent domination." Examples of the first include both the anti-imperialism of Julio César Gandarilla, in *Contra el yankee* (Against the Yankee, 1913), Enrique José Varona, and José Antonio Ramos, and the Marxism of Julio Antonio Mella and Rubén Martínez Villena. Examples of the second include the famous cry of Manuel Márquez Sterling ("Fight foreign meddling with domestic virtue"), the transculturation theories of Fernando Ortiz, the liberalism of Ramiro Guerra, and the idea of an "incomplete nation" in the work of Jorge Mañach.

U.S. INFLUENCE FROM 1959

While political and economic relations between the two countries deteriorated after 1959, the most significant development—in the discourse of the revolutionary leaders—was the suspicion that the United States intended to annex the island. As a consequence of this belief, together with revolutionary efforts to create culture and the "New Man," various practices originating in the United States were rejected and even demonized. Among these were the music of *filín* (saved from ridicule by the providential defense it received from Alejo Carpentier); the world of fashion (long hair, blue jeans, tight pants); and the subversion delivered, according to socialists, by music such as rock, jazz, and rap. Paradoxically, the musical movement known as Nueva Trova (New Song)—emblematic of the Revolution and its new culture—is permeated with U.S. musical influences: folk, rock, jazz, blues, and spirituals (Acosta).

Mirroring the hostility of four U.S. administrations (Dwight D. Eisenhower, John F. Kennedy, Lyndon B. Johnson, and Richard Nixon), a 1970 speech by Raúl Castro, then minister of the Cuban Armed Forces, defined what, from that point forward, would be known as "ideological diversionism" (Castro). This concept would be used by the State, along with Cuban political organizations and institutions, to confront the cultural influence of the United States while creating an atmosphere of friction, distortion, and extremes. With this, the old anxiety regarding U.S. culture—explicit or latent in the works of many Cuban colonial and republican intellectuals—suddenly reappeared as an ideological construct that, in conjunction with the revolutionary actions and attitudes that stood in opposition to U.S. cultural influence, affected all aspects of Cuban life, particularly the transmission of ideas.

CULTURAL IMPACTS AND STATE CONTROLS

Whatever the convulsions of the new society may have been, three facts could not be changed: Cuba is part of the Western world, it is situated only ninety miles from the United States, and a large part of the cultural repertoire of its residents (regardless of their individual political positions) is American in origin. While the Revolution initiated policies of cultural transformation, individuals maintained a zone of resistance (including customs, food habits, fashion, and ideals) that, both implicitly and more or less explicitly, opposed this change. From 1959 into the twenty-first century, models from the revolutionary government co-occurred with counteractions of citizen resistance.

The preface of the novel *Sacchario* (1970), by Miguel Cossío Woodward, takes place in a cane field during the epic "Harvest of the 1970s." Cuban exceptionalism is made apparent in the bewilderment of an extraterrestrial (behind which we can clearly identify the figure of the foreigner) trying to understand it. In the final judgment of Darío, the main character, "He was a man from another world" (Cossío 1970). However, in that world—in the invisibility or silence inherent in resistance—Cubans were listening to radio stations from the United States (WQAM, WGBS, and KAAY, among others) (Moore); taking on the fashion of long hair (or among blacks, the Afro as worn by notable African Americans such as Angela Davis and others); wearing blue jeans and sandals; dancing on Saturday nights to rock music (which was hardly broadcast at all but was played by many groups operating outside the government-sanctioned music scene); meeting to listen to the handful of imported records of Western music; passing around light magazines filled with advertisements; sharing foreign clothing (sent in gift parcels known as *paquetes* from family members in the United States); speaking a Spanish dialect riddled with Anglicisms; and even—when weather conditions permitted—enjoying television programs from the United States (building TV or FM radio antennas was a lucrative underground trade). In general, Cubans continued using those items of material culture "from before" that had survived and, most importantly, assimilating new ideas and social practices, proving Cuban acceptance of symbols, practices, and attitudes taken from the 1960s U.S. culture and counterculture.

One example of the cultural tensions in Cuba appears in a 1966 dialogue between Carlos Rafael Rodríguez, a Communist intellectual and high figure in the revolutionary government, and students of the National School of Art. At the meeting, Rodríguez confirmed the official rejection of "boys with long hair, guitars, and tight pants" and dedicated several minutes to identifying sandals as possibly homosexual (Rodríguez 1979). The Revolution's proposal for the creation of the "New Man" implied a complete change of perceptions for Cubans. At the time, the ideological battle that this entailed incorporated many objects and social practices, but particularly consumer goods and fashion. The cultural machinery of the Eastern European socialist bloc—with the Soviet Union at its head—was behind the times and imitative of higher-quality Western cultural artifacts. It was viewed as essentially foreign, boring, and even pathetic. Clearly, it was not able to fill the void or displace the enormous cultural impact Cuba experienced as a result of its proximity to the United States.

Given a generalized Cuban dissatisfaction, U.S. culture (now understood by Cubans as a lifestyle) scored a victory when—as a result of policies of normalization between Cuba and its community in exile—more than 200,000 Cubans returned to visit their country of origin between 1978 and 1980. These people brought with them their stories and possessions that revitalized the old imagery of consumption and comfort. It was no coincidence that only two years later what became known as the Crisis at the Peruvian Embassy occurred and a massive wave of so-called boat people set out for the United States in the Mariel Boatlift.

The collapse of Eastern European socialism (1989–1991) marked a second victory for U.S. culture, whereas for the Cuban leadership it meant the impossibility of finding cultural sources from other than capitalist countries (from television programs to clothing to everyday household items, as well as all types of machinery and industrial technology). With the exception of some Chinese machinery, objects, and cultural products, Cuba received only products from capitalist countries, primarily the United States, after the Soviet bloc's collapse. Audiovisual materials were shown freely in the absence of agreements between Cuba and the United States; food or other supplies came from the close and abundant U.S. market.

This cultural dependence explains why in the early 2010s Cuban television (despite its older technology) carries a virtual U.S. invasion of musicals, movies, TV series, children's programs, and science programs. The messages of these programs are potentially disruptive, since they elicit endless comparison and cultural resistance. Not surprisingly, Havana saw urban tribes appear that lay claim to the subcultures of emo and rock (the latter known as *frikis*, from *freaks*) that were in contrast to a middle-class identity based on TV images and advertisements (known as *mikis*).

Another impact of U.S. culture in Cuba takes the form of resistance associated with information technology, contemporary technologies for image recording, satellite television transmissions (subsequently distributed through neighborhood pirate networks), the expansion of communication (especially through Internet access and cell phones), and the practice of digital reproduction. U.S. entertainment products have increasingly circulated throughout the country, to the point that even people in remote rural locations wear the latest fashions and—almost like residents of the capital—consume music, films, television dramas, and other U.S. products. Many underground networks dedicated to meeting this demand have developed.

AFTER THE AFTERWARDS

In a speech given in 1910, Eliseo Giberga, an old political autonomist, said, "This island, if it manages to keep its personality and maintain and invigorate its spirit, must be, because of its unique circumstances, the blessed area in the center of the Universe where the marriage of two civilizations is celebrated" (Giberga). Considering the period in which the country came under the influence of what Andrei Sinyavsky called "the Soviet civilization" (1960–1991), then three parties, not two, were wedded in that symbolic marriage of cultures. However, cultural images from the Soviet world, increasingly displaced by capitalist products, survived only in nostalgia for a less-troubled time for Cuban socialism. In turn, the call for political independence and sovereignty—perhaps the clearest bulwark of Cuban socialism—continues to feed the country's social conscience; to put it another way, the original equation has been reconstructed.

Toward the end of the nineteenth century, when Cubans fought against Spanish colonial power and wove together the fabric of their national identity, the United States was in a position to begin a cycle of imperial influence beyond its physical borders.

Hollywood in Cuba. American entertainment products increasingly circulate throughout Cuba, to the point where it is not unusual to find Cubans, even in remote rural locations, enthusiastically consuming American music and films. The marquee in front of this Havana theater in 2007 announced: "Today, a film from the United States, Apocalypto." AP IMAGES/ GREGORY BULL

The coming to power of Fidel Castro's revolutionary movement, which introduced the socialist Revolution, coincided with the fulfillment of the promise of Theodor Adorno and Max Horkheimer in their *Dialectic of Enlightenment* (1969): The business of entertainment would thereafter remain tied to light industry to form, with the United States at the lead, the juggernaut known as the cultural industry (a world from which Cuba, although continuously experiencing its influence, remained apart). In a final dislocation at the end of the twentieth century, after the disappearance of Eastern European socialism, Cuba's resistant nationalism would once again stand in isolation, this time in a world of the Internet, iPods, computers, and cell phones, in which the chief content creator continues to be the United States.

The contradiction lives on because, as Louis Pérez Jr. said, U.S. culture is a constituent part of Cuban national identity, the "Other" with which Cubans engage in never-ending debate.

BIBLIOGRAPHY

Acosta, Leonardo. "Influencias y confluencias entre las músicas de Cuba y los Estados Unidos." In *Mirar el Niágara: Huellas culturales entre Cuba y los Estados Unidos*, edited by Rafael Hernández. Havana: Centro de Investigación y Desarrollo de la Cultura Cubana Juan Marinello, 2000.

Arocha Mariño, Carmen, Antonio Castillo Guzmán, and Benito Pérez Maza. "La organización sanitaria cubana durante las ocupaciones militares de Estados Unidos." *Revista Cubana Salud Pública* 35, no. 2 (April–June 2009). Also available from http://bvs.sld.cu/revistas.htm.

Castro Ruz, Raúl. "El diversionismo ideológico: arma sutil que esgrimen los enemigos contra la revolución." *Verde Olivo* 14, no. 30 (23 July 1972): 4–15.

Cossío Woodward, Miguel. *Sacchario*. Havana: Instituto Cubano del Libro, 1972.

Coyula, Mario. "Influencias cruzadas Cuba/Estados Unidos en el medio construido. ¿Carril dos o autopista en dos sentidos?" In *Culturas Encontradas: Cuba y los Estados Unidos*, edited by Rafael Hernandez and John Coatsworth. Havana: Centro de Investigacion y Desarrollo de la Cultura Cubana Juan Marinello and David Rockefeller Center for Latin American Studies, Harvard University, 2001.

Fariñas Borrego, Maikel. "El asociacionismo náutico en La Habana: Las prácticas socioculturales observadas desde las élites hasta las capas populares (1886–1958)." *REVISTA ESBOÇOS* (Santa Catarina, Brazil) 16, no. 21 (2009): 137–157.

Fariñas Borrego, Maikel. *Sociabilidad y cultura del ocio: Las élites habaneras y sus clubes de recreo (1902–1930)*. Havana: Fundación Fernando Ortiz, 2009.

Fattacciu, Irene. "Alexis Everett Frye y la experiencia de los maestros cubanos en Harvard en el año 1900." In *An Intimate and Contested Relation: The United States and Cuba in the Late Nineteenth and Early Twentieth Centuries/Una relacion intima y controvertida: Estados Unidos y Cuba entre los siglos XIX y XX*, compiled by Alessandra Lorini. Florence, Italy: Firenze University Press, 2005.

Fernandes, Sujatha. *Cuba Represent! Cuban Arts, State Power, and the Making of New Revolutionary Cultures*. Durham, NC: Duke University Press, 2006.

Giberga, Eliseo. *Últimos discursos*. Havana: La Moderna Poesía, 1910.

Gónzalez Pagés, Julio César. *En busca de un espacio: Historia de mujeres en Cuba*. Havana: Editorial de Ciencias Sociales, 2003.

Guerra Jova, Alberto. *¿Cocina cubana estilizada?* 10th ed. Revista Excelencias Gourmet. Available from http://www.revistasexcelencias.com/Gourmet/a(276283)-Cocina-cubana-estilizada.html.

Guía Cinematográfica, 1958–1959. Havana: Centro Católico de Orientación Cinematográfica de la Acción Católica Cubana, 1960.

Hernández, Rafael, ed. *Mirar el Niágara: Huellas culturales entre Cuba y los Estados Unidos*. Havana: Centro de Investigación y Desarrollo de la Cultura Cubana Juan Marinello, 2000.

Hernández, Rafael, and John Coatsworth, eds. *Culturas Encontradas: Cuba y los Estados Unidos*. Havana: Centro de Investigacion y Desarrollo de la Cultura Cubana Juan Marinello and David Rockefeller Center for Latin American Studies, Harvard University, 2001.

Iglesias Utset, Marial. "Imágenes en conflicto: Cuba y la presencia imperial norteamericana (1898–1902)." In *An Intimate and Contested Relation: The United States and Cuba in the Late Nineteenth and Early Twentieth Centuries/Una relacion intima y controvertida: Estados Unidos y Cuba entre los siglos XIX y XX*, compiled by A. Lorini. Florence, Italy: Firenze University Press, 2005.

Jefferson, Thomas. "To the President of the United States (James Monroe)," Monticello, 24 October 1823. Available from http://history-world.org/thomas_jefferson_on_the_monroe_d.htm

Lorini, A., comp. *An Intimate and Contested Relation: The United States and Cuba in the Late Nineteenth and Early Twentieth Centuries/Una relacion intima y controvertida: Estados Unidos y Cuba entre los siglos XIX y XX*. Florence. Italy: Firenze University Press, 2005.

Mañach, Jorge. *Teoría de la frontera*. San Juan, Puerto Rico: Editorial Universitaria, 1971.

Manduley López, Humberto. *El rock en Cuba*. Havana: Ediciones Atril Musicales, 2001.

Márquez Sterling, Manuel. "A la injerencia extraña, la virtud doméstica." *La Nación*, 13 February 1917. In *¿El abogado del diablo? Manuel Márquez Sterling: Su relación con los Estados Unidos*, by Ivette Fernández Sosa. Also available from http://librinsula.bnjm.cu/secciones/221/nombrar/221_nombrar_2.html.

Martínez Heredia, Fernando, Rebeca J. Scout, and Orlando F. García Martínez. *Espacios, silencios y los sentidos de la libertad: Cuba entre 1878 y 1912*. Havana: Ediciones UNIÓN, 2001.

Merk, Frederick, Lois Mack, and John Mack Faragher. *Manifest Destiny and Mission in American History: A Reinterpretation*. Cambridge, MA: Harvard University Press, 1995.

Miranda Bravo, Olga. "Algunas consideraciones histórico-jurídicas sobre la ocupación ilegal del territorio cubano de la base naval yanki en Guantánamo." *Revista Cubana de Derecho* 29

(June 2007). Available from http://vlex.com/vid/historico-ocupacion-territorio-yanki-50068155.

Moore, Robin D. *Music and Revolution: Cultural Change in Socialist Cuba.* Berkeley: University of California Press, 2006.

Morillas Valdés, Francisco D., and Marlene Marjorie del Valle Torres. "La influencia norteamericana en la arquitectura habanera (1898–1959)." *La Jiribilla: Revista Digital de Cultura Cubana*, 4, no. 225 (27August–2 September 2005). Also available from http://www.lajiribilla.co.cu/2005/n226_09/fuenteviva.html.

Núñez González, Niurka, and Estrella González Noriega. "Antecedentes etnohistóricos de la alimentación tradicional en Cuba." *Revista Cubana de Alimentación y Nutrición* 13, no. 2 (1999): 145–150. Also available from http://bvs.sld.cu/revistas/ali/vol13_2_99/ali10299.htm.

Perez, Louis A., Jr. *On Becoming Cuba: Identity, Nationality, and Culture.* Chapel Hill: University of North Carolina Press, 1999.

Perez, Louis A., Jr. *Ser cubano: Identidad, nacionalidad, y cultura.* Havana: Editorial Ciencias Sociales, 2007.

Pérez Pérez, Nadiezhda, and Dayami Ramírez Matos. *Anglicismos en el español hablado en Cuba.* 2004. Available from http://www.ilustrados.com/publicaciones/EEpkElAZyFRMItpUXS.php.

Pichardo, Hortensia. *Documentos para la historia de Cuba*, vol. 2. Havana: Editorial Ciencias Sociales, 1973.

Pino-Santos, Oscar. *El asalto a Cuba por la oligarquía financiera yanqui.* Havana: Casa de las Américas, 1973.

Ragano, Frank, and Selwyn Raab. "Mob Lawyer." In *The Reader's Companion to Cuba*, edited by Alan Ryan. San Diego: Harcourt Brace, 1997.

Ramos, Julio. *Desencuentros de la modernidad en América latina: Literatura y política en el siglo XIX.* Mexico City: Fondo de Cultura Económica, 1989.

Reid, Whitelaw. *Problems of Expansion, as Considered in Papers and Addresses.* New York: Century, 1900. Available from http://www.green-ebook-shop.com/ebooks/2/6/0/6/26064/26064.html.

Reig Romero, Carlos E. *YMCA de La Habana: Memorias deportivas (1905–1910).* Quito, Ecuador: Departamento de Comunicaciones, Consejo Latinoamericano de Iglesias, 2003.

Reig Romero, Carlos E. *Historia del deporte cubano: Los inicios.* San Antonio de los Baños, Cuba: Editorial Unicornio, 2007.

Rodríguez, Carlos Rafael. *Problemas del arte en la Revolución (conversatorio con los estudiantes de la Escuela Nacional de Arte [ENA]).* Havana: Editorial Letras Cubanas, 1979.

Rodríguez, Rolando. *Cuba: La forja de una nación.* Havana: Editorial de Ciencias Sociales, 2006.

Schoultz, Lars. *That Infernal Little Cuban Republic: The United States and the Cuban Revolution.* Chapel Hill: University of North Carolina Press, 2009.

Schwartz, Rosalie. *Pleasure Island: Tourism and Temptation in Cuba.* Lincoln: University of Nebraska Press, 1999.

Smith, Earl T. "Communist Threat to the United States through the Caribbean." 27–30 August 1960. Speaking before the Subcommittee to Investigate the Administration of the Internal Security Act and other Internal Security Laws. Committee on the Judiciary. Washington, D.C. 86th Cong., 2nd sess., Part 9. Washington, DC: U.S. Government Printing Office, 1960. Available from http://www.latinamericanstudies.org/us-cuba/gardner-smith.htm.

Tillmann-Weleda, Britta. *Anglicisms in Spanish from a Semantic Point of View.* 2008. Available from http://www.grin.com/e-book/154973/anglicisms-in-spanish-from-a-semantic-point-of-view#inside.

Vázquez Gálvez, Madelaine. *Apuntes sobre la historia de la cocina cubana.* Available from http://www.cubasolar.cu/Biblioteca/Energia/Energia44/HTML/Articulo10.htm.

Vega Suñol, José. *Norteamericanos en Cuba: Estudio etnohistórico.* Havana: Fundación Fernando Ortiz, 2004.

Venegas Fornias, Carlos. "La arquitectura de la Intervención (1898–1902)." In *Espacios, silencios, y los sentidos de la libertad: Cuba entre 1878 y 1912*, edited by Fernando Martínez Heredia, Rebeca J. Scout, and Orlando F. García Martínez. Havana: Ediciones UNIÓN, 2001.

Vitier, Cintio. *Lo cubano en la poesía.* Havana: Instituto del Libro, 1970.

Yaremko, Jason M. *U.S. Protestant Missions in Cuba: From Independence to Castro.* Gainesville: University Press of Florida, 2000.

THE WORLD AND CUBA: CUBA AND AFRICA

Katrin Hansing

Cuban-African relations after 1959.

The centuries-old ties between Cuba and the African continent began with the trans-Atlantic slave trade, which brought millions of Africans to the Caribbean and resulted in strong African cultural influences on Cuban culture. Apart from these historical and cultural ties, Cuban-African relations were rekindled with the Cuban Revolution in 1959, when the revolutionary government began to support many of the anticolonial and independence struggles on the African continent. Since the 1960s Cuba's provision of military, political, medical, educational, and technical aid to dozens of African countries has strengthened ties, and thousands of Cubans and Africans have travelled to each other's countries.

POLITICAL AND MILITARY RELATIONS

Despite the strong historical ties between Cuba and Africa, official political relations were almost nonexistent before 1959. At that time Egypt was the only African country with which Cuba had diplomatic relations. The new revolutionary government not only established formal diplomatic relations with many of the newly independent African nations, but also began to seek close contacts with some of the African anticolonial and independence movements.

■ See also

Che Guevara, Social and Political Thought

Cuban Thought and Cultural Identity: Socialist Thought

Economy: Special Period

Governance and Contestation: The Cuban Revolution

Health and Health Care: Medical Diplomacy and International Medical Education

Race: Race Relations after the Revolution

Given the Cold War context and Cuba's own radical stance toward the United States and imperialism, Cuba sought relations with leftist governments and movements in countries such as Algeria, Mali, the two Congos (present-day Democratic Republic of the Congo [DROC] and Republic of the Congo [ROC]), Guinea, Ghana, and the former Portuguese colonies. These relations went far beyond the purely ideological and diplomatic realms.

Starting as early as 1961 the Cuban government supplied Algeria's National Liberation Front with arms and shipped wounded fighters and war orphans to Cuba for medical treatment and education. From then until the 1990s Cuba provided military aid as well as widespread strategic and technical training and support to numerous African guerrilla groups, independence movements, and governments, including the rebel group led by Laurent Kabila, in support of independence leader Patrice Lumumba in what is present-day DROC; the African National Congress (ANC) in South Africa; the Liberation Front of Mozambique (FRELIMO); the South West Africa People's Organization (SWAPO) in Namibia; the People's Movement for the Liberation of Angola (MPLA); and the African Party for the Independence of Guinea and Cape Verde (PAIGC) in Guinea-Bissau.

Cuba's close cooperation with the PAIGC and MPLA led to the presence first of military advisors and then large numbers of combat troops. Mozambican cadres were also trained in Cuba, and Cuban guerrillas fought alongside Guineans and Cape Verdeans for the independence of Guinea Bissau and Cape Verde. Hoping to support the African Revolution, in 1965 Ernesto "Che" Guevara and one hundred Cuban troops embarked on a secret mission to train pro-Lumumbist rebels in the eastern part of what is present-day DROC. Guevara's experiences and reflections of his time in the Congo and why the mission failed were captured in his posthumously published Congo diary.

Cuba's most serious and committed military involvements in Africa were in Ethiopia and Angola. In a clear illustration of Cold War alliances, Cuba supported Soviet-backed Ethiopia against U.S.-backed Somalia during the Ogaden War from 1977 to 1978. The war ended when Somali forces retreated across the border and a truce was declared. Cuba's involvement in Angola was much longer and more intense. Starting in 1975, on the eve of Angola's independence from Portugal, Cuba launched a large-scale military intervention in support of the MPLA against the U.S.-backed invasions by South Africa and present-day DROC in support of two other liberation movements competing for power in the country, the National Liberation Front of Angola (FNLA) and National Union for the Total Independence of Angola (UNITA). Thereafter Cuban forces remained in Angola to support the Angolan government against the UNITA insurgency in the continuing Angolan Civil War.

In 1988 Cuban troops successfully intervened in an offensive by the Angolan army against South African-backed UNITA forces, leading to the Battle of Cuito Cuanavale, which was a turning point in Angola's long civil war. Because of the Cuban military enforcement, UNITA forces were severely weakened, Cuito Cuanavale was held by the Angolan army, and the South African Army withdrew into Namibia. Following the battle the ongoing peace talks were resumed, leading to the New York Accords, the eventual withdrawal of Cuban and South African forces from Angola, and Namibia's independence from South Africa.

Cuba's military engagement in Angola formally ended in 1991 (the civil war itself continued until 2002). During its fifteen-year involvement in the conflict, over 300,000 Cuban troops were stationed in Southern Africa; of these approximately 2,100 Cuban soldiers are reported to have been killed. Cuba's commitment to and support of the MPLA, its role in helping Namibia achieve independence as well as in weakening the South African apartheid regime—which eventually led to the first free and democratic elections in South Africa in 1994—has widely been recognized. Despite these successes, Cuba's involvement in Angola's brutal civil war also resulted in much loss and trauma among individual soldiers and their families. As of 2011, Cuba as a nation had yet to confront these collective wounds.

SOCIAL COLLABORATION PROGRAMS

In addition to the strong political-ideological and military relations, Cuba and many African countries have been closely linked through Cuba's social collaboration programs, in the form of education, health care, and technical development. This aid began in the early 1960s and was mainly directed at easing Africa's dire human resource problem as well as strengthening the continent's own human capital capacity by training Africans in various applied professions. With this agenda, thousands of Cuban doctors, teachers, and technicians were sent to Africa, and African students came to Cuba to study. After the 1960s Cuba offered scholarships to students from almost forty sub-Saharan African countries. As a result, more than 30,000 Africans were educated in Cuba at the primary, secondary, and tertiary levels. The first group of students came from Guinea-Conakry in 1961 to study at Cuban universities and in polytechnics. Lacking in professionals and educational infrastructure while also often enmeshed in devastating independence and civil wars, many other African countries quickly followed suit, sending their children and youth to Cuba. Most of these African countries were at one point socialist and had strong political ties to the Cuban

Fidel Castro in Tanzania, 1977. Fidel Castro (left) and Julius Nyerere (center), the president of Tanzania, chat with a Cuban worker on a visit to a Cuban-supported agricultural school in Ruvu, Tanzania, on 20 March 1977. © BETTMANN/CORBIS

government. Between the 1960s and late 1990s, the largest number of African students in Cuba came from Angola and Mozambique.

During the 1970s and 1980s thousands of primary, secondary, and pre-university foreign students were sent to the Isla de la Juventud (Isle of Youth, until 1978 called Isla de Pinos), a small island off the coast of Cuba. Based on Fidel Castro's idea to turn the island into a multinational educational project, dozens of schools and dormitories were built for students from Angola, Mozambique, Namibia, Zimbabwe, Western Sahara, Vietnam, Ghana, Nicaragua, the two Congos, Ethiopia, North Korea, Guinea-Bissau, Cape Verde, and Sao Tome and Principe, among others. Many of these students were as young as seven or eight years of age when they arrived, and many stayed in Cuba until they completed their secondary schooling or vocational or university training. Although some of these students were the children of political and revolutionary leaders, most were children of peasants and workers who had been chosen, often arbitrarily, to be trained as future cadres. Students who remained in or came to Cuba as young adults for vocational or university training joined their Cuban peers in polytechnics and universities across the island. Most were encouraged to study applied professions such as medicine, agronomy, veterinary science, engineering, and nursing so as to enable them, once they returned home, to support their country's economic and social development.

Until the early 1990s the funding for all of these programs—stipends covering tuition, room and board, school uniforms, allowances, and so on—came mainly from the Cuban government. Following the collapse of the Soviet Union in 1991 and Cuba's ensuing economic crisis, Cuba could no longer afford these stipends, resulting in a dramatic drop in the number of foreign students in Cuba. During the 1990s schools on the Isla de la Juventud were closed. Between 2000 and 2010 the number of foreign students—all at the university level, mostly attending medical school—again began to rise, in large part because African and other (mainly Latin American) governments began to pay for their students' expenses. Among the African contingent, the largest group as of 2011 was from South Africa.

After 1963, when the first Cuban medical brigade arrived in Algeria, over 140,000 Cuban technical and professional personnel—mainly doctors and nurses but also teachers, engineers, agronomists, fishing experts, and so on—served as so-called proletarian internationalists in over 150 countries on four continents. Africa in general has by far been the largest recipient of Cuba's medical assistance, with Mozambique and Angola the most significant beneficiaries. Since the 1960s over 50,000 Cuban doctors and nurses have worked on the continent. Moreover, Cuba built and staffed numerous hospitals and medical schools in several African nations. The Cuban health-care workers who go abroad are men and women between the ages of

35 and 60 who come from all parts of Cuba and represent a wide range of medical specializations. For many, the medical missions are their first time outside of Cuba and away from their families, whom they are not allowed to bring with them. They are usually sent out for an initial period of three years, during which time they are allowed to return home once a year on vacation.

As with the educational programs, Cuba paid for most of its development assistance until the early 1990s, when it began charging most countries for the medical programs it offers. Based on bilateral agreements, Cuba provides the recipient countries with the number of requested specialists in return for a fixed per-person fee, of which, however, the Cuban aid worker receives only a small percentage in the form of a stipend or salary. Despite the cost, many developing countries welcome this scheme as it is still much less expensive than importing health-care workers from elsewhere. Over the past few years, the medical aid programs have become one of Cuba's most important sources of badly needed hard currency; as a result, the number of aid programs and professionals being sent abroad has increased dramatically. In so doing the Cuban government not only profits monetarily but also has created a convenient mechanism for temporarily ridding itself of a large part of its arguably most frustrated surplus labor.

IMPACT AND ASSESSMENT OF SOCIAL COLLABORATION

Cuba's cooperation programs have generally been evaluated positively by African leaders as well as by the students, patients, and others who are the actual recipients of aid. Such positive assessments are due in part to past and some continuing political and ideological loyalties as well as economic factors (the aid, though no longer free, is still relatively inexpensive). But there are other reasons as well, beginning with the concrete results of Cuba's assistance: the treatment and cure of illnesses, care during pregnancy and birth, the building of hospitals, education and job training of young people, the building of schools, and so on. Moreover, Cuba has directed its aid toward helping other countries to strengthen their own human capital resources so that they can break out of the dependency cycle. In an age during which international aid and development has become an industry and a business, with big budgets, complex criteria and conditions, fancy jargon, and at times unclear agendas, some developing countries appreciate Cuba's relatively simple, straightforward, and effective policy.

Last but not least, it must also be remembered that Cuba's military support in Angola is a well-known and widely appreciated fact on the continent. Despite most African nations' transition from socialist to multiparty, democratic, capitalist systems, many African leaders and people still admire Cuba and especially Fidel Castro for standing up to the United States and the political and economic world order and for voicing what they themselves dare not say for fear of negative consequences, such as the suspension of trade benefits and aid packages. It is for these and other reasons that many African and other developing nations' governments and people remain indebted to Cuba. As a result, most African countries fully support the island on issues such as the U.S. embargo and the freeing of the Cuban Five (five Cuban intelligence officers convicted in 2001 on espionage and other charges in the United States) and remain conspicuously silent when it comes to Cuba's human rights abuses. The Cuban government knows full well that its best ambassadors are its doctors. In a time when the future of the Cuban Revolution seemed unclear, Cuba's medical diplomacy is expected to continue to be an important soft power tool of the island's foreign policy.

BIBLIOGRAPHY

Erisman, H. Michael, and John M. Kirk eds. *Cuban Foreign Policy Confronts a New International Order*. Boulder, CO: Lynne Rienner Publishers, 1991.

Feinsilver, Julie Margot. *Healing the Masses: Cuban Health Politics at Home and Abroad*. Berkeley: University of California Press, 1993.

Ferrer, Ada. *Insurgent Cuba: Race, Nation and Revolution, 1868–1898*. Chapel Hill: University of North Carolina Press, 1999.

Gleijeses, Piero. *Conflicting Missions: Havana, Washington and Africa, 1959–1976*. Chapel Hill: University of North Carolina Press, 2002.

Guevara, Ernesto. *The African Dream: The Diaries of the Revolutionary War in the Congo*. Translated by Patrick Camiller. New York: Grove Press, 2000.

Hansing, Katrin. "South-South Migration and Transnational Ties between Mozambique and Cuba." In *Transnational Ties: Cities, Migrations, and Identities*, edited by Michael Peter Smith and John Eade. New Brunswick, NJ: Transaction Publishers, 2008.

Kapcia, A. M. "Cuba's African Involvement: A New Perspective." *Survey* 24, no. 2 (Spring 1979): 142–159.

LeoGrande, William M. *Cuba's Policy in Africa, 1959–1980*. Berkeley: Institute of International Studies, University of California, 1980.

López Oliva, Armando. "Lazos de sangre y histora." *Verde Olivo* 21, no. 12 (1980): 12–13.

Mandela, Nelson, and Fidel Castro. *How Far We Slaves Have Come! South Africa and Cuba in Today's World*. New York: Pathfinder, 1991.

Mesa-Lago, Carmelo, and June Belkin, eds. *Cuba in Africa*. Pittsburgh: Center for Latin American Studies, University Center for International Studies, University of Pittsburgh, 1982.

Resíllez López, Antonio. *Carta desde África*. Havana: Editorial Unión de Periodistas de Cuba, 2001.

Risquet Valdés, Jorge. *40 Años de Solidaridad de Cuba con África*. Havana: Editorial SI-MAR, 1999.

THE WORLD AND CUBA: CUBA AND SOCIALIST COUNTRIES

Evgenij Haperskij

Edited by J. Preston Whitt

Cuba's place in the Cold War world.

Cuba came into the Soviet zone of economic and political interest after the success of the Revolution in January 1959; located only ninety miles from U.S. shores, it thus became a perceived threat to the United States. In the context of the Cold War, particularly given the level of hostility between the United States and the Soviet Union by late 1959, both the Soviet Union and Cuba could benefit from their relationship politically, militarily, and economically. The Soviet Union could project its military strength into the Americas and gain political prestige for its support for Third World revolutionary movements (against both the United States and China). For Cuba, Soviet support signified a powerful defense of the Cuban Revolution; cooperation with the Soviet Union could help recapture political sovereignty from the United States and break the diplomatic and economic isolation from other Latin American countries. Moreover, through access to the energy and other natural resources of the Soviet Union, Cuba could attempt to overcome its economic underdevelopment. For both countries, the alliance constituted a blow—in what Americans have traditionally referred to as their own "back yard"—to the U.S.-led imperialist system and was an opportunity to have Cuba become a showcase of socialist development in the Third World.

Cuba was neither merely a Soviet puppet nor a renegade state defying the Soviet Union. Most often, as the scholar of international relations W. Raymond Duncan argues, mutual interests determined the political relations of the two countries, rather than Soviet coercion although that was not completely absent, as for instance when the Soviet Union cut off Cuba's oil supplies in 1968 (Duncan pp. 74–75). Over the years, Soviet influence in Cuba ranged from serious concessions on how to conduct foreign policy in Latin America to a high degree of control over the economic and political affairs of the island.

CUBA TURNS TOWARD THE SOVIET UNION

The Soviet Union recognized the new Cuban government on 8 May 1960, although Soviet leader Nikita Khrushchev did not believe in the long-term success of Castro's revolutionary movement. He was cautious about engagement in the U.S. sphere of influence, particularly after the United States had demonstrated its determination to intervene in Guatemala, where President Jacobo Arbenz had launched an agrarian reform seen by the United States as menacing to U.S. corporate investments. In Cuba, American investments were far higher. In 1958, immediately prior to the Revolution, U.S. capital investments in Batista's Cuba amounted to more than $1 billion, 12 percent of all U.S. capital investments in Latin America. As a result, the best agricultural land, the biggest sugar manufacturing plants, the richest mineral reserves, significant goods-producing sectors, railroads, banks, municipal enterprises, and foreign trading were all in the hands of U.S. citizens and companies, complained Fidel Castro (pp. 79–97). After coming to power, Castro moved to nationalize U.S.-owned property. In the course of the First Agrarian Reform, launched in 1959, Castro expropriated over $912 million in U.S. petroleum, manufacturing, public utilities, and sugar holdings (Duncan p. 32), thereby earning lasting enmity and a firm reaction from the neighboring superpower.

In June 1960, the United States curtailed the sugar quota, which, months later, was totally eliminated. In October 1960, the Dwight D. Eisenhower administration imposed a partial embargo on trade with Cuba, which became a total embargo in 1962 under President John F. Kennedy. In January 1962, Cuba was suspended from the Organization of American States (OAS) under U.S. pressure (Duncan p. 35). This economic opposition directed against the Castro regime and its social, economic, and political transformation of Cuba pushed the Cubans to seek external support, which in the early Cold War could come only from the Soviet Union. Undoubtedly, U.S. behavior fulfilled Khrushchev's warning to Kennedy at the Vienna summit meeting in June 1961: "Actually, Fidel Castro is not a communist. But you could make him a communist" (Korniyenko p. 59).

In order to acquire more direct support from the Soviet Union, Castro turned the Cuban Revolution toward communism, saying after the U.S.-sponsored Bay of Pigs invasion of April 1961 that the Cuban Revolution was socialist. Then, on 2 December 1961, for the first time Castro proclaimed on Cuban television: "I am a Marxist-Leninist, and I will be one until the day I die" (Dominguez p. 30).

On 13 February 1960, the first trade agreement between the Soviet Union and Cuba was signed in Havana, in which the Soviets agreed to purchase 425,000 tons of sugar that year and one million tons annually for the following four years (Dorovtsov p. 1). In September 1962, the Soviets announced that they would supply arms to Cuba and provide technical specialists to train Cuban forces (Duncan 1985, p. 26). Also, Cuba underwent a massive political transformation: In July 1961, Fidel Castro merged his revolutionary 26th of July Movement with the existing communist Popular Socialist Party (PSP) to form the Integrated Revolutionary Organizations, the precursor to the Communist Party of Cuba (Hoffmann p. 88). In doing so, he purged those politicians of the

PSP who did not identify themselves solidly with his rule (Dinerstein pp. 169–170, 170–173). These political reforms helped Castro consolidate his power and the Revolution. Communist ideology was compatible with Cuban anti-imperialism and could help Castro defend the island from future incursions from its northern neighbor. Castro's move toward the Soviet bloc was thus a rational step to secure his regime. For Khrushchev, whose stance on Cuba was a clear-cut example of proletarian internationalism (Dorovtsov p. 1), the Cuban Revolution was a chance to reach out for expanded presence in the Western Hemisphere. In this first stage of Soviet-Cuban relationship, Khrushchev's strategy was to gain influence in the Third World through large injections of economic and military aid to Cuba (Shearman p. 1). Mutual interests formed the alliance between the two countries and affected their foreign-policy behavior.

FROM THE MISSILE CRISIS TO ECONOMIC INTEGRATION

The Cuban Missile Crisis of 1962 unsettled the relationship between Cuba and the Soviet Union. After secretly putting nuclear missiles on the island, the Soviet leader, under subsequent pressure from the United States, replaced the missiles without consultation with Castro. While students of Soviet-Cuban relations are divided on whether Khrushchev's intent in arming Cuba was to secure the island or to further Soviet strategic objectives (the United States had missiles in Turkey, which were quietly removed after the Soviet missiles were removed from Cuba), his retreat understandably cast doubt on the Soviet commitment to stand up to the United States on behalf of the Cubans and alienated the two countries. Castro, who previously was at least officially in line with Soviet policy, began to publicly criticize the Soviets, for instance accusing the leadership of giving insufficient aid to Vietnam. Furthermore, he exploited the Sino-Soviet rift, which had occurred after the Twentieth Congress of the Soviet Communist Party in 1956, at which Khrushchev criticized Stalin's rule and personality cult. Castro did not commit himself to either side, using this neutrality as leverage against the Soviet Union to gain further concessions. Most significantly, he began to insist on armed struggle as the fundamental path to change in Latin America (Duncan p. 45), a strategy opposed by the Soviets, both because of the huge supporting expenses they would be expected to incur and because of their policy of peaceful coexistence vis-à-vis the United States.

Relations between the Soviet Union and Cuba deteriorated further when Leonid Brezhnev came into power in 1964. Brezhnev regarded Khrushchev's optimistic stand toward rapid socialist development in the Third World as failed. The new Soviet leader introduced a more cautious approach, downplaying the role of armed struggle. He stressed change in Latin America and other Third World countries through peaceful means and emphasized broad united political fronts in which Latin American communist parties would participate (Duncan p. 64). In this second stage of Soviet-Cuban relationship—from mid-1960 to the early 1970s—the Soviets grew less willing to compromise with Castro, who, despite the vital need for financial and material assistance, would maintain his independent foreign policy until the end of the 1960s, calling for armed revolutionary struggle in Latin America at the Tricontinental Conference in 1966 and at the Organizacion Latinoamericana de Solidaridad (OLAS) conference in August 1967. In February 1968, Castro excluded several pro-Soviet politicians from the Integrated Revolutionary Organizations and publicly criticized the Soviet leadership. As a result, the Soviet Union cut off oil supplies to Cuba, demonstrating Cuba's growing dependence on Soviet assistance. This act of coercive power brought Cuba again in line with Soviet policy. For that reason, it is not surprising that Castro, though actually a supporter of national independence, declared his backing for the Soviet invasion of Czechoslovakia in August 1968. This was the beginning of the rapprochement between Brezhnev and Castro and a growing erosion of Castro's ability to project Cuban power internationally, at least until the mid-1970s. After the Soviet invasion of Czechoslovakia, Cuba grew more and more dependent on the Soviet Union.

In December 1970, the intergovernmental Soviet-Cuban Commission for Economic, Scientific and Technological Cooperation was established, and in July 1972 Cuba was integrated into the Soviet-directed Council for Mutual Economic Assistance (COMECON). All economic activities of the member states of COMECON were coordinated through the Soviet Union to develop multilateral economic, scientific, and technical cooperation. By 1976, total Soviet aid to Cuba reached $8.3 billion, in addition to scientific, educational, and military assistance worth several billion dollars (Duncan p. 105). By comparison, total Soviet aid to the Third World from 1954 to 1977 amounted to $13 billion.

CUBA IN THE LARGER WORLD

The island's political system underwent a substantial reorganization. A new constitution, which was approved in a national referendum in 1976, defined Cuba as a socialist republic, the Communist Party was established as the leading power, and fraternal friendship with the Soviet Union became law (Hoffmann p. 97). At the same time, this constitution consolidated Castro's power. It required that the same person be head of state and of government. That person, Fidel Castro, was also the first secretary of the Communist Party and the commander-in-chief of the armed forces (Dominguez p. 261).

In order to overcome hemispheric isolation, Castro ceased advocacy of armed struggle in Latin America, instead turning toward a pragmatic-realist policy designed to further Cuba's long-run vital interests (Duncan p. 107). This step was the key to Cuba's re-entrance into the official Latin American community. Between 1970 and 1976, eleven Caribbean and Latin American countries established diplomatic relations with Cuba. Furthermore, the OAS lifted diplomatic and commercial sanctions in July 1975. This third period of Soviet-Cuban relations saw Cuba integrated into the socialist bloc's economic system, the first such state outside Moscow's direct sphere of influence to gain admittance to COMECON. In this period Cuba was heavily dependent upon the Soviet Union for its economic survival and national security (Shearman p. 1).

Cuba's reaction to the Soviet invasion of Afghanistan illustrates its dependence. For Castro the Soviet aggression in Afghanistan in 1979 could not have been more ill-timed as far as Cuba's interests were concerned, since Cuba was enjoying its position as leader of the Non-Aligned Movement when Moscow invaded a member of that organization (Payne p. 49). Although the invasion was clearly a case of a superpower imposing its will on a Third World country through military means, Cuba voted with the socialist bloc in January 1980 at the United Nations against the U.S.-backed resolution condemning the Soviet action. Cuba was the only member of the Non-Aligned Movement to vote in this way (Bain 2006, p. 30). In doing so, Cuba lost its credibility as a supporter of Third World countries, where it had been increasingly involved.

Despite withdrawing open support of armed revolutionary struggle in Latin America, Cuba reaffirmed its proletarian internationalism in other parts of the world, such as in Africa, where diplomatic relations and military involvement without aggressive U.S. opposition have been possible. Although the Soviets rejected such uncoordinated involvement, Cubans had been involved in various African countries since the early 1960s. In the late 1970s, though, when the Soviet leadership decided to intervene (at Cuba's insistence) in Angola and later in Ethiopia, Cuban experience in Africa turned out to be of great value for the Soviet Union. Fearing direct U.S. confrontation, the Soviets provided military assistance to Cuban forces on the ground (Duncan p. 121). In both countries Soviet-Cuban joint interventions were successful, bringing the leftist movement MPLA in Angola into power against U.S.-backed groups and helping Ethiopia keep its Ogaden region against intervention by Somalia, supported by the United States. This effective cooperation in Africa encouraged Cuba and the Soviet Union to alter their policies also in the Western Hemisphere in the late 1970s and early 1980s. Both Castro and the Soviet leadership saw this as the right time for revolutionary change in Latin America and the Caribbean basin, where there were popular rebellions against U.S. interests. In the 1973–1975 period, Venezuela tried to use its leadership of the Organization of Petroleum Exporting Countries (OPEC) to raise oil prices to get more capital for Latin American oil producers. Jamaica

and Guyana nationalized Kaiser Aluminum and Reynolds Guyana Mines in 1974 and 1975. In October 1975, the Latin American Economic System (SELA) was founded, which included Cuba but excluded the United States, and thus weakened the U.S. position in the Caribbean and Latin America. In 1979, the Nicaraguan Revolution, led by the Sandinista National Liberation Front (FSLN), succeeded in overthrowing a U.S.-sponsored dictatorship (Duncan p. 174). In order to support these socialist movements, the Soviet Union increased economic and military aid to Cuba in the late 1970s and early 1980s (Duncan p. 159). Furthermore, relations between the Soviet Union and the United States deteriorated during the early years of the presidency of Ronald Reagan (1981–1989), who promoted an aggressive rollback strategy against communism. As the Cold War took a turn for the worse and because of increased Cuban leverage in the Soviet capital, Moscow supplied Cuba with state-of-the-art military hardware (Bain 2006, p. 30).

THE END OF THE COLD WAR

However, changes in the Soviet bloc in the mid-1980s marked a turning point in Soviet support for Cuba. After coming into power in 1985, Mikhail Gorbachev began a course correction of the communism of the Soviet bloc, diminishing Soviet subsidies for Cuba (Hoffmann p. 102). While Gorbachev launched his policy of *perestroika* (restructuring), Castro adapted a contrary course of *rectificación*, which reverted to the national character of the Revolution. On the economic level, the process of rectification was an antimarket reform: The economy was recentralized, farmers' markets were closed down, and, instead of economic incentives, Castro tried to motivate the workforce with moral urging in the style of Che Guevara. Sensing that socialism itself was being threatened, Castro urged a return to communist principles, epitomized by the slogan "Socialismo o muerte!" (Socialism or death!). The countries gradually grew apart, as the Soviet Union began to drastically reduce its economic subsidies, and the political changes under Gorbachev made the Cuban leadership suspicious. Furthermore, because of an improvement of relations between the Soviet Union and the United States in the mid-1980s, Cuba lost its geostrategic importance for Moscow. On 11 September 1991, Gorbachev announced the withdrawal of Soviet troops from Cuba without prior consultation with the Cubans, thereby terminating Havana's privileged position within the Soviet governing elite in Moscow (Bain 2006, p. 64). However, Gorbachev remained loyal to Cuba until the end of the Soviet Union, as he never called for the relationship to be terminated (Dominguez p. 67).

The complete breakdown of the Soviet bloc in 1990–1991 was a dramatic setback for Cuba. The collapse of the Soviet Union meant a loss of foreign trade on preferential terms, easy access to credit, the coordination of economic plans, development aid, technical

Mikahil Gorbachev (b. 1931) in Cuba, 1989. Fidel Castro and Soviet leader Mikhail Gorbachev review troops in Cuba in April 1989. After coming into power in 1985, Gorbachev reduced Soviet subsidies for Cuba, but he never called for the relationship between the two countries to end, and he remained loyal to Cuba until the dissolution of the Soviet Union. DIRCK HALSTEAD/TIME LIFE PICTURES/GETTY IMAGES

consultation, and common development projects with technological transfer. Cuba plunged into a deep economic and social crisis.

CUBA AND RUSSIA

In the early 1990s, Russia, the main successor state to the Soviet Union, immediately began to throw the switches on its traditional economic relations with Cuba. According to the Duma, the lower house of the Russian parliament, the trade between Russia and Cuba decreased from $9 billion in 1990 to $710 million three years later (Dorovtsov p. 3), resulting in the collapse of Cuba's foreign trade and a severe economic crisis.

Although Russia had reduced its cooperation with Cuba to a bare minimum, it never entirely ended the relationship and soon the deceleration was followed by tentative efforts toward rapprochement. In the early 1990s Cuba and Russia signed their first bilateral agreements. Russian critics increasingly began to voice their concerns over Russia's restrictive stance toward its former ally. However, during the rule of Boris Yeltsin (1991–1999), Cuba was not seen as being particularly important for Russian foreign policy goals.

Under the leadership of Vladimir Putin, Russia gradually changed course in its policies toward Cuba. In 2000, Putin visited and granted Castro a $50-million credit, a relatively meager financial aid package, but one that marked the resumption of an official dialogue between Cuban and Russian leadership (Isachenkov). Subsequently, trade links between Cuba and Russia increased, from $125 million in 2005 to over $231

million in 2006 and then to $285 million, with the trade turnover peaking in 2007 (Mityaev). More significant than the trade relationship between the former allies was the revival of their strategic partnership. In 2009, Russian deputy prime minister Igor Sechin signed four contracts securing oil exploration rights in Cuban territorial waters in the Gulf of Mexico (Frank).

In the early 2000s, years after the collapse of the Soviet Union and the termination of its cooperation with Cuba, Russia and Cuba worked to revive the relationship. In the new millennium mutual interests united the two countries, although divested of past ideological baggage. During his visit to Cuba in 2000, Putin emphasized that Russia had no ideological agenda in the region and instead wanted practical deals that would benefit Russian businesses ("Putin Urges"), pointing to a new globalized arena.

BIBLIOGRAPHY

Bain, Mervyn J. *Soviet-Cuban Relations, 1985 to 1991: Changing Perceptions in Moscow and Havana.* Lanham, MD: Lexington Books, 2006.

Bain, Mervyn J. *Russian-Cuban Relations since 1992: Continuing Camaraderie in a Post-Soviet World.* Lanham, MD: Lexington Books, 2008.

Castro, Fidel. "Del informe al primer congreso del Partido Comunista de Cuba." *Cuadernos Políticos* 7 (January–March 1976): 79–97. Available from http://www.cuadernospoliticos.unam.mx/cuadernos/num07.html.

Dinerstein, Herbert S. *The Making of a Missile Crisis, October 1962.* Baltimore, MD: Johns Hopkins University Press, 1976.

Domínguez, Jorge I. *To Make a World Safe for Revolution: Cuba's Foreign Policy.* Cambridge, MA: Harvard University Press, 1989.

Dorovtsov, D. E. *Rossiysko-Kubinskie Otnosheniya i Zakon "Khelmsa-Bertona"* [Russian-Cuban relations and the "Helms-Burton Act"]. Vol. 8, *Predstavitelnaya Vlact* [Representative Power]. Moscow: Lomonsov Moscow State University, 1996.

Duncan, W. Raymond. *The Soviet Union and Cuba: Interests and Influence.* New York: Praeger, 1985.

Frank, Marc. "Russia Signs Pact for Oil Exploration in Cuba." Reuters, 3 November 2009. Available from http://www.reuters.com/article/2009/11/03/us-cuba-russia-oil-idUSTRE5A25AY20091103.

Hoffmann, Bert. *Kuba.* Munich: C. H. Beck, 2002.

Isachenkov, Vladimir. "Putin Promises Friendship to Castro but Little Aid." *Miami Herald*, 15 December 2000. Available from http://www.latinamericanstudies.org/cuba/putin-promises.htm.

Korniyenko, Georgi. *Kholodnaya voina: Svidetel'stvo uchastnika* [The Cold War: A participant's testimony]. Moscow: Olma, 1994.

Mityaev, Oleg. "Kuba-Rossiya: novaya popitka sblizheniya" [Cuba-Russia: A new attempted rapprochement]. *RIA Novosti*, 31 July 2008.

Pavlov, Yuri. *Soviet-Cuban Alliance, 1959–1991.* Coral Gables, FL: North-South Center Press, 1996.

Payne, Richard J. *Opportunities and Dangers of Soviet-Cuban Expansion: Toward a Pragmatic U.S. Policy.* Albany: State University of New York Press, 1988.

"Putin Urges Revival of Russian Ties with Cuba." *Miami Herald*, 13 December 2000. Available from http://www.latinamericanstudies.org/cuba/putin.htm.

Schwab, Peter. *Cuba: Confronting the U.S. Embargo.* New York: St. Martin's Press, 1999.

Shearman, Peter. *The Soviet Union and Cuba.* London and New York: Routledge & Kegan Paul, 1987.

Staten, Clifford L. *The History of Cuba.* Westport, CT: Greenwood, 2003.

THE WORLD AND CUBA: CUBAN REVOLUTION AND LATIN AMERICA

Thomas C. Wright

The impact of the Cuban Revolution on Latin American politics, particularly its role in fomenting leftist revolutionary movements.

For three decades after Fidel Castro came to power in 1959, the Cuban Revolution was the primary driving force of Latin American politics. Castro's revolution ignited a wave of revolutionary activity that posed unprecedented levels of threat to vested interests and shook the Latin American status quo to its core in the 1960s and early 1970s. The rise of this Cuban-inspired threat of revolution, in turn, catalyzed a wave of reaction that, aided by the United States, led to heightened repression by military regimes.

In Cuba there was no debate, such as that in Russia following the Bolshevik seizure of power in 1917, over whether first to consolidate the revolution at home or to push immediately for revolution abroad. While launching the revolutionary measures that would transform the island, Castro simultaneously called for revolution throughout Latin America, famously threatening to "convert the cordillera of the Andes to the Sierra Maestra of the hemisphere" (quoted in Thomas p. 1293). Within months of coming to power, Castro organized an invasion of the Dominican Republic, then ruled by Rafael Trujillo, and aided exile attacks on other dictatorships. Over the next several years, he invited thousands of Latin Americans to visit and observe the island's transformation, in the process converting many into advocates of Cuban-style revolution. He established training facilities in Cuba for potential guerrilla fighters from around Latin America, and many availed themselves of the opportunity to prepare for insurrection. Castro also funneled aid to leftist and guerrilla groups throughout Latin America.

CUBA AS EXAMPLE

Yet while the Cuban government remained deeply involved in promoting revolution through the 1960s, Castro's exhortations and material aid were secondary to Cuba's example in inspiring Latin Americans to embrace revolution to overcome the endemic problems of poverty, illiteracy, inequality, and political exclusion. Three aspects of the Cuban Revolution were particularly appealing to many of Latin America's youth, workers, peasants, marginalized slum dwellers, and intellectuals: (1) the method of insurrection that allowed a small group to defeat a national army, (2) the economic and social revolution in Cuba, and (3) the revolution in Cuba's foreign relations.

Castro's preferred method of overthrowing President Fulgencio Batista (1933–1944, 1952–1959) was to strike direct, dramatic blows such as his assault on the Moncada Barracks in 1953 and the failed uprising in Santiago in 1956. The method that eventually worked, rural-based guerrilla warfare, was adopted in the wake of the Santiago debacle. Twenty-five months after Castro and his tiny band took refuge in the Sierra Maestra, the national army collapsed, Batista fled, and the bearded, khaki-clad guerrillas emerged from the mountains and entered Havana as heroes. By retaining the beards and khakis after taking office, the new regime sent the clear message that the rural guerrilla method had secured victory over the U.S.-trained and -equipped Cuban army. In 1960 the best-selling book by Ernesto "Che" Guevara (1928–1967), *Guerrilla Warfare,* purported to recount the Cuban experience in the form of a handbook offering step-by-step guidance for revolutionaries seeking to overthrow their

■ *See also*

Che Guevara, Social and Political Thought

Cuban Embargo

Cuban Thought and Cultural Identity: Socialist Thought

Economy: Revolutionary Period

Economy: Special Period

Guerrillero Heroico (Alberto Korda)

Health and Health Care: Medical Diplomacy and International Medical Education

governments. The combination of guerrillas in power and Che Guevara's convincing blueprint for insurrection made the rural guerrilla approach attractive and seemingly easy—deceptively so, as it turned out.

Cuba's was one of the world's most thorough and most rapidly executed revolutions. Within four years of seizing power, Castro's government had expropriated all foreign-owned properties and all but the smallest Cuban-owned businesses, establishing a socialist economy on the island. In addition, the government offered work, education, and health care to all. While these leveling measures set off an exodus of wealthy and middle-class Cubans, they created a new society based on an egalitarian model that had mass appeal in a region characterized by extremely uneven distribution of wealth, income, and opportunity. Of the measures that transformed Cuba, the one that resonated most loudly in Latin America was agrarian reform. Over half of the Latin American population in 1960 was rural, most of whom were landless in countries dominated by *latifundios* (estates), and the rapid transformation of the Cuban rural economy and society had enormous appeal to the land-starved of the hemisphere.

The third factor that accounted for the Cuban Revolution's powerful impact on Latin America was the island's break with the United States. Given Cuba's history as a U.S. protectorate from 1898 to 1933 and its economic dependence on the United States thereafter, many Cubans harbored strong anti-U.S. sentiments. As the hegemonic hemispheric power and primary source of foreign capital, the United States had created anti-American sentiments throughout Latin America, in varying degrees. When Castro began expropriating U.S.-owned land and business and refused to buckle under pressure from Washington, he became a hero to nationalists who chafed at U.S. economic and political power over their countries. When he faced and defeated the surrogate U.S. invasion force at the Bay of Pigs in April 1961, he was hailed as the liberator of Latin America, a new Bolívar.

While these accomplishments reverberated throughout Latin America, generating strong pro-Castro sentiment, other aspects of the revolution dampened enthusiasm or engendered fierce opposition. After promising a political democracy, Castro cemented his personal power and moved toward building a one-party state. He embraced Marxism-Leninism and aligned Cuba with the Soviet Union, even though at times he chose independent policies that displeased Moscow. The economy faltered and rationing had to be instituted. For many, these developments took the luster off the revolution; yet in the eyes of Latin America's have-nots, the positive changes overshadowed the revolution's shortcomings.

In addition to the concrete accomplishments, the style of leadership and the enthusiasm conveyed by the common people of Cuba further embellished the revolution's appeal. Castro was an extremely charismatic leader. Handsome, charming, and articulate, he could speak extemporaneously for hours and hold a crowd's attention, and liked to mingle with the island's common people. He was adept at using the media to his advantage. Images from Cuba also portrayed a high level of enthusiasm for and participation in the building of a socialist society. When Castro created the Comités de Defensa de la Revolución in 1960, in anticipation of the Bay of Pigs invasion, roughly half of the adult population joined. Whether it was the thousands of youth who took the literacy campaign to the remotest parts of the island or the residents of Havana building the green belt, Latin Americans saw what appeared to be massive and willing volunteer work in support of Castro's revolution.

The timing of the Cuban Revolution was another major factor in its impact. The late 1950s and early 1960s were a period of democratic ascendancy second only to the period from 1990 to the present; after the fall of several authoritarian regimes in the 1950s, only six countries—all of them small—were not governed in a mostly democratic manner. As a result, media censorship was minimal and freedom to demonstrate and to form new political groups was optimal in most of the hemisphere. The dissemination of news from Cuba was further facilitated by the advent of television and the cheap transistor radio, both of which transcended the barrier of illiteracy.

The calls for revolution, the positive accomplishments in Cuba, the style of the revolution, and the relative freedom and technology to reach out to most Latin Americans created a climate favorable to the rise of an unprecedented wave of revolutionary activity. Herbert Matthews, a *New York Times* senior editor and close observer of Cuba, described this as "something new, exciting, dangerous, and infectious [that] has come into the Western Hemisphere with the Cuban Revolution" (Matthews pp. 273–274). Some called it *fidelismo*, which amounted to acute impatience with the status quo combined with the attitude that revolution should be pursued immediately—no excuses. Castro summed up this attitude in his 1962 Second Declaration of Havana: "The duty of every revolutionary is to make revolution" (quoted in Suchlicki p. 196). As proven by the Cuban Revolution, one no longer needed to wait for the objective conditions that the Latin American communist parties argued must be in place for revolution to occur; moreover, as Che Guevara explained in addenda to *Guerrilla Warfare*, the guerrilla nucleus (*foco*, or cadre) alone could create the necessary conditions for revolution through its actions.

THE CHANGING POLITICAL LANDSCAPE

As the example of Cuba drove up demands for change, the political agenda in most countries shifted leftward, fidelista groups and publications proliferated, street demonstrations and strikes multiplied, and the slogan "Cuba sí, Yanqui no" (Cuba yes, Yankee no) was scrawled on the walls of Latin America. The impact of Cuba altered the political party landscape: The more progressive elements of mainline reformist parties such as Venezuela's Acción Democrática (AD) and Peru's Alianza Popular Revolucionaria Americana (APRA) became disillusioned with reformism and broke away, forming their own parties. Communist parties, wedded to gradualism and caution, also spun off numerous, often competing pro-Cuban groups. Inspired by the Cuban agrarian reform, landless *campesinos* (farm workers) mobilized for land reform, sometimes occupying haciendas and driving out the landowners; the Brazilian Ligas Camponesas (peasant leagues) in particular were considered a serious threat to the status quo.

Rural guerrilla movements were launched in Guatemala, Nicaragua, Venezuela, Peru, Colombia, El Salvador, and elsewhere from the early 1960s through 1980. One of these was the failed 1966–1967 movement led by Che Guevara in Bolivia. Its purpose was to train fighters from around South America in preparation for multiple guerrilla wars, but after Che's capture and execution in 1967, these fighters did not materialize. Whereas most of the guerrillas were defeated, the Frente Sandinista de Liberación Nacional (FSLN; the Sandinistas) took power in Nicaragua eighteen years after its founding. In the twenty-first century, two of the three Colombian guerrilla groups founded in the mid-1960s and early 1970s, the Fuerzas Armadas Revolucionarias de Colombia (FARC) and the Ejército de Liberación Nacional (ELN), survive despite setbacks. In El Salvador the guerrilla group Frente Farabundo Martí para la Liberación Nacional (FMLN), founded in 1980, became a political party at the end of the civil war and won the presidency in 2009. In heavily urbanized Uruguay and Argentina, powerful Cuban-inspired urban guerrilla movements appeared in the late 1960s and early 1970s.

Unprecedented degrees of radicalization and mobilization threatened the stability and even the survival of several civilian governments. As the militaries observed mounting pressures for change and civilian governments fumbling or equivocating in dealing with the rise of fidelismo, they intervened, overthrowing those governments and cracking down on dissidents in half a dozen countries by 1963. The following year, the Brazilian military deposed President João Goulart, whom they accused of pro-Castro leanings, and established a dictatorship that lasted twenty-one years and served as a precedent for later state terrorist regimes in Chile (1973–1990), Uruguay (1973–1984), and Argentina (1976–1983).

U.S. Response U.S. administrations during the 1960s viewed the fidelista threat in the hemisphere as opening a new theater in the Cold War. In 1961 President John F. Kennedy launched the Alliance for Progress, a sweeping but ultimately ineffectual program designed to promote economic development, social justice, and political democracy as antidotes to Cuban-style revolution. The United States applied escalating pressure on Cuba to curtail its ability to export revolution, establishing the trade embargo still in effect as of 2011 and persuading the Organization of American States (OAS) in 1962 to expel Cuba; two years later the OAS required member states to cut all diplomatic, commercial, and travel ties with the island. Fidel dismissed the OAS action, calling the organization the U.S. Ministry of Colonies. Mexico was the sole member country to defy the OAS by refusing to sever relations with Cuba.

Whereas the Alliance for Progress and isolation of Cuba accomplished relatively little, the U.S. military response to the Cuban threat was effective. The U.S. military taught and equipped elite units of the Latin American militaries in counterinsurgency warfare in order to defeat the guerrillas; the highest profile case of counterinsurgency versus guerrilla occurred in Bolivia, where newly formed army ranger units defeated and captured Che Guevara in 1967. The United States also instructed the Latin American officer corps in national security doctrine, or the concept that the enemy is no longer the army across the border, but Marxists and other so-called subversives inside each country's society. National security doctrine underpinned the militaries' wars against the left in several countries during the wave of reaction against the revolutionary tide.

Despite the powerful wave of revolution that swept through much of Latin America, only two revolutionary movements succeeded in taking power. (The 1968–1975 Peruvian military government applied revolutionary measures but was not a case of a revolutionary movement acceding to power.) The success of counterinsurgency against rural guerrilla movements and the urban guerrillas that succeeded them in a few countries, the effectiveness of national security doctrine in preparing the armed forces for repression, and the gradual waning of the power of Cuba to inspire revolutionary activity largely account for Castro's failure to revolutionize Latin America. And owing to both internal and external resistance, neither of the revolutionary movements that took power, the Unidad Popular coalition in Chile (1970–1973) and the Frente Sandinista de Liberación Nacional in Nicaragua (1979–1990), was able to finish the revolution that it started.

REVOLUTION IN CHILE

Chile clearly reflects the impact of the Cuban Revolution in creating a revolutionary movement. Along with Uruguay, Chile was the Latin American country with the longest and strongest democratic tradition. As a result, the impact of the Cuban Revolution on Chile was largely contained within the formal, legal political system. As a country of great rural estates, Chile was highly susceptible to the agrarian reform agenda generated by Cuba. Previously barred from recruiting in

Fidel Castro (left) and Che Guevara in Havana, 4 February 1960. Fidel Castro and Che Guevara provided an attractive and convincing blueprint for insurrection that ignited a wave of revolutionary activity throughout Latin America. © BETTMANN/ CORBIS

the countryside, urban-based labor and left party cadres redoubled their efforts after 1959 to recruit estate workers into still illegal agricultural unions and to generate demands for agrarian reform, leading the president of the Conservative Party to compare the situation to sitting on a volcano. Reflecting the success of this rural penetration, the conservative government of Jorge Alessandri (1896–1986) in 1962 enacted an agrarian reform law that, though largely ineffectual, was designed to preempt the rising mobilization for land.

Events of 1964 and 1965 further revealed the rapid unraveling of Chile's balance of power among right, center, and left parties, under pressures generated by the example of Cuba's revolution. The loss of a historically safe conservative rural congressional seat in a March 1964 special election radically altered the September presidential election of that year. Alerted that their electoral control over rural workers was in jeopardy, the right parties abandoned their presidential candidate and embraced Christian Democrat Eduardo

Frei (1911–1982). This was a desperate measure because the Christian Democratic Party had evolved in the early 1960s into a large, dynamic party whose reformist platform contained revolutionary proposals, including a thorough agrarian reform. The right calculated that in the typical three-candidate field, socialist Salvador Allende (1908–1973) would ride the wave of revolutionary sentiment into the presidential palace, and so it endorsed Frei as the lesser of the evils. Frei was elected in a contest billed by his partisans as a contest between Cuban-style revolution and "revolution in liberty"; such was the transformation of Chilean politics in the early 1960s that the two major candidates competed on the basis of their revolutionary credentials. Congressional elections the following year confirmed the eclipse of the right, which won only 7 of 45 seats in the senate and 9 of 147 in the chamber of deputies.

Frei's reformist policies pleased neither left nor right. The administration enacted an aggressive agrarian reform law and legalized rural unions in 1967, while instituting significant reforms in the urban arena. But to mobilized urban and rural workers, the pace of change was too slow and worker and campesino seizures of factories and estates escalated into what has been called a hypermobilization. Reflecting this frustration, elements of the Christian Democratic left broke away in 1969 to form the radical Movimiento de Acción Popular Unitaria (MAPU). Meanwhile, an antisystem group that embraced violence as a means to take power, the Movimiento de Izquierda Revolucionaria (MIR), was founded in 1965; two years later the Socialist Party, formerly a broad-based reformist party, declared itself Marxist Leninist and, like the MIR, accepted the validity of revolutionary violence.

The fortunes of the right revived somewhat in the 1969 congressional elections, largely in reaction to the Frei reforms, particularly those in the countryside that stripped numerous elite families of their traditional estates. Buoyed by its relative success, the right, reconstituted as the new Partido Nacional, launched its own presidential candidate for 1970, re-creating the traditional multiparty field and raising again the possibility of a left victory. Organized as the Unidad Popular coalition of the socialist and communist parties and four small groups, the left nominated Allende for the fourth time. With the Christian Democrat candidate placing third, Allende defeated the right's candidate by a narrow margin, 36.5 to 35.2 percent. Having invested heavily to stop Allende's election, the Richard M. Nixon administration tried two failed strategies to prevent his inauguration. Thus revolution reached Chile by the ballot box, far removed from Che Guevara's vision of revolutionary warfare but clearly energized by the impact of the Cuban Revolution. However, the Chilean revolution would be truncated in 1973, replaced by a military regime under General Augusto C. Pinochet (1915–2006) that was designed to eradicate, permanently, the revolutionary left in Chile, causing the torture, death, and disappearance of thousands.

REVOLUTION IN NICARAGUA

The second country where a revolutionary movement fostered by the Cuban Revolution took power was Nicaragua. With the exception of Guatemala, Central America was less affected by the Cuban Revolution in the 1960s than were the larger, more developed countries of South America. Like most of its neighbors, Nicaragua was relatively backward economically and as a result had developed few of the social groups and organizations—labor, students, and left parties—that were capable of responding to the stimuli from Cuba. Moreover, the Somoza family had run the country with an iron fist since 1936, employing censorship and repression to maintain control and discourage dissidence. The Cuban Revolution had an early and direct impact on Nicaragua—though little noticed at the time—that in the long run would bring revolution to power.

Like many Latin American leftists, Carlos Fonseca Amador, a member of Nicaragua's communist party, was invited to visit Cuba. Impressed by what he saw and discouraged by the Nicaraguan communists' gradualism, he broke with the party upon returning and, with his friends Tomás Borge and Silvio Mayorga, founded the Frente Sandinista de Liberación Nacional in 1961. Named for General Augusto C. Sandino (1895–1934), the hero of resistance to the U.S. Marines' occupation of Nicaragua in the 1920s and early 1930s, the FSLN was Marxist, fidelista, and nationalist. It adopted rural guerrilla warfare as its method of insurrection but, like most guerrilla movements that sprang up, suffered serious setbacks from the beginning.

The Sandinistas discovered through experience that Che Guevara had omitted a key element from his story of the Cuban insurrection. In Cuba, the urban resistance was so tenacious that Batista had been forced to focus his repression on it, leaving Castro's guerrilla band largely unmolested in its mountain stronghold and thus allowing it to grow, develop a liberated zone, and eventually descend onto the plains and assume power. In Nicaragua, by contrast, there was no serious urban resistance to President Luis Somoza (1922–1867) in the early 1960s. Thus Somoza's National Guard focused on the FSLN from its beginning, inflicting losses in every encounter and driving it back to safe haven in Honduras. But the Sandinistas persisted: Realizing that the guerrilla band was not creating conditions for revolution, they avoided decisive military confrontations and turned to systematic peasant recruitment in the late 1960s, referring to this approach in Maoist terms as "gathering forces in silence."

Strengthened in numbers, the Sandinistas returned to action in a dramatic way that departed from the rural guerrilla script. In 1974 they captured and held the guests at a Christmas party hosted by one of the ministers of President Anastasio Somoza (1925–1980) until Somoza freed some prisoners, paid a ransom, and agreed to have newspapers publish an FSLN communiqué. By this time the political landscape had been altered by natural and human events. After a major earthquake hit Managua in 1972, the National Guard ignored the victims while tending to their own families and openly looting damaged businesses. Somoza had made enormous profits on land and construction deals during the capital's rebuilding, virtually shutting out competitors. This behavior had significantly reduced the elites' support of the regime. When the FSLN surfaced at the Christmas party, Somoza suddenly faced dual civil and military opposition.

Frustrated by the slow pace of progress, the Sandinista's broke into three factions, pursuing different strategies: one maintained the rural guerrilla model; one opted for urban operations; and the third adopted an eclectic approach, reaching out beyond the original Marxist base. Following the January 1978 assassination of a popular opposition leader that was attributed to Somoza, riots and uprisings against the regime broke out across the country. Sensing an opportunity for victory, the FSLN factions reunited, recruited substantial numbers of new fighters, and by May 1979 announced a final offensive. Finally, after the failure of U.S. calls for Somoza's resignation and for OAS military intervention to block the Sandinista offensive, Somoza fled, the National Guard dissolved, and FSLN fighters rolled into Managua on 19 July 1979.

The Sandinista victory belatedly validated the Cuban prescription for insurrection, but with major revisions. Realizing that Che's formula would not work in Nicaragua, the Sandinistas had taken time to build a peasant base of support and proved opportunistic when new approaches appeared promising. They invested eighteen years in their quest for power, but like that of the Chilean left, their victory was pyrrhic. Although the revolution they began to implement in 1979 was moderate in comparison with Castro's, President Ronald Reagan saw it in black-and-white Cold War terms, launched a low-intensity proxy war to undermine it (incurring a death toll in the tens of thousands), and succeeded in stopping a unique exercise in social democracy. Rather than removal by military defeat or coup, the Sandinista government ended at the ballot box in 1990.

THE ECLIPSE OF CUBAN INFLUENCE

Nicaragua was not the only target of U.S. foreign policy during the administrations of presidents Reagan (1981–1989) and George H. W. Bush (1989–1993). Cuba was seen as responsible for trouble and subversion in Central America and the Caribbean, and the United States countered Cuban influence through military aid, especially to El Salvador and Guatemala, and by invading Grenada. Meanwhile, Cuba's ability to support revolutionary movements in the region was compromised by its long and costly military involvement in Angola; moreover, by the mid-1980s its relationship with the Soviet Union—then beginning to undergo political and economic reform under Communist Party leader Mikhail Gorbachev (b. 1931)—had become increasingly strained.

A number of developments in 1990 marked the end of a three-decade era during which the Cuban Revolution heavily influenced the broad sweep of Latin American politics. The end of the Soviet subsidy plunged Cuba into a severe economic crisis and forced the Castro government to look inward. The era's last South American terrorist state, Pinochet's Chile, ended in 1990, as did the only revolutionary government to take power through insurrection, the Sandinistas of Nicaragua. Moreover, most Latin American countries had reestablished diplomatic and commercial relations with the island by 1990, indicating that within Latin America the Cuban Revolution was no longer considered a threat. Meanwhile Cuba aggressively pursued trade and diplomatic relations with Latin America and the Caribbean and continued its long-standing relationship with Mexico.

With the economic crisis that ensued after the 1991 collapse of the Soviet Union, which Castro termed the "special period in peacetime," Cuba's remaining influence essentially evaporated. When leftist governments began to come to power in the late 1990s, Cuba found new allies, particularly in Hugo Chávez of Venezuela (b. 1954; elected in 1998), and its international profile rose; but while Castro sent medical specialists, teachers, and other trained personnel to Venezuela, Chávez clearly dominated the new Caracas-Havana alliance, and Cuba's apparent resuscitation as a power was limited. In the first decade of the twenty-first century, the leftward turn of additional governments (including Brazil, Ecuador, Bolivia, and Nicaragua) and the creation of the Bolivarian Alliance for the Americas (ALBA), have been hopeful signs for Cuba. But suffering ill health, Fidel handed power over to his brother Raúl in 2008. With the September 2010 announcement of far-reaching reforms that were anticipated to reduce the state's role in the economy, Cuba seemed to be turning inward again in search of economic renewal and regime survival.

BIBLIOGRAPHY

Booth, John A. *The End and the Beginning: The Nicaraguan Revolution.* 2nd ed. Boulder, CO: Westview Press, 1985.

Domínguez, Jorge I. *To Make a World Safe for Revolution: Cuba's Foreign Policy.* Cambridge, MA: Harvard University Press, 1989.

Guevara, Ernesto (Che). *Guerrilla Warfare.* 3rd ed. With case studies by Brian Loveman and Thomas M. Davies Jr. Wilmington, DE: SR Books, 1997.

Matthews, Herbert L. *The Cuban Story*. New York: George Braziller, 1961.

Suchlicki, Jaime, ed. *Cuba, Castro, and Revolution*. Coral Gables, FL: University of Miami Press, 1972.

Thomas, Hugh. *Cuba, or, The Pursuit of Freedom*. 2nd ed. New York: Da Capo Press, 1998.

Wickham-Crowley, Timothy P. *Guerrillas and Revolution in Latin America: A Comparative Study of Insurgents and Regimes since 1956*. Princeton, NJ: Princeton University Press, 1992.

Wolpin, Miles D. *Cuban Foreign Policy and Chilean Politics*. Lexington, MA: Heath Lexington Books, 1972.

Wright, Thomas C. *Latin America in the Era of the Cuban Revolution*. Rev. ed. Westport, CT: Praeger, 2001.

THE WORLD AND CUBA: CUBAN REVOLUTION AND THE NEW LEFT

Saul Landau

The Cuban Revolution's appeal to young radicals.

The term *New Left* in England and the United States referred primarily to student and professor activists in the early 1960s who wanted radical democratic changes. Unlike the Old Left Marxists (mostly the Communist Party) for whom the working class remained the historical instrument for change, New Left thinkers rejected the validity of this so-called vulgar Marxism (of economic reductionism) as well as the Cold War framework, including what the sociologist C. Wright Mills called "rabid anti-Stalinism." In the United States the New Left label was used to describe student movements such as Students for a Democratic Society (SDS), as well as civil rights activists, the anti–Vietnam War movement, and, later, members of the black liberation movement, the women's liberation movement, and the gay and lesbian rights movement.

FROM THE SIERRA TO HAVANA

On 17 February 1957 the American journalist Herbert Matthews (1900–1977) discovered young democratic idealists fighting to overthrow the U.S.-backed Fulgencio Batista government in Cuba. (Batista had seized power in a 1952 coup.) In his *New York Times* reports from the Sierra Maestra, Matthews compared the rebel leader Fidel Castro favorably with Batista's corrupt government. Some CIA cables warned of communist influence among the ragtag insurgents, but many U.S. government sources did not think that 300 guerrillas could defeat Batista's 50,000-man army, much less threaten U.S. interests and property. After all, Castro was a lawyer and previously married to an upper-class woman whose family—Diaz Balart—held powerful positions in the Batista government.

In early January 1959 major U.S. and Western European media hailed the implausible victory, but by February, a month after the revolutionaries had seized power, there was criticism of Cuba's public trials for former Batista police and military officials, followed by warnings that the rebels were not showing proper respect for U.S. property. Mainstream media echoed U.S. government criticism of Castro's so-called kangaroo courts, referring to the televised trials in the Havana Sports Stadium and some on-camera executions. These broadcasts were very popular with the Cuban public. Newsroom editors in the United States had treated the revolutionary takeover as another ho-hum change-of-Latin-American-regime-story worthy of a few days' headlines. The trials, however, provided them with truly juicy headline gore, and Cuba soon became a new bad guy on the Cold War block—in the United States' backyard.

Some American liberals took longer to change their minds—until Castro had proved his affiliation with the Communists. For the historian Theodore Draper (1912–2006), an early Castro supporter who epitomized liberal views in the United States, Castro had betrayed his stated ideals of democracy and civil liberties and turned into a communist dictator.

MILLS AND THE NEW LEFT

As the Cuban Revolution lost liberal support in the U.S. political arena and media, its leaders sought allies among radical activists and critics of mainstream opinion. C. Wright Mills (1916–1962), who had critiqued the Cold War in *Causes of World War III* (1958) and professional social scientists in *The Sociological Imagination* (1959), saw Cuba's revolution as a popular social experiment that transcended Cold War binary ideology: Revolution was neither capitalist (freedom without social justice) nor communist (social justice without freedom). Mills, the most influential academic guru of the New Left, visited Cuba in August 1960, interviewed dozens of Cubans, and spent two days with Castro. Mills saw in Cuba "realistic utopianism." *Listen Yankee* (1960), Mills's first-person narrative by an invented Cuban revolutionary, lambasted the U.S. media's ignorance and incompetence for publishing misrepresentations of the Cuban Revolution.

An editorial in *Studies on the Left* agreed with Mills: "[Defense of] Cuba presents us with an urgent task and . . . the best opportunity to expose and destroy cold war ideology" (pp. 1–16, 75–95). *Studies* had been founded by students at the University of Wisconsin in 1959, and it featured several stories on Cuba during its first year of publication, including an editorial piece titled "'Notes on the Cuban Revolution' by Commandante Ernesto 'Che' Guevara" and Saul Landau and Eleanor Hakim's reviews of Mills's *Listen Yankee* and *Cuba: Anatomy of a Revolution* (1960), by Leo Huberman and Paul Sweezy, who had concluded after visiting Cuba and conducting extensive interviews with key leaders that Cuba's revolution was socialist. The *New Left Review* in London showed similar interest in Cuba in 1960 and 1961.

THE AMERICAN LEFT CALLS FOR FAIR PLAY

Throughout 1960 Cuban leaders had responded to escalating U.S. punishments for their agenda. Washington opposed rent control, agrarian reform, and most importantly the nationalization of private U.S. corporations in Cuba without compensation. By early 1960 Cuba had accepted Soviet offers of low-priced crude oil. Washington ordered U.S. oil refineries in Cuba not to process it. Castro nationalized all U.S. property, and Eisenhower imposed an embargo that endured more than fifty years, well into the early 2000s. The Soviets responded by offering Cuba massive aid. Thus the Cold War came to the Caribbean.

As the United States aggressively responded to Cuba's handling of U.S. property, a New York–based solidarity group emerged—the Fair Play for Cuba Committee (FPCC). The FPCC was founded by Richard Gibson and former CBS newsman Bob Taber, who had interviewed Castro in 1958 in the Sierra Maestra. It had unofficial backing from the Cuban government. Notable supporters included the historian William Appleman Williams; writers and poets such as Truman Capote, Norman Mailer, Allen Ginsberg, and Lawrence Ferlinghetti (who penned "One Thousand Fearful Words for Fidel Castro" in 1961); and the Latin Americanists Waldo Frank and Carleton Beals. (Saul Landau headed the Student FPCC from late fall 1960 to early 1961.)

The African American writers Leroi Jones (Amiri Baraka) and James Baldwin toured Cuba in 1960 and responded favorably to its radical social programs and the outlawing of racial segregation. When the CIA, convinced of the Revolution's leftward turn, recruited exiles in Miami to join an armed force to "free the island from communist dictatorship," Baldwin took issue: "One has not learned anything about Castro when one says, 'He is a Communist'" (p. 44).

"The idea of 'a revolution' had been foreign to me," wrote Jones in 1960. "It was one of those inconceivably 'romantic' and/or hopeless ideas that we Norteamericanos have been taught since public school to hold up to the cold light of 'reason.' That 'reason' being whatever repugnant lie our usurious 'ruling class' had paid their journalists to disseminate" (Baraka p. 160). Robert F. Williams, the civil rights activist from North Carolina who had traveled with Baraka to Cuba, had organized black World War II and Korean War veterans into armed self-defense teams to fight Ku Klux Klan attackers in black neighborhoods—a precursor to the Black Panthers. In early 1961, with federal agents with warrants looking for him, Williams sought refuge on the island. From 1961 to 1965 Williams ran Radio Free Dixie from Cuba, playing black music and exhorting African Americans to engage in rebellion.

For New Leftists who were pacifists or practiced nonviolent civil disobedience, Cuba was an example of social transformation, even if they eschewed violence as a method of social change. Others, such as the Black Panther Party (1966), the Black Liberation Army (1970), and the Weather Underground (1969), embraced the notion of urban guerrilla warfare as a key method of struggle.

SARTRE AND CASTRO

The Revolution also hosted Jean-Paul Sartre and Simone de Beauvoir in 1960. These intellectual luminaries of the noncommunist European Left viewed the revolution historically. "Without a gesture, without a word, American imperialism, with the aid of its Cuban allies, reinforced the feudalism that its military forces had pretended to destroy. The cattlemen and planters both served the interest of the Yankees, and vice versa," wrote Sartre. "They discouraged this country from industrializing. The U.S.A. feared competition; the big landowners dreaded the rupture of the internal equilibrium. If they permitted the industrial bourgeoisie to grow, if the farm laborers left the fields to become engaged in the factories, what would happen?" (Sartre 1961). For Sartre, Cuba's agrarian reform was necessary for development, and the revolution had opened the path for proper development. "For the first time we were witnessing happiness that had been attained by violence," he declared (Reid-Henry). Sartre wondered how Cuba's leader could avoid the disease of power that had corrupted past revolutionaries of good intentions. Castro said he wanted to meet people's basic needs as they presented them.

The Cuban journalist and novelist Lisandro Otero, writing about the meeting of Sartre and Castro, commented that past revolutions had "devoured their children, incurred in terror as a form of survival. Robespierre, Saint Just, Machiavelli, and Trotsky defined violence as a resource to maintain power when power starts to deteriorate as an outcome of counterrevolutionary actions and of the pendulous action of public opinion. How could that be avoided in Cuba?" Castro rejected "coercive procedures" and offered "reason and logic" as explanation for "his long, meticulous, and didactic speeches" (Otero).

Mills's and Sartre's books painted a picture of a Cuba of collective action: housing construction for slum dwellers, literacy brigades, and access to medical care. But Cuba's nationalizing of U.S. property and developing intimacy with the Soviets, deemed necessary for revolutionary survival as the CIA prepared an invasion and Eisenhower imposed an embargo, alienated noncommunist radicals and made futile the argument of those in government and media who argued for "kissing and hugging the revolution to death" (Conversation with Herbert Matthews, February 1961). Reasoned pleas to restore common sense to United States–Cuba policy fell on deaf ears. The proverbial die had been cast.

Simone de Beauvoir and Jean-Paul Sartre in Cuba, 1960. French philosophers Simone de Beauvoir and Jean-Paul Sartre meet Ernesto "Che" Guevara (right) in Havana in 1960, an event photographed by Alberto Korda. © 2011 ARTISTS RIGHTS SOCIETY (ARS), NEW YORK/ADAGP, PARIS. RUE DES ARCHIVES/THE GRANGER COLLECTION, NEW YORK. REPRODUCED BY PERMISSION

In February 1961, two months before CIA-backed Cuban exiles invaded the island at the Bay of Pigs, even Herbert Matthews—who had been promoted to editor at the *New York Times* and no longer reported on Cuba—wrung his hands. In conversation with Saul Landau, he said, "We forced him [Castro] into the Soviets' hands" and insisted that a different U.S. policy toward the island could still deflect Castro's rapid swing toward the Soviet bloc.

By late April 1961 Mills and Sartre had begun to question their optimism about Cuba's future. Mills lunched in Paris with Sartre, Beauvoir, and K. S. Karol (author of *Guerrillas in Power*), who acted as interpreter. They shared their experiences of time spent with Castro. Mills thought that Castro's profession of Marxism-Leninism and intimacy with the Soviets had dampened the hopes of noncommunist leftists that Cuba would become a different model. Sartre and Beauvoir agreed. All would give Fidel time to see if his post–Bay of Pigs actions would translate into the Cuba they envisioned. Mills never broke formally with Cuba, but in letters to Saul Landau he repeated the pessimism he had expressed at the Sartre lunch.

THIRD WORLD LIBERATION

After the Cuban Missile Crisis (1962) Cuban-Soviet relations became strained, and in matters of foreign policy, Cuba embarked more aggressively on a path of encouraging revolutionary wars of national liberation in the Third World. On several occasions Cuba criticized the Soviet Union for not doing enough to help Vietnam. Much of this was consistent with Che Guevara's famous appeal to "create one, two, many Vietnams." By 1968 Cuba's solidarity with Vietnam brought American antiwar activists to Havana. Tom Hayden (a founder of SDS) and Dave Dellinger (a pacifist leader) met with North Vietnamese and Viet Cong delegations and with Castro.

For some American and European leftist intellectuals, their solidarity with Cuba stemmed from Cuba's support for Third World liberation. And Cuba needed allies in the West, even if they represented politically marginal publics. One important Cubaphile of the era, Regis Debray, wrote *Revolution in the Revolution?* (1967), which promoted Guevara's guerrilla war through an insurrectional nucleus (*foco* in Spanish) as the means to successful revolution. When Guevara formed his ill-fated guerrilla foco in Bolivia, Debray joined. Bolivian police arrested him and CIA agents interrogated him under conditions of extreme duress. In May 1967 Sartre spoke at a public rally in support of Debray—"Regis Debray has been arrested by the Bolivian authorities, not for having participated in guerrilla activities but for having written a book"— and he applauded Debray's efforts to promote Third World liberation (*Le Monde* 30 May 1967). After being released from jail, Debray wrote three books about Guevara and the guerrilla experience in Latin America, two of them appropriately titled *A Critique of Arms*. While remaining on the Left, Debray later published a stinging assessment of Guevara and Castro in his 1996 memoir (Debray 2007, pp. 74–109).

Lee Lockwood's 1967 *Castro's Cuba; Cuba's Fidel* presented a quite objective portrait of the Revolution and its leader. In that same year, the former Student Nonviolent Coordinating Committee (SNCC) leader and Black Panther Stokely Carmichael accompanied Castro on an island tour. Other persecuted black militants, including Eldridge Cleaver, sought refuge in Cuba. (Those who had hijacked planes, however, went to prison.) In that same year, U.S. public television presented "Report from Cuba," a program (coproduced by the author) that showed the strides Cuba had made in housing, education, and health.

In the next year, Sartre criticized Castro's August 1968 speech supporting Soviet intervention in Czechoslovakia, but he became downright irate over the 1971 arrest of the Cuban poet Heberto Padilla. In 1968 Padilla had been placed under house arrest for criticizing the Castro government in *Fuera del juego* (Out of the Game, 1968), which had won the prestigious Cuban Casa de las Americas poetry prize though it was denounced by party hardliners as counterrevolutionary. In 1971, when Padilla was imprisoned for thirty-eight days without charge, there was outcry from intellectuals around the world. Juan Arcocha, a Cuban journalist and translator who had defected to France, claimed that Padilla had been tortured. When Padilla emerged without signs of physical abuse, he spoke to fellow artists and writers in a kind of theatrical replay of the 1930s Soviet purge trial confessions. The so-called Padilla Affair ended with enduring damage to Cuba's reputation, and in 1980 Padilla left Cuba for the United States.

New Leftists in Europe who focused on promoting Third World liberation downplayed such incidents and formed alliances with the Black Panthers. Cuba also supported the Panthers, emphasizing racism in the United States and drawing international attention to the case of Angela Davis. In 1970 police had arrested Davis, a scholar and SNCC organizer, and charged her with conspiring in a failed raid on a Bay Area courtroom to free the black revolutionary George Jackson. The raid ended in the deaths of four persons, including Jackson and a judge, and guns used in the attempt were registered in Davis's name. Davis fled and was added to the FBI's most-wanted list. Later she was acquitted of the charges and became a professor at the University of California, Santa Cruz. She remained a staunch supporter of the Cuban Revolution.

The internationalist New Left continued to act in solidarity with Cuba to break the U.S. blockade with symbolic gestures. In 1969 Carol Brightman published *Viet-Report*, an antiwar periodical distinguished by scrupulous research that countered U.S. government disinformation. That same year, she helped coordinate the Venceremos Brigade, which sends American radicals to Cuba to work as volunteers for the sugar harvest. In 2010 the brigade was still active, though brigadistas have undertaken other work tasks; as the embargo continued, so did the solidarity campaign.

The Revolution also won public support from some Cuban Americans. *Areito* magazine (1974), the Antonio Maceo Brigade, and the Cuban American Committee for Normalization of Relations with Cuba (1978) emerged alongside a revived Joven Cuba (founded by Antonio Guiteras in 1934) as small counter-efforts to the hard-line anti-Castro activism that dominated the exile community. In 2011 the Venceremos Brigade, the Center for Cuban Studies, the Antonio Maceo Brigade, and Alianza Martiana still maintained their allegiance to Cuban revolutionary ideals. In addition, some of the students of the 1960s and 1970s who had called for fair play for Cuba became professors who teach and write about Cuba from a critically positive vantage. They collaborate with colleagues in other countries on Cuban Studies and U.S. foreign policy.

Although the strongest bonds between Cuba and the New Left were created in the 1960s and 1970s, Cuba's ability to survive the collapse of communism (1989) and loss of Soviet largesse continued into the early 2000s to interest those in the global justice movement, leftist ecologists, the World Social Forum, and other grassroots organizations that seek alternatives to unbridled neoliberalism. They were joined by a Latin American New Left that was voted into office in some countries (Venezuela, Bolivia, Ecuador) and by the newly created Alianza Bolivariana para los Pueblos de Nuestra América (ALBA, Bolivarian Alliance for the Americas). As Cuba prepared to undergo major reform in early 2011 in response to fifty years of U.S. government hostility, tens of thousands of Americans and Europeans remembered the heady taste of collectivity and sacrifice that prevailed on the island during its first decades of the Revolution—the possibility of building a different kind of society.

BIBLIOGRAPHY

Artaraz, Kepa. *Cuba and Western Intellectuals since 1959.* New York: Palgrave Macmillan, 2009.

Baldwin, James. "A Talk to Teachers." *Saturday Review* (21 December 1963): 42–44.

Baraka, Amiri. "Cuba Libre." In *The Leroi Jones/Amiri Baraka Reader*. Berkeley, CA: Thunder's Mouth Press, 1999.

De la Nuez, Iván. *Fantasía Roja, Los intelectuales y la Revolución cubana*. Madrid: Random House-Mondadori, 2006.

Debray, Régis. *Revolution in the Revolution?* New York: Penguin, 1967.

Debray, Régis. *Praised Be Our Lords: The Autobiography.* New York: Verso, 2007.

Draper, Theodore. *Castro's Revolution: Myths and Realities.* New York: Praeger, 1962.

Ferlinghetti, Lawrence. *One Thousand Fearful Words for Fidel Castro.* San Francisco: City Lights, 1961.

Fruchter, Norman, and Stuart Hall. "Notes on the Cuban Dilemma." *New Left Review* 1 (May–June 1961): 2–12.

Gosse, Van. *Where the Boys Are: Cuba, Cold War America, and the Making of a New Left.* New York: Verso, 1993.

Huberman, Leo, and Paul Sweezy. *Cuba: Anatomy of a Revolution.* New York: Monthly Review Press, 1960.

Landau, Saul. "Cuba, the Present Reality." *New Left Review* 1, no. 9 (1961): 33–37.

Matthews, Herbert. Conversation with author in *New York Times* office of Matthews. February 1961.

Mills, C. Wright. *Listen Yankee: The Revolution in Cuba.* New York: Ballantine Books, 1960.

Otero, Lisandro. "Sartre and Fidel Castro." July 2005. Available from http://www.cubanow.cult.cu/pages/articulo.php?sec=17&t=2&item=526.

Radosh, Ronald. *The New Cuba Paradoxes and Potentials.* New York: Morrow, 1976.

Reid-Henry, Simon. "The Last Revolutionary." *New Statesman* (5 November 2009): 28–30.

Reitan, Ruth. *The Rise and Decline of an Alliance: Cuba and African American Leaders in the 1960s.* East Lansing: Michigan State University Press, 1999.

Sartre, Jean-Paul. *Sartre on Cuba.* New York: Ballantine Books, 1961.

Scheer, Robert, and Maurice Zeitlin. *Cuba: Tragedy in Our Hemisphere.* New York: Grove Press, 1963.

Studies on the Left 1, no. 3 (1960): pp. 1–16, 75–95.

Williams, William A. *The United States, Cuba, and Castro: An Essay on the Dynamics of Revolution and the Dissolution of Empire.* New York: Monthly Review Press, 1962.

THE WORLD AND CUBA: IDEOLOGICAL STRUGGLE IN THE UNITED NATIONS

Holly Ackerman

Differing perspectives on human rights between the United States and Cuba, including the U.S. campaign to have Cuba condemned for human rights violations in the United Nations.

Few issues are as contentious as that of human and civil rights in Cuba. For those unsympathetic to the current government, including the U.S. government and some Cuban émigrés, the country is guilty of human rights abuses against its own people. To those supportive of the revolution, Cuba is a struggling Third World country that has overcome odds to deliver social justice to its people, representing an alternative to neo-liberal market fundamentalism. The sharp divide in these two perspectives has much of its roots in the countries' definitions of "rights," particularly as defined by the United Nations.

The Soviet Union and its allies, including Cuba, insisted on the need to prioritize economic, social, and cultural rights, whereas the Western capitalist countries—particularly the United States—were equally insistent on the centrality of political and civil freedoms. A pattern of mutual accusation between these two camps emerged from the very first but, in the case of Cuba, reached its zenith in the late 1980s during the U.S. administrations of Ronald Reagan and George H. W. Bush.

CUBAN PERSPECTIVE ON HUMAN RIGHTS

There is a significant philosophical difference between Western human rights scholars, Cuban intellectuals opposed to the Cuban government, and activists on the one hand, and the revolutionary government in Cuba and Cuban intellectuals aligned with the Cuban government on the other. The revolutionary government emphasizes economic, social, and cultural rights (education, health care, housing, employment and a living wage, and elimination of gender and racial discrimination), which require a greater commitment by the state so that its citizenry can enjoy them. From a human development standpoint, these are seen as nurturing capabilities that, if implemented sufficiently and sustained, provide opportunities for all citizens, and are the backbone of all other rights. Civil and political rights (the right to own property; the right to free elections; freedom of religion, speech, and association; protection from arbitrary arrest) are seen as rights that are negative in that the less the state is involved with them the better. Briefly stated, economic, social, and cultural rights, when provided in sufficient degree, support the freedom to act, whereas civil and political rights, when supported and enforced, protect freedom from a potentially oppressive government.

Cuba's notion of socialist legality and democracy implies several concepts that differ from liberal democratic notions. For example, the liberal democratic emphasis on the ownership of private property differs from Cuba's model in which the state is the primary holder of property. The Cuban model also follows a strict adherence to notions of social and economic equality as opposed to the liberal model's emphasis on individual freedom. Cuba's emphasis on economic equality, in particular, results in the practice of "unitary democracy," where the holistic welfare of society is paramount rather than the interests of the individual, as is the norm in a liberal democracy. Cuba views the Western practice of democracy as fostering social and economic inequality, stacking the deck politically to the powerful and wealthy, and that, analogously in international relationships, perpetuate or accentuate increasing disparities between wealthy and poor countries, as well as provide undue justifications to meddle in the internal affairs of developing states indirectly (through the International Monetary Fund, World Trade Organization, the United Nations) or directly through economic pressure, political coercion, or military intervention. On the other hand, critics of the actually existing Cuban model point to Cuba's economic scarcity and declining quality of education and

■ *See also*

Che Guevara, Social and Political Thought

Cuban Embargo

Cuban Thought and Cultural Identity: Socialist Thought

Governance and Contestation: The Cuban Revolution

health services where citizens cannot act independently of the state to try to improve their situation nor can they organize to demand change (outside established channels) without risking harassment or incarceration.

CUBA AND THE HUMAN RIGHTS DISCUSSION IN THE UNITED NATIONS

The primary documents used to frame international discussions of human rights and to assess progress toward universal goals are the 1948 Universal Declaration of Human Rights and two subsequent covenants passed in 1966: the United Nations International Covenant on Civil and Political Rights and the United Nations International Covenant on Economic, Social and Cultural Rights. The Declaration is a statement of general principles while the two Covenants are binding agreements that translate the Declaration into treaties, passing them into the realm of international law. The covenants were drafted and passed with great difficulty.

Whereas the Covenant on Civil and Political Rights was, from the start, accompanied by an investigative and monitoring function assigned to the UN Commission on Human Rights (UNCHR), the Covenant on Social Economic and Cultural Rights (ESCRTS) had no such body, relying on the principle of voluntary "progressive realization" until a weak monitoring committee was created in 1985. This division gave prominence and "color of law" to civil and political rights since countries accused of violating the covenant were investigated and denounced in the commission's reports, the General Assembly, the media, and world public opinion.

Until 1967 the UNCHR had operated under a strict sovereignty principle; the commission assisted in drafting treaties to join the covenant and generally promoted awareness of human rights but did not evaluate the performance of individual states. With the acceptance of the covenant, however, its role changed to encompass a six-week UNCHR annual meeting in Geneva where testimony was taken, recommendations made, and special rapporteurs could be appointed to investigate situations of particular urgency. Cuba has been a leader in the fight to return to the previous "strict sovereignty" policy.

An additional contribution to debate has come from the Non-Aligned Movement of which Cuba is a leader. The movement emphasizes the fundamental importance of self-determination, respect for cultural diversity, social justice, and the right to development. It was advocacy by the Non-Aligned Movement that brought about additional covenants which often repeated elements contained in the two principal covenants but focused squarely on issues of justice, such as racial discrimination (1965); discrimination against women (1979); against torture and degrading punishment (1984); the Right to Development (1986); and the Rights of the Child (1989). By approaching human rights through an issues-based strategy, the Non-Aligned Movement is able to focus attention on particular substantive topics of primary importance to the Global South and to detach them from debates about political/civil rights while simultaneously corralling UN resources for study and action.

The particular intensity with which these differences were felt in Cuba can be seen by the fact that the Cuban government did not become a party to either of the two conventions until 2008. Within days of Raúl Castro's ascent to the presidency, Cuba became the 166th country to sign the Convention on Political and Civil Rights and the 159th to sign the Convention on Economic Social and Political Rights. Once a country signs, it must seek ratification within its own nationally constituted treaty process and begin to bring domestic laws and practices into compliance with the conventions. At the start of 2011 Cuba had not yet ratified either. Extensive legal revision will be required for Cuba to comply, but analysis of the changes has begun within Cuba's legal and academic community (Aguado 2009).

U.S. CAMPAIGN IN THE UNITED NATIONS

In 1987, the United States mounted a campaign in the United Nations to try to mark Cuba as a severe human rights violator as part of Ronald Reagan's larger crusade to destroy the Soviet Union and its allies. The *New York Times* reported that "what seemed like an obscure U.S. sponsored motion in the United Nations to condemn Cuba for Human Rights abuses consumed much of the time and attention of top Reagan administration officials" (Sciolino p. 28A).

Reagan himself was reported to be on the phone with other world leaders; 42 U.S. ambassadors in countries seated on the UNCHR were sent to talk with their counterparts; 400 telegrams were sent to various foreign officials; UN delegates from developing nations complained that their U.S. aid shipments were threatened if they did not vote with the United States. A delegate called it a movement "marked by threats and heavy-handed lobbying" (Sciolino).

Despite these extraordinary measures, the final vote on whether to condemn Cuba's human rights situation was 19 against the U.S. motion and 18 in favor with 6 abstentions. The following year the United States increased pressure. To avoid a vote with an uncertain outcome, the Cuban delegation extended an invitation to a six-member UNCHR inspection team led by UNCHR chair Alioune Sene of Senegal to visit Cuba in 1988 and assess the rights situation for themselves (Granma; Slevin; Weissbrodt).

In an editorial to the *New York Times*, human rights advocate Aryeh Neier had warned of the dangers of Reagan's increasing manipulation of human rights for political ends. "By invoking the rhetoric of the human rights movement to promote other interests, it severely threatens the human rights movement. Unless our movement keeps its distance from those who misuse our arguments and unless we are outspoken in rejecting their efforts, we run the risk that they will deprive us of our only effective mechanism: that capacity for generating moral pressure" (*New York Times* 1986, p. A17).

INTERNATIONAL INVESTIGATION OF ALLEGATIONS IN CUBA

In 1987, Neier had a personal opportunity to measure the U.S. rhetoric against Cuban reality in advance of the visit from the UNCHR team when he was asked to participate in an invited delegation from the Institute for Policy Studies that visited six Cuban prisons of the delegation's own choosing and conducted confidential interviews with one hundred prisoners. As part of the agreement with the Institute for Policy Studies, the National Union of Cuban Jurists was to conduct a similar visit to prisons in the United States, but the U.S. government refused to issue visas to the Cubans after initially agreeing to the exchange (Neier 1988).

From Neier's point of view, the granting of access by the Cubans was significant. "A closed society opened its doors to expose some of its most secret places," he commented (Neier 1988). He saw incremental improvement in conditions made in anticipation of his visit and further changes and prisoner releases made after he left in response to his recommendations. An Amnesty International delegation followed Neier's visit and preceded the UNCHR. All resulted in improved conditions. None, including the UNCHR delegation, found evidence that outright torture, disappearances, or extrajudicial executions were being practiced in Cuba as the United States had alleged. During the UNCHR visit, the Cuban government published a phone number that citizens could use to call in complaints; fully 1,183 of the 1,600 complaints (69.5%) received by the UNCHR delegation had to do with migration issues, principally denial of exit permits by the Cuban authorities, rather than with prison conditions or other civil liberties (UNHCR 1989). The final report also included tables showing the gains in the enjoyment of economic, social, and cultural rights that have occurred since the Cuban revolution of 1961 (Brody 1989). The commission voted in 1989 to take no action on the report.

The United States continued to press its case during the George H. W. Bush administration, and in 1991 finally achieved a vote to appoint a Special Representative to meet with the government and people of Cuba to investigate the situation of human rights (Parker and Weissbrodt 1991). In 1992, this appointment was given more authority by upgrading the appointment to that of Special Rapporteur (Pitts and Weissbrodt 1993). The United States continued to achieve a vote against Cuba annually until 1998 when, following a visit to Cuba by the pope, 300 prisoners were released and Cuba was removed from the UNCHR list of countries under special scrutiny.

Throughout the period between 1991 and 1998, the Cubans countered by refusing to let the Special Rapporteur come to Cuba and by introducing an annual resolution condemning the U.S. embargo. The politicization that Neier had warned about had come to pass. As one Latin American diplomat put it, the U.S. campaign had "made us realize that this is a political forum, not a human rights forum, and we had to develop a political response" (Parker and Weissbrodt 1991). In 2010 the U.S. embargo was condemned by the General Assembly for the nineteenth consecutive time, each year by overwhelming margins with 187 in favor and 3 opposed in 2010 (Snow).

Under President George W. Bush the two-part strategy of inflammatory talk and demands for investigation of Cuba resumed. The United States succeeded in reinstating a personal representative of the High Commissioner for Human Rights on the situation of human rights in Cuba from 2003 to 2007 though the representative, French jurist Christine Chanet, was never allowed into Cuba (Chanet 2004–2007).

By 2005 the UN Secretary General Kofi Annan threw in the towel on the UNHRC saying that despite some achievements the commission had been "undermined by the politicization of its sessions and the selectivity of its work. We have reached a point at which the commission's declining credibility has cast a shadow on the reputation of the United Nations system as a whole, and where piecemeal reforms will not be enough" (Annan 2005). Annan proposed and the General Assembly enacted a new Human Rights Council to function as a standing body of the United Nations, giving the council more prominence and resources. Cuba ran for a seat on the new council in 2006 and was reelected in 2009. The United States chose not to participate during the George W. Bush administration.

The quiet diplomacy suggested by Neier and the universal periodic review adopted by the new UN Council hold promise for starting fresh. Indeed, Cuba's unilateral decision in 2010 to release dozens of political prisoners offers a point of departure (Booth and DeYoung 2010). By joining the council in 2009, the Obama administration reversed the isolationist position of the Bush administration, which is a hopeful sign. Ironically the chief opponent of renewed U.S. engagement in the UN Council came from Cuban American Representative Ileana Ros-Lehtinen, chair of the House Foreign Relations Committee who has threatened to introduce legislation to withhold funding for U.S. participation.

BIBLIOGRAPHY

Aguado, Nelia, et al. "Prácticas de los derechos humanos: un simposio cubano." *TEMAS* 59 (July–September 2009): 95–105.

Booth, William, and Karen DeYoung. "Cuba to Release 52 Political Prisoners, Catholic Church Says." *Washington Post* (8 July 2010): 1.

Brody, Reed, and David Weissbrodt. "Major Developments at the 1989 Session of the UN Commission on Human Rights." *Human Rights Quarterly* 11, 4 (1989): 586–611.

Chanet, Christine. *Situation of Human Rights in Cuba: Report*. Geneva: United Nations, 2004.

Chanet, Christine. *Situation of Human Rights in Cuba: Report*. Geneva: United Nations, 2005.

Chanet, Christine. *Situation of Human Rights in Cuba: Report*. Geneva: United Nations, 2006.

Chanet, Christine. *Situation of Human Rights in Cuba: Report*. Geneva: United Nations, 2007.

Granma 24 (21 January 26, 1988).

Neier, Aryeh. "Castro's Victims." *New York Review of Books* (17 July 1986).

Neier, Aryeh. Editorial in *New York Times* (1986): A17.

Neier, Aryeh. *In Cuban Prisons. New York Review of Books* (30 June 1988).

Parker, Penny, and David Weissbrodt. "Major Developments at the UN Commission on Human Rights in 1991." *Human Rights Quarterly* 13, 4 (November 1991): 573–613.

Pitts, Joe W., and David Weissbrodt. "Major Developments at the UN Commission on Human Rights in 1992." *Human Rights Quarterly* 15, 1 (1993): 122–196.

Sciolino, Elaine. "Reagan's Mighty Effort to Condemn Cuba." *New York Times* (24 March 1987): 28.

Slevin, Peter. "Cuba Blinked in Showdown over Rights: Wheeling, Dealing Led to Compromise." *The Miami Herald* (13 March 1988): 1.

Snow, Anita. "Cuba Embargo: UN Vote Urges U.S. to Lift Embargo." In *Christian Science Monitor* (26 October 2010). Available from http://www.csmonitor.com/World/Latest-News-Wires/2010/1026/Cuba-embargo-UN-vote-urges-US-to-lift-embargo.

United Nations Economic and Social Council. *Consideration of the Report of the Mission which Took Place In Cuba In Accordance with Commission Decision 1988/106.* New York: United Nations, 1989.

Weissbrodt, David. "Country-related and Thematic Developments at the 1988 Session of the UN Commission on Human Rights." *Human Rights Quarterly* 10, no. 4 (1988): 544–558.

THEMATIC OUTLINE

INDEX

Bold *page numbers refer to the main entry on the subject. Page numbers in italics refer to charts, figures, and tables, with c indicating a chart, f indicating a figure, and t indicating a table.*

I

N

N

0 25 50 mi.

0 25 50 km

Gulf of Mexico

24°N

Straits of Florida

Havana

San José de las Lajas

Matanzas

Cárdenas

Colorados Archipelago

Cordillera de Guaniguanico

Artemisa

Pinar del Río

Broa Gulf

Batabanó Gulf

Zapata Peninsula

Santa Clara

Guadiana Bay

Cienfuegos

22°N

Guanahacabibes Peninsula

Cape San Antonio

Nueva Gerona

Corrientes Bay

Frances Cape

San Felipe Cays

Canarreos Archipelago

Bay of Pigs

Isla de la Juventud

Cape Corrientes

Rosario Cay

Largo Cay

Trinidad

Sancti Spíritus

Sabana Archipelago

20°N

Cuba

Elevation in Feet

3,000
2,000
1,000
500
100
0

Cities

⊗ National capital

● Other city

Cayman Islands

18°N

Caribbean Sea